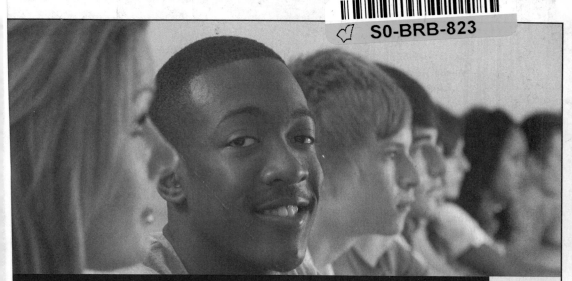

Why Do You Need This New Edition?

If you're wondering why you should buy the fifth edition of *Exploring Literature*, here are 6 great reasons!

- Your professor may assign one of several new selections, including:

  - **Two 10-minute dramas:** Galsworthy's *The Sun* and Chekhov's *Swan Song*

  - **Poetry:** Haiku poetry and a Petrarchan sonnet

  - **Graphic non-fiction:** A selection from Satrapi's "Persepolis"

- A **new mini-theme** in "Culture and Identity," which can be used for class discussion or a writing assignment, focuses on Tennessee Williams' *The Glass Menagerie* paired with/against a Christopher Durang parody, *For Whom the Southern Belle Tolls*.

- New one-page **"Brief Primer on Punctuation"** can help you with your writing by providing you with basic rules and examples for the comma, semicolon, colon, and apostrophe.

- **New student essays:** Two new student essays offer you writing models for literature.

- Fresh **theme-opening quotes** provide a historical dialogue showing the progression of thought on the theme.

- Updated literary criticism with the inclusion of a new section on **Postcolonial Criticism** in Appendix A will help you analyze literary selections in that context.

PEARSON

Media Resources to Accompany Frank Madden's *Exploring Literature* Featured in MYLITERATURELAB.COM [MLL]

FICTION

James Baldwin	*Sonny's Blues*: About the Author • Bibliography • Critical Overview • Essay Questions • Evaluation Questions • Longman Lecture • Writing Prompts • Comprehension Quiz
Toni Cade Bambara	*The Lesson*: About the Author • Longman Lecture • Essay Questions • Comprehension Quiz
Raymond Carver	*Cathedral*: About the Author • Bibliography • Critical Overview • Longman Lecture • Essay Questions • Comprehension Quiz
Kate Chopin	*The Story of an Hour*: About the Author • Bibliography • Critical Overview • Longman Lecture • Essay Questions • Comprehension Quiz
	Désirée's Baby: Critical Overview • Longman Lecture • Essay Questions • Comprehension Quiz
Sandra Cisneros	About the Author
Louise Erdrich	*The Red Convertible*: About the Author • Essay Questions • Comprehension Quiz
William Faulkner	*A Rose for Emily*: About the Author • Bibliography • Critical Overview • Critical Essay and Questions • Longman Lecture • Essay Questions • Comprehension Quiz
Charlotte Perkins Gilman	*The Yellow Wallpaper*: About the Author • Bibliography • Critical Overview • eAnthology selection • Longman Lecture • Essay Questions • Evaluation Questions • Critical Essay and Questions • Writing Prompts
Nathaniel Hawthorne	*Young Goodman Brown*: About the Author • Bibliography • Critical Overview • eAnthology selection • Longman Lecture • Essay Questions • Evaluation Questions • Writing Prompts • Comprehension Quiz
Ernest Hemingway	About the Author • Bibliography
Langston Hughes	About the Author • Bibliography
Zora Neale Hurston	*Sweat*: About the Author • eAnthology selection • Interactive Reading • Longman Lecture
James Joyce	*Araby*: About the Author • Bibliography • Critical Overview • eAnthology selection • Interactive Reading • Longman Lecture • Critical Essay and Questions • Writing Prompts • Comprehension Quiz
Jamaica Kincaid	*Girl*: About the Author • Longman Lecture • Essay Questions • Comprehension Quiz
D. H. Lawrence	*The Horse Dealer's Daughter*: About the Author • Essay Questions • Comprehension Quiz
Gabriel García Márquez	About the Author
Bobbie Ann Mason	*Shiloh*: About the Author • eAnthology selection • Longman Lecture • Essay Questions • Comprehension Questions
Joyce Carol Oates	*Where Are You Going, Where Have You Been?*: About the Author • Bibliography • Critical Overview • Longman Lecture • Essay Questions • Evaluation Questions • Writing Prompts • Comprehension Quiz
Tim O'Brien	*The Things They Carried*: About the Author • Longman Lecture • Essay Questions • Comprehension Quiz
Flannery O'Connor	*A Good Man Is Hard to Find*: About the Author • Interactive Reading • Longman Lecture • Essay Questions • Comprehension Quiz
Linda Ching Sledge	*The Road*

Amy Tan	*Two Kinds*: About the Author • Bibliography • Critical Overview • Longman Lecture • Essay Questions • Comprehension Quiz
John Updike	*A&P*: About the Author • Bibliography • Critical Overview • Interactive Reading • Evaluation Questions • Student and Critical Essay with Questions • Writing Prompts • Essay Questions • Comprehension Quiz
Alice Walker	*Everyday Use*: About the Author • Bibliography • Critical Overview • Longman Lecture • Student Essay with Questions • Essay Questions • Comprehension Quiz

POETRY

Matthew Arnold	*Dover Beach*: Audio • eAnthology selection • Critical Essay and Questions
Margaret Atwood	*you fit into me*: About the Author • Critical Essay and Questions
Elizabeth Bishop	About the Author • Bibliography
William Blake	*The Chimney Sweeper*: About the Author • eAnthology selection • Audio Essay • Critical Essay with Questions
Gwendolyn Brooks	*We Real Cool*: About the Author • Bibliography • Critical Overview • Interactive Reading • Essay Questions • Student and Critical Essay with Questions • Comprehension Quiz
Robert Browning	About the Author
Billy Collins	*Introduction to Poetry*: About the Author • Bibliography • Critical Overview • Evaluation Questions • Writing Prompts
	The Names: Critical Overview • Longman Lecture
E. E. Cummings	*anyone lived in a pretty how town*: About the Author • Bibliography • Critical Overview • Audio • Critical Essay with Questions • Essay Questions • Comprehension Quiz
Emily Dickinson	*Because I could not stop for Death*: About the Author • Bibliography • Critical Overview • Longman Lecture • Essay Questions • Comprehension Quiz
	I heard a Fly buzz—when I died: Critical Overview • Audio
	There's a certain Slant of light: Critical Overview • Video
	Wild Nights—Wild Nights!: Critical Overview • Audio
John Donne	*Death, Be Not Proud*: About the Author • Bibliography • Critical Overview • Audio • eAnthology selection
T. S. Eliot	*The Love Song of J. Alfred Prufrock*: About the Author • Bibliography • Critical Overview • eAnthology selection • Longman Lecture • Essay Questions • Student Essay with Questions • Comprehension Quiz
Robert Frost	*The Road Not Taken*: About the Author • Bibliography • Critical Overview • eAnthology selection • Evaluation Questions • Critical Essay with Questions • Writing Prompts
	Mending Wall: Critical Overview • eAnthology selection • Longman Lecture • Video • Essay Questions • Comprehension Quiz
	"Out, Out...": Critical Overview • eAnthology selection • Interactive Reading • Critical Essay and Questions
Thomas Hardy	About the Author • Bibliography
Seamus Heaney	*Digging*: About the Author • Longman Lecture • Essay Questions • Comprehension Quiz
A. E. Housman	*To an Athlete Dying Young*: About the Author • Bibliography • Critical Overview • eAnthology selection • Longman Lecture • Evaluation Questions • Writing Prompts
Langston Hughes	*The Weary Blues*: About the Author • Bibliography • Critical Overview • Longman Lecture
	Theme for English B: Critical Overview • Essay Questions • Comprehension Quiz

Edna St. Vincent Millay   *Love Is Not All*: About the Author • eAnthology selection • Audio
                             • Longman Lecture
                             What Lips My Lips Have Kissed, and Where, and Why: eAnthology
                             selection • Video Essay • Student Essay with Questions • Essay
                             Questions • Comprehension Quiz
Wilfred Owen   *Dulce et Decorum Est*: About the Author • eAnthology selection
                             • Interactive Reading • Longman Lecture • Critical Essay with
                             Questions • Essay Questions • Comprehension Quiz
Sylvia Plath   About the Author • Bibliography
Adrienne Rich   About the Author • Bibliography
Edwin Arlington Robinson   *Richard Cory*: About the Author • eAnthology selection
                             • Longman Lecture • Critical Essay with Questions • Essay
                             Questions • Comprehension Quiz
Theodore Roethke   *My Papa's Waltz*: About the Author • Longman Lecture • Essay
                             Questions • Comprehension Quiz
Anne Sexton   *Cinderella*: About the Author • Essay Questions
                             • Comprehension Quiz
William Shakespeare   *Shall I Compare Thee to a Summer's Day? (Sonnet 18)*: About the
                             Author • Bibliography • Critical Overview • Audio Essay with
                             Questions • Longman Lecture • Critical and Student Essay with
                             Questions
Percy Bysshe Shelley   *Ozymandias*: About the Author • eAnthology selection • Audio
                             • Essay Questions • Comprehension Quiz
Dylan Thomas   *Do Not Go Gentle into That Good Night*: About the Author
                             • Longman Lecture • Critical Essay with Questions • Essay
                             Questions • Comprehension Quiz
Jean Toomer   *Reapers*: About the Author • Essay Questions • Comprehension Quiz
Walt Whitman   About the Author • Bibliography
William Carlos Williams   About the Author
William Wordsworth   *Composed upon Westminster Bridge September 3, 1802*:   About the
                             Author • Bibliography • Critical Overview • Audio • eAnthology
                             selection
William Butler Yeats   *The Lake Isle of Innisfree*: About the Author • Bibliography
                             • Critical Overview • eAnthology selection • Longman Lecture
                             • Critical Essay with Questions

DRAMA

Anton Chekhov   About the Author
Susan Glaspell   *Trifles*: About the Author • Critical Overview • Bibliography
                             • Longman Lecture • Comprehension Quiz • Essay Questions
Lorraine Hansberry   *A Raisin in the Sun*: About the Author • Longman Lecture
                             • Lecture Questions • Evaluation Questions • Writing Prompts
                             • Comprehension Quiz • Essay Questions
Henrik Ibsen   *A Doll's House*: About the Author • Bibliography • Critical
                             Overview • eAnthology Selection • Longman Lecture • Essay
                             Questions • Comprehension Quiz
William Shakespeare   *Hamlet, Prince of Denmark*: About the Author • Bibliography
                             • Critical Overview • eAnthology Selection • Longman Lecture
                             • Video • Critical Essay • Essay Questions • Comprehension Quiz
Sophocles   *Antigonê*: About the Author • Bibliography • Critical Overview
                             • Longman Lecture • Essay Questions • Comprehension Quiz
Tennessee Williams   *The Glass Menagerie*: About the Author • Bibliography
                             • Critical Overview • Longman Lecture • Essay Questions
                             • Comprehension Quiz

EXPLORING

LITERATURE

EXPLORING
LITERATURE

L EXPLORING

L ITERATURE

Writing and Arguing About
Fiction, Poetry, Drama,
and the Essay

FIFTH EDITION

FRANK MADDEN
SUNY Westchester Community College

PEARSON

Boston   Columbus   Indianapolis   New York   San Francisco   Upper Saddle River   Amsterdam
Cape Town   Dubai   London   Madrid   Milan   Munich   Paris   Montréal   Toronto
Delhi   Mexico City   São Paulo   Sydney   Hong Kong   Seoul   Singapore   Taipei   Tokyo

For Suzanne and Chris;
Michelle, Bill, Sophie, Casey

Senior Acquisitions Editor: Vivian Garcia
Executive Marketing Manager: Joyce Nilsen
Senior Supplements Editor: Donna Campion
Associate Production Manager: Scarlett Lindsay
Project Coordination, Text Design, and Electronic Page Makeup: Integra
Cover Design Manager: John Callahan
Cover Designer: John Callahan
Cover Illustration: © LaVere Hutchings/Corbis
Photo Researcher: Linda Sykes
Senior Manufacturing Buyer: Dennis J. Para
Printer and Binder: Quebecor World Book Services–Taunton
Cover Printer: Lehigh Phoenix Color–Hagerstown

For permission to use copyrighted material, grateful acknowledgment is made to the copyright holders on pp. 1307–1313, which are hereby made part of this copyright page.

Library of Congress Cataloging-in-Publication Data

Madden, Frank.
   Exploring literature : writing and arguing about fiction, poetry, drama, and the essay / Frank Madden. —5th ed.
      p. cm.
Includes bibliographical references and index.
   ISBN-13: 978-0-205-18479-8
   ISBN-10: 0-205-18479-0
   1. Reader-response criticism.   2. Books and reading.   3. Literature—History and criticism—Theory, etc.   I. Title.
   PN98.R38M27 2012
   801'.95–dc22

                                                                    2011007385

1 2 3 4 5 6 7 8 9 10—QWT—14 13 12 11

ISBN-13: 978-0-205-18479-8
ISBN-10:   0-205-18479-0

BRIEF CONTENTS

DETAILED CONTENTS

CHAPTER 5
Research: Writing with Secondary Sources   184

CASE STUDY IN RESEARCH
James Joyce and "Eveline"   200

PART III   A THEMATIC ANTHOLOGY   213

Family and Friends   214

CASE STUDY IN THEATRICAL CONTEXT

Women and Men   667

Culture and Identity   892

ALTERNATE CONTENTS BY GENRE

FICTION

POETRY

DRAMA

ESSAYS

GRAPHIC NARRATIVE

PAINTINGS

PREFACE TO INSTRUCTORS

We can ask of every assignment or method or text, no matter what its short-term effectiveness: Does it get in the way of the live sense of literature? Does it make literature something to be regurgitated, analyzed, categorized, or is it a means toward making literature a more personally meaningful and self-disciplined activity?

Louise Rosenblatt, *Literature as Exploration*

This fifth edition of *Exploring Literature* remains true to the belief that literature can have an important impact on students' lives, and that this impact will only be felt when students experience the "live sense of literature"—the joy, the sorrow, the comfort, and the wisdom that literature offers.

Many students have yet to discover why literature is important. By encouraging them to see their reading and writing in the light of their own experiences, *Exploring Literature* gives students a stake in the process—a reason to care about literature—and authorizes the "meaning-making" role they play when they write about literature. Students learn that the process of crafting a persuasive argument about a work of literature requires close reading and reflection, and that the quality of their interpretation will be measured by the strength of the evidence they bring to support it.

Exploring Literature is designed for instructors who believe that a successful reading and writing experience requires students' engagement as well as analysis, not only as motivation to complete the requirements of a course but also as a prelude to a lifelong relationship with literature.

WHAT'S NEW IN THE FIFTH EDITION?

- For clarity, the term "personal response essay" replaces the term "response essay" in Chapter 2.
- To help students with their editing and proofreading, "A Brief Primer on Punctuation" has been added to Chapter 2.
- A section on Haiku Poetry and a sonnet by Petrarch have been added to the Introduction to Poetry in Chapter 3.
- An excerpt from Edith Hamilton's *The Royal House of Thebes* summarizes Sophocles's *Oedipus Rex* to introduce Sophocles's *Antigonê* in the Drama introduction in Chapter 3.
- For clarity, "Argumentative" replaces "Critical" as the term used to describe an essay that builds an argument.
- Three types of student essays about *A Doll's House*—Personal Response, Argumentative, and Research—have been included in the Women and Men theme.
- A work of graphic nonfiction from Marjane Satrapi's graphic novel, *Persepolis*, has been added to the Family and Friends theme.

- A comparison mini-theme on parody has been added to the Culture and Identity theme, with Tennessee Williams's *The Glass Menagerie* paired with a Christopher Durang parody of it, *For Whom the Southern Belle Tolls*.
- A comparison mini-theme on satire has been added to the Culture and Identity theme with Jonathan Swift's "A Modest Proposal" compared to Luis Valdez's *Los Vendidos*.
- New quotes have been added to each of the theme openers.
- Two ten-minute dramas—John Galsworthy's *The Sun* and Anton Chekhov's *The Swan Song*—have been added to the Faith and Doubt theme.
- MyLiteratureLab, Pearson's state-of-the-art, web-based, interactive learning system, has been fully integrated into this edition. Icons in the chapters lead students to film and audio clips, interactive readings, critical articles, student papers, writing prompts, and other exercises that are available on MyLiteratureLab.com, with subscription. Instructors can package access codes at no additional cost or students can purchase access individually at www.myliteraturelab.com.
- New selections have been added throughout the thematic anthology, including works from contemporary and global writers such as Colum McCann, Susan Musgrave, Sharon Olds, and Christopher Durang.
- More *Making Connections* and *Making an Argument* questions have been added throughout the anthology.
- More *Connecting Through Comparison* subtheme "clusters" provide related works of literature. Students can view similarities and differences and draw upon these works to create new ideas for critical essays.

KEY FEATURES

One of the most important skills for students to master is the ability to write an argumentative essay. Previous editions of *Exploring Literature* laid the groundwork for this often daunting task, and the fifth edition builds upon that foundation, providing more coverage of argumentation in every facet of the text.

By exploring literature as an "experience" within a world of personal responses and contextual influences, the following features encourage students to invest their emotions, to build on their knowledge and experience, and to think more critically:

- *Making Connections.* The questions and exercises in Part I, "Making Connections," are designed to sensitize students to the impact of literature in their lives. Acknowledging, reviewing, and thinking critically about the personal responses students have while reading can provide them with valuable insight into literature and themselves. These early chapters present the process of personal response as a starting point in a recursive sequence leading from engagement and reflection to formal critical tasks and literary interpretation.
- *Argumentation.* Whether reviewing their own judgments or citing evidence to support their views, students are encouraged to think critically about their responses throughout this book. Of special note is Chapter 4, "Argumentation: Writing an Argumentative Essay," which focuses directly on the process of critical thinking and argumentation and guides students through the process of choosing a topic, planning, and supporting an argument. Issues of purpose,

audience, and evidence are central to this discussion of argumentation, which culminates in writing an essay. The final section of this chapter exemplifies the process of critical thinking and argumentation by following a student's progress from initial journal entry to the final draft of an essay.

- ***The Literary Selections.*** The literature in this book, a broad selection of both classic and contemporary pieces, has been chosen for its quality, diversity, and appeal to students. Included in this edition are 40 pieces of fiction, 153 poems, 54 essays, and 13 plays. A complete list of literary selections can be found on pages xxvii–xxxiv.
- ***Writing About Literature.*** From informal journals to formal argumentative and research essays, *Exploring Literature* emphasizes writing as the means to learn about literature. Students who write about literature—and examine their own practices in reading and writing—become more self-aware, more independent, stronger readers and writers.
- ***Samples of Student Writing.*** There are thirteen student essays and many other samples of students' writing throughout the text. These models are included to assist students in formulating their ideas into coherent and cohesive writing.
- ***The Case Studies.*** A case study follows the literary selections in each thematic unit. These self-contained research projects offer a rich and provocative resource for students. The case study for Family and Friends, "**Lorraine Hansberry and A Raisin in the Sun,**" examines the life and work of Lorraine Hansberry—in her words and the words of others—and draws connections to her play, *A Raisin in the Sun.* The case study for Women and Men, "**Women in Culture and History,**" highlights speeches and written artifacts from the eighteenth and nineteenth centuries and offers a glimpse into the cultural context of that period. Accompanying the selections from Innocence and Experience, "***Hamlet and Performance***" is a case study that examines four different interpretations of a soliloquy from *Hamlet* and five critical interpretations of *Hamlet* both on television and in the movies. Following this is a mini case study, "**Case Study in Aesthetic Context: Poetry and Painting,**" that includes pairings of eight famous paintings and nine poems written about them, as well as one student's response to a particular pairing and the process involved in formulating her critical essay. The case study for Culture and Identity, "**Writers of the Harlem Renaissance,**" highlights the literature of an especially creative era in American literature. Finally, a case study for Faith and Doubt, "**The Poetry of Emily Dickinson,**" examines the life and work of this famous poet. All case studies conclude with a student essay relevant to the case study.
- ***Voice.*** The narrative "voice" of *Exploring Literature* is informal and conversational. This book is intended to be read by students—to be accessible, friendly, and informative.

FLEXIBLE ORGANIZATION

Exploring Literature can be used in many different ways. Its explanations, prompts, and literature are resources to be chosen by instructors and students as needed, in or out of sequence. Although the reading and writing activities in this book are organized in a sequence of increasing complexity, the recursive nature of both writing and responding to literature is emphasized throughout.

For instructors who want to explore personal response, have their students keep journals, or write personal response essays about literature, **Part I, "Making Connections,"** provides a rich source of material. Students are encouraged to think about the ways that their own backgrounds and personalities, their understanding of others, their knowledge of texts and contexts—their "meaning-making" processes—influence their responses to literature. Questions that accompany the literature help students clarify their responses and develop them into text-supportable hypotheses and argumentative essays. **Chapter 1, "Participation: Personal Response and Critical Thinking,"** helps students develop connections to literature through their own backgrounds and experiences. **Chapter 2, "Communication: Writing a Personal Response Essay,"** introduces students to literary craft through its discussions of voice, description, and comparison, fostering the sensitivity to language necessary for a complete experience with literature. The chapter concludes with a discussion of the writing process, samples of drafts, and a final personal response essay.

Instructors who favor a more text-based approach may move directly to **Part II, "Analysis, Argumentation, and Research." Chapter 3, "Exploration and Analysis: Genre and the Elements of Literature,"** emphasizes the importance of close reading and analysis. General introductions to fiction, poetry, drama, and the essay are followed by a comprehensive explanation of the elements that make each a distinct form. Carefully chosen literary selections illustrate and support these explanations. Wherever possible, explanations of the elements are illustrated with reference to students' experiences and are accompanied by specific examples from literature in the text.

Chapter 4, "Argumentation: Writing an Argumentative Essay," guides students through the process of critical thinking, reading, and writing. Based on the elements discussed in Chapter 3, students are provided with explanations, questions, prompts, and checklists that help them write an argumentative essay. A comprehensive discussion of argumentation suggests specific questions to ask when constructing an effective argument. The chapter concludes with an examination of a student's process and product from journal entry to final draft of an argumentative essay.

Chapter 5, "Research: Writing with Secondary Sources," completes Part II with a discussion of writing using secondary sources. Explanations and exercises help students integrate secondary sources into their writing, explore popular areas of research, organize their research, gather information from the library (both print and online) and Internet, and avoid plagiarism. The chapter concludes with a case study that provides a glimpse of how literature, culture, and their own experiences may provide a rich context for research. A student writer describes his identification with the pull of family in James Joyce's "Eveline" and investigates conditions in Ireland that prompted the vast migration of the Irish. A narrative of the student's process precedes a final essay.

Part III, "A Thematic Anthology," organizes the four genres of literature under five compelling themes: **"Family and Friends," "Innocence and Experience," "Women and Men," "Culture and Identity,"** and **"Faith and Doubt."** For those who prefer a genre approach, an alternative table of contents organizes the literature under the categories of fiction, poetry, drama, and essays. Each category includes the location of a comprehensive introduction to each of the genres. The literature in this book has been chosen for its quality, diversity, and appeal to students. These stories, poems, plays, and essays represent a broad selection of both classic and contemporary literature.

Each theme opens with a photograph and a series of short provocative quotations, a "Dialogue Across History," that provide a historical context for the literature that follows. An introductory statement about the theme and a brief statement about the literature included under that theme follow. In one thematic unit, a work of literature is highlighted and is followed by two sample student essays written from different perspectives about the selected work. These essays illustrate diversity of opinion; exemplify ways in which the literature might be "read;" and demonstrate how students' own experiences, behaviors, values, and opinions are tools for deepening their understanding and appreciation of literature. A case study follows the literature in each unit. These case studies are a resource for interpretation and biography, cultural and historical context, performance, poetry and painting, culture and research, and poetry.

Appendix A, "Critical Approaches to Literature," is a succinct discussion of major critical theories. **Appendix B, "Writing About Film,"** provides guidelines to help students make the adjustment from writing about literary works to writing about films, another outlet in the development of critical thinking skills. **Appendix C, "Documentation,"** is a guide to the correct layout and citation for a research essay. The **Glossary of Literary Terms** provides a useful reference tool.

RESOURCES FOR STUDENTS AND INSTRUCTORS

The following resources are complimentary to adopters or can be value-packed at no additional cost or at a significant discount with Madden's *Exploring Literature,* Fifth Edition. Please see your local Pearson representative for details.

Instructor's Manual (ISBN: 0-205-18486-3) An instructor's manual is available to adopters of this text. This manual includes topics, ideas, and prompts for generating student essays; frequent critical commentary about the works; useful teaching suggestions; sample syllabi; and Internet addresses for background sources and criticism for the literature and the case studies.

MyLiteratureLab (http://www.myliteraturelab.com) This password–protected Web site offers students a rich source of guidance in the key areas of reading, interpreting, writing, and research. Of special note are the distinctive Longman Lectures. These multimedia lectures, given by many of Longman's prestigious authors, including five lectures by Frank Madden, provide students with insights and support about reading and interpreting the most popular works of literature. To package *MyLiteratureLab* with *Exploring Literature* for no additional cost, use ISBN 0-205-67044-X.

The Longman Electronic Test Bank for Literature (ISBN: 0-321-14312-4) This test bank features various objective questions on the major works of fiction, short fiction, poetry, and drama. A versatile and handy resource, this easy-to-use test bank can be used for all quizzing and testing needs. Instructors can simply choose questions from the electronic test bank and then print out the complete test for distribution.

A Glossary of Literary and Critical Terms (ISBN: 0-321-12691-2) The easy-to-use glossary includes definitions and examples for over 100 literary and critical terms that students commonly encounter in their readings or hear in class. Also included are terms and explanations related to literary history, criticism, and theory.

Literature Timeline (ISBN: 0-321-14315-9) This visually appealing timeline chronicles the major literary works written throughout history. Students gain historical and contextual insights into the impact historical events have had on writers and their works, and vice versa.

Responding to Literature: A Writer's Journal (ISBN: 0-321-09542-1) This journal provides students with their own personal space for writing. Helpful writing prompts for responding to fiction, poetry, and drama are included.

Merriam Webster's Reader's Handbook: Your Complete Guide to Literary Terms (ISBN: 0-321-10541-9) Includes nearly 2,000 entries including Greek and Latin terminology; descriptions for every major genre, style, and era of writing; and assured authority from the combined resources of Merriam-Webster and Encyclopedia Britannica.

Analyzing Literature, Second Edition (ISBN: 0-321-09338-0) The critical reading strategies, writing advice, and sample essays contained in this supplement help students interpret and write about literary works in a variety of genres. Also featured are suggestions for collaborative activities and online research as well as numerous exercises and writing assignments.

Penguin Discount Program Pearson is proud to offer a large selection of Penguin paperbacks at a significant discount when packaged with any Pearson title. Penguin titles offer additional opportunities to explore contemporary and classical fiction and drama. The complete list of titles and discounted prices are available at http://www.pearsonhighered.com/penguin.

Video Program An impressive selection of videotapes is available to enrich students' experience of literature. Contact your sales representative to learn how to qualify.

Acknowledgments

I am indebted to many people over the years who have had a direct and indirect influence on my teaching philosophy—and on the writing of this book. Most notable among these teacher-scholars was Louise Rosenblatt, my teacher at NYU thirty years ago. In addition, John Clifford, Alan Purves, Peter Elbow, Wayne Booth, Robert Scholes, Ann Berthoff, Toby Fulwiler, Robert Berlin, Carl Schmidt, Cindy Onore, John Mayher, Dawn Rodrigues, Jim Slevin, Judith Stanford, Kathi Blake Yancey, and others have influenced and inspired my work. I am grateful to my generous colleagues at WCC: Bill Costanzo, who read the original manuscript with great care and contributed the Appendix, "Writing About Film"; Alan Devenish, Liz Gaffney, Linda Sledge, and Tahira Naqvi, who contributed their own work; Joanne Falinski, Richard Courage, Heather Ostman, Mira Sakrajda, Maryanne Vent, Greta Cohan, Walter Kroczak, Jillian Quinn, Richard Rodriguez, Scott Zaluda, and others who tried out the materials, contributed ideas, and/or submitted student samples. I am grateful to my students who have taught me so much about teaching and this book, especially those students who contributed their work to this volume: Janice Butwell, Dierdre Curran, Suzanne McCloskey, Michelle McAuliffe, Julie Fitzmaurice, Sara Roell, Marie Tymon, Barbara Pfister, Trisa Hayes, Alejandro Ramos, Debora VanCoughnett, Charles Chiang, William Winters, Kevin Chamberlain, Kathryn Pagano, James Militana, and others. I am indebted to President Joseph Hankin for fostering an atmosphere at WCC that made this work possible. And I am especially grateful to my brother John, who early in my life gave me a reason to care about literature, and to my wife, Sharon, my most discerning reader and loving supporter.

For their thoughtful and insightful comments on many drafts of manuscript, I am very grateful to the reviewers of the first, second, third, and fourth editions, and to the following reviewers of the fifth edition: Liz Ann Baez Aguilar, San Antonio College; Alex E. Blazer, Georgia College; Mark Sheffield Brown, Illinois Valley Community College; Cherelyn Bush, Daytona State College; Elizabeth Gaffney, SUNY Westchester Community College; Gloria Montebruno Saller, University of LaVerne; Daniel Schierenbeck, University of Central Missouri; Ken Spurlock, Northern Kentucky University; Terri L. Stricker, Washington Bible College; Karen Terrey, Sierra Nevada College; Hannah Thompson, Clarendon College.

At Pearson, I am especially grateful to Heather Vomero, Scarlett Lindsay, and Jennifer Bossert, whose skill, patience, and advice were much appreciated through the process, and to Vivian García and Joe Terry, whose vision and support made this fifth edition possible. I also wish to thank Joyce Nilsen for getting the word out about this book so effectively, and Linda Sykes and Jessica Werley for their dedication, fine work, and patience while turning a manuscript into a book.

FRANK MADDEN
SUNY Westchester Community College

◆ ABOUT THE AUTHOR ◆

Frank Madden is State University of New York Distinguished Professor and Chair of the English Department at SUNY Westchester Community College, where he also holds the Carol Russett Endowed Chair for English. He has a Ph.D. from NYU, has taught in graduate programs at City College of New York, Iona College, and the New School for Social Research, and in 1998 was Chair of the National Council of Teachers of English College Section Institute on the Teaching of Literature. He is a recipient of the SUNY Chancellor's Award for Excellence in Teaching, the SUNY Chancellor's Award for Excellence in Scholarship, the Foundation for Westchester Community College Award for Excellence in Scholarship, and the Phi Delta Kappan Educator of the Year Award from Iona College. He was awarded the 2003 Nell Ann Pickett Service Award, granted by the NCTE to an outstanding college teacher whose vision and voice have had a major impact, and who exemplifies such outstanding personal qualities as creativity, sensitivity, and leadership. He has been Chair of the College Section of the NCTE and Chair of Two-Year College English Association, and served on the Executive Committees of the NCTE, the Conference on College Composition and Communication, the MLA Association of Departments of English, the SUNY Council on Writing, as Chair of the MLA ad hoc Committee on Teaching, and as NCTE delegate to the American Council of Learned Societies. His articles, chapters, and commentary about the teaching of literature have appeared in a variety of books and journals, including *College English, PMLA, College Literature, English Journal, Computers and Composition, Computers and the Humanities,* and the *ADE Bulletin*. He is the author of two other Pearson texts, *Exploring Poetry* and *Exploring Fiction*.

EXPLORING
LITERATURE

EXPLORING
LITERATURE

PART I

MAKING
CONNECTIONS

Chapter 1

Participation
Personal Response and Critical Thinking

We begin our exploration of literature with you, the reader. Your engagement creates the literary experience. By itself, the literature in this book, as brilliantly crafted or critically acclaimed as it may be, is just words on a page. Your reading of these words through the lenses of your own experiences and beliefs brings them to life and gives them meaning, a meaning as unique as you are.

Literature reveals a possible world to us. Our engagement and involvement are the keys to enter this world and imagine its possibilities. Our backgrounds and personalities, our understanding of others, our prior experience with literature, our knowledge of the world—our sources for making meaning—are important factors in this process. And unlike our busy lives, which sometimes race forward with little time for reflection, literature awaits our examination. We can participate in it as we experience it, and analyze it as we step back and observe it.

Investing your emotions and connecting your knowledge and experience with what you read is an important first step toward our ultimate goal—an appreciation of literature and the ability to think and write critically about it. In subsequent chapters, we will build on these connections and analyze the craft with which literature is created. That analysis will require rereading and reflection, writing and revising, gathering evidence, and constructing a solid argument to support your responses.

THE PERSONAL DIMENSION OF READING LITERATURE

Most literature does not intend to convey a moral or lesson. At its best, it reveals as life reveals. But just as we *read* and react to events in our own lives, our *reading* of literature evokes our emotion and judgment. Narrators and literary characters express their beliefs in what they say or do, and as we read we compare their choices with our own, and approve or disapprove as they meet or fail to meet our expectations. While most good literature does not teach or preach, it does explore and reveal what it means to be human and provides us with a substantial opportunity for learning and self-understanding.

3

Later on in this chapter, and throughout the book, you are asked to consider how your own experiences and beliefs influence your responses to literature. Acknowledging, reviewing, and thinking critically about the judgments you make as you read may provide you with valuable insights into literature and yourself.

PERSONAL RESPONSE AND CRITICAL THINKING

Thinking critically about literature is an outgrowth of our personal responses. It is natural for us to want to comprehend what moves us or has meaning to us. Even as children, we may have tried to make sense of what we read by making connections with our experiences or other stories we read. We knew which books we liked, and even if we didn't analyze our reading systematically, we probably wondered what made those stories appealing to us.

When we think critically about literature, we build on our personal responses— recording them, reviewing them, discussing them, and supporting them. Being engaged is a crucial initial component of a complete literary experience. But once we experience this engagement and believe that literature has something to offer us, we want to know more about it, see how it triggers our responses and judgments, understand the skill with which it was created, and articulate what it means to us.

Critical thinking does not mean searching for one right answer. There may be as many answers as there are readers. *Your best answers are those that analyze and articulate your responses in light of supporting evidence.* This is critical thinking, a process that can make your opinions about literature well-informed ones.

WRITING TO LEARN

Writing is an excellent way to learn about literature. Whether you are jotting down notes, writing in a journal, or constructing a formal essay, you are learning. You learn when you struggle to choose the right words to describe your impressions, and when you revise those words because they are not quite what you mean. And you are learning when you "get it just right" and see your words match what you want to say. In short, writing your responses helps you articulate what you think and feel more clearly—an essential step in the critical thinking process.

Your First Response

When you read a work of literature for the first time, relax and give yourself enough time to experience it. Don't try too hard to figure it out. Get impressions. Notice words and phrases. Read them out loud. Listen to the rhythms. Follow the personal associations that come up. Let yourself feel the emotions connected to them. Don't be discouraged if you have difficulty understanding every word or line. Keep a dictionary handy and look up unfamiliar words. Let your unanswered questions stick with you. Write them down if you think you won't remember them. Record your responses while they're fresh. If you wait until later, you may forget. You might come away from your reading with more questions than answers. So a second or third reading with these questions in mind may clarify much that was confusing in your first reading. This *close reading* and *annotation* is addressed at greater length in the opening pages of Chapter 3.

✓ CHECKLIST: YOUR FIRST RESPONSE

❑ Write down your first impressions and questions that come to mind during and after your reading.

❑ What confuses you? What do you want to know more about? How can you find out?

❑ What words or phrases affect you most?

❑ Do any of the characters remind you of yourself or people you know? Do any of the events remind you of ones in your own life?

❑ Do these associations help or interfere with your response? If so, how?

❑ Is there anything that you don't like about the work? If so, what and why?

❑ What do you find most interesting or compelling about the work? Do any of the characters especially appeal to you or bother you? Do you find any of the events especially pleasing or disturbing? Explain.

Keeping a Reading Log

One of the best tools for exploring and thinking about your experiences with literature is a reading log. Journals and reading logs can help you view and review your ideas. Write in your most natural voice and don't worry about sounding wise. Take chances and try out ideas. Your responses, along with subsequent reading and the comments of classmates, can help you develop ideas as you write the essays required by your instructor. If you are conscientious about keeping your log, your entries will evolve naturally into the meaning you've constructed from the work. Recording your observations at this stage will provide you with much support later.

What you write in your log is your choice. You may or may not like what you read. You may find it engaging or filled with meaning. You may find it confusing or boring. Whatever your response, you'll benefit most if your entries honestly reflect your experience.

An electronic variation of the log is a designated space in an online **discussion forum** like **Blackboard.** Each posting accounts for your first impressions during and after your reading. Both your instructor and other members of your class may read and respond to your postings and use them to initiate class discussion—online or in the classroom.

There is no one correct way of keeping a log. The brief excerpts from student journals that follow are all different, but each is a start and could be built upon to develop a more formal essay. ("Araby" begins on p. 407 and "There's a Certain Slant of Light" is on p. 1249.) Even if you are not familiar with these pieces, these samples reflect the kinds of issues that might be addressed in response to any work of literature.

From confusion:

I found the story of "Araby" to be a little confusing. I couldn't really fathom what the actual point of the story was. There is a boy whose name is not mentioned, and he apparently has some sort of infatuation with a nun. He spies on her, peering through a tiny crack in his shades. He ends up talking to her and telling her that if he goes to Araby, the bazaar, he will buy her a present because she cannot go.

The last line of the story intrigued me. "Gazing up into the darkness I saw myself as a creature driven and derided by vanity; and my eyes burned with anguish and anger." I guess he said this because he did not buy her anything at Araby. I don't exactly know why.

To an appreciation of the author's artistry:

The beginning of "Araby" was written with a lot of descriptive words. As soon as I began to read sentence by sentence, the words formed pictures in my mind. I got the feeling of a painting being painted stroke by stroke. The description of the street being blind and quiet except when the school set the boys free gave me a feeling of quiet and then sudden noise, as the boys came rushing through the streets. Describing the air as cold, the space of the sky as ever-changing violet allowed me to feel the cold and see the colors.

From identification:

The first time I read the lines "There's a certain slant of light, / Winter Afternoons— / That oppresses, like the Heft / of Cathedral Tunes—" I had an immediate picture of grayish-white skies and cold, bare ground. It was almost frightening. The first stanza expresses a feeling I've had for a lifetime <u>of hideous, anxiety-filled, depressing Sunday winter afternoons</u>. From childhood, with homework unfinished and school rearing its terrifying Monday-morning head, through adulthood and its end-of-the-weekend, back to work dread, I've experienced that "Seal Despair—."

To complete frustration:

I've read this poem over and over, repeatedly, nonstop, until I finally collapsed from total exhaustion. WHAT DOES IT MEAN!? What light? The winter afternoon light? As heavy as cathedral tunes? Find a scar from what? Internal difference? Meanings? Aggggh! Help. Could the author be talking about the sun? All I have are questions when it comes to this poem. I do like the choice of words, though. They sounded grand, royal, imperial, and made me feel like there was something to grab from them. But I couldn't make sense of it.

Double-Entry Journals and Logs

Because you may be asked to read and write comments about your journal or log entries from time to time, an especially effective format is the double-entry journal. By writing on only the front side of each page (or on the right half of each page), you will leave the back of the previous page (or the left half of each page) free for subsequent commentary (new ideas, revisions, summation, etc.) while rereading and reflecting. Leaving this space, you may go back later, read through your comments, circle and make notes about entries you've made, or add additional comments based on subsequent readings or class discussion.

(Original Response)

I could relate what Joyce was saying to nowadays. I myself have felt that way. All your words and feelings are jumbled around one person. A crush. It's very stressful and exhilarating at the same time. I do have one question, though. <u>Was the object of Joyce's desire and affection a nun?</u> I didn't feel that aspect was presented too clearly. Maybe I'm misreading.

(Subsequent Comment)

She's not a nun. I found out in class that parochial schools were sometimes called convent schools back then. You didn't have to be a nun to go there. That part of the story makes much more sense to me now.

The Social Nature of Learning: Collaboration

Writing ideas down is one effective way to learn, but so much of what we learn is also learned through conversation. Sharing our responses with others, and listening to their feedback and ideas, help us build and clarify our own ideas. By articulating what you think you know and what you need to know through conversation, you may develop a clearer understanding of the literature.

Interpretive Communities   Stanley Fish, a professor and literary critic, has suggested that readers who share the same approach to literature belong to "an interpretive community." Although our interpretations are influenced by whatever collaborative group or class we are in at present, we also carry and apply our own individual values and those of many other communities (family, friends, religion) to which we belong. In this respect, we are members of many interpretive communities, and we are continually refiguring and revising our interpretations and evaluations in the light of our personal beliefs and group discussions. Throughout this text you'll be encouraged to exchange ideas and collaborate with your classmates in pairs and small groups. You may find it worthwhile and productive to keep track of this complex mix of personal response and group discussion as you write about the literature you read.

Personal, Not Private

Many of the questions that follow in this chapter prompt you to write about personal issues. These questions are not an attempt to invade your privacy or encourage you to write about aspects of your life or experience that may embarrass you or make you feel uncomfortable. What is personal or private is very different for each of us. You may choose some responses to share and other responses for your eyes only. That choice is always yours.

OURSELVES AS READERS

Our early experiences with books may have a significant influence on how we feel about reading. For many of us who enjoy reading, this joy was discovered early in our lives and outside the classroom. We felt free to read without fear of having our responses judged as right or wrong. For many who do not like to read, however, reading was often a painful chore, usually an assignment for the classroom with all the accompanying pressures of being evaluated. How often we read now may be motivated by these earlier experiences.

You might find it worthwhile to write about some of these experiences in your log or share them with others. It may be illuminating to see how much you have in common as a reader with other members of the class.

The process of reading often raises more questions than it answers. Some of the most important questions to address are the ones you have raised yourself. So before you answer the questions that follow each selection in this chapter, you may want to write down your first impressions and any questions that came to mind during and after your reading.

Different Kinds of Reading

For many of us, the different types of reading assigned in school were often treated the same way. Reading that dealt primarily with content or factual information was often not distinguished from imaginative literature. We know, however, that different types of reading material require very different kinds of involvement. Reading a science text, for example, requires that we focus on acquiring information for future use, whereas a poem, play, or work of fiction, while requiring our understanding of the facts, seeks to involve us personally in the moment—to have us share an experience, to evoke our feelings.

Read the following paragraph.

> CAUTION—NOT FOR PERSONAL USE—If splashed on skin or in eyes, rinse immediately. If accidentally taken internally give large amounts of milk or water. Call a physician. Point mouth of container away from you when removing cap. AVOID TRANSFER TO FOOD OR BEVERAGE CONTAINERS—KEEP CONTAINER UPRIGHT IN A COOL PLACE TIGHTLY CAPPED.

FIRST RESPONSES

1. What is your response to the advice in this paragraph?
2. To what extent is this warning label subject to personal interpretation?
3. Did you find yourself more engaged with the emotion or with the information in this paragraph? Explain.

Read the following poem.

PETER MEINKE [B. 1932]

ADVICE TO MY SON   [1981]

—for Tim

The trick is, to live your days
as if each one may be your last
(for they go fast, and young men lose their lives
in strange and unimaginable ways)
but at the same time, plan long range   5
(for they go slow: if you survive
the shattered windshield and the bursting shell
you will arrive
at our approximation here below
of heaven or hell).

10

To be specific, between the peony and the rose
plant squash and spinach, turnips and tomatoes;
beauty is nectar
and nectar, in a desert, saves—
but the stomach craves stronger sustenance   15
than the honied vine.
Therefore, marry a pretty girl
after seeing her mother;
speak truth to one man,
work with another;   20
and always serve bread with your wine.

But, son,
always serve wine.

FIRST RESPONSES

1. What is your response to the advice in this poem?
2. To what extent is the poem subject to personal interpretation?
3. Did you find yourself more engaged with the emotion or the information in this poem? Explain.

MAKING CONNECTIONS

Compare your response to the warning label paragraph with your response to the poem "Advice to My Son."

1. Both the poem and the warning label give advice. In what way was your reading experience with each different?
2. Did the physical appearance of each influence *how* you read it? If the warning label were written in verse form, would you have read it with different expectations?
3. To what extent can you connect the advice given in the poem to your own background or experience? To what extent can you connect the advice given in the warning label?
4. Did you learn anything from the poem? From the warning label? If so, did the *nature* of what you learned differ in each case? Explain.

MAKING CONNECTIONS WITH LITERATURE

Among the many factors that influence our response to literature is identification with characters, circumstances, and issues. Our personalities, backgrounds, and experiences can have a strong impact on these connections. Being aware of these influences can tell us much about our responses—and the works themselves.

We may identify with characters because we see elements of ourselves in them or because we admire characteristics that we lack and wish we had. We might respond negatively to characters because aspects of their personalities are different from ours or similar to ones we don't like in ourselves. We may agree or disagree with what the characters say or do, or ask ourselves if we would have behaved the same way.

Conversely, by showing us a view of life that is different from our own, we may learn from literature as we learn from life itself.

Images of Ourselves

How we view ourselves in relation to the world around us is very complex. We probably have an image of who we are that we carry within us most of the time, but we are likely to project a different personality according to the situations (home, work, school, etc.) in which we find ourselves. Depending on our relationships with them, the people we know are also likely to describe us very differently. Our families, friends, casual acquaintances, employers, and teachers may experience who we are in very different ways.

CONNECTING THROUGH EXPERIENCE

The self-images we carry with us into adulthood may be formed during childhood. Try to remember how you felt about yourself as a child and compare that self-image with how you see yourself now.

PAUL ZIMMER [B. 1934]

ZIMMER IN GRADE SCHOOL   [1983]

In grade school I wondered
Why I had been born
To wrestle in the ashy puddles,
With my square nose
Streaming mucus and blood.   5

My knuckles puffed from combat
And the old nun's ruler,
I feared everything: God,
Learning and my schoolmates.
I could not count, spell or read.   10
My report card proclaimed
These scarlet failures.
My parents wrang their loving hands.
My guardian angel wept constantly.
But I could never hide anything.   15

If I peed my pants in class
The puddle was always quickly evident.
My worst mistakes were at
The blackboard for Jesus and all
The saints to see.   20
    Even now
When I hide behind an elaborate mask
It is always known that I am Zimmer,
The one who does the messy papers
And fractures all his crayons,   25
Who spits upon the radiators
And sits all day in shame
Outside the office of the principal.

 ## MAKING CONNECTIONS

1. What did you wonder about yourself in grade school? To what extent do you still wonder the same things?
2. What does the speaker mean by "When I hide behind an elaborate mask / It is always known that I am Zimmer"? Who is Zimmer?
3. To what extent is your response to "Zimmer in Grade School" affected by your own experience?

Culture, Experience, and Values

Who we are and how we respond to literature is also influenced by many other factors. Family, religion, race, gender, friends, other influential people in our lives, and our experiences shape our views in significant ways. Once again, an awareness of these factors can help us think critically about our responses to literature—and the works themselves.

We may come from a family that is strongly connected to its ethnic roots, religious or not religious at all, closely knit or disconnected, warm and welcoming, suffocating, or cold and impersonal. Or we may not have a family at all. Our friends, too, may affect who we are, what we believe, and how we act.

We may be strongly influenced by our race, ethnic background, or gender. If we have never experienced or witnessed discrimination, we might not be able to understand its significance. If we have witnessed prejudice or had it directed against us, we know how devastating it can be. Our gender may affect the expectations others have for us, the encouragement we receive for education and career goals, marriage and family, even our involvement in sports. And it certainly influences our view of the opposite sex.

If we are deeply religious, it might be at the heart of everything we value. If we are not, our religious backgrounds may still exert a strong influence on our lives. What we do for a living, how old we are, our sexual orientation, our disabilities, or other factors may also affect how we see the world—and the literature we read.

CONNECTING THROUGH EXPERIENCE

Most of us can probably identify a person who was "always there" for us and who seemed to do the things that really mattered without being asked and who may often have been taken for granted.

Before you read the following poem, try to recall someone like that in your own life.

ROBERT HAYDEN [1913–1980]

THOSE WINTER SUNDAYS   [1962]

Sundays too my father got up early
and put his clothes on in the blueblack cold,
then with cracked hands that ached
from labor in the weekday weather made
banked fires blaze. No one ever thanked him.   5

I'd wake and hear the cold splintering, breaking.
When the rooms were warm, he'd call,
and slowly I would rise and dress,
fearing the chronic angers of that house,

Speaking indifferently to him,   10
who had driven out the cold
and polished my good shoes as well.
What did I know, what did I know
of love's austere and lonely offices?

MAKING CONNECTIONS

1. Describe the situation in the poem. Who is the speaker?
2. How does the speaker feel? Have you ever had similar feelings?
3. If you could identify a person who was "always there" for you, how does this remembrance influence your understanding of the poem?
4. What does the speaker mean by "love's austere and lonely offices"?
5. What other words, phrases, or parts of the poem had an impact on you? How so?
6. Compare this poem to Theodore Roethke's "My Papa's Waltz" (p. 274) or "Advice to My Son" on page 9.

CONNECTING THROUGH EXPERIENCE

In a world that bombards us with images from television, films, and magazines, many of us feel great pressure to look or behave in particular ways. Sometimes this pressure may even make us value our own individual strengths less favorably than what is simply more popular. See if you can recall a time when you felt pressured this way and how you reacted to that pressure.

Marge Piercy [B. 1936]

Barbie Doll   [1969]

This girlchild was born as usual
and presented dolls that did pee-pee
and miniature GE stoves and irons
and wee lipsticks the color of cherry candy.
Then in the magic of puberty, a classmate said: 5
You have a great big nose and fat legs.

She was healthy, tested intelligent,
possessed strong arms and back,
abundant sexual drive and manual dexterity.
She went to and fro apologizing.   10
Everyone saw a fat nose on thick legs.

She was advised to play coy,
exhorted to come on hearty,
exercise, diet, smile and wheedle.
Her good nature wore out   15
Like a fan belt.
So she cut off her nose and her legs
and offered them up.
In the casket displayed on satin she lay
with the undertaker's cosmetics painted on,   20
a turned-up putty nose,
dressed in a pink and white nightie.
Doesn't she look pretty? everyone said.

Consummation at last.
To every woman a happy ending.   25

MAKING CONNECTIONS

1. To what extent is your response influenced by your own experience? Could you identify with the feelings of the "girlchild" in this poem?
2. The media bombards us with images that pressure us to act or look a certain way. How does your experience with advertisements, television, movies, magazines, or newspapers influence your response to the poem?
3. Do you think a female reader is likely to respond differently to this poem than a male reader? Explain.
4. Do you think the "girlchild" is literally dead at the end of the poem? Explain.

5. What do you think "Consummation at last. / To every woman a happy ending." means?
6. What other words, phrases, or parts of the poem affected you? How so?
7. Compare this poem with "Advice to My Son" (p. 9). If Meinke's poem were called "Advice to My Daughter," do you think the advice would be the same? Explain.

BEING IN THE MOMENT

We can't get at the heart of our experience with literature by summarizing it. We might account for all that matters on the "Caution" label on the bleach bottle (p. 9) by saying, "This is a very caustic liquid and you could hurt yourself by coming in contact with it." But we couldn't get at our experience of the poem "Those Winter Sundays" (p. 13) by saying, "The poet learned to appreciate how his father expressed love for him." We read the warning label for the information we take away with us; the label seeks to inform us. Literature seeks to involve us.

A newspaper article, for example, might relate the "who, what, when, where, and why" of an event, but literature must do much more than that. It may even move us to question events in our own lives and influence us as we make our own decisions. The following newspaper account appeared in *The New York Times* the day after the racially motivated bombing of a church in Birmingham, Alabama, in 1963.

Birmingham Bomb Kills 4 Negro Girls in Church; Riots Flare; 2 Boys Slain

GUARD SUMMONED

Wallace Acts on City Plea for Help as 20 Are Injured

By CLAUDE SITTON
Special to *The New York Times*
BIRMINGHAM, Ala., Sept. 15—[1963]

A bomb severely damaged a Negro church today during Sunday school services, killing four Negro girls and setting off racial rioting and other rioting in which two Negro boys were shot to death. Fourteen Negroes were injured in the explosion. One Negro and five whites were hurt in the disorders that followed.

Some 500 National Guardsmen in battle dress stood by at armories here tonight on orders of Gov. George C. Wallace. And 300 state troopers joined the Birmingham police, Jefferson

County sheriff's deputies and other law-enforcement units in efforts to restore peace.

Governor Wallace sent the guardsmen and the troopers in response to requests from local authorities.

Sporadic gunfire sounded in Negro neighborhoods tonight, and small bands of residents roamed the streets. Aside from the patrols that cruised the city armed with riot guns, carbines and shotguns, few whites were seen.

Fire Bomb Hurled

At one point, three fires burned simultaneously in Negro sections, one at a broom and mop factory, one at a roofing company and a third in another building. An incendiary bomb was tossed into a supermarket, but the flames were extinguished swiftly. Fire marshals investigated blazes at two vacant houses to see if arson was involved.

The explosion at the 16th Street Baptist Church this morning brought hundreds of angry Negroes pouring into the streets. Some attacked the police with stones. The police dispersed them by firing shotguns over their heads. Johnny Robinson, a 16 year old Negro, was shot in the back by a policeman with a shotgun this afternoon. Officers said the victim was among a group that hurled stones at white youths driving through the area in cars flying Confederate battle flags.

When the police arrived, the youths fled, and one policeman said he had fired low but that some of the shot had struck the Robinson youth in the back.

Virgil Wade, a 13-year old Negro, was shot and killed just outside Birmingham while riding a bicycle. The Jefferson County sheriff's office said

AFTER BLAST: Rescue workers examine debris outside Negro church in Birmingham

"there apparently was no reason at all" for the killing, but indicated that it was related to the general racial disorders.

Wallace Offers Reward

Governor Wallace, at the request of city officials, offered a $5,000 reward for the arrest and conviction of the bombers.

None of the 50 bombings of Negro property here since World War II have been solved.

The four girls killed in the blast had just heard Mrs. Ellis C. Demand, their teacher, complete the Sunday School lesson for the day. The subject was "The Love That Forgives."

The blast occurred at about 10:25 A.M. (12:25 P.M. New York time).

Church members said they found the girls huddled together beneath a pile of masonry debris.

Parents of 3 Are Teachers

Both parents of each of the victims teach in the city's schools. The dead were identified by University Hospital officials as:

Cynthia Wesley, 14, the only child of Claude A. Wesley, principal of the Lewis Elementary School, and

Mrs. Wesley, a teacher there.

Denise McNair, 11, also an only child, whose parents are teachers.

Carol Robertson, 14, whose parents are teachers and whose grandmother, Mrs. Sallie Anderson, is one of the Negro members of a biracial committee established by Mayor Boutwell to deal with racial problems.

Adie Mae Collins, 14, about whom no information was immediately available.

The blast blew gaping holes through walls in the church basement. Floors of offices in the rear of the sanctuary appeared near collapse. Stairways were blocked by splintered window frames, glass, and timbers.

Chief Police Inspector W. J. Haley said the impact of the blast indicated that at least 15 sticks of dynamite might have caused it. He said the police had talked to two witnesses who reported having seen a car drive by the church, slow down and then speed away before the blast.

 FIRST RESPONSES

1. What is your response to this newspaper article?
2. Did you find yourself more engaged with the emotion or the information in this article? Explain.

Read the following poem about the same event.

DUDLEY RANDALL [B. 1914]

BALLAD OF BIRMINGHAM   [1964]

"Mother dear, may I go downtown
Instead of out to play,
And march the streets of Birmingham
In a Freedom March today?"

"No, baby, no, you may not go,   5
For the dogs are fierce and wild,
And clubs and hoses, guns and jails
Aren't good for a little child."

"But, mother, I won't be alone
Other children will go with me,   10
And march the streets of Birmingham
To make our country free."

"No, baby, no, you may not go,
For I fear those guns will fire.
But you may go to church instead   15
And sing in the children's choir."

She has combed and brushed her night-dark hair,
And bathed rose petal sweet,
And drawn white gloves on her small brown hands,
And white shoes on her feet.   20

The mother smiled to know her child
Was in that sacred place,
But that smile was the last smile
To come upon her face.

For when she heard the explosion,   25
Her eyes grew wet and wild.
She raced through the streets of Birmingham
Calling for her child.

She clawed through bits of glass and brick,
Then lifted out a shoe.   30
"O, here's the shoe my baby wore,

But, baby, where are you?"

FIRST RESPONSES

1. What is your response to this poem?
2. Did you find yourself more engaged with the emotion or the information in this poem? Explain.
3. In what way did your experience of reading the poem differ from your reading of the article?

MAKING CONNECTIONS

1. Both the newspaper article and the poem recount the bombing. What makes the poem different from the newspaper account?
2. What did you learn from the newspaper account? What did you learn from the poem? How was the *nature* of what you learned from each different?
3. To what extent is your response to "Ballad of Birmingham" influenced by your own experience?
4. How does the rhyme scheme affect your response to the poem's content? The second and fourth lines of each stanza rhyme. How does this rhyme scheme and the rhythm of the poem affect you? How might it change your response if the first and third lines rhymed instead—or as well?

PARTICIPATING, NOT SOLVING

It's essential that we are *active* participants when we read or listen to imaginative literature. But if we look for the parts of a poem before we have experienced the whole, we may shut down the emotions we need to experience it—and miss the *life* of the poem. Placing ourselves *emotionally* inside the poem, rather than examining it *rationally* from the outside, enables us to feel and sense the words and images and lets these impressions wash over us. Poetry sometimes involves an imagining that is like our dreams and reveals things to us that are not always understood in rational ways.

However, like much of the "academic" reading we do, reading poetry occurs most often in school. And school, with its right and wrong answers, has a way of making us tense and rigid (and very rational). If you had heard (studied) some of your favorite songs and music for the first time in school, you might never have loosened up enough to like them at all. Poems are not math problems—they don't have one "correct" answer. They might not even "add up." The right answer is the one that makes the most sense to you, a "sense" supported by your own imagination and the text of the poem itself. Being confused and making mistakes along the way is part of the process of finding your own right answer.

USING OUR IMAGINATIONS

When we read, the strength of our emotional involvement is based on our ability to experience scenes as if we were there. If we "surrender" ourselves, we not only imagine the details provided, we create ones that are not. We may occasionally say, or hear people say, "I liked the book better than the movie" or "I can't believe so and so was cast in that role." We probably mean, "I liked the movie of the book in my mind better than the movie on the screen" or "That actor is nothing like the character I created in my mind." Unless we complete the picture in our minds by filling in the details, we won't have a satisfying experience with literature.

Where do we get these details? Some of what we imagine is shared and comes from our cultural backgrounds. And some of what we imagine is personal and familiar and is fueled by our own experiences—the people, places, or events in our own lives. For example, it doesn't have to be summer for us to imagine the sun and heat on the beach—or winter for us to imagine snow. Through our "sense" memories, we can "recall" now what we felt and saw then. What we see in our "mind's eye" may also derive from music, television, film, other forms of media, and other things we have read.

CONNECTING THROUGH COLLABORATION

In this exercise, you may find it illuminating to share your work with a partner or a small group.

1. Take a look back through your responses and select some of your strongest reactions or impressions. For example, how did you picture the house in Robert Hayden's poem "Those Winter Sundays"? What did the mother and the little girl look like in "Ballad of Birmingham"? Think about the pictures in your mind from other poems or stories you have read.

2. Where do your pictures come from? How much of what you picture in each
    of these scenes comes from detail that the author provided and how much
    completely from your imagination?
3. Compare the pictures you've created with those of your partner or other
    classmates in your group. What is similar and what is different about their
    responses? How can you account for your differences?
4. If you wrote down details to support your own response, do those details
    adequately convey it? Do those details include specific references to the
    text?
5. Are there places where you might have clarified your response through
    a comparison (with other characters, people you know, other students'
    responses)?
6. If you did not write down supporting details or if you did not cite the text
    for support, go back to the poem(s) and see if you can.

THE WHOLE AND ITS PARTS

You've probably come across the statement "The whole is equal to the sum of
its parts." Seems to make sense, doesn't it? Well, in some areas of study it does,
but it cannot account for our response to literature. In literature and other artistic
expressions, there is a whole that is greater than the sum of its parts, a whole that
blossoms as the parts come together in our imaginations.

   We don't like our favorite music because we identify the parts and add them
up to a whole experience; we like it because we experience the sound of the instruments, the rhythms, the voices, the lyrics, all together and all at once. For all of us
that means more than the sum of the notes or words we hear, and to each of us
that means something different.

   Like music, literature cannot be reduced to its parts to account for its meaning.
But like music, there are parts, and as we become more experienced listeners or
readers—and believe that literature has something to offer us—we want to know
how those parts work together. In subsequent chapters, we will try to comprehend
the craft with which the parts are assembled.

Chapter 2

Communication
Writing a Personal Response Essay

The goal in this chapter is to develop your initial responses into an essay about literature. We begin by emphasizing the personal essay, but the habits of thinking and writing stressed in this chapter apply equally well to the argumentative essay explored in later chapters:

- Finding our writing voices;
- Developing a clear thesis statement;
- Showing what we mean through detail, illustration, and comparison;
- Citing evidence from the text.

These are core principles for writing an essay about literature. Our emphasis on analysis, argumentation, and research in Chapters 3, 4, and 5 will complement and build on our discussion in this chapter.

THE PERSONAL RESPONSE ESSAY

The purpose of a personal essay is to share our experience. Why would we want to share our experience with literature? The most compelling reason is the same one we have for sharing any other meaningful event. Why do we discuss movies, games, concerts, exhibits, or parties? Why do we chat about dates, noteworthy events in our lives, or interesting people we have met? Many of us share because we have a need to "review" or "reexperience" with others, to have them say, "I see what you mean" or "I understand why you were affected that way." We don't want advice; we want caring listeners. We share our experience, and we receive other people's understanding, affirmation, and appreciation—their participation. It's not "scoring points" or *proving* we are right.

If the voice in our writing is that of a "sharer," not a "prosecuting attorney," our essay will feel like a welcome invitation, not a summons. Readers are better able to "see" when we *show what we tell.* The strength of the readers' involvement is based on how much they care about what we share. Our voice in presenting that experience strongly influences their level of interest. For readers who accept our invitation, "I see what you mean" takes on a literal dimension. The clarity and thoughtfulness with which we write will determine how glad they are that they came.

✓ CHECKLIST: THE BASICS OF A PERSONAL ESSAY ABOUT LITERATURE

❑ Write down your impressions and whatever questions came to mind during and after your reading.

❑ What confuses you? What do you want to know more about? How can you find out?

❑ Is there anything that you don't like about the work? If so, what and why?

❑ What do you find most interesting or compelling about the work? Do any of the characters especially appeal to you or bother you? Do you find any of the events especially pleasing or disturbing? Why?

❑ Do any of the characters or events remind you of ones in your own life? Do these reminders help or interfere with your response? If so, how?

❑ Can you compare or contrast this work or its elements with another work you've read? If so, how?

❑ Are you staying anchored and "showing" what made this literature so compelling for you?

❑ What details or passages in the work or works illustrate or support your response?

Voice and Writing

We know that the tone of voice we use when speaking is likely to make an impression—that *how* we say the words out loud can convey as much meaning as the words themselves. But speech and writing are different. We can think about and revise most writing, but speech is usually spontaneous, and we don't revise what we say in normal conversation. Spontaneous speech contains lots of stops and false starts and sound fillers that would look silly in writing. Unless we say something especially memorable or inflammatory, we're confident these words won't be heard (or read) over and over again. So, what does voice have to do with writing?

Virtually all of us learned to speak before we learned to read. Throughout our lives, we've been conditioned to hear the words we read. As children, many of us said the words out loud as we read to ourselves. Even if we don't move our lips or say the words out loud now, it's difficult to read them without triggering the nerves that activate speech and help us to "subvocalize" and hear the words voiced in our minds.

So, too, readers of our writing want to hear our voices—to get a sense of who we are. As writers we are conscious of this. For example, when writing an e-mail message or a letter, our voices may change according to whom we send it, what we want, and how we want to be perceived. In a personal note to an old friend we are probably free "to be ourselves." Our friends know us, and usually we're not anxious about the impression we will make. We are confident they will recognize our voices in the words. However, when writing a letter "To the Editor," flirting with a new romantic interest, or applying for a job, our voices are likely to be quite different. We may want to convey a sense of responsibility, wisdom, wit, or whatever else we can demonstrate to make a positive impression.

What we write about may also have a strong influence on how we are heard. As you might imagine, we write with more feeling and a clearer, stronger voice about issues that move us. Here too, we write with more confidence when we are sure of our audience. Those entries that are private (and for our eyes only) are likely to be different from those we know will be read by others. Those entries written for our friends or agreeable classmates will probably be different from those written for an unknown audience.

Voice and Response to Literature

Staying Anchored in the Literature When sharing a personal response to literature, it can be very easy to see the work simply as a prompt to tell our own stories. Seeing and sharing the parallels between our own experiences and those in a work may strengthen our voices and clarify our responses, but the work on the page must remain most prominent in the presentation. To write an effective personal essay about literature, it is essential to stay "anchored" in the work and to balance references to personal experience with references to the literature itself.

Showing and Telling Most of us are best convinced when we see for ourselves. It would certainly seem risky to buy a car "sight unseen." We would probably insist on seeing it, trying it out, getting the "feel" of it before we decided to buy. When we talk with friends about a concert, game, or party, we probably would not settle for "It was great." Again, we would like to get the "feel" of it, to hear the details, to imagine ourselves there, to share the experience.

As readers, we have a similar need. We are not likely to settle for being told an issue is compelling or trivial; an event exciting, suspenseful, or sad; a character fascinating, dull, or manipulative. We want to be moved by the issue, to be present at the event, to know the character for ourselves. Writers' voices are believable when we experience characters and events with them—when the conclusions ("exciting," "sad," "dull") are ours—when we are shown, not simply told.

CONNECTING THROUGH EXPERIENCE

If you have ever been called a derogatory name because of your race, ethnic background, gender, or other factor, you know how disturbing that experience can be. If you have ever been in this position or witnessed it happening to someone else, try to recall your reaction. If you've never been in this position, try to imagine how it might make someone feel.

COUNTEE CULLEN [1903–1946]

INCIDENT   [1925]

Once riding in old Baltimore,
  Heart-filled, head-filled with glee,
I saw a Baltimorean
  Keep looking straight at me.

Now I was eight and very small,   5
  And he was no whit bigger,
And so I smiled, but he poked out
  His tongue, and called me, "Nigger."

I saw the whole of Baltimore
  From May until December: 10
Of all the things that happened there
  That's all that I remember.

MAKING CONNECTIONS

1. Can you describe an event in your life that made such a lasting impression on you?
2. If you have experienced or observed an event like the one described in "Incident," how does this influence your response? If you have not experienced or observed an event like this, how does this affect your response to the poem?
3. If the speaker were describing a racist incident he experienced as an adult, how do you think the poem would be different? Why does the speaker say, "That's all that I remember"?
4. In what way does the title of the poem fit the poem's content?
5. How does the rhyme scheme of the poem affect your response to the poem's content?

The entry that follows was written in response to Countee Cullen's "Incident." If you haven't read the poem and written your own response, you might want to do that before you read the entry below.

Janice's Response:

I have not had any experiences as powerful as what that child

experienced. I do remember being picked on by a bully when my friends and I

were walking to school and hearing him say gross things about Catholics (we

were in uniforms!), but I remember thinking he was the idiot, not us. I thought

this was a powerful little poem. I didn't see the 'n' word coming. It begins so

simply with an upbeat tone, "Heart-filled, head-filled with glee," and the sing-song quality of it remains even when the poem turns so serious. I think the rhythmic quality it has helps to remind us that this is happening to a small child. The line "That's all that I remember" I think refers more to that being all that was really memorable about the Baltimore experience, or even that that is the strongest memory. The title is perfect because that's basically what Baltimore is boiled down to in this child's eyes, "the incident" and not much more.

MAKING CONNECTIONS

1. How was Janice's response influenced by her experience?
2. Consider your response to the poem. How does it compare to hers?
3. To what extent has she stayed anchored in the poem?
4. To what extent has she "shown" what she's told?
5. How would you describe the voice in Countee Cullen's poem "Incident"? What factors make it effective?
6. In what way is "showing" a factor in both the poem and the response to it? What scenes, details, words, or phrases had the biggest impact on you?

WRITING TO DESCRIBE

You are likely to write with more feeling and a clearer, stronger voice about issues that move you, so your strongest response or impression may provide the best topic to write about; but selecting relevant details to support that response is equally important. You are describing not only how you felt, but what prompted you to feel that way.

An effective description is much more than a summary. A summary has no voice. An engaging description has our voice, impressions, and feelings, as well as relevant details. When someone asks us to describe a person we know very well (a friend, lover, spouse, parent) or a place with which we are very familiar (our home, bedroom, car, or a favorite hangout), we're not likely to respond with factual information alone. A summary of facts (dimensions, features, or colors) will not adequately convey what we feel is most important. Those details support our impression but do not replace it. Important details, however, do help the reader picture what we are describing and clarify *why* we feel the way we do.

Choosing Details

Which details we choose when describing and supporting our responses can make a big difference. Writing, "Tanya makes me feel very comfortable" by itself will not be as clear as combining it with examples or details of what she does that show it is true: "She's very soft-spoken, smiles a lot, and is a good listener." We would not include every detail ("She wants to graduate next year") unless it's relevant ("so she knows the kind of pressure I'm feeling"). Including details not important to our impression will not support, and may even dilute, the impact of ones that are.

Choosing Details from Literature

So, too, the details we choose to clarify and support our responses to literature have an important impact on readers. For example, to describe the young man's disillusionment in "Incident" and not make reference to the name he's called omits a crucial detail in this painful memory. Those details, those parts, capture the whole of a work in miniature.

CONNECTING THROUGH EXPERIENCE

From our perspectives as adults, many of the problems of childhood may seem relatively unimportant. However, what may seem unimportant to us now may have affected us very differently when we were growing up.

Can you remember what it was like to be an eleven-year-old? See if you can recall an event that you found especially humiliating or embarrassing at that age. Try to remember what you were feeling and what you found especially difficult about the experience.

▪ SANDRA CISNEROS [B. 1954]

ELEVEN   [1983]

What they don't understand about birthdays and what they never tell you is that when you're eleven, you're also ten, and nine, and eight, and seven, and six, and five, and four, and three, and two, and one. And when you wake up on your eleventh birthday you expect to feel eleven, but you don't. You open your eyes and everything's just like yesterday, only it's today. And you don't feel eleven at all. You feel like you're still ten. And you are—underneath the year that makes you eleven.

Like some days you might say something stupid, and that's the part of you that's still ten. Or maybe some days you might need to sit on your mama's lap because you're scared, and that's the part of you that's five. And maybe one day when you're all grown up maybe you will need to cry like if you're three, and that's okay. That's what I tell Mama when she's sad and needs to cry. Maybe she's feeling three.

Because the way you grow old is kind of like an onion or like the rings inside a tree trunk or like my little wooden dolls that fit one inside the other, each year inside the next one. That's how being eleven years old is.

You don't feel eleven. Not right away. It takes a few days, weeks even, sometimes even months before you say Eleven when they ask you. And you don't feel smart eleven, not until you're almost twelve. That's the way it is.

5   Only today I wish I didn't have only eleven years rattling inside me like pennies in a tin Band-Aid box. Today I wish I was one hundred and two instead of eleven because if I was one hundred and two I'd have known what to say when Mrs. Price put the red sweater on my desk. I would've known how to tell her it wasn't mine instead of just sitting there with that look on my face and nothing coming out of my mouth.

"Whose is this?" Mrs. Price says, and she holds the red sweater up in the air for all the class to see. "Whose? It's been sitting in the coatroom for a month."

"Not mine," says everybody. "Not me."

"It has to belong to somebody," Mrs. Price keeps saying, but nobody can remember. It's an ugly sweater with red plastic buttons and a collar and sleeves all stretched out like you could use them for a jump rope. It's maybe a thousand years old and even if it belonged to me I wouldn't say so.

Maybe because I'm skinny, maybe because she doesn't like me, that stupid Sylvia Saldivar says, "I think it belongs to Rachel." An ugly sweater like that, all raggedy and old, but Mrs. Price believes her; Mrs. Price takes the sweater and puts it right on my desk, but when I open my mouth nothing comes out.

10 "That's not, I don't, you're not … Not mine," I finally say in a little voice that was maybe me when I was four.

"Of course it's yours," Mrs. Price says. "I remember you wearing it once." Because she's older and the teacher, she's right and I'm not.

Not mine, not mine, not mine, but Mrs. Price is already turning to page thirty-two and math problem number four. I don't know why but all of a sudden I'm feeling sick inside, like the part of me that's three wants to come out of my eyes, only I squeeze them shut tight and bite down on my teeth real hard and try to remember today I am eleven, eleven.

Mama is making a cake for me for tonight, and when Papa comes home everybody will sing Happy birthday, happy birthday to you.

But when the sick feeling goes away and I open my eyes, the red sweater's still sitting there like a big red mountain. I move the red sweater to the corner of my desk with my ruler. I move my pencil and books and eraser as far from it as possible. I even move my chair a little to the right. Not mine, not mine, not mine.

15 In my head I'm thinking how long till lunchtime, how long till I can take the red sweater and throw it over the schoolyard fence, or leave it hanging on a parking meter, or bunch it up into a little ball and toss it in the alley. Except when math period ends Mrs. Price says loud and in front of everybody, "Now, Rachel, that's enough," because she sees I've shoved the red sweater to the tippy-tip corner of my desk and it's hanging all over the edge like a waterfall, but I don't care.

"Rachel," Mrs. Price says. She says it like she's getting mad. "You put that sweater on right now and no more nonsense."

"But it's not—"

"Now!" Mrs. Price says.

This is when I wish I wasn't eleven, because all the years inside of me—ten, nine, eight, seven, six, five, four, three, two, and one—are pushing at the back of my eyes when I put one arm through one sleeve of the sweater that smells like cottage cheese, and then the other arm through the other and stand there with my arms apart like if the sweater hurts me and it does, all itchy and full of germs that aren't even mine.

20 That's when everything I've been holding in since this morning, since when Mrs. Price put the sweater on my desk, finally lets go, and all of a sudden I'm crying in front of everybody. I wish I was invisible but I'm not. I'm eleven and it's my birthday today and I'm crying like I'm three in front of everybody. I put my head down on the desk and bury my face in my stupid clown-sweater arms. My face all hot and spit coming out of my mouth because I can't stop the little animal noises

from coming out of me, until there aren't any more tears left in my eyes, and it's just my body shaking like when you have the hiccups, and my whole head hurts like when you drink milk too fast.

But the worst part is right before the bell rings for lunch. That stupid Phyllis Lopez, who is even dumber than Sylvia Saldivar, says she remembers the red sweater is hers! I take it off right away and give it to her, only Mrs. Price pretends like everything's okay.

Today I'm eleven. There's a cake Mama's making for tonight, and when Papa comes home from work we'll eat it. There'll be candles and presents and everybody will sing Happy birthday, happy birthday to you, Rachel, only it's too late.

I'm eleven today. I'm eleven, ten, nine, eight, seven, six, five, four, three, two, and one, but I wish I was one hundred and two. I wish I was anything but eleven, because I want today to be far away already, far away like a runaway balloon, like a tiny o in the sky, so tiny-tiny you have to close your eyes to see it.

MAKING CONNECTIONS

1. If you could recall a childhood event that you found humiliating or embarrassing, how did that memory influence your response to this story?
2. How does the voice of the narrator affect your response?
3. What descriptions and what details in the story had an impact on you? How so?
4. If you find the voice of the story convincing, what features of the writing seem to make it effective? To what extent does the story "show" what is told?

CONNECTING: COLLABORATION AND PEER REVIEW

In this exercise, you may find it illuminating to share your work with a partner or a small group.

How do you respond when someone asks you to describe a work of literature that you've read? To what extent does a summary convey what you've experienced—what you feel is most important? To what extent does it seem inadequate? The following exercise may provide some insight:

a. Summarize Sandra Cisneros's "Eleven."
b. Write down your strongest impressions of the work. Write down the details—from your experience and the literature—that support or clarify those impressions.
c. What is the difference between the summary and your details and impressions?
d. Rewrite your summary with your details and impressions.
e. Compare your summary of the work with that of your partner or others in your group.

WRITING TO COMPARE

How many times are we asked to describe something, and our first reaction is "Well, it's like..." or "It reminds me of..."? In fact, it seems hard to describe anything without resorting to comparison somewhere along the way. When we think about our friends, we may compare and contrast them consciously and unconsciously with each other. When we take part in important events, we may compare them to similar events in our past: "This reminds me of the wedding I went to last year" or "My brother's graduation was done very differently."

Comparing and contrasting are also natural ways to describe our responses to literature. We might compare ourselves or others with literary characters, or our own experiences with those in a work of literature. We may compare the choices made by various characters with the choices we would make. We might even be reminded of previous reading experiences and compare the work—or elements of the work—we are reading with one we've read before. We might even compare a work of literature with a work from another form of art, like painting. A good example of both process and product is the student sample of Barbara Pfister (see p. 659), who compares van Gogh's *Starry Night* with Anne Sexton's poem about the painting.

Comparing and Contrasting Using a Venn Diagram

Sometimes it's easier to generate and organize ideas when we can see them and their relationships to one another side by side in a whole picture. One effective technique for generating and organizing ideas when writing to compare is to create a Venn diagram (Figure 2.1). This technique works equally well when comparing personal experience with the work (Figure 2.2) or comparing works or characters with one another (Figure 2.3). The three poems used as examples, "Those Winter Sundays," "Zimmer in Grade School," and "Barbie Doll," are in Chapter 1.

1. Draw two interconnecting circles. Identify each circle.
2. In the common, interconnecting area, write down what the subjects have in common.
3. In the separate sections, write down what is different.

Figure 2.1 *Venn Diagram*

"Those Winter Sundays"   A Reader's Experience

Poet's regrets

No one ever
thanked him.

Polished son's shoes

"Cracked hands"

"Blueblack cold"

Labored in the
weekday weather

Fathers both
got up early

"Chronic angers of
that house"

Don't talk
about feelings

Realized late in
life their value

Lack of
communication

I never thanked
him but I can now.

Dad's heart
attack

Our trip

Parent's visit

Coupons

A better
relationship

Figure 2.2 *Comparing Experience with Literature*

"Zimmer in
Grade School"   "Barbie
Doll"

He wondered why
he had been born.

He feared
everything.

After all these years
he still feels that
it is always known
that he is the one
who screws up.

No one seemed
to care about them.

They hated who
they were.

They are bullied
by everyone.

They don't appreciate
who they are.

She went to and
fro apologizing.

Her good nature
wore out.

She made herself
into what
they wanted.

Figure 2.3 *Comparing Two Works of Literature*

CONNECTING THROUGH EXPERIENCE

We would all probably like some things in our lives to be different. Before you read the essay that follows, see if you can think of something in your life that you wish were different. If that "something" were different, how might it change your life? Would everything be better? Might anything be worse?

ANNA QUINDLEN [B. 1953]

MOTHERS   [1988]

The two women are sitting at a corner table in the restaurant, their shopping bags wedged between their chairs and the wall: Lord & Taylor, Bloomingdale's, something from Ann Taylor for the younger one. She is wearing a bright silk shirt, some good gold jewelry; her hair is on the long side, her makeup faint. The older woman is wearing a suit, a string of pearls, a diamond solitaire, and a narrow band. They lean across the table. I imagine the conversation: Will the new blazer go with the old skirt? Is the dress really right for an afternoon wedding? How is Daddy? How is his ulcer? Won't he slow down just a little bit?

It seems that I see mothers and daughters everywhere, gliding through what I think of as the adult rituals of parent and child. My mother died when I was nineteen. For a long time, it was all you needed to know about me, a kind of vest pocket description of my emotional complexion: "Meet you in the lobby in ten minutes—I have long-brown hair, am on the short side, have on a red coat, and my mother died when I was nineteen."

That's not true anymore. When I see a mother and a daughter having lunch in a restaurant, shopping at Saks, talking together on the crosstown bus, I no longer want to murder them. I just stare a little more than is polite, hoping that I can combine my observations with a half-remembered conversation, some anecdotes, a few old dresses, a photograph or two, and re-create, like an archaeologist of the soul, a relationship that will never exist. Of course, the question is whether it would have ever existed at all. One day at lunch I told two of my closest friends that what I minded most about not having a mother was the absence of that grown-up woman-to-woman relationship that was impossible as a child or adolescent, and that my friends were having with their mothers now. They both looked at me as though my teeth had turned purple. I didn't need to ask why; I've heard so many times about the futility of such relationships, about women with business suits and briefcases reduced to whining children by their mothers' offhand comment about a man, or a dress, or a homemade dinner.

I accept the fact that mothers and daughters probably always see each other across a chasm of rivalries. But I forget all those things when one of my friends is down with the flu and her mother arrives with an overnight bag to manage her household and feed her soup.

5   So now, at the center of my heart there is a fantasy, and a mystery. The fantasy is small, and silly: a shopping trip, perhaps a pair of shoes, a walk, a talk, lunch in a good restaurant, which my mother assumes is the kind of place I eat at all the time. I pick up the check. We take a cab to the train. She reminds me of somebody's

birthday. I invite her and my father to dinner. The mystery is whether the fantasy has within it a nugget of fact. Would I really have wanted her to take care of the wedding arrangements, or come and stay for a week after the children were born? Would we have talked on the telephone about this and that? Would she have saved my clippings in a scrapbook? Or would she have meddled in my affairs, volunteering opinions I didn't want to hear about things that were none of her business, criticizing my clothes and my children? Worse still, would we have been strangers with nothing to say to each other? Is all the good I remember about us simply wishful thinking? Is all the bad self-protection? Perhaps it is at best difficult, at worst impossible for children and parents to be adults together. But I would love to be able to know that.

Sometimes I feel like one of those people searching, searching for the mother who gave them up for adoption. I have some small questions for her and I want the answers: How did she get her children to sleep through the night? What was her first labor like? Was there olive oil in her tomato sauce? Was she happy? If she had it to do over again, would she? When we pulled her wedding dress out of the box the other day to see if my sister might wear it, we were shocked to find how tiny it was. "My God," I said, "did you starve yourself to get into this thing?" But there was no one there. And if she had been there, perhaps I would not have asked in the first place. I suspect that we would have been friends, but I don't really know. I was simply a little too young at nineteen to understand the woman inside the mother.

I occasionally pass by one of those restaurant tables and I hear the bickering about nothing: You did so, I did not, don't tell me what you did or didn't do, oh, leave me alone. And I think that my fantasies are better than any reality could be. Then again, maybe not.

CONNECTING THROUGH EXPERIENCE

The desire for approval can be a very strong incentive when making important decisions. Making a decision that meets with the disapproval of our parents or others we respect can be difficult and emotionally painful—even if we believe that we've made the right choice. We may even have strong ethical reasons for taking a position, yet feel reluctant to disappoint those with whom we have emotional ties.

Try to recall an event in your life when the pressure of approval was a major factor in an important decision. Try to remember what you were feeling at the time.

 ## LANGSTON HUGHES [1902–1967]

SALVATION   [1940]

I was saved from sin when I was going on thirteen. But not really saved. It happened like this. There was a big revival at my Auntie Reed's church. Every night for weeks there had been much preaching, singing, praying, and shouting, and some very hardened sinners had been brought to Christ, and the membership of the church had grown by leaps and bounds. Then just before the revival ended, they held a special meeting for children, "to bring the young lambs to the fold."

My aunt spoke of it for days ahead. That night I was escorted to the front row and placed on the mourners' bench with all the other young sinners, who had not yet been brought to Jesus.

My aunt told me that when you were saved you saw a light, and something happened to you inside! And Jesus came into your life! And God was with you from then on! She said you could see and hear and feel Jesus in your soul. I believed her. I had heard a great many old people say the same thing and it seemed to me they ought to know. So I sat there calmly in the hot, crowded church, waiting for Jesus to come to me.

The preacher preached a wonderful rhythmical sermon, all moans and shouts and lonely cries and dire pictures of hell, and then he sang a song about the ninety and nine safe in the fold, but one little lamb was left out in the cold. Then he said: "Won't you come? Won't you come to Jesus? Young lambs, won't you come?" And he held out his arms to all us young sinners there on the mourners' bench. And the little girls cried. And some of them jumped up and went to Jesus right away. But most of us just sat there.

A great many old people came and knelt around us and prayed, old women with jet-black faces and braided hair, old men with work-gnarled hands. And the church sang a song about the lower lights are burning, some poor sinners to be saved. And the whole building rocked with prayer and song.

5   Still I kept waiting to *see* Jesus.

Finally all the young people had gone to the altar and were saved, but one boy and me. He was a rounder's son named Westley. Westley and I were surrounded by sisters and deacons praying. It was very hot in the church, and getting late now. Finally Westley said to me in a whisper: "God damn! I'm tired o' sitting here. Let's get up and be saved." So he got up and was saved.

Then I was left all alone on the mourners' bench. My aunt came and knelt at my knees and cried while prayers and song swirled all around me in the little church. The whole congregation prayed for me alone, in a mighty wail of moans and voices. And I kept waiting serenely for Jesus, waiting, waiting—but he didn't come. I wanted to see him, but nothing happened to me. Nothing! I wanted something to happen to me, but nothing happened.

I heard the songs and the minister saying: "Why don't you come? My dear child, why don't you come to Jesus? Jesus is waiting for you. He wants you. Why don't you come? Sister Reed, what is this child's name?"

"Langston," my aunt sobbed.

10   "Langston, why don't you come? Why don't you come and be saved? Oh, Lamb of God! Why don't you come?"

Now it was really getting late. I began to be ashamed of myself, holding everything up so long. I began to wonder what God thought about Westley, who certainly hadn't seen Jesus either, but who was now sitting proudly on the platform, swinging his knickerbockered legs and grinning down at me, surrounded by deacons and old women on their knees praying. God had not struck Westley dead for taking his name in vain or for lying in the temple. So I decided that maybe to save further trouble, I'd better lie, too, and say, that Jesus had come, and get up and be saved.

So I got up.

Suddenly the whole room broke into a sea of shouting, as they saw me rise. Waves of rejoicing swept the place. Women leaped in the air. My aunt threw her arms around me. The minister took me by the hand and led me to the platform.

When things quieted down, in a hushed silence, punctuated by a few ecstatic "Amens," all the new young lambs were blessed in the name of God. Then joyous singing filled the room.

15   That night, for the last time in my life but one—for I was a big boy twelve years old—I cried. I cried, in bed alone, and couldn't stop. I buried my head under the quilts, but my aunt heard me. She woke up and told my uncle I was crying because the Holy Ghost had come into my life, and because I had seen Jesus. But I was really crying because I couldn't bear to tell her that I had lied, that I had deceived everybody in the church, that I hadn't seen Jesus and that now I didn't believe there was a Jesus any more, since he didn't come to help me.

MAKING CONNECTIONS

1.   To what extent is your response to "Mothers" or "Salvation" influenced by your own experience?
2.   In "Mothers," what does Quindlen mean when she says, "My mother died when I was nineteen. For a long time, it was all you needed to know about me"? How are you affected by the description of her imagined relationship?
3.   In "Salvation," how are you affected by the description of the pressure on young Langston as the only unsaved "lamb"? Do you think young Langston made the right decision? Why?
4.   How does the voice of the narrator in each essay affect your response? In what way do the narrators "show" what they tell?
5.   What other passages in these essays affect you the most? What details help to make them effective?
6.   Can you compare your experience with that in "Mothers" or "Salvation"? Can you compare "Incident," "Eleven," "Mothers," or "Salvation" with each other? For example, "Eleven" and "Salvation" both describe a child in an embarrassing situation. How are they alike and how are they different?

CONNECTING: COLLABORATION AND PEER REVIEW

In this exercise, you may find it illuminating to share your work with a partner or a small group.

1.   If you are jotting down responses to your reading, take a look back through your entries. How many times did a work remind you of someone or something in your own life? If none did at the time you wrote your response, are there entries that bring a comparison to mind now?
2.   In a group or with a partner, choose two works from this chapter ("Incident," "Eleven," "Mothers," or "Salvation"), and construct a Venn diagram to compare them. How are they alike? How are they different?
3.   Compare your diagrams with those of other groups or partners.

Possible Worlds

The frequent comments and questions about "identifying with characters" or "connecting your experience" in the first two chapters of this text are not suggesting that it is necessary to have had similar experiences or to identify with characters to have a fulfilling experience with literature. In fact, connecting the characters and events in a work too closely with our own lives—so closely that we can't distinguish one from the other—can interfere with our ability to understand and appreciate the work.

When taking us where we have never been, literature has the power to increase the breadth and depth of our vision—to help us learn and grow in the way that all new experiences can. It is not necessary for us to have been embarrassed in school as an eleven-year-old, to have lost our mothers, or to have feigned being "saved" at a church service to be moved by "Eleven," "Mothers," or "Salvation."

The journal responses of Christine Leibowitz below to "Salvation" and "Mothers" illustrate this point. Here is Christine's response to Langston Hughes's "Salvation":

> The essay "Salvation" is wonderful! I remember being saved in ninth grade. There was this boy who went to my church and I thought that he parted the seas, so to speak. One day he invited me to go to Sunday Youth Group with him. I figured that if Shawn went then it couldn't be that bad. And, well, as my parents said, "He was such a nice boy!" So I went.
>
> This essay reminded me of that period of my life. It was funny, as was my own mission. When Langston was kneeling at the altar and everyone was waiting for him to be saved, I thought about how we used to close our eyes in church and the pastor would ask us to raise our hands if we sought salvation and were ready to give our lives to Christ. (Should I raise my hand and get it over with?) It was always a dilemma.
>
> I think Jesus forgave Langston. In fact, I believe that his true salvation was achieved when he lay in bed that night crying for not being honest. He was probably the only lamb of lambs that was truly saved on that blessed day.

Obviously, Christine's ability to identify with young Langston brought this scene vividly to life for her and intensified her reading experience, but this does not mean that she wouldn't have appreciated the essay otherwise.

Here is Christine's response to Anna Quindlen's "Mothers":

> I cannot identify with the speaker of this essay because my mother is alive and well. We share all of the things that the speaker fantasizes about. We laugh together, shop together, share stories and ideas, and give each other advice and criticism. I have a wonderful and warm relationship with my mother. She is the first person I call when something good happens in my life and when I need a shoulder to cry on.

The speaker of the essay lost her mother at age nineteen. She dreams about sharing things with her mother that I would normally take for granted. She speaks of meeting someone in the lobby and describes herself as "on the short side, have on a red coat, and my mother died when I was nineteen." That is how I think I would describe myself if I had outlived my mother. It is as if she is somehow not a complete person. She calls it "a vest pocket description of [her] emotional complexion." And for awhile "all you needed to know about [her]."

The speaker tries to rationalize that "mothers and daughters probably always see each other across a chasm of rivalries," but I think that she may be trying to compensate for her loss. I am enriched and blessed by my relationship with my mother and what happens in our lives, the love that we share transcends all.

I am so thankful to be able to read this essay knowing that my mother is just a phone call away and waiting to share with me a little bit of everything or a whole bunch of nothing.

In this response, unlike her response to "Salvation," Christine cannot identify with the plight of the speaker in "Mothers" because her own mother is still alive. However, rather than interfering with her response, her different circumstances make Quindlen's essay rich in meaning for her. The essay has taken her to a possible world. Ultimately, it is our intelligence and sensitivity to the human condition, not simply a shared experience, that help us imagine the possibilities and become engaged with the work.

CONNECTING: COLLABORATION AND PEER REVIEW

In this exercise, you may find it illuminating to share your work with a partner or a small group.

1. Take a look back through your responses and select some of your strongest reactions or impressions.
2. If you wrote down details to support your response, do those details adequately convey it? Do those details include specific references to the text?
3. Are there places where you might have clarified your response through a comparison (with other works, characters, people you know, other students' responses)?
4. If you did not write down supporting details or if you did not cite the text for support, go back to the work and see if you can.
5. Exchange your response with a partner or someone else in your group. Discuss the details and comparisons in these responses and their effectiveness.

FROM FIRST RESPONSE TO FINAL DRAFT

In the section that follows, we look at Dierdre Curran's response to Robert Hayden's "Those Winter Sundays" and follow its progress through to the final draft of her essay. Although her goal is to write a personal essay about a poem, the strategies she illustrates work equally well when planning and generating ideas for any essay.

The purpose of the strategies that follow is not to move you step-by-step through a rigid sequence. Whether you are composing a personal or argumentative essay, writing is a continuous process of moving forward and returning and moving forward again. The best way to organize an essay may occur to you early or late in the process. You may get some of your best new ideas just when you thought you were almost finished. Try to let your ideas flow freely throughout the process. Don't close out ideas by imposing a structure that will keep you from expressing what you would really like to say. Reading literature encourages a variety of responses—and perhaps more questions than answers. Generate and explore as many of your questions and ideas as possible before you decide on one direction. Free your ideas and follow them where they go. You may be surprised by what you find on your journey.

Having said that, it can be very helpful to have a plan or a process in mind that helps you to organize your ideas in developmental stages. Through the rest of this chapter—and in subsequent chapters—you will be guided through a sequential process of Using Your First Response (choosing a topic, brainstorming, freewriting, asking questions, listing, clustering, collaborating), Composing a Draft (developing a thesis statement and turning your ideas into effective paragraphs), and Revising the Essay (checking your organization and unity, support, voice, and clarity; checking for correct formatting, citation, documentation; and editing and proofreading your work effectively). And finally, having followed a student's essay through this process, you'll be presented with the product of this process—a student's final essay.

The Importance of Revision

It may seem odd to bring up revising before you generate ideas for your essay, but if you know in advance that your writing process will include revision and more than one draft, you may be more creative and explore options that you might not otherwise consider. Everything you write is temporary—until you are satisfied that you've "got it just right."

Revision is much more than proofreading. It is "re-visioning," rethinking, and rewriting. It means looking at a draft of your essay and determining how the parts you have already constructed work together to form a coherent, convincing whole. It may involve changing the structure of the essay—adding, deleting, combining, or changing the order of paragraphs and sentences. It may mean eliminating redundancies and digressions or adding details and textual support. *Most professional writers think of this part of the writing process as most important.* Many students, however, mistake revision for sentence-level editing or proofreading (e.g., correcting punctuation, sentence structure, spelling, confused words, formatting)—a process that should occur after your revision and rewriting is complete.

Using First or Third Person in Formal Essays

There is much disagreement in the academic world about the use of the first-person pronoun ("I") in formal essay writing. The student sample that follows is written in the first person. Given the nature of the personal response essay, first person is a natural fit. On the other hand, the student samples of the argumentative essay in Chapter 4 and the research essay in Chapter 5 are written in the third person—a form that works especially well with argumentation and research.

Many instructors, however, require that all essays be written in the third person. It is essential, therefore, that you find out the individual requirements of your instructor and your course before you submit your essay.

STEP 1: USING YOUR FIRST RESPONSE

If you've been keeping a journal or writing other initial responses to your reading, chances are you have already generated some good ideas for writing an essay. After you read your entries and add any comments based on rereading and class discussion, go back and underline or circle what you believe are your strongest impressions.

Let's look at Dierdre Curran's initial response to "Those Winter Sundays" (p. 13) as an example:

> I love this poem because I am totally able to relate. <u>It brought so many things back to me about my relationship with my father—some painful, some happy</u>. I grew up in a similar situation, and although there was no love verbally communicated by my gruff father, he always did little things, like getting up early to turn up the heat, digging my car out of the snow and warming it up while I dressed. The day we read this poem in class I got home to find an envelope from my still gruff, uncommunicative father (age has softened him a little). There was no card or letter, just a bunch of coupons, mostly for stuff for my cat, which is his way of sending love. Coupons. It was very nice, and I zipped off a letter of appreciation. I'm glad I still have the opportunity.

Choosing a Topic

When making a choice or choices about which idea(s) to pursue, you may want to answer two essential questions:

1. Do I care enough about this idea to pursue it further?
   You will write with your strongest voice about issues that have the most meaning to you and about which you believe you want to say something that is important for both you and your readers.

2. Is it "do-able"?

   Can you write an essay about this? No matter how compelling your idea is, you won't be able to write an essay about it unless you have enough to say, or you can support it from both your experience and the work (of literature). Remember, if the point you are trying to make is obvious, abstract, or very general, it may be impossible to develop it into an appealing essay in a reasonable amount of time.

Brainstorming

Dierdre chose the second sentence (underlined on p. 38) from her entry as the core of her response. It's obvious that she cares about this idea very much. And she feels confident that there are many lines in the poem that she can use to support the comparison between her relationship and that in the poem. But a look at her journal entry tells us that she has not identified many of them yet. Still, her essay seems very "do-able," and her journal entry has given her a start.

Dierdre has already followed her core idea with some specific support from her own experience, but she has not provided much specific support from the text of the poem itself. So if she wants to generate more ideas or extend or expand her support, there are a few other techniques she might use.

Directed Freewriting   If you don't have a journal entry or other initial response, or if you want to generate more ideas, directed freewriting can be a useful technique. The best time to do this exercise is immediately after you finish reading, while your thoughts and impressions are still fresh. The intention of this exercise is to release what you know without blocking it with pauses for reflection, punctuation, or editing.

1. Write down the name of the topic, phrase, or sentence you want to focus on.

2. Write down (nonstop) everything that comes into your mind for five or ten minutes. If punctuation or capitalization gets in the way, don't even use it.

3. Read what you have written and choose (circle or underline) your strongest responses. Here is Dierdre Curran's directed freewriting response to Robert Hayden's "Those Winter Sundays" in response to the sentence from her journal entry: It brought so many things back to me about my relationship with my father—some painful, some happy.

   My father does not express his love for us by telling us. He does things instead. Growing up was really hard. I wanted him to tell me he loved me. It has taken me years to believe that he really does, even though he never says it. Did the poet ever get to tell his own father about these things? I'll bet not. He sounds as if he regrets not understanding that his father was really expressing love in the things he did. I really like Robert Hayden's descriptions of how the house felt. My house felt the same way. Why did he have to be so cold? But not everything was as bleak as it seems now. There were good times, but it just feels not. My father is old now and had a heart attack and only now are we beginning to say what I wish we had said before. I love him so much. I only hope I will have the chance to express that before he's gone.

Dierdre's freewriting adds more detail to her earlier statement, and she was able to generate some very compelling ideas about her relationship with her father and her connections to the poem itself. By asking questions about and listing details of the selected statements, she may uncover even more specific material.

Asking Questions   Having already narrowed her choice to a particular idea, she might ask as many questions (and subquestions) as she can about some aspect of that idea. Of course, it's useful to ask only questions that will provide new information (and cannot be answered yes or no).

1. Choose an important word, phrase, or sentence from your journal entry, and write down as many related questions as you can.

2. Choose and answer the questions that will add to or clarify your support.

    <u>My father does not express his love for us by telling us.</u>

    How often do we talk?

    What do we talk about?

    How does he express his love?

    Where is the similarity in the poem?

    <u>I'm glad I still have the opportunity to express appreciation.</u>

    Did the speaker in the poem ever get to tell his father what he felt?

    How do I/will I express my appreciation?

    <u>I really like Robert Hayden's description of the house.</u>

    What language does he use?

    Why is it effective?

3. Follow up with detailed answers to these questions, and you will provide additional specific support for the original core idea.

Listing   By choosing key words or sentences from your response, and then listing as many related details and examples as you can below them, you can build the specific support you will need to justify your understanding of the literature.

1. Choose key words or sentences from your response (the name of a character, an event, an element of literature, etc.).

2. List as many related details under each as you can. By choosing some key phrases that apply to her identification with the speaker in the poem, Dierdre is able to uncover other specific details.

    <u>My father does things for me instead.</u>

    He got up early and turned up the heat.

Dug my car out of the snow and warmed it up.

Sent me envelopes with coupons.

He comforted me when my dog died.

He sometimes laughed and joked around with me and my sister.

He recently sent me the first letter I have ever received from him.

I really like Robert Hayden's description of the house in the poem.

I could feel the pain of the "blueblack cold."

I could feel and hear the cold "splintering, breaking."

Remembering getting dressed quickly in the cold.

Imagining the rooms getting warm.

The house was like their relationship.

Semantic Mapping, or Clustering

For some of us, it is easier to follow directions by looking at a map than following directions in a printed sequence. Sometimes we need to see the whole picture. When writing in response to literature, too, sometimes we can understand, see relationships, and generate and extend ideas better spatially than linearly. A technique called **semantic mapping** or **clustering** makes it possible to see ideas and relationships this way (see Figure 2.4). This is how it works:

1. Write down a question or statement in the center of a blank page in your journal or on another piece of paper. Put a circle around it.

2. Draw lines out from the circle, and write a statement or idea related to that central idea.

3. Continue to draw lines out from the central circle and the subcircles. Those from the central circle are subsets of ideas; each circle farther along each line is a level of greater specificity.

Mix and Match

The strategies above are not an end in themselves but simply the means to generate and extend ideas, ask questions, and make choices. They should be used in whatever way they work for you. There is no one "right" way to ask questions or list ideas. If a particular method is working, keep using it. If it is not, try something else. For example, you may find that only the first few circles in a mapping exercise are useful. In order to generate details quickly, you may prefer to list them instead of putting circles around them. So you might want to start with a map, get a few ideas, and then make a list to get at the details. Along with keeping a journal, you may want to freewrite as well. Different ways, combinations, and paces of writing may bring different ideas. What matters in this "prewriting" stage is that you feel free to explore in your most productive way.

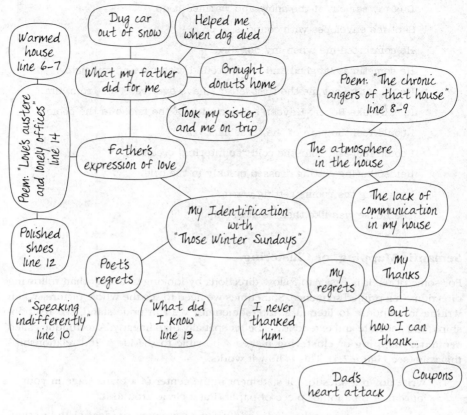

Figure 2.4 *Dierdre's Semantic Map*

Generating Ideas Through Collaboration

Sharing Responses If you are keeping a reading log or blog, you may find it useful to exchange your writing with a classmate or small group. In addition to sharing responses to the work of literature, you might comment on each other's entries. Sharing like this gives you an audience and immediate feedback.

Combining Questions After generating your own questions about a work of literature, it might be worthwhile to share these questions in pairs or with a small group. Pool everyone's questions, discuss their strengths and weaknesses, and narrow the list down to the strongest ones.

Connecting Cluster Circles You might work collaboratively on a semantic map or cluster sheet. In response to a question, topic, or character, each individual in a small group might take responsibility for a line of circles extending from the middle. Then the group might draw lines connecting one line of circles to another line of circles. By discussing these connections, new ideas, directions, and possibilities may emerge.

STEP 2: COMPOSING A DRAFT

Once you have settled on your topic and gathered supporting ideas and details, you can begin to write a draft of your essay. Even at this stage you may want to avoid forcing your writing into an inflexible outline. There may be possibilities you haven't thought of, so avoid putting walls around your work just yet.

As in earlier stages of the process, what works best for each of us may be different. Some students may work best by writing this first draft as quickly as possible without stopping and then going back to review and revise when finished. Many students (and probably most experienced writers) find that writing more reflectively at this stage works best for them. And if you have already narrowed your focus to a particular idea and generated lots of details to support it, you may want to reflect some more and review what you have written. You may want to read it out loud to hear how the wording sounds and see if the ideas are complete and clear. Evaluating your writing at this stage may give you valuable insight into where you need to go.

Developing a Thesis Statement

Once you have narrowed your focus to a particular idea and generated details in support of the idea, you are ready to create a thesis statement. Remember that the purpose of this personal essay is to share your experience with literature, so your thesis statement should reveal what you will share or show—not "prove" as argumentative and research essays will do. There is no need to "announce" what you intend to do, to show, or to share ("In this essay I will show that I am able to relate to the emotions expressed by Robert Hayden")—just do it ("I can relate to the emotions expressed by Robert Hayden" or "I can identify with Hayden's situation"). Remember, too, that you are not forced to stay with a thesis that is not working for you. While it may be important to "narrow" your topic and thesis, be flexible. If you find attractive alternatives, try them. They may take you in more productive directions.

Dierdre's tentative thesis statement (below) is "I found myself being able to fully relate to the emotions of this poem, as I have a strong personal connection with the situation that is detailed." Even though she will eventually want to make her thesis statement more succinct, for this stage of her writing process, her thesis is fine. It is not especially poignant or direct, but it's clear enough to give her a direction. After examining her draft, and in general concluding that she needed to be clearer, she revised her thesis statement to the following: "I have experienced a similar relationship, and I can relate strongly to the emotions expressed in this poem."

☑ CHECKLIST: THESIS STATEMENT

❏ Is the central thesis of the essay clearly stated?

❏ Does the title of your essay account for your thesis?

❏ Have you accounted for all parts of your thesis statement?

❏ Is the thesis in your essay fully developed?

Writing Effective Paragraphs

Even in a first draft, it's helpful to organize your thoughts into paragraphs. Each new paragraph signals a shift in direction and acts as a road sign on the reader's journey through our writing. Paragraphs are mini-versions of the essay—and as such require coherence, logical organization, and transitions. But rather than forcing preconceived ideas and an artificial structure on your essay by outlining and identifying the topic of each paragraph in advance, you might let the essay's content and structure emerge naturally.

A different approach, but an especially limiting type of formulaic writing is the five-paragraph essay. This type of essay is divided into five parts: an opening paragraph with a thesis statement that names three elements of support; second, third, and fourth paragraphs that develop each of these elements; and a concluding, summarizing paragraph. While five-paragraph essays may be effective as a "practical" response to passing timed writing exams—with little time for revision—they generally do not produce the most interesting writing.

Given adequate time to write and revise, most experienced writers do not begin with their ideas "fixed" in an unchanging outline. They have a clear objective in mind—and are sensitive to the nature of their readers—but they are confident that the ideas, supporting details, and paragraph structure of their writing will emerge as they write and revise. The key word here is "revise." What gives good writers the confidence to be creative and to explore many options is that they know they will be revising their work—perhaps several times. They know that some of their best ideas for earlier sections of their writing may occur to them later—prompted by subsequent revision and additional writing.

☑ CHECKLIST: PARAGRAPHS

❏ Do all your paragraphs relate to the central thesis?

❏ Is the organization of those paragraphs within the essay clear?

❏ Are the transitions between paragraphs effective and "seamless"?

❏ Do each of the sentences within the paragraphs relate to the central idea of each paragraph?

❏ Are the paragraphs fully developed?

Dierdre's Draft

Earlier in this section, we saw Dierdre Curran's journal entry, freewriting, listing, asking questions, and semantic map in response to Robert Hayden's "Those Winter Sundays." Let's follow up by looking at a draft of her response essay.

Twice on Sunday

The relationship between parent and child is often a significant one in literature. In his poem "Those Winter Sundays," Robert Hayden illustrates the starkness of one such relationship. The speaker in this poem is left, as an adult, feeling guilt and regret over never being able to communicate understanding and appreciation of the father's limited demonstrative abilities. I found myself being able to fully relate to the emotions of this poem, as I have a strong personal connection with the situation that is detailed.

The speaker tells of "fearing the chronic angers of that house." The house I grew up in always seemed filled with anger to me, too. The only communication that ever went on between my parents, myself, and all of my brothers and sisters involved displays of anger; we never had conversations, we had arguments and disagreements. It was a home filled with much bitterness and stress. There was nothing to ever balance it out, no tangible expressions of love from my parents... or so I thought until I got a little older and came to understand more.

The speaker tells of how the father got up early "in the blueblack cold," and then with "cracked hands that ached from labor in the weekday weather made banked fires blaze. No one ever thanked him." My Dad has always been a painfully early riser; he would get up hours before the rest of us had to. In the wintertime, he always made sure that he was up and had turned on the heat so that when the rest of us awoke it was to a warm house. In the winters of my late teens, when I needed his car to get to work, he would always go outside to start it and warm it up. Often he dug it out of a night's snowfall for me, too. I was still reeling from the trauma of my teenage years, so, seething with bitterness, I actually resented him doing me a favor. I never once thanked him for it—I was annoyed by it! My obnoxious, sullen, and ungrateful attitude led me to believe that he was only doing something he was expected to do. My behavior is well described when the speaker tells how he spoke "indifferently to him, who had driven out the cold."

The poem's speaker realizes, later in life, that although his father never outwardly expressed his love in so many words, it was expressed through a variety of gestures. Something as simple as shining his son's shoes can be interpreted as an open display of affection. When I think back on my childhood, I realize that although he is a very gruff and restrained man, my father also showed his love in the only ways he knew how.

In retrospect, I realize that my Dad has done many things over the years to convey his affection. When we were very little, I shared a room with my sister Lucy. Sometimes at night if he was in a good mood, right before we went to bed, my Dad would pretend that he was Frankenstein. He would close his eyes and stretch out his arms in front of him, walking like a fictional monster. He would chase us to our beds, approaching slowly, while we shrieked in terrified laughter, running from him. When he finally caught us, we got tickled to the point of hysteria, and then it was time for bed.

The worst day of my life was when I had to put my fifteen-year-old diabetic dog, Freebie, to sleep. The guilt has never left me. No one in my family would go with me to the vet. When my best friend, John, came to the house that morning to drive me and the dog, my mother wouldn't even come downstairs, but at least my father said goodbye to her. He was the only one that was as upset as I was, and I was crushed, only he never showed it. The day I brought her ashes back to throw around the yard, he found me in the house crying hysterically; I was totally heartbroken. The day I brought Freebie back home for the last time and fell apart in the backyard, my father's only way of acknowledging my grief was to come outside and yell at me. He just stood there and kept yelling, and I just sat there and kept crying. Finally he got quiet and told me that he missed the dog as much as me, and hadn't gone with me because he didn't have the guts to do what I had done. Then he helped me up and walked me up the driveway, hugging me for the very first time in memory.

My parents moved to Indiana. A few weeks ago, my oldest sister called to tell me that my father had suffered a heart attack. I was basically floored, and promptly drank a bottle and a half of Merlot. While I was sucking that down, I was crying hysterically. Two very long days later, I was on a plane to see him, even though he tried to tell me it was not necessary because he was doing so well. I had to see for myself. The plane trip was hellacious. It took twelve hours to get there, and the delays were torture. I made it to the hospital ten minutes before visiting hours ended on my birthday. As I rushed down the hall frantically toward his room, I heard him call out my name in excited surprise and saw him slowly hurrying toward me, pale, be-tubed and in his hospital gown. I could not believe how happy he was to see me; it made the whole trip worth it. He repeatedly held my hand and offered me his cheek for a kiss, every couple of minutes. When he asked me "what in the hell" I was doing out there, my reply was that I had the day off anyway and decided to come see him for my birthday. He had a good laugh at that one. He was a much less gruff man than the last time I had seen him.

Never in my life has my father verbally expressed his love. In younger years, I was blind to the fact that he just doesn't know how, but that he shows it in other ways. That used to make me so mad and frustrated. But he has mellowed with the coming of grandchildren and his own older age, and I have opened my eyes and learned to appreciate the gestures and to interpret their meaning. In "Those Winter Sundays," the speaker tells of the guilt of his own ignorance of "love's austere and lonely offices." While I can't imagine the day either one of us is ever able to actually say "I love you" to the other one, I am secure in the knowledge that it is mutually understood. We still don't talk about personal feelings, although now that his health has dealt him a major wake-up call, I see that changing a little. This past month has marked the first letter he ever wrote to me—three pages about the weather, constantly interjected with SO THERE! in large, capital underlined letters. I also received my very first birthday card, which not only did he sign himself, he signed it with "Love." Of course, it doesn't say "Love, Dad," it says "Love, J.C."—his initials. I laughed when I read it, and I was thrilled that he has been able to make so much progress.

The author of this poem conveys some universal feelings of guilty realization that I think all children reach as they become adults. I am just thankful that I have been given the time and opportunity in life to establish a bond with my father that I am not sure any of his other children have the privilege of sharing. I love him very much, and I have a relationship with him that may seem comparatively odd to other people, but that I treasure. Luckily I also have the sense of humor that is necessary to appreciate it.

STEP 3: REVISING THE ESSAY

Rethinking, "re-visioning," and rewriting are just as important for a response essay about literature as they are for any other kind of writing. Having discovered what you want to say, you can now focus on how well you have said it. How well is your draft organized? Does it have unnecessary or redundant information? Are there gaps that need to be filled? Are there enough details? Is there enough support from the work of literature? Have you expressed yourself as clearly as possible?

☑ CHECKLIST: REVISION

Organization and Unity

❏ Do all the paragraphs relate to the central thesis?

❏ Is the organization of those paragraphs within the essay clear?

❏ Do each of the sentences within the paragraphs relate to the central idea of the paragraph?

Support

❏ Are there enough details to support or clarify your assertions? Have you "shown" what you've told?

❏ Are there enough quotes from the work of literature to support your assertions?

❏ Are the paragraphs fully developed?

❏ Is the essay fully developed? Have you accounted for all aspects of your thesis statement?

Clarity

❏ Is the central thesis of the essay clearly stated?

❏ Does the title of your essay account for your thesis?

❏ Is the language clear?

❏ Are there redundancies, digressions, or meaningless phrases that could be cut?

❏ Is the essay written in the format required by your instructor? Have you documented your references to the text and included a list of works cited?

Voice

❏ Does the essay sound like you? When you read it out loud, can you hear your voice and emotion?

Revising Dierdre's Draft

Organization and Unity   One of the most effective ways of checking the organization of a draft is by doing an **after-draft outline.** Go back to each paragraph and find the controlling idea. List the main ideas they represent, one after the other. This should give you an outline of your draft.

Let's look at an outline of Dierdre's draft:

> Paragraph #1. Introduction and Thesis Statement—I found myself being able to fully relate to the emotions of this poem.
>
> Paragraph #2. The house I grew up in always seemed filled with anger, too.
>
> Paragraphs #3 and #4. Both my father and the poet's father expressed their love in the same way.
>
> Paragraph #5. My father has done things to express his love.
>
> Paragraph #6. The worst day of my life is also my fondest memory of my father.
>
> Paragraph #7. My parents moved to Indiana, and two weeks ago, my father had a heart attack.
>
> Paragraph #8. I didn't understand when I was younger—now I know.
>
> Paragraph #9. We still don't talk about personal feelings, but our relationship is better.
>
> Paragraph #10. Conclusion—I'm glad I've had the chance the poet missed.

When Dierdre looked at her list, she was concerned that she might have too many paragraphs. For the most part, the organization of her essay followed the pattern of the poem itself. She compared her relationship with her father to that of the poet's with his father. She took lines from the poem and then commented on how each matched her experience. *This pattern made sense to her, but it appeared that several of these paragraphs were too long and unwieldy.*

Showing Support   The support Dierdre used in this essay came from two sources: the poem and her personal experience. She supported her references to the text by quoting the poem. She supported references to her experience by giving examples. *She believed she had enough support in both cases and that her examples firmly established the connection.*

Clarity   Dierdre realized that she would have to tighten up her language by deleting unnecessary words, expressions, and sentences. After cutting and combining, she could decide if some of the paragraphs should be combined as well. *She also realized that her choice of words did not always express what she meant. In paragraphs 4 and 5 in particular, she decided that cutting, combining, and reordering some of the examples would strengthen the pace and organization of the essay.*

Her most difficult decision was what to cut. She wanted her essay to be clearly expressed and tightly organized, but she didn't want to sacrifice the concrete details and scenes that gave it a strong voice.

Voice   She believed that one of the strengths of this piece was its voice, a voice that "showed" through quotes and examples. Her biggest task was to maintain a strong voice throughout the essay while tightening up her prose overall.

FORMATTING AND DOCUMENTING YOUR ESSAY

Before you submit the final draft of your essay, check with your instructor for the format you are required to follow when you submit your essay. *For more details, see the directory of MLA Formatting and Documentation in Appendix C (p. 1289). The student essay that follows on page 53 provides examples for many of the basics listed below.*

☑ CHECKLIST: BASICS FOR A LITERARY ESSAY

❏ Are the title and heading on your first page formatted correctly? See the heading and title of the student essay on page 53.

❏ Have you double-spaced your essay and numbered your pages?

❏ Is your essay title unique to *your* essay? Does it indicate your thesis, not just the name of the work?

❏ Are the titles of works underlined or in quotations as appropriate? **Titles of shorter works** (poems, short stories, essays, one-act plays) are placed in quotation marks. **Longer works** (long plays and entire books) are underlined or italicized.

❏ Have you **stayed anchored in the work** and balanced references to your experience with references and quotes from the work?

❏ Have you **introduced quotes** with your own language—integrating them smoothly into your own writing? Used ellipses (three spaced periods) to indicate omitted material within a quotation (see p. 194). Used brackets to indicate that you have added your own language (see p. 194).

❏ Have you avoided **unnecessary plot summary?**

❏ Have you **referred to authors by their full or last names**—not their first names? Have you used **present-tense verbs** to describe the characters and events in the work?

❏ Have you acknowledged all your sources? When quoting **poetry,** have you cited line numbers (1–5)? When quoting **fiction and nonfiction prose** or **modern drama,** have you indicated page numbers: (26)? When quoting **verse drama,** have you indicated act, scene, and line numbers: (3.1.15–20)?

❑ Have you placed *periods* and *commas* **inside quotation marks**? Have you placed other punctuation outside quotation marks when appropriate?

❑ Have you cited your sources correctly in the text of your essay? Have you followed your essay with a **Work(s) Cited** to indicate the work or works you have cited in your essay? Is it in the correct format? See Appendix C.

Editing or proofreading is a crucial final step in the process of producing an essay. In addition to making any changes that did not occur to you earlier and when fine-tuning your writing, it's essential to check your essay for correct grammar, spelling, punctuation, and typos.

A Brief Primer on Punctuation

Listed below are a few basic rules of punctuaton.*

Comma

In a series of 3 or more terms with a single conjunction, use a comma after each term except the last.

For example: red, white, and blue
             gold, silver, or copper
             He opened the letter, read it, and made note of its contents.

Enclose **parenthetic expressions between commas**.

For example: Thoreau believed the best way to explore the countryside, unless he was pressed for time, was to travel on foot.

Use a comma **to separate independent clauses when they are joined by a coordinating conjunction** *(and, but, for, nor, or, so, yet).*

For example: The situation was perilous, but there was still one chance of escape.

Use a comma **to separate a dependent clause or phrase from a main clause**.

For example: After planning for two years, they finally went to Europe.

Use a comma **to separate names of geographical locations, parts of dates, etc., from the rest of the sentence.**

For example: John left Brewster, New York, at 9 AM on July 4, 2011, and arrived in Chatham, Cape Cod, Massachusetts, at 1 PM.

*These are the most common uses, but not every circumstance, where a comma, semicolon, colon, or apostrophe might be used.

*Use commas **to prevent misreading**.*

For example: After all, the snow and ice on the highways kept people from traveling.

Semicolon
*Use a semicolon **to separate independent clauses not joined by a coordinating conjunction or when independent clauses are joined by conjunctive adverbs** (however, therefore, moreover, etc.).*

For example: It is nearly half past five; we cannot reach town before dark.

*Use a semicolon **to separate the parts of a series when commas are used internally.***

For example: The flags of the three countries are red, white, and blue; green, yellow, and orange; pink, blue, and purple.

Colon
*The colon is used **to introduce a formal listing or a statement that repeats in other words or amplifies the preceding statement**.*

For example: Three runners stood at the starting line: Tanya, Bill, and Robin.

Apostrophe
*The most common use of the apostrophe is **to indicate possession**.*
*For the **possessive of a single noun, add an apostrophe**.*

For example: the play's theme

*For the **possessive of a plural noun ending in "s," add an apostrophe after the "s."***

For example: the players' union

☑ CHECKLIST: EDITING AND PROOFREADING

❑ Are all of your sentences complete sentences?

❑ Are all of your sentences punctuated appropriately?

❑ Are the words spelled correctly? Have you checked for easily confused words (*then/than, your/you're, its/it's,* etc.)?

❑ Are you sure of the meaning of all the words you've used?

❑ Are there particular errors you have a tendency to make? Have you looked for those in this essay?

Remember, computer spell checkers do not make choices about word usage. Confused words (*than/then, there/their/they're,* etc.) will not be flagged by a spell checker. You will have to use your own eyes and judgment to correct those errors.

STEP 4: DIERDRE'S REVISED ESSAY

After rewriting her introduction to make it clearer, Dierdre cut many words and phrases, combined many sentences, and shifted some of her examples. After reading this clearer, shorter version, she decided to stay with the same number of paragraphs. She could have combined several of them but decided not to. The resulting paragraphs would have been too long and much more difficult for the reader to absorb.

Dierdre Curran

Prof. Madden

English 102

September 9, 20XX

Twice on Sunday

In his poem "Those Winter Sundays," Robert Hayden illustrates the starkness of the speaker's relationship with his father. As a child, the speaker was never able to understand or appreciate what his father did for him. As an adult, he feels guilt and regret because it is too late to communicate his appreciation. I have experienced a similar relationship, and I can relate strongly to the emotions expressed in this poem.

The speaker tells of "fearing the chronic angers of that house" (9). The house I grew up in always seemed filled with anger to me, too. We never had conversations; we had arguments and disagreements. There was nothing ever to balance it out, no tangible expressions of love from my parents...or so I thought until I got a little older and came to understand more.

Hayden begins the poem by writing:

> Sundays too my father got up early
>
> and put his clothes on in the blueblack cold,
>
> then with cracked hands that ached
>
> from labor in the weekday weather made
>
> banked fires blaze. No one ever thanked him. (1–5)

In the wintertime, my dad was always up before the rest of us and had turned on the heat so that we awoke to a warm house. When I was older and needed his car to get to work, he would always go outside to start and warm it up. Often he dug it out of a night's snowfall. Reeling from the trauma of my teenage years and seething with bitterness, I actually resented his doing me a favor. I never once thanked him for it. I was annoyed and believed that he was only doing something he was expected to do. My behavior is well described when the speaker tells how he spoke "indifferently to him / who had driven out the cold" (10–11).

Later in life, the speaker realizes that while his father never expressed his love in words, he expressed it through a variety of gestures, like shining his son's shoes. When I recall my childhood, I realize that my father also showed his love in the only ways he knew how. When we were very little, I shared a room with my sister Lucy. Sometimes at night if he was in a good mood, right before we went to bed, my Dad would pretend that he was Frankenstein's monster. He would close his eyes and stretch out his arms in front of him, walking like the fictional monster, approaching slowly, while we shrieked in terrified laughter, running from him. When he finally caught us, we got tickled to the point of hysteria.

The worst day of my life is also my fondest memory of my father. It was the day I had to put my fifteen-year-old, diabetic dog Freebie to sleep. The guilt has never left me. No one in my family would go with me to the vet. At least my father said goodbye to her. He was the only one who was as upset as I was, and I was crushed. He never showed it. When I brought her ashes back to throw around the yard, he found me in the house crying hysterically. I was totally heartbroken. No one hugged me, no one said, "I'm sorry." My father's only way of acknowledging my grief was to come outside and yell at me. He just stood there and kept yelling, and I just sat there and kept crying. Finally, he got quiet and told me that he missed the dog as much as I did, and hadn't gone with me because he didn't have the guts to do what I had done. Then he helped me up and walked me up the driveway, hugging me for the first time I can remember.

After I graduated from high school, my parents moved to Indiana. A few weeks ago, my oldest sister called to tell me that my father had suffered a heart attack. I was floored. Two very long days later, I was on a plane to see him. The plane trip was horrible. It took twelve hours to get there, and the delays were torture. I didn't care about the inclement weather or the size of the plane. I didn't care about anything but getting to South Bend as soon as I could. I made it to the hospital on my birthday, ten minutes before visiting hours ended. As I rushed down the hall looking frantically for his room, I heard him call out my name in excited surprise and saw him slowly hurrying toward me, pale, be-tubed, and in his hospital gown. I could not believe how happy he was to see me. It made the whole trip worth it. He repeatedly held my hand and offered me his cheek for a kiss every couple of minutes. When he asked me "what in the hell" I was doing out there, I replied that I had the day off anyway, and decided to come see him for my birthday. He had a good laugh at that one. He seemed much less gruff than the last time I had seen him.

Never in my life has my father expressed his love verbally. In younger years I was blind to the fact that he just didn't know how, but that he showed it in other ways. That used to make me so mad and frustrated. But he has mellowed with the coming of age and grandchildren, and I have opened my eyes and learned to appreciate his gestures and to interpret their meaning. In "Those Winter Sundays," the speaker tells of the guilt of his own ignorance "of love's austere and lonely offices" (14). While I can't imagine the day when we will ever be able to actually say "I love you" to each other, I am secure in the knowledge that it is mutually understood.

We still don't talk about personal feelings, but now that his health has dealt him a major wake-up call, I see that changing a little. This past month has marked the first letter he ever wrote to me—three pages about the weather, constantly interjected with "<u>SO THERE!</u>" in large, capital, underlined letters. I also received my very first birthday card. Not only did he sign it himself, but he signed it with love. Of course, it doesn't say "Love, Dad," it says "Love, J.C."—his initials. I laughed when I read it, and I was thrilled that he has been able to make so much progress.

In "Those Winter Sundays," Hayden conveys feelings of guilt that I think most children experience as they become adults. I am just thankful that I have been given the time and the opportunity in life to establish a bond with my father. I love him very much, and I have a relationship with him that may seem comparatively odd to other people, but it's one that I treasure. Luckily, I also have the sense of humor that is necessary to appreciate it.

[New Page]

Work Cited

Hayden, Robert. "Those Winter Sundays." *Exploring Literature*. Ed. Frank Madden. 5th ed. New York: Longman, 2012. 13. Print.

PART II

ANALYSIS, ARGUMENTATION, AND RESEARCH

Chapter 3

Exploration and Analysis

Genre and the Elements of Literature

To analyze anything is to look at it closely, examine its parts, and see how it works. Our intention in this chapter, however, is not to reduce literature to its parts. *Our goal is to provide you with tools to articulate and develop your responses into effective argumentative essays.*

We know that the parts of a literary work alone cannot account for its meaning, a meaning that fully blossoms only as the parts work together. Once you've experienced the whole of the work, however, reading it carefully and analyzing its parts can tell you a great deal about it—and how it triggered your response. Analysis is an important step in interpreting or evaluating literature, and it is through this process that you may gather the support to make your opinion an informed one.

CLOSE READING

Analysis requires close reading. In a way, the term *close reading* means the opposite of what it sounds like. When we read closely, we step back. We move from being inside the work to looking at it from the outside, from participating to observing. This process requires a careful reading and a conscious examination of the elements of the work and how they contribute to its overall meaning. *A close reading is not a first reading, it is a rereading.* When you return to read the literature or your notes again after discussion in class, you are doing a close reading. You have already stepped back from your own views to hear the responses of others. You are reading your notes and the work informed by what you have learned from those discussions.

ANNOTATING THE TEXT

An effective way to do a close reading of a work is to mark up the text by underlining, circling, highlighting, or making notes in the margins. You may even find it useful to make these annotations in more than one stage. In the first stage you might want to concentrate on your understanding of the text by summarizing, noting words or passages you don't understand, and asking questions—exploring the text. Later on, as you narrow your focus, you may want to identify elements of the text, patterns, evidence, or quotations to support your thesis—analyzing the text. If you don't want to mark up the pages of your book, make a copy of the work and do your annotations on the copy. Or write your annotations on Post-it notes and attach them in the margins of the work.

The following example illustrates a two-stage process of annotating a poem.

First Annotation: Exploration

PERCY BYSSHE SHELLEY [1792–1822]

OZYMANDIAS [1818]

I met a traveler from an antique land	What does he mean "trunkless legs"?
Who said: "Two vast and trunkless legs of stone	
Stand in the desert... Near them on the sand,	Look up visage.
Half-sunk, a shattered visage lies, whose frown	"cold command"—a ruler?
And wrinkled lip, and sneer of cold command,	5
Tell that its sculptor well those passions read	A sculptor—a statue?
Which yet survive, stamped on these lifeless things,	Hand that mocked & heart that fed—How does "hand"
The <u>hand that mocked</u> them, and the <u>heart that fed</u>	differ from "heart"?
And on the pedestal these words appear	
'My name is Ozymandias, king of kings.	Summary—He met someone 10
Look on my works, ye Mighty, and despair!'	from a faraway country who
Nothing beside remains. Round the decay	saw an ancient, large, broken
Of that colossal wreck, boundless and bare	statue with an arrogant
The lone and level sands stretch far away."	statement on it.

This first annotation is an exploration of your first reading. You may clarify what you understand and ask questions about what you don't understand, or indicate what you need to know more about. You might make guesses, note impressions, summarize, and, in general, give yourself something to think about when you begin a second reading.

Second Annotation: Analysis

How does this compare with other Shelley poems I've read? What was going on in England at this time? Who was the king?

PERCY BYSSHE SHELLEY [1792–1822]

OZYMANDIAS [1818]

Why "antique" and not just "old" or "ancient"?

I met a traveler from an antique land
Who said: "Two vast and trunkless legs of stone
Stand in the desert... Near them on the sand,
Half-sunk, a shattered visage lies, whose frown
And wrinkled lip, and sneer of cold command,

The rhyme scheme: abab—"land and sand" / "stone" and "frown"?
Not just grand, but arrogant as well.

5

Tell that its sculptor well those passions read

Which yet survive, stamped on these lifeless things,

The <u>hand</u> that mocked them, and the <u>heart</u> that <u>fed</u>

And on the pedestal these words appear

'My name is Ozymandias, king of kings.

Look on my works, ye Mighty, and despair!'

Nothing beside remains. Round the decay

Of that colossal wreck, boundless and bare

The lone and level sands stretch far away."

The annotations read:

"read" and "fed" rhyme, but not "command" and "things."

The hand of the sculptor/the heart of the king?

A powerful image—decayed and worn-out grandeur and arrogance in a desert. 10

Rhymes: despair/bare—decay/away

What a powerful ironic contrast!

The second annotation is a closer reading and more analytical. Here you might look for some of the elements of literature we discuss in this chapter, try to find patterns, seek evidence to support your early conclusions, or even place the work within a larger historical, social, or biographical context.

LITERATURE IN ITS MANY CONTEXTS

Our focus on textual analysis in this chapter—on genres and their elements—is not an attempt to limit the scope of your writing to types of literature or parts of the work alone. Those parts and those works exist in a larger world—a context framed by personal, cultural, historical, biographical, and other influences. Seeing beyond the work to the contexts that influenced its writing—and your reading— may enliven and enrich your experience of the work and help you produce a more interesting essay.

Your Critical Approach

What you value most about literature, your critical stance, can be an important factor in determining what you analyze and write about when interpreting and evaluating literature. Critical approaches are broadly classified as reader based (emphasizing the reader's response and the text), text based (emphasizing the text), context based (emphasizing the background of the work), and author based (emphasizing connections to the author's life or intentions). Whatever approach you take may determine the strategy and terms you use in your writing. For a more comprehensive explanation of these approaches see Appendix A (p. 1273). Keep in mind that critical approaches may easily overlap, and critics often combine them in their analyses. The difference between one critical stance and another may be more a matter of emphasis than kind, and drawing upon several approaches can yield a rich interpretation.

READING AND ANALYZING FICTION

Telling stories and listening to stories seem to be a natural part of our lives. When we meet with friends to hear about an experience, "just the facts" won't do. We want to hear the stories that give meaning to those facts. Why do we read and listen to stories? What kind of experience do we expect to have when we sit down to read a short story or "curl up with a good book"? Many of us might say that we want to "escape" from the stress of everyday life. But in this highly complex world, there are many other ways to escape. What is it about the experience of reading a good story that makes it unique and draws us to it?

Beyond an escape, reading a story brings us to a place in our imaginations where we can live through the experience of others. Prompted by the author's words, we imagine the scenes, characters, and conflicts. We take the chances, feel the emotions, and share the insights—but without suffering the risks or consequences that living through them ourselves might bring.

Stories and storytelling have been an important part of every culture since people first roamed the earth. Before there was written language to record them, people shared stories orally and passed them down to their descendants. Even today, these stories convey the "truths" of many cultures and religions and give meaning to the lives of millions of people.

Fiction and Truth   In many ways, the designation "fiction" is misleading. Most fiction tells a story that is "made up"—or at least the specific details of the story probably did not occur in exactly the way described, in this place, at this time, to characters with these names. The most important quality of good fiction, though, is the truth or truths it tells—about being human and struggling to make sense of a complex world. The truth of fiction transcends fact. In it, we see a model of our own struggle, a model not limited by the daily news of specific time and place and fact.

NARRATION

The narrator is the storyteller, the intermediary who shapes and flavors the story for us. Try to distinguish between the author of the story and the narrator, or speaker. The narrator has been created by the author with a particular effect in mind. As you can imagine, *who* tells the story and *how* it is told can make a big difference. The same story told from a different point of view or with a different voice affects everything we experience as we read.

Point of View

Think about the last time you watched a concert or sports event on television. Can you recall how many different camera shots you were shown? When the camera gave you a distant shot, you could see a large part of the arena and most of the performers. You could see what no one performer could see. But you could not experience what it was like to be in the middle of the action. Only a close-up camera shot could help you feel the physical energy, the emotion, and give you the perspective of an individual performer. But of course, by isolating your view to one performer, you lost the larger view of the entire event. Directors, camera operators, and announcers make choices about which perspectives work best at given times. From any of these distances and angles the event we witness is the same, but the point of view we have makes our experience of it quite different.

In similar fashion, our reading of fiction is strongly influenced by the narrator's point of view. ***Point of view*** *is the perspective from which the narrator tells the story.* Generally, the pronoun that dominates the narration signals which point of view is represented. The terms most commonly used to identify point of view are first person; third-person limited, omniscient, or objective; and shifting.

Authors, like directors or camera operators, make choices about which point of view will convey the story most effectively. In Sandra Cisneros's short story "Eleven" (p. 26), for example, we experience the humiliation of the young girl from her perspective—so "close up" that we share what she thinks and feels. The author might have chosen to describe the event through a narrator who was looking on or from the viewpoint of the teacher or another student in her class. But because we see the event through the girl's eyes, we experience her pain as if it is happening to us. From any of these perspectives the event remains the same, but in each case our experience of it is quite different.

First person uses the pronoun *I* and places the narrator in the story. We see through that character (as an announcer and camera might limit what we see to the view of one performer). As readers, we will only know what this one person experiences. The short story "A&P" (p. 456) is a good example of first-person point of view. The action and the characters in this story are described solely through the eyes and mind of one character, Sammy. Because of its very limited perspective, however, we rely completely on the credibility of the narrator, so the **reliability** of that narrator is a crucial factor. Are there discrepancies between what we are being told and your own judgment of the same events or characters in the story? For example, our response to a story like "The Yellow Wallpaper" (p. 676) is very dependent on our judgment of the narrator's stability.

Third person uses the pronouns *he* or *she,* but usually limits us to one character's view. The narrator does not see through the character's eyes but focuses on the character and what he or she sees and thinks. Specifically, this is called **third-person limited point of view.** The narrative perspective of Liliana Heker's story "The Stolen Party" (p. 403) is third-person limited. The narrator describes the action and the characters from the distance of third person, but limits us to the thoughts of one character, Rosaura. **Third-person omniscient point of view** also uses the pronouns *he, she,* and *they,* but the narrator is "all knowing" and able to move in and out of the mind of more than one character, choosing what and when to share. Kate Chopin's "Désirée's Baby" (p. 902) is an example of third-person omniscient. **Third-person objective point of view** minimizes the intervention of the narrator. The setting and the action are described, and we "listen in" on the dialogue, but the narrator does not interpret for us. We must do that ourselves. Hemingway's "Hills Like White Elephants" (p. 688) is written in objective point of view. The narrator describes the setting, the characters, and the action from a distance while we seem to overhear their conversation from a neighboring table. Stories with **shifting point of view** may shift from the narrowly focused first person or third-person limited to the broad spectrum of omniscient narration.

Voice refers to the narrator's persona, the personality that seems to come alive in the words. It is quite possible to have the same point of view but very different voices. The short stories "A&P" and "The Yellow Wallpaper" both have a first-person point of view, but the voice of the brash nineteen-year-old Sammy in "A&P" is very different from that of the troubled woman in "The Yellow Wallpaper."

For a concise checklist of questions for Narration, see page 69.

SETTING

*In literature, **setting** is the location and the atmosphere of the story.* It has a direct and indirect impact on character and conflict; it supports and emphasizes the story's meaning. Its most important function is to make us feel present in the world that the characters inhabit. The more we can visualize, the more we participate, the more satisfying the experience.

In our own lives, the places and company we seek have much to do with how we want to feel. When we want to relax, we go somewhere informal and familiar. When hungry but with little time to eat, we may go to a bare and efficient place where they serve fast food. On a dinner date, however, we are more likely to seek a restaurant with a sophisticated, romantic atmosphere.

If you were asked to describe the setting you are in right now, what factors would go into your description? Would you include more than its physical features? Setting is more than just physical surroundings. It includes the atmosphere, and atmosphere changes regularly. The weather, lighting, and time of day or night may change it. The people present may change it. Who are they? What is our relationship to them? Are we or they happy or sad? Can you "cut the tension with a knife"? Permanent factors, like physical qualities, are a "shell" for this atmosphere, but those factors that vary (people, time, weather, task) strongly influence a setting, too.

Location tells us where and when the story is taking place. John Updike's "A&P" (p. 456), set in the 1960s in suburban Massachusetts, has a very different feel to it than James Joyce's "Araby" (p. 407), set in Dublin in the 1890s. Both the *where* and the *when* will strongly influence the values and behavior of the characters and color the rest of the story.

Atmosphere in a story arises from the mix of location and variable circumstances, such as the personalities present, the conflict, time of day, season, and even the weather. An effectively rendered atmosphere helps us see and experience concrete details of the setting as if we were present. It supports and complements the conflict and characters and helps to convey the story's meaning.

For a concise checklist of questions for Setting, see page 69.

CONFLICT

*In literature, **conflict** is the struggle of opposing external or internal forces.* Conflict is at the heart of every story. In fact, without it we don't have a story—at least not one most of us would want to hear or read. The impediments and complications of conflict keep us reading. The more important, challenging, believable, and coherent the conflict is, the more we are engaged by the story and want to follow it to its conclusion.

In our own lives, we spend a good portion of every day resolving conflicts. Most of them are so small we don't even think of them as conflicts. We solve them easily without much effort or anxiety. We get up in the morning when we don't feel like it. We wait patiently for the traffic light to change before we go forward. The solutions and consequences are clear. If we stay in bed, we'll lose pay or miss important information in class. If we go through the red light, we might kill someone. There is not much internal strife here. And these dilemmas are not likely to make compelling stories.

As the conflicts become more complex, however, our anxiety increases and the choices seem more difficult: "What classes will I take next semester?" "How will I get to school tomorrow?" "Should I ask that person for a date?" Increase the complexity to another level and we get: "Should I stay in school next semester?" "Will I have to buy a car?" "Should I get married?" As the stakes rise, our internal conflict increases. As you might imagine, the internal nature of conflict also has a lot to do with the personalities of the people involved. For people who are sensitive and shy, asking for a date may be a major conflict. The possibility of being rejected may cause great anxiety. For someone who is very depressed, even getting out of bed may seem like a major accomplishment.

External conflict may be physical (characters against nature) or social (characters against each other or against society). **Internal conflict** is a struggle of opposing forces within a character. The best stories contain elements of both types of conflict, but the emphasis is usually on internal conflict.

Internal conflict has much to do with the makeup of the characters in the story. Consider the personality of each character. What provokes an internal conflict in one person may go unnoticed by another. A character who is insecure and self-conscious is likely to react very differently to some situations than a character who is confident and self-absorbed.

PLOT

Plot is the structure of the story. It is the pattern of twists and turns the story takes. Most plots spring from conflict. To have a discernible plot, we must have impediments and complications for the work to take the twists and turns necessary to keep us reading.

When we share our own stories we structure them not only to convey the facts but also to have maximum impact. We might withhold information until later for the effect it will have on our listeners. We don't jump to answer the plea: So what happened!? We might say, "Hold on, I'm getting there, but you have to hear this part first to get a good sense of what happened later." We are naturally sensitive to the way that the arrangement of the details adds suspense or helps the listener "to be there" and feel the experience.

One traditional arrangement of plot in a short story follows a pattern of exposition, rising action, crisis (sometimes called climax), falling action, and resolution (sometimes called denouement or untying).

Figure 3.1 *Plot Structure*

The diagram of this structure in Figure 3.1 is a bit misleading. Even stories that contain these elements in their plots are generally not balanced so evenly. The crisis, for example, rarely falls right in the middle of the story. The bulk of most stories is spent building (exposition and rising action) to the crisis. Once the crisis is reached, the story usually winds down (falling action and resolution) quickly.

Many television shows and crime stories are classic examples of this formula. In the early days of television, Erle Stanley Gardner's *Perry Mason* mysteries were turned into a television series. As seen in the following excerpt, each episode fit this pattern especially well—so well it was easy to work in commercial breaks between stages of the plot as if they were part of the show.

> *Exposition:* A desperate client appears at the office of famous defense attorney Perry Mason, reveals that a hideous crime has been committed (usually murder), indicates that he or she is a suspect, and proclaims innocence. Perry confers with his secretary and confidant, Della Street, and calls in private detective Paul Burke. In the course of these deliberations, we (the viewers or readers) find out about the circumstances, characters, and conflict of the story. (*Commercial break*)

> *Rising Action:* The client is arrested and charged with the hideous crime. The conflict builds as a motive is established and overwhelming circumstantial evidence mounts. Meanwhile, Paul desperately seeks information and other suspects and the setting shifts to the courtroom. The conflict intensifies: the suspense increases. (*Commercial break*)

> *Crisis or Climax:* In the courtroom, the district attorney continues to build an ironclad case against the defendant. Occasionally private eye Paul enters the courtroom and passes notes to Perry. Perry occasionally sends Della on an errand. The crucial moment occurs when Perry calls the real killer (or an accomplice) to the stand and he or she breaks down under his scrutiny and the weight of the newly discovered evidence (gathered by the relentless Paul) and confesses to the crime. (*Commercial break*)

> *Falling Action:* The murderer reveals motive and method. (*Commercial break*)

> *Resolution:* Perry reveals how the good guys found out the truth and shares a joke with Della, Paul, and the grateful, relieved former defendant. Justice is done, and all return to normalcy. (*End of show*)

Consider some of your favorite television shows. Do they have predictable plot structures? Can you describe them? How well do they work?

A major impediment to finding a traditional plot structure is that it doesn't fit some of the best fiction. In many works of fiction, the crisis or climax occurs at the end of the story. Things are not wrapped up for us. There is no intention to provide us with a resolution. Life doesn't come in episodes that resolve conflict so neatly. Stories that intend to capture life as it is don't "wrap up" so neatly either. Joyce's "Araby" (p. 407), Updike's "A&P" (p. 456), Bobbie Ann Mason's "Shiloh" (p. 705), and many other stories don't fit this pattern.

Most of these stories reach their crisis or climax and end when the protagonist or central character sees beyond a comforting illusion and confronts painful reality. After this climax there is no resolution—nor would we want one.

For a concise checklist of questions for Conflict and Plot, see page 70.

CHARACTER

Do you remember the first day of class? Surrounded by unfamiliar faces, you may have wondered, Who are these people? Even the instructor may have been unfamiliar to you. By the end of that class, though, you had probably formed many impressions. You had some sense of what your classmates were like, perhaps even which ones you might like to know better. Some of those impressions may have come from *what* your classmates said about themselves and *how* they said it. But it's unlikely, even if they described themselves, that they told you what to think or feel about them. That was your decision. You probably decided what to think of them on the basis of their appearances, what they did, what they said, how they said it, and what others said about them. You wouldn't have settled for being told what to think; you wanted to see for yourself.

***Characterization** is the development of characters in a story.* At its best, the author brings characters to life and lets us "get to know them" as we know people in our own lives. While the narrator may tell us some things directly about the characters, we find out much of what we know indirectly through action and dialogue. We are not told what to think or how to feel about them. We observe the characters thinking, speaking, and doing. We hear what others say about them. They seem believable and motivated. And like our responses to people in our own lives, our reactions and judgments are based on our own observations.

The main character in a story is called the **protagonist.** When we find a character or characters who seem to be a major force in opposition to the protagonist, that character or characters is called the **antagonist** or **antagonists.** For example, the protagonist in Sandra Cisneros's short story "Eleven" (p. 26) is the young girl who narrates the story. The antagonist is Mrs. Price, who humiliates her in front of her classmates. In Ralph Ellison's "Battle Royal" (p. 421), the protagonist is the young man who narrates the story. The antagonists are "the town's leading white citizens," who degrade him at their brutally racist ceremony.

When characters lack the development that seems to bring them to life, lack the complexity that lets us know them as we know people in our own lives, and seem to represent "types" more than real personalities, they are called **flat** or **stock characters.** When they seem fully developed, with all the complexities of real people, they are described as **round characters.**

For a concise checklist of questions for Characterization, see page 70.

LANGUAGE AND STYLE

It's not possible to separate language and style from other elements. Language is the vehicle that carries narration, setting, conflict, plot, characterization, and theme to you. The formal or informal style of the language is an integral part of narration. The evocative nature of the language used to describe setting has so much to do with our visualization and response to it. The style of the language used by the characters tells us a great deal about who they are. And the symbolic nature of the language may complement and support the story's theme or meaning.

Diction

*The type of language narrators and characters use, their **diction,** tells us a lot about them and establishes their voices.* Their use of formal or informal vocabulary or nonstandard words or phrases may tell us about their education or place in society. The frequency of images and figurative language in the narration may also have an effect on our reading and response to a story.

Symbol

*A **symbol** is something that represents more than itself.* Just about anything in a story might be symbolic. In fiction, symbols are most likely to be objects, names, or places, but they might be actions, sounds, or colors as well.

Irony

Irony is a contrast between appearance/expectation and reality. The two most popular forms of irony in fiction are verbal irony and situational irony. **Verbal irony** results from the contrast between what is said by the narrator or a character and what is meant. **Irony of situation** results from the contrast between what is expected and what actually happens.

For a concise checklist of questions for Language and Style, see page 70.

THEME

Theme is the central idea expressed by the story. It is a generalization, an insight about life derived from the work as a whole. Identifying and articulating this meaning is not easy. Although our experience of the theme may be holistic or impressionistic, the analysis and support required for its articulation demand a close look at the parts—the language, events, characters, and outcome of the story.

Theme or Moral?   When writing about literature, it is tempting to reduce what it means to a moral or lesson. Good literature reveals a complex world. A statement such as "Honesty is the best policy" may seem to reverberate with truth until we examine it closely. Is honesty always the best policy? Is it always the most ethical policy? Is it "moral" to tell people things that will hurt them? Didactic stories intend to deliver a moral. A moral preaches; it teaches a lesson or a code of conduct. A theme reveals; it gives us insight into human nature.

Consider the difference between revealing and preaching. If we read a story in which John loves Mary and Mary falls in love with Bill, we might state the simplified theme of the story as: People don't necessarily fall in love with those who are in love with them. To identify this theme, we examine the particulars of the story, come to a conclusion about them, and then expand this conclusion into a generalization about life itself.

A moral, however, is a simple lesson or rule of conduct. If we tried to find a moral in the previous John-Mary-Bill example, we might write, "Fall in love only with people who love you." But we know from our experience of the world that such a statement is much too simple to account for the complex nature of this situation. Similarly, the frustration and humiliation of the protagonists in "Eleven" and "Battle Royal," or the intense emotional and ethical dilemma of the couple in "Hills Like White Elephants," cannot be reduced to clear lessons or morals. They reveal, as life reveals, complexity intact. In most modern literature, theme is not usually expressed as a moral, and it will probably take more than a few words to state the theme of a complex work.

For a concise checklist of questions for Theme, see page 70.

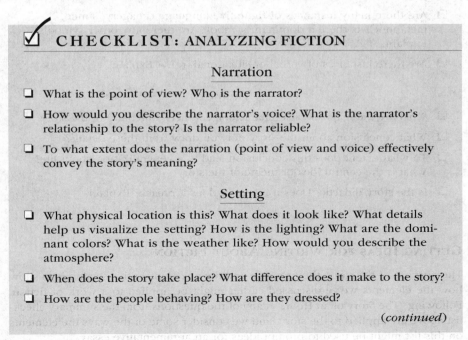

☑ CHECKLIST: ANALYZING FICTION

Narration

❑ What is the point of view? Who is the narrator?

❑ How would you describe the narrator's voice? What is the narrator's relationship to the story? Is the narrator reliable?

❑ To what extent does the narration (point of view and voice) effectively convey the story's meaning?

Setting

❑ What physical location is this? What does it look like? What details help us visualize the setting? How is the lighting? What are the dominant colors? What is the weather like? How would you describe the atmosphere?

❑ When does the story take place? What difference does it make to the story?

❑ How are the people behaving? How are they dressed?

(continued)

Conflict and Plot

❑ What is the primary external conflict? The primary internal conflict?

❑ Are there other conflicts? If so, what are they?

❑ How would you support your identification of conflict by what is in the text?

❑ To what extent do the traits of the characters lead to conflict?

❑ Can you identify the plot? Does it conform to the traditional structure? If so, how so? If not, what is the structure?

Character

❑ What is your impression of the characters? What do the characters do that makes you feel this way? What do they say? What is said about them?

❑ To what extent are the characters motivated and consistent? Believable? Flat or stock characters?

❑ Who is the protagonist? One or more antagonists?

❑ What evidence from the text of the story supports your responses?

Language and Style

❑ Is the language formal or informal? In what way does the language tell you about the narrator or characters?

❑ Are there many instances of figurative language (imagery, simile, metaphor)? Is there a dominant symbol? Are there any other symbols? Explain.

❑ Are there instances of verbal or situational irony? Explain.

Theme

❑ What are the major details (characters, conflicts, outcome) of the story?

❑ What conclusion about the story did you draw from these details?

❑ To what extent does this conclusion lead to a generalization about life? What is the central idea or theme of the story?

❑ Is the story didactic? Does it reveal or does it preach? Explain.

GETTING IDEAS FOR WRITING ABOUT FICTION

The purpose of the story, the prompts, and the questions in this section is to show how the elements we've discussed earlier might be applied to a work of fiction. Following "The Story of an Hour," many of the questions from the summary checklist above are applied to the story, and we consider some of the ways the elements on this list might be used to prompt ideas for an argumentative essay.

KATE CHOPIN [1851–1904]

THE STORY OF AN HOUR [1891]

Knowing that Mrs. Mallard was afflicted with a heart trouble, great care was taken to break to her as gently as possible the news of her husband's death.

It was her sister Josephine who told her, in broken sentences, veiled hints that revealed in half concealing. Her husband's friend Richards was there, too, near her. It was he who had been in the newspaper office when intelligence of the railroad disaster was received, with Brently Mallard's name leading the list of "killed." He had only taken the time to assure himself of its truth by a second telegram, and had hastened to forestall any less careful, less tender friend in bearing the sad message.

She did not hear the story as many women have heard the same, with a paralyzed inability to accept its significance. She wept at once, with sudden, wild abandonment, in her sister's arms. When the storm of grief had spent itself she went away to her room alone. She would have no one follow her.

There stood, facing the open window, a comfortable, roomy armchair. Into this she sank, pressed down by a physical exhaustion that haunted her body and seemed to reach into her soul.

5   She could see in the open square before her house the tops of trees that were all aquiver with the new spring life. The delicious breath of rain was in the air. In the street below a peddler was crying his wares. The notes of a distant song which some one was singing reached her faintly, and countless sparrows were twittering in the eaves.

There were patches of blue sky showing here and there through the clouds that had met and piled above the other in the west facing her window.

She sat with her head thrown back upon the cushion of the chair quite motionless, except when a sob came up into her throat and shook her, as a child who has cried itself to sleep continues to sob in its dreams.

She was young, with a fair, calm face, whose lines bespoke repression and even a certain strength. But now there was a dull stare in her eyes, whose gaze was fixed away off yonder on one of those patches of blue sky. It was not a glance of reflection, but rather indicated a suspension of intelligent thought.

There was something coming to her and she was waiting for it, fearfully. What was it? She did not know; it was too subtle and elusive to name. But she felt it, creeping out of the sky, reaching toward her through the sounds, the scents, the color that filled the air.

10   Now her bosom rose and fell tumultuously. She was beginning to recognize this thing that was approaching to possess her, and she was striving to beat it back with her will—as powerless as her two white slender hands would have been.

When she abandoned herself a little whispered word escaped her slightly parted lips. She said it over and over under her breath: "Free, free, free!" The vacant stare and the look of terror that had followed it went from her eyes. They stayed keen and bright. Her pulses beat fast, and the coursing blood warmed and relaxed every inch of her body.

She did not stop to ask if it were not a monstrous joy that held her. A clear and exalted perception enabled her to dismiss the suggestion as trivial.

She knew that she would weep again when she saw the kind, tender hands folded in death; the face that had never looked save with love upon her, fixed and gray and dead. But she saw beyond that bitter moment a long procession of years to come that would belong to her absolutely. And she opened and spread her arms out to them in welcome.

There would be no one to live for her during those coming years; she would live for herself. There would be no powerful will bending her in that blind persistence with which men and women believe they have a right to impose a private will upon a fellow creature. A kind intention or a cruel intention made the act seem no less a crime as she looked upon it in that brief moment of illumination.

15   And yet she had loved him—sometimes. Often she had not. What did it matter! What could love, the unsolved mystery, count for in face of this possession of self-assertion which she suddenly recognized as the strongest impulse of her being.

"Free! Body and soul free!" she kept whispering.

Josephine was kneeling before the closed door with her lips to the keyhole, imploring for admission. "Louise, open the door! I beg; open the door—you will make yourself ill. What are you doing, Louise? For heaven's sake open the door."

"Go away. I am not making myself ill." No; she was drinking in a very elixir of life through that open window.

Her fancy was running riot along those days ahead of her. Spring days, and summer days, and all sorts of days that would be her own. She breathed a quick prayer that life might be long. It was only yesterday she had thought with a shudder that life might be long.

20   She arose at length and opened the door to her sister's importunities. There was a feverish triumph in her eyes, and she carried herself unwittingly like a goddess of Victory. She clasped her sister's waist, and together they descended the stairs. Richards stood waiting for them at the bottom.

Some one was opening the front door with a latchkey. It was Brently Mallard who entered, a little travel-stained, composedly carrying his grip-sack and umbrella. He had been far from the scene of accident, and did not even know there had been one. He stood amazed at Josephine's piercing cry; at Richards' quick motion to screen him from the view of his wife.

But Richards was too late.

When the doctors came they said she had died of heart disease—of joy that kills.

✎ CONNECTING THROUGH WRITING

One of the best ways to get ideas for an essay is to ask and answer your own most compelling questions.

- Write down whatever questions come to mind during and after your reading. See if your answers to these questions provide topics for writing.

- Choose a compelling idea from a journal entry.

- Draw a Venn diagram to compare elements, characters, or stories (pp. 29–30), use directed freewriting (p. 39), ask questions (p. 40), list (pp. 40–41), or draw a cluster or semantic map (pp. 41–42) to loosen up ideas.

Listed below is a much more structured approach based on the elements of fiction discussed earlier in this section. Applying these questions to "The Story of an Hour" may demonstrate how the elements could be applied to any work of short fiction.

FIRST RESPONSES

1. What questions came to mind as you read "The Story of an Hour"?

2. To what extent can you connect "The Story of an Hour" to your own background or experience?

3. What do you find most compelling or provocative about the story?

NARRATION

1. Unlike the first-person narrative of Sandra Cisneros's "Eleven" in Chapter 2, this story is told from the third-person point of view. How does this narrative perspective affect your experience of the story?

2. What is the tone of the narration? What is the attitude of the narrator toward Mrs. Mallard? To what extent is the narrator reliable?

3. If the story were told in the first person by Mrs. Mallard herself, how would it change the way you experience it? Would you know any more than you do now? If so, what?

4. If the story were told by her sister Josephine, Brently Mallard, or the doctors, how would it change the way you experience the story?

SETTING

1. Describe the setting of "The Story of an Hour." In what location does the story take place? When does it occur?

2. What effect does the setting have on your response to the story?

3. The weather is described as: "...patches of blue sky showing here and there through the clouds that had met and piled above the other in the west facing her window." In what way does the weather agree with or contrast the action in the story?

4. What other details in Kate Chopin's writing were most effective in conveying the setting? Quote them from the text.

5. This story was originally published in 1891. If the story were written and published recently, would you have responded differently? Explain.

CONFLICT AND PLOT

1. What event in "The Story of an Hour" leads to the conflict?

2. How would you describe the conflict? Which elements of the conflict are external? Which ones are internal?

3. To what extent does the conflict derive from Mrs. Mallard and her beliefs?

4. What is the climax of this story? What is the resolution? To what extent are you satisfied with the resolution?

CHARACTER

1. Describe Mrs. Mallard. How does what she says and does show you who she is? Do you learn about her directly or indirectly? Explain.

2. How would you describe Mrs. Mallard's sister, Josephine? Richards? The doctors? Brently Mallard? What do they do or say that supports your description? Are they round or flat characters? Why?

3. What would you quote from the text to support your description of Mrs. Mallard?

4. To what extent does Mrs. Mallard change or develop in the story?

5. If Mrs. Mallard is the protagonist, who is the antagonist?

LANGUAGE AND STYLE

1. Is the language of "The Story of an Hour" formal or informal?

2. What does the nature of the language Mrs. Mallard uses tell you about her? The language of other characters? Cite examples.

3. How does the language of the narration affect you? For example, the description, "She sat with her head thrown back upon the cushion of the chair quite motionless, except when a sob came up into her throat and shook her, as a child who has cried itself to sleep continues to sob in its dreams," paints an especially touching picture. What other descriptions or images appeal to you and why?

4. Do you see any symbols in "The Story of an Hour"? If so, explain.

5. To what extent do you find the story ironic?

THEME

1. What conclusion do you draw from "The Story of an Hour"?

2. What details and events lead to this conclusion?

3. What is the point of the story? What is the theme?

TOPICS FOR WRITING

The following list is not exhaustive, but simply illustrative of the kinds of questions that might emerge from more specific analytical questions (and combinations of questions) like those above. Your responses to these questions might provide worthwhile topics for writing.

1. What is the effect of third-person narration on the characterization of Mrs. Mallard?

2. What would this story be like if told by Mrs. Mallard?

3. In what way is the setting a factor in "The Story of an Hour"?

4. In what way is the cultural context a factor in the outcome?

5. What were relationships or marriages between men and women like in 1891?

6. How does "The Story of an Hour" fit within the time period and culture in which it was written? To what extent would this story be told differently today?

READING AND ANALYZING POETRY

We are not likely to say of any event, "You can't write a poem about that." Birth, death, youth, old age, love, jealousy, ambition, loyalty, laughter, triumph, defeat—if we can experience it, we can write poetry about it. The more an experience moves us, the more important it seems to record the emotion, sensation, or memory with a poem. *Reading* poetry is a personal as well as a social experience. It is personal in the way it offers us a reflection of our own interior lives, our thoughts and emotions expressed in the words of others; and it is social in the way it offers us a glimpse of other people's interior lives, the shared expression of their hearts and minds.

If we reduce our reading to analysis alone, we may "figure out" the poem's structure, its rhyme scheme and rhythm, or how it might be classified, but we may miss the experience of the poem itself. That experience relies on our ability to imagine— the ability to take the "sleeping" poem from the print on the page and "wake it up" through our senses and emotions. This is not the kind of reading we might be used to doing in an academic environment, where we often read for information alone. And it may not be the style of reading we are used to in our everyday lives—in a world that bombards us with the exaggerated language of advertising, TV commercials, and talk shows, or reduces everything to sound bites. Given the lack of meaning in so much of that language, we may speed through it or ignore it altogether.

Poetry invites your engagement and comprehension. To be engaged by a poem, you need the time to read slowly and participate fully with your mind and senses. Once engaged, you have reason to analyze the poem's language, its structure, its rhymes or rhythms—to comprehend *how* it has prompted your response. Reading a poem this way involves your mind, senses, and emotions—and it has the power to change you the way that all meaningful experiences can.

Read the following poem.

BILLY COLLINS [B. 1941]

INTRODUCTION TO POETRY [1988]

I ask them to take a poem
and hold it up to the light
like a color slide
or press an ear against its hive.
I say drop a mouse into a poem   5
and watch him probe his way out,
or walk inside the poem's room
and feel the walls for a light switch.

I want them to water-ski
across the surface of a poem   10
waving at the author's name on the shore.
But all they want to do
is tie the poem to a chair with a rope
and torture a confession out of it.
They begin beating it with a hose   15
to find out what it really means.

MAKING CONNECTIONS

Collins's poem is describing students who are reading a poem. Do the students
do what he hopes they will? Do you when you read a poem? Explain.

LANGUAGE AND STYLE

Denotation and Connotation

Faced with an unfamiliar word—dictionary in hand—you might look up its definition and be reasonably satisfied with what you find. But if you are already familiar
with that word, a dictionary definition is not likely to account for everything the
word means to you. While you might not disagree with the dictionary definition,
or **denotation,** of the word, you probably won't be entirely satisfied with it, either.
Your own definitions, or **connotations,** for familiar words are flavored with personal
associations. Dictionary definitions alone cannot account for this complex response
to language.

The compressed nature of language and meaning in poetry makes word choice
crucial. Poets are very conscious of the effect that connotations, or suggested meanings, have on readers. Synonyms for the word *thin,* for example, include *slim, slender,
lean, skinny,* and *trim*—words that mean almost the same thing. But each of these
words has a different connotation and slightly different meaning for each of us—and
a different effect on us when we read it. Being conscious of word choices and patterns
of language may tell us a great deal about what makes a poem effective and how it
triggers our responses.

Voice

Be sure to differentiate between the poet and the speaker in a poem. In some
poems the poet and the speaker are virtually the same, and we can assume the
thoughts of the speaker are those of the poet as well. In Robert Hayden's poem
"Those Winter Sundays" (p. 13), the speaker's remembrance seems to be that of
the poet himself. On the other hand, the speaker (the **voice**) in a poem may use
vocabulary and express attitudes that are not characteristic of the poet. The speaker
in Robert Browning's "Porphyria's Lover" (p. 727), a demented, homicidal lover,
is clearly not the poet himself. Being able to identify the speaker, the speaker's
attitude toward the poem's content, and the speaker's intended audience helps us
read the poem more effectively.

Tone

The key to **tone** is voice. When we see or hear a poet speaking, the words, intonations, physical gestures, and facial expressions tell us the attitude of the speaker toward the subject. When we "hear" voice in our reading, we can also sense the intonations. Cues in a printed poem are not always obvious, however, and to sense the tone we must often rely on the pattern and types of words the poet chooses. Sometimes the contradictory nature of the language can give us a strong sense of that tone. For example, the repeated phrase in the Stephen Crane poem that follows is "War is kind," yet every detail he uses to describe war is anything but "kind" and indicates what he really means.

Irony

Irony is the contrast between appearance/expectation and reality. As in fiction, the two most popular forms of irony in poetry are verbal irony and situational irony. **Verbal irony** results from the contrast between what is said by a speaker and what is meant. **Irony of situation** results from the contrast between what is expected and what actually happens.

The following poem relies on an ironic tone to convey its meaning.

STEPHEN CRANE   [1871–1900]

WAR IS KIND   [1899]

Do not weep, maiden, for war is kind.
Because your lover threw wild hands toward the sky
And the affrighted steed ran on alone,
Do not weep.
War is kind.   5

    Hoarse, booming drums of the regiment,
    Little souls who thirst for fight,
    These men were born to drill and die.
    The unexplained glory flies above them,
    Great is the battle god, great, and his kingdom   10

A field where a thousand corpses lie.
Do not weep, babe, for war is kind.
Because your father tumbled in the yellow trenches,
Raged at his breast, gulped and died,
Do not weep.   15
War is kind.

    Swift blazing flag of the regiment,
    Eagle with crest of red and gold,
    These men were born to drill and die.

Point for them the virtue of slaughter,   20
Make plain for them the excellence of killing
And a field where a thousand corpses lie.

Mother whose heart hung humble as a button
On the bright splendid shroud of your son,
Do not weep.   25
War is kind.

MAKING CONNECTIONS

1. How do your feelings about war influence your response?
2. What do you think about the choice of words Crane uses to describe war?
3. With many poems, being sensitive to the voice of the speaker is crucial to our response. The tone expressed by that voice may change the meaning. How are you affected by the tone in this poem?
4. What indications of irony are there in the text of the poem? Is there a contradiction between the title "War Is Kind" and the details that Crane uses to support it?
5. How does the poet's tone and use of irony affect the meaning of "War Is Kind"?

Imagery

An **image** is a mental picture prompted by words. Images result from concrete language that appeals to our senses. "Nice image," we've heard people say about particularly striking words or phrases. But images do not exist in words on a page. They exist in our minds or "our mind's eye." The words on the page may prompt the images in our minds, but it is our own senses and memories that evoke the pictures. Experiments have shown that we use the same parts of our brains when we see or hear the word for an object as we do when looking at the object itself. It is our sense memories that bring a poet's words to life to form an image. We can see (hear, taste, touch, or smell) them in our mind's eye (ear, tongue, hand, or nose).

A variety of sense memories are evoked by the following poems.

HELEN CHASIN [B. 1938]

THE WORD *PLUM*   [1986]

The word *plum* is delicious

pout and push, luxury of
self-love, and savoring murmur

full in the mouth and falling
like fruit   5

taut skin
pierced, bitten, provoked into

juice, and tart flesh
question
and reply, lip and tongue   10
of pleasure.

 ## ROBERT BROWNING [1812–1889]

MEETING AT NIGHT   [1845]

The gray sea and the long black land:
And the yellow half-moon large and low;
And the startled little waves that leap
In fiery ringlets from their sleep,
As I gain the cove with pushing prow,   5
And quench its speed in the slushy sand.

Then a mile of warm sea-scented beach;
Three fields to cross till a farm appears;
A tap at the pane, the quick sharp scratch
And blue spurt of a lighted match,   10
And a voice less loud, through its joys and fears,
Than the two hearts beating each to each!

PARTING AT MORNING   [1845]

Round the cape of a sudden came the sea,
And the sun looked over the mountain's rim:
And straight was a path of gold for him,°
And the need of a world of men for me.

3 the sun

 ## MAKING CONNECTIONS

1. Not all poetry intends to make a serious statement. Some poems simply
   intend to engage us in an aesthetic or sensory experience. Does "The Word
   Plum" have a different effect on you than "Meeting at Night," "Parting at
   Morning," or "War Is Kind"? Explain.
2. To what extent can you connect "The Word *Plum*" and Browning's poems
   to your own experience? How does that connection affect your response to
   the imagery?
3. In "The Word *Plum*," the senses of taste and touch are primarily the senses
   we rely on to experience the images in the poem. How many senses do
   you use to experience the images in "Meeting at Night" and "Parting at
   Morning"?
4. How do these images add to the overall effect of the poems for you?

Figurative Language: Everyday Poetry

There is nothing unusual about figurative language. In fact, we would have a hard time communicating with each other without it. Comparison is at the core of "figures of speech," or figurative language. We use what is already familiar to describe something new, or we describe something familiar in a new way. Used in tandem with concrete language, similes and metaphors can lead to very striking images.

A **simile** is an announced comparison. We announce or introduce this comparison by using the words *like* or *as*. For example, "He's as quiet as a church mouse" or "She swims like a fish." Those things compared usually have only one characteristic in common. Some of the most evocative descriptions in literature are similes. James Joyce's description of a young boy's infatuation, "But my body was like a harp and her words and gestures were like fingers running upon the wires" (see "Araby," p. 407), and Marge Piercy's words, "Her good nature wore out like a fan belt" (see "Barbie Doll," p. 14), are vivid examples of how simile can evoke lasting images in our minds.

Simile is the dominant poetic effect in the two poems that follow.

LANGSTON HUGHES [1902–1967]

A DREAM DEFERRED   [1951]

What happens to a dream deferred?

Does it dry up
like a raisin in the sun?
Or fester like a sore—
And then run?   5
Does it stink like rotten meat?
Or crust and sugar over—
like a syrupy sweet?
Maybe it just sags
like a heavy load.   10

Or does it explode?

N. SCOTT MOMADAY [B. 1934]

SIMILE   [1974]

What did we say to each other
that now we are as the deer
who walk in single file
with heads high
with ears forward   5
with eyes watchful
with hooves always placed on firm ground
in whose limbs there is latent flight

MAKING CONNECTIONS

1. Each of these poems relies on comparison to make its point. To what extent do these comparisons bring personal experiences to mind?
2. There are five announced comparisons (similes) and one implied comparison (metaphor) in "A Dream Deferred." What are they? What images do they prompt in you? What senses do you use to experience them?
3. As its title suggests, there is one announced comparison in "Simile." What is it? What image does it prompt in you?
4. To what extent are you affected differently by the many brief similes of "A Dream Deferred" in comparison to the one extended simile in "Simile"?
5. What is the point of each poem? In each case, how do the similes present it effectively?
6. To what extent is "A Dream Deferred" similar to Hughes's short story "One Friday Morning" (p. 1076)?

A **metaphor** is a more direct and more complete comparison than a simile. A metaphor does not announce itself; it states that something *is* something else (My love is a red rose) or implies it (My love has red petals and sharp thorns). Our everyday language is filled with metaphors. We call attractive-looking people hunks and foxes. Businesses use implied metaphors to name their products. We buy an antiperspirant named Arrid, soap named Irish Spring, laptop computers named Macbooks, and cars named Jaguars. Sometimes, however, people get carried away and mix metaphors, with confusing rather than clarifying results. A baseball manager once remarked about a suspended player that "The ball was in his court now [tennis], so he better not step out of bounds [basketball], or he'd be down for the count [boxing]." Try to picture that!

Note the metaphor in the following poem.

CARL SANDBURG [1878–1967]

FOG   [1916]

The fog comes
on little cat feet.
It sits looking
over harbor and city
on silent haunches   5
and then moves on.

Personification is a frequently used form of metaphor. To personify is to give human characteristics or qualities to something not human. Consider how often you personify objects in your everyday use of language. The following poem illustrates personification.

JAMES STEPHENS [1882–1950]

THE WIND [1915]

The wind stood up and gave a shout.
He whistled on his fingers and

Kicked the withered leaves about
And thumped the branches with his hand

And said he'd kill and kill and kill,   5
And so he will and so he will.

MAKING CONNECTIONS

1. To what extent is your response to "Fog" or "The Wind" influenced by your own experience? Support your explanation with reference to the poems.
2. What are the metaphors in each poem?
3. What images do they prompt in you?
4. What senses do you use to experience them?
5. How do these images add to the overall effect of the poems?

Symbol

*A **symbol** is something that represents more than itself.* Every word we speak is a symbol. Government flags, religious objects, and logos on college sweatshirts are all symbols. We have personal symbols (meaningful objects, special songs), public symbols (flags), and conventional symbols (a road as the journey of life, seasons to represent the stages of our lives). Symbols are subject to personal interpretation. A nation's flag may symbolize truth and justice to one person, but deceit and oppression to another. Note the symbol in the following poem.

 # ROBERT FROST [1874–1963]

THE ROAD NOT TAKEN [1915]

Two roads diverged in a yellow wood
And sorry I could not travel both
And be one traveler, long I stood
And looked down one as far as I could
To where it bent in the undergrowth;   5

Then took the other, as just as fair,
And having perhaps the better claim,
Because it was grassy and wanted wear,
Though as for that the passing there
Had worn them really about the same.   10

And both that morning equally lay
In leaves no step had trodden black.
Oh, I kept the first for another day!
Yet knowing how way leads on to way,
I doubted if I should ever come back.   15

I shall be telling this with a sigh
somewhere ages and ages hence:
Two roads diverged in a wood, and I—
I took the one less traveled by,
And that has made all the difference.   20

MAKING CONNECTIONS

1. To what extent is your response to "The Road Not Taken" influenced by
   your own experience?
2. What is the symbol in "The Road Not Taken"?
3. What images does the poem prompt in you?
4. What senses do you use to experience these images?
5. How does the symbolism add to the overall effect of the poem for you?

For a concise checklist of questions for Language and Style, see page 91.

SOUND AND STRUCTURE

Long before we had the ability to speak, we enjoyed making and listening to
sounds. As newcomers to the world, we were probably soothed or frightened
by the sound of the adult voices around us. The sounds we made helped us
develop our vocal cords, but there was much more to it than that. We listened
to the sounds we made and adjusted them until we got them just right. We
made the leap from gurgles and hisses to new sounds with syllables like ba-ba,
ma-ma, da-da.

The amazing thing is that this happened before we could speak or comprehend
the adult language that surrounded us. Those sounds were a universal language we
shared with children all over the world. And those sounds, like music, seemed to
have an appeal in and of themselves—an appeal we haven't forgotten. Sometimes
we listen to songs and sing along or sing the songs to ourselves—even when we
don't know all the words. And sometimes we like the sounds of the words and the
rhymes and rhythms of poems just as much as their meanings.

Alliteration, Assonance, and Rhyme

As kids in school, we may have used rhymes to memorize the number of days in
each month or the names of the states or presidents. The most obvious rhymes
come at ends of lines when final vowel and consonant sounds in a word at the end
of one line match vowel and consonant sounds at the end of another (l*and* and
s*and,* th*ings* and k*ings,* b*are* and desp*air*).

Less obvious are repeated initial consonant sounds ("*do* or *die*," "*s*ink or *s*wim," "*s*uffering *s*uccotash"), which is called **alliteration.**

Less obvious still are **assonance,** or repeated vowel sounds (t*i*me l*i*ne, fr*ee* and *ea*sy), and **consonance,** or repeated consonant sounds (sho*rt* and sma*rt,* st*ru*ts and f*re*ts).

When we listen to music, we are moved along (in spirit and time) and can anticipate structure by patterns and combinations of repeated tones. If we listen sensitively to rhyme and rhythm in poetry, we are likely to have a similar experience.

Look at the following quatrains (units of four lines) from two different William Blake poems. This quatrain has an *ab, ab* rhyme scheme:

From "London"

In every cry of every Man,	(*a*)
In every Infant's cry of fear,	(*b*)
In every voice, in every ban,	(*a*)
The mind-forg'd manacles I hear.	(*b*)

This quatrain has an *aa, bb* rhyme scheme:

From "The Tyger"

In what distant deeps or skies	(*a*)
Burnt the fire of thine eyes?	(*a*)
On what wings dare he aspire?	(*b*)
What the hand dare seize the fire?	(*b*)

Recite each quatrain out loud several times. How does the ordering of rhyme affect your pace? How does it affect the content of the lines and the units of thought you remember?

Examine other poems in this section. For example, Robert Browning's "Meeting at Night" and Robert Frost's "The Road Not Taken" have very different rhyme schemes. Read them out loud and see how the rhyme scheme affects how you hear and organize the content of the poems.

Rhyme and Rhythm: Limericks

A light, usually humorous, form of poetry that is helpful for getting the feel of rhyme and rhythm is the **limerick.** Limericks are very common and almost always anonymous (usually for good reason), and we're just as likely to see them scrawled on a wall as on paper.

There was a young maid who said, "Why	(*a*)
Can't I look in my ear with my eye?	(*a*)
If I put my mind to it,	(*b*)
I'm sure I can do it.	(*b*)
You never can tell till you try."	(*a*)

Read it out loud several times. Listen to the rhythm. Look at the rhyme pattern or scheme. Which lines rhyme? What is the rhythm like? Can you describe the pattern of a limerick? If you need to, read it out loud again.

Limericks have five lines. The first, second, and fifth lines rhyme (*aaa,* above) and so do the third and fourth (*bb,* above). The first, second, and fifth have approximately the same verbal rhythm (**meter**) and length, and so do the third and fourth.

Haiku Poetry

A more sophisticated poetic form that relies on sounds is the *haiku*. The haiku has a long tradition in its native Japanese, but a much briefer history in English. For much of its early history in Japan, haiku was a short section of a longer poem called a *haikai*. The traditional haiku is an unrhymed poem consisting of seventeen "sounds," or characters representing sounds (we refer to these in English as syllables), distributed over three lines (line 1—five sounds, line 2—seven sounds, line 3—five sounds). The goal of a Haiku poem is compression of meaning—and by nature of its seventeen syllables, conciseness. Here are some examples:

CHIYOJO*   [1703–1775]

Whether astringent
I do not know. This is my first
Persimmon picking.

*Translated by Daniel Crump Buchanan

BASHO*   [1644–1694]

A village without bells—
how do they live?
spring dusk.

*Translated by Robert Hass

BUSON*   [1716–1783]

Listening to the moon,
gazing at the croaking of frogs
in a field of ripe rice.

*Translated by Robert Hass

Modern Haiku in English

JENNIFER BRUTSCHY [B. 1960]

BORN AGAIN

Born Again
she speaks excitedly
of death

A particularly sad and poignant use of haiku poetry was the work of interned Japanese Americans. In the 1940s, in a shameful act, the U.S. government branded Japanese Americans as "enemy aliens" and interned them in concentration camps. A number of those interned turned to haiku poetry to express their pain. See one of these below.

SUIKO MATSUSHITA

RAIN SHOWER FROM MOUNTAIN*

Rain shower from mountain
quietly soaking
barbed wire fence

*Translated by Violet Kazue de Cristoforo

MAKING CONNECTIONS

If you want to write some haiku poems, poet and translator X. J. Kennedy has suggested that you should "make every word matter," "set your poem in the present," and "confine your poem" to the five senses.

1. Do you "get" (understand) the point of these poems? Explain.
2. Haiku is often used to introduce poetry to children. Do you find these poems harder or easier to comprehend (or to write) than other forms? Explain.
3. Write a haiku. In what way does your poem "qualify" as a haiku?

Meter

Rhythm in poetry is often described by the word *meter*. Meter refers to the pattern of stressed (/) and unstressed (˘) syllables in a line. The group of syllables making up one metrical unit is called a foot. The metrical feet most commonly used are iambic (unstressed, stressed), trochaic (stressed, unstressed), anapestic (two unstressed, one stressed), and dactylic (one stressed, two unstressed).

The number of feet in each line is described as **monometer** (one foot), **dimeter** (two feet), **trimeter** (three feet), **tetrameter** (four feet), **pentameter** (five feet), **hexameter** (six feet), **heptameter** (seven feet), and **octameter** (eight feet).

The most common form of meter in poetry written in English is **iambic** (unstressed, stressed) **pentameter** (five feet).

The pair of lines from two sonnets written over three hundred years apart are examples of iambic pentameter (five feet of iambic per line):

Dĕsír\ĭng thís\ măn's aŕt \ănd thát\ măn's scópe
Wĭth whát\ Ĭ móst\ ĕnjóy\ cŏntént\ĕd leást;

  —William Shakespeare [1609]

Nŏr ýet\ă flóat\ĭng spár\ tŏ mén\ thăt sínk
Ănd riśe\ ănd sínk\ ănd riśe\ ănd sínk\ ăgaín;

  —Edna St. Vincent Millay [1931]

Formal Verse: The Sonnet

One of the most popular and enduring formal verse structures is the sonnet. Sonnets are fourteen lines long and are usually written in iambic pentameter. Rhyme schemes will vary according to type. The oldest form of the sonnet is the Italian, or Petrarchan, sonnet (named for its greatest practitioner, Petrarch). Its rhyme scheme is usually an octave (eight lines) and a sestet (six lines). The octave usually follows a pattern of *abbaabba*. The concluding sestet may be *cdecde* or *cdcdcd* or *cdedce*.

FRANCIS PETRARCH [1304–1374]

THE EYES THAT DREW FROM ME* [1348]

The eyes that drew from me with such fervent praise. (*a*)
The arms and hands and feet and countenance. (*b*)
Which made me a stranger in my own romance. (*b*)
And set me apart from the well trodden ways; (*a*)
The gleaming golden curly hair, the rays. (*a*)   5
Flashing from a smiling angel's glance. (*b*)
Which moved the world in paradisal dance (*b*)
Are grains of dust, insensibilities. (*a*)
And I live on, but in grief and self contempt. (*c*)
Left here without the light I loved so much, (*d*)   10
In a great tempest and with shrouds unkempt. (*c*)
No more love songs, then, I have done with such; (*d*)
My old skill now runs thin at each attempt. (*c*)
And years are heard within the heart by touch. (*d*)

*Translated by Edwin Morgan

In English, the most popular form is the English, or Shakespearean, sonnet (named for its greatest practitioner, Shakespeare, who wrote 154 of them), so we use it here to illustrate formal verse. The Shakespearean sonnet is a fourteen-line poem of three quatrains (four-line units) and a final couplet (a two-line unit) in the rhyme scheme *abab cdcd efef gg*. It is a structure that presents the content of the poem in predictable ways. The first two quatrains often present a problem. The third quatrain is often pivotal and begins a reversal. The final couplet most often suggests a solution.

 ## WILLIAM SHAKESPEARE [1564–1616]

WHEN, IN DISGRACE WITH FORTUNE AND MEN'S EYES (SONNET 29) [1609]

When, in disgrace with Fortune and men's eyes, (*a*)
I all alone beweep my outcast state, (*b*)
And trouble deaf heaven with my bootless° cries, (*a*)
And look upon myself, and curse my fate, (*b*)
Wishing me like to one more rich in hope, (*c*)   5

3 bootless useless

Featured like him, like him with friends possessed, (*d*)
Desiring this man's art and that man's scope, (*c*)
With what I most enjoy contented least; (*d*)
Yet in these thoughts myself almost despising, (*e*)
Haply I think on thee—and then my state, (*f*)   10
Like to the lark at break of day arising (*e*)
From sullen earth, sings hymns at heaven's gate; (*f*)
For thy sweet love remembered such wealth brings (*g*)
That then I scorn to change my state with kings. (*g*)

⟋MAKING CONNECTIONS

1. Describe the emotions of the speakers in both the Petrarch and Shakespeare sonnets.
2. Do their situations bring to mind any of your own experiences? Would you describe love in the same way? How does that affect your response?
3. In what way does the sonnet structure of each affect your response? To what extent does the form (the structure and rhyme scheme) of each sonnet deliver the substance?

Blank Verse

Another popular form is **blank verse.** Blank verse is unrhymed but follows a regular verse form, usually iambic pentameter. Some of the greatest epic poems and plays (including Milton's *Paradise Lost* and Shakespeare's plays) have been written in blank verse, and it is still a very popular form today.

Here are the first four lines from Robert Frost's "Mending Wall." The entire poem is forty-five lines long (see p. 280).

Something there is that doesn't love a wall
That sends the frozen ground swell under it
And spills the upper boulders in the sun,
And makes gaps even two can pass abreast.

While it does not rhyme, the iambic pentameter still moves us from line to line in a regular, predictable rhythm and influences our "hearing" of the poem. Read it out loud several times and see if you can hear and feel the regular beat.

Iambic pentameter is the dominant pattern in blank verse, but every word and every line may not conform to this pattern. For example, "Something," the first word of Frost's poem above, with its emphasis on the first syllable, is trochaic (stressed, unstressed), not iambic (unstressed, stressed). So, too, while the dominant pattern of Shakespeare's sonnets and plays is blank verse, not every foot is iambic, nor every line pentameter. You will find a number of exceptions to this pattern in the sonnets and *Hamlet* (p. 495) in this text.

Free or Open Form Verse

As its name implies, this is verse that is not constrained by an imposed form. **Free** or **open form verse** does not have a rhyme scheme or regular rhythm. It is not formless, however, but relies on its own words and content to determine its best form. The poem that follows was written by Walt Whitman, a celebrated pioneer of free-verse writing.

 # WALT WHITMAN [1819–1892]

WHEN I HEARD THE LEARN'D ASTRONOMER   [1865]

When I heard the learn'd astronomer,
When the proofs, the figures, were ranged in columns before me,
When I was shown the charts and diagrams, to add, divide, and measure them,
When I sitting heard the astronomer where he lectured with applause in the
    lecture-room,
How soon unaccountable I became tired and sick,   5
Till rising and gliding out I wander'd off by myself,
In the mystical moist night-air, and from time to time,
Look'd up in perfect silence at the stars.

 ## MAKING CONNECTIONS

1. Have you ever been in a situation where the explanation of the experience paled in comparison to the experience itself? Explain.
2. What does the speaker mean when he says, "How soon unaccountable I became tired and sick"?
3. How does the free verse affect your response to the poem?

For a concise checklist of questions for Sound and Structure, see page 91.

Interpretation: What Does the Poem Mean?

Theme is the meaning we construct from the poem. It is an insight about life that we derive from the poem as a whole. Identifying and articulating this meaning is not an easy task. While our experience of the poem may be holistic or impression-istic, the analysis and support required for its articulation demand a close look at the parts—the language, events, and outcome of the poem.

As with fiction, be wary of reducing what the poem means to a moral or lesson. Good literature reveals a complex world. A moral preaches; it teaches us a lesson or a code of conduct. A theme reveals; it gives us insight into human nature.

Explication

An **explication** involves a line-by-line analysis of a text. Since works of fiction or drama are usually long, an explication would take quite a bit of time and space and would probably be better left to a lengthy term paper. Most poems, however, are relatively brief and by their nature "packed with meaning." So they present a good opportunity for a very close reading and examination—an opportunity to look closely at sounds, words, images, lines, and how they all work together to deliver the poem's meaning. An explication is not just a summary or translation of the poet's language into your own; it is a detailed interpretation of *how* and *what* you believe the poem means.

Like other forms of literature, poems are not problems to be solved. They don't have one correct answer or interpretation. Remember, what makes an interpretation convincing or defensible is your ability to support it.

For a concise checklist of questions for Interpretation and Theme, see page 91.

TYPES OF POETRY

For the sake of clarification and simplification, poetry may be classified into two types: lyric and narrative. As with other forms of literature, classifications of this kind are not exclusive. There is overlap between the designations lyric and narrative. Poems in each of these categories may have elements characteristic of the other. And both lyric and narrative poetry have dramatic qualities.

Lyric Poetry

Lyric poetry is the most popular form of poetry written today. Lyric poems are characterized by the expression of the speaker's innermost feelings, thoughts, and imagination. The word *lyric* is taken from a stringed musical instrument called the lyre, which was used in classical and medieval times to accompany a singer. In addition to the very subjective stance of the speaker, lyric poems are melodic—a melody derived not from a lyre but from words and their arrangement. It's not mere coincidence that the words that accompany the melody in a song are called lyrics. Most of the poetry in this text can be classified as lyric poetry, and a specific example of this type is Edna St. Vincent Millay's "Love Is Not All" (p. 739).

One kind of lyric poetry that deserves special mention is the **dramatic monologue.** In a dramatic monologue, the poet, like an actor in a play, assumes a different persona and speaks to us through the voice and personality of another person. Robert Browning's "Porphyria's Lover" (p. 727) is an example of a dramatic monologue.

Narrative Poetry

A narrative poem tells a story. The poet takes on a role similar to that of a narrator in a work of fiction. The oldest stories were recorded in poetry and recited by "bards," who used the rhythms of the verse to help them memorize their lines. One difference between the narratives of short stories and those of narrative poems is length. With the exception of epic poems—book-length narrative poems with lots of room for development of conflict and character—the length of most narrative poems limits the development of conflict and character. The brevity of the poems allows little space for exposition, and the poem usually moves quickly to the "chase," or crisis, beginning virtually in the middle of the story (or *in medias res*). Dudley Randall's "Ballad of Birmingham" (p. 17) and Seamus Heaney's "Mid-Term Break" (p. 481) are examples of narrative poems.

For a concise checklist of questions for Types of Poetry, see page 91.

☑ CHECKLIST: ANALYZING POETRY

Language and Style

❏ How are you affected by the speaker's voice?

❏ Is there anything ironic in the poem? How so?

❏ What images do you experience? Are there similes or metaphors? Is there symbolism? If so, identify them in the poem.

❏ How do voice, irony, imagery, figurative language, and/or symbolism affect your response?

Sound and Structure

❏ Is there a rhyme scheme in the poem? If so, what is its pattern? How does the rhyme scheme add to the overall effect of the poem?

❏ Are there other sound devices (alliteration, assonance, consonance)? If so, identify them and indicate how they affect your response.

❏ Is there a regular pattern to the verse? If so, describe it. How does it add to the effect of the poem? If there is no regular pattern, how does the unique form of the poem match the content? How did it affect your response?

Interpretation and Theme

❏ What are the major details (images, symbols, rhymes, rhythms, etc.) of the poem?

❏ What conclusion can you draw from these details?

❏ To what extent does this conclusion lead to a generalization about life? What is the central idea expressed by the poem?

Types of Poetry

❏ Is the poem an expression of the poet's thoughts and feelings, or is it telling a story? Is it a narrative or lyric poem?

GETTING IDEAS FOR WRITING ABOUT POETRY

The purpose of the poem, the prompts, and the questions in this section is to show how the elements we've discussed earlier might be applied to poetry. Following "Pigeon Woman," many of the questions from the summary checklist above are applied to the poem, and we consider some of the ways the elements discussed in this section might be used to prompt ideas for an essay.

MAY SWENSON [1919–1989]

PIGEON WOMAN   [1958]

Slate, or dirty-marbled-colored,
or rusty-iron-colored, the pigeons
on the flagstones in front of the
Public Library make a sharp lake

into which the pigeon woman wades   5
at exactly 1:30. She wears a
plastic pink raincoat with a round
collar (looking like a little

girl, so gay) and flat gym shoes,
her hair square-cut, orange.   10
Wide-apart feet carefully enter
the spinning, crooning waves

(as if she'd just learned how
to walk, each step conscious,
an accomplishment); blue knots in the   15
calves of her bare legs (uglied marble),

age in angled cords of jaw
and neck, her pimento-colored hair,
hanging in thin tassels, is gray
around a balding crown.   20

The day-old bread drops down
from her veined hand dipping out
of a paper sack. Choppy, shadowy ripples,
the pigeons strike around her legs.

Sack empty, she squats and seems to rinse   25
her hands in them—the rainy greens and
oily purples of their necks. Almost
they let her wet thirsty fingertips—

but drain away in an untouchable tide.
A make-believe trade   30
she has come to, in her lostness
of illness or age—to treat the motley

city pigeons at 1:30 every day, in all
weathers. It is for them she colors her own
feathers. Ruddy-footed   35
on the lime stained paving,

purling to meet her when she comes,
they are a lake of love. Retreating
from her hands as soon as empty
they are the flints of love.   40

CONNECTING THROUGH WRITING

One of the best ways to get ideas for an essay is to ask and answer your own most compelling questions.

- Write down whatever questions come to mind during and after your reading. See if your answers to these questions provide topics for writing.
- Choose a compelling idea from a journal entry.
- Draw a Venn diagram to compare elements, characters, or stories (pp. 29–30), use directed freewriting (p. 39), ask questions (p. 40), list (pp. 40–41), or draw a cluster or semantic map (pp. 41–42) to loosen up ideas.

Listed below is a more structured approach based on the elements of poetry discussed earlier in this section. Applying these questions to "Pigeon Woman" may demonstrate how the elements might be applied to any poem.

FIRST RESPONSES

1. What questions came to mind as you read "Pigeon Woman"?

2. What words or expressions are not clear to you?

3. To what extent can you connect "Pigeon Woman" to your own background or experience?

4. What do you find most compelling or provocative about the poem?

LANGUAGE AND STYLE

1. Who is the speaker in "Pigeon Woman"? What kind of voice does she have? What is the speaker's tone? What is the speaker's attitude toward the woman being described?

2. One image in the poem describes the pigeons as making "a sharp lake into which the pigeon woman wades." Where else in the poem is that image supported?

3. What other images in the poem have an effect on you? To what senses do the images appeal?

4. What similes or metaphors do you find in the poem? How do they contribute to the imagery?

5. How does the figurative language in "Pigeon Woman" help to convey its meaning?

6. Is there symbolism in the poem? Explain.

SOUND AND STRUCTURE

1. This poem does not have an obvious rhyme scheme. How does that affect your response?

2. What instances of alliteration or assonance can you identify?

3. To what extent does "Pigeon Woman" have a rhythm or a regular pattern to the verse? How does that influence your reading?

4. How does the form of "Pigeon Woman" match its content? To what extent does it help to convey its meaning?

INTERPRETATION AND THEME

1. What does the last line, "they are the flints of love," mean?

2. What are the major details of the poem?

3. What conclusion can you draw from the details? What is the poem about?

4. To what extent does this conclusion lead to a generalization about life?

5. What is the theme of "Pigeon Woman"?

TYPES OF POETRY

1. Is "Pigeon Woman" expressing the poet's innermost thoughts and feelings, or is it telling a story? Is it a narrative or lyric poem? Explain.

TOPICS FOR WRITING

The following list is not exhaustive, but simply illustrative of the kinds of questions that might emerge from the more specific analytical questions (and combinations of questions) like those above. Your responses to these questions might provide worthwhile topics for writing.

1. To what extent is "Pigeon Woman" a love story?

2. Some poems paint pictures; some make statements. In what way does this poem do both?

3. How do the structure, images, and sounds of the poem convey the meaning of "Pigeon Woman"?

4. To what extent is this poem a comment about human relationships?

5. It is not unusual to see lonely old people looking for companionship. In what way does "Pigeon Woman" enable us to "be there" and experience what that means?

6. Many people rely on the company of "nature's creatures" for companionship. To what extent is this a poem about this kind of mutual dependency?

7. How necessary was it to understand the social circumstances of the woman to make sense of the poem?

8. Can you compare this poem or the woman in it to another work or character in that work? Explain.

9. This poem was written in 1958. Does it still make sense today? How so?

10. Are you familiar with other poems of May Swenson? If so, how does this poem compare with them?

READING AND ANALYZING DRAMA

Since earliest times, people have had the need to act out and witness stories. Telling them and hearing them was important, too, but witnessing the drama of the story as it happened was a different kind of experience. Ancient hunters wore masks of the animals they hunted because they believed that by mimicking their behavior they would come to know, understand, and honor them—and, of course, hunt them more effectively. From the time of the ancient Greeks to the present, however, we have shared a somewhat more idealistic goal. We've believed that by acting out and witnessing the struggle of other human beings, we are enlightened about the nature of our own lives.

To look at the history of drama, and its development, is to learn a great deal about who people were and what they valued at different times in history. Whatever technological, social, or political developments have changed us over the last several thousand years, it is clear that there are important ties at the core of human experience that still bind us with our ancient ancestors.

Although we have seen dramatists' definitions of a hero or protagonist change over the years, from Aristotle's "characters of a higher type" to Arthur Miller's "common man [and woman]," the focus of drama remains the struggle of characters to face life with a sense of purpose and dignity. From the Greeks to the present, characters struggle with the gods, themselves, each other, and society. They rise to heroic heights or fall from them. Of noble birth, they may fail to be humble, and fall. Of humble birth, they may struggle to be noble, and triumph.

As we witness drama at its best from any period, we see ourselves and recollect the struggle of our own lives. And most of all, we are reminded of the human drama outside the theater, where joy and suffering, courage and cowardice, have been acted out for no audience in particular for thousands of years.

Reading a Play

Drama is meant to be seen and heard, so attending a good performance of a play is almost always preferable to reading it. In addition to what you see and hear onstage, the sense of community you share with the audience can be an integral part of your experience. If you are reading a play, though, there are a few strategies that may enhance your experience.

To read a play effectively, try to create the stage in your mind. Imagine you are sitting in a theater watching a performance. If there are stage directions, read them carefully. Try to imagine the set, props, and action, and hear the voices. Be conscious of what the characters say and how their words can help you picture the scene. If you are not sure who a character is, you may need to go back from time to time to read the list of characters or reread the dialogue.

Point of View

A play does not usually have a narrator to interpret the action for us. Most often we see the play through our own eyes. We observe the actions of the characters, hear what they say and what is said about them, and make our own judgments.

In Greek drama, however, it is the function of the chorus and *Choragos* (the leader of the chorus) to address the audience from time to time to remind us about the cultural and historical context of the play and the significance of the action and dialogue. In Shakespearean drama, the characters themselves will sometimes speak directly to us in asides or soliloquies. In the play *Hamlet,* for example, the character Hamlet shares his thoughts directly with us at important times throughout the play. And occasionally in a modern play a character acts as narrator and comments on the action at timely intervals. Such is the role that Tom plays in Tennessee Williams's *The Glass Menagerie* (p. 966). But generally, whether attending a performance or reading a play, we are on our own.

For a concise checklist of questions for Point of View, see page 108.

Set and Setting

In drama, the immediate setting is the set itself. When attending a play, it's often the first part of the drama we experience. It draws us into another world. We know it's not real, but we are prepared to forget that once the action starts. As we look at the set and wonder what the action will be like, we are already beginning to experience the play.

As in fiction, setting is more than the place and time period of the play. It has a direct and indirect impact on character and conflict. It supports and emphasizes the play's meaning. *Its most important function is to make us feel present in the world that the characters inhabit.*

In the history of theater, sets and settings have varied widely. Greek and Shakespearean plays were originally performed on a bare set, and the setting was sometimes described by the characters themselves or by a narrator, but always imagined by the audience. Over the years, both Greek and Shakespearean drama have often been performed with elaborate sets (particularly in videos and films). In most modern plays, the nature of the setting is spelled out in detail in the script. For example, the printed texts in this volume of the Greek play *Antigonê* (p. 113) and the Shakespearean play *Hamlet* (p. 495) contain little indication of the nature of the setting beyond a broad reference to location. On the other hand, the texts of modern plays like *A Doll's House* (p. 803), *The Glass Menagerie* (p. 966), and *A Raisin in the Sun* (p. 310) contain very specific details about the nature of the set and setting.

Location tells us where and when the story is taking place. Both the *where* and the *when* will strongly influence the values and behavior of the characters and color the rest of the play. **Atmosphere** is the mix of location and more changeable circumstances, such as conflict, the characters present, the time of day, the season, and the weather. Its overall effect supports and complements conflict and character and helps to convey the play's meaning.

For a concise checklist of questions for Set and Setting, see pages 108–109.

Conflict

Conflict is at the heart of every play. The impediments and complications the characters must overcome keep us watching or reading. The more important, challenging, believable, and coherent a conflict is, the more we are engaged by the action and dialogue, and the greater our desire to follow it to its conclusion.

Internal and External Conflict   **External conflict** may be physical (characters against nature) or social (characters against each other or against society). **Internal conflict** is a struggle of opposing forces within a character. The best drama contains elements of both types of conflict, but the emphasis is usually on the internal elements.

Conflict and Characterization   As in fiction, who the characters are, how they feel about themselves, and how they behave are at the core of both external and internal conflict.

Plot

Plot is the structure of the play. It is the pattern of twists and turns that the play takes. Most plots spring from conflict. To have a discernible plot, we must have impediments, complications, and opposition.

The traditional arrangement of plot in drama is virtually the same as it is in fiction. It follows a pattern of exposition, rising action, crisis (sometimes called climax), falling action, and resolution (sometimes called denouement or untying).

The fundamental difference between plot in fiction and drama is how we experience the plot. Without the benefit of a narrator, we are limited to action and dialogue, so the plot must develop entirely through what we see and hear onstage.

> *Exposition:* We learn what we need to know about the circumstances, characters, and the potential conflict through dialogue and action.
>
> *Rising Action:* An event occurs that builds the conflict, and our emotional involvement intensifies.
>
> *Crisis, or Climax:* The main character is in the moment of truth. The turning point of the conflict (sometimes called a reversal) begins.
>
> *Falling Action:* The conflict is beyond the crisis, the intensity subsides, and the outcome seems inevitable.
>
> *Resolution:* The details are wrapped up and we are returned to normalcy.

Applying this pattern to drama can be problematic. Modern playwrights in particular do not limit their work to conform to a pattern that wraps the conflict up so neatly. The structure of many modern plays emerges naturally from the content of the play and bears little resemblance to this classical pattern.

The Poetics

The Poetics of Aristotle is the earliest surviving work of literary criticism in the Western world. Written between 335 and 322 BCE, more than one hundred years after the works of Aeschylus, Sophocles, and Euripides were first produced, it was modeled on plays that Aristotle liked best. It is our earliest written set of standards for dramatic art, and it continues to be influential today. The plays of Sophocles were particularly favored by Aristotle, so Sophocles's *Antigonê* in this text is a good model of these standards.

Tragedy

The Poetics defines tragedy as the imitation of an action that is serious and of sufficient magnitude, that is expressed in artistic language, that is performed through drama instead of narration, and that accomplishes catharsis through the arousal of pity and fear. Aristotle emphasizes the nature of the **tragic hero** and the importance of plot in tragedy. He defines his tragic hero as a character of noble stature who is admired by society but flawed. The flaw (often excessive pride, or hubris) leads directly to a reversal of good fortune (catastrophe). But the punishment usually exceeds the crime, and the character deserves our pity. The tragic fall is not a complete loss, as the character gains in wisdom and self-knowledge. Finally, there is a recognition of the causes and consequences of this reversal, and a resolution returns things to normal. The audience, enlightened by the play, experiences **catharsis** (emotional purging or cleansing).

Comedy

Aristotle does not have as much to say about comedy, which he considers a lower form of drama. The traditional plot of comedy is the reverse of tragedy. The protagonist, usually an ordinary person, faces a dilemma. The plot of the play is an extrication from this dilemma and an improvement of circumstances. The reversal of fortune, therefore, is from bad to good; the falling action becomes a rising action with a happy ending. Aristotle suggests that "characters of a higher type" are fit subjects for tragedy, but "persons inferior" are appropriate for comedy.

Although these classifications of tragedy and comedy have been in place since the age of Greek drama, most plays since that time have not strictly conformed to these requirements. Modern plays in particular often contain elements of both tragedy and comedy, a classification called tragicomedy, which is discussed later in the chapter.

For a concise checklist of questions for Conflict and Plot, see page 109.

Characterization

*As in fiction, **characterization** in drama is the development of characters.* But unlike fiction, where some characterization is done through description, characterization in most drama is limited to action and dialogue. We find out about the characters indirectly. We are not told what to think or feel about them. We observe them speaking and doing. We hear what other characters have to say about them. If they are well developed, they seem believable and motivated. Like our response to people in our lives, our response to them and our judgments about them are based on our own observations.

The same terms in both drama and fiction are used to describe characters. The main character in a drama is called the *protagonist*. A character who seems to be a major force in opposition to the protagonist is called an *antagonist*. When characters are not fully developed but seem to represent "types" more than real personalities, we call them *flat*, or *stock, characters*. When they seem fully developed with the complexities of real people, they are described as *round characters*.

For a concise checklist of questions for Characterization, see page 109.

LANGUAGE AND STYLE

Language is the vehicle that carries the characters to us. The style of language used by the characters tells us a lot about them. And the symbolic nature of the language may complement and support the story's theme or meaning.

Greek and Shakespearean plays are written in verse. This very formal style has a very different effect on the audience than the informal vernacular used in modern drama.

Diction

An important element in establishing characters is the kind of language they use to express themselves. This is especially important in drama because what we know is usually limited to dialogue and action. Characters are often defined as much by *how* they say something as *what* they say. Diction is particularly important in the naturalistic speech of modern drama, where it tells us a great deal about class and cultural distinctions.

Symbol

A **symbol** *is something that represents more than itself*. In drama, the set, costumes, and props are often used symbolically. The set (the furniture, the size of the room, the light, the color, etc.) often reflects the content of the play itself. The props (the objects onstage and those used by the characters) often reflect the conflict, characters, and theme of the play. The costumes tell us a great deal about the characters themselves.

Irony

Irony *is the contrast between appearance/expectation and reality*. As in fiction and poetry, the two most popular forms of irony in drama are verbal irony and situational irony. **Verbal irony** results from the contrast between what is said by characters and what is meant. **Irony of situation** results from the contrast between what is expected and what actually happens.

For a concise checklist of questions for Language and Style, see page 109.

THEME

As in fiction and poetry, *theme is the central idea expressed by the play*. It is a generalization, an insight about life, that we derive from the play as a whole. Identifying and articulating this meaning is not an easy task. While our experience of the theme may be holistic or impressionistic, the analysis and support required for its articulation demand a close look at the parts—the language, events, characters, and outcome of the play.

Like fiction and poetry, plays do not have one correct answer or interpretation. What makes an interpretation convincing or defensible is your ability to support it. Your belief about what the play means may change as you move back and forth through the stages of your reading or viewing experience. The first time you experience a play, you may feel one way, but writing down your reflections, rereading the play, and discussing it with others may lead to a different, better-informed understanding and interpretation.

Theme or Moral?   It is tempting when writing about literature to reduce what it means to a moral or lesson. Good literature reveals a complex world. A moral preaches; it teaches us a lesson or a code of conduct. A theme reveals; it gives us an insight into human nature.

One of the functions of classical drama is to illuminate the audience spiritually, so it's almost certain that we will be left with a clear message by the end of a play. In this respect, Greek plays tend to be **didactic,** or lesson-giving, in a way that most drama since the time of Shakespeare is not.

For a concise checklist of questions for Theme, see page 109.

PERIODS OF DRAMA: A BRIEF BACKGROUND

Greek Drama

Ancient Greece was a remarkable place. It was a democratic society flourishing in the midst of totalitarian regimes and foreign wars. It was also a place where achievements in art, literature, and philosophy were so great that they are still revered as models today, thousands of years after their creation.

Greek drama emerged from religious rituals of the time, but Greek religion bore little resemblance to the dominant religions of the modern Western world. Modern Western religions acknowledge a single, just, and benevolent God, whereas Greek religion was polytheistic and recognized many gods—deities who were just as likely to be arbitrary and nasty as to be just and benevolent. For the ancient Greeks, their world was a microcosm, or smaller version, of the divine world. And since the deities themselves were capable of both good and evil, the existence of evil in their world did not contradict these beliefs.

The Greeks believed that they had little control of their fate but had much control of and responsibility for how they faced up to it. This view, which espoused dignity and humility in the face of adversity, is at the core of most Greek drama. The Greeks saw life as a series of struggles to be faced with courage and humility.

During the fifth century BCE, dramatic or religious festivals were held each spring to celebrate Dionysus, the god of wine and fertility. These festivals are thought to be the origin of Greek tragedy. Playwrights from all over Greece competed for prizes awarded by wealthy citizens, with each competing playwright presenting a trilogy of tragic plays. Though we know the names of more than 150 of these ancient writers, we have only a small sample of their work. Of the almost three hundred plays from the three most prominent playwrights of this period, Euripides, Aeschylus, and Sophocles, only thirty-two remain. Given the quality of these plays, it is sad to imagine the treasures that have been lost.

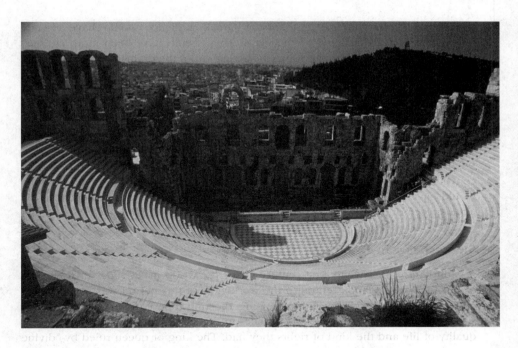

Staging and Acting   The word *theater* is taken from the Greek *theatron* or "seeing-place," a term used to describe the huge open-air amphitheater that seated the audience during performances. Despite their huge dimensions, these theaters had excellent acoustics that were aided by small megaphones in the actors' masks and a style of acting more in keeping with religious ritual than real life. The number of actors with individual roles onstage at once was limited to two or three. The set was bare and the actors were stationary. All the roles were played by males who wore ornate costumes and large masks to reflect the mood of the play and represent types as much as individuals. Though the dialogue itself and the choral odes contained references to and descriptions of violent actions, no violence was actually shown.

The Chorus   The chorus entered during the **parodos** (the choral ode) and remained onstage throughout the play. The role of the chorus came directly from drama as religious ritual, and dates to a time when there were no individual actors. What the chorus said about the action reflected the traditional values of an Athenian audience. When a passage of dialogue was finished, the characters left the stage and the chorus came forward to comment on it. They chanted their lines together and moved as a unit in one direction, then the other. The chorus explained the action, built anticipation for the upcoming scene, and reminded the audience about the significance of the action or dialogue and the cultural or historical context of the play.

The **choragos** was the leader of the chorus. He acted and spoke as the group's representative, and he was free to speak with both the chorus and the other characters onstage.

Audience Participation   An ancient Greek audience would have already known the myths that inspired the plays. They would have been more curious, then, about the play's dramatization (the acting out of the dramatic moments) than the story line. Suspense was based on the tension of the crises, not on the outcome of the plot. According to Aristotle, the tragic nature of a play should not leave its audience depressed or disheartened. Instead, the audience should be enlightened and inspired by what they had witnessed.

The Language of the Script   Because the text is a translation into modern English, you should not have too much trouble reading it. The verse form was a convention of the time and a requirement. It is not written as people of this time would have spoken to one another. The diction is formal and represents the exalted speech of nobility.

Shakespearean Drama

It is difficult in the twenty-first century to see the world in the light (or darkness) of Elizabethan England. Central to the worldview of this period was the idea of a vertical hierarchy (God superior to the king, the king superior to nobles, the nobles superior to peasants, etc.). People's places in this hierarchy directly affected their quality of life and the kind of rights they had. The king or queen ruled by "divine right," not as elected leaders "through the consent of the governed." Although we regularly make claims for equal opportunity as guaranteed by law today, the idea of peasants in the sixteenth century claiming equal rights with people above their rank would have seemed outrageous. People were not free to worship as they chose. They were not even free to dress as they chose. Though the "sumptuary laws" were not always enforced, they prohibited peasants from dressing in other than coarse fabrics and dull colors, with fine fabrics and bright colors reserved for the nobility. What we call science was nonexistent; very little was known about the cause or spread of disease, and very little could be done for those who became ill. For much of the population, the sole means of transportation was on foot, and life was difficult and short.

And yet, life had never been better. Early modern* England was emerging as a world power. Trade had opened up with the Continent, providing an exchange of goods, culture, language, and literature never seen before. The printing press was mass-producing pamphlets and books, and literacy among the general public was improving dramatically.

It is into this atmosphere that Shakespeare was born in 1564, the year the great Renaissance artist Michelangelo died. It is fitting that Shakespeare was born late in the Renaissance. The Renaissance was a "rebirth"—a revival of a golden age—a triumph of classical creation. Shakespeare's art is distinguished by a looking forward. Like the explorers of his time, his is a genius of discovery. He explores what is most essential to individual human experience. Rather than types, he discovers and reveals highly individualized characters who struggle with each

*Early modern. Refers to period in Western European history (circa 1500–1800).

other and themselves, not with fate, the gods, or heredity. But most of all, he discovers language to express these characters and their struggles in verse unparalleled for the quality of its poetry and insight.

Staging and Acting   Before the late sixteenth century, acting companies traveled from town to town and rented space in yards of local inns. Plays were produced on a platform at one end of the yard and the audience gathered around the platform. Wealthier members of the audience viewed the action from the balconies of the surrounding rooms of the inn. The major advantages of this arrangement were its informal, festive atmosphere; the attendance of all classes; and the intimate actor-audience relationship that it encouraged. The close proximity of actor and audience allowed for direct eye contact, an ideal situation for the many soliloquies and asides that playwrights of this period included in their plays.

The Globe Theatre, where most of Shakespeare's plays were performed, was built in 1599 and reflected the kind of space that actors were used to—a space that maintained the intimate atmosphere of the innyards. The Globe was typical of theaters of its kind: a tight, enclosed structure with galleries around the periphery, a projecting platform (about as deep as it was wide) with two upstage entrances, and at least one balcony. The stage itself was almost bare, with only a few simple props or a table, chair, or throne when appropriate. It was a very versatile acting area; there were two exit and entrance doors in the rear of the platform; a curtained alcove between them; a second-story balcony above the stage; a third-story balcony for musicians; a ceiling or heavens extending over the platform, supported by two pillars on the stage; and a trapdoor in the stage platform from which ghosts or devils might emerge.

Although the costumes were elaborate, they reflected current fashion and were not designed to convey the actual clothing of the different countries or times in history depicted in the plays. As in ancient Greece, all parts were played by males. Violence was depicted onstage and quite realistically. Public executions and an abundance of brutal entertainment gave Elizabethans particular expectations. Actors did their best to meet them.

Audience Participation   Audience members who paid the highest admission prices sat in the three stories of covered galleries that enclosed the theater. Here they were protected from the often inclement English weather. Those who paid the lowest prices stood in the open area below and around the stage and were called groundlings, a term meant to disparage their social standing as much as to describe their location in the theater.

Throughout his plays, Shakespeare created opportunities for characters to speak directly with the audience. Delivered by a character alone onstage, these **soliloquies** are a "thinking out loud"; true to the speaker, they range from philosophical to diabolical in nature. And they are often the highlights of Shakespeare's plays. Sometimes characters address the audience while not alone onstage. These brief comments, usually in the midst of ongoing dialogue, are called **asides.** The close proximity of actor and audience in an Elizabethan theater made both types of "confidences" particularly effective.

Tips on Reading the Language of Shakespeare

Most of the verse in Shakespeare's plays is written in unrhymed iambic pentameter or blank verse (see p. 88 for a detailed description). This pattern of rhythm (alternating unstressed and stressed syllables) is the natural way English is spoken. The predictability of the pattern made it easier for actors of this period to memorize their lines.

Shakespeare wrote in modern English, but it was a relatively early form of modern English. Some of the words he used have disappeared from the language, some have different meanings today, and many of his sentences have a syntax, or word order, we no longer recognize.

Look at the following passage from Shakespeare's play *Othello* (Act III, Scene 4).

OTHELLO: That's a fault.

> That handkerchief
> Did an Egyptian to my mother give;
> She was a charmer, and could almost read
> The thoughts of people: she told her, while she kept it,   5
> 'Twould make her amiable and subdue my father

Entirely to her love, but if she lost it
Or made a gift of it, my father's eye
Should hold her loathed and his spirits should hunt
After new fancies: she, dying, gave it me;   10
And bid me, when my fate would have me wive,
To give it her.

The plays are written in blank verse, but don't let the capital letters at the beginning of each line affect your reading. Don't stop at the end of each verse line unless it has punctuation. Use the punctuation to create pauses or stops as you would with language in prose. Let's look at one of the sentences above in prose form, with the capitals removed:

She told her, while she kept it, 'twould make her amiable and subdue my father entirely to her love, but if she lost it or made a gift of it, my father's eye should hold her loathed and his spirits should hunt after new fancies.

Even in prose, this is a long sentence and requires patience and concentration to understand. But by reading it as prose, you can focus on the punctuation. Some of the phrases might still seem a bit elusive, but read it a few times and see if it is easier to understand.

Reading Out Loud

Good actors help the audience understand the language by the intonations and pacing of their voices. But when you are reading from the text of the play, you won't have the benefit of hearing an actor's voice. Reading the lines aloud may help. When you read silently, you subvocalize and hear the words in your brain. But the sound and sense of these words will be clearer if you say and hear the word combinations out loud.

Read the verse passage from *Othello* above aloud and see what you learn about its meaning (and your understanding) in the process.

Word Order

Getting used to the language of Shakespeare means adjusting our expectations for word order in a sentence. In today's English, we generally express ourselves in a subject-verb-object pattern. For example: "A girl hit that ball to her brother." But earlier forms of English sometimes used a word order with the verb at the end. In this earlier form our sentence would read: "That ball did a girl to her brother hit." Takes a little longer to figure out, doesn't it? We need to read the whole sentence to get to the verb. And it is only after we get to the verb that we understand what is being said.

If you look at the first sentence of the quote from *Othello* (above), "That handkerchief / Did an Egyptian to my mother give," you'll see the same pattern. If those words were written in the subject-verb-object pattern we are used to, they would read: "An Egyptian gave that handkerchief to my mother." Made sense much faster, didn't it? You've seen this older verb pattern before in language carried down through the ages for meaningful rituals, like the marriage ceremony (e.g., "With this ring I thee wed" and "'Til death do us part").

Most often, the key to reading unusual word order is patience. The meaning may not be clear until you reach the last word of the sentence—and even then you may have to pause to unravel it.

Words, Words, Words

While many other modern languages still have them, English dropped the second-person "familiar" pronoun form some time ago, and uses the "you" form exclusively. When Shakespeare wrote his plays, however, *thou, thee, thy,* and *thine* were the second-person singular "familiar" versions of *you, your,* and *yours*. In general, they indicated a caring relationship with the person addressed—a lover, family member, servant. Dropped as well are verb endings like *st* that agreed with these familiar pronouns (thou dost, thou shalt, thou goest). Other third-person verb endings like *th* ("It *hath* made me ill"; "It *doth* give me heartburn") have simply become obsolete.

It is not unusual to see letters replaced with apostrophes occasionally. ("Whether *'tis* nobler"; "*'twould* make her amiable"; "*o'erstep* not the modesty of nature"). By leaving a letter out, Shakespeare often managed to eliminate a beat and keep the blank verse intact. In these cases, the context of the statement will usually tell you that *'tis* means "it is," *'twould* means "it would," and *o'erstep* means "overstep."

In other cases, entire words seem to be left out ("Let's [?] to bed knight"; "My father had a daughter [?] loved a man"). Again in these cases the context of the sentence should tell you that *go* and *who* are the words assumed to be understood.

Shakespeare was a master of making up words too (*assassinate, dislocate, obscene, reliance, submerged,* and hundreds of others we still use), and changing words from one part of speech to another, for example, in the above quote from *Othello,* the use of *wive* instead of *marry:* "And bid me, when my fate would have me wive, / To give it her." So don't be surprised when you come across a verb that you're used to being a noun. The meaning is likely to be what you think it is.

You may notice that when a king speaks, he often uses the pronouns *our, us,* and *we* to refer to himself. In the first line of his opening speech in Act I, Scene 2 of *Hamlet,* Claudius refers to himself this way: "Though yet of Hamlet *our* dear brother's death / The memory be green." This use of the "royal plural," or "imperial we," was common among royalty, who saw themselves as personifying the kingdom and everyone in it.

Finally, it is very helpful to read the notes that accompany the text. You'll need help with words no longer in use and words that had a different meaning than they do now. It will take a little longer to read the text, but remember that patience is a key to having a successful experience with Shakespeare's work.

Modern Drama

Modern drama, like so much else "modern," was born in the nineteenth century. Its emergence was a natural outgrowth and reflection of the profound social, political, and technological changes taking place around it. Like so many other modern movements, it arose as a reaction—to the content, staging, and acting of the neoclassical drama and romantic melodrama so popular in the era that preceded it. As this reaction ran its course, virtually every aspect of theater changed.

The preceding seventeenth and eighteenth centuries were dominated early by neoclassicism (or new classicism), which was notable for its rigid adherence to the forms of classical drama. While there were a number of highly successful comedies, the power and passion of ancient tragedy was missing in an age that seemed to prefer form over substance. Later in this period, melodramas with elaborate but oversimplified plots, flat characters, excessive sentiment, and happy endings were most popular. The physical layout of the theater changed during this period, too, and theaters moved indoors. The stage was recessed behind and framed by a **proscenium arch** at the end of a long room or hall. The audience was seated directly in front of the stage and in the surrounding galleries. This layout is the one we still see today in most school auditoriums and many theaters. Settings for each play were painted on canvas backdrops behind the acting area. A scene could be changed simply by changing the backdrop. Both the audience and the actors behaved with great flamboyance. The audience came to the theater as much to be seen as to see the action onstage. Consequently, both audience and actors spent much money on elaborate costumes. And as the size of theaters increased, so did the volume of the actors' voices and the exaggeration of their gestures.

A transformation to what we recognize as modern drama came slowly, and it took much of the nineteenth century to make real progress. But that change and that movement toward **realism** in both content and technique would affect every aspect of drama. Writers depicted the reality of struggling, ordinary people. Set designers produced authentic settings onstage. Actors spoke and behaved like real people.

But even as realism was becoming established, it was generating reactions to its own form and objective view of reality. In the twentieth century, **symbolism** would seek its truth in symbols, myths, and dreams; **expressionism** in the subjectivity of perception; and **surrealism** in the irrationality of the unconscious mind.

Modern drama is a synthesis of many forms and philosophies. More than a single approach, it is characterized by variety and diversity—diversity of content, perspective, and staging. The traditional categories of tragedy and comedy are inadequate to classify most modern drama. Tragic, comic, and absurd views of life often mix together in the same script, side by side, back to back. This diverse combination of views and styles is described as **tragicomedy.**

Staging and Acting   In general, theaters built today have better acoustical, visual, and spatial arrangements than ever before. Interiors with rising tiers of seats give audiences clear sight lines and encourage a more naturalistic style of acting. In many ways the era of modern drama began with the development of the **box set**—a set composed of **flats,** or connected walls enclosing three sides of the stage, with an invisible "fourth wall" open to the audience. Through this invisible fourth wall the audience sees the action and eavesdrops on the conversations of characters, who occupy a room with authentic furniture, rugs, hanging fixtures, and other realistic props.

Today, there are many types of stages. Several variations of the proscenium stage with enclosed box set have evolved. And since the 1940s, thrust stages—a throwback to the Elizabethan platform that extends into the audience—and the arena stage, or theater in the round—a circular acting area surrounded by the audience—have been designed to bring audiences closer to the actors.

Artificial light and sound create realistic stage settings. Lighting can project times, places, and moods, and can even divide the stage into different acting areas. Computerized light boards control hundreds of lights and lighting combinations. Electronic amplification and portable microphones make it easier for actors to speak in their natural voices. Authentic costumes complement the set, support historical authenticity, and enrich characterization.

As the twentieth century approached and the demands for realism increased, the training of actors changed, too. The work of Constantine Stanislavski epitomized this movement. Stanislavski's *method* required that actors express the interior lives of the characters they played—to live the role by finding the character's emotions and motivation in themselves. More than a century after he developed his method, it is still the most popular approach used by actors to prepare their roles.

Audience Participation   While realistic staging and lighting highlight a real setting peopled by real characters, they put the audience literally in the dark. Though the box set in particular encourages actors to move more deeply into "character," its fourth wall maintains a distance from the audience. The actors move on a lighted stage very visible to the audience, but the audience often sits in the dark invisible to the actors.

The Language and Style of the Script   Characters in modern drama almost always speak in colloquial language, not verse. What they say sounds like everyday speech. Following the lead of fiction writers in the late nineteenth century, dramatists began to write dialogue in the regional speech of the characters. Having "an ear" for dialogue, for realistic speech and how it sounds, is a crucial skill for any dramatist today.

Stage directions in the text of modern plays are more detailed than ever before. Descriptions of the set, props, movements of the actors, and the lighting are often specified in the script and integrated with action and characterization.

 CHECKLIST: ANALYZING DRAMA

Point of View

❑ Does the play have a narrator? If so, who is it and what effect does this narration have on your response?

Set and Setting

❑ When is the play set? What role does the setting have? What physical location is this? The country? The city? What does the set look like? What props are present?

❏ Can you describe the atmosphere? What time of day is this? What is the lighting? What are the dominant colors? What is the weather like? Who is present? How are they dressed?

❏ Does the setting support and emphasize the story's meaning?

Conflict and Plot

❏ What is the primary external conflict in the play? The primary internal conflict? Are there other conflicts? If so, what are they?

❏ Support your identification of conflict by citing action and dialogue in the text.

❏ In what way do the personality traits of the characters lead to conflict?

❏ Can you identify the plot? Does it conform to the traditional structure? If so, how? If not, what is the structure?

❏ Is it a tragedy or a comedy? Explain.

Characterization

❏ How do you feel about the characters? What do the characters do to make you feel this way? What do the characters say to make you feel this way? What is said about the characters to make you feel this way?

❏ Are the characters motivated and consistent? Are they believable? Are there flat, or stock, characters in the play? Explain.

❏ Who is the protagonist? The antagonist(s)?

❏ Support your responses to the characters by citing action and dialogue in the play.

Language and Style

❏ Is the language used in the play formal or informal? What does the nature of their language use tell you about the characters?

❏ Are there any symbols? Is the set symbolic? Are the props or the costumes symbolic? If so, how do they connect to or support the story?

❏ Are there instances of verbal or situational irony? Explain.

Theme

❏ What are the major details (characters, conflicts, outcome) of the play?

❏ What conclusion about the play did you draw from these details? What generalization about life does this conclusion lead to?

❏ What is the central idea expressed by the play? What is its theme? Does the play reveal or does it preach? Explain.

GETTING IDEAS FOR WRITING ABOUT DRAMA

The purpose of the play, the prompts, and the questions in this section is to show how the elements we've discussed earlier might be applied to drama. Following *Antigonê*, many of the questions from the summary checklist above are applied to the play, and we consider some of the ways the elements discussed in this section might be used to prompt ideas for an essay.

An Introduction to Sophocles and *Antigonê*

EDITH HAMILTON   [1867–1963]

FROM *THE ROYAL HOUSE OF THEBES*   [1942]

"OEDIPUS"

I have taken this story entirely from Sophocles' play of that name except for the riddle of the Sphinx which Sophocles merely alludes to. It is given by many writers, always in substantially the same form.

King Laius of Thebes was the third in descent from Cadmus. He married a distant cousin, Jocasta. With their reign Apollo's oracle at Delphi began to play a leading part in the family's fortunes.

Apollo was the God of Truth. Whatever the priestess at Delphi said would happen infallibly came to pass. To attempt to act in such a way that the prophecy would be made void was as futile as to set oneself against the decrees of fate. Nevertheless, when the oracle warned Laius that he would die at the hands of his son he determined that this should not be. When the child was born he bound its feet together and had it exposed on a lonely mountain where it must soon die. He felt no more fear; he was sure that on this point he could foretell the future better than the god. His folly was not brought home to him. He was killed, indeed, but he thought the man who attacked him was a stranger. He never knew that in his death he had proved Apollo's truth.

When he died he was away from home and many years had passed since the baby had been left on the mountain. It was reported that a band of robbers had slain him together with his attendants, all except one, who brought the news home. The matter was not carefully investigated because Thebes was in sore straits at the time. The country around was beset by a frightful monster, the Sphinx, a creature shaped like a winged lion, but with the breast and face of a woman. She lay in wait for the wayfarers along the roads to the city and whomever she seized she put a riddle to, telling him if he could answer it, she would let him go. No one could, and the horrible creature devoured man after man until the city was in a state of siege. The seven great gates which were the Thebans' pride remained closed, and famine drew near to the citizens.

So matters stood when there came into the stricken country a stranger, a man of great courage and great intelligence, whose name was Oedipus. He had left his home, Corinth, where he was held to be the son of the King, Polybus, and the reason for his self-exile was another Delphic oracle. Apollo had declared that he was fated to kill his father. He, too, like Laius, thought to make it impossible for the oracle to come true; he resolved never to see Polybus again. In his lonely wanderings he came into the country around Thebes and he heard what was happening there. He was a homeless, friendless man to whom life meant little and he determined to seek the Sphinx out and try to solve the riddle. "What creature," the Sphinx asked him, "goes on four feet in the morning, on two at noonday, on three in the evening?" "Man," answered Oedipus. "In childhood he creeps on hands and feet; in manhood he walks erect; in old age he helps himself with a staff." It was the right answer. The Sphinx, inexplicably, but most fortunately, killed herself; the Thebans were saved. Oedipus gained all and more than he had left. The grateful citizens made him their King and he married the dead King's wife, Jocasta. For many years they lived happily. It seemed that in this case Apollo's words had been proved to be false.

5   But when their two sons had grown to manhood Thebes was visited by a terrible plague. A blight fell upon everything. Not only were men dying throughout the country, the flocks and herds and the fruits of the field were blasted as well. Those who were spared death by disease faced death by famine. No one suffered more than Oedipus. He regarded himself as the father of the whole state; the people in it were his children; the misery of each one was his too. He dispatched Jocasta's brother Creon to Delphi to implore the god's help.

Creon returned with good news. Apollo had declared that the plague would be stayed upon one condition: whoever had murdered King Laius must be punished. Oedipus was enormously relieved. Surely the men or the man could be found even after all these years, and they would know well how to punish him. He proclaimed to the people gathered to hear the message Creon brought back: –

...Let no one of this land
  Give shelter to him. Bar him from your homes,
As one defiled, companioned by pollution.
And solemnly I pray, may he who killed
  Wear out his life in evil, being evil.

Oedipus took the matter in hand with energy. He sent for Teiresias, the old blind prophet, the most revered of Thebans. Had he any means of finding out, he asked him, who the guilty were? To his amazement and indignation the seer at first refused to answer. "For the love of God," Oedipus implored him. "If you have knowledge—" "Fools," Teiresias said. "Fools all of you. I will not answer." But when Oedipus went so far as to accuse him of keeping silence because he had himself taken part in the murder, the prophet in his turn was angered and words he had meant never to speak fell heavily from his lips: "You are yourself the murderer you seek." To Oedipus the old man's mind was wandering; what he said was sheer madness. He ordered him out of his sight and never again to appear before him.

Jocasta too treated the assertion with scorn. "Neither prophets nor oracles have any sure knowledge," she said. She told her husband how the priestess at Delphi had prophesied that Laius should die at the hand of his son and how he and she together had seen to it that this should not happen by having the child killed. "And Laius was murdered by robbers, where three roads meet on the way to Delphi," she concluded triumphantly. Oedipus gave her a strange look. "When did this happen?" he asked slowly. "Just before you came to Thebes," she said.

"How many were with him?" Oedipus asked. "They were five in all," Jocasta spoke quickly, "all killed but one." "I must see that man," he told her. "Send for him." "I will," she said. "At once. But I have a right to know what is in your mind." "You shall know all that I know," he answered. "I went to Delphi just before I came here because a man had flung it in my face that I was not the son of Polybus. I went to ask the god. He did not answer me, but he told me horrible things—that I should kill my father, marry my mother, and have children men would shudder to look upon. I never went back to Corinth. On my way from Delphi, at a place where three roads met, I came upon a man with four attendants. He tried to force me from the path; he struck me with his stick. Angered I fell upon them and I killed them. Could it be the leader was Laius?" "The one man left alive brought back a tale of robbers," Jocasta said. "Laius was killed by robbers, not by his son—the poor innocent who died upon the mountain."

10   As they talked a further proof seemed given them that Apollo could speak falsely. A messenger came from Corinth to announce to Oedipus the death of Polybus. "O oracle of the god," Jocasta cried, "where are you now? The man died, but not by his son's hand." The messenger smiled wisely. "Did the fear of killing your father drive you from Corinth?" he asked. "Ah, King, you were in error. You never had reason to fear—for you were not the son of Polybus. He brought you up as though you were his, but he took you from my hands." "Where did you get me?" Oedipus asked. "Who were my father and mother?" "I know nothing of them," the messenger said. "A wandering shepherd gave you to me, a servant of Laius."

Jocasta turned white; a look of horror was on her face. "Why waste a thought upon what such a fellow says?" she cried. "Nothing he says can matter." She spoke hurriedly, yet fiercely. Oedipus could not understand her. "My birth does not matter?" he asked. "For God's sake, go no further," she said. "My misery is enough." She broke away and rushed into the palace.

At that moment an old man entered. He and the messenger eyed each other curiously. "The very man. O King," the messenger cried. "The shepherd who gave you to me." "And you," Oedipus asked the other, "do you know him as he knows you?" The old man did not answer, but the messenger insisted. "You must remember. You gave me once a little child you had found – and the King here is that child." "Curse you," the other muttered. "Hold your tongue." "What!" Oedipus said angrily. "You would conspire with him to hide from me what I desire to know? There are ways, be sure, to make you speak."

The old man wailed, "Oh, do not hurt me. I did give him the child, but do not ask more, master, for the love of God." "If I have to order you a second time to tell me where you got him, you are lost," Oedipus said. "Ask your lady," the old man cried. "She can tell you best." "She gave him to you?" asked Oedipus. "Oh, yes, oh, yes," the other groaned. "I was to kill the child. There was a prophecy—" "A prophecy!" Oedipus repeated. "That he should kill his father?" "Yes," the old man whispered.

A cry of agony came from the King. At last he understood. "All true! Now shall my light be changed to darkness. I am accursed." He had murdered his father, he had married his father's wife, his own mother. There was no help for him, for her, for their children. All were accursed.

15   Within the palace Oedipus wildly sought for his wife that was his mother. He found her in her chamber. She was dead. When the truth broke upon her she had killed herself. Standing beside her he too turned his hand against himself, but not to end his life. He changed his light to darkness. He put out his eyes. The black world of blindness was a refuge; better to be there than to see with strange shamed eyes the old world that had been so bright.

Tips on Reading the Text of *Antigonê*

To prepare for reading *Antigonê,* be sure to read the section on Greek Drama (pp. 102–02) and the preceding Edith Hamilton summary of *Oedipus Rex*—the play that serves as the foundation of the Oedipus Trilogy and that *leads to Antigonê.* Since this is an ancient play and some of its conventions may seem unusual to you, give yourself enough time to read (and reread) it. The translation that follows is in modern English, so you should have no trouble understanding the language. But you may be a bit confused by the verse form and the choral odes, so here are two suggestions to make your reading easier:

1. *Read the verse lines as if they are prose.* Instead of stopping at the end of each verse line, read right through the caps at the beginning of the next line and stop or pause at the punctuation. Each verse line does not contain a complete thought, but the sentences do.

2. *The first time you read the play, skip the choral odes* (parodos). They are not intended to advance the action but to comment upon it. After your first reading, go back and read the choral odes informed by your understanding of what has happened in the play.

MLL # SOPHOCLES   [CA. 496–406 BCE]

*Considered during his lifetime one of the three great Athenian tragic playwrights (the other two being Aeschylus and Euripides), Sophocles is believed to have written over 120 plays, although only seven of his tragedies have survived to modern times (*Ajax, Antigonê, Oedipus the King, Electra, Philoctetes, The Trachinian Women, *and* Oedipus at Colonus*). A popular figure throughout his long life, he served in a series of public offices, including those of general and priest, during a*

century that witnessed Athens's rise to power and its subsequent decline. The play has been held in high esteem since ancient times, when Aristotle cited his work as the perfect example of tragedy in his famous treatise on poetry, The Poetics.

ANTIGONÊ

[CA. 441 BCE]

AN ENGLISH VERSION BY DUDLEY FITTS AND ROBERT FITZGERALD

CHARACTERS
ANTIGONÊ
ISMENÊ
EURYDICÊ
CREON
HAIMON
TEIRESIAS
A SENTRY
A MESSENGER
CHORUS

SCENE: *Before the palace of* CREON *King of Thebes. A central double door, and two lateral doors. A platform extends the length of the facade, and from this platform three steps lead down into the orchestra, or chorus-ground.*

TIME: *Dawn of the day after the repulse of the Argive army from the assault on Thebes.*

PROLOGUE

ANTIGONÊ *and* ISMENÊ *enter from the central door of the palace.*

ANTIGONÊ: Ismenê, dear sister,
    You would think that we had already suffered enough
    For the curse on Oedipus:°
    I cannot imagine any grief
    That you and I have not gone through. And now—   5
    Have they told you of the new decree of our King Creon?

ISMENÊ: I have heard nothing: I know
    That two sisters lost two brothers, a double death
    In a single hour; and I know that the Argive army
    Fled in the night; but beyond this, nothing.   10

ANTIGONÊ: I thought so. And that is why I wanted you
    To come out here with me. There is something we must do.

---

3 Oedipus the father of Antigonê, Ismenê, and their brothers Polyneicês and Eteoclês, and former king of Thebes. Oedipus unknowingly killed his father, Laios, and married his mother, Iocastê. When he discovered the truth, he blinded himself and left Thebes. After Oedipus abdicated the throne, the two brothers ruled. But they quarreled. Polyneicês was defeated but returned to attack Thebes. Both brothers were killed in battle. Creon, who became king, ordered that Polyneicês remain unburied.

ISMENÊ: Why do you speak so strangely?

ANTIGONÊ: Listen, Ismenê:

    Creon buried our brother Eteoclês   15
    With military honors, gave him a soldier's funeral,
    And it was right that he should; but Polyneicês,
    Who fought as bravely and died as miserably,—
    They say that Creon has sworn
    No one shall bury him, no one mourn for him,   20
    But his body must lie in the fields, a sweet treasure
    For carrion birds to find as they search for food.
    That is what they say, and our good Creon is coming here
    To announce it publicly; and the penalty—
    Stoning to death in the public square!   25
                  There it is,
    And now you can prove what you are:
    A true sister, or a traitor to your family.

ISMENÊ: Antigonê, you are mad! What could I possibly do?

ANTIGONÊ: You must decide whether you will help me or not.   30

ISMENÊ: I do not understand you. Help you in what?

ANTIGONÊ: Ismenê, I am going to bury him. Will you come?

ISMENÊ: Bury him! You have just said the new law forbids it.

ANTIGONÊ: He is my brother. And he is your brother, too.

ISMENÊ: But think of the danger! Think what Creon will do!   35

ANTIGONÊ: Creon is not strong enough to stand in my way.

ISMENÊ: Ah sister!

    Oedipus died, everyone hating him
    For what his own search brought to light, his eyes
    Ripped out by his own hand; and Iocastê died,   40
    His mother and wife at once: she twisted the cords
    That strangled her life; and our two brothers died,
    Each killed by the other's sword. And we are left:
    But oh, Antigonê,
    Think how much more terrible than these   45
    Our own death would be if we should go against Creon
    And do what he has forbidden! We are only women,
    We cannot fight with men, Antigonê!
    The law is strong, we must give in to the law
    In this thing, and in worse. I beg the Dead   50
    To forgive me, but I am helpless: I must yield
    To those in authority. And I think it is dangerous business
    To be always meddling.

ANTIGONÊ: If that is what you think,

    I should not want you, even if you asked to come.   55
    You have made your choice, you can be what you want to be.
    But I will bury him; and if I must die,
    I say that this crime is holy: I shall lie down

With him in death, and I shall be as dear
   To him as he to me.
               It is the dead,   60
Not the living, who make the longest demands:
We die for ever...
                You may do as you like,
Since apparently the laws of the gods mean nothing to you.   65
ISMENÊ: They mean a great deal to me; but I have no strength
   To break laws that were made for the public good.
ANTIGONÊ: That must be your excuse, I suppose. But as for me,
   I will bury the brother I love.
ISMENÊ: Antigonê,   70
   I am so afraid for you!
ANTIGONÊ: You need not be:
   You have yourself to consider, after all.
ISMENÊ: But no one must hear of this, you must tell no one!
   I will keep it a secret, I promise!   75
ANTIGONÊ: O tell it! Tell everyone!
   Think how they'll hate you when it all comes out
   If they learn that you knew about it all the time!
ISMENÊ: So fiery! You should be cold with fear.
ANTIGONÊ: Perhaps. But I am doing only what I must.   80
ISMENÊ: But you can do it? I say that you cannot.
ANTIGONÊ: Very well: when my strength gives out,
   I shall do no more.
ISMENÊ: Impossible things should not be tried at all.
ANTIGONÊ: Go away, Ismenê: 85
   I shall be hating you soon, and the dead will too,
   For your words are hateful. Leave me my foolish plan:
   I am not afraid of the danger; if it means death,
   It will not be the worst of deaths—death without honor.
ISMENÊ: Go then, if you feel that you must.   90
   You are unwise,
   But a loyal friend indeed to those who love you.

       Exit into the palace. ANTIGONÊ *goes off, left. Enter the Chorus.*

PARODOS°

Strophe 1°

CHORUS: Now the long blade of the sun, lying
   Level east to west, touches with glory
   Thebes of the Seven Gates. Open, unlidded

Parodos the entrance song of the chorus   **Strophe** sung as the chorus moves
from stage right to stage left

Eye of golden day! O marching light
Across the eddy and rush of Dircê's stream°   5
Striking the white shields of the enemy
Thrown headlong backward from the blaze of morning!
CHORAGOS°:   Polyneicês their commander
Roused them with windy phrases,
He the wild eagle screaming   10
Insults above our land,
His wings their shields of snow,
His crest their marshalled helms.

Antistrophe 1°

CHORUS: Against our seven gates in a yawning ring
The famished spears came onward in the night;   15
But before his jaws were sated with our blood,
Or pinefire took the garland of our towers,
He was thrown back; and as he turned, great Thebes—
No tender victim for his noisy power—
Rose like a dragon behind him, shouting war.   20

CHORAGOS: For God hates utterly
The bray of bragging tongues;
And when he beheld their smiling,
Their swagger of golden helms,
The frown of his thunder blasted   25
Their first man from our walls.

Strophe 2

CHORUS: We heard his shout of triumph high in the air
Turn to a scream; far out in a flaming arc
He fell with his windy torch, and the earth struck him.
And others storming in fury no less than his   30
Found shock of death in the dusty joy of battle.

CHORAGOS: Seven captains at seven gates
Yielded their clanging arms to the god
That bends the battle-line and breaks it.
These two only, brothers in blood,   35
Face to face in matchless rage,
Mirroring each the other's death,
Clashed in long combat.

5 Dircê's stream a river near Thebes   **8 Choragos** the leader of the chorus   **Antistrophe**
sung as the chorus moves from stage left to stage right

Antistrophe 2

CHORUS: But now in the beautiful morning of victory
>   Let Thebes of the many chariots sing for joy!   40
>   With hearts for dancing we'll take leave of war:
>   Our temples shall be sweet with hymns of praise,
>   And the long night shall echo with our chorus.

SCENE I

CHORAGOS: But now at last our new King is coming:
>   Creon of Thebes, Menoikeus' son.
>   In this auspicious dawn of his reign
>   What are the new complexities
>   That shifting Fate has woven for him?   5
>   What is his counsel? Why has he summoned
>   The old men to hear him?

>   *Enter* CREON *from the palace, center. He addresses the Chorus*
>   *from the top step.*

CREON: Gentlemen: I have the honor to inform you that our Ship of State,
which recent storms have threatened to destroy, has come safely to
harbor at last, guided by the merciful wisdom of Heaven. I have sum-   10
moned you here this morning because I know that I can depend upon
you: your devotion to King Laïos was absolute; you never hesitated
in your duty to our late ruler Oedipus; and when Oedipus died, your
loyalty was transferred to his children. Unfortunately, as you know, his
two sons, the princes Eteoclês and Polyneicês, have killed each other   15
in battle; and I, as the next in blood, have succeeded to the full power
of the throne.

   I am aware, of course, that no Ruler can expect complete loyalty
from his subjects until he has been tested in office. Nevertheless, I
say to you at the very outset that I have nothing but contempt for the   20
kind of Governor who is afraid, for whatever reason, to follow the
course that he knows is best for the State; and as for the man who
sets private friendship above the public welfare,—I have no use for
him, either. I call God to witness that if I saw my country headed for
ruin, I should not be afraid to speak out plainly; and I need hardly   25
remind you that I would never have any dealings with an enemy of
the people. No one values friendship more highly than I; but we must
remember that friends made at the risk of wrecking our Ship are not
real friends at all.

   These are my principles, at any rate, and that is why I have made   30
the following decision concerning the sons of Oedipus: Eteoclês, who
died as a man should die, fighting for his country, is to be buried
with full military honors, with all the ceremony that is usual when the

greatest heroes die; but his brother Polyneicês who broke his exile to
come back with fire and sword against his native city and the shrines   35
of his fathers' gods, whose one idea was to spill the blood of his blood
and sell his own people into slavery—Polyneicês, I say, is to have no
burial: no man is to touch him or say the least prayer for him; he shall
lie on the plain, unburied; and the birds and the scavenging dogs can
do with him whatever they like.   40

    This is my command, and you can see the wisdom behind it. As
long as I am King, no traitor is going to be honored with the loyal man.
But whoever shows by word and deed that he is on the side of the
State,—he shall have my respect while he is living, and my reverence
when he is dead.   45

CHORAGOS: If that is your will, Creon son of Menoikeus,
    You have the right to enforce it: we are yours.
CREON: That is my will. Take care that you do your part.
CHORAGOS: We are old men: let the younger ones carry it out.
CREON: I do not mean that: the sentries have been appointed.   50
CHORAGOS: Then what is it that you would have us do?
CREON: You will give no support to whoever breaks this law.
CHORAGOS: Only a crazy man is in love with death!
CREON: And death it is, yet money talks, and the wisest
    Have sometimes been known to count a few coins too many.   55

Enter SENTRY *from left.*

SENTRY: I'll not say that I'm out of breath from running, King, because every
    time I stopped to think about what I have to tell you, I felt like going
    back. And all the time a voice kept saying, "You fool, don't you know
    you're walking straight into trouble?"; and then another voice: "Yes,
    but if you let somebody else get the news to Creon first, it will be even   60
    worse than that for you!" But good sense won out, at least I hope it was
    good sense, and here I am with a story that makes no sense at all; but
    I'll tell it anyhow, because, as they say, what's going to happen's going
    to happen and—
CREON: Come to the point. What have you to say?   65
SENTRY: I did not do it. I did not see who did it. You must not punish me for
    what someone else has done.
CREON: A comprehensive defense! More effective, perhaps,
    If I knew its purpose. Come: what is it?
SENTRY: A dreadful thing... I don't know how to put it—   70
CREON: Out with it!
SENTRY: Well, then;
    The dead man—
        Polyneicês—

Pause. The SENTRY *is overcome, fumbles for words.* CREON *waits impassively.*

        out there—   75
            someone,—

New dust on the slimy flesh!

Pause. No sign from CREON.

Someone has given it burial that way, and
Gone...

Long pause. CREON *finally speaks with deadly control.*

CREON: And the man who dared do this?   80
SENTRY: I swear I
Do not know! You must believe me!
                                          Listen:
The ground was dry, not a sign of digging, no,
Not a wheeltrack in the dust, no trace of anyone.   85
It was when they relieved us this morning: and one of them,
The corporal, pointed to it.
                                There it was,
The strangest—
                    Look: 90
The body, just mounded over with light dust: you see?
Not buried really, but as if they'd covered it
Just enough for the ghost's peace. And no sign
Of dogs or any wild animal that had been there.
And then what a scene there was! Every man of us   95
Accusing the other: we all proved the other man did it,
We all had proof that we could not have done it.
We were ready to take hot iron in our hands,
Walk through fire, swear by all the gods,
It was not I!   100
I do not know who it was, but it was not I!

CREON'S *rage has been mounting steadily, but the* SENTRY *is too intent
upon his story to notice it.*

And then, when this came to nothing, someone said
A thing that silenced us and made us stare
Down at the ground: you had to be told the news,
And one of us had to do it! We threw the dice,   105
And the bad luck fell to me. So here I am,
No happier to be here than you are to have me:
Nobody likes the man who brings bad news.
CHORAGOS: I have been wondering, King: can it be that the gods have done this?
CREON [*furiously*]:   Stop!   110
Must you doddering wrecks
Go out of your heads entirely? "The gods"!
Intolerable!
The gods favor this corpse? Why? How had he served them?
Tried to loot their temples, burn their images,   115

Yes, and the whole State, and its laws with it!
Is it your senile opinion that the gods love to honor bad men?
A pious thought!—
                    No, from the very beginning
There have been those who have whispered together,   120
Stiff-necked anarchists, putting their heads together,
Scheming against me in alleys. These are the men,
And they have bribed my own guard to do this thing.
[*Sententiously.*] Money!
There's nothing in the world so demoralizing as money.   125
Down go your cities,
Homes gone, men gone, honest hearts corrupted,
Crookedness of all kinds, and all for money!

                              To SENTRY.

                    But you—!
I swear by God and by the throne of God,   130
The man who has done this thing shall pay for it!
Find that man, bring him here to me, or your death
Will be the least of your problems: I'll string you up
Alive, and there will be certain ways to make you
Discover your employer before you die;   135
And the process may teach you a lesson you seem to have missed:
The dearest profit is sometimes all too dear:
That depends on the source. Do you understand me?
A fortune won is often misfortune.
SENTRY: King, may I speak?   140
CREON: Your very voice distresses me.
SENTRY: Are you sure that it is my voice, and not your conscience?
CREON: By God, he wants to analyze me now!
SENTRY: It is not what I say, but what has been done, that hurts you.
CREON: You talk too much.   145
SENTRY: Maybe; but I've done nothing.
CREON: Sold your soul for some silver: that's all you've done.
SENTRY: How dreadful it is when the right judge judges wrong!
CREON: Your figures of speech
                    May entertain you now; but unless you bring me the man,   150
                    You will get little profit from them in the end.
                              Exit CREON *into the palace.*

SENTRY: "Bring me the man"—!
I'd like nothing better than bringing him the man!
But bring him or not, you have seen the last of me here.
At any rate, I am safe!   155
                              Exit SENTRY.

ODE I

Strophe 1

CHORUS: Numberless are the world's wonders, but none
    More wonderful than man; the stormgray sea
    Yields to his prows, the huge crests bear him high;
    Earth, holy and inexhaustible, is graven
    With shining furrows where his plows have gone   5
    Year after year, the timeless labor of stallions.

Antistrophe 1

    The lightboned birds and beasts that cling to cover,
    The lithe fish lighting their reaches of dim water,
    All are taken, tamed in the net of his mind;
    The lion on the hill, the wild horse windy-maned,   10
    Resign to him; and his blunt yoke has broken
    The sultry shoulders of the mountain bull.

Strophe 2

    Words also, and thought as rapid as air,
    He fashions to his good use; statecraft is his,
    And his the skill that deflects the arrows of snow,   15
    The spears of winter rain: from every wind
    He has made himself secure—from all but one:
    In the late wind of death he cannot stand.

Antistrophe 2

    O clear intelligence, force beyond all measure!
    O fate of man, working both good and evil!   20
    When the laws are kept, how proudly his city stands!
    When the laws are broken, what of his city then?
    Never may the anárchic man find rest at my hearth,
    Never be it said that my thoughts are his thoughts.

SCENE II

Reenter SENTRY *leading* ANTIGONÊ.

CHORAGOS: What does this mean? Surely this captive woman
    Is the Princess, Antigonê. Why should she be taken?
SENTRY: Here is the one who did it! We caught her
    In the very act of burying him—Where is Creon?
CHORAGOS: Just coming from the house.   5

Enter CREON, *center.*

CREON: What has happened?
    Why have you come back so soon?
SENTRY [*expansively*]:   O King,

A man should never be too sure of anything:
I would have sworn   10
That you'd not see me here again: your anger
Frightened me so, and the things you threatened me with;
But how could I tell then
That I'd be able to solve the case so soon?
No dice-throwing this time: I was only too glad to come!   15
Here is this woman. She is the guilty one:
We found her trying to bury him.
Take her, then; question her; judge her as you will.
I am through with the whole thing now, and glad of it.

CREON: But this is Antigonê! Why have you brought her here?   20

SENTRY: She was burying him, I tell you!

CREON   [*severely*]:   Is this the truth?

SENTRY: I saw her with my own eyes. Can I say more?

CREON: The details: come, tell me quickly!

SENTRY: It was like this: 25
After those terrible threats of yours, King,
We went back and brushed the dust away from the body.
The flesh was soft by now, and stinking,
So we sat on a hill to windward and kept guard.
No napping this time! We kept each other awake.   30
But nothing happened until the white round sun
Whirled in the center of the round sky over us:
Then, suddenly,
A storm of dust roared up from the earth, and the sky
Went out, the plain vanished with all its trees   35
In the stinging dark. We closed our eyes and endured it.
The whirlwind lasted a long time, but it passed;
And then we looked, and there was Antigonê!
I have seen
A mother bird come back to a stripped nest, heard   40
Her crying bitterly a broken note or two
For the young ones stolen. Just so, when this girl
Found the bare corpse, and all her love's work wasted,
She wept, and cried on heaven to damn the hands
That had done this thing.   45
                        And then she brought more dust
And sprinkled wine three times for her brother's ghost.
We ran and took her at once. She was not afraid,
Not even when we charged her with what she had done.
She denied nothing.   50
                        And this was a comfort to me,
And some uneasiness: for it is a good thing
To escape from death, but it is no great pleasure
To bring death to a friend.

Yet I always say   55
There is nothing so comfortable as your own safe skin!

CREON   [*slowly, dangerously*]:   And you, Antigonê,
You with your head hanging,—do you confess this thing?

ANTIGONÊ: I do. I deny nothing.

CREON   [*to* SENTRY]:   You may go.   60

Exit SENTRY.

[*to* ANTIGONÊ] Tell me, tell me briefly:
Had you heard my proclamation touching this matter?

ANTIGONÊ: It was public. Could I help hearing it?

CREON: And yet you dared defy the law.

ANTIGONÊ: I dared.   65
It was not God's proclamation. That final Justice
That rules the world below makes no such laws.

Your edict, King, was strong,
But all your strength is weakness itself against
The immortal unrecorded laws of God.   70
They are not merely now: they were, and shall be,
Operative for ever, beyond man utterly.

I knew I must die, even without your decree:
I am only mortal. And if I must die
Now, before it is my time to die,   75
Surely this is no hardship: can anyone
Living, as I live, with evil all about me,
Think Death less than a friend? This death of mine
Is of no importance; but if I had left my brother
Lying in death unburied, I should have suffered.   80
Now I do not.
              You smile at me. Ah Creon,
Think me a fool, if you like; but it may well be
That a fool convicts me of folly.

CHORAGOS: Like father, like daughter: both headstrong, deaf to reason!   85
She has never learned to yield.

CREON: She has much to learn.
The inflexible heart breaks first, the toughest iron
Cracks first, and the wildest horses bend their necks
At the pull of the smallest curb.   90
Pride? In a slave?
This girl is guilty of a double insolence,
Breaking the given laws and boasting of it.
Who is the man here,
She or I, if this crime goes unpunished?
Sister's child, or more than sister's child,   95
Or closer yet in blood—she and her sister
Win bitter death for this!

[*to* SERVANTS]

Go, some of you,
Arrest Ismenê. I accuse her equally.   100
Bring her: you will find her sniffling in the house there.

Her mind's a traitor: crimes kept in the dark
Cry for light, and the guardian brain shudders;
But how much worse than this
Is brazen boasting of barefaced anarchy!   105

ANTIGONÊ: Creon, what more do you want than my death?
CREON: Nothing.
That gives me everything.
ANTIGONÊ: Then I beg you: kill me.
This talking is a great weariness: your words   110
Are distasteful to me, and I am sure that mine
Seem so to you. And yet they should not seem so:
I should have praise and honor for what I have done.
All these men here would praise me
Were their lips not frozen shut with fear of you.   115
[*Bitterly.*] Ah the good fortune of kings,
Licensed to say and do whatever they please!
CREON: You are alone here in that opinion.
ANTIGONÊ: No, they are with me. But they keep their tongues in leash.
CREON: Maybe. But you are guilty, and they are not.   120
ANTIGONÊ: There is no guilt in reverence for the dead.
CREON: But Eteoclês—was he not your brother too?
ANTIGONÊ: My brother too.
CREON: And you insult his memory?
ANTIGONÊ [*softly*]:   The dead man would not say that I insult it.   125
CREON: He would: for you honor a traitor as much as him.
ANTIGONÊ: His own brother, traitor or not, and equal in blood.
CREON: He made war on his country. Eteoclês defended it.
ANTIGONÊ: Nevertheless, there are honors due all the dead.
CREON: But not the same for the wicked as for the just.   130
ANTIGONÊ: Ah Creon, Creon,
Which of us can say what the gods hold wicked?
CREON: An enemy is an enemy, even dead.
ANTIGONÊ: It is my nature to join in love, not hate.
CREON [*finally losing patience*]:   Go join them, then; if you must have your love, 135
Find it in hell!
CHORAGOS: But see, Ismenê comes:

Enter ISMENÊ, *guarded.*

Those tears are sisterly, the cloud
That shadows her eyes rains down gentle sorrow.
CREON   You too, Ismenê,   140
Snake in my ordered house, sucking my blood

Stealthily—and all the time I never knew
That these two sisters were aiming at my throne!
                                        Ismenê,
Do you confess your share in this crime, or deny it?   145
Answer me.

ISMENÊ: Yes, if she will let me say so. I am guilty.

ANTIGONÊ [*coldly*]:   No, Ismenê. You have no right to say so.
You would not help me, and I will not have you help me.

ISMENÊ: But now I know what you meant; and I am here   150
To join you, to take my share of punishment.

ANTIGONÊ: The dead man and the gods who rule the dead
Know whose act this was. Words are not friends.

ISMENÊ: Do you refuse me, Antigonê? I want to die with you:
I too have a duty that I must discharge to the dead.   155

ANTIGONÊ: You shall not lessen my death by sharing it.

ISMENÊ: What do I care for life when you are dead?

ANTIGONÊ: Ask Creon. You're always hanging on his opinions.

ISMENÊ: You are laughing at me. Why, Antigonê?

ANTIGONÊ: It's a joyless laughter, Ismenê.   160

ISMENÊ: But can I do nothing?

ANTIGONÊ: Yes. Save yourself. I shall not envy you.
There are those who will praise you; I shall have honor, too.

ISMENÊ: But we are equally guilty!

ANTIGONÊ: No more, Ismenê.   165
You are alive, but I belong to Death.

CREON [*to the Chorus*]:   Gentlemen, I beg you to observe these girls:
One has just now lost her mind; the other,
It seems, has never had a mind at all.

ISMENÊ: Grief teaches the steadiest minds to waver, King.   170

CREON: Yours certainly did, when you assumed guilt with the guilty!

ISMENÊ: But how could I go on living without her?

CREON: You are.
She is already dead.

ISMENÊ: But your own son's bride!   175

CREON: There are places enough for him to push his plow.
I want no wicked women for my sons!

ISMENÊ: O dearest Haimon, how your father wrongs you!

CREON: I've had enough of your childish talk of marriage!

CHORAGOS: Do you really intend to steal this girl from your son?   180

CREON: No; Death will do that for me.

CHORAGOS: Then she must die?

CREON [*ironically*]:   You dazzle me.
                         —But enough of this talk!
[*to* GUARDS] You, there, take them away and guard them well: 185
For they are but women, and even brave men run
When they see Death coming.

                   Exeunt ISMENÊ, ANTIGONÊ, *and* GUARDS.

ODE II

Strophe 1

CHORUS: Fortunate is the man who has never tasted God's vengeance!
Where once the anger of heaven has struck, that house is shaken
For ever: damnation rises behind each child
Like a wave cresting out of the black northeast,
When the long darkness under sea roars up   5
And bursts drumming death upon the windwhipped sand.

Antistrophe 1

I have seen this gathering sorrow from time long past
Loom upon Oedipus' children: generation from generation
Takes the compulsive rage of the enemy god.
So lately this last flower of Oedipus' line   10
Drank the sunlight! but now a passionate word
And a handful of dust have closed up all its beauty.

Strophe 2

What mortal arrogance
Transcends the wrath of Zeus?
Sleep cannot lull him nor the effortless long months   15
Of the timeless gods: but he is young for ever,
And his house is the shining day of high Olympos.
All that is and shall be,
And all the past, is his.
No pride on earth is free of the curse of heaven.   20

Antistrophe 2

The straying dreams of men
May bring them ghosts of joy:
But as they drowse, the waking embers burn them;
Or they walk with fixed eyes, as blind men walk.
But the ancient wisdom speaks for our own time: 25
Fate works most for woe
With Folly's fairest show.
Man's little pleasure is the spring of sorrow.

SCENE III

CHORAGOS: But here is Haimon, King, the last of all your sons.
Is it grief for Antigonê that brings him here,
And bitterness at being robbed of his bride?

Enter HAIMON.

CREON: We shall soon see, and no need of diviners.
                                              —Son,   5
You have heard my final judgment on that girl:

Have you come here hating me, or have you come
With deference and with love, whatever I do?
HAIMON: I am your son, father. You are my guide.
You make things clear for me, and I obey you.
No marriage means more to me than your continuing wisdom.   10
CREON   Good. That is the way to behave: subordinate
Everything else, my son, to your father's will.
This is what a man prays for, that he may get
Sons attentive and dutiful in his house,   15
Each one hating his father's enemies,
Honoring his father's friends. But if his sons
Fail him, if they turn out unprofitably,
What has he fathered but trouble for himself
And amusement for the malicious?   20
                            So you are right
Not to lose your head over this woman.
Your pleasure with her would soon grow cold, Haimon,
And then you'd have a hellcat in bed and elsewhere.
Let her find her husband in Hell!   25
Of all the people in this city, only she
Has had contempt for my law and broken it.

Do you want me to show myself weak before the people?
Or to break my sworn word? No, and I will not.
The woman dies.   30
I suppose she'll plead "family ties." Well, let her.
If I permit my own family to rebel,
How shall I earn the world's obedience?
Show me the man who keeps his house in hand,
He's fit for public authority.   35
                            I'll have no dealings
With law-breakers, critics of the government:
Whoever is chosen to govern should be obeyed—
Must be obeyed, in all things, great and small,
Just and unjust! O Haimon,   40
The man who knows how to obey, and that man only,
Knows how to give commands when the time comes.
You can depend on him, no matter how fast
The spears come: he's a good soldier, he'll stick it out.

Anarchy, anarchy! Show me a greater evil!   45
This is why cities tumble and the great houses rain down,
This is what scatters armies!
No, no: good lives are made so by discipline.
We keep the laws then, and the lawmakers,
And no woman shall seduce us. If we must lose,   50
Let's lose to a man, at least! Is a woman stronger than we?

CHORAGOS: Unless time has rusted my wits,
  What you say, King, is said with point and dignity.
HAIMON   [*boyishly earnest*]:   Father:
  Reason is God's crowning gift to man, and you are right   55
  To warn me against losing mine. I cannot say—
  I hope that I shall never want to say!—that you
  Have reasoned badly. Yet there are other men
  Who can reason, too; and their opinions might be helpful.
  You are not in a position to know everything   60
  That people say or do, or what they feel:
  Your temper terrifies them—everyone
  Will tell you only what you like to hear.
  But I, at any rate, can listen; and I have heard them
  Muttering and whispering in the dark about this girl.   65
  They say no woman has ever, so unreasonably,
  Died so shameful a death for a generous act:
  "She covered her brother's body. Is this indecent?
  She kept him from dogs and vultures. Is this a crime?
  Death?—She should have all the honor that we can give her!" 70

  This is the way they talk out there in the city.

  You must believe me:
  Nothing is closer to me than your happiness.
  What could be closer? Must not any son
  Value his father's fortune as his father does his?   75
  I beg you, do not be unchangeable:
  Do not believe that you alone can be right.
  The man who thinks that,
  The man who maintains that only he has the power
  To reason correctly, the gift to speak, the soul—   80
  A man like that, when you know him, turns out empty.

  It is not reason never to yield to reason!

  In flood time you can see how some trees bend,
  And because they bend, even their twigs are safe,
  While stubborn trees are torn up, roots and all.   85
  And the same thing happens in sailing:
  Make your sheet fast, never slacken,—and over you go,
  Head over heels and under: and there's your voyage.
  Forget you are angry! Let yourself be moved!
  I know I am young; but please let me say this: 90
  The ideal condition
  Would be, I admit, that men should be right by instinct;
  But since we are all too likely to go astray,
  The reasonable thing is to learn from those who can teach.

CHORAGOS: You will do well to listen to him, King,   95
            If what he says is sensible. And you, Haimon,
            Must listen to your father.—Both speak well.

CREON: You consider it right for a man of my years and experience
         To go to school to a boy?

HAIMON: It is not right,   100
         If I am wrong. But if I am young, and right,
         What does my age matter?

CREON: You think it right to stand up for an anarchist?

HAIMON: Not at all. I pay no respect to criminals.

CREON: Then she is not a criminal?   105

HAIMON: The City would deny it, to a man.

CREON: And the City proposes to teach me how to rule?

HAIMON: Ah. Who is it that's talking like a boy now?

CREON: My voice is the one voice giving orders in this City!

HAIMON: It is no City if it takes orders from one voice.   110

CREON: The State is the King!

HAIMON: Yes, if the State is a desert.

                        Pause.

CREON: This boy, it seems, has sold out to a woman.

HAIMON: If you are a woman: my concern is only for you.

CREON: So? Your "concern"! In a public brawl with your father!   115

HAIMON: How about you, in a public brawl with justice?

CREON: With justice, when all that I do is within my rights?

HAIMON: You have no right to trample on God's right.

CREON: [*completely out of control*]: Fool, adolescent fool! Taken in by a woman!

HAIMON: You'll never see me taken in by anything vile.   120

CREON: Every word you say is for her!

HAIMON [*quietly, darkly*]:   And for you.
         And for me. And for the gods under the earth.

CREON: You'll never marry her while she lives.

HAIMON: Then she must die.—But her death will cause another.   125

CREON: Another?
         Have you lost your senses? Is this an open threat?

HAIMON: There is no threat in speaking to emptiness.

CREON: I swear you'll regret this superior tone of yours!
         You are the empty one!   130

HAIMON: If you were not my father,
         I'd say you were perverse.

CREON: You girlstruck fool, don't play at words with me!

HAIMON: I am sorry. You prefer silence.

CREON: Now, by God—!   135
         I swear, by all the gods in heaven above us,
         You'll watch it, I swear you shall!

[*To the* SERVANTS.]

Bring her out!

Bring the woman out! Let her die before his eyes!

Here, this instant, with her bridegroom beside her!   140

HAIMON: Not here, no; she will not die here, King.

And you will never see my face again.

Go on raving as long as you've a friend to endure you.

Exit HAIMON.

CHORAGOS: Gone, gone.

Creon, a young man in a rage is dangerous!   145

CREON: Let him do, or dream to do, more than a man can.

He shall not save these girls from death.

CHORAGOS: These girls?

You have sentenced them both?

CREON: No, you are right.   150

I will not kill the one whose hands are clean.

CHORAGOS: But Antigonê?

CREON [*somberly*]:   I will carry her far away

Out there in the wilderness, and lock her

Living in a vault of stone. She shall have food,   155

As the custom is, to absolve the State of her death.

And there let her pray to the gods of hell:

They are her only gods:

Perhaps they will show her an escape from death,

Or she may learn,   160

though late,

That piety shown the dead is pity in vain.

Exit CREON.

ODE III

Strophe

CHORUS   Love, unconquerable

Waster of rich men, keeper

Of warm lights and all-night vigil

In the soft face of a girl:

Sea-wanderer, forest-visitor!   5

Even the pure Immortals cannot escape you,

And mortal man, in his one day's dusk,

Trembles before your glory.

Antistrophe

Surely you swerve upon ruin

The just man's consenting heart,   10

As here you have made bright anger

Strike between father and son—

And none has conquered but Love!
A girl's glance working the will of heaven:
Pleasure to her alone who mocks us,   15
Merciless Aphroditê.°

SCENE IV

CHORAGOS [*as* ANTIGONÊ *enters guarded*]:   But I can no longer stand in
          awe of this,
     Nor, seeing what I see, keep back my tears.
     Here is Antigonê, passing to that chamber
     Where all find sleep at last.   5

Strophe 1

ANTIGONÊ: Look upon me, friends, and pity me
     Turning back at the night's edge to say
     Good-by to the sun that shines for me no longer;
     Now sleepy Death
     Summons me down to Acheron°, that cold shore: 10
     There is no bridesong there, nor any music.
CHORUS   Yet not unpraised, not without a kind of honor,
     You walk at last into the underworld;
     Untouched by sickness, broken by no sword.
     What woman has ever found your way to death?   15

Antistrophe 1

ANTIGONÊ: How often I have heard the story of Niobê,
     Tantalos's wretched daughter, how the stone
     Clung fast about her, ivy-close: and they say
     The rain falls endlessly
     And sifting soft snow; her tears are never done.   20
     I feel the loneliness of her death in mine.
CHORUS   But she was born of heaven, and you
     Are woman, woman-born. If her death is yours,
     A mortal woman's, is this not for you
     Glory in our world and in the world beyond?   25

Strophe 2

ANTIGONÊ   You laugh at me. Ah, friends, friends,
     Can you not wait until I am dead? O Thebes,
     O men many-charioted, in love with Fortune,
     Dear springs of Dircê, sacred Theban grove,
     Be witnesses for me, denied all pity,   30
     Unjustly judged! and think a word of love

---

16 Aphroditê the goddess of love   **10 Acheron** a river of the underworld where death
reigns

For her whose path turns
Under dark earth, where there are no more tears.
CHORUS: You have passed beyond human daring and come at last
Into a place of stone where Justice sits.   35
I cannot tell
What shape of your father's guilt appears in this.

Antistrophe 2

ANTIGONÊ: You have touched it at last: that bridal bed
Unspeakable, horror of son and mother mingling:
Their crime, infection of all our family!   40
O Oedipus, father and brother!
Your marriage strikes from the grave to murder mine.
I have been a stranger here in my own land:
All my life
The blasphemy of my birth has followed me.   45
CHORUS: Reverence is a virtue, but strength
Lives in established law: that must prevail.
You have made your choice,
Your death is the doing of your conscious hand.

Epode

ANTIGONÊ: Then let me go, since all your words are bitter,   50
And the very light of the sun is cold to me.
Lead me to my vigil, where I must have
Neither love nor lamentation; no song, but silence.

CREON *interrupts impatiently.*

CREON: If dirges and planned lamentations could put off death,
Men would be singing for ever.   55

[*to the* SERVANTS]

Take her, go!
You know your orders: take her to the vault
And leave her alone there. And if she lives or dies,
That's her affair, not ours: our hands are clean.
ANTIGONÊ: O tomb, vaulted bride bed in eternal rock,   60
Soon I shall be with my own again
Where Persephonê° welcomes the thin ghosts underground:
And I shall see my father again, and you, mother,
And dearest Polyneicês—
                              dearest indeed   65

62 Persephonê the queen of the underworld

To me, since it was my hand
That washed him clean and poured the ritual wine:
And my reward is death before my time!

And yet, as men's hearts know, I have done no wrong,
I have not sinned before God. Or if I have,   70
I shall know the truth in death. But if the guilt
Lies upon Creon who judged me, then, I pray,
May his punishment equal my own.
CHORAGOS: O passionate heart,
   Unyielding, tormented still by the same winds!   75
CREON: Her guards shall have good cause to regret their delaying.
ANTIGONÊ: Ah! That voice is like the voice of death!
CREON: I can give you no reason to think you are mistaken.
ANTIGONÊ: Thebes, and you my fathers' gods,
   And rulers of Thebes, you see me now, the last   80
   Unhappy daughter of a line of kings,
   Your kings, led away to death. You will remember
   What things I suffer, and at what men's hands,
   Because I would not transgress the laws of heaven.
   [*To the* GUARDS, *simply.*] Come: let us wait no longer.   85

Exit ANTIGONÊ, *left, guarded.*

ODE IV

Strophe 1
CHORUS: All Danaê's beauty was locked away
   In a brazen cell where the sunlight could not come:
   A small room still as any grave, enclosed her.
   Yet she was a princess too,
   And Zeus in a rain of gold poured love upon her.   5
   O child, child,
   No power in wealth or war
   Or tough sea-blackened ships
   Can prevail against untiring Destiny!

Antistrophe 1
   And Dryas' son° also, that furious king,   10
   Bore the god's prisoning anger for his pride:
   Sealed up by Dionysos in deaf stone,
   His madness died among echoes.
   So at the last he learned what dreadful power
   His tongue had mocked: 15
   For he had profaned the revels,

10 Dryas' son Lycurgus, king of Thrace

And fired the wrath of the nine
Implacable Sisters° that love the sound of the flute.

Strophe 2

And old men tell a half-remembered tale
Of horror where a dark ledge splits the sea   20
And a double surf beats on the gray shores:
How a king's new woman,° sick
With hatred for the queen he had imprisoned,
Ripped out his two sons' eyes with her bloody hands
While grinning Arês° watched the shuttle plunge   25
Four times: four blind wounds crying for revenge,

Antistrophe 2

Crying, tears and blood mingled.—Piteously born,
Those sons whose mother was of heavenly birth!
Her father was the god of the North Wind
And she was cradled by gales,   30
She raced with young colts on the glittering hills
And walked untrammeled in the open light:
But in her marriage deathless Fate found means
To build a tomb like yours for all her joy.

SCENE V

Enter blind TEIRESIAS, *led by a boy. The opening speeches of* TEIRESIAS
should be in singsong contrast to the realistic lines of CREON.

TEIRESIAS: This is the way the blind man comes, Princes, Princes, Lockstep, two
heads lit by the eyes of one.

CREON: What new thing have you to tell us, old Teiresias?

TEIRESIAS: I have much to tell you: listen to the prophet, Creon.

CREON: I am not aware that I have ever failed to listen.   5

TEIRESIAS: Then you have done wisely, King, and ruled well.

CREON: I admit my debt to you. But what have you to say?

TEIRESIAS: This, Creon: you stand once more on the edge of fate.

CREON: What do you mean? Your words are a kind of dread.

TEIRESIAS: Listen Creon: 10
I was sitting in my chair of augury, at the place
Where the birds gather about me. They were all a-chatter,
As is their habit, when suddenly I heard
A strange note in their jangling, a scream, a
Whirring fury; I knew that they were fighting,   15
Tearing each other, dying

18 Implacable Sisters the Muses of poetry and music, arts and sciences   **22 king's
new woman** Eidothea, second wife of King Phineas, blinded her stepsons after the king
had imprisoned their mother in a cave   **25 Arês** the god of war who loves bloodshed

In a whirlwind of wings clashing. And I was afraid.
I began the rites of burnt-offering at the altar,
But Hephaistos° failed me: instead of bright flame,
There was only the sputtering slime of the fat thigh-flesh   20
Melting: the entrails dissolved in gray smoke,
The bare bone burst from the welter. And no blaze!

This was a sign from heaven. My boy described it,
Seeing for me as I see for others.

I tell you, Creon, you yourself have brought   25
This new calamity upon us. Our hearths and altars
Are stained with the corruption of dogs and carrion birds
That glut themselves on the corpse of Oedipus' son.
The gods are deaf when we pray to them, their fire
Recoils from our offering, their birds of omen   30
Have no cry of comfort, for they are gorged
With the thick blood of the dead.

                        O my son,
These are no trifles! Think: all men make mistakes,
But a good man yields when he knows his course is wrong,   35

Give in to the dead man, then: do not fight with a corpse—
What glory is it to kill a man who is dead?
Think, I beg you:
It is for your own good that I speak as I do.
You should be able to yield for your own good.   40
CREON: It seems that prophets have made me their especial province.
All my life long
I have been a kind of butt for the dull arrows
Of doddering fortune-tellers!

                     No, Teiresias: 45
If your birds—if the great eagles of God himself
Should carry him stinking bit by bit to heaven,
I would not yield. I am not afraid of pollution:
No man can defile the gods.

                  Do what you will,   50
Go into business, make money, speculate
In India gold or that synthetic gold from Sardis,
Get rich otherwise than by my consent to bury him.
Teiresias, it is a sorry thing when a wise man
Sells his wisdom, lets out his words for hire!   55
TEIRESIAS: Ah Creon! Is there no man left in the world—
CREON: To do what?—Come, let's have the aphorism!
TEIRESIAS: No man who knows that wisdom outweighs any wealth?
CREON: As surely as bribes are baser than any baseness.

19 Hephaistos the god of fire

TEIRESIAS: You are sick, Creon! You are deathly sick!   60

CREON: As you say: it is not my place to challenge a prophet.

TEIRESIAS: Yet you have said my prophecy is for sale.

CREON: The generation of prophets has always loved gold.

TEIRESIAS: The generation of kings has always loved brass.

CREON: You forget yourself! You are speaking to your King.   65

TEIRESIAS: I know it. You are a king because of me.

CREON: You have a certain skill; but you have sold out.

TEIRESIAS: King, you will drive me to words that—

CREON: Say them, say them!

   Only remember: I will not pay you for them.   70

TEIRESIAS: No, you will find them too costly.

CREON: No doubt. Speak:

   Whatever you say, you will not change my will.

TEIRESIAS: Then take this, and take it to heart!

   The time is not far off when you shall pay back   75

   Corpse for corpse, flesh of your own flesh.

   You have thrust the child of this world into living night,

   You have kept from the gods below the child that is theirs:

   The one in a grave before her death, the other,

   Dead, denied the grave. This is your crime: 80

   And the Furies and the dark gods of Hell

   Are swift with terrible punishment for you.

   Do you want to buy me now, Creon?

                                                 Not many days,

   And your house will be full of men and women weeping,   85

   And curses will be hurled at you from far

   Cities grieving for sons unburied, left to rot

   Before the walls of Thebes.

   These are my arrows, Creon: they are all for you.

[*To boy.*] But come, child: lead me home.   90

   Let him waste his fine anger upon younger men.

   Maybe he will learn at last

   To control a wiser tongue in a better head.

                                 Exit TEIRESIAS.

CHORAGOS: The old man has gone, King, but his words

   Remain to plague us. I am old, too,   95

   But I cannot remember that he was ever false.

CREON: That is true.... It troubles me.

   Oh it is hard to give in! but it is worse

   To risk everything for stubborn pride.

CHORAGOS: Creon: take my advice.   100

CREON: What shall I do?

CHORAGOS: Go quickly: free Antigonê from her vault

   And build a tomb for the body of Polyneicês.

CREON: You would have me do this!

CHORAGOS: Creon, yes!   105
 And it must be done at once: God moves
 Swiftly to cancel the folly of stubborn men.
CREON: It is hard to deny the heart! But I
 Will do it: I will not fight with destiny.
CHORAGOS: You must go yourself, you cannot leave it to others.   110
CREON: I will go.
    —Bring axes, servants:
 Come with me to the tomb. I buried her,
 Will set her free.
     Oh quickly!   115
 My mind misgives—
 The laws of the gods are mighty, and a man must serve them
 To the last day of his life!

     Exit CREON.

PAEAN°

Strophe 1

CHORAGOS: God of many names
CHORUS   O Iacchos°
       son
 of Kadmeian Sémelê°
     O born of the Thunder!   5
 Guardian of the West
     Regent
 of Eleusis' plain
     O Prince of maenad° Thebes
 and the Dragon Field by rippling Ismenos.°   10

Antistrophe 1

CHORAGOS: God of many names
CHORUS: the flame of torches
 flares on our hills
    the nymphs of Iacchos
 dance at the spring of Castalia.°   15
 from the vine-close mountain
     come ah come in ivy:
 Evohé evohé! sings through the streets of Thebes

Strophe 2

CHORAGOS: God of many names
CHORUS: Iacchos of Thebes   20
 heavenly Child

Paean a triumphant song **2 Iacchos** also called Bacchos or Dionysos, god of wine
and revelry **4 Sémelê** mother of Iacchos, consort of Zeus **9 Maenad** female worshipper,
attendant of Iacchos **10 Ismenos** a river near Thebes where, legend has it, the ancestors of Thebes sprang from a dragon's teeth **15 Castalia** a spring on Mount Parnassus

of Sémelê bride of the Thunderer!
The shadow of plague is upon us:
come
with clement feet   25
oh come from Parnasos
down the long slopes
across the lamenting water

Antistrophe 2

CHORAGOS: Iô Fire! Chorister of the throbbing stars!
O purest among the voices of the night!   30
Thou son of God, blaze for us!
CHORUS: Come with choric rapture of circling Maenads
Who cry *Iô Iacche!*

God of many names!

EXODOS

Enter MESSENGER *from left.*

MESSENGER: Men of the line of Kadmos,° you who live
Near Amphion's citadel,°
I cannot say
Of any condition of human life "This is fixed,
This is clearly good, or bad." Fate raises up,   5
And Fate casts down the happy and unhappy alike:
No man can foretell his Fate.
Take the case of Creon:
Creon was happy once, as I count happiness:
Victorious in battle, sole governor of the land,   10
Fortunate father of children nobly born.
And now it has all gone from him! Who can say
That a man is still alive when his life's joy fails?
He is a walking dead man. Grant him rich,
Let him live like a king in his great house: 15
If his pleasure is gone, I would not give
So much as the shadow of smoke for all he owns.
CHORAGOS: Your words hint at sorrow: what is your news for us?
MESSENGER: They are dead. The living are guilty of their death.
CHORAGOS: Who is guilty? Who is dead? Speak!   20
MESSENGER: Haimon.
Haimon is dead; and the hand that killed him
Is his own hand.
CHORAGOS: His father's? or his own?

---

1 Kadmos sowed the dragon's teeth and founded Thebes   **2 Amphion's citadel** Amphion's lyre playing was so beautiful that he charmed stones to form a wall around Thebes

MESSENGER:	His own, driven mad by the murder his father had done.	25
CHORAGOS:	Teiresias, Teiresias, how clearly you saw it all!	
MESSENGER:	This is my news: you must draw what conclusions you can from it.	
CHORAGOS:	But look: Eurydicê, our Queen:	

Has she overheard us?

Enter EURYDICÊ *from the palace, center.*

EURYDICÊ: I have heard something, friends: 30
     As I was unlocking the gate of Pallas'° shrine,
     For I needed her help today, I heard a voice
     Telling of some new sorrow. And I fainted
     There at the temple with all my maidens about me.
     But speak again: whatever it is, I can bear it: 35
     Grief and I are no strangers.
MESSENGER: Dearest Lady.
     I will tell you plainly all that I have seen.
     I shall not try to comfort you: what is the use,
     Since comfort could lie only in what is not true?   40
     The truth is always best.
                         I went with Creon
     To the outer plain where Polyneicês was lying,
     No friend to pity him, his body shredded by dogs.

     We made our prayers in that place to Hecatê°   45
     And Pluto,° that they would be merciful. And we bathed
     The corpse with holy water, and we brought
     Fresh-broken branches to burn what was left of it,
     And upon the urn we heaped up a towering barrow
     Of the earth of his own land.   50
                         When we were done, we ran
     To the vault where Antigonê lay on her couch of stone.
     One of the servants had gone ahead,
     And while he was yet far off he heard a voice
     Grieving within the chamber, and he came back   55
     And told Creon. And as the King went closer,
     The air was full of wailing, the words lost,
     And he begged us to make all haste. "Am I a prophet?"
     He said, weeping, "And must I walk this road,
     The saddest of all that I have gone before?   60
     My son's voice calls me on. Oh quickly, quickly!
     Look through the crevice there, and tell me
     If it is Haimon, or some deception of the gods!"

---

31 Pallas Athena, the goddess of wisdom   **45 Hecatê** the goddess of witchcraft
46 Pluto king of the underworld

We obeyed; and in the cavern's farthest corner
We saw her lying: 65
She had made a noose of her fine linen veil
And hanged herself. Haimon lay beside her,
His arms about her waist, lamenting her,
His love lost under ground, crying out
That his father had stolen her away from him.   70
When Creon saw him the tears rushed to his eyes
And he called to him: "What have you done, child? Speak to me.
What are you thinking that makes your eyes so strange?
O my son, my son, I come to you on my knees!"
But Haimon spat in his face. He said not a word,   75
Staring—
            And suddenly drew his sword
And lunged. Creon shrank back, the blade missed; and the boy,
Desperate against himself, drove it half its length
Into his own side, and fell. And as he died   80
He gathered Antigonê close in his arms again,
Choking, his blood bright red on her white cheek.
And now he lies dead with the dead, and she is his
At last, his bride in the houses of the dead.

> *Exit* EURYDICÊ *into the palace.*

CHORAGOS: She has left us without a word. What can this mean?   85
MESSENGER: It troubles me, too; yet she knows what is best,
Her grief is too great for public lamentation,
And doubtless she has gone to her chamber to weep
For her dead son, leading her maidens in his dirge.

> *Pause.*

CHORAGOS: It may be so: but I fear this deep silence.   90
MESSENGER: I will see what she is doing. I will go in.

> *Exit* MESSENGER *into the palace.*
> *Enter* CREON *with attendants, bearing* HAIMON'S *body.*

CHORAGOS: But here is the king himself: oh look at him,
Bearing his own damnation in his arms.
CREON: Nothing you say can touch me any more.
My own blind heart has brought me   95
From darkness to final darkness. Here you see
The father murdering, the murdered son—
And all my civic wisdom!

Haimon my son, so young, so young to die,
I was the fool, not you; and you died for me.   100
CHORAGOS: That is the truth; but you were late in learning it.
CREON: This truth is hard to bear. Surely a god
Has crushed me beneath the hugest weight of heaven,

And driven me headlong a barbaric way
To trample out the thing I held most dear.   105

The pains that men will take to come to pain!

Enter MESSENGER *from the palace.*

MESSENGER: The burden you carry in your hands is heavy,
    But it is not all: you will find more in your house.
CREON: What burden worse than this shall I find there?
MESSENGER: The Queen is dead.   110
CREON: O port of death, deaf world,
    Is there no pity for me? And you, Angel of evil,
    I was dead, and your words are death again.
    Is it true, boy? Can it be true?
    Is my wife dead? Has death bred death?   115
MESSENGER: You can see for yourself.

The doors are opened and the body of EURYDICÊ *is disclosed within.*

CREON: Oh pity!
    All true, all true, and more than I can bear!
    O my wife, my son!
MESSENGER: She stood before the altar, and her heart   120
    Welcomed the knife her own hand guided,
    And a great cry burst from her lips for Megareus° dead,
    And for Haimon dead, her sons; and her last breath
    Was a curse for their father, the murderer of her sons.
    And she fell, and the dark flowed in through her closing eyes.   125
CREON: O God, I am sick with fear.
    Are there no swords here? Has no one a blow for me?
MESSENGER: Her curse is upon you for the deaths of both.
CREON: It is right that it should be. I alone am guilty.
    I know it, and I say it. Lead me in,   130
    Quickly, friends.
    I have neither life nor substance. Lead me in.
CHORAGOS: You are right, if there can be right in so much wrong.
    The briefest way is best in a world of sorrow.
CREON: Let it come,   135
    Let death come quickly, and be kind to me.
    I would not ever see the sun again.
CHORAGOS: All that will come when it will; but we, meanwhile,
    Have much to do. Leave the future to itself.
CREON: All my heart was in that prayer!   140
CHORAGOS: Then do not pray any more: the sky is deaf.
CREON: Lead me away. I have been rash and foolish.
    I have killed my son and my wife.

122 Megareus the other son of Eurydicê and Creon who had sacrificed himself to Arês
to save Thebes from the seven who attacked it

I look for comfort; my comfort lies here dead.
Whatever my hands have touched has come to nothing.   145
Fate has brought all my pride to a thought of dust.

As CREON *is being led into the house, the* CHORAGOS *advances and speaks directly to the audience.*

CHORAGOS: There is no happiness where there is no wisdom;
    No wisdom but in submission to the gods.
    Big words are always punished,
    And proud men in old age learn to be wise.   150

CONNECTING THROUGH WRITING

One of the best ways to get ideas for an essay is to ask and answer your own most compelling questions.

- Write down whatever questions come to mind during and after your reading. See if your answers to these questions provide topics for writing.

- Choose a compelling idea from a journal entry.

- Draw a Venn diagram to compare elements, characters, or stories (pp. 29–30), use directed freewriting (p. 39), ask questions (p. 40), list (p. 40–41), or draw a cluster or semantic map (pp. 41–42) to loosen up ideas.

Listed below is a more structured approach based on the elements of drama discussed earlier in this section. Applying these questions to *Antigonê* may demonstrate how the elements might be applied to any work of drama.

FIRST RESPONSES

1. To what extent is your response to *Antigonê* influenced by your own experience?

2. If you were placed in their positions, would you behave the same way as Antigonê? Creon? Haimon? Ismenê? Explain.

3. Which do you think is more important, loyalty to your family, religion, or country? Explain.

LANGUAGE AND STYLE

1. How does the formal language and verse form of the play affect you?

2. What does Creon's use of language tell you about him?

3. Is there symbolism in this play? Explain.

NARRATION

1. How are you affected by the comments of Choragos and the chorus?

2. How does the nature of what they say differ from what the individual characters say?

3. How does the role of Choragos differ from that of the other characters?

SETTING

1. When and where is *Antigonê* set?

2. What is the atmosphere in this play?

3. How does the setting influence the conflict between Antigonê and Creon?

4. To what extent does the setting support and emphasize the play's meaning?

5. There are very few stage directions in *Antigonê*. To what extent did that affect your reading of the play?

CONFLICT AND PLOT

1. What is the main conflict in the play? Is it external or internal? Explain.

2. How many other conflicts are there?

3. In what way are they related to the main conflict?

4. To what extent does the plot follow a traditional structure?

CHARACTER

1. How does what Antigonê, Ismenê, Creon, and Haimon say tell you about them?

2. How does what they do tell you about them?

3. What is the function of Teiresias in this play?

4. To what extent is conflict in *Antigonê* connected to characterization?

5. Who is the protagonist and who is the antagonist in this play?

THEME

1. What is the theme of *Antigonê*?

2. How do setting, conflict, and character contribute to this theme?

3. To what extent does the play preach as well as reveal?

TOPICS FOR WRITING

The following list is not exhaustive, but simply illustrative of the kinds of questions that might emerge from the more specific analytical questions (and combinations of questions) like those above. Your responses might provide worthwhile topics for writing.

1. Compare the characterizations of Antigonê and Creon. To what extent are they alike or different?

2. To what extent was it possible for Antigonê to achieve the burial of her brother through different means?

3. Is Creon powerless to respond differently to her behavior? Explain.

4. What is the role of Ismenê? To what extent can you justify her behavior?

5. What is the impact of power on the characters in *Antigonê*?

6. What is the impact of pride on the characters in this play?

7. How important is it that a woman broke the law? What does the play tell us about the place of women in that society?

8. What is the connection between the choral odes and the play's meaning?

9. To what extent is *Antigonê* typical of the work of Sophocles? How does this play compare with Edith Hamilton's summary of the Oedipus myth?

10. How does it compare to the work of other Greek dramatists of this period?

11. How well does *Antigonê* fulfill Aristotle's requirements for tragedy?

    a. In the light of Aristotle's definition of a tragic hero on page 98, write a comparison of Antigonê and Creon. Are they both tragic heroes? Cite the text of *Antigonê* for support.

12. In what way is this play a reflection of the cultural beliefs of ancient Greece?

13. In what way does the conflict in *Antigonê* transcend that period and speak to us now?

READING AND ANALYZING ESSAYS

Of all forms of literature, you are probably most familiar with the essay. You have read them in newspapers and magazines most of your life. And you have had lots of practice writing them. If reading and writing essays has been a good experience, you already know why they are important. They let us express who we are and what we think—our personal stories, impressions, feelings, ideas, and opinions. They let us know who other people are and what they think. They spring from a basic human need to communicate.

In late-sixteenth-century France, Michel de Montaigne, the first modern essay writer, introduced his book *Essais* by writing, "I am myself the subject of my book." Whatever form the essay has taken since then, Montaigne's statement is still at the heart of effective essay writing. Both of the earliest popular essay writers, Montaigne and his English counterpart Francis Bacon, were personal and informal. They wrote about whatever intrigued them, usually in a light, speculative way. They didn't write about the strange or unusual; they wrote about everyday topics—conversation, education, friendship, gardening. But they wrote about these topics in such an entertaining and insightful way that their voices, as if in conversation with us, come back to life when we read them three hundred years later. Since that time some of our most prominent writers have expanded the scope of the essay to moral, social, and political criticism, and its tone from bawdy humor and biting satire to great solemnity.

Most of our favorite essay writers today write in newspapers, magazines, and on the Internet. We may call them columnists, op-ed writers, bloggers, or sports writers, but they are in fact essay writers. They don't tell us the news; they tell us what they think of the news. They are emotional, outspoken, and opinionated in predictable ways—and very much the inheritors of Montaigne's "I." They have strong "voices," and we have gotten to know them. Whether we agree or disagree with them, we usually look forward to reading what they have to say.

When you're reading an essay for the first time, imagine you're in a conversation, that the writer is talking to you. Relax and listen. And talk back from time to time by writing down your responses.

TYPES OF ESSAYS

There is no easy or entirely accurate way to classify essays. Instead of giving a clear picture of how each category is different, the discussion of types below blurs distinctions. After all, narrative and expository essays may be argumentative; exposition and argumentation may use narrative to make or to prove their points. Basically, the intention of all essays is to be persuasive, to have readers respond by thinking, "I see what you mean" or "Yes, you're right."

It may be helpful to think of the designations "narrative," "expository," and "argumentative" as degrees of emphasis rather than discrete or exclusive types.

Narrative

Narrative essays tell a story. Most essays of this type spring from an event or experience in the writer's life. Beyond sharing an aspect of the writer's life, however, their intention is to make a point, present an idea, or make an argument. They not only recount what's happened, they emphasize the importance of the occurrence. This narration is often "seasoned" with personal comment, reflection, and opinion.

Voice is crucial to this kind of essay. All of the personal narratives in this text rely heavily on the narrator as a participant who feels frustration, pain, or joy; who experiences insight and earns the right to tell the story.

Among the narrative essays in this text are "Salvation" (p. 32) and "The Learning Curve" (p. 487).

Expository

Expository essays share, explain, suggest, or explore information, emotion, and ideas. You might ask, "What else is there?" This is the broadest category. Many of these essays may seem to be narrative or argumentative; they may use stories as examples or may imply an argument or position. The key to exposition is the emphasis on showing and sharing insight—not primarily on telling a story or making an argument.

A few examples of exposition in this text are Quindlen's "Mothers" (p. 31) and Bettelheim's "Cinderella" (p. 753).

Argumentative

The intention of a formal argumentative essay is to prove a point by supporting it with evidence. Note that proving and persuading are not the same thing. Proving may persuade or convince us if we are open-minded and have not formed a contrary opinion. If we feel differently about an issue, the amount of logical evidence might not matter. People are often persuaded by advertisements that offer little or no evidence but appeal almost exclusively to their emotions or sense of style.

The most effective argumentative essays do not rely on evidence alone to convince us. While facts and statistics may lie at the foundation of a strong persuasive argument, examples and personal anecdotes often do the real convincing. We think with our heads, but we pay attention with our hearts. When we look at some of the essays in this book that make convincing arguments, we see that they appeal to both head and heart.

Two wide-ranging examples of argumentative essays in this text are "I Have a Dream" (p. 1051) and "A Modest Proposal" (p. 1025).

For a concise checklist of questions for Types of Essays, see page 149.

LANGUAGE, STYLE, AND STRUCTURE

Formal or Informal

Formal essays are usually about a serious topic; they have a fairly tight, clear structure and strategy. Their narrative perspective emphasizes objectivity, and the writer's voice is often impersonal and detached. This type of essay is more likely to gather its support from facts, data, or statistics, and to use formal language, not everyday words or phrases.

Though many formal essays have a complex structure, the classic structure of a formal essay has an introduction that involves the reader and states the thesis, a middle that gives details and examples, and a conclusion that restates support for the thesis and (if successful) leaves the reader enlightened and convinced.

Informal essays deal with both lighthearted and serious topics. They generally rely on detail, emotion, narrative, and personal examples for support. The choice of words and sentence structure is more likely to be conversational and informal, with everyday phrases, dialogue, narration, imagery, and figurative language. The overall structure of an informal essay is likely to emerge from the subject matter rather than adhere to a predetermined structure.

Voice

Voice refers to the individual personality that comes alive in the words. It is the key to **tone,** and tone is not always easy to pick up. When we see or hear a person speaking words, their intonations, physical gestures, and facial expressions tell us the attitude of the speaker toward the subject. When we hear "voice" in our reading, too, we can also sense the intonations. Cues in a printed text are not always obvious, however, and we must often rely on the pattern and types of words the writer chooses to sense the tone.

Irony

Irony is the contrast between appearance/expectation and reality. As in other forms of literature, the two most popular forms of irony in essays are verbal irony and situational irony. **Verbal irony** results from the contrast between what is said by the writer and what is meant. **Irony of situation** results from the contrast between what is expected and what actually happens. Jonathan Swift's "A Modest Proposal" (p. 1025) is a classic example of an essay that relies on verbal irony to make its point.

Word Choice and Style

Choice of language is an important element in creating voice in an essay. Figurative language brings the writing to life. Concrete details and evocative images pull us into the text. Formal vocabulary evokes a different response from us than informal or nonstandard words. So, too, the frequency of images and figurative language has an effect on our reading and response. Using what you already know about language in fiction, poetry, and drama tells you much about imagery, figurative language, syntax, rhythm, and sound in essays as well.

For a concise checklist of questions for Language, Style, and Structure, see page 149.

Theme: What's the Point?

The theme of an essay is the insight the writer shares, or the point the writer wants to teach, prove, or convince us of. Because they often have a tight structure and direct writing style, it may be easier to identify and to articulate the theme in a formal essay than in a narrative or informal one.

The Aims of an Essay: Inform, Preach, or Reveal

Many formal, expository essays intend to inform or teach us. Likewise, it's the intention of many formal, argumentative essays to teach a lesson or convince us of a particular moral view. Essays of this type are often written in response to a perceived political or social problem. In this respect they have a moral, or message.

At the beginning of the essay, writers of formal essays often announce what they intend to prove or to explain and then remind us again at the end. The predictability of the structure itself is designed to make it clear. Like other forms of literature, however, most good narrative and informal essays share or reveal something insightful about human nature. Our experience of the theme, however, may be holistic or impressionistic—and a bit more elusive.

Regardless of the type of essay, what makes your interpretation convincing or defensible is your ability to support it. Your belief about what the essay means may change as you move back and forth through the stages of your reading experience. The first time you read an essay, you may feel one way. Writing down your reflections, rereading the essay, and discussing it with others may lead to a different, better-informed understanding and interpretation.

For a concise checklist of questions for Theme, see below.

✓ CHECKLIST: ANALYZING ESSAYS

Types of Essays

❑ Would you classify the essay as narrative, expository, or argumentative? Explain. Is the classification clear? If not, why?

Language, Style, and Structure

❑ In general, is the essay formal or informal? How so?

❑ How would you describe the writer's voice? Do you find the author believable? Why?

❑ Was the voice of the author effective in conveying the essay's meaning? Why?

❑ Is the language formal or informal? What does the nature of the language tell you about the essay?

❑ Are there many instances of imagery and figurative language (simile, metaphor)? If so, how do they connect to or support the essay?

Theme

❑ What is the intention of the essay? Is it trying to inform us of something? To prove or convince us of something? To share an insight?

❑ What is its theme?

GETTING IDEAS FOR WRITING ABOUT THE ESSAY

The purpose of the essay, the prompts, and the questions in this section is to show how the elements we discussed earlier might be applied to an essay. Following "Mother Tongue," many of the questions from the summary checklist above are applied to the essay, and we consider some of the ways the elements discussed in this section might be used to prompt ideas for your own argumentative essay.

AMY TAN [B. 1952]

MOTHER TONGUE [1990]

I am not a scholar of English or literature. I cannot give you much more than personal opinions on the English language and its variations in this country or others. I am a writer. And by that definition, I am someone who has always loved language. I am fascinated by language in daily life. I spend a great deal of my time thinking about the power of language—the way it can evoke an emotion, a visual image, a complex idea, or a simple truth. Language is the tool of my trade. And I use them all—all the Englishes I grew up with.

Recently, I was made keenly aware of the different Englishes I do use. I was giving a talk to a large group of people, the same talk I had already given to half a dozen other groups. The nature of the talk was about my writing, my life, and my book, *The Joy Luck Club*. The talk was going along well enough, until I remembered one major difference that made the whole talk sound wrong. My mother was in the room. And it was perhaps the first time she had heard me give a lengthy speech, using the kind of English I have never used with her. I was saying things like, "The intersection of memory upon imagination" and "There is an aspect of my fiction that relates to thus-and-thus"—a speech filled with carefully wrought grammatical phrases, burdened, it suddenly seemed to me, with nominalized forms, past perfect tenses, conditional phrases, all the forms of standard English that I had learned in school and through books, the forms of English I did not use at home with my mother.

Just last week, I was walking down the street with my mother, and I again found myself conscious of the English I was using, the English I do use with her. We were talking about the price of new and used furniture and I heard myself saying this: "Not waste money that way." My husband was with us as well, and he didn't notice any switch in my English. And then I realized why. It's because over the twenty years we've been together I've often used that same kind of English with him, and sometimes he even uses it with me. It has become our language of intimacy, a different sort of English that relates to family talk, the language I grew up with.

So you'll have some idea of what this family talk I heard sounds like, I'll quote what my mother said during a recent conversation which I videotaped and then transcribed. During this conversation, my mother was talking about a political gangster in Shanghai who had the same last name as her family's, Du, and how the gangster in his early years wanted to be adopted by her family, which was rich by comparison. Later, the gangster became more powerful, far richer than my mother's family, and one day showed up at my mother's wedding to pay his respects. Here's what she said in part:

5   Du-Yusong having business like fruit stand. Like off the street kind. He is Du like Du Zong but not Tsung-ming Island people. The local people call put-ong, the river east side, he belong to that side local people. That man want to ask Du Zong father take him in like become own family. Du Zong father wasn't look down on him, but didn't take seriously, until that man big like become a mafia. Now important person, very hard to inviting him. Chinese

way, came only to show respect, don't stay for dinner. Respect for making big celebration, he shows up. Mean gives lots of respect. Chinese custom. Chinese social life that way. If too important won't have to stay too long. He come to my wedding. I didn't see, I heard it. I gone to boy's side, they have YMCA dinner. Chinese age I was nineteen.

You should know that my mother's expressive command of English belies how much she actually understands. She reads the *Forbes* report, listens to *Wall Street Week,* converses daily with her stockbroker, reads all of Shirley MacLaine's books with ease—all kinds of things I can't begin to understand. Yet some of my friends tell me they understand 50 percent of what my mother says. Some say they understand 80 to 90 percent. Some say they understand none of it, as if she were speaking pure Chinese. But to me, my mother's English is perfectly clear, perfectly natural. It's my mother tongue. Her language, as I hear it, is vivid, direct, full of observation and imagery. That was the language that helped shape the way I saw things, expressed things, made sense of the world.

Lately, I've been giving more thought to the kind of English my mother speaks. Like others, I have described it to people as "broken" or "fractured" English. But I wince when I say that. It has always bothered me that I can think of no way to describe it other than "broken," as if it were damaged and needed to be fixed, as if it lacked a certain wholeness and soundness. I've heard other terms used, "limited English," for example. But they seem just as bad, as if everything is limited, including people's perceptions of the limited English speaker.

I know this for a fact, because when I was growing up, my mother's "limited" English limited my perception of her. I was ashamed of her English. I believed that her English reflected the quality of what she had to say. That is, because she expressed them imperfectly her thoughts were imperfect. And I had plenty of empirical evidence to support me: the fact that people in department stores, at banks, and at restaurants did not take her seriously, did not give her good service, pretended not to understand her, or even acted as if they did not hear her.

My mother had long realized the limitations of her English as well. When I was fifteen, she used to have me call people on the phone to pretend I was she. In this guise, I was forced to ask for information or even to complain and yell at people who had been rude to her. One time it was a call to her stockbroker in New York. She had cashed out her small portfolio and it just so happened we were going to go to New York the next week, our very first trip outside California. I had to get on the phone and say in an adolescent voice that was not very convincing, "This is Mrs. Tan."

10   And my mother was standing in the back whispering loudly, "Why he don't send me check, already two weeks late. So mad he lie to me, losing me money."

And then I said in perfect English, "Yes, I'm getting rather concerned. You had agreed to send the check two weeks ago, but it hasn't arrived."

Then she began to talk more loudly. "What he want, I come to New York tell him front of his boss, you cheating me?" And I was trying to calm her down, make her be quiet, while telling the stockbroker, "I can't tolerate any more excuses. If I don't receive the check immediately, I am going to have to speak to your manager when I'm in New York next week." And sure enough, the following week there we were in front of this astonished stockbroker, and I was sitting there red-faced and quiet, and my mother, the real Mrs. Tan, was shouting at his boss in her impeccable broken English.

We used a similar routine just five days ago, for a situation that was far less humorous. My mother had gone to the hospital for an appointment, to find out about a benign brain tumor a CAT scan had revealed a month ago. She said she had spoken very good English, her best English, no mistakes. Still, she said, the hospital did not apologize when they said they had lost the CAT scan and she had come for nothing. She said they did not seem to have any sympathy when she told them she was anxious to know the exact diagnosis, since her husband and son had both died of brain tumors. She said they would not give her any more information until the next time and she would have to make another appointment for that. So she said she would not leave until the doctor called her daughter. She wouldn't budge. And when the doctor finally called her daughter, me, who spoke in perfect English—lo and behold—we had assurances the CAT scan would be found, promises that a conference call on Monday would be held, and apologies for any suffering my mother had gone through for a most regrettable mistake.

I think my mother's English almost had an effect on limiting my possibilities in life as well. Sociologists and linguists probably will tell you that a person developing language skills is more influenced by peers. But I do think that the language spoken in the family, especially in immigrant families which are more insular, plays a large role in shaping the language of the child. And I believe that it affected my results on achievement tests, IQ tests, and the SAT. While my English skills were never judged as poor, compared to math, English could not be considered my strong suit. In grade school I did moderately well, getting perhaps B's, sometimes B-pluses, in English and scoring perhaps in the sixtieth or seventieth percentile on achievement tests. But those scores were not good enough to override the opinion that my true abilities lay in math and science, because in those areas I achieved A's and scored in the ninetieth percentile or higher.

15   This was understandable. Math is precise; there is only one correct answer. Whereas, for me at least, the answers on English tests were always a judgment call, a matter of opinion and personal experience. Those tests were constructed around items like fill-in-the-blank sentence completion, such as, "Even though Tom was—, Mary thought he was—." And the correct answer always seemed to be the most bland combinations of thoughts, for example, "Even though Tom was shy, Mary thought he was charming," with the grammatical structure "even though" limiting the correct answer to some sort of semantic opposites, so you wouldn't get answers like, "Even though Tom was foolish, Mary thought he was ridiculous." Well, according to my mother, there were very few limitations as to what Tom could have been and what Mary might have thought of him. So I never did well on tests like that.

The same was true with word analogies, pairs of words in which you were supposed to find some sort of logical, semantic relationship—for example,

"*Sunset* is to *nightfall* as—is to—." And here you would be presented with a list of four possible pairs, one of which showed the same kind of relationship: *red* is to *stoplight, bus* is to *arrival, chills* is to *fever, yawn* is to *boring.* Well, I could never think that way. I knew what the tests were asking, but I could not block out of my mind the images already created by the first pair, "*sunset* is to *nightfall*"—and I would see a burst of colors against a darkening sky, the moon rising, the lowering of a curtain of stars. And all the other pairs of words—red, bus, stoplight, boring—just threw up a mass of confusing images, making it impossible for me to sort out something as logical as saying: "A sunset precedes nightfall" is the same as "a chill precedes a fever." The only way I would have gotten that answer right would have been to imagine an associative situation, for example, my being disobedient and staying out past sunset, catching a chill at night, which turns into feverish pneumonia as punishment, which indeed did happen to me.

I have been thinking about all this lately, about my mother's English, about achievement tests. Because lately I've been asked, as a writer, why there are not more Asian Americans represented in American literature. Why are there few Asian Americans enrolled in creative writing programs? Why do so many Chinese students go into engineering? Well, these are broad sociological questions I can't begin to answer. But I have noticed in surveys—in fact, just last week—that Asian students, as a whole, always do significantly better on math achievement tests than in English. And this makes me think that there are other Asian-American students whose English spoken in the home might also be described as "broken" or "limited." And perhaps they also have teachers who are steering them away from writing and into math and science, which is what happened to me.

Fortunately, I happen to be rebellious in nature and enjoy the challenge of disproving assumptions made about me. I became an English major my first year in college, after being enrolled as pre-med. I started writing nonfiction as a freelancer the week after I was told by my former boss that writing was my worst skill and I should hone my talents toward account management.

But it wasn't until 1985 that I finally began to write fiction. And at first I wrote using what I thought to be wittily crafted sentences, sentences that would finally prove I had mastery over the English language. Here's an example from the first draft of a story that later made its way into *The Joy Luck Club,* but without this line: "That was my mental quandary in its nascent state." A terrible line, which I can barely pronounce.

20   Fortunately, for reasons I won't get into today, I later decided I should envision a reader for the stories I would write. And the reader I decided upon was my mother, because these were stories about mothers. So with this reader in mind—and in fact she did read my early drafts—I began to write stories using all the Englishes I grew up with: the English I spoke to my mother, which for lack of a better term might be described as "simple"; the English she used with me, which for lack of a better term might be described as "broken"; my translation of her Chinese, which could certainly be described as "watered down"; and what I imagined to be her translation of her Chinese if she could speak in perfect English, her internal language, and for that I sought to preserve the

essence, but neither an English nor a Chinese structure. I wanted to capture what language ability tests can never reveal: her intent, her passion, her imagery, the rhythms of her speech and the nature of her thoughts.

Apart from what any critic had to say about my writing, I knew I had succeeded where it counted when my mother finished reading my book and gave me her verdict: "So easy to read."

CONNECTING THROUGH WRITING

One of the best ways to get ideas for an essay is to ask and answer your own most compelling questions.

- Write down whatever questions come to mind during and after your reading. See if your answers to these questions provide topics for writing.

- Choose a compelling idea from a journal entry.

- Draw a Venn diagram to compare elements, characters, or stories (pp. 29–30), use directed freewriting (p. 39), ask questions (p. 40), list (pp. 40–41), or draw a cluster or semantic map (pp. 41–42) to loosen up ideas.

Listed below is a more structured approach based on the elements discussed earlier in this section. Applying these questions to "Mother Tongue" may demonstrate how the elements might be applied to any essay.

FIRST RESPONSES

1. To what extent is your response to "Mother Tongue" influenced by your own background or experience?

2. What questions came to mind as you read the essay?

3. What do you find most provocative or compelling about the essay?

TYPE OF ESSAY

1. How does the voice of the writer influence your response?

2. Amy Tan opens her essay by writing "I am not a scholar of English or literature." How does that influence your response to her?

3. Would you classify this as a narrative, expository, or argumentative essay? Why? To what extent is the classification clear?

LANGUAGE, STYLE, AND STRUCTURE

1. In general, is "Mother Tongue" formal or informal? How so?

2. Is Amy Tan's use of language formal or informal?

3. Are there many instances of imagery and figurative language (simile, metaphor)? If so, how do they connect to or support the essay?

4. How would you describe Amy Tan's voice? Do you find her believable? Why?

5. Was she effective in conveying the essay's meaning? How so?

THEME

1. Do you gain any insights about yourself or your writing from this essay? If so, explain.

2. What is the intention of the essay? Is it trying to inform us of something? To prove or convince us of something? To share an insight?

3. What do you think the author is trying to say? What is the essay's theme?

TOPICS FOR WRITING

The following list is not exhaustive, but simply illustrative of the kinds of questions that might emerge from the more specific analytical questions (and combinations of questions) like those above. Your responses to these questions might provide worthwhile topics for writing.

1. How does the way people use language influence other people's opinion of them?

2. Amy Tan writes, "the language spoken in the family, especially in immigrant families which are more insular, plays a large role in shaping the language of the child." Do you think this is true? Explain.

3. In what way is it possible for someone to be articulate and not have a formal command of the language?

4. To what extent is there an advantage to using "different Englishes" for different occasions?

5. Do you think many people have a "mother tongue"? Do you? Explain.

6. Do you think everyone should learn to use standard English correctly? Why?

Chapter 4

Argumentation
Writing an Argumentative Essay

The goal in this chapter is to develop your writing and analysis into an argumentative essay. Building an argument is a natural extension of your earlier work. At their best, your essays should continue to express, in your strongest voice, what you believe is important. There is no need for you to become completely formal or use complicated terminology. But writing an argumentative essay will require:

- Reading and rereading a text carefully;

- Gathering textual evidence;

- Building observations into an interpretation or evaluation;

- Articulating a sound argument.

Convincing others requires clear thinking and writing. We may write with a stronger voice when we feel passionate about an issue, but it is our ability to *explain why with evidence,* not just our passion, that gives clarity and credibility to our arguments.

AN ARGUMENTATIVE ESSAY

The difference between a personal response essay and an argumentative essay is a matter of emphasis rather than kind. A personal essay describes our experience with literature—how we are individually affected by the work. The primary intention of a personal essay is to share our personal experience, not to argue for a position.

An **argumentative essay,** while motivated by our experience with literature, *shifts the emphasis toward the work itself and builds an argument for what the work or some aspect of it means (an interpretation), or its worth (an evaluation), or both.* In addition to analyzing or explicating the text of a work, or making comparisons, an argumentative essay may evaluate philosophically or ethically, or view a work or its elements within a variety of historical, cultural, biographical, or other contexts (see Appendix A on p. 1273 for an explanation of these approaches).

156

Beyond sharing your experience, you must be prepared to offer arguments in support of your views and state them clearly and persuasively. The following response may give you an insight into the difference between a personal and an argumentative response.

Suzanne's Response to *Antigonê*

The central focus throughout the play seems to be public policy vs. individual conscience. I found it very interesting that even though *Antigonê* was written so long ago, it dealt with civil disobedience, which remains a major social issue to this day. I liked the way Antigonê stood up for what she felt was right instead of letting Creon force her to live with something she felt was morally wrong. Creon's sexist attitude became his downfall. At first I thought Haimon would side with his father, so I was pretty surprised when they found him dead in Antigonê's cave. Everyone tried to reason with Creon, and he had plenty of chances to change his mind, so I thought he got what he deserved. I really liked this play, and I thought it was very well written.

Suzanne comments about how the play affected her, but she has taken her comments a step further. When she writes, "The central focus throughout the play seems to be public policy vs. individual conscience," she is stating what she believes the play is about—the subject (or issue) of the play. By going one step further and stating what she believes the play is saying about this subject, she may have a strong proposition, or thesis statement, for an argumentative essay.

When she writes, "I thought it was very well written," she is making an evaluative statement about the quality of writing in the play. Again, if she defines what she means by "well written," and indicates how *Antigonê* fulfills that description, she may have a good proposition, or thesis statement, for an argumentative essay.

In each case, her support for these propositions (not the propositions themselves) is the crucial factor in building either of these statements into a clear thesis statement and effective essay. In both cases, she would have to build an argument by gathering support from the text. To support her interpretation of what *Antigonê* is saying about "public policy vs. individual conscience," she would have to define what she means by these terms, cite evidence, and identify connecting patterns of this theme in the text of the play. To support her evaluation that "it was very well written," she would have to define her standards for "well written" and show—with reference to the text—how the play matches them.

INTERPRETATION AND EVALUATION

Like many other classifications in literature, *interpretation* and *evaluation* are not separate and distinct. In our reading, both often occur at the same time. When we write about our reading, however, we can make choices about which to emphasize.

Do we want to interpret what the work, or an aspect of it, means or its worth? While each is a different emphasis, it may be difficult to separate them, and many essays are a combination of both.

Interpretation: What Does It Mean?

The idea of coming up with an interpretation may seem a bit overwhelming, but in our everyday lives we hear and respond to this request regularly. "What do you make of that?" "What was that all about?" and "What's your read on that?" are among the many ways we might be asked for an interpretation. At the core of all these questions is a basic request for an explanation of "meaning." When we construct and articulate that meaning, we are giving our interpretation.

What goes into our explanation of meaning, of course, has a lot to do with who we are. Our interpretations are influenced by many personal factors, but *what makes an interpretation convincing or credible is our ability to explain why—a why not based on unsupported personal opinion but on support with evidence.*

An interpretation of literature may involve almost any aspect of a work, from the meaning of a single word, image, character, or place to a statement of its overall meaning. It may even involve more than one work, so don't feel that you must limit yourself to choosing from the possibilities discussed here. The first time you read a work you may feel one way, but writing down your reflections, rereading the text, and discussing it with others—doing a close reading—may lead to a different, better-informed understanding and interpretation.

Evaluation: How Well Does It Work?

You've been evaluating literature since you first started reading. You like it or don't like it, believe it's good or bad. How specific you are about "why" may depend on your experience as a reader. Those of us who read often have probably given some thought to why we like to read some things more than others. Experienced readers are likely to respond to "why" by pointing to particular qualities that are present or absent. Those of us who don't read very much might simply say, "I couldn't get into it" or "It was boring" and leave it at that.

We live in the world that literature reveals. Our standards, the principles by which we evaluate literature, tend to be developed through experience and over time. We make judgments about the nature of that world—people's biases, our surroundings, difficult circumstances, and the authenticity of people we meet. In this way we have already experienced and developed standards about point of view, setting, conflict, character, and other aspects of the literary experience.

The standards we have for evaluating literature are also affected by our expectations. Is the primary purpose of this literature to thrill or entertain? To make a social comment? To reveal something essential about the human condition? All of these? Some of these? It would be unfair to apply the same standards to a mystery thriller that we would to "Araby." On the other hand, applying our "thrill and entertain" standards to a story that intends to give insight into the human condition seems equally unfair.

CONNECTING THROUGH COLLABORATION

You may find it interesting to share your responses to the prompts that follow with other members of the class in pairs or small groups.

1. Choose a topic you know a lot about (music, dance, sports, cars, computers, etc.). How did you learn about it? By yourself? Did someone show you or teach you? Why do you think you know a lot about it?

2. What are your standards or criteria for evaluating the topic you chose in question 1? See if you can make a list and explain the importance of each standard.

3. Think back to a large purchase you made recently (clothes, car, computer, stereo, etc.). What were your standards or criteria for evaluation? Make a list and explain the importance of each of these standards.

4. Do you feel as if you know a lot about literature? How do you feel when someone asks you to evaluate a poem, story, play, or essay? Explain.

5. What are your standards for evaluating literature? See if you can make a list and explain the importance of each one.

6. If you had trouble coming up with a list or explanations, read the Options for an Argument below for help.

OPTIONS FOR AN ARGUMENT: PROCESS AND PRODUCT

The following checklist is an outline of five types of argumentative essays: analytical, comparative, thematic, philosophical or ethical evaluation, and contextual. Most of the terms in the checklist have been explained in Chapter 3 and should already be familiar to you. Brief explanations of each type with examples follow the checklist.

   CHECKLIST: OPTIONS FOR AN ARGUMENT

An Analytical Essay (explanations/examples on pp. 161–163)

Language and Form

❏ In what ways are diction, imagery, figurative language, or symbolism important to the work and your understanding of it? Do rhyme, rhythm, or verse form play a role in the work?

❏ To what extent does the language prompt your imagination, engage your emotions, and convey the work's meaning?

Narration: Point of View and Voice

❏ To what extent do point of view and voice affect what you know about the setting, conflict, or characters, and support the work's meaning?

(continued)

Setting

❏ How effective is the setting in presenting concrete details and enabling you to feel like you're present?

❏ To what extent does the setting complement conflict and character and support the work's meaning?

Conflict

❏ How important is the conflict? How believable are the internal and external conflicts? How challenging is the struggle?

❏ How unified is the conflict? How well do the minor conflicts complement each other and support the major conflict?

❏ In what ways do setting and characterization support the conflict?

Plot

❏ What is the plot structure? To what extent does the plot structure convey the conflict and the work's meaning?

Characterization

❏ How effectively are the characters developed? To what extent are you shown, not told, who they are? How believable are the characters? How complex? How motivated and consistent? Does their behavior make sense?

❏ To what extent do narration, setting, or conflict influence characterization?

❏ In what ways does characterization affect the work's meaning?

Theme

❏ What conclusion can you draw from what happens in the work?

❏ What comment about the human condition—what generalization about life—does this conclusion lead to? What is the central idea expressed by the work? What is its theme?

❏ Is this generalization always true? To what extent is it limited by time, place, and circumstances? Does this theme *reveal* or does it *preach*? Is it an insight about life or a lesson?

Explication

❏ Can you do, and is this work brief enough to do, a line-by-line interpretation of *how* and *what* the work or some portion of it means?

A Comparative Essay (explanation/examples on p. 163)

❏ Can you compare characters in the work with each other?

❏ Can you compare the work or characters or elements in it with those in another work?

A Thematic Essay (explanation/example on p. 164)

❑ Is there a theme or topic common to two or more works that you can write about?

A Philosophical or Ethical Evaluation (explanation/ examples on p. 164)

❑ What beliefs are expressed by the narrator or characters in the work and how does what they say or do exemplify these beliefs or actions?

❑ Can you write about whether you agree or disagree with these beliefs or actions?

A Contextual Essay (explanation/examples on p. 164)

❑ How much do you know about the contextual background of the work? What do you need to know? How will you find out more?

❑ How is the work influenced by historical, cultural, biographical, or other contextual factors? Can you write about the work in the light of these contextual factors?

An Analytical Essay

To analyze a work of literature is to look closely at how it works—to examine its parts or elements as they contribute to the work's meaning. Our brief discussion of these elements below is a carryover from a more comprehensive explanation of these terms in Chapter 3. *If you have unanswered questions about these elements, you may find it helpful to refer to that discussion beginning on page 59.*

Language and **form** are the vehicles that carry literature to us. The diction of the narrator or characters, concrete images, similes, metaphors, and symbols may all contribute in crucial ways to the meaning of a work. The sounds and structures of rhyme, rhythm, and verse may play a vital role in conveying a work's meaning. When language is used effectively, it prompts our imaginations and provides us with clear images, rhythm, and insight. Form complements content and effectively conveys meaning to us.

For example, you might write about the powerful, concrete imagery in Robert Hayden's "Those Winter Sundays" (p. 13) or Marge Piercy's "Barbie Doll" (p. 14). You could address the impact of Sammy's slang and concrete descriptions in John Updike's "A&P" (p. 456). You could write about the rhymes, rhythms, and verse form in Countee Cullen's "Incident" (p. 24) or Dudley Randall's "Ballad of Birmingham" (p. 17)—or in other pieces you've read.

Narration includes *point of view,* the perspective from which the narrator speaks to us, and *voice,* the personality behind the words. This narrative "lens" controls what we see and know about the setting, the characters, or the conflict in a work. When point of view and voice are used effectively, we see the characters, setting, and events from a perspective and with a flavor that help us experience the overall meaning of a work.

Here, you might write about point of view by addressing Mama's up close, first-person narration and its influence on your interpretation of Alice Walker's "Everyday Use" (p. 933). Or you might write about the impact of the distanced, third-person narration on Ernest Hemingway's "Hills Like White Elephants" (p. 688).

Setting includes location, time, atmosphere, and mood and has a direct and indirect impact on character and conflict. It supports and emphasizes the story's meaning. An effective setting will help us see and experience the concrete details of a work's environment. We "sense" the sights, sounds, and emotions of the atmosphere as if we were really there.

As an example, you might write about the dreary, dark atmosphere in James Joyce's "Araby" (p. 407) and how it contrasts with the warmth of the boy's feelings for Mangan's sister.

Conflict is the struggle of opposing external or internal forces. Most good literature contains both types of conflict, but places greater emphasis on the internal component. In many cases, it is our ability to identify with the *internal nature* (the anxiety, frustration, and disappointment) of the conflict that gives us a feel for it. We may never have faced this kind of external dilemma, but other experiences we have had may give us an idea of what the dilemma feels like inside. We won't care about the conflict if it's not important to the characters and to us. As we know from our own lives, a conflict doesn't need to be a life-and-death struggle to have an impact on us. Well-developed conflict, like a game between two evenly matched teams or players, keeps us involved until the outcome is decided.

To write about conflict, you might address the extraordinary external and internal conflicts in the brutal, racist humiliation experienced by the young man in Ralph Ellison's "Battle Royal" (p. 421), or write about the ordinary but painful internal conflict that results from the young girl's humiliation in Sandra Cisneros's "Eleven" (p. 26).

Plot is the structure of the story. Think about the plots of stories you've read. How and how well does the structure of each work convey the setting, the conflict, the characters, and ultimately the story's meaning?

Characterization is the creation and development of characters in a work. In our own lives, we react to people on the basis of how they look and what they say and do. In most good literature, we're able to observe characters thinking, speaking, and doing—and judge who they are for ourselves. Effective characters seem lifelike. Like real people, they are not simple, but have depth and complexity. We "see" and experience them through their words and actions and what others have to say about them.

To write about characterization, you might address how much you learn about the characters Antigonê and Ismenê solely from their conversation in the Prologue of Sophocles's *Antigonê* (p. 113), or write about the description, actions, and reactions of Nora as her character grows up in Ibsen' s *A Doll's House.* The narration, conversations, settings, and conflicts all provide opportunities for us to witness these characters thinking, saying, and doing.

Theme is the central idea expressed by a work. What conclusion can you draw from what happens in the work? Can you expand your conclusion into a generalization or idea that addresses the human condition? When literature preaches or teaches a lesson, it doesn't usually account for the complexities of the real world. An effective theme transcends the time and place of its setting. It has universal qualities that make it applicable to human nature in any time or place.

For example, the final draft of Suzanne McCloskey's sample essay at the end of this chapter (p. 181) argues for what she believes is the theme of *Antigonê*: "The arrogance of political power cannot defeat moral justice, for conscience and the will of the gods will always triumph."

Explication is a detailed analysis, a line-by-line interpretation of *how* and *what* a short work (or brief section of a larger work) means. Because they are longer pieces, works of fiction, drama, and essays usually don't lend themselves to such close reading. Most poems, however, are relatively brief, and by their nature packed with meaning. Poetry presents a good opportunity for a very close reading and an examination of sounds, words, images, and lines, and how they all work together to deliver the work's meaning. An explication is not just a summary or translation of the author's language into your own; it is a detailed explanation of *how* the work conveys meaning.

There is a good example on page 624, where Charles Chiang explicates the text of the "To be or not to be" soliloquy from Shakespeare's *Hamlet* by closely examining each line of the speech and building it into an interpretation of Hamlet's character and Shakespeare's intended effect on the audience.

A Comparative Essay

To what extent is the work or some aspect of it comparable to other works or aspects of them? In what way are characters or other aspects of this work comparable to each other? The objective of a comparison is not just to list similarities and differences but to reveal something important about whatever is being compared. Which details you choose as the basis of this comparison can make a difference. To give yourself a clear direction, and an overview of what you have, it may be helpful to make separate lists of similarities and differences before you start to write. Ask yourself what's worth comparing and what's not—and how this comparison might yield an effective essay. One useful method of lining up similarities and differences is the Venn diagram, described in Chapter 2 on pages 29–30.

William Winters exemplifies this approach in his essay on page 1101, where he compares Langston Hughes's "Theme for English B" with Countee Cullen's "Incident" and concludes that both poems reflect Hughes's views as expressed in "The Negro Artist and Racial Mountain." And on page 662, Barbara Pfister compares two different types of art—a van Gogh painting, *Starry Night,* and an Anne Sexton poem written in response to it.

A Thematic Essay

A variation of both the comparative essay and the contextual essay (below) is a thematic essay. A **thematic essay** compares several works that treat the same theme or topic (such as "family and friends," "innocence and experience," or "faith and doubt"), and may include works from different genres (poems, stories, plays). In addition to writing about the literature, it is essential that you explore the theme or topic and state why—and in what ways—the literature exemplifies the topic so well.

For example, you might address the theme of sibling relationships in Sophocles's *Antigonê* (p. 113), Louise Erdrich's "The Red Convertible" (p. 241), and Tennessee Williams's *The Glass Menagerie* (p. 966).

A Philosophical or Ethical Evaluation

Narrators and literary characters often express their beliefs in what they say or do, and it's natural for us to judge their words and actions through our own values. Based on your own clearly stated criteria, you might interpret the wisdom or virtue of their actions and beliefs or build an argument for or against them. Before you evaluate the beliefs or actions of the narrator or characters, be clear about what they are and be clear about your own standards for judging them. Only when you have clarified both will you be able to take a position and build an argument.

Here, you might write about the beliefs or actions (or potential actions) expressed by the man or the woman in Ernest Hemingway's "Hills Like White Elephants" (p. 688). Or you could address the beliefs expressed by the narrator/protagonist in Langston Hughes's "Salvation" (p. 32). The student essays of Michelle McAuliffe (p. 461) and Julie Fitzmaurice (p. 463) about John Updike's "A&P" illustrate this type of response. Both students comment on the protagonist's decision to quit his job, but they disagree about the wisdom of his decision. Michelle criticizes his decision and believes that he will regret it because of the consequences it will have for him and his family. Julie, however, sees his action as an inspiring statement that he will refuse to sell out and live his life like the store manager in the story.

A Contextual Essay

To write about literature in context is to consider the work within a framework of cultural, historical, biographical, or other factors, and articulate the influence that context has on the work or an element of the work. If you're not very knowledgeable about this background, it may be necessary to do additional reading and research before you write your essay.

For example, in her personal essay on page 874, Trisa Hayes critiques Ibsen's *A Doll's House* and Kate Chopin's "The Story of an Hour" within the historical and social framework of the nineteenth century. And Kevin Chamberlain's essay about James Joyce's "Eveline" on page 208 examines the cultural imperatives of late-nineteenth-century Ireland as they seem to determine the fate of the story's protagonist.

For a more comprehensive explanation of these approaches (including historical, gender, political-economic, psychoanalytic, archetypal, postcolonial, and biographical criticism), see Appendix A: Critical Approaches to Literature, on page 1273.

ARGUMENTATION: WRITING AN ESSAY

There are many different ways to plan and structure an argumentative essay. The suggestions that follow represent one approach (see three other approaches below). The purpose of this discussion is not to move you step-by-step through a rigid sequence. Constructing an argument is a continuous process of moving forward and returning and moving forward again. The strongest thesis, the most convincing evidence, the most effective structure may occur to you early or late. Let your ideas flow freely throughout the process. Some of your best ideas may come to you when you think you're almost finished.

Other Models: Classical, Toulmin, and Rogerian

The Classical or Aristotelian approach is derived from the rhetorical strategies of orators in ancient Greece and Rome. Classical argumentation requires (1) the identification of a core issue, (2) a clear thesis statement indicating the writer's/orator's position on the issue, (3) the presentation of evidence in support of that position, (4) recognition of opposing views—in order to refute them, (5) if appropriate, recommendations for improvement, and finally (6) concluding/summarizing thoughts.

A modern rendering of this approach is based on the work of English philosopher and scientist Stephen Toulmin, who categorizes the stages of this process with the terms "issue," "claim," "reason," and "assumption" or "warrant." For those already familiar with these terms—and for those who might find it helpful to learn them—they are indicated on the pages that follow in parentheses next to or below their equivalents.

Rogerian rhetoric is based on the work of psychologist Carl Rogers, and its objective and strategy differ from the Classical and Toulmin approaches in one fundamental way: Rogerian rhetoric seeks common ground with the reader in order to "find truth" rather than win an argument. A core assumption is that traditional approaches—instead of encouraging a cooperative spirit of seeking truth—foster an atmosphere of competitive antagonism. Facing an onslaught of one-sided evidence, readers believe their differing opinions are not respected, and however convincing the logic of the writer's argument, remain steadfast in their views. A Rogerian approach requires (1) an open-minded understanding of opposing views and the ability to articulate them, (2) finding common ground with the reader while addressing points of difference, (3) evidence expressed in terms the reader will respect, and (4) a conclusion that is respectful of opposing views.

The Shape of an Argument

The subject

(The issue)

The proposition about the subject (thesis)

(The claim)

The evidence that supports the proposition about the subject

(The reasons)

The explanation that connects the evidence to the proposition about the subject

(The warrant or assumption)

 CHECKLIST: WRITING AN ARGUMENTATIVE ESSAY
(For detailed explanations, see pp. 168–175)

Planning Your Argument

Determine Its Feasibility

❏ Can you write an essay about this?

❏ Do you have enough to say, and can you find enough evidence to support your case?

Consider Your Motivation

❏ Will this topic sustain your interest long enough for you to do a good job?

Clarify Your Thesis (The Claim)

❏ Do you have a clear understanding of the thesis you want to argue? Can you articulate it in a thesis statement?

Know Your Readers

❏ What assumptions can you make about your readers? Are they likely to agree or disagree with your thesis?

Supporting Your Argument

Arrange Your Support Effectively

❏ Is the support for your thesis arranged in the most effective way? Is it more effective to develop your argument by stating your thesis first and then supporting it with evidence, or by allowing the evidence to build into your thesis?

Support Your Thesis with Facts from the Text (The Reasons)

❑ Is your support based on facts or opinions? Have you supported your opinions with facts and quotes from the text?

Account for All the Evidence (The Reasons)

❑ Have you accounted for *all* the evidence in the text? Have you accounted for evidence that may not support your thesis?

Explain the Connections (The Warrant or Assumption)

❑ Have you explained *how* the evidence you've chosen supports your thesis?

Opening, Closing, and Revising

Write or Rewrite Your Introduction After Your First Draft

❑ Is your introduction clear, informative, and interesting?

❑ If appropriate, does it map out the journey for the reader?

Close Your Argument Reasonably

❑ Have you explained the connections between the thesis and your support?

❑ Have you claimed anything for which you haven't delivered evidence?

Revise with a Fresh View

❑ Have you reread and reviewed your essay?

❑ How well is your draft organized? Does the sequence make sense? Are there gaps that need to be filled? Is there enough support?

❑ Have you explained the connections between your support and your thesis?

❑ Have you expressed those connections as clearly as possible?

❑ Have you maintained a consistent "voice" throughout the essay?

Review Your Intentions and Organization

❑ Is the central thesis of the essay clearly stated? Does the title account for your thesis?

❑ Is the essay fully developed? Have you accounted for all aspects of your thesis statement? Are there enough details to support or clarify your thesis? Have you *shown* what you've told?

❑ Are there enough quotes from the work to support your thesis? Do all the paragraphs relate to your thesis? Is the essay fully developed? Is the organization of the paragraphs within the essay clear? Are the paragraphs fully developed? Do each of the sentences within the paragraphs relate to the paragraph's central idea?

❑ Is the language clear? Are there redundancies, digressions, or meaningless phrases that could be cut?

(continued)

Check for Logical Fallacies (see explanations on pp. 174–175)

❑ Are any of your arguments based on non sequiturs—or directed against the person ("ad hominem"), not the issue?

❑ Are there any "unsupported or hasty generalizations"—or ("red herrings") premature shifts away from arguments before they are concluded?

❑ Have you "begged the question" by simply rewording the question as your answer? Have you inappropriately attributed a "cause and effect" relationship where there is no evidence that one thing caused another?

❑ Have you assumed in any of your arguments that there are only two possibilities to resolving an issue when there may be more?

❑ Are any of your comparisons inappropriate, or are any of your analogies based on distorted or exaggerated comparisons?

❑ Have you relied on evidence from sources that are not clearly identified or are not reliable?

❑ Are any of your conclusions based on ignorance or what is *not* known?

Proofread Carefully

❑ Are all your sentences complete sentences? Are all your sentences punctuated appropriately?

❑ Have you checked for easily confused words (*then/than, your/you're, its/it's,* etc.)? Are you sure of the meaning of all the words you've used?

❑ Are the titles of works underlined or in quotations, as appropriate?

❑ Are there particular errors that you have a tendency to make? Have you looked for those in this essay?

❑ Is the essay written in the format required by your instructor? Have you documented your references to the text and included a list of works cited?

Planning Your Argument

Determine the Argument's Feasibility (The Issue)   Can you write an essay about this? No matter how compelling your proposition, you cannot write an essay about it unless you have enough to say and can find enough evidence to support your argument. If the point you want to make is obvious, abstract, or very general, it may be impossible to come up with a solid argument and develop it into a convincing essay in a reasonable amount of time.

Consider Your Own Motivation   How much do you care about the subject? Will it sustain your enthusiasm long enough for you to complete the essay? Can you identify strongly with the situation in the work? Do you approve or disapprove of a character's action? Do you believe the work has helped you to understand yourself or inspired you to act in a particular way? Have you learned something about your own life through your experience of the work? Finally, do you feel strongly about your ability to convince an audience of your argument?

You will work with more enthusiasm and write with a stronger voice when you care about the subject.

Clarify Your Proposition: Write a Thesis Statement (The Claim)   Do you have a clear understanding of the proposition you are trying to prove? If you don't, you won't be able to express it in a form your readers will understand. Try to put your proposition into the form of a complete sentence that connects it to the subject. This thesis statement will sit at the core of your argument. Everything in your argument must relate back to and support this thesis statement. If you've put it in a form that you and your readers clearly understand, you will know if the evidence you've gathered adequately supports it.

If your thesis is an interpretation, define what you mean by the terms of the proposition or thesis. In her journal entry at the beginning of this chapter, Suzanne has identified the subject of *Antigonê* as "public policy vs. individual conscience." Her proposition about this subject, her thesis statement (what she believes the play is saying about public policy and individual conscience), will not be clear unless she spells out what she means by those terms. What "public policy" and "individual conscience" mean to her may be different from what they mean to other readers.

If your thesis is an evaluation, define your standards. If (like Suzanne) you believe *Antigonê* is well written, what are your standards for a well written play? If you believe the characters are well developed, what are your standards for effective characterization?

Be careful to distinguish between the *subject* or issue of your essay and your *proposition* or claim about the subject—your thesis statement. Suzanne's subject is "public policy vs. individual conscience." What she believes the play, *Antigonê,* is saying about this subject—her thesis statement—(as reflected in the final draft of her essay) is "The arrogance of political power cannot defeat moral justice, for conscience and the will of the gods will always triumph."

As you consider the evidence you have and gather new evidence, you may discover that your thesis statement must be adjusted to accommodate this new information. Be flexible. Match the statement to the evidence, and the evidence to the statement. Until you submit your final draft, it's never too late to make adjustments to strengthen your thesis.

Know Your Readers   What can you assume about your readers? If you're writing this essay to be read by those in your class, you may already have some idea what your classmates and instructor think about your opinion. If so, does your thesis statement agree with the majority of responses you've heard? If not, it's important to "speak to" these contrary views when you present your own view.

No matter how convincing your evidence may be, if you don't address their contrary position, your readers will always wonder, "Yes, but what about...?" This doesn't mean you must change their minds, but it does mean that you must account for all the evidence, especially the evidence that may seem (to some) to go against your thesis statement. If you cannot account for it, it may be time to reexamine your original proposition.

Remember, a number of interpretations may be acceptable. The strength of your thesis is in its support, not the thesis itself. So don't offend your readers by being inflexible and suggesting that anyone holding a different view is ignorant. Feeling strongly about what you want to prove gives you a stronger voice, but insulting or overpowering your readers is not likely to be persuasive.

Supporting Your Argument: Induction and Substantiation

Have you ever watched a toddler discover the world? The child crawls through the grass, stops to examine it blade by blade, picks it up, feels it, shakes it, tastes it. The child explores the surroundings and tests them piece by piece, and after several tries, probably comes to a conclusion: Grass is good for crawling but not so great for eating. When someone offers you a type of food you've never eaten before, how do you respond? How do you discover if you like it or not? Well, you probably ask for a taste. If you like the taste, you might ask for more. If you don't like the taste, you may or may not try more. This kind of examining, testing, making tentative observations, retesting, and concluding is a fairly common process in our lives. It is called **inductive reasoning.**

When you think or write inductively, you move from specific observations to conclusions. If you try a new food and like it, the next time it's offered you can respond with more certainty. You've tested it and can come to a tentative conclusion. Each subsequent tasting gives you more information and solidifies your conclusion: I like sushi; it tastes good.

Once you arrive at your conclusion, you are ready to make a generalization: Sushi tastes good or not. The process of supporting this generalization is called **substantiation.** When we substantiate, we support our conclusion with specific observations. This brings the process full circle. We discover how much we like or don't like sushi through specific tastings. We explain why sushi is good with support from those tastings: "This sushi sits lightly on my tongue; it's soft and moist with a full seafood flavor and pleasant smell." We arrive at our conclusion inductively; we support, defend, and explain it through substantiation.

In many ways, writing about literature follows a similar induction and substantiation pattern. As we initially read, respond, discuss, and write about our experience with literature, we build on our specific observations of the text and arrive at our conclusions inductively. With those conclusions in hand, we substantiate them with reference to our specific observations of the text.

Arrange Your Support Effectively   You substantiate your argument when you place the thesis statement or proposition at the beginning of the essay and lay out evidence in the rest of the essay to support it. You begin with a generalization and support it with specific examples as evidence. You immediately make it clear to your readers what you intend to prove. Your thesis remains in their minds as they encounter each piece of subsequent evidence. In fact, if what you propose at the outset is interesting enough, your thesis statement may act as a "hook" for your readers and pull them into the essay.

Substantiation

$(a = b + b + b + b + b)$

(Your thesis equals the sum of the evidence.)

This approach may not work well if you are trying to convince skeptical readers, that is, readers who have already made up their minds and hold a contrary view. Encountering a proposition they disagree with at the beginning may interfere with their response through the rest of the essay. Once they know what you want to prove, they may not give you an open-minded reading. They may be predisposed to disagree with you no matter how compelling your evidence.

Inductive argumentation moves from specific examples to a generalization or conclusion. It mimics the process you probably went through when you came up with your proposition to begin with. As the specifics of the work built up in your mind, they moved you toward a conclusion and a proposition. A more effective strategy to convince a skeptical reader may be to withhold your proposition until the end. By first providing support before readers know what your position is, they may withhold judgment and be more likely to accept your thesis when it comes as the natural conclusion of strong evidence.

Induction

$(b + b + b + b + b + b = a)$

(The sum of the evidence equals your thesis.)

And, of course, there are variations of these strategies. For example, if you're stating your thesis up front, you may want to provide background information to "educate" the reader before you present your thesis, and then follow with supporting evidence. If you are using an inductive approach, you may want to build your support to a natural conclusion, and then discuss why this conclusion makes sense. In any case, you should consider your audience and your intentions before you decide which strategy will work best.

Support Your Thesis with Facts from the Text (The Reasons)   All of us have probably been criticized at some time for not being objective or for allowing our personal feelings to influence our judgment. It's not possible, of course, to be entirely objective—to separate the facts from who we are and how we see them. In the course of our daily lives, we're not usually required to justify our feelings or our opinions. But writing an effective argumentative essay requires a rationale for our judgments—reasons derived not only from our feelings and values but also from ingredients in the work of literature that prompt those judgments. Although there is no guarantee that everyone will agree with our conclusions, we can make sure that our evidence is recognized and respected as valid.

Facts are verifiable. You can cite them in the text. They should be the core of the evidence that supports your argument. For example, it is a fact that in John Updike's poem "Ex-Basketball Player" (p. 961), Flick Webb was a high school basketball star. You can verify this fact by citing the text of the poem:

Once Flick played for the high-school team, the Wizards.
He was good: in fact, the best. In '46
He bucketed three hundred ninety points,
A county record still. The ball loved Flick.

And you can verify the fact of his current employment by citing the text:

He never learned a trade, he just sells gas,
Checks oil, and changes flats.

But if (based on these few facts) you say that Flick is an "unhappy loser," you are expressing an opinion, not a fact. You may hold this opinion for any number of personal reasons, prompted by a few facts in the poem. But if you want to build an argument to support this opinion, you will need to connect most or all the facts in the poem in a convincing way, and logically demonstrate how they lead to this conclusion. A good argumentative essay requires reasons for your judgments, factual support derived not only from your feelings and values but also from ingredients in the text that logically combine to prompt them. There is no guarantee, of course, that everyone will agree with your conclusions, but you should make sure that your evidence is recognized and respected as valid.

Account for All the Evidence (The Reasons)   A strong thesis is constructed from all the evidence, not just the parts that agree with your conclusion. A discerning reader sees contrary evidence whether you point it out or not. For example, it is a fact that the speaker in Robert Frost's "The Road Not Taken" (p. 82) has taken the road less traveled, as suggested in the first two lines of this stanza:

Then took the other, as just as fair,
And having perhaps the better claim,
Because it was grassy and wanted wear:
Though as for that the passing there
Had worn them really about the same.

To suggest that one road was very different from the other, though, is to ignore the last two lines. It is a fact that he says his choice will make a difference in his life:

I shall be telling this with a sigh
Somewhere ages and ages hence:
Two roads diverged in a wood, and I—
I took the one less traveled by,
And that has made all the difference.

But suggesting that the speaker knows that this choice was the best one and has made him happiest is to ignore other lines in this last stanza that seem to indicate uncertainty. Do we know that "all the difference" means a positive difference? How would you support that from the text?

So too, in Alice Walker's "Everyday Use" (p. 933), if you ignore the fact that the story is told by Dee's mother, you fail to account for the subjectivity of her descriptions. By addressing her subjectivity, however, and demonstrating that she is a reliable narrator by matching her descriptions to Dee's actions in the story, you may establish credibility for her narration and what she tells you.

None of this is to say that the personal meaning you derive from the work is not the most important meaning for you—a meaning that is often based on many factors beyond the text. But for the purposes of an argument, you must rely heavily on the text and its factual support to make a convincing case for your reader.

Explain the Connections (The Warrant or Assumption)   Sometimes what seems self-evident to us is not so evident to our readers. In addition to highlighting the facts to support your argument, explain the connections. Explicitly show your readers *how* the chosen evidence supports your conclusion. For example, if your proposition about the play *Antigonê* is that "Ismenê is not as courageous as Antigonê," and your evidence is that Ismenê says, "...I have no strength / To break laws that were made for the public good," it is still necessary to explain the connection between the evidence (what Ismenê has said) and the proposition (that Ismenê is not as courageous as Antigonê).

Consider the explanation: "While Antigonê is willing to accept the consequences of her action and suffer death if necessary, Ismenê indicates that she is afraid of Creon's directive and will not join her sister in the burial." This explanation shows the connection between the proposition and the quoted evidence and makes your logic clear to the reader.

Opening, Closing, and Revising Your Argument

Write Your Introduction After You Know Your Argument   It may seem strange to wait until you're almost finished with the first draft of an essay before writing its introduction. However, introducing an essay is a bit like introducing a person. In both cases, you can make a more effective introduction when you know who or what you are introducing. This does not mean you have to mention everything you know. It means that you know your subject well enough to say the essential things.

Make your introduction interesting. You want the reader to continue reading beyond the first paragraph. Remember what seemed so interesting to you about the work, and try to pass that interest on to the reader. Make sure that what you say flows smoothly and maintains the same voice used in the rest of the essay. If you're developing your argument through substantiation, this is the place to state your thesis as clearly as possible.

Close Your Argument Reasonably   Although there is no need to summarize your essay in the conclusion, it may be helpful to remind the reader of the logic of your argument and explain the basic connections between your support and your thesis. Avoid being too ambitious. Only make claims or take credit for connections you've actually established.

If you've developed your argument inductively, this is the place where you want to state your thesis. Remember not to overstate your case. If you've proved your point, the evidence will carry it.

Revise with a Fresh View   If you really want to "re-vision" your essay, to see it again from a fresh perspective, it's best to let some time pass. Try to place yourself in the position of the reader who is reading your essay for the first time.

As with any other essay, it can be very useful to do an after-draft outline. Go back and identify the point of each paragraph. List those points. This should give you a pretty good overview of your essay. How well is your draft organized? Does the sequence make sense? Are there gaps that need to be filled? Is there enough support?

Within the body of the essay, have you explained the connections between your support and your thesis? Have you expressed those connections as clearly as possible? Have you maintained a consistent voice throughout the essay?

Check Against Your Intentions and Organization   State your thesis clearly. Support and clarify your thesis with enough details and examples from the work of literature. *Show* what you have stated. Give the essay a title based on your thesis. If you're having trouble thinking of a title, it may be an indication that the thesis itself is not clear. Make sure that your essay is fully developed. Account for all aspects of your thesis statement.

All your paragraphs must relate to that central thesis, and the organization of those paragraphs within the essay should be clear. Each paragraph should be fully developed, too; each of the sentences within your paragraphs should relate to the central idea of each paragraph. All your statements should add something to the essay. Are there redundancies, digressions, or meaningless phrases that could be cut?

Beware of Logical Fallacies   No argument is foolproof, so it's essential that your arguments and evidence are logical. But sometimes what seems like logic to us is a misjudgment. The following logical fallacies can sometimes seem "reasonable" until we take a closer look.

- **Non Sequitur** or "It does not follow"—The reason given for the event, the action, the behavior, etc., is not related logically to what we say it causes. **Ad Hominem** (Against the person) is a non sequitur based on an attack on the person rather than the person's view or position on an issue. As you've probably noticed, this type of logical fallacy is very popular among competing politicians.

- **An Unsupported Generalization** is a conclusion without evidence to support it. Presenting convincing evidence for any generalizations or conclusions we state is crucial to effective argumentation and to our credibility as writers. **A Hasty Generalization** is a generalization or conclusion based on insufficient evidence.

- **A Red Herring** is an attempt to avoid dealing with an argument by shifting the discussion in a new, irrelevant direction.

- **Begging the Question** is coming to a conclusion or an answer that is nothing more than a rewording of the question.

- **Post Hoc Ergo Propter Hoc** (After the fact, therefore because of the fact) is incorrectly attributing a cause and effect relationship to proximity in time or order of occurrence.

- **A False Dichotomy** (Limited to one or the other) is the assumption that there are only two possibilities to resolving an issue—when, in fact, most issues are more complex than that, and there may be many positions in between.

- **Inappropriate Comparison** (You may have heard this described as "comparing apples and oranges") is comparing two things that are not of the same "type" and lack a clear basis for comparison.

- **False or Faulty Analogy** is an analogy that distorts or exaggerates the nature of what is being compared.

- **Vague or Questionable Authority** is reliance on evidence from sources that are not clearly identified or are not reliable. Be cautious especially when citing secondary sources from the Internet. Your evidence is only as good as the sources that support it.

- **An Appeal to Ignorance** is coming to a conclusion on the basis of what is *not* known about something rather than what is known.

Proofread Carefully   Proofreading is a crucial final step in the process of producing an essay. In addition to making any changes that did not occur to you earlier and fine-tuning your writing, check your essay for correct grammar, spelling, punctuation, and typos. Make sure all your sentences are complete and punctuated appropriately. Check to see that all of your words are spelled correctly. Check for easily confused words (*then/than, your/you're, its/it's,* etc.), which computerized spell checkers do not pick up. Check on the meaning of any words you are not sure of. Make sure the titles of works are underlined or in quotations, as appropriate.

If there are types of errors you personally have a tendency to make, look carefully for them. Finally, make sure you've followed the *MLA Handbook for Writers of Research Papers* or another documentation format recommended by your instructor. Have you cited and documented your sources correctly? Do you have a "Work(s) Cited" section at the end of your essay?

THE DEVELOPMENT OF AN ARGUMENTATIVE ESSAY

Step 1: Using Your First Response

The same processes that are so useful in generating ideas for a personal essay are just as valuable for giving you ideas and narrowing your topic for an argument. Reading literature encourages a variety of responses—and perhaps raises more questions than answers. It is a good idea to generate and explore as many of your questions and ideas as possible before you decide on a topic. Below is a quick review of strategies to get started. For a detailed explanation of these techniques, with examples, see Chapter 2, pages 29–42.

- *Using directed freewriting* can generate ideas. The best time to do this exercise is immediately after you finish reading, while your thoughts and impressions are still fresh. The intention of this exercise is to release what you know without blocking it with pauses for reflection, punctuation, or editing.

- *Asking questions about a general topic* is likely to provide you with new information. Responding with detailed answers to these questions may provide you with ideas for a narrowed thesis and specific support for that thesis.

- By *choosing a few key words or phrases* that apply to your topic and then *listing* as many related details under each as you can, you should be able to generate many concrete details and much specific support for your ideas.

- *Clustering your ideas* or drawing a semantic map may help you discover and understand relationships, and generate and extend ideas better by seeing them spatially rather than linearly.

Earlier in this chapter, we looked at Suzanne's journal response to Sophocles's *Antigonê* in Chapter 3. Let's follow up as she develops this response into an argumentative essay.

Suzanne's Proposition (The Issue? Or the Claim?) Suzanne's proposition in her first draft was that the focus of *Antigonê* is public policy versus individual conscience. In addition, she wanted to address Creon's sexism as a feature of that policy.

Feasibility During her own reading and in class discussion, she saw much support for this thesis. Several statements in the play immediately came to mind that would support this idea, and she felt confident that this evidence would provide her with a strong argument.

Motivation Suzanne had strong motivation to write about this issue. She liked the play and felt strongly about its issues, especially individual conscience and women's equality.

Clarity of the Thesis Statement (The Claim) Her thesis statement, "The theme of *Antigonê* is public policy versus individual conscience," seems clear. But, as we will see when she revises, this statement identifies the subject of the play, not what the play is saying about this subject.

Audience Based on general class discussion and the response of her small group, she was confident about her position. Occasionally, someone would sympathize with Creon's position, but in general her classmates were supportive of her views and believed that there was ample evidence to support her position.

Step 2: Composing a Draft

Arranging Support (The Reasons)   In class discussion, Suzanne had already received a generally sympathetic response. She was not trying to convince a hostile audience, so she believed that it would be most effective to state her position at the beginning and substantiate that position with support from the text.

Her plan was to introduce her thesis as clearly as possible, state and connect her beliefs about Creon and Antigonê with support from the play, and conclude by reaffirming her belief and how the text supported it.

Deriving Factual Support from the Text (The Reasons)   She derived her support from two basic sources: first, her description and interpretation of the actions of Creon and Antigonê; second, what Creon, Antigonê, and Haimon said that confirmed her judgments and her thesis statement.

Accounting for All the Evidence   In addition to the evidence that favored her views, she considered views that were more sympathetic to Creon's position. The argument most sympathetic to Creon was that Antigonê put him in an impossible position through her aggressive stance, that had she approached him in a more reasonable way, he might have listened. She intended to use Haimon's experience with Creon to counter this argument.

Explaining the Connections (The Warrant or Assumption)   Suzanne knew that she would have to explain the connections between her support (the quotes from the text and the actions of the characters) and her proposition, which was that Creon and Antigonê were representative of "public policy" and "individual conscience," respectively.

Suzanne's Draft

Based on her journal entry and notes, Suzanne wrote the following draft:

Might Against Right

Antigonê is a tragic story that deals with the struggles between public policy and individual conscience, and on a lesser level, a woman's conflict with a man. Sophocles broaches the issues of might against right and civil disobedience in this shockingly tragic play.

In this play, Creon stands for public policy and Antigonê symbolizes the individual conscience. The major conflict lies between these two headstrong figures. Creon has just been made king of Thebes because his nephews have killed each other in battle. Creon decreed that Eteocles, who died defending Thebes in battle, should be buried with full military honors. Polyneices was to be left to rot in the fields because Creon believed him to be a traitor who didn't deserve to be honored. Creon's law was clear: whoever disobeyed him and buried Polyneices was sentenced to be stoned to death in the public square. Creon is more concerned with forcing everyone to obey his decree than whether or not he has done the right thing. He seems to be an extremely headstrong and stubborn man who has a very hard time admitting that he's wrong. It is these very qualities that cause the chain reaction that dictates the downfall of Creon and all whom he loves.

Antigonê is the sister of Eteocles and Polyneices, and she decides that she cannot abide by Creon's law. Polyneices was her brother just as much as Eteocles was, and to leave him to rot in the fields was wrong according to her conscience and God's law. She felt that Creon had no right to try to overstep God's boundaries; kings shouldn't presume to dictate who is privileged enough for a burial. Burial is supposed to be a universal right given to all of mankind. When Creon is informed that it is Antigonê who has defied his law, he explodes. Not only has Antigonê blatantly disregarded his wishes, she is both smug and righteous about the whole situation: "It was not God's proclamation. That final Justice that rules the world below makes no such laws." This shows the strength of Antigonê's convictions. She knows that she will die for what she has done, but she stands firmly behind her decision and just wants it to be over with.

Creon is doubly enraged; Antigonê has deliberately defied him and she is a woman. Women are supposed to be timid, weak, and docile creatures who need to be guided by men and their laws. Creon might have considered revoking his decree if it had been anyone else, but a woman has defied him and he can't let a mere woman get the better of him. This has now become, to a smaller degree, a battle of the sexes: "This girl is guilty of a double insolence, breaking the given laws and boasting of it. Who is the man here, she or I, if this crime goes unpunished?" This quote illustrates the lengths to which Creon would go to triumph over Antigonê. Antigonê defied a man's law and now a man is going to teach her a lesson. Creon's sense was being affected by his discriminatory and condescending attitude toward women. His irrationality is further proven when his son, Haimon, tries to reason with him. Haimon points out the validity of Antigonê's actions and the fear that prevents any of the other citizens to voice their support of her: "I have heard them muttering and whispering in the dark about this girl. They say no woman has ever, so unreasonably, died so shameful a death for a generous act: 'She covered her brother's body. Is this indecent? She kept him from dogs and vultures. Is this a crime? Death?—She should have all the honor that we can give her!'"

The citizens of Thebes are starting to discreetly voice their disapproval of Creon's condemnation of Antigonê's act of mercy. Creon interprets Haimon's speech as a sign that Haimon has chosen Antigonê over him and forces Haimon to denounce his own father. This further alienates Creon from his subjects, and the play's atmosphere begins to change. Creon is not in complete control anymore. A woman has managed to disrupt his reign and turn his most precious son against him. Creon is going to force Antigonê to regret her actions against him by sentencing her to a slow, painful death in a sealed cave with no food or water. A quick death would be too easy. Creon wants her to suffer. From this point on, the atmosphere of the play continues to spiral into a whirlwind of chaos and tragedy.

Teiresias, the old prophet who's never wrong, comes to warn Creon that the wrath of the gods will be upon him if he doesn't right his wrongs: "The time is not far off when you shall pay back corpse for corpse, flesh of your own flesh." But by then it's too late. By the time he sees the error of his ways, Creon's course of destruction is already set and the damage has already been done.

Creon's foolish superiority complex led to the downfall of everyone he cared about and his credibility as a king. He let his attitude toward women and his thirst for absolute power cloud his judgment and drove his family into the arms of death and tragedy. Antigonê's fight against the unjust decree of the king could be characterized as the beginnings of civil disobedience. She is driven by her firm belief in God's laws and her own views on right and wrong. Antigonê believed that a law is not right just because it's a law and that God's law outweighs public policy every time.

Step 3: Revising the Essay

Introduction   While Suzanne's introductory paragraph was adequate to keep her focused throughout the draft, it would have to be revised to integrate Creon's sexism. In addition, she has not defined what she means by "public policy" and "individual conscience." This would be an appropriate place to define her terms.

Finally, she realizes that her "public policy versus individual conscience" statement is only identifying the subject (the issue) of the play, not *what the play is saying* about that subject or issue. She must come up with a thesis statement that more clearly represents the theme of the play. She changes her thesis statement (her claim) to

"Sophocles' message is clear: the arrogance of political power cannot defeat

moral justice, for conscience and the will of the gods will always triumph."

Closing   Her closing could be more inclusive of her whole argument. Her statement about the "beginnings of civil disobedience" is a nice touch and will leave readers with a sense of its relevance to today.

After-Draft Outline   When Suzanne examined the structure of her draft by creating an after-draft outline from her paragraphs, it took the following form:

Paragraph #1—Introduction (a brief statement of the thesis and comment about Creon's sexism). A statement about the subject (public policy vs. individual conscience) but not what the play was saying about that subject (a thesis statement)

Paragraph #2—Creon's stance as public policy and summary of the major conflict

Paragraph #3—Antigonê's position

Paragraph #4—Creon's sexism

Paragraph #5—Haimon's reasonable approach, Creon's response, and Teiresias's prophecy

Paragraph #6—Conclusion (a brief statement summarizing the conflict, Antigonê's motivation, and its significance then and now)

For the most part, her draft contained the information and support she needed, but the thesis statement could be clearer, some of the paragraphs more tightly structured, and the essay's organization more coherent. By combining her first two paragraphs into a more substantial introduction concluding in a thesis statement, and combining and reorganizing subsequent paragraphs, she came up with the following revised outline:

Paragraph #1—Introduction (explains the basic conflict, defines the terms, and states the thesis). That thesis now reads: "Sophocles's message is clear: the arrogance of political power cannot defeat moral justice, for conscience and the will of the gods will always triumph."

Paragraph #2—Fleshes out the conflict

Paragraph #3—Antigonê's position

Paragraph #4—Creon's response and its motivation (to include sexism)

Paragraph #5—Haimon's reasoned approach

Paragraph #6—Creon's response

Paragraph #7—The warning and prophecy of Teiresias

Paragraph #8—Conclusion (a more inclusive summary and reminder of the play's thesis)

Checking Against Intentions   Suzanne's intentions were to explain and support her now clearer thesis that the play's theme is "The arrogance of political power cannot defeat moral justice, for conscience and the will of the gods will always triumph," and that part of Creon's motivation for condemning Antigonê was sexist. She believed that this reorganization and integration would accomplish her goal.

Proofreading   In addition to correcting a few minor problems, she would have to cite the line sources of her textual support, format it correctly, and add a "Work Cited" section at the end of her essay.

Step 4: Suzanne's Revised Essay

Suzanne McCloskey

Dr. Madden

English 102

November 3, 20XX

Might Against Right

Sophocles' tragic play *Antigonê* is a powerful example of the struggle between public policy and individual conscience. Throughout history, rulers have imposed and enforced laws for what they claimed was the best interest of the public. At times, courageous individuals have refused to obey these laws, despite the consequences, because these policies interfered with their own consciences. Creon stands for public policy in this play, and Antigonê represents individual conscience, loyalty to the gods, and civil disobedience. Sophocles' message is clear: the arrogance of political power cannot defeat moral justice, for conscience and the will of the gods will always triumph.

The major conflict in this play is between Creon and Antigonê. Creon has just been made king of Thebes because his nephews have killed each other in battle. He decrees that Eteocles, who died defending Thebes, will be buried with full military honors. The body of Polyneices, however, will be left to rot in the fields. Creon believes that Polyneices was a traitor who doesn't deserve to be honored. His law is clear: whoever disobeys him and buries Polyneices is to be stoned to death in the public square. Creon, however, seems more concerned with forcing everyone to obey his decree than whether or not he has done the right thing. He is an extremely headstrong and stubborn man who has a very hard time admitting that he is wrong. It is these personal weaknesses that begin the chain reaction that will destroy Creon and those he loves.

Antigonê is the sister of Eteocles and Polyneices, and she decides that she cannot abide by Creon's law. Polyneices was her brother, just as much as Eteocles was. According to her conscience and the laws of the gods, leaving his body to rot in the fields is wrong. She feels that Creon has no right to overstep the boundaries of what the gods decreed. Kings shouldn't presume to dictate who is privileged enough for a burial. Burial is a universal right given to all humanity. When Creon is informed that Antigonê has defied his law, he explodes in anger. Not only has Antigonê blatantly disregarded his wishes, she is smug and righteous about it. She says, "It was not God's proclamation. That final Justice / That rules the world below makes no such laws" (2. 66–67). Her statement shows the strength of her convictions. She knows that she will die for what she has done, but she stands firmly behind her decision.

Creon is doubly enraged; Antigonê has deliberately defied him, and she is a woman. In Creon's view, women are timid, weak, and docile creatures who need to be guided by men and their laws. He can't let a mere woman get the better of him. He says, "This girl is guilty of a double insolence, / Breaking the given laws and boasting of it. / Who is the man here, / She or I, if this crime goes unpunished?" (2. 92–95). Creon's statement illustrates the lengths to which he will go to triumph over Antigonê. Antigonê has defied a man's law, and now a man is going to teach her a lesson. His judgment is clearly affected by his discriminatory and condescending attitude toward women.

Creon's blind stubbornness is demonstrated further when his son, Haimon, tries to reason with him. Haimon points out the validity of Antigonê's actions and the fear that prevents any of the other citizens from voicing their support of her:

> HAIMON.   I have heard them
> Muttering and whispering in the dark about this girl.
> They say no woman has ever, so unreasonably,
> Died so shameful a death for a generous act:
> "She covered her brother's body. Is this indecent?
> She kept him from dogs and vultures. Is this a crime?
> Death?—She should have all the honor that we can give her!" (3. 64–70)

The citizens of Thebes are discreetly voicing their disapproval of Creon's condemnation of Antigonê's act of mercy. Creon interprets Haimon's speech as a sign that Haimon has chosen Antigonê over him and forces his own son to denounce him. This further alienates Creon from his subjects, and the play's atmosphere begins to change. Creon is not in complete control anymore. A woman has managed to disrupt his reign and even turn his son against him. He tries to make Antigonê regret her actions by sentencing her to a slow, painful death in a sealed cave with no food or water. A quick death would be too easy. Creon wants her to suffer.

From this point on, the atmosphere of the play continues to spiral into a whirlwind of chaos and tragedy. Teiresias, the old prophet who is never wrong, comes to warn Creon that the wrath of the gods will be upon him if he doesn't right his wrongs: "The time is not far off when you shall pay back / Corpse for corpse, flesh of your own flesh" (5. 76–77). But by then it's too late. By the time Creon sees the error of his ways, his course of destruction is already set and the damage has been done.

Creon's "public policy" destroys his credibility as a king and everyone he cares about. He lets his thirst for absolute power and his condescending attitude toward women cloud his judgment and drive his family into the arms of death and tragedy. Antigonê's fight against the unjust decree of the king is an act of civil disobedience. She is driven by her firm belief in her religion and her own views on right and wrong. Antigonê believes that a law is not right just because it is a law. Individual conscience and the laws of the gods must always outweigh public policy.

[New Page]

Work Cited

Sophocles. *Antigonê*. Trans. Dudley Fitts and Robert Fitzgerald. *Exploring Literature*. Ed. Frank Madden. 5th ed. New York: Longman, 2012. 114–143. Print.

Chapter 5

Research
Writing with Secondary Sources

Our goal in this chapter is to build on the work you've done in previous chapters and to develop your ideas and your writing into a research essay. Making connections, analyzing the work and its influences, gathering evidence, and constructing an argument are also essential components of writing a research essay. In the pages that follow, however, we will expand our focus to include:

• Choosing your research topic;
• Conducting your search;
• Evaluating your sources;
• Integrating secondary source research into your writing;
• Documenting your sources and avoiding plagiarism.

THE RESEARCH ESSAY

Research is probably a commonplace event in your life. When you call a friend to seek advice about hooking up your computer or stereo, you are doing research. When you look up the spelling or meaning of a word, you are doing research. When you ask the opinion of a classmate about a poem, you are doing research. So despite any ominous connotations the word might have for you in an academic setting, it's a familiar activity.

For the most part, writing a research essay about literature is not a new activity for you either. You are doing research whenever you go to the text of the work itself, the **primary source,** to support your opinions and interpretations. But a *research essay expands the range of your research to include **secondary sources**—sources beyond the text of the work and your classroom—sources that may help to clarify, enrich, or add clout to your interpretation.* By going to secondary sources, you expand the scope of your writing. You might, for example, consult articles, books, or online sites that were written about the work or its author. You might consult sources that were written about the cultural or historical period in which the work was written. Or you might explore any number of other possibilities. The choices are limited only by your time and imagination.

CREATING, EXPANDING, AND JOINING INTERPRETIVE COMMUNITIES

We have discussed how your classmates and collaborative groups become interpretive communities, groups of readers who help to shape your views about how and what literature means. Your initial responses to literature are based on many factors. And through the social and intellectual exchanges of your groups, you confirm, supplement, or change these responses. In this respect, you already belong to many interpretive communities. By using secondary sources, however, you join new communities and share the views of many other readers and writers across hundreds of years and around the world.

IT IS YOUR INTERPRETATION

Regardless of how much research you do, this essay should be *your* interpretation in *your* own voice. Remember, what makes an interpretation convincing or defensible is your ability to support it. Doing research continues this process and adds to your support. In the same way that writing down your reflections, rereading the text, and discussing it with others informs your response, seeking information and ideas from secondary sources may lead you to a different, better-informed understanding and interpretation. Integrating these sources into your own writing style, however, is not always easy and may take some practice.

CONNECTING THROUGH COLLABORATION

1. Look back through your writing and pick out a work of literature that you discussed in class.
2. Try to remember what others in your class said about it.
   a. Did any of their comments help you to see the work in a different way?
   b. Did you disagree with any of their comments?
3. Write a response that includes their comments and your reactions to them.
4. Read your response.
   a. Does it accurately reflect your experience of the group's discussion?
   b. Were you able to integrate others' comments comfortably into your own writing?
   c. If not, what problems did you encounter?

GETTING STARTED

Choosing a Topic

If you are choosing your own topic, you might begin by asking yourself the same questions you would ask about any other kind of essay. If you are keeping a journal or other notes, you've probably jotted down potential topics for your research. Look back at your entries. Make sure you feel confident about the details and your understanding of the work. What did you find most interesting about the work? What would you like to know more about?

Remember, you are seeking information from other sources. You are not limited to what you already know. So be flexible. You don't have to decide on your final thesis right away. Share your early ideas with other students. They may give you ideas you haven't considered. In the process of putting your ideas into words and getting feedback, try out and develop the language and strategies you will use later in the essay itself.

Some Popular Areas of Literary Research

A Particular Work, Features of a Work, or Different Critical Views of a Work   A research essay on a single work is similar to the argumentative essays you have been writing, but by going to secondary sources you can tap the views of critics who may give you insights you haven't considered. For example, Sophocles's *Antigonê* (p. 113) contains several complex external and internal conflicts; the attitudes and behavior of Nora and Mrs. Linde in Ibsen's *A Doll's House* (p. 803) raise compelling questions about the role of women; the strong narrator in Alice Walker's "Everyday Use" (p. 933) might provide an interesting study of the effect of point of view.

A Particular Author or the Relationship Between the Author's Life and Work   Is there something about the work that makes you curious about the person who wrote it? Or about the connection of that person's life to the work? For example, Robert Hayden's "Those Winter Sundays" (p. 13), James Joyce's "Araby" (p. 407), and Liliana Heker's "The Stolen Party" (p. 403) are personal pieces about growing up. When you read them you may wonder how closely they are tied to the authors' own experiences. It might be interesting to explore the authors' lives in search of these connections.

The Social, Historical, or Cultural Background of a Work   When was the work written? Under what circumstances was it written? What impact did this background have on the work and its reception by the public? For example, when you read or see *A Doll's House,* it may make you curious about the marriage customs that existed when the play was written. You may wonder how audiences of 1879 responded to the play. Lorraine Hansberry's *A Raisin in the Sun* or Dudley Randall's "Ballad of Birmingham" may arouse your interest in race relations in America in the 1950s and 1960s.

Political, Philosophical, and Artistic Influences on the Author's Work
What political, philosophical, and artistic sources influenced the work or its author? In what way was the author influenced? How did the work of this author influence other authors? For example, how did the philosophical or political atmosphere of the time influence W. H. Auden's "The Unknown Citizen"? How did Sophocles's plays influence Aristotle's writing of *The Poetics*?

A Theme or Characters Compared Across Two or More Works   Is there a common theme that is shared by two or more works? Are there characters in different works who share similar traits? How are they alike? How are they different? How do secondary sources describe this theme or these characters? For example, you might address the theme of sibling relationships in Tennessee Williams's *The Glass Menagerie* (p. 966), Louise Erdrich's "The Red Convertible" (p. 241), and Sophocles's *Antigonê* (p. 113). To fully account for the complexity of these relationships, you could do research about the very different times, places, and cultures from which these pieces and their characters sprang.

YOUR SEARCH

Peer Support

Sometimes the best sources to start with are people. If you are struggling to find a topic, share your struggle with your friends and classmates. When you have chosen a topic, explain why you think it's interesting. See what your peers think. They may be able to give you ideas you hadn't considered, and they may spot problems. Use them for support, and cite them in your essay. Writing our ideas down is one way to learn, but we can also learn through conversation with our peers. Sharing our responses with others, and listening to their feedback and ideas, help us build and clarify our own ideas.

The Library

Again, your best initial source here may be people themselves, the librarians. Librarians know about the library's resources. They not only want to help you find what you need for this project, they want to help you learn how to use the library for future projects. Go to the library's information desk. Most libraries have one just inside the front door. Ask if there is a library map or information guide. Learn the location of the reference desk. The reference librarian can help you find the resources you need and show you how to use them.

Once you have some idea about what you're looking for, go to the library's online catalog. Most academic libraries list their resources in an online public access catalog. Here you can look for information under the author's name, the title of the book or other resource, its subject, or key words in its title. Most library systems are computerized and share resources with other libraries, so you not only have access to the listings in your library, but in other libraries as well. You can find most college and university libraries on the Internet and tap into their online public access catalogs. If you find the sources you are looking for, you can request them through interlibrary loan. Many libraries also have their own Web pages that will show you how to access their reference works or useful databases through your computer.

Reference Works

A particularly valuable source in your search for literary criticism is the *MLA International Bibliography*. It lists scholarly books and articles published each year, and it's organized by period and author. Most academic libraries have both the CD-ROM and hard copies of it. An especially useful computerized database for literary research is the Gale Group's *Literature Resource Center,* which has an enormous collection of critical, biographical, and historical information. Reference works like *The Oxford Companion to English Literature, The Oxford Companion to American Literature,* and *The Reader's Encyclopedia* can also be good places to start. *The New York Times* index may be very useful for book and play reviews. Even the *Reader's Guide to Periodical Literature* may contain useful reviews located in popular magazines like *The Atlantic Monthly, Time, Newsweek,* and *The New Yorker.*

Selected Sources Useful for Literary Research

Abstracts

Abstracts of English Studies

American Literature Abstracts

Bibliographies

Annual Bibliography of English Language and Literature

MLA International Bibliography

New Cambridge Bibliography of English Literature Biographies

Biographies

Black Writers

Contemporary Authors

Contemporary Dramatists

Contemporary Novelists

Contemporary Poets

Oxford Guide to British Women Writers

Dictionaries

Biographical Dictionary of Irish Writers

Columbia Dictionary of Modern European Literature

Dictionary of British Folk-Tales in the English Language

Dictionary of Celtic Myth and Legend

Dictionary of Celtic Mythology

Dictionary of Concepts in Literary Criticism and Theory

Dictionary of Literary Biography

Dictionary of Mythology, Folklore, and Symbols

Dictionary of Native American Mythology

Funk and Wagnall's Standard Dictionary of Folklore, Mythology and Legend

Encyclopedias

Cassell's Encyclopedia of World Literature

Encyclopedia of Contemporary Literary Theory

Encyclopedia of Continental Women Writers

Encyclopedia of Literature and Criticism

Encyclopedia of World Literature in the Twentieth Century

Encyclopedia of World Theater

Larousse Encyclopedia of Mythology

McGraw-Hill Encyclopedia of World Drama

New Princeton Encyclopedia of Poetry and Poetics

Reader's Encyclopedia of World Drama

The Reader's Encyclopedia

Indices

Centennial Index

Cumulated Dramatic Index 1909–1949

Play Index

Short Story Index

Oxford Companions

Oxford Companion to American Literature

Oxford Companion to American Theatre

Oxford Companion to Canadian Literature

Oxford Companion to Children's Literature

Oxford Companion to Classical Literature

Oxford Companion to the Theatre

Miscellaneous

Contemporary Literary Criticism

Handbook to Literature

Larousse World Mythology

Literary History of England

Literary History of the United States

Mythology of All Races

New York Times Theater Reviews, 1920–1970

Year's Work in English Studies

Most of these reference works now come in CD-ROM form or are available online. Most libraries have periodical databases on CD-ROM that are updated frequently.

Humanities Index is one such database that is very useful for literary research. CD-ROMs are also available that contain the complete texts of literary works along with critical commentary, historical and biographical information, and dramatic readings by the authors. Check with your librarian to see what electronic resources are available.

Finding Sources on the Internet

The Internet can be an excellent source of information for your research. But while most indexes and other library sources of information about books and periodicals are organized in alphabetical or chronological order, the Internet is not. The World Wide Web is a hypertext system that moves you from one source to another. It finds the connections you request between pieces of information and helps to generate new ones. By typing in key words or phrases, you request the combinations. Instead of choosing an item on a menu, you use your mouse to click on a highlighted term or topic on a Web page.

Web Browsers and Search Engines   Most Internet systems provide access to Web browsers such as Microsoft Explorer, Netscape Navigator, Safari, Mozilla Firefox, and Google Chrome. Web browsers give you access to search engines and make it easy for you to save or print the information you uncover. Search engines such as Google, Yahoo!, Bing, AltaVista, Excite, HotBot, Go, and Lycos act as directories and create indexes of key words that help you to find the information you seek. They provide a long, horizontal box in which you type a key word or words that describe your subject. In order to work as efficiently as possible, it is essential to narrow the field of your search.

Add plus or minus signs to key words to narrow your search. If you add plus signs before each word (+Shakespeare +"The Tempest" +Prospero), a search engine like Google will come up with only those sites that include all three key words. If you wish to look at sites that exclude one of these elements, use a minus sign in front of the key word you wish to exclude (+Shakespeare +"The Tempest" −Prospero), and only Web sites without Prospero's name will come up.

Use quotation marks to keep key words together and narrow your search. If you place quotation marks around the information you seek (e.g., "William Shakespeare The Tempest"), the search engine will only come up with instances of that exact combination. If you don't use quotation marks, it will yield every instance of related and unrelated material bearing those terms (e.g., The tempest over Frank Shakespeare was explained by William Smith).

Type in more key words to narrow your field; otherwise your search will come up with many more sources than you will have time to examine.

Type in fewer or different key words to broaden your field. If your search comes up with very few items, it may be necessary to cut down on the number of key terms or try different ones with a similar meaning.

Discussion Groups, Listservs, and Newsgroups   Two resources for direct online communication with other people who have similar interests are discussion groups, listservs, and newsgroups. You can join a discussion or chat group by subscribing to a mailing list and receiving messages via e-mail. Newsgroups are like bulletin boards: everyone in the group reads the same messages. They provide information similar to discussion groups but don't send messages to individuals. Users can post and read messages without subscribing to a list. Newsgroups are joined through a newsreader or a World Wide Web browser.

Internet Sources Useful for Literary Research

Literary Resources on the Net: {http://ethnicity.rutgers.edu/~jlynch/Lit}

American Literature Gateway: {http://www.academicinfo.net/amlit.html}

English Literature Links: {http://www.academicinfo.net/englitmeta.html}

Bartleby.com: Great Books online: {http://www.bartleby.com}

The Voice of the Shuttle: {http://vos.ucsb.edu}

Justin's Theatre Links Page: {http://www.theatrelinks.com}

Shakespeare and the Internet: {http://shakespeare.palomar.edu}

Electronic Shakespeare: {http://www.wfu.edu/%7Etedforrl/shakespeare}

Evaluating Internet Sources

Prior to publication, books and articles in scholarly journals are usually reviewed and carefully edited by those with expertise in the field. So, too, editors at reputable newspapers and magazines usually ask writers to verify the accuracy of their sources before they will publish their work. But anyone can put information on the Internet, and it may not be screened for accuracy. Thus, you always need to check the source of any information you take from the Internet. Look for biographical or other data that might tell you something about the author or the author's academic or scholarly affiliation. If the author provides links to other sources, check them out to verify the accuracy of the information. Look for publication or revision dates. As with any source, make sure the assertions made are supported with evidence, and be sure that you give credit to the author and correctly cite the information when you quote or paraphrase from a Web site.

Remember, you—not an unknown and potentially unreliable source on the Internet—are responsible for the accuracy of your support information.

 CHECKLIST: EVALUATING INTERNET SOURCES

❑ Make sure that the author of the document or the person or group responsible for the Web site is identified. Is this person or group a credible source? How is this verifiable? Is there a phone number or postal address?

(continued)

❑ Is the page well written? Is it well organized? If not, it may have been constructed by a child or an unreliable source.

❑ Is there a link to a page describing the purpose of the sponsoring organization? Is this information provided as a public service? Might there be reasons for bias or prejudice? How will that affect the accuracy of the information?

❑ What kind of Web site is indicated? Addresses that end in *.edu* are educational institutions; *.gov* is a government site; *.mil* is military; *.com* and *.net* are commercial sites; and *.org* is a nonprofit organization. Being aware of this may tell you about the potential biases of these sources.

❑ Check to see that the work's sources are indicated. Is there a list of works cited? Does the list seem sufficient?

❑ Are there links to other sources indicated? Do they seem reliable?

❑ Check the dates of the sources. Are they current? Is there a different date for an earlier print source? Have the sources been revised?

TAKING NOTES

Whether you use slips of paper, note cards, or a computer, you should be able to rearrange your information according to your needs. Cards are easier to move around and rearrange, so you may find it convenient to use 3" × 5" or 4" × 6" file or note cards to record documentation information and notes, usually with a separate source on each card.

Using a computer to take notes and record bibliographic information will save you time later: You can open a separate file for bibliographic entries and copy and paste this information directly into your essay. You can organize your notes into separate files—placing quotation marks around direct quotes and noting their sources—then copy and paste as you write and revise.

Be selective when you go through your sources. Keep the focus of your essay in mind as you take notes. Ignore irrelevant material. Sources that are particularly valuable may provide you with much information and point you to additional sources as well. As you read, be sure to jot down your own ideas as they occur to you. If you wait until later, you may forget them.

Don't forget to copy all the information you will need for documentation, including page numbers. Whether you are using note cards or a computer, it is a good idea to record the bibliographic information of your print or electronic resources in the form you will be using on the Works Cited page of your essay. You will then have the appropriate format ready, and you can simply rearrange the sources in alphabetical order when listing your Works Cited.

Integrating Sources into Your Writing

Even though you listen to the views of others in your class, you can claim your final interpretation as your own. You might refer to someone else's view to support your opinion—or comment on others' views as a point of disagreement. But your interpretation and the support behind it are still yours; this is your essay, not the views of other students and the instructor strung together. An essay that uses secondary sources for support should be no different. But it's not always easy to integrate secondary sources into your writing without sounding too artificial or making the essay look like a list of other people's statements pasted together.

Be selective about using direct quotes from secondary sources. Sometimes a summary or paraphrase (see pp. 193–194) will be a more effective fit with your own writing style. When you quote, make sure that you introduce the quote so that its relevance to your argument is clear. You may be able to integrate the quote smoothly into your own writing style by quoting only those words that are relevant and by using an ellipsis (see p. 194) to indicate omitted material or brackets (see p. 194) to indicate you have included your own word(s) for clarification.

What Must Be Documented

- Information that is not common knowledge—knowledge that you or most others would not have without reference to this or a similar source.

- Information or ideas from another source (text or interview) that you have paraphrased (rephrased in your own words) or summarized (reduced to its essential points).

- Direct quotations from another source (text or interview).

Where and How to Document

- In the text of the essay itself, you must indicate the author and page number(s) of borrowed information or quotations.

- On a separate page at the end of the essay, you must include an alphabetized list of all the sources you have used in the text.

Paraphrasing and Summarizing

Most of your notes should paraphrase or summarize rather than quote directly the author's exact words. In addition to helping you comprehend what you read, putting the material into your own words (your own writing style, your own voice) will clarify your ideas and help you build the language you will need when you write your essay.

Paraphrasing   To paraphrase, you must thoroughly understand what the author has written and then rewrite that material in your own words and sentences. If you use any of the author's language, you must enclose it in quotation marks. (See example on p. 195.)

Summarizing To summarize, you must understand what the author has written and then condense the source material to its main points. If you use any of the author's language, you must enclose it in quotation marks. (See example on p. 195.)

Quoting

This is *your* essay, *your* argument or the point *you* want to express. Bring in secondary sources only when you need them. Use direct quotes only when the language in your source makes an impact that your wording would not. Be sure to surround any quotes you use with sufficient support. Introduce them and explain how they work as evidence. Work quotes smoothly into your writing style. Combine what you paraphrase and summarize with brief quotations.

When you quote most (but not all) of a sentence, or you leave out unnecessary parts of a long sentence, an **ellipsis** signals to the reader that the quoted material does not include all of its original sentence. For example, if you wanted to describe some of the physical characteristics of Maggie in Alice Walker's "Everyday Use," but you did not want to quote an entire sentence, you might write:

> In contrast to her attractive and confident sister Dee, Maggie is described as "…homely and ashamed of the burn scars down her arms and legs…" (983).

When you add your own word or words to the quote for integration and clarification, **brackets** [ ] tell the reader that this is your language, not that of the source material:

> It is hard to tell what Dee thought when she looked at "the burn scars down [Maggie's] arms and legs…" (983).

Avoiding Plagiarism

Plagiarism is taking someone else's ideas or words and passing them off as your own. The most basic rule of all documentation is that direct quotations, summarized or paraphrased information, or ideas from another source must be appropriately credited. This includes information that is not common knowledge (information that you would not have without reference to this or a similar source).

In the text of the essay, you must indicate the author and page number(s) of borrowed information or quotations. On a separate page at the end of the essay, you must include an alphabetized list (Works Cited) of all the sources you have used in the text.

You must always make it clear which words and ideas are yours and which ones come from other sources. Before you submit your essay, check your paraphrases and summaries against the original sources. Make sure that the words and sentences are your own and that they accurately reflect the meaning of the source material. *To use other people's words and ideas and not give them credit is plagiarism, a serious academic offense.*

Examples of Paraphrasing, Summarizing, Quoting, and Plagiarizing

The Original Source
(From Shulevitz, Judith. "The Hall of Fame." Rev. of *Genius*, by Harold Bloom. *New York Times Book Review,* 27 Oct. 2002.)

Bloom is not so easily dismissed, however. His style may be disheveled and his book shockingly attuned to the demands of the marketplace, but both have a virtue that trumps those flaws. Bloom's focus on genius is not just commercial opportunism, the usual blather about the moral import of cultural literacy or part of the national obsession with success, though critics will find all three if they go looking for them.

Summarizing
Shulevitz says Bloom's book is stylistically "disheveled" and market-driven, but these may be greater strengths than weaknesses. She believes critics will reduce it to these weaknesses if they want to, but the book has greater value than that (11).

Paraphrasing
Shulevitz says Bloom's work remains important even though it seems a bit "disheveled" in style and market driven. She asserts that these features of his writing are actually greater strengths than weaknesses, and that this work is not just an attempt to make money by taking advantage of the public's desire for books about cultural literacy or success. But she believes that critics will be able to reduce the book to these weaknesses if they want to and ignore its qualities (11).

Quoting
Shulevitz says Bloom's work remains important and adds, "His style may be disheveled and his book shockingly attuned to the demands of the market-place, but both have a virtue that trumps those flaws" (11).

Plagiarizing
Shulevitz insists that Bloom is not so easily dismissed. He may have a disheveled style and his book is shockingly attuned to the marketplace, but both of these things have a virtue that trumps those flaws.

See Appendix C (p. 1289) for a Directory of MLA Formatting and Documentation.

From First Response to Research Essay

The same processes that are so useful in generating ideas for personal or argumentative essays may be just as valuable for giving you ideas and narrowing your topic for a research essay. Reading literature encourages a variety of responses and perhaps raises more questions than it answers. It is a good idea to generate and explore as many of your questions and ideas as possible before you decide on one direction. Here is a quick review of strategies to get started. For a detailed explanation of these techniques, with examples, see Chapter 2, pages 29–42.

- Employing directed freewriting can be a useful technique for loosening up ideas. The best time to do this exercise is immediately after you finish reading, while your thoughts and impressions are fresh. The intention of directed freewriting is to release what you know without blocking it with pauses for reflection, punctuation, or editing.

- Asking questions about a general topic is likely to provide you with new information. Responding with detailed answers to these questions may provide you with ideas for a narrowed thesis and specific support for that thesis.

- Choosing a few key words or phrases that apply to your topic and then listing as many related details as you can under each should help you generate many concrete details and much specific support for your ideas.

- Clustering your ideas or drawing a semantic map may help you understand, generate, extend, and see relationships between ideas better by looking at them spatially rather than linearly.

- Your peers can be a terrific resource. If you are struggling with your topic, or you are not sure that you've expressed what you wanted to say clearly, exchange your draft with a classmate or with a small group. Have them read it and tell you what they think. They may be able to give you ideas you hadn't considered, and they may spot problems and inconsistencies. Use your peers for support. When you take their advice, have them read your revision to see if you've nailed it. Writing our ideas down by ourselves is one way to learn, but getting constructive criticism from supportive peers gives us a sense of audience and tells us more about the impact of our writing and our ideas than we can possibly know in isolation.

☑ CHECKLIST: WRITING A RESEARCH ESSAY

Planning Your Essay

Consider Your Motivation

❑ Will this topic sustain your interest long enough for you to do a good job?

Determine Its Feasibility

❑ Can you write a research essay about this subject? Do you have enough to say and can you find enough evidence to support your case?

Secondary Sources

❑ Can you find appropriate secondary sources? Where will you get them? Are you sure of their reliability?

Taking Notes

❑ Do you have an effective system to organize your notes? What is it? Can you use a computer to save time later?

❑ Have you copied down all the information you will need to document your sources?

❑ Have you decided which sources to summarize, paraphrase, and quote?

Clarify Your Thesis

❑ Do you have a clear understanding of the thesis you want to argue? Can you articulate it in a thesis statement?

Know Your Readers

❑ What assumptions can you make about your readers? Are they likely to agree or disagree with your thesis?

Supporting Your Argument

Arrange Your Support Effectively

❑ Is the support for your thesis arranged in the most effective way? Is it more effective to develop your argument by stating your thesis first and then supporting it with evidence or by allowing the evidence to build into your thesis?

Integrating Secondary Sources

❑ How can you effectively and smoothly integrate your secondary sources into your own writing style? What should be paraphrased? What should be quoted? Why?

Support Your Thesis with Facts from the Text and Secondary Sources

❑ Is your support based on facts or opinions? Have you supported your opinions with facts and quotes from the text?

❑ Do your secondary sources support your view? How?

Account for All the Evidence

❑ Have you accounted for *all* the evidence in the text? Have you accounted for evidence that may not support your thesis? Have you accounted for secondary source material that may not support your thesis?

(continued)

Explain the Connections

❏ Have you explained *how* the evidence you have chosen supports your thesis?

❏ Are the connections between your secondary sources and your thesis clear?

Opening, Closing, and Revising

Write or Rewrite Your Introduction After Your First Draft

❏ Is your introduction clear, informative, and interesting?

❏ If appropriate, does it map out the journey for the reader?

Close Your Argument Reasonably

❏ Have you explained the connections between the thesis and your primary and secondary source support? Have you claimed only what you have delivered?

Revise with a Fresh View

❏ Have you reread and reviewed your essay?

❏ How well is your draft organized? Does the sequence make sense?

❏ Are there gaps that need to be filled? Is there enough support? Have you explained the connections between your support and your thesis? Have you expressed those connections as clearly as possible?

❏ Have you maintained a consistent voice throughout the essay?

Review Your Intentions and Organization

❏ Is the central thesis of the essay clearly stated? Does the title of your essay account for your thesis?

❏ Is the essay fully developed? Have you accounted for all aspects of your thesis statement?

❏ Do all the paragraphs relate to your thesis? Is the organization of those paragraphs within the essay clear? Are the paragraphs fully developed? Do each of the sentences within the paragraphs relate to the central idea of the paragraph?

❏ Are there enough details to support or clarify your proposition? Have you "shown" what you've "told"? Are there enough quotes from both primary and secondary sources to support your thesis?

❏ Are there redundancies, digressions, or meaningless phrases that could be cut?

Proofread Carefully

❑ Are all of your sentences complete sentences? Are all of your sentences punctuated appropriately?

❑ Are all the words spelled correctly? Have you checked for easily confused words (*then/than, your/you're, its/it's,* etc.)?

❑ Are you sure of the meaning of all the words you've used?

❑ Are the titles of works underlined or in quotation marks as appropriate?

❑ Are there particular errors you have a tendency to make? Have you looked for those in this essay?

❑ Is the essay written in the format required by your instructor? Have you documented your references to the text and included a list of works cited?

CASE STUDY
IN RESEARCH

James Joyce and "Eveline"

STEP 1: USING YOUR FIRST RESPONSE

The purpose of the Case Study that follows is to provide a model of one student's process as he moved from an initial idea to a research essay. In many ways, what kept this student's interest alive—and gave him the energy to pursue his goal to the finish—was the personally compelling nature of his topic. Having such a topic will not guarantee a successful research experience, but it's a good place to start.

As we have emphasized throughout this book, writing an effective essay is not always a straightforward process. Many factors may influence the choices we make along the way. This is particularly true when using secondary source research in our writing. One possible topic, and a rich source for research, may be the connection we find between our own backgrounds or culture and that presented in the work. The best research springs from our need to know more—to fill in the gaps in our knowledge. This research is not imposed on our writing but evolves naturally from it.

On the next page is James Joyce's short story "Eveline" and questions to prompt your own response. Following the story and questions is the commentary of Prof. Alan Devenish, and the research essay of his student Kevin Chamberlain. Prof. Devenish recalls their conferences and the process Kevin experienced while writing his research essay. He explains that Kevin did not set out to do research. While reading James Joyce's short story "Eveline," Kevin found similarities between himself and the protagonist. He started to write a response essay, but his interest in the protagonist inspired him to want to know more. He sought information about the conditions of her background. This, in turn, led him to do research about the author and to read more of Joyce's work. What began as a personal response developed naturally into an informative and personally meaningful research essay.

JAMES JOYCE [1882–1941]

James Joyce was one of ten children born into a middle-class family of declining fortunes in a suburb of Dublin, Ireland. In spite of an unhappy childhood dominated by a drunken father, Joyce managed to receive a thorough classical education, first in Jesuit schools and then at University College, Dublin. Though he spent most of his adult life living outside Ireland, Dublin is the backdrop for nearly all of his work. His three innovative novels, Portrait of the Artist as a Young Man *(1916),* Ulysses *(1922), and* Finnegans Wake *(1939), established him as one of the greatest writers of modern times. "Eveline" (below) and "Araby" (p. 407) are taken from his collection of short stories,* Dubliners, *which appeared in 1914 after an eight-year battle with publishers who feared it would offend important residents of the city.*

EVELINE

[1914]

She sat at the window watching the evening invade the avenue. Her head was leaned against the window curtains and in her nostrils was the odour of dusty cretonne. She was tired.

Few people passed. The man out of the last house passed on his way home; she heard his footsteps clacking along the concrete pavement and afterwards crunching on the cinder path before the new red houses. One time there used to be a field there in which they used to play every evening with other people's children. Then a man from Belfast bought the field and built houses in it—not like their little brown houses but bright brick houses with shining roofs. The children of the avenue used to play together in that field—the Devines, the Waters, the Dunns, little Keogh the cripple, she and her brothers and sisters. Ernest, however, never played: he was too grown up. Her father used often to hunt them in out of the field with his blackthorn stick; but usually little Keogh used to keep *nix* and call out when he saw her father coming. Still they seemed to have been rather happy then. Her father was not so bad then; and besides, her mother was alive. That was a long time ago; she and her brothers and sisters were all grown up; her mother was dead. Tizzie Dunn was dead, too, and the Waters had gone back to England. Everything changes. Now she was going to go away like the others, to leave her home.

Home! She looked around the room, reviewing all its familiar objects which she had dusted once a week for so many years, wondering where on earth all the dust came from. Perhaps she would never see again those familiar objects from which she had never dreamed of being divided. And yet during all those years she had never found out the name of the priest whose yellowing photograph hung on the wall above the broken harmonium beside the coloured print of the promises made to Blessed Margaret Mary Alacoque. He had been a school friend of her father. Whenever he showed the photograph to a visitor her father used to pass it with a casual word:

　　—He is in Melbourne now.

5　　She had consented to go away, to leave her home. Was that wise? She tried to weigh each side of the question. In her home anyway she had shelter and food; she had those whom she had known all her life about her. Of course she had to work hard both in the house and at business. What would they say of her in the Stores when they found out that she had run away with a fellow? Say she was a fool, perhaps; and her place would be filled up by advertisement. Miss Gavan would be glad. She had always had an edge on her, especially whenever there were people listening.

　　—Miss Hill, don't you see these ladies are waiting?

　　—Look lively, Miss Hill, please.

She would not cry many tears at leaving the Stores.

But in her new home, in a distant unknown country, it would not be like that. Then she would be married—she, Eveline. People would treat her with respect then. She would not be treated as her mother had been. Even now, though she was over nineteen, she sometimes felt herself in danger of her father's violence. She knew it was that that had given her the palpitations.

When they were growing up he had never gone for her, like he used to go for Harry and Ernest, because she was a girl; but latterly he had begun to threaten her and say what he would do to her only for her dead mother's sake. And now she had nobody to protect her. Ernest was dead and Harry, who was in the church decorating business, was nearly always down somewhere in the country. Besides, the invariable squabble for money on Saturday nights had begun to weary her unspeakably. She always gave her entire wages—seven shillings—and Harry always sent up what he could but the trouble was to get any money from her father. He said she used to squander the money, that she had no head, that he wasn't going to give her his hard-earned money to throw about the streets, and much more, for he was usually fairly bad of a Saturday night. In the end he would give her the money and ask her had she any intention of buying Sunday's dinner. Then she had to rush out as quickly as she could and do her marketing, holding her black leather purse tightly in her hand as she elbowed her way through the crowds and returning home late under her load of provisions. She had hard work to keep the house together and to see that the two young children who had been left to her charge went to school regularly and got their meals regularly. It was hard work—a hard life—but now that she was about to leave it she did not find it a wholly undesirable life.

10   She was about to explore another life with Frank. Frank was very kind, manly, open-hearted. She was to go away with him by the night-boat to be his wife and to live with him in Buenos Ayres where he had a home waiting for her. How well she remembered the first time she had seen him; he was lodging in a house on the main road where she used to visit. It seemed a few weeks ago. He was standing at the gate, his peaked cap pushed back on his head and his hair tumbled forward over a face of bronze. Then they had come to know each other. He used to meet her outside the Stores every evening and see her home. He took her to see *The Bohemian Girl* and she felt elated as she sat in an unaccustomed part of the theatre with him. He was awfully fond of music and sang a little. People knew that they were courting and, when he sang about the lass that loves a sailor, she always felt pleasantly confused. He used to call her Poppens out of fun. First of all it had been an excitement for her to have a fellow and then she had begun to like him. He had tales of distant countries. He had started as a deck boy at a pound a month on a ship of the Allan Line going out to Canada. He told her the names of the ships he had been on and the names of the different services. He had sailed through the Straits of Magellan and he told her stories of the terrible Patagonians. He had fallen on his feet in Buenos Ayres, he said, and had come over to the old country just for a holiday. Of course, her father had found out the affair and had forbidden her to have anything to say to him.

—I know these sailor chaps, he said.

One day he had quarreled with Frank and after that she had to meet her lover secretly.

The evening deepened in the avenue. The white of two letters in her lap grew indistinct. One was to Harry; the other was to her father. Ernest had been her favourite but she liked Harry too. Her father was becoming old lately, she noticed; he would miss her. Sometimes he could be very nice. Not long before, when she had been laid up for a day, he had read her out a ghost story and made toast for her at the fire. Another day, when their mother was alive, they had all gone for a picnic to the Hill of Howth. She remembered her father putting on her mother's bonnet to make the children laugh.

Her time was running out but she continued to sit by the window, leaning her head against the window curtain, inhaling the odour of dusty cretonne. Down far in the avenue she could hear a street organ playing. She knew the air. Strange that it should come that very night to remind her of the promise to her mother, her promise to keep the home together as long as she could. She remembered the last night of her mother's illness; she was again in the close dark room at the other side of the hall and outside she heard a melancholy air of Italy. The organ-player had been ordered to go away and given sixpence. She remembered her father strutting back into the sickroom saying.

15 —Damned Italians! Coming over here!

As she mused the pitiful vision of her mother's life laid its spell on the very quick of her being—that life of commonplace sacrifices closing in final craziness. She trembled as she heard again her mother's voice saying constantly with foolish insistence:

—Derevaun Seraun! Derevaun Seraun!*

She stood up in a sudden impulse of terror. Escape! She must escape! Frank would save her. He would give her life, perhaps love, too. But she wanted to live. Why should she be unhappy? She had a right to happiness. Frank would take her in his arms, fold her in his arms. He would save her.

She stood among the swaying crowd in the station at the North Wall. He held her hand and she knew that he was speaking to her, saying something about the passage over and over again. The station was full of soldiers with brown baggages. Through the wide doors of the sheds she caught a glimpse of the black mass of the boat, lying in beside the quay wall, with illumined portholes. She answered nothing. She felt her cheek pale and cold and, out of a maze of distress, she prayed to God to direct her, to show her what was her duty. The boat blew a long mournful whistle into the mist. If she went, to-morrow she would be on the sea with Frank, steaming towards Buenos Ayres. Their passage had been booked. Could she still draw back after all he had done for her? Her distress awoke a nausea in her body and she kept moving her lips in silent fervent prayer.

20 A bell clanged upon her heart. She felt him seize her hand:
—Come!

All the seas of the world tumbled about her heart. He was drawing her into them: he would drown her. She gripped with both hands at the iron railing.
—Come!

*(Gaelic) "The end of pleasure is pain."

No! No! No! It was impossible. Her hands clutched the iron in frenzy. Amid the seas she sent a cry of anguish!

25   —Eveline! Evvy!

He rushed beyond the barrier and called to her to follow. He was shouted at to go on but he still called to her. She set her white face to him, passive, like a helpless animal. Her eyes gave him no sign of love or farewell or recognition.

MAKING CONNECTIONS

1. To what extent is your response to this story influenced by your own background or experience?
2. Were you hoping that Eveline would leave or stay? Why?
3. Describe Frank. What does he represent to Eveline?
4. To what extent is Eveline a prisoner of her setting? Of her own culture?
5. Do you think Eveline really has a choice at the end of the story? Explain.

MAKING AN ARGUMENT

1. At the end of the story, Eveline decides to stay with her father. Citing the text of the story and/or other pertinent sources for support, write an essay that argues for or against her decision.

STEP 2: COMPOSING A DRAFT

All readers may not have a strong personal identification with the work or, like Kevin, follow up their reading of one work by reading other works by the same author. But the process Kevin followed is a strong model for anyone doing secondary source research. He did not begin by gathering all the information he could and refashioning it into an essay. He began by writing a draft of his own response. In the process, he identified the issues he wanted to explore and generated the questions he needed to answer to make this exploration successful. The objective of his search was not to gather the most information, but to gather answers to his questions. His search was motivated by his "need to know," and it was only through his early writing and reflection that *what* he needed to know became clear to him.

Professor Devenish's Commentary

Before beginning my commentary on his essay "Leaving Home," I met with Kevin Chamberlain to discuss his paper. In preparation for our informal interview I asked him to write a short "process reflection" describing the researching, writing, and revising of his essay. I am tempted to delete this last phrase—"researching, writing, and revising"—because Kevin's actual process did not follow this neat, if unnatural, progression of discrete steps or stages. His process was rich in recursions and excursions, in rethinkings that led to new inquiries, which in turn led to further thinking and writing. The finished essay is not the one Kevin thought he was going to write when he started out.

So, how *did* he start out? Why did he choose to write on James Joyce's "Eveline," a story about a young woman's unsuccessful struggle to leave home, when he had any number of literary works and authors from which to select?

Kevin's Motivation and Process

"I was drawn to this story because I, too, am attached to my home and family," Kevin writes in his process reflection. "I have lived in the same house all of my life and I often dread the thought of leaving." Kevin adds similarly: "I was able to empathize with Eveline because I am at a similar point in my life—too long in the nest." Kevin's impetus for this paper was at heart a personal one. He responded emotionally to the title character's fears and desires, to the terrible conflict between home and self. Kevin also notes that he had read other works by Joyce and enjoyed his "writing style." Clearly, however, "Eveline" struck a special chord.

In our conversation, Kevin spoke of his initial impatience with the character Eveline, how he felt "anxious to push this person out of her home—to do what I would do." On further reading and research, however, he tempered this impulse, as he looked more closely at the conditions and culture that gave rise to Eveline's quandary. Reading Joyce's *Portrait of the Artist as a Young Man* and *Dubliners,* along with relevant critical research on the author and Ireland itself, brought Kevin to a more complex and empathetic understanding of the character. No doubt, too, rereading the story reminded Kevin of his own unresolved tensions between loyalties to home and family on one hand, and change and "beginning my own life" on the other.

Along with Kevin's intimate connection with the story's protagonist must be added another: culture. Eveline is not only a person struggling with fierce inner conflicts, she is a person living in a particular place and time, Ireland of the early twentieth century. Again, in his process, Kevin writes of "being part Irish" and how this cultural heritage leads him to share similar values with Eveline in regard to family, religion, and change. At the same time, he realized that he needed to know more of the particular Ireland of Joyce's "Eveline" and how the author "intertwines political, social, religious, and economic themes into his writing...That is where the research began."

Cultural relevance, then, became a starting point for inquiry into the important complexities that form the backdrop of Joyce's story. Interestingly, Kevin did not presume that his own Irish heritage gave him a satisfactory understanding of the character or story. Being part Irish did, however, stir his interest in the Ireland that gave rise to Eveline, and indeed to Joyce himself. In our interview, Kevin made the surprising assertion that in Joyce the characters are "the least important things in the story. The characters show one whole side of life, are representative of a whole class of people." What Kevin meant by this, I believe, is that "Eveline," far from being the idiosyncratic story of a particularly troubled young woman, is the story of many an Irish woman of Joyce's day, these Evelines holding fast to the dock railing as their figurative or real ships left for distant ports. In his essay, Kevin makes amply clear the enormous historical, economic, religious, and familial forces that converged into a sort of paralysis in Eveline and so many like her, and how these selfsame forces acted more centrifugally on Joyce and others like him who broke from home, and "the old sow" of Ireland "that eats her farrow," as Kevin quotes Joyce's biting indictment. Most notable in this analysis is that Kevin undertook his research from a need to know more of the very culture whose personal relevance first connected him to the story.

STEP 3: REVISING THE ESSAY

Here I would like to quote Kevin's description of how his initial intent to write an interpretive essay relying solely on his reading of "Eveline" evolved rather organically into a more complex inquiry:

> My first step was to respond to the story, writing an essay that examined the primary source [the story "Eveline"] without any outside influences such as literary criticism. Once the draft was completed, I made a list of things in the story that I did not understand but felt were important to understanding the work as a whole... By making a list of things I did not understand, I had something to look for in the outside sources... Once I felt I had enough information to revise my first draft, I added in the research to my already existing essay... without letting my research write the paper for me. I simply used the research to support my already existing thesis.

Clearly, Kevin did not start out with either the requirement or the intention of writing a research paper. His method was not to get books out of the library and then figure out a way to incorporate all the research into a readable—or writable—essay. Rather, as his process reflection here and his finished essay demonstrate, he *grew* into the research, beginning with that important personal connection, that moment of recognition between himself and the text. He saw something of himself in Eveline, as he did in the Ireland that lived in her. From this recognition he wrote his first draft, a draft that led him to other questions. These questions, in turn, led him to further reading and writing, thereby strengthening the original connection between himself and the story. He repeated this process through several revisions, each time returning to the library when he felt "there were things that were still not strong enough," until he had satisfied the questions raised by his reading and writing. What started, then, as a response to a short story related to his own life grew to a larger inquiry into cultural contexts, literary criticism, and the author's work. That initial personal response, however, was not simply a starting point for the "real" work of research and writing. From Kevin's process reflections, as from his completed essay, I am convinced that his ongoing—indeed deepened—connection with the character and culture of this story sustained his research, writing, and revision throughout.

By citing Kevin's approach to writing about a literary work I am not claiming that students need to share a cultural identity with an author or text, or find exact parallels with the circumstances of their own lives. What I do believe Kevin's example illustrates is the importance of a personal connection with the work. Clearly, Kevin did not need a male protagonist in a familiar, contemporary setting in order to "relate." He did, however, feel a need to find in the work something that touched him. As it happened, he found this through cultural and psychological perspectives. More important, he then broadened these perspectives, questioning what he read and wrote, adding to it, seeing what was previously unseen. In the process, he learned about women in Joyce's Ireland; he read other works by the author; he saw historical and political patterns in Eveline's painful stasis; he deciphered religious references as significant symbols; he studied the human heart through the particulars of one fictive but very human creation. As important, I think, is that Kevin came to experience this story and his response to it as integral to his own life.

STEP 4: KEVIN'S REVISED ESSAY

Kevin Chamberlain

Dr. Devenish

English 102

March 20, 20XX

Leaving Home

James Joyce's short story "Eveline" is the story of a girl who turns down a marriage proposal because of her attachment to her home and family. This story still has relevance today. Many young adults live in the homes they grew up in and often dread the thought of leaving. These adult children and their parents depend on each other emotionally and financially, and moving out would alter their lives significantly. Eveline, the main character in Joyce's story, is faced with a similar dilemma. Should she abandon her father and begin her own life? Or should she stay home and take care of her father, but give up her own future in the process?

Eveline's devotion to her father stems from a promise to her deceased mother to keep her home together. Even after the home falls apart, Eveline feels that she must stay. On the surface, it is Eveline's tale of how and why she cannot leave. Beneath the surface, the story is a metaphor for women's conditions in turn-of-the-century Ireland. Many factors influence Eveline's decision, but the most compelling are religion, family, and fear of change.

There is not much to the story on the surface. It appears to be nothing more than the story of a girl who makes a bad decision, but Joyce has neatly interwoven a metaphor for what keeps Irish people in an idle state. He is using his story to point out how Irish people, especially women, let themselves be trapped. He does not entirely blame the individual because conditions gave people a poor foundation to build on. Finally, when there is some certainty, they cling to it and are reluctant to change. This is the plight of Eveline.

In the 1890s, when this story was set, Ireland was still suffering the effects of the potato famine of the 1840s. Around this time, the country had lost millions of its people to starvation and emigration. The people left behind suffered many effects. "For a full century after 1845, poverty was widespread, jobs few and precarious, salaries meager, and opportunities for advancement rare" (Walzl 33). This was especially true for women, who were relegated to more traditional roles.

Lack of financial resources led people to put off marriage. Postponing marriages kept women with their families longer, causing them to become dependent on that lifestyle. As one becomes more devoted to family, the option of marriage becomes less likely. Eveline's chance to marry Frank, her fiancée, is important because it may be her only chance to marry and leave the country. By deciding not to marry Frank, she identifies herself as one woman who will not leave her homeland. In this sense, Eveline is representative of many of her fellow citizens. "Even when emigration had become established as an almost automatic part of rural life, it conflicted sharply with the high value that Irish country people put upon communalism, kinship and a sense of place. To leave here meant a psychic disruption" (Foster 351).

The story opens with Eveline sitting motionless, contemplating leaving the home she has known. After her mother's death, Eveline takes over her duties in the home and tends to her abusive father: "…growing up he had never gone for her,…but latterly he had begun to threaten her" (203). Usually, his rage is about money and the idea that she squanders it. The truth is that after working at her job all week, she gives her wages to him, ultimately to support his drinking habit. A family that has a minimal income should treat alcohol as a luxury, yet "he was usually fairly bad of a Saturday night" (203).

This kind of life should create a fear of remaining at home, yet Eveline feels that the unknown is much more frightening. It is clear that her social paralysis is self-inflicted and reinforced by her beliefs. Perhaps it is the thought that her father cannot survive without her that keeps her from leaving. She expends herself and her earnings just to support him. In a way she is acting more like a wife or mother than like a daughter: "...she had to work hard both in the house and at business" (202), but her marriage to Frank would change all that. He offers to take her to Buenos Aires, where she could live a comfortable life, but she finally chooses not to go with him because of her attachment to the life she has known. She is paralyzed by her fear of change and her devotion to her family.

During the scene that depicts her mother's final moments, when the promise to keep the home together is made, Eveline muses that her mother's life is a "life of commonplace sacrifices closing in final craziness" (204). This describes Eveline's life as well. Her own commonplace sacrifice is staying in her home and tending to her father. To her, it is a necessary sacrifice for her family's sake not to take interest in her own future. Her final craziness happens when she tries to escape. In the final scene at the station, she "clutched the iron [railing] in frenzy" trying to hold on to the life she has known (205). Her decision could mark the end of her social existence. She will probably never have this kind of opportunity again. Even if the opportunity again were to arise, she would most likely act the same way.

It is obvious that religion plays a role in Eveline's decision as well. In his description of her home, Joyce includes a "coloured print of the promises made to Blessed Margaret Mary Alacoque" (201). This is a symbol of devotion to home and family in the Catholic Church. The promises that are made by Jesus himself include, "I will establish peace in their homes. / I will comfort them in all their afflictions. / I will be their secure refuge during life, and above all in death" (Gifford 49). Joyce refers to this in his narration because Eveline's promise to her mother parallels these promises. He does this to show how religion only increases the guilt felt by someone who leaves home to make a life for herself. Since Eveline's promise was to keep her family together, it becomes impossible for her to leave. In the final scene, she stands at the station, unable to board the boat: "she prayed to God to direct her, to show her what was her duty" (204). It is clear that she feels it is her duty to stay at home and give up her only chance at starting a life of her own.

There is great emphasis on the promise that Eveline made to her mother, "to keep the home together as long as she could" (204). This might be seen, metaphorically, as the people of Ireland promising to stay together as long as possible because their own country has been taken from them. Weakened by the famine and exploited by the British, the country was in shambles. Although Ireland did not have control of its own government, the people maintained collective unity.

During this time, one of the country's worst periods, people depended on each other to survive. Afterward, the people had trouble getting back on their feet and relied mostly on religion to guide them. Joyce reacted against this. He felt that people should get out of Ireland and writes that "Ireland is the old sow that eats her farrow" (Joyce, *Portrait* 220). He makes his feelings very clear in this story by drawing on Eveline's promise to her mother.

Throughout the story, Eveline is tormented by the thought of leaving her home, and it ultimately consumes her. Her home life is not at all desirable, yet she stays. It is a condition often depicted by Joyce in his stories: "[Joyce] expresses the fragmentation experienced by individuals unable to rely on old certainties, whether religious, economic, or political" (Werner 27). It is these certainties that Eveline and many others are unable to part with. Her faith and bond to her family help instill a fear of change that, for her, is too great to overcome.

One of the main reasons that many young adults still live at home is that they are dependent on the security and simplicity of being where they have always been. By living with their families, they know that they will never go hungry or worry about where they will sleep. They are secure in their surroundings. There may be the proud fear that their families cannot survive without them, and the belittling fear that they can't survive without their families. Perhaps it is one or both of these fears that influence Eveline's actions and ultimately control them.

[New Page]

Works Cited

Foster, Roy F. *Modern Ireland, 1600–1972*. London: Penguin, 1988. Print.

Gifford, Don. *Joyce Annotated*. Berkeley: U of California P, 1982. 48–52.
Print.

Joyce, James. "Eveline." *Exploring Literature*. Ed. Frank Madden. 5th ed.
New York: Longman, 2012. 201–05. Print.

---. *Portrait of the Artist as a Young Man*. New York: Penguin, 1987. Print.

Walzl, Florence L. "Dubliners: Women in Irish Society." *Women in Joyce*.
Ed. Suzette Hanke and Elaine Unkless. Champaign-Urbana: U of Illinois P,
1982. 31–54. Print.

Werner, Craig Hansen. *Dubliners: A Student's Companion to the Stories*.
Ed. Robert Lecker. Boston: Twayne, 1988. Print.

PART III

A THEMATIC
ANTHOLOGY

Family & Friends

Family & Friends
A DIALOGUE ACROSS HISTORY

Friends have all things in common.
— Plato, 428–348 BCE, *Dialogues*

He who has a thousand friends has not a / Friend to spare. / And he who has one enemy will meet him / Everywhere.
— Ali ibn-Abi-Talib, c. 602–661

Hold a true friend with both your hands.
— Nigerian proverb

In the misfortune of our best friends we often find something that is not displeasing.
— La Rochefouchaud, *Maxims,* 1665

It is impossible to please all the world and one's father.
— Jean de la Fontaine, 1668

I lay it down as fact that if all men knew what others say of them, there would not be four friends in the world.
— Blaise Pascal, *Pensées,* 1670

Fate chooses our relatives, we choose our friends.
— Jacques Delille, *Malheur et Pitie,* 1803

The only way to have a friend is to be one.
— Ralph Waldo Emerson, *Friendship,* 1841

A friend is a person with whom I may be sincere. Before him, I may think aloud.
— Ralph Waldo Emerson, *Friendship,* 1841

Give a little love to a child, and you get a great deal back.
— John Ruskin, *The Crown of Wild Olive,* 1866

Happy families are all alike; every unhappy family is unhappy in its own way.
— Leo Tolstoy, *Anna Karenina,* 1877

So long as we serve; so long as we are loved by others, I would almost say that we are indispensable; and no man is useless while he has a friend.
  —Robert Louis Stevenson, *Across the Plains,* 1892

The little world of childhood with its familiar surroundings is a model of the greater world. The more intensely the family has stamped its character upon the child, the more it will tend to feel and see its earlier miniature world again in the bigger world of adult life.
  —Carl Jung, *The Theory of Psychoanalysis,* 1913

Home is the place where, when you have to / go there, / They have to take you in.
  —Robert Frost, *The Death of the Hired Man,* 1914

Each friend represents a world in us, a world possibly not born until they arrive, and it is only by this meeting that a new world is born.
  —Anaïs Nin, 1937

The more people have studied different methods of bringing up children the more they have come to the conclusion that what good mothers and fathers instinctively feel like doing for their babies is the best after all.
  —Benjamin Spock, *The Common Sense Book of Baby and Child Care,* 1946

Don't walk in front of me, I may not follow / Don't walk behind me / I may not lead / Just walk beside me and be my friend.
  —Attributed to Albert Camus

If we were to see the family as a wealthy source of traditions, stories, characters and values, we might not feel so alone and abandoned to a life that has to be manufactured every day.
  —Thomas Moore, *Soul Mates,* 1994

Every parent knows that raising children requires bicycle pumps, Beanie babies, notebook paper, prayers, skill, and plain dumb luck. But what many of us don't ever come to grips with is this: we must take responsibility for the world our children inhabit. We make the world for them. We give it to them. And if we fail them, they will break our hearts ten different ways.
  —Amy Dickinson, *Time,* 1999

If you as parents cut corners, your children will too. If you lie, they will too. If you spend all your money on yourselves and tithe no portion of it for charities, colleges, churches, synagogues, and civic causes, your children won't either. And if parents snicker at racial and gender jokes, another generation will pass on the poison adults still have not had the courage to snuff out.
  —Marian Wright Edelman, 1993

FAMILY AND FRIENDS: EXPLORING YOUR OWN VALUES AND BELIEFS

A look at depictions of family life over the last fifty years shows us how much the public image of family has changed. It is a long journey from the stable, wise, supportive families of television shows of fifty years ago to the chaotic, unstable families depicted in current shows like *The Simpsons*. We live in an age that bombards us with traditional "family values" while urging our recovery from "dysfunctional family" experiences. Our families may be large and extend to distant relations or be as small as a single parent and child. Until we have the opportunity to form our own families, we don't have much choice about family membership. "Home," as Robert Frost writes, may be "the place where, when you have to / go there, / They have to take you in." And this same sense of responsibility may also compel us to love our brothers or sisters, even when we don't like them very much.

For many of us, friends are a chosen family. We rely on friends to provide the kind of stability, wisdom, and support that make us think of them as "family" in the most favorable sense of the word. We confide in our friends or ask for their help when we're in trouble, and we selflessly rush to help and comfort them when they are most in need.

Our families and friends can have a powerful effect on our lives. They influence and shape our values, our behavior, our aspirations. We may be happy in their company and so attached to them that we have difficulty pulling away. We may be unhappy and disconnected from them and yearn for the warmth we believe we're missing. How important have family and/or friends been in the formation of your beliefs and values? As we experience the issues of family and friends that we encounter in literature, we will naturally compare them to similar circumstances in our own lives.

READING AND WRITING ABOUT FAMILY AND FRIENDS

Exploring your beliefs and values and connecting your experience with what you read is an important first step toward our ultimate goal—an appreciation of literature and the ability to think and write critically about it. Critical analysis will require rereading and reflection, writing and revising, gathering evidence, and constructing a solid argument to support your responses.

At least one aspect of the many stories, poems, plays, and essays in this section is about the impact that family and/or friends have on characters: the heartbreaking father–son conflict over tradition and values in Chinua Achebe's short story "Marriage Is a Private Affair"; the realization and application of a gift handed down from his father in Li-Young Lee's poem "The Gift"; the struggle of the Younger family to realize their dreams in Lorraine Hansberry's *A Raisin in the Sun*; and the lifelong lessons learned by bell hooks in her essay "Inspired Eccentricity." The brief quotes that open this section also give you some idea of the number of compelling views that are connected to family and friends. Issues of parent–child tension, mutual support, loneliness, loyalty, comfort, personal growth, and parental responsibility head a long list of concerns. Any of these or other related issues might provide a fine topic for building an argument and writing an essay.

♦ FICTION ♦

Connecting Through Comparison: Sibling Relationships

The two stories that follow address a subtheme of this section: sibling relationships. In both stories, the narrator is a brother who is trying to help a troubled sibling. The Baldwin story is told from the point of view of an older brother, but it's a younger brother who narrates "The Red Convertible." Read and discussed together, these stories invite comparison and connections—not only with each other, but with similar experiences of your own.

James Baldwin [1924–1987]

James Baldwin grew up in poverty in Harlem with his mother, eight half-brothers and -sisters, and a stepfather whom he hated. He became a preacher at the age of fourteen, but after graduating from high school he left the ministry disillusioned. Turning to writing, he struggled for over ten years to complete his first novel, the autobiographical Go Tell It on the Mountain *(1953), a publication that instantly made Baldwin one of the most important American writers of his time. In his subsequent work, which included numerous novels, plays, and essays, Baldwin continually explored issues of racial and sexual identity and the civil rights movement, often writing of his own experiences of his family and Harlem. Unhappy with racial conditions in the United States, Baldwin spent most of his adult life in Paris, returning to the United States only occasionally.*

Sonny's Blues   [1957]

I read about it in the paper, in the subway, on my way to work. I read it, and I couldn't believe it, and I read it again. Then perhaps I just stared at it, at the newsprint spelling out his name, spelling out the story. I stared at it in the swinging lights of the subway car, and in the faces and bodies of the people, and in my own face, trapped in the darkness which roared outside.

It was not to be believed and I kept telling myself that, as I walked from the subway station to the high school. And at the same time I couldn't doubt it. I was scared, scared for Sonny. He became real to me again. A great block of ice got settled in my belly and kept melting there slowly all day long, while I taught my classes algebra. It was a special kind of ice. It kept melting, sending trickles of ice water all up and down my veins, but it never got less. Sometimes it hardened and seemed to expand until I felt my guts were going to come spilling out or that I was going to choke or scream. This would always be at a moment when I was remembering some specific thing Sonny had once said or done.

When he was about as old as the boys in my classes his face had been bright and open, there was a lot of copper in it; and he'd had wonderfully direct brown eyes, and great gentleness and privacy. I wondered what he looked like now. He had been picked up, the evening before, in a raid on an apartment downtown, for peddling and using heroin.

I couldn't believe it: but what I mean by that is that I couldn't find any room for it anywhere inside me. I had kept it outside me for a long time. I hadn't wanted to know. I had had suspicions, but I didn't name them, I kept putting them away. I told myself that Sonny was wild, but he wasn't crazy. And he'd always been a good boy, he hadn't ever turned hard or evil or disrespectful, the way kids can, so quick, so quick, especially in Harlem. I didn't want to believe that I'd ever see my brother going down, coming to nothing, all that light in his face gone out, in the condition I'd already seen so many others. Yet it had happened and here I was, talking about algebra to a lot of boys who might, every one of them for all I knew, be popping off needles every time they went to the head. Maybe it did more for them than algebra could.

5 I was sure that the first time Sonny had ever had horse,[1] he couldn't have been much older than these boys were now. These boys, now, were living as we'd been living then, they were growing up with a rush and their heads bumped abruptly against the low ceiling of their actual possibilities. They were filled with rage. All they really knew were two darknesses, the darkness of their lives, which was now closing in on them, and the darkness of the movies, which had blinded them to that other darkness, and in which they now, vindictively, dreamed, at once more together than they were at any other time, and more alone.

When the last bell rang, the last class ended, I let out my breath. It seemed I'd been holding it for all that time. My clothes were wet—I may have looked as though I'd been sitting in a steam bath, all dressed up, all afternoon. I sat alone in the classroom a long time. I listened to the boys outside, downstairs, shouting and cursing and laughing. Their laughter struck me for perhaps the first time. It was not the joyous laughter which—God knows why—one associates with children. It was mocking and insular, its intent was to denigrate. It was disenchanted, and in this, also, lay the authority of their curses. Perhaps I was listening to them because I was thinking about my brother and in them I heard my brother. And myself.

One boy was whistling a tune, at once very complicated and very simple, it seemed to be pouring out of him as though he were a bird, and it sounded very cool and moving through all that harsh, bright air, only just holding its own through all those other sounds.

I stood up and walked over to the window and looked down into the courtyard. It was the beginning of the spring and the sap was rising in the boys. A teacher passed through them every now and again, quickly, as though he or she couldn't wait to get out of that courtyard, to get those boys out of their sight and off their minds. I started collecting my stuff. I thought I'd better get home and talk to Isabel.

The courtyard was almost deserted by the time I got downstairs. I saw this boy standing in the shadow of a doorway, looking just like Sonny. I almost called his name. Then I saw that it wasn't Sonny, but somebody we used to know, a boy from around our block. He'd been Sonny's friend. He'd never been mine, having been too young for me, and, anyway, I'd never liked him. And now, even though he was a grown-up man, he still hung around that block, still spent hours on the street corners, was always high and raggy. I used to run into him from time to time

---

[1]**horse** heroin

and he'd often work around to asking me for a quarter or fifty cents. He always had some real good excuse, too, and I always gave it to him, I don't know why.

But now, abruptly, I hated him. I couldn't stand the way he looked at me, partly like a dog, partly like a cunning child. I wanted to ask him what the hell he was doing in the school courtyard.

He sort of shuffled over to me, and he said, "I see you got the papers. So you already know about it."

"You mean about Sonny? Yes, I already know about it. How come they didn't get you?"

He grinned. It made him repulsive and it also brought to mind what he'd looked like as a kid. "I wasn't there. I stay away from them people."

"Good for you." I offered him a cigarette and I watched him through the smoke. "You come all the way down here just to tell me about Sonny?"

"That's right." He was sort of shaking his head and his eyes looked strange, as though they were about to cross. The bright sun deadened his damp dark brown skin and it made his eyes look yellow and showed up the dirt in his kinked hair. He smelled funky. I moved a little away from him and I said, "Well, thanks. But I already know about it and I got to get home."

"I'll walk you a little ways," he said. We started walking. There were a couple of kids still loitering in the courtyard and one of them said goodnight to me and looked strangely at the boy beside me.

"What're you going to do?" he asked me. "I mean, about Sonny?"

"Look. I haven't seen Sonny for over a year, I'm not sure I'm going to do anything. Anyway, what the hell *can* I do?"

"That's right," he said quickly, "ain't nothing you can do. Can't much help old Sonny no more, I guess."

It was what I was thinking and so it seemed to me he had no right to say it.

"I'm surprised at Sonny, though," he went on—he had a funny way of talking, he looked straight ahead as though he were talking to himself—"I thought Sonny was a smart boy, I thought he was too smart to get hung."

"I guess he thought so too," I said sharply, "and that's how he got hung. And how about you? You're pretty goddamn smart, I bet."

Then he looked directly at me, just for a minute. "I ain't smart," he said. "If I was smart, I'd have reached for a pistol a long time ago."

"Look. Don't tell *me* your sad story, if it was up to me, I'd give you one." Then I felt guilty—guilty, probably, for never having supposed that the poor bastard *had* a story of his own, much less a sad one, and I asked, quickly, "What's going to happen to him now?"

He didn't answer this. He was off by himself some place. "Funny thing," he said, and from his tone we might have been discussing the quickest way to get to Brooklyn, "when I saw the papers this morning, the first thing I asked myself was if I had anything to do with it. I felt sort of responsible."

I began to listen more carefully. The subway station was on the corner, just before us, and I stopped. He stopped, too. We were in front of a bar and he ducked slightly, peering in, but whoever he was looking for didn't seem to be there. The juke box was blasting away with something black and bouncy and I half watched the barmaid as she danced her way from the juke box to her place behind the bar. And I watched her face as she laughingly responded to something someone said to her, still keeping time to the music. When she smiled one saw the little girl, one sensed the doomed, still-struggling woman beneath the battered face of the semiwhore.

"I never *give* Sonny nothing," the boy said finally, "but a long time ago I come to school high and Sonny asked me how it felt." He paused, I couldn't bear to watch him, I watched the barmaid, and I listened to the music which seemed to be causing the pavement to shake. "I told him it felt great." The music stopped, the barmaid paused and watched the juke box until the music began again. "It did."

All this was carrying me some place I didn't want to go. I certainly didn't want to know how it felt. It filled everything, the people, the houses, the music, the dark, quicksilver barmaid, with menace; and this menace was their reality.

"What's going to happen to him now?" I asked again.

30   "They'll send him away some place and they'll try to cure him." He shook his head. "Maybe he'll even think he's kicked the habit. Then they'll let him loose"—he gestured, throwing his cigarette into the gutter. "That's all."

"What do you mean, that's *all?*"

But I knew what he meant.

"I *mean,* that's *all.*" He turned his head and looked at me, pulling down the corners of his mouth. "Don't you know what I mean?" he asked, softly.

"How the hell *would* I know what you mean?" I almost whispered it, I don't know why.

35   "That's right," he said to the air, "how would *he* know what I mean?" He turned toward me again, patient and calm, and yet I somehow felt him shaking, shaking as though he were going to fall apart. I felt that ice in my guts again, the dread I'd felt all afternoon; and again I watched the barmaid, moving about the bar, washing glasses, and singing. "Listen. They'll let him out and then it'll just start all over again. That's what I mean."

"You mean—they'll let him out. And then he'll just start working his way back in again. You mean he'll never kick the habit. Is that what you mean?"

"That's right," he said, cheerfully. "*You* see what I mean."

"Tell me," I said at last, "why does he want to die? He must want to die, he's killing himself, why does he want to die?"

He looked at me in surprise. He licked his lips. "He don't want to die. He wants to live. Don't nobody want to die, ever."

40   Then I wanted to ask him—too many things. He could not have answered, or if he had, I could not have borne the answers. I started walking. "Well, I guess it's none of my business."

"It's going to be rough on old Sonny," he said. We reached the subway station. "This is your station?" he asked. I nodded. I took one step down. "Damn!" he said, suddenly. I looked up at him. He grinned again. "Damn it if I didn't leave all my money home. You ain't got a dollar on you, have you? Just for a couple of days, is all."

All at once something inside gave and threatened to come pouring out of me. I didn't hate him any more. I felt that in another moment I'd start crying like a child.

"Sure," I said. "Don't sweat." I looked in my wallet and didn't have a dollar, I only had a five. "Here," I said. "That hold you?"

He didn't look at it—he didn't want to look at it. A terrible closed look came over his face, as though he were keeping the number on the bill a secret from him and me. "Thanks," he said, and now he was dying to see me go. "Don't worry about Sonny. Maybe I'll write him or something."

45 "Sure," I said. "You do that. So long."

"Be seeing you," he said. I went on down the steps.

And I didn't write Sonny or send him anything for a long time. When I finally did, it was just after my little girl died, he wrote me back a letter which made me feel like a bastard.

Here's what he said:

Dear brother,

You don't know how much I needed to hear from you. I wanted to write you many a time but I dug how much I must have hurt you and so I didn't write. But now I feel like a man who's been trying to climb up out of some deep, real deep and funky hole and just saw the sun up there, outside. I got to get outside.

50 I can't tell you much about how I got here. I mean I don't know how to tell you. I guess I was afraid of something or I was trying to escape from something and you know I have never been very strong in the head (smile). I'm glad Mama and Daddy are dead and can't see what's happened to their son and I swear if I'd known what I was doing I would never have hurt you so, you and a lot of other fine people who were nice to me and who believed in me.

I don't want you to think it had anything to do with me being a musician. It's more than that. Or maybe less than that. I can't get anything straight in my head down here and I try not to think about what's going to happen to me when I get outside again. Sometime I think I'm going to flip and *never* get outside and sometime I think I'll come straight back. I tell you one thing, though, I'd rather blow my brains out than go through this again. But that's what they all say, so they tell me. If I tell you when I'm coming to New York and if you could meet me, I sure would appreciate it. Give my love to Isabel and the kids and I was sure sorry to hear about little Gracie. I wish I could be like Mama and say the Lord's will be done, but I don't know it seems to me that trouble is the one thing that never does get stopped and I don't know what good it does to blame it on the Lord. But maybe it does some good if you believe it.

Your brother,
Sonny

Then I kept in constant touch with him and I sent him whatever I could and I went to meet him when he came back to New York. When I saw him many things I thought I had forgotten came flooding back to me. This was because I had begun, finally, to wonder about Sonny, about the life that Sonny lived inside. This life, whatever it was, had made him older and thinner and it had deepened the distant stillness in which he had always moved. He looked very unlike my baby brother. Yet, when he smiled, when we shook hands, the baby brother I'd never known looked out from the depths of his private life, like an animal waiting to be coaxed into the light.

"How you been keeping?" he asked me.

"All right. And you?"

55   "Just fine." He was smiling all over his face. "It's good to see you again."

"It's good to see you."

The seven years' difference in our ages lay between us like a chasm: I wondered if these years would ever operate between us as a bridge. I was remembering, and it made it hard to catch my breath, that I had been there when he was born; and I had heard the first words he had ever spoken. When he started to walk, he walked from our mother straight to me. I caught him just before he fell when he took the first steps he ever took in this world.

"How's Isabel?"

"Just fine. She's dying to see you."

60   "And the boys?"

"They're fine, too. They're anxious to see their uncle."

"Oh, come on. You know they don't remember me."

"Are you kidding? Of course they remember you."

He grinned again. We got into a taxi. We had a lot to say to each other, far too much to know how to begin.

65   As the taxi began to move, I asked, "You still want to go to India?"

He laughed. "You still remember that. Hell, no. This place is Indian enough for me."

"It used to belong to them," I said.

And he laughed again. "They damn sure knew what they were doing when they got rid of it."

Years ago, when he was around fourteen, he'd been all hipped on the idea of going to India. He read books about people sitting on rocks, naked, in all kinds of weather, but mostly bad, naturally, and walking barefoot through hot coals and arriving at wisdom. I used to say that it sounded to me as though they were getting away from wisdom as fast as they could. I think he sort of looked down on me for that.

70   "Do you mind," he asked, "if we have the driver drive alongside the park? On the west side—I haven't seen the city in so long."

"Of course not," I said. I was afraid that I might sound as though I were humoring him, but I hoped he wouldn't take it that way.

So we drove along, between the green of the park and the stony, lifeless elegance of hotels and apartment buildings, toward the vivid, killing streets of our childhood. These streets hadn't changed, though housing projects jutted up out of them now like rocks in the middle of a boiling sea. Most of the houses in which we had grown up had vanished, as had the stores from which we had stolen, the basements in which we had first tried sex, the rooftops from which we had hurled tin cans and bricks. But houses exactly like the houses of our past yet dominated the landscape, boys exactly like the boys we once had been found themselves smothering in these houses, came down into the streets for light and air and found themselves encircled by disaster. Some escaped the trap, most didn't. Those who got out always left something of themselves behind, as some animals amputate a leg and leave it in the trap. It might be said, perhaps, that I had escaped, after all, I was a school teacher; or that Sonny had, he hadn't lived in Harlem for years. Yet, as the cab moved uptown through streets which seemed, with a rush, to darken with dark people, and as I covertly studied Sonny's face, it came to me that what we both were seeking through our separate cab windows was that part of ourselves which had been left behind. It's always at the hour of trouble and confrontation that the missing member aches.

We hit 110th Street and started rolling up Lenox Avenue. And I'd known this avenue all my life, but it seemed to me again, as it had seemed on the day I'd first heard about Sonny's trouble, filled with a hidden menace which was its very breath of life.

"We almost there," said Sonny.

75 "Almost." We were both too nervous to say anything more.

We live in a housing project. It hasn't been up long. A few days after it was up it seemed uninhabitably new, now, of course, it's already rundown. It looks like a parody of the good, clean, faceless life—God knows the people who live in it do their best to make it a parody. The beat-looking grass lying around isn't enough to make their lives green, the hedges will never hold out the streets, and they know it. The big windows fool no one, they aren't big enough to make space out of no space. They don't bother with the windows, they watch the TV screen instead. The playground is most popular with the children who don't play at jacks, or skip rope, or roller skate, or swing, and they can be found in it after dark. We moved in partly because it's not too far from where I teach, and partly for the kids; but it's really just like the houses in which Sonny and I grew up. The same things happen, they'll have the same things to remember. The moment Sonny and I started into the house I had the feeling that I was simply bringing him back into the danger he had almost died trying to escape.

Sonny has never been talkative. So I don't know why I was sure he'd be dying to talk to me when supper was over the first night. Everything went fine, the oldest boy remembered him, and the youngest boy liked him, and Sonny had remembered to bring something for each of them; and Isabel, who is really much nicer than I am, more open and giving, had gone to a lot of trouble about dinner and was genuinely glad to see him. And she's always been able to tease Sonny in a way that I haven't. It was nice to see her face so vivid again and to hear her laugh and watch her make Sonny laugh. She wasn't, or, anyway, she didn't seem to be, at all uneasy or embarrassed. She chatted as though there were no subject which had to be avoided and she got Sonny past his first, faint stiffness. And thank God she was there, for I was filled with that icy dread again. Everything I did seemed awkward to me, and everything I said sounded freighted with hidden meaning. I was trying to remember everything I'd heard about dope addiction and I couldn't help watching Sonny for signs. I wasn't doing it out of malice. I was trying to find out something about my brother. I was dying to hear him tell me he was safe.

"Safe!" my father grunted, whenever Mama suggested trying to move to a neighborhood which might be safer for children. "Safe, hell! Ain't no place safe for kids, nor nobody."

He always went on like this, but he wasn't, ever, really as bad as he sounded, not even on weekends, when he got drunk. As a matter of fact, he was always on the lookout for "something a little better," but he died before he found it. He died suddenly, during a drunken weekend in the middle of the war, when Sonny was fifteen. He and Sonny hadn't ever got on too well. And this was partly because Sonny was the apple of his father's eye. It was because he loved Sonny so much and was frightened for him, that he was always fighting with him. It doesn't do any good to fight with Sonny. Sonny just moves back, inside himself, where he can't be reached. But the principal reason that they never hit it off is that they were so much alike. Daddy was big and rough and loud-talking, just the opposite of Sonny, but they both had—that same privacy.

80   Mama tried to tell me something about this, just after Daddy died. I was home on leave from the army.

This was the last time I ever saw my mother alive. Just the same, this picture gets all mixed up in my mind with pictures I had of her when she was younger. The way I always see her is the way she used to be on a Sunday afternoon, say, when the old folks were talking after the big Sunday dinner. I always see her wearing pale blue. She'd be sitting on the sofa. And my father would be sitting in the easy chair, not far from her. And the living room would be full of church folks and relatives. There they sit, in chairs all around the living room, and the night is creeping up outside, but nobody knows it yet. You can see the darkness growing against the windowpanes and you hear the street noises every now and again, or maybe the jangling beat of a tambourine from one of the churches close by, but it's real quiet in the room. For a moment nobody's talking, but every face looks darkening, like the sky outside. And my mother rocks a little from the waist, and my father's eyes are closed. Everyone is looking at something a child can't see. For a minute they've forgotten the children. Maybe a kid is lying on the rug, half asleep. Maybe somebody's got a kid in his lap and is absentmindedly stroking the kid's head. Maybe there's a kid, quiet and big-eyed, curled up in a big chair in the corner. The silence, the darkness coming, and the darkness in the faces frightens the child obscurely. He hopes that the hand which strokes his forehead will never stop—will never die. He hopes that there will never come a time when the old folks won't be sitting around the living room, talking about where they've come from, and what they've seen, and what's happened to them and their kinfolk.

But something deep and watchful in the child knows that this is bound to end, is already ending. In a moment someone will get up and turn on the light. Then the old folks will remember the children and they won't talk any more that day. And when light fills the room, the child is filled with darkness. He knows that every time this happens he's moved just a little closer to that darkness out-side. The darkness outside is what the old folks have been talking about. It's what they've come from. It's what they endure. The child knows that they won't talk any more because if he knows too much about what's happened to *them,* he'll know too much too soon, about what's going to happen to *him*.

The last time I talked to my mother, I remember I was restless. I wanted to get out and see Isabel. We weren't married then and we had a lot to straighten out between us.

There Mama sat, in black, by the window. She was humming an old church song, *Lord, you brought me from a long ways off.* Sonny was out somewhere. Mama kept watching the streets.

85   "I don't know," she said, "if I'll ever see you again, after you go off from here. But I hope you'll remember the things I tried to teach you."

"Don't talk like that," I said, and smiled. "You'll be here a long time yet."

She smiled, too, but she said nothing. She was quiet for a long time. And I said, "Mama, don't you worry about nothing. I'll be writing all the time, and you be getting the checks...."

"I want to talk to you about your brother," she said, suddenly. "If anything happens to me he ain't going to have nobody to look out for him."

"Mama," I said, "ain't nothing going to happen to you *or* Sonny. Sonny's all right. He's a good boy and he's got good sense."

90   "It ain't a question of his being a good boy," Mama said, "nor of his having good sense. It ain't only the bad ones, nor yet the dumb ones that gets sucked un-der." She stopped, looking at me. "Your Daddy once had a brother," she said, and she smiled in a way that made me feel she was in pain. "You didn't never know that, did you?"

"No," I said, "I never knew that," and I watched her face.

"Oh, yes," she said, "your Daddy had a brother." She looked out of the window again. "I know you never saw your Daddy cry. But I did—many a time, through all these years."

I asked her, "What happened to his brother? How come nobody's ever talked about him?"

This was the first time I ever saw my mother look old.

95   "His brother got killed," she said, "when he was just a little younger than you are now. I knew him. He was a fine boy. He was maybe a little full of the devil, but he didn't mean nobody no harm."

Then she stopped and the room was silent, exactly as it had sometimes been on those Sunday afternoons. Mama kept looking out into the streets.

"He used to have a job in the mill," she said, "and, like all young folks, he just liked to perform on Saturday nights. Saturday nights, him and your father would drift around to different places, go to dances and things like that, or just sit around with people they knew, and your father's brother would sing, he had a fine voice, and play along with himself on his guitar. Well, this particular Sat-urday night, him and your father was coming home from some place, and they were both a little drunk and there was a moon that night, it was bright like day. Your father's brother was feeling kind of good, and he was whistling to himself, and he had his guitar slung over his shoulder. They was coming down a hill and beneath them was a road that turned off from the highway. Well, your father's brother, being always kind of frisky, decided to run down this hill, and he did, with that guitar banging and clanging behind him, and he ran across the road, and he was making water behind a tree. And your father was sort of amused at him and he was still coming down the hill, kind of slow. Then he heard a car motor and that same minute his brother stepped from behind the tree, into the road, in the moonlight. And he started to cross the road. And your father started to run down the hill, he says he don't know why. This car was full of white men. They was all drunk, and when they seen your father's brother they let out a great whoop and holler and they aimed the car straight at him. They was having fun, they just wanted to scare him, the way they do sometimes, you know. But they was drunk. And I guess the boy, being drunk, too, and scared, kind of lost his head. By the time he jumped it was too late. Your father says he heard his brother scream when the car rolled over him, and he heard the wood of that guitar when it give, and he heard them strings go flying, and he heard them white men shouting, and the car kept on a-going and it ain't stopped till this day. And, time your father got down the hill, his brother weren't nothing but blood and pulp."

Tears were gleaming on my mother's face. There wasn't anything I could say.

"He never mentioned it," she said, "because I never let him mention it before you children. Your Daddy was like a crazy man that night and for many a night thereafter. He says he never in his life seen anything as dark as that road after the lights of that car had gone away. Weren't nothing, weren't nobody on that road, just your Daddy and his brother and that busted guitar. Oh, yes. Your Daddy never did really get right again. Till the day he died he weren't sure but that every white man he saw was the man that killed his brother."

100   She stopped and took out her handkerchief and dried her eyes and looked at me.

"I ain't telling you all this," she said, "to make you scared or bitter or to make you hate nobody. I'm telling you this because you got a brother. And the world ain't changed."

I guess I didn't want to believe this. I guess she saw this in my face. She turned away from me, toward the window again, searching those streets.

"But I praise my Redeemer," she said at last, "that He called your Daddy home before me. I ain't saying it to throw no flowers at myself, but, I declare, it keeps me from feeling too cast down to know I helped your father get safely through this world. Your father always acted like he was the roughest, strongest man on earth. And everybody took him to be like that. But if he hadn't had *me* there—to see his tears!"

She was crying again. Still, I couldn't move. I said, "Lord, Lord, Mama, I didn't know it was like that."

105   "Oh, honey," she said, "there's a lot that you don't know. But you are going to find it out." She stood up from the window and came over to me. "You got to hold on to your brother," she said, "and don't let him fall, no matter what it looks like is happening to him and no matter how evil you gets with him. You

going to be evil with him many a time. But don't you forget what I told you, you hear?"

"I won't forget," I said. "Don't you worry, I won't forget. I won't let nothing happen to Sonny."

My mother smiled as though she were amused at something she saw in my face. Then, "You may not be able to stop nothing from happening. But you got to let him know you's *there.*"

Two days later I was married, and then I was gone. And I had a lot of things on my mind and I pretty well forgot my promise to Mama until I got shipped home on a special furlough for her funeral.

And, after the funeral, with just Sonny and me alone in the empty kitchen, I tried to find out something about him.

110   "What do you want to do?" I asked him.

"I'm going to be a musician," he said.

For he had graduated, in the time I had been away, from dancing to the juke box to finding out who was playing what, and what they were doing with it, and he had bought himself a set of drums.

"You mean, you want to be a drummer?" I somehow had the feeling that being a drummer might be all right for other people but not for my brother Sonny.

"I don't think," he said, looking at me very gravely, "that I'll ever be a good drummer. But I think I can play a piano."

115   I frowned. I'd never played the role of the older brother quite so seriously before, had scarcely ever, in fact, *asked* Sonny a damn thing. I sensed myself in the presence of something I didn't really know how to handle, didn't understand. So I made my frown a little deeper as I asked: "What kind of musician do you want to be?"

He grinned. "How many kinds do you think there are?"

"Be *serious,*" I said.

He laughed, throwing his head back, and then looked at me. "I *am* serious."

"Well, then, for Christ's sake, stop kidding around and answer a serious question. I mean, do you want to be a concert pianist, you want to play classical music and all that, or—or what?" Long before I finished he was laughing again. "For Christ's *sake,* Sonny!"

120   He sobered, but with difficulty. "I'm sorry. But you sound so—*scared!*" and he was off again.

"Well, you may think it's funny now, baby, but it's not going to be so funny when you have to make your living at it, let me tell you *that.*" I was furious because I knew he was laughing at me and I didn't know why.

No," he said, very sober now, and afraid, perhaps, that he'd hurt me, "I don't want to be a classical pianist. That isn't what interests me. I mean—" he paused, looking hard at me, as though his eyes would help me to understand, and then gestured helplessly, as though perhaps his hand would help—"I mean, I'll have a lot of studying to do, and I'll have to study *everything,* but, I mean, I want to play *with*—jazz musicians." He stopped. "I want to play jazz," he said.

Well, the word had never before sounded as heavy, as real, as it sounded that afternoon in Sonny's mouth. I just looked at him and I was probably frowning a real frown by this time. I simply couldn't see why on earth he'd want to spend his time hanging around nightclubs, clowning around on bandstands, while people pushed each other around a dance floor. It seemed—beneath him, somehow. I had never thought about it before, had never been forced to, but I suppose I had always put jazz musicians in a class with what Daddy called "good-time people."

"Are you *serious*?"

125   "Hell, *yes,* I'm serious."

He looked more helpless than ever, and annoyed, and deeply hurt.

I suggested, helpfully: "You mean—like Louis Armstrong?"

His face closed as though I'd struck him. "No. I'm not talking about none of that old-time, down home crap."

"Well, look, Sonny, I'm sorry, don't get mad. I just don't altogether get it, that's all. Name somebody—you know, a jazz musician you admire."

130   "Bird."

"Who?"

"Bird! Charlie Parker! Don't they teach you nothing in the goddamn army?"

I lit a cigarette. I was surprised and then a little amused to discover that I was trembling. "I've been out of touch," I said. "You'll have to be patient with me. Now. Who's this Parker character?"

"He's just one of the greatest jazz musicians alive," said Sonny, sullenly, his hands in his pockets, his back to me. "Maybe *the* greatest," he added, bitterly, "that's probably why you never heard of him."

135   "All right," I said, "I'm ignorant. I'm sorry. I'll go out and buy all the cat's records right away, all right?"

"It don't," said Sonny, with dignity, "make any difference to me. I don't care what you listen to. Don't do me no favors."

I was beginning to realize that I'd never seen him so upset before. With another part of my mind I was thinking that this would probably turn out to be one of those things kids go through and that I shouldn't make it seem important by pushing it too hard. Still, I didn't think it would do any harm to ask: "Doesn't all this take a lot of time? Can you make a living at it?"

He turned back to me and half leaned, half sat, on the kitchen table. "Everything takes time," he said, "and—well, yes, sure, I can make a living at it. But what I don't seem to be able to make you understand is that it's the only thing I want to do."

"Well, Sonny," I said, gently, "you know people can't always do exactly what they *want* to do—"

140   "*No,* I don't know that," said Sonny, surprising me. "I think people *ought* to do what they want to do, what else are they alive for?"

"You getting to be a big boy," I said desperately, "it's time you started thinking about your future."

"I'm thinking about my future," said Sonny, grimly. "I think about it all the time."

I gave up. I decided, if he didn't change his mind, that we could always talk about it later. "In the meantime," I said, "you got to finish school." We had already decided that he'd have to move in with Isabel and her folks. I knew this wasn't the ideal arrangement because Isabel's folks are inclined to be dicty and they hadn't especially wanted Isabel to marry me. But I didn't know what else to do. "And we have to get you fixed up at Isabel's."

There was a long silence. He moved from the kitchen table to the window. "That's a terrible idea. You know it yourself."

145   "Do you have a *better* idea?"

He just walked up and down the kitchen for a minute. He was as tall as I was. He had started to shave. I suddenly had the feeling that I didn't know him at all.

He stopped at the kitchen table and picked up my cigarettes. Looking at me with a kind of mocking, amused defiance, he put one between his lips. "You mind?"

"You smoking already?"

He lit the cigarette and nodded, watching me through the smoke. "I just wanted to see if I'd have the courage to smoke in front of you." He grinned and blew a great cloud of smoke to the ceiling. "It was easy." He looked at my face. "Come on, now. I bet you was smoking at my age, tell the truth."

150   I didn't say anything but the truth was on my face, and he laughed. But now there was something very strained in his laugh. "Sure. And I bet that ain't all you was doing."

He was frightening me a little. "Cut the crap," I said. "We already decided that you was going to go and live at Isabel's. Now what's got into you all of a sudden?"

"*You* decided it," he pointed out. "*I* didn't decide nothing." He stopped in front of me, leaning against the stove, arms loosely folded. "Look, brother. I don't want to stay in Harlem no more, I really don't." He was very earnest. He looked at me, then over toward the kitchen window. There was something in his eyes I'd never seen before, some thoughtfulness, some worry all his own. He rubbed the muscle of one arm. "It's time I was getting out of here."

"Where do you want to go, Sonny?"

"I want to join the army. Or the navy, I don't care. If I say I'm old enough, they'll believe me."

155   Then I got mad. It was because I was so scared. "You must be crazy. You goddamn fool, what the hell do you want to go and join the *army* for?"

"I just told you. To get out of Harlem."

"Sonny, you haven't even finished *school*. And if you really want to be a musician, how do you expect to study if you're in the *army*?"

He looked at me, trapped, and in anguish. "There's ways. I might be able to work out some kind of deal. Anyway, I'll have the G.I. Bill when I come out."

"*If* you come out." We stared at each other. "Sonny, please. Be reasonable. I know the setup is far from perfect. But we got to do the best we can."

160   "I ain't learning nothing in school," he said. "Even when I go." He turned away from me and opened the window and threw his cigarette out into the narrow alley. I watched his back. "At least, I ain't learning nothing you'd want me to learn." He slammed the window so hard I thought the glass would fly out, and turned back to me. "And I'm sick of the stink of these garbage cans!"

"Sonny," I said, "I know how you feel. But if you don't finish school now, you're going to be sorry later that you didn't." I grabbed him by the shoulders. "And you only got another year. It ain't so bad. And I'll come back and I swear I'll help you do *whatever* you want to do. Just try to put up with it till I come back. Will you please do that? For me?"

He didn't answer and he wouldn't look at me.

"Sonny. You hear me?"

He pulled away. "I hear you. But you never hear anything I say."

165   I didn't know what to say to that. He looked out of the window and then back at me. "OK," he said, and sighed. "I'll try."

Then I said, trying to cheer him up a little, "They got a piano at Isabel's. You can practice on it."

And as a matter of fact, it did cheer him up for a minute. "That's right," he said to himself. "I forgot that." His face relaxed a little. But the worry, the thoughtfulness, played on it still, the way shadows play on a face which is staring into the fire.

But I thought I'd never hear the end of that piano. At first, Isabel would write me, saying how nice it was that Sonny was so serious about his music and how, as soon as he came in from school, or wherever he had been when he was supposed to be at school, he went straight to that piano and stayed there until suppertime. And, after supper, he went back to that piano and stayed there until everybody went to bed. He was at the piano all day Saturday and all day Sunday. Then he bought a record player and started playing records. He'd play one record over and over again, all day long sometimes, and he'd improvise along with it on the piano. Or he'd play one section of the record, one chord, one change, one progression, then he'd do it on the piano. Then back to the record. Then back to the piano.

Well, I really don't know how they stood it. Isabel finally confessed that it wasn't like living with a person at all, it was like living with sound. And the sound didn't make any sense to her, didn't make any sense to any of them—naturally. They began, in a way, to be afflicted by this presence that was living in their home. It was as though Sonny were some sort of god, or monster. He moved in an atmosphere which wasn't like theirs at all. They fed him and he ate, he washed himself, he walked in and out of their door; he certainly wasn't nasty or unpleasant or rude, Sonny isn't any of those things; but it was as though he were all wrapped up in some cloud, some fire, some vision all his own; and there wasn't any way to reach him.

170   At the same time, he wasn't really a man yet, he was still a child, and they had to watch out for him in all kinds of ways. They certainly couldn't throw him out. Neither did they dare to make a great scene about that piano because even they dimly sensed, as I sensed, from so many thousands of miles away, that Sonny was at that piano playing for his life.

But he hadn't been going to school. One day a letter came from the school board and Isabel's mother got it—there had, apparently, been other letters but

Sonny had torn them up. This day, when Sonny came in, Isabel's mother showed him the letter and asked where he'd been spending his time. And she finally got it out of him that he'd been down in Greenwich Village, with musicians and other characters, in a white girl's apartment. And this scared her and she started to scream at him and what came up, once she began—though she denies it to this day—was what sacrifices they were making to give Sonny a decent home and how little he appreciated it.

Sonny didn't play the piano that day. By evening, Isabel's mother had calmed down but then there was the old man to deal with, and Isabel herself. Isabel says she did her best to be calm but she broke down and started crying. She says she just watched Sonny's face. She could tell, by watching him, what was happening with him. And what was happening was that they penetrated his cloud, they had reached him. Even if their fingers had been a thousand times more gentle than human fingers ever are, he could hardly help feeling that they had stripped him naked and were spitting on that nakedness. For he also had to see that his presence, that music, which was life or death to him, had been torture for them and that they had endured it, not at all for his sake, but only for mine. And Sonny couldn't take that. He can take it a little better today than he could then but he's still not very good at it and, frankly, I don't know anybody who is.

The silence of the next few days must have been louder than the sound of all the music ever played since time began. One morning, before she went to work, Isabel was in his room for something and she suddenly realized that all of his records were gone. And she knew for certain that he was gone. And he was. He went as far as the navy would carry him. He finally sent me a postcard from some place in Greece and that was the first I knew that Sonny was still alive. I didn't see him any more until we were both back in New York and the war had long been over.

He was a man by then, of course, but I wasn't willing to see it. He came by the house from time to time, but we fought almost every time we met. I didn't like the way he carried himself, loose and dreamlike all the time, and I didn't like his friends, and his music seemed to be merely an excuse for the life he led. It sounded just that weird and disordered.

175   Then we had a fight, a pretty awful fight, and I didn't see him for months. By and by I looked him up, where he was living, in a furnished room in the Village, and I tried to make it up. But there were lots of people in the room and Sonny just lay on his bed, and he wouldn't come downstairs with me, and he treated these other people as though they were his family and I weren't. So I got mad and then he got mad, and then I told him that he might just as well be dead as live the way he was living. Then he stood up and he told me not to worry about him any more in life, that he *was* dead as far as I was concerned. Then he pushed me to the door and the other people looked on as though nothing were happening, and he slammed the door behind me. I stood in the hallway, staring at the door. I heard somebody laugh in the room and then the tears came to my eyes. I started down the steps, whistling to keep from crying, I kept whistling to myself, *You going to need me, baby, one of these cold, rainy days.*

I read about Sonny's trouble in the spring. Little Grace died in the fall. She was a beautiful little girl. But she only lived a little over two years. She died of polio and she suffered. She had a slight fever for a couple of days, but it didn't seem like anything and we just kept her in bed. And we would certainly have called the doctor, but the fever dropped, she seemed to be all right. So we thought it had just been a cold. Then, one day, she was up, playing, Isabel was in the kitchen fixing lunch for the two boys when they'd come in from school, and she heard Grace fall down in the living room. When you have a lot of children you don't always start running when one of them falls, unless they start screaming or something. And, this time, Grace was quiet. Yet, Isabel says that when she heard that *thump* and then that silence, something happened in her to make her afraid. And she ran to the living room and there was little Grace on the floor, all twisted up, and the reason she hadn't screamed was that she couldn't get her breath. And when she did scream, it was the worst sound, Isabel says, that she'd ever heard in all her life, and she still hears it sometimes in her dreams. Isabel will sometimes wake me up with a low, moaning, strangled sound and I have to be quick to awaken her and hold her to me and where Isabel is weeping against me seems a mortal wound.

I think I may have written Sonny the very day that little Grace was buried. I was sitting in the living room in the dark, by myself, and I suddenly thought of Sonny. My trouble made his real.

One Saturday afternoon, when Sonny had been living with us, or, anyway, been in our house, for nearly two weeks, I found myself wandering aimlessly about the living room, drinking from a can of beer, and trying to work up the courage to search Sonny's room. He was out, he was usually out whenever I was home, and Isabel had taken the children to see their grandparents. Suddenly I was standing still in front of the living room window, watching Seventh Avenue. The idea of searching Sonny's room made me still. I scarcely dared to admit to myself what I'd be searching for. I didn't know what I'd do if I found it. Or if I didn't.

On the sidewalk across from me, near the entrance to a barbecue joint, some people were holding an old-fashioned revival meeting. The barbecue cook, wearing a dirty white apron, his conked hair reddish and metallic in the pale sun, and a cigarette between his lips, stood in the doorway, watching them. Kids and older people paused in their errands and stood there, along with some older men and a couple of very tough-looking women who watched everything that happened on the avenue, as though they owned it, or were maybe owned by it. Well, they were watching this, too. The revival was being carried on by three sisters in black, and a brother. All they had were their voices and their Bibles and a tambourine. The brother was testifying and while he testified two of the sisters stood together, seeming to say, amen, and the third sister walked around with the tambourine outstretched and a couple of people dropped coins into it. Then the brother's testimony ended and the sister who had been taking up the collection dumped the coins into her palm and transferred them to the pocket of her long black robe. Then she raised both hands, striking the tambourine against the air, and then against one hand, and she started to sing. And the two other sisters and the brother joined in.

180   It was strange, suddenly, to watch, though I had been seeing these street meetings all my life. So, of course, had everybody else down there. Yet, they paused and watched and listened and I stood still at the window. *"Tis the old ship of Zion,"* they sang, and the sister with the tambourine kept a steady, jangling beat, *"it has rescued many a thousand!"* Not a soul under the sound of their voices was hearing this song for the first time, not one of them had been rescued. Nor had they seen much in the way of rescue work being done around them. Neither did they especially believe in the holiness of the three sisters and the brother, they knew too much about them, knew where they lived, and how. The woman with the tambourine, whose voice dominated the air, whose face was bright with joy, was divided by very little from the woman who stood watching her, a cigarette between her heavy, chapped lips, her hair a cuckoo's nest, her face scarred and swollen from many beatings, and her black eyes glittering like coal. Perhaps they both knew this, which was why, when, as rarely, they addressed each other, they addressed each other as Sister. As the singing filled the air the watching, listening faces underwent a change, the eyes focusing on something within; the music seemed to soothe a poison out of them; and time seemed, nearly, to fall away from the sullen, belligerent, battered faces, as though they were fleeing back to their first condition, while dreaming of their last. The barbecue cook half shook his head and smiled, and dropped his cigarette and disappeared into his joint. A man fumbled in his pockets for change and stood holding it in his hand impatiently, as though he had just remembered a pressing appointment further up the avenue. He looked furious. Then I saw Sonny, standing on the edge of the crowd. He was carrying a wide, flat notebook with a green cover, and it made him look, from where I was standing, almost like a schoolboy. The coppery sun brought out the copper in his skin, he was very faintly smiling, standing very still. Then the singing stopped, the tambourine turned into a collection plate again. The furious man dropped in his coins and vanished, so did a couple of the women, and Sonny dropped some change in the plate, looking directly at the woman with a little smile. He started across the avenue, toward the house. He has a slow, loping walk, something like the way Harlem hipsters walk, only he's imposed on this his own half-beat. I had never really noticed it before.

I stayed at the window, both relieved and apprehensive. As Sonny disappeared from my sight, they began singing again. And they were still singing when his key turned in the lock.

"Hey," he said.

"Hey, yourself. You want some beer?"

"No. Well, maybe." But he came up to the window and stood beside me, looking out. "What a warm voice," he said.

185   They were singing *If I could only hear my mother pray again!*

"Yes," I said, "and she can sure beat that tambourine."

"But what a terrible song," he said, and laughed. He dropped his notebook on the sofa and disappeared into the kitchen. "Where's Isabel and the kids?"

"I think they went to see their grandparents. You hungry?"

"No." He came back into the living room with his can of beer. "You want to come some place with me tonight?"

190   I sensed, I don't know how, that I couldn't possibly say no. "Sure. Where?"

He sat down on the sofa and picked up his notebook and started leafing through it. "I'm going to sit in with some fellows in a joint in the Village."

"You mean, you're going to play, tonight?"

"That's right." He took a swallow of his beer and moved back to the window. He gave me a sidelong look. "If you can stand it."

"I'll try," I said.

195   He smiled to himself and we both watched as the meeting across the way broke up. The three sisters and the brother, heads bowed, were singing *God be with you till we meet again*. The faces around them were very quiet. Then the song ended. The small crowd dispersed. We watched the three women and the lone man walk slowly up the avenue.

"When she was singing before," said Sonny, abruptly, "her voice reminded me for a minute of what heroin feels like sometimes—when it's in your veins. It makes you feel sort of warm and cool at the same time. And distant. And—and sure." He sipped his beer, very deliberately not looking at me. I watched his face. "It makes you feel—in control. Sometimes you've got to have that feeling."

"Do you?" I sat down slowly in the easy chair.

"Sometimes." He went to the sofa and picked up his notebook again. "Some people do."

"In order," I asked, "to play?" And my voice was very ugly, full of contempt and anger.

200   "Well"—he looked at me with great, troubled eyes, as though, in fact, he hoped his eyes would tell me things he could never otherwise say—"they *think* so. And *if* they think so—!"

"And what do *you* think?" I asked.

He sat on the sofa and put his can of beer on the floor. "I don't know," he said, and I couldn't be sure if he were answering my question or pursuing his thoughts. His face didn't tell me. "It's not so much to *play*. It's to *stand* it, to be able to make it at all. On any level." He frowned and smiled: "In order to keep from shaking to pieces."

"But these friends of yours," I said, "they seem to shake themselves to pieces pretty goddamn fast."

"Maybe." He played with the notebook. And something told me that I should curb my tongue, that Sonny was doing his best to talk, that I should listen. "But of course you only know the ones that've gone to pieces. Some don't—or at least they haven't *yet* and that's just about all *any* of us can say." He paused. "And then there are some who just live, really, in hell, and they know it and they see what's happening and they go right on. I don't know." He sighed, dropped the notebook, folded his arms. "Some guys, you can tell from the way they play, they on something *all* the time. And you can see that, well, it makes something real for them. But of course," he picked up his beer from the floor and sipped it and put the can down again, "they *want* to, too, you've got to see that. Even some of them that say they don't—*some*, not all."

205   "And what about you?" I asked—I couldn't help it. "What about you? Do *you* want to?"

He stood up and walked to the window and remained silent for a long time. Then he sighed. "Me," he said. Then: "While I was downstairs before, on my way here, listening to that woman sing, it struck me all of a sudden how much suffering she must have had to go through—to sing like that. It's *repulsive* to think you have to suffer that much."

I said: "But there's no way not to suffer—is there, Sonny?"

"I believe not," he said and smiled, "but that's never stopped anyone from trying." He looked at me. "Has it?" I realized, with this mocking look, that there stood between us, forever, beyond the power of time or forgiveness, the fact that I had held silence—so long!—when he had needed human speech to help him. He turned back to the window. "No, there's no way not to suffer. But you try all kinds of ways to keep from drowning in it, to keep on top of it, and to make it seem—well, like *you*. Like you did something, all right, and now you're suffering for it. You know?" I said nothing. "Well you know," he said, impatiently, "Why *do* people suffer? Maybe it's better to do something to give it a reason, *any* reason."

"But we just agreed," I said, "that there's no way not to suffer. Isn't it better, then, just to—take it?"

210   "But nobody just takes it," Sonny cried, "that's what I'm telling you! *Everybody* tries not to. You're just hung up on the *way* some people try—it's not *your* way!"

The hair on my face began to itch, my face felt wet. "That's not true," I said, "that's not true. I don't give a damn what other people do, I don't even care how they suffer. I just care how *you* suffer." And he looked at me. "Please believe me," I said, "I don't want to see you—die—trying not to suffer."

"I won't," he said, flatly, "die trying not to suffer. At least, not any faster than anybody else."

"But there's no need," I said, trying to laugh, "is there? in killing yourself."

I wanted to say more, but I couldn't. I wanted to talk about will power and how life could be—well, beautiful. I wanted to say that it was all within; but was it? or, rather, wasn't that exactly the trouble? And I wanted to promise that I would never fail him again. But it would all have sounded—empty words and lies.

215   So I made the promise to myself and prayed that I would keep it.

"It's terrible sometimes, inside," he said, "that's what's the trouble. You walk these streets, black and funky and cold, and there's not really a living ass to talk to, and there's nothing shaking, and there's no way of getting it out—that storm inside. You can't talk it and you can't make love with it, and when you finally try to get with it and play it, you realize *nobody's* listening. So *you've* got to listen. You got to find a way to listen."

And then he walked away from the window and sat on the sofa again, as though all the wind had suddenly been knocked out of him. "Sometimes you'll do *anything* to play, even cut your mother's throat." He laughed and looked at me. "Or your brother's." Then he sobered. "Or your own." Then: "Don't worry. I'm all right now and I think I'll *be* all right. But I can't forget where I've been.

I don't mean just the physical place I've been, I mean where I've *been*. And *what* I've been."

"What have you been, Sonny?" I asked.

He smiled—but sat sideways on the sofa, his elbow resting on the back, his fingers playing with his mouth and chin, not looking at me. "I've been something I didn't recognize, didn't know I could be. Didn't know anybody could be." He stopped, looking inward, looking helplessly young, looking old. "I'm not talking about it now because I feel *guilty* or anything like that—maybe it would be better if I did, I don't know. Anyway, I can't really talk about it. Not to you, not to anybody," and now he turned and faced me. "Sometimes, you know, and it was actually when I was most *out* of the world, I felt that I was in it, that I was *with* it, really, and I could play or I didn't really have to *play,* it just came out of me, it was there. And I don't know how I played, thinking about it now, but I know I did awful things, those times, sometimes, to people. Or it wasn't that I *did* anything to them—it was that they weren't real." He picked up the beer can; it was empty; he rolled it between his palms: "And other times—well, I needed a fix, I needed to find a place to lean, I needed to clear a space to *listen*—and I couldn't find it, and I—went crazy, I did terrible things to *me,* I was terrible *for* me." He began pressing the beer can between his hands, I watched the metal begin to give. It glittered, as he played with it, like a knife, and I was afraid he would cut himself, but I said nothing. "Oh well. I can never tell you. I was all by myself at the bottom of something, stinking and sweating and crying and shaking, and I smelled it, you know? *my* stink, and I thought I'd die if I couldn't get away from it and yet, all the same, I knew that everything I was doing was just locking me in with it. And I didn't know," he paused, still flattening the beer can, "I didn't know, I still *don't* know, something kept telling me that maybe it was good to smell your own stink, but I didn't think that *that* was what I'd been trying to do— and—who can stand it?" and he abruptly dropped the ruined beer can, looking at me with a small, still smile, and then rose, walking to the window as though it were the lodestone rock. I watched his face, he watched the avenue. "I couldn't tell you when Mama died—but the reason I wanted to leave Harlem so bad was to get away from drugs. And then, when I ran away, that's what I was running from—really. When I came back, nothing had changed, I hadn't changed, I was just—older." And he stopped, drumming with his fingers on the windowpane. The sun had vanished, soon darkness would fall. I watched his face. "It can come again," he said, almost as though speaking to himself. Then he turned to me. "It can come again," he repeated. "I just want you to know that."

220 "All right," I said, at last. "So it can come again. All right."

He smiled, but the smile was sorrowful. "I had to try to tell you," he said.

"Yes," I said. "I understand that."

"You're my brother," he said, looking straight at me, and not smiling at all.

"Yes," I repeated, "yes. I understand that."

225 He turned back to the window, looking out. "All that hatred down there," he said, "all that hatred and misery and love. It's a wonder it doesn't blow the avenue apart."

We went to the only nightclub on a short, dark street, downtown. We squeezed through the narrow, chattering, jam-packed bar to the entrance of the big room, where the bandstand was. And we stood there for a moment, for the lights were very dim in this room and we couldn't see. Then, "Hello, boy," said a voice and an enormous black man, much older than Sonny or myself, erupted out of all that atmospheric lighting and put an arm around Sonny's shoulder. "I been sitting right here," he said, "waiting for you."

He had a big voice, too, and heads in the darkness turned toward us.

Sonny grinned and pulled a little away, and said, "Creole, this is my brother. I told you about him."

Creole shook my hand. "I'm glad to meet you, son," he said, and it was clear that he was glad to meet me *there,* for Sonny's sake. And he smiled, "You got a real musician in *your* family," and he took his arm from Sonny's shoulder and slapped him, lightly, affectionately, with the back of his hand.

230   "Well. Now I've heard it all," said a voice behind us. This was another musician, and a friend of Sonny's, a coal-black, cheerful-looking man, built close to the ground. He immediately began confiding to me, at the top of his lungs, the most terrible things about Sonny, his teeth gleaming like a lighthouse and his laugh coming up out of him like the beginning of an earthquake. And it turned out that everyone at the bar knew Sonny, or almost everyone; some were musicians, working there, or nearby, or not working, some were simply hangers-on, and some were there to hear Sonny play. I was introduced to all of them and they were all very polite to me. Yet, it was clear that, for them, I was only Sonny's brother. Here, I was in Sonny's world. Or, rather: his kingdom. Here, it was not even a question that his veins bore royal blood.

They were going to play soon and Creole installed me, by myself, at a table in a dark corner. Then I watched them, Creole, and the little black man, and Sonny, and the others, while they horsed around, standing just below the bandstand. The light from the bandstand spilled just a little short of them and, watching them laughing and gesturing and moving about, I had the feeling that they, nevertheless, were being most careful not to step into that circle of light too suddenly: that if they moved into the light too suddenly, without thinking, they would perish in flame. Then, while I watched, one of them, the small, black man, moved into the light and crossed the bandstand and started fooling around with his drums. Then—being funny and being, also, extremely ceremonious—Creole took Sonny by the arm and led him to the piano. A woman's voice called Sonny's name and a few hands started clapping. And Sonny, also being funny and being ceremonious, and so touched, I think, that he could have cried, but neither hiding it nor showing it, riding it like a man, grinned, and put both hands to his heart and bowed from the waist.

Creole then went to the bass fiddle and a lean, very bright-skinned brown man jumped up on the bandstand and picked up his horn. So there they were, and the atmosphere on the bandstand and in the room began to change and tighten. Someone stepped up to the microphone and announced them. Then there were all kinds of murmurs. Some people at the bar shushed others. The waitress ran around, frantically getting in the last orders, guys and chicks got closer to each other, and the lights on the bandstand, on the quartet, turned to a kind of indigo. Then they all looked different there. Creole looked about him for the last time, as though he were making certain that all his chickens were in the coop, and then he—jumped and struck the fiddle. And there they were.

All I know about music is that not many people ever really hear it. And even then, on the rare occasions when something opens within, and the music enters, what we mainly hear, or hear corroborated, are personal, private, vanishing evocations. But the man who creates the music is hearing something else, is dealing with the roar rising from the void and imposing order on it as it hits the air. What is evoked in him, then, is of another order, more terrible because it has no words, and triumphant, too, for that same reason. And his triumph, when he triumphs, is ours. I just watched Sonny's face. His face was troubled, he was working hard, but he wasn't with it. And I had the feeling that, in a way, everyone on the bandstand was waiting for him, both waiting for him and pushing him along. But as I began to watch Creole, I realized that it was Creole who held them all back. He had them on a short rein. Up there, keeping the beat with his whole body, wailing on the fiddle, with his eyes half closed, he was listening to everything, but he was listening to Sonny. He was having a dialogue with Sonny. He wanted Sonny to leave the shoreline and strike out for the deep water. He was Sonny's witness that deep water and drowning were not the same thing—he had been there, and he knew. And he wanted Sonny to know. He was waiting for Sonny to do the things on the keys which would let Creole know that Sonny was in the water.

And, while Creole listened, Sonny moved, deep within, exactly like someone in torment. I had never before thought of how awful the relationship must be between the musician and his instrument. He has to fill it, this instrument, with the breath of life, his own. He has to make it do what he wants it to do. And a piano is just a piano. It's made out of so much wood and wires and little hammers and big ones, and ivory. While there's only so much you can do with it, the only way to find this out is to try; to try and make it do everything.

235   And Sonny hadn't been near a piano for over a year. And he wasn't on much better terms with his life, not the life that stretched before him now. He and the piano stammered, started one way, got scared, stopped; started another way, panicked, marked time, started again; then seemed to have found a direction, panicked again, got stuck. And the face I saw on Sonny I'd never seen before. Everything had been burned out of it, and, at the same time, things usually hidden were being burned in, by the fire and fury of the battle which was occurring in him up there.

Yet, watching Creole's face as they neared the end of the first set, I had the feeling that something had happened, something I hadn't heard. Then they finished, there was scattered applause, and then, without an instant's warning, Creole started into something else, it was almost sardonic, it was *Am I Blue*. And, as though he commanded, Sonny began to play. Something began to happen. And Creole let out the reins. The dry, low, black man said something awful on the drums, Creole answered, and the drums talked back. Then the horn insisted, sweet and high, slightly detached perhaps, and Creole listened, commenting now and then, dry, and driving, beautiful and calm and old. Then they all came together again, and Sonny was part of the family again. I could tell this from his face. He seemed to have found, right there beneath his fingers, a damn brand-new piano. It seemed that he couldn't get over it. Then, for awhile, just being happy with Sonny, they seemed to be agreeing with him that brand-new pianos certainly were a gas.

Then Creole stepped forward to remind them that what they were playing was the blues. He hit something in all of them, he hit something in me, myself, and the music tightened and deepened, apprehension began to beat the air. Creole began to tell us what the blues were all about. They were not about anything very new. He and his boys up there were keeping it new, at the risk of ruin, destruction, madness, and death, in order to find new ways to make us listen. For, while the tale of how we suffer, and how we are delighted, and how we may triumph is never new, it always must be heard. There isn't any other tale to tell, it's the only light we've got in all this darkness.

And this tale, according to that face, that body, those strong hands on those strings, has another aspect in every country, and a new depth in every generation. Listen, Creole seemed to be saying, listen. Now these are Sonny's blues. He made the little black man on the drums know it, and the bright, brown man on the horn. Creole wasn't trying any longer to get Sonny in the water. He was wishing him Godspeed. Then he stepped back, very slowly, filling the air with the immense suggestion that Sonny speak for himself.

Then they all gathered around Sonny and Sonny played. Every now and again one of them seemed to say, amen. Sonny's fingers filled the air with life, his life. But that life contained so many others. And Sonny went all the way back, he really began with the spare, flat statement of the opening phrase of the song. Then he began to make it his. It was very beautiful because it wasn't hurried and it was no longer a lament. I seemed to hear with what burning he had made it his, with what burning we had yet to make it ours, how we could cease lamenting. Freedom lurked around us and I understood, at last, that he could help us to be free if we would listen, that he would never be free until we did. Yet, there was no battle in his face now. I heard what he had gone through, and would continue to go through until he came to rest in earth. He had made it his: that long line, of which we knew only Mama and Daddy. And he was giving it back, as everything must be given back, so that, passing through death, it can live forever. I saw my mother's face again, and felt, for the first time, how the stones of the road she had walked on must have bruised her feet. I saw the moonlit road where my father's brother died. And it brought something else back to me, and carried me past it. I saw my little girl again and felt Isabel's tears again, and I felt my own tears begin to rise. And I was yet aware that this was only a moment, that the world waited outside, as hungry as a tiger, and that trouble stretched above us, longer than the sky.

240   Then it was over. Creole and Sonny let out their breath, both soaking wet, and grinning. There was a lot of applause and some of it was real. In the dark, the girl came by and I asked her to take drinks to the bandstand. There was a long pause, while they talked up there in the indigo light and after awhile I saw the girl put a Scotch and milk on top of the piano for Sonny. He didn't seem to notice it, but just before they started playing again, he sipped from it and looked toward me, and

nodded. Then he put it back on top of the piano. For me, then, as they began to play again, it glowed and shook above my brother's head like the very cup of trembling.

LOUISE ERDRICH [B. 1954]

The daughter of a Chippewa Indian mother and a German-American father, Louise Erdrich was raised in Wahpeton, North Dakota, near the Turtle Mountain Reservation. Her parents both worked in the Bureau of Indian Affairs boarding school. From an early age, she was encouraged to write stories (she says: "My father used to give me a nickel for every story I wrote"). Following graduation from Dartmouth College in 1976, she earned an M.A. _____ *University in 1979. Her works includ* _____ *expanded edition in 1993);* The Beet Queen *(19* _____ *f Columbus (1991), which she coauthored with h* _____ The Bingo Palace *(1994);* The Antelope Wife *(19* _____ *Club (2003);* The Painted Drum *(2005); and* The P _____ *recent novel,* Shadow Tag, *was published in 2010.*

THE RED CONVERTIBLE   [1984]

Lyman Lamartine

I was the first one to drive a conve _____ course it was red, a red Olds. I owned that car a _____ or. We owned it together until his boots filled w _____ e bought out my share. Now Henry owns the wh _____ Lyman (that's myself), Lyman walks everywhere _____

How did I earn enough money _____ My own talent was I could always make money. _____ hippewa. From the first I was different that way, a _____ e only kid they let in the American Legion Hall to _____ Christmas I sold spiritual bouquets for the mission door to door. The nuns let me ___ep a percentage. Once I started, it seemed the more money I made the easier the money came. Everyone encouraged it. When I was fifteen I got a job washing dishes at the Joliet Café, and that was where my first big break happened.

It wasn't long before I was promoted to busing tables, and then the order-order cook quit and I was hired to take her place. No sooner than you know it I was managing the Joliet. The rest is history. I went on managing. I soon became part owner, and of course there was no stopping me then. It wasn't long before the whole thing was mine.

After I'd owned the Joliet for one year, it blew over in the worst tornado ever seen around here. The whole operation was smashed to bits. A total loss. The fryalator was up in a tree, the grill torn in half like it was paper. I was only sixteen. I had it all in my mother's name, and I lost it quick, but before I lost it

I had every one of my relatives, and their relatives, to dinner, and I also bought that red Olds I mentioned, along with Henry.

5   The first time we saw it! I'll tell you when we first saw it. We had gotten a ride up to Winnipeg, and both of us had money. Don't ask me why, because we never mentioned a car or anything, we just had all our money. Mine was cash, a big bank-roll from the Joliet's insurance. Henry had two checks—a week's extra pay for being laid off, and his regular check from the Jewel Bearing Plant.

We were walking down Portage anyway, seeing the sights, when we saw it. There it was, parked, large as life. Really as *if* it was alive. I thought of the word *repose,* because the car wasn't simply stopped, parked, or whatever. That car re-posed, calm and gleaming, a FOR SALE sign in its left front window. Then, before we had thought it over at all, the car belonged to us and our pockets were empty. We had just enough money for gas back home.

We went places in that car, me and Henry. We took off driving all one whole summer. We started off toward the Little Knife River and Mandaree in Fort Berthold and then we found ourselves down in Wakpala somehow, and then suddenly we were over in Montana on the Rocky Boy, and yet the summer was not even half over. Some people hang on to details when they travel, but we didn't let them bother us and just lived our everyday lives here to there.

I do remember this one place with willows. I remember I laid under those trees and it was comfortable. So comfortable. The branches bent down all around me like a tent or a stable. And quiet, it was quiet, even though there was a pow-wow close enough so I could see it going on. The air was not too still, not too windy either. When the dust rises up and hangs in the air around the dancers like that, I feel good. Henry was asleep with his arms thrown wide. Later on, he woke up and we started driving again. We were somewhere in Montana, or maybe on the Blood Reserve—it could have been anywhere. Anyway it was where we met the girl.

All her hair was in buns around her ears, that's the first thing I noticed about her. She was posed alongside the road with her arm out, so we stopped. That girl was short, so short her lumber shirt looked comical on her, like a nightgown. She had jeans on and fancy moccasins and she carried a little suitcase.

10   "Hop on in," says Henry. So she climbs in between us.

"We'll take you home," I says. "Where do you live?"

"Chicken," she says.

"Where the hell's that?" I ask her.

"Alaska."

15   "Okay," says Henry, and we drive.

We got up there and never wanted to leave. The sun doesn't truly set there in summer, and the night is more of soft dusk. You might doze off, sometimes, but be-fore you know it you're up again, like an animal in nature. You never feel like you have to sleep hard or put away the world. And things would grow up there. One day just dirt or moss, the next day flowers and long grass. The girl's name was Susy. Her family really took to us. They fed us and put us up. We had our own tent to live in by their house, and the kids would be in and out of there all day and night. They couldn't get over me and Henry being brothers, we looked so different. We told them we know we had the same mother, anyway.

One night Susy came in to visit us. We sat around in the tent talking of this and that. The season was changing. It was getting darker by that time, and the cold was even getting just a little mean. I told her it was time for us to go. She stood up on a chair.

"You never seen my hair," Susy said.

That was true. She was standing on a chair, but still, when she unclipped her buns the hair reached all the way to the ground. Our eyes opened. You couldn't tell how much hair she had when it was rolled up so neatly. Then my brother Henry did something funny. He went up to the chair and said, "Jump on my shoulders." So she did that, and her hair reached down past his waist, and he started twirling, this way and that, so her hair was flung out from side to side.

20   "I always wondered what it was like to have long pretty hair," Henry says. Well we laughed. It was a funny sight, the way he did it. The next morning we got up and took leave of those people.

On to greener pastures, as they say. It was down through Spokane and across Idaho then Montana and very soon we were racing the weather right along under the Canadian border through Columbus, Des Lacs, and then we were in Bottineau County and soon home. We'd made most of the trip, that summer, without putting up the car hood at all. We got home just in time, it turned out, for the army to remember Henry had signed up to join it.

I don't wonder that the army was so glad to get my brother that they turned him into a Marine. He was built like a brick outhouse anyway. We liked to tease him that they really wanted him for his Indian nose. He had a nose big and sharp as a hatchet, like the nose on Red Tomahawk, the Indian who killed Sitting Bull, whose profile is on signs all along the North Dakota highways. Henry went off to training camp, came home once during Christmas, then the next thing you know we got an overseas letter from him. It was 1970, and he said he was stationed up in the northern hill country. Whereabouts I did not know. He wasn't such a hot letter writer, and only got off two before the enemy caught him. I could never keep it straight, which direction those good Vietnam soldiers were from.

I wrote him back several times, even though I didn't know if those letters would get through. I kept him informed all about the car. Most of the time I had it up on blocks in the yard or half taken apart, because that long trip did a hard job on it under the hood.

I always had good luck with numbers, and never worried about the draft myself. I never even had to think about what my number was. But Henry was never lucky in the same way as me. It was at least three years before Henry came home. By then I guess the whole war was solved in the government's mind, but for him it would keep on going. In those years I'd put his car into almost perfect shape. I always thought of it as his car while he was gone, even though when he left he said, "Now it's yours," and threw me his key.

25   "Thanks for the extra key," I'd said. "I'll put it up in your drawer just in case I need it." He laughed.

When he came home, though, Henry was very different, and I'll say this: the change was no good. You could hardly expect him to change for the better, I know. But he was quiet, so quiet, and never comfortable sitting still anywhere but always up and moving around. I thought back to times we'd sat still for whole afternoons, never moving a muscle, just shifting our weight along the ground, talking to whoever sat with us, watching things. He'd always had a joke, then, too, and now you couldn't get him to laugh, or when he did it was more the sound of a man choking, a sound that stopped up the throats of other people around him. They got to leaving him alone most of the time, and I didn't blame them. It was a fact: Henry was jumpy and mean.

I'd bought a color TV set for my mom and the rest of us while Henry was away. Money still came very easy. I was sorry I'd ever bought it though, because of Henry. I was also sorry I'd bought color, because with black-and-white pictures seem older and farther away. But what are you going to do? He sat in front of it, watching it, and that was the only time he was completely still. But it was the kind of stillness that you see in a rabbit when it freezes and before it will bolt. He was not easy. He sat in his chair gripping the armrests with all his might, as if the chair itself was moving at a high speed and if he let go at all he would rocket forward and maybe crash right through the set.

Once I was in the room watching TV with Henry and I heard his teeth click at something. I looked over, and he'd bitten through his lip. Blood was going down his chin. I tell you right then I wanted to smash that tube to pieces. I went over to it but Henry must have known what I was up to. He rushed from his chair and shoved me out of the way, against the wall. I told myself he didn't know what he was doing.

My mom came in, turned the set off real quiet, and told us she had made something for supper. So we went and sat down. There was still blood going down Henry's chin, but he didn't notice it and no one said anything, even though every time he took a bite of his bread his blood fell onto it until he was eating his own blood mixed in with the food.

30   While Henry was not around we talked about what was going to happen to him. There were no Indian doctors on the reservation, and my mom couldn't come around to trusting the old man, Moses Pillager, because he courted her long ago and was jealous of her husbands. He might take revenge through her son. We were afraid that if we brought Henry to a regular hospital they would keep him.

"They don't fix them in those places," Mom said; "they just give them drugs."

"We wouldn't get him there in the first place," I agree, "so let's just forget about it."

Then I thought about the car.

Henry had not even looked at the car since he'd gotten home, though like I said, it was in tip-top condition and ready to drive. I thought the car might bring the old Henry back somehow. So I bided my time and waited for my chance to interest him in the vehicle.

35   One night Henry was off somewhere. I took myself a hammer. I went out to that car and I did a number on its underside. Whacked it up. Bent the tail pipe double. Ripped the muffler loose. By the time I was done with the car it looked

worse than any typical Indian car that has been driven all its life on reservation roads, which they always say are like government promises—full of holes. It just about hurt me, I'll tell you that! I threw dirt in the carburetor and I ripped all the electric tape off the seats. I made it look just as beat up as I could. Then I sat back and waited for Henry to find it.

Still, it took him over a month. That was all right, because it was just getting warm enough, not melting, but warm enough to work outside.

"Lyman," he says, walking in one day, "that red car looks like shit."

"Well it's old," I says. "You got to expect that."

"No way!" says Henry. "That car's a classic! But you went and ran the piss right out of it, Lyman, and you know it don't deserve that. I kept that car in A-one shape. You don't remember. You're too young. But when I left, that car was running like a watch. Now I don't even know if I can get it to start again, let alone get it anywhere near its old condition."

40   "Well you try," I said, like I was getting mad, "but I say it's a piece of junk."

Then I walked out before he could realize I knew he'd strung together more than six words at once.

After that I thought he'd freeze himself to death working on that car. He was out there all day, and at night he rigged up a little lamp, ran a cord out the window, and had himself some light to see by while he worked. He was better than he had been before, but that's still not saying much. It was easier for him to do the things the rest of us did. He ate more slowly and didn't jump up and down during the meal to get this or that or look out the window. I put my hand in the back of the TV set, I admit, and fiddled around with it good, so that it was almost impossible now to get a clear picture. He didn't look at it very often anyway. He was always out with that car or going off to get parts for it. By the time it was really melting outside, he had it fixed.

I had been feeling down in the dumps about Henry around this time. We had always been together before. Henry and Lyman. But he was such a loner now that I didn't know how to take it. So I jumped at the chance one day when Henry seemed friendly. It's not that he smiled or anything. He just said, "Let's take that old shitbox for a spin." Just the way he said it made me think he could be coming around.

We went out to the car. It was spring. The sun was shining very bright. My only sister, Bonita, who was just eleven years old, came out and made us stand together for a picture. Henry leaned his elbow on the red car's windshield, and he took his other arm and put it over my shoulder, very carefully, as though it was heavy for him to lift and he didn't want to bring the weight down all at once.

45   "Smile," Bonita said, and he did.

That picture. I never look at it anymore. A few months ago, I don't know why, I got his picture out and tacked it on the wall. I felt good about Henry at the time, close to him. I felt good having his picture on the wall, until one night when I was looking at television. I was a little drunk and stoned. I looked up at the wall and Henry was staring at me. I don't know what it was, but his smile had changed, or maybe it was gone. All I know is I couldn't stay in the same room with that picture. I was shaking. I got up, closed the door, and went into the kitchen. A little later my friend Ray came over and we both went back into that room. We put the picture in a brown bag, folded the bag over and over tightly, then put it way back in a closet.

I still see that picture now, as if it tugs at me, whenever I pass that closet door. The picture is very clear in my mind. It was so sunny that day Henry had to squint against the glare. Or maybe the camera Bonita held flashed like a mirror, blinding him, before she snapped the picture. My face is right out in the sun, big and round. But he might have drawn back, because the shadows on his face are deep as holes. There are two shadows curved like little hooks around the ends of his smile, as if to frame it and try to keep it there—that one, first smile that looked like it might have hurt his face. He has his field jacket on and the worn-in clothes he'd come back in and kept wearing ever since. After Bonita took the picture, she went into the house and we got into the car. There was a full cooler in the trunk. We started off, east, toward Pembina and the Red River because Henry said he wanted to see the high water.

The trip over there was beautiful. When everything starts changing, drying up, clearing off, you feel like your whole life is starting. Henry felt it, too. The top was down and the car hummed like a top. He'd really put it back in shape, even the tape on the seats was very carefully put down and glued back in layers. It's not that he smiled again or even joked, but his face looked to me as if it was clear, more peaceful. It looked as though he wasn't thinking of anything in particular except the bare fields and windbreaks and houses we were passing.

The river was high and full of winter trash when we got there. The sun was still out, but it was colder by the river. There were still little clumps of dirty snow here and there on the banks. The water hadn't gone over the banks yet, but it would, you could tell. It was just at its limit, hard swollen, glossy like an old gray scar. We made ourselves a fire, and we sat down and watched the current go. As I watched it I felt something squeezing inside me and tightening and trying to let go all at the same time. I knew I was not just feeling it myself; I knew I was feeling what Henry was going through at that moment. Except that I couldn't stand it, the closing and opening. I jumped to my feet. I took Henry by the shoulders and I started shaking him. "Wake up," I says, "wake up, wake up, wake up!" I didn't know what had come over me. I sat down beside him again.

50   His face was totally white and hard. Then it broke, like stones break all of a sudden when water boils up inside them.

"I know it," he says. "I know it. I can't help it. It's no use."

We start talking. He said he knew what I'd done with the car. It was obvious it had been whacked out of shape and not just neglected. He said he wanted to give the car to me for good now, it was no use. He said he'd fixed it just to give it back and I should take it.

"No way," I says. "I don't want it."

"That's okay," he says, "you take it."

55   "I don't want it, though," I says back to him, and then to emphasize, just to emphasize, you understand, I touch his shoulder. He slaps my hand off.

"Take that car," he says.

"No," I say. "Make me," I say, and then he grabs my jacket and rips the arm loose. That jacket is a class act, suede with tags and zippers. I push Henry backwards, off the log. He jumps up and bowls me over. We go down in a clinch and come up swinging hard, for all we're worth, with our fists. He socks my jaw so hard I feel like it swings loose. Then I'm at his rib cage and land a good one under his chin so his head snaps back. He's dazzled. He looks at me and I look at him and then his eyes are full of tears and blood and at first I think he's crying. But no, he's laughing. "Ha! Ha!" he says. "Ha! Ha! Take good care of it."

"Okay," I says. "Okay, no problem. Ha! Ha!"

I can't help it, and I start laughing, too. My face feels fat and strange, and after a while I get a beer from the cooler in the trunk, and when I hand it to Henry he takes his shirt and wipes my germs off. "Hoof and mouth disease," he says. For some reason this cracks me up, and so we're really laughing for a while, and then we drink all the rest of the beers one by one and throw them in the river and see how far, how fast, the current takes them before they fill up and sink.

60   "You want to go on back?" I ask after a while. "Maybe we could snag a couple nice Kashpaw girls."

He says nothing. But I can tell his mood is turning again.

"They're all crazy, the girls up here, every damn one of them."

"You're crazy too," I say, to jolly him up. "Crazy Lamartine boys!"

He looks as though he will take this wrong at first. His face twists, then clears. And he jumps up on his feet. "That's right!" he says. "Crazier 'n hell. Crazy Indians!"

65   I think it's the old Henry again. He throws off his jacket and starts springing his legs up from the knees like a fancy dancer. He's doing something between a grass dance and a bunny hop, no kind of dance I ever saw before, but neither has anyone else on all this green growing earth. He's wild. He wants to pitch whoopee! He's up and at me and all over. All this time I'm laughing so hard, so hard my belly is getting tied up in a knot.

"Got to cool me off!" he shouts all of a sudden. Then he runs over to the river and jumps in.

There's boards and other things in the current. It's so high. No sound comes from the river after the splash he makes, so I run right over. I look around. It's getting dark. I see he's halfway across the water already, and I know he didn't swim there but the current took him. It's far. I hear his voice, though, very clearly across it.

"My boots are filling," he says.

He says this in a normal voice, like he just noticed and he doesn't know what to think of it. Then he's gone. A branch comes by. Another branch. And I go in.

70   By the time I get out of the river, off the snag I pulled myself onto, the sun is down. I walk back to the car, turn on the high beams, and drive it up the bank. I put it in first gear and then I take my foot off the clutch. I get out, close the door, and watch it plow softly into the water. The headlights reach in as they go down, searching, still lighted even after the water swirls over the back end. I wait. The wires short out. It is all finally dark. And then there is only the water, the sound of it going and running and going and running and running.

MAKING CONNECTIONS

1. In "Sonny's Blues," who is the narrator? What kind of relationship does he have with Sonny?
2. How does the tale of the narrator's father and his father's brother shed light on this story?
3. Why do you think the narrator writes to Sonny after his daughter, Grace, dies? What does he mean, "My trouble made his real"?
4. Describe the relationship between Sonny and his music. Why does it mean so much to him?
5. The relationship between Sonny and his brother changes. What helps the narrator to understand Sonny better? Find passages in the story to indicate that.
6. In what way do you think "Sonny's Blues" is an appropriate title for this story?
7. In the first paragraph of "The Red Convertible" the narrator, Lyman, says of the car: "We owned it together until his boots filled with water." Were you puzzled by this comment? In what way does it make sense at the end of the story, literally and metaphorically?
8. Why do you suppose Lyman refers to himself in the third person at the end of the first paragraph?
9. What do you think happened to Henry in Vietnam that changed him?
10. Why does Lyman push the car into the water after Henry?

MAKING AN ARGUMENT

1. To what extent is darkness symbolic throughout "Sonny's Blues"? Interpret and write about the statement: "All they really knew were two darknesses, the darkness of their lives, which was now closing in on them, and the darkness of the movies, which had blinded them to that other darkness." Cite the text and quote other passages in the story for support.
2. Write an essay comparing the narration and the relationship of the brothers in "Sonny's Blues" (p. 218) with that in "The Red Convertible" (p. 241). In "Sonny's Blues," it is the older brother who narrates, but in "The Red Convertible," it is the younger brother. What difference does relative age make to each relationship and to the voice and tone of the narration? Cite the text of each story for support.
3. To what extent is the car in "The Red Convertible" a central symbol in the story? In what way do the changes the car goes through seem to reflect the changes in Lyman and Henry and their relationship? Write about symbolism in this story. Cite the text of the story to support your view.
4. Identify a common thread and write about sibling relationships as exemplified by "The Red Convertible," "Sonny's Blues," and other works in the text, such as "How to Watch Your Brother Die" (p. 736). Consider narration, setting, characterization, and conflict as elements to be addressed. Cite the text of each work for support.

CHINUA ACHEBE [B. 1930]

The son of a mission schoolteacher, Chinua Achebe was born and raised in eastern Nigeria, a British colony that later became the Republic of Nigeria after gaining independence in 1963. Educated both in Africa and England, he first burst into prominence with his 1958 novel Things Fall Apart, *a moving portrayal of the conflicts between traditional tribal customs and European culture in colonial Africa. He has since become one of the most influential African voices of his generation. Much of his later work, including the novels* Man of the People *(1966) and* Anthills of the Savannah *(1988), explores the corruption and conflicts of contemporary Nigeria. His most recent works are* Home and Exile *(2000) and* Collected Poems *(2004). In 2007, he was awarded the Man Booker International Prize for Fiction. He is currently Charles P. Stevenson Professor of Languages and Literature at Bard College.*

MARRIAGE IS A PRIVATE AFFAIR   [1972]

"Have you written to your dad yet?" asked Nene one afternoon as she sat with Nnaemeka in her room at 16 Kasanga Street, Lagos.

"No. I've been thinking about it. I think it's better to tell him when I get home on leave!"

"But why? Your leave is such a long way off yet—six whole weeks. He should be let into our happiness now."

Nnaemeka was silent for a while, and then began very slowly as if he groped for his words: "I wish I were sure it would be happiness to him."

5   "Of course it must," replied Nene, a little surprised. "Why shouldn't it?"

"You have lived in Lagos all your life, and you know very little about people in remote parts of the country."

"That's what you always say. But I don't believe anybody will be so unlike other people that they will be unhappy when their sons are engaged to marry."

"Yes. They are most unhappy if the engagement is not arranged by them. In our case it's worse—you are not even an Ibo."

This was said so seriously and so bluntly that Nene could not find speech immediately. In the cosmopolitan atmosphere of the city it had always seemed to her something of a joke that a person's tribe could determine whom he married.

10   At last she said, "You don't really mean that he will object to your marrying me simply on that account? I had always thought you Ibos were kindly disposed to other people."

"So we are. But when it comes to marriage, well, it's not quite so simple. And this," he added, "is not peculiar to the Ibos. If your father were alive and lived in the heart of Ibibio-land he would be exactly like my father."

"I don't know. But anyway, as your father is so fond of you, I'm sure he will forgive you soon enough. Come on then, be a good boy and send him a nice lovely letter..."

"It would not be wise to break the news to him by writing. A letter will bring it upon him with a shock. I'm quite sure about that."

"All right, honey, suit yourself. You know your father."

15   As Nnaemeka walked home that evening he turned over in his mind the different ways of overcoming his father's opposition, especially now that he had gone and found a girl for him. He had thought of showing his letter to Nene but decided on second thought not to, at least for the moment. He read it again when he got home and couldn't help smiling to himself. He remembered Ugoye quite well, an Amazon of a girl who used to beat up all the boys, himself included, on the way to the stream, a complete dunce at school.

I have found a girl who will suit you admirably—Ugoye Nweke, the eldest daughter of our neighbor, Jacob Nweke. She has a proper Christian upbringing. When she stopped schooling some years ago her father (a man of sound judgment) sent her to live in the house of a pastor where she has received all the training a wife could need. Her Sunday School teacher has told me that she reads her Bible very fluently. I hope we shall begin negotiations when you come home in December.

On the second evening of his return from Lagos Nnaemeka sat with his father under a cassia tree. This was the old man's retreat where he went to read his Bible when the parching December sun had set and a fresh, reviving wind blew on the leaves.

"Father," began Nnaemeka suddenly, "I have come to ask forgiveness."

"Forgiveness? For what, my son?" he asked in amazement.

"It's about this marriage question!"

20   "Which marriage question?"

"I can't—we must—I mean it is impossible for me to marry Nweke's daughter."

"Impossible? Why?" asked his father.

"I don't love her."

"Nobody said you did. Why should you?" he asked.

25   "Marriage today is different..."

"Look here, my son," interrupted his father, "nothing is different. What one looks for in a wife are a good character and a Christian background."

Nnaemeka saw there was no hope along the present line of argument.

"Moreover," he said, "I am engaged to marry another girl who has all of Ugoye's good qualities, and who..."

His father did not believe his ears. "What did you say?" he asked slowly and disconcertingly.

30   "She is a good Christian," his son went on, "and a teacher in a girls' school in Lagos."

"Teacher, did you say? If you consider that a qualification for a good wife I should like to point out to you, Emeka, that no Christian woman should teach. St. Paul in his letter to the Corinthians says that women should keep silence." He rose slowly from his seat and paced forwards and backwards. This was his pet subject, and he condemned vehemently those church leaders who encouraged women to teach in their schools. After he had spent his emotion on a long homily, he at last came back to his son's engagement, in a seemingly milder tone.

"Whose daughter is she, anyway?"

"She is Nene Atang."

"What!" All the mildness was gone again. "Did you say Neneatang? What does that mean?"

35   "Nene Atang from Calabar. She is the only girl I can marry." This was a very rash reply and Nnaemeka expected the storm to burst. But it did not. His father merely walked away into his room. This was most unexpected and perplexed Nnaemeka. His father's silence was infinitely more menacing than a flood of threatening speech. That night the old man did not eat.

When he sent for Nnaemeka a day later he applied all possible ways of dissuasion. But the young man's heart was hardened, and his father eventually gave him up as lost.

"I owe it to you, my son, as a duty to show you what is right and what is wrong. Whoever put this idea into your head might as well have cut your throat. It is Satan's work." He waved his son away.

"You will change your mind, Father, when you know Nene."

"I shall never see her," was the reply. From that night the father scarcely spoke to his son. He did not, however, cease hoping that he would realize how serious was the danger he was heading for. Day and night he put him in his prayers.

40   Nnaemeka, for his own part, was very deeply affected by his father's grief. But he kept hoping that it would pass away. If it had occurred to him that never in the history of his people had a man married a woman who spoke a different tongue, he might have been less optimistic. "It has never been heard," was the verdict of an old man speaking a few weeks later. In that short sentence he spoke for all of his people. This man had come with others to commiserate with Okeke when news went round about his son's behavior. By that time the son had gone back to Lagos.

"It has never been heard," said the old man again with a sad shake of his head.

"What did Our Lord say?" asked another gentleman. "Sons shall rise against their Fathers; it is there in the Holy Book."

"It is the beginning of the end," said another.

The discussion thus tending to become theological, Madubogwu, a highly practical man, brought it down once more to the ordinary level.

45   "Have you thought of consulting a native doctor about your son?" he asked Nnaemeka's father.

"He isn't sick," was the reply.

"What is he then? The boy's mind is diseased and only a good herbalist can bring him back to his right senses. The medicine he requires is *Amalile*, the same that women apply with success to recapture their husbands' straying affection."

"Madubogwu is right," said another gentleman. "This thing calls for medicine."

"I shall not call in a native doctor." Nnaemeka's father was known to be obstinately ahead of his more superstitious neighbors in these matters. "I will not be another Mrs. Ochuba. If my son wants to kill himself let him do it with his own hands. It is not for me to help him."

50   "But it was her fault," said Madubogwu. "She ought to have gone to an honest herbalist. She was a clever woman, nevertheless."

"She was a wicked murderess," said Jonathan who rarely argued with his neighbors because, he often said, they were incapable of reasoning. "The medicine was prepared for her husband, it was his name they called in its preparation and I am sure it would have been perfectly beneficial to him. It was wicked to put it into the herbalist's food, and say you were only trying it out."

Six months later, Nnaemeka was showing his young wife a short letter from his father:

It amazes me that you could be so unfeeling as to send me your wedding picture. I would have sent it back. But on further thought I decided just to cut off your wife and sent it back to you because I have nothing to do with her. How I wish that I had nothing to do with you either.

When Nene read through this letter and looked at the mutilated picture her eyes filled with tears, and she began to sob.

"Don't cry, my darling," said her husband. "He is essentially good natured and will one day look more kindly on our marriage." But years passed and that one day did not come.

55   For eight years, Okeke would have nothing to do with his son, Nnaemeka. Only three times (when Nnaemeka asked to come home and spend his leave) did he write to him.

"I can't have you in my house," he replied on one occasion. "It can be of no interest to me where or how you spend your leave—or your life, for that matter."

The prejudice against Nnaemeka's marriage was not confined to his little village In Lagos, especially among his people who worked there, it showed itself in a different way. Their women, when they met at their village meeting were not hostile to Nene. Rather, they paid her such excessive deference as to make her feel she was not one of them. But as time went on, Nene gradually broke through some of this prejudice and even began to make friends among them. Slowly and grudgingly they began to admit that she kept her home much better than most of them.

The story eventually got to the little village in the heart of the Ibo country that Nnaemeka and his young wife were a most happy couple. But his father was one of the few people who knew nothing about this. He always displayed so much temper whenever his son's name was mentioned that everyone avoided it in his presence. By a tremendous effort of will he had succeeded in pushing his son to the back of his mind. The strain had nearly killed him but he had persevered, and won.

Then one day he received a letter from Nene, and in spite of himself he began to glance through it perfunctorily until all of a sudden the expression on his face changed and he began to read more carefully.

...Our two sons, from the day they learnt that they have a grandfather, have insisted on being taken to him. I find it impossible to tell them that you will not see them. I implore you to allow Nnaemeka to bring them home for a short time during his leave next month. I shall remain here in Lagos...

60   The old man at once felt the resolution he had built up over so many years falling in. He was telling himself that he must not give in. He tried to steel his heart against all emotional appeals. It was a reenactment of that other struggle. He leaned against a window and looked out. The sky was overcast with heavy black clouds and a high wind began to blow filling the air with dust and dry leaves. It was one of those rare occasions when even Nature takes a hand in a human fight. Very soon it began to rain, the first rain in the year. It came down in large sharp drops and was accompanied by the lightning and thunder which mark a change of season. Okeke was trying hard not to think of his two grandsons. But he knew he was now fighting a losing battle. He tried to hum a favorite hymn but the pattering of large rain drops on the roof broke up the tune. His mind immediately returned to the children. How could he shut his door against them? By a curious mental process he imagined them standing, sad and forsaken, under the harsh angry weather—shut out from his house.

That night he hardly slept, from remorse—and a vague fear that he might die without making it up to them.

MAKING CONNECTIONS

1. At the start of the story, Nnaemeka has a letter from his father that he doesn't share with Nene. Why does he conceal its contents? Is he justified in not sharing such information with his fiancée?
2. Nnaemeka's father objects to his marriage to Nene because she is not an Ibo. Are there any groups whose members it would be difficult for you to marry? Explain.
3. It is commonly assumed that marriages are based upon love, but even in our society people marry for reasons other than love. Is marriage for a motive other than love justifiable? Might it even be preferable? Explain.
4. What do you think of the way that Okeke treats his son and daughter-in-law? Is it ever appropriate to disown a child? Explain.
5. Do you think the rain near the end of the story is symbolic? Explain.
6. Throughout the story, Nnaemeka seems optimistic that his father will come to accept his marriage. To what extent do Okeke's reactions to Nene's letter at the end of the story validate his son's optimism? Why?
7. To what extent does this story exemplify the Jean de la Fontaine adage "It is impossible to please all the world and one's father"?

MAKING AN ARGUMENT

1. Write about the characterization of father and son and its relationship to the conflict in this story. What are the cultural values of father and son in this story? Despite their differences over the marriage, in what ways are they alike? To what extent does their conflict result from who they are as individuals as much as what they believe in? Cite evidence from the text of the story for support.

JOHN CHEEVER [1912–1982]

John Cheever was born in Quincy, Massachusetts, and published his first story, "Expelled," in the New Republic *shortly after he was expelled from prep school at the age of eighteen. Instead of attending college, Cheever moved to New York City and devoted himself to writing. His stories, which often appeared in* The New Yorker, *gradually earned him a reputation as a master short-story writer, and, as they were usually set among upper-middle-class suburbanites, led one critic to dub Cheever the "Chekhov of the Suburbs." Though his reputation rests mainly on his short stories, Cheever published a number of well-received novels, most notably* The Wapshot Scandal *(1965), which won the National Book Award. His best-selling* Stories of John Cheever *was awarded the Pulitzer Prize in 1978.*

REUNION   [1962]

The last time I saw my father was in Grand Central Station. I was going from my grandmother's in the Adirondacks to a cottage on the Cape that my mother had rented,—and I wrote my father that I would be in New York between trains for an hour and a half, and asked if we could have lunch together. His secretary wrote to say that he would meet me at the information booth at noon, and at twelve o'clock sharp I saw him coming through the crowd. He was a stranger to me—my mother divorced him three years ago and I hadn't been with him since—but as soon as I saw him I felt that he was my father, my flesh and blood, my future and my doom. I knew that when I was grown I would be something like him; I would have to plan my campaigns within his limitations. He was a big, good-looking man, and I was terribly happy to see him again. He struck me on the back and shook my hand. "Hi, Charlie," he said. "Hi, boy. I'd like to take you up to my club, but it's in the Sixties, and if you have to catch an early train I guess we'd better get something to eat around here." He put his arm around me, and I smelled my father the way my mother sniffs a rose. It was a rich compound of whiskey, after-shave lotion, shoe polish, woolens, and the rankness of a mature male. I hoped that someone would see us together. I wished that we could be photographed. I wanted some record of our having been together.

We went out of the station and up a side street to a restaurant. It was still early, and the place was empty. The bartender was quarreling with a delivery boy, and there was one very old waiter in a red coat down by the kitchen door. We sat down, and my father hailed the waiter in a loud voice. *"Kellner!"* he shouted. *"Garcon! Cameriere! You!"* His boisterousness in the empty restaurant seemed out of place. "Could we have a little service here!" he shouted. "Chop-chop." Then he clapped his hands. This caught the waiter's attention, and he shuffled over to our table.

"Were you clapping your hands at me?" he asked.

"Calm down, calm down, *sommelier,*" my father said. "If it isn't too much to ask of you—if it wouldn't be too much above and beyond the call of duty, we would like a couple of Beefeater Gibsons."

5   "I don't like to be clapped at," the waiter said.

"I should have brought my whistle," my father said. "I have a whistle that is audible only to the ears of old waiters. Now, take out your little pad and your little pencil and see if you can get this straight: two Beefeater Gibsons. Repeat after me: two Beefeater Gibsons."

"I think you'd better go somewhere else," the waiter said quietly.

"That," said my father, "is one of the most brilliant suggestions I have ever heard. Come on, Charlie, let's get the hell out of here."

I followed my father out of that restaurant into another. He was not so boisterous this time. Our drinks came, and he cross-questioned me about the baseball season. He then struck the edge of his empty glass with his knife and began shouting again. "Garcon! Kellner! Cameriere! *You!* Could we trouble you to bring us two more of the same."

10   "How old is the boy?" the waiter asked.

"That," my father said, "is none of your God-damned business."

"I'm sorry, sir," the waiter said, "but I won't serve the boy another drink."

"Well, I have some news for you," my father said. "I have some very interesting news for you. This doesn't happen to be the only restaurant in New York. They've opened another on the corner. Come on, Charlie."

He paid the bill, and I followed him out of that restaurant into another. Here the waiters wore pink jackets like hunting coats and there was a lot of horse tack on the walls. We sat down, and my father began to shout again. "Master of the hounds! Tallyhoo and all that sort of thing. We'd like a little something in the way of a stirrup cup. Namely, two Bibson Geefeaters."

15   "Two Bibson Geefeaters?" the waiter asked, smiling.

"You know damned well what I want," my father said angrily. "I want two Beefeater Gibsons, and make it snappy. Things have changed in jolly old England. So my friend the duke tells me. Let's see what England can produce in the way of a cocktail."

"This isn't England," the waiter said.

"Don't argue with me," my father said. "Just do as you're told."

"I just thought you might like to know where you are," the waiter said.

20   "If there is one thing I cannot tolerate," my father said, "it is an impudent domestic. Come on, Charlie."

The fourth place we went to was Italian. *"Buon giorno,"* my father said. *"Per favore, possiamo avere due cocktail americani, forti, forti. Molto gin, poco vermut."*

"I don't understand Italian," the waiter said.

"Oh, come off it," my father said. "You understand Italian, and you know damned well you do. *Vogliamo due cocktail americani. Subito."*

The waiter left us and spoke with the captain, who came over to our table and said, "I'm sorry, sir, but this table is reserved."

25   "All right," my father said. "Get us another table."

"All the tables are reserved," the captain said.

"I get it," my father said, "You don't desire our patronage. Is that it? Well, the hell with you. *Vada all'inferno.* Let's go, Charlie."

"I have to get my train," I said.

"I'm sorry, sonny," my father said. "I'm terribly sorry." He put his arm around me and pressed me against him. "I'll walk you back to the station. If there had only been time to go up to my club."

30   "That's all right, Daddy," I said.

"I'll get you a paper," he said. "I'll get you a paper to read on the train."

Then he went up to a newsstand and said, "Kind sir, will you be good enough to favor me with one of your God-damned, no-good, ten-cent afternoon papers?" The clerk turned away from him and stared at a magazine cover. "Is it asking too much, kind sir," my father said, "is it asking too much for you to sell me one of your disgusting specimens of yellow journalism?"

"I have to go, Daddy," I said. "It's late."

"Now, just wait a second, sonny," he said. "Just wait a second. I want to get a rise out of this chap."

35   "Goodbye, Daddy," I said, and I went down the stairs and got my train, and that was the last time I saw my father.

MAKING CONNECTIONS

1. Characterize the father and his behavior. What do you think is motivating him to behave as he does? Do you think the son should have said something to him about his behavior? Explain.
2. Were you surprised by the last line of the story? Do you think that he will ever want to see his father again? Would you in this situation?

MAKING AN ARGUMENT

1. Narrated by the son in the past tense, "Reunion" begins with a brief descriptive paragraph, but most of what follows is heated dialogue in a series of quick encounters with waiters—and a quick good-bye. To what extent does this style adequately convey the characterization of the father and the son—their relationship—and the conflict in the story? What is not said by the narrator? Do you think more should have been said? Write about the effectiveness of the writing style in this story. Cite the text of the story for support.

LINDA CHING SLEDGE [B. 1944]

Born in Hawaii, Linda Ching Sledge holds a B.A. from the University of California at Berkeley and a Ph.D. in English Literature from the City University of New York. She has written two award-winning historical novels, Empire of Heaven *(Bantam, 1990) and* A Map of Paradise *(Bantam, 1997), as well as* Shivering Babe, Victorious Lord *(Eerdmans, 1981), a literary history. She is Professor Emerita of English at SUNY Westchester Community College.*

The story below is taken from A Map of Paradise, *a historical novel set in nineteenth-century Hawaii, which depicts the struggle of emigrants from south China as they lay claim to their new island home. In this episode, a Chinese father clashes with his son over the boy's desperate longing to abandon the family's lucrative construction business to enter an all-white mission school. The domestic crisis unfolds against the background of a rapidly changing Hawaii torn by forces of Hawaiian court politics, American sugar interests, Chinese labor, and rival immigrant clans.*

THE ROAD   [1997]

The hurricane proved a boon for Pao An. His was not the kind of inventory that could be spoiled by wind or rain, and now everyone needed hammers and wire nails, lumber and coral stone to rebuild. Roads, dikes, dams, fishponds also needed repairing, thus prompting the king to auction off contracts for a massive public works scheme across Oahu. The grass shacks and wooden tenements built in Queen Emma's reign[1] were proving woefully inadequate to house the foreigners flocking to Hawaii's shores; and King Kalakaua, having already depleted his treasury in the building of his brick and iron frame palace, intended to do still more to reshape Honolulu into the commercial center of the islands. His next plan was to construct a road encircling the island so that a man might go from Waianae Beach to Honolulu in less than half a day. With the cost of construction soaring and pitting him against a reluctant legislature, Kalakaua had turned to Claus Spreckels[2] to bail him out of his gambling debts.

By skillfully underbidding his rivals, Pao An was granted a lucrative contract for the building of a section of the road and promptly hired a crew of Chinamen and *kanakas*[3] to dig the windward end. With his adopted son Lincoln as surveyor and a road crew led by three Tang men[4] who had blasted tunnels through the Sierras for the railroad, Pao An began by reducing the lava cliffs to rubble, then leveling the roadbed with drag sledges pulled by oxen. On the bluffs, the soil was porous and ashy, the residue of a long-dormant volcano called Kaimana-hila, or Diamond Hill, for the false hopes sparked decades before by crystalline fragments that occasionally winked in the rock. The grading was as tedious as dredging the heavy, waterlogged peat of the deltas of China or California by hand. Although Pao An fell easily into the familiar task of moving earth, he could no longer discount the changes that age and toil had wrought on the powerful body that had once been his pride; his broad back was beginning to bend, and after a day of hauling rock his ribs, knees, and shoulders had pains that sleep could not cure.

Yet despite the cost to his body, moving rock was finally earning Pao An the prosperity for which he had labored so long. Squinting into the harsh light from

[1]**Queen Emma (reigned 1856–1863) and King David Kalakaua (1874–1891)** two popular native rulers of the Kingdom of Hawaii. Kalakaua was the second-to-the-last monarch of Hawaii before its annexation by the United States in 1898.   [2]**Claus Spreckels** California sugar magnate who controlled sugar manufacturing in the islands and had the ear of King Kalakaua.   [3]*kanaka* native term for people of Hawaiian ancestry.   [4]**Tang men** Chinese immigrants from southern China (Guangdong Province) call themselves "people of Tang" after the Tang dynasty (CE 618–907) in which the South achieved particular distinction.

under the brim of his conical straw hat, he saw the distant shape of Maui across the channel; behind him rose Kaimana-hila blanketed by clouds. Generations of Chens in On Ting village[5] had spent their lives tilling their few square miles of Delta earth before laying their bones there. Yet he, an outcast son of the village, had walked from the southern tip of the empire to the very outskirts of Peking. He, the poorest boy in On Ting, was now turning the red earth of a land his kin knew only in talk story, the place they called *Fusan,* the Blessed Isles. Given a chance, Pao An thought proudly, even he, the humblest of Tang men, might accomplish feats worthy of an emperor. In its own way, the building of this road was as grandiose a project as the wall the first Chin emperor had made to safeguard his empire from northern invaders.

One day, his vendors would travel this road from his lumberyards to small fishing villages on the coast to bring tools and lumber to any man who wanted a store or restaurant or cottage of his own. By then, roads would crisscross the island and buildings made from the Chens' stone and lumber would dot the horizon. He envisioned an Oahu furnished with dwellings to suit every purpose: one-story plantation cottages stuck side by side on stilts so that workers need not sleep like animals penned in a barn but live decently with wives and children and a vegetable garden of their own, dwellings made from clapboard or adobe and thatch like those he had seen along the levees in California, stately edifices of lava stone where bankers and merchants came to trade.

5   "Some day," he told Lincoln, gesturing at imaginary roads and canals and dwellings as if he were presenting the boy a kingdom, "this business will be yours. Something for you and your sons."

In truth, Lincoln didn't want what his father proffered. At least, not this way. He revered the man who had taken him in, but he hated reducing himself to a mindless thing of sinew and bone. He hated the mud and the sweat and the agony of pitting himself against the relentless drift of earth and sea. The summer before, he had steeped himself in the writings of Emerson, Wordsworth, and Rousseau and come away convinced that by meditation, one could cross over at will from the real world into a veritable paradise of the mind. Escape from the drudgery of each day came as easily as thought. He had discovered that any rhythmical activity performed for prolonged periods—the swinging of a pickax, the steady contemplation of the swell of the waves—would create answering interior rhythms that would send his mind soaring above his aching body. In those moments of "transcendings," Lincoln neither heard the cacophony of animals and men nor felt the soreness in his muscles nor remembered his despair.

The Widow had won a contract too, a lucrative franchise to supply the workers' canteen, a natural extension of her fish and vegetable markets. Because her provisions were abundant and cheap, she was soon supplying food to road gangs all over the island. For an extra fee, a laborer might buy a packet of opium, which

[5]**On Ting village** a village in the Pearl River Delta in Guangdong Province, the region where nineteenth-century immigrants to Hawaii and California came from.

the Widow's vendors, all brothers of the *tong*,[6] hid inside covered baskets of rice. Pao An had forbidden opium on the job; even so, the Widow managed to do a thriving clandestine business in the drug. The day was coming, she foresaw, when the bankrupt kingdom would reissue the lucrative opium license and assess taxes on the smoking of dirt as other kings had done before. Having heard that the king's advisers were pressing Kalakaua to reintroduce the opium license, the Widow was spending a fortune on bribes. When the license was issued, she would be ready for trade.

A week after the crew broke ground, the Widow ordered her driver to take her in an ancient rig to various construction sites to oversee the midday distribution of food. She came dressed in a shiny coat of embroidered black satin and a black Buddhist headband encrusted with seed pearls, making a great show of scolding her workers for not being liberal enough with portions of food.

Pao An saw her coming from the hillock where he was helping Lincoln mark off the section of land for the next day's blasting. His immediate response was to throw her off the site. Yet one glimpse of the Widow fanning herself in the rig while her menservants scurried like puppies to do her bidding brought back a disturbing recollection. He remembered her at their first meeting, a girl of fourteen borne aloft on her wedding palanquin and he a stone-stupid youth teasing the bride on her way along the levee road. When she had peeked fearfully out of her covered palanquin and raised her veil to look at him, he had been struck dumb by her beauty and felt for the first time the meanness of his estate. He was a paddy boy too poor and dirty to touch the hem of her garment and as much an ox as the one he drove through the mud. The realization that he was still mucking about in mud made him ashamed. Rather than face her, he grabbed up his pickax and shovel and headed up the road toward the sea.

10   The Widow, however, had come to waylay someone else. For some time, she had been gathering reports on Lincoln, who inspected the food baskets and calculated the invoices from her cooks and suppliers. Her overseers had been grumbling about the scrupulousness of his tallying. Now she watched the tall, rawboned youth oversee the apportioning of food; he had not yet lost the clumsiness of boyhood and was covered with red dirt as dry as powder.

"You, boy," the Widow called. "Come here."

Lincoln sauntered over, preparing himself for a fight. The Widow had her driver pull into the shade of a *hala* tree, the only one in that barren section of rocky ground. "You like crawling through the dirt like a gecko in this heat?" the Widow asked, fanning herself as she reclined under the canopy of her buggy. "Give me a stool in a Chinatown shop any day." She was rewarded by Lincoln's rueful smile. "This work is fit only for *gu li,*" she said vehemently. "You are not a 'rough man.' Why do you stay?"

"My father needs me," Lincoln replied with what courtesy he could muster. He wondered why others thought this small woman with her pretentious city accent so formidable. Still, the Widow was sensible enough to divine his dislike of dirt and stone and his unease among the rough, crude men. For he did indeed miss the order of the shop, the clean floors and polished wooden countertops, the logic of commerce and inventory and the smooth abacus beads under his fingers.

[6]***tong*** a club or society of immigrants whose activities ranged from financing illegal operations such as gambling or opium to charitable operations for indigents.

"How is your father going to pay you?" She prodded, "In Kalakaua dollars?"[7] She laughed at her own joke. The newly minted coins stamped with the king's head were considered worthless by the Chinese, who would not accept wages or trade goods in them. Claus Spreckels had beguiled the king into creating the new coinage as a means of skimming money off the treasury.

15　"My father's coins are as good as his word," Lincoln replied.

The Widow went on reprovingly, "Not your father by blood! You're more filial to this stranger than his own daughter!" Suddenly the Widow leaned over and said in a conspiratorial tone, "Quit this job and come to me! I could use a bookkeeper who speaks English and Hawaiian as well as you. And I pay in American money!"

"There are twenty Tang boys at the Fort Street Mission who can figure as well as I," Lincoln replied.

"Perhaps, but you are shrewd and my men fear you. So if you decide to do something better than smash stone for a living, come see me."

"I am already learning a trade."

20　"Pah! Crushing rock is not a trade for an educated man. And any apprenticeship can be bought off," the Widow retorted. "You're old enough to make your own way. How will you get a wife if you have no decent livelihood? And do not tell me you intend to muck about in mud, for you are not built along your father's lines. You would surely fail at his business!"

Lincoln shifted his feet self-consciously and looked down at the ground. The Widow was nosy and impertinent, yet she was putting into words the same doubts that had plagued him for months.

"I will pay you five hundred Yankee dollars a year to keep my company's books and oversee the food concessions." When his eyes widened at the princely sum, she continued with a smile, "Tell your father about my offer. See if he puts your interests above his own!"

"My place is with him," Lincoln affirmed.

Anger blazed up in her eyes. "*Aiya, I* see you are the consummate businessman," she snapped, "one who intends to set the pace of the bargaining. Well, every man has his price, and I mean to discover yours."

25　Lincoln left feeling soiled and guilty. The Widow had a way of reaching into the recesses of his mind and dragging out his secret fears.

"The Chens have no breeding, no appreciation for the scholarly mind. I tell you, they are wasting that boy's gifts," the Widow told the *tong* council, which was meeting that morning on one of their charitable schemes to impress the government. This time, they were selecting the most worthy youth for further study at a private high school. The training would be at their expense, for any youth who lifted himself up did the same for all Tang people in the islands. It was a shrewd investment too, for if the boy were a brother bound by oath to the *tong,* he would eventually be in a position to pay them back handsomely in the form of favors. "Even the *kanaka* teacher at the common school says Lin Kong should not be apprenticed. A scholar should use his brains, not his back."

---

[7]**Kalakaua dollars** Hawaiian silver coinage minted in Kalakaua's reign, the source of much scandal and economic havoc.

The council brother with the smoothest tongue was delegated to convey the news to Pao An that Lincoln had been selected as that year's scholar. But the man had uttered no more than a few sentences before Pao An drove him out of his shop for interfering in matters that were not the *tong*'s concern.

In bed that night, Pao An raged at his wife. The man was undoubtedly sent by the Widow who was trying to entice the boy into her employ, for the *tong* emissary had implied that Pao An treated Lincoln too harshly. No man had done more for the boy than he! Didn't these fools know, moreover, that they were sowing the seeds of their own destruction by sending Tang boys to school with the *bak kuei?*[8] The day was coming when there would be no more brave Tang men laboring in earthworks or plantations or fishing boats up and down the coast of California or in the port cities of the Hawaiian kingdom. The builders and the dreamers would be gone. Soon they would all be talking in the strangled accents of the deceivers!

Back at the digging, Pao An saw that Lincoln had pushed the road ahead another mile along the mountain. Yet Pao An was short-tempered and rude to the boy, unable to praise. To mollify his father, Lincoln talked about the prospects the road presented for cross-island trade, but Pao An snapped at him, saying that the road would never be completed if he could not stop chattering long enough to lift a spade. When the cook boys came with buckets of hot rice and tea, Pao An saw Lincoln take his bowl to eat rice with the men. The boy was angry with him. And angry at himself too, Pao An concluded ruefully, for pretending an enthusiasm for the work he did not feel. Had never felt.

30   They worked side by side in edgy silence. Lincoln's anger had burned itself off in the heat of the afternoon. Now memories of his father's past kindnesses returned to haunt him: he remembered drinking from his father's cup when they worked together on the farm in Antioch. Another time, his father had fed him from his own bowl during one lean season on the levees. The memories were as painful as a magistrate's bamboo on the frail flesh of an unfilial son.

"Where have you hidden the book?" Pao An asked Lincoln that night. He had returned to their tent after visiting the privy to find the coal oil lamp relit, the flame turned down low.

Lincoln's face fell, embarrassed for having been caught yet again. "Here," Lincoln said, holding out a well-thumbed copy of Edward Everett's orations from beneath his blanket as if it were an excrescence.

Outside the tent, the men were playing a noisy game of *fan-tan* around the fire. Pao An turned the small volume over in his big leathery hand. "What is in this book?"

"Grand phrases, big ideas," Lincoln muttered. "I don't always know what they mean but I like the sound."

35   "You would rather read than sleep, wouldn't you?" Pao An asked.

"I don't read while I am working," Lincoln said defensively.

"I know you don't," Pao An growled. "You work hard. You are the best man of all my crew."

[8]***bak kuei*** "white devil"; Chinese term for a Caucasian.

Lincoln inclined his head. His father's praise was rare and therefore precious.

"You prefer books to anything, especially this... the rock, mud, noise, oxen... the *fan-tan* game. The road." The words were more statement than accusation.

40   The lamp threw Pao An's craggy features into cruel relief—the corners of eyes and mouth dragged down by disappointment, the cheeks sagging from exhaustion and care. Seated on his cot, Lincoln raised a hand in mute resignation. He was convinced that his father was seething at having raised a boy to manhood only to have him scorn the legacy of sweat and tears constructed on his behalf.

"So, boy," Pao An said gruffly, throwing the book down upon the cot, "I am taking you off the job."

"Why?" Lincoln wailed, a frightened child again. "How have I failed you, father?"

"You have not failed me. I am the one to blame. I have taken away the thing you love."

"No!"

45   "Tomorrow you leave me. I will get another boy to take your apprenticeship. Go to Bethel Mission or Fort Street Mission or Mills Institute or wherever clever Tang boys go these days to turn themselves into scholars. But be forewarned. Take what you wish from them but believe nothing the *bak kuei* say."

"But you need me!" the boy insisted.

"No. Not now, not anymore." With a gesture of finality, Pao An reached over and turned the little metal knob that stopped the flow of coal oil. The flame instantly shrank and died.

The next day, after Lincoln had departed, Pao An composed a poem, the first he had made in Hawaii, for the urge to make poems had vanished with his domestic responsibilities. Now faced with the dissolution of his house, he felt words welling up like tears.

The son I have is not my own
Only a shadow, myself in miniature,
Hiding, always hiding.

I offer him the earth,
But he refuses, longing instead for the sky.
I ask nothing of him.

We went together, he and I,
Two warriors to tame a mountain.
Side by side, we thrust shovel and pike into the red rock.

I cannot begin to tell you
What it was that
Made him lay a trail toward the west.
I want a sword
To carve out the mountain before him.

An arrow to mark the distance
He must travel
Away from me.

MAKING CONNECTIONS

1. Discuss Pao An's poem at the end of the story. What does it mean? What do you think he is saying about the future of his relationship with his son?

2. Why does Pao An change his mind at the end of this story? Do you think it is natural for fathers to want sons to follow in their footsteps? Explain.

3. Compare this story with "For My Father" on page 272. If Lincoln were writing a poem about his relationship with his father, what might he write about?

MAKING AN ARGUMENT

1. There are a number of works in this text that address father-son relationships, but the narration in poems like "Those Winter Sundays" (p. 13), "My Papa's Waltz" (p. 274), and "Digging" (p. 281), and the story "Reunion" (p. 254) is from the son's view. The third-person narration of "The Road" shows us more of the father's view than these other pieces. Write about the impact of this shift in narrative perspective as it affects characterization and conflict in this story. Cite the texts of "The Road" and other works for support.

CONNECTING THROUGH COMPARISON: PARENTS AND CHILDREN

The story and three poems that follow address a subtheme of this section: parents and children. They address relationships between mothers and daughters, father and daughter, and father and son. Each of them seems to have a source of tension added to the usual relationship between parent and child. Read and discussed together, they invite comparison, contrasts, and connections—with each other, and with your own experiences growing up.

AMY TAN [B. 1952]

Amy Tan was born in Oakland, California, several years after her mother and father emigrated from China. Upon the deaths of her brother and father in 1967 and 1968, the family began a haphazard journey through Europe, before settling in Switzerland. For the next seven years, Tan attended five schools before graduating with honors from San Jose State University, where she later earned an M.A. in Linguistics. In 1989, The Joy Luck Club *(from which "Two Kinds" is taken) was published and, through word-of-mouth endorsements by independent booksellers, became a surprise best seller. Though Tan wrote the book as a collection of linked short stories, reviewers enthusiastically and erroneously referred to the book as an intricately woven "novel." It was nominated for the National Book Award and the National Book Critics Award and was adapted into a film for Hollywood Pictures in 1994 with Tan as a co-screenwriter.* The Kitchen God's Wife *was published in 1991, followed by* The Hundred Secret Senses *in 1995, and*

The Bonesetter's Daughter *in 2001. Her short stories and essays have appeared in* The Atlantic, Harper's, The New Yorker, *and other publications. Her essay "Mother Tongue" (in this text on p. 150) was chosen for* The Best American Essays 1991, *and she was the guest editor for* The Best American Short Stories 1999. *Her latest book,* Saving Fish from Drowning, *was published in 2006.*

Two Kinds   [1989]

My mother believed you could be anything you wanted to be in America. You could open a restaurant. You could work for the government and get good retirement. You could buy a house with almost no money down. You could become rich. You could become instantly famous.

"Of course you can be prodigy, too," my mother told me when I was nine. "You can be best anything. What does Auntie Lindo know? Her daughter, she is only best tricky."

America was where all my mother's hopes lay. She had come here in 1949 after losing everything in China: her mother and father, her family home, her first husband, and two daughters, twin baby girls. But she never looked back with regret. There were so many ways for things to get better.

We didn't immediately pick the right kind of prodigy. At first my mother thought I could be a Chinese Shirley Temple. We'd watch Shirley's old movies on TV as though they were training films. My mother would poke my arm and say, "*Ni kan.*"—You watch. And I would see Shirley tapping her feet, or singing a sailor song, or pursing her lips into a very round O while saying "Oh, my goodness."

5   "*Ni kan,*" said my mother as Shirley's eyes flooded with tears. "You already know how. Don't need talent for crying!"

Soon after my mother got this idea about Shirley Temple, she took me to a beauty training school in the Mission district and put me in the hands of a student who could barely hold the scissors without shaking. Instead of getting big fat curls, I emerged with an uneven mass of crinkly black fuzz. My mother dragged me off to the bathroom and tried to wet down my hair.

"You look like Negro Chinese," she lamented, as if I had done this on purpose.

The instructor of the beauty training school had to lop off these soggy clumps to make my hair even again. "Peter Pan is very popular these days," the instructor assured my mother. I now had hair the length of a boy's, with straight-across bangs that hung at a slant two inches above my eyebrows. I liked the haircut and it made me actually look forward to my future fame.

In fact, in the beginning, I was just as excited as my mother, maybe even more so. I pictured this prodigy part of me as many different images, trying each one on for size. I was a dainty ballerina girl standing by the curtains, waiting to hear the music that would send me floating on my tiptoes. I was like the Christ child lifted out of the straw manger, crying with holy indignity. I was Cinderella stepping from her pumpkin carriage with sparkly cartoon music filling the air.

10   In all of my imaginings, I was filled with a sense that I would soon become *perfect.* My mother and father would adore me. I would be beyond reproach. I would never feel the need to sulk for anything.

But sometimes the prodigy in me became impatient. "If you don't hurry up and get me out of here, I'm disappearing for good," it warned. "And then you'll always be nothing."

Every night after dinner, my mother and I would sit at the Formica kitchen table. She would present new tests, taking her examples from stories of amazing children she had read in *Ripley's Believe It or Not,* or *Good Housekeeping, Reader's Digest,* and a dozen other magazines she kept in a pile in our bathroom. My mother got these magazines from people whose houses she cleaned. And since she cleaned many houses each week, we had a great assortment. She would look through them all, searching for stories about remarkable children.

The first night she brought out a story about a three-year-old boy who knew the capitals of all the states and even most of the European countries. A teacher was quoted as saying the little boy could also pronounce the names of the foreign cities correctly.

"What's the capital of Finland?" my mother asked me, looking at the magazine story.

15   All I knew was the capital of California, because Sacramento was the name of the street we lived on in Chinatown. "Nairobi!" I guessed, saying the most foreign word I could think of. She checked to see if that was possibly one way to pronounce "Helsinki" before showing me the answer.

The tests got harder—multiplying numbers in my head, finding the queen of hearts in a deck of cards, trying to stand on my head without using my hands, predicting the daily temperatures in Los Angeles, New York, and London.

One night I had to look at a page from the Bible for three minutes and then report everything I could remember. "Now Jehoshaphat had riches and honor in abundance and... that's all I remember, Ma," I said.

And after seeing my mother's disappointed face once again, something inside of me began to die. I hated the tests, the raised hopes and failed expectations. Before going to bed that night, I looked in the mirror above the bathroom sink and when I saw only my face staring back—and that it would always be this ordinary face—I began to cry. Such a sad, ugly girl! I made high-pitched noises like a crazed animal, trying to scratch out the face in the mirror.

And then I saw what seemed to be the prodigy side of me—because I had never seen that face before. I looked at my reflection, blinking so I could see more clearly. The girl staring back at me was angry, powerful. This girl and I were the same. I had new thoughts, willful thoughts, or rather thoughts filled with lots of won'ts. I won't let her change me, I promised myself. I won't be what I'm not.

20   So now on nights when my mother presented her tests, I performed listlessly, my head propped on one arm. I pretended to be bored. And I was. I got so bored I started counting the bellows of the foghorns out on the bay while my mother drilled me in other areas. The sound was comforting and reminded me of the cow jumping over the moon. And the next day, I played a game with myself, seeing if my mother would give up on me before eight bellows. After a while I usually counted only one, maybe two bellows at most. At last she was beginning to give up hope.

Two or three months had gone by without any mention of my being a prodigy again. And then one day my mother was watching *The Ed Sullivan Show* on TV. The TV was old and the sound kept shorting out. Every time my mother got halfway up from the sofa to adjust the set, the sound would go back on and Ed would be talking. As soon as she sat down, Ed would go silent again. She got up, the TV broke into loud piano music. She sat down. Silence. Up and down, back and forth, quiet and loud. It was like a stiff embraceless dance between her and the TV set. Finally she stood by the set with her hand on the sound dial.

She seemed entranced by the music, a little frenzied piano piece with this mesmerizing quality, sort of quick passages and then teasing lilting ones before it returned to the quick playful parts.

"*Ni kan,*" my mother said, calling me over with hurried hand gestures, "look here."

I could see why my mother was fascinated by the music. It was being pounded out by a little Chinese girl, about nine years old, with a Peter Pan haircut. The girl had the sauciness of a Shirley Temple. She was proudly modest like a proper Chinese child. And she also did this fancy sweep of a curtsy, so that the fluffy skirt of her white dress cascaded slowly to the floor like the petals of a large carnation.

25   In spite of these warning signs, I wasn't worried. Our family had no piano and we couldn't afford to buy one, let alone reams of sheet music and piano lessons. So I could be generous in my comments when my mother bad-mouthed the little girl on TV.

"Play note right, but doesn't sound good! No singing sound," my mother complained.

"What are you picking on her for?" I said carelessly. "She's pretty good. Maybe she's not the best, but she's trying hard." I knew almost immediately I would be sorry I said that.

"Just like you," she said. "Not the best. Because you not trying." She gave a little huff as she let go of the sound dial and sat down on the sofa.

The little Chinese girl sat down also to play an encore of "Anitra's Dance," by Grieg. I remember the song, because later on I had to learn how to play it.

30   Three days after watching *The Ed Sullivan Show,* my mother told me what my schedule would be for piano lessons and piano practice. She had talked to Mr. Chong, who lived on the first floor of our apartment building. Mr. Chong was a retired piano teacher and my mother had traded housecleaning services for weekly lessons and a piano for me to practice on every day, two hours a day, from four until six.

When my mother told me this, I felt as though I had been sent to hell. I whined and then kicked my foot a little when I couldn't stand it anymore.

"Why don't you like me the way I am? I'm *not* a genius! I can't play the piano. And even if I could, I wouldn't go on TV if you paid me a million dollars!" I cried.

My mother slapped me. "Who ask you be genius?" she shouted. "Only ask you be your best. For you sake. You think I want you be genius? Hnnh! What for! Who ask you!"

"So ungrateful," I heard her mutter in Chinese. "If she had as much talent as she has temper, she would be famous now."

35   Mr. Chong, whom I secretly nicknamed Old Chong, was very strange, always tapping his fingers to the silent music of an invisible orchestra. He looked ancient in my eyes. He had lost most of the hair on top of his head and he wore thick glasses and had eyes that always looked tired and sleepy. But he must have been younger than I thought, since he lived with his mother and was not yet married.

I met Old Lady Chong once and that was enough. She had this peculiar smell like a baby that had done something in its pants. And her fingers felt like a dead person's, like an old peach I once found in the back of the refrigerator; the skin just slid off the meat when I picked it up.

I soon found out why Old Chong had retired from teaching piano. He was deaf. "Like Beethoven!" he shouted to me. "We're both listening only in our head!" And he would start to conduct his frantic silent sonatas.

Our lessons went like this. He would open the book and point to different things, explaining their purpose: "Key! Treble! Bass! No sharps or flats! So this is C major! Listen now and play after me!"

And then he would play the C scale a few times, a simple chord, and then, as if inspired by an old, unreachable itch, he gradually added more notes and running trills and a pounding bass until the music was really something quite grand.

40   I would play after him, the simple scale, the simple chord, and then I just played some nonsense that sounded like a cat running up and down on top of garbage cans. Old Chong smiled and applauded and then said, "Very good! But now you must learn to keep time!"

So that's how I discovered that Old Chong's eyes were too slow to keep up with the wrong notes I was playing. He went through the motions in half-time. To help me keep rhythm, he stood behind me, pushing down on my right shoulder for every beat. He balanced pennies on top of my wrists so I would keep them still as I slowly played scales and arpeggios. He had me curve my hand around an apple and keep that shape when playing chords. He marched stiffly to show me how to make each finger dance up and down, staccato like an obedient little soldier.

He taught me all these things, and that was how I also learned I could be lazy and get away with mistakes, lots of mistakes. If I hit the wrong notes because I hadn't practiced enough, I never corrected myself. I just kept playing in rhythm. And Old Chong kept conducting his own private reverie.

So maybe I never really gave myself a fair chance. I did pick up the basics pretty quickly, and I might have become a good pianist at that young age. But I was so determined not to try, not to be anybody different that I learned to play only the most ear-splitting preludes, the most discordant hymns.

Over the next year I practiced like this, dutifully in my own way. And then one day I heard my mother and her friend Lindo Jong both talking in a loud bragging tone of voice so others could hear. It was after church, and I was leaning against the brick wall wearing a dress with stiff white petticoats. Auntie Lindo's daughter, Waverly, who was about my age, was standing farther down the wall about five feet away. We had grown up together and shared all the closeness of two sisters squabbling over crayons and dolls. In other words, for the most part, we hated each other. I thought she was snotty. Waverly Jong had gained a certain amount of fame as "Chinatown's Littlest Chinese Chess Champion."

45   "She bring home too many trophy," lamented Auntie Lindo that Sunday. "All day she play chess. All day I have no time do nothing but dust off her winnings." She threw a scolding look at Waverly, who pretended not to see her.

    "You lucky you don't have this problem," said Auntie Lindo with a sigh to my mother.

    And my mother squared her shoulders and bragged: "Our problem worser than yours. If we ask Jing-mei wash dish, she hear nothing but music. It's like you can't stop this natural talent."

    And right then, I was determined to put a stop to her foolish pride.

    A few weeks later, Old Chong and my mother conspired to have me play in a talent show which would be held in the church hall. By then, my parents had saved up enough to buy me a secondhand piano, a black Wurlitzer spinet with a scarred bench. It was the showpiece of our living room.

50   For the talent show, I was to play a piece called "Pleading Child" from Schumann's *Scenes from Childhood.* It was a simple, moody piece that sounded more difficult than it was. I was supposed to memorize the whole thing, playing the repeat parts twice to make the piece sound longer. But I dawdled over it, playing a few bars and then cheating, looking up to see what notes followed. I never really listened to what I was playing. I daydreamed about being somewhere else, about being someone else.

    The part I liked to practice best was the fancy curtsy: right foot out, touch the rose on the carpet with a pointed foot, sweep to the side, left leg bends, look up and smile.

    My parents invited all the couples from the Joy Luck Club to witness my debut. Auntie Lindo and Uncle Tin were there. Waverly and her two older brothers had also come. The first two rows were filled with children both younger and older than I was. The littlest ones got to go first. They recited simple nursery rhymes, squawked out tunes on miniature violins, twirled Hula Hoops, pranced in pink ballet tutus, and when they bowed or curtsied, the audience would sigh in unison, "Awww," and then clap enthusiastically.

    When my turn came, I was very confident. I remember my childish excitement. It was as if I knew, without a doubt, that the prodigy side of me really did exist. I had no fear whatsoever, no nervousness. I remember thinking to myself, This is it! This is it! I looked out over the audience, at my mother's blank face, my father's yawn, Auntie Lindo's stiff-lipped smile, Waverly's sulky expression. I had on a white dress layered with sheets of lace, and a pink bow in my Peter Pan haircut. As I sat down I envisioned people jumping to their feet and Ed Sullivan rushing up to introduce me to everyone on TV.

    And I started to play. It was so beautiful. I was so caught up in how lovely I looked that at first I didn't worry how I would sound. So it was a surprise to me when I hit the first wrong note and I realized something didn't sound quite right. And then I hit another and another followed that. A chill started at the top of my head and began to trickle down. Yet I couldn't stop playing, as though my hands were bewitched. I kept thinking my fingers would adjust themselves back, like a train switching to the right track. I played this strange jumble through two repeats, the sour notes staying with me all the way to the end.

55   When I stood up, I discovered my legs were shaking. Maybe I had just been nervous and the audience, like Old Chong, had seen me go through the right motions

and had not heard anything wrong at all. I swept my right foot out, went down on my knee, looked up and smiled. The room was quiet, except for Old Chong, who was beaming and shouting, "Bravo! Bravo! Well done!" But then I saw my mother's face, her stricken face. The audience clapped weakly, and as I walked back to my chair, with my whole face quivering as I tried not to cry, I heard a little boy whisper loudly to his mother, "That was awful," and the mother whispered back, "Well, she certainly tried."

And now I realized how many people were in the audience, the whole world it seemed. I was aware of eyes burning into my back. I felt the shame of my mother and father as they sat stiffly throughout the rest of the show.

We could have escaped during intermission. Pride and some strange sense of honor must have anchored my parents to their chairs. And so we watched it all: the eighteen-year-old boy with a fake moustache who did a magic show and juggled flaming hoops while riding a unicycle. The breasted girl with white makeup who sang from *Madame Butterfly* and got honorable mention. And the eleven-year-old boy who won first prize playing a tricky violin song that sounded like a busy bee.

After the show, the Hsus, the Jongs, and the St. Clairs from the Joy Luck Club, came up to my mother and father.

"Lots of talented kids," Auntie Lindo said vaguely, smiling broadly.

60 "That was somethin' else," said my father, and I wondered if he was referring to me in a humorous way, or whether he even remembered what I had done.

Waverly looked at me and shrugged her shoulders. "You aren't a genius like me," she said matter-of-factly. And if I hadn't felt so bad, I would have pulled her braids and punched her stomach.

But my mother's expression was what devastated me: a quiet, blank look that said she had lost everything. I felt the same way, and it seemed as if everybody were now coming up, like gawkers at the scene of an accident, to see what parts were actually missing. When we got on the bus to go home, my father was humming the busy-bee tune and my mother was silent. I kept thinking she wanted to wait until we got home before shouting at me. But when my father unlocked the door to our apartment, my mother walked in and then went to the back, into the bedroom. No accusations. No blame. And in a way, I felt disappointed. I had been waiting for her to start shouting, so I could shout back and cry and blame her for all my misery.

I assumed my talent-show fiasco meant I never had to play the piano again. But two days later, after school, my mother came out of the kitchen and saw me watching TV.

"Four clock," she reminded me as if it were any other day. I was stunned, as though she were asking me to go through the talent-show torture again. I wedged myself more tightly in front of the TV.

65 "Turn off TV," she called from the kitchen five minutes later.

I didn't budge. And then I decided. I didn't have to do what my mother said anymore. I wasn't her slave. This wasn't China. I had listened to her before and look what happened. She was the stupid one.

She came out from the kitchen and stood in the arched entryway of the living room. "Four clock," she said once again, louder.

"I'm not going to play anymore," I said nonchalantly. "Why should I? I'm not a genius."

She walked over and stood in front of the TV. I saw her chest was heaving up and down in an angry way.

70   "No!" I said, and I now felt stronger, as if my true self had finally emerged. So this was what had been inside me all along.

"No! I won't!" I screamed.

She yanked me by the arm, pulled me off the floor, snapped off the TV. She was frighteningly strong, half pulling, half carrying me toward the piano as I kicked the throw rugs under my feet. She lifted me up and onto the hard bench. I was sobbing by now, looking at her bitterly. Her chest was heaving even more and her mouth was open, smiling crazily as if she were pleased I was crying.

"You want me to be someone that I'm not!" I sobbed. "I'll never be the kind of daughter you want me to be!"

"Only two kinds of daughters," she shouted in Chinese. "Those who are obedient and those who follow their own mind! Only one kind of daughter can live in this house. Obedient daughter!"

75   "Then I wish I wasn't your daughter. I wish you weren't my mother," I shouted. As I said these things I got scared. It felt like worms and toads and slimy things crawling out of my chest, but it also felt good, as if this awful side of me had surfaced, at last.

"Too late change this," said my mother shrilly.

And I could sense her anger rising to its breaking point. I wanted to see it spill over. And that's when I remembered the babies she had lost in China, the ones we never talked about. "Then I wish I'd never been born!" I shouted. "I wish I were dead! Like them."

It was as if I had said the magic words. Alakazam!—and her face went blank, her mouth closed, her arms went slack, and she backed out of the room, stunned, as if she were blowing away like a small brown leaf, thin, brittle, lifeless.

It was not the only disappointment my mother felt in me. In the years that followed, I failed her so many times, each time asserting my own will, my right to fall short of expectations. I didn't get straight As. I didn't become class president. I didn't get into Stanford. I dropped out of college.

80   For unlike my mother, I did not believe I could be anything I wanted to be. I could only be me.

And for all those years, we never talked about the disaster at the recital or my terrible accusations afterward at the piano bench. All of that remained unchecked, like a betrayal that was now unspeakable. So I never found a way to ask her why she had hoped for something so large that failure was inevitable.

And even worse, I never asked her what frightened me the most: Why had she given up hope?

For after our struggle at the piano, she never mentioned my playing again. The lessons stopped. The lid to the piano was closed, shutting out the dust, my misery, and her dreams.

So she surprised me. A few years ago, she offered to give me the piano, for my thirtieth birthday. I had not played in all those years. I saw the offer as a sign of forgiveness, a tremendous burden removed.

85   "Are you sure?" I asked shyly. "I mean, won't you and Dad miss it?"

"No, this your piano," she said firmly. "Always your piano. You only one can play."

"Well, I probably can't play anymore," I said. "It's been years."

"You pick up fast," said my mother, as if she knew this was certain. "You have natural talent. You could been genius if you want to."

"No I couldn't."

90 "You just not trying," said my mother. And she was neither angry nor sad. She said it as if to announce a fact that could never be disproved. "Take it," she said.

But I didn't at first. It was enough that she had offered it to me. And after that, every time I saw it in my parents' living room, standing in front of the bay windows, it made me feel proud, as if it were a shiny trophy I had won back.

Last week I sent a tuner over to my parents' apartment and had the piano reconditioned, for purely sentimental reasons. My mother had died a few months before and I had been getting things in order for my father, a little bit at a time. I put the jewelry in special silk pouches. The sweaters she had knitted in yellow, pink, bright orange—all the colors I hated—I put those in moth-proof boxes. I found some old Chinese silk dresses, the kind with little slits up the sides. I rubbed the old silk against my skin, then wrapped them in tissue and decided to take them home with me.

After I had the piano tuned, I opened the lid and touched the keys. It sounded even richer than I remembered. Really, it was a very good piano. Inside the bench were the same exercise notes with handwritten scales, the same secondhand music books with their covers held together with yellow tape.

I opened up the Schumann book to the dark little piece I had played at the recital. It was on the left-hand side of the page, "Pleading Child." It looked more difficult than I remembered. I played a few bars, surprised at how easily the notes came back to me.

95 And for the first time, or so it seemed, I noticed the piece on the right-hand side. It was called "Perfectly Contented." I tried to play this one as well. It had a lighter melody but the same flowing rhythm and turned out to be quite easy. "Pleading Child" was shorter but slower; "Perfectly Contented" was longer, but faster. And after I played them both a few times, I realized they were two halves of the same song.

◆ POETRY ◆

JULIA ALVAREZ [B. 1950]

Though Julia Alvarez was born in New York City, she spent her childhood in the Dominican Republic. When she was ten, she returned with her parents to New York City, where she attended public schools. Confused and lonely (she spoke only Spanish), she struggled until high school, where she encountered an English teacher who encouraged her to write of her experiences as a stranger to the United States and its language. This experience was transforming, and she discovered her love of writing. She went on to study at Middlebury College, where she currently teaches, and later earned an M.F.A. from Syracuse University. She has published three books of poetry, Homecoming

(1984), The Other Side/El Otro Lado *(1995), and* The Woman I Kept to Myself *(2004), and four novels,* How the Garcia Girls Lost Their Accents *(1991),* In the Time of the Butterflies *(1994),* ¡Yo! *(1996), and* In the Name of Salome *(2000). Her latest book is a young adult novel,* Return to Sender *(2009).*

DUSTING   [1984]

Each morning I wrote my name
On the dusty cabinet, then crossed
The dining table in script, scrawled
In capitals on the backs of chairs,
Practicing signatures like scales   5
While mother followed, squirting
Linseed from a burping can
Into a crumpled-up flannel.

She erased my fingerprints
From the bookshelf and rocker,   10
Polished mirrors on the desk
Scribbled with my alphabets.
My name was swallowed in the towel
With which she jewelled the table tops.
The grain surfaced in the oak   15
And the pine grew luminous.
But I refused with every mark
To be like her, anonymous.

JANICE MIRIKITANI [B. 1938]

Like many Japanese-Americans of her generation, Janice Mirikitani was incarcerated with her family in an internment camp during World War II. She was educated at UCLA and the University of California of Berkeley, where she first developed her interests in the arts, from both creative and administrative perspectives. During her career, she has managed numerous social and arts programs, public and private, including San Francisco's famous Glide Foundation. She has published four collections of poetry: Awake in the River *(1978),* Shedding Silence *(1987),* We, the Dangerous *(1994), and* Love Works *(2002).*

FOR MY FATHER   [1987]

He came over the ocean
carrying Mt. Fuji on
his back/Tule Lake on his chest

hacked through the brush
of deserts   5
and made them grow
strawberries

we stole berries
from the stem
we could not afford them   10
for breakfast

his eyes held
nothing
as he whipped us
for stealing.   15

the desert had dried
his soul.

wordless
he sold
the rich,   20
full berries
to hakujin°
whose children
pointed at our eyes

they ate fresh   25
strawberries
on corn flakes.
Father,
i wanted to scream
at your silence.   30
Your strength
was a stranger
i could never touch.

iron
in your eyes   35
to shield
the pain
to shield desert-like wind
from patches
of strawberries   40
grown
from
tears.

22 hakujin white people

THEODORE ROETHKE [1908–1963]

Theodore Roethke was a native of Saginaw, Michigan, where his father owned a greenhouse. After graduating from the University of Michigan, he did graduate work at Harvard, taught at a number of universities and became a poet-in-residence at the University of Washington in 1948. The poem "My Papa's Waltz" is taken from his second volume of poems, The Lost Son *(1948). During the course of a long career, he won two National Book Awards, and in 1954* received the Pulitzer Prize for his book of poems, The Waking: Poems 1933–1953.

MY PAPA'S WALTZ   [1942]

The whiskey on your breath
Could make a small boy dizzy;
But I hung on like death
Such waltzing was not easy.

We romped until the pans   5
Slid from the kitchen shelf;
My mother's countenance
Could not unfrown itself.

The hand that held my wrist
Was battered on one knuckle;   10
At every step you missed
My right ear scraped a buckle.

You beat time on my head
With a palm caked hard by dirt,
Then waltzed me off to bed   15
Still clinging to your shirt.

CATHY SONG [B. 1955]

Cathy Song was born in Honolulu, Hawaii, to a Korean father and a Chinese mother. She graduated from Welles-ley College in 1975, and received an M.A. from Boston Col-lege in 1981. She currently lives in Hawaii, when she is not teaching creative writing on the mainland. Her first book, The Picture Bride, *from which "The Youngest Daughter" is taken, was published in 1983.* Frameless Windows, Squares of Light, *her second book, was published in 1991.* School Figures *appeared in 1994 and* The Land of Bliss *in 2001, and her latest collection of poems,* Cloud Moving Hands, *was published in 2007.*

THE YOUNGEST DAUGHTER

[1983]

The sky has been dark
for many years.
My skin has become as damp
and pale as rice paper
and feels the way   5
mother's used to before the drying sun
parched it out there in the fields.
Lately, when I touch my eyelids,
my hands react as if
I had just touched something   10
hot enough to burn.
My skin, aspirin colored,
tingles with migraine. Mother
has been massaging the left side of my face
especially in the evenings   15
when the pain flares up.

This morning
her breathing was graveled,
her voice gruff with affection
when I wheeled her into the bath.   20
She was in a good humor,
making jokes about her great breasts,
floating in the milky water
like two walruses,
flaccid and whiskered around the nipples.   25
I scrubbed them with a sour taste
in my mouth, thinking:
six children and an old man
have sucked from these brown nipples.

I was almost tender   30
when I came to the blue bruises
that freckle her body,
places where she has been injecting insulin
for thirty years. I soaped her slowly,
she sighed deeply, her eyes closed.   35
It seems it has always
been like this: the two of us
in this sunless room,
the splashing of the bathwater.

In the afternoons   40
when she has rested,
she prepares our ritual of tea and rice,
garnished with a shred of gingered fish,

a slice of pickled turnip,
a token for my white body.   45
We eat in the familiar silence.
She knows I am not to be trusted,
even now planning my escape.
As I toast to her health
with the tea she has poured,   50
a thousand cranes curtain the window,
fly up in a sudden breeze.

MAKING CONNECTIONS

1. To what extent does your own experience affect your response to the mother-daughter relationship in Amy Tan's "Two Kinds"?

2. The narrator, Jing-mei, is the protagonist in this story. How does her point of view affect how and what we are told?

3. Describe Jing-mei. What is the primary conflict she struggles with? Is it external? Internal? Both? Explain. Why is she so resistant to her mother's wishes?

4. Describe her mother. How would she characterize Jing-mei? What does she want for her daughter? How does her own background influence that?

5. When Jing-mei shouts at her mother that she wishes she was not her daughter, she recalls, "As I said [this] I got scared. It felt like worms and toads and slimy things crawling out of my chest, but it also felt good, as if this awful side of me had surfaced, at last." What do you think she means?

6. After her mother dies, Jing-mei is reunited with her piano. What does she realize about herself, her mother, and their relationship?

7. In Julia Alvarez's "Dusting," the speaker's attitude toward her mother seems to be revealed in the poem's final word. What effect did the speaker's final comment have on you? Were you expecting the poem to end this way?

8. In what sense is the mother "anonymous"? Why do you think the speaker refuses to be like her?

9. Compare this poem with "The Youngest Daughter" on page 275.

10. The speaker in "For My Father" says that her father "came over the ocean / carrying Mt. Fuji on / his back." What do you think she means?

11. Later in the poem, she addresses her father directly and says, "Your strength / was a stranger / I could never touch." What do you think she is saying about their relationship? What has she been missing?

12. Have you ever had this kind of response to a parent or authority figure in your life? Explain.

13. Compare this poem to the parent-child relationship in "Those Winter Sundays" (p. 13) or "The Road" (p. 256).

14. In "My Papa's Waltz," do you think this is a good or bad memory for the speaker? Explain. To what extent is your response to this poem affected by your own experience with a parent?

15. What is the mother's response to the dancing, and why does she respond this way?
16. How does this father compare with the fathers in other poems in the text (e.g., "Those Winter Sundays" on p. 13 or "For My Father" on p. 272)?
17. What does the speaker in "The Youngest Daughter" mean by "She knows I am not to be trusted, / even now planning my escape"? Do you think the narrator should be having these feelings? Explain.
18. Describe the speaker's reciprocal relationship with her mother. What keeps the mother and daughter bound to each other? What power do they have over each other? What lines in the poem support your view?
19. Compare this mother-daughter relationship with other poems in this subtheme and "35/10" on page 285.

MAKING AN ARGUMENT

1. To what extent do cultural differences lead to the central conflict in "Two Kinds"? To what extent are these differences generational or based on the differing circumstances of where the mother and daughter grew up? Write about the impact of cultural and generational differences on the relationship of mother and daughter in this story. Cite the text of the story for support.
2. Based on the description in "Dusting," write a different ending for this poem. Generate a list of different words that could have been used to describe the mother. Write about the ways that these words change the overall effect of the poem and its meaning. Carefully cite the original language of the poem for support.
3. "My Papa's Waltz" is written in the past tense and contains a number of strong images. Is the adult speaker angry or appreciative? Based on the content of the poem, what do you believe he feels? Is there a clear message here? Write about the narrative tone and imagery in this poem and its effectiveness in conveying the poem's meaning. Cite the text of the poem for support.
4. The speaker in "My Papa's Waltz" narrates in the past tense—not from the perspective of the small boy in the poem. If it were told from the perspective of the small boy, how would it change? Write about the effectiveness of narration and imagery in this poem. Cite the text of the poem for support.
5. One of the most striking images in "The Youngest Daughter" coincides with the speaker's toast to her mother's health in the same stanza, and is contained in the lines, "a thousand cranes curtain the window, / fly up in a sudden breeze." How does that image compare with other images the speaker presents? Write about the effectiveness of the imagery in this poem and the impact it has on the poem's meaning. Cite the text of the poem for support.

MARGARET ATWOOD [B. 1939]

Margaret Atwood was born in Ottawa, Canada, and took extensive trips during her childhood through the wilds of Canada with her father, an entomologist. In 1962, the same year she graduated from the University of Toronto, she published her first book of poetry, Double Persephone. *She has since published numerous works of fiction, poetry, and criticism, including the novels* Surfacing *(1972),* Cat's Eye *(1988), and the futuristic* The Handmaid's Tale *(1985), which was made into a film. Her most recent book is a novel,* The Year of the Flood *(2009). A fierce proponent of Canadian literature as well as an ardent feminist, Atwood has been instrumental in forging a Canadian cultural identity separate from that of England and the United States. She told an interviewer in* Ms. *magazine, "I began as a profoundly apolitical writer, but then I began to do what all novelists and some poets do: I began to describe the world around me."*

SIREN SONG   [1974]

This is the one song everyone
would like to learn: the song
that is irresistible:

the song that forces men
to leap overboard in squadrons   5
even though they see in the beached skulls

the song nobody knows
because anyone who has heard it
is dead, and others can't remember.

Shall I tell you the secret   10
and if I do, will you get me
out of this bird suit?

I don't enjoy it here
squatting on this island
looking picturesque and mythical   15

with these two feathery maniacs.
I don't enjoy singing
this trio, fatal and valuable.

I will tell the secret to you,
to you, only to you.   20
Come closer. This song

is a cry for help: Help me!
Only you, only you can,
you are unique

at last. Alas   25
it is a boring song
but it works every time.

MAKING CONNECTIONS

1. "Siren Song" alludes to Greek mythology. Who were the Sirens?
2. Who is the speaker in this version? What is her "siren song"?
3. Do you agree that the song she describes is "irresistible"? Explain.

MAKING AN ARGUMENT

1. Identify the theme of this poem, and write an essay comparing it to "The
    Horse Dealer's Daughter" on page 693. Cite the text of both the poem and
    the story for support.

ROBERT FROST [1874–1963]

Robert Frost was born in San Francisco, California, to a
headmaster and schoolteacher who met at a tiny private
school in Pennsylvania. When his father died of tubercu-
losis in 1885, his mother returned the family to New Eng-
land. Frost attended a local high school where, together
with the woman he would eventually marry, Elinor White,
he served as class valedictorian. It was in high school,
where he was known as the class poet, that Frost seriously
began writing poetry. In the many years that followed, Frost continued to write
while he attended college (short stints at Dartmouth and Harvard) and held a
series of odd jobs, including work as a cobbler, journalist, and teacher, and at
a cotton mill. From 1900 to 1905, he lived on a farm in Derry, New Hampshire,
purchased for him by his grandfather, but financial hardships—he and Elinor
had five children by this point—forced him to return to teaching. In 1912, frus-
trated by his inability to publish in the United States, Frost moved his family to
England, where he published his first two books of poetry: A Boy's Will *(1913)*
and North of Boston *(1914). By the time he returned to the United States in*
1915, he was well on his way to becoming the most famous American poet of
the century. In 1961, an infirm Frost read his poem "The Gift Outright" at the
inauguration of President John F. Kennedy. His poetry, which takes much of its
inspiration from the countryside of New England, is often deceptively simple, as
it artfully and effortlessly weaves together traditional metrical forms with col-
loquial American speech.

MENDING WALL

[1914]

Something there is that doesn't love a wall,
That sends the frozen-ground-swell under it,
And spills the upper boulders in the sun;
And makes gaps even two can pass abreast.
The work of hunters is another thing: 5
I have come after them and made repair
Where they have left not one stone on a stone,
But they would have the rabbit out of hiding,
To please the yelping dogs. The gaps I mean,
No one has seen them made or heard them made,   10
But at spring mending-time we find them there.
I let my neighbor know beyond the hill;
And on a day we meet to walk the line
And set the wall between us once again.
We keep the wall between us as we go.   15
To each the boulders that have fallen to each.
And some are loaves and some so nearly balls
We have to use a spell to make them balance:
"Stay where you are until our backs are turned!"
We wear our fingers rough with handling them.   20
Oh, just another kind of outdoor game,
One on a side. It comes to little more:
There where it is we do not need the wall:
He is all pine and I am apple orchard.
My apple trees will never get across   25
And eat the cones under his pines, I tell him.
He only says, "Good fences make good neighbors."
Spring is the mischief in me, and I wonder
If I could put a notion in his head:
"*Why* do they make good neighbors? Isn't it   30
Where there are cows? But here there are no cows.
Before I built a wall I'd ask to know
What I was walling in or walling out,
And to whom I was like to give offense.
Something there is that doesn't love a wall,   35
That wants it down." I could say "Elves" to him,
But it's not elves exactly, and I'd rather
He said it for himself. I see him there
Bringing a stone grasped firmly by the top
In each hand, like an old-stone savage armed.   40
He moves in darkness as it seems to me,
Not of woods only and the shade of trees.
He will not go behind his father's saying,

And he likes having thought of it so well
He says again, "Good fences make good neighbors."   45

MAKING CONNECTIONS

1.   Have you ever felt walled in or out? Explain.
2.   To what extent is the wall in this poem symbolic?
3.   What is the "Something" in "Something there is that doesn't love a wall"?
4.   How would you interpret the line "He moves in darkness as it seems to me"?

MAKING AN ARGUMENT

1.   Does the speaker in the poem agree that "Good fences make good neigh-
     bors"? He says of his neighbor: "He moves in darkness as it seems to me." But
     why does he remind his neighbor when it's time to mend the wall? Write an
     interpretation of this poem. Carefully cite the text of the poem for support.

SEAMUS HEANEY [B. 1939]

*Sometimes referred to as Ireland's greatest poet since Yeats,
Seamus Heaney was born on a farm in County Derry in
Northern Ireland. He graduated from Queen's University
in Belfast in 1961. He published his first book of poetry,
Eleven Poems, in 1965; Electric Light (2001) is his most
recent. He was awarded the Nobel Prize in Literature in
1995. Currently he divides his time between Dublin and
the United States, where he holds a teaching position at
Harvard University. The rich, and often violent, history of
Ireland and its people is the concern of much of his poetry. His critically acclaimed
verse translation of Beowulf was published in 2000. The Burial at Thebes, a version of Sophocles's Antigonê, was published in 2004. And his latest collection of
poetry, Spelling It Out, was published in 2009.*

DIGGING   [1965]

Between my finger and my thumb
The squat pen rests; snug as a gun.

Under my window, a clean rasping sound
When the spade sinks into gravelly ground:
My father, digging. I look down   5

Till his straining rump among the flowerbeds
Bends low, comes up twenty years away

Stooping in rhythm through potato drills
Where he was digging.

The coarse boot nestled on the lug, the shaft   10
Against the inside knee was levered firmly.
He rooted out tall tops, buried the bright edge deep
To scatter new potatoes that we picked
Loving their cool hardness in our hands.

By God, the old man could handle a spade.   15
Just like his old man.

My grandfather cut more turf in a day
Than any other man on Toner's bog.
Once I carried him milk in a bottle
Corked sloppily with paper. He straightened up   20
To drink it, then fell to right away

Nicking and slicing neatly, heaving sods
Over his shoulder, going down and down
For the good turf. Digging.

The cold smell of potato mould, the squelch and slap   25
Of soggy peat, the curt cuts of an edge
Through living roots awaken in my head.
But I've no spade to follow men like them.

Between my finger and my thumb
The squat pen rests.   30
I'll dig with it.

▌MAKING CONNECTIONS

1. What kind of work did the speaker's father and grandfather do? To what
   extent is your response to this poem influenced by the work of your parents
   or grandparents?
2. The speaker begins the poem by saying, "The squat pen rests; snug as a
   gun." But in the last stanza he says of the squat pen, "I'll dig with it." What
   kind of work does he do, and what does he mean?

▌MAKING AN ARGUMENT

1. Do you think the speaker in the poem is suggesting that "we should define
   ourselves by the work we do"? Write about the extent to which this poem
   suggests that and whether or not you think it's appropriate. Cite the text of
   the poem for support.

PHILIP LARKIN [1922–1985]

Philip Larkin was born to a working-class family in Coventry, an industrial city in northern England. He attended Oxford University on a scholarship, and afterward served for many years as the librarian at the University of Hull. Though he wrote novels and was an astute critic of both music—jazz, in particular—and literature, Larkin is remembered today as one of England's most influential postwar poets. In his poems, which are often called anti-Romantic, Larkin takes a witty, sophisticated, and tough-minded approach to traditional poetic subjects.

THIS BE THE VERSE   [1971]

They fuck you up, your mum and dad.
    They may not mean to, but they do.
They fill you with the faults they had
    And add some extra, just for you.

But they were fucked up in their turn   5
    By fools in old-style hats and coats,
Who half the time were soppy-stern
    And half at one another's throats.

Man hands on misery to man.
    It deepens like a coastal shelf.   10
Get out as early as you can.
    And don't have any kids yourself.

MAKING CONNECTIONS

1. What is the tone of this poem? Were you surprised by it, and the message? Why?
2. Discuss the effect of the rhythm and rhyme scheme on the content of the poem. Do you think it helps to convey its meaning? How so?

MAKING AN ARGUMENT

1. Take a position in response to the conclusion of this whimsical but provocative poem. To what extent is the advice at the end of the poem realistic? Do you agree with it? If yes, why? If not, write an ending you believe is more realistic, and explain why you prefer it. Cite the text of the poem for support.

LI-YOUNG LEE [B. 1957]

*Li-Young Lee was born in Jakarta, Indonesia. He came
to the United States in 1964 at the age of seven, when his
father, a physician and minister, was forced to flee Indonesia due to political persecution. He attended the University of Pittsburgh, the University of Arizona, and the State
University of New York at Brockport. His volumes of poetry
include* Rose *(1986) and* The City in Which I Love You
(1990). In 1994, be published a book of his memoirs, The
Winged Seed. *His most recent book of poems,* Behind My Eyes, *was published in
2008. He lives in Chicago.*

THE GIFT   [1986]

To pull the metal splinter from my palm
my father recited a story in a low voice.
I watched his lovely face and not the blade.
Before the story ended he removed
the iron sliver I thought I'd die from.   5

I can't remember the tale
but hear his voice still, a well
of dark water, a prayer.
And I recall his hands,
two measures of tenderness   10
he laid against my face,
the flames of discipline
he raised above my head.

Had you entered that afternoon
you would have thought you saw a man   15
planting something in a boy's palm,
a silver tear, a tiny flame.
Had you followed that boy
you would have arrived here,
where I bend over my wife's right hand.   20

Look how I shave her thumbnail down
so carefully she feels no pain.
Watch as I lift the splinter out.
I was seven when my father
took my hand like this,   25
and I did not hold that shard
between my fingers and think,
Metal that will bury me,
christen it Little Assassin,
Ore Going Deep for My Heart,   30
And I did not lift up my wound and cry,

Death visited here!
I did what a child does
when he's given something to keep,
I kissed my father.   35

MAKING CONNECTIONS

1. What is "the gift"? Can you remember a time when someone gave you a "gift" like this? Explain.

2. How do you think the italicized phrases *"Metal that will bury me"* and *"Death visited here!"* fit in this poem? Are there any other phrases that stand out for you?

MAKING AN ARGUMENT

1. Like "Those Winter Sundays" (p. 13), "My Papa's Waltz" (p. 274), and "The Road" (p. 257), this poem is about a father-son relationship. On the surface, its tone and conclusion seem quite different, yet there is one similarity they all share. Each of these sons has been "given something to keep." Write about what each son has been given, and cite the text of each work to support your view.

SHARON OLDS [B. 1942]

Born in San Francisco, California, Sharon Olds graduated from Stanford University in 1964 and earned a Ph.D. from Columbia University in 1972. She published her first book of poetry, Satan Says, *in 1980, but it was not until her second,* The Dead and the Living, *which won the National Book Critics Circle Award in 1985, that her reputation as an important voice was firmly established. Her poetry, which is often intensely personal, is noted for its candor and power. Her book of poems,* Blood, Tin, and Straw, *was published in 1999 and her latest book of poems,* One Secret Thing, *in 2008. She teaches creative writing at New York University.*

35/10   [1984]

Brushing out my daughter's dark
silken hair before the mirror
I see the grey gleaming on my head,
the silver-haired servant behind her. Why is it
just as we begin to go   5
they begin to arrive, the fold in my neck
clarifying as the fine bones of her
hips sharpen? As my skin shows
its dry pitting, she opens like a small
pale flower on the tip of a cactus;   10
as my last chances to bear a child

are falling through my body, the duds among them,
her purse of eggs, round and
firm as hard-boiled yolks, is about
to snap its clasp. I brush her tangled   15
fragrant hair at bedtime. It's an old
story—the oldest we have on our planet—
the story of replacement.

MAKING CONNECTIONS

1. What does the title of the poem refer to? How do the numbers "35/10" match the specific comparisons of the poem?

2. In what way is it "an old / story—the oldest we have on our planet"? How does it play itself out in your own life?

3. Compare this mother-daughter relationship with that in "Dusting" on page 272.

SUSAN MUSGRAVE [B. 1951]

Raised on Vancouver Island in British Columbia, Canada, Susan Musgrave has spent extended periods of time living in Ireland, England, the Queen Charlotte Islands, Panama, and Colombia. She travels widely, both abroad and in Canada, to give speeches, writing workshops, and poetry readings. She has held Writer-in-Residence positions at the University of Waterloo and the University of Western Ontario, and was awarded the Presidential Writer-in-Residence Fellowship at the University of Toronto. She has worked online with over *a thousand high school students across Canada through the Writers in Electronic Residence Programme, and she has served as Chair of the Writers' Union of Canada. In addition to her poetry, Musgrave has published several children's books, works of fiction, and collections of essays.*

YOU DIDN'T FIT   [1985]

for my father

You wouldn't fit in your coffin
but to me it was no surprise.
All your life you had never fit in
anywhere; you saw no reason to
begin fitting now.   5

When I was little I remember
a sheriff coming. You were
taken to court because your
false teeth didn't fit and you
wouldn't pay the dentist. It was   10
your third set, you said none of them

fit properly. I was afraid then
that something would take you from me
as it has done now: death
with a bright face and teeth that   15
fit perfectly.

A human smile that shuts me out.
The Court, I remember, returned
your teeth, now marked an exhibit.
You were dismissed with costs—   20
I never understood. The teeth were
terrible. We liked you better
without them.

We didn't fit, either, into your
life or your loneliness, though you   25
tried, and we did too. Once
I wanted to marry you, and then left;
I'm still the child who won't fit
into the arms of anyone, but is
always reaching.   30

I was awkward for years, my bones
didn't fit in my body but stuck out
like my heart—people used to comment
on it. They said I was very good
at office parties where you took me   35
and let others do the talking—the
crude jokes, the corny men—I saw
how they hurt you and I loved you
harder than ever.

Because neither of us fit. Later you   40
blamed me, said "You must fit in,"
but I didn't and I still think
it made you secretly happy.

Like I am now: you won't fit in your
coffin. My mother, after a life   45
of it, says, "This is the last straw."
And it is. We're all clutching.

MAKING CONNECTIONS

1. Based on your own experience, do you think "not fitting in" is a problem? Explain.
2. What is the tone of this poem? Does the speaker think "not fitting in" is a problem? Explain.
3. In response to the mother's declaration "this is the last straw," what does the speaker mean when she says, "we're all clutching."

MAKING AN ARGUMENT

1. Do you think there is a price to be paid for not fitting in? Is it worth it? Explain. Compare this poem to "Barbie Doll" on page 14.

WILLIAM STAFFORD [1914–1993]

William Stafford was raised during the Great Depression and spent the majority of his childhood moving from place to place while his family searched for work. Despite such hardships, he earned a bachelor's degree from the University of Kansas in 1937 and began to work on his master's degree, until he was drafted by the Army. Stafford was classified as a conscientious objector and assigned to alternative service, working on forestry and soil-conservation efforts.

He recorded this experience in his 1947 memoir, Down My Heart. *Stafford's first major work of poetry,* Traveling through the Dark, *won the National Book Award in 1963. In 1970, he became the Consultant in Poetry to the Library of Congress, a position that we know today as the U.S. Poet Laureate. Stafford's poetry is typically short and deceptively simple, often revealing a complex outlook on man's relationship with nature.*

FRIENDS   [1982]

How far friends are! They forget you,
most days. They have to, I know; but still,
it's lonely just being far and a friend.
I put my hand out—this chair, this table—
so near: touch, that's how to live.   5
Call up a friend? All right, but the phone
itself is what loves you, warm on your ear,
on your hand. Or, you lift a pen
to write—it's not that far person
but this familiar pen that comforts.   10
Near things: Friend, here's my hand.

MAKING CONNECTIONS

1. What is the speaker saying about friendship? Do you agree or disagree? Why?
2. How important is proximity to friendship? Have you been able to maintain friendships with your high school classmates? Has it been challenging?
3. Describe the imagery used by the author. How does it differ from the way poets usually describe friendship?

MAKING AN ARGUMENT

1. How do you think this speaker would feel about a long-distance relationship? Take a position and defend it using citations from the text of the poem for support.

CONNECTING THROUGH COMPARISON: REMEMBRANCE

The two poems that follow address a subtheme of this section: remembrance of family and friends. In each of the poems that follow, the speaker expresses regret about past events. In one case, the memory is prompted by objects from her past. In the other, the speaker seems to seek the memory on his own. Read and discussed together, these poems invite comparison and connections—not only with each other, but with similar experiences of your own.

ELIZABETH GAFFNEY [B. 1953]

Elizabeth Gaffney's poems have appeared in Wordsmith, Southern Poetry Review, College English, Descant, Wind, *and other publications. A graduate of Fordham University, she has a Ph.D. from the State University of New York at Stony Brook and teaches at SUNY Westchester Community College. She lives in Pelham, New York, with her husband and three children.*

LOSSES THAT TURN UP IN DREAMS [1992]

The notebook I left on a windowsill
in Keating Hall two years ago
floats back to me full of poems.
The silver pin shaped like a bird's wings,
my mother's gold chain   5
stolen with the burnished purse I loved,
its leather worn to smoothness
from years of use—in dreams
appear again my homing pigeons.

Their familiar feel reassures me   10
that nothing's ever gone for good;
the sunglasses, pens, umbrellas,
the scarf of red and blue challis,
the lost socks, the trivial objects
I weep for are losses so palpable,   15

all equal in the land of dreams,
where the baby I lost one October night
comes home to nest, poor ghost,
and my mother, grandmother, uncles
crowd small rooms, and I am one   20
with the tree that bloomed on my birthday,
a daughter, filling up with milk and love.

WILLIAM SHAKESPEARE   [1564–1616]

(See biography on p. 495)

WHEN TO THE SESSIONS OF SWEET SILENT THOUGHT (SONNET 30)

[1609]

When to the sessions° of sweet silent thought
I summon° up remembrance of things past,
I sigh the lack of many a thing I sought,
And with old woes new wail my dear times waste:
Then can I drown an eye (un-used to flow)   5
For precious friends hid in death's dateless° night,
And weep afresh love's long since canceled° woe,
And moan the expense of many a vanished sight,
Then can I grieve at grievances foregone,
And heavily from woe to woe tell o'er   10
The sad account of fore-bemoaned moan,
Which I new pay, as if not paid before.
But the while I think on thee (dear friend)
All losses are restored, and sorrows end.

MAKING CONNECTIONS

1. In "Losses That Turn Up in Dreams," what losses is the speaker talking about?
2. In what way are the objects that she mentions "homing pigeons"? Can you think of objects in your own life that are "homing pigeons"?
3. What does she mean by "I am one / with the tree that bloomed on my birthday"?
4. In "Sonnet 30," what does the speaker mean by "weep afresh love's long since canceled woe"?
5. To what extent do either or both poems remind you of your own experience? Compare the two poems. How are they alike? How different?

MAKING AN ARGUMENT

1. While both poems address a similar topic, they were written nearly four hundred years apart, and their structures, rhythm and rhyme, diction, and use of poetic language are quite different. Write about the differences and similarities of these elements in these poems and their impact on content. Cite the language of both poems for support.

1 sessions as in court sessions
2 summon as in a legal summons
6 dateless endless
7 canceled as in a paid-up debt

◆ **E S S A Y** ◆

BELL HOOKS [B. 1952]

A prolific prose writer and poet who was born as Gloria Jean Watkins, bell hooks took the name of her progressive, outspoken great-grandmother. An outspoken commentator herself on issues of race, class, and gender, her books include Ain't I a Woman *(1981),* Talking Back: Thinking Feminist, Thinking Black *(1989),* Yearning: Race, Gender and Cultural Studies *(1990),* Outlaw Culture: Resisting Representation *(1994),* Bone Black: Memories of Girlhood *(1996),* Remembered Rapture: The Writer at Work *(1999), and* Communion: The Female Search for Love *(2003). Her latest book,* Teaching Critical Thinking: Practical Wisdom, *was published in 2010. She has taught at Yale University, Oberlin College, and CCNY (Community College of New York).*

INSPIRED ECCENTRICITY   [1996]

There are family members you try to forget and ones that you always remember, that you can't stop talking about. They may be dead—long gone—but their presence lingers and you have to share who they were and who they still are with the world. You want everyone to know them as you did, to love them as you did.

All my life I have remained enchanted by the presence of my mother's parents, Sarah and Gus Oldham. When I was a child they were already old. I did not see that then, though. They were Baba and Daddy Gus, together for more than seventy years at the time of his death. Their marriage fascinated me. They were strangers and lovers—two eccentrics who created their own world.

More than any other family members, together they gave me a worldview that sustained me during a difficult and painful childhood. Reflecting on the eclectic writer I have become, I see in myself a mixture of these two very different but equally powerful figures from my childhood. Baba was tall, her skin so white and her hair so jet black and straight that she could have easily "passed," denying all traces of blackness. Yet the man she married was short and dark, and sometimes his skin looked like the color of soot from burning coal. In our childhood the fireplaces burned coal. It was bright heat, luminous and fierce. If you got too close it could burn you.

Together Baba and Daddy Gus generated a hot heat. He was a man of few words, deeply committed to silence—so much so that it was like a religion to him. When he spoke you could hardly hear what he said. Baba was just the opposite. Smoking an abundance of cigarettes a day, she talked endlessly. She preached. She yelled. She fussed. Often her vitriolic rage would heap itself on Daddy Gus, who would sit calmly in his chair by the stove, as calm and still as the Buddha sits. And when he had enough of her words, he would reach for his hat and walk.

5   Neither Baba nor Daddy Gus drove cars. Rarely did they ride in them. They preferred walking. And even then their styles were different. He moved slow, as though carrying a great weight; she with her tall, lean, boyish frame moved swiftly, as though there was never time to waste. Their one agreed-upon passion was fishing. Though they did not do even that together. They lived close but they created separate worlds.

In a big two-story wood frame house with lots of rooms they constructed a world that could contain their separate and distinct personalities. As children one of the first things we noticed about our grandparents was that they did not sleep in the same room. This arrangement was contrary to everything we understood about marriage. While Mama never wanted to talk about their separate worlds, Baba would tell you in a minute that Daddy Gus was nasty, that he smelled like tobacco juice, that he did not wash enough, that there was no way she would want him in her bed. And while he would say nothing nasty about her, he would merely say why would he want to share somebody else's bed when he could have his own bed to himself, with no one to complain about anything.

I loved my granddaddy's smells. Always, they filled my nostrils with the scent of happiness. It was sheer ecstasy for me to be allowed into his inner sanctum. His room was a small Van Gogh–like space off from the living room. There was no door. Old-fashioned curtains were the only attempt at privacy. Usually the curtains were closed. His room reeked of tobacco. There were treasures everywhere in that small room. As a younger man Daddy Gus did odd jobs, and sometimes even in his old age he would do a chore for some needy lady. As he went about his work, he would pick up found objects, scraps. All these objects would lie about his room, on the dresser, on the table near his bed. Unlike all other grown-ups he never cared about children looking through his things. Anything we wanted he gave to us.

Daddy Gus collected beautiful wooden cigar boxes. They held lots of the important stuff—the treasures. He had tons of little diaries that he made notes in. He gave me my first wallet, my first teeny little book to write in, my first beautiful pen, which did not write for long, but it was still a found and shared treasure. When I would lie on his bed or sit close to him, sometimes just standing near, I would feel all the pain and anxiety of my troubled childhood leave me. His spirit was calm. He gave me the unconditional love I longed for.

"Too calm," his grown-up children thought. That's why he had let this old woman rule him, my cousin BoBo would say. Even as children we knew that grown-ups felt sorry for Daddy Gus. At times his sons seemed to look upon him as not a "real man." His refusal to fight in wars was another sign to them of weakness. It was my grandfather who taught me to oppose war. They saw him as a man controlled by the whims of others, by this tall, strident, demanding woman he had married. I saw him as a man of profound beliefs, a man of integrity. When he heard their putdowns—for they talked on and on about his laziness—he merely muttered that he had no use for them. He was not gonna let anybody tell him what to do with his life.

10   Daddy Gus was a devout believer, a deacon at his church; he was one of the right-hand men of God. At church, everyone admired his calmness. Baba had no

use for church. She liked nothing better than to tell us all the ways it was one big hypocritical place: "Why, I can find God anywhere I want to—I do not need a church." Indeed, when my grandmother died, her funeral could not take place in a church, for she had never belonged. Her refusal to attend church bothered some of her daughters, for they thought she was sinning against God, setting a bad example for the children. We were not supposed to listen when she began to damn the church and everybody in it.

Baba loved to "cuss." There was no bad word she was not willing to say. The improvisational manner in which she would string those words together was awesome. It was the goddamn sons of bitches who thought that they could fuck with her when they could just kiss her black ass. A woman of strong words and powerful metaphors, she could not read or write. She lived in the power of language. Her favorite sayings were a prelude for storytelling. It was she who told me, "Play with a puppy, he'll lick you in the mouth." When I heard this saying, I knew what was coming—a long polemic about not letting folks get too close, 'cause they will mess with you.

Baba loved to tell her stories. And I loved to hear them. She called me Glory. And in the midst of her storytelling she would pause to say, "Glory, are ya listenin'. Do you understand what I'm telling ya." Sometimes I would have to repeat the lessons I had learned. Sometimes I was not able to get it right and she would start again. When Mama felt I was learning too much craziness "over home" (that is what we called Baba's house), my visits were curtailed. As I moved into my teens I learned to keep to myself all the wisdom of the old ways I picked up over home.

Baba was an incredible quilt maker, but by the time I was old enough to really understand her work, to see its beauty; she was already having difficulty with her eyesight. She could not sew as much as in the old days, when her work was on everybody's bed. Unwilling to throw anything away, she loved to make crazy quilts, 'cause they allowed every scrap to be used. Although she would one day order patterns and make perfect quilts with colors that went together, she always collected scraps.

Long before I read Virginia Woolf's *A Room of One's Own* I learned from Baba that a woman needed her own space to work. She had a huge room for her quilting. Like every other space in the private world she created upstairs, it had her treasures, an endless array of hatboxes, feathers, and trunks filled with old clothes she had held on to. In room after room there were feather tick mattresses; when they were pulled back, the wooden slats of the bed were revealed, lined with exquisite hand-sewn quilts.

15   In all these trunks, in crevices and drawers were braided tobacco leaves to keep away moths and other insects. A really hot summer could make cloth sweat, and stains from tobacco juice would end up on quilts no one had ever used. When I was a young child, a quilt my grandmother had made kept me warm, was my solace and comfort. Even though Mama protested when I dragged that old raggedy quilt from Kentucky to Stanford, I knew I needed that bit of the South, of Baba's world, to sustain me.

Like Daddy Gus, she was a woman of her word. She liked to declare with pride, "I mean what I say and I say what I mean." "Glory," she would tell me, "nobody is better than their word—if you can't keep ya word you ain't worth nothin' in this world." She would stop speaking to folk over the breaking of their word, over lies. Our mama was not given to loud speech or confrontation. I learned all those things from Baba—"to stand up and speak up" and not to "give a good goddamn" what folk who "ain't got a pot to pee in" think. My parents were concerned with their image in the world. It was pure blasphemy for Baba to teach that it did not matter what other folks thought—"Ya have to be right with yaself in ya own heart—that's all that matters." Baba taught me to listen to my heart—to follow it. From her we learned as small children to remember our dreams in the night and to share them when we awakened. They would be interpreted by her. She taught us to listen to the knowledge in dreams. Mama would say this was all nonsense, but she too was known to ask the meaning of a dream.

In their own way my grandparents were rebels, deeply committed to radical individualism. I learned how to be myself from them. Mama hated this. She thought it was important to be liked, to conform. She had hated growing up in such an eccentric, otherworldly household. This world where folks made their own wine, their own butter, their own soap; where chickens were raised, and huge gardens were grown for canning everything. This was the world Mama wanted to leave behind. She wanted store-bought things.

Baba lived in another time, a time when all things were produced in the individual household. Everything the family needed was made at home. She loved to tell me stories about learning to trap animals, to skin, to soak possum and coon in brine, to fry up a fresh rabbit. Though a total woman of the outdoors who could shoot and trap as good as any man, she still believed every woman should sew—she made her first quilt as a girl. In her world, women were as strong as men because they had to be. She had grown up in the country and knew that country ways were the best ways to live. Boasting about being able to do anything that a man could do and better, this woman who could not read or write was confident about her place in the universe.

My sense of aesthetics came from her. She taught me to really look at things, to see underneath the surface, to see the different shades of red in the peppers she had dried and hung in the kitchen sunlight. The beauty of the ordinary, the everyday, was her feast of light. While she had no use for the treasures in my granddaddy's world, he too taught me to look for the living spirit in things—the things that are cast away but still need to be touched and cared for. Picking up a found object he would tell me its story or tell me how he was planning to give it life again.

20   Connected in spirit but so far apart in the life of everydayness, Baba and Daddy Gus were rarely civil to each other. Every shared talk begun with goodwill ended in disagreement and contestation. Everyone knew Baba just loved to fuss. She liked a good war of words. And she was comfortable using words to sting and hurt, to punish. When words would not do the job, she could reach for the strap, a long piece of black leather that would leave tiny imprints on the flesh.

There was no violence in Daddy Gus. Mama shared that he had always been that way, a calm and gentle man, full of tenderness. I remember clinging to his tenderness when nothing I did was right in my mother's eyes, when I was constantly punished. Baba was not an ally. She advocated harsh punishment. She had no use for children who would not obey. She was never ever affectionate. When we entered her house, we gave her a kiss in greeting and that was it. With Daddy Gus we could cuddle, linger in his arms, give as many kisses as desired. His arms and heart were always open.

In the back of their house were fruit trees, chicken coops, and gardens, and in the front were flowers. Baba could make anything grow. And she knew all about herbs and roots. Her home remedies healed our childhood sicknesses. Of course she thought it crazy for anyone to go to a doctor when she could tell them just what they needed. All these things she had learned from her mother, Bell Blair Hooks, whose name I would choose as my pen name. Everyone agreed that I had the temperament of this great-grandmother I would not remember. She was a sharp-tongued woman. Or so they said. And it was believed I had inherited my way with words from her.

Families do that. They chart psychic genealogies that often overlook what is right before our eyes. I may have inherited my great-grandmother Bell Hook's way with words, but I learned to use those words listening to my grandmother. I learned to be courageous by seeing her act without fear. I learned to risk because she was daring. Home and family were her world. While my grandfather journeyed downtown, visited at other folks' houses, went to church, and conducted affairs in the world, Baba rarely left home. There was nothing in the world she needed. Things out there violated her spirit.

As a child I had no sense of what it would mean to live a life, spanning so many generations, unable to read or write. To me Baba was a woman of power. That she would have been extraordinarily powerless in a world beyond 1200 Broad Street was a thought that never entered my mind. I believed that she stayed home because it was the place she liked best. Just as Daddy Gus seemed to need to walk—to roam.

25   After his death it was easier to see the ways that they complemented and completed each other. For suddenly, without him as a silent backdrop, Baba's spirit was diminished. Something in her was forever lonely and could not find solace. When she died, tulips, her favorite flower, surrounded her. The preacher told us that her death was not an occasion for grief, for "it is hard to live in a world where your choicest friends are gone." Daddy Gus was the companion she missed most. His presence had always been the mirror of memory. Without it there was so much that could not be shared. There was no witness.

Seeing their life together, I learned that it was possible for women and men to fashion households arranged around their own needs. Power was shared. When there was an imbalance, Baba ruled the day. It seemed utterly alien to me to learn about black women and men not making families and homes together. I had not been raised in a world of absent men. One day I knew I would fashion a life using the patterns I inherited from Baba and Daddy Gus. I keep treasures in my cigar box, which still smells after all these years. The quilt that covered me as a child remains, full of ink stains and faded colors. In my trunks are braided tobacco leaves, taken from over home. They keep evil away—keep bad spirits from crossing the threshold, like the ancestors they guard and protect.

MAKING CONNECTIONS

1. Can you think of family members from whom you've learned lessons that will last a lifetime? Explain.
2. To what extent does the author "show," not just tell you about, her grandparents and the influence they have had on her? Pick out specific details that support her description of them and the role they played in her life; discuss their effectiveness.
3. Compare this essay to Philip Larkin's poem "This Be the Verse" on page 283 and Li-Young Lee's poem "The Gift" on page 284.

MAKING AN ARGUMENT

1. In the opening section of this theme, Carl Jung is quoted as saying that "The little world of childhood with its familiar surroundings is a model of the greater world." In "Inspired Eccentricity," bell hooks seems to agree when she says, "One day I knew I would fashion a life using the patterns I inherited from Baba and Daddy Gus." Using this essay and other works from Family and Friends, build an argument in support of or against the view that the family provides us a model of the greater world—and that we "fashion" our lives "using the patterns" we've learned at home.

◆ GRAPHIC NARRATIVE ◆

The selection below is taken from a genre that is often called a graphic novel. But literary critic, Hillary Chute, says that *graphic novel* is a misnomer—that these works "aren't novels at all" but rather "rich works of non-fiction." The term she uses, "graphic narrative," fits the autobiographical work of Marjane Satrapi especially well.

MARJANE SATRAPI [B. 1969]

The author was born in Iran and was still a child when the fundamentalist Islamic regime took over the country. In order to protect her, her family moved her to Austria. She studied illustration in France and combined her writing and drawing talents to construct what is essentially a graphic autobiographical novel, told from her point of view as a child. The final chapter of that story, called "The Dowry" is below. Persepolis *was so successful that it has a sequel,* Persepolis 2, *that is the story of her return to Iran.*

"The Dowry" (Excerpt from *Persepolis*) [2003]

 THE DOWRY

AFTER THE DEATH OF NEDA BABA-LEVY, MY LIFE TOOK A NEW TURN. IN 1984, I WAS FOURTEEN AND A REBEL. NOTHING SCARED ME ANYMORE.

I'VE TOLD YOU A HUNDRED TIMES THAT IT IS STRICTLY FORBIDDEN TO WEAR JEWELRY AND JEANS!

WHAT ARE YOU DOING WITH THAT BRACELET? GIVE IT TO ME RIGHT NOW!

OVER MY DEAD BODY! IT WAS A GIFT FROM MY MOM.

I HAD LEARNED THAT YOU SHOULD ALWAYS SHOUT LOUDER THAN YOUR AGGRESSOR.

IF YOU'RE STILL WEARING JEWELRY TOMORROW...

YEAH, I KNOW!

AND THE NEXT DAY...

LET ME SEE YOUR WRIST.

WHAT FOR?

LET ME SEE IT, I'M TELLING YOU.

WITH ALL THE JEWELRY YOU STEAL FROM US, YOU MUST BE MAKING A PILE OF MONEY.

WHAT HAPPENED?

MARJI HIT THE PRINCIPAL

SHE'S FINISHED!

EXCUSE ME! I DIDN'T MEAN IT!

SATRAPI, YOU'RE EXPELLED!

AFTER I WAS EXPELLED, IT WAS A REAL STRUGGLE TO FIND ANOTHER SCHOOL THAT WOULD ACCEPT ME. HITTING THE PRINCIPAL WAS A VERITABLE CRIME. BUT THANKS TO MY AUNT, WHO KNEW SOME BUREAUCRATS IN THE EDUCATION SYSTEM, THEY MANAGED TO PLACE ME IN ANOTHER SCHOOL. AND THERE...

SINCE THE ISLAMIC REPUBLIC WAS FOUNDED, WE NO LONGER HAVE POLITICAL PRISONERS.

MA'AM!

MY UNCLE WAS IMPRISONED BY THE SHAH'S REGIME, BUT IT WAS THE ISLAMIC REGIME THAT ORDERED HIS EXECUTION.

YOU SAY THAT WE DON'T HAVE POLITICAL PRISONERS ANYMORE. BUT WE'VE GONE FROM 3000 PRISONERS UNDER THE SHAH TO 300,000 UNDER YOUR REGIME.

HOW DARE YOU LIE TO US LIKE THAT?

OH, SATRAPI!

CLAP!
CLAP!
CLAP!
CLAP!
CLAP!
CLAP!
CLAP!
CLAP!
CLAP!

OBVIOUSLY, THAT EVENING MY FATHER GOT A PHONE CALL.

YES. OF COURSE...YES...

WHO IS IT?

IT WAS THE PRINCIPAL OF MARJI'S SCHOOL. APPARENTLY SHE TOLD OFF THE RELIGION TEACHER. SHE GETS THAT FROM HER UNCLE.

MAYBE YOU'D LIKE HER TO END UP LIKE HIM TOO? EXECUTED?

YOU KNOW WHAT THEY DO TO THE YOUNG GIRLS THEY ARREST?

YOU KNOW WHAT HAPPENED TO NILOUFAR? THE GIRL YOU MET AT KHOSRO'S HOUSE? THE MAN WHO MADE PASSPORTS?

YOU KNOW THAT IT'S AGAINST THE LAW TO KILL A VIRGIN...

SO A GUARDIAN OF THE REVOLUTION MARRIES HER...

...AND TAKES HER VIRGINITY BEFORE EXECUTING HER. DO YOU UNDERSTAND WHAT THAT MEANS???

IF SOMEONE SO MUCH AS TOUCHES A HAIR ON YOUR HEAD, I'LL KILL HIM!

BUT HOW DO YOU KNOW THAT FOR SURE? MAYBE THEY JUST EXECUTED HER!

NO. YOUR MOTHER'S RIGHT. TRADITIONALLY, WHEN A GIRL GETS MARRIED, THE HUSBAND IS SUPPOSED TO PAY HER A DOWRY.

IF THE GIRL DIES, THE HUSBAND HAS TO GIVE THE DOWRY TO HER FAMILY.

THAT'S WHAT HAPPENED WITH NILOUFAR. AFTER SHE WAS EXECUTED, TO MAKE SURE HER AWFUL FATE WAS UNDERSTOOD, THEY SENT 500 TUMANS* TO HER PARENTS.

500 TUMANS FOR THE LIFE AND VIRGINITY OF AN INNOCENT GIRL.

I HAD NO IDEA.

*EQUIVALENT TO $5.00

ALL NIGHT LONG, I THOUGHT OF THAT PHRASE: "TO DIE A MARTYR IS TO INJECT BLOOD INTO THE VEINS OF SOCIETY." NILOUFAR WAS A REAL MARTYR, AND HER BLOOD CERTAINLY DID NOT FEED OUR SOCIETY'S VEINS.

ONE WEEK LATER...

MARJI, CAN YOU COME HERE FOR A FEW MINUTES? WE WANT TO TALK TO YOU.

I WENT TO SEE THE PRINCIPAL TODAY. SHE ASSURED ME THAT SHE HAD NOT SENT A REPORT THIS TIME. BUT CONSIDERING THE PERSON YOU ARE AND THE EDUCATION YOU'VE RECEIVED, WE THOUGHT THAT IT WOULD BE BETTER IF YOU LEFT IRAN.

WHAT?

YOUR MOTHER AND I HAVE DECIDED TO SEND YOU TO AUSTRIA.

WHY AUSTRIA?

FIRST OF ALL, BECAUSE IT'S EASIER TO GET AN AUSTRIAN VISA, AND SECOND BECAUSE MY BEST FRIEND LIVES IN VIENNA. DO YOU REMEMBER HER? ZOZO? SHERINE'S MOM?

YEAH, YEAH. BUT I DON'T SPEAK GERMAN!

THERE'S A FRENCH SCHOOL IN VIENNA. ONE OF THE BEST IN EUROPE!

AND WHAT ARE YOU GOING TO DO THERE?

YOU'RE GOING ON AHEAD OF US. WE HAVE SOME BUSINESS TO TAKE CARE OF. WE'LL JOIN YOU A FEW MONTHS FROM NOW!

BUT I'M ONLY FOURTEEN! YOU TRUST ME?

YOU'RE FOURTEEN AND I KNOW HOW I BROUGHT YOU UP. ABOVE ALL, I TRUST YOUR EDUCATION.

YOU'RE THE SAME PERSON WHO WENT ON VACATION TO FRANCE ALL BY YOURSELF, REMEMBER?

BEFORE THE REVOLUTION, MY PARENTS SENT ME TO SUMMER CAMP IN FRANCE. MY MOTHER DIDN'T WANT ME TO GROW UP LIKE AN ONLY CHILD.

IT'S TRUE, THAT WAS GREAT...REAL INDEPENDENCE.

WE LOVE YOU SO MUCH THAT WE WANT YOU TO GO.

WE FEEL IT'S BETTER FOR YOU TO BE FAR AWAY AND HAPPY THAN CLOSE BY AND MISERABLE. JUDGING BY THE SITUATION HERE, YOU'LL BE BETTER OFF SOMEWHERE ELSE.

AT THAT POINT, I STARTED TO HAVE MY DOUBTS. WHY SAY THOSE THINGS IF THEY WERE COMING TOO?

WE ADORE YOU!

DON'T EVER FORGET WHO YOU ARE!

NO. I WON'T EVER FORGET.

I REPEATED WHAT THEY HAD TOLD ME OVER AND OVER IN MY HEAD. I WAS PRETTY SURE THEY WEREN'T COMING TO VIENNA.

I STAYED UP ALL NIGHT AND WONDERED IF THE MOON SHONE AS BRIGHTLY IN VIENNA.

THE NEXT DAY I FILLED A JAR WITH SOIL FROM OUR GARDEN. IRANIAN SOIL.

I TOOK DOWN ALL OF MY POSTERS.

I INVITED MY GIRLFRIENDS OVER TO SAY GOODBYE.

HERE. I'M GIVING YOU MY MOST PRECIOUS THINGS, SO THAT YOU WON'T FORGET ME.

I NEVER REALIZED HOW MUCH THEY LOVED ME.

AND I UNDERSTOOD HOW IMPORTANT THEY WERE TO ME.

ON THE EVE OF MY DEPARTURE, MY GRANDMOTHER CAME TO SPEND THE NIGHT AT OUR HOUSE.

CAN I SLEEP WITH YOU?

THAT'S WHY I'M HERE!

I WATCHED MY GRANDMA UNDRESS. EACH MORNING, SHE PICKED JASMINE FLOWERS TO PUT IN HER BRA SO THAT SHE WOULD SMELL NICE. WHEN SHE UNDRESSED, YOU COULD SEE THE FLOWERS FALL FROM HER BREASTS.

IT WAS SOMETHING TO SEE

GRANDMA, HOW DO YOU HAVE SUCH ROUND BREASTS AT YOUR AGE?

EVERY MORNING AND NIGHT, I SOAK THEM IN A BOWL OF ICE WATER FOR TEN MINUTES.

SHE ACTUALLY DID, AND I KNEW IT. I JUST WANTED TO HEAR HER SAY IT.

I'LL MISS YOU.

OH, I'LL COME SEE YOU.

SHE TOO WAS LYING TO ME.

LISTEN, I DON'T WANT TO PREACH, BUT LET ME GIVE YOU SOME ADVICE THAT WILL ALWAYS HELP YOU.

IN LIFE YOU'LL MEET A LOT OF JERKS. IF THEY HURT YOU, TELL YOURSELF THAT IT'S BECAUSE THEY'RE STUPID. THAT WILL HELP KEEP YOU FROM REACTING TO THEIR CRUELTY. BECAUSE THERE IS NOTHING WORSE THAN BITTERNESS AND VENGEANCE... ALWAYS KEEP YOUR DIGNITY AND BE TRUE TO YOURSELF.

I SMELLED MY GRANDMA'S BOSOM. IT SMELLED GOOD. I'LL NEVER FORGET THAT SMELL.

AND THE NEXT MORNING.

WAKE UP! IT'S SEVEN O'CLOCK, WE'VE GOT TO GO.

?

I WILL ALWAYS BE TRUE TO MYSELF.

I'M NOT COMING ALONG.

DON'T EVER FORGET WHAT I TOLD YOU.

GRANDMA

HERE WE ARE!

THERE WAS A HUGE LINE. LOTS OF PEOPLE WERE LEAVING THE COUNTRY.

ESPECIALLY YOUNG BOYS. CONSIDERED FUTURE SOLDIERS, THEY WERE FORBIDDEN TO LEAVE THE COUNTRY AFTER THEY TURNED THIRTEEN.

MEHRABAD AIRPORT

MAKING CONNECTIONS

1. Imagine that you grew up under these conditions, would you have objected so vehemently—and so loudly—to the treatment you received, even if your life was threatened? Explain.
2. Iran is often in the news these days. How does your knowledge of Iran influence your response to the story? If you don't know much about Iran, were you able to learn much by reading the story? Explain.
3. Does Marji remind you of any other characters you've encountered in your reading? Explain.
4. Why is this last chapter called "The Dowry." If this word is not familiar to you, look it up.
5. How were you influenced by the drawings? Did they help to pull you into the story? Did they convey anything that the words could have done just as well? Explain.

MAKING AN ARGUMENT

1. Choose another work that you have read and compare it to "The Dowry." Imagine that this work was also illustrated. Would that make it better or worse? Is it better to have illustrations accompanying literature or does it interfere with or limit our imaginations? Explain.

CASE STUDY IN BIOGRAPHICAL CONTEXT

Lorraine Hansberry and *A Raisin in the Sun*

The purpose of this Case Study is to provide you with biographical, historical, and cultural material for a self-contained research unit. As indicated in Chapter 5, one popular area of literary research is inquiry into an author's life or the relationship between the author's life and work. The materials that follow contain a primary source—the play *A Raisin in the Sun*—and a number of secondary sources—a brief biography, the author's words, interviews, and articles about her and the play. Individually or in combination with other sources, they provide good resources for a research essay.

Knowing about the author's life or intentions is not a prerequisite for understanding and appreciating a work of literature. Good literature stands on its own and appeals to us through its own merit. Of greatest importance, for our purposes, is reading and interpreting these texts. But discovering and exploring connections between an author's background and the literature may enrich and expand your response.

Our focus in this Case Study is on playwright Lorraine Hansberry. Her story is both inspiring and tragically sad. By the time she was twenty-nine years old, *A Raisin in the Sun* was an award-winning play on Broadway, and this brilliant young playwright seemed to have a remarkable future in front of her. Before she was thirty-five years old, however, she died of cancer.

The passages that follow her brief biography and the play contain the comments of both Lorraine Hansberry and others about her life and work. Many of her own comments, taken largely from interviews and public presentations, were organized and reprinted by her husband in a production and publication called *To Be Young, Gifted, and Black (YGB)*. The rest of her comments are taken from speeches and television interviews with Mike Wallace and Studs Terkel shortly after the Broadway debut of *A Raisin in the Sun*. The commentary of others includes a biographical tribute by friend and fellow writer James Baldwin and critical and biographical commentary about the play by Julius Lester, Anne Cheney, Steven R. Carter, and Margaret B. Wilkerson. This casebook concludes with a 1999 article by Michael Anderson that celebrates the fortieth anniversary of the play's opening.

How has Lorraine Hansberry's background, her artistic philosophy, and the influence of other writers affected her writing of *A Raisin in the Sun*? Does the play seem to fulfill her own artistic requirements? Do the characters have within them the "elements of profundity, of profound anguish"? Does the play seem to "tell the truth about people"? How do her own comments about herself compare with what others say? Is there anything in her background, for example, that may account for what Steven R. Carter in his comments calls her "artistic misstep"?

LORRAINE HANSBERRY [1930–1965]

Lorraine Hansberry was born in Chicago, Illinois, to middle-class black parents who lived on the city's South Side. When she was still a child, her father was barred from purchasing a house in a white neighborhood. He sued and pursued the case all the way to the Supreme Court, which ruled in his favor. Hansberry attended the University of Wisconsin as an undergraduate. Following college, she pursued a career as a painter, studying at the Art Institute of Chicago and in Mexico before she decided to move to New York to pursue her interest in writing. There she wrote for Freedom, *a magazine founded by the great singer-actor-turned-political-activist Paul Robeson. When her first play,* A Raisin in the Sun, *premiered at the Ethel Barrymore Theater in 1959, it was the first play written by an African American woman to be performed on Broadway. She wrote only one other play,* The Sign in Sidney Brustien's Window *(1965), before she died of cancer at the age of thirty-four. The title of* A Raisin in the Sun *is taken from the poem "A Dream Deferred" by Langston Hughes (p. 80).*

A RAISIN IN THE SUN   [1958]

CHARACTERS IN ORDER OF APPEARANCE
RUTH YOUNGER *Walter's wife, about thirty*
TRAVIS YOUNGER *her son and Walter's*
WALTER LEE YOUNGER *(brother) Ruth's husband, mid-thirties*
BENEATHA YOUNGER *Walter's sister, about twenty*
LENA YOUNGER *(Mama) mother of Walter and Beneatha*
JOSEPH ASAGAI *Nigerian, Beneatha's suitor*
GEORGE MURCHISON *Beneatha's date, wealthy*
KARL LINDNER *white, chairman of the Clybourne Park New Neighbors Orientation Committee*
BOBO *one of Walter's business partners*
MOVING MEN
The action of the play is set in Chicago's South Side, sometime between World War II and the present.

ACT I
Scene 1. Friday morning
Scene 2. The following morning

ACT II

Scene 1. Later, the same day
Scene 2. Friday night, a few weeks later
Scene 3. Moving day, one week later

ACT III

An hour later

ACT I

SCENE 1

The Younger living room would be a comfortable and well-ordered room if it were not for a number of indestructible contradictions to this state of being. Its furnishings are typical and undistinguished and their primary feature now is that they have clearly had to accommodate the living of too many people for too many years—and they are tired. Still, we can see that at some time, a time probably no longer remembered by the family (except perhaps for MAMA*) the furnishings of this room were actually selected with care and love and even hope—and brought to this apartment and arranged with taste and pride.*

That was a long time ago. Now the once loved pattern of the couch upholstery has to fight to show itself from under acres of crocheted doilies and couch covers which have themselves finally come to be more important than the upholstery. And here a table or a chair has been moved to disguise the worn places in the carpet; but the carpet has fought back by showing its weariness, with depressing uniformity, elsewhere on its surface.

Weariness has, in fact, won in this room. Everything has been polished, washed, sat on, used, scrubbed too often. All pretenses but living itself have long since vanished from the very atmosphere of this room.

Moreover, a section of this room, for it is not really a room unto itself, though the landlord's lease would make it seem so, slopes backward to provide a small kitchen area, where the family prepares the meals that are eaten in the living room proper, which must also serve as dining room. The single window that has been provided for these "two" rooms is located in this kitchen area. The sole natural light the family may enjoy in the course of a day is only that which fights its way through this little window.

At left, a door leads to a bedroom which is shared by MAMA *and her daughter,* BENEATHA. *At right, opposite, is a second room (which in the beginning of the life of this apartment was probably a breakfast room) which serves as a bedroom for* WALTER *and his wife,* RUTH.

TIME: *Sometime between World War II and the present.*

PLACE: *Chicago's South Side.*

AT RISE: *It is morning dark in the living room.* TRAVIS *is asleep on the make-down bed at center. An alarm clock sounds from within the bedroom at right, and presently* RUTH *enters from that room and closes the door behind her. She crosses sleepily toward the window. As she passes her sleeping son she reaches down and shakes him a little. At the window she raises the shade and a dusky South Side morning light comes in feebly. She fills a pot with water and puts it on to boil. She calls to the boy, between yawns, in a slightly muffled voice.*

RUTH *is about thirty. We can see that she was a pretty girl, even exceptionally so, but now it is apparent that life has been little that she expected, and disappointment has already begun to hang in her face. In a few years, before thirty-five even, she will be known among her people as a "settled woman."*

She crosses to her son and gives him a good, final, rousing shake.

RUTH: Come on now, boy, it's seven thirty! [*Her son sits up at last, in a stupor of sleepiness.*] I say hurry up, Travis! You ain't the only person in the world got to use a bathroom! [*The child, a sturdy, handsome little boy of ten or eleven, drags himself out of the bed and almost blindly takes his towels and "today's clothes" from drawers and a closet and goes out to the bathroom, which is in an outside hall and which is shared by another family or families on the same floor.* RUTH *crosses to the bedroom door at right and opens it and calls in to her husband.*] Walter Lee! . . . It's after seven thirty! Lemme see you do some waking up in there now! [*She waits.*] You better get up from there, man! It's after seven thirty I tell you. [*She waits again.*] All right, you just go ahead and lay there and next thing you know Travis be finished and Mr. Johnson'll be in there and you'll be fussing and cussing round here like a mad man! And be late too! [*She waits, at the end of patience.*] Walter Lee—it's time for you to get up! [*She waits another second and then starts to go into the bedroom, but is apparently satisfied that her husband has begun to get up. She stops, pulls the door to, and returns to the kitchen area. She wipes her face with a moist cloth and runs her fingers through her sleep-disheveled hair in a vain effort and ties an apron around her housecoat. The bedroom door at right opens and her husband stands in the doorway in his pajamas, which are rumpled and mismated. He is a lean, intense young man in his middle thirties, inclined to quick nervous movements and erratic speech habits—and always in his voice there is a quality of indictment.*]

WALTER: Is he out yet?

RUTH: What you mean *out*? He ain't hardly got in there good yet.

WALTER [*wandering in, still more oriented to sleep than to a new day*]:   Well, what was you doing all that yelling for if I can't even get in there yet? [*stopping and thinking*] Check coming today?

RUTH: They *said* Saturday and this is just Friday and I hopes to God you ain't going to get up here first thing this morning and start talking to me 'bout no money—'cause I 'bout don't want to hear it.

WALTER: Something the matter with you this morning?

RUTH: No—I'm just sleepy as the devil. What kind of eggs you want?

WALTER: Not scrambled. [RUTH *starts to scramble eggs.*] Paper come? [RUTH *points impatiently to the rolled up the Tribune on the table, and he gets it and spreads it out and vaguely reads the front page.*] Set off another bomb yesterday.

RUTH [*maximum indifference*]:   Did they?

WALTER [*looking up*]:   What's the matter with you?

RUTH: Ain't nothing the matter with me. And don't keep asking me that this morning.

WALTER: Ain't nobody bothering you. [*reading the news of the day absently again*] Say Colonel McCormick is sick.

RUTH [*affecting tea-party interest*]:   Is he now? Poor thing.

WALTER [*sighing and looking at his watch*]:   Oh, me. [*He waits.*] Now what is that boy doing in that bathroom all this time? He just going to have to start getting up earlier. I can't be being late to work on account of him fooling around in there.

RUTH [*turning on him*]:   Oh, no he ain't going to be getting up earlier no such thing! It ain't his fault that he can't get to bed no earlier nights 'cause he got a bunch of crazy good-for-nothing clowns sitting up running their mouths in what is supposed to be his bedroom after ten o'clock at night...

WALTER: That's what you mad about, ain't it? The things I want to talk about with my friends just couldn't be important in your mind, could they? [*He rises and finds a cigarette in her handbag on the table and crosses to the little window and looks out, smoking and deeply enjoying this first one.*]

RUTH [*almost matter of factly, a complaint too automatic to deserve emphasis*]:   Why you always got to smoke before you eat in the morning?

WALTER [*at the window*]:   Just look at 'em down there. ...Running and racing to work... [*He turns and faces his wife and watches her a moment at the stove, and then, suddenly.*] You look young this morning, baby.

RUTH [*indifferently*]:   Yeah?

WALTER: Just for a second—stirring them eggs. It's gone now—just for a second it was—you looked real young again. [*then, drily*] It's gone now—you look like yourself again.

RUTH: Man, if you don't shut up and leave me alone.

WALTER [*looking out to the street again*]:   First thing a man ought to learn in life is not to make love to no colored woman first thing in the morning. You all some evil people at eight o'clock in the morning. [TRAVIS *appears in the hall doorway, almost fully dressed and quite wide awake now, his towels and pajamas across his shoulders. He opens the door and signals for his father to make the bathroom in a hurry.*]

TRAVIS [*watching the bathroom*]:   Daddy, come on! [WALTER *gets his bathroom utensils and flies out to the bathroom.*]

RUTH: Sit down and have your breakfast, Travis.

TRAVIS: Mama, this is Friday. [*gleefully*] Check coming tomorrow, huh?

RUTH: You get your mind off money and eat your breakfast.

TRAVIS [*eating*]:   This is the morning we supposed to bring the fifty cents to school.

RUTH: Well, I ain't got no fifty cents this morning.

TRAVIS: Teacher say we have to.

RUTH: I don't care what teacher say. I ain't got it. Eat your breakfast, Travis.

TRAVIS: I *am* eating.

RUTH: Hush up now and just eat! [*The boy gives her an exasperated look for her lack of understanding, and eats grudgingly.*]

TRAVIS: You think Grandmama would have it?

RUTH: No! And I want you to stop asking your grandmother for money, you hear me?

TRAVIS [*outraged*]:   Gaaaleee! I don't ask her, she just gimme it sometimes!

RUTH: Travis Willard Younger—I got too much on me this morning to be—

TRAVIS: Maybe Daddy—

RUTH: *Travis!* [*The boy hushes abruptly. They are both quiet and tense for several seconds.*]

TRAVIS [*presently*]:   Could I maybe go carry some groceries in front of the supermarket for a little while after school then?

RUTH: Just hush, I said. [TRAVIS *jabs his spoon into his cereal bowl viciously, and rests his head in anger upon his fists.*] If you through eating, you can get over there and make up your bed. [*The boy obeys stiffly and crosses the room, almost mechanically, to the bed and more or less carefully folds the covering. He carries the bedding into his mother's room and returns with his books and cap.*]

TRAVIS [*sulking and standing apart from her unnaturally*]:   I'm gone.

RUTH [*looking up from the stove to inspect him automatically*]:   Come here. [*He crosses to her and she studies his head.*] If you don't take this comb and fix this here head, you better! [TRAVIS *puts down his books with a great sigh of oppression, and crosses to the mirror. His mother mutters under her breath about his "stubbornness."*] 'Bout to march out of here with that head looking just like chickens slept in it! I just don't know where you get your stubborn ways... And get your jacket, too. Looks chilly out this morning.

TRAVIS [*with conspicuously brushed hair and jacket*]:   I'm gone.

RUTH: Get carfare and milk money—[*waving one finger*]—and not a single penny for no caps, you hear me?

TRAVIS [*with sullen politeness*]:   Yes'm. [*He turns in outrage to leave. His mother watches after him as in his frustration he approaches the door almost comically. When she speaks to him, her voice has become a very gentle tease.*]

RUTH [*mocking, as she thinks he would say it*]:   Oh, Mama makes me so mad sometimes, I don't know what to do! [*She waits and continues to his back as he stands stock-still in front of the door.*] I wouldn't kiss that woman good-bye for nothing in this world this morning! [*The boy finally turns around and rolls his eyes at her, knowing the mood has changed and he is vindicated; he does not, however, move toward her yet.*] Not for nothing in this world! [*She finally laughs aloud at him and holds out her arms to him and we see that it is a way between them, very old and practiced. He crosses to her and allows her to embrace him warmly but keeps his face fixed with masculine rigidity. She holds him back from her presently and looks at him and runs her fingers over the features of his face. With utter gentleness—*] Now—whose little old angry man are you?

TRAVIS [*The masculinity and gruffness start to fade at last.*]:   Aw gaalee—Mama...

RUTH [*mimicking*]   Aw—gaaaaalleeeee, Mama! [*She pushes him, with rough playfulness and finality, toward the door.*] Get on out of here or you going to be late.

TRAVIS [*in the face of love, new aggressiveness*]:   Mama, could I *please* go carry groceries?

RUTH: Honey, it's starting to get so cold evenings.

WALTER [*coming in from the bedroom and drawing a make-believe gun from a make-believe holster and shooting at his son*]:   What is it he wants to do?

RUTH: Go carry groceries after school at the supermarket.

WALTER: Well, let him go...

TRAVIS [*quickly, to the ally*]:   I *have* to—she won't gimme the fifty cents...

WALTER [*to his wife only*]:   Why not?

RUTH [*simply, and with flavor*]:   'Cause we don't have it.

WALTER [*to RUTH only*]:   What you tell the boy things like that for? [*reaching down into his pants with a rather important gesture*] Here, son—[*He hands the boy the coin, but his eyes are directed to his wife's.* TRAVIS *takes the money happily.*]

TRAVIS: Thanks, Daddy. [*He starts out.* RUTH *watches both of them with murder in her eyes.* WALTER *stands and stares back at her with defiance, and suddenly reaches into his pocket again on an afterthought.*]

WALTER [*without even looking at his son, still staring hard at his wife*]:   In fact, here's another fifty cents... Buy yourself some fruit today—or take a taxicab to school or something!

TRAVIS: Whoopee—[*He leaps up and clasps his father around the middle with his legs, and they face each other in mutual appreciation; slowly* WALTER LEE *peeks around the boy to catch the violent rays from his wife's eyes and draws his head back as if shot.*]

WALTER: You better get down now—and get to school, man.

TRAVIS [*at the door*]:   O.K. Good-bye. [*He exits.*]

WALTER [*after him, pointing with pride*]:   That's *my* boy. [*She looks at him in disgust and turns back to her work.*] You know what I was thinking 'bout in the bathroom this morning?

RUTH: No.

WALTER: How come you always try to be so pleasant!

RUTH: What is there to be pleasant 'bout!

WALTER: You want to know what I was thinking 'bout in the bathroom or not!

RUTH: I know what you thinking 'bout.

WALTER [*ignoring her*]:   'Bout what me and Willy Harris was talking about last night.

RUTH [*immediately—a refrain*]:   Willy Harris is a good-for-nothing loudmouth.

WALTER: Anybody who talks to me has got to be a good-for-nothing loudmouth, ain't he? And what you know about who is just a good-for-nothing loudmouth? Charlie Atkins was just a "good-for-nothing loudmouth" too, wasn't he! When he wanted me to go in the dry-cleaning business with him. And now—he's grossing a hundred thousand a year. A hundred thousand dollars a year! You still call *him* a loudmouth!

RUTH [*bitterly*]:   Oh, Walter Lee... [*She folds her head on her arms over the table.*]

WALTER [*rising and coming to her and standing over her*]:   You tired, ain't you? Tired of everything. Me, the boy, the way we live—this beat-up hole—everything. Ain't you? [*She doesn't look up, doesn't answer.*] So tired—moaning and groaning all the time, but you wouldn't do nothing to help, would you? You couldn't be on my side that long for nothing, could you?

RUTH: Walter, please leave me alone.

WALTER: A man needs for a woman to back him up…

RUTH: Walter—

WALTER: Mama would listen to you. You know she listen to you more than she do me and Bennie. She think more of you. All you have to do is just sit down with her when you drinking your coffee one morning and talking 'bout things like you do and—[*He sits down beside her and demonstrates graphically what he thinks her methods and tone should be.*]—you just sip your coffee, see, and say easy like that you been thinking 'bout that deal Walter Lee is so interested in, 'bout the store and all, and sip some more coffee, like what you saying ain't really that important to you—And the next thing you know, she be listening good and asking you questions and when I come home—I can tell her the details. This ain't no fly-by-night proposition, baby. I mean we figured it out, me and Willy and Bobo.

RUTH [*with a frown*]:   Bobo?

WALTER: Yeah. You see, this little liquor store we got in mind cost seventy-five thousand and we figured the initial investment on the place be 'bout thirty thousand, see. That be ten thousand each. Course, there's a couple of hundred you got to pay so's you don't spend your life just waiting for them clowns to let your license get approved—

RUTH: You mean graft?

WALTER [*frowning impatiently*]:   Don't call it that. See there, that just goes to show you what women understand about the world. Baby, don't *nothing* happen for you in this world 'less you pay *somebody* off!

RUTH: Walter, leave me alone! [*She raises her head and stares at him vigorously—then says, more quietly*] Eat your eggs, they gonna be cold.

WALTER [*straightening up from her and looking off*]:   That's it. There you are. Man say to his woman: I got me a dream. His woman say: Eat your eggs. [*sadly, but gaining in power*] Man say: I got to take hold of this here world, baby! And a woman will say: Eat your eggs and go to work. [*passionately now*] Man say: I got to change my life, I'm choking to death, baby! And his woman say—[*in utter anguish as he brings his fists down on his thighs*]—Your eggs is getting cold!

RUTH [*softly*]:   Walter, that ain't none of our money.

WALTER [*not listening at all or even looking at her*]:   This morning, I was lookin' in the mirror and thinking about it… I'm thirty-five years old; I been married eleven years and I got a boy who sleeps in the living room—[*very, very quietly*]—and all I got to give him is stories about how rich white people live…

RUTH: Eat your eggs, Walter.

WALTER: *Damn my eggs… damn all the eggs that ever was!*

RUTH: Then go to work.

WALTER [*looking up at her*]:   See—I'm trying to talk to you 'bout myself—[*shaking his head with the repetition*]—and all you can say is eat them eggs and go to work.

RUTH [*wearily*]:   Honey, you never say nothing new. I listen to you every day, every night and every morning, and you never say nothing new. [*shrugging*] So you would rather *be* Mr. Arnold than be his chauffeur. So—I would *rather* be living in Buckingham Palace.

WALTER: That is just what is wrong with the colored woman in this world... Don't understand about building their men up and making 'em feel like they somebody. Like they can do something.

RUTH [*drily, but to hurt*]:   There *are* colored men who do things.

WALTER: No thanks to the colored woman.

RUTH: Well, being a colored woman, I guess I can't help myself none. [*She rises and gets the ironing board and sets it up and attacks a huge pile of rough-dried clothes, sprinkling them in preparation for the ironing and then rolling them into tight fat balls.*]

WALTER [*mumbling*]:   We one group of men tied to a race of women with small minds. [*his sister* BENEATHA *enters. She is about twenty, as slim and intense as her brother. She is not as pretty as her sister-in-law, but her lean, almost intellectual face has a handsomeness of its own. She wears a bright-red flannel nightie, and her thick hair stands wildly about her head. Her speech is a mixture of many things; it is different from the rest of the family's insofar as education has permeated her sense of English—and perhaps the Midwest rather than the South has finally—at last—won out in her inflection; but not altogether, because over all of it is a soft slurring and transformed use of vowels which is the decided influence of the South Side. She passes through the room without looking at either* RUTH *or* WALTER *and goes to the outside door and looks, a little blindly, out to the bathroom. She sees that it has been lost to the Johnsons. She closes the door with a sleepy vengeance and crosses to the table and sits down a little defeated.*]

BENEATHA: I am going to start timing those people.

WALTER: You should get up earlier.

BENEATHA [*Her face in her hands. She is still fighting the urge to go back to bed*]:   Really—would you suggest dawn? Where's the paper?

WALTER [*pushing the paper across the table to her as he studies her almost clinically, as though he has never seen her before*]:   You a horrible-looking chick at this hour.

BENEATHA [*drily*]:   Good morning, everybody.

WALTER [*senselessly*]:   How is school coming?

BENEATHA [*in the same spirit*]:   Lovely, Lovely. And you know, biology is the greatest. [*looking up at him*] I dissected something that looked just like you yesterday.

WALTER: I just wondered if you've made up your mind and everything.

BENEATHA [*gaining in sharpness and impatience*]:   And what did I answer yesterday morning—and the day before that?

RUTH [*from the ironing board, like someone disinterested and old*]:   Don't be so nasty, Bennie.

BENEATHA [*still to her brother*]:   And the day before that and the day before that!

WALTER [*defensively*]:   I'm interested in you. Something wrong with that? Ain't many girls who decide—

WALTER AND BENEATHA [*in unison*]:   —"to be a doctor." [*silence*]

WALTER: Have we figured out yet just exactly how much medical school is going to cost?

RUTH: Walter Lee, why don't you leave that girl alone and get out of here to work?

BENEATHA [*exits to the bathroom and bangs on the door*]:   Come on out of there, please! [*She comes back into the room.*]

WALTER [*looking at his sister intently*]:   You know the check is coming tomorrow.

BENEATHA [*turning on him with a sharpness all her own*]:   That money belongs to Mama, Walter, and it's for her to decide how she wants to use it. I don't care if she wants to buy a house or a rocket ship or just nail it up somewhere and look at it. It's hers. Not ours—hers.

WALTER [*bitterly*]:   Now ain't that fine! You just got your mother's interest at heart, ain't you, girl? You such a nice girl—but if Mama got that money she can always take a few thousand and help you through school too—can't she?

BENEATHA: I have never asked anyone around here to do anything for me!

WALTER: No! And the line between asking and just accepting when the time comes is big and wide—ain't it!

BENEATHA [*with fury*]:   What do you want from me, Brother—that I quit school or just drop dead, which!

WALTER: I don't want nothing but for you to stop acting holy 'round here. Me and Ruth done made some sacrifices for you—why can't you do something for the family?

RUTH: Walter, don't be dragging me in it.

WALTER: You are in it—Don't you get up and go work in somebody's kitchen for the last three years to help put clothes on her back?

RUTH: Oh, Walter—that's not fair...

WALTER: It ain't that nobody expects you to get on your knees and say thank you, Brother; thank you, Ruth; thank you, Mama—and thank you, Travis, for wearing the same pair of shoes for two semesters—

BENEATHA [*dropping to her knees*]:   Well—I do—all right?—thank everybody...and forgive me for ever wanting to be anything at all... forgive me, forgive me!

RUTH: Please stop it! Your mama'll hear you.

WALTER: Who the hell told you you had to be a doctor? If you so crazy 'bout messing 'round with sick people—then go be a nurse like other women—or just get married and be quiet...

BENEATHA: Well—you finally got it said... It took you three years but you finally got it said. Walter, give up; leave me alone—it's Mama's money.

WALTER: *He was my father, too!*

BENEATHA: So what? He was mine, too—and Travis' grandfather—but the insurance money belongs to Mama. Picking on me is not going to make her give it to you to invest in any liquor stores—[*under breath, dropping into a chair*]— and I for one say, God bless Mama for that!

WALTER [*to* RUTH]:   See—did you hear? Did you hear!

RUTH: Honey, please go to work.

WALTER: Nobody in this house is ever going to understand me.

BENEATHA: Because you're a nut.

WALTER: Who's a nut?

BENEATHA: You—you are a nut. Thee is mad, boy.

WALTER [*looking at his wife and his sister from the door, very sadly*]:   The world's most backward race of people, and that's a fact.

BENEATHA [*turning slowly in her chair*]:   And then there are all those prophets who would lead us out of the wilderness—[WALTER *slams out of the house.*]—into the swamps!

RUTH: Bennie, why you always gotta be pickin' on your brother? Can't you be a little sweeter sometimes? [*Door opens.* WALTER *walks in.*]

WALTER [*to* RUTH]:   I need some money for carfare.

RUTH [*looks at him, then warms; teasing, but tenderly*]:   Fifty cents? [*She goes to her bag and gets money.*] Here, take a taxi. [WALTER *exits.* MAMA *enters. She is a woman in her early sixties, full-bodied and strong. She is one of those women of a certain grace and beauty who wear it so unobtrusively that it takes a while to notice. Her dark-brown face is surrounded by the total whiteness of her hair, and, being a woman who has adjusted to many things in life and overcome many more, her face is full of strength. She has, we can see, wit and faith of a kind that keep her eyes lit and full of interest and expectancy. She is, in a word, a beautiful woman. Her bearing is perhaps most like the noble bearing of the women of the Hereros of Southwest Africa—rather as if she imagines that as she walks she still bears a basket or a vessel upon her head. Her speech, on the other hand, is as careless as her carriage is precise—she is inclined to slur everything—but her voice is perhaps not so much quiet as simply soft.*]

MAMA: Who that 'round here slamming doors at this hour? [*She crosses through the room, goes to the window, opens it, and brings in a feeble little plant growing doggedly in a small pot on the window sill. She feels the dirt and puts it back out.*]

RUTH: That was Walter Lee. He and Bennie was at it again.

MAMA: My children and they tempers. Lord, if this little old plant don't get more sun than it's been getting it ain't never going to see spring again. [*She turns from the window.*] What's the matter with you this morning, Ruth? You looks right peaked. You aiming to iron all them things? Leave some for me. I'll get to 'em this afternoon. Bennie honey, it's too drafty for you to be sitting 'round half dressed. Where's your robe?

BENEATHA: In the cleaners.

MAMA: Well, go get mine and put it on.

BENEATHA: I'm not cold, Mama, honest.

MAMA: I know—but you so thin...

BENEATHA [*irritably*]:   Mama, I'm not cold.

MAMA [*seeing the make-down bed as* TRAVIS *has left it*]:   Lord have mercy, look at that poor bed. Bless his heart—he tries, don't he? [*She moves to the bed* TRAVIS *has sloppily made up.*]

RUTH: No—he don't half try at all 'cause he knows you going to come along behind him and fix everything. That's just how come he don't know how to do nothing right now—you done spoiled that boy so.

MAMA: Well—he's a little boy. Ain't supposed to know 'bout housekeeping. My baby, that's what he is. What you fix for his breakfast this morning?

RUTH [*angrily*]:   I feed my son, Lena!

MAMA: I ain't meddling—[*under breath, busy-bodyish*]: I just noticed all last week he had cold cereal, and when it starts getting this chilly in the fall a child ought to have some hot grits or something when he goes out in the cold—

RUTH [*furious*]:   I gave him hot oats—is that all right!

MAMA: I ain't meddling. [*pause*] Put a lot of nice butter on it? [RUTH *shoots her an angry look and does not reply.*] He likes lots of butter.

RUTH [*exasperated*]:   Lena—

MAMA [*To* BENEATHA: MAMA *is inclined to wander conversationally sometimes*]: What was you and your brother fussing 'bout this morning?

BENEATHA: It's not important, Mama. [*She gets up and goes to look out at the bathroom, which is apparently free, and she picks up her towels and rushes out.*]

MAMA: What was they fighting about?

RUTH: Now you know as well as I do.

MAMA [*shaking her head*]:   Brother still worrying hisself sick about that money?

RUTH: You know he is.

MAMA: You had breakfast?

RUTH: Some coffee.

MAMA: Girl, you better start eating and looking after yourself better. You almost thin as Travis.

RUTH: Lena—

MAMA: Uh-hunh?

RUTH: What are you going to do with it?

MAMA: Now don't you start, child. It's too early in the morning to be talking about money. It ain't Christian.

RUTH: It's just that he got his heart set on that store—

MAMA: You mean that liquor store that Willy Harris want him to invest in?

RUTH: Yes—

MAMA: We ain't no business people, Ruth. We just plain working folks.

RUTH: Ain't nobody business people till they go into business. Walter Lee say colored people ain't never going to start getting ahead till they start gambling on some different kinds of things in the world—investments and things.

MAMA: What done got into you, girl? Walter Lee done finally sold you on investing.

RUTH: No. Mama, something is happening between Walter and me. I don't know what it is—but he needs something—something I can't give him any more. He needs this chance, Lena.

MAMA [*frowning deeply*]:   But liquor, honey—

RUTH: Well—like Walter say—I spec people going to always be drinking themselves some liquor.

MAMA: Well—whether they drinks it or not ain't none of my business. But whether I go into business selling it to 'em is, and I don't want that on my ledger this late in life. [*stopping suddenly and studying her daughter-in-law*] Ruth Younger, what's the matter with you today? You look like you could fall over right there.

RUTH: I'm tired.

MAMA: Then you better stay home from work today.

RUTH: I can't stay home. She'd be calling up the agency and screaming at them, "My girl didn't come in today—send me somebody! My girl didn't come in!" Oh, she just have a fit...

MAMA: Well, let her have it. I'll just call her up and say you got the flu—

RUTH [*laughing*]: Why the flu?

MAMA: 'Cause it sounds respectable to 'em. Something white people get, too. They know 'bout the flu. Otherwise they think you been cut up or something when you tell 'em you sick.

RUTH: I got to go in. We need the money.

MAMA: Somebody would of thought my children done all but starved to death the way they talk about money here late. Child, we got a great big old check coming tomorrow.

RUTH [*sincerely, but also self-righteously*]: Now that's your money. It ain't got nothing to do with me. We all feel like that—Walter and Bennie and me—even Travis.

MAMA [*thoughtfully, and suddenly very far away*]: Ten thousand dollars—

RUTH: Sure is wonderful.

MAMA: Ten thousand dollars.

RUTH: You know what you should do, Miss Lena? You should take yourself a trip somewhere. To Europe or South America or someplace—

MAMA [*throwing up her hands at the thought*]: Oh, child!

RUTH: I'm serious. Just pack up and leave! Go on away and enjoy yourself some. Forget about the family and have yourself a ball for once in your life—

MAMA [*drily*]: You sound like I'm just about ready to die. Who'd go with me? What I look like wandering 'round Europe by myself?

RUTH: Shoot—these here rich white women do it all the time. They don't think nothing of packing up they suitcases and piling on one of them big steamships and—swoosh!—they gone, child.

MAMA: Something always told me I wasn't no rich white woman.

RUTH: Well—what are you going to do with it then?

MAMA: I ain't rightly decided. [*Thinking. She speaks now with emphasis.*] Some of it got to be put away for Beneatha and her schoolin'—and ain't nothing going to touch that part of it. Nothing. [*She waits several seconds, trying to make up her mind about something, and looks at* RUTH *a little tentatively before going on.*] Been thinking that we maybe could meet the notes on a little old two-story somewhere, with a yard where Travis could play in the summertime, if we use part of the insurance for a down payment and everybody kind of pitch in. I could maybe take on a little day work again, few days a week—

RUTH [*studying her mother-in-law furtively and concentrating on her ironing, anxious to encourage without seeming to*]: Well, Lord knows, we've put enough rent into this here rat trap to pay for four houses by now...

MAMA [*looking up at the words "rat trap" and then looking around and leaning back and sighing—in a suddenly reflective mood—*]: "Rat trap"—yes, that's all it is. [*smiling*] I remember just as well the day me and Big Walter moved in here. Hadn't been married but two weeks and wasn't planning on living here no more than a year. [*She shakes her head at the dissolved dream.*] We was going to set away, little by little, don't you know, and buy a little place out in

Morgan Park. We had even picked out the house. [*chuckling a little*] Looks right dumpy today. But Lord, child, you should know all the dreams I had 'bout buying that house and fixing it up and making me a little garden in the back—[*She waits and stops smiling.*] And didn't none of it happen. [*dropping her hands in a futile gesture*]

RUTH [*keeps her head down, ironing*]: Yes, life can be a barrel of disappointments, sometimes.

MAMA: Honey, Big Walter would come in here some nights back then and slump down on that couch there and just look at the rug, and look at me and look at the rug and then back at me—and I'd know he was down then...really down. [*After a second very long and thoughtful pause; she is seeing back to times that only she can see.*] And then, Lord, when I lost that baby—little Claude—I almost thought I was going to lose Big Walter too. Oh, that man grieved hisself! He was one man to love his children.

RUTH: Ain't nothin' can tear at you like losin' your baby.

MAMA: I guess that's how come that man finally worked hisself to death like he done. Likely he was fighting his own war with this here world that took his baby from him.

RUTH: He sure was a fine man, all right. I always liked Mr. Younger.

MAMA: Crazy 'bout his children! God knows there was plenty wrong with Walter Younger—hard-headed, mean, kind of wild with women—plenty wrong with him. But he sure loved his children. Always wanted them to have some-thing—be something. That's where Brother gets all these notions, I reckon. Big Walter used to say, he'd get right wet in the eyes sometimes, lean his head back with the water standing in his eyes and say, "Seem like God didn't see fit to give the black man nothing but dreams—but He did give us children to make them dreams seem worth while." [*She smiles.*] He could talk like that, don't you know.

RUTH: Yes, he sure could. He was a good man, Mr. Younger.

MAMA: Yes, a fine man—just couldn't never catch up with his dreams, that's all. [BENEATHA *comes in, brushing her hair and looking up to the ceiling, where the sound of a vacuum cleaner has started up.*]

BENEATHA: What could be so dirty on that woman's rugs that she has to vacuum them every single day?

RUTH: I wish certain young women 'round here who I could name would take inspiration about certain rugs in a certain apartment I could also mention.

BENEATHA [*shrugging*]: How much cleaning can a house need, for Christ's sakes?

MAMA [*not liking the Lord's name used thus*]: Bennie!

RUTH: Just listen to her—just listen!

BENEATHA: Oh, God!

MAMA: If you use the Lord's name just one more time—

BENEATHA [*a bit of a whine*]: Oh, Mama—

RUTH: Fresh—just fresh as salt, this girl!

BENEATHA [*drily*]: Well—if the salt loses its savor—

MAMA: Now that will do. I just ain't going to have you 'round here reciting the scriptures in vain—you hear me?

BENEATHA: How did I manage to get on everybody's wrong side by just walking into a room?

RUTH: If you weren't so fresh—

BENEATHA: Ruth, I'm twenty years old.

MAMA: What time you be home from school today?

BENEATHA: Kind of late. [*with enthusiasm*] Madeline is going to start my guitar lessons today. [MAMA *and* RUTH *look up with the same expression.*]

MAMA: Your *what* kind of lessons?

BENEATHA: Guitar.

RUTH: Oh, Father!

MAMA: How come you done taken it in your mind to learn to play the guitar?

BENEATHA: I just want to, that's all.

MAMA [*smiling*]:   Lord, child, don't you know what to do with yourself? How long it going to be before you get tired of this now—like you got tired of that little play-acting group you joined last year? [*looking at* RUTH] And what was it the year before that?

RUTH: The horseback-riding club for which she bought that fifty-five-dollar riding habit that's been hanging in the closet ever since!

MAMA [*to* BENEATHA]:   Why you got to flit so from one thing to another, baby?

BENEATHA [*sharply*]:   I just want to learn to play the guitar. Is there anything wrong with that?

MAMA: Ain't nobody trying to stop you. I just wonders sometimes why you has to flit so from one thing to another all the time. You ain't never done nothing with all that camera equipment you brought home—

BENEATHA: I don't flit! I—I experiment with different forms of expression—

RUTH: Like riding a horse?

BENEATHA: —People have to express themselves one way or another.

MAMA: What is it you want to express?

BENEATHA [*angrily*]:   Me! [MAMA *and* RUTH *look at each other and burst into raucous laughter*] Don't worry—I don't expect you to understand.

MAMA [*to change the subject*]:   Who you going out with tomorrow night?

BENEATHA [*with displeasure*]:   George Murchison again.

MAMA [*pleased*]:   Oh—you getting a little sweet on him?

RUTH: You ask me, this child ain't sweet on nobody but herself—[*under breath*] Express herself! [*They laugh.*]

BENEATHA: Oh—I like George all right, Mama. I mean I like him enough to go out with him and stuff, but—

RUTH [*for devilment*]:   What does and stuff mean?

BENEATHA: Mind your own business.

MAMA: Stop picking at her now, Ruth. [*a thoughtful pause, and then a suspicious sudden look at her daughter as she turns in her chair for emphasis*] What does it mean?

BENEATHA [*wearily*]:   Oh, I just mean I couldn't ever really be serious about George. He's—he's so shallow.

RUTH: Shallow—what do you mean he's shallow? He's *Rich!*

MAMA: Hush, Ruth.

BENEATHA: I know he's rich. He knows he's rich, too.

RUTH: Well—what other qualities a man got to have to satisfy you, little girl?

BENEATHA: You wouldn't even begin to understand. Anybody who married Walter could not possibly understand.

MAMA [*outraged*]:   What kind of way is that to talk about your brother?

BENEATHA: Brother is a flip—let's face it.

MAMA [*to* RUTH, *helplessly*]:   What's a flip?

RUTH [*glad to add kindling*]:   She's saying he's crazy.

BENEATHA: Not crazy. Brother isn't really crazy yet—he—he's an elaborate neurotic.

MAMA: Hush your mouth!

BENEATHA: As for George. Well. George looks good—he's got a beautiful car and he takes me to nice places and, as my sister-in-law says, he is probably the richest boy I will ever get to know and I even like him sometimes—but if the Youngers are sitting around waiting to see if their little Bennie is going to tie up the family with the Murchisons, they are wasting their time.

RUTH: You mean you wouldn't marry George Murchison if he asked you someday? That pretty, rich thing? Honey, I knew you was odd—

BENEATHA: No I would not marry him if all I felt for him was what I feel now. Besides, George's family wouldn't really like it.

MAMA: Why not?

BENEATHA: Oh, Mama—The Murchisons are honest-to-God-real-*live*-rich colored people, and the only people in the world who are more snobbish than rich white people are rich colored people. I thought everybody knew that. I've met Mrs. Murchison. She's a scene!

MAMA: You must not dislike people 'cause they well off, honey.

BENEATHA: Why not? It makes just as much sense as disliking people 'cause they are poor, and lots of people do that.

RUTH [*a wisdom-of-the-ages manner. To* MAMA]:   Well, she'll get over some of this—

BENEATHA: Get over it? What are you talking about, Ruth? Listen, I'm going to be a doctor. I'm not worried about who I'm going to marry yet—if I ever get married.

MAMA AND RUTH: *If!*

MAMA: Now, Bennie—

BENEATHA: Oh, I probably will...but first I'm going to be a doctor, and George, for one, still thinks that's pretty funny. I couldn't be bothered with that. I am going to be a doctor and everybody around here better understand that!

MAMA [*kindly*]:   'Course you going to be a doctor, honey, God willing.

BENEATHA [*drily*]:   God hasn't got a thing to do with it.

MAMA: Beneatha—that just wasn't necessary.

BENEATHA: Well—neither is God. I get sick of hearing about God.

MAMA: Beneatha!

BENEATHA: I mean it! I'm just tired of hearing about God all the time. What has He got to do with anything? Does he pay tuition?

MAMA: You 'bout to get your fresh little jaw slapped!

RUTH: That's just what she needs, all right!

BENEATHA: Why? Why can't I say what I want to around here, like everybody else?

MAMA: It don't sound nice for a young girl to say things like that—you wasn't brought up that way. Me and your father went to trouble to get you and Brother to church every Sunday.

BENEATHA: Mama, you don't understand. It's all a matter of ideas, and God is just one idea I don't accept. It's not important. I am not going out and be immoral or commit crimes because I don't believe in God. I don't even think about it. It's just that I get tired of Him getting credit for all the things the human race achieves through its own stubborn effort. There simply is no blasted God— there is only man and it is he who makes miracles! [MAMA *absorbs this speech, studies her daughter and rises slowly and crosses to* BENEATHA *and slaps her powerfully across the face. After, there is only silence and the daughter drops her eyes from her mother's face, and* MAMA *is very tall before her.*]

MAMA: Now—you say after me, in my mother's house there is still God. [*There is a long pause and* BENEATHA *stares at the floor wordlessly.* MAMA *repeats the phrase with precision and cool emotion.*] In my mother's house there is still God.

BENEATHA: In my mother's house there is still God. [*a long pause*]

MAMA [*Walking away from* BENEATHA, *too disturbed for triumphant posture. Stopping and turning back to her daughter.*]:   There are some ideas we ain't going to have in this house. Not long as I am at the head of this family.

BENEATHA: Yes, ma'am. [MAMA *walks out of the room.*]

RUTH [*almost gently, with profound understanding*]:   You think you a woman, Bennie—but you still a little girl. What you did was childish—so you got treated like a child.

BENEATHA: I see. [*quietly*] I also see that everybody thinks it's all right for Mama to be a tyrant. But all the tyranny in the world will never put a God in the heavens! [*She picks up her books and goes out.*]

RUTH [*goes to* MAMA's *door*]:   She said she was sorry.

MAMA [*coming out, going to her plant*]:   They frightens me, Ruth. My children.

RUTH: You got good children, Lena. They just a little off sometimes—but they're good.

MAMA: No—There's something come down between me and them that don't let us understand each other and I don't know what it is. One done almost lost his mind thinking 'bout money all the time and the other done commence to talk about things I can't seem to understand in no form or fashion. What is it that's changing, Ruth?

RUTH [*soothingly, older than her years*]:   Now…you taking it all too seriously. You just got strong-willed children and it takes a strong woman like you to keep 'em in hand.

MAMA [*looking at her plant and sprinkling a little water on it*]:   They spirited all right, my children. Got to admit they got spirit—Bennie and Walter. Like this little old plant that ain't never had enough sunshine or nothing—and look at it… [*She has her back to* RUTH, *who has had to stop ironing and lean against something and put the back of her hand to her forehead.*]

RUTH [*trying to keep Mama from noticing*]:   You…sure…loves that little old thing, don't you?…

MAMA: Well, I always wanted me a garden like I used to see sometimes at the back of the houses down home. This plant is close as I ever got to having one.

[*She looks out of the window as she replaces the plant.*] Lord, ain't nothing as dreary as the view from this window on a dreary day, is there? Why ain't you singing this morning, Ruth? Sing that "No Ways Tired." That song always lifts me up so—[*She turns at last to see that* RUTH *has slipped quietly into a chair, in a state of semiconsciousness.*] Ruth! Ruth honey—what's the matter with you... Ruth!

Curtain

SCENE 2

It is the following morning; a Saturday morning, and house cleaning is in progress at the Youngers. Furniture has been shoved hither and yon and MAMA *is giving the kitchen-area walls a washing down.* BENEATHA, *in dungarees, with a handkerchief tied around her face, is spraying insecticide into the cracks in the walls. As they work, the radio is on and a South Side disk jockey program is inappropriately filling the house with a rather exotic saxophone blues.* TRAVIS, *the sole idle one, is leaning on his arms, looking out of the window.*

TRAVIS: Grandmama, that stuff Bennie is using smells awful. Can I go downstairs, please?

MAMA: Did you get all them chores done already? I ain't seen you doing much.

TRAVIS: Yes'm—finished early. Where did Mama go this morning?

MAMA [*looking at* BENEATHA]:   She had to go on a little errand.

TRAVIS: Where?

MAMA: To tend to her business.

TRAVIS: Can I go outside then?

MAMA: Oh, I guess so. You better stay right in front of the house, though... and keep a good lookout for the postman.

TRAVIS: Yes'm. [*He starts out and decides to give his* AUNT BENEATHA *a good swat on the legs as he passes her.*] Leave them poor little old cockroaches alone, they ain't bothering you none. [*He runs as she swings the spray gun at him both viciously and playfully.* WALTER *enters from the bedroom and goes to the phone.*]

MAMA: Look out there, girl, before you be spilling some of that stuff on that child!

TRAVIS [*teasing*]:   That's right—look out now! [*He exits.*]

BENEATHA [*drily*]:   I can't imagine that it would hurt him—it has never hurt the roaches.

MAMA: Well, little boys' hides ain't as tough as South Side roaches.

WALTER [*into phone*]:   Hello—Let me talk to Willy Harris.

MAMA: You better get over there behind the bureau. I seen one marching out of there like Napoleon yesterday.

WALTER: Hello, Willy? It ain't come yet. It'll be here in a few minutes. Did the lawyer give you the papers?

BENEATHA: There's really only one way to get rid of them, Mama—

MAMA: How?

BENEATHA: Set fire to this building.

WALTER: Good. Good. I'll be right over.

BENEATHA: Where did Ruth go, Walter?

WALTER: I don't know. [*He exits abruptly.*]

BENEATHA: Mama, where did Ruth go?

MAMA [*looking at her with meaning*]:   To the doctor, I think.

BENEATHA: The doctor? What's the matter? [*They exchange glances.*] You don't think—

MAMA [*with her sense of drama*]:   Now I ain't saying what I think. But I ain't never been wrong 'bout a woman neither. [*The phone rings.*]

BENEATHA [*at the phone*]:   Hay-lo... [*pause, and a moment of recognition*] Well— when did you get back!... And how was it?... Of course I've missed you—in my way... This morning? No...house cleaning and all that and Mama hates it if I let people come over when the house is like this... You *have?* Well, that's different... What is it—Oh, what the hell, come on over... Right, see you then.

[*She hangs up.*]

MAMA [*who has listened vigorously, as is her habit*]:   Who is that you inviting over here with this house looking like this? You ain't got the pride you was born with!

BENEATHA: Asagai doesn't care how houses look, Mama—he's an intellectual.

MAMA: *Who?*

BENEATHA: Asagai—Joseph Asagai. He's an African boy I met on campus. He's been studying in Canada all summer.

MAMA: What's his name?

BENEATHA: Asagai, Joseph. Ah-sah-guy... He's from Nigeria.

MAMA: Oh, that's the little country that was founded by slaves way back...

BENEATHA: No, Mama—that's Liberia.

MAMA: I don't think I never met no African before.

BENEATHA: Well, do me a favor and don't ask him a whole lot of ignorant questions about Africans. I mean, do they wear clothes and all that—

MAMA: Well, now, I guess if you think we so ignorant 'round here maybe you shouldn't bring your friends here—

BENEATHA: It's just that people ask such crazy things. All anyone seems to know about when it comes to Africa is Tarzan—

MAMA [*indignantly*]:   Why should I know anything about Africa?

BENEATHA: Why do you give money at church for the missionary work?

MAMA: Well, that's to help save people.

BENEATHA: You mean save them from *heathenism*—

MAMA [*innocently*]:   Yes.

BENEATHA: I'm afraid they need more salvation from the British and the French.

[RUTH *comes in forlornly and pulls off her coat with dejection. They both turn to look at her.*]

RUTH [*dispiritedly*]:   Well, I guess from all the happy faces—everybody knows.

BENEATHA: You pregnant?

MAMA: Lord have mercy, I sure hope it's a little old girl. Travis ought to have a sister.

[BENEATHA *and* RUTH *give her a hopeless look for this grandmotherly enthusiasm.*]

BENEATHA: How far along are you?

RUTH: Two months.

BENEATHA: Did you mean to? I mean did you plan it or was it an accident?

MAMA: What do you know about planning or not planning?

BENEATHA: Oh, Mama.

RUTH [*wearily*]:   She's twenty years old, Lena.

BENEATHA: Did you plan it, Ruth?

RUTH: Mind your own business.

BENEATHA: It is my business—where is he going to live, on the roof? [*There is silence following the remark as the three women react to the sense of it.*] Gee—I didn't mean that, Ruth, honest. Gee, I don't feel like that at all. I—I think it is wonderful.

RUTH [*dully*]:   Wonderful.

BENEATHA: Yes—really.

MAMA [*looking at* RUTH, *worried*]:   Doctor say everything going to be all right?

RUTH [*far away*]:   Yes—she says everything is going to be fine...

MAMA [*immediately suspicious*]:   "She"—What doctor you went to? [RUTH *folds over, near hysteria*]

MAMA [*worriedly hovering over* RUTH]:   Ruth, honey—what's the matter with you—you sick? [RUTH *has her fists clenched on her thighs and is fighting hard to suppress a scream that seems to be rising in her.*]

BENEATHA: What's the matter with her, Mama?

MAMA [*working her fingers in* RUTH's *shoulder to relax her*]:   She be all right. Women gets right depressed sometimes when they get her way. [*speaking softly, expertly, rapidly*] Now you just relax. That's right...just lean back, don't think 'bout nothing at all...nothing at all—

RUTH: I'm all right... [*The glassy-eyed look melts and then she collapses into a fit of heavy sobbing. The bell rings.*]

BENEATHA: Oh, my God—that must be Asagai.

MAMA [*to* RUTH]:   Come on now, honey. You need to lie down and rest awhile... then have some nice hot food. [*They exit,* RUTH's *weight on her mother-in-law.* BENEATHA, *herself profoundly disturbed, opens the door to admit a rather dramatic-looking young man with a large package.*]

ASAGAI: Hello, Alaiyo—

BENEATHA [*holding the door open and regarding him with pleasure*]:   Hello... [*long pause*] Well—come in. And please excuse everything. My mother was very upset about my letting anyone come here with the place like this.

ASAGAI [*coming into the room*]:   You look disturbed too... Is something wrong?

BENEATHA [*still at the door, absently*]:   Yes... we've all got acute ghetto-itus. [*She smiles and comes toward him, finding a cigarette and sitting.*] So—sit down! How was Canada?

ASAGAI [*a sophisticate*]:   Canadian.

BENEATHA [*looking at him*]:   I'm very glad you are back.

ASAGAI [*looking back at her in turn*]:   Are you really?

BENEATHA: Yes—very.

ASAGAI: Why—you were quite glad when I went away. What happened?

BENEATHA: You went away.

ASAGAI: Ahhhhhhhh.

BENEATHA: Before—you wanted to be so serious before there was time.

ASAGAI: How much time must there be before one knows what one feels?

BENEATHA [*Stalling this particular conversation. Her hands pressed together, in a deliberately childish gesture*]:   What did you bring me?

ASAGAI [*handing her the package*]:   Open it and see.

BENEATHA [*eagerly opening the package and drawing out some records and the colorful robes of a Nigerian woman*]:   Oh, Asagai!... You got them for me!... How beautiful...and the records too! [*She lifts out the robes and runs to the mirror with them and holds the drapery up in front of herself.*]

ASAGAI [*coming to her at the mirror*]:   I shall have to teach you how to drape it properly. [*He flings the material about her for the moment and stands back to look at her.*] Ah—Oh-pay-gay-day, oh-gbah-mu-shay. [*a Yoruba exclamation for admiration*] You wear it well... very well... mutilated hair and all.

BENEATHA [*turning suddenly*]:   My hair—what's wrong with my hair?

ASAGAI [*shrugging*]:   Were you born with it like that?

BENEATHA [*reaching up to touch it*]:   No... of course not. [*She looks back to the mirror, disturbed.*]

ASAGAI [*smiling*]:   How then?

BENEATHA: You know perfectly well how...as crinkly as yours...that's how.

ASAGAI: And it is ugly to you that way?

BENEATHA [*quickly*]:   Oh, no—not ugly...[*more slowly, apologetically*] But it's so hard to manage when it's, well—raw.

ASAGAI: And so to accommodate that—you mutilate it every week?

BENEATHA: It's not mutilation!

ASAGAI [*laughing aloud at her seriousness*]:   Oh...please! I am only teasing you because you are so very serious about these things. [*He stands back from her and folds his arms across his chest as he watches her pulling at her hair and frowning in the mirror.*] Do you remember the first time you met me at school?... [*He laughs.*] You came up to me and said—and I thought you were the most serious little thing I had ever seen—you said: [*He imitates her.*] "Mr. Asagai— I want very much to talk with you. About Africa. You see, Mr. Asagai, I am looking for my *identity!*" [*He laughs.*]

BENEATHA [*turning to him, not laughing*]:   Yes—[*Her face is quizzical, profoundly disturbed.*]

ASAGAI [*still teasing and reaching out and taking her face in his hands and turning her profile to him*]:   Well... it is true that this is not so much a profile of a Hollywood queen as perhaps a queen of the Nile—[*a mock dismissal of the importance of the question*] But what does it matter? Assimilationism is so popular in your country.

BENEATHA [*wheeling, passionately, sharply*]:   I am not an assimilationist!

ASAGAI [*The protest hangs in the room for a moment and* ASAGAI *studies her, his laughter fading.*]:   Such a serious one. [*There is a pause.*] So—you like the robes? You must take excellent care of them—they are from my sister's personal wardrobe.

BENEATHA [*with incredulity*]:   You—you sent all the way home—for me?

ASAGAI [*with charm*]:   For you—I would do much more... Well, that is what I came for. I must go.

BENEATHA: Will you call me Monday?

ASAGAI: Yes... We have a great deal to talk about. I mean about identity and time and all that.

BENEATHA: Time?

ASAGAI: Yes. About how much time one needs to know what one feels.

BENEATHA: You never understood that there is more than one kind of feeling which can exist between a man and a woman—or, at least, there should be.

ASAGAI [*shaking his head negatively but gently*]:   No. Between a man and a woman there need be only one kind of feeling. I have that for you... Now even... right this moment...

BENEATHA: I know—and by itself—it won't do. I can find that anywhere.

ASAGAI: For a woman it should be enough.

BENEATHA: I know—because that's what it says in all the novels that men write. But it isn't. Go ahead and laugh—but I'm not interested in being someone's little episode in America or—[*with feminine vengeance*]—one of them! [ASAGAI *has burst into laughter again.*] That's funny as hell, huh!

ASAGAI: It's just that every American girl I have known has said that to me. White— black—in this you are all the same. And the same speech, too!

BENEATHA [*angrily*]:   Yuk, yuk, yuk!

ASAGAI: It's how you can be sure that the world's most liberated women are not liberated at all. You all talk about it too much! [MAMA *enters and is immediately all social charm because of the presence of a guest.*]

BENEATHA: Oh—Mama—this is Mr. Asagai.

MAMA: How do you do?

ASAGAI [*total politeness to an elder*]:   How do you do, Mrs. Younger. Please forgive me for coming at such an outrageous hour on a Saturday.

MAMA: Well, you are quite welcome. I just hope you understand that our house don't always look like this. [*chatterish*] You must come again. I would love to hear all about—[*not sure of the name*]—your country. I think it's so sad the way our American Negroes don't know nothing about Africa 'cept Tarzan and all that. And all that money they pour into these churches when they ought to be helping you people over there drive out them French and Englishmen done taken away your land. [*The mother flashes a slightly superior look at her daughter upon completion of the recitation.*]

ASAGAI [*taken aback by this sudden and acutely unrelated expression of sympathy*]:   Yes...yes...

MAMA [*smiling at him suddenly and relaxing and looking him over*]:   How many miles is it from here to where you come from?

ASAGAI: Many thousands.

MAMA [*looking at him as she would* WALTER]:   I bet you don't half look after yourself, being away from your mama either. I spec you better come 'round here from time to time and get yourself some decent home-cooked meals...

ASAGAI [*moved*]:   Thank you. Thank you very much. [*They are all quiet, then—*] Well... I must go. I will call you Monday, Alaiyo.

MAMA: What's that he call you?

ASAGAI: Oh—"Alaiyo." I hope you don't mind. It is what you would call a nickname, I think. It is a Yoruba word. I am a Yoruba.

MAMA [*looking at Beneatha*]:   I—I thought he was from—

ASAGAI [*understanding*]:   Nigeria is my country. Yoruba is my tribal origin—

BENEATHA: You didn't tell us what Alaiyo means...for all I know, you might be calling me Little Idiot or something...

ASAGAI: Well...let me see... I do not know how just to explain it... The sense of a thing can be so different when it changes languages.

BENEATHA: You're evading.

ASAGAI: No—really it is difficult...[*thinking*] It means...it means One for Whom Bread—Food—Is Not Enough. [*He looks at her.*] Is that all right?

BENEATHA [*understanding, softly*]:   Thank you.

MAMA [*looking from one to the other and not understanding any of it*]:   Well... that's nice.... You must come see us again—Mr.—

ASAGAI: Ah-sah-guy....

MAMA: Yes... Do come again.

ASAGAI: Good-bye. [*He exits.*]

MAMA [*after him*]:   Lord, that's a pretty thing just went out here! [*insinuatingly, to her daughter*] Yes, I guess I see why we done commence to get so interested in Africa 'round here. Missionaries my aunt Jenny! [*She exits.*]

BENEATHA: Oh, Mama!... [*She picks up the Nigerian dress and holds it up to her in front of the mirror again. She sets the headdress on haphazardly and then notices her hair again and clutches at it and then replaces the headdress and frowns at herself. Then she starts to wriggle in front of the mirror as she thinks a Nigerian woman might.* TRAVIS *enters and regards her.*]

TRAVIS: You cracking up?

BENEATHA: Shut up. [*She pulls the headdress off and looks at herself in the mirror and clutches at her hair again and squinches her eyes as if trying to imagine something. Then, suddenly, she gets her raincoat and kerchief and hurriedly prepares for going out.*]

MAMA [*coming back into the room*]:   She's resting now. Travis, baby, run next door and ask Miss Johnson to please let me have a little kitchen cleanser. This here can is empty as Jacob's kettle.

TRAVIS: I just came in.

MAMA: Do as you told. [*He exits and she looks at her daughter.*] Where you going?

BENEATHA [*halting at the door*]:   To become a queen of the Nile! [*She exits in a breathless blaze of glory.* RUTH *appears in the bedroom doorway.*]

MAMA: Who told you to get up?

RUTH: Ain't nothing wrong with me to be lying in no bed for. Where did Bennie go?

MAMA [*drumming her fingers*]:   Far as I could make out—to Egypt. [RUTH *just looks at her.*] What time is it getting to?

RUTH: Ten twenty. And the mailman going to ring that bell this morning just like he done every morning for the last umpteen years. [TRAVIS *comes in with the cleanser can.*]

TRAVIS: She say to tell you that she don't have much.

MAMA [*angrily*]:   Lord, some people I could name sure is tight-fisted! [*directing her grandson*] Mark two cans of cleanser down on the list there. If she that hard up for kitchen cleanser, I sure don't want to forget to get her none!

RUTH: Lena—maybe the woman is just short on cleanser—

MAMA [*not listening*]:   —Much baking powder as she done borrowed from me all these years, she could of done gone into the baking business! [*The bell sounds suddenly and sharply and all three are stunned—serious and silent—mid-speech. In spite of all the other conversation and distractions of the morning, this is what they have been waiting for, even* TRAVIS, *who looks helplessly from his mother to his grandmother.* RUTH *is the first to come to life again.*]

RUTH [*to* TRAVIS]:   Get down them steps, boy! [TRAVIS *snaps to life and flies out to get the mail.*]

MAMA [*her eyes wide, her hand to her breast*]:   You mean it done really come?

RUTH [*excited*]:   Oh, Miss Lena!

MAMA [*collecting herself*]:   Well... I don't know what we all so excited about 'round here for. We known it was coming for months.

RUTH: That's a whole lot different from having it come and being able to hold it in your hands... a piece of paper worth ten thousand dollars... [TRAVIS *bursts back into the room. He holds the envelope high above his head, like a little dancer, his face is radiant and he is breathless. He moves to his grandmother with sudden slow ceremony and puts the envelope into her hands. She accepts it, and then merely holds it and looks at it.*] Come on! Open it... Lord have mercy, I wish Walter Lee was here!

TRAVIS: Open it, Grandmama!

MAMA [*staring at it*]:   Now you all be quiet. It's just a check.

RUTH: Open it...

MAMA [*still staring at it*]:   Now don't act silly... We ain't never been no people to act silly 'bout no money—

RUTH [*swiftly*]:   We ain't never had none before—*open it!* [MAMA *finally makes a good strong tear and pulls out the thin blue slice of paper and inspects it closely. The boy and his mother study it raptly over* MAMA's *shoulders.*]

MAMA: Travis! [*She is counting off with doubt.*] Is that the right number of zeros?

TRAVIS: Yes'm... ten thousand dollars. Gaalee, Grandmama, you rich.

MAMA [*She holds the check away from her, still looking at it. Slowly her face sobers into a mask of unhappiness.*]:   Ten thousand dollars. [*She hands it to* RUTH.] Put it away somewhere, Ruth. [*She does not look at* RUTH; *her eyes seem to be seeing something somewhere very far off.*] Ten thousand dollars they give you. Ten thousand dollars.

TRAVIS [*to his mother, sincerely*]:   What's the matter with Grandmama—don't she want to be rich?

RUTH [*distractedly*]:   You go on out and play now, baby. [TRAVIS *exits.* MAMA *starts wiping dishes absently, humming intently to herself.* RUTH *turns to her, with kind exasperation.*] You've gone and got yourself upset.

MAMA [*not looking at her*]:   I spec if it wasn't for you all... I would just put that money away or give it to the church or something.

RUTH: Now what kind of talk is that. Mr. Younger would just be plain mad if he could hear you talking foolish like that.

MAMA [*stopping and staring off*]:   Yes…he sure would. [*sighing*] We got enough to do with that money, all right. [*She halts then, and turns and looks at her daughter-in-law hard;* RUTH *avoids her eyes and* MAMA *wipes her hands with finality and starts to speak firmly to* RUTH.] Where did you go today, girl?

RUTH: To the doctor.

MAMA [*impatiently*]:   Now, Ruth…you know better than that. Old Doctor Jones is strange enough in his way but there ain't nothing 'bout him make somebody slip and call him "she"—like you done this morning.

RUTH: Well, that's what happened—my tongue slipped.

MAMA: You went to see that woman, didn't you?

RUTH [*defensively, giving herself away*]:   What woman you talking about?

MAMA [*angrily*]:   That woman who—[WALTER *enters in great excitement.*]

WALTER: Did it come?

MAMA [*quietly*]:   Can't you give people a Christian greeting before you start asking about money?

WALTER [*to* RUTH]:   Did it come? [RUTH *unfolds the check and lays it quietly before him, watching him intently with thoughts of her own.* WALTER *sits down and grasps it close and counts off the zeros.*] Ten thousand dollars—[*He turns suddenly, frantically to his mother and draws some papers out of his breast pocket.*] Mama—look. Old Willy Harris put everything on paper—

MAMA: Son—I think you ought to talk to your wife… I'll go on out and leave you alone if you want—

WALTER: I can talk to her later—Mama, look—

MAMA: Son—

WALTER: WILL SOMEBODY PLEASE LISTEN TO ME TODAY!

MAMA [*quietly*]:   I don't 'low no yellin' in this house, Walter Lee, and you know it—[WALTER *stares at them in frustration and starts to speak several times.*] And there ain't going to be no investing in no liquor stores. I don't aim to have to speak on that again. [*a long pause*]

WALTER: Oh—so you don't aim to have to speak on that again? So you have decided… [*crumpling his papers*] Well, *you* tell that to my boy tonight when you put him to sleep on the living-room couch… [*turning to* MAMA *and speaking directly to her*]: Yeah—and tell it to my wife, Mama, tomorrow when she has to go out of here to look after somebody else's kids. And tell it to *me*, mama, every time we need a new pair of curtains and I have to watch *you* go out and work in somebody's kitchen. Yeah, you tell me then! [WALTER *starts out*]

RUTH: Where you going?

WALTER: I'm going out!

RUTH: Where?

WALTER: Just out of this house somewhere—

RUTH [*getting her coat*]:   I'll come too.

WALTER: I don't want you to come!

RUTH: I got something to talk to you about, Walter.

WALTER: That's too bad.

MAMA [*still quietly*]:   Walter Lee—[*She waits and he finally turns and looks at her.*]
Sit down.

WALTER: I'm a grown man, Mama.

MAMA: Ain't nobody said you wasn't grown. But you still in my house and my presence. And as long as you are—you'll talk to your wife civil. Now sit down.

RUTH [*suddenly*]:   Oh, let him go on out and drink himself to death! He makes me
sick to my stomach! [*She flings her coat against him.*]

WALTER [*violently*]:   And you turn mine, too, baby! [RUTH *goes into their bedroom
and slams the door behind her.*] That was my greatest mistake—

MAMA [*still quietly*]:   Walter, what is the matter with you?

WALTER: Matter with me? Ain't nothing the matter with *me!*

MAMA: Yes there is. Something eating you up like a crazy man. Something more than
me not giving you this money. The past few years I been watching it happen to
you. You get all nervous acting and kind of wild in the eyes—[WALTER *jumps up
impatiently at her words.*] I said sit there now, I'm talking to you!

WALTER: Mama—I don't need no nagging at me today.

MAMA: Seem like you getting to a place where you always tied up in some kind
of knot about something. But if anybody ask you 'bout it you just yell at 'em
and bust out the house and go out and drink somewheres. Walter Lee, people
can't live with that. Ruth's a good, patient girl in her way—but you getting to
be too much. Boy, don't make the mistake of driving that girl away from you.

WALTER: Why—what she do for me?

MAMA: She loves you.

WALTER: Mama—I'm going out. I want to go off somewhere and be by myself for
a while.

MAMA: I'm sorry 'bout your liquor store, son. It just wasn't the thing for us to do.
That's what I want to tell you about—

WALTER: I got to go out, Mama—[*He rises.*]

MAMA: It's dangerous, son.

WALTER: What's dangerous?

MAMA: When a man goes outside his home to look for peace.

WALTER [*beseechingly*]:   Then why can't there never be no peace in this house then?

MAMA: You done found it in some other house?

WALTER: No—there ain't no woman! Why do women always think there's a woman somewhere when a man gets restless. [*coming to her*] Mama—Mama—I
want so many things...

MAMA: Yes, son—

WALTER: I want so many things that they are driving me kind of crazy... Mama—
look at me.

MAMA: I'm looking at you. You a good-looking boy. You got a job, a nice wife, a
fine boy and—

WALTER: A job. [*looks at her*] Mama, a job? I open and close car doors all day long. I
drive a man around in his limousine and I say, "Yes, sir; no, sir; very good, sir;
shall I take the Drive, sir?" Mama, that ain't no kind of job...that ain't nothing
at all. [*very quietly*] Mama, I don't know if I can make you understand.

MAMA: Understand what, baby?

WALTER [*quietly*]:   Sometimes it's like I can see the future stretched out in front of me—just plain as day. The future, Mama. Hanging over there at the edge of my days. Just waiting for me—a big, looming blank space—full of *nothing.* Just waiting for *me.* [*pause*] Mama—sometimes when I'm downtown and I pass them cool, quiet-looking restaurants where them white boys are sitting back and talking 'bout things . . . sitting there turning deals worth millions of dollars . . . sometimes I see guys don't look much older than me—

MAMA: Son—how come you talk so much 'bout money?

WALTER [*with immense passion*]:   Because it is life, Mama!

MAMA [*quietly*]:   Oh—[*very quietly*] So now it's life. Money is life. Once upon a time freedom used to be life—now it's money. I guess the world really do change . . .

WALTER: No—it was always money, Mama. We just didn't know about it.

MAMA: No . . . something has changed. [*She looks at him.*] You something new, boy. In my time we was worried about not being lynched and getting to the North if we could and how to stay alive and still have a pinch of dignity too . . . Now here come you and Beneatha—talking 'bout things we ain't never even thought about hardly, me and your daddy. You ain't satisfied or proud of nothing we done. I mean that you had a home; that we kept you out of trouble till you was grown; that you don't have to ride to work on the back of nobody's streetcar— You my children—but how different we done become.

WALTER: You just don't understand, Mama, you just don't understand.

MAMA: Son—do you know your wife is expecting another baby? [WALTER *stands, stunned, and absorbs what his mother has said.*] That's what she wanted to talk to you about. [WALTER *sinks down into a chair.*] This ain't for me to be telling—but you ought to know. [*She waits*] I think Ruth is thinking 'bout getting rid of that child.

WALTER [*slowly understanding*]:   No—no—Ruth wouldn't do that.

MAMA: When the world gets ugly enough—a woman will do anything for her family. *The part that's already living.*

WALTER: You don't know Ruth, Mama, if you think she would do that. [RUTH *opens the bedroom door and stands there a little limp.*]

RUTH [*beaten*]:   Yes I would too, Walter, [*pause*] I gave her a five-dollar down payment. [*There is total silence as the man stares at his wife and the mother stares at her son.*]

MAMA [*presently*]:   Well—[*tightly*] Well—son, I'm waiting to hear you say something . . . I'm waiting to hear how you be your father's son. Be the man he was . . . [*pause*] Your wife say she going to destroy your child. And I'm waiting to hear you talk like him and say we a people who give children life, not who destroys them—[*She rises.*] I'm waiting to see you stand up and look like your daddy and say we done give up one baby to poverty and that we ain't going to give up nary another one . . . I'm waiting.

WALTER: Ruth—

MAMA: If you a son of mine, tell her! [WALTER *turns, looks at her and can say nothing. She continues, bitterly.*] You . . . you are a disgrace to your father's memory. Somebody get me my hat.

Curtain

ACT II
SCENE 1

TIME: *Later the same day.*

AT RISE: RUTH *is ironing again. She has the radio going. Presently* BENEATHA'S *bedroom door opens and* RUTH'S *mouth falls and she puts down the iron in fascination.*

RUTH: What have we got on tonight!

BENEATHA [*emerging grandly from the doorway so that we can see her thoroughly robed in the costume* ASAGAI *brought.*]: You are looking at what a well-dressed Nigerian woman wears—[*She parades for* RUTH, *her hair completely hidden by the headdress; she is coquettishly fanning herself with an ornate oriental fan, mistakenly more like Butterfly than any Nigerian that ever was.*] Isn't it beautiful? [*She promenades to the radio and, with an arrogant flourish, turns off the good loud blues that is playing.*] Enough of this assimilationist junk! [RUTH *follows her with her eyes as she goes to the phonograph and puts on a record and turns and waits ceremoniously for the music to come up. Then with a shout*—] OCOMOGOSIAY! [RUTH *jumps. The music comes up, a lovely Nigerian melody.* BENEATHA *listens, enraptured, her eyes far away—"back to the past." She begins to dance.* RUTH *is dumbfounded.*]

RUTH: What kind of dance is that?

BENEATHA: A folk dance.

RUTH [*Pearl Bailey*]: What kind of folks do that, honey?

BENEATHA: It's from Nigeria. It's a dance of welcome.

RUTH: Who you welcoming?

BENEATHA: The men back to the village.

RUTH: Where they been?

BENEATHA: How should I know—out hunting or something. Anyway, they are coming back now...

RUTH: Well, that's good.

BENEATHA: [*with the record*]: Alundi, alundi
Alundi alunya
Jop pu a jeepua
Ang gu soooooooooo
Ai yai yae...

Ayehaye—alundi...[WALTER *comes in during this performance; he has obviously been drinking. He leans against the door heavily and watches his sister, at first with distaste. Then his eyes look off—"back to the past"—as he lifts both his fists to the roof, screaming.*]

WALTER: YEAH... AND ETHIOPIA STRETCH FORTH HER HANDS AGAIN!...

RUTH [*drily, looking at him*]: Yes—and Africa sure is claiming her own tonight. [*She gives them both up and starts ironing again.*]

WALTER [*all in a drunken, dramatic shout*]: Shut up!... I'm digging them drums... them drums move me!... [*He makes his weaving way to his wife's face and leans in close to her.*] In my heart of hearts—[*He thumps his chest.*]—I am much warrior!

RUTH [*without even looking up*]: In your heart of hearts you are much drunkard.

WALTER [*coming away from her and starting to wander around the room, shouting*]: Me and Jomo... [*Intently, in his sister's face. She has stopped dancing to watch him in this unknown mood.*] That's my man, Kenyatta. [*Shouting and thumping his chest.*] FLAMING SPEAR! HOT DAMN! [*He is suddenly in posses-sion of an imaginary spear and actively spearing enemies all over the room.*] OCOMOGOSIAY... THE LION IS WAKING... OWIMOWEH! [*He pulls his shirt open and leaps up on a table and gestures with his spear. The bell rings. RUTH goes to answer.*]

BENEATHA [*to encourage WALTER, thoroughly caught up with this side of him*]: OCOMOGOSIAY, FLAMING SPEAR!

WALTER [*On the table, very far gone, his eyes pure glass sheets. He sees what we can-not, that he is a leader of his people, a great chief, a descendant of Chaka, and that the hour to march has come.*]:   Listen, my black brothers—

BENEATHA: OCOMOGOSIAY!

WALTER: —Do you hear the waters rushing against the shores of the coastlands—

BENEATHA: OCOMOGOSIAY!

WALTER: —Do you hear the screeching of the cocks in yonder hills beyond where the chiefs meet in council for the coming of the mighty war—

BENEATHA: OCOMOGOSIAY!

WALTER: —Do you hear the beating of the wings of the birds flying low over the mountains and the low places of our land—[RUTH *opens the door,* GEORGE MURCHISON *enters.*]

BENEATHA: OCOMOGOSIAY!

WALTER: —Do you hear the singing of the women, singing the war songs of our fathers to the babies in the great houses... singing the sweet war songs? OH, DO YOU HEAR, MY BLACK BROTHERS?

BENEATHA [*completely gone*]:   We hear you, Flaming Spear—

WALTER: Telling us to prepare for the greatness of the time—[*to* GEORGE] Black Brother! [*He extends his hand for the fraternal clasp.*]

GEORGE: Black Brother, hell!

RUTH [*having had enough, and embarrassed for the family*]:   Beneatha, you got company—what's the matter with you? Walter Lee Younger, get down off that table and stop acting like a fool... [WALTER *comes down off the table suddenly and makes a quick exit to the bathroom.*]

RUTH: He's had a little to drink... I don't know what her excuse is.

GEORGE [*to* BENEATHA]:   Look honey, we're going *to* the theatre—we're not going to be *in* it... so go change, huh?

RUTH: You expect this boy to go out with you looking like that?

BENEATHA [*looking at* GEORGE]:   That's up to George. If he's ashamed of his heritage—

GEORGE: Oh, don't be so proud of yourself, Bennie—just because you look eccentric.

BENEATHA: How can something that's natural be eccentric?

GEORGE: That's what being eccentric means—being natural. Get dressed.

BENEATHA: I don't like that, George.

RUTH: Why must you and your brother make an argument out of everything people say?

BENEATHA: Because I hate assimilationist Negroes!

RUTH: Will somebody please tell me what assimila-who-ever means!

GEORGE: Oh, it's just a college girl's way of calling people Uncle Toms—but that isn't what it means at all.

RUTH: Well, what does it mean?

BENEATHA [*cutting* GEORGE *off and staring at him as she replies to* RUTH]:   It means someone who is willing to give up his own culture and submerge himself completely in the dominant, and in this case, *oppressive* culture!

GEORGE: Oh, dear, dear, dear! Here we go! A lecture on the African past! On our Great West African Heritage! In one second we will hear all about the great Ashanti empires; the great Songhay civilizations; and the great sculpture of Benin—and then some poetry in the Bantu—and the whole monologue will end with the word *heritage!* [*nastily*] Let's face it, baby, your heritage is nothing but a bunch of raggedy-assed spirituals and some grass huts!

BENEATHA: *Grass huts!* [RUTH *crosses to her and forcibly pushes her toward the bedroom.*] See there . . . you are standing there in your splendid ignorance talking about people who were the first to smelt iron on the face of the earth! [RUTH *is pushing her through the door.*] The Ashanti were performing surgical operations when the English—[RUTH *pulls the door to, with* BENEATHA *on the other side, and smiles graciously at* GEORGE. BENEATHA *opens the door and shouts the end of the sentence defiantly at* GEORGE.]—were still tattooing themselves with blue dragons . . . [*She goes back inside.*]

RUTH: Have a seat, George. [*They both sit.* RUTH *folds her hands rather primly on her lap, determined to demonstrate the civilization of the family.*] Warm, ain't it? I mean for September. [*pause*] Just like they always say about Chicago weather: If it's too hot or cold for you, just wait a minute and it'll change. [*She smiles happily at this cliché of clichés.*] Everybody say it's got to do with them bombs and things they keep setting off. [*pause*] Would you like a nice cold beer?

GEORGE: No, thank you. I don't care for beer. [*He looks at his watch.*] I hope she hurries up.

RUTH: What time is the show?

GEORGE: It's an eight-thirty curtain. That's just Chicago, though. In New York standard curtain time is eight forty. [*He is rather proud of this knowledge.*]

RUTH [*properly appreciating it*]:   You get to New York a lot?

GEORGE [*offhand*]:   Few times a year.

RUTH: Oh—that's nice. I've never been to New York. [WALTER *enters. We feel he has relieved himself, but the edge of unreality is still with him.*]

WALTER: New York ain't got nothing Chicago ain't. Just a bunch of hustling people all squeezed up together—being "Eastern." [*He turns his face into a screw of displeasure.*]

GEORGE: Oh—you've been?

WALTER: Plenty of times.

RUTH [*shocked at the lie*]:   Walter Lee Younger!

WALTER [*staring her down*]:   Plenty! [*pause*] What we got to drink in this house? Why don't you offer this man some refreshment. [*to* GEORGE] They don't know how to entertain people in this house, man.

GEORGE: Thank you—I don't really care for anything.

WALTER [*feeling his head; sobriety coming*]:   Where's Mama?

RUTH: She ain't come back yet.

WALTER [*looking* MURCHISON *over from head to toe, scrutinizing his carefully casual tweed sports jacket over cashmere V-neck sweater over soft eyelet shirt and tie, and soft slacks, finished off with white buckskin shoes*]:   Why all you college boys wear them fairyish-looking white shoes?

RUTH: Walter Lee! [GEORGE MURCHISON *ignores the remark.*]

WALTER [*to* RUTH]:   Well, they look crazy as hell—white shoes, cold as it is.

RUTH [*crushed*]:   You have to excuse him—

WALTER: No he don't! Excuse me for what? What you always excusing me for! I'll excuse myself when I needs to be excused! [*a pause*] They look as funny as them black knee socks Beneatha wears out of here all the time.

RUTH: It's the college *style*, Walter.

WALTER: Style, hell. She looks like she got burnt legs or something!

RUTH: Oh, Walter—

WALTER [*an irritable mimic*]:   Oh, Walter! Oh, Walter! [*to* MURCHISON] How's your old man making out? I understand you all going to buy that big hotel on the Drive?[1] [*He finds a beer in the refrigerator, wanders over to* MURCHISON, *sipping and wiping his lips with the back of his hand, and straddling a chair backwards to talk to the other man.*] Shrewd move. Your old man is all right, man. [*tapping his head and half winking for emphasis*] I mean he knows how to operate. I mean he thinks big, you know what I mean, I mean for a home,[2] you know? But I think he's kind of running out of ideas now. I'd like to talk to him. Listen, man, I got some plans that could turn this city upside down. I mean I think like he does. *Big.* Invest big, gamble big, hell, lose *big* if you have to, you know what I mean. It's hard to find a man on this whole Southside who understands my kind of thinking—you dig? [*He scrutinizes* MURCHISON *again, drinks his beer, squints his eyes and leans in close, confidential, man to man.*] Me and you ought to sit down and talk sometimes, man. Man, I got me some ideas...

GEORGE [*with boredom*]:   Yeah—sometimes we'll have to do that, Walter.

WALTER [*understanding the indifference, and offended*]:   Yeah—well, when you get the time, man. I know you a busy little boy.

RUTH: Walter, please—

WALTER [*bitterly, hurt*]:   I know ain't nothing in this world as busy as you colored college boys with your fraternity pins and white shoes...

RUTH [*covering her face with humiliation*]:   Oh, Walter Lee—

WALTER: I see you all all the time—with the books tucked under your arms—going to your [*British accent—a mimic*] "clahsses." And for what! What the hell you learning over there? Filling up your heads—[*counting off on his fingers*]—with the sociology and the psychology—but they teaching you how to be a man? How to take over and run the world? They teaching you how to run a rubber plantation or a steel mill? Naw—just to talk proper and read books and wear white shoes...

---

[1]**Drive** Chicago's Outer Drive running along Lake Michigan
[2]**home** home-boy; one of us

GEORGE [*looking at him with distaste, a little above it all*]:   You're all wacked up
    with bitterness, man.

WALTER [*intently, almost quietly, between the teeth, glaring at the boy*]:   And
    you—ain't you bitter, man? Ain't you just about had it yet? Don't you see
    no stars gleaming that you can't reach out and grab? You happy?—You
    contented son-of-a-bitch—you happy? You got it made? Bitter? Man, I'm
    a volcano. Bitter? Here I am a giant—surrounded by ants! Ants who can't
    even understand what it is the giant is talking about.

RUTH [*passionately and suddenly*]:   Oh, Walter—ain't you with nobody!

WALTER [*violently*]:   No! 'Cause ain't nobody with me! Not even my own mother!

RUTH: Walter, that's a terrible thing to say! [BENEATHA *enters, dressed for the evening
    in a cocktail dress and earrings.*]

GEORGE: Well—hey, you look great.

BENEATHA: Let's go, George. See you all later.

RUTH: Have a nice time.

GEORGE: Thanks. Good night. [*to* WALTER, *sarcastically*] Good night, *Prometheus.*
    [BENEATHA *and* GEORGE *exit.*]

WALTER [*to* RUTH]:   Who is Prometheus?

RUTH: I don't know. Don't worry about it.

WALTER [*in fury, pointing after* GEORGE]:   See there—they get to a point where
    they can't insult you man to man—they got to go talk about something ain't
    nobody never heard of!

RUTH: How do you know it was an insult? [*to humor him*] Maybe Prometheus is
    a nice fellow.

WALTER: Prometheus! I bet there ain't even no such thing! I bet that simpleminded
    clown—

RUTH: Walter—[*She stops what she is doing and looks at him.*]

WALTER [*yelling*]:   Don't start!

RUTH: Start what?

WALTER: Your nagging! Where was I? Who was I with? How much money did I spend?

RUTH [*plaintively*]:   Walter Lee—why don't we just try to talk about it...

WALTER [*not listening*]:   I been out talking with people who understand me. People
    who care about the things I got on my mind.

RUTH [*wearily*]:   I guess that means people like Willy Harris.

WALTER: Yes, people like Willy Harris.

RUTH [*with a sudden flash of impatience*]:   Why don't you all just hurry up and go
    into the banking business and stop talking about it!

WALTER: Why? You want to know why? 'Cause we all tied up in a race of people
    that don't know how to do nothing but moan, pray and have babies! [*The line
    is too bitter even for him and he looks at her and sits down.*]

RUTH: Oh, Walter... [*softly*] Honey, why can't you stop fighting me?

WALTER [*without thinking*]:   Who's fighting you? Who even cares about you? [*This
    line begins the retardation of his mood.*]

RUTH: Well—[*She waits a long time, and then with resignation starts to put
    away her things.*] I guess I might as well go on to bed... [*more or less to
    herself*] I don't know where we lost it...but we have... [*Then, to him.*]

I—I'm sorry about this new baby, Walter. I guess maybe I better go on and do what I started... I guess I just didn't realize how bad things was with us... I guess I just didn't really realize—[*She starts out to the bedroom and stops.*] You want some hot milk?

WALTER: Hot milk?

RUTH: Yes—hot milk.

WALTER: Why hot milk?

RUTH: 'Cause after all that liquor you come home with you ought to have something hot in your stomach.

WALTER: I don't want no milk.

RUTH: You want some coffee then?

WALTER: No, I don't want no coffee. I don't want nothing hot to drink. [*almost plaintively*] Why you always trying to give me something to eat?

RUTH [*standing and looking at him helplessly*]:   What else can I give you, Walter Lee Younger? [*She stands and looks at him and presently turns to go out again. He lifts his head and watches her going away from him in a new mood which began to emerge when he asked her, "Who cares about you?"*]

WALTER: It's been rough, ain't it, baby? [*She hears and stops but does not turn around and he continues to her back.*] I guess between two people there ain't never as much understood as folks generally thinks there is. I mean like between me and you—[*She turns to face him.*] How we gets to the place where we scared to talk softness to each other. [*He waits, thinking hard himself.*] Why you think it got to be like that? [*He is thoughtful, almost as a child would be.*] Ruth, what is it gets into people ought to be close?

RUTH: I don't know, honey. I think about it a lot.

WALTER: On account of you and me, you mean? The way things are with us. The way something done come down between us.

RUTH: There ain't so much between us, Walter... Not when you come to me and try to talk to me. Try to be with me... a little even.

WALTER [*total honesty*]:   Sometimes... sometimes... I don't even know how to try.

RUTH: Walter—

WALTER: Yes?

RUTH [*coming to him, gently and with misgiving, but coming to him*]:   Honey...life don't have to be like this. I mean sometimes people can do things so that things are better... You remember how we used to talk when Travis was born...about the way we were going to live...the kind of house... [*She is stroking his head.*] Well, it's all starting to slip away from us... [MAMA *enters, and* WALTER *jumps up and shouts at her.*]

WALTER: Mama, where have you been?

MAMA: My—them steps is longer than they used to be. Whew! [*She sits down and ignores him.*] How you feeling this evening, Ruth! [RUTH *shrugs, disturbed some at having been prematurely interrupted and watching her husband knowingly.*]

WALTER: Mama, where have you been all day?

MAMA [*still ignoring him and leaning on the table and changing to more comfortable shoes*]:   Where's Travis?

RUTH: I let him go out earlier and he ain't come back yet. Boy, is he going to get it!

WALTER: Mama!

MAMA [*as if she has heard him for the first time*]:   Yes, son?

WALTER: Where did you go this afternoon?

MAMA: I went downtown to tend to some business that I had to tend to.

WALTER: What kind of business?

MAMA: You know better than to question me like a child, Brother.

WALTER [*rising and bending over the table*]:   Where were you, Mama? [*bringing his fists down and shouting*] Mama, you didn't go do something with that insurance money, something crazy? [*The front door opens slowly, interrupting him, and* TRAVIS *peeks his head in, less than hopefully.*]

TRAVIS [*to his mother*]:   Mama, I—

RUTH: "Mama I" nothing! You're going to get it, boy! Get on in that bedroom and get yourself ready!

TRAVIS: But I—

MAMA: Why don't you all never let the child explain hisself.

RUTH: Keep out of it now, Lena. [MAMA *clamps her lips together, and* RUTH *advances toward her son menacingly.*]

RUTH: A thousand times I have told you not to go off like that—

MAMA [*holding out her arms to her grandson*]:   Well—at least let me tell him something. I want him to be the first one to hear... Come here, Travis. [*the boy obeys, gladly*] Travis—[*She takes him by the shoulder and looks into his face.*]—you know that money we got in the mail this morning?

TRAVIS: Yes'm—

MAMA: Well—what you think your grandmama gone and done with that money?

TRAVIS: I don't know, Grandmama.

MAMA [*putting her finger on his nose for emphasis*]:   She went out and she bought you a house! [*The explosion comes from* WALTER *at the end of the revelation and he jumps up and turns away from all of them in a fury.* MAMA *continues, to* TRAVIS.] You glad about the house? It's going to be yours when you get to be a man.

TRAVIS: Yeah—I always wanted to live in a house.

MAMA: All right, gimme some sugar then—[TRAVIS *puts his arms around her neck as she watches her son over the boy's shoulder. Then, to* TRAVIS, *after the embrace.*] Now when you say your prayers tonight, you thank God and your grandfather—'cause it was him who give you the house—in his way.

RUTH [*taking the boy from* MAMA *and pushing him toward the bedroom*]:   Now you get out of here and get ready for your beating.

TRAVIS: Aw, Mama—

RUTH: Get on in there—[*closing the door behind him and turning radiantly to her mother-in-law*] So you went and did it!

MAMA [*quietly, looking at her son with pain*]:   Yes, I did.

RUTH [*raising both arms classically*]:   Praise God! [*Looks at* WALTER *a moment, who says nothing. She crosses rapidly to her husband.*] Please, honey—let me be glad...you be glad too. [*She has laid her hands on his shoulders, but he shakes himself free of her roughly, without turning to face her.*] Oh, Walter...

a home...*a home.* [*She comes back to* MAMA.] Well—where is it? How big is
it? How much it going to cost?

MAMA: Well—

RUTH: When we moving?

MAMA [*smiling at her*]:   First of the month.

RUTH [*throwing back her head with jubilance*]:   *Praise God!*

MAMA [*tentatively, still looking at her son's back turned against her and* RUTH]:   It's—
it's a nice house too... [*She cannot help speaking directly to him. An imploring quality in her voice, her manner, makes her almost like a girl now.*] Three
bedrooms—nice big one for you and Ruth... Me and Beneatha still have to
share our room, but Travis have one of his own—and [*with difficulty*] I figure
if the—new baby—is a boy, we could get one of them double-decker out-
fits... And there's a yard with a little patch of dirt where I could maybe get
to grow me a few flowers... And a nice big basement....

RUTH: Walter honey, be glad—

MAMA [*still to his back, fingering things on the table*]:   'Course I don't want to make
it sound fancier than it is.... It's just a plain little old house—but it's made
good and solid—and it will be *ours.* Walter Lee—it makes a difference in a
man when he can walk on floors that belong to *him....*

RUTH: Where is it?

MAMA [*frightened at this telling*]:   Well—well—it's out there in Clybourne Park—
[RUTH's *radiance fades abruptly, and* WALTER *finally turns slowly to face his
mother with incredulity and hostility.*]

RUTH: Where?

MAMA [*matter-of-factly*]:   Four o six Clybourne Street, Clybourne Park.

RUTH: Clybourne Park? Mama, there ain't no colored people living in Clybourne
Park.

MAMA [*almost idiotically*]:   Well, I guess there's going to be some now.

WALTER [*bitterly*]:   So that's the peace and comfort you went out and bought for
us today!

MAMA [*raising her eyes to meet his finally*]:   Son—I just tried to find the nicest place
for the least amount of money for my family.

RUTH [*trying to recover from the shock*]:   Well—well—'course I ain't one never been
'fraid of no crackers, mind you—but—well, wasn't there no other houses
nowhere?

MAMA: Them houses they put up for colored in them areas way out all seem to
cost twice as much as other houses. I did the best I could.

RUTH [*Struck senseless with the news, in its various degrees of goodness and trouble,
she sits a moment, her fists propping her chin in thought, and then she starts
to rise, bringing her fists down with vigor, the radiance spreading from cheek
to cheek again.*]:   Well—well!—All I can say is—if this is my time in life—
my time—to say good-bye—[*And she builds with momentum as she starts to
circle the room with an exuberant, almost tearfully happy release.*]—to these
Goddamned cracking walls!—[*She pounds the walls*]—and these marching
roaches!—[*She wipes at an imaginary army of marching roaches.*]—and this
cramped little closet which ain't now or never was no kitchen!...then I say it

loud and good, *Hallelujah! and good-bye misery* . . . *I don't never want to see your ugly face again!* [*She laughs joyously, having practically destroyed the apartment, and flings her arms up and lets them come down happily, slowly, reflectively, over her abdomen, aware for the first time perhaps that the life therein pulses with happiness and not despair.*] Lena?

MAMA [*moved, watching her happiness*]:   Yes, honey?

RUTH [*looking off*]:   Is there—is there a whole lot of sunlight?

MAMA [*understanding*]:   Yes, child, there's a whole lot of sunlight. [*long pause*]

RUTH [*collecting herself and going to the door of the room* TRAVIS *is in*]:   Well—I guess I better see 'bout Travis. [*to* MAMA] Lord, I sure don't feel like whipping nobody today! [*she exits*]

MAMA [*The mother and son are left alone now and the mother waits a long time, considering deeply, before she speaks.*]:   Son—you—you understand what I done, don't you? [WALTER *is silent and sullen.*] I—I just seen my family falling apart today . . . just falling to pieces in front of my eyes . . . We couldn't of gone on like we was today. We was going backwards 'stead of forwards—talking 'bout killing babies and wishing each other was dead . . . When it gets like that in life—you just got to do something different, push on out and do something bigger . . . [*She waits.*] I wish you say something, son . . . I wish you'd say how deep inside you you think I done the right thing—

WALTER [*crossing slowly to his bedroom door and finally turning there and speaking measuredly*]:   What you need me to say you done right for? You the head of this family. You run our lives like you want to. It was your money and you did what you wanted with it. So what you need for me to say it was all right for? [*bitterly, to hurt her as deeply as he knows is possible*] So you butchered up a dream of mine—you—who always talking 'bout your children's dreams . . .

MAMA: Walter Lee—[*He just closes the door behind him.* MAMA *sits alone, thinking heavily.*]

Curtain

SCENE 2

TIME: *Friday night. A few weeks later.*

AT RISE: *Packing crates mark the intention of the family to move.* BENEATHA *and* GEORGE *come in, presumably from an evening out again.*

GEORGE: O.K. . . . O.K., whatever you say . . . [*They both sit on the couch. He tries to kiss her. She moves away.*] Look, we've had a nice evening; let's not spoil it, huh? . . . [*He again turns her head and tries to nuzzle in and she turns away from him, not with distaste but with momentary lack of interest; in a mood to pursue what they were talking about.*]

BENEATHA: I'm trying to talk to you.

GEORGE: We always talk.

BENEATHA: Yes—and I love to talk.

GEORGE [*exasperated; rising*]:   I know it and I don't mind it sometimes... I want
   you to cut it out, see—The moody stuff, I mean. I don't like it. You're a nice-
   looking girl...all over. That's all you need, honey, forget the atmosphere.
   Guys aren't going to go for the atmosphere—they're going to go for what
   they see. Be glad for that. Drop the Garbo routine. It doesn't go with you.
   As for myself, I want a nice—[*groping*]—simple [*thoughtfully*]—sophisticated
   girl...not a poet—O.K.? [*She rebuffs him again and he starts to leave.*]
BENEATHA: Why are you angry?
GEORGE: Because this is stupid! I don't go out with you to discuss the nature of
   "quiet desperation" or to hear all about your thoughts—because the world
   will go on thinking what it thinks regardless—
BENEATHA: Then why read books? Why go to school?
GEORGE [*with artificial patience, counting on his fingers*]:   It's simple. You read
   books—to learn facts—to get grades—to pass the course—to get a degree.
   That's all—it has nothing to do with thoughts. [*a long pause*]
BENEATHA: I see. [*a longer pause as she looks at him*] Good night, George. [GEORGE
   looks at her a little oddly, and starts to exit. He meets MAMA *coming in.*]
GEORGE: Oh—hello, Mrs. Younger.
MAMA: Hello, George, how you feeling?
GEORGE: Fine—fine, how are you?
MAMA: Oh, a little tired. You know them steps can get you after a day's work. You
   all have a nice time tonight?
GEORGE: Yes—a fine time. Well, good night.
MAMA: Good night. [*He exits.* MAMA *closes the door behind her.*] Hello, honey. What
   you sitting like that for?
BENEATHA: I'm just sitting.
MAMA: Didn't you have a nice time?
BENEATHA: No.
MAMA: No? What's the matter?
BENEATHA: Mama, George is a fool—honest. [*She rises.*]
MAMA [*Hustling around unloading the packages she has entered with. She stops.*]:
   Is he, baby?
BENEATHA: Yes. [BENEATHA *makes up* TRAVIS' *bed as she talks.*]
MAMA: You sure?
BENEATHA: Yes.
MAMA: Well—I guess you better not waste your time with no fools. [BENEATHA
   *looks up at her mother, watching her put groceries in the refrigerator. Finally
   she gathers up her things and starts into the bedroom. At the door she stops
   and looks back at her mother.*]
BENEATHA: Mama—
MAMA: Yes, baby—
BENEATHA: Thank you.
MAMA: For what?
BENEATHA: For understanding me this time. [*She exits quickly and the mother stands,
   smiling a little, looking at the place where* BENEATHA *had stood.* RUTH *enters.*]
RUTH: Now don't you fool with any of this stuff, Lena—

MAMA: Oh, I just thought I'd sort a few things out. [*The phone rings.* RUTH *answers.*]

RUTH [*at the phone*]:   Hello—Just a minute. [*goes to door*] Walter, it's Mrs. Arnold. [*Waits. Goes back to the phone. Tense.*] Hello. Yes, this is his wife speaking... He's lying down now. Yes...well, he'll be in tomorrow. He's been very sick. Yes—I know we should have called, but we were so sure he'd be able to come in today. Yes—yes, I'm very sorry. Yes... Thank you very much. [*She hangs up.* WALTER *is standing in the doorway of the bedroom behind her.*] That was Mrs. Arnold.

WALTER [*indifferently*]:   Was it?

RUTH: She said if you don't come in tomorrow that they are getting a new man...

WALTER: Ain't that sad—ain't that crying sad.

RUTH: She said Mr. Arnold has had to take a cab for three days... Walter, you ain't been to work for three days! [*This is a revelation to her.*] Where you been, Walter Lee Younger? [WALTER *looks at her and starts to laugh.*] You're going to lose your job.

WALTER: That's right...

RUTH: Oh, Walter, and with your mother working like a dog every day—

WALTER: That's sad too—Everything is sad.

MAMA: What you been doing for these three days, son?

WALTER: Mama—you don't know all the things a man what got leisure can find to do in this city... What's this—Friday night? Well—Wednesday I borrowed Willy Harris' car and I went for a drive...just me and myself and I drove and drove... Way out...way past South Chicago, and I parked the car and I sat and looked at the steel mills all day long. I just sat in the car and looked at them big black chimneys for hours. Then I drove back and I went to the Green Hat. [*pause*] And Thursday—Thursday I borrowed the car again and I got in it and I pointed it the other way and I drove the other way—for hours—way, way up to Wisconsin, and I looked at the farms. I just drove and looked at the farms. Then I drove back and I went to the Green Hat. [*pause*] And today—today I didn't get the car. Today I just walked. All over the Southside. And I looked at the Negroes and they looked at me and finally I just sat down on the curb at Thirty-ninth and South Parkway and I just sat there and watched the Negroes go by. And then I went to the Green Hat. You all sad? You all depressed? And you know where I am going right now—[RUTH *goes out quietly.*].

MAMA: Oh, Big Walter, is this the harvest of our days?

WALTER: You know what I like about the Green Hat? [*He turns the radio on and a steamy, deep blues pours into the room.*] I like this little cat they got there who blows a sax... He blows. He talks to me. He ain't but 'bout five feet tall and he's got a conked head and his eyes is always closed and he's all music—

MAMA [*rising and getting some papers out of her handbag*]:   Walter—

WALTER: And there's this other guy who plays the piano... and they got a sound. I mean they can work on some music... They got the best little combo in the world in the Green Hat... You can just sit there and drink and listen to them three men play and you realize that don't nothing matter worth a damn, but just being there—

MAMA: I've helped do it to you, haven't I, son? Walter, I been wrong.

WALTER: Naw—you ain't never been wrong about nothing, Mama.

MAMA: Listen to me, now. I say I been wrong, son. That I been doing to you what
the rest of the world been doing to you. [*She stops and he looks up slowly at
her and she meets his eyes pleadingly.*] Walter—what you ain't understood is
that I ain't got nothing, don't own nothing, ain't never really wanted nothing that wasn't for you. There ain't nothing as precious to me... There ain't
nothing worth holding on to, money, dreams, nothing else—if it means—if
it means it's going to destroy my boy. [*She puts her papers in front of him
and he watches her without speaking or moving.*] I paid the man thirty-five
hundred dollars down on the house. That leaves sixty-five hundred dollars.
Monday morning I want you to take this money and take three thousand dollars and put it in a savings account for Beneatha's medical schooling. The rest
you put in a checking account—with your name on it. And from now on any
penny that come out of it or that go in it is for you to look after. For you to
decide. [*She drops her hands a little helplessly.*] It ain't much, but it's all I got
in the world and I'm putting it in your hands. I'm telling you to be the head
of this family from now on like you supposed to be.

WALTER [*stares at the money*]:   You trust me like that, Mama?

MAMA: I ain't never stop trusting you. Like I ain't never stop loving you. [*She goes
out, and* WALTER *sits looking at the money on the table as the music continues
in its idiom, pulsing in the room. Finally, in a decisive gesture, he gets up,
and, in mingled joy and desperation, picks up the money. At the same moment,* TRAVIS *enters for bed.*]

TRAVIS: What's the matter, Daddy? You drunk?

WALTER [*sweetly, more sweetly than we have ever known him*]:   No, Daddy ain't
drunk. Daddy ain't going to never be drunk again....

TRAVIS: Well, good night, Daddy. [*The father has come from behind the couch and
leans over, embracing his son.*]

WALTER: Son, I feel like talking to you tonight.

TRAVIS: About what?

WALTER: Oh, about a lot of things. About you and what kind of man you going
to be when you grow up.... Son—son, what do you want to be when you
grow up?

TRAVIS: A bus driver.

WALTER [*laughing a little*]:   A what? Man, that ain't nothing to want to be!

TRAVIS: Why not?

WALTER: 'Cause, man—it ain't big enough—you know what I mean.

TRAVIS: I don't know then. I can't make up my mind. Sometimes Mama asks me
that too. And sometimes when I tell her I just want to be like you—she says
she don't want me to be like that and sometimes she says she does...

WALTER [*gathering him up in his arms*]:   You know what, Travis? In seven years
you going to be seventeen years old. And things is going to be very different
with us in seven years, Travis.... One day when you are seventeen I'll come
home—home from my office downtown somewhere—

TRAVIS: You don't work in no office, Daddy.

WALTER: No—but after tonight. After what your daddy gonna do tonight, there's
going to be offices—a whole lot of offices....

TRAVIS: What you gonna do tonight, Daddy?

WALTER: You wouldn't understand yet, son, but your daddy's gonna make a transaction... a business transaction that's going to change our lives... That's how
come one day when you 'bout seventeen years old I'll come home and I'll be
pretty tired, you know what I mean, after a day of conferences and secretar-
ies getting things wrong the way they do... 'cause an executive's life is hell,
man—[*The more he talks the farther away he gets.*] And I'll pull the car up on
the driveway... just a plain black Chrysler, I think, with white walls—no—black
tires. More elegant. Rich people don't have to be flashy...though I'll have to
get something a little sportier for Ruth—maybe a Cadillac convertible to do her
shopping in.... And I'll come up the steps to the house and the gardener will be
clipping away at the hedges and he'll say, "Good evening, Mr. Younger." And
I'll say, "Hello, Jefferson, how are you this evening?" And I'll go inside and Ruth
will come downstairs and meet me at the door and we'll kiss each other and
she'll take my arm and we'll go up to your room to see you sitting on the floor
with the catalogues of all the great schools in America around you.... All the
great schools in the world! And—and I'll say, all right son—it's your seventeenth
birthday, what is it you've decided?... Just tell me where you want to go to
school and you'll *go.* Just tell me, what it is you want to be—and you'll be it....
Whatever you want to be—Yessir! [*He holds his arms open for* TRAVIS.] You just
name it, son... [TRAVIS *leaps into them*] and I hand you the world! [WALTER's *voice
has risen in pitch and hysterical promise and on the last line he lifts* TRAVIS *high.*]

Blackout

SCENE 3

TIME: *Saturday, moving day, one week later.*

Before the curtain rises, RUTH'S *voice, a strident, dramatic church alto, cuts
through the silence.*

*It is, in the darkness, a triumphant surge, a penetrating statement of expec-
tation; "Oh, Lord, I don't feel no ways tired! Children, oh, glory hallelujah!"*

As the curtain rises we see that RUTH *is alone in the living room, finishing
up the family's packing. It is moving day. She is nailing crates and tying cartons.*
BENEATHA *enters, carrying a guitar case, and watches her exuberant sister-in-law.*

RUTH: Hey!

BENEATHA [*putting away the case*]:   Hi.

RUTH [*pointing at a package*]:   Honey—look in that package there and see what I
found on sale this morning at the South Center. [RUTH *gets up and moves to
the package and draws out some curtains.*] Lookahere—hand-turned hems!

BENEATHA: How do you know the window size out there?

RUTH [*who hadn't thought of that*]:   Oh—Well, they bound to fit something in the
whole house. Anyhow, they was too good a bargain to pass up. [RUTH *slaps*

her head, suddenly remembering something.] Oh, Bennie—I meant to put a special note on that carton over there. That's your mama's good china and she wants 'em to be very careful with it.

BENEATHA: I'll do it. [BENEATHA *finds a piece of paper and starts to draw large letters on it.*]

RUTH: You know what I'm going to do soon as I get in that new house?

BENEATHA: What?

RUTH: Honey—I'm going to run me a tub of water up to here... [*with her fingers practically up to her nostrils*] And I'm going to get in it—and I am going to sit...and sit...and sit in that hot water and the first person who knocks to tell *me* to hurry up and come out—

BENEATHA: Gets shot at sunrise.

RUTH [*laughing happily*]:   You said it, sister! [*noticing how large* BENEATHA *is absent-mindedly making the note*] Honey, they ain't going to read that from no airplane.

BENEATHA [*laughing herself*]:   I guess I always think things have more emphasis if they are big, somehow.

RUTH [*looking up at her and smiling*]:   You and your brother seem to have that as a philosophy of life. Lord, that man—done changed so 'round here. You know—you know what we did last night? Me and Walter Lee?

BENEATHA: What?

RUTH [*smiling to herself*]:   We went to the movies. [*looking at* BENEATHA *to see if she understands*] We went to the movies. You know the last time me and Walter went to the movies together?

BENEATHA: No.

RUTH: Me neither. That's how long it been. [*smiling again*] But we went last night. The picture wasn't much good, but that didn't seem to matter. We went—and we held hands.

BENEATHA: Oh, Lord!

RUTH: We held hands—and you know what?

BENEATHA: What?

RUTH: When we come out of the show it was late and dark and all the stores and things was closed up...and it was kind of chilly and there wasn't many people on the streets...and we was still holding hands, me and Walter.

BENEATHA: You're killing me. [WALTER *enters with a large package. His happiness is deep in him; he cannot keep still with his new-found exuberance. He is singing and wiggling and snapping his fingers. He puts his package in a corner and puts a phonograph record, which he has brought in with him, on the record player. As the music comes up he dances over to* RUTH *and tries to get her to dance with him. She gives in at last to his raunchiness and in a fit of giggling allows herself to be drawn into his mood and together they deliberately burlesque an old social dance of their youth.*]

BENEATHA [*Regarding them a long time as they dance, then drawing in her breath for a deeply exaggerated comment which she does not particularly mean.*]:   Talk about—olddddddddddd—fashioneddddddddd—Negroes!

WALTER [*stopping momentarily*]:   What kind of Negroes? [*He says this in fun. He is not angry with her today, nor with anyone. He starts to dance with his wife again.*]

BENEATHA: Old-fashioned.

WALTER [*as he dances with* RUTH]:   You know, when these *New Negroes* have their convention—[*pointing at his sister*]—that is going to be the chairman of the Committee on Unending Agitation. [*He goes on dancing, then stops.*] Race, race, race!... Girl, I do believe you are the first person in the history of the entire human race to successfully brainwash yourself. [BENEATHA *breaks up and he goes on dancing. He stops again, enjoying his tease.*] Damn, even the N double A C P takes a holiday sometimes! [BENEATHA *and* RUTH *laugh. He dances with* RUTH *some more and starts to laugh and stops and pantomimes someone over an operating table.*] I can just see that chick someday looking down at some poor cat on an operating table before she starts to slice him, saying... [*pulling his sleeves back maliciously*] "By the way, what are your views on civil rights down there?..." [*He laughs at her again and starts to dance happily. The bell sounds.*]

BENEATHA: Sticks and stones may break my bones but... words will never hurt me! [BENEATHA *goes to the door and opens it as* WALTER *and* RUTH *go on with the clowning.* BENEATHA *is somewhat surprised to see a quiet-looking middle-aged white man in a business suit holding his hat and a briefcase in his hand and consulting a small piece of paper.*]

MAN: Uh—how do you do, miss. I am looking for a Mrs.—[*He looks at the slip of paper.*] Mrs. Lena Younger?

BENEATHA [*smoothing her hair with slight embarrassment*]:   Oh—yes, that's my mother. Excuse me. [*She closes the door and turns to quiet the other two.*] Ruth! Brother! Somebody's here. [*Then she opens the door. The man casts a curious quick glance at all of them.*] Uh—come in please.

MAN [*coming in*]:   Thank you.

BENEATHA: My mother isn't here just now. Is it business?

MAN: Yes... well, of a sort.

WALTER [*freely, the Man of the House*]:   Have a seat. I'm Mrs. Younger's son. I look after most of her business matters. [RUTH *and* BENEATHA *exchange amused glances.*]

MAN [*regarding* WALTER, *and sitting*]:   Well—My name is Karl Lindner...

WALTER [*stretching out his hand*]:   Walter Younger. This is my wife—[RUTH *nods politely.*]—and my sister.

LINDNER: How do you do.

WALTER [*amiably, as he sits himself easily on a chair, leaning with interest forward on his knees and looking expectantly into the newcomer's face*]:   What can we do for you, Mr. Lindner!

LINDNER [*some minor shuffling of the hat and briefcase on his knees*]:   Well—I am a representative of the Clybourne Park Improvement Association—

WALTER [*pointing*]:   Why don't you sit your things on the floor?

LINDNER: Oh—yes. Thank you. [*He slides the briefcase and hat under the chair.*] And as I was saying—I am from the Clybourne Park Improvement Association—and we have had it brought to our attention at the last meeting that you people—or at least your mother—has bought a piece of residential property at—[*He digs for the slip of paper again.*]—four o six at Clybourne Street...

WALTER: That's right. Care for something to drink? Ruth, get Mr. Lindner a beer.

LINDNER [*upset for some reason*]:   Oh—no, really, I mean thank you very much, but no thank you.

RUTH [*innocently*]:   Some coffee?

LINDNER: Thank you, nothing at all. [BENEATHA *is watching the man carefully.*]

LINDNER: Well, I don't know how much you folks know about our organization. [*He is a gentle man; thoughtful and somewhat labored in his manner.*] It is one of these community organizations set up to look after—oh, you know, things like block upkeep and special projects and we also have what we call our New Neighbors Orientation Committee...

BENEATHA [*drily*]:   Yes—and what do they do?

LINDNER [*turning a little to her and then returning the main force to* WALTER]:   Well— it's what you might call a sort of welcoming committee, I guess. I mean they, we, I'm the chairman of the committee—go around and see the new people who move into the neighborhood and sort of give them the lowdown on the way we do things out in Clybourne Park.

BENEATHA [*with appreciation of the two meanings, which escape* RUTH *and* WALTER]:   Uh-huh.

LINDNER: And we also have the category of what the association calls—[*He looks elsewhere.*]—uh—special community problems...

BENEATHA: Yes—and what are some of those?

WALTER: Girl, let the man talk.

LINDNER [*with understated relief*]:   Thank you. I would sort of like to explain this thing in my own way. I mean I want to explain to you in a certain way.

WALTER: Go ahead.

LINDNER: Yes. Well. I'm going to try to get right to the point. I'm sure we'll all appreciate that in the long run.

BENEATHA: Yes.

WALTER: Be still now!

LINDNER: Well—

RUTH [*still innocently*]:   Would you like another chair—you don't look comfortable.

LINDNER [*more frustrated than annoyed*]:   No, thank you very much. Please. Well— to get right to the point I—[*a great breath, and he is off at last*] I am sure you people must be aware of some of the incidents which have happened in vari- ous parts of the city when colored people have moved into certain areas— [BENEATHA: *exhales heavily and starts tossing a piece of fruit up and down in the air.*] Well—because we have what I think is going to be a unique type of organization in American community life—not only do we deplore that kind of thing—but we are trying to do something about it. [BENEATHA *stops tossing and turns with a new and quizzical interest to the man.*] We feel—[*gaining confidence in his mission because of the interest in the faces of the people he is talking to*]—we feel that most of the trouble in this world, when you come right down to it—[*He hits his knee for emphasis.*]—most of the trouble exists because people just don't sit down and talk to each other.

RUTH [*nodding as she might in church, pleased with the remark*]:   You can say that again, mister.

LINDNER [*more encouraged by such affirmation*]:   That we don't try hard enough in this world to understand the other fellow's problem. The other guy's point of view.

RUTH: Now that's right. [BENEATHA *and* WALTER *merely watch and listen with genuine interest.*]

LINDNER: Yes—that's the way we feel out in Clybourne Park. And that's why I was elected to come here this afternoon and talk to you people. Friendly like, you know, the way people should talk to each other and see if we couldn't find some way to work this thing out. As I say, the whole business is a matter of caring about the other fellow. Anybody can see that you are a nice family of folks, hard working and honest I'm sure. [BENEATHA *frowns slightly, quizzically, her head tilted regarding him.*] Today everybody knows what it means to be on the outside of *something*. And of course, there is always somebody who is out to take the advantage of people who don't always understand.

WALTER: What do you mean?

LINDNER: Well—you see our community is made of people who've worked hard as the dickens for years to build up that little community. They're not rich and fancy people; just hardworking, honest people who don't really have much but those little homes and a dream of the kind of community they want to raise their children in. Now, I don't say we are perfect and there is a lot wrong in some of the things they want. But you've got to admit that a man, right or wrong, has the right to want to have the neighborhood he lives in a certain kind of way. And at the moment the overwhelming majority of our people out there feel that people get along better, take more of a common interest in the life of the community, when they share a common background. I want you to believe me when I tell you that race prejudice simply doesn't enter into it. It is a matter of the people of Clybourne Park believing, rightly or wrongly, as I say, that for the happiness of all concerned that our Negro families are happier when they live in their *own* communities.

BENEATHA [*with a grand and bitter gesture*]:   This, friends, is the Welcoming Committee!

WALTER [*dumbfounded, looking at* LINDNER]:   Is this what you came marching all the way over here to tell us?

LINDNER: Well, now we've been having a fine conversation. I hope you'll hear me all the way through.

WALTER [*tightly*]:   Go ahead, man.

LINDNER: You see—in the face of all the things I have said, we are prepared to make your family a very generous offer...

BENEATHA: Thirty pieces and not a coin less!

WALTER: Yeah?

LINDNER [*putting on his glasses and drawing a form out of the briefcase*]:   Our association is prepared, through the collective effort of our people, to buy the house from you at a financial gain to your family.

RUTH: Lord have mercy, ain't this the living gall!

WALTER: All right, you through?

LINDNER: Well, I want to give you the exact terms of the financial arrangement—

WALTER: We don't want to hear no exact terms of no arrangements. I want to know if you got any more to tell us 'bout getting together?

LINDNER [*taking off his glasses*]:   Well—I don't suppose that you feel...

WALTER: Never mind how I feel—you got any more to say 'bout how people ought to sit down and talk to each other?... Get out of my house, man. [*He turns his back and walks to the door.*]

LINDNER [*looking around at the hostile faces and reaching and assembling his hat and briefcase*]:   Well—I don't understand why you people are reacting this way. What do you think you are going to gain by moving into a neighborhood where you just aren't wanted and where some elements—well—people can get awful worked up when they feel that their whole way of life and everything they've ever worked for is threatened.

WALTER: Get out.

LINDNER [*at the door, holding a small card*]:   Well—I'm sorry it went like this.

WALTER: Get out.

LINDNER [*almost sadly regarding* WALTER]:   You just can't force people to change their hearts, son. [*He turns and puts his card on a table and exits.* WALTER *pushes the door to with stinging hatred, and stands looking at it.* RUTH *just sits and* BENEATHA *just stands. They say nothing.* MAMA *and* TRAVIS *enter.*]

MAMA: Well—this all the packing got done since I left out of here this morning. I testify before God that my children got all the energy of the dead. What time the moving men due?

BENEATHA: Four o'clock. You had a caller, Mama. [*She is smiling, teasingly.*]

MAMA: Sure enough—who?

BENEATHA [*her arms folded saucily*]:   The Welcoming Committee. [WALTER *and* RUTH *giggle.*]

MAMA [*innocently*]:   Who?

BENEATHA: The Welcoming Committee. They said they're sure going to be glad to see you when you get there.

WALTER [*devilishly*]:   Yeah, they said they can't hardly wait to see your face. [*laughter*]

MAMA [*sensing their facetiousness*]:   What's the matter with you all?

WALTER: Ain't nothing the matter with us. We just telling you 'bout the gentleman who came to see you this afternoon. From the Clybourne Park Improvement Association.

MAMA: What he want?

RUTH [*in the same mood as* BENEATHA *and* WALTER]:   To welcome you, honey.

WALTER: He said they can't hardly wait. He said the one thing they don't have, that they just dying to have out there is a fine family of colored people! [*to* RUTH *and* BENEATHA] Ain't that right!

RUTH AND BENEATHA [*mockingly*]:   Yeah! He left his card in case—[*They indicate the card, and* MAMA *picks it up and throws it on the floor—understanding and looking off as she draws her chair up to the table on which she has put her plant and some sticks and some cord.*]

MAMA: Father, give us strength. [*knowingly—and without fun*] Did he threaten us?

BENEATHA: Oh—Mama—they don't do it like that any more. He talked Brotherhood. He said everybody ought to learn how to sit down and hate each other with good Christian fellowship. [*She and* WALTER *shake hands to ridicule the remark.*]

MAMA [*sadly*]:   Lord, protect us...

RUTH: You should hear the money those folks raised to buy the house from us. All we paid and then some.

BENEATHA: What they think we going to do—eat 'em?

RUTH: No, honey, marry 'em.

MAMA [*shaking her head*]:   Lord, Lord, Lord...

RUTH: Well—that's the way the crackers crumble. Joke.

BENEATHA [*laughingly noticing what her mother is doing*]:   Mama, what are you doing?

MAMA: Fixing my plant so it won't get hurt none on the way...

BENEATHA: Mama, you going to take that to the new house?

MAMA: Un-huh—

BENEATHA: That raggedy-looking old thing?

MAMA [*stopping and looking at her*]:   It expresses *me*.

RUTH [*with delight, to* BENEATHA]:   So there, Miss Thing! [WALTER *comes to* MAMA *suddenly and bends down behind her and squeezes her in his arms with all his strength. She is overwhelmed by the suddenness of it and, though delighted, her manner is like that of* RUTH *with* TRAVIS.]

MAMA: Look out now, boy! You make me mess up my thing here!

WALTER [*His face lit, he slips down on his knees beside her, his arms still about her.*]:   Mama...you know what it means to climb up in the chariot?

MAMA [*gruffly, very happy*]:   Get on away from me now...

RUTH [*near the gift-wrapped package, trying to catch* WALTER'S *eye*]:   Psst—

WALTER: What the old song say, Mama...

RUTH: Walter—Now? [*She is pointing at the package.*]

WALTER [*speaking the lines, sweetly, playfully, in his mother's face*]:
    I got wings... you got wings...
    All God's children got wings...

MAMA: Boy—get out of my face and do some work...

WALTER: *When I get to heaven gonna put on my wings, Gonna fly all over God's heaven...*

BENEATHA [*teasingly, from across the room*]:   Everybody talking 'bout heaven ain't going there!

WALTER [*to* RUTH, *who is carrying the box across to them*]:   I don't know, you think we ought to give her that... Seems to me she ain't been very appreciative around here.

MAMA [*eying the box, which is obviously a gift*]:   What is that?

WALTER [*taking it from* RUTH *and putting it on the table in front of* MAMA]:   Well— what you all think? Should we give it to her?

RUTH: Oh—she was pretty good today.

MAMA: I'll good you—[*She turns her eyes to the box again.*]

BENEATHA: Open it, Mama. [*She stands up, looks at it, turns and looks at all of them, and then presses her hands together and does not open the package.*]

WALTER [*sweetly*]:   Open it, Mama. It's for you. [MAMA *looks in his eyes. It is the first present in her life without its being Christmas. Slowly she opens her package and lifts out, one by one, a brand-new sparkling set of gardening tools.* WALTER *continues, prodding.*] Ruth made up the note—read it...

MAMA [*picking up the card and adjusting her glasses*]:   "To our own Mrs. Miniver— Love from Brother, Ruth and Beneatha." Ain't that lovely...

TRAVIS [*tugging at his father's sleeve*]:   Daddy, can I give her mine now?

WALTER: All right, son. [TRAVIS *flies to get his gift.*] Travis didn't want to go in with the rest of us, Mama. He got his own. [*somewhat amused*] We don't know what it is...

TRAVIS [*racing back in the room with a large hatbox and putting it in front of his grandmother*]:   Here!

MAMA: Lord have mercy, baby. You done gone and bought your grandmother a hat?

TRAVIS [*very proud*]:   Open it! [*She does and lifts out an elaborate, but very elaborate, wide gardening hat, and all the adults break up at the sight of it.*]

RUTH: Travis, honey, what is that?

TRAVIS [*who thinks it is beautiful and appropriate*]:   It's a gardening hat! Like the ladies always have on in the magazines when they work in their gardens.

BENEATHA [*giggling fiercely*]:   Travis—we were trying to make Mama Mrs. Miniver— not Scarlett O'Hara!

MAMA [*indignantly*]:   What's the matter with you all! This here is a beautiful hat! [*absurdly*] I always wanted me one just like it! [*She pops it on her head to prove it to her grandson, and the hat is ludicrous and considerably oversized.*]

RUTH: Hot dog! Go, Mama!

WALTER [*doubled over with laughter*]:   I'm sorry, Mama—but you look like you ready to go out and chop you some cotton sure enough! [*They all laugh except* MAMA, *out of deference to* TRAVIS'S *feelings.*]

MAMA [*gathering the boy up to her*]:   Bless your heart—this is the prettiest hat I ever owned—[WALTER, RUTH *and* BENEATHA *chime in—noisily, festively and insincerely congratulating* TRAVIS *on his gift.*] What are we all standing around here for? We ain't finished packin' yet. Bennie, you ain't packed one book. [*The bell rings.*]

BENEATHA: That couldn't be the movers... it's not hardly two o'clock yet—[BENEATHA *goes into her room.* MAMA *starts for the door.*]

WALTER [*turning, stiffening*]:   Wait—wait—I'll get it. [*He stands and looks at the door.*]

MAMA: You expecting company, son?

WALTER [*just looking at the door*]:   Yeah—yeah... [MAMA *looks at* RUTH, *and they exchange innocent and unfrightened glances.*]

MAMA [*not understanding*]:   Well, let them in, son.

BENEATHA [*from her room*]:   We need some more string.

MAMA: Travis—you run to the hardware and get me some string cord. [MAMA *goes out and* WALTER *turns and looks at* RUTH. TRAVIS *goes to a dish for money.*]

RUTH: Why don't you answer the door, man?

WALTER [*suddenly bounding across the floor to her*]:   'Cause sometimes it hard to let the future begin! [*stooping down in her face*]

> *I got wings! You got wings!*
> *All God's children got wings!*

[*He crosses to the door and throws it open. Standing there is a very slight little man in a not too prosperous business suit and with haunted frightened eyes and a hat pulled down tightly, brim up, around his forehead.* TRAVIS *passes between the men and exits.* WALTER *leans deep in the man's face, still in his jubilance.*]

> *When I get to heaven gonna put on my wings,*
> *Gonna fly all over God's heaven . . .*
> [*The little man just stares at him*]
> *Heaven—*
> [*Suddenly he stops and looks past the little man into the empty hallway.*] Where's Willy, man?

BOBO: He ain't with me.

WALTER [*not disturbed*]:   Oh—come on in. You know my wife.

BOBO [*dumbly, taking off his hat*]:   Yes—h'you, Miss Ruth.

RUTH [*quietly, a mood apart from her husband already, seeing* BOBO]:   Hello, Bobo.

WALTER: You right on time today . . . Right on time. That's the way! [*He slaps* BOBO *on his back.*] Sit down . . . lemme hear. [RUTH *stands stiffly and quietly in back of them, as though somehow she senses death, her eyes fixed on her husband.*]

BOBO [*his frightened eyes on the floor, his hat in his hands*]:   Could I please get a drink of water, before I tell you about it, Walter Lee? [WALTER *does not take his eyes off the man.* RUTH *goes blindly to the tap and gets a glass of water and brings it to* BOBO.]

WALTER: There ain't nothing wrong, is there?

BOBO: Lemme tell you—

WALTER: Man—didn't nothing go wrong?

BOBO: Lemme tell you—Walter Lee. [*Looking at* RUTH *and talking to her more than to* WALTER.] You know how it was. I got to tell you how it was. I mean first I got to tell you how it was all the way . . . I mean about the money I put in, Walter Lee . . .

WALTER [*with taut agitation now*]:   What about the money you put in?

BOBO: Well—it wasn't much as we told you—me and Willy—[*He stops.*] I'm sorry, Walter. I got a bad feeling about it. I got a real bad feeling about it . . .

WALTER: Man, what you telling me about all this for? . . . Tell me what happened in Springfield . . .

BOBO: Springfield.

RUTH [*like a dead woman*]:   What was supposed to happen in Springfield?

BOBO [*to her*]:   This deal that me and Walter went into with Willy—Me and Willy was going to go down to Springfield and spread some money 'round so's we wouldn't have to wait so long for the liquor license . . . That's what we were going to do. Everybody said that was the way you had to do, you understand, Miss Ruth?

WALTER: Man—what happened down there?

BOBO [*a pitiful man, near tears*]:   I'm trying to tell you, Walter.

WALTER [*screaming at him suddenly*]:   THEN TELL ME, GODDAMMIT... WHAT'S THE MATTER WITH YOU?

BOBO: Man... I didn't go to no Springfield, yesterday.

WALTER [*halted, life hanging in the moment*]:   Why not?

BOBO [*the long way, the hard way to tell*]:   'Cause I didn't have no reasons to...

WALTER: Man, what are you talking about!

BOBO: I'm talking about the fact that when I got to the train station yesterday morning—eight o'clock like we planned... Man—*Willy didn't never show up.*

WALTER: Why... where was he... where is he?

BOBO: That's what I'm trying to tell you... I don't know... I waited six hours... I called his house...and I waited... six hours... I waited in that train station six hours... [*breaking into tears*] That was all the extra money I had in the world... [*looking up at* WALTER *with the tears running down his face*] Man, *Willy is gone.*

WALTER: Gone, what you mean Willy is gone? Gone where? You mean he went by himself. You mean he went off to Springfield by himself—to take care of getting the license—[*turns and looks anxiously at* RUTH] You mean maybe he didn't want too many people in on the business down there? [*looks to* RUTH *again, as before*] You know Willy got his own ways. [*looks back to* BOBO] Maybe you was late yesterday and he just went on down there without you. Maybe—maybe—he's been callin' you at home tryin' to tell you what happened or something. Maybe—maybe—he just got sick. He's somewhere—he's got to be somewhere. We just got to find him—me and you got to find him. [*grabs* BOBO *senselessly by the collar and starts to shake him*] We got to!

BOBO [*in sudden angry, frightened agony*]:   What's the matter with you, Walter! *When a cat take off with your money he don't leave you no maps!*

WALTER [*turning madly, as though he is looking for* WILLY *in the very room*]:   Willy!... Willy...don't do it... Please don't do it... Man, not with that money... Man, please, not with that money... Oh, God... Don't let it be true... [*He is wandering around, crying out for* WILLY *and looking for him or perhaps for help from God.*] Man... I trusted you... Man, I put my life in your hands... [*He starts to crumple down on the floor as* RUTH *just covers her face in horror,* MAMA *opens the door and comes into the room, with* BENEATHA *behind her.*] Man... [*He starts to pound the floor with his fists, sobbing wildly.*] *That money is made out of my father's flesh...*

BOBO [*standing over him helplessly*]:   I'm sorry, Walter... [*Only* WALTER'S *sobs reply.* BOBO *puts on his hat.*] I had my life staked on this deal, too... [*He exits.*]

MAMA [*to* WALTER]:   Son—[*She goes to him, bends down to him, talks to his bent head.*] Son... Is it gone? Son, I gave you sixty-five hundred dollars. Is it gone? All of it? Beneatha's money too?

WALTER [*lifting his head slowly*]:   Mama... I never...went to the bank at all.

MAMA [*not wanting to believe him*]:   You mean...your sister's school money...you used that too... Walter?...

WALTER: Yessss!... All of it... It's all gone...

[*There is total silence.* RUTH *stands with her face covered with her hands;* BENEATHA *leans forlornly against a wall, fingering a piece of red ribbon from the mother's gift.* MAMA *stops and looks at her son without recognition and then, quite without thinking about it, starts to beat him senselessly in the face.* BENEATHA *goes to them and stops it.*]

BENEATHA: Mama! [MAMA *stops and looks at both of her children and rises slowly and wanders vaguely, aimlessly away from them.*]

MAMA: I seen...him...night after night...come in...and look at that rug...and then look at me...the red showing in his eyes...the veins moving in his head... I seen him grow thin and old before he was forty...working and working and working like somebody's old horse...killing himself...and you—you give it all away in a day...

BENEATHA: Mama—

MAMA: Oh, God... [*She looks up to Him.*] Look down here—and show me the strength.

BENEATHA: Mama—

MAMA [*folding over*]:   Strength...

BENEATHA [*plaintively*]:   MAMA...

MAMA: Strength!

Curtain

ACT III

An hour later.

At curtain, there is a sullen light of gloom in the living room, gray light not unlike that which began the first scene of Act I. At left we can see WALTER within his room, alone with himself. He is stretched out on the bed, his shirt out and open, his arms under his head. He does not smoke, he does not cry out, he merely lies there, looking up at the ceiling, much as if he were alone in the world.

In the living room BENEATHA sits at the table, still surrounded by the now almost ominous packing crates. She sits looking off. We feel that this is a mood struck perhaps an hour before, and it lingers now, full of the empty sound of profound disappointment. We see on a line from her brother's bedroom the sameness of their attitudes. Presently the bell rings and BENEATHA rises without ambition or interest in answering. It is ASAGAI, smiling broadly, striding into the room with energy and happy expectation and conversation.

ASAGAI: I came over... I had some free time. I thought I might help with the packing. Ah, I like the look of packing crates! A household in preparation for a journey! It depresses some people... but for me... it is another feeling. Something full of the flow of life, do you understand? Movement, progress... It makes me think of Africa.

BENEATHA: Africa!

ASAGAI: What kind of a mood is this? Have I told you how deeply you move me?

BENEATHA: He gave away the money, Asagai...

ASAGAI: Who gave away what money?

BENEATHA: The insurance money. My brother gave it away.

ASAGAI: Gave it away?

BENEATHA: He made an investment! With a man even Travis wouldn't have trusted.

ASAGAI: And it's gone?

BENEATHA: Gone!

ASAGAI: I'm very sorry... And you, now?

BENEATHA: Me?... Me?... Me, I'm nothing... Me. When I was very small...we used to take our sleds out in the wintertime and the only hills we had were the ice-covered stone steps of some houses down the street. And we used to fill them in with snow and make them smooth and slide down them all day... and it was very dangerous you know...far too steep...and sure enough one day a kid named Rufus came down too fast and hit the sidewalk...and we saw his face just split open right there in front of us... And I remember standing there looking at his bloody open face thinking that was the end of Rufus. But the ambulance came and they took him to the hospital and they fixed the broken bones and they sewed it all up...and the next time I saw Rufus he just had a little line down the middle of his face... I never got over that... [WALTER *sits up, listening on the bed. Throughout this scene it is important that we feel his reaction at all times, that he visibly respond to the words of his sister and* ASAGAI.]

ASAGAI: What?

BENEATHA: That that was what one person could do for another, fix him up—sew up the problem, make him all right again. That was the most marvelous thing in the world... I wanted to do that. I always thought it was the one concrete thing in the world that a human being could do. Fix up the sick, you know— and make them whole again. This was truly being God...

ASAGAI: You wanted to be God?

BENEATHA: No—I wanted to cure. It used to be so important to me. I wanted to cure. It used to matter. I used to care. I mean about people and how their bodies hurt...

ASAGAI: And you've stopped caring?

BENEATHA: Yes—I think so.

ASAGAI: Why? [WALTER *rises, goes to the door of his room and is about to open it, then stops and stands listening, leaning on the door jamb.*]

BENEATHA: Because it doesn't seem deep enough, close enough to what ails mankind—I mean this thing of sewing up bodies or administering drugs. Don't you understand? It was a child's reaction to the world. I thought that doctors had the secret to all the hurts... That's the way a child sees things—or an idealist.

ASAGAI: Children see things very well sometimes—and idealists even better.

BENEATHA: I know that's what you think. Because you are still where I left off— you still care. This is what you see for the world, for Africa. You with the dreams of the future will patch up all Africa—you are going to cure the Great Sore of colonialism with Independence—

ASAGAI: Yes!

BENEATHA: Yes—and you think that one word is the penicillin of the human spirit: "Independence!" But then what?

ASAGAI: That will be the problem for another time. First we must get there.

BENEATHA: And where does it end?

ASAGAI: End? Who even spoke of an end? To life? To living?

BENEATHA: An end to misery!

ASAGAI [*smiling*]:   You sound like a French intellectual.

BENEATHA: No! I sound like a human being who just had her future taken right out of her hands! While I was sleeping in my bed in there, things were happening in this world that directly concerned me—and nobody asked me, consulted me—they just went out and did things—and changed my life. Don't you see there isn't any real progress, Asagai, there is only one large circle that we march in, around and around, each of us with our own little picture—in front of us—our own little mirage that we think is the future.

ASAGAI: That is the mistake.

BENEATHA: What?

ASAGAI: What you just said—about the circle. It isn't a circle—it is simply a long line—as in geometry, you know, one that reaches into infinity. And because we cannot see the end—we also cannot see how it changes. And it is very odd but those who see the changes are called "idealists"—and those who cannot, or refuse to think, they are the "realists." It is very strange, and amusing too, I think.

BENEATHA: You—you are almost religious.

ASAGAI: Yes... I think I have the religion of doing what is necessary in the world— and of worshipping man—because he is so marvelous, you see.

BENEATHA: Man is foul! And the human race deserves its misery!

ASAGAI: You see: *you* have become the religious one in the old sense. Already, and after such a small defeat, you are worshipping despair.

BENEATHA: From now on, I worship the truth—and the truth is that people are puny, small and selfish...

ASAGAI: Truth? Why is it that you despairing ones always think that only you have the truth? I never thought to see *you* like that. You! Your brother made a stupid, childish mistake—and you are grateful to him. So that now you can give up the ailing human race on account of it. You talk about what good is struggle; what good is anything? Where are we all going? And why are we bothering?

BENEATHA: *And you cannot answer it!* All your talk and dreams about Africa and Independence. Independence and then what? What about all the crooks and petty thieves and just plain idiots who will come into power to steal and plunder the same as before—only now they will be black and do it in the name of the new Independence—You cannot answer that.

ASAGAI [*shouting over her*]:   *I live the answer!* [*pause*] In my village at home it is the exceptional man who can even read a newspaper... or who ever *sees* a book at all. I will go home and much of what I will have to say will seem strange to the people of my village.... But I will teach and work and things will happen, slowly and swiftly. At times it will seem that nothing changes at all...and then again... the sudden dramatic events which make history leap into the future. And then quiet again. Retrogression even. Guns, murder, revolution. And I even will have moments when I wonder if the quiet was not better than all that death and hatred. But I will look about my village at the illiteracy and disease and ignorance and I will not wonder long. And perhaps...perhaps I will be a great man... I mean perhaps I will hold on to the substance of truth and find my way always with the right course...and perhaps for it I will be butchered in my bed some night by the servants of empire...

BENEATHA: *The martyr!*

ASAGAI: ... or perhaps I shall live to be a very old man, respected and esteemed in my new nation... And perhaps I shall hold office and this is what I'm trying to tell you, Alaiyo; perhaps the things I believe now for my country will be wrong and outmoded, and I will not understand and do terrible things to have things my way or merely to keep my power. Don't you see that there will be young men and women, not British soldiers then, but my own black countrymen...to step out of the shadows some evening and slit my then useless throat? Don't you see they have always been there... that they always will be. And that such a thing as my own death will be an advance? They who might kill me even... actually replenish me!

BENEATHA: Oh, Asagai, I know all that.

ASAGAI: Good! Then stop moaning and groaning and tell me what you plan to do.

BENEATHA: Do?

ASAGAI: I have a bit of a suggestion.

BENEATHA: What?

ASAGAI [*rather quietly for him*]: That when it is all over—that you come home with me—

BENEATHA [*slapping herself on the forehead with exasperation born of misunderstanding*]: Oh—Asagai—at this moment you decide to be romantic!

ASAGAI [*quickly understanding the misunderstanding*]: My dear, young creature of the New World—I do not mean across the city—I mean across the ocean; home—to Africa.

BENEATHA [*slowly understanding and turning to him with murmured amazement*]: To—to Nigeria?

ASAGAI: Yes!... [*smiling and lifting his arms playfully*]. Three hundred years later the African Prince rose up out of the seas and swept the maiden back across the middle passage over which her ancestors had come—

BENEATHA [*unable to play*]: Nigeria?

ASAGAI: Nigeria. Home. [*coming to her with genuine romantic flippancy*] I will show you our mountains and our stars; and give you cool drinks from gourds and teach you the old songs and the ways of our people—and, in time, we will pretend that—[*very softly*]—you have only been away for a day—[*She turns her back to him, thinking. He swings her around and takes her full in his arms in a long embrace which proceeds to passion.*]

BENEATHA [*pulling away*]: You're getting me all mixed up—

ASAGAI: Why?

BENEATHA: Too many things—too many things have happened today. I must sit down and think. I don't know what I feel about anything right this minute. [*She promptly sits down and props her chin on her fist.*]

ASAGAI [*charmed*]: All right, I shall leave you. No—don't get up. [*touching her, gently, sweetly*] Just sit awhile and think... Never be afraid to sit awhile and think. [*He goes to door and looks at her.*] How often I have looked at you and said, "Ah—so this is what the New World hath finally wrought..." [*He exits. BENEATHA sits on alone. Presently WALTER enters from his room and starts to rummage through things, feverishly looking for something. She looks up and turns in her seat.*]

BENEATHA [*hissingly*]: Yes—just look at what the New World hath wrought!... Just look! [*She gestures with bitter disgust.*] There he is! *Monsieur le petit bougeois noir*—himself! There he is—Symbol of a Rising Class! Entrepreneur! Titan of the system! [*WALTER ignores her completely and continues frantically and destructively looking for something and hurling things to the floor and tearing things out of their place in his search. BENEATHA ignores the eccentricity of his actions and goes on with the monologue of insult.*] Did you dream of yachts on Lake Michigan, Brother? Did you see yourself on that Great Day sitting down at the Conference Table, surrounded by all the mighty bald-headed men in America? All halted, waiting, breathless, waiting for your pronouncements on industry? Waiting for you—Chairman of the Board? [*WALTER finds what he is looking for—a small piece of white paper—and pushes it in his pocket and puts on his coat and rushes out without ever having looked at her. She shouts after him.*] I look at you and I see the final triumph of stupidity in the world! [*The door slams and she returns to just sitting again. RUTH comes quickly out of MAMA's room.*]

RUTH: Who was that?

BENEATHA: Your husband.

RUTH: Where did he go?

BENEATHA: Who knows—maybe he has an appointment at U.S. Steel.

RUTH [*anxiously, with frightened eyes*]: You didn't say nothing bad to him, did you?

BENEATHA: Bad? Say anything bad to him? No—I told him he was a sweet boy and full of dreams and everything is strictly peachy keen, as the ofay[3] kids say!

[*MAMA enters from her bedroom. She is lost, vague, trying to catch hold, to make some sense of her former command of the world, but it still eludes her. A sense of waste overwhelms her gait; a measure of apology rides on her shoulders. She goes to her plant, which has remained on the table, looks at it, picks it up and takes it to the window sill and sets it outside, and she stands and looks at it a long moment. Then she closes the window, straightens her body with effort and turns around to her children.*]

MAMA: Well—ain't it a mess in here, though? [*a false cheerfulness, a beginning of something*] I guess we all better stop moping around and get some work done. All this unpacking and everything we got to do. [*RUTH raises her head*

---

[3]**ofay** white (pig Latin meaning "foe")

slowly in response to the sense of the line; and BENEATHA *in similar manner turns very slowly to look at her mother.*] One of you all better call the moving people and tell 'em not to come.

RUTH: Tell 'em not to come?

MAMA: Of course, baby. Ain't no need in 'em coming all the way here and having to go back. They charges for that too. [*She sits down, fingers to her brow, thinking.*] Lord, ever since I was a little girl, I always remembers people saying, "Lena—Lena Eggleston, you aims too high all the time. You needs to slow down and see life a little more like it is. Just slow down some." That's what they always used to say down home—"Lord, that Lena Eggleston is a high-minded thing. She'll get her due one day!"

RUTH: No, Lena...

MAMA: Me and Big Walter just didn't never learn right.

RUTH: Lena, no! We gotta go. Bennie—tell her... [*She rises and crosses to* BENEATHA *with her arms outstretched.* BENEATHA *doesn't respond.*] Tell her we can still move...the notes ain't but a hundred and twenty-five a month. We got four grown people in this house—we can work...

MAMA [*to herself*]:   Just aimed too high all the time—

RUTH [*turning and going to* MAMA *fast—the words pouring out with urgency and desperation*]:   Lena—I'll work... I'll work twenty hours a day in all the kitchens in Chicago... I'll strap my baby on my back if I have to and scrub all the floors in America and wash all the sheets in America if I have to—but we got to move... We got to get out of here... [MAMA *reaches out absently and pats* RUTH's *hand.*]

MAMA: No—I sees things differently now. Been thinking 'bout some of the things we could do to fix this place up some. I seen a second-hand bureau over on Maxwell Street just the other day that could fit right there. [*She points to where the new furniture might go.* RUTH *wanders away from her.*] Would need some new handles on it and then a little varnish and then it look like something brand-new. And—we can put up them new curtains in the kitchen... Why this place be looking fine. Cheer us all up so that we forget trouble ever came... [*to* RUTH] And you could get some nice screens to put up in your room round the baby's bassinet... [*She looks at both of them, pleadingly.*] Sometimes you just got to know when to give up some things... and hold on to what you got. [WALTER *enters from the outside, looking spent and leaning against the door, his coat hanging from him.*]

MAMA: Where you been, son?

WALTER [*breathing hard*]:   Made a call.

MAMA: To who, son?

WALTER: To the Man.

MAMA: What man, baby?

WALTER: The Man, Mama. Don't you know who The Man is?

RUTH: Walter Lee?

WALTER: *The Man.* Like the guys in the street say—*the Man.* Captain Boss—Mistuh Charley... Old Captain Please Mr. Bossman...

BENEATHA [*suddenly*]:   Lindner!

WALTER: That's right! That's good. I told him to come right over.

BENEATHA [*fiercely, understanding*]:   For what? What do you want to see him for?

WALTER [*looking at his sister*]:   We are going to do business with him.

MAMA: What you talking 'bout, son?

WALTER: Talking 'bout life, Mama. You all always telling me to see life like it is. Well—I laid in there on my back today... and I figured it out. Life just like it is. Who gets and who don't get. [*He sits down with his coat on and laughs.*] Mama, you know it's all divided up. Life is. Sure enough. Between the takers and the "tooken." [*He laughs.*] I've figured it out finally. [*He looks around at them.*] Yeah. Some of us always getting "tooken." [*He laughs.*] People like Willy Harris, they don't never get "tooken." And you know why the rest of us do? 'Cause we all mixed up. Mixed up bad. We get to looking 'round for the right and the wrong; and we worry about it and cry about it and stay up nights trying to figure out 'bout the wrong and the right of things all the time... And all the time, man, them takers is out there operating, just taking and taking. Willy Harris? Shoot—Willy Harris don't even count. He don't even count in the big scheme of things. But I'll say one thing for old Willy Harris... he's taught me something. He's taught me to keep my eye on what counts in this world. Yeah—[*shouting out a little*] Thanks, Willy!

RUTH: What did you call that man for, Walter Lee!

WALTER: Called him to tell him to come on over to the show. Gonna put on a show for the man. Just what he wants to see. You see, Mama, the man came here today and he told us that them people out there where you want us to move—well they so upset they willing to pay us not to move out there. [*He laughs again.*] And—and oh, Mama—you would of been proud of the way me and Ruth and Bennie acted. We told him to get out... Lord have mercy! We told the man to get out. Oh, we was some proud folks this afternoon, yeah. [*He lights a cigarette.*] We were still full of that old-time stuff...

RUTH [*coming toward him slowly*]:   You talking 'bout taking them people's money to keep us from moving in that house?

WALTER: I ain't just talking 'bout it, baby—I'm telling you that's what's going to happen.

BENEATHA: Oh, God! Where is the bottom! Where is the real honest-to-God bottom so he can't go any farther!

WALTER: See—that's the old stuff. You and that boy that was here today. You all want everybody to carry a flag and a spear and sing some marching songs, huh? You wanna spend your life looking into things and trying to find the right and the wrong part, huh? Yeah. You know what's going to happen to that boy someday—he'll find himself sitting in a dungeon, locked in forever—and the takers will have the key! Forget it, baby! There ain't no causes—there ain't nothing but taking in this world, and he who takes most is smartest—and it don't make a damn bit of difference *how*.

MAMA: You making something inside me cry, son. Some awful pain inside me.

WALTER: Don't cry, Mama. Understand. That white man is going to walk in that door able to write checks for more money than we ever had. It's important to him and I'm going to help him... I'm going to put on the show, Mama.

MAMA: Son—I come from five generations of people who was slaves and share-croppers—but ain't nobody in my family never let nobody pay 'em no money that was a way of telling us we wasn't fit to walk the earth. We ain't never been that poor. [*raising her eyes and looking at him*] We ain't never been that dead inside.

BENEATHA: Well—we are dead now. All the talk about dreams and sunlight that goes on in this house. All dead.

WALTER: What's the matter with you all! I didn't make this world! It was give to me this way! Hell, yes, I want me some yachts someday! Yes, I want to hang some real pearls 'round my wife's neck. Ain't she supposed to wear no pearls? Somebody tell me—tell me, who decides which women is suppose to wear pearls in this world. I tell you I am a *man*—and I think my wife should wear some pearls in this world! [*This last line hangs a good while and* WALTER *begins to move about the room. The word "Man" has penetrated his conscious-ness; he mumbles it to himself repeatedly between strange agitated pauses as he moves about.*]

MAMA: Baby, how you going to feel on the inside?

WALTER: Fine!... Going to feel fine... a man....

MAMA: You won't have nothing left then, Walter Lee.

WALTER [*coming to her*]:   I'm going to feel fine, Mama. I'm going to look that son-of-a-bitch in the eyes and say—[*He falters.*]—and say, "All right, Mr. Lind-ner—[*He falters even more.*]—that's your neighborhood out there. You got the right to keep it like you want. You got the right to have it like you want. Just write the check and—the house is yours." And, and I am going to say—[*His voice almost breaks.*] And you—you people just put the money in my hand and you won't have to live next to this bunch of stinking niggers!... [*He straightens up and moves away from his mother, walking around the room.*] Maybe—maybe I'll just get down on my black knees... [*He does so;* RUTH *and* BENNIE *and* MAMA *watch him in frozen horror.*] Captain, Mistuh, Bossman. [*He starts crying.*] A-hee-hee-hee! [*wringing his hands in pro-foundly anguished imitation*] Yasssssuh! Great White Father, just gi' ussen de money, fo' God's sake, and we's ain't gwine come out deh and dirty up yo' white folks neighborhood... [*He breaks down completely, then gets up and goes into the bedroom.*]

BENEATHA: That is not a man. That is nothing but a toothless rat.

MAMA: Yes—death done come in this here house. [*She is nodding, slowly, reflec-tively.*] Done come walking in my house. On the lips of my children. You what supposed to be my beginning again. You—what supposed to be my harvest. [*to* BENEATHA] You—you mourning your brother?

BENEATHA: He's no brother of mine.

MAMA: What you say?

BENEATHA: I said that that individual in that room is no brother of mine.

MAMA: That's what I thought you said. You feeling like you better than he is today? [BENEATHA *does not answer.*] Yes? What you tell him a minute ago? That he wasn't a man? Yes? You give him up for me? You done wrote his epitaph too—like the rest of the world? Well, who give you the privilege?

BENEATHA: Be on my side for once! You saw what he just did, Mama! You saw him—down on his knees. Wasn't it you who taught me—to despise any man who would do that? Do what he's going to do.

MAMA: Yes—I taught you that. Me and your daddy. But I thought I taught you something else too... I thought I taught you to love him.

BENEATHA: Love him? There is nothing left to love.

MAMA: There is always something left to love. And if you ain't learned that, you ain't learned nothing. [*looking at her*] Have you cried for that boy today? I don't mean for yourself and for the family 'cause we lost the money. I mean for him; what he been through and what it done to him. Child, when do you think is the time to love somebody the most; when they done good and made things easy for everybody? Well then, you ain't through learning—because that ain't the time at all. It's when he's at his lowest and can't believe in hisself 'cause the world done whipped him so. When you starts measuring somebody, measure him right, child, measure him right. Make sure you done taken into account what hills and valleys he come through before he got to wherever he is. [TRAVIS *bursts into the room at the end of the speech, leaving the door open.*]

TRAVIS: Grandmama—the moving men are downstairs! The truck just pulled up.

MAMA [*turning and looking at him*]:   Are they, baby? They downstairs? [*She sighs and sits.* LINDNER *appears in the doorway. He peers in and knocks lightly, to gain attention, and comes in. All turn to look at him.*]

LINDNER [*hat and briefcase in hand*]:   Uh—hello... [RUTH *crosses mechanically to the bedroom door and opens it and lets it swing open freely and slowly as the lights come up on* WALTER *within, still in his coat, sitting at the far corner of the room. He looks up and out through the room to* LINDNER.]

RUTH: He's here. [*A long minute passes and* WALTER *slowly gets up.*]

LINDNER [*coming to the table with efficiency, putting his briefcase on the table and starting to unfold papers and unscrew fountain pens*]:   Well, I certainly was glad to hear from you people. [WALTER *has begun the trek out of the room, slowly and awkwardly, rather like a small boy, passing the back of his sleeve across his mouth from time to time.*] Life can really be so much simpler than people let it be most of the time. Well—with whom do I negotiate? You, Mrs. Younger, or your son here? [MAMA *sits with her hands folded on her lap and her eyes closed as* WALTER *advances.* TRAVIS *goes close to* LINDNER *and looks at the papers curiously.*] Just some official papers, sonny.

RUTH: Travis, you go downstairs.

MAMA [*opening her eyes and looking into* WALTER'S]:   No. Travis, you stay right here. And you make him understand what you doing. Walter Lee. You teach him good. Like Willy Harris taught you. You show where our five generations done come to. Go ahead, son—

WALTER [*Looks down into his boy's eyes.* TRAVIS *grins at him merrily and* WALTER *draws him beside him with his arm lightly around his shoulders.*]:   Well, Mr. Lindner. [BENEATHA *turns away.*] We called you—[*There is a profound, simple groping quality in his speech.*]—because, well, me and my family [*He looks around and shifts from one foot to the other.*] Well—we are very plain people....

LINDNER: Yes—

WALTER: I mean—I have worked as a chauffeur most of my life—and my wife here, she does domestic work in people's kitchens. So does my mother. I mean—we are plain people....

LINDNER: Yes, Mr. Younger—

WALTER [*really like a small boy, looking down at his shoes and then up at the man*]:   And—uh—well, my father, well, he was a laborer most of his life.

LINDNER [*absolutely confused*]:   Uh, yes—

WALTER [*looking down at his toes once again*]:   My father almost beat a man to death once because this man called him a bad name or something, you know what I mean?

LINDNER: No, I'm afraid I don't.

WALTER [*finally straightening up*]:   Well, what I mean is that we come from people who had a lot of pride. I mean—we are very proud people. And that's my sister over there and she's going to be a doctor—and we are very proud—

LINDNER: Well—I am sure that is very nice, but—

WALTER [*starting to cry and facing the man eye to eye*]:   What I am telling you is that we called you over here to tell you that we are very proud and that this is—this is my son, who makes the sixth generation of our family in this country, and that we have all thought about your offer and we have decided to move into our house because my father—my father—he earned it. [MAMA *has her eyes closed and is rocking back and forth as though she were in church, with her head nodding the amen yes.*] We don't want to make no trouble for nobody or fight no causes—but we will try to be good neighbors. That's all we got to say. [*He looks the man absolutely in the eyes.*] We don't want your money. [*He turns and walks away from the man.*]

LINDNER [*looking around at all of them*]:   I take it then that you have decided to occupy.

BENEATHA: That's what the man said.

LINDNER [*to* MAMA *in her reverie*]:   Then I would like to appeal to you, Mrs. Younger. You are older and wiser and understand things better I am sure...

MAMA [*rising*]:   I am afraid you don't understand. My son said we was going to move and there ain't nothing left for me to say. [*Shaking her head with double meaning.*] You know how these young folks is nowadays, mister. Can't do a thing with 'em. Good-bye.

LINDNER [*folding up his materials*]:   Well—if you are that final about it... There is nothing left for me to say. [*He finishes. He is almost ignored by the family, who are concentrating on* WALTER LEE. *At the door* LINDNER *halts and looks around.*] I sure hope you people know what you're doing. [*He shakes his head and exits.*]

RUTH [*looking around and coming to life*]:   Well, for God's sake—if the moving men are here—LET'S GET THE HELL OUT OF HERE!

MAMA [*into action*]:   Ain't it the truth! Look at all this here mess. Ruth, put Travis' good jacket on him... Walter Lee, fix your tie and tuck your shirt in, you look just like somebody's hoodlum. Lord have mercy, where is my plant? [*She flies to get it amid the general bustling of the family, who are deliberately trying to ignore the nobility of the past moment.*] You all start on down... Travis child, don't go empty-handed... Ruth, where did I put that box with my skillets in it? I want to be in charge of it myself... I'm going to make us the biggest dinner we ever ate tonight... Beneatha, what's the matter with them stockings? Pull them things up, girl... [*The family starts to file out as two moving men appear and begin to carry out the heavier pieces of furniture, bumping into the family as they move about.*]

BENEATHA: Mama, Asagai—asked me to marry him today and go to Africa—

MAMA [*in the middle of her getting-ready activity*]:   He did? You ain't old enough to marry nobody—[*Seeing the* MOVING MEN *lifting one of her chairs precariously.*] Darling, that ain't no bale of cotton, please handle it so we can sit in it again. I had that chair twenty-five years... [*The movers sigh with exasperation and go on with their work.*]

BENEATHA [*girlishly and unreasonably trying to pursue the conversation*]:   To go to Africa, Mama—be a doctor in Africa...

MAMA [*distracted*]:   Yes, baby—

WALTER: Africa! What he want to go to Africa for?

BENEATHA: To practice there...

WALTER: Girl, if you don't get all them silly ideas out your head! You better marry yourself a man with some loot...

BENEATHA [*angrily, precisely as in the first scene of the play*]:   What have you got to do with who I marry!

WALTER: Plenty. Now I think George Murchison—[*He and* BENEATHA *go out yelling at each other vigorously;* BENEATHA *is heard saying that she would not marry* GEORGE MURCHISON *if he were Adam and she were Eve, etc. The anger is loud and real till their voices diminish.* RUTH *stands at the door and turns to* MAMA *and smiles knowingly.*]

MAMA [*fixing her hat at last*]:   Yeah—they something all right, my children...

RUTH: Yeah—they're something. Let's go, Lena.

MAMA [*stalling, starting to look around at the house*]:   Yes—I'm coming. Ruth—

RUTH: Yes?

MAMA [*quietly, woman to woman*]:   He finally come into his manhood today, didn't he? Kind of like a rainbow after the rain...

RUTH [*biting her lip lest her own pride explode in front of* MAMA]:   Yes, Lena. [WALTER'S *voice calls for them raucously.*]

MAMA [*waving* RUTH *out vaguely*]:   All right, honey—go on down. I be down directly.

[RUTH *hesitates, then exits.* MAMA *stands, at last alone in the living room, her plant on the table before her as the lights start to come down. She looks around at all the walls and ceilings and suddenly, despite herself, while the children call below, a great heaving thing rises in her and she puts her fist to her mouth, takes a final desperate look, pulls her coat about her, pats her hat and goes out. The lights dim down. The door opens and she comes back in, grabs her plant, and goes out for the last time.*]

Curtain

MAKING CONNECTIONS

1. The title of the play is taken from a line in Langston Hughes's poem "A Dream Deferred" (p. 80). Do you think *A Raisin in the Sun* is an appropriate title? Explain.

2. How are sunlight and Mama's plant used as symbols in this play? How do these objects also serve to set the mood?

3. The main characters all have different plans for the insurance money. What do you think of the process the Youngers follow in making the decision? Do you think the decision might have been made differently?

4. Does the Younger family share a common heritage with Asagai? Explain your answer with examples from the play.

5. What purpose do the scenes between George and Beneatha serve? Compare their different ideas about education, race, heritage, and the future.

6. Do you think it is necessary for Mama to entrust Walter with all the money? Why doesn't she split the money, giving Beneatha her share?

7. Do you agree with Walter's decision at the end of the play? What does he gain? What would be gained or lost by selling to Lindner? What kind of life do you expect the Youngers to find in Clybourne Park?

8. Ruth is very eager for the family to move into a house. Have you ever lived somewhere that you didn't consider a home? How does that affect a person—or a family—psychologically?

9. To what extent are the family's problems a question of bad luck, bad timing, or forces beyond their control? Provide examples.

10. Compare the relationships within the Younger family with those in other works you've read.

MAKING AN ARGUMENT

1. Characterization is one of the play's great strengths. Consider the dreams of Mama, Walter, Ruth, and Beneatha. Beyond specific goals—like owning a liquor store—what do their dreams represent for them? What would achieving these dreams give them that seems to be missing from their lives? How does the insurance payment increase or ease the frustration they feel? To what extent are the characters themselves—in addition to the setting and their economic circumstances—responsible for the central conflict?

   Write an argumentative essay about the relationship between characterization and conflict in this play. Cite the text of the play to support your views.

■ LORRAINE HANSBERRY

IN HER OWN WORDS

On Growing Up "I was born May 19, 1930, the last of four children. Of love and my parents there is little to be written: their relationship to their children was utilitarian. We were fed and housed and dressed and outfitted with more cash than our associates and that was all. We were also vaguely taught certain vague absolutes: that we were better than no one but infinitely superior to everyone; that we were products of the proudest and most mistreated of the races of man; that there was nothing enormously difficult about life; that one succeeded as a matter of course."

"Life was not a struggle—it was something that one *did*. One won an argument because, if facts gave out, one invented them—with color! The only sinful people in the world were dull people. And above all, there were two things which were never to be betrayed: the family and the race. But of love, there was nothing ever said." (*YGB*, pp. 17–18)

"Seven years separated the nearest of my brothers and sisters and myself; I wear, I am sure, the earmarks of that familial station to this day. Little has been written or thought to my knowledge about children who occupy that place: the last born separated by an uncommon length of time from the next youngest. I suspect we are probably a race apart." (*YGB*, p. 18)

"I was given, during my grade school years, one-half the amount of education prescribed by the Board of Education of my city. This was so because the children of the Chicago ghetto were jammed into a segregated school system. I am a product of that system and one result is that—to this day—I cannot count properly. I do not add, subtract, or multiply with ease. Our teachers, devoted and indifferent alike, had to sacrifice something to make the system work at all—and in my case it was arithmetic that got put aside most often. Thus, the mind which was able to grasp university-level reading materials in the sixth and seventh grades had not been sufficiently exposed to elementary arithmetic to make even simple change in a grocery store."

"This is what is meant when we speak of the scars, the marks that the ghettoized child carries through life. To be imprisoned in the ghetto is to be forgotten— or deliberately cheated of one's birthright—at best." (*YGB*, p. 36)

"But we are all shaped, are we not, by that particular rim of the soup bowl where we swim, and I have remained throughout the balance of my life a creature formed in a community atmosphere where I was known as a 'rich' girl."

"In any case, my mother sent me to kindergarten in white fur in the middle of the depression; the kids beat me up; and I think it was from that moment I became— a rebel..." (*YGB*, p. 36)

"Above all, there had been an aspect of the society of the kids from the ghetto which demanded utmost respect: they fought. The girls as well as the boys. THEY FOUGHT. If you were not right with them, or sometimes even if you were, there they were of an afternoon after school, standing waiting for you in the sunshine; a little gang of them in their gym shoes, milling close together, blocking off the sidewalk, daring you to break for it and try to run to the other side of the street where, if luck prevailed, one might gain the protection of some chance passing adult. That, ultimately, was the worst thing of all to do because they always got you after that. *Always.* It was better to continue on right in their midst, feigning the courage or at least nonchalance." (*YGB,* p. 38)

"[My father] was the sort of a man who put a great deal of his money, a great deal of his extraordinary talents, and a great deal of passion into everything that we say is the American way of going after gold. He moved his family into a restricted area where no Negroes were supposed to live and proceeded to fight the case in the courts, all the way to the Supreme Court of the United States. This cost a great deal of money and involved the assistance of the NAACP attorneys and so on. It is the way of struggling that everyone says is the proper way. And it individually resulted in a decision against restrictive covenance, which is a famous case known as Hansberry vs. Lee." (From a speech at Town Hall, New York City, 1964)

On Her Motivation to Become a Playwright "My high school yearbook bears the dedication: "Englewood High trains for citizenship in a world of many different peoples. Who could better appreciate this wonderful country than our forefathers who traveled hundreds of miles from every known nation, seeking a land of freedom from discrimination of race, color, or creed." And in illustration, there is this:

The Great Branches of Man at Englewood High: in front, Mangolia Ali of East Indian Mohammedan descent; second couple, Nancy Diagre and Harold Bradley, Negroid; middle couple, Rosalind Sherr and William Krugman, Jewish religion, not a racial stock; next, Eleanor Trester and Theodore Flood, Caucasoid; extreme right, Lois Lee and Barbara Nomura, Mongoloid; rear, left, Mr. Thompson, principal.

I was reminded of Englewood by a questionnaire which came from *Show* magazine the other day...

THE SHAKESPEAREAN EXPERIENCE
SHOW POLL #5, FEBRUARY 1964

Some Questions Answered by: Robert Bolt, Jean Cocteau, T. S. Eliot, Tyrone Guthrie, Lorraine Hansberry, Joan Littlewood, Harold Pinter, Alain Robbe-Grillet, Igor Stravinsky, Harry S. Truman

QUESTION: *What was your first contact with Shakespeare?*

High school English literature classwork. We had to read and memorize speeches from *Macbeth* and *Julius Caesar* all under the auspices of a strange and bewigged teacher who we, after this induction, naturally and cruelly christened "Pale Hecate"— God rest her gentle, enraptured and igniting soul!

PALE HECATE *enters, ruler in hand, and takes her place in the classroom. She surveys the class. They come to attention as her eye falls on each in turn.*

PALE HECATE: Y'do not read, nor speak, nor write the English language! I suspect that y'do not even *think* in it! God only knows in what language y'do think, or if you think at all. 'Tis true that the *English* have done little enough with the tongue, but being the English I expect it was the best they could do. [*They giggle.*] In any case, I'll have it learned properly before a living one of y'll pass out of this class. That I will! [*Waving a composition book and indicating the grade marked in red at the top*] As for you, Miss—as for you, indeed, surely you will recognize the third letter of the alphabet, when y'have seen it?

STUDENT: *C.*

PALE HECATE: Aye, a *C* it 'tis! You're a bright and clever one now after all, aren't y'lass? [*The class snickers.*] And now, my brilliance, would you also be inform-ing us as to what a grade signifies when it is thus put upon the page?

STUDENT: Average.

PALE HECATE: "Average." Yes, yes—and what else in your case, my iridescence? Well then, I'll be tellin' you in fine order. It stands for "cheat," my luminous one! [*The class sobers.*] For them that will do *half* when *all* is called for; for them that will slip and slide through life at the edge of their minds, never once pushing into the interior to see what wonders are hiding there—content to drift along on whatever gets them by, *cheating* themselves, *cheating* the world, *cheating* Nature! That is what the *C* means, my dear child—[*She smiles.*]—my pet [*they giggle; in rapid order she raps each on the head with her ruler.*]—my laziest *Queen of the Ethiopes!*

She exits or dims out.

QUESTION: *Which is your favorite Shakespeare play and why?*

"Favorite? It is like choosing the 'superiority' of autumn days; mingling titles permits a reply: *Othello* and *Hamlet.* Why? There is a sweetness in the former that lingers long after the tragedy is done. A kind of possibility that we suspect in man wherein even its flaw is a tribute. The latter because there remains a depth in the prince that, as we all know, constantly reengages as we mature. And it does seem that the wit remains the brightest and most instructive in all dramatic literature."

QUESTION: *What is the most important result of your familiarity with Shakespeare? What has he given you?*

"Comfort and agitation so bound together that they are inseparable. Man, as set down in the plays, is large. Enormous. Capable of anything at all. And yet fragile, too, this view of the human spirit; one feels it ought be respected and protected and loved rather fiercely.

Rollicking times, Shakespeare has given me. I love to laugh and his humor is that of everyday; of every man's foible at no man's expense. Language. At thirteen a difficult and alien tedium, those Elizabethan cadences; but soon a balm, a thrilling source of contact with life." (*YGB,* pp. 43–44)

On the Influence of Sean O'Casey (At seventeen years old, sitting in on a rehearsal of Sean O'Casey's *Juno and the Paycock*) "I remember rather clearly that my coming had been an accident. Also that I sat in the orchestra close to the stage: the orches-tra of the great modern building which is the main theater plant of the University of Wisconsin. The woman's voice, the howl, the shriek of misery fitted to a wail of poetry that consumed all my senses and all my awareness of human pain, endurance and the futility of it—'Now Mrs. Madigan reappeared with her compassionate shawl and the wail rose and hummed through the tenement, through Dublin, through Ireland itself and then mingled with seas and became something born of the Irish wail that was all of us.' I remember sitting there stunned with a melody that I thought might have been sung in a different meter. The play was *Juno,* the writer Sean O'Casey—but the melody was one that I had known for a very long while."

"I was seventeen and I did not think then of *writing* the melody as *I* knew it—in a different key; but I believe it entered my consciousness and stayed there... " (*YGB,* p. 65)

"I love Sean O'Casey. This, to me, is the playwright of the twentieth century accepting and using the most obvious instruments of Shakespeare, which is the human personality in its totality. O'Casey never fools you about the Irish, you see... the Irish drunkard, the Irish braggart, the Irish liar... and the genuine heroism which must naturally emerge when you tell the truth about people. This, to me, is the height of artistic perception and is the most rewarding kind of thing that can happen in drama, because when you believe people so completely—because *everybody* has their drunkards and their braggarts and their cowards, you know—then you also believe them in their moments of heroic assertion; you don't doubt them." (*YGB,* p. 69)

On Drama as a Medium "I happen to believe that the most ordinary human being... has within him elements of profundity, of profound anguish. You don't have to go to the kings and queens of the earth—I think the Greeks and the Elizabethans did this because it was a logical concept—but every human being is in enormous conflict about something, even if it's how to get to work in the morning and all that... " (Studs Terkel interview, 1959)

"I'm particularly attracted to a medium where not only do you get to do what we do in life every day—you know, talk to people—but to be very selective about the nature of the conversation. It's an opportunity to treat character in the most absolute relief, one against the other, so that everything, sympathy and conflict, is played so sharply, you know—even a little more than a novel. And I suppose it's my own private sense of drama that makes *that* appeal to me." (Studs Terkel interview, 1959)

"There's no contradiction between protest art and good art. That's an artificial argument. You either write a good play or bad play. It doesn't have too much to do with what it is about. People say that this or that minority group is so preoccupied with their problem that it diminishes their art. I've always been very pleased, and my husband also, to note that for the last two hundred years the only writers in the English language we've had to boast about are the Irish writers—who reflect an oppressed culture." (Mike Wallace interview, 1959)

On A Raisin in the Sun "Months before I had turned the last page out of the typewriter and pressed all the sheets neatly together in a pile, and gone and stretched

out face down on the living room floor. I had finished a play; a play I had no reason to think or not think would ever be done; a play that I was sure no one would
quite understand...."

"I cannot any longer remember if I liked it or not. I have said to some that it
was not my 'kind' of play; and yet it moved me to read it sometimes—and once I
wept at a performance."

"I have been tongue-tied and glib and fatuous trying to answer questions
which must always seem strange to a writer: 'Why did you write it?' and 'How did
it come to be?'"

"The truly relevant and revealing answers are always too diffuse, too vague in
time and place and specific meaning to quite try and share with people. I know—
but how can I tell it." (*YGB*, p. 104)

Hotel Taft
New Haven, Conn.
January 19, 1959

Dear Mother:

Well—here we are. I am sitting alone in a nice hotel room in New Haven,
Conn. Downstairs, next door in the Shubert Theatre, technicians are putting the
finishing touches on a living room that is supposed to be a Chicago living room.
Wednesday the curtain goes up at 8 P.M. The next day the New Haven papers will
say what they think of our efforts. A great deal of money has been spent and a lot
of people have done some hard, hard work, and it may be the beginning of many
different careers.

The actors are very good and the director is a very talented man—so if it is a
poor show I won't be able to blame a soul but your youngest daughter.

Mama, it is a play that tells the truth about people, Negroes and life and I think
it will help a lot of people to understand how we are just as complicated as they
are—and just as mixed up—but above all, that we have among our miserable and
downtrodden ranks—people who are the very essence of human dignity. That is
what, after all the laughter and tears, the play is supposed to say. I hope it will
make you very proud. See you soon. Love to all. (*YGB*, p. 91)

QUESTION: *Is there a character in the play who represents Lorraine Hansberry?*

"The college student—Beneatha. I had a great deal of fun with this character. First
of all I knew if the play ever got to Broadway, she would be the kind of character
that people had never seen before—a Negro girl with actual pretensions of any
sort—it's just unknown to theater and I also had a great deal of fun making fun of
her a little bit because it's a pleasure to sit back eight years later and see yourself as
you think you were. What she reflects symbolically is a very legitimate and active
sentiment among American Negro intellectuals and among much larger sections of
Negro life, that repudiates much of what has come to us through cultural experience and historical experience that we think is not necessarily as valid as we have

been told that it is. And since the 1930s there has been quite a movement that feels that what we want now is a recognition of the beauty of things African and the beauty of things black, and this girl represents part of this development—as I do, I think." (Mike Wallace interview, 1959)

On Walter Lee's Comment: "We're all tied up in a race of people who don't know how to do nothing but moan, pray and have babies." "He's an individual. He's one character in a play—representative of a good many people. This is inner group bitterness. When one can't speak against anyone else, one indicts one's own. It's very common. People have done this always. And he means this to hurt. It's a line that's directed toward his wife in the play. It's a way of turning the attack within for his own personal reasons. I think if you had a conversation with Walter Lee Younger, he'd have other things to tell you. But in that moment, he is trying to hurt her." (Mike Wallace interview, 1959)

On What People of Any Race Can Learn from This Play "I have a suspicion of the universal humanity of all people. I think it is possible to reach it. And I think in the moment when they are sitting in the theater and they murmur in favor of the family and they applaud a particular action, I believe that almost every human being there genuinely wishes it to happen. To what extent that any member of the audience comes out of the theater at any time and retains the emotion of a moment within the theater I certainly couldn't begin to guess. In a much larger way, it may have affirmative effects." (Mike Wallace interview, 1959)

On the Affirmative Ending of the Play "For me this is one of the most affirmative periods in history. I'm very pleased that those peoples in the world that I feel closest to, the colonial peoples, the African peoples, the Asian peoples, are in an insurgent mood. They are in the process of transforming the world, and I think for the better. I can't quite understand pessimism at this moment. Unless, of course, one is wedded to things that are dying out like colonialism, like racism. Walter Lee Younger and his family are necessarily tied to this international movement, whether they have consciousness of it or not, they belong to an affirmative movement in history. Anything that he does that is the least positive has implications that embrace all of us. I feel that his moving into the new house, his decision, is in a way a reply to those who say all guilt is equal, all questions lack clarity, that it's hard to know what you should fight for or against, that there are things to do—that the new house has many shapes, and we must make some decisions in this country as this man does." (Mike Wallace interview, 1959)

On MAMA "This is a very strong woman. This is a woman who keeps her authority in any way that she has to, emotionally, physically, however. I think she's a great woman. But she can be wrong—terribly wrong." (Mike Wallace interview, 1959)

On What Joseph Asagai Represents in This Play "He represents two things: he represents, first of all, the true intellectual. This is a young man who is so absolutely confident in his understanding and his perception about the world that he has no need of any of the façade of pseudo intellectuality—for any of the pretenses and the nonsense. He can already kid about all the features of intense nationalism because he's been there and he understands beyond that point. He's already concerned about the human race on a new level. He's a true, genuine intellectual. So that he doesn't have time or interest except for amusement in useless passion, in useless promenading of ideas. That's partially what he represents. The other thing that he represents is much more overt. I was aware that on a Broadway stage they have never seen an African who didn't have his shoes hanging around his neck and a bone through his nose or his ears or something. And I thought that even just theatrically speaking this would most certainly be refreshing, and what this fellow represents in the play is the emergence of an articulate and deeply conscious colonial intelligentsia in the world." (Studs Terkel interview, 1959)

In Others' Words

 James Baldwin

Sweet Lorraine   [1969]

That's the way I always felt about her, and so I won't apologize for calling her that now. *She* understood it: in that far too brief a time when we walked and talked and laughed and drank together, sometimes in the streets and bars and restaurants of the Village, sometimes at her house, sometimes at my house, sometimes gracelessly fleeing the houses of others; and sometimes seeming, for anyone who didn't know us, to be having a knockdown, drag-out battle. We spent a lot of time arguing about history and tremendously related subjects in her Bleecker Street and, later Waverly Place flat. And often, just when I was certain that she was about to throw me out, as being altogether too rowdy a type, she would stand up, her hands on her hips (for these down-home sessions she always wore slacks) and pick up my empty glass as though she intended to throw it at me. Then she would walk into the kitchen, saying, with a haughty toss of her head, "Really, Jimmy. You ain't *right,* child!" With which stern put down, she would hand me another drink and launch into a brilliant analysis of just why I wasn't "right." I would often stagger down her stairs as the sun came up, usually in the middle of a paragraph and always in the middle of a laugh. That marvelous laugh. That marvelous face. I loved her, she was my sister and my comrade. Her going did not so much make me lonely as make me realize how lonely we were. We had that respect for each other which perhaps is only felt by people on the same side of the barricades, listening to the accumulating thunder of the hooves of horses and the threads of tanks.

　　The first time I ever saw Lorraine was at the Actors' Studio, in the winter of '57–58. She was there as an observer of the Workshop Production of *Giovanni's Room.*[1] She was way up in the bleachers, taking on some of the biggest names in the American theater because she had liked the play and they, in the main, hadn't. I was enormously grateful to her, she seemed to speak for me; and afterwards she

[1] *Giovanni's Room* a novel by James Baldwin published in 1956

talked to me with a gentleness and generosity never to be forgotten. A small, shy, determined person, with that strength dictated by absolutely impersonal ambition: she was not trying to "make it"—she was trying to keep the faith.

We really met, however, in Philadelphia, in 1959, when *A Raisin in the Sun* was at the beginning of its amazing career. Much has been written about this play; I personally feel that it will demand a far less guilty and constricted people than the present-day Americans to be able to assess it at all; as an historical achievement, anyway, no one can gainsay its importance. What is relevant here is that I had never in my life seen so many black people in the theater. And the reason was that never before, in the entire history of the American theater, had so much of the truth of black people's lives been seen on the stage. Black people ignored the theater because the theater had always ignored them.

But, in *Raisin,* black people recognized that house and all the people in it—the mother, the son, the daughter, and the daughter-in-law, and supplied the play with an interpretative element which could not be present in the minds of white people: a kind of claustrophobic terror, created not only by their knowledge of the house but by their knowledge of the streets. And when the curtain came down, Lorraine and I found ourselves in the backstage alley, where she was immediately mobbed. I produced a pen and Lorraine handed me her handbag and began signing autographs. "It only happens once," she said. I stood there and watched. I watched the people, who loved Lorraine for what she had brought to them; and watched Lorraine, who loved the people for what they brought to *her.* It was not, for her, a matter of being admired. She was being corroborated and confirmed. She was wise enough and honest enough to recognize that black American artists are a very special case. One is not merely an artist and one is not judged merely as an artist: the black people crowding around Lorraine, whether or not they considered her an artist, assuredly considered her a witness. This country's concept of art and artists has the effect, scarcely worth mentioning by now, of isolating the artist from the people. One can see the effect of this in the irrelevance of so much of the work produced by celebrated white artists; but the effect of this isolation on a black artist is absolutely fatal. He *is,* already, as a black American citizen, isolated from most of his white countrymen. At the crucial hour, he can hardly look to his artistic peers for help, for they do not know enough about him to be able to correct him. To continue to grow, to remain in touch with himself, he needs the support of that community from which, however, all of the pressures of American life incessantly conspire to remove him. And when he is effectively removed, he falls silent—and the people have lost another hope.

5   Much of the strain under which Lorraine worked was produced by her knowledge of this reality, and her determined refusal to be destroyed by it. She was a very young woman, with an overpowering vision, and fame had come to her early—she must certainly have wished, often enough, that fame had seen fit to drag its feet a little. For fame and recognition are not synonymous, especially not here, and her fame was to cause her to be criticized very harshly, very loudly, and very often by both black and white people who were unable to believe, apparently, that

a really serious intention could be contained in so glamorous a frame. She took it all with a kind of astringent good humor, refusing, for example, even to consider defending herself when she was being accused of being a "slum-lord" because of her family's real-estate holdings in Chicago. I called her during that time, and all she said—with a wry laugh—was, "My God, Jimmy, do you realize you're only the second person who's called me today? And you know how my phone kept ringing *before!*" She was not surprised. She was devoted to the human race, but she was not romantic about it.

JULIUS LESTER

THE HEROIC DIMENSION IN A RAISIN IN THE SUN   [1972]

A Raisin in the Sun is no intellectual abstraction about upward mobility and conspicuous consumption. It goes right to the core of practically every black family in the ghettos of Chicago, New York, Los Angeles, and elsewhere. Whether they have a picture of Jesus, Martin Luther King, or Malcolm X on the lead-painted walls of their rat-infested tenement, all of them want to get the hell out of there as quickly as they can. Maybe black militants don't know it, or don't want to admit it, but Malcolm X made a down payment on a house in a suburban community a few weeks before he was murdered. And one surely can't accuse Malcolm of bourgeois aspirations. He merely wanted what every black wants—a home of his own adequate to his needs, at a minimum, and the fulfillment of his desires, at the most....*A Raisin in the Sun* is most definitely about "human dignity" because Lorraine Hansberry is concerned with the attitude we must have toward material things if we are to be their master and not their slave. Is that attitude to be Mama's? Or is it to be Walter's? And, for blacks, locked out from these things for so long, the question is a crucial one. As blacks acquire more and more of America's material offerings, are they, too, going to be transformed by their acquisitions into mindless consumers like the majority of whites? Or are they going to continue to walk in the path of righteousness like their forebears? Lorraine Hansberry summarized it well when, in a letter, she wrote of the play:

> ...we cannot...very well succumb to monetary values and know the survival of certain interior aspects of man which...must remain if we are to loom larger than other creatures on this planet.... Our people fight daily and magnificently for a more comfortable material base for their lives; they desperately need and hourly sacrifice for clean homes, decent food, personal and group dignity and the abolition of terroristic violence as their children's heritage. So, in that sense, I am certainly a materialist in the first order.

However, the distortion of this aspiration surrounds us in the form of an almost maniacal lusting for "acquisitions." It seems to have absorbed the national mentality and Negroes, to be sure, have certainly been affected by it. The young man in the play, Walter Lee, is meant to symbolize their number. Consequently, in the beginning, he dreams not so much of being comfortable and imparting the most meaningful gifts to his son (education in depth, humanist values, a worship of dignity) but merely of being what it seems to him the "success" portion of humankind is—"rich." Toward this end he is willing to make an old trade; urgently willing. On the fact that some aspect of his society has brought him to this point, the core of the drama hangs.

Walter blames himself, his wife, and his mother for what he sees as his personal failure. And only at the end of the play does it become possible for him to realize that there is a puppeteer manipulating him, a puppeteer who brought him dangerously close to destroying his family and himself.

The climax of the play comes after Walter's deal to get a liquor license falls through. Mama Younger has made a $3,500 down payment on a house and gives the remaining money to Walter to do with as he wishes after he deposits $2,500 in a savings account for Beneatha's education. Walter, however, takes the entire $6,500 and gives it to one of his two future "partners." One of the "partners" absconds with the money. A Mr. Lindner, a white man from the neighborhood into which they are to move, comes and offers to buy the house from them for more than they would eventually pay. The whites in the neighborhood do not want a black family moving in. Previously, Walter had scornfully turned the man down. However, when he learns that his money has been stolen, he calls Mr. Lindner on the phone and tells him that they will sell the house. Mr. Lindner comes over and Walter finds that he is unable to go through with it. There is something in him—a little bit of self-respect is still left; he tells Mr. Lindner that they are going to move in. And with Walter making his first step toward being a man, a *black* man, the play ends.

Few see the heroism in Walter's simple act of assertion. Indeed, how many who have seen the play or the movie have not thought that Walter was a fool for *not* accepting the money? How one views Walter's act is a direct reflection of how much one accepts the American dream. And there is the significance of the fact that the play ends with the Youngers moving into a "white" neighborhood. To see this as a confirmation of the American dream is to accept the myth that blacks have wanted nothing more than to be integrated with whites. In actuality, the fact that the neighborhood is white is the least important thing about it. It merely happened to be the neighborhood in which Mama Younger could find a nice house she could afford. And it is this simple, practical element which has always been mistaken by whites as a desire on the part of blacks to be "integrated." But why, the question could be raised, would the Youngers persist in moving into a neighborhood where they are not wanted, where they may be subjected to harassment or even physical violence? They persist, as all blacks persist, not because it is any great honor to live among whites, but because one cannot consider himself a human being as long as he acquiesces to restrictions placed upon him by others, particularly if those restrictions are based solely on race or religion. If Walter had accepted the money, he would have been saying, in graphic language, You are right, we are niggers and don't have the right to live where we can afford to. But, with that earthy eloquence of a black still close to his roots, Walter says, "We have decided to move into our house because my father—my father—he earned it." And, in that realization, Walter learns also that it was not a black woman who castrated him. It was America and his own acceptance of America's values. No woman can make him a man. He has to do it himself.

5   He is a hero, a twentieth-century hero. We still long, of course, for the heroes who seemed to ride history as if it were a bronco and they were champion rodeo riders. But those heroes—if they were ever real—come from a time when life, perhaps, was somewhat less complex. But the problems that face man in the latter twentieth century are large, larger than any one of us, and the sword of a knight in armor is laughable to the dragons roaming our countryside. Our heroes are more difficult to recognize only because they appear so small beside the overwhelming enemies they must slay. But because they appear small does not mean that they are, and it does not make their acts less heroic. Walter Lee Younger has his contemporary historic counterpart in the person of a small, quiet black woman named Rosa Parks who refused to get out of a seat on a bus in Montgomery, Alabama. It would have been so easy for her to have relinquished her seat to a white person that day—as it would have been easy for Walter to have taken the money. But something in her, as in him, said No. And in that quiet dissent, both of them said Yes to human dignity. They said No to those who would define them and thereby deny their existence, and by saying No, they began to define themselves. There have been many Rosa Parks, but few of them have mysteriously set in motion a whole movement for social change. Walter Lee Younger is one of those whose act probably set nothing in motion. And that only increases its heroic dimension. In an article in *The Village Voice,* which compared Walter to Willy Loman, Lorraine Hansberry described the hero she saw in Walter Younger.

> For if there are no waving flags and marching songs at the barricades as Walter marches out with his little battalion, it is not because the battle lacks nobility. On the contrary, he has picked up in his way, still imperfect and wobbly in his small view of human destiny, what I believe Arthur Miller once called "the golden thread of history." He becomes, in spite of those who are too intrigued with despair and hatred of man to see it, King Oedipus refusing to tear out his eyes, but attacking the Oracle instead. He is that last Jewish patriot manning his rifle in the burning ghetto at Warsaw; he is that young girl who swam into sharks to save a friend a few weeks ago; he is Anne Frank, still believing in people; he is the nine small heroes of Little Rock; he is Michelangelo creating David, and Beethoven bursting forth with the Ninth Symphony. He is all those things because he has finally reached out in his tiny moment and caught that sweet essence which is human dignity, and it shines like the old star-touched dream that is in his eyes.

ANNE CHENEY

The African Heritage in A Raisin in the Sun   [1984]

A moving testament to the strength and endurance of the human spirit, *A Raisin in the Sun* is a quiet celebration of the black family, the importance of African roots, the equality of women, the vulnerability of marriage, the true value of money, the survival of the individual, and the nature of man's dreams. A well-made play, *Raisin* at first seems a plea for racial tolerance or a fable of man's overcoming an insensitive society, but the simple eloquence of the characters elevates the play into a universal representation of all people's hopes, fears, and dreams.

On January 19, 1959, a timid Lorraine Hansberry wrote her mother about *Raisin:* "Mama, it is a play that tells the truth about people, Negroes and life and I think it will help a lot of people to understand how we are just as complicated as they are... people who are the very essence of human dignity.... I hope it will make you very proud." Indeed, *A Raisin in the Sun* made not only Nannie Perry Hansberry proud but also artists—both black and white. *Raisin* was the first play by a black writer ever to win the prestigious New York Drama Critics' Circle Award. The play would become "an American classic, published and produced in some thirty languages abroad and in thousands of productions across the country.... James Baldwin [said]: "Never before in the entire history of the American theatre had so much of the truth of Black people's lives been seen on the stage." Despite the earlier contributions of Langston Hughes, David Littlejohn wrote, "It would not be unfair in dating the emergence of a serious and mature Negro theatre in America from 1959, the date of Lorraine Hansberry's *A Raisin in the Sun....* "

Today some black critics feel that *A Raisin in the Sun* is a play whose time has passed—a simplistic, halting treatment of race relations. Some are confused by Hansberry's professed nationalism, when she seems to favor integration. Harold Cruse even calls *Raisin* a "cleverly written piece of glorified soap opera." Hansberry used the traditional form of the well-made play in *Raisin,* especially observing the unities of action, place, and time. The action of the play is carefully delineated: act 1 serves as the beginning, act 2 as the middle, and act 3 as the tightly knit end. Furthermore, all action is carefully and causally related. Hansberry strictly abides by the unity of place: all action transpires in one room of the Youngers' South Side Chicago apartment. Stretching the unity of time from one day to one month (not unusual for a modern dramatist), Hansberry still maintains unity of impression with the central emotional concerns of the Younger family: Walter's search for a dream, Lena's faith in God and the family, Beneatha's hope for a new world.

Hansberry needed this rather traditional form to control the innovative ideas and themes of *Raisin.* Far from being a stereotyped or romanticized treatment of black life, the play embodies ideas that have been uncommon on the Broadway stage in any period. Resurrecting the ideas of the Harlem renaissance and anticipating the new thinking of the 1960s, Hansberry examines the importance of African roots, traditional versus innovative women, the nature of marriage, the real meaning of money, the search for human dignity. Most significantly, she addresses the sensitive question of to what extent people, in liberating themselves from the burdens of discrimination, should aspire to a white middle-class way of life.

5   During her *Freedom* years, Lorraine Hansberry continued to study African history with encouragement from Paul Robeson, W. E. B. Du Bois, and Louis Burnham. "She had spent hours of her younger years poring over maps of the African continent.... She was at one, texture, blood... with the sound of a mighty Congo drum." She imaginatively knew the lions, drumbeats, quiet sandy nights, respected the antiquity of Ethiopia founded in 1000 BCE Stirred by Kenya and Ghana wresting control from Europe and England, Hansberry inevitably incorporated her knowledge of Africa in

her first play. More than earlier playwrights, Hansberry made Africa a serious, yet natural, issue on Broadway.

In *Raisin* even George Murchison, Beneatha's beau, has an awareness of his African past. In the fever of Walter Lee's and Beneatha's mock African dance in act 2, George remarks sarcastically: "In one second we will hear all about the great Ashanti empires; the great Songhay civilizations; and the great sculpture of Benin—and then some poetry in the Bantu." George had probably learned in a college atmosphere that the Songhai empire was a powerful western African kingdom, which garnered wealth from its export of ivory and gold between 850 and 1500 A.D. (Mali and Ghana—not to be confused with the modern state of Ghana— were equally old and powerful empires.) Along the coast of Nigeria, Benin was another expansive empire, noted for its bronze and gold art objects, that came to power around 1500. Coming to power about 1700, Ashanti was still another western kingdom famous for its heroic warriors.

In the stage direction, Hansberry writes that Lena has "the noble bearing of the women of the Hereros of Southwest Africa," who were essentially a pastoral people. Thus Hansberry identifies Lena as an "earth mother," one who nurtures both her family and her plant as well as she can. But Lena reveals her total ignorance of African history by a parroting of Beneatha's earlier remarks in her politely naïve, unwittingly humorous speech to Joseph Asagai, the young Nigerian visitor: "I think it's so sad the way our American Negroes don't know nothing about Africa 'cept Tarzan and all that. And all that money they pour into these churches when they ought to be helping you people over there drive out them French and Englishmen done taken away your Land."

Most of the African material in *A Raisin in the Sun,* however, surfaces in conversations between Beneatha and Joseph Asagai. Touched by Beneatha's beauty and idealism, Asagai lovingly nicknames her Alaiyo—a Yoruban word for "One for Whom Bread—Food—Is Not Enough." In act 3, after Walter Lee has been duped out of his $6,500, Asagai visits an embittered, distraught Beneatha. Speaking of his beloved Nigeria, Asagai reveals his basic philosophy of life, of Africa: "A household in preparation of a journey...it is another feeling. Something full of the flow of life.... Movement, progress.... It makes me think of Africa." Perhaps he sees in Beneatha a microcosmic America—one struggling to overthrow the limitations imposed on her by an alien culture.

Asagai's village in Nigeria is one where most people cannot read, where many have not even seen a book. In the village, there are mountains and stars, cool drinks from gourds at the well, old songs, people who move slowly, anciently. But Nigeria also has guns, murder, revolution, illiteracy, disease, ignorance. Asagai understands the inevitability of change and progress in Africa; he imagines for a moment the consequences should he betray the movement. "Don't you see that...young men and women...my own black countrymen...[may]...step out of the shadows some evening and slit my then useless throat?" Rebuking Beneatha for becoming discouraged over one small frustration (Walter's losing the money), Asagai views his possible death as an advance toward freedom for himself and his people. "They who might kill me even...actually replenish me." Asagai's beliefs certainly contribute to Beneatha's transition from brittle idealist to a more tolerant human being.

10   In an interview with Studs Terkel (Chicago, May 2, 1959), Lorraine Hansberry referred to Joseph Asagai as her "favorite character" in *Raisin*. He represents the "true intellectual" with no pretense, no illusions. A revolutionary and nationalist, he realizes that initially black African leaders may be as corrupt as their white predecessors (Idi Amin of Uganda bore out this theory in the 1970s). Nevertheless, he shares Hansberry's conviction that "before you can start talking about what's wrong with independence, get it." More the idealist than the practical, effective leader—compared to Kenyatta and Nkrumah—Asagai is willing to die at the hands of his countrymen for the general good and freedom. (Harold Isaacs suggests that his name derives from the Zulu word *asegai,* "sawed-off spear.") On a more obvious level, Asagai certainly refutes the stage stereotype of the African with "a bone through his nose, or his ears."

In *A Raisin in the Sun,* then, Africa becomes a symbol of a proud heritage and a troublesome but hopeful future. To Hansberry's great credit, Africa is a natural, at times humorous, element in the Younger family—as Walter Lee shouts "HOT DAMN! FLAMING SPEAR," as Beneatha dresses in Nigerian robes, as Mama speaks of Tarzan, churches, and Englishmen.

STEVEN R. CARTER

HANSBERRY'S ARTISTIC MISSTEP   [1994]

Unfortunately, Hansberry's vigorous, sharp, and usually intriguing characterization of Beneatha is slightly marred by her one serious artistic misstep in *A Raisin in the Sun*. This occurs when Beneatha tells Lena and Ruth about the guitar lessons she has just started and they remind her about "the horseback-riding club for which she bought that fifty-five dollar riding habit that's been hanging in the closet ever since!" On the whole, this scene portrays Beneatha's striving for self-expression with warm humor and a touch of self-mockery that almost always pleases the audiences. The problem is that only a short time earlier Walter had angrily demanded that Beneatha show more gratitude for the financial sacrifices he and Ruth have made for her, and Ruth had denied her son the fifty cents he requested for school. It is inconceivable that a woman who could refuse such a small sum to a dearly beloved son would so casually accept the squandering of a much larger contribution to a mere sister-in-law, and even if, by some miracle, she were able to accept it out of an all-embracing feminist sisterhood (which doesn't fit Ruth's overall character), she could not do so with such ease. Worse still, lightly tossing away all this money in the face of the family's dire need makes Beneatha seem monstrously selfish rather than mildly selfish as Hansberry had intended. Granted, Hansberry's main concern in the scene was the general relationship between the two older women and Beneatha, particularly their fond amusement at the younger woman's forms of self-expression, which are so different from anything they have ever done, and their vicarious delight at her ability to break free from restrictions, including that of having to weigh the cost of everything. However, on this rare occasion, by concentrating exclusively on the moment and neglecting to see its relation to previous parts of the play, Hansberry, to a small but disconcerting extent, damages the whole.

MARGARET B. WILKERSON

HANSBERRY'S AWARENESS OF CULTURE AND GENDER   [1994]

As a black writer, Hansberry was caught in a paradox of expectations. She was expected to write about that which she "knew best," the black experience, and yet that expression was doomed to be called parochial and narrow. Hansberry, however, challenged these facile categories and forced a redefinition of the term "universality," one which would include the dissonant voice of an oppressed American minority. As a young college student, she had wandered into a rehearsal of Sean O'Casey's *Juno and the Paycock.* Hearing in the wails and moans of the Irish characters a universal cry of human misery, she determined to capture that sound in the idiom of her own people—so that it could be heard by all. "One of the most sound ideas in dramatic writing," she would later conclude, "is that in order to create the universal, you must pay very great attention to the specific. Universality, I think, emerges from truthful identity of what is.... In other words, I think people, to the extent we accept them and believe them as who they're supposed to be, to that extent they can become everybody." Such a choice by a black writer posed an unusual challenge to the literary establishment and a divided society ill-prepared to comprehend its meaning.

"All art is ultimately social: that which agitates and that which prepares the mind for slumber," Hansberry argued, attacking another basic tenet held by traditional critics. One of the most fundamental illusions of her time and culture, she believed, is the idea that art is not and should not make a social statement. The belief in "l'art pour l'art" permeates literary and theatrical criticism, denying the integral relationship between society and art. "The writer is deceived who thinks he has some other choice. The question is not whether one will make a social statement in one's work—but only *what* the statement will say, for if it says anything at all, it will be social."

It would have been impossible for a person of her background and sensitivity to divorce herself from the momentous social and political events of the 1950s and 1960s. This period witnessed the beginning of a Cold War between the U.S. and Soviet superpowers, a rising demand by blacks for civil rights at home, and a growing intransigence by colonized peoples throughout the world. Isolation is the enemy of black writers, Hansberry believed; they are obligated to participate in the intellectual and social affairs of humankind everywhere.

This abhorrence for narrowness and parochialism led her to examine the hidden alliance between racism and sexism long before it was popular to do so, and to shape a vision cognizant of the many dimensions of colonialism and oppression. Anticipating the women's movement of the 1970s, Hansberry was already aware of the peculiar oppression under which women lived and the particular devastation visited upon women of color.

5   With the statement "I was born black and a female," Hansberry immediately established the basis for a tension that informed her world view. Her consciousness, of both ethnicity and gender from the very beginning, brought awareness of two key forces of conflict and oppression in the contemporary world. Because she embraced

these dual truths despite their implicit competition for her attention (a competition exacerbated by external pressures), her vision was expansive enough to contain and even synthesize what to others would be contradictions. Thus, she was amused in 1955 at progressive friends who protested whenever she posed "so much as an itsy-bitsy analogy between the situation, say, of the Negro people in the U.S.—and women." She was astonished to be accused by a woman of being bitter and of thinking that men are beasts simply because she expressed the view that women are oppressed. "Must I hate 'men' any more than I hate 'white people'—because some of them are savage and others commit savage acts," she asked herself. "Of course not!" she answered vehemently.

This recognition of the tension implicit in her blackness and femaleness was the starting point for her philosophical journey from the South Side of Chicago to the world community. The following quote charts the journey and the expansion of Hansberry's consciousness, which is unconstrained by culture and gender, but which at the same time refuses to diminish the importance of either.

> I was born on the South Side of Chicago. I was born black and a female. I was born in a depression after one world war, and came into my adolescence during another. While I was still in my teens the first atom bombs were dropped on human beings at Nagasaki and Hiroshima. And by the time I was twenty-three years old, my government and that of the Soviet Union had entered actively into the worst conflict of nerves in human history—the Cold War.
>
> I have lost friends and relatives through cancer, lynching, and war. I have been personally the victim of physical attack which was the offspring of racial and political hysteria. I have worked with the handicapped and seen the ravages of congenital diseases that we have not yet conquered, because we spend our time and ingenuity in far less purposeful wars; I have known persons afflicted with drug addiction and alcoholism and mental illness. I see daily on the streets of New York, street gangs and prostitutes and beggars. I have, like all of you, on a thousand occasions seen indescribable displays of man's very real inhumanity to man, and I have come to maturity, as we all must, knowing that greed and malice and indifference to human misery and bigotry and corruption, brutality, and perhaps above all else, ignorance—the prime ancient and persistent enemy of man—abound in this world.
>
> I say all of this to say that one cannot live with sighted eyes and feeling heart and not know and react to the miseries which afflict this world.

10   Her "sighted eyes and feeling heart" were what enabled her to hear the wail of her own people in O'Casey's *Juno and the Paycock,* a play steeped in Irish history and tradition. And those eloquent moans sent her forth to capture that collective cry in a black idiom.

Hansberry's cognizance of being black and female formed the basis for her comprehensive world view. Just as she could accept fully the implications and responsibility of both blackness and femaleness, so was she also aware of the many other competing and equally legitimate causes which grow out of humankind's misery. The one issue that deeply concerned her but that she did not address publicly was homosexuality. The repressive atmosphere of the 1950s, coupled with the homophobia of the general society, including politically left organizations, caused her to suppress her writings that explored issues of sexuality and gender relations. Nevertheless, she pushed and teased boundaries by probing the nature of the individual within the specifics of culture, ethnicity, and gender. In the midst of her expansiveness, she refused to diminish the pain, suffering, or truths of any one group in order to benefit another, a factor which made her plays particularly rich and her characters thoroughly complex. Hence, she could write authentically about a black family in *A Raisin in the Sun* and yet produce, in the same instance, a play which appealed to both blacks and whites, bridging for a moment the historical and cultural gaps between them.

Her universalism, which redefines that much abused term, grew out of a deep, complex encounter with the specific terms of human experience as it occurs for blacks, women, whites, and many other groups of people. Her universalism was not facile, nor did it gloss over the things that divide people. She engaged those issues, worked through them to find whatever may be, *a priori,* the human commonality that lies beneath. It was as if she believed that one can understand and embrace the human family (with all its familial warfare) only to the extent that one can engage the truths (however partisan they may seem) of a social, cultural individual. "We must turn our eyes outward," she wrote, "but to do so we must also turn them inward toward our people and their complex and still transitory culture." When she turned inward, she saw not only color but gender as well—a prism of humanity.

MICHAEL ANDERSON

A RAISIN IN THE SUN: *A LANDMARK LESSON IN BEING BLACK*   [1999]

They had never seen anything like it. The theater critics, hurrying down the aisles under the pressure of deadline, paused at the rear of the Ethel Barrymore Theater. The date was March 11, 1959. For a few moments they stopped considering the words with which they would salute this poetically named play, *A Raisin in the Sun*. Instead, they watched the first-night audience deliver its own verdict: on its feet and willing to applaud, it seemed, for eternity.

The cast took its curtain calls—Sidney Poitier, Claudia McNeil, Ruby Dee, Diana Sands, Lonne Elder 3d, Lou Gossett Jr., Ivan Dixon, Glynn Turman, John Fiedler, Ed Hall, Douglas Turner—as the applause engulfed the theater. The stage manager opened and closed the curtain. The director, Lloyd Richards, joined his players, but the ovations swelled ever louder and more insistent: "Author! Author! Author!"

Finally, Mr. Poitier descended to a fourth-row aisle seat, where the twenty-eight-year-old playwright sat, thrilled rigid at the reception of her first produced play. On the arm of her leading man, Lorraine Hansberry took the stage.

"It was as if the audience that night uniquely understood that they had not just seen a play but had attended a historical event," the play's coproducer, Philip Rose, said recently, reminiscing about the opening on the eve of its fortieth anniversary this Thursday.

5   In that remarkable theatrical season of 1958–59, Broadway had seen Paul Newman and Geraldine Page open (the previous night) in Tennessee Williams's

Sweet Bird of Youth, directed by Elia Kazan; Helen Hayes and Kim Stanley in *A Touch of the Poet* by Eugene O'Neill, directed by Harold Clurman; and Christopher Plummer and Raymond Massey in Archibald MacLeish's *J.B.,* also directed by Mr. Kazan.

But until that evening, Broadway had never seen a play written by a black woman, nor a play with a black director, nor a commercially produced drama about black life, rather than musicals or comedy. The Broadway premiere of *A Raisin in the Sun* was as much a milestone in the nation's social history as it was in American theater. "Never before," commented James Baldwin, "had so much of the truth of black people's lives been seen onstage."

Hansberry's story—about the black Younger family's decision to risk moving from their "rat-trap" on the South Side of Chicago to a three-bedroom house in an all-white neighborhood—interwove prescient observations about identity, feminism, and personal ethics. Unlike the wooden "problem plays" about blacks that preceded it, *A Raisin in the Sun* seemed steeped in human drama. The cruelties of racism—"What happens to a dream deferred/ Does it dry up/ Like a raisin in the sun?" in the words of the Langston Hughes poem that gave the play its title—are illuminated through the dynamics of conflict and love between mother and son, husband and wife, brother and sister.

Kenneth Tynan remarked in his review of *A Raisin in the Sun* in *The New Yorker* that "a play is not an entity in itself, it is a part of history." In that sense, the presence of the play on Broadway appeared to be a triumph of determined idealism for those involved. The 1960s would see productions of *The Blacks,* the drama by Jean Genet about racism, as well as works by the black playwrights LeRoi Jones (later Amiri Baraka) and Ed Bullins. Lonne Elder 3rd would go on to write the acclaimed 1969 play *Ceremonies in Dark Old Men.*

But in the 1950s, before the acclaim that greeted *A Raisin in the Sun,* "Broadway was not ready for a play about a black family," Mr. Richards, the director, said.

10   What Broadway knew about black people, Hansberry once told a reporter, involved "cardboard characters, cute dialect bits, or hip-swinging musicals from exotic scores." (And few enough of those: in the seventy-seven productions of the 1958–59 season, Actors Equity reported that the number of Broadway parts for black actors totaled twenty-four.)

The inspiration for *A Raisin in the Sun,* its author said, came after she had seen a play in 1956 that left her "disgusted with a whole body of material about Negroes." That night, she told her husband, Robert Nemiroff, "I'm going to write a social drama about Negroes that will be good art." But since devoting herself full-time to playwriting in 1955, she had accomplished little—drafts of three plays had gone nowhere beyond sympathetic readings by her husband and friends.

She expected much the same in the late summer of 1957, when she and Nemiroff invited company for a dinner of spaghetti and banana cream pie to their fourth-floor walk-up on Bleecker Street in Greenwich Village.

Then Nemiroff began to read from the work that had possessed his wife for nearly a year. This time it was different. "The feeling was one of excitement," Mr. Rose said, during an interview in his office on the Upper West Side of Manhattan. After an animated discussion that went on into the night, Mr. Rose called Hansberry early the next morning. "I told her," he said, " 'this play has to get done, and it has to get done on Broadway.' "

Mr. Rose would end up as a producer of nearly two dozen plays, including *Purlie Victorious* (1961), *The Owl and the Pussycat* (1964), and the musical *Shenandoah* (1975). But at the time, he was thirty-six years old and in the music business, producing and publishing. He said he had assumed that there would be difficulties in getting a work by a first-time playwright on the boards, but not that raising the money would take nearly fifteen agonizing months.

15   Networking among his friends brought a response "somewhere between admiration and pity," he said, along with donations of $50 toward what they regarded as a lost cause. Established theatrical backers were equally skeptical. "Much as some expressed admiration," Nemiroff wrote in his introduction to the Modern Library edition of *A Raisin in the Sun,* the play "was turned down by virtually every established name in the business."

The conventional wisdom was that "nobody was going to pay those prices to see "a bunch of Negroes emoting," Hansberry later said in a letter included in *To Be Young, Gifted and Black,* a collection of her writings. (Nemiroff assembled the book after Hansberry's death from cancer at thirty-four in 1965, during the run of her second Broadway play, *The Sign in Sidney Brustein's Window;* Nemiroff died in 1991.)

"Very often, the professionals were respectful, even admiring that I would think of trying to get the play on," said Mr. Rose, who is writing a book about the production. "However, they could not see where it would make any money."

He did have one ace: his friend Sidney Poitier. Already a movie star, the actor had agreed to join the cast after being "overwhelmed by the power of the material," as he wrote in his own memoir, *This Life.* "Without Sidney Poitier," Mr. Rose said, "the play would never have seen the light of day."

Mr. Poitier was also responsible for the director. "I had a pact with Sidney Poitier," Mr. Richards said in an interview at his home on the Upper West Side. It dated to their time as students of the director and drama teacher Paul Mann. "One day, after class, Sidney said, 'If I ever do anything on Broadway, I want you to direct it.'"

20   In December 1957, Mr. Poitier introduced Mr. Richards, already known as an actor, teacher, and director, to Mr. Rose and Hansberry. They clicked.

"There was no question that I wanted to do the play," Mr. Richards said, remembering that when he and his wife first read it, "We laughed and cried; it was a wonderful evening reading." Still, it was the work of a neophyte, and he and Hansberry struggled until opening night to develop her script. Although not autobiographical, the story originated from an incident in Hansberry's childhood.

Her parents, politically and socially prominent in Chicago's black upper-middle class, agreed in 1938 to take the lead in the fight against housing segregation by buying a home in an all-white neighborhood near the University of Chicago. Hansberry would always remember being an eight-year-old who was "spat at, cursed and pummeled in the daily trek to and from school." She also remembered the nights her mother patrolled their house with a loaded pistol against the "literally howling mobs" that surrounded their home and once threw bricks through their windows.

But the real story of the play, Mr. Rose said, was not the family's move to the unreceptive white neighborhood but Walter Lee Younger, the character portrayed by Mr. Poitier, "and his development, his being able to accept certain responsibilities." With this as the goal, playwright and director began their work.

Meanwhile, the tasks of production went on, including casting.

25   "*Raisin* was a big breakthrough," said Ruby Dee. "The mainstream was not welcoming for African-American actors." She signed on even though she would not have the ingenue role of Walter Lee's sister that she desired; Diana Sands got the part, while Claudia McNeil portrayed his mother. Instead, Ms. Dee would play his wife, Ruth. "Another one of those put-upon wives. And they always seemed to be named Ruth!" But, she added: "I dusted off my disappointment. This was very important. It was going to be a Broadway show."

It would be, that is, if the money could be raised. Throughout 1958, Mr. Rose sought big-money angels. "The smart money on Broadway was not involved and would not be involved," Mr. Richards said. The $75,000 budget (equivalent to more than $420,000 today) would eventually come from a group of 147 investors—"more than any play on Broadway had had up to that time," Mr. Richards said. Mr. Poitier's wife, Juanita, invested $4,000 and "about two or three people, including Harry Belafonte, put in $2,000 each," Mr. Rose said. But the most significant investor was the playwright William Gibson, whose *Two for the Seesaw* had opened a successful run with Anne Bancroft and Henry Fonda in January 1958.

"I sent him the play," Mr. Rose recalled. "He called me and said: 'This play must get on Broadway.'" With that endorsement (and Mr. Gibson's own stake of $750), his tax consultant, David J. Cogan, a previous Broadway investor who initially had rejected *A Raisin in the Sun,* signed on as coproducer, and the financing was complete. Rehearsals began on December 27, 1958.

There was only one problem: no theater on Broadway would agree to rent to *A Raisin in the Sun.* The same arguments were repeated: a white audience would not pay to see a nonmusical about blacks. The possibility of black theatergoers was dismissed out of hand. And if they did come, would white patrons stay away—perhaps even boycott other shows? In 1958, the Supreme Court's landmark school desegregation decision was four years old; not until February 1960 would the student sit-ins put the racial equality movement permanently before the nation's conscience. Even in the relatively urbane climate of the Village, an interracial couple like Hansberry and Nemiroff could expect stares and denial of service in some restaurants.

Mr. Rose said he was advised to terminate the production until he could obtain a theater. Instead, he took a gamble: he booked the traditional tryout theaters in New Haven and Philadelphia. "And I prayed a lot," he said. "But I knew if we didn't do it, nothing was going to get done. The hope was that we had something so spectacular, Broadway couldn't ignore us." His daring paid off. The rave reviews for the four-night engagement in New Haven were matched during the two-week run in Philadelphia.

30   *A Raisin in the Sun* ended up playing for nineteen months at the Ethel Barrymore on Broadway. Hansberry won the New York Drama Critics Circle Award for best play, and most of the original cast starred in the 1961 film version, directed by Daniel Petrie. The 1973 musical *Raisin* was adapted from the play and produced by Nemiroff. The play has been translated into thirty languages.

In retrospect, Mr. Rose can joke that during the prolonged incubation of *A Raisin in the Sun* he was discouraged "only about half the time." But his explanation for his stubborn determination is simple: "I believed in it. I loved the play."

A Student's Research Essay

In the research essay that follows, Sara Roell's thesis at the end of the first paragraph describes the mixed reaction of the African American community to Hansberry's play—as a "disagreement...about the motivation and the goals that Lorraine Hansberry had in mind when she wrote the play." Her thesis is, however, that Hansberry's intentions are clear. What makes this a research essay is not extensive research but rather the presence of secondary sources. In addition to her primary source, *A Raisin in the Sun,* Sara cites only five secondary sources—three from the casebook on the preceding pages, one from an academic journal, and one from a book. But those "outside" sources take Sara beyond her response to the play into a broader interpretive community and include her reaction to the response of other critics.

Sara Roell

Dr. Madden

English 102

December 12, 20XX

The Realism of A Raisin in the Sun

The issue of racism and the emergence of civil rights among black men and women is evident in Lorraine Hansberry's *A Raisin in the Sun*. The play, written in 1957, is an inspiring but at times wrenching depiction of a black family's struggle to achieve the American dream and escape the constraints of poverty. When the play first opened in the early years of the civil rights movement, there was a strong reaction by some in the black community to its harsh depiction of black family life and by others to the Youngers' desire to move into a white community. A black family moving into an all-white neighborhood was not common before this time period. And disagreement exists about the motivation and the goals Lorraine Hansberry had in mind when she wrote the play. Hansberry has been praised by many critics, but a number of critics write that they are uncomfortable with Hansberry's intentions.

Harold Cruse questions Hansberry's motivation for writing the play. He insists, "She intended to write a Negro play because she could not make her stage debut with anything else" (270). During that time the theater with his idealized self that he is unable to alter his plan even when faced with his mother's moral reservations. While Walter seems superficial on one level, it is understandable how this newfound insurance money contributes to his dreams of providing for himself and his family. He wants to provide pearls for his wife, Ruth, as other men do for their wives and says in frustration: "...who decides which women is supposed to wear pearls in this world. I tell you I am a *man*..." (Hansberry 365).

Racism in this play is expressed through the white character, Lindner, who represents the white majority of the time and, in all likelihood, many whites even now. A less obvious representation of the impact of racism is portrayed in the internal racial conflicts of the black characters themselves, especially Walter Lee Younger and his untrustworthy friend, Willy.

Walter's growth is evident as his focus changes from materialism to a conviction that his family should move into an all-white neighborhood where blacks aren't wanted. At this juncture, Walter realizes that what really gives his life worth is standing up for the principle that should be basic to all people, that all individuals have a basic right to choose where and how they live. Walter's decision to go forward with the move to the all-white neighborhood represents a victory for himself as a person and as a black male.

Walter finally tells Lindner that his family will move despite protests and monetary incentives. "Few see the heroism in Walter's simple act of assertion" in rejecting the white neighborhood association's offer to buy them out (Lester 379). Lindner is representative of the white majority of this time period. However, in his initial meeting with the Younger family his discomfort is evident when he realizes that the family members are open and likable. An example of this is when Ruth says, "Would you like another chair—you don't look comfortable" (Hansberry 351). Lindner has been stumbling on his words and cannot get directly to the point. It is interesting that Hansberry portrays this character as polite and unthreatening, although his message is racially motivated. Given the climate of the times and the subsequent racial strife that occurred in the United States during the 1960s, creating a character in this way took what could have been an even more politically charged issue and softened it so that a white majority could be more reflective about their own prejudices.

Although we never see or meet him, we know that Willy has a background similar to Walter's: he is a black man living in a racially oppressed ghetto. Despite the fact that he has a similar background, and has the same wants and needs as his friends, he steals the money. Racism and poverty provoke thinking like this by clouding a person's vision and making him feel entitled to have something he has never had an opportunity to acquire. Willy has no illusions about getting rich through Walter's liquor store. "You know Willy got his own ways" (Hansberry 357). He is street smart and is not bound by traditional moral codes or religious ideals that probably never worked in the past for him anyway. He lives in a neighborhood where if you need something, for the most part, you either do without it or get it any way you can.

These three characters, Walter Younger, Lindner, and Willy, are all dealing with racial issues that impact on them both globally and individually. In some ways, Willy and Lindner are more similar to each other than to Walter. They have learned to negotiate the racism in their environments differently, but both with narrow focus. Walter Younger, while initially focused on escaping his situation and the effect that racism has on it, ultimately rises to hurdle his internal conflicts and stand up for beliefs that give him his individual worth.

"*A Raisin in the Sun* is most definitely about 'human dignity,'" writes Julius Lester. "Lorraine Hansberry is concerned with the attitude we must have toward material things if we are to be their master and not their slave" (378). The play was introduced into a society just beginning to become aware of its many flaws, and people were challenged to change their actions and feelings about the controversial issue of race relations. The debatable issues surrounding this play are not important when considering the issues within the play, issues that are universal.

The struggle of Walter Lee and his family can be understood by everyone. The public reaction to the play when it was first produced is evidence of the ignorance that people had toward its issues. The embarrassing issue of racism was something America didn't want to face, but civil rights leaders, dramatists like Hansberry, and the people themselves who were suffering from it forced members of the white community to see what they didn't want to see. Anne Cheney suggests how Americans should view *A*

Raisin in the Sun: "Raisin at first seems a plea for racial tolerance or a fable of man's overcoming an insensitive society, but the simple eloquence of the characters elevates the play into a universal representation of all people's hopes, fears, and dreams" (380–81). And the realism in the play has stood the test of time. On the fortieth anniversary of the play's opening, Michael Anderson reminds us what James Baldwin said that first night: "Never before, had so much of the truth of black people's lives been seen onstage" (381). A Raisin in the Sun is a notable achievement in the history of realistic drama.

[New Page]

Works Cited

Adams, George R. "Black Literature: Black Militant Drama." *American Imago.*
    Vol. 28, No. 2. New York: Association for Applied Psychoanalysis, 1971.
    107–128. Print.

Anderson, Michael. "*A Raisin in the Sun:* A Landmark Lesson in Being
    Black." Madden 386–90.

Cheney, Anne. "The African Heritage in *A Raisin in the Sun.*" Madden 380–83.

Cruse, Harold. *Lorraine Hansberry: The Crisis of the Negro Intellectual.* New
    York: William Morrow & Company, Inc., 1967. 267–284. Print.

Hansberry, Lorraine. *A Raisin in the Sun.* Madden 310–69.

———. *To Be Young, Gifted and Black.* Adapted by Robert Nemiroff. New York:
    Vintage Books, 1969.

Lester, Julius. "The Heroic Dimension in *A Raisin in the Sun.*" Madden 378–80.

Madden, Frank, ed. *Exploring Literature.* 5th ed. New York: Longman,
    2012. Print.

EXPLORING THE LITERATURE OF FAMILY AND FRIENDS: OPTIONS FOR MAKING CONNECTIONS, BUILDING ARGUMENTS, AND USING RESEARCH

MAKING CONNECTIONS

1. Consider the ways in which your family or friends have affected your life. Do any of the stories, poems, plays, or essays in this section remind you of your relationships with family or friends?

    Choose one or more of these works and write a response essay that compares your experience or circumstances with those in the literature.

2. Our families and friends can influence and shape our values, our behavior, our aspirations. These values can also strongly influence our response to literature. We may agree or disagree with what an author says or what characters say or do. So, too, literature may influence us and the formation of our values about family and friends.

   Choose one or more works in this section and write an essay about the ways in which this literature either provoked your moral judgment or enabled you to learn something that influenced your values.

MAKING AN ARGUMENT

1. In his *Theory of Psychoanalysis,* Carl Jung, a pioneer and influential theorist in the field of psychology, wrote: "The little world of childhood with its familiar surroundings is a model of the greater world. The more intensely the family has stamped its character upon the child, the more it will tend to feel and see its earlier miniature world again in the bigger world of adult life."

   Consider this quote and write an argumentative essay about the way in which one or more works in this section exemplify the way that early family experiences influence how we see and experience the world.

2. Over two thousand years ago, Plato wrote in *Dialogues:* "Friends have all things in common." What do you think he meant?

   Are any of the selections in this section good examples of this adage about friendship? Write an argumentative essay about this quote and its application to one or more works in this section.

3. Choose a quote (or quotes) in the introduction to this section, Family and Friends (pp. 215–16), and pair it (or them) with one of the longer pieces in this section that either supports it or argues against it. For example, Benjamin Spock's statement about the instincts of parents to do what is best for their children might be paired with John Cheever's "Reunion," which might be seen as an argument against it. If we chose Jean de la Fontaine's comment about the impossibility of pleasing all the world and one's father, we might choose Janice Mirikitani's poem "For My Father" to qualify and to support de la Fontaine's statement.

   Write an essay that compares or contrasts a quote (or quotes) from the introduction with a story, poem, play, or essay that supports or argues against it.

USING RESEARCH

Janice Mirikitani's poem "For My Father," Marjane Satrapi's graphic narrative "The Dowry," and bell hooks's essay "Inspired Eccentricity" all have something important to say about family and friends. However insightful each of these pieces is by itself, expanding our exploration of literature by seeking, using, and citing relevant secondary sources can add support and credibility to our writing.

1. At the time she wrote *A Raisin in the Sun,* Lorraine Hansberry said that being the youngest sibling in her family had more of an impact on her life and attitude toward the world than being a woman or an African American. Choose one or more of the works in this section that address sibling relationships, and write an essay that includes secondary source material to support its argument. What does research say about birth order and sibling relationships in families? To what extent do "Sonny's Blues," "The Red Convertible," or *A Raisin in the Sun* support or contradict this research?

2. Consider Phillip Larkin's "This Be the Verse," and its concluding line "... don't have any kids yourself." Do you agree that, in general, parents mess up their kids' lives—whether they intend to or not? Explore the topic of "child rearing" and/or "parent-child" relationships and see what the research says. Write about one or more of the works in this section that deal with parent-child relationships, and support your argument by citing not only the literature in this section but also the secondary sources that support your interpretation.

3. The works in this section that deal directly with friendship seem to define it in a variety of ways. For example, Margaret Atwood's "Siren Song" seems to take a cynical view of "attachment," whereas William Stafford's "Friends" seems to view friendship in a more positive light. Beyond the works in this section, what research has been done to measure the importance of friends in our lives? Take a position of your own on the importance of friendship to a happy and healthy life, and write an essay that cites both the literature in this section and secondary sources.

Writing About Connections Across Themes

Most of the literature in the text has been organized into theme sections, but good literature is much too complex to be reduced to a single broad theme. Many of the works included under Family and Friends could just as easily fit under other themes—and in many cases works arranged in other themes could fit here as well.

Choose one or more of the following works from earlier chapters or other themes and consider how they can be linked to Family and Friends—and how this combination of the work with more than one theme provides additional insight into the literature and fresh topics for writing.

From Chapter 1
"Advice to My Son"—p. 9
"Those Winter Sundays"—p. 13
From Chapter 2
"Mothers"—p. 31
"Salvation"—p. 32

Collaboration: Writing and Revising with Your Peers

In addition to applying your own values and standards to writing about the literature in this section, you may find it beneficial to share and discuss your work with classmates. Getting feedback from others can help you generate and clarify your ideas and revise and edit your writing more effectively.

Choose a work, a topic, or one of the options for writing about family and friends above, and work with a partner or in a small group. Exchange journal entries or response sheets, generate questions together, do a group semantic map (see p. 41), or simply share and respond to each other's ideas.

After you have written a rough draft of your essay, share it with a partner or your group. Respondents should function primarily as sensitive readers and give honest, constructive responses. They should try to be aware of each writer's purpose, discuss concerns particular to each writer, and comment on the effectiveness of the essay's organization, support, clarity, and voice (for a checklist for revision, see p. 48).

In the final stage of your writing, editing and proofreading might be done in a similar fashion. A partner or group of readers might help you check for correct grammar, spelling, punctuation, and typos (a checklist for editing is on p. 52).

A Writing/Research Portfolio Option

A portfolio is a collection of your work, related materials, and commentary about your work collected over time. Gathering materials in a portfolio will provide you with resources for research and development. You can use your portfolio to collect your writing about the literature in this section, find a topic to write about, revise or add to your work, or keep multiple drafts and monitor the changes you make as you revise. Among the resources you might include:

- Your responses to the quotes and prompts about family and friends at the beginning of this section, the questions you had right after you finished reading each piece of literature, or your journal entries.

- What your classmates, instructor, or published critics had to say about the literature and how their comments may have influenced your interpretation.

- Information you have gathered from the library and the Internet about the historical, social, and political context of the work or its author.

Innocence & Experience

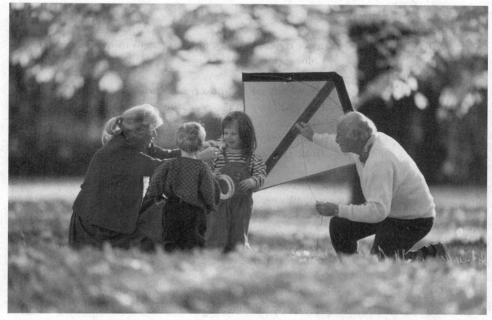

Innocence & Experience

A DIALOGUE ACROSS HISTORY

Experience is a comb which nature gives us when we are bald.
   —Chinese proverb

The life which is unexamined is not worth living.
   —Plato, 428–348 BCE, *Symposium*

The mind is always the dupe of the heart.
   —Duke Francois de La Rochefoucauld, *Maxims,* 1665

*Crime like virtue has its degrees; and timid innocence was never
known to blossom suddenly into extreme license.*
   —Jean Racine, *Phedre,* 1677

We live and learn, but not the wiser grow.
   —John Pomfret, *Reason,* 1702

*I have but one lamp by which my feet are guided, and that is the
lamp of experience, [judging] the future by the past.*
   —Patrick Henry, speech, 1775

Ignorance is not innocence but sin.
   —Robert Browning, *The Inn Album,* 1875

*Education is an admirable thing, but it is well to remember from
time to time that nothing worth knowing can be taught.*
   —Oscar Wilde, "The Critic as Artist," 1890

A man's errors are his portals of discovery.
   —James Joyce, 1882–1941, Irish novelist

You cannot create experience, you undergo it.
   —Albert Camus, 1935–1942, *Notebooks*

I used to be Snow White—but I drifted.
   —Mae West, *The Wit and Wisdom of Mae West*

The turning point in the process of growing up is when you discover the core of strength within you that survives all hurt.
    —Max Lerner, *The Unfinished Country*, 1950

Experience is not what happens to you; it is what you do with what happens to you.
    —Aldous Huxley, *Reader's Digest*, 1956

Experience is a hard teacher because [it] gives the test first, the lesson after.
    —Vernon Law, *This Week*, 1960

Tis e'er the lot of the innocent in the world to fly to the wolf for succor from the lion.
    —John Barth, *The Sot-Weed Factor*, 1960

How many roads must a man walk down / Before you call him a man?
    —Bob Dylan, "Blowin' in the Wind," 1962

All I Really Need To Know I Learned in Kindergarten
    —Robert Fulghum, book title, 1993

Our genetic heritage endows each of us with a series of emotional setpoints that determines our temperament. But the brain circuitry involved is extraordinarily malleable....
This means that childhood and adolescence are critical windows of opportunity for setting down the essential emotional habits that will govern our lives.
    —Daniel Goleman, *Emotional Intelligence*, 1995

INNOCENCE AND EXPERIENCE: EXPLORING YOUR OWN VALUES AND BELIEFS

What comes to mind when you hear the word *innocence*? Do you think of innocence as being "good"? Or do you think of innocence as being naïve, uninformed, or inexperienced? Is the "loss" of innocence really a loss—or is it a gain of knowledge? Does experience bring wisdom? Or is it what we do with our experiences—in ourselves and in the world—that brings wisdom? Must we learn from all experiences? Or should we try to forget some experiences and move on as best we can?

Innocence is most often associated with childhood and growing up. The world is relatively new to us as children, and our understanding of the world is relatively simple. We are very impressionable, and our hopes and expectations are often measured against the ideals that we have learned from the well-intentioned adults around us. As we make the passage from child to adult, however, we realize through experience—often abruptly and painfully—that the world is a much more complex, uncertain, and hostile place than we had imagined as children.

Our experiences remain with us for the duration of our lives. The nature of those experiences—especially our experiences growing up—can have a powerful impact on us. For better or worse, they will influence our values and our behavior. We may feel crushed and defeated by them or enlightened and strengthened by them. And as we encounter issues of innocence and experience in the literature we read, we will naturally compare them to similar circumstances in our own lives. As a preparation for reading the literature in this section, you may want to think about the way that important personal experiences have shaped your own values and beliefs.

READING AND WRITING ABOUT INNOCENCE AND EXPERIENCE

Exploring your beliefs and values and connecting your experiences with what you read is an important first step toward our ultimate goal—an appreciation of literature and the ability to think and write critically about it. Critical analysis will require rereading and reflection, writing and revising, gathering evidence, and constructing a solid argument to support your responses.

At least one aspect of the many stories, poems, plays, and essays in this section is about the impact that an experience or the loss of innocence has on characters: a young boy's overwhelming crush on his friend's older sister—and subsequent disappointment—in James Joyce's short story "Araby," a young girl's disillusionment as she realizes her "place" at a birthday party in Liliana Heker's short story "The Stolen Party," a young man's experience of the death of a sibling in Seamus Heaney's poem "Mid-Term Break," and the humor with which David Sedaris describes his first experience teaching writing. The quotes that open this section also give you some idea of the number of compelling emotions that are connected to innocence and experience. Issues of unrequited love, disillusionment, loneliness, loyalty, comfort, and self-realization head a long list of concerns. Any of these or other related issues might provide a fine topic for an essay.

◆ FICTION ◆

CONNECTING THROUGH COMPARISON: ILLUSION AND DISILLUSION

The two stories that follow are about two different topics. Liliana Heker's "The Stolen Party" addresses the issue of social and economic class, whereas James Joyce's "Araby" is a story about young infatuation. Both, however, explore what it means to experience an epiphany—a moment when both characters see the truth of their situations. Read and discussed together they invite comparisons and connections, not only with each other—but with your own experience of disillusionment.

LILIANA HEKER [B. 1943]

Liliana Heker is a native of Argentina. She was editor in chief of two literary magazines, the Escarahajo de Oro, *and the* Ornitorrinco *("The Platypus"), for over twenty-five years—an era that coincided with Argentina's descent into chaos under military dictatorships. Her works include* Those That Saw the Bramble *(1966),* Zona de Clivage *(1988),* The Edges of the Real Thing *(1991), and* The Aim of History *(1996). "The Stolen Party" was published in Spanish in 1982 and translated into English by Alberto Manguel. It was also published in 1985 in a collection of short stories,* Other Fires: Short Fiction by Latin American Women. *Her latest book,* La Crueldad de La Vida, *was published in 2001.*

THE STOLEN PARTY   [1982]

As soon as she arrived she went straight to the kitchen to see if the monkey was there. It was: what a relief! She wouldn't have liked to admit that her mother had been right. *Monkeys at a birthday?* her mother had sneered. *Get away with you, believing any nonsense you're told!* She was cross, but not because of the monkey, the girl thought; it's just because of the party.

"I don't like you going," she told her. "It's a rich people's party."

"Rich people go to Heaven too," said the girl, who studied religion at school.

"Get away with Heaven," said the mother. "The problem with you, young lady, is that you like to fart higher than your ass."

5   The girl didn't approve of the way her mother spoke. She was barely nine, and one of the best in her class.

"I'm going because I've been invited," she said. "And I've been invited because Luciana is my friend. So there."

"Ah yes, your friend," her mother grumbled. She paused. "Listen, Rosaura," she said at last. "That one's not your friend. You know what you are to them? The maid's daughter, that's what."

Rosaura blinked hard: she wasn't going to cry. Then she yelled: "Shut up! You know nothing about being friends!"

Every afternoon she used to go to Luciana's house and they would both finish their homework while Rosaura's mother did the cleaning. They had their tea in the kitchen and they told each other secrets. Rosaura loved everything in the big house, and she also loved the people who lived there.

10 "I'm going because it will be the most lovely party in the whole world, Luciana told me it would. There will be a magician, and he will bring a monkey and everything."

The mother swung around to take a good look at her child, and pompously put her hands on her hips.

"Monkeys at a birthday?" she said. "Get away with you, believing any nonsense you're told!"

Rosaura was deeply offended. She thought it unfair of her mother to accuse other people of being liars simply because they were rich. Rosaura too wanted to be rich, of course. If one day she managed to live in a beautiful palace, would her mother stop loving her? She felt very sad. She wanted to go to that party more than anything else in the world.

"I'll die if I don't go," she whispered, almost without moving her lips.

15 And she wasn't sure whether she had been heard, but on the morning of the party she discovered that her mother had starched her Christmas dress. And in the afternoon, after washing her hair, her mother rinsed it in apple vinegar so that it would be all nice and shiny. Before going out, Rosaura admired herself in the mirror, with her white dress and glossy hair, and thought she looked terribly pretty.

Señora Ines also seemed to notice. As soon as she saw her, she said:

"How lovely you look today, Rosaura."

Rosaura gave her starched skirt a slight toss with her hands and walked into the party with a firm step. She said hello to Luciana and asked about the monkey. Luciana put on a secretive look and whispered into Rosaura's ear: "He's in the kitchen. But don't tell anyone, because it's a surprise."

Rosaura wanted to make sure. Carefully she entered the kitchen and there she saw it: deep in thought, inside its cage. It looked so funny that the girl stood there for a while, watching it, and later, every so often, she would slip out of the party unseen and go and admire it. Rosaura was the only one allowed into the kitchen. Señora Ines had said: "You yes, but not the others, they're much too boisterous, they might break something." Rosaura had never broken anything. She even managed the jug of orange juice, carrying it from the kitchen into the dining room. She held it carefully and didn't spill a single drop. And Señora Ines had said: "Are you sure you can manage a jug as big as that?" Of course she could manage. She wasn't a butterfingers, like the others. Like that blonde girl with the bow in her hair. As soon as she saw Rosaura, the girl with the bow had said:

20 "And you? Who are you?"

"I'm a friend of Luciana," said Rosaura.

"No," said the girl with the bow, "you are not a friend of Luciana because I'm her cousin and I know all her friends. And I don't know you."

"So what," said Rosaura. "I come here every afternoon with my mother and we do our homework together."

"You and your mother do your homework together?" asked the girl, laughing.

25   "I and Luciana do our homework together," said Rosaura, very seriously.
       The girl with the bow shrugged her shoulders.
       "That's not being friends," she said. "Do you go to school together?"
       "No."
       "So where do you know her from?" said the girl, getting impatient.
30   Rosaura remembered her mother's words perfectly. She took a deep breath.
       "I'm the daughter of the employee," she said.
       Her mother had said very clearly: "If someone asks, you say you're the daughter
of the employee; that's all." She also told her to add: "And proud of it." But Rosaura
thought that never in her life would she dare say something of the sort.
       "What employee?" said the girl with the bow. "Employee in a shop?"
       "No," said Rosaura angrily. "My mother doesn't sell anything in any shop, so
there."
35   "So how come she's an employee?" said the girl with the bow.
       Just then Señora Ines arrived saying *shh shh,* and asked Rosaura if she wouldn't
mind helping serve out the hotdogs, as she knew the house so much better than
the others.
       "See?" said Rosaura to the girl with the bow, and when no one was looking she
kicked her in the shin.
       Apart from the girl with the bow, all the others were delightful. The one she
liked best was Luciana, with her golden birthday crown; and then the boys.
Rosaura won the sack race, and nobody managed to catch her when they played
tag. When they split into two teams to play charades, all the boys wanted her
for their side. Rosaura felt she had never been so happy in all her life.
       But the best was still to come. The best came after Luciana blew out the
candles. First the cake. Señora Ines had asked her to help pass the cake around,
and Rosaura had enjoyed the task immensely, because everyone called out to her,
shouting "Me, me!" Rosaura remembered a story in which there was a queen who
had the power of life or death over her subjects. She had always loved that, having
the power of life or death. To Luciana and the boys she gave the largest pieces, and
to the girl with the bow she gave a slice so thin one could see through it.
40   After the cake came the magician, tall and bony, with a fine red cape. A true
magician: he could untie handkerchiefs by blowing on them and make a chain
with links that had no openings. He could guess what cards were pulled out from
a pack, and the monkey was his assistant. He called the monkey "partner." "Let's
see here, partner," he would say, "turn over a card." And, "Don't run away, partner:
time to work now."
       The final trick was wonderful. One of the children had to hold the monkey in
his arms and the magician said he would make him disappear.
       "What, the boy?" they all shouted.
       "No, the monkey!" shouted back the magician.
       Rosaura thought that this was truly the most amusing party in the whole world.
45   The magician asked a small fat boy to come and help, but the small fat boy
got frightened almost at once and dropped the monkey on the floor. The magician
picked him up carefully, whispered something in his ear, and the monkey nodded
almost as if he understood.

"You mustn't be so unmanly, my friend," the magician said to the fat boy.

"What's unmanly?" said the fat boy.

The magician turned around as if to look for spies.

"A sissy," said the magician. "Go sit down."

50   Then he stared at all the faces, one by one. Rosaura felt her heart tremble.

"You, with the Spanish eyes," said the magician. And everyone saw that he was pointing at her.

She wasn't afraid. Neither holding the monkey, nor when the magician made him vanish; not even when, at the end, the magician flung his red cape over Rosaura's head and uttered a few magic words...and the monkey reappeared, chattering happily, in her arms. The children clapped furiously. And before Rosaura returned to her seat, the magician said:

"Thank you very much, my little countess."

She was so pleased with the compliment that a while later, when her mother came to fetch her, that was the first thing she told her.

55   "I helped the magician and he said to me, 'Thank you very much, my little countess.' "

It was strange because up to then Rosaura had thought that she was angry with her mother. All along Rosaura had imagined that she would say to her: "See that the monkey wasn't a lie?" But instead she was so thrilled that she told her mother all about the wonderful magician.

Her mother tapped her on the head and said: "So now we're a countess!"

But one could see that she was beaming.

And now they both stood in the entrance, because a moment ago Señora Ines, smiling, had said: "Please wait here a second."

60   Her mother suddenly seemed worried.

"What is it?" she asked Rosaura.

"What is what?" said Rosaura. "It's nothing; she just wants to get the presents for those who are leaving, see?"

She pointed at the fat boy and at a girl with pigtails who were also waiting there, next to their mothers. And she explained about the presents. She knew, because she had been watching those who left before her. When one of the girls was about to leave, Señora Ines would give her a bracelet. When a boy left, Señora Ines gave him a yo-yo. Rosaura preferred the yo-yo because it sparkled, but she didn't mention that to her mother. Her mother might have said: "So why don't you ask for one, you blockhead?" That's what her mother was like. Rosaura didn't feel like explaining that she'd be horribly ashamed to be the odd one out. Instead she said:

"I was the best-behaved at the party."

65   And she said no more because Señora Ines came out into the hall with two bags, one pink and one blue.

First she went up to the fat boy, gave him a yo-yo out of the blue bag, and the fat boy left with his mother. Then she went up to the girl and gave her a bracelet out of the pink bag, and the girl with the pigtails left as well.

Finally she came up to Rosaura and her mother. She had a big smile on her face and Rosaura liked that. Señora Ines looked down at her, then looked up at her mother, and then said something that made Rosaura proud:

"What a marvelous daughter you have, Herminia."

For an instant, Rosaura thought that she'd give her two presents: the bracelet and the yo-yo. Señora Ines bent down as if about to look for something. Rosaura also leaned forward, stretching out her arm. But she never completed the movement.

70   Señora Ines didn't look in the pink bag. Nor did she look in the blue bag. Instead she rummaged in her purse. In her hand appeared two bills.

"You really and truly earned this," she said handing them over. "Thank you for all your help, my pet."

Rosaura felt her arms stiffen, stick close to her body, and then she noticed her mother's hand on her shoulder. Instinctively she pressed herself against her mother's body. That was all. Except her eyes. Rosaura's eyes had a cold, clear look that fixed itself on Señora Ines's face.

Señora Ines, motionless, stood there with her hand outstretched. As if she didn't dare draw it back. As if the slightest change might shatter an infinitely delicate balance.

JAMES JOYCE [1882–1941]

(See biography on p. 201.)

ARABY   [1914]

North Richmond Street, being blind, was a quiet street except at the hour when the Christian Brothers' School set the boys free. An uninhabited house of two stories stood at the blind end, detached from its neighbors in a square ground. The other houses of the street, conscious of decent lives within them, gazed at one another with brown imperturbable faces.

The former tenant of our house, a priest, had died in the back drawing-room. Air, musty from having been long enclosed, hung in all the rooms, and the waste room behind the kitchen was littered with old useless papers. Among these I found a few paper-covered books, the pages of which were curled and damp: *The Abbot,*[1] by Walter Scott, *The Devout Communicant*[2] and *The Memoirs of Vidocq.*[3] I liked the last best because its leaves were yellow. The wild garden behind the house contained a central apple-tree and a few straggling bushes under one of which I found the late tenant's rusty bicycle-pump. He had been a very charitable priest; in his will he had left all his money to institutions and the furniture of his house to his sister.

When the short days of winter came dusk fell before we had well eaten our dinners. When we met in the street the houses had grown sombre. The space of sky above us was the colour of ever-changing violet and towards it the lamps of the street lifted their feeble lanterns. The cold air stung us and we played till our bodies glowed. Our shouts echoed in the silent street. The career of our play brought us through the dark muddy lanes behind the houses where we

---

[1]*The Abbot* an early-nineteenth-century romantic novel   [2]*The Devout Communicant* a religious text   [3]*The Memoirs of Vidocq* the memoirs of a French secret service agent

ran the gauntlet of the rough tribes from the cottages, to the back doors of the dark dripping gardens where odours arose from the ashpits, to the dark odorous stables where a coachman smoothed and combed the horse or shook music from the buckled harness. When we returned to the street light from the kitchen windows had filled the areas. If my uncle was seen turning the corner we hid in the shadow until we had seen him safely housed. Or if Mangan's sister came out on the doorstep to call her brother in to his tea we watched her from our shadow peer up and down the street. We waited to see whether she would remain or go in and, if she remained, we left our shadow and walked up to Mangan's steps resignedly. She was waiting for us, her figure defined by the light from the half-opened door. Her brother always teased her before he obeyed and I stood by the railings looking at her. Her dress swung as she moved her body and the soft rope of her hair tossed from side to side.

Every morning I lay on the floor in the front parlour watching her door. The blind was pulled down to within an inch of the sash so that I could not be seen. When she came out on the doorstep my heart leaped. I ran to the hall, seized my books and followed her. I kept her brown figure always in my eye and, when we came near the point at which our ways diverged, I quickened my pace and passed her. This happened morning after morning. I had never spoken to her, except for a few casual words, and yet her name was like a summons to all my foolish blood.

5   Her image accompanied me even in places the most hostile to romance. On Saturday evenings when my aunt went marketing I had to go to carry some of the parcels. We walked through the flaring streets, jostled by drunken men and bargaining women, amid the curses of labourers, the shrill litanies of shop-boys who stood on guard by the barrels of pigs' cheeks, the nasal chanting of street-singers, who sang a *come-all-you* about O'Donovan Rossa, or a ballad about the troubles in our native land. These noises converged in a single sensation of life for me: I imagined that I bore my chalice safely through a throng of foes. Her name sprang to my lips at moments in strange prayers and praises which I myself did not understand. My eyes were often full of tears (I could not tell why) and at times a flood from my heart seemed to pour itself out into my bosom. I thought little of the future. I did not know whether I would ever speak to her or not or, if I spoke to her, how I could tell her of my confused adoration. But my body was like a harp and her words and gestures were like fingers running upon the wires.

One evening I went into the back drawing-room in which the priest had died. It was a dark rainy evening and there was no sound in the house. Through one of the broken panes I heard the rain impinge upon the earth, the fine incessant needles of water playing in the sodden beds. Some distant lamp or lighted window gleamed below me. I was thankful that I could see so little. All my senses seemed to desire to veil themselves and, feeling that I was about to slip from them, I pressed the palms of my hands together until they trembled, murmuring: "*O love! O love!*" many times.

At last she spoke to me. When she addressed the first words to me I was so confused that I did not know what to answer. She asked me was I going to Araby.

I forget whether I answered yes or no. It would be a splendid bazaar, she said; she would love to go.

"And why can't you?" I asked.

While she spoke she turned a silver bracelet round and round her wrist. She could not go, she said, because there would be a retreat that week in her convent.[4] Her brother and two other boys were fighting for their caps and I was alone at the railings. She held one of the spikes, bowing her head towards me. The light from the lamp opposite our door caught the white curve of her neck, lit up her hair that rested there and, falling, lit up the hand upon the railing. It fell over one side of her dress and caught the white border of a petticoat, just visible as she stood at ease.

10   "It's well for you," she said.

"If I go," I said, "I will bring you something."

What innumerable follies laid waste my waking and sleeping thoughts after that evening! I wished to annihilate the tedious intervening days. I chafed against the work of school. At night in my bedroom and by day in the classroom her image came between me and the page I strove to read. The syllables of the word *Araby* were called to me through the silence in which my soul luxuriated and cast an Eastern enchantment over me. I asked for leave to go to the bazaar on Saturday night. My aunt was surprised and hoped it was not some Freemason affair. I answered few questions in class. I watched my master's face pass from amiability to sternness; he hoped I was not beginning to idle. I could not call my wandering thoughts together. I had hardly any patience with the serious work of life which, now that it stood between me and my desire, seemed to me child's play, ugly monotonous child's play.

On Saturday morning I reminded my uncle that I wished to go to the bazaar in the evening. He was fussing at the hall-stand, looking for the hat-brush, and answered me curtly:

"Yes, boy, I know."

15   As he was in the hall I could not go into the front parlour and lie at the window. I left the house in bad humour and walked slowly towards the school. The air was pitilessly raw and already my heart misgave me.

When I came home to dinner my uncle had not yet been home. Still it was early. I sat staring at the clock for some time and, when its ticking began to irritate me, I left the room. I mounted the staircase and gained the upper part of the house. The high cold empty gloomy rooms liberated me and I went from room to room singing. From the front window I saw my companions playing below in the street. Their cries reached me weakened and indistinct and, leaning my forehead against the cool glass, I looked over at the dark house where she lived. I may have stood there for an hour, seeing nothing but the brown-clad figure cast by my imagination, touched discreetly by the lamplight at the curved neck, at the hand upon the railings and at the border below the dress.

When I came downstairs again I found Mrs. Mercer sitting at the fire. She was an old garrulous woman, a pawnbroker's widow, who collected used stamps

[4]**convent** in this case a parochial school for girls

for some pious purpose. I had to endure the gossip of the tea-table. The meal was prolonged beyond an hour and still my uncle did not come. Mrs. Mercer stood up to go: she was sorry she couldn't wait any longer, but it was after eight o'clock and she did not like to be out late, as the night air was bad for her. When she had gone I began to walk up and down the room, clenching my fists. My aunt said:

"I'm afraid you may put off your bazaar for this night of Our Lord."

At nine o'clock I heard my uncle's latchkey in the halldoor. I heard him talking to himself and heard the hallstand rocking when it had received the weight of his overcoat. I could interpret these signs. When he was midway through his dinner I asked him to give me the money to go to the bazaar. He had forgotten.

20   "The people are in bed and after their first sleep now," he said.

I did not smile. My aunt said to him energetically:

"Can't you give him the money and let him go? You've kept him late enough as it is."

My uncle said he was very sorry he had forgotten. He said he believed in the old saying: "All work and no play makes Jack a dull boy." He asked me where I was going and, when I had told him a second time he asked me did I know *The Arab's Farewell to His Steed*. When I left the kitchen he was about to recite the opening lines of the piece to my aunt.

I held a florin tightly in my hand as I strode down Buckingham Street towards the station. The sight of the streets thronged with buyers and glaring with gas recalled to me the purpose of my journey. I took my seat in a third-class carriage of a deserted train. After an intolerable delay the train moved out of the station slowly. It crept onward among ruinous houses and over the twinkling river. At Westland Row Station a crowd of people pressed to the carriage doors; but the porters moved them back, saying that it was a special train for the bazaar. I remained alone in the bare carriage. In a few minutes the train drew up beside an improvised wooden platform. I passed out on to the road and saw by the lighted dial of a clock that it was ten minutes to ten. In front of me was a large building which displayed the magical name.

25   I could not find any sixpenny entrance and, fearing that the bazaar would be closed, I passed in quickly through a turnstile, handing a shilling to a weary-looking man. I found myself in a big hall girdled at half its height by a gallery. Nearly all the stalls were closed and the greater part of the hall was in darkness. I recognized a silence like that which pervades a church after a service. I walked into the center of the bazaar timidly. A few people were gathered about the stalls which were still open. Before a curtain, over which the words *Café Chantant* were written in coloured lamps, two men were counting money on a salver. I listened to the fall of the coins.

Remembering with difficulty why I had come I went over to one of the stalls and examined porcelain vases and flowered tea-sets. At the door of the stall a young lady was talking and laughing with two young gentlemen. I remarked their English accents and listened vaguely to their conversation.

"O, I never said such a thing!"

"O, but you did!"

"O, but I didn't!"

30   "Didn't she say that?"

"Yes. I heard her."

"O, there's a...fib!"

Observing me the young lady came over and asked me did I wish to buy any-thing. The tone of her voice was not encouraging; she seemed to have spoken to me out of a sense of duty. I looked humbly at the great jars that stood like eastern guards at either side of the dark entrance to the stall and murmured:

"No, thank you."

35   The young lady changed the position of one of the vases and went back to the two young men. They began to talk of the same subject. Once or twice the young lady glanced at me over her shoulder.

I lingered before her stall, though I knew my stay was useless, to make my in-terest in her wares seem the more real. Then I turned away slowly and walked down the middle of the bazaar. I allowed the two pennies to fall against the sixpence in my pocket. I heard a voice call from one end of the gallery that the light was out. The upper part of the hall was now completely dark.

Gazing up into the darkness I saw myself as a creature driven and derided by vanity; and my eyes burned with anguish and anger.

MAKING CONNECTIONS: ILLUSION AND DISILLUSION

1. Discuss the relationship between Rosaura and her mother in "The Stolen Party." Do you think it's a good one? Do they learn anything from each other? Pick out passages in the story that illustrate their relationship.

2. Why do you think the story is called "The Stolen Party"? What has been "stolen"? Explain.

3. What is the point of view of this story? What impact does this narrative perspective have on the story? If the story were told by Señora Ines, how would it be different?

4. To what extent does your own experience with a crush influence your response to James Joyce's "Araby"?

5. Describe the setting of the story. How are you affected by the personification in the first paragraph? Is North Richmond street "blind" only because it's a dead-end street? Do you think the setting is an appropriate background for the boy's feelings? To what extent are the changes in setting related to his emotions?

6. Who is the narrator? How old is he at the time of the story? Is the story told in the "voice" of a child or an adult? What difference does that make in the telling and in your response?

7. What aspects of the boy's reactions illustrate his feelings for Mangan's sister? Do you think the boy's crush is believable? Do people behave like this when they are "smitten"? Explain.

8. To what extent is the Araby bazaar symbolic of the boy's crush on Mangan's sister? What other symbols can you find?

MAKING AN ARGUMENT

1. Is Señora Ines a rich snob? Or is she just trying to be nice to Rosaura? Or something else? Take a position and write an essay that interprets the characters, the conflict, and the theme of this story. Cite the text of the story for support.

2. At the end of "Araby," the boy sees himself "as a creature driven and derided by vanity." Why? Is this a loss of innocence? Was he really in love? Is his disappointment only about love? Write an essay that interprets this story in light of Joyce's characterization of the boy, the conflict, and the outcome. Cite the text of the story for support.

3. Compare "The Stolen Party" with "Araby." In both stories the protagonists experience an epiphany—a moment when they see the "truth" of their situations. But these stories are about very different topics. In what way are the stories alike? In what way different? Support your views with evidence from the text.

JULIA ALVAREZ [b. 1954]

(See biography on pp. 271–272.)

SNOW   [1991]

Our first year in New York we rented a small apartment with a Catholic school nearby, taught by the Sisters of Charity, hefty women in long black gowns and bonnets that made them look peculiar, like dolls in mourning. I liked them a lot, especially my grandmotherly fourth grade teacher, Sister Zoe. I had a lovely name, she said, and she had me teach the whole class how to pronounce it. *Yo-lan-da.* As the only immigrant in my class, I was put in a special seat in the first row by the window, apart from the other children so that Sister Zoe could tutor me without disturbing them. Slowly, she enunciated the new words I was to repeat: *laundromat, cornflakes, subway, snow.*

Soon I picked up enough English to understand holocaust was in the air. Sister Zoe explained to a wide-eyed classroom what was happening in Cuba. Russian missiles were being assembled, trained supposedly on New York City. President Kennedy, looking worried too, was on the television at home, explaining we might have to go to war against the Communists. At school, we had air-raid drills: an ominous bell would go off and we'd file into the hall, fall to the floor, cover our heads with our coats, and imagine our hair falling out, the bones in our arms going soft. At home, Mami and my sisters and I said a rosary for world peace. I heard new vocabulary: *nuclear bomb, radioactive fallout, bomb shelter.* Sister Zoe explained how it would happen. She drew a picture of a mushroom on the blackboard and dotted a flurry of chalkmarks for the dusty fallout that would kill us all.

The months grew cold, November, December. It was dark when I got up in the morning, frosty when I followed my breath to school. One morning as I sat at my desk daydreaming out the window, I saw dots in the air like the ones Sister Zoe had drawn—random at first, then lots and lots. I shrieked, "Bomb! Bomb!" Sister

Zoe jerked around, her full black skirt ballooning as she hurried to my side. A few girls began to cry.

But then Sister Zoe's shocked look faded. "Why, Yolanda dear, that's snow!" She laughed. "Snow."

5   "Snow," I repeated. I looked out the window warily. All my life I had heard about the white crystals that fell out of American skies in the winter. From my desk I watched the fine powder dust the sidewalk and parked cars below. Each flake was different, Sister Zoe said, like a person, irreplaceable and beautiful.

MAKING CONNECTIONS

1. Why is the snowfall such a shocking experience for the narrator? What does she think is falling from the sky?
2. This story is told from the first-person point of view. How would it change if told in the third person?
3. At the end of this brief story, Sister Zoe tries to calm Yolanda by telling her each snowflake "was different…like a person, irreplaceable and beautiful." Do you think her explanation of snow is comforting? Why?
4. What has the narrator learned, and how has she learned it?

MAKING AN ARGUMENT

1. Both "Snow" and Sandra Cisneros's "Eleven" on page 26 are stories of classroom experiences told in the first person, but one narrator is an adult looking back and the other is a child "in the moment." Compare their narrative voices and write about the effectiveness of narration in each story. Cite the language of both stories for support.

TONI CADE BAMBARA [1939–1995]

Toni Cade Bambara was born in New York City and raised in the impoverished neighborhoods of Harlem and Bedford-Stuyvesant, New York, and Jersey City, New Jersey. Born Toni Cade, she added the name Bambara after discovering it as part of a signature in her great-grandmother's sketchbook. She attended Queens College, where she majored in Theater Arts and English, graduating in 1959. Before turning to writing, she worked for the New York Department of Welfare, served as a director of recreation in a psychiatric ward, studied theater at the famous Commedia dell'Arte in Italy, ran a local community center, and earned an M.A. from the City University of New York. She began her writing career editing anthologies of black women writers and African American stories, but first attracted attention with her collections of short stories Gorilla, My Love *(1972) and* The Sea Birds Are Still Alive *(1977). She died of cancer in 1995. Her most recent publication,* Deep Sightings and Rescue Missions: Fiction, Essays, and Conversations *(1996), was published posthumously. In an interview in* Black Women Writers at Work, *she said: "It's a*

tremendous responsibility—responsibility and honor—to be a writer, an artist, a cul-
tural worker…One's got to see what the factory worker sees, what the prisoner sees,
what the welfare children see, what the scholar sees, got to see what the ruling-class
mythmakers see as well, in order to tell the truth and not get trapped."

THE LESSON   [1972]

Back in the days when everyone was old and stupid or young and foolish and me
and Sugar were the only ones just right, this lady moved on our block with nappy
hair and proper speech and no makeup. And quite naturally we laughed at her,
laughed the way we did at the junk man who went about his business like he was
some big-time president and his sorryass horse his secretary. And we kinda hated
her too, hated the way we did the winos who cluttered up our parks and pissed on
our handball walls and stank up our hallways and stairs so you couldn't-halfway
play hide-and-seek without a goddamn gas mask. Miss Moore was her name. The
only woman on the block with no first name. And she was black as hell, cept for
her feet, which were fish-white and spooky. And she was always planning these
boring-ass things for us to do, us being my cousin, mostly, who lived on the block
cause we all moved North the same time and to the same apartment then spread
out gradual to breathe. And our parents would yank our heads into some kinda
shape and crisp up our clothes so we'd be presentable for travel with Miss Moore,
who always looked like she was going to church, though she never did. Which is
just one of the things the grownups talked about when they talked behind her back
like a dog. But when she came calling, with some sachet she'd sewed up or some
gingerbread she'd made or some book, why then they'd still be too embarrassed to
turn her down and we'd get handed over all spruced up. She'd been to college and
said it was only right that she should take responsibility for the young ones' education, and she not even related by marriage or blood. So they'd go for it. Specially
Aunt Gretchen. She was the main gofer in the family. You got some ole dumb shit
foolishness you want somebody to go for, you send for Aunt Gretchen. She been
screwed into the go-along for so long, it's a blood-deep natural thing with her.
Which is how she got saddled with me and Sugar and junior in the first place while
our mothers were in a la-de-da apartment up the block having a good ole time.

So this one day Miss Moore rounds us all up at the mailbox and it's puredee
hot and she's knockin herself out about arithmetic. And school suppose to let up in
summer I heard, but she don't never let up. And the starch in my pinafore scratching the shit outta me and I'm really hating this nappy-head bitch and her goddamn
college degree. I'd much rather go to the pool or to the show where it's cool. So
me and Sugar leaning on the mailbox being surly, which is a Miss Moore word. And
Flyboy checking out what everybody brought for lunch. And Fat Butt already wasting his peanut butter-and-jelly sandwich like the pig he is. And Junebug punchin
on Q.T.'s arm for potato chips. And Rosie Giraffe shifting from one hip to the other
waiting for somebody to step on her foot or ask her if she from Georgia so she can
kick ass, preferably Mercedes'. And Miss Moore asking us do we know what money
is, like we a bunch of retards. I mean real money, she say, like it's only poker chips
or monopoly papers we lay on the grocer. So right away I'm tired of this and say

so. And would much rather snatch Sugar and go to the Sunset and terrorize the West Indian kids and take their hair ribbons and their money too. And Miss Moore files that remark away for next week's lesson on brotherhood, I can tell. And finally I say we oughta get to the subway cause it's cooler and besides we might meet some cute boys. Sugar done swiped her mama's lipstick, so we ready.

So we heading down the street and she's boring us silly about what things cost and what our parents make and how much goes for rent and how money ain't divided up right in this country. And then she gets to the part about we all poor and live in the slums, which I don't feature. And I'm ready to speak on that, but she steps out in the street and hails two cabs just like that. Then she hustles half the crew in with her and hands me a five-dollar bill and tells me to calculate 10 percent tip for the driver. And we're off. Me and Sugar and Junebug and Flyboy hangin out the window and hollering to everybody, putting lipstick on each other cause Flyboy a faggot anyway, and making farts with our sweaty armpits. But I'm mostly trying to figure how to spend this money. But they all fascinated with the meter ticking and Junebug starts laying bets as to how much it'll read when Flyboy can't hold his breath no more. Then Sugar lays bets as to how much it'll be when we get there. So I'm stuck. Don't nobody want to go for my plan, which is to jump out at the next light and run off to the first bar-b-que we can find. Then the driver tells us to get the hell out cause we there already. And the meter reads eighty-five cents. And I'm stalling to figure out the tip and Sugar say give him a dime. And I decide he don't need it bad as I do, so later for him. But then he tries to take off with Junebug foot still in the door so we talk about his mama something ferocious. Then we check out that we on Fifth Avenue and everybody dressed up in stockings. One lady in a fur coat, hot as it is. White folks crazy.

"This is the place," Miss Moore say, presenting it to us in the voice she uses at the museum. "Let's look in the windows before we go in."

5   "Can we steal?" Sugar asks very serious like she's getting the ground rules squared away before she plays. "I beg your pardon," say Miss Moore, and we fall out. So she leads us around the windows of the toy store and me and Sugar screamin, "This is mine, that's mine, I gotta have that, that was made for me, I was born for that," till Big Butt drowns us out.

"Hey, I'm going to buy that there."

"That there? You don't even know what it is, stupid."

"I do so," he say punchin on Rosie Giraffe. "It's a microscope."

"Whatcha gonna do with a microscope, fool?"

10   "Look at things."

"Like what, Ronald?" ask Miss Moore. And Big Butt ain't got the first notion. So here go Miss Moore gabbing about the thousands of bacteria in a drop of water and the somethin or other in a speck of blood and the million and one living things in the air around us is invisible to the naked eye. And what she say that for? Junebug go to town on that "naked" and we rolling. Then Miss Moore ask what it cost. So we all jam into the window smudgin it up and the price tag say $300. So then she ask how long'd take for Big Butt and Junebug to save up their allowances. "Too long," I say. "Yeh," adds Sugar, "outgrown it by that time." And, Miss Moore say no, you never outgrow learning instruments. "Why, even medical students and interns and," blah, blah, blah. And we ready to choke Big Butt for bringing it up in the first damn place.

"This here costs four hundred eighty dollars," say Rosie Giraffe. So we pile up all over her to see what she pointin out. My eyes tells me it's a chunk of glass cracked with something heavy, and different-color inks dripped into the splits, then the whole thing put into a oven or something. But for $480 it don't make sense.

"That's a paperweight made of semi-precious stones fused together under tremendous pressure," she explains slowly, with her hands doing the mining and all the factory work.

"So what's a paperweight?" asks Rosie Giraffe.

15   "To weigh paper with, dumbbell," say Flyboy, the wise man from the East.

"Not exactly," say Miss Moore, which is what she say when you warm or way off too. "It's to weigh paper down so it won't scatter and make your desk untidy." So right away me and Sugar curtsy to each other and then to Mercedes who is more the tidy type.

"We don't keep paper on top of the desk in my class," say Junebug, figuring Miss Moore crazy or lyin one.

"At home, then," she say. "Don't you have a calendar and a pencil case and a blotter and a letter-opener on your desk at home where you do your homework?" And she know damn well what our homes look like cause she nosys around in them every chance she gets.

"I don't even have a desk," say Junebug. "Do we?"

20   "No. And I don't get no homework neither," says Big Butt.

"And I don't even have a home," say Flyboy like he do at school to keep the white folks off his back and sorry for him. Send this poor kid to camp posters, is his specialty.

"I do," says Mercedes. "I have a box of stationery on my desk and a picture of my cat. My godmother bought the stationery and the desk. There's a big rose on each sheet and the envelopes smell like roses."

"Who wants to know about your smelly-ass stationery," say Rosie Giraffe fore I can get my two cents in.

"It's important to have a work area all your own so that..."

25   "Will you look at this sailboat, please," say Flyboy, cuttin her off and pointin to the thing like it was his.

So once again we tumble all over each other to gaze at this magnificent thing in the toy store which is just big enough to maybe sail two kittens across the pond if you strap them to the posts tight. We all start reciting the price tag like we in assembly. "Hand-crafted sailboat of fiberglass at one thousand one hundred ninety-five dollars."

"Unbelievable," I hear myself say and am really stunned. I read it again for myself just in case the group recitation put me in a trance. Same thing. For some reason this pisses me off. We look at Miss Moore and she lookin at us, waiting for I dunno what.

"Who'd pay all that when you can buy a sailboat set for a quarter at Pop's, a tube of glue for a dime, and a ball of string for eight cents? It must have a motor and a whole lot else besides," I say. "My sailboat cost me about fifty cents."

"But will it take water?" say Mercedes with her smart ass.

30   "Took mine to Alley Pond Park once," say Flyboy. "String broke. Lost it. Pity."
        "Sailed mine in Central Park and it keeled over and sank. Had to ask my father for another dollar."
        "And you got the strap," laugh Big Butt. "The jerk didn't even have a string on it. My old man wailed on his behind."
        Little Q.T. was staring hard at the sailboat and you could see he wanted it bad. But he too little and somebody'd just take it from him. So what the hell. "This boat for kids, Miss Moore?"
        "Parents silly to buy something like that just to get all broke up," say Rosie Giraffe.
35   "That much money it should last forever," I figure.
        "My father'd buy it for me if I wanted it."
        "Your father, my ass," say Rosie Giraffe getting a chance to finally push Mercedes.
        "Must be rich people shop here," say Q.T.
        "You are a very bright boy," say Flyboy. "What was your first clue?" And he rap him on the head with the back of his knuckles, since Q.T. the only one he could get away with. Though Q.T. liable to come up behind you years later and get his licks in when you half expect it.
40   "What I want to know is," I says to Miss Moore though I never talk to her, I wouldn't give the bitch that satisfaction, "is how much a real boat costs? I figure a thousand'd get you a yacht any day."
        "Why don't you check that out," she says, "and report back to the group?" Which really pains my ass. If you gonna mess up a perfectly good swim day least you could do is have some answers. "Let's go in," she say like she got something up her sleeve. Only she don't lead the way. So me and Sugar turn the corner to where the entrance is, but when we get there I kinda hang back. Not that I'm scared, what's there to be afraid of, just a toy store. But I feel funny, shame. But what I got to be shamed about? Got as much right to go in as anybody. But somehow I can't seem to get hold of the door, so I step away for Sugar to lead. But she hangs back too. And I look at her and she looks at me and this is ridiculous. I mean, damn, I have never ever been shy about doing nothing or going nowhere. But then Mercedes steps up and then Rosie Giraffe and Big Butt crowd in behind and shove, and next thing we all stuffed into the doorway with only Mercedes squeezing past us, smoothing out her jumper and walking right down the aisle. Then the rest of us tumble in like a glued-together jigsaw done all wrong. And people lookin at us. And it's like the time me and Sugar crashed into the Catholic church on a dare. But once we got in there and everything so hushed and holy and the candles and the bowin and the handkerchiefs on all the drooping heads, I just couldn't go through with the plan. Which was for me to run up to the altar and do a tap dance while Sugar played the nose flute and messed around in the holy water. And Sugar kept given me the elbow. Then later teased me so bad I tied her up in the shower and turned it on and locked her in. And she'd be there till this day if Aunt Gretchen hadn't finally figured I was lyin about the boarder takin a shower.
        Same thing in the store. We all walkin on tiptoe and hardly touchin the games and puzzles and things. And I watched Miss Moore who is steady watchin us like

she waitin for a sign. Like Mama Drewery watches the sky and sniffs the air and takes note of just how much slant is in the bird formation. Then me and Sugar bump smack into each other, so busy gazing at the toys, 'specially the sailboat. But we don't laugh and go into our fat-lady bump-stomach routine. We just stare at that price tag. Then Sugar run a finger over the whole boat. And I'm jealous and want to hit her. Maybe not her, but I sure want to punch somebody in the mouth.

"Watcha bring us here for, Miss Moore?"

"You sound angry, Sylvia. Are you mad about something?" Given me one of them grins like she tellin a grown-up joke that never turns out to be funny. And she's lookin very closely at me like maybe she plannin to do my portrait from memory. I'm mad, but I won't give her that satisfaction. So I slouch around the store bein very bored and say, "Let's go."

45   Me and Sugar at the back of the train watchin the tracks whizzin by large then small then gettin gobbled up in the dark. I'm thinkin about this tricky toy I saw in the store. A clown that somersaults on a bar then does chin-ups just cause you yank lightly at his leg. Cost $35. I could see me askin my mother for a $35 birthday clown. "You wanna who that costs what?" she'd say, cocking her head to the side to get a better view of the hole in my head. Thirty-five dollars could buy new bunk beds for junior and Gretchen's boy. Thirty-five dollars and the whole household could go visit Granddaddy Nelson in the country. Thirty-five dollars would pay for the rent and the piano bill too. Who are these people that spend that much for performing clowns and $1000 for toy sailboats? What kinda work they do and how they live and how come we ain't in on it? Where we are is who we are, Miss Moore always pointin out. But it don't necessarily have to be that way, she always adds then waits for somebody to say that poor people have to wake up and demand their share of the pie and don't none of us know what kind of pie she talking about in the first damn place. But she ain't so smart cause I still got her four dollars from the taxi and she sure ain't gettin it. Messin up my day with this shit. Sugar nudges me in my pocket and winks.

Miss Moore lines us up in front of the mailbox where we started from, seem like years ago, and I got a headache for thinkin so hard. And we lean all over each other so we can hold up under the draggy-ass lecture she always finishes us off with at the end before we thank her for borin us to tears. But she just looks at us like she readin tea leaves. Finally she say, "Well, what did you think of F.A.O. Schwartz?"

Rosie Giraffe mumbles, "White folks crazy."

"I'd like to go there again when I get my birthday money," says Mercedes, and we shove her out the pack so she has to lean on the mailbox by herself.

"I'd like a shower. Tiring day," say Flyboy.

50   Then Sugar surprises me by sayin, "You know, Miss Moore, I don't think all of us here put together eat in a year what that sailboat costs." And Miss Moore lights up like somebody goosed her. "And?" she say, urging Sugar on. Only I'm standin on her foot so she don't continue.

"Imagine for a minute what kind of society it is in which some people can spend on a toy what it would cost to feed a family of six or seven. What do you think?"

"I think," say Sugar pushing me off her feet like she never done before, cause I whip her ass in a minute, "that this is not much of a democracy if you ask me. Equal chance to pursue happiness means an equal crack at the dough, don't it?"

Miss Moore is beside herself and I am disgusted with Sugar's treachery. So I stand on her foot one more time to see if she'll shove me. She shuts up, and Miss Moore looks at me, sorrowfully I'm thinkin. And somethin weird is goin on, I can feel it in my chest.

"Anybody else learn anything today?" lookin dead at me. I walk away and Sugar has to run to catch up and don't even seem to notice when I shrug her arm off my shoulder.

"Well, we got four dollars anyway," she says.

55   "Uh hunh."

"We could go to Hascombs and get half a chocolate layer and then go to the Sunset and still have plenty money for potato chips and ice cream sodas."

"Uh hunh."

"Race you to Hascombs," she say.

We start down the block and she gets ahead which is O.K. by me cause I'm going to the West End and then over to the Drive to think this day through. She can run if she want to and even run faster. But ain't nobody gonna beat me at nuthin.

MAKING CONNECTIONS

1. Have you ever learned a lesson in school or elsewhere that was not necessarily intended but has given you an insight you would not have otherwise had? Explain.

2. You might say that this story is told from the point of view of a "hostile witness." How did you respond to the speaker? To the events she describes? How would the story change if told from Miss Moore's point of view?

3. Describe the narrator's relationship to Sugar. In what ways is this relationship important to the narrator? How is the relationship developed throughout the story?

4. Think about the final paragraph of the story. Has the narrator changed? If so, why? What does she tell us about herself and her future?

5. What is it that Miss Moore wants these children to experience? Why does she bring poor inner-city adolescents to a store where they can't afford anything? What has been learned in this story, and how was it learned? Explain.

MAKING AN ARGUMENT

1. In the quotations that open this theme, Aldous Huxley is quoted as saying: "Experience is not what happens to you; it is what you do with what happens to you." Do you agree? What difference would that distinction make for the children in the story? What could they "do" with this experience? Write about this quote as it applies to this story. Cite the text of the story for support.

2. Both this story and "Snow" on page 412 are about learning experiences that are prompted by the "setting" of the story. Compare these stories, and write about the way that setting contributes to their impact, meaning, or emotion.

THOMAS BULFINCH [1796–1867]

Thomas Bulfinch was born in Newton, Massachusetts, the son of one of the most prominent architects of the time. During most of his life he worked as a clerk at the Merchant's Bank of Boston, a post that allowed him the leisure to pursue his many other interests, which included writing. His most enduring works are his three collections of myths and fables, The Age of Fables *(1855),* The Age of Chivalry *(1858), and* Legends of Charlemagne *(1863), which are now reprinted under the title* Bulfinch's Mythology. *Bulfinch's approach to the ancient myths may seem dated by twenty-first-century standards, but his learned and vigorous retellings of these tales remain timeless.*

THE MYTH OF DAEDALUS AND ICARUS   [1855]

The labyrinth from which Theseus escaped, by means of the clew of Ariadne was built by Daedalus, a most skilful artificer. It was an edifice with numberless winding passages and turnings opening into one another, and seeming to have neither beginning nor end, like the river Maeander, which returns on itself, and flows now onward, now backward, in its course to the sea. Daedalus built the labyrinth for King Minos, but afterwards lost the favor of the king, and was shut up in a tower. He contrived to make his escape from his prison, but could not leave the island by sea, as the king kept strict watch on all the vessels, and permitted none to sail without being carefully searched. "Minos may control the land and sea," said Daedalus, "but not the regions of the air. I will try that way." So he set to work to fabricate wings for himself and his young son Icarus. He wrought feathers together, beginning with the smallest and adding larger, so as to form an increasing surface. The larger ones he secured with thread and the smaller with wax, and gave the whole a gentle curvature like the wings of a bird. Icarus, the boy, stood and looked on, sometimes running to gather up the feathers which the wind had blown away, and then handling the wax and working it over with his fingers, by his play impeding his father in his labors. When at last the work was done, the artist, waving his wings, found himself buoyed upward, and hung suspended, poising himself on the beaten air. He next equipped his son in the same manner, and taught him how to fly, as a bird tempts her young ones from the lofty nest into the air. When all was prepared for flight he said, "Icarus, my son, I charge you to keep at a moderate height, for if you fly too low the damp will clog your wings, and if too high the heat will melt them. Keep near me and you will be safe." While he gave him these instructions and fitted the wings to his shoulders, the face of the father was wet with tears, and his hands trembled. He kissed the boy, not knowing that it was for the last time. Then rising on his wings, he flew off, encouraging him to follow, and looked back from his own flight to see how his son managed his wings. As they flew the ploughman stopped his work to gaze, and the shepherd leaned on his staff and watched them, astonished at the sight, and thinking they were gods who could thus cleave the air.

They passed Samos and Delos on the left and Lebynthos on the right, when the boy, exulting in his career, began to leave the guidance of his companion and soar upward as if to reach heaven. The nearness of the blazing sun softened the wax which held the feathers together, and they came off. He fluttered with his arms, but no feathers remained to hold the air. While his mouth uttered cries to his father it was submerged in the blue waters of the sea, which thenceforth was called by his name. His father cried, "Icarus, Icarus, where are you?" At last he saw the feathers floating on the water, and bitterly lamenting his own arts, he buried the body and called the land Icaria in memory of his child. Daedalus arrived safe in Sicily where he built a Temple to Apollo, and hung up his wings, an offering to the gods.

MAKING CONNECTIONS

1. Is there a lesson to be learned in this myth? Explain.
2. Daedalus warned Icarus about flying too high. Why does he bitterly lament his own arts?

MAKING AN ARGUMENT

1. Look at Brueghel's painting of this myth, *Landscape with the Fall of Icarus,* on page 644 and the two poems written in response to the painting. Does the painting capture what you felt after reading "The Myth of Daedalus and Icarus"? Do the poems? Identify the theme of the myth, and write an essay comparing the effectiveness of each medium in conveying that theme. Cite the texts of the myth and the poems for support.

RALPH ELLISON [1914–1994]

Ralph Waldo Ellison was born in Oklahoma and was named after the famous nineteenth-century writer Ralph Waldo Emerson. He was educated at the Tuskegee Institute where he majored in music. The short story below, "Battle Royal," is an excerpt from his novel Invisible Man, *which won the National Book Award in 1953 and was widely praised for its depiction of the plight of African Americans. In addition to his fiction writing, Ellison frequently wrote essays (many of them about music), gave interviews about race relations, and was Albert Schweitzer Professor of the Humanities at New York University.*
The Collected Essays of Ralph Ellison *was published in 1995, and an unfinished novel,* Juneteenth *(completed by John Callahan), was published in 1999.*

BATTLE ROYAL   [1953]

It goes a long way back, some twenty years. All my life I had been looking for something, and everywhere I turned someone tried to tell me what it was. I accepted their answers too, though they were often in contradiction and even self-contradictory.

I was naïve. I was looking for myself and asking everyone except myself questions which I, and only I, could answer. It took me a long time and much painful boomer-anging of my expectations to achieve a realization everyone else appears to have been born with: That I am nobody but myself. But first I had to discover that I am an invisible man!

And yet I am no freak of nature, nor of history. I was in the cards, other things having been equal (or unequal) eighty-five years ago. I am not ashamed of my grandparents for having been slaves. I am only ashamed of myself for having at one time been ashamed. About eighty-five years ago they were told that they were free, united with others of our country in everything pertaining to the com-mon good, and, in everything social, separate like the fingers of the hand. And they believed it. They exulted in it. They stayed in their place, worked hard, and brought up my father to do the same. But my grandfather is the one. He was an odd old guy, my grandfather, and I am told I take after him. It was he who caused the trouble. On his deathbed he called my father to him and said, "Son, after I'm gone I want you to keep up the good fight. I never told you, but our life is a war and I have been a traitor all my born days, a spy in the enemy's country ever since I give up my gun back in the Reconstruction. Live with your head in the lion's mouth. I want you to overcome 'em with yeses, undermine 'em with grins, agree 'em to death and destruction, let 'em swoller you till they vomit or bust wide open." They thought the old man had gone out of his mind. He had been the meekest of men. The younger children were rushed from the room, the shades drawn and the flame of the lamp turned so low that it sputtered on the wick like the old man's breathing. "Learn it to the younguns," he whispered fiercely; then he died.

But my folks were more alarmed over his last words than over his dying. It was as though he had not died at all, his words caused so much anxiety. I was warned emphatically to forget what he had said and, indeed, this is the first time it has been mentioned outside the family circle. It had a tremendous effect upon me, however. I could never be sure of what he meant. Grandfather had been a quiet old man who never made any trouble, yet on his deathbed he had called himself a traitor and a spy, and he had spoken of his meekness as a dangerous activity. It became a constant puzzle which lay unanswered in the back of my mind. And whenever things went well for me I remembered my grandfather and felt guilty and uncomfortable. It was as though I was carrying out his advice in spite of myself. And to make it worse, everyone loved me for it. I was praised by the most lily-white men of the town. I was considered an example of desirable conduct—just as my grandfather had been. And what puzzled me was that the old man had defined it as *treachery*. When I was praised for my conduct I felt a guilt that in some way I was doing something that was really against the wishes of the white folks, that if they had understood they would have desired me to act just the opposite, that I should have been sulky and mean, and that that really would have been what they wanted, even though they were fooled and thought they wanted me to act as I did. It made me afraid that some day they would look upon me as a traitor and I would be lost. Still I was more afraid to act any other way because they didn't like that at all. The old man's words were like a curse. On my graduation day I delivered an oration in which I showed that humility was the secret, indeed, the very essence of progress. (Not that I believed this—how could I, remembering my grandfather?—I only believed that it worked.) It was a great success. Everyone praised me and I was invited to give the speech at a gathering of the town's leading white citizens. It was a triumph for our whole community.

It was in the main ballroom of the leading hotel. When I got there I discovered that it was on the occasion of a smoker, and I was told that since I was to be there anyway I might as well take part in the battle royal to be fought by some of my schoolmates as part of the entertainment. The battle royal came first.

5   All of the town's big shots were there in their tuxedoes, wolfing down the buffet foods, drinking beer and whiskey and smoking black cigars. It was a large room with a high ceiling. Chairs were arranged in neat rows around three sides of a portable boxing ring. The fourth side was clear, revealing a gleaming space of polished floor. I had some misgivings over the battle royal, by the way. Not from a distaste for fighting, but because I didn't care too much for the other fellows who were to take part. They were tough guys who seemed to have no grandfather's curse worrying their minds. No one could mistake their toughness. And besides, I suspected that fighting a battle royal might detract from the dignity of my speech. In those pre-invisible days I visualized myself as a potential Booker T. Washington. But the other fellows didn't care too much for me either, and there were nine of them. I felt superior to them in my way, and I didn't like the manner in which we were all crowded together into the servants' elevator. Nor did they like my being there. In fact, as the warmly lighted floors flashed past the elevator we had words over the fact that I, by taking part in the fight, had knocked one of their friends out of a night's work.

We were led out of the elevator through a rococo hall into an anteroom and told to get into our fighting togs. Each of us was issued a pair of boxing gloves and ushered out into the big mirrored hall, which we entered looking cautiously about us and whispering, lest we might accidentally be heard above the noise of the room. It was foggy with cigar smoke. And already the whiskey was taking effect. I was shocked to see some of the most important men of the town quite tipsy. They were all there—bankers, lawyers, judges, doctors, fire chiefs, teachers, merchants. Even one of the more fashionable pastors. Something we could not see was going on up front. A clarinet was vibrating sensuously and the men were standing up and moving eagerly forward. We were a small tight group, clustered together, our bare upper bodies touching and shining with anticipatory sweat; while up front the big shots were becoming increasingly excited over something we still could not see. Suddenly I heard the school superintendent, who had told me to come, yell. "Bring up the shines, gentlemen! Bring up the little shines!"

We were rushed up to the front of the ballroom, where it smelled even more strongly of tobacco and whiskey. Then we were pushed into place. I almost wet my pants. A sea of faces, some hostile, some amused, ringed around us, and in the center, facing us, stood a magnificent blonde—stark naked. There was dead silence. I felt a blast of cold air chill me. I tried to back away, but they were behind me and around me. Some of the boys stood with lowered heads, trembling. I felt a wave of irrational guilt and fear. My teeth chattered, my skin turned to goose flesh, my knees knocked. Yet I was strongly attracted and looked in spite of myself. Had the price of looking been blindness, I would have looked. The hair was yellow like that of a circus kewpie doll, the face heavily powdered and rouged, as though to form an abstract mask, the eyes hollow and smeared a cool blue, the color of a baboon's butt. I felt a desire to spit upon her as my eyes brushed slowly over her body. Her breasts were firm and round as the domes of East Indian temples, and I stood so close as to see the fine skin texture and beads of pearly perspiration glistening like dew around the pink and erected buds of her nipples. I wanted at one and the same time to run from the room, to sink through the floor, or go to her and cover her from my eyes and the eyes of the others with my body; to feel the soft thighs, to caress her and destroy her, to love her and murder her, to hide from her, and yet to stroke where below the small American flag tattooed upon her belly her thighs formed a capital V. I had a notion that of all in the room she saw only me with her impersonal eyes.

And then she began to dance, a slow sensuous movement; the smoke of a hundred cigars clinging to her like the thinnest of veils. She seemed like a fair bird-girl girdled in veils calling to me from the angry surface of some gray and threatening sea. I was transported. Then I became aware of the clarinet playing and the big shots yelling at us. Some threatened us if we looked and others if we did not. On my right I saw one boy faint. And now a man grabbed a silver pitcher from a table and stepped close as he dashed ice water upon him and stood him up and forced two of us to support him as his head hung and moans issued from his thick bluish lips. Another boy began to plead to go home. He was the largest of the group, wearing dark red fighting trunks much too small to conceal the erection which projected from him as though in answer to the insinuating low-registered moans of the clarinet. He tried to hide himself with his boxing gloves.

And all the while the blonde continued dancing, smiling faintly at the big shots who watched her with fascination, and faintly smiling at our fear. I noticed a certain merchant who followed her hungrily, his lips loose and drooling. He was a large man who wore diamond studs in a shirtfront which swelled with the ample paunch underneath, and each time the blonde swayed her undulating hips he ran his hand through the thin hair of his bald head and, with his arms upheld, his posture clumsy like that of an intoxicated panda, wound his belly in a slow and obscene grind. This creature was completely hypnotized. The music had quickened. As the dancer flung herself about with a detached expression on her face, the men began reaching out to touch her. I could see their beefy fingers sink into her soft flesh. Some of the others tried to stop them and she began to move around the floor in graceful circles, as they gave chase, slipping and sliding over the polished floor. It was mad. Chairs went crashing, drinks were spilt, as they ran laughing and howling after her. They caught her just as she reached a door, raised her from the floor, and tossed her as college boys are tossed at a hazing, and above her red, fixed-smiling lips I saw the terror and disgust in her eyes, almost like my own terror and that which I saw in some of the other boys. As I watched, they tossed her twice and her soft breasts seemed to flatten against the air and her legs flung wildly as she spun. Some of the more sober ones helped her to escape. And I started off the floor, heading for the anteroom with the rest of the boys.

10   Some were still crying and in hysteria. But as we tried to leave we were stopped and ordered to get into the ring. There was nothing to do but what we were told.

All ten of us climbed under the ropes and allowed ourselves to be blindfolded with broad bands of white cloth. One of the men seemed to feel a bit sympathetic and tried to cheer us up as we stood with our backs against the ropes. Some of us tried to grin. "See that boy over there?" one of the men said. "I want you to run across at the bell and give it to him right in the belly. If you don't get him, I'm going to get you. I don't like his looks." Each of us was told the same. The blindfolds were put on. Yet even then I had been going over my speech. In my mind each word was as bright as flame. I felt the cloth pressed into place, and frowned so that it would be loosened when I relaxed.

But now I felt a sudden fit of blind terror. I was unused to darkness. It was as though I had suddenly found myself in a dark room filled with poisonous cotton-mouths. I could hear the bleary voices yelling insistently for the battle royal to begin.

"Get going in there!"

"Let me at that big nigger!"

I strained to pick up the school superintendent's voice, as though to squeeze some security out of that slightly more familiar sound.

15   "Let me at those black sonsabitches!" someone yelled.

"No, Jackson, no!" another voice yelled. "Here, somebody, help me hold Jack."

"I want to get at that ginger-colored nigger. Tear him limb from limb," the first voice yelled.

I stood against the ropes trembling. For in those days I was what they called ginger-colored, and he sounded as though he might crunch me between his teeth like a crisp ginger cookie.

Quite a struggle was going on. Chairs were being kicked about and I could hear voices grunting as with a terrific effort. I wanted to see, to see more desperately than ever before. But the blindfold was as tight as a thick skin-puckering scab and when I raised my gloved hands to push the layers of white aside a voice yelled, "Oh, no you don't, black bastard! Leave that alone!"

20   "Ring the bell before Jackson kills him a coon!" someone boomed in the sudden silence. And I heard the bell clang and the sound of the feet scuffling forward.

A glove smacked against my head. I pivoted, striking out stiffly as someone went past, and felt the jar ripple along the length of my arm to my shoulder. Then it seemed as though all nine of the boys had turned upon me at once. Blows pounded me from all sides while I struck out as best I could. So many blows landed upon me that I wondered if I were not the only blindfolded fighter in the ring, or if the man called Jackson hadn't succeeded in getting me after all.

Blindfolded, I could no longer control my motions. I had no dignity. I stumbled about like a baby or a drunken man. The smoke had become thicker and with each new blow it seemed to sear and further restrict my lungs. My saliva became like hot bitter glue. A glove connected with my head, filling my mouth with warm blood. It was everywhere. I could not tell if the moisture I felt upon my body was sweat or blood. A blow landed hard against the nape of my neck. I felt myself going over, my head hitting the floor. Streaks of blue light filled the black world behind the blindfold. I lay prone, pretending that I was knocked out, but felt myself seized by hands and yanked to my feet. "Get going, black boy! Mix it up!" My arms were like lead, my head smarting from blows. I managed to feel my way to the ropes and held on, trying to catch my breath. A glove landed in my midsection and I went over again, feeling as though the smoke had become a knife jabbed into my guts. Pushed this way and that by the legs milling around me, I finally pulled erect and discovered that I could see the black, sweat-washed forms weaving in the smoky-blue atmosphere like drunken dancers weaving to the rapid drum-like thuds of blows.

Everyone fought hysterically. It was complete anarchy. Everybody fought everybody else. No group fought together for long. Two, three, four, fought one, then turned to fight each other, were themselves attacked. Blows landed below the belt and in the kidney, with the gloves open as well as closed, and with my eye partly opened now there was not so much terror. I moved carefully, avoiding blows, although not too many to attract attention, fighting from group to group. The boys groped about like blind, cautious crabs crouching to protect their mid-sections, their heads pulled in short against their shoulders, their arms stretched nervously before them, with their fists testing the smoke-filled air like the knobbed feelers of hypersensitive snails. In one corner I glimpsed a boy violently punching the air and heard him scream in pain as he smashed his hand against a ring post. For a second I saw him bent over holding his hand, then going down as a blow caught his unprotected head. I played one group against the other, slipping and throwing a punch then stepping out of range while pushing the others into the melee to take the blows blindly aimed at me. The smoke was agonizing and there were no rounds, no bells at three minute intervals to relieve our exhaustion. The room spun round me, a swirl of lights, smoke, sweating bodies surrounded by tense white faces. I bled from both nose and mouth, the blood spattering upon my chest.

The men kept yelling, "Slug him, black boy! Knock his guts out!"

25   "Uppercut him! Kill him! Kill that big boy!"

Taking a fake fall, I saw a boy going down heavily beside me as though we were felled by a single blow, saw a sneaker-clad foot shoot into his groin as the two who had knocked him down stumbled upon him. I rolled out of range, feeling a twinge of nausea.

The harder we fought the more threatening the men became. And yet, I had begun to worry about my speech again. How would it go? Would they recognize my ability? What would they give me?

I was fighting automatically and suddenly I noticed that one after another of the boys was leaving the ring. I was surprised, filled with panic, as though I had been left alone with an unknown danger. Then I understood. The boys had arranged it among themselves. It was the custom for the two men left in the ring to slug it out for the winner's prize. I discovered this too late. When the bell sounded two men in tuxedoes leaped into the ring and removed the blindfold. I found myself facing Tatlock, the biggest of the gang. I felt sick at my stomach. Hardly had the bell stopped ringing in my ears than it clanged again and I saw him moving swiftly toward me. Thinking of nothing else to do I hit him smash on the nose. He kept coming, bringing the rank sharp violence of stale sweat. His face was a black bank of a face, only his eyes alive—with hate of me and aglow with a feverish terror from what had happened to us all. I became anxious. I wanted to deliver my speech and he came at me as though he meant to beat it out of me. I smashed him again and again, taking his blows as they came. Then on a sudden impulse I struck him lightly as we clinched, I whispered, "Fake like I knocked you out, you can have the prize."

"I'll break your behind," he whispered hoarsely.

30   "For *them?*"

"For *me,* sonofabitch!"

They were yelling for us to break it up and Tatlock spun me half around with a blow, and as a joggled camera sweeps in a reeling scene, I saw the howling red faces crouching tense beneath the cloud of blue-gray smoke. For a moment the world wavered, unraveled, flowed, then my head cleared and Tatlock bounced before me. That fluttering shadow before my eyes was his jabbing left hand. Then falling forward, my head against his damp shoulder, I whispered,

"I'll make it five dollars more."

"Go to hell!"

35   But his muscles relaxed a trifle beneath my pressure and I breathed, "Seven!"

"Give it to your ma," he said, ripping me beneath the heart.

And while I still held him I butted him and moved away. I felt myself bombarded with punches. I fought back with hopeless desperation. I wanted to deliver my speech more than anything else in the world, because I felt that only these men could judge truly my ability, and now this stupid clown was ruining my chances. I began fighting carefully now, moving in to punch him and out again with my greater speed. A lucky blow to his chin and I had him going too—until I heard a loud voice yell, "I got my money on the big boy."

Hearing this, I almost dropped my guard. I was confused: Should I try to win against the voice out there? Would not this go against my speech, and was not this a moment for humility, for nonresistance? A blow to my head as I danced about sent my right eye popping like a jack-in-the-box and settled my dilemma. The room went red as I fell. It was a dream fall, my body languid and fastidious as to where to land, until the floor became impatient and smashed up to meet me. A moment later I came to. An hypnotic voice said FIVE emphatically. And I lay there, hazily watching a dark red spot of my own blood shaping itself into a butterfly, glistening and soaking into the soiled gray world of the canvas.

When the voice drawled TEN I was lifted up and dragged to a chair. I sat dazed. My eye pained and swelled with each throb of my pounding heart and I wondered if now I would be allowed to speak. I was wringing wet, my mouth still bleeding. We were grouped along the wall now. The other boys ignored me as they congratulated Tatlock and speculated as to how much they would be paid. One boy whimpered over his smashed hand. Looking up front, I saw attendants in white jackets rolling the portable ring away and placing a small square rug in the vacant space surrounded by chairs. Perhaps, I thought, I will stand on the rug to deliver my speech.

40   Then the M.C. called to us, "Come on up here boys and get your money." We ran forward to where the men laughed and talked in their chairs, waiting. Everyone seemed friendly now.

"There it is on the rug," the man said. I saw the rug covered with coins of all dimensions and a few crumpled bills. But what excited me, scattered here and there, were the gold pieces.

"Boys, it's all yours," the man said. "You get all you grab."

"That's right, Sambo," a blond man said, winking at me confidentially.

I trembled with excitement, forgetting my pain. I would get the gold and the bills, I thought. I would use both hands. I would throw my body against the boys nearest me to block them from the gold.

45   "Get down around the rug now," the man commanded, "and don't anyone touch it until I give the signal."

"This ought to be good," I heard.

As told, we got around the square rug on our knees. Slowly the man raised his freckled hand as we followed it upward with our eyes.

I heard, "These niggers look like they're about to pray!"

Then, "Ready," the man said. "Go!"

50   I lunged for a yellow coin lying on the blue design of the carpet, touching it and sending a surprised shriek to join those rising around me. I tried frantically to remove my hand but could not let go. A hot, violent force tore through my body, shaking me like a wet rat. The rug was electrified. The hair bristled up on my head as I shook myself free. My muscles jumped, my nerves jangled, writhed. But I saw that this was not stopping the other boys. Laughing in fear and embarrassment, some were holding back and scooping up the coins knocked off by the painful contortions of the others. The men roared above us as we struggled.

"Pick it up, goddamnit, pick it up!" someone called like a bass-voiced parrot. "Go on, get it!"

I crawled rapidly around the floor, picking up the coins, trying to avoid the coppers and to get greenbacks and the gold. Ignoring the shock by laughing, as I brushed the coins off quickly, I discovered that I could contain the electricity—a contradiction, but it works. Then the men began to push us onto the rug. Laughing embarrassedly, we struggled out of their hands and kept after the coins. We were all wet and slippery and hard to hold. Suddenly I saw a boy lifted into the air, glistening with sweat like a circus seal, and dropped, his wet back landing flush upon the charged rug, heard him yell and saw him literally dance upon his back, his elbows beating a frenzied tattoo upon the floor, his muscles twitching like the flesh of a horse stung by many flies. When he finally rolled off, his face was gray and no one stopped him when he ran from the floor amid booming laughter.

"Get the money," the M.C. called. "That's good hard American cash!"

And we snatched and grabbed, snatched and grabbed. I was careful not to come too close to the rug now, and when I felt the hot whiskey breath descend upon me like a cloud of foul air I reached out and grabbed the leg of a chair. It was occupied and I held on desperately.

55   "Leggo, nigger! Leggo!"

The huge face wavered down to mine as he tried to push me free. But my body was slippery and he was too drunk. It was Mr. Colcord, who owned a chain of movie houses and "entertainment palaces." Each time he grabbed me I slipped out of his hands. It became a real struggle. I feared the rug more than I did the drunk, so I held on, surprising myself for a moment by trying to topple *him* upon the rug. It was such an enormous idea that I found myself actually carrying it out. I tried not to be obvious, yet when I grabbed his leg, trying to tumble him out of the chair, he raised up roaring with laughter, and, looking at me with soberness dead in the eye, kicked me viciously in the chest. The chair leg flew out of my hand. I felt myself going and rolled. It was as though I had rolled through a bed of hot coals. It seemed a whole century would pass before I would roll free, a century in which I was seared through the deepest levels of my body to the fearful breath within me and the breath seared and heated to the point of explosion. It'll all be over in a flash, I thought as I rolled clear. It'll all be over in a flash.

But not yet, the men on the other side were waiting, red faces swollen as though from apoplexy as they bent forward in their chairs. Seeing their fingers coming toward me I rolled away as a fumbled football rolls off the receiver's fingertips, back into the coals. That time I luckily sent the rug sliding out of place and heard the coins ringing against the floor and the boys scuffling to pick them up and the M.C. calling, "All right, boys, that's all. Go get dressed and get your money."

I was limp as a dish rag. My back felt as though it had been beaten with wires.

When we had dressed the M.C. came in and gave us each five dollars, except Tatlock, who got ten for being the last in the ring. Then he told us to leave. I was not to get a chance to deliver my speech, I thought. I was going out into the dim alley in despair when I was stopped and told to go back. I returned to the ballroom, where the men were pushing back their chairs and gathering in groups to talk.

60   The M.C. knocked on a table for quiet. "Gentlemen," he said, "we almost forgot an important part of the program. A most serious part, gentlemen. This boy was brought here to deliver a speech which he made at his graduation yesterday...."

"Bravo!"

"I'm told that he is the smartest boy we've got out there in Greenwood. I'm told that he knows more big words than a pocket-sized dictionary."

Much applause and laughter.

"So now, gentlemen, I want you to give him your attention."

65   There was still laughter as I faced them, my mouth dry, my eye throbbing. I began slowly, but evidently my throat was tense, because they began shouting, "Louder! Louder!"

"We of the younger generation extol the wisdom of that great leader and educator," I shouted, "who first spoke these flaming words of wisdom: 'A ship lost at sea for many days suddenly sighted a friendly vessel. From the mast of the unfortunate vessel was seen a signal: "Water, water; we die of thirst!" The answer from the friendly vessel came back: "Cast down your bucket where you are." The captain of the distressed vessel, at last heeding the injunction, cast down his bucket, and it came up full of fresh sparkling water from the mouth of the Amazon River.' And like him I say, and in his words. 'To those of my race who depend upon bettering their condition in a foreign land, or who underestimate the importance of cultivating friendly relations with the Southern white man, who is his next-door neighbor, I would say: "Cast down your bucket where you are"— cast it down in making friends in every manly way of the people of all races by whom we are surrounded....'"

I spoke automatically and with such fervor that I did not realize that the men were still talking and laughing until my dry mouth, filling up with blood from the cut, almost strangled me. I coughed, wanting to stop and go to one of the tall brass, sand-filled spittoons to relieve myself, but a few of the men, especially the superintendent, were listening and I was afraid. So I gulped it down, blood, saliva and all, and continued. (What powers of endurance I had during those days! What enthusiasm! What a belief in the rightness of things!) I spoke even louder in spite of the pain. But still they talked and still they laughed, as though deaf with cotton in dirty ears. So I spoke with greater emotional emphasis. I closed my ears and swallowed blood until I was nauseated. The speech seemed a hundred times as long as before, but I could not leave out a single word. All had to be said, each memorized nuance considered, rendered. Nor was that all. Whenever I uttered a word of three or more syllables a group of voices would yell for me to repeat it. I used the phrase "social responsibility" and they yelled:

"What's the word you say, boy?"

"Social responsibility," I said.

70   "What?"

"Social ..."

"Louder."

"... responsibility."

"More!"

75   "Respon—"

"Repeat!"

"—sibility."

The room filled with the uproar of laughter until, no doubt, distracted by having to gulp down my blood, I made a mistake and yelled a phrase I had often seen denounced in newspaper editorials, heard debated in private.

"Social ..."

80   "What?" they yelled.

"... equality—"

The laughter hung smokelike in the sudden stillness. I opened my eyes, puzzled. Sounds of displeasure filled the room. The M.C. rushed forward. They shouted hostile phrases at me. But I did not understand.

A small dry mustached man in the front row blared out, "Say that slowly, son!"

"What sir?"

85   "What you just said!"

"Social responsibility, sir," I said.

"You weren't being smart, were you, boy?" he said, not unkindly.

"No, sir!"

"You sure that about 'equality' was a mistake?"

90   "Oh, yes, sir," I said. "I was swallowing blood."

"Well, you had better speak more slowly so we can understand. We mean to do right by you, but you've got to know your place at all times. All right, now, go on with your speech."

I was afraid. I wanted to leave but I wanted also to speak and I was afraid they'd snatch me down.

"Thank you, sir," I said, beginning where I had left off, and having them ignore me as before.

Yet when I finished there was a thunderous applause. I was surprised to see the superintendent come forth with a package wrapped in white tissue paper, and gesturing for quiet, address the men.

95   "Gentlemen, you see that I did not overpraise this boy. He makes a good speech and some day he'll lead his people in the proper paths. And I don't have to tell you that that is important in these days and times. This is a good, smart boy, and so to encourage him in the right direction, in the name of the Board of Education I wish to present him a prize in the form of this..."

He paused, removing the tissue paper and revealing a gleaming calfskin brief case. "...in the form of this first-class article from Shad Whitmore's shop."

"Boy," he said, addressing me, "take this prize and keep it well. Consider it a badge of office. Prize it. Keep developing as you are and some day it will be filled with important papers that will help shape the destiny of your people."

I was so moved that I could hardly express my thanks. A rope of bloody saliva forming a shape like an undiscovered continent drooled upon the leather and I wiped it quickly away. I felt an importance that I had never dreamed.

100   "Open it and see what's inside," I was told.

My fingers a-tremble, I complied, smelling the fresh leather and finding an official-looking document inside. It was a scholarship to the state college for Negroes. My eyes filled with tears and I ran awkwardly off the floor.

I was overjoyed; I did not even mind when I discovered that the gold pieces I had scrambled for were brass pocket tokens advertising a certain make of automobile.

When I reached home everyone was excited. Next day the neighbors came to congratulate me. I even felt safe from grandfather, whose deathbed curse usually spoiled my triumphs. I stood beneath his photograph with my brief case in hand and smiled triumphantly into his stolid black peasant's face. It was a face that fascinated me. The eyes seemed to follow everywhere I went.

That night I dreamed I was at a circus with him and that he refused to laugh at the clowns no matter what they did. Then later he told me to open my brief case and read what was inside and I did, finding an official envelope stamped with the state seal; and inside the envelope I found another and another, endlessly, and I thought I would fall of weariness. "Them's years," he said. "Now open that one." And I did and in it I found an engraved document containing a short message in letters of gold. "Read it," my grandfather said. "Out loud."

105   "To Whom It May Concern," I intoned. "Keep This Nigger-Boy Running."

I awoke with the old man's laughter ringing in my ears.

(It was a dream I was to remember and dream again for many years after. But at the time I had no insight into its meaning. First I had to attend college.)

MAKING CONNECTIONS

1. Have you ever found yourself in a humiliating circumstance but didn't want to protest—and wanted the approval of those who were humiliating you? If so, how did that experience affect your response to this story?

2. The narrator is the protagonist. In what way does this point of view influence how you experience the story?

3. What is the role of the naked dancer in the story?

4. To what extent is the narrator's act of delivering the speech more important to him than its message or the citizens to whom it is delivered? Why do you think he feels this way?

5. Describe the setting of the story. What aspects of the description were most effective in conveying the atmosphere?

6. Why does the audience react so strongly to the narrator's use of the terms "social responsibility" and "social equality"?

7. What is the primary conflict in the story? Is it external, internal, both? Explain.

MAKING AN ARGUMENT

1. Interpret the narrator's dream in terms of the "battle" he has just fought. What do you think the declaration in the dream "Keep This Nigger-Boy Running" means? Write an essay about the relationship between the "battle royal" the narrator has just experienced and his dream at the end. Cite the text of the story for support.

HARUKI MURAKAMI [B. 1949]

Born in postwar Kyoto, Murakami spent most of his child-hood in Kobe, where his parents taught Japanese literature. From an early age, Murakami was attracted to Western culture, and its influence features heavily in his work. After some early successes, he received widespread popularity in his native Japan with the publication of Norwegian Wood *(2000). Soon after, he began a period of traveling throughout Europe and the United States, during which he wrote three novels:* Dance, Dance, Dance; South of the Border, West of the Sun; *and* The Wind-up Bird Chronicle *(2003). Shaken by the Kobe earthquake and the Tokyo subway gas attack, Murakami returned to Japan and penned two works focusing on the events. In 2006, he was awarded the Kafka Prize for his novel,* Kafka on the Shore. *Murakami currently lives in Tokyo.*

ON SEEING THE 100% PERFECT GIRL ONE BEAUTIFUL APRIL MORNING*

[1993]

One beautiful April morning, on a narrow side street in Tokyo's fashionable Harajuku neighborhood, I walk past the 100% perfect girl.

Tell you the truth, she's not that good-looking. She doesn't stand out in any way. Her clothes are nothing special. The back of her hair is still bent out of shape from sleep. She isn't young, either—must be near thirty, not even close to a "girl," properly speaking. But still, I know from fifty yards away: She's the 100% perfect girl for me. The moment I see her, there's a rumbling in my chest, and my mouth is as dry as a desert.

*Translated by Jay Rabin.

Maybe you have your own particular favorite type of girl—one with slim ankles, say, or big eyes, or graceful fingers, or you're drawn for no good reason to girls who take their time with every meal. I have my own preferences, of course. Sometimes in a restaurant I'll catch myself staring at the girl at the table next to mine because I like the shape of her nose.

But no one can insist that his 100% perfect girl correspond to some preconceived type. Much as I like noses, I can't recall the shape of hers—or even if she had one. All I can remember for sure is that she was no great beauty. It's weird.

5   "Yesterday on the street I passed the 100% perfect girl," I tell someone.

"Yeah?" he says. "Good-looking?"

"Not really."

"Your favorite type, then?"

"I don't know. I can't seem to remember anything about her—the shape of her eyes or the size of her breasts."

10   "Strange."

"Yeah. Strange."

"So anyhow," he says, already bored, "what did you do? Talk to her? Follow her?"

"Nah. Just passed her on the street."

She's walking east to west, and I west to east. It's a really nice April morning.

15   Wish I could talk to her. Half an hour would be plenty: just ask her about herself, tell her about myself, and—what I'd really like to do—explain to her the complexities of fate that have led to our passing each other on a side street in Harajuku on a beautiful April morning in 1981. This was something sure to be crammed full of warm secrets, like an antique clock built when peace filled the world.

After talking, we'd have lunch somewhere, maybe see a Woody Allen movie, stop by a hotel bar for cocktails. With any kind of luck, we might end up in bed.

Potentiality knocks on the door of my heart.

Now the distance between us has narrowed to fifteen yards.

How can I approach her? What should I say?

20   "Good morning, miss. Do you think you could spare half an hour for a little conversation?"

Ridiculous. I'd sound like an insurance salesman.

"Pardon me, but would you happen to know if there is an all-night cleaners in the neighborhood?"

No, this is just as ridiculous. I'm not carrying any laundry, for one thing. Who's going to buy a line like that?

Maybe the simple truth would do. "Good morning. You are the 100% perfect girl for me."

25   No, she wouldn't believe it. Or even if she did, she might not want to talk to me. Sorry, she could say, I might be the 100% perfect girl for you, but you're not the 100% perfect boy for me. It could happen. And if I found myself in that situation, I'd probably go to pieces. I'd never recover from the shock. I'm thirty-two, and that's what growing older is all about.

We pass in front of a flower shop. A small, warm air mass touches my skin. The asphalt is damp, and I catch the scent of roses. I can't bring myself to speak to her. She wears a white sweater, and in her right hand she holds a crisp white envelope lacking only a stamp. So: She's written somebody a letter, maybe spent the whole night writing, to judge from the sleepy look in her eyes. The envelope could contain every secret she's ever had.

I take a few more strides and turn: She's lost in the crowd.

Now, of course, I know exactly what I should have said to her. It would have been a long speech, though, far too long for me to have delivered it properly. The ideas I come up with are never very practical.

Oh, well. It would have started "Once upon a time" and ended "A sad story, don't you think?"

30   Once upon a time, there lived a boy and a girl. The boy was eighteen and the girl sixteen. He was not unusually handsome, and she was not especially beautiful. They were just an ordinary lonely boy and an ordinary lonely girl, like all the others. But they believed with their whole hearts that somewhere in the world there lived the 100% perfect boy and the 100% perfect girl for them. Yes, they believed in a miracle. And that miracle actually happened.

One day the two came upon each other on the corner of a street.

"This is amazing," he said. "I've been looking for you all my life. You may not believe this, but you're the 100% perfect girl for me."

"And you," she said to him, "are the 100% perfect boy for me, exactly as I'd pictured you in every detail. It's like a dream."

They sat on a park bench, held hands, and told each other their stories hour after hour. They were not lonely anymore. They had found and been found by their 100% perfect other. What a wonderful thing it is to find and be found by your 100% perfect other. It's a miracle, a cosmic miracle.

35   As they sat and talked, however, a tiny, tiny sliver of doubt took root in their hearts: Was it really all right for one's dreams to come true so easily?

And so, when there came a momentary lull in their conversation, the boy said to the girl, "Let's test ourselves—just once. If we really are each other's 100% perfect lovers, then sometime, somewhere, we will meet again without fail. And when that happens, and we know that we are the 100% perfect ones, we'll marry then and there. What do you think?"

"Yes," she said, "that is exactly what we should do."

And so they parted, she to the east, and he to the west.

The test they had agreed upon, however, was utterly unnecessary. They should never have undertaken it, because they really and truly were each other's 100% perfect lovers, and it was a miracle that they had ever met. But it was impossible for them to know this, young as they were. The cold, indifferent waves of fate proceeded to toss them unmercifully.

40   One winter, both the boy and the girl came down with the season's terrible influenza, and after drifting for weeks between life and death they lost all memory of their earlier years. When they awoke, their heads were as empty as the young D. H. Lawrence's piggy bank.

They were two bright, determined young people, however, and through their unremitting efforts they were able to acquire once again the knowledge and feeling that qualified them to return as full-fledged members of society. Heaven be praised, they became truly upstanding citizens who knew how to transfer from one subway line to another; who were fully capable of sending a special-delivery letter at the post office. Indeed, they even experienced love again, sometimes as much as 75% or even 85% love.

Time passed with shocking swiftness, and soon the boy was thirty-two, the girl thirty.

One beautiful April morning, in search of a cup of coffee to start the day, the boy was walking from west to east, while the girl, intending to send a special-delivery letter, was walking from east to west, both along the same narrow street in the Harajuku neighborhood of Tokyo. They passed each other in the very center of the street. The faintest gleam of their lost memories glimmered for the briefest moment in their hearts. Each felt a rumbling in the chest. And they knew:

She is the 100% perfect girl for me.

45   He is the 100% perfect boy for me.

But the glow of their memories was far too weak, and their thoughts no longer had the clarity of fourteen years earlier. Without a word, they passed each other, disappearing into the crowd. Forever.

A sad story, don't you think?

Yes, that's it, that is what I should have said to her.

MAKING CONNECTIONS

1. Have you ever felt strongly connected to a stranger? Did you act on the feeling? Why or why not?
2. What was your first response to this story? Should the boy have spoken to the girl? Was it foolish to let her pass or would it have been more foolish to speak to her?
3. Why does the narrator continually draw attention to the girl's ordinary appearance?
4. What initially attracts the narrator to the girl on the street? How can he feel so strongly that this stranger is his 100% perfect girl?
5. Why can't the narrator remember what his 100% perfect girl looks like?
6. The narrator comments, "The ideas I come up with are never very practical." Do you think the boy could have told this story to the girl? What are some of her probable reactions?
7. Is the boy saying anything about age? In his story, why are the boy and girl able to speak to each other in their teens, but not in their thirties?
8. Murakami ends his story, "that is what I should have said..." What does this ending say to you about the narrator's desire, dreams, and ideals?

MAKING AN ARGUMENT

1. Murakami's style has been described as having a heavy Western influence. Write an essay that identifies and analyzes this influence as it manifests in the story.
2. The boy cannot remember anything about his 100% perfect girl, but through his narration we learn much about the boy himself. Using examples from

the text that serve to characterize the boy, write an essay that describes the 100% perfect girl for him.

3. Did the boy make a mistake by letting the girl pass by without speaking? Using evidence from the text, defend one of the following positions. (a) The boy made a mistake by not speaking to the girl; he will always wonder about her and regret the decision. (b) The boy made the right decision by not speaking to the girl; she probably would not have lived up to his idea of her and that would have ruined his memory of her.

JOYCE CAROL OATES [B. 1938]

Joyce Carol Oates was born into a blue-collar family in Lockport, New York, and even as a child, she was a prolific writer. Her best-known works include A Garden of Earthly Delights *(1967), the National Book Award–winning* Them *(1969), and* On Boxing *(1987). Oates currently lives in suburban New Jersey and is the Berlind Distinguished Professor of Humanities at Princeton University. Many critics have complained about the graphic violence that is often present in her work. Oates has responded:* "The more violent the murders in Macbeth, *the more relief one can feel at not having to perform them. Great art is cathartic; it is always moral." "Where Are You Going, Where Have You Been?" first appeared in* The Wheel and Love and Other Stories *(1970) and was the basis for the 1985 film,* Smooth Talk. *She is the author of more than thirty books, and her most recent book is* A Widow's Story *(2011), a memoir about her husband's death. In 2011, she received a National Humanities Medal from President Obama.*

WHERE ARE YOU GOING, WHERE HAVE YOU BEEN?   [1970]

For Bob Dylan

Her name was Connie. She was fifteen and she had a quick nervous giggling habit of craning her neck to glance into mirrors, or checking other people's faces to make sure her own was all right. Her mother, who noticed everything and knew everything and who hadn't much reason any longer to look at her own face, always scolded Connie about it. "Stop gawking at yourself, who are you? You think you're so pretty?" she would say. Connie would raise her eyebrows at these familiar complaints and look right through her mother, into a shadowy vision of herself as she was right at that moment: she knew she was pretty and that was everything. Her mother had been pretty once too, if you could believe those old snapshots in the album, but now her looks were gone and that was why she was always after Connie.

"Why don't you keep your room clean like your sister? How've you got your hair fixed—what the hell stinks? Hair spray? You don't see your sister using that junk."

Her sister June was twenty-four and still lived at home. She was a secretary in the high school Connie attended, and if that wasn't bad enough—with her in the same building—she was so plain and chunky and steady that Connie had to hear her praised all the time by her mother and her mother's sisters. June did this, June did that, she saved money and helped clean the house and cooked and Connie couldn't do a thing, her mind was all filled with trashy daydreams. Their father was away at work most of the time and when he came home he wanted supper and he read the newspaper at supper and after supper he went to bed. He didn't bother talking much to them, but around his bent head Connie's mother kept picking at her until Connie wished her mother was dead and she herself was dead and it was all over. "She makes me want to throw up sometimes," she complained to her friends. She had a high, breathless, amused voice which made everything she said sound a little forced, whether it was sincere or not.

There was one good thing: June went places with girl friends of hers, girls who were just as plain and steady as she, and so when Connie wanted to do that her mother had no objections. The father of Connie's best girl friend drove the girls the three miles to town and left them off at a shopping plaza, so that they could walk through the stores or go to a movie, and when he came to pick them up again at eleven he never bothered to ask what they had done.

5   They must have been familiar sights, walking around that shopping plaza in their shorts and flat ballerina slippers that always scuffed the sidewalk, with charm bracelets jingling on their thin wrists; they would lean together to whisper and laugh secretly if someone passed by who amused or interested them. Connie had long dark blond hair that drew anyone's eye to it, and she wore part of it pulled up on her head and puffed out and the rest of it she let fall down her back. She wore a pull-over jersey blouse that looked one way when she was at home and another way when she was away from home. Everything about her had two sides to it, one for home and one for anywhere that was not home: her walk that could be childlike and bobbing, or languid enough to make anyone think she was hearing music in her head, her mouth which was pale and smirking most of the time, but bright and pink on these evenings out, her laugh which was cynical and drawling at home— "Ha, ha, very funny"—but high-pitched and nervous anywhere else, like the jingling of the charms on her bracelet.

Sometimes they did go shopping or to a movie, but sometimes they went across the highway, ducking fast across the busy road, to a drive-in restaurant where older kids hung out. The restaurant was shaped like a big bottle, though squatter than a real bottle, and on its cap was a revolving figure of a grinning boy who held a hamburger aloft. One night in mid-summer they ran across, breathless with daring, and right away someone leaned out a car window and invited them over, but it was just a boy from high school they didn't like. It made them feel good to be able to ignore him. They went up through the maze of parked and cruising cars to the bright-lit, fly-infested restaurant, their faces pleased and expectant as if they were entering a sacred building that loomed out of the night to give them what haven and what blessing they yearned for. They sat at the counter and crossed their legs at the ankles, their thin shoulders rigid with excitement, and listened to the music that made everything so good: the music was always in the background like music at a church service, it was something to depend upon.

A boy named Eddie came in to talk with them. He sat backwards on his stool, turning himself jerkily around in semi-circles and then stopping and turning again, and after a while he asked Connie if she would like something to eat. She said she did and so she tapped her friend's arm on her way out—her friend pulled her face up into a brave droll look—and Connie said she would meet her at eleven, across the way. "I just hate to leave her like that," Connie said earnestly, but the boy said that she wouldn't be alone for long. So they went out to his car and on the way Connie couldn't help but let her eyes wander over the windshields and faces all around her, her face gleaming with a joy that had nothing to do with Eddie or even this place; it might have been the music. She drew her shoulders up and sucked in her breath with the pure pleasure of being alive, and just at that moment she happened to glance at a face just a few feet from hers. It was a boy with shaggy black hair, in a convertible jalopy painted gold. He stared at her and then his lips widened into a grin. Connie slit her eyes at him and turned away, but she couldn't help glancing back and there he was still watching her. He wagged a finger and laughed and said, "Gonna get you, baby," and Connie turned away again without Eddie noticing anything.

She spent three hours with him, at the restaurant where they ate hamburgers and drank Cokes in wax cups that were always sweating, and then down an alley a mile or so away, and when he left her off at five to eleven only the movie house was still open at the plaza. Her girl friend was there, talking with a boy. When Connie came up the two girls smiled at each other and Connie said, "How was the movie?" and the girl said, "*You* should know." They rode off with the girl's father, sleepy and pleased, and Connie couldn't help but look at the darkened shopping plaza with its big empty parking lot and its signs that were faded and ghostly now, and over at the drive-in restaurant where cars were still circling tirelessly. She couldn't hear the music at this distance.

Next morning June asked her how the movie was and Connie said, "So-so."

10   She and that girl and occasionally another girl went out several times a week that way, and the rest of the time Connie spent around the house—it was summer vacation—getting in her mother's way and thinking, dreaming, about the boys she met. But all the boys fell back and dissolved into a single face that was not even a face, but an idea, a feeling, mixed up with the urgent insistent pounding of the music and the humid night air of July. Connie's mother kept dragging her back to the daylight by finding things for her to do or saying, suddenly, "What's this about the Pettinger girl?"

And Connie would say nervously, "Oh, her. That dope." She always drew thick clear lines between herself and such girls, and her mother was simple and kindly enough to believe her. Her mother was so simple, Connie thought, that it was maybe cruel to fool her so much. Her mother went scuffling around the house in old bedroom slippers and complained over the telephone to one sister about the other, then the other called up and the two of them complained about the third one. If June's name was mentioned her mother's tone was approving, and if Connie's name was mentioned it was disapproving. This did not really mean she disliked Connie and actually Connie thought that her mother preferred her to June because she was prettier, but the two of them kept up a pretense of exasperation, a sense that they were tugging and struggling over something of little value to either of them. Sometimes, over coffee, they were almost friends, but something would come up—some vexation that was like a fly buzzing suddenly around their heads—and their faces went hard with contempt.

One Sunday Connie got up at eleven—none of them bothered with church— and washed her hair so that it could dry all day long, in the sun. Her parents and sister were going to a barbecue at an aunt's house and Connie said no, she wasn't interested, rolling her eyes to let her mother know just what she thought of it. "Stay home alone then," her mother said sharply. Connie sat out back in a lawn chair and watched them drive away, her father quiet and bald, hunched around so that he could back the car out, her mother with a look that was still angry and not at all softened through the windshield, and in the back seat poor old June all dressed up as if she didn't know what a barbecue was, with all the running yelling kids and the flies. Connie sat with her eyes closed in the sun, dreaming and dazed with the warmth about her as if this were a kind of love, the caresses of love, and her mind slipped over onto thoughts of the boy she had been with the night before and how nice he had been, how sweet it always was, not the way someone like June would suppose but sweet, gentle, the way it was in movies and promised in songs; and when she opened her eyes she hardly knew where she was, the back yard ran off into weeds and a fence-line of trees and behind it the sky was perfectly blue and still. The asbestos "ranch house" that was now three years old startled her—it looked small. She shook her head as if to get awake.

It was too hot. She went inside the house and turned on the radio to drown out the quiet. She sat on the edge of her bed, barefoot, and listened for an hour and a half to a program called XYZ Sunday Jamboree, record after record of hard, fast, shrieking songs she sang along with, interspersed by exclamations from "Bobby King": "An' look here you girls at Napoleon's—Son and Charley want you to pay real close attention to this song coming up!"

And Connie paid close attention herself, bathed in a glow of slow-pulsed joy that seemed to rise mysteriously out of the music itself and lay languidly about the airless little room, breathed in and breathed out with each gentle rise and fall of her chest.

15   After a while she heard a car coming up the drive. She sat up at once, startled, because it couldn't be her father so soon. The gravel kept crunching all the way in from the road—the driveway was long—and Connie ran to the window. It was a car she didn't know. It was an open jalopy, painted a bright gold that caught the sunlight opaquely. Her heart began to pound and her fingers snatched at her hair, checking it, and she whispered "Christ. Christ," wondering how bad she looked. The car came to a stop at the side door and the horn sounded four short taps as if this were a signal Connie knew.

She went into the kitchen and approached the door slowly, then hung out the screen door, her bare toes curling down off the step. There were two boys in the car and now she recognized the driver: he had shaggy, shabby black hair that looked crazy as a wig and he was grinning at her.

"I ain't late, am I?" he said.

"Who the hell do you think you are?" Connie said.

"Toldja I'd be out, didn't I?"

20   "I don't even know who you are."

She spoke sullenly, careful to show no interest or pleasure, and he spoke in a fast bright monotone. Connie looked past him to the other boy, taking her time. He had fair brown hair, with a lock that fell onto his forehead. His sideburns gave him a fierce, embarrassed look, but so far he hadn't even bothered to glance at her. Both boys wore sunglasses. The driver's glasses were metallic and mirrored everything in miniature.

"You wanta come for a ride?" he said.

Connie smirked and let her hair fall loose over one shoulder.

"Don'tcha like my car? New paint job," he said. "Hey."

25   "What?"

"You're cute."

She pretended to fidget, chasing flies away from the door.

"Don'tcha believe me, or what?" he said.

"Look, I don't even know who you are," Connie said in disgust.

30   "Hey, Ellie's got a radio, see. Mine's broke down." He lifted his friend's arm and showed her the little transistor the boy was holding, and now Connie began to hear the music. It was the same program that was playing inside the house.

"Bobby King?" she said.

"I listen to him all the time. I think he's great."

"He's kind of great," Connie said reluctantly.

"Listen, that guy's *great*. He knows where the action is."

35   Connie blushed a little, because the glasses made it impossible for her to see just what this boy was looking at. She couldn't decide if she liked him or if he was just a jerk, and so she dawdled in the doorway and wouldn't come down or go back inside. She said, "What's all that stuff painted on your car?"

"Can'tcha read it?" He opened the door very carefully, as if he was afraid it might fall off. He slid out just as carefully, planting his feet firmly on the ground, the tiny metallic world in his glasses slowing down like gelatin hardening and in the midst of it Connie's bright green blouse. "This here is my name, to begin with," he said. ARNOLD FRIEND was written in tarlike black letters on the side, with a drawing of a round grinning face that reminded Connie of a pumpkin, except it wore sunglasses. "I wanta introduce myself, I'm Arnold Friend and that's my real name and I'm gonna be your friend, honey, and inside the car's Ellie Oscar, he's kinda shy." Ellie brought his transistor radio up to his shoulder and balanced it there. "Now these numbers are a secret code, honey," Arnold Friend explained. He read off the numbers 33, 19, 17 and raised his eyebrows at her to see what she thought of that, but she didn't think much of it. The left rear fender had been smashed and around it was written, on the gleaming gold background: DONE BY CRAZY WOMAN DRIVER. Connie had to laugh at that. Arnold Friend was pleased at her laughter and looked up at her. "Around the other side's a lot more—you wanta come and see them?"

"No."

"Why not?"

"Why should I?"

40   "Don'tcha wanta see what's on the car? Don'tcha wanta go for a ride?"

"I don't know."

"Why not?"

"I got things to do."

"Like what?"

45   "Things."

He laughed as if she had said something funny. He slapped his thighs. He was standing in a strange way, leaning back against the car as if he were balancing himself. He wasn't tall, only an inch or so taller than she would be if she came down to him. Connie liked the way he was dressed, which was the way all of them dressed: tight faded jeans stuffed into black, scuffed boots, a belt that pulled his waist in and showed how lean he was, and a white pull-over shirt that was a little soiled and showed the hard small muscles of his arms and shoulders. He looked as if he probably did hard work, lifting and carrying things. Even his neck looked muscular. And his face was a familiar face, somehow: the jaw and chin and cheeks slightly darkened, because he hadn't shaved for a day or two, and the nose long and hawk-like, sniffing as if she were a treat he was going to gobble up and it was all a joke.

"Connie, you ain't telling the truth. This is your day set aside for a ride with me and you know it," he said, still laughing. The way he straightened and recovered from his fit of laughing showed that it had been all fake.

"How do you know what my name is?" she said suspiciously.

"It's Connie."

50   "Maybe and maybe not."

"I know my Connie," he said, wagging his finger. Now she remembered him even better, back at the restaurant, and her cheeks warmed at the thought of how she sucked in her breath just at the moment she passed him—how she must have looked to him. And he had remembered her. "Ellie and I come out here especially for you," he said. "Ellie can sit in back. How about it?"

"Where?"

"Where what?"

"Where're we going?"

55   He looked at her. He took off the sunglasses and she saw how pale the skin around his eyes was, like holes that were not in shadow but instead in light. His eyes were chips of broken glass that catch the light in an amiable way. He smiled. It was as if the idea of going for a ride somewhere, to some place, was a new idea to him.

"Just for a ride, Connie sweetheart."

"I never said my name was Connie," she said.

"But I know what it is. I know your name and all about you, lots of things," Arnold Friend said. He had not moved yet but stood still leaning back against the side of his jalopy. "I took a special interest in you, such a pretty girl, and found out all about you like I know your parents and sister are gone somewheres and I know where and how long they're going to be gone, and I know who you were with last night, and your best girl friend's name is Betty. Right?"

He spoke in a simple lilting voice, exactly as if he were reciting the words to a song. His smile assured her that everything was fine. In the car Ellie turned up the volume on his radio and did not bother to look around at them.

60   "Ellie can sit in the back seat," Arnold Friend said. He indicated his friend with a casual jerk of his chin, as if Ellie did not count and she should not bother with him.

"How'd you find out all that stuff?" Connie said.

"Listen: Betty Schultz and Tony Fitch and Jimmy Pettinger and Nancy Pettinger," he said, in a chant. "Raymond Stanley and Bob Hutter—"

"Do you know all those kids?"

"I know everybody."

65   "Look, you're kidding. You're not from around here."

"Sure."

"But—how come we never saw you before?"

"Sure you saw me before," he said. He looked down at his boots, as if he were a little offended. "You just don't remember."

"I guess I'd remember you," Connie said.

70   "Yeah?" He looked up at this, beaming. He was pleased. He began to mark time with the music from Ellie's radio, tapping his fists lightly together. Connie looked away from his smile to the car, which was painted so bright it almost hurt her eyes to look at it. She looked at that name, ARNOLD FRIEND. And up at the front fender was an expression that was familiar—MAN THE FLYING SAUCERS. It was an expression kids had used the year before, but didn't use this year. She looked at it for a while as if the words meant something to her that she did not yet know.

"What're you thinking about? Huh?" Arnold Friend demanded. "Not worried about your hair blowing around in the car, are you?"

"No."

"Think I maybe can't drive good?"

"How do I know?"

75   "You're a hard girl to handle. How come?" he said. "Don't you know I'm your friend? Didn't you see me put my sign in the air when you walked by?"

"What sign?"

"My sign." And he drew an X in the air, leaning out toward her. They were maybe ten feet apart. After his hand fell back to his side the X was still in the air, almost visible. Connie let the screen door close and stood perfectly still inside it, listening to the music from her radio and the boy's blend together. She stared at Arnold Friend. He stood there so stiffly relaxed, pretending to be relaxed, with one hand idly on the door handle as if he were keeping himself up that way and had no intention of ever moving again. She recognized most things about him, the tight jeans that showed his thighs and buttocks and the greasy leather boots and the tight shirt, and even that slippery friendly smile of his, that sleepy dreamy smile that all the boys used to get across ideas they didn't want to put into words. She recognized all this and also the singsong way he talked, slightly mocking, kidding, but serious and a little melancholy, and she recognized the way he tapped one fist against the other in homage to the perpetual music behind him. But all these things did not come together.

She said suddenly, "Hey, how old are you?"

His smile faded. She could see then that he wasn't a kid, he was much older— thirty, maybe more. At this knowledge her heart began to pound faster.

80   "That's a crazy thing to ask. Can'tcha see I'm your own age?"

"Like hell you are."

"Or maybe a coupla years older, I'm eighteen."

"Eighteen?" she said doubtfully.

He grinned to reassure her and lines appeared at the corners of his mouth. His teeth were big and white. He grinned so broadly his eyes became slits and she saw how thick the lashes were, thick and black as if painted with a black tarlike material. Then he seemed to become embarrassed, abruptly, and looked over his shoulder at Ellie. "*Him,* he's crazy," he said. "Ain't he a riot, he's a nut, a real character." Ellie was still listening to the music. His sunglasses told nothing about what he was thinking. He wore a bright orange shirt unbuttoned halfway to show his chest, which was a pale, bluish chest and not muscular like Arnold Friend's. His shirt collar was turned up all around and the very tips of the collar pointed out past his chin as if they were protecting him. He was pressing the transistor radio up against his ear and sat there in a kind of daze, right in the sun.

85   "He's kinda strange," Connie said.

"Hey, she says you're kinda strange! Kinda strange!" Arnold Friend cried. He pounded on the car to get Ellie's attention. Ellie turned for the first time and Connie saw with shock that he wasn't a kid either—he had a fair, hairless face, cheeks reddened slightly as if the veins grew too close to the surface of his skin, the face of a forty-year-old baby. Connie felt a wave of dizziness rise in her at this sight and she stared at him as if waiting for something to change the shock of the moment, make it all right again. Ellie's lips kept shaping words, mumbling along, with the words blasting in his ear.

"Maybe you two better go away," Connie said faintly.

"What? How come?" Arnold Friend cried. "We come out here to take you for a ride. It's Sunday." He had the voice of the man on the radio now. It was the same voice, Connie thought. "Don'tcha know it's Sunday all day and honey, no matter who you were with last night today you're with Arnold Friend and don't you forget it!—Maybe you better step out here," he said, and this last was in a different voice. It was a little flatter, as if the heat was finally getting to him.

"No. I got things to do."

90   "Hey."

"You two better leave."

"We ain't leaving until you come with us."

"Like hell I am—"

"Connie, don't fool around with me. I mean, I mean, don't fool *around,*" he said, shaking his head. He laughed incredulously. He placed his sunglasses on top of his head, carefully, as if he were indeed wearing a wig, and brought the stems down behind his ears. Connie stared at him, another wave of dizziness and fear rising in her so that for a moment he wasn't even in focus but was just a blur, standing there against his gold car, and she had the idea that he had driven up the driveway all right but had come from nowhere before that and belonged nowhere and that everything about him and even about the music that was so familiar to her was only half real.

95   "If my father comes and sees you—"

"He ain't coming. He's at the barbecue."

"How do you know that?"

"Aunt Tillie's. Right now they're—uh—they're drinking. Sitting around," he said vaguely, squinting as if he were staring all the way to town and over to Aunt Tillie's backyard. Then the vision seemed to get clear and he nodded energetically. "Yeah. Sitting around. There's your sister in a blue dress, huh? And high heels, the poor sad bitch—nothing like you, sweetheart! And your mother's helping some fat woman with the corn, they're cleaning the corn—husking the corn—"

"What fat woman?" Connie cried.

100   "How do I know what fat woman. I don't know every goddam fat woman in the world!" Arnold Friend laughed.

"Oh, that's Mrs. Hornby....Who invited her?" Connie said. She felt a little light-headed. Her breath was coming quickly.

"She's too fat. I don't like them fat. I like them the way you are, honey," he said, smiling sleepily at her. They stared at each other for a while, through the screen door. He said softly, "Now what you're going to do is this: you're going to come out that door. You're going to sit up front with me and Ellie's going to sit in the back, the hell with Ellie, right? This isn't Ellie's date. You're my date. I'm your lover, honey."

"What? You're crazy—"

"Yes, I'm your lover. You don't know what that is but you will," he said. "I know that too. I know all about you. But look: it's real nice and you couldn't ask for nobody better than me, or more polite. I always keep my word. I'll tell you how it is, I'm always nice at first, the first time. I'll hold you so tight you won't think you have to try to get away or pretend anything because you'll know you can't. And I'll come inside you where it's all secret and you'll give in to me and you'll love me—"

105   "Shut up! You're crazy!" Connie said. She backed away from the door. She put her hands against her ears as if she'd heard something terrible, something not meant for her. "People don't talk like that, you're crazy," she muttered. Her heart was almost too big now for her chest and its pumping made sweat break out all over her. She looked out to see Arnold Friend pause and then take a step toward the porch lurching. He almost fell. But, like a clever drunken man, he managed to catch his balance. He wobbled in his high boots and grabbed hold of one of the porch posts.

"Honey?" he said. "You still listening?"

"Get the hell out of here!"

"Be nice, honey. Listen."

"I'm going to call the police—"

110   He wobbled again and out of the side of his mouth came a fast spat curse, an aside not meant for her to hear. But even this "Christ!" sounded forced. Then he began to smile again. She watched this smile come, awkward as if he were smiling from inside a mask. His whole face was a mask, she thought wildly, tanned down onto his throat but then running out as if he had plastered make-up on his face but had forgotten about his throat.

"Honey—? Listen, here's how it is. I always tell the truth and I promise you this: I ain't coming in that house after you."

"You better not! I'm going to call the police if you—if you don't—"

"Honey," he said, talking right through her voice, "honey, I'm not coming in there but you are coming out here. You know why?"

She was panting. The kitchen looked like a place she had never seen before, some room she had run inside but which wasn't good enough, wasn't going to help her. The kitchen window had never had a curtain, after three years, and there were dishes in the sink for her to do—probably—and if you ran your hand across the table you'd probably feel something sticky there.

115   "You listening, honey? Hey?"

"—going to call the police—"

"Soon as you touch the phone I don't need to keep my promise and can come inside. You won't want that."

She rushed forward and tried to lock the door. Her fingers were shaking. "But why lock it," Arnold Friend said gently, talking right into her face. "It's just a screen door. It's just nothing." One of his boots was at a strange angle, as if his foot wasn't in it. It pointed out to the left, bent at the ankle. "I mean, anybody can break through a screen door and glass and wood and iron or anything else if he needs to, anybody at all and specially Arnold Friend. If the place got lit up with a fire honey you'd come running out into my arms, right into my arms and safe at home—like you knew I was your lover and'd stopped fooling around. I don't mind a nice shy girl but I don't like no fooling around." Part of those words were spoken with a slight rhythmic lilt, and Connie somehow recognized them—the echo of a song from last year, about a girl rushing into her boy friend's arms and coming home again—

Connie stood barefoot on the linoleum floor, staring at him. "What do you want?" she whispered.

120   "I want you," he said.

"What?"

"Seen you that night and thought, that's the one, yes sir. I never needed to look any more."

"But my father's coming back. He's coming to get me. I had to wash my hair first—" She spoke in a dry, rapid voice, hardly raising it for him to hear.

"No, your daddy is not coming and yes, you had to wash your hair and you washed it for me. It's nice and shining and all for me, I thank you, sweetheart," he said, with a mock bow, but again he almost lost his balance. He had to bend and adjust his boots. Evidently his feet did not go all the way down; the boots must have been stuffed with something so that he would seem taller. Connie stared out at him and behind him Ellie in the car, who seemed to be looking off toward Connie's right, into nothing. This Ellie said, pulling the words out of the air one after another as if he were just discovering them, "You want me to pull out the phone?"

125   "Shut your mouth and keep it shut," Arnold Friend said, his face red from bending over or maybe from embarrassment because Connie had seen his boots. "This ain't none of your business."

"What—what are you doing? What do you want?" Connie said. "If I call the police they'll get you, they'll arrest you—"

"Promise was not to come in unless you touch that phone, and I'll keep that promise," he said. He resumed his erect position and tried to force his shoulders back. He sounded like a hero in a movie, declaring something important. He spoke too loudly and it was as if he were speaking to someone behind Connie. "I ain't made plans for coming in that house where I don't belong but just for you to come out to me, the way you should. Don't you know who I am?"

"You're crazy," she whispered. She backed away from the door but did not want to go into another part of the house, as if this would give him permission to come through the door. "What do you ... You're crazy, you ... "

"Huh? What're you saying, honey?"

130   Her eyes darted everywhere in the kitchen. She could not remember what it was, this room.

"This is how it is, honey: you come out and we'll drive away, have a nice ride. But if you don't come out we're gonna wait till your people come home and then they're all going to get it."

"You want that telephone pulled out?" Ellie said. He held the radio away from his ear and grimaced, as if without the radio the air was too much for him.

"I toldja shut up, Ellie," Arnold Friend said, "you're deaf, get a hearing aid, right? Fix yourself up. This little girl's no trouble and's gonna be nice to me, so Ellie keep to yourself, this ain't your date—right? Don't hem in on me. Don't hog. Don't crush. Don't bird dog. Don't trail me," he said in a rapid meaningless voice, as if he were running through all the expressions he'd learned but was no longer sure which one of them was in style, then rushing on to new ones, making them up with his eyes closed, "Don't crawl under my fence, don't squeeze in my chipmunk hole, don't sniff my glue, suck my popsicle, keep your own greasy fingers on yourself!" He shaded his eyes and peered in at Connie, who was backed against the kitchen table. "Don't mind him honey he's just a creep. He's a dope. Right? I'm the boy for you and like I said you come out here nice like a lady and give me your hand, and nobody else gets hurt, I mean, your nice old bald-headed daddy and your mummy and your sister in her high heels. Because listen: why bring them in this?"

"Leave me alone," Connie whispered.

135   "Hey, you know that old woman down the road, the one with the chickens and stuff—you know her?"

"She's dead!"

"Dead? What? You know her?" Arnold Friend said.

"She's dead—"

"Don't you like her?"

140   "She's dead—she's—she isn't here any more—"

"But don't you like her, I mean, you got something against her? Some grudge or something?" Then his voice dipped as if he were conscious of a rudeness. He touched the sunglasses perched on top of his head as if to make sure they were still there. "Now you be a good girl."

"What are you going to do?"

"Just two things, or maybe three," Arnold Friend said. "But I promise it won't last long and you'll like me that way you get to like people you're close to. You will. It's all over for you here, so come on out. You don't want your people in any trouble, do you?"

She turned and bumped against a chair or something, hurting her leg, but she ran into the back room and picked up the telephone. Something roared in her ear, a tiny roaring, and she was so sick with fear that she could do nothing but listen to it—the telephone was clammy and very heavy and her fingers groped down to the dial but were too weak to touch it. She began to scream into the phone, into the roaring. She cried out, she cried for her mother, she felt her breath start jerking back and forth in her lungs as if it were something Arnold Friend were stabbing her with again and again with no tenderness. A noisy sorrowful wailing rose all about her and she was locked inside it the way she was locked inside the house.

145   After a while she could hear again. She was sitting on the floor with her wet back against the wall.

Arnold Friend was saying from the door, "That's a good girl. Put the phone back."

She kicked the phone away from her.

"No, honey. Pick it up. Put it back right."

She picked it up and put it back. The dial tone stopped.

150   "That's a good girl. Now come outside."

She was hollow with what had been fear, but what was now just an emptiness. All that screaming had blasted it out of her. She sat, one leg cramped under her, and deep inside her brain was something like a pinpoint of light that kept going and would not let her relax. She thought, I'm not going to see my mother again. She thought, I'm not going to sleep in my bed again. Her bright green blouse was all wet.

Arnold Friend said, in a gentle-loud voice that was like a stage voice, "The place where you came from ain't there any more, and where you had in mind to go is cancelled out. This place you are now—inside your daddy's house—is nothing but a cardboard box I can knock down any time. You know that and always did know it. You hear me?"

She thought, I have got to think. I have to know what to do.

"We'll go out to a nice field, out in the country here where it smells so nice and it's sunny," Arnold Friend said. "I'll have my arms around you so you won't need to try to get away and I'll show you what love is like, what it does. The hell with this house! It looks solid all right," he said. He ran a fingernail down the screen and the noise did not make Connie shiver, as it would have the day before. "Now put your hand on your heart, honey. Feel that? That feels solid too but we know better, be nice to me, be sweet like you can because what else is there for a girl like you but to be sweet and pretty and give in?—and get away before her people come back?"

155   She felt her pounding heart. Her hand seemed to enclose it. She thought for the first time in her life that it was nothing that was hers, that belonged to her, but just a pounding, living thing inside this body that wasn't really hers either.

"You don't want them to get hurt," Arnold Friend went on. "Now get up, honey. Get up all by yourself."

She stood up.

"Now turn this way. That's right. Come over here to me—Ellie, put that away, didn't I tell you? You dope. You miserable creepy dope," Arnold Friend said. His words were not angry but only part of an incantation. The incantation was kindly. "Now come out through the kitchen to me honey and let's see a smile, try it, you're a brave sweet little girl and now they're eating corn and hot-dogs cooked to bursting over an outdoor fire, and they don't know one thing about you and never did and honey you're better than them because not a one of them would have done this for you."

Connie felt the linoleum under her feet; it was cool. She brushed her hair back out of her eyes. Arnold Friend let go of the post tentatively and opened his arms for her, his elbows pointing in toward each other and his wrists limp, to show that this was an embarrassed embrace and a little mocking, he didn't want to make her self-conscious.

160   She put out her hand against the screen. She watched herself push the door slowly open as if she were safe back somewhere in the other doorway, watching this body and this head of long hair moving out into the sunlight where Arnold Friend waited.

"My sweet little blue-eyed girl," he said, in a half-sung sigh that had nothing to do with her brown eyes but was taken up just the same by the vast sunlit reaches of the land behind him and on all sides of him, so much land that Connie had never seen before and did not recognize except to know that she was going to it.

MAKING CONNECTIONS

1. Describe Connie. Why is she so irked by her mother's criticism and comparisons to her older sister? What is her social life like?

2. Music is a recurrent image in this story. To what kinds of music does the narrator refer and in what settings? The narrator says that for the girls, "music was something to depend on." Do you think it is? Explain.

3. Describe Arnold Friend. What is your reaction to him? If he called on you, would you go with him? Explain.

4. Why does Connie eventually go with him? To what extent does she go voluntarily and to what extent is she coerced by his threat to kill her family? Does Connie have any idea what will happen to her if she goes with Friend? Explain.

MAKING AN ARGUMENT

1. Arnold Friend says to Connie, "What else is there for a girl like you but to be sweet and pretty and give in?" Do you think he's right? Interpret the characterization of Connie, and make a case for why she gives in and goes with Arnold Friend. Cite the text of the story for support.

COLUM MCCANN [B. 1965]

Born in Dublin, Ireland, Colum McCann is an award-winning author who received the Irish Novel of The Year in 2003 for Dancer, *a fictional portrait of dancer Rudolf Nureyev. Among his other novels is* This Side of Brightness, *which he researched by living with the homeless in the subway tunnels of Manhattan. His most recent novel is* Let the Great World Spin *(2009). Colum McCann teaches creative writing at Hunter College at the City University of New York. He is also a contributor to* The New York Times, The New Yorker, *and* GQ, *among other publications. In 2009, he was awarded the National Book Award for fiction. He lives in New York with his wife and children.*

EVERYTHING IN THIS COUNTRY MUST   [2004]

It was a summer flood when our draft horse was caught in the river and the river smashed against stones. The sound of it to me was like the turning of locks. It was silage time, and the water smelled of grass. The draft horse, Father's favorite, had stepped in the river for a sniff maybe, and she was caught, couldn't move, her foreleg trapped between rocks. Father found her and called, *Katie!* above the wailing of the rain. I was in the barn, waiting for drips on my tongue from the ceiling hole. I ran out past the farmhouse into the field. At the river the horse stared wild through the rain; maybe she remembered me. Father moved slow and scared, like someone traveling deep in snow except there was no snow, just flood, and Father was frightened of water, always frightened. Father told me, *Out on the rock there, girl.* He gave me the length of rope with the harness clip, and I knew what to do. I am taller than Father since my last birthday, fifteen. I stretched wide like love and put one foot on the rock in the river middle and one hand on the tree branch above it and swung out over the river flood.

Behind me Father said, *Careful now hai.* The water ran warm and fast, like girl blood, and I held the tree branch, still able to lean down from the rock and put the rope to the halter of the lovely draft horse.

The trees went down to the river in a whispering, and they hung their long branches over the water, and the horse jerked quick and sudden, and I felt there would be a dying, but I pulled the rope up to keep her neck above water.

Father was shouting, *Hold it, girl!* and I could see his teeth clenched and his eyes wide and all the traveling of veins in his neck, the same as when he walks the ditches of our farm, many cows, hedgerows, fences. Father is always full of ditches and fright for the losing of Mammy and Fiachra and now his horse, his favorite, a big Belgian mare that cut fields once in the peaceful dark soil of long ago.

5   The river split at the rock and jumped fast into sprays coming up above my feet into my dress. But I held tight to the rope, held it like Father sometimes holds his last Sweet Afton cigarette at mealtime before prayers. Father was shouting, *Keep it there, girl, good!* He was looking at the water as if Mammy was there, as if Fiachra was there, and he gulped air and down he went in the water and he was gone so

long he made me wail to the sky for being alone. He kept a strong hold of one tree root but all the rest of his body went away under the quick brown water.

The night had started stars. They were up through the branches. The river was spraying in them.

Father came up splutter spluttering for air with his eyes all horsewild and his cap lost down the river. The rope was jumping in my hands and burning like oven rings, and he was shouting, *Hold it, girl, hold it, for the love of God hold it, please!*

Father went down in the water again but came up early, no longer enough in his lungs to keep down. He stayed in the river holding the root, and the water was hitting his shoulders and he was sad watching the draft horse die like everything does, but still I pulled on the halter rope so it would not, because Molly in the sweet shop told me it is not always so.

One more try, Father said in a sad voice like his voice over Mammy and Fiachra's coffins long ago.

10   Father dipped under and he stayed down as long as yesterday's yesterday, and then some headlights came sweeping up the town road. The lights made a painting of the rain way up high and they put shadows on the hedgerows and ditches. Father's head popped out of the water and he was breathing heavy, so he didn't see the light. His chest was wide and jumping. He looked at the draft horse and then at me. I pointed up the road and he turned in the flood and stared. Father smiled, maybe thinking it was Mack Devlin with his milk truck or Molly coming home from the sweet shop or someone come to help save his favorite horse. He dragged on the tree root and out-struggled from the river and stood on the bank, and his arms went up in the air like he was waving, shouting, *Over here over here hai!*

Father's shirt was wet under his overalls and it was very white when the headlights hit it. The lights got close close closer, and in the brightening we heard shouts and then the voices came clear. They sounded like they had swallowed things I never swallowed. I looked at Father and he looked at me all of a sudden with the strangest of faces, like he was lost, like he was punched, like he was the river cap floating, like he was a big alone tree desperate for forest. Someone shouted out, *Hey, mate, what's goin' on?* in a strange strange way, and Father said, *Nothing*, and his head dropped to his chest and he looked across the river at me and I think what he was telling me was *Drop the rope, girl*, but I didn't. I kept it tight, holding the draft horse's neck above the water, and all the time Father was saying but not saying, *Drop it, please, Katie, drop it, let her drown.*

They came right quick through the hedge, with no regard for the uniforms that hide them. One took off his helmet while he was running, and his hair was the color of winter ice. One had a moustache that looked like long grasses, and one had a scar on his cheek like the bottom end of Father's barn hay knife.

HayKnife was first to the edge of the river, and his rifle banged against his hip when he jumped out to the rock where I was halter-holding. *Okay, love, you're all right now*, he said to me, and his hand was rain-wet at my back, and he took the halter and shouted things to the other soldiers, what to do, where to stand. He kept ahold of the halter and passed me back to LongGrasses, who caught my hand and brought me safely to the riverbank. There were six of them now, all guns and helmets. Father didn't move. His eyes were steady looking at the river, maybe seeing Mammy and Fiachra in each eye of the draft horse, staring back.

One soldier was talking to him loud and fast, but Father was like a Derry shopwindow dummy, and the soldier threw up his arms and turned away through the rain and spat a big spit into the wind.

15   HayKnife was all balance on the rock with the halter, and he didn't even hold the branch above his head. IceHair was taking off his boots and gun and shirt and he looked not like boys from town who come to the barn for love, he looked not like Father when Father cuts hay without his shirt, no, he looked not like anybody; he was very skinny and strong with ribs like sometimes a horse has after a long day in the field. He didn't dive like I think now I would have liked him to, he just stepped into the water very slow and not show-offy and began making his way across, arms high in the air getting lower. But the river got too deep and HayKnife shouted from the rock, saying, *Stay high, Stevie, stay high side, mate.*

And Stevie gave a thumb up to HayKnife and then he was down under the water and the last thing was the kick of the feet.

LongGrasses was standing beside me and he put Stevie's jacket on my shoulders to warm me, but then Father came over and pushed LongGrasses away. Father pushed hard. He was smaller than LongGrasses, but LongGrasses bashed against the trunk of the tree. LongGrasses took a big breath and stared hard at him. Father said, *Leave her alone, can't you see she's just a child?* I covered my face for shame, like in school when they put me in class at a special desk bigger than the rest, not the wooden ones with lifting lids, except I don't go to school anymore since Mammy and Fiachra died. I felt shame like the shame of that day, and I covered my face and peeped through my fingers.

Father was giving a bad look to LongGrasses. LongGrasses stared at Father for a long time too and then shook his head and walked away to the riverbank where Stevie was still down in the water.

Father's hands were on my shoulders, keeping me warm, and he said, *It'll be all right now, love,* but I was only thinking about Stevie and how long he was under water. HayKnife was shouting at the top of his voice and staring down into the water, and I looked up and saw the big army truck coming through the hedgerow fence and the hedge was broken open with a big hole and Father screamed *No!* The extra lights of the truck were on and they were lighting up all the river. Father screamed again, *No!* but stopped when one of the soldiers stared at him. *Your horse or your bloody hedge, mate.*

20   Father sat down on the riverbank and said, *Sit down, Katie,* and I could hear in Father's voice more sadness than when he was over Mammy's and Fiachra's coffins, more sadness than the day after they were hit by the army truck down near the Glen, more sadness than the day the judge said, *Nobody is guilty, it's just a tragedy,* more sadness than even that day and all the other days that follow.

Bastards, Father said in a whisper, *bastards,* and he put his arm around me and sat watching until Stevie came up from the water swimming against the current to stay in one place. He shouted up at HayKnife, *Her leg's trapped,* and then,

I'm gonna try and get the hoof out. Stevie took four big gulps of air and HayKnife was pulling on the halter rope and the draft horse was screaming like I never heard a horse before or after. Father was quiet and I wanted to be back in the barn alone, waiting for drips on my tongue. I was wearing Stevie's jacket but I was shivering and wet and cold and scared, because Stevie and the draft horse were going to die, since everything in this country must.

Father likes his tea without bags, like Mammy used to make, and so there is a special way for me to make it. Put cold cold water in the kettle, and only cold, and boil it, and then put a little boiling water in the teapot and swish it around until the bottom of the teapot is warm. Then put in tea leaves, not bags, and then the boiling water, and stir it all very slowly and put on the tea cozy and let it stew on the stove for five minutes, making sure the flame is not too high so the tea cozy doesn't catch flame and burn. Then pour milk into the cups and then the tea, followed at last by the sugar all spooned around into a careful mixture.

My tea fuss made the soldiers smile, even Stevie, who had a head full of blood pouring down from where the draft horse kicked him above his eye. Father's face went white when Stevie smiled, but Stevie was very polite. He took a towel from me because he said he didn't want to get blood on the chair. He smiled at me two times when I put my head around the kitchen door, and held up one finger, meaning *One sugar, please*, and a big O from fingers for *No milk, please*. Some blood was drying in his hair, and his eyes were bright like the sky should be, and I could feel my belly sink way down until it was there like love in the barn, and he smiled at me number three.

Everyone felt good for saving a life, even a horse life, maybe even Father, but Father was silent in the corner. He was angry at me for asking the soldiers to tea, and his chin was long to his chest and there was a puddle at his feet. Everybody was towel-drying except Father and me, because we had not enough towels.

25   LongGrasses sat in the armchair and said, *Good thing ya had heat lamps, guvnor.*

Father just nodded.

How was it under the water, Stevie? LongGrasses said.

Wet, Stevie said, and everybody laughed but not Father. He stared at Stevie and then looked away.

The living room is always dark with Father grim, but it was brighter now. I liked the green of the uniforms and even the red of Stevie's blood. But Stevie's head from the horse kick must have been very sore. The other soldiers were talking about how maybe the army truck should take Stevie straight off to hospital and not get dry, just get stitches, and not get tea, just come back later to see about the draft horse if she survives under the heat lamps. But Stevie said, *I'm okay, guys, it's just a scrape. I'd kill for a cuppa.*

30   The tea was good-tasting from long brewing, and we had biscuits for special visitors. I fetched them from the pantry. I tasted one to make sure they were fresh-tasting and I carried out the tray.

I was sneezing but I was very careful to sneeze away from the tray so as to have politeness like Stevie. Stevie said, *God bless you* in his funny funny way, and we were all quiet as we sipped on the tea, but I sneezed again three four five times, and HayKnife said, *You should change out of them wet clothes, love.*

Father put down his teacup very heavy on the saucer and it was very quiet.

Everyone, even the soldiers, looked at the floor, and the mantelpiece clock was ticking and Mammy's picture was staring down from the wall, and Fiachra when he was playing football, and the soldiers didn't see them but Father did. The long silence was longer and longer until Father called me over, *Come here, Katie*, and he stood me by the window and he took the long curtain in his hands. He turned me around and wrapped the curtain around me and he took my hair and started rubbing not tender but hard. Father is good; he was just wanting to dry my hair because I was shivering even in Stevie's jacket. From under the curtain I could see the soldiers and I could see most of all Stevie. He sipped from his tea and smiled at me, and Father coughed real loud and the clock ticked some more until HayKnife said, *Here, guv, why don't you use my towel for her?*

Father said, *No, thanks.*

35   HayKnife said, *Go on, guv*, and he put the towel in a ball and made about to throw it.

Father said, *No!*

Stevie said, *Take it easy.*

Take it easy? Hay Knife said.

Maybe you should all leave, Father said.

40   HayKnife changed his face and threw the towel on the ground at Father's feet, and HayKnife's cheeks were outpuffing and he was breathing hard and he was saying, *Fat lot of fuckin thanks we get from your sort, mister.*

HayKnife was up on his feet now and pointing at Father, and the light shone off his boots well polished, and his face was twitching so the scar looked like it was cutting his face. LongGrasses and Stevie stood up from the chairs and were holding HayKnife back, but HayKnife was saying, *Risk our fuckin lives and save your fuckin horse and that's all the thanks we get, eh?*

Father held me very tight with the curtain wrapped around me, and he seemed scared and small and trembly. HayKnife was shouting lots and his face was red and scrunched. Stevie kept him back. Stevie's face was long and sad and I knew he knew because he kept looking at Mammy and Fiachra on the mantelpiece beside the ticking clock. Stevie dragged HayKnife out from the living room and at the kitchen door he let go. HayKnife turned over Stevie's shoulder one last time and looked at Father with his face all twisted, but Stevie grabbed him again and said, *Forget it, mate.*

Stevie took HayKnife out through the kitchen door and into the yard toward the army truck, and still the rain was coming down outside, and then the living room was quiet except for the clock.

I heard the engine of the army truck start.

45   Father stood away from me and put his head on the mantelpiece near the photos. I stayed at the window still in Stevie's jacket, which Stevie forgot and hasn't come back for yet.

I watched the truck as it went down the laneway, and the red lights on the green gate as it stopped and then turned into the road past where the draft horse was lifted from the river. I didn't hear anything then, just Father starting low noises in his throat, and I didn't turn from the window because I knew he would be angry for me to see him. Father was sniff sniffling. Maybe he forgot I was there. It was going right down into him and it came in big gulps like I never heard before. I stayed still, but Father was trembling big and fast. He took out a handkerchief and moved away from the mantelpiece. I didn't watch him because I knew he would be shamed for his crying.

The army truck was near out of sight, red lights on the hedgerows.

I heard the living room door shut, then the kitchen door, then the pantry door where Father keeps his hunting rifle, then the front door, and I heard the sounds of the clicker on the rifle and him still crying going farther and farther away until they were gone, and he must have been in the courtyard standing in the rain.

The clock on the mantelpiece sounded very loud, so did the rain, so did my breathing, and I looked out the window.

50   It was all near empty on the outside road, and the soldiers were going around the corner when I heard the sounds, not like bullets, more like pops one two three and the echo of them came loud to me.

The clock still ticked.

It ticked and ticked and ticked.

The curtain was wet around me, but I pulled it tight. I was scared, I couldn't move. I waited it seemed like forever.

When Father came in from outside I knew what it was. His face was like it was cut from a stone and he was not crying anymore and he didn't even look at me, just went to sit in the chair. He picked up his teacup and it rattled in his fingers, so he put it down again and put his face in his hands and stayed like that. The ticking was gone from my mind, and all was quiet everywhere in the world, and I held the curtain like I held the sound of the bullets going into the draft horse's head, his favorite, in the barn, one two three, and I stood at the window in Stevie's jacket and looked and waited and still the rain kept coming down outside one two three one two three one two three and I was thinking oh, what a small sky for so much rain.

MAKING CONNECTIONS

1.   The narrative perspective of this story is first person and through the consciousness of a teenage child. How were you affected by that? How would the story be different if told through the father? Or through one of the soldiers?

2.   As the story moves on, it's clear that the narrator must choose between loyalty to her father and gratitude to the British soldiers who have saved the family's horse. Where does your sympathy lie? What, if anything, would you like to know about this situation before you would pass judgment?

3.   Take a close look at the narrator's descriptions. For example, immediately following the powerful drama of the drowning horse, the next paragraph begins: "Father likes his tea without bags, like mammy used to make." How does this shift from terrifying spectacle to domestic tranquility affect you. Is it effective in conveying something important about the story? Explain.

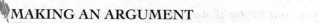

MAKING AN ARGUMENT

1. What difference does cultural context make to this story? If you are not familiar with the "troubles" in Northern Ireland, do some research and read the story again. Does your knowledge of the background help to make the motivation of the characters clearer? Does it change your mind in any way? Gather evidence from both your research and the text of the story to justify your view.

TWO READERS ∿ TWO DIFFERENT VIEWS

EXPLORING "A&P" AND MAKING CONNECTIONS

There is nothing extraordinary about the setting, the characters, or the conflict of John Updike's short story "A&P." The setting, an A&P supermarket in suburban Massachusetts in the 1960s, is as commonplace as it gets. And we experience this setting and the story's conflict through the eyes and mind of the protagonist, Sammy, an ordinary young man enduring the monotony of working a checkout slot. But Sammy checks out more than groceries. Through his narration we view the customers and employees of the supermarket, and witness his conflict, an ordinary conflict, but one that leaves him feeling "how hard the world was going to be to me hereafter."

What is extraordinary about this story is the quality of John Updike's description and his characterization of Sammy and his dilemma. Sammy, the supermarket, the customers, his boss, and his parents come to life for us. Whether we agree or disagree with Sammy's decision, we are reminded of our own choices and their consequences. In the tradition of some of the best fiction, Updike finds the "extraordinary in the ordinary" and reveals a great deal about the hard choices of growing up.

Your Experiences and Beliefs   Before you read "A&P," it may be helpful to think about your own experiences and beliefs in relation to issues that emerge from this story: pleasing or disappointing parents, teachers, employers, or other people you respect; staying in a job, in school, or in a relationship to avoid disappointing others; or taking responsibility for your actions. If you have ever worked in a supermarket, department store, fast-food restaurant, or similar business, try to remember what that experience was like for you. If you have ever been in charge of other employees, try to recall how that responsibility made you feel.

JOHN UPDIKE [1932–2009]

John Updike was born in Shillington, Pennsylvania. His father was a teacher, and his mother a writer. After graduating from Harvard University in 1954, Updike spent two years in England, where he studied at the Ruskin School of Drawing and Fine Art. After returning to the United States in 1955, he worked as a reporter for The New Yorker, *leaving the magazine two years later to become a full-time writer. Though he was an accomplished critic, essayist, and poet, Updike is best known for his novels, which include* The Centaur *(1963),*

Couples *(1968),* S. *(1988), and* Rabbit Is Rich, *which was awarded the Pulitzer Prize in 1982. His novel,* The Witches of Eastwick *(1984), was turned into a film starring Susan Sarandon and Jack Nicholson in 1987. His last novel,* Terrorist, *was published in 2006. Michiko Kakutani, a longtime critic for* The New York Times, *has said of Updike's fiction: "His heroes over the years, have all suffered from 'the tension and guilt of being human.' Torn between vestigial spiritual yearnings and the new imperatives of self-fulfillment, they hunger for salvation even as they submit to importunate demands of the flesh."*

A&P   [1962]

In walks these three girls in nothing but bathing suits. I'm in the third check-out slot, with my back to the door, so I don't see them until they're over by the bread. The one that caught my eye first was the one in the plaid green two-piece. She was a chunky kid, with a good tan and a sweet broad soft-looking can with those two crescents of white just under it, where the sun never seems to hit, at the top of the backs of her legs. I stood there with my hand on a box of HiHo crackers trying to remember if I rang it up or not. I ring it up again and the customer starts giving me hell. She's one of these cash-register-watchers, a witch about fifty with rouge on her cheekbones and no eyebrows, and I know it made her day to trip me up. She'd been watching cash registers for fifty years and probably never seen a mistake before.

By the time I got her feathers smoothed and her goodies into a bag—she gives me a little snort in passing, if she'd been born at the right time they would have burned her over in Salem—by the time I get her on her way the girls had circled around the bread and were coming back, without a pushcart, back my way along the counters, in the aisle between the check-outs and the Special bins. They didn't even have shoes on. There was this chunky one, with the two-piece—it was bright green and the seams on the bra were still sharp and her belly was still pretty pale so I guessed she just got it (the suit)—there was this one, with one of those chubby berry-faces, the lips all bunched together under her nose, this one, and a tall one, with black hair that hadn't quite frizzed right, and one of these sunburns right across under the eyes, and a chin that was too long—you know, the kind of girl other girls think is very "striking" and "attractive" but never quite makes it, as they very well know, which is why they like her so much—and then the third one, that wasn't quite so tall. She was the queen. She kind of led them, the other two peeking around and making their shoulders round. She didn't look around, not this queen, she just walked straight on slowly, on these long white prima donna legs. She came down a little hard on her heels, as if she didn't walk in her bare feet that much, putting down her heels and then letting the weight move along to her toes as if she was testing the floor with every step, putting a little deliberate, extra action into it. You never know for sure how girls' minds work (do you really think it's a mind in there or just a little buzz like a bee in a glass jar?), but you got the idea she had talked the other two into coming in here with her, and now she was showing them how to do it, walk slow and hold yourself straight.

She had on a kind of dirty-pink—beige maybe, I don't know—bathing suit with a little nubble all over it and, what got me, the straps were down. They were off her shoulders looped loose around the cool tops of her arms, and I guess as a result the suit had slipped a little on her, so all around the top of the cloth there was this shining rim. If it hadn't been there you wouldn't have known there could have been anything whiter than those shoulders. With the straps pushed off, there was nothing between the top of the suit and the top of her head except just *her,* this clean bare plane of the top of her chest down from the shoulder bones like a dented sheet of metal tilted in the light. I mean, it was more than pretty.

She had sort of oaky hair that the sun and salt had bleached, done up in a bun that was unraveling, and a kind of prim face. Walking into the A&P with your straps down, I suppose it's the only kind of face you *can* have. She held her head so high her neck, coming up out of those white shoulders, looked kind of stretched, but I didn't mind. The longer her neck was, the more of her there was.

5   She must have felt in the corner of her eye me and over my shoulder Stokesie in the second slot watching, but she didn't tip. Not this queen. She kept her eyes moving across the racks, and stopped, and turned so slow it made my stomach rub the inside of my apron, and buzzed to the other two, who kind of huddled against her for relief, and they all three of them went up the cat-and-dog-food-breakfast-cereal-macaroni-rice-raisins-seasonings-spreads-spaghetti-soft-drinks-crackers-and-cookies aisle. From the third slot I look straight up this aisle to the meat counter, and I watched them all the way. The fat one with the tan sort of fumbled with the cookies, but on second thought she put the packages back. The sheep pushing their carts down the aisle—the girls were walking against the usual traffic (not that we have one-way signs or any-thing)—were pretty hilarious. You could see them, when Queenie's white shoulders dawned on them, kind of jerk, or hop, or hiccup, but their eyes snapped back to their own baskets and on they pushed. I bet you could set off dynamite in an A&P and the people would by and large keep reaching and checking oatmeal off their lists and muttering "Let me see, there was a third thing, began with A, asparagus, no, ah yes, applesauce!" or whatever it is they do mutter. But there was no doubt, this jiggled them. A few houseslaves in pin curlers even looked around after pushing their carts past to make sure what they had seen was correct.

You know, it's one thing to have a girl in a bathing suit down on the beach, where what with the glare nobody can look at each other much anyway, and another thing in the cool of the A&P, under the fluorescent lights, against all those stacked packages, with her feet paddling along naked over our checkerboard green-and-cream rubber-tile floor.

"Oh Daddy," Stokesie said beside me. "I feel so faint."

"Darling," I said. "Hold me tight." Stokesie's married, with two babies chalked up on his fuselage already, but as far as I can tell that's the only difference. He's twenty-two, and I was nineteen this April.

"Is it done?" he asks, the responsible married man finding his voice. I forgot to say he thinks he's going to be manager some sunny day, maybe in 1990 when it's called the Great Alexandrov and Petrooshki Tea Company or something.

10   What he meant was, our town is five miles from a beach, with a big summer colony out on the Point, but we're right in the middle of town, and the women

generally put on a shirt or shorts or something before they get out of the car into the street. And anyway these are usually women with six children and varicose veins mapping their legs and nobody, including them, could care less. As I say, we're right in the middle of town, and if you stand at our front doors you can see two banks and the Congregational church and the newspaper store and three real-estate offices and about twenty-seven old freeloaders tearing up Central Street because the sewer broke again. It's not as if we're on the Cape; we're north of Boston and there's people in this town haven't seen the ocean for twenty years.

The girls had reached the meat counter and were asking McMahon something. He pointed, they pointed, and they shuffled out of sight behind a pyramid of Diet Delight peaches. All that was left for us to see was old McMahon patting his mouth and looking after them sizing up their joints. Poor kids, I began to feel sorry for them, they couldn't help it.

Now here comes the sad part of the story, at least my family says it's sad but I don't think it's sad myself. The store's pretty empty, it being Thursday afternoon, so there was nothing much to do except lean on the register and wait for the girls to show up again. The whole store was like a pinball machine and I didn't know which tunnel they'd come out of. After a while they come around out of the far aisle, around the light bulbs, records at discount of the Caribbean Six or Tony Martin Sings or some such gunk you wonder they waste the wax on, sixpacks of candy bars, and plastic toys done up in cellophane that fall apart when a kid looks at them anyway. Around they come, Queenie still leading the way, and holding a little gray jar in her hand. Slots Three through Seven are unmanned, and I could see her wondering between Stokes and me, but Stokesie with his usual luck, draws an old party in baggy gray pants who stumbles up with four giant cans of pineapple juice (what do these bums *do* with all that pineapple juice? I've often asked myself) so the girls come to me. Queenie puts down the jar and I take it into my fingers icy cold. Kingfish Fancy Herring Snacks in Pure Sour Cream: 49¢. Now her hands are empty, not a ring or a bracelet, bare as God made them, and I wonder where the money's coming from. Still with that prim look she lifts a folded dollar bill out of the hollow at the center of her nubbled pink top. The jar went heavy in my hand. Really, I thought that was so cute.

Then everybody's luck begins to run out. Lengel comes in from haggling with a truck full of cabbages on the lot and is about to scuttle into that door marked MANAGER behind which he hides all day when the girls touch his eye. Lengel's pretty dreary, teaches Sunday school and the rest, but he doesn't miss that much. He comes over and says, "Girls, this isn't the beach."

Queenie blushes, though maybe it's just a brush of sunburn I was noticing for the first time, now that she was so close. "My mother asked me to pick up a jar of herring snacks." Her voice kind of startled me, the way voices do when you see the people first, coming out so flat and dumb yet kind of tony, too, the way it ticked over "pick up" and "snacks." All of a sudden I slid right down her voice into her living room. Her father and the other men were standing around in ice-cream coats and bow ties and the women were in sandals picking up herring snacks on toothpicks off a big plate and they were all holding drinks the color of water with olives and sprigs of mint in them. When my parents have somebody over they get lemonade and if it's a real racy affair Schlitz in tall glasses with "They'll Do It Every Time" cartoons stenciled on.

15   "That's all right," Lengel said. "But this isn't the beach." His repeating this struck me as funny, as if it had just occurred to him, and he had been thinking all these years the A&P was a great big dune and he was the head lifeguard. He didn't like my smiling—as I say he doesn't miss much—but he concentrates on giving the girls that sad Sunday-school-superintendent stare.

Queenie's blush is no sunburn now, and the plump one in plaid, that I liked better from the back—a really sweet can—pipes up, "We weren't doing any shopping. We just came in for the one thing."

"That makes no difference," Lengel tells her, and I could see from the way his eyes went that he hadn't noticed she was wearing a two-piece before. "We want you decently dressed when you come in here."

"We *are* decent," Queenie says suddenly, her lower lip pushing, getting sore now that she remembers her place, a place from which the crowd that runs the A&P must look pretty crummy. Fancy Herring Snacks flashed in her very blue eyes.

"Girls, I don't want to argue with you. After this come in here with your shoulders covered. It's our policy." He turns his back. That's policy for you. Policy is what the kingpins want. What the others want is juvenile delinquency.

20   All this while, the customers had been showing up with their carts but, you know, sheep, seeing a scene, they had all bunched up on Stokesie, who shook open a paper bag as gently as peeling a peach, not wanting to miss a word. I could feel in the silence everybody getting nervous, most of all Lengel, who asks me, "Sammy, have you rung up this purchase?"

I thought and said, "No" but it wasn't about that I was thinking. I go through the punches, 4, 9, GROC, TOT—it's more complicated than you think, and after you do it often enough, it begins to make a little song, that you hear words to, in my case "Hello (*bing*) there, you (*gung*) hap-py pee-pul (*splat*)!"—the splat being the drawer flying out. I uncrease the bill, tenderly as you may imagine, it just having come from between the two smoothest scoops of vanilla I had ever known were there, and pass a half and a penny into her narrow pink palm, and nestle the herrings in a bag and twist its neck and hand it over, all the time thinking.

The girls, and who'd blame them, are in a hurry to get out, so I say "I quit" to Lengel quick enough for them to hear, hoping they'll stop and watch me, their unsuspected hero. They keep right on going, into the electric eye; the door flies open and they flicker across the lot to their car, Queenie and Plaid and Big Tall Goony-Goony (not that as raw material she was so bad), leaving me with Lengel and a kink in his eyebrow.

"Did you say something, Sammy?"

"I said I quit."

25   "I thought you did."

"You didn't have to embarrass them."

"It was they who were embarrassing us."

I started to say something that came out "Fiddle-de-doo." It's a saying of my grandmother's, and I know she would have been pleased.

30   "I don't think you know what you're saying," Lengel said.

"I know you don't," I said. "But I do." I pull the bow at the back of my apron and start shrugging it off my shoulders. A couple customers that had been heading for my slot begin to knock against each other, like scared pigs in a chute.

Lengel sighs and begins to look very patient and old and gray. He's been a friend of my parents for years. "Sammy, you don't want to do this to your Mom and Dad," he tells me. It's true, I don't. But it seems to me that once you begin a gesture it's fatal not to go through with it. I fold the apron, "Sammy" stitched in red on the pocket, and put it on the counter, and drop the bow tie on top of it. The bow tie is theirs, if you've ever wondered. "You'll feel this for the rest of your life," Lengel says, and I know that's true, too, but remembering how he made that pretty girl blush makes me so scrunchy inside I punch the No Sale tab and the machine whirs "pee-pul" and the drawer splats out. One advantage to this scene taking place in summer, I can follow this up with a clean exit, there's no fumbling around getting your coat and galoshes, I just saunter into the electric eye in my white shirt that my mother ironed the night before, and the door heaves itself open, and outside the sunshine is skating around on the asphalt.

I look around for my girls, but they're gone, of course. There wasn't anybody but some young married screaming with her children about some candy they didn't get by the door of a powder-blue Falcon station wagon. Looking back in the big windows, over the bags of peat moss and aluminum lawn furniture stacked on the pavement, I could see Lengel in my place in the slot, checking the sheep through. His face was dark gray and his back stiff, as if he'd just had an injection of iron, and my stomach kind of fell as I felt how hard the world was going to be to me hereafter.

MAKING CONNECTIONS

1. To what extent can you connect "A&P" with your own background and experience? How did this influence your response? If you were in Sammy's position, would you have made the same decision? Explain.

2. How would you describe Sammy? What is your reaction to his description of the girls and what he says about the customers?

3. How are you affected by the concrete description of the setting? What is the relationship between the setting and the conflict in the story or between the time period in which this is set and the conflict?

4. What do you think Sammy means when he says, "Now here comes the sad part of the story, at least my family says it's sad but I don't think it's sad myself"?

MAKING AN ARGUMENT

1. At the end of the story Sammy says, "...my stomach kind of fell as I felt how hard the world was going to be to me hereafter." What does he mean? What do you think he has learned from this experience? Do you think he's a hero or has simply behaved immaturely? Write an essay that makes a case for what Sammy has or has not learned from this experience—and what he does with it. Cite the text of the story for support.

TWO STUDENT ESSAYS ⌇ TWO DIFFERENT VIEWS

Depending on your experience of it, "A&P" is a story about many different things. You may experience it as a story about family pressure, rebellion, loss of innocence, immaturity, or any number of other issues.

In the student essays that follow, Michelle and Julie both emphasize the importance of Sammy's decision to quit, but come to different conclusions about what it means. Michelle sees it as a loss of innocence—and a realization by Sammy that his actions will have negative consequences for him and his family. Julie also sees Sammy's action as significant, but as a defining moment for the rest of his life, a clear statement that Sammy will refuse to live his life like Lengel.

Michelle McAuliffe

Dr. Madden

English 102

April 10, 20XX

Ironed Shirts and Bathing Suits

We all have moments in our lives when we find ourselves alone and forced to see the world and ourselves in a new and painful light. In the short story "A&P," John Updike illustrates how a seemingly unimportant experience becomes this kind of moment in the life of his main character, Sammy.

Sammy is a lively, cynical young guy who seems more than familiar with the grocery sciences, anatomy of the store, and psychology of the customer mind: "The girls had circled around the bread and were coming back, without a pushcart, back my way along the counters, in the aisle between the check-outs and the Special bins" (456). Sammy spends a lot of time analyzing the store and the people in it: "I bet you could set off dynamite in an A&P and the people would by and large keep reaching and checking oatmeal off their lists and muttering 'Let me see, there was a third thing, began with A, asparagus, no, ah yes, applesauce!' or whatever it is they do mutter" (457). He doesn't hesitate to pass judgment on them either: "What do these bums *do* with all that pineapple juice?" (458). This seems to be the primary mental activity of his day.

On this particular day, Sammy's focus is on three young girls who enter the store wearing bathing suits. Besides ogling their every move, he gets a kick out of how they are dressed and people's reactions to it: "You could see them, when Queenie's white shoulders dawned on them, kind of jerk, or hop, or hiccup, but their eyes snapped back to their own baskets and on they pushed" (457). But Lengel, the store manager, is not so amused. He exclaims, "Girls, this isn't the beach" (458). And the fun begins.

When the confrontation with the girls and the manager occurs, Sammy sees it as time to act instead of watching passively. We can't really say what motivates his action. It may be something noble, or simply an excuse to be rid of a stifling job. Even Sammy might not be able to tell us. He has the initial urge to quit in the presence of the girls, but when they're gone, he still feels strongly about something. Once he says he quits, it's too late to turn back. Even though Lengel, the store manager, is giving him the chance to stay, "You don't want to do this to your Mom and Dad" (460), his decision is final. Sammy admits to us that he doesn't want to do this to his parents, but he adds, "It seems to me that once you begin a gesture it's fatal not to go through with it" (460). He has his personal dignity to consider. Lengel speaks prophetically when he says, "'You'll feel this for the rest of your life'" (460). Sammy knows this too, but feels his decision is one of liberation. He even likes the idea of this taking place in the summertime, so he can make a quick exit.

Sammy, however, is also aware of Lengel's reaction. He notices that "Lengel sighs and begins to look very patient and old and gray" (460). Sammy's need for a quick exit is a result of feeling some shame and guilt in the face of a family friend and understanding man. When Sammy gets outside, the desolation of the parking lot takes away the glory of his act in the war between youth and responsibility. His righteous decision is not so simple anymore. Without something to rebel against, he feels alone. Sammy may be expressing his sympathy for Lengel when he says, "I could see Lengel in my place in the slot, checking the sheep through. His face was dark gray and his back stiff, as if he'd just had an injection of iron, and my stomach kind of fell as I felt how hard the world was going to be to me hereafter" (460). He feels that Lengel and his parents, and perhaps the entire adult world, must be disappointed in him. He has let them down.

Although we can't say what immediate consequence Sammy will face, we know that he recognizes the effects of his action beyond himself. This realization of how we affect others through our actions is not a lesson to be learned in books; we must experience it. We are often surprised when we see how what we do, say, or think affects others. At moments like this we know we have learned something valuable. Although we don't always understand it, we know that it's something that will influence our outlook on life. At the end of this story, Sammy is all alone to contemplate a decision and thoughts that only a half hour before were very far from his mind. Such is the introduction of insight and wisdom into our lives—when we least expect it, and in the most unlikely situations.

[New Page]

Work Cited

Updike, John. "A&P." *Exploring Literature*. Ed. Frank Madden. 5th ed. New
    York: Longman, 2012. 456–460. Print.

Julie Fitzmaurice

Dr. Madden

English 102

April 6, 20XX

What Makes Sammy Quit?

In John Updike's short story "A&P," we see the world through the eyes of a nineteen-year-old. Sammy, the main character, is also the narrator, and his narration creates the tone and atmosphere of the story. When Sammy quits his job for no obvious reason, we are left with a question: Why? Was it his impatience with older people, rebellion against authority, or just boredom? It was not one of these reasons alone that made him quit, but the synergy they created, once established, could not be denied.

First let us consider Sammy and what we learn about his character in the story. Updike doesn't give us many details about him. From the text we learn that Sammy is nineteen years old and lives in a small town north of Boston, five miles from the beach. The most important key to Sammy's character, however, is how he sees everyone else.

Virtually everything we learn in this story, we learn through Sammy's thoughts. Sammy comes from a working-class background: "When my parents have somebody over they get lemonade and if it's a real racy affair Schlitz in tall glasses with 'They'll Do It Every Time' cartoons stenciled on" (458–459). Another indication of a working-class background is in his comment, "Now here comes the sad part of the story, at least my family says it's sad, but I don't think it's sad myself" (458). This statement tells us that Sammy's parents placed importance on his job at the A&P.

His comments about Lengel tell us more about Sammy than they do about his boss at the A&P. Lengel is older and the manager of the A&P. He teaches Sunday school and has been a friend of Sammy's parents for years. Sammy thinks Lengel is "pretty dreary," and "doesn't miss that much" (458), and describes him as giving the girls that "sad Sunday-school-superintendent stare" (459). His descriptions of the customers also tell us a lot about him: "one of these cash-register-watchers, a witch about fifty" (456), "The sheep pushing their carts down the aisle" (457), and "A few houseslaves in pin curlers" (457). These comments reveal Sammy's impatience with adults and his rebellious streak.

Sammy's description of the A&P itself turns the store into a quasi character. The A&P has its own pulse and comes alive for us. He tells us what the store looks and sounds like. The cash register even sings a song as Sammy tediously pushes its keys: "Hello (*bing*) there, you (*gung*) hap-py pee-pul (*splat*)!" (459). Almost everyone has experienced the setting of a food store; there is a certain universality about them. But Sammy's description of the "cat-and-dog-food-breakfast-cereal-macaroni-rice-raisins-seasonings-spreads-spaghetti-soft-drinks-crackers-and-cookies aisle" (457) brings this familiar place to dull but fresh life.

Sammy goes into great detail about the girls, too. If he were busy he would not notice so much about them. The store is slow, and Sammy leans on the register looking at the girls. He is so bored that he sees the store as a pinball machine. The girls are the balls, and the aisles are the chutes that the balls travel through.

His detailed description has a strong impact on our reading of the story. It makes it easy for us to imagine being nineteen and working in a store on a hot summer day. Sammy describes what the atmosphere is like: "The store's pretty empty, it being Thursday afternoon, so there was nothing much to do except lean on the register and wait for the girls to show up again" (458).

At the climax of the story, when Lengel confronts the girls about their bathing suits, Sammy is already bored and frustrated to exhaustion. He thinks that Lengel is a pompous bag of wind, so he says, "'I quit'" (459). He says this to Lengel to save himself, not the girls. The girls are simply the final impetus for Sammy's quitting: he needs them as his excuse. He would like to have the girls think that he is quitting his job in indignation over the way Lengel treated them.

At this moment, Lengel is everything that Sammy detests. He represents all the things that Sammy wants to rebel against: age, authority, his working-class background, Sunday school teachers, and the voice of righteousness. He realizes that if he stays at the A&P he will become a Lengel. In one brief moment all his emotions synergize. The two words "I quit" leave his lips, and Sammy changes the course of his life forever.

[New Page]

Work Cited

Updike, John. "A&P." *Exploring Literature.* Ed. Frank Madden. 5th ed. New
    York: Longman, 2012. 456–460. Print.

◆ POETRY ◆

CONNECTING THROUGH COMPARISON: THE CITY

Throughout history, cities have been identified as a prime source of sophistication, experience, loss of innocence—and, sometimes, evil. Is there something about cities that attracts evil people and activities? Is the countryside healthier physically and morally? The two poems that follow address a subtheme of this section: the city. Read and discussed together, they invite comparisons and connections—not only with each other—but with your own experience of the evils—or positive forces—of city life.

WILLIAM BLAKE [1757–1827]

The son of a London haberdasher, William Blake received very little formal education. When he was ten, he entered a drawing school, and later studied for a few months at the Royal Academy of Art. At the age of fourteen, he was apprenticed to an engraver, and, after seven years, he was able to earn his living illustrating books. From his early twenties to his sixties, when he chose to devote himself exclusively to pictorial art, Blake produced books of his own poetry, which were painstakingly illustrated and hand colored, often with the help of his wife. His early books of poetry, Songs of Innocence *(1789) and* Songs of Experience *(1794), from which "London" and both versions of "The Chimney Sweeper" are taken, express Blake's rage at the social injustices of England. His later work, the so-called* Prophetic Works, *are much more difficult. In these highly symbolic and often cryptic poems, Blake created his own complicated mythological system based*

on his deeply held religious and spiritual beliefs. (His wife said of him: "I have very little of Mr. Blake's company; he is always in Paradise.") His now-famous verses were not very well known during his lifetime, and it is only in the past century that he has earned a wider readership.

LONDON [1794]

I wander through each chartered street,
Near where the chartered Thames does flow,
And mark in every face I meet
Marks of weakness, marks of woe.

In every cry of every man,   5
In every infant's cry of fear,
In every voice, in every ban,
The mind-forged manacles I hear.

How the chimney-sweeper's cry
Every black'ning church appalls   10
And the hapless soldier's sigh
Runs in blood down palace walls.

But most through midnight streets I hear
How the youthful harlot's curse
Blasts the new born infant's tear   15
And blights with plagues the marriage hearse.

WILLIAM WORDSWORTH [1770–1850]

William Wordsworth was born in Cockermouth on the northern tip of England's Lake District and spent much of his childhood exploring the natural sights of this region, which later served as the setting for many of his greatest poems. In 1791, after attending Cambridge University, he traveled to France, where he became a supporter of the French Revolution and met and fell in love with a French woman, Annette Vallon, with whom he had a daughter. Due to the political situation, Wordsworth was forced to flee France, and the couple never married. Together with his sister Dorothy, an accomplished writer herself and later his editor, Wordsworth settled first in a rent-free cottage in Dorsetshire, and then moved to Somersetshire to be near his friend, the poet Samuel Taylor Coleridge. In 1798, the two men collaborated to produce Lyrical Ballads *(which Wordsworth revised in 1800), a collection of poetry credited with bringing the Romantic movement to England. The enormously influential volume was a commercial success, and Wordsworth and his sister were able to live comfortably for the rest of their lives. In 1843, he was appointed poet laureate. Today, Wordsworth is best remembered for his deeply felt depiction of the English countryside and of the customs and common speech of its people.*

COMPOSED UPON WESTMINSTER BRIDGE, SEPTEMBER 3, 1802   [1807]

Earth has not anything to show more fair:
Dull would he be of soul who could pass by
A sight so touching in its majesty;
This City now doth, like a garment, wear
The beauty of the morning; silent, bare,   5
Ships, towers, domes, theaters, and temples lie
Open unto the fields, and to the sky;
All bright and glittering in the smokeless air.
Never did sun more beautifully steep
In his first splendor, valley, rock, or hill;   10
Ne'er saw I, never felt, a calm so deep!
The river glideth at his own sweet will:
Dear God! the very houses seem asleep;
And all that mighty heart is lying still!

MAKING CONNECTIONS

1. In "London," what are "mind-forged manacles"? Can you think of any "mind-forged manacles" that exist today?
2. What is the "youthful harlot's curse," and what does it have to do with blasting "the new born infant's tear" or plaguing "the marriage hearse"?
3. Much of Wordsworth's verse depicts the countryside, but this is a city scene in early morning. To what extent is the beauty depicted here just as majestic as—but different from—nature?
4. Have you ever been so "taken" by a "human-made" sight? Explain.

MAKING AN ARGUMENT

1. Most cities have changed to some degree for the better since the days of Blake and Wordsworth, but many of the positive and negative elements described in these poems still remain. Compare and contrast Wordsworth's vision of the city with that of Blake as expressed in "London." Bring that vision forward two hundred years and write about their views as they might apply to a modern city. Cite the text of the poems for support.

CONNECTING THROUGH COMPARISON: THE CHIMNEY SWEEPERS

The next two poems by William Blake address the same subject—the chimney sweeper mentioned in his poem "London" above. One poet, but the speakers in both poems seem to experience the same role—a chimney sweeper—very differently. Or do they? Read and discussed together, they invite comparisons and connections with the poem "London" and each other.

MLL WILLIAM BLAKE [1757–1827]

(See biography on pp. 456–466.)
"Chimney-sweeps" were usually small children (small enough to slide down chimneys)
who either had been sold by their poverty-stricken parents or were orphans or illegiti-
mate children. They were overworked, inadequately clothed—and often suffered from
burns, a permanent coating of soot, deformed limbs, black lung disease, or cancer.

THE CHIMNEY SWEEPER (FROM SONGS OF INNOCENCE)   [1789]

When my mother died I was very young,
And my father sold me while yet my tongue
Could scarcely cry weep weep weep weep
So your chimneys I sweep & in soot I sleep.

There's little Tom Dacre, who cried when his head   5
That curl'd like a lambs back, was shav'd, so I said:
Hush Tom never mind it, for when your head's bare
You know that the soot cannot spoil your white hair.

And so he was quiet, & that very night,
As Tom was sleeping he had such a sight,   10
That thousands of sweepers Dick, Joe, Ned & Jack
Were all of them lock'd up in coffins of black,

And by came an Angel who had a bright key,
And he open'd the coffins & set them all free.
Then down a green plain leaping laughing they run   15
And wash in a river and shine in the Sun.

Then naked & white, all their bags left behind
They rise upon clouds, and sport in the wind
And the Angel told Tom if he'd be a good boy,
He'd have God for his father & never want joy.   20

And so Tom awoke and we rose in the dark
And got with our bags & our brushes to work
Tho' the morning was cold, Tom was happy & warm
So if all do their duty they need not fear harm.

THE CHIMNEY SWEEPER (FROM SONGS OF EXPERIENCE)   [1794]

A little black thing among the snow:
Crying weep, weep, in notes of woe!
Where are thy father & mother? say?
They are both gone up to the church to pray.

Because I was happy upon the heath   5
And smil'd among the winters snow:

Etching of "The Chimney Sweeper" from *Songs of Innocence*

Etching of "The Chimney Sweeper" from *Songs of Experience*

They clothed me in the clothes of death,
And taught me to sing the notes of woe.

And because I am happy & dance & sing,
They think they have done me no injury: 10
And are gone to praise God & his Priest & King
Who make up a heaven of our misery.

MAKING CONNECTIONS

1. How does the structure and rhyme-scheme of each poem influence your response?
2. Identify the images in both poems, and write about their effectiveness in establishing the speaker's tone in each poem. Is there a difference in tone between the two? Explain.
3. Blake composed his *Songs of Innocence* and *Songs of Experience* using a method called "relief etching." Examine his illustrations on the previous page, and write a brief essay that explores how they reflect the poems' differing content.

MAKING AN ARGUMENT

1. Write a comparison of "London" and the two versions of "The Chimney Sweeper." Is there a difference in tone among the poems? Why is the first version of "The Chimney Sweeper" a "song of innocence" and the second one a "song of experience"? Cite text from all three poems for support.

A. E. HOUSMAN   [1859–1936]

An important scholar of Latin as well as a celebrated poet, A[lfred] E[dward] Housman was born in the village of Fockbury in Worcestershire, England. A brilliant student at Oxford University, Housman inexplicably failed his final exams. Determined to redeem himself after his poor show-ing, he wrote scholarly articles while working at night as a civil servant in the patent office. His brilliant scholarship eventually won him positions at the University of London and Cambridge University. During his life he published only two slim volumes of poetry, A Shropshire Lad *(1898) and* Last Poems *(1922). His poems are tinged with melancholy, often dealing with themes of lost love and youth. His* Complete Poems, *which includes verses released posthumously, was published in 1956.*

WHEN I WAS ONE-AND-TWENTY   [1898]

When I was one-and-twenty
    I heard a wise man say,
'Give crowns and pounds and guineas
    But not your heart away;
Give pearls away and rubies   5
    But keep your fancy free.'

But I was one-and-twenty,
   No use to talk to me.

When I was one-and-twenty
   I heard him say again,   10
'The heart out of the bosom
   Was never given in vain;
'Tis paid with sighs a plenty
   And sold for endless rue.'
And I am two-and-twenty,   15
   And oh, 'tis true, 'tis true.

MAKING CONNECTIONS

1. What do you think of the wise man's advice in the first stanza?
2. Would you have taken his advice? Explain.
3. What happened to the speaker? Does he regret his decision? Would you?

MAKING AN ARGUMENT

1. This poem and Edna St. Vincent Millay's "What Lips My Lips Have Kissed, and Where, and Why" on page 739 and "Love Is Not All" on page 739 are love poems. Do you think the speakers in Millay's poems would agree with the view of the speaker in this poem? Write an essay in response to that question and cite the texts of all three poems for support.

ALBERTO RIOS [B. 1952]

A bilingual native of Nogales, Arizona (where he could stand with one foot in the United States and the other in Mexico at the same time), Alberto Rios's father came from Mexico and his mother from England. He has received Guggenheim and National Endowment for the Arts Fellowships, and his books of poetry include Whispering to Fool the Wind *(1981), for which he won the Walt Whitman Award;* The Live Orchard Woman *(1990);* Pig Cookies and Other Stories *(1995);* The Smallest Muscle in the Human Body *(2002); and* The Dangerous Shirt *(2009). He is the Regents Professor of English at Arizona State University, where he teaches creative writing.*

IN SECOND GRADE MISS LEE I PROMISED NEVER TO FORGET YOU AND I NEVER DID
                                                 [2002]

In a letting-go moment
Miss Lee the Teacher
Who was not married
And who the next year was not at school,
Said to us, her second grade,   5
French lovers in the morning
Keep an apple next to the bed,

Each taking a bite
On first waking, to take away
The blackish breath of the night,
You know the kind.   10
A bite and then kissing,
And kissing like that was better.

I saw her once more
When she came to sell encyclopedias.
I was always her favorite—   15
The erasers, and the way she looked at me.
I promised, but not to her face,
Never to forget
The story of the apples.
Miss Lee all blond hair and thin,   20
Like *a real movie star*
If she would have just combed herself more.
Miss Lee, I promised,
I would keep apples
For you.   25

MAKING CONNECTIONS

1. Why did Miss Lee's story make such an impression on the speaker?
2. How did the speaker feel about Miss Lee when he was in the second grade?
   How does he feel about her now?
3. Does the poem tell us anything about Miss Lee's teaching abilities? Can we
   infer anything about her?

MAKING AN ARGUMENT

1. From the poem, we know that Miss Lee is a young teacher. Write an essay
   that compares Miss Lee's classroom with that of another inexperienced
   teacher, David Sedaris in "The Learning Curve" (p. 486). Sedaris's essay
   is meant to be satirically funny. Do you think Rios is making fun of Miss
   Lee? What types of impressions does each teacher seem to leave with their
   students? Cite examples from the texts in your essay.

EDWIN ARLINGTON ROBINSON [1869–1935]

*Born into a wealthy New England family, Edwin Arlington
Robinson was raised in Gardiner, Maine, a small town that
later served as the model for "Tilbury Town," the setting for
many of his most famous poems. Encouraged by a neighbor,
he developed an interest in poetry and wrote numerous original poems, as well as diligently translated the great Greek
and Roman poets. He spent two years at Harvard University,
and after failing to get his poems published he decided to*

print copies of his first collection, The Torrent and The Night Before *(1896), himself. He mailed copies to publishers and received some favorable responses, though some found his subject matter bleak. Encouraged, he published* The Children of the Night *(1896), which contained many of what were to become his best-known Tilbury poems (including "Richard Cory"). The collection was considered a failure, and Robinson descended into poverty and alcoholism. In 1902, in a stroke of luck, President Theodore Roosevelt stumbled onto a copy of* The Children of the Night *and was taken with it, saying, "I am not sure I understand... but I'm entirely sure that I like it." Roosevelt found Robinson a post with very few duties in the customs office in New York City, and Robinson was free to devote himself to his poetry. He stepped down from the post following the success of his 1910 collection,* The Town Down the River. *In 1921, Robinson was awarded the first Pulitzer Prize for poetry for his* Collected Poems *and was awarded two more for* The Man Who Died Twice *(1924) and* Tristam *(1927). After Robinson's death in 1935, Robert Frost, who listed Robinson as one of his greatest influences, wrote of him and his often unhappy life: "His theme was unhappiness itself, but his skill was as happy as it was playful. There is that comforting thought for those who suffered to see him suffer."*

RICHARD CORY   [1896]

Whenever Richard Cory went downtown,
We people on the pavement looked at him;
He was a gentleman from sole to crown,
Clean favored, and imperially slim,

And he was always quietly arrayed,   5
And he was always human when he talked;
But still he fluttered pulses when he said,
"Good-morning," and he glittered when he walked.

And he was rich—yes, richer than a king—
And admirably schooled in every grace: 10
In fine, we thought that he was everything
To make us wish that we were in his place.

So on we worked, and waited for the light,
And went without the meat, and cursed the bread;
And Richard Cory, one calm summer night,   15
Went home and put a bullet through his head.

MAKING CONNECTIONS

1. Who is the speaker in this poem?
2. Who are "we"? Who is Richard Cory to us? What lines in the poem indicate these things?
3. What effect does the last line have on you? Were you surprised? Was it effective to wait until the last line to tell you that he killed himself? Why?

MAKING AN ARGUMENT

1. We know very little about Richard Cory from the description in this poem. Based on the little you have from the poem, tap your imagination and write a history of Richard Cory up to the last line of the poem. Who was he? How did he feel about himself and why? What motivated him to kill himself? Cite the text of the poem for support.

ANNE SEXTON [1928–1974]

Born and raised in New England, Anne Sexton attended Garland Junior College and was married at the age of twenty. She suffered the first of many mental breakdowns following the birth of her first child in 1954. After a break-down following the birth of her second child, she began writing poetry at the suggestion of a therapist. To Bedlam and Part Way Back, *her first book of poems, was published in 1960. Her 1967 volume,* Live or Die, *was awarded the Pulitzer Prize. Though she became extraordinarily successful, Sexton continually struggled with depression. Following her divorce, she committed suicide in 1974. Like her contemporary Sylvia Plath, Sexton's powerful and often startling work has been characterized as confessional poetry, in which deeply personal topics once considered taboo in modern poetry—mental illness, religious guilt, therapy—are openly discussed.*

PAIN FOR A DAUGHTER   [1966]

Blind with love, my daughter
has cried nightly for horses,
those long-necked marchers and churners
that she has mastered, any and all,
reigning them in like a circus hand—   5
the excitable muscles and the ripe neck;
tending this summer, a pony and a foal.
She who is too squeamish to pull
a thorn from the dog's paw,
watched her pony blossom with distemper,   10
the underside of the jaw swelling
like an enormous grape.
Gritting her teeth with love,
she drained the boil and scoured it
with hydrogen peroxide until pus   15
ran like milk on the barn floor.

Blind with loss all winter,
in dungarees, a ski jacket and a hard hat,

she visits the neighbor's stable,
our acreage not zoned for barns;   20
they who own the flaming horses
and the swan-whipped thoroughbred
that she tugs at and cajoles,
thinking it will burn like a furnace
under her small-hipped English seat.   25

Blind with pain she limps home.
The thoroughbred has stood on her foot.
He rested there like a building.
He grew into her foot until they were one.
The marks of the horseshoe printed   30
into her flesh, the tips of her toes
ripped off like pieces of leather,
three toenails swirled like shells
and left to float in blood in her riding boot.

Blind with fear, she sits on the toilet,   35
her foot balanced over the washbasin,
her father, hydrogen peroxide in hand,
performing the rites of the cleansing.
She bites on a towel, sucked in breath,
sucked in and arched against the pain,   40
her eyes glancing off me where
I stand at the door, eyes locked
on the ceiling, eyes of a stranger,
and then she cries...
Oh my God, help me!   45
Where a child would have cried *Mama!*
Where a child would have believed *Mama!*
she bit the towel and called on God
and I saw her life stretch out...
I saw her torn in childbirth,   50
and I saw her, at that moment,
in her own death and I knew that she
knew.

MAKING CONNECTIONS

1. Do you think the title of the poem refers to the daughter's or the mother's pain—or both? Explain.
2. The poem seems to be divided into four sections: love, loss, pain, and fear. How are each of these emotions described in the poem?
3. At the end of the poem, the speaker says, "I knew that she / knew." What do you think the daughter knows that she did not before?

MAKING AN ARGUMENT

1. The speaker in the poem is the mother. Do you think a daughter would
   have the same understanding of this event? Imagine you are the daughter
   in this poem. Using the information and images in the poem, write about
   this experience from your perspective. What have you learned from this
   experience and why? Cite the text of the poem to support your views.

WALT WHITMAN   [1819–1892]

*Walt Whitman was born on an impoverished farm near the
town of Huntington on Long Island, New York, and moved
with his family to the then-independent city of Brooklyn. For
many years, he worked in the printing trade, taking occasional writing jobs, until he landed a position as an editor of
a Brooklyn newspaper. Dismissed from his editorial position
because of his politics, Whitman supported himself working
as a carpenter and contractor, while he wrote in his spare
time. In 1855, he published his own book of poetry,* Leaves of Grass, *a collection of
twelve poems (including* Song of Myself*), which Whitman continually expanded
and revised throughout his life, publishing a final "death bed" edition in 1892. His
work as a volunteer nurse during the Civil War inspired his next collection of verse,*
Drum Taps *(1865), as well as his famous elegy for Abraham Lincoln, "When Lilacs
Last in the Dooryard Bloom'd." Whitman spent his later years as a revered figure
in Camden, New Jersey, where he was the center of a devoted band of disciples and
visited by many writers from around the world. His strikingly original poetry, with
its boldness of form, scope, and subject matter, has influenced generations of poets.
The selection below is taken from* Song of Myself *(1855), Whitman's longest (it runs
over two thousand lines) and perhaps greatest poem.*

THERE WAS A CHILD WENT FORTH   [1855]

There was a child went forth every day,
And the first object he looked upon, that object he
    became,
And that object became part of him for the day or a
    certain part of the day,
Or for many years or stretching cycles of years.

The early lilacs became part of this child,   5
And grass and white and red morning-glories, and
    white and red clover, and the song of the
    phoebe-bird,
And the Third-month° lambs and the sow's pink-
    faint litter, and the mare's foal and the cow's
    calf,

7 Third-month March

And the noisy brood of the barnyard or by the mire
    of the pond-side,
And the fish suspending themselves so curiously below there,
    and the beautiful curious liquid,
And the water-plants with their graceful flat heads,   10
    all became part of him.

The field-sprouts of Fourth-month and Fifth-month
    became part of him,
Winter-grain sprouts and those of the light-yellow
    corn, and the esculent° roots of the garden,
And the apple-trees covered with blossoms and the
    fruit afterward, and wood-berries, and the commonest
    weeds by the road,
And the old drunkard staggering home from the outhouse
    of the tavern whence he had lately risen,
And the schoolmistress that passed on her way to   15
    the school,
And the friendly boys that passed, and the quarrel-
    some boys,
And the tidy and fresh-cheeked girls, and the bare-
    foot negro boy and girl,
And all the changes of city and country wherever he
    went.

His own parents, he that had fathered him and she
    that had conceived him in her womb and
    birthed him,
They gave this child more of themselves than that,   20
They gave him afterward every day, they became
    part of him.

The mother at home quietly placing the dishes on
    the supper-table,
The mother with mild words, clean her cap and
    gown, a wholesome odor falling off her person
    and clothes as she walks by,
The father, strong, self-sufficient, manly, mean, angered,
    unjust,
The blow, the quick loud word, the tight bargain, the crafty lure,   25
The family usages, the language, the company, the
    furniture, the yearning and swelling heart,
Affection that will not be gainsayed,° the sense of
    what is real, the thought if after all it should
    prove unreal,

12 esculent edible   **27 gainsayed** denied

The doubts of day-time and the doubts of night-
    time, the curious whether and how,
Whether that which appears so is so, or is it all
    flashes and specks?
Men and women crowding fast in the streets, if they   30
    are not flashes and specks what are they?
The streets themselves and the façades of houses,
    and goods in the windows,
Vehicles, teams, the heavy-planked wharves,
    the huge crossing at the ferries,
The village on the highland seen from afar at sunset,
    the river between,
Shadows, aureola° and mist, the light falling
    on roofs and gables of white or brown two miles off,
The schooner near by sleepily dropping down the   35
    tide, the little boat slack-towed astern,
The hurrying tumbling waves, quick-broken crests,
    slapping,
The strata of colored clouds, the long bar of maroon-
    tint away solitary by itself, the spread of
    purity it lies motionless in,
The horizon's edge, the flying sea-crow, the fragrance
    of salt marsh and shore mud,
These became part of that child who went forth
    every day, and who now goes, and will always
    go forth every day.

MAKING CONNECTIONS

1. The first six lines of the poem serve as an introduction. What do they say this poem is about? Do you agree that we become objects that we look upon—and that those objects become part of us? Explain.

2. What follows in the poem is a long list of objects, people, and events the child encounters. To what extent does each of the encounters represent something different? If you recall your own childhood, can you come up with a similar list?

MAKING AN ARGUMENT

1. Compare the style and the content of this poem with Whitman's *Song of Myself* 6 on page 1164 and "When I Heard the Learn'd Astronomer" on page 89. Make believe that you have not seen Whitman's name on the poems. Analyze the three poems carefully, and write an argument that makes the case that all three poems were written by the same author. Cite the text of all three for support.

34 aureola bands of light

STEPHEN CRANE [1871–1900]

Stephen Crane was the youngest of fourteen children born to a Methodist minister in Newark, New Jersey. After briefly attending LaFayette College and Syracuse University, Crane moved to New York City to work as a freelance journalist. He lived an often impoverished existence and came to know life in the slums firsthand. These experiences inspired his first novel, Maggie, a Girl of the Streets, *which he published at his own expense under a pseudonym. The novel impressed members of New York's literary elite and set the stage for the publication of his second novel,* The Red Badge of Courage *(1895). In 1895, Crane also published a book of short poems,* The Black Riders. *In 1899,* Other Lines, *and another collection of poems,* War Is Kind, *would prove influential after his death. Crane died of tuberculosis when he was only twenty-eight.*

THE WAYFARER   [1895]

The wayfarer,
Perceiving the pathway to truth,
Was struck with astonishment.
It was thickly grown with weeds.
"Ha," he said   5
"I see that none has passed here
In a long time."
Later he saw that each weed was a singular knife.
"Well," he mumbled at last,
"Doubtless there are other roads."   10

MAKING CONNECTIONS

1. Why is the wayfarer "struck with astonishment"?
2. Why does he change his mind about following the path? Do you find this ironic? Explain.

MAKING AN ARGUMENT

1. Compare this poem with Matthew Arnold's "Dover Beach" on page 1160. How do both poems play on this book's themes of Faith and Doubt? Innocence and Experience?

CONNECTING THROUGH COMPARISON: THE DEATH OF A CHILD

One of the most heart-wrenching moments we can experience is the death of a child. Can we justify the death of a child? Is it fair that an innocent child should die when evil people sometimes live long and prosperous lives? The two poems that follow address this subtheme of innocence and experience. Read and discussed together, they invite comparisons and connections—not only with each other, but with your own experience of this topic and other poems about death in this textbook.

ROBERT FROST   [1874–1963]

(See biography on p. 279.)

"OUT, OUT..."   [1916]

The buzz saw snarled and rattled in the yard
And made dust and dropped stove-length sticks of wood,
Sweet-scented stuff when the breeze drew across it.
And from there those that lifted eyes could count
Five mountain ranges one behind the other   5
Under the sunset far into Vermont.
And the saw snarled and rattled, snarled and rattled,
As it ran light, or had to bear a load.
And nothing happened: day was all but done.
Call it a day, I wish they might have said   10
To please the boy by giving him the half hour
That a boy counts so much when saved from work.
His sister stood beside them in her apron
To tell them "Supper." At the word, the saw,
As if to prove saws knew what supper meant,   15
Leaped out at the boy's hand, or seemed to leap—
He must have given the hand. However it was,
Neither refused the meeting. But the hand!
The boy's first outcry was a rueful laugh,
As he swung toward them holding up the hand,   20
Half in appeal, but half as if to keep
The life from spilling. Then the boy saw all—
Since he was old enough to know, big boy
Doing a man's work, though a child at heart—
He saw all spoiled. "Don't let him cut my hand off—   25
The doctor, when he comes. Don't let him, sister!"
So. But the hand was gone already.
The doctor put him in the dark of ether.
He lay and puffed his lips out with his breath.
And then—the watcher at his pulse took fright.   30
No one believed. They listened at his heart.
Little—less—nothing!—and that ended it.
No more to build on there. And they, since they
Were Not The One Dead, Turned To Their Affairs

SEAMUS HEANEY [B. 1939]

(See biography on p. 281.)

MID-TERM BREAK   [1965]

I sat all morning in the college sick bay
Counting bells knelling classes to a close.
At two o'clock our neighbors drove me home.

In the porch I met my father crying—
He had always taken funerals in his stride—   5
And Big Jim Evans saying it was a hard blow.

The baby cooed and laughed and rocked the pram
When I came in, and I was embarrassed
By old men standing up to shake my hand

And tell me they were "sorry for my trouble."   10
Whispers informed strangers I was the eldest,
Away at school, as my mother held my hand

In hers and coughed out angry tearless sighs.
At ten o'clock the ambulance arrived
With the corpse, stanched and bandaged by the nurses.   15

Next morning I went up into the room. Snowdrops
And candles soothed the bedside; I saw him
For the first time in six weeks. Paler now,

Wearing a poppy bruise on his left temple.
He lay in the four foot box as in his cot.   20
No gaudy scars, the bumper knocked him clear

A four foot box, a foot for every year.

MAKING CONNECTIONS

1. To what extent does your own experience with the death of someone young affect your response to "Out, Out..."?
2. In what way does the setting of the sawmill in the poem emphasize what happens to the boy?
3. At the end of the poem, the speaker says, "And they, since they / Were not the one dead, turned to their affairs." Do you think "they" are being heartless? Why or why not?
4. In "Mid-Term Break, " the boy is told by the old men that they are "sorry for my trouble." What trouble is that? What's happened here?
5. To what extent is your response to this poem affected by your own experience with the death of someone very young?
6. The last line of the poem, "A four foot box, a foot for every year," stands by itself. What is your reaction to it? In what ways is it appropriate to wrap up the poem?

MAKING AN ARGUMENT

1. The title "Out, Out..." is taken from Shakespeare's play *Macbeth*. When he receives the news that his young wife is dead, Macbeth begins a soliloquy that includes the line "Out, out, brief candle!" Get a copy of the play, read the entire soliloquy (*Macbeth*, Act V, Sc. 5), and write about the appropriateness of Frost's title and its allusion to the soliloquy by comparing and contrasting the poem with the soliloquy.

2. Both Heaney's "Mid-Term Break" and Frost's "Out, Out..." address the death of a boy. How each one addresses this premature death, however, seems quite different. Analyze and interpret both poems, and write a comparison of their treatment of young death. Cite the text of both poems for support.

◆ ESSAYS ◆

JUDITH ORTIZ COFER [B. 1952]

The daughter of a Puerto Rican mother and a U.S. mainland father, Judith Ortiz Cofer was born in Puerto Rico but immigrated to the mainland in 1956. Educated at Augusta College and Florida Atlantic University, Cofer worked as an English teacher and bilingual instructor in Florida. Because of her bilingual upbringing, much of Cofer's work is concerned with the power of language and its uses. She has published a number of volumes of poetry, novels, and *memoirs. Her latest poetry collection is* A Love Story Beginning in Spanish *(2005). The essay below is taken from her memoir,* Silent Dancing.

I FELL IN LOVE, OR MY HORMONES AWAKENED [1990]

I fell in love, or my hormones awakened from their long slumber in my body, and suddenly the goal of my days was focused on one thing: to catch a glimpse of my secret love. And it had to remain secret, because I had, of course, in the great tradition of tragic romance, chosen to love a boy who was totally out of my reach. He was not Puerto Rican; he was Italian and rich. He was also an older man. He was a senior at the high school when I came in as a freshman. I first saw him in the hall, leaning casually on a wall that was the border line between girlside and boyside for underclassmen. He looked extraordinarily like a young Marlon Brando—down to the ironic little smile. The total of what I knew about the boy who starred in every one of my awkward fantasies was this: that he was the nephew of the man who owned the supermarket on my block; that he often had parties at his parents' beautiful home in the suburbs which I would hear about; that his family had money (which came to our school in many ways)—and this fact made my knees weak: and that he worked at the store near my apartment building on weekends and in the summer.

My mother could not understand why I became so eager to be the one sent out on her endless errands. I pounced on every opportunity from Friday to late Saturday afternoon to go after eggs, cigarettes, milk (I tried to drink as much of it as possible, although I hated the stuff)—the staple items that she would order from the "American" store.

Week after week I wandered up and down the aisles, taking furtive glances at the stock room in the back, breathlessly hoping to see my prince. Not that I had a plan. I felt like a pilgrim waiting for a glimpse of Mecca. I did not expect him to notice me. It was sweet agony.

One day I did see him. Dressed in a white outfit like a surgeon: white pants and shirt, white cap, and (gross sight, but not to my love-glazed eyes) blood-smeared butcher's apron. He was helping to drag a side of beef into the freezer storage area of the store. I must have stood there like an idiot, because I remember that he did see me, he even spoke to me! I could have died. I think he said, "Excuse me," and smiled vaguely in my direction.

5   After that, I *willed* occasions to go to the supermarket. I watched my mother's pack of cigarettes empty ever so slowly. I wanted her to smoke them fast. I drank milk and forced it on my brother (although a second glass for him had to be bought with my share of Fig Newton cookies which we both liked, but we were restricted to one row each). I gave my cookies up for love, and watched my mother smoke her L&M's with so little enthusiasm that I thought (God, no!) that she might be cutting down on her smoking or maybe even giving up the habit. At this crucial time!

I thought I had kept my lonely romance a secret. Often I cried hot tears on my pillow for the things that kept us apart. In my mind there was no doubt that he would never notice me (and that is why I felt free to stare at him—I was invisible). He could not see me because I was a skinny Puerto Rican girl, a freshman who did not belong to any group he associated with.

At the end of the year I found out that I had not been invisible. I learned one little lesson about human nature—adulation leaves a scent, one that we are all equipped to recognize, and no matter how insignificant the source, we seek it.

In June the nuns at our school would always arrange for some cultural extravaganza. In my freshman year it was a Roman banquet. We had been studying Greek drama (as a prelude to church history—it was at a fast clip that we galloped through Sophocles and Euripides toward the early Christian martyrs), and our young, energetic Sister Agnes was in the mood for spectacle. She ordered the entire student body (it was a small group of under 300 students) to have our mothers make us togas out of sheets. She handed out a pattern on mimeo pages fresh out of the machine. I remember the intense smell of the alcohol on the sheets of paper, and how almost everyone in the auditorium brought theirs to their noses and inhaled deeply—mimeographed handouts were the school-day buzz that the new Xerox generation of kids is missing out on. Then, as the last couple of weeks of school dragged on, the city of Paterson becoming a concrete oven, and us wilting in our uncomfortable uniforms, we labored like frantic Roman slaves to build a splendid banquet hall in our small auditorium. Sister Agnes wanted a raised dais where the host and hostess would be regally enthroned.

She had already chosen our Senator and Lady from among our ranks. The Lady was to be a beautiful new student named Sophia, a recent Polish immigrant, whose English was still practically unintelligible, but whose features, classically perfect without a trace of makeup, enthralled us. Everyone talked about her gold hair cascading past her waist, and her voice which could carry a note right up to heaven in choir. The nuns wanted her for God. They kept saying that she had vocation. We just looked at her in awe, and the boys seemed afraid of her. She just smiled and did as she was told. I don't know what she thought of it all. The main privilege of beauty is that others will do almost everything for you, including thinking.

10   Her partner was to be our best basketball player, a tall, red-haired senior whose family sent its many offspring to our school. Together, Sophia and her senator looked like the best combination of immigrant genes our community could produce. It did not occur to me to ask then whether anything but their physical beauty qualified them for the starring roles in our production. I had the highest average in the church history class, but I was given the part of one of many "Roman Citizens." I was to sit in front of the plastic fruit and recite a greeting in Latin along with the rest of the school when our hosts came into the hall and took their places on their throne.

On the night of our banquet, my father escorted me in my toga to the door of our school. I felt foolish in my awkwardly draped sheet (blouse and skirt required underneath). My mother had no great skill as a seamstress. The best she could do was hem a skirt or a pair of pants. That night I would have traded her for a peasant woman with a golden needle. I saw other Roman ladies emerging from their parents' cars looking authentic in sheets of material that folded over their bodies like the garments on a statue by Michelangelo. How did they do it? How was it that I always got it just slightly wrong, and worse, I believed that other people were just too polite to mention it. "The poor little Puerto Rican girl," I could hear them thinking. But in reality, I must have been my worst critic, self-conscious as I was.

Soon, we were all sitting at our circle of tables joined together around the dais. Sophia glittered like a golden statue. Her smile was beatific: a perfect, silent Roman lady. Her "senator" looked uncomfortable, glancing around at his buddies, perhaps waiting for the ridicule that he would surely get in the locker room later. The nuns in their black habits stood in the background watching us. What were they supposed to be, the Fates? Nubian slaves? The dancing girls did their modest little dance to tinny music from their finger cymbals, then the speeches were made. Then the grape juice "wine" was raised in a toast to the Roman Empire we all knew would fall within the week—before finals anyway.

All during the program I had been in a state of controlled hysteria. My secret love sat across the room from me looking supremely bored. I watched his every move, taking him in gluttonously. I relished the shadow of his eyelashes on his ruddy cheeks, his pouty lips smirking sarcastically at the ridiculous sight of our little play. Once he slumped down on his chair, and our sergeant-at-arms nun came over and tapped him sharply on his shoulder. He drew himself up slowly, with disdain. I loved his rebellious spirit. I believed myself still invisible to him in my "nothing" status as I looked upon my beloved. But toward the end of the evening, as we stood chanting our farewells in Latin, he looked straight across the room and into my eyes! How did I survive the killing power of those dark pupils? I trembled in a new way. I was not cold—I was burning! Yet I shook from the inside out, feeling light-headed, dizzy.

The room began to empty and I headed for the girls' lavatory. I wanted to relish the miracle in silence. I did not think for a minute that anything more would follow. I was satisfied with the enormous favor of a look from my beloved. I took my time, knowing that my father would be waiting outside for me, impatient, perhaps glowing in the dark in his phosphorescent white Navy uniform. The others would ride home. I would walk home with my father, both of us in costume. I wanted as few witnesses as possible. When I could no longer hear the crowds in the hallway, I emerged from the bathroom, still under the spell of those mesmerizing eyes.

15   The lights had been turned off in the hallway and all I could see was the lighted stairwell, at the bottom of which a nun would be stationed. My father would be waiting just outside. I nearly screamed when I felt someone grab me by the waist. But my mouth was quickly covered by someone else's mouth. I was being kissed. My first kiss and I could not even tell who it was. I pulled away to see that face not two inches away from mine. It was he. He smiled down at me. Did I have a silly expression on my face? My glasses felt crooked on my nose. I was unable to move or to speak. More gently, he lifted my chin and touched his lips to mine. This time I did not forget to enjoy it. Then, like the phantom lover that he was, he walked away into the darkened corridor and disappeared.

I don't know how long I stood there. My body was changing right there in the hallway of a Catholic school. My cells were tuning up like musicians in an orchestra, and my heart was a chorus. It was an opera I was composing, and I wanted to stand very still and just listen. But, of course, I heard my father's voice talking to the nun. I was in trouble if he had had to ask about me. I hurried down the stairs making up a story on the way about feeling sick. That would explain my flushed face and it would buy me a little privacy when I got home.

The next day Father announced at the breakfast table that he was leaving on a six month tour of Europe with the Navy in a few weeks and that at the end of the school year my mother, my brother, and I would be sent to Puerto Rico to stay for half a year at Mamá's (my mother's mother) house. I was devastated. This was the usual routine for us. We had always gone to Mamá's to stay when Father was away for long periods. But this year it was different for me. I was in love, and…my heart knocked against my bony chest at this thought…he loved me too? I broke into sobs and left the table.

In the next week I discovered the inexorable truth about parents. They can actually carry on with their plans right through tears, threats, and the awful spectacle of a teenager's broken heart. My father left me to my mother who impassively packed while I explained over and over that I was at a crucial time in my studies and that if I left my entire life would be ruined. All she would say was, "You are an intelligent girl, you'll catch up." Her head was filled with visions of *casa*[1] and family reunions, long gossip sessions with her mamá and sisters. What did she care that I was losing my one chance at true love?

[1]*casa* home

In the meantime I tried desperately to see him. I thought he would look for me too. But the few times I saw him in the hallway, he was always rushing away. It would be long weeks of confusion and pain before I realized that the kiss was nothing but a little trophy for his ego. He had no interest in me other than as his adorer. He was flattered by my silent worship of him, and he had *bestowed* a kiss on me to please himself, and to fan the flames. I learned a lesson about the battle of the sexes then that I have never forgotten: the object is not always to win, but most times simply to keep your opponent (synonymous at times with "the loved one") guessing.

20   But this is too cynical a view to sustain in the face of that overwhelming rush of emotion that is first love. And in thinking back about my own experience with it, I can be objective only to the point where I recall how sweet the anguish was, how caught up in the moment I felt, and how every nerve in my body was involved in this salute to life. Later, much later, after what seemed like an eternity of dragging the weight of unrequited love around with me, I learned to make myself visible and to relish the little battles required to win the greatest prize of all. And much later, I read and understood Camus'[2] statement about the subject that concerns both adolescent and philosopher alike: if love were easy, life would be too simple.

MAKING CONNECTIONS

1. Can you recall a similar experience? If so, what did you learn from it?
2. Toward the end of the essay, the author writes: "I learned to make myself visible and to relish the little battles required to win the greatest prize of all." What do you think she means?

MAKING AN ARGUMENT

1. Both this essay and James Joyce's short story "Araby" on page 407 describe the painful experience and realization of unrequited love. Write a comparison of the two with special attention to narration, characterization, and the development of the conflict to its resolution.

DAVID SEDARIS [B. 1956]

David Sedaris is a humorist, playwright, former elf, apartment cleaner, and regular contributor to National Public Radio. His books include Barrel Fever *(1994),* Naked *(1997),* Holidays on Ice *(1998), and* Me Talk Pretty One Day *(2000), from which the essay below is taken. In 2001, he received the title "Humorist of the Year" from* Time *magazine and the Thurber Prize for American Humor. His latest book,* Squirrel Seeks Chipmunk: A Modest Bestiary, *was published in 2010.*

[2]**Albert Camus** (1913–1960), French novelist and philosopher

The Learning Curve   [2000]

A year after my graduation from the School of the Art Institute of Chicago, a terrible mistake was made and I was offered a position teaching a writing workshop. I had never gone to graduate school, and although several of my stories had been Xeroxed and stapled, none of them had ever been published in the traditional sense of the word.

Like branding steers or embalming the dead, teaching was a profession I had never seriously considered. I was clearly unqualified, yet I accepted the job without hesitation, as it would allow me to wear a tie and go by the name of Mr. Sedaris. My father went by the same name, and though he lived a thousand miles away, I liked to imagine someone getting the two of us confused. "Wait a minute," this someone might say, "are you talking about Mr. Sedaris the retired man living in North Carolina, or Mr. Sedaris the distinguished academic?"

The position was offered at the last minute, when the scheduled professor found a better-paying job delivering pizza. I was given two weeks to prepare, a period I spent searching for a briefcase and standing before my full-length mirror, repeating the words "Hello, class, my name is Mr. Sedaris." Sometimes I'd give myself an aggressive voice and firm, athletic timbre. This was the masculine Mr. Sedaris, who wrote knowingly of flesh wounds and tractor pulls. Then there was the ragged bark of the newspaper editor, a tone that coupled wisdom with an unlimited capacity for cruelty. I tried sounding businesslike and world-weary, but when the day eventually came, my nerves kicked in and the true Mr. Sedaris revealed himself. In a voice reflecting doubt, fear, and an unmistakable desire to be loved, I sounded not like a thoughtful college professor but, rather, like a high-strung twelve-year-old girl; someone named Brittany.

My first semester I had only nine students. Hoping they might view me as professional and well prepared, I arrived bearing name tags fashioned in the shape of maple leaves. I'd cut them myself out of orange construction paper and handed them out along with a box of straight pins. My fourth-grade teacher had done the same thing, explaining that we were to take only one pin per person. This being college rather than elementary school, I encouraged my students to take as many pins as they liked. They wrote their names upon their leaves, fastened them to their breast pockets, and bellied up to the long oak table that served as our communal desk.

5   "All right then," I said. "Okay, here we go." I opened my briefcase and realized that I'd never thought beyond this moment. The orange leaves were the extent of my lesson plan, but still I searched the empty briefcase, mindful that I had stupidly armed my audience with straight pins. I guess I'd been thinking that, without provocation, my students would talk, offering their thoughts and opinions on the issues of the day. I'd imagined myself sitting on the edge of the desk, overlooking a forest of raised hands. The students would simultaneously shout to be heard, and I'd pound on something in order to silence them. "Whoa people," I'd yell. "Calm down, you'll all get your turn. One at a time, one at a time."

The error of my thinking yawned before me. A terrible silence overtook the room, and seeing no other option, I instructed my students to pull out their notebooks and write a brief essay related to the theme of profound disappointment.

I'd always hated it when a teacher forced us to invent something on the spot. Aside from the obvious pressure, it seemed that everyone had his or her own little way of doing things, especially when it came to writing. Maybe someone needed a particular kind of lamp or pen or typewriter. In my experience, it was hard to write without your preferred tools, but impossible to write without a cigarette.

I made a note to bring in some ashtrays and then I rooted through the waste-paper basket for a few empty cans. Standing beneath the prominently displayed NO SMOKING sign, I distributed the cans and cast my cigarettes upon the table, encouraging my students to go at it. This, to me, was the very essence of teaching, and I thought I'd made a real breakthrough until the class asthmatic raised his hand, saying that, to the best of his knowledge, Aristophanes had never smoked a cigarette in his life. "Neither did Jane Austen," he said. "Or the Brontës."

I jotted these names into my notebook alongside the word *Troublemaker,* and said I'd look into it. Because I was the writing teacher, it was automatically assumed that I had read every leather-bound volume in the Library of Classics. The truth was that I had read none of those books, nor did I intend to. I bluffed my way through most challenges with dim memories of the movie or miniseries based upon the book in question, but it was an exhausting exercise and eventually I learned it was easier to simply reply with a question, saying, "I know what Flaubert means to *me,* but what do *you* think of her?"

10 As Mr. Sedaris I lived in constant fear. There was the perfectly understandable fear of being exposed as a fraud, and then there was the deeper fear that my students might hate me. I imagined them calling their friends on the phone. "Guess who *I* got stuck with," they'd say. Most dull teachers at least had a few credentials to back them up. They had a philosophy and a lesson plan and didn't need to hide behind a clip-on tie and an empty briefcase.

Whenever I felt in danger of losing my authority, I would cross the room and either open or close the door. A student needed to ask permission before regulating the temperature or noise level, but I could do so whenever I liked. It was the only activity sure to remind me that I was in charge, and I took full advantage of it.

"There he goes again," my students would whisper. "What's up with him and that door?"

The asthmatic transferred to another class, leaving me with only eight students. Of these, four were seasoned smokers who took long, contemplative drags and occasionally demonstrated their proficiency by blowing ghostly concentric rings that hovered like halos above their bowed heads. The others tried as best they could, but it wasn't pretty. By the end of the second session, my students had produced nothing but ashes. Their hacking coughs and complete lack of output suggested that, for certain writers, smoking was obviously not enough.

Thinking that a clever assignment might help loosen them up, I instructed my students to write a letter to their mothers in prison. They were free to determine both the crime and the sentence, and references to cellmates were strongly encouraged.

15 The group set to work with genuine purpose and enthusiasm, and I felt proud of myself, until the quietest member of the class handed in her paper, whispering that both her father and her uncle were currently serving time on federal racketeering charges.

"I just never thought of my mom going off as well," she said. "This was just a really...depressing assignment."

I'd never known what an actual child-to-parent prison letter might be like, but now I had a pretty clear idea. I envisioned two convicts sharing a cell. One man stood at the sink while the other lay on a bunk, reading his mail.

"Anything interesting?" the standing man asked.

"Oh, it's from my daughter," the other man said. "She's just started college, and apparently her writing teacher is a real asshole."

20   That was the last time I asked my students to write in class. From that point on all their stories were to be written at home on the subject of their choice. If I'd had my way, we would have all stayed home and conducted the class through smoke signals. As it was, I had to find some way to pass the time and trick my students into believing that they were getting an education. The class met twice a week for two hours a day. Filling an entire session with one activity was out of the question, so I began breaking each session into a series of brief, regularly scheduled discussion periods. We began each day with Celebrity Corner. This was an opportunity for the students to share interesting bits of information provided by friends in New York or Los Angeles who were forever claiming firsthand knowledge of a rock band's impending breakup or movie star's dark sexual secret. Luckily everyone seemed to have such a friend, and we were never short of material.

Celebrity Corner was followed by the Feedbag Forum, my shameless call for easy, one-pot dinner recipes, the type favored by elderly aunts and grandmothers whose dental status demanded that all meat fall from the bone without provocation. When asked what Boiled Beef Arkansas had to do with the craft of writing, I did not mention my recent purchase of a Crock-Pot; rather, I lied through my rotten teeth, explaining that it wasn't the recipe itself but the pacing that was of interest to the writer.

After the Feedbag Forum it was time for Pillow Talk, which was defined as "an opportunity for you to discuss your private sex lives in a safe, intellectual environment." The majority of my students were reluctant to share their experiences, so arrangements were made with the audiovisual department. I then took to wheeling in a big color television so that we might spend an hour watching *One Life to Live.* This was back when Victoria Buchanan passed out at her twentieth high-school reunion and came to remembering that rather than graduating with the rest of her class, she had instead hitchhiked to New York City, where she'd coupled with a hippie and given birth to a long-lost daughter. It sounds far-fetched, but like a roast forsaken in the oven or a rescheduled dental appointment, childbirth is one of those minor details that tends to slip the minds of most soap opera characters. It's a personality trait you've just got to accept.

On *General Hospital* or *Guiding Light* a similar story might come off as trite or even laughable. This, though, was *One Life to Live,* and no one could suddenly recall the birth of a child quite like Erika Slezak, who played both Victoria Buchanan and her alternate personality, Nicole Smith. I'd been in the habit of taping the show and watching it every night while eating dinner. Now that I was an academic, I could watch it in class and use the dinner hour to catch up on *All My Children.* A few students grumbled, but again I assured them that this was all part of my master plan.

Word came from the front office that there had been some complaints regarding my use of class time. This meant I'd have to justify my daily screenings with a homework assignment. Now the students were to watch an episode and write what I referred to as a "guessay," a brief prediction of what might take place the following day.

25   "Remember that this is not Port Charles or Pine Valley," I said. "This is Llanview, Pennsylvania, and we're talking about the Buchanan family."

It actually wasn't a bad little assignment. While the dialogue occasionally falters, you have to admire daytime dramas for their remarkable attention to plot. Yes, there were always the predictable kidnappings and summer love triangles, but a good show could always surprise you with something as simple as the discovery of an underground city. I'd coached my students through half a dozen episodes, giving them background information and explaining that missing children do not just march through the door ten minutes after the critical delivery flashback. The inevitable reunion must unfold delicately and involve at least two-thirds of the cast.

I thought I'd effectively conveyed the seriousness of the assignment. I thought that in my own way I had actually taught them something, so I was angry when their papers included such predictions as "the long-lost daughter turns out to be a vampire" and "the next day Vicki chokes to death while eating a submarine sandwich." The vampire business smacked of *Dark Shadows* reruns, and I refused to take it seriously. But choking to death on a sandwich, that was an insult. Victoria was a Buchanan and would never duck into a sub shop, much less choke to death in a single episode. Especially on a Wednesday. Nobody dies on a Wednesday—hadn't these people learned anything?

In the past I had tried my hardest to be understanding, going so far as to allow the conjugation of nouns and the use of such questionable words as *whatever-ishly*. This though, was going too far. I'd taught the Buchanans' Llanview just as my colleagues had taught Joyce's Dublin or Faulkner's Mississippi, but that was over now. Obviously certain people didn't deserve to watch TV in the middle of the afternoon. If my students wanted to stare at the walls for two hours a day, then fine, from here on out we'd just stick to the basics.

I don't know who invented the template for the standard writing workshop, but whoever it was seems to have struck the perfect balance between sadism and masochism. Here is a system designed to eliminate pleasure for everyone involved. The idea is that a student turns in a story, which is then read and thoughtfully critiqued by everyone in the class. In my experience the process worked, in that the stories were occasionally submitted, Xeroxed, and distributed hand to hand. They were folded into purses and knapsacks, but here the system tended to break down. Come critique time, most students behaved as if the assignment had been to confine the stories in a dark, enclosed area and test their reaction to sensory deprivation. Even if the papers were read out loud in class, the discussions were usually brief, as the combination of good manners and complete lack of interest kept most workshop participants from expressing their honest opinions.

30   With a few notable exceptions, most of the stories were thinly veiled accounts of the author's life as he or she attempted to complete the assignment.
Roommates were forever stepping out of showers, and waitresses appeared
out of nowhere to deliver the onion rings and breakfast burritos that stained
the pages of the manuscripts. The sloppiness occasionally bothered me, but I
had no room to complain. This was an art school, and the writing workshop
was commonly known as the easiest way to fulfill one's mandatory English
credits. My students had been admitted because they could admirably paint or
sculpt or videotape their bodies in exhausting detail, and wasn't that enough?
They told funny, compelling stories about their lives, but committing the details to paper was, for them, a chore rather than an aspiration. The way I saw it,
if my students were willing to pretend I was a teacher, the least I could do was
return the favor and pretend that they were writers. Even if someone had used
his real name and recounted, say, a recent appointment with an oral surgeon,
I would accept the story as pure fiction, saying, "So tell us, Dean, how did you
come up with this person?"

        The student might mumble, pointing to the bloodied cotton wad packed
against his swollen gum, and I'd ask, "When did you decide that your character
should seek treatment for his impacted molar?" This line of questioning allowed
the authors to feel creative and protected anyone who held an unpopular political
opinion.

        "Let me get this straight," one student said. "You're telling me that if I say
something out loud, it's me saying it, but if I write the exact same thing on
paper, it's somebody else, right?"

        "Yes," I said. "And we're calling that fiction."

        The student pulled out his notebook, wrote something down, and handed
me a sheet of paper that read, "That's the stupidest fucking thing I ever heard
in my life."

35   They were a smart group.

        As Mr. Sedaris I made it a point to type up a poorly spelled evaluation of
each submitted story. I'd usually begin with the high points and end, a page or
two later, by dispensing such sage professional advice as "Punctuation never
hurt anyone" or "Think verbs!" I tended to lose patience with some of the longer dream sequences, but for the most part we all got along, and the students
either accepted or politely ignored my advice.

        Trouble arose only when authors used their stories to vindicate themselves
against a great hurt or perceived injustice. This was the case with a woman
whom the admissions office would have labeled a "returning student," meaning
that her social life did not revolve around the cafeteria. The woman was a good
fifteen years older than me and clearly disapproved of my teaching methods.
She never contributed to Pillow Talk or the Feedbag Forum, and I had good
reason to suspect it was she who had complained about the *One Life to Live*
episodes. With the teenage freshmen, I stood a chance, but there was nothing
I could do to please someone who regularly complained that she'd wasted
enough time already. The class was divided into two distinct groups, with her

on one side and everyone else on the other. I'd tried everything except leg irons, but nothing could bring the two sides together. It was a real problem.

The returning student had recently come through a difficult divorce, and because her pain was significant, she wrongly insisted that her writing was significant as well. Titled something along the lines of "I Deserve Another Chance," her story was not well received by the class. Following the brief group discussion, I handed her my written evaluation, which she quietly skimmed over before raising her hand.

"Yes," she said. "If you don't mind, I have a little question." She lit a cigarette and spent a moment identifying with the smoldering match. "Who are *you*," she asked. "I mean, just who in the hell are you to tell *me* that *my* story has no ending?"

40   It was a worthwhile question that was bound to be raised sooner or later. I'd noticed that her story had ended in midsentence, but that aside, who was I to offer criticism to anyone, especially in regard to writing? I'd meant to give the issue some serious thought, but there had been shirts to iron and name tags to make and, between one thing and another, I managed to put it out of my mind.

The woman repeated the question, her voice breaking. "Just who . . . in the stinking hell do you think . . . you are?"

"Can I give you an answer tomorrow?" I asked.

"No," she barked. "I want to know now. Who do you think you are?"

Judging from their expressions, I could see that the other side of the class was entertaining the same question. Doubt was spreading through the room like the cold germs seen in one of those slow-motion close-ups of a sneeze. I envisioned myself burning on a pyre of dream sequences, and then the answer came to me.

45   "Who am I?" I asked. "I am the only one who is paid to be in this room." This was nothing I'd necessarily want to embroider on a pillow, but still, once the answer left my mouth, I embraced it as a perfectly acceptable teaching philosophy. My previous doubts and fears evaporated, as now I knew that I could excuse anything. The new Mr. Sedaris would never again back down or apologize. From here on out, I'd order my *students* to open and close the door and let *that* remind me that I was in charge. We could do whatever I wanted because I was a certified professional—it practically said so right there on my paycheck. My voice deepened as I stood to straighten my tie. "All right then," I said. "Does anyone else have a stupid question for Mr. Sedaris?"

The returning student once again raised her hand. "It's a personal question, I know, but exactly how much is the school paying you to be in this room?"

I answered honestly, and then, for the first time since the beginning of the school year, my students came together as one. I can't recall which side started it, I remember only that the laughter was so loud, so violent and prolonged that Mr. Sedaris had to run and close the door so that the real teachers could conduct their business in peace.

❧MAKING CONNECTIONS

1. The title of this humorous essay is "The Learning Curve." What is a "learning curve"? How does it fit this piece?
2. It is not as easy to pick up humor in print as it is when you actually see or hear the person telling the story. When did you first realize the author was not "serious"? What cues in the text indicate that? Is there a consistent style to this humor that helps you anticipate or appreciate the humor? Explain.
3. To what extent does your own experience as a writing student help you appreciate the plight of the teacher and students? Pick out the events that you thought were especially funny and explain what made them humorous to you.

❧MAKING AN ARGUMENT

1. To what extent is it possible to make serious points in a humorous essay? Most authors treat the passage from innocence to experience seriously. This essay treats it humorously. Which do you prefer? Write about your preference as it applies to this work and other works in this section. Cite the texts of the work(s) for support.

CASE STUDY
IN THEATRICAL
CONTEXT

Hamlet and Performance

INTERPRETATION AND PERFORMANCE

The purpose of this Case Study is to present Hamlet *in the context of commentary about the play and several of its productions—and to demonstrate the possibility of multiple interpretations.* It has been an emphasis throughout this book that literature prompts multiple interpretations. Nowhere is this more apparent than in great works of drama and in the process actors go through as they prepare to "interpret" the characters they play.

As readers of literature, we may interpret characters by asking who they are and what they say and do. We can distance ourselves from the work, examine the facts, judge the characters and their actions, and see them as part of a coherent whole. Actors, too, may begin with an objective analysis of characters they play, but rather than distancing themselves from the action and observing characters from outside, they must move inside the play and the characters and immerse themselves in the action.

For an actor, reading a play requires a much closer look—so close that it means looking from the inside out. Questions about characterization shift from "Who is he or she?" to "Who am I?" "When is this occurring in my life?" "How do I feel about being here?" "What do I want?" Answering questions like these requires a great deal of work, but it results in a comprehensive analysis and thorough interpretation of character—an interpretation that links actor and playwright in the creative process.

Multiple Interpretations of *Hamlet*

It is hard to imagine any character in dramatic literature who is discussed, interpreted, or performed more often than Hamlet. And yet no two Hamlets are identical. From the time of Shakespeare and the first actor who played the role, Richard Burbage, to the present, we are just as likely to identify the character Hamlet with the actor playing the role as with the playwright. Hamlet's words may belong to

Shakespeare, but the interpretation of the character belongs to Laurence Olivier, Derek Jacobi, Mel Gibson, Kenneth Branagh, and many other actors who have played the role. While we are likely to say that we prefer one or some of these interpretations more than others, we are not likely to say that one interpretation is right and the others wrong. In this respect, examining different but supportable interpretations can give us an insight into the many views possible when reading other forms of literature as well.

WILLIAM SHAKESPEARE [1564–1616]

Though William Shakespeare is the most famous writer ever to have written in English, details of his life are surprisingly sketchy. It is known that he was born in the town of Stratford-on-Avon, where he probably attended the local grammar school, and that he married Anne Hathaway in 1582. By 1592, he was an actor and playwright in London, associated with the Lord Chamberlain's Men, the most successful acting troupe of the time. In 1593 and 1594, he published two long mythological poems, Venus and Adonis *and* The Rape of Lucrece. *His astonishing sequence of sonnets, some of the most beautiful poetry ever created, were published in 1609, though they were probably written from 1592 to 1594, when the theaters were shut because of the plague. By 1597, he was able to buy a large house in Stratford and apparently retired there in 1610. His works for the theater, which were not published until after his death, number thirteen comedies (including* A Midsummer's Night Dream, Twelfth Night, *and* The Merchant of Venice), *ten tragedies (including* Romeo and Juliet, Macbeth, Julius Caesar, Othello, *and* Hamlet), *ten history plays, and four romances (including* The Tempest). *Ben Jonson, a playwright who was Shakespeare's contemporary and rival, wrote of him: "He was not of an age, but for all time!"*

HAMLET, PRINCE OF DENMARK

DRAMATIS PERSONAE
GHOST *of Hamlet, the former King of Denmark*
CLAUDIUS, *King of Denmark, the former King's brother*
GERTRUDE, *Queen of Denmark, widow of the former King and now wife
    of Claudius*
HAMLET, *Prince of Denmark, son of the late King and of Gertrude*
POLONIUS, *councillor to the King*
LAERTES, *his son*
OPHELIA, *his daughter*
REYNALDO, *his servant*
HORATIO, *Hamlet's friend and fellow student*

VOLTIMAND,
CORNELIUS,
ROSENCRANTZ,
GUILDENSTERN,   } *members of the Danish court*
OSRIC,
A GENTLEMAN,
A LORD,

BERNARDO,
FRANCISCO,   } *officers and soldiers on watch*
MARCELLUS,

FORTINBRAS, *Prince of Norway*
CAPTAIN *in his army*
THREE OR FOUR PLAYERS, *taking the roles of* PROLOGUE, PLAYER KING, PLAYER
        QUEEN, *and* LUCIANUS
TWO MESSENGERS
FIRST SAILOR
TWO CLOWNS, *a gravedigger and his companion*
PRIEST
FIRST AMBASSADOR *from England*
*Lords, Soldiers, Attendants, Guards, other Players, Followers of Laertes, other Sailors,
        another Ambassador or Ambassadors from England*

SCENE: *Denmark*

[Act 1.1 *Enter* BERNARDO *and* FRANCISCO, *two sentinels (meeting)*].°
BERNARDO: Who's there?
FRANCISCO: Nay, answer me.° Stand and unfold yourself.°
BERNARDO: Long live the King!
FRANCISCO: Bernardo?
BERNARDO: He.
FRANCISCO: You come most carefully upon your hour.   5
BERNARDO: 'Tis now struck twelve. Get thee to bed, Francisco.
FRANCISCO: For this relief much thanks. 'Tis bitter cold,
        And I am sick at heart.
BERNARDO: Have you had quiet guard?
FRANCISCO: Not a mouse stirring.   10
BERNARDO: Well, good night.
        If you do meet Horatio and Marcellus,
        The rivals° of my watch, bid them make haste.

1.1s.d. Location: Elsinore castle. A guard platform.   2 me (Francisco emphasizes
that he is the sentry currently on watch.)   **unfold yourself** reveal your identity   **14 rivals**
partners

[*Enter* HORATIO *and* MARCELLUS.]

FRANCISCO:	I think I hear them.—Stand, ho! Who is there?	15

HORATIO: Friends to this ground.°

MARCELLUS: And liegemen to the Dane.°

FRANCISCO: Give° you good night.

MARCELLUS: O, farewell, honest soldier. Who hath relieved you?

FRANCISCO: Bernardo hath my place. Give you good night.   20

[*Exit* FRANCISCO.]

MARCELLUS: Holla! Bernardo!

BERNARDO: Say, what, is Horatio there?

HORATIO: A piece of him.

BERNARDO: Welcome, Horatio. Welcome, good Marcellus.

HORATIO: What, has this thing appeared again tonight?   25

BERNARDO: I have seen nothing.

MARCELLUS: Horatio says 'tis but our fantasy,°
            And will not let belief take hold of him
            Touching this dreaded sight twice seen of us.
            Therefore I have entreated him along°   30
            With us to watch° the minutes of this night,
            That if again this apparition come
            He may approve° our eyes and speak to it.

HORATIO: Tush, tush, 'twill not appear.

BERNARDO: Sit down awhile,   35
            And let us once again assail your ears,
            That are so fortified against our story,
            What° we have two nights seen.

HORATIO: Well, sit we down,
            And let us hear Bernardo speak of this.   40

BERNARDO: Last night of all,°
            When yond same star that's westward from the pole°
            Had made his° course t' illume° that part of heaven
            Where now it burns, Marcellus and myself,
            The bell then beating one—   45

[*Enter* GHOST.]

MARCELLUS: Peace, break thee off! Look where it comes again!

BERNARDO: In the same figure like the King that's dead.

---

16 ground country, land   **17 liegemen to the Dane** men sworn to serve the Danish king
18 Give i.e., may God give   **27 fantasy** imagination   **30 along** to come along   **31 watch**
keep watch during   **33 approve** corroborate   **38 What** with what   **41 Last…all** i.e., this
very last night (Emphatic.)   **42 pole** polestar, north star   **43 his** its   **illume** illuminate

MARCELLUS: Thou art a scholar.° Speak to it, Horatio.

BERNARDO: Looks 'a° not like the King? Mark it, Horatio.

HORATIO: Most like. It harrows me with fear and wonder.   50

BERNARDO: It would be spoke to.°

MARCELLUS: Speak to it, Horatio.

HORATIO: What art thou that usurp'st° this time of night,

    Together with that fair and warlike form

    In which the majesty of buried Denmark°   55

    Did sometime° march? By heaven, I charge thee, speak!

MARCELLUS: It is offended.

BERNARDO: See, it stalks away.

HORATIO: Stay! Speak, speak! I charge thee, speak!

[*Exit* GHOST.]

MARCELLUS: 'Tis gone and will not answer.   60

BERNARDO: How now, Horatio? You tremble and look pale.

    Is not this something more than fantasy?

    What think you on 't?°

HORATIO: Before my God, I might not this believe

    Without the sensible° and true avouch°   65

    Of mine own eyes.

MARCELLUS: Is it not like the King?

HORATIO: As thou art to thyself.

    Such was the very armor he had on

    When he the ambitious Norway° combated.   70

    So frowned he once when, in an angry parle,°

    He smote the sledded° Polacks° on the ice.

    'Tis strange.

MARCELLUS: Thus twice before, and jump° at this dead hour,

    With martial stalk° hath he gone by our watch.   75

HORATIO: In what particular thought to work° I know not,

    But in the gross and scope° of mine opinion

    This bodes some strange eruption to our state.

MARCELLUS: Good now° sit down, and tell me, he that knows,

    Why this same strict and most observant watch

    So nightly toils° the subject° of the land,   80

48 scholar one learned enough to know how to question a ghost properly   **49 'a** he
51 It...to (It was commonly believed that a ghost could not speak until spoken to.)
53 usurp'st wrongfully takes over   **55 buried Denmark** the buried King of Denmark
56 sometime formerly   **63 on 't** of it   **65 sensible** confirmed by the senses   **avouch**
warrant, evidence   **70 Norway** King of Norway   **71 parle** parley   **72 sledded** traveling
on sleds   **Polacks** Poles   **74 jump** exactly   **75 stalk** stride   **76 to work** i.e., to collect
my thoughts and try to understand this   **77 gross and scope** general drift   **79 Good now**
(An expression denoting entreaty or expostulation.)   **81 toils** causes to toil   **subject** subjects

And why such daily cast° of brazen cannon
And foreign mart° for implements of war,
Why such impress° of shipwrights, whose sore task
Does not divide the Sunday from the week.   85
What might be toward,° that this sweaty haste
Doth make the night joint-laborer with the day?
Who is 't that can inform me?

HORATIO: That can I;
At least, the whisper goes so. Our last king,   90
Whose image even but now appeared to us,
Was, as you know, by Fortinbras of Norway,
Thereto pricked on° by a most emulate° pride,°
Dared to the combat; in which our valiant Hamlet—
For so this side of our known world° esteemed him—   95
Did slay this Fortinbras; who by a sealed° compact
Well ratified by law and heraldry
Did forfeit, with his life, all those his lands
Which he stood seized° of, to the conqueror;
Against the° which a moiety competent°   100
Was gagèd° by our king, which had returned°
To the inheritance° of Fortinbras
Had he been vanquisher, as, by the same cov'nant°
And carriage of the article designed,°
His fell to Hamlet. Now, sir, young Fortinbras,   105
Of unimprovèd mettle° hot and full,
Hath in the skirts° of Norway here and there
Sharked up° a list° of lawless resolutes°
For food and diet° to some enterprise°
That hath a stomach° in 't, which is no other—   110
As it doth well appear unto our state—
But to recover of us, by strong hand
And terms compulsatory, those foresaid lands

---

82 cast casting   **83 mart** buying and selling   **84 impress** impressment, conscription
86 toward in preparation   **93 pricked on** incited   **emulate** emulous, ambitious   **Thereto...
pride** (Refers to old Fortinbras, not the Danish King.)   **95 this...world** i.e., all Europe,
the Western world   **96 sealed** certified, confirmed   **99 seized** possessed   **100 Against
the** in return for   **moiety** competent corresponding portion   **101 gagèd** engaged, pledged
had returned would have passed   **102 inheritance** possession   **103 cov'nant** i.e., the sealed
compact of line 90   **104 carriage...designed** carrying out of the article or clause drawn
up to cover the point   **106 unimprovèd mettle** untried, undisciplined spirits   **107 skirts**
outlying regions, outskirts   **108 Sharked up** gathered up, as a shark takes fish   **list**
i.e., troop   **resolutes** desperadoes   **109 For food and diet** i.e., they are to serve as
food, or "*means,*" *to* **some enterprise** also they serve in return for the rations they get
110 stomach (1) a spirit of daring (2) an appetite that is fed by the *lawless resolutes*

So by his father lost. And this, I take it,
Is the main motive of our preparations,   115
The source of this our watch, and the chief head°
Of this posthaste and rummage° in the land.

BERNARDO: I think it be no other but e'en so.
Well may it sort° that this portentous figure
Comes arméd through our watch so like the King   120
That was and is the question° of these wars.

HORATIO   A mote° it is to trouble the mind's eye.
In the most high and palmy° state of Rome,
A little ere the mightiest Julius fell,
The graves stood tenantless, and the sheeted° dead   125
Did squeak and gibber in the Roman streets;
As° stars with trains° of fire and dews of blood,
Disasters° in the sun; and the moist star°
Upon whose influence Neptune's° empire stands
Was sick almost to doomsday° with eclipse.   130
And even the like precurse° of feared events,
As harbingers° preceding still° the fates
And prologue to the omen° coming on,
Have heaven and earth together demonstrated
Unto our climatures° and countrymen.   135

[*Enter* GHOST.]

But soft,° behold! Lo, where it comes again!
I'll cross° it, though it blast° me. [*It spreads his° arms.*]
    Stay, *illusion!*
If thou hast any sound or use of voice,
Speak to me!
If there be any good thing to be done   140
That may to thee do ease and grace to me,
Speak to me!
If thou art privy to° thy country's fate,
Which, happily,° foreknowing may avoid,   145

116 **head** source   117 **rummage** bustle, commotion   119 **sort** suit   121 **question** focus
of contention   122 **mote** speck of dust   123 **palmy** flourishing   125 **sheeted** shrouded
127 **As** (This abrupt transition suggests that matter is possibly omitted between lines 120
and 121.)   **trains** trails   128 **Disasters** unfavorable signs or aspects   **moist star** *i.e.,*
moon, governing tides   129 **Neptune** god of the sea   **stands** depends   130 **sick...dooms-**
day (See Matthew 24:29 and Revelation 6:12.)   131 **precurse** heralding, foreshadowing
132 **harbingers** forerunners   **still** continually   133 **omen** calamitous event   135 **climatures**
regions   136 **soft** *i.e.,* enough, break off   137 **cross** stand in its path, confront   **blast** wither,
strike with a curse   **s.d. his** its   144 **privy to** in on the secret of   145 **happily** haply, perchance

O, speak!
Or if thou hast uphoarded in thy life
Extorted treasure in the womb of earth,
For which, they say, you spirits oft walk in death,
Speak of it! [*The cock crows.*] Stay and speak!—Stop it, Marcellus.   150

MARCELLUS: Shall I strike at it with my partisan?°

HORATIO: Do, if it will not stand. [*They strike at it.*]

BERNARDO: 'Tis here!

HORATIO: 'Tis here!

[*Exit* GHOST.]

MARCELLUS: 'Tis gone.   155
We do it wrong, being so majestical,
To offer it the show of violence,
For it is as the air invulnerable,
And our vain blows malicious mockery.

BERNARDO: It was about to speak when the cock crew.   160

HORATIO: And then it started like a guilty thing
Upon a fearful summons. I have heard
The cock, that is the trumpet° to the morn,
Doth with his lofty and shrill-sounding throat
Awake the god of day, and at his warning,   165
Whether in sea or fire, in earth or air,
Th' extravagant and erring° spirit hies°
To his confine; and of the truth herein
This present object made probation.°

MARCELLUS: It faded on the crowing of the cock.   170
Some say that ever 'gainst° that season comes
Wherein our Savior's birth is celebrated,
This bird of dawning singeth all night long,
And then, they say, no spirit dare stir abroad;
The nights are wholesome, then no planets strike,°   175
No fairy takes,° nor witch hath power to charm,
So hallowed and so gracious° is that time.

HORATIO: So have I heared and do in part believe it.
But, look, the morn in russet mantle clad
Walks o'er the dew of yon high eastward hill.   180
Break we our watch up, and by my advice

---

151 partisan long-handled spear   **163 trumpet** trumpeter   **167 extravagant and erring** wandering beyond bounds (The words have similar meaning.)   **hies** hastens   **169 probation** proof   **171 'gainst** just before   **175 strike** destroy by evil influence   **176 takes** bewitches   **177 gracious** full of grace

Let us impart what we have seen tonight
Unto young Hamlet; for upon my life,
This spirit, dumb to us, will speak to him.
Do you consent we shall acquaint him with it,   185
As needful in our loves, fitting our duty?
MARCELLUS: Let's do 't, I pray, and I this morning know
Where we shall find him most conveniently.

[*Exeunt.*]

[**Act 1.2** *Flourish. Enter* CLAUDIUS, *King of Denmark,* GERTRUDE *the Queen, the
Council, as*° POLONIUS *and his son* LAERTES, HAMLET, *cum aliis*° *(including*
VOLTIMAND *and* CORNELIUS*).*]

KING: Though yet of Hamlet our° dear brother's death
The memory be green, and that it us befitted
To bear our hearts in grief and our whole kingdom
To be contracted in one brow of woe,
Yet so far hath discretion fought with nature   5
That we with wisest sorrow think on him
Together with remembrance of ourselves.
Therefore our sometime° sister, now our queen,
Th' imperial jointress° to this warlike state,
Have we, as 'twere with a defeated joy—   10
With an auspicious and a dropping eye,°
With mirth in funeral and with dirge in marriage,
In equal scale weighing delight and dole°—
Taken to wife: Nor have we herein barred
Your better wisdoms, which have freely gone   15
With this affair along. For all, our thanks.
Now follows that you know° young Fortinbras,
Holding a weak supposal° of our worth,
Or thinking by our late dear brother's death
Our state to be disjoint and out of frame,   20
Co-leaguèd with° this dream of his advantage,°
He hath not failed to pester us with message
Importing° the surrender of those lands
Lost by his father, with all bonds° of law,

1.2 s.d. Location: The castle. as i.e., such as, including   **cum aliis** with others   **1 our**
my (The royal "we"; also in the following lines.)   **8 sometime** former   **9 jointress** woman
possessing property with her husband   **11 With…eye** with one eye smiling and the other
weeping   **13 dole** grief   **17 that you know** what you know already, that; or, that you be
informed as follows   **18 weak supposal** low estimate   **21 Co-leaguèd with** joined to, allied
with   **dream…advantage** illusory hope of having the advantage (His only ally is this hope.)
23 Importing pertaining to   **24 bonds** contracts

To our most valiant brother. So much for him.   25
Now for ourself and for this time of meeting.
Thus much the business is: we have here writ
To Norway, uncle of young Fortinbras—
Who, impotent° and bed-rid, scarcely hears
Of this his nephew's purpose—to suppress   30
His° further gait° herein, in that the levies,
The lists, and full proportions are all made
Out of his subject;° and we here dispatch
You, good Cornelius, and you, Voltimand,
For bearers of this greeting to old Norway,   35
Giving to you no further personal power
To business with the King more than the scope
Of these dilated° articles allow. [*He gives a paper.*]
Farewell, and let your haste commend your duty.°

CORNELIUS, VOLTIMAND: In that, and all things, will we show our duty.   40

KING: We doubt it nothing.° Heartily farewell.

[*Exeunt* VOLTIMAND *and* CORNELIUS.]

And now, Laertes, what's the news with you?
You told us of some suit; what is 't, Laertes?
You cannot speak of reason to the Dane
And lose your voice.° What wouldst thou beg, Laertes,   45
That shall not be my offer, not thy asking?
The head is not more native° to the heart,
The hand more instrumental° to the mouth,
Than is the throne of Denmark to thy father.
What wouldst thou have, Laertes?   50

LAERTES: My dread lord,
Your leave and favor° to return to France,
From whence though willingly I came to Denmark
To show my duty in your coronation,
Yet now I must confess, that duty done,   55
My thoughts and wishes bend again toward France
And bow them to your gracious leave and pardon.°

---

29 impotent helpless   **31 His** i.e., Fortinbras'   **gait** proceeding   **33 31–33 in that...sub-ject** since the levying of troops and supplies is drawn entirely from the King of Norway's own subjects   **38 dilated** set out at length   **39 let...duty** let your swift obeying of orders, rather than mere words, express your dutifulness   **41 nothing** not at all   **44 the Dane** the Danish king   **45 lose your voice** waste your speech   **47 native** closely connected, related   **48 instrumental** serviceable   **52 leave and favor** kind permission   **57 bow...pardon** entreatingly make a deep bow, asking your permission to depart

KING: Have you your father's leave? What says Polonius?

POLONIUS: H'ath,° my lord, wrung from me my slow leave
  By laborsome petition, and at last   60
  Upon his will I sealed° my hard° consent.
  I do beseech you, give him leave to go.

KING: Take thy fair hour,° Laertes. Time be thine,
  And thy best graces spend it at thy will!°
  But now, my cousin° Hamlet, and my son—   65

HAMLET: A little more than kin, and less than kind.°

KING: How is it that the clouds still hang on you?

HAMLET: Not so, my lord. I am too much in the sun.°

QUEEN: Good Hamlet, cast thy nighted color° off,
  And let thine eye look like a friend on Denmark.°   70
  Do not forever with thy vailèd lids°
  Seek for thy noble father in the dust.
  Thou know'st 'tis common,° all that lives must die,
  Passing through nature to eternity.

HAMLET: Ay, madam, it is common.   75

QUEEN: If it be,
  Why seems it so particular° with thee?

HAMLET: Seems, madam? Nay, it is. I know not "seems."
  'Tis not alone my inky cloak, good Mother,
  Nor customary° suits of solemn black,   80
  Nor windy suspiration° of forced breath,
  No, nor the fruitful° river in the eye,
  Nor the dejected havior° of the visage,
  Together with all forms, moods,° shapes of grief,
  That can denote me truly. These indeed seem,   85
  For they are actions that a man might play.
  But I have that within which passes show;
  These but the trappings and the suits of woe.

---

59 **H'ath** he has   61 **sealed** (as if sealing a legal document)   **hard** reluctant   63 **Take thy fair hour** enjoy your time of youth   64 **And...will** and may your finest qualities guide the way you choose to spend your time   65 **cousin** any kin not of the immediate family   66 **A little...kind** i.e., closer than an ordinary nephew (since I am stepson), and yet more separated in natural feeling (with pun on *kind* meaning "affectionate" and "natural," "lawful." This line is often read as an aside, but it need not be. The King chooses perhaps not to respond to Hamlet's cryptic and bitter remark.)   68 **the sun** i.e., the sunshine of the King's royal favor (with pun on *son*)   69 **nighted color** (1) mourning garments of black (2) dark melancholy   70 **Denmark** the King of Denmark   71 **vailèd lids** lowered eyes   73 **common** of universal occurrence (But Hamlet plays on the sense of "vulgar" in line 74.)   77 **particular** personal   80 **customary** (1) socially conventional (2) habitual with me   81 **suspiration** sighing   82 **fruitful** abundant   83 **havior** expression   84 **moods** outward expression of feeling

KING: 'Tis sweet and commendable in your nature, Hamlet,
To give these mourning duties to your father. 90
But you must know your father lost a father,
That father lost, lost his, and the survivor bound
In filial obligation for some term
To do obsequious° sorrow. But to persever°
In obstinate condolement° is a course 95
Of impious stubbornness. 'Tis unmanly grief.
It shows a will most incorrect to heaven,
A heart unfortified,° a mind impatient,
An understanding simple° and unschooled.
For what we know must be and is as common 100
As any the most vulgar thing to sense,°
Why should we in our peevish opposition
Take it to heart? Fie, 'tis a fault to heaven,
A fault against the dead, a fault to nature,
To reason most absurd, whose common theme 105
Is death of fathers, and who still° hath cried,
From the first corpse° till he that died today,
"This must be so." We pray you, throw to earth
This unprevailing° woe and think of us
As of a father; for let the world take note, 110
You are the most immediate° to our throne,
And with no less nobility of love
Than that which dearest father bears his son
Do I impart toward° you. For° your intent
In going back to school° in Wittenberg,° 115
It is most retrograde° to our desire,
And we beseech you bend you° to remain
Here in the cheer and comfort of our eye,
Our chiefest courtier, cousin, and our son.
QUEEN: Let not thy mother lose her prayers, Hamlet. 120
I pray thee, stay with us, go not to Wittenberg.
HAMLET: I shall in all my best° obey you, madam.

94 obsequious suited to obsequies or funerals   **persever** persevere   **95 condolement**
sorrowing   **98 unfortified** i.e., against adversity   **99 simple** ignorant   **101 As...sense**
as the most ordinary experience   **106 still** always   **107 the first corpse** (Abel's)   **109**
unprevailing unavailing, useless   **111 most immediate** next in succession   **114 impart**
toward i.e., bestow my affection on   **For** as for   **115 to school** i.e., to your studies   **Wit-**
tenberg famous German university founded in 1502   **116 retrograde** contrary   **117 bend**
you incline yourself   **122 in all my best** to the best of my ability

KING: Why, 'tis a loving and a fair reply.
         Be as ourself in Denmark. Madam, come.
         This gentle and unforced accord of Hamlet   125
         Sits smiling to° my heart, in grace° whereof
         No jocund° health that Denmark drinks today
         But the great cannon to the clouds shall tell,
         And the King's rouse° the heaven shall bruit again,°
         Respeaking earthly thunder.° Come away.   130

[Flourish. Exeunt all but HAMLET.]

HAMLET: O, that this too too sullied° flesh would melt,
         Thaw, and resolve itself into a dew!
         Or that the Everlasting had not fixed
         His canon° 'gainst self-slaughter! O God, God,
         How weary, stale, flat, and unprofitable   135
         Seem to me all the uses° of this world!
         Fie on 't, ah fie! 'Tis an unweeded garden
         That grows to seed. Things rank and gross in nature
         Possess it merely.° That it should come to this!
         But two months dead—nay, not so much, not two.   140
         So excellent a king, that was to° this
         Hyperion° to a satyr,° so loving to my mother
         That he might not beteem° the winds of heaven
         Visit her face too roughly. Heaven and earth,
         Must I remember? Why, she would hang on him   145
         As if increase of appetite had grown
         By what it fed on, and yet within a month—
         Let me not think on 't; frailty, thy name is woman!—
         A little month, or ere° those shoes were old
         With which she followed my poor father's body,   150
         Like Niobe;° all tears, why she, even she—
         O God, a beast, that wants discourse of reason,°
         Would have mourned longer—married with my uncle,
         My father's brother, but no more like my father

126 to i.e., at   **grace** thanksgiving   **127 jocund** merry   **129 rouse** drinking of a draft of liquor   **bruit again** loudly echo   **130 thunder** i.e., of trumpet and kettledrum, sounded when the King drinks; see 1.4.8–12   **131 sullied** defiled (The early quartos read *sallied;* the Folio, *solid.*)   **134 canon** law   **136 all the uses** the whole routine   **139 merely** completely   **141 to** in comparison to   **142 Hyperion** Titan sun-god, father of Helios   **satyr** a lecherous creature of classical mythology, half-human but with a goat's legs, tail, ears, and horns   **143 beteem** allow   **149 or ere** even before   **151 Niobe** Tantalus' daughter, Queen of Thebes, who boasted that she had more sons and daughters than Leto; for this, Apollo and Artemis, children of Leto, slew her fourteen children. She was turned by Zeus into a stone that continually dropped tears.   **152 wants...reason** lacks the faculty of reason

Than I to Hercules. Within a month,   155
Ere yet the salt of most unrighteous tears
Had left the flushing in her gallèd° eyes,
She married. O, most wicked speed, to post°
With such dexterity to incestuous° sheets!
It is not, nor it cannot come to good.   160
But break, my heart, for I must hold my tongue.

[*Enter* HORATIO, MARCELLUS *and* BERNARDO.]

HORATIO: Hail to your lordship!
HAMLET: I am glad to see you well.
   Horatio!—or I do forget myself.
HORATIO: The same, my lord, and your poor servant ever.   165
HAMLET: Sir, my good friend; I'll change that name° with you.
   And what make you from° Wittenberg, Horatio?
   Marcellus.
MARCELLUS: My good lord.
HAMLET: I am very glad to see you. [*To* BERNARDO.] Good even, sir.—   170
   But what in faith make you from Wittenberg?
HORATIO: A truant disposition, good my lord.
HAMLET: I would not hear your enemy say so,
   Nor shall you do my ear that violence
   To make it truster of your own report   175
   Against yourself. I know you are no truant.
   But what is your affair in Elsinore?
   We'll teach you to drink deep ere you depart.
HORATIO: My lord, I came to see your father's funeral.
HAMLET: I prithee, do not mock me, fellow student;   180
   I think it was to see my mother's wedding.
HORATIO: Indeed, my lord, it followed hard° upon.
HAMLET: Thrift, thrift, Horatio! The funeral baked meats°
   Did coldly° furnish forth the marriage tables.
   Would I had met my dearest° foe in heaven   185
   Or ever° I had seen that day, Horatio!
   My father!—Methinks I see my father.
HORATIO: Where, my lord?
HAMLET: In my mind's eye, Horatio.
HORATIO: I saw him once. 'A° was a goodly king.   190

---

157 gallèd irritated, inflamed   **158 post** hasten   **159 incestuous** (In Shakespeare's day, the marriage of a man like Claudius to his deceased brother's wife was considered incestuous.)   **166 change that name** i.e., give and receive reciprocally the name of "friend" (rather than talk of "servant")   **167 make you from** are you doing away from   **182 hard** close   **183 baked meats** meat pies   **184 coldly** i.e., as cold leftovers   **185 dearest** closest (and therefore deadliest)   **186 Or ever** before   **190 'A** he

HAMLET: 'A was a man. Take him for all in all,
    I shall not look upon his like again.
HORATIO: My lord, I think I saw him yesternight.
HAMLET: Saw? Who?
HORATIO: My lord, the King your father.   195
HAMLET: The King my father?
HORATIO: Season your admiration° for a while
    With an attent° ear till I may deliver,
    Upon the witness of these gentlemen,
    This marvel to you.   200
HAMLET: For God's love, let me hear!
HORATIO: Two nights together had these gentlemen,
    Marcellus and Bernardo, on their watch,
    In the dead waste° and middle of the night,
    Been thus encountered. A figure like your father,   205
    Armèd at point° exactly, cap-á-pie,°
    Appears before them, and with solemn march
    Goes slow and stately by them. Thrice he walked
    By their oppressed and fear-surprisèd eyes
    Within his truncheon's° length, whilst they, distilled°   210
    Almost to jelly with the act° of fear,
    Stand dumb and speak not to him. This to me
    In dreadful° secrecy impart they did,
    And I with them the third night kept the watch,
    Where, as they had delivered, both in time,   215
    Form of the thing, each word made true and good,
    The apparition comes. I knew your father;
    These hands are not more like.
HAMLET: But where was this?
MARCELLUS: My lord, upon the platform where we watch.   220
HAMLET: Did you not speak to it?
HORATIO: My lord, I did,
    But answer made it none. Yet once methought
    It lifted up its head and did address
    Itself to motion, like as it would speak;°
    But even then° the morning cock crew loud,   225

---

197 Season your admiration restrain your astonishment   **198 attent** attentive   **204 dead waste** desolate stillness   **206 at point** correctly in every detail   **cap-á-pie** from head to foot   **210 truncheon** officer's staff   **distilled** dissolved   **211 act** action, operation   **213 dreadful** full of dread   **225 did...speak** began to move as though it were about to speak   **226 even then** at that very instant

And at the sound it shrunk in haste away
And vanished from our sight.

HAMLET: 'Tis very strange.

HORATIO: As I do live, my honored lord, 'tis true,   230
And we did think it writ down in our duty
To let you know of it.

HAMLET: Indeed, indeed, sirs. But this troubles me.
Hold you the watch tonight?

ALL: We do, my lord.   235

HAMLET: Armed, say you?

ALL: Armed, my lord.

HAMLET: From top to toe?

ALL: My lord, from head to foot.

HAMLET: Then saw you not his face?   240

HORATIO: O, yes, my lord, he wore his beaver° up.

HAMLET: What° looked he, frowningly?

HORATIO: A countenance more in sorrow than in anger.

HAMLET: Pale or red?

HORATIO: Nay, very pale.   245

HAMLET: And fixed his eyes upon you?

HORATIO: Most constantly.

HAMLET: I would I had been there.

HORATIO: It would have much amazed you.

HAMLET: Very like, very like. Stayed it long?   250

HORATIO: While one with moderate haste might tell° a hundred.

MARCELLUS, BERNARDO: Longer, longer.

HORATIO: Not when I saw 't.

HAMLET: His beard was grizzled°—no?

HORATIO: It was, as I have seen it in his life,   255
A sable silvered.°

HAMLET: I will watch tonight.
Perchance 'twill walk again.

HORATIO: I warrant° it will.

HAMLET: If it assume my noble father's person,   260
I'll speak to it though hell itself should gape
And bid me hold my peace. I pray you all,
If you have hitherto concealed this sight,
Let it be tenable° in your silence still,
And whatsoever else shall hap tonight,   265

---

241 beaver visor on the helmet   **242 What** how   **251 tell** count   **254 grizzled** gray
256 sable silvered black mixed with white   **259 warrant** assure you   **264 tenable** held

Give it an understanding but no tongue.
I will requite your loves. So, fare you well.
Upon the platform twixt eleven and twelve
I'll visit you.

ALL: Our duty to your honor.   270

HAMLET: Your loves, as mine to you. Farewell.

[*Exeunt (all but* HAMLET).]

My father's spirit in arms! All is not well.
I doubt° some foul play. Would the night were come!
Till then sit still, my soul. Foul deeds will rise,
Though all the earth o'erwhelm them, to men's eyes.   275

[*Exit.*]

[**Act 1.3** *Enter* LAERTES *and* OPHELIA, *his sister.*]°

LAERTES: My necessaries are embarked. Farewell.
And, sister, as the winds give benefit
And convoy is assistant,° do not sleep
But let me hear from you.

OPHELIA: Do you doubt that?   5

LAERTES: For Hamlet, and the trifling of his favor,
Hold it a fashion and a toy in blood,°
A violet in the youth of primy° nature,
Forward,° not permanent, sweet, not lasting,
The perfume and suppliance° of a minute—   10
No more.

OPHELIA: No more but so?

LAERTES: Think it no more.
For nature crescent° does not grow alone
In thews° and bulk, but as this temple° waxes   15
The inward service of the mind and soul
Grows wide withal.° Perhaps he loves you now,
And now no soil° nor cautel° doth besmirch
The virtue of his will,° but you must fear,
His greatness weighed,° his will is not his own.   20
For he himself is subject to his birth.
He may not, as unvalued persons do,

---

273 doubt suspect   **1.3 s.d. Location:** Polonius' chambers   **3 convoy is assistant**
means of conveyance are available   **7 toy in blood** passing amorous fancy   **8 primy** in
its prime, springtime   **9 Forward** precocious   **10 suppliance** supply, filler   **14 crescent**
growing, waxing   **15 thews** bodily strength   **temple** i.e., body   **17 Grows wide withal**
grows along with it   **18 soil** blemish   **cautel** deceit   **19 will** desire   **20 His greatness
weighed** if you take into account his high position

Carve° for himself, for on his choice depends
The safety and health of this whole state,
And therefore must his choice be circumscribed   25
Unto the voice and yielding° of that body
Whereof he is the head. Then if he says he loves you,
It fits your wisdom so far to believe it
As he in his particular act and place°
May give his saying deed, which is no further   30
Than the main voice° of Denmark goes withal.°
Then weigh what loss your honor may sustain
If with too credent° ear you list° his songs,
Or lose your heart, or your chaste treasure open
To his unmastered importunity.   35
Fear it, Ophelia, fear it, my dear sister,
And keep you in the rear of your affection,°
Out of the shot and danger of desire.
The chariest° maid is prodigal enough
If she unmask° her beauty to the moon.°   40
Virtue itself scapes not calumnious strokes.
The canker galls° the infants of the spring
Too oft before their buttons° be disclosed,°
And in the morn and liquid dew° of youth
Contagious blastments° are most imminent.   45
Be wary then; best safety lies in fear.
Youth to itself rebels,° though none else near.

OPHELIA: I shall the effect of this good lesson keep
As watchman to my heart. But, good my brother,
Do not, as some ungracious° pastors do,   50
Show me the steep and thorny way to heaven,
Whiles like a puffed° and reckless libertine
Himself the primrose path of dalliance treads,
And recks° not his own rede.°

[*Enter* POLONIUS.]

23 **Carve** i.e., choose   26 **voice and yielding** assent, approval   29 **in…place** in his particular restricted circumstances   31 **main voice** general assent   **withal** along with   33 **credent** credulous   **list** listen to   37 **keep…affection** don't advance as far as your affection might lead you (A military metaphor.)   39 **chariest** most scrupulously modest   40 **If she unmask** if she does no more than show her beauty   **moon** (Symbol of chastity.)   42 **canker galls** canker-worm destroys   43 **buttons** buds   **disclosed** opened   44 **liquid dew** i.e., time when dew is fresh and bright   45 **blastments** blights   47 **Youth…rebels** youth is inherently rebellious   50 **ungracious** ungodly   52 **puffed** bloated, or swollen with pride   54 **recks** heeds   **rede** counsel

LAERTES: O, fear me not.°   55
    I stay too long. But here my father comes.
    A double° blessing is a double grace;
    Occasion smiles upon a second leave.°
POLONIUS: Yet here, Laertes? Aboard, aboard, for shame!
    The wind sits in the shoulder of your sail,   60
    And you are stayed for. There—my blessing with thee!
    And these few precepts in thy memory
    Look° thou character.° Give thy thoughts no tongue,
    Nor any unproportioned° thought his° act.
    Be thou familiar,° but by no means vulgar.°   65
    Those friends thou hast, and their adoption tried,°
    Grapple them unto thy soul with hoops of steel,
    But do not dull thy palm° with entertainment
    Of each new-hatched, unfledged courage.° Beware
    Of entrance to a quarrel, but being in,   70
    Bear 't that° th' opposèd may beware of thee.
    Give every man thy ear, but few thy voice;
    Take each man's censure,° but reserve thy judgment.
    Costly thy habit° as thy purse can buy,
    But not expressed in fancy;° rich, not gaudy,   75
    For the apparel oft proclaims the man,
    And they in France of the best rank and station
    Are of a most select and generous chief in that.°
    Neither a borrower nor a lender be,
    For loan oft loses both itself and friend,   80
    And borrowing dulleth edge of husbandry.°
    This above all: to thine own self be true,
    And it must follow, as the night the day,
    Thou canst not then be false to any man.
    Farewell. My blessing season° this in thee!   85

---

55 fear me not don't worry on my account   **57 double** (Laertes has already bid his father good-bye.)   **58 Occasion...leave** happy is the circumstance that provides a second leave-taking (The goddess Occasion, or Opportunity, smiles.)   **63 Look** be sure that   **character** inscribe   **64 unproportioned** badly calculated, intemperate   **his** its   **65 familiar** sociable   **vulgar** common   **66 and their adoption tried** and also their suitability for adoption as friends having been tested   **68 dull thy palm** i.e., shake hands so often as to make the gesture meaningless   **69 courage** young man of spirit   **71 Bear 't that** manage it so that   **73 censure** opinion, judgment   **74 habit** clothing   **75 fancy** excessive ornament, decadent fashion   **78 Are...that** are of a most refined and well-bred preeminence in choosing what to wear   **81 husbandry** thrift   **85 season** mature

LAERTES: Most humbly do I take my leave, my lord.

POLONIUS: The time invests° you. Go, your servants tend.°

LAERTES: Farewell, Ophelia, and remember well
  What I have said to you.

OPHELIA: 'Tis in my memory locked,   90
  And you yourself shall keep the key of it.

LAERTES: Farewell.

[*Exit* LAERTES.]

POLONIUS: What is 't, Ophelia, he hath said to you?

OPHELIA: So please you, something touching the Lord Hamlet.

POLONIUS: Marry,° well bethought.   95
  'Tis told me he hath very oft of late
  Given private time to you, and you yourself
  Have of your audience been most free and bounteous.
  If it be so—as so 'tis put on° me,
  And that in way of caution—I must tell you   100
  You do not understand yourself so clearly
  As it behooves° my daughter and your honor.
  What is between you? Give me up the truth.

OPHELIA: He hath, my lord, of late made many tenders°
  Of his affection to me.   105

POLONIUS: Affection? Pooh! You speak like a green girl,
  Unsifted° in such perilous circumstance.
  Do you believe his tenders, as you call them?

OPHELIA: I do not know, my lord, what I should think.

POLONIUS: Marry, I will teach you. Think yourself a baby   110
  That you have ta'en these tenders for true pay
  Which are not sterling.° Tender° yourself more dearly,
  Or—not to crack the wind° of the poor phrase,
  Running it thus—you'll tender me a fool.°

OPHELIA: My lord, he hath importuned me with love   115
  In honorable fashion.

POLONIUS: Ay, fashion° you may call it. Go to,° go to.

---

87 invests besieges, presses upon   **tend** attend, wait   **95 Marry** i.e., by the Virgin Mary
(A mild oath.)   **99 put on** impressed on, told to   **102 behooves** befits   **103 tenders**
offers   **107 Unsifted** i.e., untried   **112 sterling** legal currency   **Tender** hold, look after,
offer   **112 crack the wind** i.e., run it until it is broken-winded   **114 tender me a fool** (1)
show yourself to me as a fool (2) show me up as a fool (3) present me with a grandchild
(*Fool* was a term of endearment for a child.)   **117 fashion** mere form, pretense   **Go to**
(An expression of impatience.)

OPHELIA: And hath given countenance° to his speech, my lord,
     With almost all the holy vows of heaven.

POLONIUS: Ay, springes° to catch woodcocks.° I do know,   120
     When the blood burns, how prodigal° the soul
     Lends the tongue vows. These blazes, daughter,
     Giving more light than heat, extinct in both
     Even in their promise as it° is a-making,
     You must not take for fire. From this time   125
     Be something° scanter of your maiden presence.
     Set your entreatments° at a higher rate
     Than a command to parle.° For Lord Hamlet,
     Believe so much in him° that he is young,
     And with a larger tether may he walk   130
     Than may be given you. In few,° Ophelia,
     Do not believe his vows, for they are brokers,°
     Not of that dye° which their investments° show,
     But mere implorators° of unholy suits,
     Breathing° like sanctified and pious bawds,   135
     The better to beguile. This is for all:°
     I would not, in plain terms, from this time forth
     Have you so slander° any moment° leisure
     As to give words or talk with the Lord Hamlet.
     Look to 't, I charge you. Come your ways.°   140

OPHELIA: I shall obey, my lord.

[*Exeunt.*]

[**Act 1.4** *Enter* HAMLET, HORATIO, *and* MARCELLUS.]°

HAMLET: The air bites shrewdly,° it is very cold.

HORATIO: It is a nipping and an eager° air.

HAMLET: What hour now?

HORATIO: I think it lacks of° twelve.

MARCELLUS: No, it is struck.   5

---

118 countenance credit, confirmation **120 springes** snares **woodcocks** birds easily caught; here used to connote gullibility **121 prodigal** prodigally **124 it** i.e., the promise **126 something** somewhat **127 entreatments** negotiations for surrender (A military term.) **128 parle** discuss terms with the enemy (Polonius urges his daughter, in the metaphor of military language, not to meet with Hamlet and consider giving in to him merely because he requests an interview.) **129 so...him** this much concerning him **131 In few** briefly **132 brokers** go-betweens, procurers **133 dye** color or sort **investments** clothes (The vows are not what they seem.) **134 mere implorators** out and out solicitors **135 Breathing** speaking **136 for all** once for all, in sum **137 slander** abuse, misuse **moment** moment's **140 Come your ways** come along **1.4 s.d. Location: The guard platform** **1 shrewdly** keenly, sharply **2 eager** biting **4 lacks of** is just short of

HORATIO: Indeed? I heard it not.
        It then draws near the season°
        Wherein the spirit held his wont° to walk.

[*A flourish of trumpets, and two pieces° go off (within)*.]

        What does this mean, my lord?   10
HAMLET: The King doth wake° tonight and takes his rouse,°
        Keeps wassail,° and the swaggering upspring° reels,°
        And as he drains his drafts of Rhenish° down,
        The kettledrum and trumpet thus bray out
        The triumph of his pledge.°   15
HORATIO: It is a custom?
HAMLET: Ay, marry, is 't,
        But to my mind, though I am native here
        And to the manner° born, it is a custom
        More honored in the breach than the observance.°   20
        This heavy-headed revel east and west°
        Makes us traduced and taxed of° other nations.
        They clepe° us drunkards, and with swinish phrase°
        Soil our addition;° and indeed it takes
        From our achievements, though performed at height,°   25
        The pith and marrow of our attribute.°
        So, oft it chances in particular men,
        That for° some vicious mole of nature° in them,
        As in their birth—wherein they are not guilty,
        Since nature cannot choose his° origin—   30
        By their o'ergrowth of some complexion,°
        Oft breaking down the pales° and forts of reason,
        Or by some habit that too much o'erleavens°
        The form of plausive° manners, that these men,
        Carrying, I say, the stamp of one defect,   35
        Being nature's livery° or fortune's star,°

---

7 season time   **8 held his wont** was accustomed   **s.d. pieces** i.e., of ordnance, cannon
11 wake stay awake and hold revel   **takes his rouse** carouses   **12 wassail** carousal
upspring wild German dance   **reels** dances   **13 Rhenish** Rhine wine   **15 The**
triumph...pledge i.e., his feat in draining the wine in a single draft   **19 manner** custom (of
drinking)   **20 More...observance** better neglected than followed   **21 east and west** i.e.,
everywhere   **22 taxed of** censured by   **23 clepe** call   **with swinish phrase** i.e., by calling
us swine   **24 addition** reputation   **25 at height** outstandingly   **26 The pith...attribute**
the essence of the reputation that others attribute to us   **28 for** on account of   **mole**
of nature natural blemish in one's constitution   **30 his** its   **31 their o'ergrowth...**
complexion the excessive growth in individuals of some natural trait   **32 pales** palings,
fences (as of a fortification)   **33 o'erleavens** induces a change throughout (as yeast works
in dough)   **34 plausive** pleasing   **36 nature's livery** sign of one's servitude to nature
fortune's star the destiny that chance brings

His virtues else,° be they as pure as grace,

As infinite as man may undergo,°

Shall in the general censure° take corruption

From that particular fault. The dram of evil   40

Doth all the noble substance often dout

To his own scandal.°

[*Enter* GHOST.]

HORATIO: Look, my lord, it comes!

HAMLET: Angels and ministers° of grace defend us!

Be thou° a spirit of health° or goblin damned,   45

Bring° with thee airs from heaven or blasts from hell,

Be thy intents° wicked or charitable,

Thou com'st in such a questionable° shape

That I will speak to thee. I'll call thee Hamlet,

King, father, royal Dane. O, answer me!   50

Let me not burst in ignorance, but tell

Why thy canonized° bones, hearsèd° in death,

Have burst their cerements;° why the sepulcher

Wherein we saw thee quietly inurned°

Hath oped his ponderous and marble jaws   55

To cast thee up again. What may this mean,

That thou, dead corpse, again in complete steel,°

Revisits thus the glimpses of the moon,°

Making night hideous, and we fools of nature°

So horridly to shake our disposition°   60

With thoughts beyond the reaches of our souls?

Say, why is this? Wherefore? What should we do?

[*The* GHOST *beckons* HAMLET.]

HORATIO: It beckons you to go away with it,

As if it some impartment° did desire

To you alone.   65

---

37 His virtues else i.e., the other qualities of *these men* (line 30)   **38 may undergo** can sustain   **39 general censure** general opinion that people have of him   **42 The dram...scandal** i.e., the small drop of evil blots out or works against the noble substance of the whole and brings it into disrepute. To *dout* is to blot out. (A famous crux.)   **44 ministers of grace** messengers of God   **45 Be thou** whether you are   **spirit of health** good angel   **46 Bring** whether you bring   **47 Be thy intents** whether your intentions are   **48 questionable** inviting question   **52 canonized** buried according to the canons of the church   **hearsèd** coffined   **53 cerements** grave clothes   **54 inurned** entombed   **57 complete steel** full armor   **58 glimpses of the moon** pale and uncertain moonlight   **59 fools of nature** mere men, limited to natural knowledge and subject to nature   **60 So...disposition** to distress our mental composure so violently   **64 impartment** communication

MARCELLUS: Look with what courteous action
    It wafts you to a more removèd ground.
    But do not go with it.
HORATIO: No, by no means.
HAMLET: It will not speak. Then I will follow it.   70
HORATIO: Do not, my lord!
HAMLET: Why, what should be the fear?
    I do not set my life at a pin's fee,°
    And for my soul, what can it do to that,
    Being a thing immortal as itself?   75
    It waves me forth again. I'll follow it.
HORATIO: What if it tempt you toward the flood,° my lord,
    Or to the dreadful summit of the cliff
    That beetles o'er° his° base into the sea,
    And there assume some other horrible form   80
    Which might deprive your sovereignty of reason°
    And draw you into madness? Think of it.
    The very place puts toys of desperation,°
    Without more motive, into every brain
    That looks so many fathoms to the sea   85
    And hears it roar beneath.
HAMLET: It wafts me still.—Go on, I'll follow thee.
MARCELLUS: You shall not go, my lord.   [*They try to stop him.*]
HAMLET: Hold off your hands!
HORATIO: Be ruled. You shall not go.   90
HAMLET: My fate cries out,°
    And makes each petty° artery° in this body
    As hardy as the Nemean lion's° nerve.°
    Still am I called. Unhand me, gentlemen.
    By heaven, I'll make a ghost of him that lets° me!   95
    I say, away!—Go on, I'll follow thee.
[*Exeunt* GHOST *and* HAMLET.]

HORATIO: He waxes desperate with imagination.
MARCELLUS: Let's follow. 'Tis not fit thus to obey him.

---

73 fee value   **77 flood** sea   **79 beetles o'er** overhangs threateningly (like bushy eye-brows)   **his** its   **81 deprive...reason** take away the rule of reason over your mind   **83 toys of desperation** fancies of desperate acts, i.e., suicide   **91 My fate cries out** my destiny summons me   **92 petty** weak   **artery** (through which the vital spirits were thought to have been conveyed)   **93 Nemean lion** one of the monsters slain by Hercules in his twelve labors   **nerve** sinew   **95 lets** hinders

HORATIO: Have after.° To what issue° will this come?

MARCELLUS: Something is rotten in the state of Denmark.   100

HORATIO: Heaven will direct it.°

MARCELLUS: Nay, let's follow him.

[*Exeunt.*]

[**Act 1.5** *Enter* GHOST *and* HAMLET.]°

HAMLET: Whither wilt thou lead me? Speak. I'll go no further.

GHOST: Mark me.

HAMLET: I will.

GHOST: My hour is almost come,

When I to sulfurous and tormenting flames   5

Must render up myself.

HAMLET: Alas, poor ghost!

GHOST: Pity me not, but lend thy serious hearing

To what I shall unfold.

HAMLET: Speak. I am bound° to hear.   10

GHOST: So art thou to revenge, when thou shalt hear.

HAMLET: What?

GHOST: I am thy father's spirit,

Doomed for a certain term to walk the night,

And for the day confined to fast° in fires,   15

Till the foul crimes° done in my days of nature°

Are burnt and purged away. But that° I am forbid

To tell the secrets of my prison house,

I could a tale unfold whose lightest word

Would harrow up° thy soul, freeze thy young blood,   20

Make thy two eyes like stars start from their spheres,°

Thy knotted and combinèd locks° to part,

And each particular hair to stand on end

Like quills upon the fretful porcupine.

But this eternal blazon° must not be   25

To ears of flesh and blood. List, list, O, list!

If thou didst ever thy dear father love—

99 Have after let's go after him   **issue** outcome   **101 it** i.e., the outcome   **1.5 s.d. Location: The battlements of the castle 10 bound** (1) ready (2) obligated by duty and fate (The Ghost, in line 8, answers in the second sense.)   **15 fast** do penance by fasting   **16 crimes** sins   **of nature** as a mortal   **17 But that** were it not that   **20 harrow up** lacerate, tear   **21 spheres** i.e., eye-sockets, here compared to the orbits or transparent revolving spheres in which, according to Ptolemaic astronomy, the heavenly bodies were fixed   **22 knotted…locks** hair neatly arranged and confined   **25 eternal blazon** revelation of the secrets of eternity

HAMLET: O God!

GHOST: Revenge his foul and most unnatural murder.

HAMLET: Murder?   30

GHOST: Murder most foul, as in the best° it is,

But this most foul, strange, and unnatural.

HAMLET: Haste me to know't, that I, with wings as swift

As meditation or the thoughts of love,

May sweep to my revenge.   35

GHOST: I find thee apt;

And duller shouldst thou be° than the fat° weed

That roots itself in ease on Lethe° wharf,

Wouldst thou not stir in this. Now, Hamlet, hear.

'Tis given out that, sleeping in my orchard,°   40

A serpent stung me. So the whole ear of Denmark

Is by a forgèd process° of my death

Rankly abused.° But know, thou noble youth,

The serpent that did sting thy father's life

Now wears his crown.   45

HAMLET: O, my prophetic soul! My uncle!

GHOST: Ay, that incestuous, that adulterate° beast,

With witchcraft of his wit, with traitorous gifts°—

O wicked wit and gifts, that have the power

So to seduce!—won to his shameful lust   50

The will of my most seeming-virtuous queen.

O Hamlet, what a falling off was there!

From me, whose love was of that dignity

That it went hand in hand even with the vow°

I made to her in marriage, and to decline   55

Upon a wretch whose natural gifts were poor

To° those of mine!

But virtue, as it° never will be moved,

Though lewdness court it in a shape of heaven,°

So lust, though to a radiant angel linked,   60

Will sate itself in a celestial bed°

And prey on garbage.

But soft, methinks I scent the morning air.

---

31 in the best even at best   **37 shouldst thou be** you would have to be   **fat** torpid, lethargic   **38 Lethe** the river of forgetfulness in Hades   **40 orchard** garden   **42 forgèd process** falsified account   **43 abused** deceived   **47 adulterate** adulterous   **48 gifts** (1) talents (2) presents   **54 even with the vow** with the very vow   **57 To** compared to   **58 virtue, as it** as virtue   **59 shape of heaven** heavenly form   **61 sate...bed** cease to find sexual pleasure in a virtuously lawful marriage

Brief let me be. Sleeping within my orchard,
My custom always of the afternoon,   65
Upon my secure° hour thy uncle stole,
With juice of cursèd hebona° in a vial,
And in the porches of my ears° did pour
The leprous distillment,° whose effect
Holds such an enmity with blood of man   70
That swift as quicksilver it courses through
The natural gates and alleys of the body,
And with a sudden vigor it doth posset°
And curd, like eager° droppings into milk,
The thin and wholesome blood. So did it mine,   75
And a most instant tetter° barked° about,
Most lazar-like,° with vile and loathsome crust,
All my smooth body.
Thus was I, sleeping, by a brother's hand
Of life, of crown, of queen at once dispatched,°   80
Cut off even in the blossoms of my sin,
Unhouseled,° disappointed,° unaneled,°
No reckoning° made, but sent to my account
With all my imperfections on my head.
O, horrible! O, horrible, most horrible!   85
If thou hast nature° in thee, bear it not.
Let not the royal bed of Denmark be
A couch for luxury° and damnèd incest.
But, howsoever thou pursues this act,
Taint not thy mind nor let thy soul contrive   90
Against thy mother aught. Leave her to heaven
And to those thorns that in her bosom lodge,
To prick and sting her. Fare thee well at once.
The glowworm shows the matin° to be near,
And 'gins to pale his° uneffectual fire.   95
Adieu, adieu, adieu! Remember me.

[*Exit.*]

---

66 secure confident, unsuspicious   **67 hebona** a poison (The word seems to be a form of *ebony*, though it is thought perhaps to be related to *henbane*, a poison, or to *ebenus*, "yew.") **68 porches of my ears** ears as a porch or entrance of the body   **69 leprous distillment** distillation causing leprosylike disfigurement   **73 posset** coagulate, curdle   **74 eager** sour, acid **76 tetter** eruption of scabs   **barked** recovered with a rough covering, like bark on a tree **77 lazar-like** leperlike   **80 dispatched** suddenly deprived   **82 Unhouseled** without having received the Sacrament   **disappointed** unready (spiritually) for the last journey   **unaneled** without having received extreme unction   **83 reckoning** settling of accounts   **86 nature** i.e., the promptings of a son   **88 luxury** lechery   **94 matin** morning   **95 his** its

HAMLET: O all you host of heaven! O earth! What else?
　　　　 And shall I couple° hell? O, fie! Hold,° hold, my heart,
　　　　 And you, my sinews, grow not instant° old,
　　　　 But bear me stiffly up. Remember thee?　　　　　　　　　　　100
　　　　 Ay, thou poor ghost, whiles memory holds a seat
　　　　 In this distracted globe.° Remember thee?
　　　　 Yea, from the table° of my memory
　　　　 I'll wipe away all trivial fond° records,
　　　　 All saws° of books, all forms,° all pressures° past　　　　　105
　　　　 That youth and observation copied there,
　　　　 And thy commandment all alone shall live
　　　　 Within the book and volume of my brain,
　　　　 Unmixed with baser matter. Yes, by heaven!
　　　　 O most pernicious woman!　　　　　　　　　　　　　　　　110
　　　　 O villain, villain, smiling, damnèd villain!
　　　　 My tables°—meet it is° I set it down
　　　　 That one may smile, and smile, and be a villain.
　　　　 At least I am sure it may be so in Denmark.

[*Writing.*]

　　　　 So uncle, there you are.° Now to my word:　　　　　　　　115
　　　　 It is "Adieu, adieu! Remember me."
　　　　 I have sworn't.

[*Enter* HORATIO *and* MARCELLUS.]

HORATIO: My lord, my lord!
MARCELLUS: Lord Hamlet!
HORATIO: Heavens secure him!°　　　　　　　　　　　　　　　　120
HAMLET: So be it.
MARCELLUS: Hilo, ho, ho, my lord!
HAMLET: Hilo, ho, ho, boy! Come, bird, come.°
MARCELLUS: How is 't, my noble lord?
HORATIO: What news, my lord?　　　　　　　　　　　　　　　125
HAMLET: O, wonderful!
HORATIO: Good my lord, tell it.
HAMLET: No, you will reveal it.

98 couple add　　**Hold** hold together　　**99 instant** instantly　　**102 globe** (1) head (2)
world　　**103 table** tablet, slate　　**104 fond** foolish　　**105 saws** wise sayings　　**forms**
shapes or images copied onto the slate; general ideas　　**pressures** impressions stamped
112 tables writing tablets　　**meet it is** it is fitting　　**115 there you are** i.e., there, I've
written that down against you　　**120 secure him** keep him safe　　**123 Hilo...come**
(A falconer's call to a hawk in air. Hamlet mocks the hallooing as though it were a part
of hawking.)

HORATIO: Not I, my lord, by heaven.

MARCELLUS: Nor I, my lord.   130

HAMLET: How say you, then, would heart of man once° think it?

But you'll be secret?

HORATIO, MARCELLUS: Ay, by heaven, my lord.

HAMLET: There's never a villain dwelling in all Denmark

But he's an arrant° knave.   135

HORATIO: There needs no ghost, my lord, come from the grave

To tell us this.

HAMLET: Why, right, you are in the right.

And so, without more circumstance° at all,

I hold it fit that we shake hands and part,   140

You as your business and desire shall point you—

For every man hath business and desire,

Such as it is—and for my own poor part,

Look you, I'll go pray,

HORATIO: These are but wild and whirling words, my lord.   145

HAMLET: I am sorry they offend you, heartily;

Yes, faith, heartily.

HORATIO: There's no offense, my lord.

HAMLET: Yes, but Saint Patrick,° but there is, Horatio,

And much offense° too. Touching this vision here,   150

It is an honest ghost,° that let me tell you.

For your desire to know what is between us,

O'ermaster 't as you may. And now, good friends,

As you are friends, scholars, and soldiers,

Give me one poor request.   155

HORATIO: What is 't, my lord? We will.

HAMLET: Never make known what you have seen tonight.

HORATIO, MARCELLUS: My lord, we will not.

HAMLET: Nay, but swear 't.

HORATIO: In faith, my lord, not I.°   160

MARCELLUS: Nor I, my lord, in faith.

HAMLET: Upon my sword.°   [*He holds out his sword.*]

---

131 once ever   **135 arrant** thoroughgoing   **139 circumstance** ceremony, elaboration
149 Saint Patrick The keeper of Purgatory and patron saint of all blunders and confusion.   **150 offense** (Hamlet deliberately changes Horatio's "no offense taken" to "an offense against all decency.")   **151 an honest ghost** i.e., a real ghost and not an evil spirit
160 In faith...I i.e., I swear not to tell what I have seen (Horatio is not refusing to swear.)
162 sword i.e., the hilt in the form of a cross

MARCELLUS: We have sworn, my lord, already.°
HAMLET: Indeed, upon my sword, indeed.
GHOST [*cries under the stage*]:   Swear.   165
HAMLET: Ha, ha, boy, sayst thou so? Art thou there, truepenny?°
      Come on, you hear this fellow in the cellarage.
      Consent to swear.
HORATIO: Propose the oath, my lord.
HAMLET: Never to speak of this that you have seen,   170
      Swear by my sword.
GHOST [*beneath*]:   Swear.   [*They swear.*°]
HAMLET: *Hic et ubique?°* Then we'll shift our ground.

[*He moves to another spot.*]

      Come hither, gentlemen,
      And lay your hands again upon my sword.
      Swear by my sword   175
      Never to speak of this that you have heard.
GHOST [*beneath*]:   Swear by his sword.   [*They swear.*]
HAMLET: Well said, old mole. Canst work i' th' earth so fast?
      A worthy pioneer!°—Once more removed, good friends.   180

[*He moves again.*]

HORATIO: O day and night, but this is wondrous strange!
HAMLET: And therefore as a stranger° give it welcome.
      There are more things in heaven and earth, Horatio,
      Than are dreamt of in your philosophy.°
      But come;   185
      Here, as before, never, so help you mercy,°
      How strange or odd soe'er I bear myself—
      As I perchance hereafter shall think meet
      To put an antic° disposition on—
      That you, at such times seeing me, never shall,   190

163 We...already i.e., we swore in *faith*   **166 truepenny** honest old fellow   **173 *Hic et ubique*** here and everywhere (Latin.)   **172 s.d. They swear** (Seemingly they swear here, and at lines 170 and 190, as they lay their hands on Hamlet's sword. Triple oaths would have particular force; these three oaths deal with what they have seen, what they have heard, and what they promise about Hamlet's *antic disposition*.   **180 pioneer** foot soldier assigned to dig tunnels and excavations   **182 as a stranger** i.e., needing your hospitality   **184 your philosophy** this subject called "natural philosophy" or "science" that people talk about   **186 so help you mercy** as you hope for God's mercy when you are judged   **189 antic** fantastic

With arms encumbered° thus, or this headshake,
Or by pronouncing of some doubtful phrase
As "Well, we know," or "We could, an if° we would,"
Or "If we list° to speak," or "There be, an if they might,"
Or such ambiguous giving out,° to note   195
That you know aught° of me—this do swear,
So grace and mercy at your most need help you.

GHOST [*beneath*]:   Swear.   [*They swear.*]
HAMLET: Rest, rest, perturbèd spirit! So, gentlemen,
With all my love I do commend me to you;°   200
And what so poor a man as Hamlet is
May do t' express his love and friending° to you,
God willing, shall not lack.° Let us go in together,
And still° your fingers on your lips, I pray.
The time° is out of joint. O cursèd spite°   205
That ever I was born to set it right!

[*They wait for him to leave first.*]

Nay, come, let's go together.°

[*Exeunt.*]

[**Act 2.1** *Enter old* POLONIUS *with his man* (REYNALDO).]°

POLONIUS: Give him this money and these notes, Reynaldo.

[*He gives money and papers.*]

REYNALDO: I will, my lord.
POLONIUS: You shall do marvelous° wisely, good Reynaldo,
Before you visit him, to make inquire°
Of his behavior.   5
REYNALDO: My lord, I did intend it.
POLONIUS: Marry, well said, very well said. Look you, sir,
Inquire me first what Danskers° are in Paris,
And how, and who, what means,° and where they keep,°

---

191 encumbered folded   **193 an if** if   **194 list** wished   **There…might** i.e., there are
people here (we, in fact) who could tell news if we were at liberty to do so   **195 giving out** intimation   **note** draw attention to the fact   **196 aught** i.e., something secret
200 do…you entrust myself to you   **202 friending** friendliness   **203 lack** be lacking   **204 still** always   **205 The time** the state of affairs   **spite** i.e., the spite of Fortune
207 let's go together (Probably they wait for him to leave first, but he refuses this
ceremoniousness.)   **2.1 s.d. Location: Polonius' chambers 3 marvelous** marvelously
4 inquire inquiry   **8 Danskers** Danes   **9 what means** what wealth (they have)
keep dwell

What company, at what expense; and finding   10
By this encompassment° and drift° of question
That they do know my son, come you more nearer
Than your particular demands will touch it.°
Take you,° as 'twere, some distant knowledge of him,
As thus, "I know his father and his friends,   15
And in part him." Do you mark this, Reynaldo?

REYNALDO: Ay, very well, my lord.

POLONIUS: "And in part him, but," you may say, "not well.
But if 't be he I mean, he's very wild,
Addicted so and so," and there put on° him   20
What forgeries° you please—marry, none so rank°
As may dishonor him, take heed of that,
But, sir, such wanton,° wild, and usual slips
As are companions noted and most known
To youth and liberty.   25

REYNALDO: As gaming, my lord.

POLONIUS: Ay, or drinking, fencing, swearing,
Quarreling, drabbing°—you may go so far.

REYNALDO: My lord, that would dishonor him.

POLONIUS: Faith, no, as you may season° it in the charge.   30
You must not put another scandal on him
That he is open to incontinency;°
That's not my meaning. But breathe his faults so quaintly°
That they may seem the taints of liberty,°
The flash and outbreak of a fiery mind,   35
A savageness in unreclaimèd blood,
Of general assault.°

REYNALDO: But, my good lord—

POLONIUS: Wherefore should you do this?

REYNALDO: Ay, my lord, I would know that.   40

POLONIUS: Marry, sir, here's my drift,
And I believe it is a fetch of warrant.°
You laying these slight sullies on my son,

---

11 encompassment roundabout talking   **drift** gradual approach or course   **13 come...it**
you will find out more this way than by asking pointed questions (*particular demands*)
14 Take you assume, pretend   **20 put on** impute to   **21 forgeries** invented tales   **rank** gross
23 wanton sportive, unrestrained   **28 drabbing** whoring   **30 season** temper, soften   **32 incontinency** habitual sexual excess   **33 quaintly** artfully, subtly   **34 taints of liberty** faults resulting
from free living   **37 A savageness...assault** a wildness in untamed youth that assails all indiscriminately   **42 fetch of warrant** legitimate trick

As 'twere a thing a little soiled wi' the working,°
Mark you,
Your party in converse,° him you would sound,°   45
Having ever° seen in the prenominate crimes°
The youth you breathe° of guilty, be assured
He closes with you in this consequence:°
"Good sir," or so, or "friend," or "gentleman,"
According to the phrase or the addition°   50
Of man and country.

REYNALDO: Very good, my lord.

POLONIUS: And then, sir, does 'a this—'a does—what was I about to say?
By the Mass, I was about to say something. Where did I leave?   55

REYNALDO: At "closes in the consequence."

POLONIUS: At "closes in the consequence," ay, marry.
He closes thus: "I know the gentleman,
I saw him yesterday," or "th' other day,"
Or then, or then, with such or such, "and as you say,   60
There was 'a gaming," "there o'ertook in 's rouse,"°
"There falling out° at tennis," or perchance
"I saw him enter such a house of sale,"
Videlicet° a brothel, or so forth. See you now,
Your bait of falsehood takes this carp° of truth;   65
And thus do we of wisdom and of reach,°
With windlasses° and with assays of bias,°
By indirections find directions° out.
So by my former lecture and advice
Shall you my son. You have° me, have you not?   70

REYNALDO: My lord, I have.

POLONIUS: God b' wi'° ye; fare ye well.

REYNALDO: Good my lord.

POLONIUS: Observe his inclination in yourself.°

REYNALDO: I shall, my lord.   75

---

44 soiled wi' the working soiled by handling while it is being made, i.e., by involvement in the ways of the world   **46 converse** conversation   **sound** i.e., sound out   **47 Having ever** if he has ever   **prenominate crimes** before-mentioned offenses   **48 breathe** speak   **49 closes...consequence** takes you into his confidence in some fashion, as follows   **51 addition** title   **61 o'er-took in 's rouse** overcome by drink   **62 falling out** quarreling   **63 Videlicet** namely   **65 carp** a fish   **66 reach** capacity, ability   **67 windlasses** i.e., circuitous paths. (Literally, circuits made to head off the game in hunting.)   **assays of bias** attempts through indirection (like the curving path of the bowling ball, which is biased or weighted to one side)   **68 directions** i.e., the way things really are   **70 have** understand   **72 b' wi'** be with   **74 in yourself** in your own person (as well as by asking questions)

POLONIUS: And let him ply his music.

REYNALDO: Well, my lord.

POLONIUS: Farewell.

[*Exit* REYNALDO.]

[*Enter* OPHELIA.]

                      How now, Ophelia, what's the matter?

OPHELIA: O my lord, my lord, I have been so affrighted!   80

POLONIUS: With what, i' the name of God?

OPHELIA: My lord, as I was sewing in my closet,°

    Lord Hamlet, with his doublet° all unbraced,°

    No hat upon his head, his stockings fouled,

    Ungartered, and down-gyvèd° to his ankle,   85

    Pale as his shirt, his knees knocking each other,

    And with a look so piteous in purport°

    As if he had been loosèd out of hell

    To speak of horrors—he comes before me.

POLONIUS: Mad for thy love?   90

OPHELIA: My lord, I do not know,

    But truly I do fear it.

POLONIUS: What said he?

OPHELIA: He took me by the wrist and held me hard.

    Then goes he to the length of all his arm,   95

    And, with his other hand thus o'er his brow

    He falls to such perusal of my face

    As° 'a would draw it. Long stayed he so.

    At last, a little shaking of mine arm

    And thrice his head thus waving up and down,   100

    He raised a sigh so piteous and profound

    As it did seem to shatter all his bulk°

    And end his being. That done, he lets me go,

    And with his head over his shoulder turned

    He seemed to find his way without his eyes,   105

    For out o' doors he went without their helps,

    And to the last bended their light on me.

POLONIUS: Come, go with me. I will go seek the King.

    This is the very ecstasy° of love,

---

82 closet private chamber   **83 doublet** close-fitting jacket   **unbraced** unfastened   **85 down-gyvèd** fallen to the ankles (like gyves or fetters)   **87 in purport** in what it expressed   **98 As** as if (also in line 97)   **102 bulk** body   **109 ecstasy** madness

Whose violent property° fordoes° itself   110
And leads the will to desperate undertakings
As oft as any passion under heaven
That does afflict our natures. I am sorry.
What, have you given him any hard words of late?

OPHELIA: No, my good lord, but as you did command   115
I did repel his letters and denied
His access to me.

POLONIUS: That hath made him mad.
I am sorry that with better heed and judgment
I had not quoted° him. I feared he did but trifle   120
And meant to wrack° thee. But beshrew my jealousy!°
By heaven, it is as proper to our age°
To cast beyond° ourselves in our opinions
As it is common for the younger sort
To lack discretion. Come, go we to the King.   125
This must be known,° which, being kept close,° might move
More grief to hide than hate to utter love.°
Come.

[*Exeunt.*]

[**Act 2.2** *Flourish. Enter* KING *and* QUEEN, ROSENCRANTZ, *and* GUILDENSTERN
(with others).]°

KING: Welcome, dear Rosencrantz and Guildenstern.
Moreover that° we much did long to see you,
The need we have to use you did provoke
Our hasty sending. Something have you heard
Of Hamlet's transformation—so call it,   5
Sith nor° th' exterior nor the inward man
Resembles that° it was. What it should be,
More than his father's death, that thus hath put him
So much from th' understanding of himself,
I cannot dream of. I entreat you both   10
That, being of so young days° brought up with him,

---

110 property nature **fordoes** destroys **120 quoted** observed **121 wrack** ruin, seduce
beshrew my jealousy a plague upon my suspicious nature **122 proper...age** characteristic of us (old) men **123 cast beyond** overshoot, miscalculate (A metaphor from hunting.)
126 known made known (to the King) **close** secret **127 might...love** i.e., might cause
more grief (because of what Hamlet might do) by hiding the knowledge of Hamlet's strange
behavior to Ophelia than unpleasantness by telling it **2.2 s.d. Location: The castle 2
Moreover that** besides the fact that **6 Sith nor** since neither **7 that** what **11 of...days**
from such early youth

And sith so neighbored to° his youth and havior,°
That you vouchsafe your rest° here in our court
Some little time, so by your companies
To draw him on to pleasures, and to gather   15
So much as from occasion° you may glean,
Whether aught to us unknown afflicts him thus
That, opened,° lies within our remedy.

QUEEN: Good gentlemen, he hath much talked of you,
And sure I am two men there is not living   20
To whom he more adheres. If it will please you
To show us so much gentry° and good will
As to expend your time with us awhile
For the supply and profit of our hope,°
Your visitation shall receive such thanks   25
As fits a king's remembrance.°

ROSENCRANTZ: Both Your Majesties
Might, by the sovereign power you have of° us,
Put your dread° pleasures more into command
Than to entreaty.   30

GUILDENSTERN: But we both obey,
And here give up ourselves in the full bent°
To lay our service freely at your feet,
To be commanded.

KING: Thanks, Rosencrantz and gentle Guildenstern.   35

QUEEN: Thanks, Guildenstern and gentle Rosencrantz.
And I beseech you instantly to visit
My too much changèd son. Go, some of you,
And bring these gentlemen where Hamlet is.

GUILDENSTERN: Heavens make our presence and our practices°   40
Pleasant and helpful to him!

QUEEN: Ay, amen!

[*Exeunt* ROSENCRANTZ *and* GUILDENSTERN *(with some attendants).*]

[*Enter* POLONIUS.]

POLONIUS: Th' ambassadors from Norway, my good lord,
Are joyfully returned.

KING: Thou still° hast been the father of good news.   45

---

12 And sith so neighbored to and since you are (or, and since that time you are) intimately
acquainted with   **havior** demeanor   **13 vouchsafe your rest** please to stay   **16 occasion**
opportunity   **18 opened** being revealed   **22 gentry** courtesy   **24 supply...hope** aid and
furtherance of what we hope for   **26 As fits...remembrance** as would be a fitting gift of a
king who rewards true service   **27 of** over   **29 dread** inspiring awe   **32 in...bent** to the
utmost degree of our capacity (An archery metaphor.)   **40 practices** doings   **45 still** always

POLONIUS: Have I, my lord? I assure my good liege
    I hold° my duty, as° I hold my soul,
    Both to my God and to my gracious king;
    And I do think, or else this brain of mine
    Hunts not the trail of policy° so sure   50
    As it hath used to do, that I have found
    The very cause of Hamlet's lunacy.

KING: O, speak of that! That do I long to hear.

POLONIUS: Give first admittance to th' ambassadors.
    My news shall be the fruit° to that great feast.   55

KING: Thyself do grace° to them and bring them in.

[*Exit* POLONIUS.]

    He tells me, my dear Gertrude, he hath found
    The head and source of all your son's distemper.

QUEEN: I doubt° it is no other but the main,°
    His father's death and our o'erhasty marriage.   60

[*Enter Ambassadors* VOLTIMAND *and* CORNELIUS, *with* POLONIUS.]

KING: Well, we shall sift him.°—Welcome, my good friends!
    Say, Voltimand, what from our brother° Norway?

VOLTIMAND: Most fair return of greetings and desires.°
    Upon our first,° he sent out to suppress
    His nephew's levies, which to him appeared   65
    To be a preparation 'gainst the Polack,
    But, better looked into, he truly found
    It was against Your Highness. Whereat grieved
    That so his sickness, age, and impotence°
    Was falsely borne in hand,° sends out arrests°   70
    On Fortinbras, which he, in brief, obeys,
    Receives rebuke from Norway, and in fine°
    Makes vow before his uncle never more
    To give th' assay° of arms against Your Majesty.
    Whereon old Norway, overcome with joy,   75
    Gives him three thousand crowns in annual fee
    And his commission to employ those soldiers,

---

47 hold maintain **as** firmly as **50 policy** sagacity **55 fruit** dessert **56 grace** honor (punning on *grace* said before a *feast,* line 52) **59 doubt** fear, suspect **main** chief point, principal concern **61 sift him** question Polonius closely **62 brother** fellow king **63 desires** good wishes **64 Upon our first** at our first words on the business **69 impotence** helplessness **70 borne in hand** deluded, taken advantage of **arrests** orders to desist **72 in fine** in conclusion **74 give th' assay** make trial of strength, challenge

So levied as before, against the Polack,
With an entreaty, herein further shown, [*giving a paper*]
That it might please you to give quiet pass   80
Through your dominions for this enterprise
On such regards of safety and allowance°
As therein are set down.

KING: It likes° us well,
And at our more considered° time we'll read,   85
Answer, and think upon this business.
Meantime we thank you for your well-took labor.
Go to your rest; at night we'll feast together.
Most welcome home!

                                        [*Exeunt* AMBASSADORS.]

POLONIUS: This business is well ended.   90
My liege, and madam, to expostulate°
What majesty should be, what duty is,
Why day is day, night night, and time is time,
Were nothing but to waste night, day, and time.
Therefore, since brevity is the soul of wit,°   95
And tediousness the limbs and outward flourishes,
I will be brief. Your noble son is mad.
Mad call I it, for, to define true madness.
What is 't but to be nothing else but mad?
But let that go.   100

QUEEN: More matter, with less art.
POLONIUS: Madam. I swear I use no art at all.
That he's mad, 'tis true; 'tis true 'tis pity.
And pity 'tis 'tis true—a foolish figure,°
But farewell it, for I will use no art.   105
Mad let us grant him, then, and now remains
That we find out the cause of this effect,
Or rather say, the cause of this defect,
For this effect defective comes by cause.°
Thus it remains, and the remainder thus.   110
Perpend.°
I have a daughter—have while she is mine—
Who, in her duty and obedience, mark,

82 On...allowance i.e., with such considerations for the safety of Denmark and permission for Fortinbras **84 likes** pleases **85 considered** suitable for deliberation **91 expostulate** expound, inquire into **95 wit** sense or judgment **104 figure** figure of speech **110 For...cause** i.e., for this defective behavior, this madness, has a cause **111 Perpend** consider

Hath given me this. Now gather and surmise.°

[*He reads the letter.*] "To the celestial and my soul's idol, the most   115
beautified Ophelia"—

That's an ill phrase, a vile phrase; "beautified" is a vile phrase. But
you shall hear. Thus: [*He reads.*]

"In her excellent white bosom,° these,° etc."

QUEEN: Came this from Hamlet to her?   120

POLONIUS: Good madam, stay° awhile, I will be faithful.°   [*He reads.*]

"Doubt thou the stars are fire,
    Doubt that the sun doth move,
Doubt° truth to be a liar,
    But never doubt I love.   125

O dear Ophelia, I am ill at these numbers.° I have not art to
reckon° my groans. But that I love thee best, O most best, believe it.
Adieu.

Thine evermore, most dear lady, whilst this machine° is to him,

                                                Hamlet."   130

This in obedience hath my daughter shown me,
And, more above,° hath his solicitings,
As they fell out° by° time, by means, and place,
All given to mine ear.°

KING: But how hath she   135
Received his love?

POLONIUS: What do you think of me?

KING: As of a man faithful and honorable.

POLONIUS: I would fain° prove so. But what might you think,
When I had seen this hot love on the wing—   140
As I perceived it, I must tell you that,
Before my daughter told me—what might you,
Or my dear Majesty your queen here, think,
If I had played the desk or table book,°
Or given my heart a winking,° mute and dumb,   145
Or looked upon this love with idle sight?°
What might you think? No, I went round° to work,

114 gather and surmise draw your own conclusions   **119 In…bosom** (The letter is
poetically addressed to her heart.)   **these** i.e., the letter   **121 stay** wait   **faithful** i.e., in
reading the letter accurately   **124 Doubt** suspect   **126 ill…numbers** unskilled at writing verses   **127 reckon** (1) count (2) number metrically, scan   **129 machine** i.e., body
132 more above moreover   **133 fell out** occurred   **by** according to   **134 given…ear** i.e.,
told me about   **139 fain** gladly   **144 played…table book** i.e., remained shut up, concealing the information   **145 given…winking** closed the eyes of my heart to this   **146 with
idle sight** complacently or incomprehendingly   **147 round** roundly, plainly

And my young mistress thus I did bespeak:°
"Lord Hamlet is a prince out of thy star;°
This must not be." And then I prescripts° gave her,   150
That she should lock herself from his resort,°
Admit no messengers, receive no tokens.
Which done, she took the fruits of my advice;
And he, repellèd—a short tale to make—
Fell into a sadness, then into a fast,   155
Thence to a watch,° thence into a weakness,
Thence to a lightness,° and by this declension°
Into the madness wherein now he raves,
And all we° mourn for.

KING [*to the* QUEEN]:   Do you think 'tis this?   160
QUEEN: It may be, very like.
POLONIUS: Hath there been such a time—I would fain know that—
That I have positively said "'Tis so,"
When it proved otherwise?
KING: Not that I know.   165
POLONIUS: Take this from this,° if this be otherwise.
If circumstances lead me, I will find
Where truth is hid, though it were hid indeed
Within the center.°
KING: How may we try° it further?   170
POLONIUS: You know sometimes he walks four hours together
Here in the lobby.
QUEEN: So he does indeed.
POLONIUS: At such a time I'll loose° my daughter to him.
Be you and I behind an arras° then.   175
Mark the encounter. If he love her not
And be not from his reason fall'n thereon,°
Let me be no assistant for a state,
But keep a farm and carters.°
KING: We will try it.   180

[*Enter* HAMLET *(reading on a book)*.]

---

148 bespeak address   **149 out of thy star** above your sphere, position   **150 prescripts**
orders   **151 his resort** his visits   **156 watch** state of sleeplessness   **157 lightness** light-
headedness   **declension** decline, deterioration (with a pun on the grammatical sense)
159 all we all of us, or, into everything that we   **166 Take this from this** (The actor probably gestures, indicating that he means his head from his shoulders, or his staff of office
or chain from his hands or neck, or something similar.)   **169 center** middle point of the
earth (which is also the center of the Ptolemaic universe)   **170 try** test, judge   **174 loose**
(as one might release an animal that is being mated)   **175 arras** hanging, tapestry   **177
thereon** on that account   **179 carters** wagon drivers

QUEEN: But look where sadly° the poor wretch comes reading.

POLONIUS: Away, I do beseech you both, away.

I'll board° him presently.° O, give me leave.°

[*Exeunt* KING *and* QUEEN *(with attendants)*.]

How does my good Lord Hamlet?

HAMLET: Well, God-a-mercy.°   185

POLONIUS: Do you know me, my lord?

HAMLET: Excellent well. You are a fishmonger.°

POLONIUS: Not I, my lord.

HAMLET: Then I would you were so honest a man.

POLONIUS: Honest, my lord?   190

HAMLET: Ay, sir. To be honest, as this world goes, is to be one man picked
out of ten thousand.

POLONIUS: That's very true, my lord.

HAMLET: For if the sun breed maggots in a dead dog, being a good kissing
carrion°—Have you a daughter?   195

POLONIUS: I have, my lord.

HAMLET: Let her not walk i' the sun.° Conception° is a blessing, but as your
daughter may conceive, friend, look to 't.

POLONIUS [*aside*]:   How say you by that? Still harping on my daughter. Yet he
knew me not at first; 'a° said I was a fishmonger. 'A is far gone. And   200
truly in my youth I suffered much extremity for love, very near this. I'll
speak to him again.—What do you read, my lord?

HAMLET: Words, words, words.

POLONIUS: What is the matter,° my lord?

HAMLET: Between who?   205

POLONIUS: I mean, the matter that you read, my lord.

HAMLET: Slanders, sir; for the satirical rogue says here that old men have gray
beards, that their faces are wrinkled, their eyes purging° thick amber° and
plum-tree gum, and that they have a plentiful lack of wit,° together with
most weak hams. All which, sir, though I most powerfully and potently   210
believe, yet I hold it not honesty° to have it thus set down, for yourself,
sir, shall grow old° as I am, if like a crab you could go backward.

---

181 sadly seriously   **183 board** accost   **presently** at once   **give me leave** i.e., excuse
me, leave me alone (Said to those he hurries offstage, including the King and Queen.)
185 God-a-mercy God have mercy, i.e., thank you   **187 fishmonger** fish merchant
195 a good kissing carrion i.e., a good piece of flesh for kissing, or for the sun to
kiss   **197 i' the sun** in public (with additional implication of the sunshine of princely
favors)   **Conception** (1) understanding (2) pregnancy   **200 'a** he   **204 matter** substance
(But Hamlet plays on the sense of "basis for a dispute.")   **208 purging** discharging
amber i.e., resin, like the resinous   **209 wit** understanding   **211 honesty** decency,
decorum   **212 old** as old

POLONIUS [*aside*]:   Though this be madness, yet there is method in 't.—Will
    you walk out of the air,° my lord?

HAMLET: Into my grave.   215

POLONIUS: Indeed, that's out of the air. [*Aside.*] How pregnant° sometimes his
    replies are! A happiness° that often madness hits on, which reason and
    sanity could not so prosperously° be delivered of. I will leave him and sud-
    denly° contrive the means of meeting between him and my daughter.—My
    honorable lord, I will most humbly take my leave of you.   220

HAMLET: You cannot, sir, take from me anything that I will more willingly
    part withal°—except my life, except my life, except my life.

[*Enter* GUILDENSTERN *and* ROSENCRANTZ.]

POLONIUS: Fare you well, my lord.

HAMLET: These tedious old fools!°

POLONIUS: You go to seek the Lord Hamlet. There he is.   225

ROSENCRANTZ [*to* POLONIUS]:   God save you, sir!

[*Exit* POLONIUS.]

GUILDENSTERN: My honored lord!

ROSENCRANTZ: My most dear lord!

HAMLET: My excellent good friends! How dost thou, Guildenstern? Ah,
    Rosencrantz! Good lads, how do you both?   230

ROSENCRANTZ: As the indifferent° children of the earth.

GUILDENSTERN: Happy in that we are not overhappy.
    On Fortune's cap we are not the very button.

HAMLET: Nor the soles of her shoe?

ROSENCRANTZ: Neither, my lord.   235

HAMLET: Then you live about her waist, or in the middle of her favors?°

GUILDENSTERN: Faith, her privates we.°

HAMLET: In the secret parts of Fortune? O, most true, she is a strumpet.°
    What news?

ROSENCRANTZ: None, my lord, but the world's grown honest.   240

HAMLET: Then is doomsday near. But your news is not true. Let me question
    more in particular. What have you, my good friends, deserved at the
    hands of Fortune that she sends you to prison hither?

---

214 out of the air (The open air was considered dangerous for sick people.)   **216 pregnant**
quick-witted, full of meaning   **217 happiness** felicity of expression   **218 prosperously** successfully   **219 suddenly** immediately   **222 withal** with   **224 old fools** i.e., old men like
Polonius   **231 indifferent** ordinary, at neither extreme of fortune or misfortune   **236 favors**
i.e., sexual favors   **237 her privates we** i.e., (1) we are sexually intimate with Fortune,
the fickle goddess who bestows her favors indiscriminately (2) we are her private citizens
238 strumpet prostitute (A common epithet for indiscriminate Fortune; see line 452.)

GUILDENSTERN: Prison, my lord?

HAMLET: Denmark's a prison.   245

ROSENCRANTZ: Then is the world one.

HAMLET: A goodly one, in which there are many confines,° wards,° and
dungeons, Denmark being one o' the worst.

ROSENCRANTZ: We think not so, my lord.

HAMLET: Why then 'tis none to you, for there is nothing either good or bad   250
but thinking makes it so. To me it is a prison.

ROSENCRANTZ: Why then, your ambition makes it one. 'Tis too narrow for
your mind.

HAMLET: O God, I could be bounded in a nutshell and count myself a king   255
of infinite space, were it not that I have bad dreams.

GUILDENSTERN: Which dreams indeed are ambition, for the very substance of
the ambitious° is merely the shadow of a dream.

HAMLET: A dream itself is but a shadow.

ROSENCRANTZ: Truly, and I hold ambition of so airy and light a quality that it
is but a shadow's shadow.   260

HAMLET: Then are our beggars bodies,° and our monarchs and outstretched°
heroes the beggars' shadows. Shall we to the court? For, by my fay,° I
cannot reason.

ROSENCRANTZ, GUILDENSTERN: We'll wait upon° you.

HAMLET: No such matter. I will not sort° you with the rest of my ser-   265
vants, for, to speak to you like an honest man, I am most dreadfully
attended.° But, in the beaten way° of friendship, what make° you at
Elsinore?

ROSENCRANTZ: To visit you, my lord, no other occasion.

HAMLET: Beggar that I am, I am even poor in thanks; but I thank you, and   270
sure, dear friends, my thanks are too dear a halfpenny.° Were you not
sent for? Is it your own inclining? Is it a free° visitation? Come, come,
deal justly with me. Come, come. Nay, speak.

GUILDENSTERN: What should we say; my lord?

---

247 confines places of confinement **wards** cells **256–257 the very...ambitious** that
seemingly very substantial thing that the ambitious pursue **261 bodies** i.e., solid substanc-
es rather than shadows (since beggars are not ambitious) **outstretched** (1) far-reaching in
their ambition (2) elongated as shadows **262 fay** faith **264 wait upon** accompany, attend
(But Hamlet uses the phrase in the sense of providing menial service.) **265 sort** class,
categorize **266–267 dreadfully attended** waited upon in slovenly fashion **268 beaten
way** familiar path, tried-and-true course **make** do **271 too dear a halfpenny** (1) too
expensive at even a halfpenny, i.e., of little worth (2) too expensive *by* a halfpenny in return
for worthless kindness **272 free** voluntary

HAMLET: Anything but to the purpose.° You were sent for, and there is a   275
    kind of confession in your looks which your modesties° have not craft
    enough to color.° I know the good King and Queen have sent for you.

ROSENCRANTZ: To what end, my lord?

HAMLET: That you must teach me. But let me conjure° you, by the rights of
    our fellowship, by the consonancy of our youth,° by the obligation of   280
    our ever-preserved love, and by what more dear a better° proposer
    could charge° you withal, be even° and direct with me whether you
    were sent for or no.

ROSENCRANTZ [*aside to* GUILDENSTERN]:   What say you?

HAMLET [*aside*]:   Nay, then, I have an eye of° you.—If you love me, hold not off.°   285

GUILDENSTERN: My lord, we were sent for.

HAMLET: I will tell you why; so shall my anticipation prevent your discovery,°
    and your secrecy to the King and Queen molt no feather,° I have of late—
    but wherefore I know not—lost all my mirth, forgone all custom of exer-
    cises; and indeed it goes so heavily with my disposition that this goodly   290
    frame, the earth, seems to me a sterile promontory; this most excellent can-
    opy, the air, look you, this brave° o'erhanging firmament, this majestical
    roof fretted° with golden fire, why, it appeareth nothing to me but a foul
    and pestilent congregation° of vapors. What a piece of work° is a man!
    How noble in reason, how infinite in faculties, in form and moving how   295
    express° and admirable, in action how like an angel, in apprehension°
    how like a god! The beauty of the world, the paragon of animals! And yet,
    to me, what is this quintessence° of dust? Man delights not me—no, nor
    woman neither, though by your smiling you seem to say so.

ROSENCRANTZ: My lord, there was no such stuff in my thoughts.   300

HAMLET: Why did you laugh, then, when I said man delights not me?

ROSENCRANTZ: To think, my lord, if you delight not in man, what Lenten
    entertainment° the players shall receive from you. We coted° them
    on the way, and hither are they coming to offer you service.

275 Anything but to the purpose anything except a straightforward answer (said ironically.)   **276 modesties** sense of shame   **277 color** disguise   **279 conjure** adjure, entreat   **280 the consonancy of our youth** our closeness in our younger days   **281 better**
more skillful   **282 charge** urge   **even** straight, honest   **285 of** on   **hold not off** don't
hold back   **287 so...discovery** in that way my saying it first will spare you from revealing
the truth   **288 molt no feather** i.e., not diminish in the least   **292 brave** splendid   **293
fretted** adorned (with fretwork, as in a vaulted ceiling)   **294 congregation** mass   **piece
of work** masterpiece   **296 express** well-framed, exact, expressive   **296–297 apprehension** power of comprehending   **298 quintessence** the fifth essence of ancient philosophy, beyond earth, water, air, and fire, supposed to be the substance of the heavenly
bodies and to be latent in all things   **302–303 Lenten entertainment** meager reception
(appropriate to Lent)   **coted** overtook and passed by

HAMLET: He that plays the king shall be welcome; His Majesty shall have   305
tribute° of° me. The adventurous knight shall use his foil and target,°
the lover shall not sigh gratis,° the humorous man° shall end his part in
peace,° the clown shall make those laugh whose lungs are tickle o' the
sear,° and the lady shall say her mind freely, or the blank verse shall
halt° for 't. What players are they?   310

ROSENCRANTZ: Even those you were wont to take such delight in, the trage-
dians° of the city.

HAMLET: How chances it they travel? Their residence,° both in reputation
and profit, was better both ways.

ROSENCRANTZ: I think their inhibition° comes by the means of the late°   315
innovation.°

HAMLET: Do they hold the same estimation they did when I was in the city?
Are they so followed?

ROSENCRANTZ: No, indeed are they not.

HAMLET: How comes it? Do they grow rusty?   320

ROSENCRANTZ: Nay, their endeavor keeps° in the wonted° pace. But there is, sir,
an aerie° of children, little eyases,° that cry out on the top of question°
and are most tyrannically° clapped for 't. These are now the fashion, and
so berattle° the common stages°—so they call them—that many wearing
rapiers° are afraid of goose quills° and dare scarce come thither.   325

HAMLET: What, are they children? Who maintains 'em? How are they escoted?°
Will they pursue the quality° no longer than they can sing?° Will they not
say afterwards, if they should grow themselves to common° players—
as it is most like,° if their means are no better°—their writers do them
wrong to make them exclaim against their own succession?°   330

305–306 **tribute** (1) applause (2) homage paid in money **of** from **foil and target** sword and shield **307 gratis** for nothing **humorous man** eccentric character, dominated by one trait or "humor" **in peace** i.e., with full license **308 tickle
o' the sear** easy on the trigger, ready to laugh easily (A sear is part of a gunlock.)
309 halt limp **311–312 tragedians** actors **313 residence** remaining in their usual
place, i.e., in the city **315 inhibition** formal prohibition (from acting plays in the city)
late recent **316 innovation** i.e., the new fashion in satirical plays performed by
boy actors in the "private" theaters; or possibly a political uprising; or the strict limitations set on the theaters in London in 1600 **321 keeps** continues **wonted** usual
322 aerie nest **eyases** young hawks **cry...question** speak shrilly, dominating the controversy (in decrying the public theaters) **323 tyrannically** outrageously **324 berattle**
berate, clamor against **common stages** public theaters **325 many wearing rapiers**
i.e., many men of fashion, afraid to patronize the common players for fear of being
satirized by the poets writing for the boy actors **goose quills** i.e., pens of satirists **326
escoted** maintained **327 quality** (acting) profession **no longer...sing** i.e., only until
their voices change **328 common** regular, adult **if...better** if they find no better way
to support themselves **329 like** likely **330 succession** i.e., future careers

ROSENCRANTZ: Faith, there has been much to-do° on both sides, and the
nation holds it no sin to tar° them to controversy. There was for a while
no money bid for argument unless the poet and the player went to cuffs
in the question.°

HAMLET: Is 't possible?   335

GUILDENSTERN: O, there has been much throwing about of brains.

HAMLET: Do the boys carry it away?°

ROSENCRANTZ: Ay, that they do, my lord—Hercules and his load too.°

HAMLET: It is not very strange; for my uncle is King of Denmark, and those
that would make mouths° at him while my father lived give twenty, forty,   340
fifty, a hundred ducats° apiece for his picture in little.° 'Sblood,° there
is something in this more than natural, if philosophy° could find it out.

[*A flourish (of trumpets within).*]

GUILDENSTERN: There are the players.

HAMLET: Gentlemen, you are welcome to Elsinore. Your hands, come then. Th'
appurtenance° of welcome is fashion and ceremony. Let me comply° with   345
you in this garb,° lest my extent° to the players, which, I tell you, must
show fairly outwards,° should more appear like entertainment° than yours.
You are welcome. But my uncle-father and aunt-mother are deceived.

GUILDENSTERN: In what, my dear lord?

HAMLET: I am but mad north-north-west.° When the wind is southerly I   350
know a hawk from a handsaw.°

[*Enter* POLONIUS.]

POLONIUS: Well be with you, gentlemen!

HAMLET: Hark you, Guildenstern, and you too; at each ear a hearer. That
great baby you see there is not yet out of his swaddling clouts.°

---

331 to-do ado   **332 tar** set on (as dogs)   **333–334 There...question** i.e., for a while,
no money was offered by the acting companies to playwrights for the plot to a play
unless the satirical poets who wrote for the boys and the adult actors came to blows in
the play itself   **337 carry it away** i.e., win the day   **338 Hercules...load** (Thought
to be an allusion to the sign of the Globe Theatre, which was Hercules bearing the
world on his shoulders.)   **326–338 How...load too** (The passage, omitted from the
early quartos, alludes to the so-called War of the Theaters, 1599–1602, the rivalry between the children's companies and the adult actors.)   **340 mouths** faces   **341 ducats**
gold coins   **in little** in miniature   **'Sblood** by God's (Christ's) blood   **342 philosophy**
i.e., scientific inquiry   **345 appurtenance** proper accompaniment   **comply** observe the
formalities of courtesy   **346 garb** i.e., manner   **my extent** that which I extend, i.e.,
my polite behavior   **347 show fairly outwards** show every evidence of cordiality
entertainment a (warm) reception   **350 north-north-west** just off true north, only partly
351 hawk...handsaw i.e., two very different things, though also perhaps meaning a
mattock (or *back*) and a carpenter's cutting tool, respectively; also birds, with a play on
bernsbaw, or heron   **354 swaddling clouts** cloths in which to wrap a newborn baby

ROSENCRANTZ: Haply° he is the second time come to them, for they say an   355
old man is twice a child.

HAMLET: I will prophesy he comes to tell me of the players. Mark it.—You
say right, sir, o' Monday morning, 'twas then indeed.

POLONIUS: My lord, I have news to tell you.

HAMLET: My lord, I have news to tell you. When Roscius° was an actor in Rome—   360

POLONIUS: The actors are come hither, my lord.

HAMLET: Buzz,° buzz!

POLONIUS: Upon my honor—

HAMLET: Then came each actor on his ass.

POLONIUS: The best actors in the world, either for tragedy, comedy, history,   365
pastoral, pastoral-comical, historical-pastoral, tragical-historical, tragical-
comical-historical-pastoral, scene individable,° or poem unlimited.°
Seneca° cannot be too heavy, nor Plautus° too light. For the law of writ
and the liberty,° these° are the only men.

HAMLET: O Jephthah, judge of Israel,° what a treasure hadst thou!   370

POLONIUS: What a treasure had he, my lord?

HAMLET: Why,

"One fair daughter, and no more,
The which he loved passing° well."

POLONIUS [*aside*]:   Still on my daughter.   375

HAMLET: Am I not i' the right, old Jephthah?

POLONIUS: If you call me Jephthah, my lord, I have a daughter that I love
passing well.

HAMLET: Nay, that follows not.

POLONIUS: What follows then, my lord?   380

HAMLET: Why,

"As by lot,° God wot,"°

and then, you know,

"It came to pass, as most like° it was"—

the first row° of the pious chanson° will show you more, for look   385
where my abridgement° comes.

355 Haply perhaps **360 Roscius** a famous Roman actor who died in 62 BCE
362 Buzz (An interjection used to denote stale news.)   **367 scene individable** a play
observing the unity of place; or perhaps one that is unclassifiable, or performed without intermission   **poem unlimited** a play disregarding the unities of time and place;
one that is all-inclusive   **368 Seneca** writer of Latin tragedies   **Plautus** writer of Latin
comedy   **368–369 law...liberty** dramatic composition both according to the rules and
disregarding the rules   **these** i.e., the actors   **370 Jephthah...Israel** (Jephthah had to
sacrifice his daughter; see Judges 11. Hamlet goes on to quote from a ballad on the
theme.)   **374 passing** surpassingly   **382 lot** chance   **wot** knows   **384 like** likely, probable   **385 row** stanza   **chanson** ballad, song   **386 my abridgment** something that cuts
short my conversation; also, a diversion

[*Enter the* PLAYERS.]

You are welcome, masters; welcome, all. I am glad to see thee well. Welcome, good friends. O, old friend! Why, thy face is valanced° since I saw thee last. Com'st thou to beard° me in Denmark? What, my young lady° and mistress! By 'r Lady,° your ladyship is nearer to heaven than when   390
I saw you last, by the altitude of a chopine.° Pray God your voice, like a piece of uncurrent° gold, be not cracked within the ring.° Masters, you are all welcome. We'll e'en to 't° like French falconers, fly at anything we see. We'll have a speech straight.° Come, give us a taste of your quality.° Come, a passionate speech.   395

FIRST PLAYER: What speech, my good lord?
HAMLET: I heard thee speak me a speech once, but it was never acted, or if it was, not above once, for the play, I remember, pleased not the million; 'twas caviar to the general.° But it was—as I received it, and others, whose judgments in such matters cried in the top of° mine—an excellent play,   400
well digested° in the scenes, set down with as much modesty° as cunning.° I remember one said there were no sallets° in the lines to make the matter savory, nor no matter in the phrase that might indict° the author of affectation, but called it an honest method, as wholesome as sweet, and by very much more handsome° than fine.° One speech in 't I chiefly loved: 'twas   405
Aeneas' tale to Dido, and thereabout of it especially when he speaks of Priam's slaughter.° If it live in your memory, begin at this line: let me see, let me see—
    "The rugged Pyrrhus,° like th' Hyrcanian beast"°—
'Tis not so. It begins with Pyrrhus: 410
    "The rugged° Pyrrhus, he whose sable° arms,

---

388 valanced fringed (with a beard)   **389 beard** confront, challenge (with obvious pun)
young lady i.e., boy playing women's parts   **390 By 'r Lady** by Our Lady
391 chopine thick-soled shoe of Italian fashion   **392 uncurrent** not passable as lawful
coinage   **cracked...ring** i.e., changed from adolescent to male voice, no longer suitable
for women's roles (Coins featured rings enclosing the sovereign's head; if the coin was
cracked within this ring, it was unfit for currency.)   **393 e'en to 't** go at it   **394 straight** at
once   **quality** professional skill   **399 caviar to the general** caviar to the multitude, i.e., a
choice dish too elegant for coarse tastes   **400 cried in the top of** i.e., spoke with greater
authority than   **401 digested** arranged, ordered   **modesty** moderation, restraint   **cunning** skill   **402 sallets** i.e., something savory, spicy improprieties   **403 indict** convict
405 handsome well-proportioned   **fine** elaborately ornamented, showy   **407 Priam's slaughter** the slaying of the ruler of Troy, when the Greeks finally took the city
409 Pyrrhus a Greek hero in the Trojan War, also known as Neoptolemus, son of Achilles—another avenging son   **Hyrcanian beast** i.e., tiger (On the death of Priam, see Virgil,
Aeneid, 2.506 ff.; compare the whole speech with Marlowe's *Dido Queen of Carthage,*
2.1.214. ff. On the Hyrcanian tiger, see *Aeneid,* 4.366–367. Hyrcania is on the Caspian
Sea.)   **411 rugged** shaggy, savage   **sable** black (for reasons of camouflage during the
episode of the Trojan horse)

Black as his purpose, did the night resemble
When he lay couchèd° in the ominous horse,°
Hath now this dread and black complexion smeared
With heraldry more dismal.° Head to foot   415
Now is he total gules,° horridly tricked°
With blood of fathers, mothers, daughters, sons,
Baked and impasted° with the parching streets,°
That lend a tyrannous° and a damnèd light
To their lord's° murder. Roasted in wrath and fire,   420
And thus o'ersizèd° with coagulate gore,
With eyes like carbuncles,° the hellish Pyrrhus
Old grandsire Priam seeks."
    So proceed you.

POLONIUS: 'Fore God, my lord, well spoken, with good accent and good   425
discretion.

FIRST PLAYER: "Anon he finds him
Striking too short at Greeks. His antique° sword,
Rebellious to his arm, lies where it falls,
Repugnant° to command. Unequal matched,   430
Pyrrhus at Priam drives, in rage strikes wide,
But with the whiff and wind of his fell° sword
Th' unnervèd° father falls. Then senseless Ilium,°
Seeming to feel this blow, with flaming top
Stoops to his° base, and with a hideous crash   435
Takes prisoner Pyrrhus' ear. For, lo! His sword,
Which was declining° on the milky° head
Of reverend Priam, seemed i' th' air to stick.
So as a painted° tyrant Pyrrhus stood,
And, like a neutral to his will and matter,°   440
Did nothing.
But as we often see against° some storm
A silence in the heavens, the rack° stand still,

412 **couchèd** concealed **ominous horse** fateful Trojan horse, by which the Greeks gained access to Troy   415 **dismal** ill-omened   416 **total gules** entirely red (A heraldic term.) **tricked** spotted and smeared (Heraldic.)   418 **impasted** crusted, like a thick paste **with...streets** by the parching heat of the streets (because of the fires everywhere)   419 **tyrannous** cruel   420 **their lord's** i.e., Priam's   421 **o'ersizèd** covered as with size or glue   422 **carbuncles** large fiery-red precious stones thought to emit their own light   428 **antique** ancient, long-used   430 **Repugnant** disobedient, resistant   432 **fell** cruel   433 **unnervèd** strengthless **senseless Ilium** inanimate citadel of Troy   435 **his** its   437 **declining** descending **milky** white-haired   439 **painted** i.e., painted in a picture   440 **like...matter** i.e., as though suspended between his intention and its fulfillment   442 **against** just before   443 **rack** mass of clouds

The bold winds speechless, and the orb° below
As hush as death, anon the dreadful thunder   445
Doth rend the region,° so, after Pyrrhus' pause,
A rousèd vengeance sets him new a-work
And never did the Cyclops'° hammers fall
On Mars's armor forged for proof eterne°
With less remorse° than Pyrrhus' bleeding sword   450
Now falls on Priam.
Out, out, thou strumpet Fortune! All you gods
In general synod° take away her power!
Break all the spokes and fellies° from her wheel,
And bowl the round nave° down the hill of heaven°   455
As low as to the fiends!"

POLONIUS: This is too long.

HAMLET: It shall to the barber's with your beard.—Prithee, say on. He's
for a jig° or a tale of bawdry, or he sleeps. Say on; come to
Hecuba.°   460

FIRST PLAYER: "But who, ah woe! had° seen the moblèd° queen"—

HAMLET: "The moblèd queen"?

POLONIUS: That's good. "Moblèd queen" is good.

FIRST PLAYER: "Run barefoot up and down, threat'ning the flames°
With bisson rheum,° a clout° upon that head   465
Where late° the diadem stood, and, for a robe,
About her lank and all o'erteemèd° loins
A blanket, in the alarm of fear caught up—
Who this had seen, with tongue in venom steeped,
'Gainst Fortune's state° would treason have pronounced.°   470
But if the gods themselves did see her then
When she saw Pyrrhus make malicious sport
In mincing with his sword her husband's limbs,
The instant burst of clamor that she made,
Unless things mortal move them not at all,   475
Would have made milch° the burning eyes of heaven,°
And passion° in the gods."

---

444 orb globe, earth   **446 region** sky   **448 Cyclops** giant armor makers in the smithy of Vulcan   **449 proof eterne** eternal resistance to assault   **450 remorse** pity   **453 synod** assembly   **454 fellies** pieces of wood forming the rim of a wheel   **455 nave** hub   **hill of heaven** Mount Olympus   **459 jig** comic song and dance often given at the end of a play   **460 Hecuba** wife of Priam   **461 who...had** anyone who had (also in line 456)   **moblèd** muffled   **464 threat'ning the flames** i.e., weeping hard enough to dampen the flames   **465 bisson rheum** blinding tears   **clout** cloth   **466 late** lately   **467 all o'erteemèd** utterly worn out with bearing children   **470 state** rule, managing   **pronounced** proclaimed   **476 milch** milky, moist with tears   **burning eyes of heaven** i.e., heavenly bodies   **477 passion** overpowering emotion

POLONIUS: Look whe'er° he has not turned his color and has tears in 's eyes.
Prithee, no more.

HAMLET: 'Tis well; I'll have thee speak out the rest of this soon.—Good my   480
lord, will you see the players well bestowed?° Do you hear, let them
be well used, for they are the abstract° and brief chronicles of the time.
After your death you were better have a bad epitaph than their ill report
while you live.

POLONIUS: My lord, I will use them according to their desert.   485

HAMLET: God's bodikin,° man, much better. Use every man after his desert, and
who shall scape whipping? Use them after° your own honor and dignity.
The less they deserve, the more merit is in your bounty. Take them in.

POLONIUS: Come, sirs.

[*Exit.*]

HAMLET: Follow him, friends. We'll hear a play tomorrow. [*As they start to*   490
leave, HAMLET *detains the* FIRST PLAYER.] Dost thou hear me, old friend?
Can you play *The Murder of Gonzago?*

FIRST PLAYER: Ay, my lord.

HAMLET: We'll ha 't° tomorrow night. You could, for a need, study° a speech
of some dozen or sixteen lines which I would set down and insert in 't,   495
could you not?

FIRST PLAYER: Ay, my lord.

HAMLET: Very well. Follow that lord, and look you mock him not.

[*Exeunt* PLAYERS.] My good friends, I'll leave you till night. You are
welcome to Elsinore.
                                                                             500

ROSENCRANTZ: Good my lord!

[*Exeunt* ROSENCRANTZ *and* GUILDENSTERN.]

HAMLET: Ay, so, goodbye to you.—Now I am alone.
O, what a rogue and peasant slave am I!
Is it not monstrous that this player here,
But° in a fiction, in a dream of passion,   505
Could force his soul so to his own conceit°
That from her working° all his visage wanned,°
Tears in his eyes, distraction in his aspect,°
A broken voice, and his whole function suiting

---

478 whe'er whether   **481 bestowed** lodged   **482 abstract** summary account   **486 God's
bodikin** by God's (Christ's) little body, *bodykin* (Not to be confused with *bodkin*, "dagger.")
487 after according to   **494 ha 't** have it   **study** memorize   **505 But** merely   **506 force…
conceit** bring his innermost being so entirely into accord with his conception (of the
role)   **507 from her working** as a result of, or in response to, his soul's activity   **wanned**
grew pale   **508 aspect** look, glance

With forms to his conceit?° And all for nothing!   510
For Hecuba!
What's Hecuba to him, or he to Hecuba,
That he should weep for her? What would he do
Had he the motive and the cue for passion
That I have? He would drown the stage with tears   515
And cleave the general ear° with horrid° speech,
Make mad the guilty and appall° the free,°
Confound the ignorant,° and amaze° indeed
The very faculties of eyes and ears. Yet I,
A dull and muddy-mettled° rascal, peak°   520
Like John-a-dreams,° unpregnant of° my cause,
And can say nothing—no, not for a king
Upon whose property° and most dear life
A damned defeat° was made. Am I a coward?
Who calls me villain? Breaks my pate° across?   525
Plucks off my beard and blows it in my face?
Tweaks me by the nose? Gives me the lie i' the throat°
As deep as to the lungs? Who does me this?
Ha, 'swounds,° I should take it; for it cannot be
But I am pigeon-livered° and lack gall   530
To make oppression bitter,° or ere this
I should ha' fatted all the region kites°
With this slave's offal.° Bloody, bawdy villain!
Remorseless,° treacherous, lecherous, kindless° villain!
O, vengeance!   535
Why, what an ass am I! This is most brave,°
That I, the son of a dear father murdered,
Prompted to my revenge by heaven and hell,
Must like a whore unpack my heart with words
And fall a-cursing, like a very drab,°   540

---

510 his whole...conceit all his bodily powers responding with actions to suit his thought   **516 the general ear** everyone's ear   **horrid** horrible   **517 appall** (literally, make pale)   **free** innocent   **518 Confound the ignorant** i.e., dumbfound those who know nothing of the crime that has been committed   **amaze** stun   **520 muddy-mettled** dull-spirited   **peak** mope, pine   **521 John-a-dreams** a sleepy, dreaming idler   **unpregnant of** not quickened by   **523 property** i.e., the crown; also character, quality   **524 damned defeat** damnable act of destruction   **525 pate** head   **527 Gives...throat** calls me an out-and-out liar **529 'swounds** by his (Christ's) wounds   **530 pigeon-livered** (The pigeon or dove was popularly supposed to be mild because it secreted no gall.)   **531 bitter** i.e., bitter to me **532 region kites** kites (birds of prey) of the air   **533 offal** entrails   **534 Remorseless** pitiless   **kindless** unnatural   **536 brave** fine, admirable (said ironically.)   **540 drab** whore

A scullion!° Fie upon 't, foh! About,° my brains!

Hum, I have heard

That guilty creatures sitting at a play

Have by the very cunning° of the scene°

Been struck so to the soul that presently°   545

They have proclaimed their malefactions;

For murder, though it have no tongue, will speak

With most miraculous organ. I'll have these players

Play something like the murder of my father

Before mine uncle. I'll observe his looks;   550

I'll tent° him to the quick.° If 'a do blench,°

I know my course. The spirit that I have seen

May be the devil, and the devil hath power

T' assume a pleasing shape; yea, and perhaps,

Out of my weakness and my melancholy,   555

As he is very potent with such spirits,°

Abuses° me to damn me. I'll have grounds

More relative° than this. The play's the thing

Wherein I'll catch the conscience of the King.

[*Exit.*]

[**Act 3.1** *Enter* KING, QUEEN, POLONIUS, OPHELIA, ROSENCRANTZ, GUILDERNSTERN, *lords.*]°

KING: And can you by no drift of conference°

Get from him why he puts on this confusion,

Grating so harshly all his days of quiet

With turbulent and dangerous lunacy?

ROSENCRANTZ: He does confess he feels himself distracted,   5

But from what cause 'a will by no means speak.

GUILDENSTERN   Nor do we find him forward° to be sounded,°

But with a crafty madness keeps aloof

When we would bring him on to some confession

Of his true state.   10

QUEEN: Did he receive you well?

ROSENCRANTZ: Most like a gentleman.

GUILDENSTERN: But with much forcing of his disposition.°

---

541 scullion menial kitchen servant (apt to be foul-mouthed) **About** about it, to work **544 cunning** art, skill **scene** dramatic presentation **545 presently** at once **551 tent** probe **the quick** the tender part of a wound, the core **blench** quail, flinch **556 spirits** humors (of melancholy) **557 Abuses** deludes **558 relative** cogent, pertinent **3.1 s.d. Location: The castle 1 drift of conference** directing of conversation **7 forward** willing **sounded** questioned **13 disposition** inclination

ROSENCRANTZ: Niggard° of question,° but of our demands
 Most free in his reply.   15

QUEEN: Did you assay° him
 To any pastime?

ROSENCRANTZ: Madam, it so fell out that certain players
 We o'erraught° on the way. Of these we told him,
 And there did seem in him a kind of joy   20
 To hear of it. They are here about the court,
 And, as I think, they have already order
 This night to play before him.

POLONIUS: 'Tis most true,
 And he beseeched me to entreat Your Majesties   25
 To hear and see the matter.

KING: With all my heart, and it doth much content me
 To hear him so inclined.
 Good gentlemen, give him a further edge°
 And drive his purpose into these delights.   30

ROSENCRANTZ: We shall, my lord.

[*Exeunt* ROSENCRANTZ *and* GUILDENSTERN.]

KING: Sweet Gertrude, leave us too,
 For we have closely° sent for Hamlet hither,
 That he, as 'twere by accident, may here
 Affront° Ophelia.   35
 Her father and myself, lawful espials,°
 Will so bestow ourselves that seeing, unseen,
 We may of their encounter frankly judge,
 And gather by him, as he is behaved,
 If 't be th' affliction of his love or no   40
 That thus he suffers for.

QUEEN: I shall obey you.
 And for your part, Ophelia, I do wish
 That your good beauties be the happy cause
 Of Hamlet's wildness. So shall I hope your virtues   45
 Will bring him to his wonted° way again,
 To both your honors.

OPHELIA: Madam, I wish it may.

[*Exit* QUEEN.]

---

14 Niggard stingy   **question** conversation   **15 assay** try to win   **18 o'erraught** overtook
33 closely privately   **35 Affront** confront, meet   **36 espials** spies   **46 wonted** accustomed

POLONIUS: Ophelia, walk you here.—Gracious,° so please you,
　　　We will bestow° ourselves. [*To* OPHELIA.] Read on this book,　　　50

　　　　　　　　　　　　　　　　　　[*giving her a book*]

　　　That show of such an exercise° may color°
　　　Your loneliness.° We are oft to blame in this—
　　　'Tis too much proved°—that with devotion's visage
　　　And pious action we do sugar o'er
　　　The devil himself.　　　55
KING [*aside*]:   O 'tis too true!
　　　How smart a lash that speech doth give my conscience!
　　　The harlot's cheek, beautied with plastering art,
　　　Is not more ugly to° the thing° that helps it
　　　Than is my deed to my most painted word.　　　60
　　　O heavy burden!
POLONIUS: I hear him coming. Let's withdraw, my lord.

[*The* KING *and* POLONIUS *withdraw.*°]

[*Enter* HAMLET. (OPHELIA *pretends to read a book.*)]

HAMLET: To be, or not to be, that is the question:
　　　Whether 'tis nobler in the mind to suffer
　　　The slings° and arrows of outrageous fortune,　　　65
　　　Or to take arms against a sea of troubles
　　　And by opposing end them. To die, to sleep—
　　　No more—and by a sleep to say we end
　　　The heartache and the thousand natural shocks
　　　That flesh is heir to. 'Tis a consummation　　　70
　　　Devoutly to be wished. To die, to sleep;
　　　To sleep, perchance to dream. Ay, there's the rub,°
　　　For in that sleep of death what dreams may come,
　　　When we have shuffled° off this mortal coil,°
　　　Must give us pause. There's the respect°　　　75
　　　That makes calamity of so long life.°

26 edge incitement   **49 Gracious** Your Grace (i.e., the King)   **50 bestow** conceal
51 exercise religious exercise (The book she reads is one of devotion.)   **color** give a
plausible appearance to   **52 loneliness** being alone   **53 too much proved** too often
shown to be true, too often practiced   **59 to** compared to   **the thing** i.e., the cosmetic
s.d. withdraw (The King and Polonius may retire behind an arras. The stage directions specify that they "enter" again near the end of the scene.)   **65 slings** missiles
72 rub (Literally, an obstacle in the game of bowls.)   **74 shuffled** sloughed, cast   **coil**
turmoil   **75 respect** consideration   **76 of...life** so long-lived, something we willingly
endure for so long (also suggesting that long life is itself a calamity)

For who would bear the whips and scorns of time,
Th' oppressor's wrong, the proud man's contumely,°
The pangs of disprized° love, the law's delay,
The insolence of office,° and the spurns°   80
That patient merit of th' unworthy takes,°
When he himself might his quietus° make
With a bare bodkin?° Who would fardels° bear,
To grunt and sweat under a weary life,
But that the dread of something after death,   85
The undiscovered country from whose bourn°
No traveler returns, puzzles the will,
And makes us rather bear those ills we have
Than fly to others that we know not of?
Thus conscience does make cowards of us all;   90
And thus the native hue° of resolution
Is sicklied o'er with the pale cast° of thought,
And enterprises of great pitch° and moment°
With this regard° their currents° turn awry
And lose the name of action.—Soft you° now,   95
The fair Ophelia. Nymph, in thy orisons°
Be all my sins remembered.

OPHELIA: Good my lord,
How does your honor for this many a day?

HAMLET: I humbly thank you; well, well, well.   100

OPHELIA: My lord, I have remembrances of yours,
That I have longèd long to redeliver.
I pray you, now receive them.   [*She offers tokens.*]

HAMLET: No, not I, I never gave you aught.

OPHELIA: My honored lord, you know right well you did,   105
And with them words of so sweet breath composed
As made the things more rich. Their perfume lost,
Take these again, for to the noble mind
Rich gifts wax poor when givers prove unkind.
There, my lord.   [*She gives tokens.*]   110

HAMLET: Ha, ha! Are you honest?°

---

78 contumely insolent abuse   **79 disprized** unvalued   **80 office** officialdom   **spurns** insults   **81 of...takes** receives from unworthy persons   **76 quietus** acquittance; here, death   **83 a bare bodkin** a mere dagger, unsheathed   **fardels** burdens   **86 bourn** frontier, boundary   **91 native hue** natural color, complexion   **92 cast** tinge, shade of color   **93 pitch** height (as of a falcon's flight)   **moment** importance   **94 regard** respect, consideration   **currents** courses   **95 Soft you** i.e., wait a minute, gently   **96 orisons** prayers   **111 honest** (1) truthful (2) chaste

OPHELIA: My lord?

HAMLET: Are you fair?°

OPHELIA: What means your lordship?

HAMLET: That if you be honest and fair, your honesty° should admit no dis-   115
course° to your beauty.

OPHELIA: Could beauty, my lord, have better commerce° than with honesty?

HAMLET: Ay, truly, for the power of beauty will sooner transform honesty
from what it is to a bawd than the force of honesty can translate beauty
into his° likeness. This was sometime° a paradox,° but now the time°   120
gives it proof. I did love you once.

OPHELIA: Indeed, my lord, you made me believe so.

HAMLET: You should not have believed me, for virtue cannot so inoculate°
our old stock but we shall relish of it.° I loved you not.

OPHELIA: I was the more deceived.   125

HAMLET: Get thee to a nunnery.° Why wouldst thou be a breeder of sinners? I am myself indifferent honest,° but yet I could accuse me of such
things that it were better my mother had not borne me: I am very proud,
revengeful, ambitious, with more offenses at my beck° than I have
thoughts to put them in, imagination to give them shape, or time to act   130
them in. What should such fellows as I do crawling between earth and
heaven? We are arrant knaves all; believe none of us. Go thy ways to a
nunnery. Where's your father?

OPHELIA: At home, my lord.

HAMLET: Let the doors be shut upon him, that he may play the fool nowhere   135
but in 's own house. Farewell.

OPHELIA: O, help him, you sweet heavens!

HAMLET: If thou dost marry, I'll give thee this plague for thy dowry: be thou
as chaste as ice, as pure as snow, thou shalt not escape calumny. Get
thee to a nunnery, farewell. Or, if thou wilt needs marry, marry a fool,   140
for wise men know well enough what monsters° you° make of them.
To a nunnery, go, and quickly too. Farewell.

OPHELIA: Heavenly powers, restore him!

HAMLET: I have heard of your paintings too, well enough. God hath given you
one face, and you make yourselves another. You jig,° you amble,° and you   145

---

113 fair (1) beautiful (2) just, honorable   **115 your honesty** your chastity   **116
discourse** to familiar dealings with   **117 commerce** dealings, intercourse   **120 his**
its   **sometime** formerly   **a paradox** a view opposite to commonly held opinion
the time the present age   **123 inoculate** graft, be engrafted to   **124 but...it** that
we do not still have about us a taste of the old stock (i.e., retain our sinfulness)
126 nunnery convent (with possibly an awareness that the word was also used
derisively to denote a brothel)   **127 indifferent honest** reasonably virtuous   **129
beck** command   **141 monsters** (An allusion to the horns of a cuckold.)   **you** i.e., you
women   **145 jig** dance   **amble** move coyly

lisp, you nickname God's creatures,° and make your wantonness your ignorance.° Go to, I'll no more on 't;° it hath made me mad. I say we will have
no more marriage. Those that are married already—all but one—shall live.
The rest shall keep as they are. To a nunnery, go.

[*Exit.*]

OPHELIA: O, what a noble mind is here o'erthrown!   150
    The courtier's, soldier's, scholar's, eye, tongue, sword,
    Th' expectancy° and rose° of the fair state,
    The glass of fashion and the mold of form,°
    Th' observed of all observers,° quite, quite down!
    And I, of ladies most deject and wretched,   155
    That sucked the honey of his music° vows,
    Now see that noble and most sovereign reason
    Like sweet bells jangled out of tune and harsh,
    That unmatched form and feature of blown° youth
    Blasted° with ecstasy.° O, woe is me,   160
    T' have seen what I have seen, see what I see!

[*Enter* KING *and* POLONIUS.]

KING: Love? His affections° do not that way tend;
    Nor what he spake, though it lacked form a little,
    Was not like madness. There's something in his soul
    O'er which his melancholy sits on brood,°   165
    And I do doubt° the hatch and the disclose°
    Will be some danger; which for to prevent,
    I have in quick determination
    Thus set it down:° he shall with speed to England
    For the demand of° our neglected tribute.   170
    Haply the seas and countries different
    With variable objects° shall expel
    This something-settled matter in his heart,°

---

146 you nickname...creatures i.e., you give trendy names to things in place of their
God-given names   **146 make...ignorance** i.e., excuse your affectation on the grounds
of pretended ignorance   **147 on 't** of it   **152 expectancy** hope   **rose** ornament
153 The glass...form the mirror of true fashioning and the pattern of courtly behavior
154 Th' observed...observers i.e., the center of attention and honor in the court
156 music musical, sweetly uttered   **159 blown** blooming   **160 Blasted** withered
ecstasy madness   **161 affections** emotions, feelings   **165 sits on brood** sits like a bird
on a nest, about to *hatch* mischief (line 166)   **166 doubt** fear   **disclose** disclosure, hatch-
ing   **169 set it down** resolved   **170 For...of** to demand   **172 variable objects** various
sights and surroundings to divert him   **173 This something...heart** the strange matter
settled in his heart

Whereon his brains still° beating puts him thus
From fashion of himself.° What think you on 't   175
POLONIUS: It shall do well. But yet do I believe
The origin and commencement of his grief
Sprung from neglected love.—How now, Ophelia?
You need not tell us what Lord Hamlet said;
We heard it all.—My lord, do as you please,   180
But, if you hold it fit, after the play
Let his queen-mother° all alone entreat him
To show his grief. Let her be round° with him;
And I'll be placed, so please you, in the ear
Of all their conference. If she find him not,°   185
To England send him, or confine him where
Your wisdom best shall think.
KING: It shall be so.
Madness in great ones must not unwatched go.

[*Exeunt.*]

[**Act 3.2** *Enter* HAMLET *and three of the* PLAYERS.]°

HAMLET: Speak the speech, I pray you, as I pronounced it to you, trippingly
on the tongue. But if you mouth it, as many of our players° do, I had as
lief° the town crier spoke my lines. Nor do not saw the air too much with
your hand, thus, but use all gently; for in the very torrent, tempest, and,
as I may say, whirlwind of your passion, you must acquire and beget a   5
temperance that may give it smoothness. O, it offends me to the soul to
hear a robustious° periwig-pated° fellow tear a passion to tatters, to very
rags, to split the ears of the groundlings,° who for the most part are capable of° nothing but inexplicable dumb shows° and noise. I would have
such a fellow whipped for o'erdoing Termagant.° It out-Herods Herod.°   10
Pray you, avoid it.
FIRST PLAYER: I warrant your honor.

---

174 still continually   **175 From...himself** out of his natural manner   **182 queen-mother**
queen and mother   **183 round** blunt   **185 find him not** fails to discover what is troubling
him   **3.2 s.d. Location: The castle 2 our players** players nowadays   **I had as lief** I would
just as soon   **7 robustious** violent, boisterous   **periwig-pated** wearing a wig   **8 groundlings** spectators who paid least and stood in the yard of the theater   **8–9 capable of** able to
understand   **9 dumb shows** mimed performances, often used before Shakespeare's time to
precede a play or each act   **10 Termagant** a supposed deity of the Mohammedans, not found
in any English medieval play but elsewhere portrayed as violent and blustering   **Herod** Herod
of Jewry (A character in *The Slaughter of the Innocents* and other cycle plays. The part was
played with great noise and fury.)

HAMLET: Be not too tame neither, but let your own discretion be your tutor. Suit the action to the word, the word to the action, with this special observance, that you o'erstep not the modesty° of nature. For anything so   15
o'erdone is from° the purpose of playing, whose end, both at the first and now, was and is to hold as 't were the mirror up to nature, to show virtue her feature, scorn° her own image, and the very age and body of the time° his° form and pressure.° Now this overdone or come tardy off,° though it makes the unskillful° laugh, cannot but make the judicious grieve, the   20
censure of the which one° must in your allowance° o'erweigh a whole theater of others. O, there be players that I have seen play, and heard others praise, and that highly, not to speak it profanely,° that, neither having th' accent of Christians° nor the gait of Christian, pagan, nor man,° have so strutted and bellowed that I have thought some of nature's journey-   25
men° had made men and not made them well, they imitated humanity so abominably.°

FIRST PLAYER: I hope we have reformed that indifferently° with us, sir.

HAMLET: O, reform it altogether. And let those that play your clowns speak no more than is set down for them; for there be of them° that will themselves   30
laugh, to set on some quantity of barren° spectators to laugh too, though in the meantime some necessary question of the play be then to be considered. That's villainous, and shows a most pitiful ambition in the fool that uses it. Go make you ready.

[*Exeunt* PLAYERS.]

[*Enter* POLONIUS, GUILDENSTERN *and* ROSENCRANTZ.]

How now, my lord, will the King hear this piece of work?   35

POLONIUS: And the Queen too, and that presently.°

HAMLET: Bid the players make haste.

[*Exit* POLONIUS.]

Will you two help to hasten them?

ROSENCRANTZ: Ay, my lord.

[*Exeunt they two.*]

---

15 modesty restraint, moderation   **16 from** contrary to   **18 scorn** i.e., something foolish and deserving of scorn   **the very...time** i.e., the present state of affairs   **19 his** its   **pressure** stamp, impressed character   **come tardy off** inadequately done   **20 the unskillful** those lacking in judgment   **20–21 the censure...one** the judgment of even one of whom   **21 your allowance** your scale of values   **23 not...profanely** (Hamlet anticipates his idea in lines 25–27 that some men were not made by God at all.)   **24 Christians** i.e., ordinary decent folk   **nor man** i.e., nor any human being at all   **25 journeymen** laborers who are not yet masters in their trade   **27 abominably** (Shakespeare's usual spelling, *abbominably,* suggests a literal though etymologically incorrect meaning, "removed from human nature.")   **28 indifferently** tolerably   **30 of them** some among them   **31 barren** i.e., of wit   **36 presently** at once

HAMLET: What ho, Horatio!   40

[*Enter* HORATIO.]

HORATIO: Here, sweet lord, at your service.

HAMLET: Horatio, thou art e'en as just a man

As e'er my conversation coped withal.°

HORATIO: O, my dear lord—

HAMLET: Nay, do not think I flatter,   45

For what advancement may I hope from thee

That no revenue hast but thy good spirits

To feed and clothe thee? Why should the poor be flattered?

No, let the candied° tongue lick absurd pomp,

And crook the pregnant° hinges of the knee   50

Where thrift° may follow fawning. Dost thou hear?

Since my dear soul was mistress of her choice

And could of men distinguish her election,°

Sh' hath sealed thee° for herself, for thou hast been

As one, in suffering all, that suffers nothing,   55

A man that Fortune's buffets and rewards

Hast ta'en with equal thanks; and blest are those

Whose blood° and judgment are so well commeddled°

That they are not a pipe for Fortune's finger

To sound what stop° she please. Give me that man   60

That is not passion's slave, and I will wear him

In my heart's core, ay, in my heart of heart,

As I do thee.—Something too much of this.—

There is a play tonight before the King.

One scene of it comes near the circumstance   65

Which I have told thee of my father's death.

I prithee, when thou seest that act afoot,

Even with the very comment of thy soul°

Observe my uncle. If his occulted° guilt

Do not itself unkennel° in one speech,   70

It is a damnèd° ghost that we have seen,

And my imaginations are as foul

As Vulcan's stithy.° Give him heedful note,

---

43 my...withal my dealings encountered   **49 candied** sugared, flattering   **50 pregnant** compliant   **51 thrift** profit   **52 could...election** could make distinguishing choices among persons   **53 sealed thee** (Literally, as one would seal a legal document to mark possession.)   **58 blood** passion   **commeddled** commingled   **60 stop** hole in a wind instrument for controlling the sound   **68 very...soul** your most penetrating observation and consideration   **69 occulted** hidden   **70 unkennel** (As one would say of a fox driven from its lair.)   **71 damnèd** in league with Satan   **72 stithy** smithy, place of stiths (anvils)

For I mine eyes will rivet to his face,
And after we will both our judgments join   75
In censure of his seeming.°

HORATIO: Well, my lord.
If 'a steal aught° the whilst this play is playing
And scape detecting, I will pay the theft.

[*(Flourish.) Enter trumpets and kettledrums,* KING, QUEEN, POLONIUS OPHELIA,
(ROSENCRANTZ, GUILDENSTERN, *and other lords, with guards carrying torches).*]

HAMLET: They are coming to the play. I must be idle.°   80
Get you a place. [*The* KING, QUEEN, *and courtiers sit.*]

KING: How fares our cousin° Hamlet?

HAMLET: Excellent, i' faith, of the chameleon's dish:° I eat the air, promise-
crammed. You cannot feed capons° so.

KING: I have nothing with° this answer, Hamlet. These words are not mine.°   85

HAMLET: No, nor mine now.° [*To* POLONIUS.] My lord, you played once i' th'
university, you say?

POLONIUS: That did I, my lord, and was accounted a good actor.

HAMLET: What did you enact?

POLONIUS: I did enact Julius Caesar. I was killed i' the Capitol; Brutus killed me.   90

HAMLET: It was a brute° part° of him to kill so capital a calf° there.—Be the
players ready?

ROSENCRANTZ: Ay, my lord. They stay upon° your patience.

QUEEN: Come hither, my dear Hamlet, sit by me.

HAMLET: No, good Mother, here's metal° more attractive.   95

POLONIUS: [*to the* KING] O, ho, do you mark that?

HAMLET: Lady, shall I lie in your lap?

[*Lying down at* OPHELIA'S *feet.*]

OPHELIA: No, my lord.

HAMLET: I mean, my head upon your lap?

OPHELIA: Ay, my lord.   100

---

76 censure of his seeming judgment of his appearance or behavior   **78 If 'a steal
aught** if he gets away with anything   **80 idle** (1) unoccupied (2) mad   **82 cousin** i.e.,
close relative   **83 chameleon's dish** (Chameleons were supposed to feed on air. Hamlet
deliberately misinterprets the King's *fares* as "feeds." By his phrase *eat the air* he also
plays on the idea of feeding himself with the promise of succession, of being the
heir.)   **84 capons** roosters castrated and *crammed* with feed to make them succulent
85 have...with make nothing of, or gain nothing from   **are not mine** do not respond
to what I asked   **86 nor mine now** (Once spoken, words are proverbially no longer the
speaker's own—and hence should be uttered warily.)   **91 brute** (The Latin meaning of
brutus, "stupid," was often used punningly with the name Brutus.)   **part** (1) deed (2)
role   **calf** fool   **93 stay upon** await   **95 metal** substance that is attractive, i.e., magnetic,
but with suggestion also of *mettle,* "disposition"

HAMLET: Do you think I meant country matters?°

OPHELIA: I think nothing, my lord.

HAMLET: That's a fair thought to lie between maids' legs.

OPHELIA: What is, my lord?

HAMLET: Nothing.°   105

OPHELIA: You are merry, my lord.

HAMLET: Who, I?

OPHELIA: Ay, my lord.

HAMLET: O God, your only jig maker.° What should a man do but be merry?
For look you how cheerfully my mother looks, and my father died   110
within 's° two hours.

OPHELIA: Nay, 'tis twice two months, my lord.

HAMLET: So long? Nay then, let the devil wear black, for I'll have a suit of
sables.° O heavens! Die two months ago, and not forgotten yet? Then
there's hope a great man's memory may outlive his life half a year.   115
But, by 'r Lady, 'a must build churches, then, or else shall 'a suffer not
thinking on,° with the hobbyhorse, whose epitaph is "For O, for O, the
hobbyhorse is forgot."°

[*The trumpets sound. Dumb show follows.*]

[*Enter a King and a Queen (very lovingly); the Queen embracing him, and he
her. (She kneels, and makes show of protestation unto him.) He takes her up, and
declines his head upon her neck. He lies him down upon a bank of flowers. She,
seeing him asleep, leaves him. Anon comes in another man, takes off his crown,
kisses it, pours poison in the sleeper's ears, and leaves him. The Queen returns,
finds the King dead, makes passionate action. The Poisoner with some three or
four come in again, seem to condole with her. The dead body is carried away.
The Poisoner woos the Queen with gifts; she seems harsh awhile, but in the end
accepts love.*]

[*Exeunt* PLAYERS.]

100 country matters sexual intercourse (making a bawdy pun on the first syllable of *country*)
105 Nothing the figure zero or naught, suggesting the female sexual anatomy. (*Thing* not
infrequently has a bawdy connotation of male or female anatomy, and the reference here
could be male.)   **109 only jig maker** very best composer of jigs, i.e., pointless merriment
(Hamlet replies sardonically to Ophelia's observation that he is merry by saying, "If you're
looking for someone who is really merry, you've come to the right person.")   **111 within 's**
within this (i.e., these)   **113–114 suit of sables** garments trimmed with the fur of the
sable and hence suited for a wealthy person, not a mourner (but with a pun on *sable*,
"black," ironically suggesting mourning once again)   **116–117 suffer...on** undergo oblivion
117–118 For...forgot (verse of a song occurring also in *Love's Labor's Lost*, 3.1.27–28. The
hobbyhorse was a character made up to resemble a horse and rider, appearing in the morris dance and such May-game sports. This song laments the disappearance of such customs
under pressure from the Puritans.)

OPHELIA: What means this, my lord?

HAMLET: Marry, this' miching mallico;° it means mischief.   120

OPHELIA: Belike° this show imports the argument° of the play.

[*Enter* PROLOGUE.]

HAMLET: We shall know by this fellow. The players cannot keep counsel;°
    they'll tell all.

OPHELIA: Will 'a tell us what this show meant?

HAMLET: Ay, or any show that you will show him. Be not you° ashamed to   125
    show, he'll not shame to tell you what it means.

OPHELIA: You are naught,° you are naught. I'll mark the play.

PROLOGUE: For us, and for our tragedy,
    Here stooping° to your clemency,
    We beg your hearing patiently.   130

[*Exit.*]

HAMLET: Is this a prologue, or the posy of a ring?°

OPHELIA: 'Tis brief, my lord.

HAMLET: As woman's love.

[*Enter (two* PLAYERS *as) King and Queen.*]

PLAYER KING: Full thirty times hath Phoebus' cart° gone round
    Neptune's salt wash° and Tellus'° orbèd ground,   135
    And thirty dozen moons with borrowed° sheen
    About the world have times twelve thirties been,
    Since love our hearts and Hymen° did our hands
    Unite commutual° in most sacred bands.°

PLAYER QUEEN: So many journeys may the sun and moon   140
    Make us again count o'er ere love be done!
    But, woe is me, you are so sick of late,
    So far from cheer and from your former state,
    That I distrust° you. Yet, though I distrust,
    Discomfort° you, my lord, it nothing° must.   145
    For women's fear and love hold quantity;°

---

120 this' miching mallico this is sneaking mischief   **121 Belike** probably   **argu-ment** plot   **122 counsel** secret   **125 Be not you** provided you are not   **127 naught** indecent (Ophelia is reacting to Hamlet's pointed remarks about not being ashamed to show all.)   **129 stooping** bowing   **131 posy...ring** brief motto in verse inscribed in a ring   **134 Phoebus' cart** the sun-god's chariot, making its yearly cycle   **135 salt wash** the sea   **Tellus** goddess of the earth, of the *orbèd ground*   **136 borrowed** i.e., reflect-ed   **138 Hymen** god of matrimony   **139 commutual** mutually   **bands** bonds   **144 distrust** am anxious about   **145 Discomfort** distress   **nothing** not at all   **146 hold quantity** keep proportion with one another

In neither aught, or in extremity.°
Now, what my love is, proof° hath made you know,
And as my love is sized,° my fear is so.
Where love is great, the littlest doubts are fear;   150
Where little fears grow great, great love grows there.
PLAYER KING: Faith, I must leave thee, love, and shortly too;
My operant powers° their functions leave to do.°
And thou shalt live in this fair world behind, °
Honored, beloved; and haply one as kind   155
For husband shalt thou—
PLAYER QUEEN: O, confound the rest!
Such love must needs be treason in my breast.
In second husband let me be accurst!
None° wed the second but who° killed the first.   160
HAMLET: Wormwood,° wormwood.
PLAYER QUEEN: The instances° that second marriage move°
Are base respects of thrift,° but none of love.
A second time I kill my husband dead
When second husband kisses me in bed.   165
PLAYER KING: I do believe you think what now you speak,
But what we do determine oft we break.
Purpose is but the slave to memory,°
Of violent birth, but poor validity,°
Which° now, like fruit unripe, sticks on the tree,   170
But fall unshaken when they mellow be.
Most necessary 'tis that we forget
To pay ourselves what to ourselves is debt.°
What to ourselves in passion we propose,
The passion ending, doth the purpose lose.   175
The violence of either grief or joy
Their own enactures° with themselves destroy.
Where joy most revels, grief doth most lament;

---

147 In...extremity i.e., women fear and love either too little or too much, but the
two, fear and love, are equal in either case   148 proof experience   149 sized in size
153 operant powers vital functions   leave to do cease to perform   154 behind after
I have gone   161 None i.e., let no woman   but who except the one who   161 Wormwood
i.e., how bitter. (Literally, a bitter-tasting plant.)   162 instances motives   move motivate
163 base...thrift ignoble considerations of material prosperity   168 Purpose...
memory our good intentions are subject to forgetfulness   169 validity strength, durability
170 Which i.e., purpose   172–173 Most...debt it's inevitable that in time we forget the
obligations we have imposed on ourselves   177 enactures fulfillments

Grief joys, joy grieves, on slender accident.°

This world is not for aye,° nor 'tis not strange　　　　180

That even our loves should with our fortunes change;

For 'tis a question left us yet to prove,

Whether love lead fortune, or else fortune love.

The great man down,° you mark his favorite flies;

The poor advanced makes friends of enemies.°　　　　185

And hitherto° doth love on fortune tend;°

For who not needs° shall never lack a friend,

And who in want° a hollow friend doth try°

Directly seasons him° his enemy.

But, orderly to end where I begun,　　　　190

Our wills and fates do so contrary run°

That our devices still° are overthrown;

Our thoughts are ours, their ends° none of our own.

So think thou wilt no second husband wed,

But die thy thoughts when thy first lord is dead.　　　　195

PLAYER QUEEN:　Nor° earth to me give food, nor heaven light,

Sport and repose lock from me day and night,°

To desperation turn my trust and hope,

An anchor's cheer° in prison be my scope!°

Each opposite that blanks° the face of joy　　　　200

Meet what I would have well and it destroy!°

Both here and hence° pursue me lasting strife

If, once a widow, ever I be wife!

HAMLET:　If she should break it now!

PLAYER KING:　'Tis deeply sworn. Sweet, leave me here awhile;　　　　205

My spirits° grow dull, and fain I would beguile

The tedious day with sleep.

178–179 Where...accident the capacity for extreme joy and grief go together, and often one extreme is instantly changed into its opposite on the slightest provocation　**180 aye** ever　**184 down** fallen in fortune　**185 The poor...enemies** when one of humble station is promoted, you see his enemies suddenly becoming his friends　**186 hitherto** up to this point in the argument, or, to this extent　**tend** attend　**187 who not needs** he who is not in need (of wealth)　**188 who in want** he who, being in need　**try** test (his generosity)　**189 seasons him** ripens him into　**191 Our...run** what we want and what we get go so contrarily　**192 devices still** intentions continually　**193 ends** results　**196 Nor** let neither　**197 Sport...night** may day deny me its pastimes and night its repose　**199 anchor's cheer** anchorite's or hermit's fare　**my scope** the extent of my happiness　**200 blanks** causes to blanch or grow pale　**200–201 Each...destroy** may every adverse thing that causes the face of joy to turn pale meet and destroy everything that I desire to see prosper　**202 hence** in the life hereafter　**206 spirits** vital spirits

PLAYER QUEEN: Sleep rock thy brain,
  And never come mischance between us twain!

[*(He sleeps.) Exit* (PLAYER QUEEN).]

HAMLET: Madam, how like you this play?   210

QUEEN: The lady doth protest too much,° methinks.

HAMLET: O, but she'll keep her word.

KING: Have you heard the argument?° Is there no offense in 't?

HAMLET: No, no, they do but jest,° poison in jest. No offense° i' the world.

KING: What do you call the play?   215

HAMLET: *The Mousetrap.* Marry, how? Tropically.° This play is the image of
  a murder done in Vienna. Gonzago is the Duke's° name, his wife, Bap-
  tista. You shall see anon. 'Tis a knavish piece of work, but what of that?
  Your Majesty, and we that have free° souls, it touches us not. Let the
  galled jade° wince, our withers° are unwrung.°   220

[*Enter* LUCIANUS.]

  This is one Lucianus, nephew to the King.

OPHELIA: You are as good as a chorus,° my lord.

HAMLET: I could interpret° between you and your love, if I could see the puppets dallying.°

OPHELIA: You are keen,° my lord, you are keen.   225

HAMLET: It would cost you a groaning to take off mine edge.

OPHELIA: Still better, and worse.°

HAMLET: So° you mis-take° your husbands. Begin, murder; leave thy damnable faces and begin. Come, the croaking raven doth bellow for revenge.

211 doth...much makes too many promises and protestations   **213 argument** plot
214 jest make believe   **213–214 offense...offense** cause for objection...actual injury,
crime   **216 Tropically** figuratively (The First Quarto reading, *trapically,* suggests a pun
on *trap* in *Mousetrap.*)   **217 Duke's** i.e., King's (A slip that may be due to Shakespeare's possible source, the alleged murder of the Duke of Urbino by Luigi Gonzaga
in 1538.)   **219 free** guiltless   **219–220 galled jade** horse whose hide is rubbed by
saddle or harness   **220 withers** the part between the horse's shoulder blades
unwrung not rubbed sore   **222 chorus** (In many Elizabethan plays, the forthcoming
action was explained by an actor known as the "chorus"; at a puppet show, the actor who
spoke the dialogue was known as an "interpreter," as indicated by the lines following.)
223 interpret (1) ventriloquize the dialogue, as in puppet show (2) act as pander
224 puppets dallying (With suggestion of sexual play, continued in *keen,* "sexually
aroused," *groaning,* "moaning in pregnancy," and *edge,* "sexual desire" or "impetuos-
ity.")   **225 keen** sharp, bitter   **227 Still...worse** more keen, always *bettering* what
other people say with witty wordplay, but at the same time more offensive   **228 So**
even thus (in marriage)   **mis-take** take falseheartedly and cheat on (The marriage vows
say "for better, for worse.")

LUCIANUS: Thoughts black, hands apt, drugs fit, and time agreeing,   230
  Confederate season,° else° no creature seeing,°
  Thou mixture rank, of midnight weeds collected,
  With Hecate's ban° thrice blasted, thrice infected,
  Thy natural magic and dire property°
  On wholesome life usurp immediately.   235

[*He pours the poison into the sleeper's ear.*]

HAMLET: 'A poisons him i' the garden for his estate.° His° name's Gonzago. The
  story is extant, and written in very choice Italian. You shall see anon how
  the murderer gets the love of Gonzago's wife.

[CLAUDIUS *rises.*]

OPHELIA: The King rises.

HAMLET: What, frighted with false fire?°   240

QUEEN: How fares my lord?

POLONIUS: Give o'er the play.

KING: Give me some light. Away!

POLONIUS: Lights, lights, lights!

[*Exeunt all but* HAMLET *and* HORATIO.]

HAMLET: "Why, let the strucken deer go weep,   245
   The hart ungallèd° play.
  For some must watch,° while some must sleep;
   Thus runs the world away."°
  Would not this,° sir, and a forest of feathers°—if the rest of my fortunes
  turn Turk with° me—with two Provincial roses° on my razed° shoes, get   250
  me a fellowship in a cry° of players?°

HORATIO: Half a share.

HAMLET: A whole one, I.
  "For thou dost know, O Damon° dear,

---

231 Confederate season the time and occasion conspiring (to assist the murderer)   **else**
otherwise   **seeing** seeing me   **233 Hecate's ban** the curse of Hecate, the goddess of
witchcraft   **234 dire property** baleful quality   **236 estate** i.e., the kingship   **His** i.e.,
the King's   **240 false fire** the blank discharge of a gun loaded with powder but no
shot   **246 ungallèd** unafflicted   **247 watch** remain awake   **248 Thus...away** thus the
world goes   **245–248 Why...away** (Probably from an old ballad, with allusion to the
popular belief that a wounded deer retires to weep and die; compare with *As You Like
It,* 2.1.33–66.)   **249 this** i.e., the play   **feathers** (Allusion to the plumes that Elizabethan actors were fond of wearing.)   **250 turn Turk with** turn renegade against, go back
on   **Provincial roses** rosettes of ribbon, named for roses grown in a part of France   **razed**
with ornamental slashing   **251 cry** pack (of hounds)   **fellowship...players** partnership
in a theatrical company   **254 Damon** the friend of Pythias, as Horatio is friend of Hamlet;
or, a traditional pastoral name

This realm dismantled° was   255

Of Jove himself, and now reigns here

A very, very—pajock."°

HORATIO: You might have rhymed.

HAMLET: O good Horatio, I'll take the ghost's word for a thousand pound.   260
Didst perceive?

HORATIO: Very well, my lord.

HAMLET: Upon the talk of the poisoning?

HORATIO: I did very well note him.

[*Enter* ROSENCRANTZ *and* GUILDENSTERN.]

HAMLET: Aha! Come, some music! Come, the recorders.°

"For if the King like not the comedy,   265

Why then, belike, he likes it not, perdy."°

Come, some music.

GUILDENSTERN: Good my lord, vouchsafe me a word with you.

HAMLET: Sir, a whole history.

GUILDENSTERN: The King, sir—   270

HAMLET: Ay, sir, what of him?

GUILDENSTERN: Is in his retirement° marvelous distempered.°

HAMLET: With drink, sir?

GUILDENSTERN: No, my lord, with choler.°

HAMLET: Your wisdom should show itself more richer to signify this to the   275
doctor, for me to put him to his purgation° would perhaps plunge him
into more choler.

GUILDENSTERN: Good my lord, put your discourse into some frame° and start°
not so wildly from my affair.

HAMLET: I am tame, sir. Pronounce.   280

GUILDENSTERN: The Queen, your mother, in most great affliction of spirit, hath
sent me to you.

HAMLET: You are welcome.

---

255 dismantled stripped, divested   **255–257 This realm...pajock** i.e., Jove, representing divine authority and justice, has abandoned this realm to its own devices, leaving in his stead only a peacock or vain pretender to virtue (though the rhyme-word expected in place of *pajock* or "peacock" suggests that the realm is now ruled over by an "ass")   **264 recorders** wind instruments of the flute kind   **266 perdy** (A corruption of the French *par dieu*, "by God")   **272 retirement** withdrawal to his chambers **distempered** out of humor (But Hamlet deliberately plays on the wider application to any illness of mind or body, as in line 272, especially to drunkenness.)   **274 choler** anger (But Hamlet takes the word in its more basic humoral sense of "bilious disorder.")   **276 purgation** (Hamlet hints at something going beyond medical treatment to bloodletting and the extraction of confession.)   **278 frame** order   **start** shy or jump away (like a horse; the opposite of *tame* in line 279)

GUILDENSTERN: Nay, good my lord, this courtesy is not of the right breed.° If it
     shall please you to make me a wholesome answer, I will do your mother's   285
     commandment; if not, your pardon° and my return shall be the end of
     my business.
HAMLET: Sir, I cannot.
ROSENCRANTZ: What, my lord?
HAMLET: Make you a wholesome answer; my wit's diseased. But, sir, such an-   290
     swer as I can make, you shall command, or rather, as you say, my mother.
     Therefore no more, but to the matter. My mother, you say—
ROSENCRANTZ: Then thus she says: your behavior hath struck her into amaze-
     ment and admiration.°
HAMLET: O wonderful son, that can so stonish a mother! But is there no sequel   295
     at the heels of this mother's admiration? Impart.
ROSENCRANTZ: She desires to speak with you in her closet° ere you go to bed.
HAMLET: We shall obey, were she ten times our mother. Have you any further
     trade with us?
ROSENCRANTZ: My lord, you once did love me.   300
HAMLET: And do still, by these pickers and stealers.°
ROSENCRANTZ: Good my lord, what is your cause of distemper? You do surely
     bar the door upon your own liberty° if you deny° your griefs to your
     friend.
HAMLET: Sir, I lack advancement.   305
ROSENCRANTZ: How can that be, when you have the voice of the King himself
     for your succession in Denmark?
HAMLET: Ay, sir, but "While the grass grows"°—the proverb is something°
     musty.

[*Enter the* PLAYERS° *with recorders.*]

     O, the recorders. Let me see one. [*He takes a recorder.*]   310
     To withdraw° with you: why do you go about to recover the wind° of
     me, as if you would drive me into a toil?°
GUILDENSTERN: O, my lord, if my duty be too bold, my love is too unmannerly.°
HAMLET: I do not well understand that.° Will you play upon this pipe?

---

284 breed (1) kind (2) breeding, manners   **286 pardon** permission to depart   **294 admiration** bewilderment   **297 closet** private chamber   **301 pickers and stealers** i.e., hands
(So called from the catechism, "to keep my hands from picking and stealing.")   **303 liberty**
i.e., being freed from *distemper,* line 301; but perhaps with a veiled threat as well   **deny**
refuse to share   **308 While...grows** (The rest of the proverb is "the silly horse starves";
Hamlet may not live long enough to succeed to the kingdom.)   **something** somewhat
s.d. Players actors   **311 withdraw** speak privately   **recover the wind** get to the
windward side (thus driving the game into the *toil,* or "net")   **312 toil** snare   **313 If...
unmannerly** if I am using an unmannerly boldness, it is my love that occasion it
314 I...that i.e., I don't understand how genuine love can be unmannerly

GUILDENSTERN: My lord, I cannot.   315

HAMLET: I pray you.

GUILDENSTERN: Believe me, I cannot.

HAMLET: I do beseech you.

GUILDENSTERN: I know no touch of it, my lord.

HAMLET: It is as easy as lying. Govern these ventages° with your fingers and   320
thumb, give it breath with your mouth, and it will discourse most eloquent
music. Look you, these are the stops.

GUILDENSTERN: But these cannot I command to any utterance of harmony. I
have not the skill.

HAMLET: Why, look you now, how unworthy a thing you make of me! You   325
would play upon me, you would seem to know my stops, you would
pluck out the heart of my mystery, you would sound° me from my lowest
note to the top of my compass,° and there is much music, excellent voice,
in this little organ,° yet cannot you make it speak. 'Sblood, do you think I
am easier to be played on than a pipe? Call me what instrument you will,   330
though you can fret° me, you cannot play upon me.

[*Enter* POLONIUS.]

God bless you, sir!

POLONIUS: My lord, the Queen would speak with you, and presently.°

HAMLET: Do you see yonder cloud that's almost in shape of a camel?

POLONIUS: By the Mass and 'tis, like a camel indeed.   335

HAMLET: Methinks it is like a weasel.

POLONIUS: It is backed like a weasel.

HAMLET: Or like a whale.

POLONIUS: Very like a whale.

HAMLET: Then I will come to my mother by and by.° [*Aside.*] They fool me°   340
to the top of my bent.°—I will come by and by.

POLONIUS: I will say so.

[*Exit.*]

HAMLET: "By and by" is easily said. Leave me, friends.

[*Exeunt all but* HAMLET.]

'Tis now the very witching time° of night,
When churchyards yawn and hell itself breathes out   345

---

320 ventages finger-holes or *stops* (line 325) of the recorder   **327 sound** (1) fathom
(2) produce sound in   **328 compass** range (of voice)   **329 organ** musical instrument   **331 fret** irritate (with a quibble on *fret,* meaning the piece of wood, gut, or metal
that regulates the fingering on an instrument)   **333 presently** at once   **340 by and by**
quite soon   **fool me** trifle with me, humor my fooling   **341 top of my bent** limit of my
ability or endurance (Literally, the extent to which a bow may be bent.)   **344 witching
time** time when spells are cast and evil is abroad

Contagion to this world. Now could I drink hot blood
And do such bitter business as the day
Would quake to look on. Soft, now to my mother.
O heart, lose not thy nature!° Let not ever
The soul of Nero° enter this firm bosom.   350
Let me be cruel, not unnatural;
I will speak daggers to her, but use none.
My tongue and soul in this be hypocrites:
How in my words soever° she be shent,°
To give them seals° never my soul consent!   355

[*Exit.*]

[**Act 3.3** *Enter* KING, ROSENCRANTZ, *and* GUILDENSTERN.]°

KING: I like him° not, nor stands it safe with us
To let his madness range. Therefore prepare you.
I your commission will forthwith dispatch,°
And he to England shall along with you.
The terms of our estate° may not endure   5
Hazard so near 's as doth hourly grow
Out of his brows.°

GUILDENSTERN: We will ourselves provide.
Most holy and religious fear° it is
To keep those many many bodies safe   10
That live and feed upon Your Majesty.

ROSENCRANTZ: The single and peculiar° life is bound
With all the strength and armor of the mind
To keep itself from noyance,° but much more
That spirit upon whose weal depends and rests   15
The lives of many. The cess° of majesty
Dies not alone, but like a gulf° doth draw
What's near it with it; or it is a massy° wheel
Fixed on the summit of the highest mount,
To whose huge spokes ten thousand lesser things   20
Are mortised° and adjoined, which, when it falls,°

---

349 nature natural feeling   **350 Nero** murderer of his mother, Agrippina   **354 How...
soever** however much by my words   **shent** rebuked   **355 give them seals** i.e., confirm
them with deeds   **3.3 s.d. Location: The castle 1 him** i.e., his behavior   **3 dispatch**
prepare, cause to be drawn up   **5 terms of our estate** circumstances of my royal position
7 Out of his brows i.e., from his brain, in the form of plots and threats   **9 religious
fear** sacred concern   **12 single and peculiar** individual and private   **14 noyance** harm
16 cess decease, cessation   **17 gulf** whirlpool   **18 massy** massive   **21 mortised** fastened
(as with a fitted joint)   **when it falls** i.e., when it descends, like the wheel of Fortune,
bringing a king down with it

Each small annexment, petty consequence,°
Attends° the boisterous ruin. Never alone
Did the King sigh, but with a general groan.

KING: Arm° you, I pray you, to this speedy voyage,   25
For we will fetters put about this fear,
Which now goes too free-footed.

ROSENCRANTZ: We will haste us.

[*Exeunt gentlemen* (ROSENCRANTZ *and* GUILDENSTERN).]

[*Enter* POLONIUS.]

POLONIUS: My lord, he's going to his mother's closet.
Behind the arras° I'll convey myself   30
To hear the process.° I'll warrant she'll tax him home,°
And, as you said—and wisely was it said—
'Tis meet° that some more audience than a mother,
Since nature makes them partial, should o'erhear
The speech, of vantage.° Fare you well, my liege.   35
I'll call upon you ere you go to bed
And tell you what I know.

KING: Thanks, dear my lord.

[*Exit* POLONIUS.]

O, my offense is rank! It smells to heaven.
It hath the primal eldest curse° upon 't,   40
A brother's murder. Pray can I not,
Though inclination be as sharp as will;°
My stronger guilt defeats my strong intent,
And like a man to double business bound°
I stand in pause where I shall first begin,   45
And both neglect. What if this cursèd hand
Were thicker than itself with brother's blood,
Is there not rain enough in the sweet heavens
To wash it white as snow? Whereto serves mercy

---

22 Each...consequence i.e., every hanger-on and unimportant person or thing connected with the King   **23 Attends** participates in   **25 Arm** prepare   **30 arras** screen or tapestry placed around the walls of household apartments (On the Elizabethan stage, the arras was presumably over a door or discovery space in the tiring-house façade.)   **31 process** proceedings   **tax him home** reprove him severely   **33 meet** fitting   **35 of vantage** from an advantageous place, or, in addition   **40 the primal eldest curse** the curse of Cain, the first murderer; he killed his brother Abel   **42 Though...will** though my desire is as strong as my determination   **44 bound** (1) destined (2) obliged (The King wants to repent and still enjoy what he has gained.)

But to confront the visage of offense?°   50
And what's in prayer but this twofold force,
To be forestallèd° ere we come to fall,
Or pardoned being down? Then I'll look up.
My fault is past. But O, what form of prayer
Can serve my turn? "Forgive me my foul murder"?   55
That cannot be, since I am still possessed
Of those effects for which I did the murder:
My crown, mine own ambition, and my Queen.
May one be pardoned and retain th' offense?°
In the corrupted currents° of this world   60
Offense's gilded hand° may shove by° justice,
And oft 'tis seen the wicked prize° itself
Buys out the law. But 'tis not so above.
There° is no shuffling,° there the action lies°
In his° true nature, and we ourselves compelled,   65
Even to the teeth and forehead° of our faults,
To give in° evidence. What then? What rests?°
Try what repentance can. What can it not?
Yet what can it, when one cannot repent?
O wretched state, O bosom black as death,   70
O limèd° soul that, struggling to be free,
Art more engaged!° Help, angels! Make assay.°
Bow, stubborn knees, and heart with strings of steel,
Be soft as sinews of the newborn babe!
All may be well.   75

[*He kneels.*]

[*Enter* HAMLET.]

HAMLET: Now might I do it pat,° now 'a is a-praying;
        And now I'll do 't. [*He draws his sword.*] And so 'a goes to heaven,
        And so am I revenged. That would be scanned:°
        A villain kills my father, and for that,

50 Whereto...offense what function does mercy serve other than to meet sin face to face?   **52 forestallèd** prevented (from sinning)   **59 th' offense** the thing for which one offended   **60 currents** courses   **61 gilded hand** hand offering gold as a bribe   **shove by** thrust aside   **62 wicked prize** prize won by wickedness   **64 There** i.e., in heaven   **shuffling** escape by trickery   **the action lies** the accusation is made manifest (A legal metaphor.)   **65 his** its   **66 to the teeth and forehead** face to face, concealing nothing   **67 give in** provide   **rests** remains   **71 limèd** caught as with birdlime, a sticky substance used to ensnare birds   **72 engaged** entangled   **assay** trial (Said to himself.)   **76 pat** opportunely   **78 would be scanned** needs to be looked into, or, would be interpreted as follows

I, his sole son, do this same villain send   80
To heaven.
Why, this is hire and salary, not revenge.
'A took my father grossly, full of bread,°
With all his crimes broad blown,° as flush° as May;
And how his audit° stands who knows save° heaven?   85
But in our circumstance and course of thought°
'Tis heavy with him. And am I then revenged,
To take him in the purging of his soul,
When he is fit and seasoned° for his passage?
No!   90
Up, sword, and know thou a more horrid hent.°

                                        [*He puts up his sword.*]

When he is drunk asleep, or in his rage,°
Or in th' incestuous pleasure of his bed,
At game,° a-swearing, or about some act
That has no relish° of salvation in 't—   95
Then trip him, that his heels may kick at heaven,
And that his soul may be as damned and black
As hell, whereto it goes. My mother stays.°
This physic° but prolongs thy sickly days.

[*Exit.*]

KING: My words fly up, my thoughts remain below.   100
Words without thoughts never to heaven go.

[*Exit.*]

[**Act 3.4** *Enter* (QUEEN) GERTRUDE *and* POLONIUS.]°

POLONIUS: 'A will come straight. Look you lay home° to him.
Tell him his pranks have been too broad° to bear with,
And that Your Grace hath screened and stood between

---

83 grossly, full of bread i.e., enjoying his worldly pleasures rather than fasting (See Ezekiel 16:49.)   **84 crimes broad blown** sins in full bloom   **flush** vigorous   **85 audit** account   **save** except for   **86 in...thought** as we see it from our mortal perspective   **89 seasoned** matured, readied   **91 know...hent** await to be grasped by me on a more horrid occasion   **hent** act of seizing   **92 drunk...rage** dead drunk, or in a fit of sexual passion   **94 game** gambling   **95 relish** trace, savor   **98 stays** awaits (me)   **99 physic** purging (by prayer), or, Hamlet's postponement of the killing   **3.4 s.d. Location: The Queen's private chamber 1 lay home** thrust to the heart, reprove him soundly   **2 broad** unrestrained

Much heat° and him. I'll shroud° me even here.

Pray you, be round° with him.   5

HAMLET [*within*]: Mother, Mother, Mother!

QUEEN: I'll warrant you, fear me not.

Withdraw, I hear him coming.

[POLONIUS *hides behind the arras.*]

[*Enter* HAMLET.]

HAMLET: Now, Mother, what's the matter?

QUEEN: Hamlet, thou hast thy father° much offended.   10

HAMLET: Mother, you have my father much offended.

QUEEN: Come, come, you answer with an idle° tongue.

HAMLET: Go, go, you question with a wicked tongue.

QUEEN: Why, how now, Hamlet?

HAMLET: What's the matter now?   15

QUEEN: Have you forgot me?°

HAMLET: No, by the rood,° not so:

You are the Queen, your husband's brother's wife,

And—would it were not so!—you are my mother.

QUEEN: Nay, then, I'll set those to you that can speak.°   20

HAMLET: Come, come, and sit you down; you shall not budge.

You go not till I set you up a glass

Where you may see the inmost part of you.

QUEEN: What wilt thou do? Thou wilt not murder me?

Help, ho!   25

POLONIUS [*behind the arras*]:   What ho! Help!

HAMLET [*drawing*]:   How now? A rat? Dead for a ducat,° dead!

[*He thrusts his rapier through the arras.*]

POLONIUS [*behind the arras*]:   O, I am slain!   [*He falls and dies.*]

QUEEN: O me, what hast thou done?

HAMLET: Nay, I know not. Is it the King?   30

QUEEN: O, what a rash and bloody deed is this!

HAMLET: A bloody deed—almost as bad, good Mother,

As kill a King, and marry with his brother.

QUEEN: As kill a King!

---

4 Much heat i.e., the King's anger   **shroud** conceal (with ironic fitness to Polonius'
imminent death. The word is only in the First Quarto: the Second Quarto and the Folio
read "silence.")   **5 round** blunt   **10 thy father** i.e., your stepfather, Claudius   **12 idle**
foolish   **14 forgot me** i.e., forgotten that I am your mother   **17 rood** cross of Christ
20 speak i.e., to someone so rude   **27 Dead for a ducat** i.e., I bet a ducat he's dead; or,
a ducat is his life's fee

HAMLET: Ay, lady, it was my word.   35

[*He parts the arras and discovers* POLONIUS.]

Thou wretched, rash, intruding fool, farewell!
I took thee for thy better. Take thy fortune.
Thou find'st to be too busy° is some danger.—
Leave wringing of your hands. Peace, sit you down,
And let me wring your heart, for so I shall,   40
If it be made of penetrable stuff,
If damnèd custom° have not brazed° it so
That it be proof° and bulwark against sense.°

QUEEN: What have I done, that thou dar'st wag thy tongue
In noise so rude against me?   45

HAMLET: Such an act
That blurs the grace and blush of modesty,
Calls virtue hypocrite, takes off the rose
From the fair forehead of an innocent love
And sets a blister° there, makes marriage vows   50
As false as dicers' oaths. O, such a deed
As from the body of contraction° plucks
The very soul, and sweet religion makes°
A rhapsody° of words. Heaven's face does glow
O'er this solidity and compound mass   55
With tristful visage, as against the doom,
Is thought-sick at the act.°

QUEEN: Ay me, what act,
That roars so loud and thunders in the index?°

HAMLET [*showing her two likenesses*]:   Look here upon this picture, and on this,   60
The counterfeit presentment° of two brothers.
See what a grace was seated on this brow:
Hyperion's° curls, the front° of Jove himself,
An eye like Mars° to threaten and command,
A station° like the herald Mercury°   65
New-lighted° on a heaven-kissing hill—

---

38 busy nosey   **42 damnèd custom** habitual wickedness   **brazed** brazened, hardened
43 proof armor   **sense** feeling   **50 sets a blister** i.e., brands as a harlot   **52 contraction**
the marriage contract   **53 sweet religion makes** i.e., makes marriage vows   **54 rhapsody**
senseless string   **54–57 Heaven's…act** heaven's face blushes at this solid world compounded of the various elements, with sorrowful face as though the day of doom were near, and is sick with horror at the deed (i.e., Gertrude's marriage)   **59 index** table of contents, prelude or preface   **61 counterfeit presentment** portrayed representation   **63 Hyperion's** the sungod's   **front** brow   **64 Mars** god of war   **65 station** manner of standing   **Mercury** winged messenger of the gods   **66 New-lighted** newly alighted

A combination and a form indeed
Where every god did seem to set his seal°
To give the world assurance of a man.
This was your husband. Look you now what follows: 70
Here is your husband, like a mildewed ear,°
Blasting° his wholesome brother. Have you eyes?
Could you on this fair mountain leave° to feed
And batten° on this moor?° Ha, have you eyes?
You cannot call it love, for at your age   75
The heyday° in the blood° is tame, it's humble,
And waits upon the judgment, and what judgment
Would step from this to this? Sense,° sure, you have,
Else could you not have motion, but sure that sense
Is apoplexed,° for madness would not err,°   80
Nor sense to ecstasy was ne'er so thralled,
But° it reserved some quantity of choice
To serve in such a difference.° What devil was 't
That thus hath cozened° you at hoodman-blind?°
Eyes without feeling, feeling without sight,   85
Ears without hands or eyes, smelling sans° all,
Or but a sickly part of one true sense
Could not so mope.° O shame, where is thy blush?
Rebellious hell,
If thou canst mutine° in a matron's bones,   90
To flaming youth let virtue be as wax
And melt in her own fire.° Proclaim no shame
When the compulsive ardor gives the charge,
Since frost itself as actively doth burn,
And reason panders will.°   95

68 set his seal i.e., affix his approval   **71 ear** i.e., of grain   **72 Blasting** blighting
73 leave cease   **74 batten** gorge   **moor** barren or marshy ground (suggesting also
"dark-skinned")   **76 heyday** state of excitement   **blood** passion   **78 Sense** perception
through the five senses (the functions of the middle or sensible soul)   **80 apoplexed**
paralyzed (Hamlet goes on to explain that, without such a paralysis of will, mere madness would not so err, nor would the five senses so enthrall themselves to ecstasy or
lunacy; even such deranged states of mind would be able to make the obvious choice
between Hamlet Senior and Claudius.)   **err** so err   **82 But** but that   **83 To…difference**
to help in making a choice between two such men   **84 cozened** cheated   **hoodman-
blind** blindman's buff (In this game, says Hamlet, the devil must have pushed Claudius
toward Gertrude while she was blindfolded.)   **86 sans** without   **88 mope** be dazed, act
aimlessly   **90 mutine** incite mutiny   **91–92 be as wax…fire** melt like a candle or stick
of sealing wax held over the candle flame   **92–95 Proclaim…will** call it no shameful
business when the compelling ardor of youth delivers the attack, i.e., commits lechery,
since the *frost* of advanced age burns with as active a fire of lust and reason perverts itself
by fomenting lust rather than restraining it

QUEEN: O Hamlet, speak no more!
    Thou turn'st mine eyes into my very soul,
    And there I see such black and grainèd° spots
    As will not leave their tinct.°

HAMLET: Nay, but to live   100
    In the rank sweat of an enseamèd° bed,
    Stewed° in corruption, honeying and making love
    Over the nasty sty!

QUEEN: O, speak to me no more!
    These words like daggers enter in my ears.   105
    No more, sweet Hamlet!

HAMLET: A murderer and a villain,
    A slave that is not twentieth part the tithe°
    Of your precedent lord,° a vice° of kings,
    A cutpurse of the empire and the rule,   110
    That from a shelf the precious diadem stole
    And put it in his pocket!

QUEEN: No more!

[*Enter* GHOST *(in his nightgown).*]

HAMLET: A king of shreds and patches°—
    Save me, and hover o'er me with your wings,   115
    You heavenly guards! What would your gracious figure?

QUEEN: Alas, he's mad!

HAMLET: Do you not come your tardy son to chide,
    That, lapsed° in time and passion, lets go by
    Th' important° acting of your dread command?   120
    O, say!

GHOST: Do not forget. This visitation
    Is but to whet thy almost blunted purpose.
    But look, amazement° on thy mother sits.
    O, step between her and her fighting soul!   125
    Conceit° in weakest bodies strongest works.
    Speak to her, Hamlet.

HAMLET: How is it with you, lady?

---

98 grainèd dyed in grain, indelible   **99 leave their tinct** surrender their color
101 enseamèd saturated in the grease and filth of passionate lovemaking   **102 Stewed**
soaked, bathed (with a suggestion of "stew," brothel)   **108 tithe** tenth part   **109 prec-
edent lord** former husband   **vice** buffoon (A reference to the Vice of the morality
plays.)   **114 shreds and patches** i.e., motley, the traditional costume of the clown
or fool   **119 lapsed** delaying   **120 important** importunate, urgent   **124 amazement**
distraction   **126 Conceit** imagination

QUEEN: Alas, how is 't with you,

    That you do bend your eye on vacancy, 130

    And with th' incorporal° air do hold discourse?

    Forth at your eyes your spirits wildly peep,

    And, as the sleeping soldiers in th' alarm,°

    Your bedded° hair, like life in excrements,°

    Start up and stand on end. O gentle son, 135

    Upon the heat and flame of thy distemper°

    Sprinkle cool patience. Whereon do you look?

HAMLET: On him, on him! Look you how pale he glares!

    His form and cause conjoined,° preaching to stones,

    Would make them capable.°—Do not look upon me, 140

    Lest with this piteous action you convert

    My stern effects.° Then what I have to do

    Will want true color—tears perchance for blood.°

QUEEN: To whom do you speak this?

HAMLET: Do you see nothing there? 145

QUEEN: Nothing at all, yet all that is I see.

HAMLET: Nor did you nothing hear?

QUEEN: No, nothing but ourselves.

HAMLET: Why, look you there, look how it steals away!

    My father, in his habit° as° he lived! 150

    Look where he goes even now out at the portal!

[*Exit* GHOST.]

QUEEN: This is the very° coinage of your brain.

    This bodiless creation ecstasy

    Is very cunning in.°

HAMLET: Ecstasy? 155

    My pulse as yours doth temperately keep time,

    And makes as healthful music. It is not madness

    That I have uttered. Bring me to the test,

    And I the matter will reword,° which madness

---

131 incorporal immaterial **133 as...alarm** like soldiers called out of sleep by an alarm **134 bedded** laid flat **like life in excrements** i.e., as though hair, an outgrowth of the body, had a life of its own (Hair was thought to be lifeless because it lacks sensation, and so its standing on end would be unnatural and ominous.) **136 distemper** disorder **139 His...conjoined** his appearance joined to his cause for speaking **140 capable** receptive **141–142 convert...effects** divert me from my stern duty **143 want... blood** lack plausibility so that (with a play on the normal sense of *color*) I shall shed colorless tears instead of blood **150 habit** clothes **as** as when **152 very** mere **153–154 This...in** madness is skillful in creating this kind of hallucination **159 reword** repeat word for word

Would gambol° from. Mother, for love of grace,   160
Lay not that flattering unction° to your soul
That not your trespass but my madness speaks.
It will but skin° and film the ulcerous place,
Whiles rank corruption, mining° all within,
Infects unseen. Confess yourself to heaven,   165
Repent what's past, avoid what is to come,
And do not spread the compost° on the weeds
To make them ranker. Forgive me this my virtue;°
For in the fatness° of these pursy° times
Virtue itself of vice must pardon beg,   170
Yea, curb° and woo for leave° to do him good.

QUEEN: O Hamlet, thou hast cleft my heart in twain.

HAMLET: O, throw away the worser part of it,
And live the purer with the other half.
Good night. But go not to my uncle's bed;   175
Assume a virtue, if you have it not.
That monster, custom, who all sense doth eat,°
Of habits devil,° is angel yet in this,
That to the use of actions fair and good
He likewise gives a frock or livery°   180
That aptly° is put on. Refrain tonight,
And that shall lend a kind of easiness
To the next abstinence; the next more easy;
For use° almost can change the stamp of nature,°
And either°...the devil, or throw him out   185
With wondrous potency. Once more, good night;
And when you are desirous to be blest,
I'll blessing beg of you.° For this same lord,

                          [*pointing to* POLONIUS]
I do repent; but heaven hath pleased it so
To punish me with this, and this with me,   190

---

160 gambol skip away   **161 unction** ointment   **163 skin** grow a skin for   **164 mining** working under the surface   **167 compost** manure   **168 this my virtue** my virtuous talk in reproving you   **169 fatness** grossness   **pursy** flabby, out of shape   **171 curb** bow, bend the knee   **leave** permission   **177 who...eat** which consumes all proper or natural feeling, all sensibility   **178 Of habits devil** devil-like in prompting evil habits   **180 livery** an outer appearance, a customary garb (and hence a predisposition easily assumed in time of stress)   **181 aptly** readily   **184 use** habit   **the stamp of nature** our inborn traits   **185 And either** (A defective line, usually emended by inserting the word *master* after *either,* following the Fourth Quarto and early editors.)   **187–188 when... you** i.e., when you are ready to be penitent and seek God's blessing, I will ask your blessing as a dutiful son should

That I must be their scourge and minister.°
I will bestow° him, and will answer° well
The death I gave him. So, again, good night.
I must be cruel only to be kind.
This° bad begins, and worse remains behind.°   195
One word more, good lady.

QUEEN: What shall I do?

HAMLET: Not this by no means that I bid you do:
Let the bloat° King tempt you again to bed,
Pinch wanton° on your cheek, call you his mouse,   200
And let him, for a pair of reechy° kisses,
Or paddling° in your neck with his damned fingers,
Make you to ravel all this matter out°
That I essentially am not in madness,
But mad in craft.° 'Twere good° you let him know,   205
For who that's but a Queen, fair, sober, wise,
Would from a paddock,° from a bat, a gib,°
Such dear concernings° hide? Who would do so?
No, in despite of sense and secrecy,°
Unpeg the basket° on the house's top,   210
Let the birds fly, and like the famous ape,°
To try conclusions,° in the basket creep
And break your own neck down.°

QUEEN: Be thou assured, if words be made of breath,
And breath of life, I have no life to breathe   215
What thou hast said to me.

HAMLET: I must to England. You know that?

QUEEN: Alack,
I had forgot. 'Tis so concluded on.

HAMLET: There's letters sealed, and my two schoolfellows,   220
Whom I will trust as I will adders fanged,

191 their scourge and minister i.e., agent of heavenly retribution (By *scourge,* Hamlet also suggests that he himself will eventually suffer punishment in the process of fulfilling heaven's will.)   **192 bestow** stow, dispose of   **answer** account or pay for   **195 This** i.e., the killing of Polonius   **behind** to come   **199 bloat** bloated   **200 Pinch wanton** i.e., leave his love pinches on your cheeks, branding you as wanton   **201 reechy** dirty, filthy   **202 paddling** fingering amorously   **203 ravel...out** unravel, disclose   **205 in craft** by cunning   **good** (Said sarcastically; also the following eight lines.)   **207 paddock** toad   **gib** tomcat   **208 dear concernings** important affairs   **209 sense and secrecy** secrecy that common sense requires   **210 Unpeg the basket** open the cage, i.e., let out the secret   **211 famous ape** (In a story now lost.)   **212 try conclusions** test the outcome (in which the ape apparently enters a cage from which birds have been released and then tries to fly out of the cage as they have done, falling to its death)   **213 down** in the fall; utterly

They bear the mandate; they must sweep my way
And marshal me to knavery.° Let it work.°
For 'tis the sport to have the enginer°
Hoist with° his own petard,° and 't shall go hard   225
But I will° delve one yard below their mines°
And blow them at the moon. O, 'tis most sweet
When in one line° two crafts° directly meet.
This man shall set me packing.°
I'll lug the guts into the neighbor room.   230
Mother, good night indeed. This counselor
Is now most still, most secret, and most grave,
Who was in life a foolish prating knave.—
Come, sir, to draw toward an end° with you.—
Good night, Mother.   235

[*Exeunt (separately,* HAMLET *dragging in* POLONIUS*).*]

[**Act 4.1** *Enter* KING *and* QUEEN,° *with* ROSENCRANTZ *and* GUILDENSTERN.]°

KING: There's matter° in these sighs, these profound heaves.°
            You must translate; 'tis fit we understand them.
            Where is your son?

QUEEN: Bestow this place on us a little while.

[*Exeunt* ROSENCRANTZ *and* GUILDENSTERN.]

            Ah, mine own lord, what have I seen tonight!   5

KING: What, Gertrude? How does Hamlet?

QUEEN: Mad as the sea and wind when both contend
            Which is the mightier. In his lawless fit,
            Behind the arras hearing something stir,
            Whips out his rapier, cries, "A rat, a rat!"   10

222–223 sweep...knavery sweep a path before me and conduct me to some *knavery* or treachery prepared for me   **223 work** proceed   **224 enginer** maker of military contrivances   **225 Hoist with** blown up by   **petard** an explosive used to blow in a door or make a breach   **225–226 't shall...will** unless luck is against me, I will   **226 mines** tunnels used in warfare to undermine the enemy's emplacements; Hamlet will countermine by going under their mines   **228 in one line** i.e., mines and countermines on a collision course, or the countermines directly below the mines   **crafts** acts of guile, plots   **229 set me packing** set me to making schemes, and set me to lugging (him), and, also, send me off in a hurry   **234 draw...end** finish up (with a pun on *draw,* "pull")   **4.1 s.d Location: The castle   s.d. Enter...Queen** (Some editors argue that Gertrude never exits in 3.4 and that the scene is continuous here, as suggested in the Folio, but the Second Quarto marks an entrance for her and at line 35 Claudius speaks of Gertrude's *closet* as though it were elsewhere. A short time has elapsed, during which the King has become aware of her highly wrought emotional state.)   **1 matter** significance   **heaves** heavy sighs

And in this brainish apprehension° kills
The unseen good old man.
KING: O heavy° deed!
It had been so with us,° had we been there.
His liberty is full of threats to all—   15
To you yourself, to us, to everyone.
Alas, how shall this bloody deed be answered?°
It will be laid to us, whose providence°
Should have kept short,° restrained, and out of haunt°
This mad young man. But so much was our love,   20
We would not understand what was most fit,
But, like the owner of a foul disease,
To keep it from divulging,° let it feed
Even on the pith of life. Where is he gone?
QUEEN: To draw apart the body he hath killed,   25
O'er whom his very madness, like some ore°
Among a mineral° of metals base,
Shows itself pure: 'a weeps for what is done.
KING: O Gertrude, come away!
The sun no sooner shall the mountains touch   30
But we will ship him hence, and this vile deed
We must with all our majesty and skill
Both countenance° and excuse.—Ho, Guildenstern!

[*Enter* ROSENCRANTZ *and* GUILDENSTERN.]

Friends both, go join you with some further aid.
Hamlet in madness hath Polonius slain,   35
And from his mother's closet hath he dragged him.
Go seek him out, speak fair, and bring the body
Into the chapel. I pray you, haste in this.

[*Exeunt* ROSENCRANTZ *and* GUILDENSTERN.]

Come, Gertrude, we'll call up our wisest friends
And let them know both what we mean to do   40
And what's untimely done°

---

11 brainish apprehension headstrong conception   **13 heavy** grievous   **14 us** i.e., me
(The royal "we"; also in line 14.)   **17 answered** explained   **18 providence** foresight
19 short i.e., on a short tether   **out of haunt** secluded   **23 divulging** becoming
evident   **26 ore** vein of gold   **27 mineral** mine   **33 countenance** put the best face on
41 And...done (A defective line; conjectures as to the missing words include *So, haply,
slander* [Capell and others]; *For, haply, slander* [Theobald and others]; and *So envious
slander* [Jenkins].)

Whose whisper o'er the world's diameter,°
As level° as the cannon to his blank,°
Transports his poisoned shot, may miss our name
And hit the woundless° air. O, come away!   45
My soul is full of discord and dismay.

[*Exeunt.*]

[**Act 4.2** *Enter* HAMLET.]°

HAMLET: Safely stowed.

ROSENCRANTZ, GUILDENSTERN [*within*]:   Hamlet! Lord Hamlet!

HAMLET: But soft, what noise? Who calls on Hamlet? O, here they come.

[*Enter* ROSENCRANTZ *and* GUILDENSTERN.]

ROSENCRANTZ: What have you done, my lord, with the dead body?

HAMLET: Compounded it with dust, whereto 'tis kin.   5

ROSENCRANTZ: Tell us where 'tis, that we may take it thence
     And bear it to the chapel.

HAMLET: Do not believe it.

ROSENCRANTZ: Believe what?

HAMLET: That I can keep your counsel and not mine own.° Besides, to be   10
     demanded of° a sponge, what replication° should be made by the son
     of a king?

ROSENCRANTZ: Take you me for a sponge, my lord?

HAMLET: Ay, sir, that soaks up the King's countenance,° his rewards, his
     authorities.° But such officers do the King best service in the end.   15
     He keeps them, like an ape, an apple, in the corner of his jaw, first
     mouthed to be last swallowed. When he needs what you have gleaned,
     it is but squeezing you, and, sponge, you shall be dry again.

ROSENCRANTZ: I understand you not, my lord.

HAMLET: I am glad of it. A knavish speech sleeps in° a foolish ear.   20

ROSENCRANTZ: My lord, you must tell us where the body is and go with us
     to the King.

HAMLET: The body is with the King, but the King is not with the body.°
     The King is a thing—

---

42 diameter extent from side to side   **43 As level** with as direct aim   **his blank** its target
at point-blank range   **45 woundless** invulnerable   **4.2 s.d. Location: The castle**   **10
That...own** i.e., that I can follow your advice (by telling where the body is) and still keep
my own secret   **11 demanded of** questioned by   **replication** reply   **14 countenance**
favor   **15 authorities** delegated power, influence   **20 sleeps in** has no meaning to   **23
The...body** (Perhaps alludes to the legal commonplace of "the king's two bodies," which
drew a distinction between the sacred office of kingship and the particular mortal who
possessed it at any given time. Hence, although Claudius' body is necessarily a part of him,
true kingship is not contained in it. Similarly, Claudius will have Polonius' body when it is
found, but there is no kingship in this business either.)

GUILDENSTERN: A thing, my lord?   25

HAMLET: Of nothing.° Bring me to him. Hide fox, and all after!°

[*Exeunt (running).*]

[**Act 4.3** *Enter* KING, *and two or three.*]°

KING: I have sent to seek him, and to find the body.

How dangerous is it that this man goes loose!

Yet must not we put the strong law on him.

He's loved of° the distracted° multitude,

Who like not in their judgment, but their eyes,°   5

And where 'tis so, th' offender's scourge° is weighed,°

But never the offense. To bear all smooth and even,°

This sudden sending him away must seem

Deliberate pause.° Diseases desperate grown

By desperate appliance° are relieved,   10

Or not at all.

[*Enter* ROSENCRANTZ, GUILDENSTERN, *and all the rest.*]

How now, what hath befall'n?

ROSENCRANTZ: Where the dead body is bestowed, my lord,

We cannot get from him.

KING: But where is he?   15

ROSENCRANTZ: Without, my lord; guarded, to know your pleasure.

KING: Bring him before us.

ROSENCRANTZ: Ho! Bring in the lord.

[*They enter (with* HAMLET).]

KING: Now, Hamlet, where's Polonius?

HAMLET: At supper.   20

KING: At supper? Where?

HAMLET: Not where he eats, but where 'a is eaten. A certain convocation of
politic worms° are e'en° at him. Your worm° is your only emperor for
diet.° We fat all creatures else to fat us, and we fat ourselves for maggots. Your fat king and your lean beggar is but variable service°—two   25
dishes, but to one table. That's the end.

---

26 Of nothing (1) of no account (2) lacking the essence of kingship, as in lines 23–24 and
note   **Hide…after** (An old signal cry in the game of hide-and-seek, suggesting that Hamlet now runs away from them.)   **4.3 s.d. Location: The castle   4 of** by   **distracted** fickle,
unstable   **5 Who…eyes** who choose not by judgment but by appearance   **6 scourge** punishment (Literally, blow with a whip.)   **weighed** sympathetically considered   **7 To…even**
to manage the business in an unprovocative way   **9 Deliberate pause** carefully considered
action   **10 appliance** remedies   **23 politic worms** crafty worms (suited to a master spy like
Polonius)   **e'en** even now   **Your worm** your average worm (Compare *your fat king and your
lean beggar* in line 25.)   **24 diet** food, eating (with a punning reference to the Diet of Worms,
a famous *convocation* held in 1521)   **25 variable service** different courses of a single meal

KING: Alas, alas!

HAMLET: A man may fish with the worm that hath eat° of a king, and eat of the
fish that hath fed of that worm.

KING: What dost thou mean by this?   30

HAMLET: Nothing but to show you how a king may go a progress° through
the guts of a beggar.

KING: Where is Polonius?

HAMLET: In heaven. Send thither to see. If your messenger find him not there,
seek him i' th' other place yourself. But if indeed you find him not within   35
this month, you shall nose him as you go up the stairs into the lobby.

KING: [*to some attendants*] Go seek him there.

HAMLET: 'A will stay till you come.

[*Exeunt attendants.*]

KING: Hamlet, this deed, for thine especial safety—
Which we do tender,° as we dearly° grieve   40
For that which thou hast done—must send thee hence
With fiery quickness. Therefore prepare thyself.
The bark° is ready, and the wind at help,
Th' associates tend,° and everything is bent°
For England.   45

HAMLET: For England!

KING: Ay, Hamlet.

HAMLET: Good.

KING: So is it, if thou knew'st our purposes.

HAMLET: I see a cherub° that sees them. But come, for England!   50
Farewell, dear mother.

KING: Thy loving father, Hamlet.

HAMLET: My mother. Father and mother is man and wife, man and wife is
one flesh, and so, my mother. Come, for England!

[*Exit.*]

KING: Follow him at foot;° tempt him with speed aboard.   55
Delay it not. I'll have him hence tonight.
Away! For everything is sealed and done
That else leans on° th' affair. Pray you, make haste.

[*Exeunt all but the* KING.]

---

28 eat eaten (Pronounced et.)   **31 progress** royal journey of state   **40 tender** regard, hold
dear   **dearly** intensely   **43 bark** sailing vessel   **44 tend** wait   **bent** in readiness   **50 cherub**
(Cherubim are angels of knowledge. Hamlet hints that both he and heaven are onto Claudius'
tricks.)   **55 at foot** close behind, at heel   **58 leans on** bears upon, is related to

And, England,° if my love thou hold'st at aught°—
As my great power thereof may give thee sense,°   60
Since yet thy cicatrice° looks raw and red
After the Danish sword, and thy free awe°
Pays homage to us—thou mayst not coldly set°
Our sovereign process,° which imports at full,°
By letters congruing° to that effect,   65
The present° death of Hamlet. Do it, England,
For like the hectic° in my blood he rages,
And thou must cure me. Till I know 'tis done,
Howe'er my haps,° my joys were ne'er begun.

[*Exit.*]

[**Act 4.4** *Enter* FORTINBRAS *with his army over the stage.*]°

FORTINBRAS: Go, Captain, from me greet the Danish king.
    Tell him that by his license° Fortinbras
    Craves the conveyance of° a promised march
    Over his kingdom. You know the rendezvous.
    If that His Majesty would aught with us,   5
    We shall express our duty° in his eye;°
    And let him know so.
CAPTAIN: I will do 't, my lord.
FORTINBRAS: Go softly° on.

[*Exeunt all but the* CAPTAIN.]

[*Enter* HAMLET, ROSENCRANTZ, GUILDENSTERN, *etc.*]

HAMLET: Good sir, whose powers° are these?   10
CAPTAIN: They are of Norway, sir.
HAMLET: How purposed, sir, I pray you?
CAPTAIN: Against some part of Poland.
HAMLET: Who commands them, sir?
CAPTAIN: The nephew to old Norway, Fortinbras.   15
HAMLET: Goes it against the main° of Poland, sir,
    Or for some frontier?

---

59 England i.e., King of England   **at aught** at any value   **60 As…sense** for so my great power may give you a just appreciation of the importance of valuing my love   **61 cicatrice** scar   **62 free awe** voluntary show of respect   **63 coldly set** regard with indifference **64 process** command   **imports at full** conveys specific directions for   **65 congruing** agreeing   **66 present** immediate   **67 hectic** persistent fever   **69 haps** fortunes **4.4 s.d. Location: The coast of Denmark 2 license** permission   **3 the conveyance of** escort during   **6 duty** respect   **eye** presence   **9 softly** slowly, circumspectly   **10 powers** forces   **16 main** main part

CAPTAIN: Truly to speak, and with no addition,°
    We go to gain a little patch of ground
    That hath in it no profit but the name.   20
    To pay° five ducats, five, I would not farm it;°
    Nor will it yield to Norway or the Pole
    A ranker° rate, should it be sold in fee.°
HAMLET: Why, then the Polack never will defend it.
CAPTAIN: Yes, it is already garrisoned.   25
HAMLET: Two thousand souls and twenty thousand ducats
    Will not debate° the question of this straw.°
    This is th' impostume° of much wealth and peace,
    That inward breaks, and shows no cause without
    Why the man dies. I humbly thank you, sir.   30
CAPTAIN: God b' wi' you, sir.

[*Exit.*]

ROSENCRANTZ: Will 't please you go, my lord?
HAMLET: I'll be with you straight. Go a little before.

                                     [*Exeunt all except* HAMLET.]

    How all occasions do inform against° me
    And spur my dull revenge! What is a man,   35
    If his chief good and market of° his time
    Be but to sleep and feed? A beast, no more.
    Sure he that made us with such large discourse,°
    Looking before and after,° gave us not
    That capability and godlike reason   40
    To fust° in us unused. Now, whether it be
    Bestial oblivion,° or some craven° scruple
    Of thinking too precisely° on th' event°—
    A thought which, quartered, hath but one part wisdom
    And ever three parts coward—I do not know   45
    Why yet I live to say "This thing's to do,"
    Sith° I have cause, and will, and strength, and means
    To do 't. Examples gross° as earth exhort me:
    Witness this army of such mass and charge,°
    Led by a delicate and tender° prince,   50

---

18 addition exaggeration   **21 To pay** i.e., for a yearly rental of   **farm it** take a lease of it   **23 ranker** higher   **in fee** fee simple, outright   **27 debate...straw** settle this trifling matter   **28 impostume** abscess   **34 inform against** denounce, betray; take shape against **36 market of** profit of, compensation for   **38 discourse** power of reasoning   **39 Looking before and after** able to review past events and anticipate the future   **41 fust** grow moldy **42 oblivion** forgetfulness   **craven** cowardly   **43 precisely** scrupulously   **event** outcome **47 Sith** since   **48 gross** obvious   **49 charge** expense   **50 delicate and tender** of fine and youthful qualities

Whose spirit with divine ambition puffed
Makes mouths° at the invisible event,°
Exposing what is mortal and unsure
To all that fortune, death, and danger dare,°
Even for an eggshell. Rightly to be great   55
Is not to stir without great argument,
But greatly to find quarrel in a straw
When honor's at the stake.° How stand I, then,
That have a father killed, a mother stained,
Excitements of° my reason and my blood,   60
And let all sleep, while to my shame I see
The imminent death of twenty thousand men
That for a fantasy° and trick° of fame
Go to their graves like beds, fight for a plot°
Whereon the numbers cannot try the cause,°   65
Which is not tomb enough and continent°
To hide the slain? O, from this time forth
My thoughts be bloody or be nothing worth!

[*Exit.*]

[**Act 4.5** *Enter* HORATIO, (QUEEN) GERTRUDE, *and a* GENTLEMAN.]°

QUEEN: I will not speak with her.
GENTLEMAN: She is importunate,
Indeed distract.° Her mood will needs be pitied.
QUEEN: What would she have?
GENTLEMAN: She speaks much of her father, says she hears   5
There's tricks° i' the world, and hems,° and beats her heart,°
Spurns enviously at straws,° speaks things in doubt°
That carry but half sense. Her speech is nothing,
Yet the unshapèd use° of it doth move
The hearers to collection;° they yawn° at it,   10
And botch° the words up fit to their own thoughts,

52 Makes mouths makes scornful faces **invisible event** unforeseeable outcome
54 dare could do (to him) **55–58 Rightly...stake** true greatness does not normally
consist of rushing into action over some trivial provocation; however, when one's honor
is involved, even a trifling insult requires that one respond greatly **58 at the stake**
(A metaphor from gambling or bear-baiting.) **60 Excitements of** promptings by
63 fantasy fanciful caprice, illusion **trick** trifle, deceit **64 plot** plot of ground
65 Whereon...cause on which there is insufficient room for the soldiers needed to
engage in a military contest **66 continent** receptacle; container **4.5 s.d. Location: The
castle 3 distract** distracted **5 tricks** deceptions **hems** makes "hmm" sounds **heart**
i.e., breast **7 Spurns...straws** kicks spitefully, takes offense at trifles **in doubt**
obscurely **9 unshapèd use** incoherent manner **10 collection** inference, a guess at
some sort of meaning **yawn** gape, wonder; grasp (The Folio reading, *aim,* is possible.)
11 botch patch

Which,° as her winks and nods and gestures yield° them,
Indeed would make one think there might be thought,°
Though nothing sure, yet much unhappily.°

HORATIO: 'Twere good she were spoken with, for she may strew   15
Dangerous conjectures in ill-breeding° minds.

QUEEN: Let her come in.   [*Exit* GENTLEMAN.]
[*Aside*.] To my sick soul, as sin's true nature is,
Each toy° seems prologue to some great amiss.°
So full of artless jealousy is guilt,   20
It spills itself in fearing to be spilt.°

[*Enter* OPHELIA° *(distracted)*.]

OPHELIA: Where is the beauteous majesty of Denmark?

QUEEN: How now, Ophelia?

OPHELIA [*she sings*]:
      "How should I your true love know   25
            From another one?
      By his cockle hat° and staff,
            And his sandal shoon."°

QUEEN: Alas, sweet lady, what imports this song?

OPHELIA: Say you? Nay, pray you, mark.   30
      "He is dead and gone, lady,   [*Song*.]
         He is dead and gone;
      At his head a grass-green turf,
         At his heels a stone."
      O, ho!   35

QUEEN: Nay, but Ophelia—

OPHELIA: Pray you, mark.   [*Sings*.]
      "White his shroud as the mountain snow"—

[*Enter* KING.]

QUEEN: Alas, look here, my lord.

OPHELIA: "Larded° with sweet flowers;   [*Song*.]   40
      Which bewept to the ground did not go
            With true-love showers."°

KING: How do you, pretty lady?

---

12 Which which words   **yield** deliver, represent   **13 thought** intended   **14 unhappily** unpleasantly near the truth, shrewdly   **16 ill-breeding** prone to suspect the worst and to make mischief   **19 toy** trifle   **amiss** calamity   **20–21 So...split** guilt is so full of suspicion that it unskillfully betrays itself in fearing betrayal   **s.d. Enter Ophelia** (In the First Quarto, Ophelia enters, "playing on a lute, and her hair down, singing.")   **27 cockle hat** hat with cockle-shell stuck in it as a sign that the wearer had been a pilgrim to the shrine of Saint James of Compostela in Spain   **28 shoon** shoes   **40 Larded** decorated   **42 showers** i.e., tears

OPHELIA: Well, God 'ild° you! They say the owl° was a baker's daughter.
  Lord, we know what we are, but know not what we may be. God be 45
  at your table!

KING: Conceit° upon her father.

OPHELIA: Pray let's have no words of this; but when they ask you what it
  means, say you this:

   "Tomorrow is Saint Valentine's day,   [*Song.*] 50
    All in the morning betime,°
  And I a maid at your window,
    To be your Valentine.
  Then up he rose, and donned his clothes,
    And dupped° the chamber door,   55
  Let in the maid, that out a maid
    Never departed more."

KING: Pretty Ophelia—

OPHELIA: Indeed, la, without an oath, I'll make an end on 't: [*Sings.*]
   "By Gis° and by Saint Charity,   60
    Alack, and fie for shame!
  Young men will do 't, if they come to 't;
    By Cock,° they are to blame.
  Quoth she, 'Before you tumbled me,
    You promised me to wed.' "   65
  He answers:
   " 'So would I ha' done, by yonder sun,
    An° thou hadst not come to my bed.' "

KING: How long hath she been thus?

OPHELIA: I hope all will be well. We must be patient, but I cannot choose but 70
  weep to think they would lay him i' the cold ground. My brother shall
  know of it. And so I thank you for your good counsel. Come, my coach!
  Good night, ladies, good night, sweet ladies, good night, good night.

[*Exit.*]

KING [*to* HORATIO]:   Follow her close. Give her good watch, I pray you.

                  [*Exit* HORATIO.]

  O, this is the poison of deep grief; it springs   75
  All from her father's death—and now behold!
  O Gertrude, Gertrude,
  When sorrows come, they come not single spies,°

---

44 God 'ild God yield or reward **owl** (Refers to a legend about a baker's daughter who was turned into an owl for being ungenerous when Jesus begged a loaf of bread.) **47 Conceit** brooding **51 betime** early **55 dupped** did up, opened **60 Gis** Jesus **63 Cock** (A perversion of "God" in oaths; here also with a quibble on the slang word for penis.) **68 An** if **78 spies** scouts sent in advance of the main force

But in battalions. First, her father slain;
Next, your son gone, and he most violent author   80
Of his own just remove;° the people muddied,°
Thick and unwholesome in their thoughts and whispers
For good Polonius' death—and we have done but greenly,°
In hugger-mugger° to inter him; poor Ophelia
Divided from herself and her fair judgment,   85
Without the which we are pictures or mere beasts;
Last, and as much containing° as all these,
Her brother is in secret come from France,
Feeds on this wonder, keeps himself in clouds,°
And wants° not buzzers° to infect his ear   90
With pestilent speeches of his father's death,
Wherein necessity,° of matter beggared,°
Will nothing stick our person to arraign
In ear and ear.° O my dear Gertrude, this,
Like to a murdering piece,° in many places   95
Gives me superfluous death.°   [*A noise within.*]

QUEEN: Alack, what noise is this?
KING: Attend!°
Where is my Switzers?° Let them guard the door.

[*Enter* MESSENGER.]

What is the matter?   100
MESSENGER: Save yourself, my lord!
The ocean, overpeering of his list,°
Eats not the flats° with more impetuous° haste
Than young Laertes, in a riotous head,°
O'erbears your officers. The rabble call him lord,   105
And, as° the world were now but to begin,
Antiquity forgot, custom not known,
The ratifiers and props of every word,°

81 **remove** removal   **muddied** stirred up, confused   83 **greenly** in an inexperienced way, foolishly   84 **hugger-mugger** secret haste   87 **as much containing** as full of serious matter   89 **Feeds…clouds** feeds his resentment or shocked grievance, holds himself inscrutable and aloof amid all this rumor   90 **wants** lacks   **buzzers** gossipers, informers   92 **necessity** i.e., the need to invent some plausible explanation   **of matter beggared** unprovided with facts   93–94 **Will…ear** will not hesitate to accuse my (royal) person in everybody's ears   93 **murdering piece** cannon loaded so as to scatter its shot   96 **Gives…death** kills me over and over   98 **Attend** i.e., guard me   99 **Switzers** Swiss guards, mercenaries   102 **overpeering of his list** overflowing its shore, boundary   103 **flats** i.e., flatlands near shore   **impetuous** violent (perhaps also with the meaning of *impiteous* [*impitious*, Q2], "pitiless.")   104 **head** insurrection   106 **as** as if   108 **The ratifiers…word** i.e., *antiquity* (or tradition) and *custom* ought to confirm (*ratify*) and underprop our every word or promise

They cry, "Choose we! Laertes shall be king!"

Caps,° hands, and tongues applaud it to the clouds,   110

"Laertes shall be king, Laertes king!"

QUEEN: How cheerfully on the false trail they cry!   [*A noise within.*]

O, this is counter,° you false Danish dogs!

[*Enter* LAERTES *with others.*]

KING: The doors are broke.

LAERTES: Where is this King?—Sirs, stand you all without.   115

ALL: No, let's come in.

LAERTES: I pray you, give me leave.

ALL: We will, we will.

LAERTES: I thank you. Keep the door. [*Exeunt followers.*] O thou vile king,

Give me my father!   120

QUEEN [*restraining him*]:   Calmly, good Laertes.

LAERTES: That drop of blood that's calm proclaims me bastard,

Cries cuckold to my father, brands the harlot

Even here, between° the chaste unsmirchèd brow

Of my true mother.   125

KING: What is the cause, Laertes,

That thy rebellion looks so giantlike?

Let him go, Gertrude. Do not fear our° person.

There's such divinity doth hedge° a king

That treason can but peep to what it would,°   130

Acts little of his will.° Tell me, Laertes,

Why thou art thus incensed. Let him go, Gertrude.

Speak, man.

LAERTES: Where is my father?

KING: Dead.   135

QUEEN: But not by him.

KING: Let him demand his fill.

LAERTES: How came he dead? I'll not be juggled with.°

To hell, allegiance! Vows, to the blackest devil!

Conscience and grace, to the profoundest pit!   140

I dare damnation. To this point I stand,°

That both the worlds I give to negligence,°

---

110 Caps (The caps are thrown in the air.)   **113 counter** (A hunting term, meaning to follow the trail in a direction opposite to that which the game has taken.)   **128 fear our** fear for my   **129 hedge** protect, as with a surrounding barrier   **130 can...would** can only peep to what it would intend   **131 Acts...will** (but) performs little of what it intends   **138 juggled with** cheated, deceived   **141 To...stand** I am resolved in this   **142 both...negligence** i.e., both this world and the next are of no consequence to me

Let come what comes, only I'll be revenged
Most throughly° for my father.

KING: Who shall stay you?   145

LAERTES: My will, not all the world's.°
And for° my means, I'll husband them so well
They shall go far with little.

KING: Good Laertes,
If you desire to know the certainty   150
Of your dear father, is 't writ in your revenge
That, swoopstake,° you will draw both friend and foe,
Winner and loser?

LAERTES: None but his enemies.

KING: Will you know them, then?   155

LAERTES: To his good friends thus wide I'll ope my arms,
And like the kind life-rendering pelican°
Repast° them with my blood.

KING: Why, now you speak
Like a good child and a true gentleman.   160
That I am guiltless of your father's death,
And am most sensibly° in grief for it,
It shall as level° to your judgment 'pear
As day does to your eye.   [*A noise within.*]

LAERTES: How now, what noise is that?   165

[*Enter* OPHELIA.]

KING: Let her come in.

LAERTES: O heat, dry up my brains! Tears seven times salt
Burn out the sense and virtue° of mine eye!
By heaven, thy madness shall be paid with weight°
Till our scale turn the beam.° O rose of May!   170
Dear maid, kind sister, sweet Ophelia!
O heavens, is 't possible a young maid's wits
Should be as mortal as an old man's life?
Nature is fine in° love, and where 'tis fine
It sends some precious instance° of itself   175
After the thing it loves.°

---

144 **throughly** thoroughly   146 **My will...world's** I'll stop (stay) when my will is accomplished, not for anyone else's   147 **for** as for   152 **swoopstake** i.e., indiscriminately (Literally, taking all stakes on the gambling table at once. *Draw* is also a gambling term, meaning "take from.")   157 **pelican** (Refers to the belief that the female pelican fed its young with its own blood.)   158 **Repast** feed   162 **sensibly** feelingly   163 **level** plain   168 **virtue** faculty, power   169 **paid with weight** repaid, avenged equally or more   170 **beam** crossbar of a balance   174 **fine in** refined by   175 **instance** token   176 **After... loves** i.e., into the grave, along with Polonius

OPHELIA: [*Song.*]

> "They bore him barefaced on the bier,
>   Hey non nonny, nonny, hey nonny,
>   And in his grave rained many a tear—"
> Fare you well, my dove!   180

LAERTES: Hadst thou thy wits and didst persuade° revenge,
    It could not move thus.

OPHELIA: You must sing "A-down a-down," and you "call him a-down-a."°
    O, how the wheel° becomes it! It is the false steward° that stole his
    master's daughter.   185

LAERTES: This nothing's more than matter.°

OPHELIA: There's rosemary,° that's for remembrance; pray you, love, remember.
    And there is pansies;° that's for thoughts.

LAERTES: A document° in madness, thoughts and remembrance fitted.

OPHELIA: There's fennel° for you, and columbines.° There's rue° for you,   190
    and here's some for me; we may call it herb of grace o' Sundays. You
    must wear your rue with a difference.° There's a daisy.°
    I would give you some violets,° but they withered all when my father
    died. They say 'a made a good end—
    [*Sings.*] "For bonny sweet Robin is all my joy."   195

LAERTES: Thought° and affliction, passion,° hell itself,
    She turns to favor° and to prettiness.

OPHELIA: [*Song.*]

> "And will 'a not come again?
> And will 'a not come again?
>   No, no, he is dead.   200
>   Go to thy deathbed,
> He never will come again.
> "His beard was as white as snow,
> All flaxen was his poll.°

---

181 persuade argue cogently for   **183 You...a-down-a** (Ophelia assigns the singing
of refrains, like her own "Hey non nonny," to others present.)   **184 wheel** spinning
wheel as accompaniment to the song, or refrain   **false steward** (The story is unknown.)
186 This...matter this seeming nonsense is more eloquent than sane utterance
187 rosemary (Used as a symbol of remembrance both at weddings and at funerals.)
188 pansies (Emblems of love and courtship; perhaps from French *pensées*,
"thoughts.")   **189 document** instruction, lesson   **190 fennel** (Emblem of flattery.)
columbines (Emblems of unchastity or ingratitude.)   **rue** (Emblem of repentance—a sig-
nification that is evident in its popular name, *herb of grace*.)   **192 with a difference** (A
device used in heraldry to distinguish one family from another on the coat of arms, here
suggesting that Ophelia and the others have different causes of sorrow and repentance;
perhaps with a play on rue in the sense of "ruth," "pity.")   **daisy** (Emblem of dissem-
bling, faithlessness.)   **193 violets** (Emblems of faithfulness.)   **196 Thought** melancholy
passion suffering   **197 favor** grace, beauty   **204 poll** head

> He is gone, he is gone,   205
> And we cast away moan.
> God ha' mercy on his soul!"
> And of all Christian souls, I pray God. God b' wi' you.

[*Exit, followed by* GERTRUDE.]

LAERTES: Do you see this, O God?

KING: Laertes, I must commune with your grief,   210
  Or you deny me right. Go but apart,
  Make choice of whom° your wisest friends you will,
  And they shall hear and judge twixt you and me.
  If by direct or by collateral hand°
  They find us touched,° we will our kingdom give,   215
  Our crown, our life, and all that we call ours
  To you in satisfaction; but if not,
  Be you content to lend your patience to us,
  And we shall jointly labor with your soul
  To give it due content.   220

LAERTES: Let this be so.
  His means of death, his obscure funeral—
  No trophy,° sword, nor hatchment° o'er his bones,
  No noble rite, nor formal ostentation°—
  Cry to be heard, as 'twere from heaven to earth,   225
  That° I must call 't in question.°

KING: So you shall,
  And where th' offense is, let the great ax fall.
  I pray you, go with me.

[*Exeunt.*]

[**Act 4.6** *Enter* HORATIO *and others.*]°

HORATIO: What are they that would speak with me?

GENTLEMAN: Seafaring men, sir. They say they have letters for you.

HORATIO: Let them come in.

                                                    [*Exit* GENTLEMAN.]

  I do not know from what part of the world
  I should be greeted, if not from Lord Hamlet.   5

[*Enter* SAILORS.]

---

212 whom whichever of   **214 collateral hand** indirect agency   **215 us touched** me implicated   **223 trophy** memorial   **hatchment** tablet displaying the armorial bearings of a deceased person   **224 ostentation** ceremony   **226 That** so that   **call 't in question** demand an explanation   **4.6 s.d. Location: The castle**

FIRST SAILOR: God bless you, sir.

HORATIO: Let him bless thee too.

FIRST SAILOR: 'A shall, sir, an 't° please him. There's a letter for you, sir—it
came from th' ambassador° that was bound for England—if your name
be Horatio, as I am let to know it is.   [*He gives a letter.*]   10

HORATIO [*reads*]:   "Horatio, when thou shalt have overlooked° this, give these
fellows some means° to the King; they have letters for him. Ere we were
two days old at sea, a pirate of very warlike appointment° gave us chase.
Finding ourselves too slow of sail, we put on a compelled valor, and in
the grapple I boarded them. On the instant they got clear of our ship, so   15
I alone became their prisoner. They have dealt with me like thieves of
mercy,° but they knew what they did: I am to do a good turn for them.
Let the King have the letters I have sent, and repair° thou to me with as
much speed as thou wouldest fly death. I have words to speak in thine
ear will make thee dumb, yet are they much too light for the bore° of   20
the matter. These good fellows will bring thee where I am. Rosencrantz
and Guildenstern hold their course for England. Of them I have much
to tell thee. Farewell.

                         He that thou knowest thine, Hamlet."

Come, I will give you way° for these your letters,   25
And do 't the speedier that you may direct me
To him from whom you brought them.

[*Exeunt.*]

[**Act 4.7** *Enter* KING *and* LAERTES.]°

KING: Now must your conscience my acquittance seal,°
And you must put me in your heart for friend,
Sith° you have heard, and with a knowing ear,
That he which hath your noble father slain
Pursued my life.   5

LAERTES: It well appears. But tell me
Why you proceeded not against these feats°
So crimeful and so capital° in nature,
As by your safety, greatness, wisdom, all things else,
You mainly° were stirred up.   10

---

8 an't if it   **9 th' ambassador** (Evidently Hamlet. The sailor is being circumspect.)
11 overlooked looked over   **12 means** means of access   **13 appointment** equi-
page   **16–17 thieves of mercy** merciful thieves   **18 repair** come   **20 bore** caliber, i.e.,
importance   **25 way** means of access   **4.7 s.d.** Location: The castle   **1 my acquittance
seal** confirm or acknowledge my innocence   **3 Sith** since   **7 feats** acts   **8 capital** pun-
ishable by death   **10 mainly** greatly

KING: O, for two special reasons,
   Which may to you perhaps seem much unsinewed,°
   But yet to me they're strong. The Queen his mother
   Lives almost by his looks, and for myself—
   My virtue or my plague, be it either which—   15
   She is so conjunctive° to my life and soul
   That, as the star moves not but in his° sphere,°
   I could not but by her. The other motive
   Why to a public count° I might not go
   Is the great love the general gender° bear him,   20
   Who, dipping all his faults in their affection,
   Work° like the spring° that turneth wood to stone,
   Convert his gyves° to graces, so that my arrows,
   Too slightly timbered° for so loud° a wind,
   Would have reverted° to my bow again   25
   But not where I had aimed them.

LAERTES: And so have I a noble father lost,
   A sister driven into desperate terms,°
   Whose worth, if praises may go back° again,
   Stood challenger on mount° of all the age   30
   For her perfections. But my revenge will come.

KING: Break not your sleeps for that. You must not think
   That we are made of stuff so flat and dull
   That we can let our beard be shook with danger
   And think it pastime. You shortly shall hear more.   35
   I loved your father, and we love ourself;
   And that, I hope, will teach you to imagine—

[*Enter* MESSENGER *with letters.*]

   How now? What news?

MESSENGER: Letters, my lord, from Hamlet:
   This to Your Majesty, this to the Queen.   40

[*He gives letters.*]

---

12 unsinewed weak **16 conjunctive** closely united (An astronomical metaphor.) **17 his** its **sphere** one of the hollow spheres in which, according to Ptolematic astronomy, the planets were supposed to move **19 count** account, reckoning, indictment **20 general gender** common people **22 Work** operate, act **spring** i.e., a spring with such a concentration of lime that it coats a piece of wood with limestone, in effect gilding and petrifying it **23 gyves** fetters (which, gilded by the people's praise, would look like badges of honor) **24 slightly timbered** light **24 loud** (suggesting public outcry on Hamlet's behalf) **25 reverted** returned **28 terms** state, condition **29 go back** i.e., recall what she was **30 on mount** set up on high

KING: From Hamlet? Who brought them?

MESSENGER: Sailors, my lord, they say. I saw them not.
They were given me by Claudio. He received them
Of him that brought them.

KING: Laertes, you shall hear them.—   45
Leave us.

[*Exit* MESSENGER.]

[*He reads.*] "High and mighty, you shall know I am set naked° on your
kingdom. Tomorrow shall I beg leave to see your kingly eyes, when I
shall, first asking your pardon,° thereunto recount the occasion of my
sudden and more strange return.   Hamlet."   50
What should this mean? Are all the rest come back?
Or is it some abuse,° and no such thing?°

LAERTES: Know you the hand?

KING: 'Tis Hamlet's character.° "Naked!"
And in a postscript here he says "alone."   55
Can you devise° me?

LAERTES: I am lost in it, my lord. But let him come.
It warms the very sickness in my heart
That I shall live and tell him to his teeth,
"Thus didst thou."°   60

KING: If it be so, Laertes—
As how should it be so? How otherwise?°—
Will you be ruled by me?

LAERTES: Ay, my lord,
So° you will not o'errule me to a peace.   65

KING: To thine own peace. If he be now returned,
As checking at° his voyage, and that° he means
No more to undertake it, I will work him
To an exploit, now ripe in my device,°
Under the which he shall not choose but fall;   70
And for his death no wind of blame shall breathe,
But even his mother shall uncharge the practice°
And call it accident.

LAERTES: My lord, I will be ruled,

---

47 naked destitute, unarmed, without following   **49 pardon** permission   **502 abuse**
deceit   **no such thing** not what it appears   **54 character** handwriting   **56 devise**
explain to   **60 Thus didst thou** i.e., here's for what you did to my father   **61 As...
otherwise** how can this (Hamlet's return) be true? Yet how otherwise than true (since we
have the evidence of his letter)?   **65 So** provided that   **67 checking at** i.e., turning aside
from (like a falcon leaving the quarry to fly at a chance bird)   **that** if   **69 device** devising,
invention   **72 uncharge the practice** acquit the stratagem of being a plot

The rather if you could devise it so   75
That I might be the organ.°

KING: It falls right.
You have been talked of since your travel much,
And that in Hamlet's hearing, for a quality
Wherein they say you shine. Your sum of parts°   80
Did not together pluck such envy from him
As did that one, and that, in my regard,
Of the unworthiest siege.°

LAERTES: What part is that, my lord?

KING: A very ribbon in the cap of youth,   85
Yet needful too, for youth no less becomes°
The light and careless livery that it wears
Than settled age his sables° and his weeds°
Importing health and graveness.° Two months since
Here was a gentleman of Normandy.   90
I have seen myself, and served against, the French,
And they can well° on horseback, but this gallant
Had witchcraft in 't; he grew unto his seat,
And to such wondrous doing brought his horse
As had he been incorpsed and demi-natured°   95
With the brave beast. So far he topped° my thought
That I in forgery° of shapes and tricks
Come short of what he did.

LAERTES: A Norman was 't?

KING: A Norman.   100

LAERTES: Upon my life, Lamord.

KING: The very same.

LAERTES: I know him well. He is the brooch° indeed
And gem of all the nation.

KING: He made confession° of you,   105
And gave you such a masterly report
For art and exercise in your defense,°
And for your rapier most especial,

76 organ agent, instrument   **80 Your…parts** i.e., all your other virtues   **83 unworthiest siege** least important rank   **86 no less becomes** is no less suited by   **88 his sables**
its rich robes furred with sable   **weeds** garments   **89 Importing…graveness** signifying
a concern for health and dignified prosperity; also, giving an impression of comfortable
prosperity   **92 can well** are skilled   **95 As…demi-natured** as if he had been of one
body and nearly of one nature (like the centaur)   **96 topped** surpassed   **97 forgery**
imagining   **103 brooch** ornament   **105 confession** testimonial, admission of superiority   **107 For…defense** with respect to your skill and practice with your weapon

That he cried out 'twould be a sight indeed
If one could match you. Th' escrimers° of their nation,   110
He swore, had neither motion, guard, nor eye
If you opposed them. Sir, this report of his
Did Hamlet so envenom with his envy
That he could nothing do but wish and beg
Your sudden° coming o'er, to play° with you.   115
Now, out of this—

LAERTES: What out of this, my lord?

KING: Laertes, was your father dear to you?
Or are you like the painting of a sorrow,
A face without a heart?   120

LAERTES: Why ask you this?

KING: Not that I think you did not love your father,
But that I know love is begun by time,°
And that I see, in passages of proof,°
Time qualifies° the spark and fire of it.   125
There lives within the very flame of love
A kind of wick or snuff° that will abate it,
And nothing is at a like goodness still,°
For goodness, growing to a pleurisy,°
Dies in his own too much.° That° we would do,   130
We should do when we would; for this "would" changes
And hath abatements° and delays as many
As there are tongues, are hands, are accidents,°
And then this "should" is like a spendthrift sigh,°
That hurts by easing.° But, to the quick o' th' ulcer:°   135
Hamlet comes back. What would you undertake
To show yourself in deed your father's son
More than in words?

LAERTES: To cut his throat i' the church.

---

110 escrimers fencers   **115 sudden** immediate   **play** fence   **123 begun by time**
i.e., created by the right circumstance and hence subject to change   **124 passages of**
proof actual instances that prove it   **125 qualifies** weakens, moderates   **127 snuff**
the charred part of a candlewick   **128 nothing...still** nothing remains at a constant
level of perfection   **129 pleurisy** excess, plethora (Literally, a chest inflammation.)
130 in...much of its own excess   **That** that which   **132 abatements** diminutions
133 As...accidents as there are tongues to dissuade, hands to prevent, and chance
events to intervene   **134 spendthrift sigh** (An allusion to the belief that sighs draw
blood from the heart.)   **135 hurts by easing** i.e., costs the heart blood and wastes precious opportunity even while it affords emotional relief   **quick o' th' ulcer i.e.,** heart
of the matter

KING: No place, indeed, should murder sanctuarize;°   140
   Revenge should have no bounds. But good Laertes,
   Will you do this,° keep close within your chamber.
   Hamlet returned shall know you are come home.
   We'll put on those shall° praise your excellence
   And set a double varnish on the fame   145
   The Frenchman gave you, bring you in fine° together,
   And wager on your heads. He, being remiss,°
   Most generous,° and free from all contriving,
   Will not peruse the foils, so that with ease,
   Or with a little shuffling, you may choose   150
   A sword unbated,° and in a pass of practice°
   Requite him for your father.

LAERTES: I will do 't,
   And for that purpose I'll anoint my sword.
   I bought an unction° of a mountebank°   155
   So mortal that, but dip a knife in it,
   Where it draws blood no cataplasm° so rare,
   Collected from all simples° that have virtue°
   Under the moon,° can save the thing from death
   That is but scratched withal. I'll touch my point   160
   With this contagion, that if I gall° him slightly,
   It may be death.

KING: Let's further think of this,
   Weigh what convenience both of time and means
   May fit us to our shape.° If this should fail,   165
   And that our drift look through our bad performance,°
   'Twere better not assayed. Therefore this project
   Should have a back or second, that might hold
   If this did blast in proof.° Soft, let me see.
   We'll make a solemn wager on your cunnings°—   170
   I ha 't!

---

140 sanctuarize protect from punishment (Alludes to the right of sanctuary with which certain religious places were invested.) **142 Will you do this** if you wish to do this **144 put on those shall** arrange for some to **146 in fine** finally **147 remiss** negligently unsuspicious **148 generous** noble-minded **151 unbated** not blunted, having no button **pass of practice** treacherous thrust **155 unction** ointment **mountebank** quack doctor **157 cataplasm** plaster or poultice **158 simples** herbs **virtue** potency **159 Under the moon** i.e., anywhere (with reference perhaps to the belief that herbs gathered at night had a special power) **161 gall** graze, wound **165 shape** part we propose to act **166 drift...performance** intention should be made visible by our bungling **169 blast in proof** burst in the test (like a cannon) **170 cunnings** respective skills

When in your motion you are hot and dry—
As° make your bouts more violent to that end—
And that he calls for drink, I'll have prepared him
A chalice for the nonce,° whereon but sipping,   175
If he by chance escape your venomed stuck,°
Our purpose may hold there. [*A cry within.*] But stay, what noise?

[*Enter* QUEEN.]

QUEEN: One woe doth tread upon another's heel,
So fast they follow. Your sister's drowned, Laertes.
LAERTES: Drowned! O, where?   180
QUEEN: There is a willow grows askant° the brook,
That shows his hoar leaves° in the glassy stream;
Therewith fantastic garlands did she make
Of crowflowers, nettles, daisies, and long purples,°
That liberal° shepherds give a grosser name,°   185
But our cold° maids do dead men's fingers call them.
There on the pendent° boughs her crownet° weeds
Clamb'ring to hang, an envious sliver° broke,
When down her weedy° trophies and herself
Fell in the weeping brook. Her clothes spread wide,   190
And mermaidlike awhile they bore her up,
Which time she chanted snatches of old lauds,°
As one incapable of° her own distress,
Or like a creature native and endued°
Unto that element. But long it could not be   195
Till that her garments, heavy with their drink,
Pulled the poor wretch from her melodious lay
To muddy death.
LAERTES: Alas, then she is drowned?
QUEEN: Drowned, drowned.   200
LAERTES: Too much of water hast thou, poor Ophelia,
And therefore I forbid my tears. But yet
It is our trick;° nature her custom holds,

---

173 As i.e., and you should   **175 nonce** occasion   **176 stuck** thrust (From *stoccado,*
a fencing term.)   **181 askant** aslant   **182 hoar leaves** white or gray undersides of
the leaves   **184 long purples** early purple orchids   **185 liberal** free-spoken   **a
grosser name** (The testicle-resembling tubers of the orchid, which also in some cases resemble *dead men's fingers,* have earned various slang names like "dogstones" and
"cullions.")   **186 cold** chaste   **187 pendent** over-hanging   **crownet** made into a chaplet
or coronet   **188 envious sliver** malicious branch   **189 weedy** i.e., of plants   **192 lauds**
hymns   **193 incapable of** lacking capacity to apprehend   **194 endued** adapted by nature   **203 It is our trick** i.e., weeping is our natural way (when sad)

Let shame say what it will. [*He weeps.*] When these are gone,
The woman will be out.° Adieu, my lord.   205
I have a speech of fire that fain would blaze,
But that this folly douts° it.   [*Exit.*]

KING: Let's follow, Gertrude.
How much I had to do to calm his rage!
Now fear I this will give it start again;   210
Therefore let's follow.

[*Exeunt.*]

[**Act 5.1** *Enter two* CLOWNS° *(with spades and mattocks).*]°

FIRST CLOWN: Is she to be buried in Christian burial, when she willfully seeks
her own salvation?°

SECOND CLOWN: I tell thee she is; therefore make her grave straight.° The
crowner° hath sat on her,° and finds it° Christian burial.

FIRST CLOWN: How can that be, unless she drowned herself in her own defense?   5

SECOND CLOWN: Why, 'tis found so.°

FIRST CLOWN: It must be *se offendendo*,° it cannot be else. For here lies the
point: if I drown myself wittingly, it argues an act, and an act hath
three branches—it is to act, to do, and to perform. Argal,° she drowned
herself wittingly.   10

SECOND CLOWN: Nay, but hear you, goodman° delver—

FIRST CLOWN: Give me leave. Here lies the water; good. Here stands the man;
good. If the man go to this water and drown himself, it is, will he, nill
he,° he goes, mark you that. But if the water come to him and drown
him, he drowns not himself. Argal, he that is not guilty of his own death   15
shortens not his own life.

SECOND CLOWN: But is this law?

FIRST CLOWN: Ay, marry, is 't—crowner's quest° law.

SECOND CLOWN: Will you ha' the truth on 't? If this had not been a gentle-
woman, she should have been buried out o' Christian burial.   20

204–205 When...out when my tears are all shed, the woman in me will be expended,
satisfied   **207 douts** extinguishes (The Second Quarto reads "drowns.")   **5.1 s.d. Location: A churchyard Clowns** rustics   **2 salvation** (A blunder for "damnation," or perhaps
a suggestion that Ophelia was taking her own shortcut to heaven.)   **3 straight** straightway, immediately (But with a pun on *strait*, "narrow.")   **4 crowner** coroner   **sat on her**
conducted an inquest on her case   **finds it** gives his official verdict that her means of
death was consistent with   **6 found so** determined so in the coroner's verdict   **7 *se offendendo*** (A comic mistake for *se defendendo*, a term used in verdicts of justifiable homicide.)   **9 Argal** (Corruption of *ergo*, "therefore.")   **11 goodman** (An honorific title often
used with the name of a profession or craft.)   **13–14 will he, nill he** whether he will or
no, willy-nilly   **18 quest** inquest

FIRST CLOWN: Why, there thou sayst.° And the more pity that great folk should have countenance° in this world to drown or hang themselves, more than their even-Christian.° Come, my spade. There is no ancient° gentlemen but gardeners, ditchers, and grave makers. They hold up° Adam's profession.   25

SECOND CLOWN: Was he a gentleman?

FIRST CLOWN: 'A was the first that ever bore arms.°

SECOND CLOWN: Why, he had none.

FIRST CLOWN: What, art a heathen? How dost thou understand the Scripture? The Scripture says Adam digged. Could he dig without arms?° I'll put   30 another question to thee. If thou answerest me not to the purpose, confess thyself°—

SECOND CLOWN: Go to.

FIRST CLOWN: What is he that builds stronger than either the mason, the ship-wright, or the carpenter?   35

SECOND CLOWN: The gallows maker, for that frame° outlives a thousand tenants.

FIRST CLOWN: I like thy wit well, in good faith. The gallows does well.° But how does it well? It does well to those that do ill. Now thou dost ill to say the gallows is built stronger than the church. Argal, the gallows may do well to thee. To 't again, come.   40

SECOND CLOWN: "Who builds stronger than a mason, a shipwright, or a carpenter?"

FIRST CLOWN: Ay, tell me that, and unyoke.°

SECOND CLOWN: Marry, now I can tell.

FIRST CLOWN: To 't.   45

SECOND CLOWN: Mass,° I cannot tell.

[*Enter* HAMLET *and* HORATIO *(at a distance).*]

FIRST CLOWN: Cudgel thy brains no more about it, for your dull ass will not mend his pace with beating; and when you are asked this question next, say "a grave maker." The houses he makes lasts till doomsday. Go get thee in and fetch me a stoup° of liquor.   50

[*Exit* SECOND CLOWN. FIRST CLOWN *digs.*]

[*Song.*]

---

21 there thou sayst i.e., that's right   **22 countenance** privilege   **23 even-Christian** fellow Christians   **ancient** going back to ancient times   **24 hold up** maintain   **27 bore arms** (To be entitled to bear a coat of arms would make Adam a gentleman, but as one who bore a spade, our common ancestor was an ordinary delver in the earth.)   **30 arms** i.e., the arms of the body   **32 confess thyself** (The saying continues, "and be hanged.")   **36 frame** (1) gallows (2) structure   **37 does well** (1) is an apt answer (2) does a good turn   **43 unyoke** i.e., after this great effort, you may unharness the team of your wits   **46 Mass** by the Mass   **50 stoup** two-quart measure

"In youth, when I did love, did love,°
    Methought it was very sweet,
        To contract—O—the time for—a—my behove,°
    O, methought there—a—was nothing—a—meet."°

HAMLET: Has this fellow no feeling of his business, 'a° sings in gravemaking?   55

HORATIO: Custom hath made it in him a property of easiness.°

HAMLET: 'Tis e'en so. The hand of little employment hath the daintier sense.°

FIRST CLOWN: [*Song.*]

    "But age with his stealing steps
        Hath clawed me in his clutch,
        And hath shipped me into the land,°   60
        As if I had never been such."

[*He throws up a skull.*]

HAMLET: That skull had a tongue in it and could sing once. How the knave
    jowls° it to the ground, as if 'twere Cain's jawbone, that did the first
    murder! This might be the pate of a politician,° which this ass now
    o'er-reaches,° one that would circumvent God, might it not?   65

HORATIO: It might, my lord.

HAMLET: Or of a courtier, which could say, "Good morrow, sweet lord! How
    dost thou, sweet lord?" This might be my Lord Such-a-one, that praised
    my Lord Such-a-one's horse when 'a meant to beg it, might it not?

HORATIO: Ay, my lord.   70

HAMLET: Why, e'en so, and now my Lady Worm's, chapless,° and knocked
    about the mazard° with a sexton's spade. Here's fine revolution,° an°
    we had the trick to see° 't. Did these bones cost no more the breeding
    but° to play at loggets° with them? Mine ache to think on 't.

FIRST CLOWN: [*Song.*]

    "A pickax and a spade, a spade,   75
        For and° a shrouding sheet;
        O, a pit of clay for to be made
        For such a guest is meet."

51 In…love (This and the two following stanzas, with nonsensical variations, are from a poem attributed to Lord Vaux and printed in *Tottel's Miscellany,* 1557. The *O* and *a* [for "ah"] seemingly are the grunts of the digger.) **53 To contract…behove** i.e., to shorten the time for my own advantage (Perhaps he means to *prolong* it.) **54 meet** suitable, i.e., more suitable **55 'a** that he **56 property of easiness** something he can do easily and indifferently **57 daintier sense** more delicate sense of feeling **60 into the land** i.e., toward my grave (But note the lack of rhyme in *steps, land.*) **63 jowls** dashes (with a pun on *jowl,* "jawbone") **64 politician** schemer, plotter **65 o'erreaches** circumvents, gets the better of (with a quibble on the literal sense) **71 chapless** having no lower jaw **72 mazard** i.e., head (Literally, a drinking vessel.) **revolution** turn of Fortune's wheel, change **an** if **73 trick to see** knack of seeing **cost…but** involve so little expense and care in upbringing that we may **74 loggets** a game in which pieces of hard wood shaped like Indian clubs or bowling pins are thrown to lie as near as possible to a stake **76 For and** and moreover

[*He throws up another skull.*]

HAMLET: There's another. Why may not that be the skull of a lawyer? Where
be his quiddities° now, his quillities,° his cases, his tenures,° and his   80
tricks? Why does he suffer this mad knave now to knock him about the
sconce° with a dirty shovel, and will not tell him of his action of battery?° Hum, this fellow might be in 's time a great buyer of land, with his
statutes, his recognizances,° his fines, his double° vouchers,° his recoveries.° Is this the fine of his fines and the recovery of his recoveries, to   85
have his fine pate full of fine dirt?° Will his vouchers vouch him no more
of his purchases, and double ones too, than the length and breadth of a
pair of indentures?° The very conveyances° of his lands will scarcely lie
in this box,° and must th' inheritor° himself have no more, ha?

HORATIO: Not a jot more, my lord.   90

HAMLET: Is not parchment made of sheepskins?

HORATIO: Ay, my lord, and of calves' skins too.

HAMLET: They are sheep and calves which seek out assurance in that.° I will
speak to this fellow.—Whose grave's this, sirrah?°

FIRST CLOWN: Mine, sir.   [*Sings.*]   95
"O, pit of clay for to be made
For such a guest is meet."

HAMLET: I think it be thine, indeed, for thou liest in 't.

FIRST CLOWN: You lie out on 't, sir, and therefore 'tis not yours. For my part,
I do not lie in 't, yet it is mine.   100

HAMLET: Thou dost lie in 't, to be in 't and say it is thine. 'Tis for the dead,
not for the quick;° therefore thou liest.

FIRST CLOWN: 'Tis a quick lie, sir; 'twill away again from me to you.

HAMLET: What man dost thou dig it for?

FIRST CLOWN: For no man, sir.   105

HAMLET: What woman, then?

80 quiddities subtleties, quibbles (From Latin *quid,* "a thing.") **quillities** verbal
niceties, subtle distinctions (Variation of *quiddities.*) **tenures** the holding of a piece of
property or office, or the conditions or period of such holding   **82 sconce** head   **82
action of battery** lawsuit about physical assault   **84 statutes...recognizances** legal
documents guaranteeing a debt by attaching land and property   **84 double** signed by
two signatories   **vouchers** guarantees of the legality of a title to real estate   **fines...
recoveries** ways of converting entailed estates into "fee simple" or freehold   **85–86
fine of his fines...fine pate...fine dirt** end of his legal maneuvers...elegant head...
minutely sifted dirt   **88 pair of indentures** legal document drawn up in duplicate on a
single sheet and then cut apart on a zigzag line so that each pair was uniquely matched
(Hamlet may refer to two rows of teeth or dentures.)   **88 conveyances** deeds   **89 box** (1)
deed box (2) coffin ("Skull" has been suggested.)   **89 inheritor** possessor, owner
93 assurance in that safety in legal parchments   **94 sirrah** (A term of address to inferi-
ors.)   **102 quick** living

FIRST CLOWN: For none, neither.

HAMLET: Who is to be buried in 't?

FIRST CLOWN: One that was a woman, sir, but, rest her soul, she's dead.

HAMLET: How absolute° the knave is! We must speak by the card,° or   110
equivocation° will undo us. By the Lord, Horatio, this three years I
have took° note of it: the age is grown so picked° that the toe of the
peasant comes so near the heel of the courtier, he galls his kibe.°—
How long hast thou been grave maker?

FIRST CLOWN: Of all the days i' the year, I came to 't that day that our last king   115
Hamlet overcame Fortinbras.

HAMLET: How long is that since?

FIRST CLOWN: Cannot you tell that? Every fool can tell that. It was that very
day that young Hamlet was born—he that is mad and sent into England.

HAMLET: Ay, marry, why was he sent into England?   120

FIRST CLOWN: Why, because 'a was mad. 'A shall recover his wits there, or if
'a do not, 'tis no great matter there.

HAMLET: Why?

FIRST CLOWN: 'Twill not be seen in him there. There the men are as mad as he.

HAMLET: How came he mad?   125

FIRST CLOWN: Very strangely, they say.

HAMLET: How strangely?

FIRST CLOWN: Faith, e'en with losing his wits.

HAMLET: Upon what ground?°

FIRST CLOWN: Why, here in Denmark. I have been sexton here, man and boy,   130
thirty years.

HAMLET: How long will a man lie i' th' earth ere he rot?

FIRST CLOWN: Faith, if 'a be not rotten before 'a die—as we have many pocky°
corpses nowadays, that will scarce hold the laying in°—'a will last you°
some eight year or nine year. A tanner will last you nine year.   135

HAMLET: Why he more than another?

FIRST CLOWN: Why, sir, his hide is so tanned with his trade that 'a will keep
out water a great while, and your water is a sore° decayer of your

---

110 absolute strict, precise **by the card** i.e., with precision (Literally, by the mariner's
compass-card, on which the points of the compass were marked.) **111 equivocation**
ambiguity in the use of terms **112 took** taken **picked** refined, fastidious **113 galls his
kibe** chafes the courtier's chilblain **129 ground** cause (But, in the next line, the gravedigger takes the word in the sense of "land," "country.") **133 pocky** rotten, diseased
(Literally, with the pox, or syphilis.) **134 hold the laying in** hold together long enough
to be interred **134 last you** last (*You* is used colloquially here and in the following
lines.) **138 sore** i.e., terrible, great

whoreson° dead body. [*He picks up a skull.*] Here's a skull now hath
lien you° i'th' earth three-and-twenty years.   140

HAMLET: Whose was it?

FIRST CLOWN: A whoreson mad fellow's it was. Whose do you think it was?

HAMLET: Nay, I know not.

FIRST CLOWN: A pestilence on him for a mad rogue! 'A poured a flagon of
Rhenish° on my head once. This same skull, sir, was, sir, Yorick's skull,   145
the King's jester.

HAMLET: This?

FIRST CLOWN: E'en that.

HAMLET: Let me see. [*He takes the skull.*] Alas, poor Yorick! I knew him, Horatio, a fellow of infinite jest, of most excellent fancy. He hath bore° me on   150
his back a thousand times, and now how abhorred in my imagination it
is! My gorge rises° at it. Here hung those lips that I have kissed I know
not how oft. Where be your gibes now? Your gambols, your songs, your
flashes of merriment that were wont° to set the table on a roar? Not one
now, to mock your own grinning?° Quite chopfallen?° Now get you to my   155
lady's chamber and tell her, let her paint an inch thick, to this favor° she
must come. Make her laugh at that. Prithee, Horatio, tell me one thing.

HORATIO: What's that, my lord?

HAMLET: Dost thou think Alexander looked o' this fashion i' th' earth?

HORATIO: E'en so.   160

HAMLET: And smelt so? Pah! [*He throws down the skull.*]

HORATIO: E'en so, my lord.

HAMLET: To what base uses we may return, Horatio! Why may not imagination
trace the noble dust of Alexander till 'a find it stopping a bunghole?°

HORATIO: 'Twere to consider too curiously° to consider so.   165

HAMLET: No, faith, not a jot, but to follow him thither with modesty° enough,
and likelihood to lead it. As thus: Alexander died, Alexander was buried, Alexander returneth to dust, the dust is earth, of earth we make
loam,° and why of that loam whereto he was converted might they not
stop a beer barrel?   170
Imperious° Caesar, dead and turned to clay,

---

139 whoreson i.e., vile, scurvy   **140 lien you** lain (See the note at line 134.)   **145
Rhenish** Rhine wine   **150 bore** borne   **152 My gorge rises** i.e., I feel nauseated   **154 were wont** used   **155 mock your own grinning** mock at the way your skull
seems to be grinning (just as you used to mock at yourself and those who grinned at
you)   **chopfallen** (1) lacking the lower jaw (2) dejected   **156 favor** aspect, appearance   **164 bunghole** hole for filling or emptying a cask   **165 curiously** minutely
166 modesty plausible moderation   **169 loam** mortar consisting chiefly of moistened
clay and straw   **171 Imperious** imperial

Might stop a hole to keep the wind away.

O, that that earth which kept the world in awe

Should patch a wall t' expel the winter's flaw!°

[*Enter* KING, QUEEN, LAERTES, *and the corpse (of* OPHELIA, *in procession, with* PRIEST, *lords, etc.).*]

But soft,° but soft awhile! Here comes the King,   175

The Queen, the courtiers. Who is this they follow?

And with such maimèd° rites? This doth betoken

The corpse they follow did with desperate hand

Fordo° its own life. 'Twas of some estate.°

Couch we° awhile and mark.   180

[*He and* HORATIO *conceal themselves.* OPHELIA's *body is taken to the grave.*]

LAERTES: What ceremony else?

HAMLET: [*to* HORATIO]: That is Laertes, a very noble youth. Mark.

LAERTES: What ceremony else?

PRIEST: Her obsequies have been as far enlarged

As we have warranty.° Her death was doubtful,   185

And but that great command o'ersways the order°

She should in ground unsanctified been lodged°

Till the last trumpet. For° charitable prayers,

Shards,° flints, and pebbles should be thrown on her.

Yet here she is allowed her virgin crants,°   190

Her maiden strewments,° and the bringing home

Of bell and burial.°

LAERTES: Must there no more be done?

PRIEST: No more be done.

We should profane the service of the dead   195

To sing a requiem and such rest° to her

As to peace-parted souls.°

LAERTES: Lay her i' th' earth,

And from her fair and unpolluted flesh

May violets° spring! I tell thee, churlish priest,   200

---

174 **flaw** gust of wind   175 **soft** i.e., wait, be careful   177 **maimèd** mutilated, incomplete   179 **Fordo** destroy   **estate** rank   180 **Couch we** let's hide, lie low   185 **warranty** i.e., ecclesiastical authority   186 **great...order** orders from on high overrule the prescribed procedures   187 **She should...lodged** she should have been buried in unsanctified ground   188 **For** in place of   189 **Shards** broken bits of pottery   190 **crants** garlands betokening maidenhood   191 **strewments** flowers strewn on a coffin   191–192 **bringing...burial** laying the body to rest, to the sound of the bell   196 **such rest** i.e., to pray for such rest   197 **peace-parted souls** those who have died at peace with God   200 **violets** (See 4.5.183 and note.)

A ministering angel shall my sister be
When thou liest howling.°
HAMLET [*to* HORATIO]:   What, the fair Ophelia!
QUEEN [*scattering flowers*]:   Sweets to the sweet! Farewell.
　　I hoped thou shouldst have been my Hamlet's wife.   205
　　I thought thy bride-bed to have decked, sweet maid,
　　And not t' have strewed thy grave.
LAERTES: O, treble woe
　　Fall ten times treble on that cursèd head
　　Whose wicked deed thy most ingenious sense°   210
　　Deprived thee of! Hold off the earth awhile,
　　Till I have caught her once more in mine arms.
[*He leaps into the grave and embraces* OPHELIA.]
　　Now pile your dust upon the quick and dead,
　　Till of this flat a mountain you have made
　　T' o'ertop old Pelion or the skyish head   215
　　Of blue Olympus.°
HAMLET [*coming forward*]:   What is he whose grief
　　Bears such an emphasis,° whose phrase of sorrow
　　Conjures the wandering stars° and makes them stand
　　Like wonder-wounded° hearers? This is I,
　　Hamlet the Dane.°   220
LAERTES [*grappling with him*°]:   The devil take thy soul!
HAMLET: Thou pray'st not well.
　　I prithee, take thy fingers from my throat,
　　For though I am not splenitive° and rash,   225
　　Yet have I in me something dangerous,
　　Which let thy wisdom fear. Hold off thy hand.
KING: Pluck them asunder.
QUEEN: Hamlet, Hamlet!
ALL: Gentlemen!   230

---

202 howling i.e., in hell   **210 ingenious sense** a mind that is quick, alert, of fine qualities   **215–216 Pelion...Olympus** sacred mountains in the north of Thessaly; see also
Ossa, below, at line 245   **218 emphasis** i.e., rhetorical and florid emphasis (*Phrase* has
a similar rhetorical connotation.)   **219 wandering stars** planets   **220 wonder-wounded**
struck with amazement   **221 the Dane** (This title normally signifies the King; see 1.1.17
and note.)   **s.d. grappling with him** The testimony of the First Quarto that "*Hamlet leaps
in after Laertes*" and the "Elegy on Burbage" ("Oft have I seen him leap into the grave")
seem to indicate one way in which this fight was staged; however, the difficulty of fitting
two contenders and Ophelia's body into a confined space (probably the trapdoor) suggests to many editors the alternative, that Laertes jumps out of the grave to attack Hamlet.)
225 splenitive quick-tempered

HORATIO: Good my lord, be quiet.

[HAMLET *and* LAERTES *are parted*.]

HAMLET: Why, I will fight with him upon this theme
     Until my eyelids will no longer wag.°

QUEEN: O my son, what theme?

HAMLET: I loved Ophelia. Forty thousand brothers   235
     Could not with all their quantity of love
     Make up my sum. What wilt thou do for her?

KING: O, he is mad, Laertes.

QUEEN: For love of God, forbear him.°

HAMLET: 'Swounds,° show me what thou'lt do.   240
     Woo 't° weep? Woo 't fight? Woo 't fast? Woo 't tear thyself?
     Woo 't drink up° eisel?° Eat a crocodile?°
     I'll do 't. Dost come here to whine?
     To outface me with leaping in her grave?
     Be buried quick° with her, and so will I.   245
     And if thou prate of mountains, let them throw
     Millions of acres on us, till our ground,
     Singeing his pate° against the burning zone,°
     Make Ossa° like a wart! Nay, an° thou'lt mouth,°
     I'll rant as well as thou.   250

QUEEN: This is mere° madness,
     And thus awhile the fit will work on him;
     Anon, as patient as the female dove
     When that her golden couplets° are disclosed,°
     His silence will sit drooping.   255

HAMLET: Hear you, sir,
     What is the reason that you use me thus?
     I loved you ever. But it is no matter.
     Let Hercules himself do what he may,
     The cat will mew, and dog will have his day.°   260

[*Exit* HAMLET.]

---

233 wag move (A fluttering eyelid is a conventional sign that life has not yet gone.)   **239 forbear him** leave him alone   **240 'Swounds** by His (Christ's) wounds   **241 Woo 't** wilt thou   **242 drink up** drink deeply   **eisel** vinegar   **crocodile** (Crocodiles were tough and dangerous, and were supposed to shed hypocritical tears.)   **245 quick** alive   **248 his pate** its head, i.e., top   **burning zone** zone in the celestial sphere containing the sun's orbit, between the tropics of Cancer and Capricorn   **249 Ossa** another mountain in Thessaly (In their war against the Olympian gods, the giants attempted to heap Ossa on Pelion to scale Olympus.)   **an if**   **mouth** i.e., rant   **251 mere** utter   **254 golden couplets** two baby pigeons, covered with yellow down   **disclosed** hatched   **259–260 Let…day** i.e., (1) even Hercules couldn't stop Laertes' theatrical rant (2) I, too, will have my turn; i.e., despite any blustering attempts at interference, every person will sooner or later do what he or she must do

KING: I pray thee, good Horatio, wait upon him.

[*Exit* HORATIO.]

    [*To* LAERTES.] Strengthen your patience in° our last night's speech;
    We'll put the matter to the present push.°—
    Good Gertrude, set some watch over your son.—
    This grave shall have a living° monument.   265
    An hour of quiet° shortly shall we see;
    Till then, in patience our proceeding be.

[*Exeunt.*]

[**Act 5.2** *Enter* HAMLET *and* HORATIO.]°

HAMLET: So much for this, sir; now shall you see the other.°
    You do remember all the circumstance?

HORATIO: Remember it, my lord!

HAMLET: Sir, in my heart there was a kind of fighting
    That would not let me sleep. Methought I lay   5
    Worse than the mutines° in the bilboes.° Rashly,°
    And praised be rashness for it—let us know°
    Our indiscretion° sometimes serves us well
    When our deep plots do pall,° and that should learn° us
    There's a divinity that shapes our ends,   10
    Rough-hew° them how we will—

HORATIO: That is most certain.

HAMLET: Up from my cabin,
    My sea-gown° scarfed° about me, in the dark
    Groped I to find out them,° had my desire,
    Fingered° their packet, and in fine° withdrew   15
    To mine own room again, making so bold,
    My fears forgetting manners, to unseal
    Their grand commission; where I found, Horatio—
    Ah, royal knavery!—an exact command,   20
    Larded° with many several° sorts of reasons
    Importing° Denmark's health and England's too,

---

262 in i.e., by recalling **263 present push** immediate test **265 living** lasting (For Laertes' private understanding, Claudius also hints that Hamlet's death will serve as such a monument.) **266 hour of quiet** time free of conflict **5.2 s.d. Location: The castle 1 see the other** hear the other news **6 mutines** mutineers **bilboes** shackles **rashly** on impulse (This adverb goes with lines 12 ff.) **7 know** acknowledge **8 indiscretion** lack of foresight and judgment (not an indiscreet act) **9 pall** fail, falter, go stale **learn** teach **11 Rough-hew** shape roughly **14 sea-gown** seaman's coat **scarfed** loosely wrapped **15 them** i.e., Rosencrantz and Guildenstern **16 Fingered** pilfered, pinched **in fine** finally, in conclusion **21 Larded** garnished **several** different **22 Importing** relating to

With, ho! such bugs° and goblins in my life,°
That on the supervise,° no leisure bated,°
No, not to stay° the grinding of the ax,   25
My head should be struck off.

HORATIO: Is 't possible?

HAMLET [*giving a document*]:   Here's the commission. Read it at more leisure.
But wilt thou hear now how I did proceed?

HORATIO: I beseech you.   30

HAMLET: Being thus benetted round with villainies—
Ere I could make a prologue to my brains,
They had begun the play°—I sat me down,
Devised a new commission, wrote it fair.°
I once did hold it, as our statists° do,   35
A baseness° to write fair, and labored much
How to forget that learning; but, sir, now
It did me yeoman's° service. Wilt thou know
Th' effect° of what I wrote?

HORATIO: Ay, good my lord.   40

HAMLET: An earnest conjuration° from the King,
As England was his faithful tributary,
As love between them like the palm° might flourish,
As peace should still° her wheaten garland° wear
And stand a comma° 'tween their amities,   45
And many suchlike "as"es° of great charge,°
That on the view and knowing of these contents,
Without debatement further more or less,
He should those bearers put to sudden death,
Not shriving time° allowed.   50

HORATIO: How was this sealed?

HAMLET: Why, even in that was heaven ordinant.°
I had my father's signet° in my purse,
Which was the model° of that Danish seal;
Folded the writ° up in the form of th' other,   55

---

23 bugs bugbears, hobgoblins   **in my life** i.e., to be feared if I were allowed to live
24 supervise reading   **leisure bated** delay allowed   **25 stay** await   **33 Ere . . . play** before
I could consciously turn my brain to the matter, it had started working on a plan   **34 fair**
in a clear hand   **35 statists** statesmen   **36 baseness** i.e., lower-class trait   **38 yeoman's**
i.e., substantial, faithful, loyal   **39 effect** purport   **41 conjuration** entreaty   **43 palm**
(An image of health; see Psalm 92:12.)   **44 still** always   **wheaten garland** (Symbolic
of fruitful agriculture, of peace and plenty.)   **45 comma** (Indicating continuity, link.)
46 "as"es (1) the "whereases" of a formal document (2) asses   **charge** (1) import (2) burden
(appropriate to asses)   **50 shriving time** time for confession and absolution   **52 ordinant**
directing   **53 signet** small seal   **54 model** replica   **55 writ** writing

Subscribed° it, gave 't th' impression,° placed it safely,
The changeling° never known. Now, the next day
Was our sea fight, and what to this was sequent°
Thou knowest already.

HORATIO: So Guildenstern and Rosencrantz go to 't.   60

HAMLET: Why, man, they did make love to this employment.
They are not near my conscience. Their defeat°
Does by their own insinuation° grow.
'Tis dangerous when the baser° nature comes
Between the pass° and fell° incensèd points   65
Of mighty opposites.°

HORATIO: Why, what a king is this!

HAMLET: Does it not, think thee, stand me now upon°—
He that hath killed my king and whored my mother,
Popped in between th' election° and my hopes,   70
Thrown out his angle° for my proper° life,
And with such cozenage°—is 't not perfect conscience
To quit° him with this arm? And is 't not to be damned
To let this canker° of our nature come
In° further evil?   75

HORATIO: It must be shortly known to him from England
What is the issue of the business there.

HAMLET: It will be short. The interim is mine,
And a man's life's no more than to say "one."°
But I am very sorry, good Horatio,   80
That to Laertes I forgot myself,
For by the image of my cause I see
The portraiture of his. I'll court his favors.
But, sure, the bravery° of his grief did put me
Into a tow'ring passion.   85

HORATIO: Peace, who comes here?

[*Enter a Courtier* (OSRIC).]

OSRIC: Your lordship is right welcome back to Denmark.

56 Subscribed signed (with forged signature) **impression** i.e., with a wax seal **57 changeling** i.e., substituted letter (Literally, a fairy child substituted for a human one.) **58 was sequent** followed **63 defeat** destruction **63 insinuation** intrusive intervention, sticking their noses in my business **64 baser** of lower social station **65 pass** thrust **fell** fierce **66 opposites** antagonists **68 stand me now upon** become incumbent on me now **70 election** (The Danish monarch was "elected" by a small number of high-ranking electors.) **71 angle** fishhook **proper** very **72 cozenage** trickery **73 quit** requite, pay back **74 canker** ulcer **75 come In** grow into **79 a man's..."one"** one's whole life occupies such a short time, only as long as it takes to count to 1 **84 bravery** bravado

HAMLET: I humbly thank you, sir. [*To* HORATIO.] Dost know this water fly?

HORATIO: No, my good lord.

HAMLET: Thy state is the more gracious, for 'tis a vice to know him. He hath   90
much land, and fertile. Let a beast be lord of beasts, and his crib° shall
stand at the King's mess.° 'Tis a chuff,° but, as I say, spacious in the
possession of dirt.

OSRIC: Sweet lord, if your lordship were at leisure, I should impart a thing to
you from His Majesty.   95

HAMLET: I will receive it, sir, with all diligence of spirit.
Put your bonnet° to his° right use; 'tis for the head.

OSRIC: I thank your lordship, it is very hot.

HAMLET: No, believe me, 'tis very cold. The wind is northerly.

OSRIC: It is indifferent° cold, my lord, indeed.   100

HAMLET: But yet methinks it is very sultry and hot for my complexion.°

OSRIC: Exceedingly, my lord. It is very sultry, as 'twere—I cannot tell how.
My lord, His Majesty bade me signify to you that 'a has laid a great
wager on your head. Sir, this is the matter—

HAMLET: I beseech you, remember.   105

[*Hamlet moves him to put on his hat.*]

OSRIC: Nay, good my lord; for my ease,° in good faith. Sir, here is newly come to
court Laertes—believe me, an absolute° gentleman, full of most excellent
differences,° of very soft society° and great showing.° Indeed, to speak
feelingly° of him, he is the card° or calendar° of gentry,° for you shall find
in him the continent of what part a gentleman would see.°   110

HAMLET: Sir, his definement° suffers no perdition° in you,° though I know to
divide him inventorially° would dozy° th' arithmetic of memory, and yet
but yaw° neither° in respect of° his quick sail. But, in the verity of extol-
ment,° I take him to be a soul of great article,° and his infusion° of such

---

91 crib manger   **91–92 Let...mess** i.e., if a man, no matter how beastlike, is as rich in
livestock and possessions as Osric, he may eat at the King's table   **92 chuff** boor, churl
(The Second Quarto spelling, *chough,* is a variant spelling that also suggests the meaning
here of "chattering jackdaw.")   **97 bonnet** any kind of cap or hat   **his** its   **100 indifferent** somewhat   **101 complexion** temperament   **106 for my ease** (A conventional reply
declining the invitation to put his hat back on.)   **107 absolute** perfect   **108 differences**
special qualities   **soft society** agreeable manners   **great showing** distinguished appearance   **109 feelingly** with just perception   **card** chart, map   **calendar** guide   **gentry**
good breeding   **110 the continent...see** one who contains in him all the qualities a
gentleman would like to see (A *continent* is that which contains.)   **111 definement** definition (Hamlet proceeds to mock Osric by throwing his lofty diction back at him.)   **perdi-
tion** loss, diminution   **you** your description   **112 divide him inventorially** enumerate
his graces   **dozy** dizzy   **113 yaw** swing unsteadily off course (Said of a ship.)   **neither**
for all that   **in respect of** in comparison with   **113–114 in...extolment** in true praise
(of him)   **114 of great article** one with many articles in his inventory   **infusion** essence,
character infused into him by nature

dearth and rareness° as, to make true diction° of him, his semblable° is his   115
mirror and who else would trace° him his umbrage,° nothing more.

OSRIC: Your lordship speaks most infallibly of him.

HAMLET: The concernancy,° sir? Why do we wrap the gentleman in our more
rawer breath?°

OSRIC: Sir?   120

HORATIO: Is 't not possible to understand in another tongue?° You will do 't,°
sir, really.

HAMLET: What imports the nomination° of this gentleman?

OSRIC: Of Laertes?

HORATIO [*To* HAMLET]: His purse is empty already; all 's golden words are spent.   125

HAMLET: Of him, sir.

OSRIC: I know you are not ignorant—

HAMLET: I would you did, sir. Yet in faith if you did, it would not much ap-
prove° me. Well, sir?

OSRIC: You are not ignorant of what excellence Laertes is—   130

HAMLET: I dare not confess that, lest I should compare with him in excellence.
But to know a man well were to know himself.°

OSRIC: I mean, sir, for° his weapon; but in the imputation laid on him by
them,° in his meed° he's unfellowed.°

HAMLET: What's his weapon?   135

OSRIC: Rapier and dagger.

HAMLET: That's two of his weapons—but well.°

OSRIC: The King, sir, hath wagered with him six Barbary horses, against the
which he° has impawned,° as I take it, six French rapiers and poniards,°
with their assigns,° as girdle, hangers,° and so.° Three of the carriages,°   140
in faith, are very dear to fancy,° very responsive° to the hilts, most deli-
cate° carriages, and of very liberal conceit.°

115 dearth and rareness rarity   **make true diction** speak truly   **semblable** only true
likeness   **116 who…trace** any other person who would wish to follow   **umbrage** shadow   **118 concernancy** import, relevance   **119 rawer breath** unrefined speech that can
only come short in praising him   **121 to understand…tongue** i.e., for you, Osric, to
understand when someone else speaks your language. (Horatio twits Osric for not being
able to understand the kind of flowery speech he himself uses, when Hamlet speaks in
such a vein. Alternatively, all this could be said to Hamlet.)   **You will do 't** i.e., you
can if you try, or, you may well have to try (to speak plainly)   **123 nomination** naming
128 approve commend   **131–132 I dare…himself** I dare not boast of knowing
Laertes' excellence lest I seem to imply a comparable excellence in myself. Certainly,
to know another person well, one must know oneself.   **133 for** i.e., with   **133–134
imputation…them** reputation given him by others   **134 meed** merit   **unfellowed**
unmatched   **137 but well** but never mind   **139 he** i.e., Laertes   **impawned** staked, wagered   **poniards** daggers   **140 assigns** appurtenances   **hangers** straps on the sword
belt (*girdle*), from which the sword hung   **and so** and so on   **carriages** (An affected
way of saying *hangers;* literally, gun carriages.)   **141 dear to fancy** delightful to the
fancy   **responsive** corresponding closely, matching or well adjusted   **delicate** (i.e., in
workmanship.)   **142 liberal conceit** elaborate design

HAMLET: What call you the carriages?

HORATIO [*to* HAMLET]:   I knew you must be edified by the margent° ere you
    had done.   145

OSRIC: The carriages, sir, are the hangers.

HAMLET: The phrase would be more germane to the matter if we could carry
    a cannon by our sides; I would it might be hangers till then. But, on:
    six Barbary horses against six French swords, their assigns, and three
    liberal-conceited carriages; that's the French bet against the Danish.   150
    Why is this impawned, as you call it?

OSRIC: The King, sir, hath laid,° sir, that in a dozen passes° between yourself
    and him, he shall not exceed you three hits. He hath laid on twelve
    for nine, and it would come to immediate trial, if your lordship would
    vouchsafe the answer.°   155

HAMLET: How if I answer no?

OSRIC: I mean, my lord, the opposition of your person in trial.

HAMLET: Sir, I will walk here in the hall. If it please His Majesty, it is the
    breathing time° of day with me. Let° the foils be brought, the gentle-
    man willing, and the King hold his purpose. I will win for him an I can;   160
    if not, I will gain nothing but my shame and the odd hits.

OSRIC: Shall I deliver you° so?

HAMLET: To this effect, sir—after what flourish your nature will.

OSRIC: I commend° my duty to your lordship.

HAMLET: Yours, yours. [*Exit* OSRIC.] 'A does well to commend it himself; there   165
    are no tongues else for 's turn.°

HORATIO: This lapwing° runs away with the shell on his head.

HAMLET: 'A did comply with his dug° before 'a sucked it. Thus has he—and
    many more of the same breed that I know the drossy° age dotes on—
    only got the tune° of the time and, out of an habit of encounter,° a   170
    kind of yeasty° collection,° which carries them through and through the

---

144 margent margin of a book, place for explanatory notes   **152 laid** wagered   **passes**
bouts (The odds of the betting are hard to explain. Possibly the King bets that Hamlet will
win at least five out of twelve, at which point Laertes raises the odds against himself by
betting he will win nine.)   **155 vouchsafe the answer** be so good as to accept the challenge (Hamlet deliberately takes the phrase in its literal sense of replying.)   **157 breathing
time** exercise period   **Let** i.e., if   **162 deliver you** report what you say   **164 commend**
commit to your favor (A conventional salutation, but Hamlet wryly uses a more literal
meaning, "recommend," "praise," in line 159.)   **166 for 's turn** for his purposes, i.e., to
do it for him   **167 lapwing** (A proverbial type of youthful forwardness. Also, a bird that
draws intruders away from its nest and was thought to run about with its head in the shell
when newly hatched; a seeming reference to Osric's hat.)   **168 comply...dug** observe
ceremonious formality toward his nurse's or mother's teat   **169 drossy** laden with scum
and impurities, frivolous   **170 tune** temper, mood, manner of speech   **an habit of
encounter** a demeanor in conversing (with courtiers of his own kind)   **171 yeasty**
frothy   **collection** i.e., of current phrases

most fanned and winnowed opinions;° and do° but blow them to their
trial, the bubbles are out.°   [*Enter a* LORD.]

LORD: My lord, His Majesty commended him to you by young Osric, who
brings back to him that you attend him in the hall. He sends to know   175
if your pleasure hold to play with Laertes, or that° you will take longer
time.

HAMLET: I am constant to my purposes; they follow the King's pleasure. If
his fitness speaks, mine is ready;° now or whensoever, provided I be
so able as now.   180

LORD: The King and Queen and all are coming down.

HAMLET: In happy time.°

LORD: The Queen desires you to use some gentle entertainment° to Laertes
before you fall to play.

HAMLET: She well instructs me.   185

                                                   [*Exit* LORD.]

HORATIO: You will lose, my lord.

HAMLET: I do not think so. Since he went into France, I have been in continual practice; I shall win at the odds. But thou wouldst not think how
ill all's here about my heart; but it is no matter.

HORATIO: Nay, good my lord—   190

HAMLET: It is but foolery, but it is such a kind of gaingiving° as would perhaps
trouble a woman.

HORATIO: If your mind dislike anything, obey it. I will forestall their repair°
hither and say you are not fit.

HAMLET: Not a whit, we defy augury. There is special providence in the fall   195
of a sparrow. If it be now, 'tis not to come; if it be not to come, it will
be now; if it be not now, yet it will come. The readiness is all. Since
no man of aught he leaves knows, what is 't to leave betimes? Let be.°

[*A table prepared. (Enter) trumpets, drums, and officers with cushions;* KING, QUEEN,
(OSRIC,) *and all the state; foils, daggers, (and wine borne in;) and* LAERTES.]

KING: Come, Hamlet, come and take this hand from me.

[The KING *puts* LAERTES' *hand into* HAMLET's.]

---

172 carries...opinions sustains them right through the scrutiny of persons whose opinions are select and refined (Literally, like grain separated from its chaff. Osric is both the
chaff and the bubbly froth on the surface of the liquor that is soon blown away.)   **and
do** yet do   **172–173 blow...out** test them by merely blowing on them, and their bubbles
burst   **176 that** if   **179 If...ready** if he declares his readiness, my convenience waits on
his   **182 In happy time** (A phrase of courtesy indicating that the time is convenient.)   **183
entertainment** greeting   **191 gaingiving** misgiving   **193 repair** coming   **197–198
Since...Let be** since no one has knowledge of what he is leaving behind, what does an
early death matter after all? Enough; don't struggle against it.

HAMLET [*to* LAERTES]:   Give me your pardon, sir. I have done you wrong,   200
    But pardon 't as you are a gentleman.
    This presence° knows,
    And you must needs have heard, how I am punished°
    With a sore distraction. What I have done
    That might your nature, honor, and exception°   205
    Roughly awake, I here proclaim was madness.
    Was 't Hamlet wronged Laertes? Never Hamlet.
    If Hamlet from himself be ta'en away,
    And when he's not himself does wrong Laertes,
    Then Hamlet does it not, Hamlet denies it.   210
    Who does it, then? His madness. If 't be so,
    Hamlet is of the faction° that is wronged;
    His madness is poor Hamlet's enemy.
    Sir, in this audience
    Let my disclaiming from a purposed evil   215
    Free me so far in your most generous thoughts
    That I have° shot my arrow o'er the house
    And hurt my brother.
LAERTES: I am satisfied in nature,°
    Whose motive° in this case should stir me most   220
    To my revenge. But in my terms of honor
    I stand aloof, and will no reconcilement
    Till by some elder masters of known honor
    I have a voice° and precedent of peace°
    To keep my name ungored.° But till that time   225
    I do receive your offered love like love,
    And will not wrong it.
HAMLET: I embrace it freely,
    And will this brothers' wager frankly° play.—
    Give us the foils. Come on.   230
LAERTES: Come, one for me.
HAMLET: I'll be your foil,° Laertes. In mine ignorance
    Your skill shall, like a star i' the darkest night,
    Stick fiery off° indeed.
LAERTES: You mock me, sir.   235
HAMLET: No, by this hand.

202 presence royal assembly   **203 punished** afflicted   **205 exception** disapproval
212 faction party   **217 That I have** as if I had   **219 in nature** i.e., as to my personal
feelings   **220 motive** prompting   **224 voice** authoritative pronouncement   **of peace** for
reconciliation   **225 name ungored** reputation unwounded   **229 frankly** without ill feeling or the burden of rancor   **232 foil** thin metal background which sets a jewel off (with
pun on the blunted rapier for fencing)   **234 Stick fiery off** stand out brilliantly

KING: Give them the foils, young Osric. Cousin Hamlet,
     You know the wager?

HAMLET: Very well, my lord.
     Your Grace has laid the odds o'° the weaker side.   240

KING: I do not fear it; I have seen you both.
     But since he is bettered,° we have therefore odds.

LAERTES: This is too heavy. Let me see another.

[*He exchanges his foil for another.*]

HAMLET: This likes me° well. These foils have all a length?

[*They prepare to play.*]

OSRIC: Ay, my good lord.   245

KING: Set me the stoups of wine upon that table.
     If Hamlet give the first or second hit,
     Or quit in answer of the third exchange,°
     Let all the battlements their ordnance fire.
     The King shall drink to Hamlet's better breath,°   250
     And in the cup an union° shall he throw
     Richer than that which four successive kings
     In Denmark's crown have worn. Give me the cups,
     And let the kettle° to the trumpet speak,
     The trumpet to the cannoneer without,   255
     The cannons to the heavens, the heaven to earth,
     "Now the King drinks to Hamlet." Come, begin.

                                 [*Trumpets the while.*]

     And you, the judges, bear a wary eye.

HAMLET: Come on, sir.

LAERTES: Come, my lord.   [*They play.* HAMLET *scores a hit.*]   260

HAMLET: One.

LAERTES: No.

HAMLET: Judgment.

OSRIC: A hit, a very palpable hit.

[*Drum, trumpets, and shot. Flourish. A piece goes off.*]

LAERTES: Well, again.   265

KING: Stay, give me drink. Hamlet, this pearl is thine.

        [*He drinks, and throws a pearl in* HAMLET'S *cup.*]

     Here's to thy health. Give him the cup.

---

240 laid the odds o' bet on, backed   **242 is bettered** has improved; is the odds-on favorite (Laertes' handicap is the "three hits" specified in line 147.)   **244 likes me** pleases me   **248 Or...exchange** i.e., or requites Laertes in the third bout for having won the first two   **250 better breath** improved vigor   **251 union** pearl (So called, according to Pliny's *Natural History,* 9, because pearls are *unique,* never identical.)   **254 kettle** kettledrum

HAMLET: I'll play this bout first. Set it by awhile.
    Come. [*They play.*] Another hit; what say you?
LAERTES: A touch, a touch, I do confess 't.   270
KING: Our son shall win.
QUEEN: He's fat° and scant of breath.
    Here, Hamlet, take my napkin,° rub thy brows.
    The Queen carouses° to thy fortune, Hamlet.
HAMLET: Good, madam!   275
KING: Gertrude, do not drink.
QUEEN: I will, my lord, I pray you pardon me.   [*She drinks.*]
KING [*aside*]:   It is the poisoned cup. It is too late.
HAMLET: I dare not drink yet, madam; by and by.
QUEEN: Come, let me wipe thy face.   280
LAERTES [*to* KING]:   My lord, I'll hit him now.
KING: I do not think 't.
LAERTES [*aside*]:   And yet it is almost against my conscience.
HAMLET: Come, for the third, Laertes. You do but dally.
    I pray you, pass° with your best violence;   285
    I am afeard you make a wanton of me.°
LAERTES: Say you so? Come on.   [*They play.*]
OSRIC: Nothing neither way.
LAERTES: Have at you now!
[LAERTES *wounds* HAMLET; *then, in scuffling, they change rapiers,° and* HAMLET
wounds LAERTES.]
KING: Part them! They are incensed.   290
HAMLET: Nay, come, again.   [*The* QUEEN *falls.*]
OSRIC: Look to the Queen there, ho!
HORATIO: They bleed on both sides. How is it, my lord?
OSRIC: How is 't, Laertes?
LAERTES: Why, as a woodcock° to mine own springe,° Osric;   295
    I am justly killed with mine own treachery.
HAMLET: How does the Queen?
KING: She swoons to see them bleed.
QUEEN: No, no, the drink, the drink—O my dear Hamlet—
    The drink, the drink! I am poisoned.   [*She dies.*]   300
HAMLET: O villainy! Ho, let the door be locked!
    Treachery! Seek it out.

---

272 fat not physically fit, out of training   **273 napkin** handkerchief   **274 carouses**
drinks a toast   **285 pass** thrust   **286 make...me** i.e., treat me like a spoiled child, trifle
with me   **s.d. in scuffling, they change rapiers** (This stage direction occurs in the Folio.
According to a widespread stage tradition, Hamlet receives a scratch, realizes that Laertes'
sword is unbated, and accordingly forces an exchange.)   **295 woodcock** a bird, a type of
stupidity or as a decoy   **springe** trap, snare

[LAERTES *falls. Exit* OSRIC.]

LAERTES: It is here, Hamlet. Hamlet, thou art slain.
No med'cine in the world can do thee good;
In thee there is not half an hour's life.   305
The treacherous instrument is in thy hand,
Unbated° and envenomed. The foul practice°
Hath turned itself on me. Lo, here I lie,
Never to rise again. Thy mother's poisoned.
I can no more. The King, the King's to blame.   310

HAMLET: The point envenomed too? Then, venom, to thy work.

[*He stabs the* KING.]

ALL: Treason! Treason!

KING: O, yet defend me, friends! I am but hurt.

HAMLET [*forcing the* KING *to drink.*]:
Here, thou incestuous, murderous, damnèd Dane,
Drink off this potion. Is thy union° here?   315
Follow my mother.   [*The* KING *dies.*]

LAERTES: He is justly served.
It is a poison tempered° by himself.
Exchange forgiveness with me, noble Hamlet.
Mine and my father's death come not upon thee,   320
Nor thine on me!   [*He dies.*]

HAMLET: Heaven make thee free of it! I follow thee.
I am dead, Horatio. Wretched Queen, adieu!
You that look pale and tremble at this chance,°
That are but mutes° or audience to this act,   325
Had I but time—as this fell° sergeant,° Death,
Is strict° in his arrest°—O, I could tell you—
But let it be. Horatio, I am dead;
Thou livest. Report me and my cause aright
To the unsatisfied.   330

HORATIO: Never believe it.
I am more an antique Roman° than a Dane.
Here's yet some liquor left.

[*He attempts to drink from the poisoned cup.* HAMLET *prevents him.*]

---

307 Unbated not blunted with a button   **practice** plot   **315 union** pearl (See line 251;
with grim puns on the word's other meanings: marriage, shared death.)   **318 tempered**
mixed   **324 chance** mischance   **325 mutes** silent observers (Literally, actors with non-
speaking parts.)   **326 fell** cruel   **sergeant** sheriffs officer   **327 strict** (1) severely just
(2) unavoidable   **arrest** (1) taking into custody (2) stopping my speech   **332 Roman**
(Suicide was an honorable choice for many Romans as an alternative to a dishonorable life.)

HAMLET: As thou'rt a man,
    Give me the cup! Let go! By heaven, I'll ha 't.   335
    O God, Horatio, what a wounded name,
    Things standing thus unknown, shall I leave behind me!
    If thou didst ever hold me in thy heart,
    Absent thee from felicity awhile,
    And in this harsh world draw thy breath in pain   340
    To tell my story.   [*A march afar off (and a volley within)*.]
    What warlike noise is this?

[*Enter* OSRIC.]

OSRIC: Young Fortinbras, with conquest come from Poland,
    To th' ambassadors of England gives
    This warlike volley.   345
HAMLET: O, I die, Horatio!
    The potent poison quite o'ercrows° my spirit.
    I cannot live to hear the news from England,
    But I do prophesy th' election lights
    On Fortinbras. He has my dying voice.°   350
    So tell him, with th' occurents° more and less
    Which have solicited°—the rest is silence.   [*He dies.*]
HORATIO: Now cracks a noble heart. Good night, sweet prince,
    And flights of angels sing thee to thy rest!

               [*March within.*]

    Why does the drum come hither?   355
[*Enter* FORTINBRAS, *with the (English)* AMBASSADORS *(with drum, colors, and attendants)*.]

FORTINBRAS: Where is this sight?
HORATIO: What is it you would see?
    If aught of woe or wonder, cease your search.
FORTINBRAS: This quarry° cries on havoc.° O proud Death,
    What feast° is toward° in thine eternal cell,   360
    That thou so many princes at a shot
    So bloodily hast struck?
FIRST AMBASSADOR: The sight is dismal,
    And our affairs from England come too late.
    The ears are senseless that should give us hearing,   365
    To tell him his commandment is fulfilled,

---

347 o'ercrows triumphs over (like the winner in a cockfight)   **350 voice** vote   **351 occurrents** events, incidents   **352 solicited** moved, urged (Hamlet doesn't finish saying what the events have prompted—presumably, his acts of vengeance, or his reporting of those events to Fortinbras.)   **359 quarry** heap of dead   **cries on havoc** proclaims a general slaughter   **360 feast** i.e., Death feasting on those who have fallen   **toward** in preparation

That Rosencrantz and Guildenstern are dead.
Where should we have our thanks?

HORATIO: Not from his° mouth,
Had it th' ability of life to thank you.   370
He never gave commandment for their death.
But since, so jump° upon this bloody question,°
You from the Polack wars, and you from England,
And here arrived, give order that these bodies
High on a stage° be placèd to the view,   375
And let me speak to th' yet unknowing world
How these things came about. So shall you hear
Of carnal, bloody, and unnatural acts,
Of accidental judgments,° casual° slaughters,
Of deaths put on° by cunning and forced cause,°   380
And, in this upshot, purposes mistook
Fall'n on th' inventors' heads. All this can I
Truly deliver.

FORTINBRAS: Let us haste to hear it,
And call the noblest to the audience.   385
For me, with sorrow I embrace my fortune.
I have some rights of memory° in this kingdom,
Which now to claim my vantage° doth invite me.

HORATIO: Of that I shall have also cause to speak,
And from his mouth whose voice will draw on more.°   390
But let this same be presently° performed,
Even while men's minds are wild, lest more mischance
On° plots and errors happen.

FORTINBRAS: Let four captains
Bear Hamlet, like a soldier, to the stage,   395
For he was likely, had he been put on,°
To have proved most royal; and for his passage,°
The soldiers' music and the rite of war
Speak° loudly for him.
Take up the bodies. Such a sight as this   400
Becomes the field,° but here shows much amiss.
Go bid the soldiers shoot.

[*Exeunt (marching, bearing off the dead bodies; a peal of ordnance is shot off).*]

369 his i.e., Claudius' **372 jump** precisely, immediately **question** dispute, affair
375 stage platform **379 judgments** retributions **casual** occurring by chance **380 put
on** instigated **forced cause** contrivance **387 of memory** traditional, remembered, un-
forgotten **388 vantage** favorable opportunity **390 voice...more** vote will influence
still others **391 presently** immediately **393 On** on the basis of; on top of **396 put
on** i.e., invested in royal office and so put to the test **397 passage** i.e., from life to
death **399 Speak** (let them) speak **401 Becomes the field** suits the field of battle

MAKING CONNECTIONS

1. What is your reaction to Hamlet at the beginning of the play? Do you think his response to his father's death and mother's marriage is excessive? Explain.

2. If you were in his situation, do you think you would have responded in the same way? Why or why not?

3. What is your response to Claudius at the beginning of the play? Does he seem to be an effective leader, loving stepfather to Hamlet, loving husband to Gertrude? Explain.

4. What is your response to Hamlet's mother, Gertrude? Does she seem to be a loving mother to Hamlet? Do you think she understands why he is so angry? Explain.

5. Describe Polonius, Laertes, and Ophelia. To what extent is this a loving family? A dysfunctional family?

6. Pick out Hamlet's soliloquies throughout the play. Is there a pattern in what Hamlet says about himself and his dilemma?

7. Do you think Hamlet procrastinates too much? Is the play he arranges necessary? Should he have killed Claudius at his first opportunity? Explain.

8. Is Hamlet all good? Do you think that his treatment of Ophelia was fair? Are any of his other actions questionable? Explain.

9. At the beginning of the play we are told, "Something is rotten in the state of Denmark." Is all well at the end of the play? Explain.

10. Choose a scene from the play and discuss why it is important in light of the whole play.

MAKING AN ARGUMENT

1. Read the Ernest Jones essay "Hamlet's Oedipus Complex" on page 627, and write an argument in support of it or against it. Carefully cite both the article and the text of the play in support of your view.

2. Like Shakespeare's other plays, most of this play is dramatic poetry. Choose examples of poetic language from *Hamlet* that are particularly effective in prompting strong emotion, developing character, building conflict, or advancing the plot. Write an essay that describes why the language is so effective. Cite the text of the play for support.

Desperately Seeking *Hamlet*: Four Interpretations

Over the past sixty years, some of the best performances of *Hamlet* have been recorded on film and video. Perhaps the four most popular of these productions are Laurence Olivier's 1948 film, which won the Academy Award for best picture; Derek Jacobi's 1979 *Hamlet,* produced as part of the monumental BBC Shakespeare series; Mel Gibson's portrayal in a popular 1990 Franco Zeffirelli production; and Kenneth Branagh's 1996 star-studded extravaganza. Their performances—their different, but justifiable interpretations—illustrate the complexities of the character and demonstrate the validity of multiple perspectives.

Let's look briefly at these four versions and examine each actor's interpretation of the famous "To be, or not to be" soliloquy. Because this soliloquy is so familiar to the general public, even to those who have never seen the play, it is a major challenge for an actor. Like the role of Hamlet itself, this soliloquy demands a unique interpretation. Both actors and audience often recognize in its rendering a microcosm of the character himself.

Olivier's **Hamlet**   The oldest, but not the most traditional, of these versions is Laurence Olivier's 1948 film. Revered by many purists as the definitive version, it is in many ways the least pure. The film opens with a reductive voice-over that claims, "This is the story of a man who could not make up his mind." While it is not unusual for directors to cut lines in this four-hour-long play, Olivier has, in addition, cut two important characters, Rosencrantz and Guildenstern. The fog-shrouded setting and powerful orchestral music seem omnipresent. And instead of preceding Hamlet's encounter with Ophelia with his "To be, or not to be" soliloquy, Olivier has switched the order of Shakespeare's text. In this version, Hamlet's speech follows and seems influenced by their painful meeting.

We move into his soliloquy as we move away from a sobbing, disconsolate Ophelia, who has thrown herself at the foot of the castle steps where Hamlet has just exited. The camera follows the path of her extended arm up the winding, cold stone stairs—higher and higher—as the music rises and we are hurled into the swirling dark clouds above the castle, then down to the crashing sea and jagged rocks below. The camera shifts slowly to the back of Hamlet's head and seems to bore deeper and deeper into his skull as we hear powerful string music and see an impression of the pulsing, swirling chaos of the sea embedded on the lobes of his brain. And he has not even begun to speak.

When he does speak, he is accompanied by the sounds of the chaotic sea below and powerful orchestral music in the background. He delivers the first part of the speech looking out over the castle wall to the sea below and seems mesmerized by what he sees and says. He produces a dagger and closes his eyes while we hear the "To die, to sleep…" section as a voice-over. He snaps out of his reverie when he cries out, "perchance to dream." The music stops and he delivers the rest of the soliloquy to the crashing of the waves beneath him. While he speaks he peruses the sea and points the dagger at himself. As he concludes the soliloquy, he drops the dagger and it falls ominously to the rocks far below. He rises from his precarious perch on the castle wall, finishes the speech, and walks off into the fog.

Jacobi's **Hamlet**   The BBC video production of 1979 is a very complete version of the play and follows the original order of Shakespeare's text. For Derek Jacobi, this means starting the "To be, or not to be" soliloquy from scratch without the momentum of the previous scene to build on. As he begins his soliloquy, therefore, Hamlet remains unaware of the interloping Polonius and Claudius and the "by chance" encounter with Ophelia they have planned for him.

Jacobi enters a quiet, empty room, notices us (the audience), and approaches to speak with us. There is no music in the background—just Jacobi and Shakespeare's words. He looks at us, confides in us. He is earnest and philosophical. He seems to ask questions with his statements and to seek answers while feeling our concern. His is a youthful sadness and confusion—not a deep obsessive depression like Olivier's. Halfway through the soliloquy, we catch a glimpse of Ophelia approaching in the background. But Jacobi's eyes remain on us throughout. Like Olivier, he shows us his dagger as he contemplates death but looks, too, at the picture of his dead father.

On "lose the name of action," he returns the dagger to its case and greets the "fair Ophelia"—first with enthusiasm and affection, then with disappointment and suspicion as he notices the book she is reading is upside down.

***Gibson's* Hamlet**   Like Olivier's *Hamlet,* Franco Zeffirelli's 1989 film of the play with Mel Gibson as Hamlet takes a few liberties with Shakespeare's text. Here too, the Ophelia encounter and the "To be, or not to be" soliloquy are reversed from their original order. Hamlet's painful scene with Ophelia precedes his speech, and his realization that "it hath made me mad" seems to say more about his anger than his sanity.

Mel Gibson takes his soliloquy "on the run"—busying himself with other tasks while he speaks to us—not entirely surprising for an actor who is not used to doing Shakespeare. Perhaps the most difficult task in performing Shakespeare's work is delivering a soliloquy head-on with the audience—with nothing between the actor and the audience but the words. Having Gibson keep physically busy while he relates his thoughts fits the energy of this Hamlet. His is a visceral, physical Hamlet who doesn't sit still for much. As he enters a large family crypt below the castle, his perusal of the tombs seems "to give him pause" even before he speaks. Rather than confiding in us as Jacobi does, he seems to be thinking out loud to himself. While he speaks and moves, he pauses to view and touch the reclining statues on top of the tombs. He leans against them, kneels at them, sits on the floor by them as he ponders the big questions of life and death. He seems energized by his musings and almost bounds up the stairs toward the light as he finishes his soliloquy and leaves the crypt.

***Branagh's* Hamlet**   Kenneth Branagh's 1996 four-hour-long production of *Hamlet* is lavish. The play is set in the nineteenth century at a magnificent palace (actually, England's Blenheim Palace). The indoor scenes include a throne room surrounded by mirrored walls, overlooked by a gallery, and divided by an elevated walkway. There are two-way mirrors and concealed chambers and corridors. There are movie stars galore. And this production definitely answers the question "Was Ophelia sleeping with Hamlet?" by showing Ophelia sleeping with Hamlet.

Like the production itself, the setting for Branagh's "To be, or not to be" soliloquy is opulent—a glorious mirrored-in throne room. Like

Shakespeare's text and the BBC production, and unlike the Olivier and Zeffirelli versions, this scene precedes the Ophelia encounter. Branagh enters the huge, empty room and walks slowly across it, footsteps echoing loudly. He turns, looks directly at a mirror—behind which Claudius and Polonius are hiding to listen in on the subsequent Ophelia encounter. He speaks quickly but clearly, his voice almost a whisper. He moves closer and closer to the mirror as he speaks—thus moving closer and closer to the hiding interlopers, who see him clearly through the two-way mirror. Is he speaking to himself or to them? He unsheaths a dagger on "bare bodkin" and points it at his reflection in the mirror and Claudius on the other side of the mirror—now only a hand's length away. Claudius shudders.

As the soliloquy ends, Ophelia crosses the long hall. Hamlet approaches her with affection and a gentle hug and kiss, which gradually turns to anger as she tries to return his gifts and he suspects her duplicity.

From Part to Whole, from Whole to Part

Thinking about and analyzing the interpretations of these actors and directors can tell us much about interpreting literature. Many legitimate interpretations are possible. We would not say that one was correct and the others wrong. We might say that we preferred one to the others—or preferred a different one to any presented here.

But we might also conclude that no one scene could show us all of a character. Olivier's interpretation of this soliloquy seems to show us an obsessed, deeply depressed Hamlet close to suicide. Though we can say that this speech tells us a lot about Hamlet, we cannot say that that is all there is to this Hamlet unless we place the speech in the context of all his other speeches and actions. And so it is with Jacobi's earnest and likable Hamlet, Gibson's energetic and sad Hamlet, or Branagh's quick and angry Hamlet. If we characterize any of these Hamlets solely on his behavior as he delivers this one soliloquy, we may be ignoring evidence in other parts of the play that tells us about aspects of the character not revealed in this scene.

So, too, our interpretation of this soliloquy, like an actor's preparation and interpretation of this speech, should be informed by our whole vision of Hamlet— the whole character as we have seen him throughout the play.

A Student's Argumentative Essay—Explication/Analysis of the "To be, or not to be" Soliloquy

In the argumentative essay that follows, Charles Chiang's thesis addresses the appeal of Hamlet to a broad audience. He says that Hamlet's "To be, or not to be" soliloquy finds common ground with the audience—even to the point of fabricating experiences that a prince would never encounter personally. It is an argumentative essay because Charles's analysis or "explication" of the soliloquy is a line-by-line reading. His exploration of the soliloquy is based completely on his own interpretation and does not refer to secondary sources for support.

Charles Chiang

Dr. Madden

English 102

November 16, 20XX

Hamlet: Connecting with the Audience

The emotional impact of Hamlet's death on the audience results less from his nobility than from his fragility and humanity. It is the human side of Hamlet that touches us and makes his death seem more tragic. Shakespeare creates empathy between Hamlet and the audience in a number of ways but accomplishes the task best with the "To be, or not to be" soliloquy. In this speech, which best demonstrates Hamlet's humanity, Shakespeare connects Hamlet to his audience with thoughts that cross the mind of every person at one time or another.

Even without the obvious closeness between the character of Hamlet and the audience that comes from the very nature of the soliloquy, the "To be, or not to be" soliloquy is so ingeniously crafted to appeal to the audience that we ignore the minor discrepancies that might come from careful analysis.

> For who would bear the whips and scorns of time,
>
> Th' oppressor's wrong, the proud man's contumely,
>
> The pangs of disprized love, the law's delay,
>
> The insolence of office, and the spurns
>
> That patient merit of th' unworthy takes. (3.1.77–81)

In this passage, Shakespeare (through Hamlet) is able to connect with us by using the tactic of a common denominator. Unreturned love ("disprized love"), injustice ("law's delay"), and bureaucracy ("insolence of office") are all experiences that are familiar even to us today. However, are these really experiences that Hamlet has suffered himself? The answer is no.

Hamlet was the prince of Denmark and lived a life of privilege. His only known romantic interest was Ophelia, who obviously returned his affections. Throughout the play almost every request he makes is granted. People are constantly doting on him and waiting on him hand and foot. While this may seem to be a burden to him, it is one the average person is unfamiliar with and one that would naturally distance Hamlet from us. Yet we ignore this reality because the soliloquy is written so well.

Shakespeare first manages to manipulate us with the brilliant introduction of the soliloquy:

> To be, or not to be, that is the question:
> Whether 'tis nobler in the mind to suffer
> The slings and arrows of outrageous fortune,
> Or to take arms against a sea of troubles
> And by opposing, end them. (3.1.63–67)

When first contemplating the subject, Hamlet considers factors involved in suicide. For instance, there are "the slings and arrows of outrageous fortune," which we probably interpret as the death of Hamlet's father, the subsequent marriage of his uncle and mother, the appearance of the ghost, and the revelation that his uncle killed his father.

This series of events, added to the betrayal of Hamlet's childhood friends Rosencrantz and Guildenstern, would qualify as both "outrageous fortune" and "a sea of troubles" to most people because they are not everyday occurrences for anyone. However, there is no resemblance between these events and the common experiences described in the passage above, yet Shakespeare is somehow able to join these two sets of experiences together and create a bond between Hamlet and the audience.

Shakespeare does this by using logic and a subtle shift in language in the intervening passage between the two sections:

> To die, to sleep—
> No more—and by a sleep to say we end
> The heartache and the thousand natural shocks
> That flesh is heir to. 'Tis a consummation
> Devoutly to be wished. To die, to sleep;
> To sleep, perchance to dream. Ay, there's the rub,
> For in that sleep of death what dreams may come,
> When we have shuffled off this mortal coil,
> Must give us pause. There's the respect
> That makes calamity of so long life. (3.1.67–76)

First, Shakespeare has Hamlet take a commonsense and almost childlike approach to suicide by comparing it to sleep, an everyday experience. We buy into this argument because death is like a "no more" sleep, a sleep without any waking. Hamlet continues with his logic by asking: If death is like sleep, are there dreams in death? Moreover, he implies there might be nightmares in death, thereby making suicide not an escape from unpleasant experiences.

However, in this progression of logic, Hamlet takes a more familiar tone with the audience. It is not "I" but "we," and Hamlet is no longer ending "the slings and arrows of outrageous fortune" or "a sea of troubles," but now refers to the end of "the heartache and the thousand natural shocks that flesh is heir to." Thus Shakespeare has shifted our thoughts from Hamlet's situation and mortality to our own.

As if he is still trying to distract us from the true topic, himself, Hamlet continues with the logic and reasoning of suicide:

> But that the dread of something after death,
> The undiscovered country from whose bourn
> No traveler returns, puzzles the will,
> And makes us rather bear those ills we have
> Than fly to others that we know not of?
> Thus conscience does make cowards of us all;
> And thus the native hue of resolution
> Is sicklied o'er with the pale cast of thought,
> And enterprises of great pitch and moment
> With this regard their currents turn awry
> And lose the name of action. (3.1.85–95)

Hamlet, like the audience, is afraid of the great unknown of death and that is why he will not commit suicide. However, Hamlet does suspect what death is like because of his experience with his father's ghost. If Hamlet does kill himself without first avenging his father's death, a terrible fate may await him in the afterlife. Though not addressed in this speech, there is also the Christian taboo against suicide and the punishment of going to hell for committing the sin.

It can be suggested that Hamlet knows that death is a fate worse than living, and that his true dilemma lies with deciding to act or to go against his uncle. Instead, Hamlet is trying in a roundabout way to tell us that he is a coward for not acting. Like a real person trying to reveal a personal secret and shame, Hamlet hems and haws around the topic, hints at, and then hopes we can guess what he is really talking about. With either explanation, Hamlet still connects and bonds with us.

What the "To be, or not to be" soliloquy accomplishes is to bring Hamlet to the level of the audience by allowing both audience and prince to connect with a common interest—suicide. When subtext and nuances are combined, the audience (and reader) is able to sympathize with the character, thereby making his death seem more tragic.

Hamlet's death, unlike the deaths of most fictional characters, and even some real people, evokes an authentic response from us because of the emotional and personal connection. This was best demonstrated in our class, where our initial response to the ending was more numbness than sadness. This reaction was like the initial reaction to a real death—numbness, disbelief, and denial.

Despite the fact that the play is a tragedy, there is a sense of disbelief and denial when Hamlet dies, and not because he dies so senselessly. Shakespeare defies the conventions of the time and his own standards because Hamlet lacked the tragic flaw that doomed other tragic heroes. Hamlet's only flaw was to be human. So if Hamlet can die just because he is all too human, isn't Shakespeare forcing us to confront our own mortality? In "denying" Hamlet's death, the audience is denying its own mortality as if a real person has died.

[New Page]

Work Cited

Shakespeare, William. *Hamlet. Exploring Literature.* Ed. Frank Madden.

5th ed. New York: Longman, 2012. 495–619. Print.

A Critic's Influential Interpretation

ERNEST JONES

HAMLET'S OEDIPUS COMPLEX

In short, the whole picture presented by Hamlet, his deep depression, the hopeless note in his attitude towards the world and towards the value of life, his dread of death, his repeated reference to bad dreams, his self-accusations, his desperate efforts to get away from the thoughts of his duty, and his vain attempts to find an excuse for his procrastination: all this unequivocally points to a *tortured conscience,* to some hidden ground for shirking his task, a ground which he dare not or cannot avow to himself.

Extensive studies of the past half century, inspired by Freud, have taught us that a psychoneurosis means a state of mind where the person is unduly, and often painfully, driven or thwarted by the "unconscious" part of his mind, that buried part that was once the infant's mind and still lives on side by side with the adult mentality that has developed out of it and should have taken its place. It signifies *internal* mental conflict. We have here the reason why it is impossible to discuss intelligently the state of mind of anyone suffering from a psychoneurosis, whether the description is of a living person or an imagined one, without correlating the manifestations with what must have operated in his infancy and is *still operating*. That is what I propose to attempt here.

For some deep-seated reason, which is to him unacceptable, Hamlet is plunged into anguish at the thought of his father being replaced in his mother's affections by someone else. It is as if his devotion to his mother had made him so jealous for her affection that he had found it hard enough to share this even with his father and could not endure to share it with still another man. Against this thought, however, suggestive as it is, may be urged three objections. First, if it were in itself a full statement of the matter, Hamlet would have been aware of the jealousy, whereas we have concluded that the mental process we are seeking is hidden from him. Secondly, we see in it no evidence of the arousing of an old and forgotten memory. And, thirdly, Hamlet is being deprived by Claudius of no greater share in the Queen's affection than he had been by his own father, for the two brothers made exactly similar claims in this respect—namely, those of a loved husband. The last-named objection, however, leads us to the heart of the situation. How if, in fact, Hamlet had in years gone by, as a child, bitterly resented having had to share his mother's affection even with his own father, had regarded him as a rival, and had secretly wished him out of the way so that he might enjoy undisputed and undisturbed the monopoly of that affection? If such thoughts had been present in his mind in childhood days they evidently would have been "repressed," and all traces of them obliterated, by filial piety and other educative influences. The actual realization of his early wish in the death of his father at the hands of a jealous rival would then have stimulated into activity these "repressed" memories, which would have produced, in the form of depression and other suffering, an obscure aftermath of his childhood's conflict. This is at all events the mechanism that is actually found in the real Hamlets who are investigated psychologically.

The explanation, therefore, of the delay and self-frustration exhibited in the endeavour to fulfil his father's demand for vengeance is that to Hamlet the thought of incest and parricide combined is too intolerable to be borne. One part of him tries to carry out the task, the other flinches inexorably from the thought of it. How fain would he blot it out in that "bestial oblivion" which unfortunately for him his conscience contemns. He is torn and tortured in an insoluble inner conflict.

5   Now comes the father's death and the mother's second marriage. The association of the idea of sexuality with his mother, buried since infancy, can no longer be concealed from his consciousness. As Bradley well says: "Her son was forced to see in her action not only an astounding shallowness of feeling, but an eruption of coarse sensuality, 'rank and gross,' speeding post-haste to its horrible delight." Feelings which once, in the infancy of long ago, were pleasurable desires can now,

because of his repressions, only fill him with repulsion. The long "repressed" desire to take his father's place in his mother's affection is stimulated to unconscious activity by the sight of someone usurping this place exactly as he himself had once longed to do. More, this someone was a member of the same family, so that the actual usurpation further resembled the imaginary one in being incestuous. Without his being in the least aware of it these ancient desires are ringing in his mind, are once more struggling to find conscious expression, and need such an expenditure of energy again to "repress" them that he is reduced to the deplorable mental state he himself so vividly depicts.

There follows the Ghost's announcement that the father's death was a willed one, was due to murder. Hamlet, having at the moment his mind filled with natural indignation at the news, answers normally enough with the cry (Act I, Sc. 5):

> Haste me to know't, that I with wings as swift
> As meditation or the thoughts of love,
> May sweep to my revenge.

The momentous words follow revealing who was the guilty person, namely a relative who had committed the deed at the bidding of lust. Hamlet's second guilty wish had thus also been realized by his uncle, namely to procure the fulfilment of the first—the possession of the mother—by a personal deed, in fact by murder of the father. The two recent events, the father's death and the mother's second marriage, seemed to the world to have no inner causal relation to each other, but they represented ideas which in Hamlet's unconscious phantasy had always been closely associated. These ideas now in a moment forced their way to conscious recognition in spite of all "repressing forces," and found immediate expression in his almost reflex cry: "O my prophetic soul! My uncle?" The frightful truth his unconscious had already intuitively divined, his consciousness had now to assimiliate as best it could. For the rest of the interview Hamlet is stunned by the effect of the internal conflict thus re-awakened, which from now on never ceases, and into the essential nature of which he never penetrates.

HAMLET ON SCREEN

BERNICE W. KLIMAN

THE BBC HAMLET

With *Hamlet,* the producers of the BBC Shakespeare Plays have finally met the demands of Shakespeare-on-television by choosing a relatively bare set, conceding only a few richly detailed movable panels and props to shape key locales. By avoiding both location and realistic settings, they point up the natural affinity between Shakespeare's stage and the undisguised sound set. This starkness of setting admits poetry, heightened intensity—and "what not that's sweet and happy."

The producers have thus made a valid choice from among television's three faces: one, broadcast films whether made for television or not, which exploit location settings, long shots, and all the clichés we associate with movies, including sudden shifts of space and time and full use of distance, from the most extreme long shots to "eyes only" closeups; two, studio-shot television drama with naturalistic settings, such as the hospital corridors and middle-class living rooms of sitcoms and soap operas, mostly in mid- to close-shots, often interspersed, to be sure, with a bit of stock footage of highways and skylines to establish a realistic environment. This second style varies from a close representation of real action to frankly staged action, where canned laughter or even shadowy glimpses of the studio audience can heighten the staged effect. Three, there is bare space with little or no effort made to disguise that this is a televised activity with a television crew out of sight but nearby. News broadcasts, talk shows and some television drama fit into this third category. Because of its patently unrepresentational quality, this last type offers the most freedom in shooting style. To all three kinds of settings we bring particular expectations in response to their conventions.

Shakespeare's plays work best in the last kind of television space, I believe, because it avoids the clash between realism and poetry, between the unity often expected in realistic media and the disunity and ambiguity of many of the plays, especially *Hamlet*. Yet, while closest to the kind of stage Shakespeare wrote for, the bare television set can be stretched through creative camera work. For example, when Hamlet follows the ghost in the BBC play, the two repeatedly walk across the frame and out of it, first from one direction, then from another; framing fosters the illusion of extended space. Freeing this *Hamlet* from location (as in the BBC *As You Like It*) and from realistic sets (as in the BBC *Measure for Measure*—however well those sets worked for that play) allows the play to be as inconsistent as it is, with, as Bernard Beckerman has so brilliantly explained in *Shakespeare at the Globe, 1599–1609,* a rising and falling action in each individual scene rather than through the course of the drama as a whole. It also allows for acting, the bravura kind that Derek Jacobi is so capable of.

Although gradually coalescing like the pointillism of impressionistic paintings into a subtly textured portrait, at first his mannerisms suggesting madness seem excessive. It is to be expected, perhaps, that Hamlet is a bit unhinged after the ghost scene, but Jacobi's rapid, hard blows to his forehead with the flat of his hand as he says "My tables" recall the desperation of Lear's cry: "O, let me not be mad, not mad, sweet heaven." And soon after, following the last couplet of the scene, Hamlet, maniacally playful, widens his eyes and points, pretending to see the ghost again, then guffaws at Marcellus's fears. Even more unsettling is his laughter when he is alone, as while he is saying "The play's the thing / Wherein I'll catch the conscience of the King." More significantly, he breaks up his own "Mousetrap" by getting right into the play, destroying the distance between audience and stage (a very real raked proscenium-arch stage), spoiling it as a test, because Claudius has a right to be incensed at Hamlet's behavior. Of course, Hamlet does so because Claudius never gives himself away, an unusual and provocative but not impossible interpretation. Thus, Claudius can only have the court's sympathy as he calmly calls for light and uses it to examine Hamlet closely. Hamlet, in response, covers his face, then laughs.

5   Hamlet himself thinks he is mad. To Ophelia he says, as if the realization had suddenly struck him, "It *hath* made me mad [emphasis his]" (III.i.147). To his

mother he stresses the word "essentially" in "I *essentially* am not in madness" (III. iv.187). That is, in all essential matters he can be considered sane, though mad around the edges. This indeed turns out to be the explanation.

However doubtful about Hamlet's sanity Jacobi's acting leaves us, in this production this question does not seem to make a difference because it does not have a bearing on the tragedy, and this is true at least partly because in each scene on this nonrealistic set we seem to start anew, ready to let Hamlet's behavior tell us if he is mad or not. Moreover, if Hamlet is mad, it is not so totally as to obscure reason or sensibility. Far from it. It is more as if exacerbated reason and sensibility sometimes tip him into madness. This madness is no excuse for action or delay; it is simply part of the suffering that Hamlet is heir to.

Hamlet, then, is left to struggle against himself—surely where Shakespeare intended the struggle to abide. One of the conflicts in this Hamlet results from his affinity, perhaps, more to the bureaucratic Claudius who handles war-scares with diplomacy and who sits at a desk while brooding over his sins than to the warlike King Hamlet who comes in full armor. Hamlet may admire Fortinbras but is himself more like the bookish Horatio. Through nuance of gesture, through body movement, through a face that is indeed a map of all emotions, Jacobi shapes a Hamlet who loves his father too much to disregard his command, yet who cannot hate his step-father enough to attend to it. Because Jacobi conveys so fully Hamlet's aloneness and vulnerability, one could be struck, for the first time, by the ghost's silence about his son. There is no declaration of love, no concern about Hamlet's ascension to the throne. Hamlet is doomed, it seems, to care about those who consistently care more for others than for him.

All of this production's richness and suggestiveness was realized not only because Jacobi is a marvelous actor—as indeed he is—but also because within the set's spareness that acting could unfold, an acting style that subsumes and transcends the "real." This production's space tells us what is possible for television presentations of Shakespeare. The more bare the set, it seems, the more glowing the words, the more immediate our apprehension of the enacted emotion.

CLAIRE BLOOM

PLAYING GERTRUDE ON TELEVISION

It's very hard to play because strangely enough Gertrude has very few lines; I've always known it was a wonderful part and it *is,* but when you come to play it you realise you have to find many ways around the fact that she in actual fact says little!

You come to rehearse a part like this with certain preconceived notions, which you usually leave! I can only describe them as a battering ram—you knock down the first wall then what is inside is something quite different from what you'd imagined. I was convinced that she was guilty, not of the murder, but certainly that she had found out from Claudius that he had killed her husband. But there's nothing in the text that bears that out and many things that contradict it. I had thought it would make her less of a victim, more of a performer in the world, but [she laughs at herself] it isn't so. Like anyone if you live with a man, she must know there was something more, but I now believe that when Hamlet confronts her with "as kill a king...ay, madam, it was my word," it's the first time she's realised. I think from then on she knows and she must accept the fact that Claudius did it, and there is a change in their relationship. But there isn't a break—you don't break with someone suddenly like that. It changes; perhaps if they'd lived another twenty years they would have drifted apart. But there isn't a complete withdrawal. The hold they have on each other is too strong for that to happen. That caused me great difficulty; the scene after the closet scene is with Claudius, when he repeats twice "Gertrude, come away," and she doesn't reply. It's very mysterious. It's a kind of underwritten scene until you realise, or I realised, that there is no real choice for her. For the moment she doesn't go with him, but the next day she does. Hamlet knows it when he says, "Go not to my uncle's bed." She never replies and says "I won't"; she just says, "Thou hast cleft my heart in twain." She's a woman who goes with whatever is happening at the time. She's a weak-willed woman, but most of us are weak-willed if we're in the power of somebody who is very strong—and Claudius and Hamlet are both pretty strong fellows.

The "mysterious" scene with Claudius was one of the hardest to deal with in rehearsal....We tried backwards, forwards, upside down and inside out and didn't really find it until a couple of days before we shot it. The minute we found it we knew it was the right one, but at other times we'd go away saying, "We've got it," then both Patrick and I would come in the next day depressed and say to Rodney, "Could we please do that scene again because it doesn't make sense when you think about it." There are questions that I'm sure have been asked by every cast of every *Hamlet* since Burbage[1] and for Gertrude they are: Was there a decision to go with Claudius or not to go with Claudius? How far was she lying about Hamlet's madness? I do think part of her believes he's mad, but when she says to the king "He's mad," I think that's protection, or overstating a fact she believes is possibly true. And of course she withholds information from Claudius; she says, "Behind the arras hearing something stir...[he] kills the unseen good old man," but she *doesn't* say he said "Is it the king?" That is a very important bit of information which she certainly doesn't pass on!

STANLEY KAUFFMANN

BRANAGH'S HAMLET

Kenneth Branagh wins two victories in *Hamlet* (Castle Rock [1996]). He has made a vital, exciting film; and he has triumphed over the obstacles he put in his own way.

Let's first rejoice in the virtues. Branagh confirms what was known from the opening shot of *Henry V*: he has fine cinematic skills. His directing keeps *Hamlet* flowing, endows scenes that might become static with germane movement. Many of his touches illuminate. One of them: Hamlet comes into a huge mirrored room in the palace, sees himself full-length and, after a moment, begins "To be or not to be." Two selves speak that speech and give it an added edge.

[1]**Burbage** Richard Burbage (c. 1567–1619), the first actor to play Shakepeare's Hamlet.

Then there's the text itself. Branagh has used the complete First Folio text, has included a scene from the Second Quarto that is not in the Folio, to make a film that runs four hours plus intermission. I could find only a few alterations, trifles compared with the chopped, twisted, insulting text that Olivier used in his 155-minute version. Branagh's film looks splendid. He sets it in the mid-nineteenth century—with Blenheim Palace serving as the exterior of Elsinore—and Alex Byrne's costumes fully exploit the period. The cinematographer, Alex Thomson, using 70-mm widescreen format, has nonetheless created lighting that seems naturally evolved from the hundreds of candles. And as for the music, Patrick Doyle again does wonders. He wrote the scores for Branagh's two previous Shakespeare films, and here again he provides music that rises unobtrusively to benefit scene after scene.

Every supporting role of significance has been superbly cast and is superbly played. I can't imagine a better Claudius than Derek Jacobi, who brings to it force and cunning and manipulative charm. The sequences in which he converts the furious Laertes from enemy to accomplice are masterpieces of guile manifested as honesty. (Jacobi, by the way, was the first Hamlet that Branagh ever saw; and years later Jacobi directed Branagh in a theater production.)

5   Jacobi is no surprise: Julie Christie is. This Golden Girl of the 1960s virtually disappeared for a while, then reappeared in a London production of Pinter's *Old Times*. She was so dull that I thought she was being used just for her name. But here, as Gertrude, she is emotionally rich. She brings to the role the apt quality of overblown sex object, and, presumably with Branagh's help, she completely fulfills the woman. In Gertrude's key moment, the closet scene, Christie bursts with the frightened despair of a guilty woman who thinks that her behavior may have driven her son mad.

Kate Winslet, dear to us already through *Sense and Sensibility* and *Jude,* gives Ophelia the kind of vulnerability that almost invites the man she loves to wound her. Polonius gets the obtuse officiousness that he needs from Richard Briers. It's immediately clear why Horatio, done by Nicholas Farrell, is Hamlet's dearest friend; anybody would want him for a friend. Laertes, a role always in danger of being as much of a blowhard as his father, Polonius, is realized in his confusions by Michael Maloney. Branagh, as he did in *Much Ado About Nothing,* has sprinkled some American actors through his cast. The best of these is Charlton Heston as the Player King, sounding and (even) looking plummy, home at last.

Hamlet is unique in Shakespeare. I can think of no other role in the plays in which an actor is so compelled, commanded, to present *himself*. Macbeth, Othello, Iago, the Richards and the Henrys—run through the roster, and always the actor selects and nurtures what there is in his imagination and experience and technique that will make the man come alive. No such selections for Hamlet. The whole actor is the whole character. So, when we see a Hamlet, we are looking at an actor in a unique way.

Branagh's Hamlet—or, one might say, Hamlet's Branagh—is attractive, keen, nobly intended, tender with regret for Ophelia, torn with disgust for the chicaneries of the world, fiery, quite susceptible to cracking into frenzy. (In appearance, he is fair—not Olivier's platinum blond—with a somewhat darker moustache and goatee.)

This is a man we could meet and understand. What this Hamlet lacks is what possibly we could not understand: his sense of falling upward into the metaphysical. This is what is sometimes called the "poetic" nature of Hamlet, this linkage with a spirit walking the earth in quest of purgation; and this linkage, in mystery and awe and uncertainty, leads to what Granville Barker called "a tragedy of inaction." Branagh's Hamlet doesn't attain this quality; it doesn't quite seem to be in him. Not long ago Ralph Fiennes, burdened with an unworthy director and cast, nevertheless did a Hamlet on Broadway that took us out into the spheres. Not Branagh. Every word he speaks is true. But in Hamlet that is not quite enough.

10   Now the lesser aspects of the film. First, the obverse side of Branagh's directing skill. He is too eager for spectacle, even if it's pointless or harmful. When Gertrude and Claudius exit at the end of the first court scene, confetti rains down on them. For the moment, it's startling, pretty. Then we wonder who planned it and who threw it. Answer: the director. When the Ghost speaks to Hamlet, the earth splits and flames leap. Is this God overseeing unpurged souls? Or the special effects department? Rosencrantz and Guildenstern arrive on a toy locomotive. Who put that model train and tracks on the palace grounds? Old King Hamlet? Claudius? Or the director? When Hamlet and Laertes duel, the civilized sport explodes into Errol Flynn antics, with ropes and chandeliers—another directorial intrusion. Branagh sets the whole film in winter, which allows for some breathtaking vistas but makes us wonder why the old king was sleeping outdoors in his snow-covered orchard on the afternoon of his murder and how the brookside flowers could be present when Ophelia drowns.

Another obverse side, one that may sound odd: the use of the complete text. Admirable though it is in Branagh to aim at "classic" status, not every word is helpful today, especially in a film. To hear Marcellus discourse on "the bird of dawning" at Christmastime, just after the Ghost's second appearance, is a soft indulgence in Elizabethan folklore. To hear Gertrude include a small dirty joke, about "long purples," when she tells Laertes of his sister's death is to coddle the lad from Stratford who couldn't always keep rustic humor out of his plays. And the sad fact is that, when Shakespeare takes time out from drama for moral commentary, the result is sometimes mere homiletics. Hamlet's speech about "the dram of evil" is not only a brusque lapse in the action, it captures perfectly the quality in Shakespeare that Bernard Shaw called "the atmosphere of the rented pew."

Sex. Branagh has searched for chances to get it into the film. While Polonius is warning Ophelia to be careful in her behavior with Hamlet, to avoid the prince completely, Branagh includes flashback shots of her and Hamlet naked in bed together. Presumably Branagh takes his license from the bawdy song that Ophelia later sings when she is mad—"Young men will do't if they come to't," etc.—a song that is usually viewed as the raving of a sexually repressed virgin. Whether or not Hamlet and Ophelia actually had an affair is possibly arguable, but what seems clear is that, if they have made love, it detracts considerably from the fierce, Savonarola-like outburst of the "get thee to a nunnery" passages.

Then, too, Polonius is given a visiting whore in the scene with Reynaldo, who is apparently her pimp. (Ophelia bursts in without knocking—fortuitously, just after Reynaldo and the whore leave.) Branagh's purpose is to lend irony to the old man's instructions to Reynaldo, about checking on Laertes's behavior in Paris, but the episode smacks of opportunism.

Politics. Of course *Hamlet* is, among other elements, a political play. One cause for Hamlet's hatred of Claudius is that his uncle has "popp'd in between th'election and my hopes." Branagh's use of the mid-century period affords the ambiance of the "Age of Metternich," but it misplaces in time the Denmark-England-Norway-Poland relationships of the original. Further, Branagh distorts the political action of the closing scenes. Early in the play we learn that the young Fortinbras of Norway wants to reconquer some lands that his country lost to Denmark, but the Norwegian king dissuades him. Fortinbras swears never to attack Denmark, but he will ask for the right of passage through Denmark to attack Poland. Toward the end of the play Fortinbras leads an army into Denmark and sends a messenger to Claudius to ask for that right of passage.

15   Incomprehensibly, in Branagh's film, Fortinbras then attacks Elsinore. (Real reason: Branagh wants to heat up the film's closing moments.) Shots of this violence are intercut with the Hamlet-Laertes duel. Just as Hamlet dies, the Norwegian soldiers burst into the court, destroying as they come. Fortinbras ought to feel a bit foolish, not only having broken his word but to find out that, just before Hamlet expired, the prince named him as his successor. ("He has my dying voice.") Instead, Fortinbras is shown as a glowering conqueror moderately disturbed by the prince's death. The very last shot is of old King Hamlet's statue being toppled and smashed. Why did Branagh choose that shot as the moment toward which the entire film moved?

Some other points might be called matters of interpretation—Claudius's slapping of Hamlet in anger at the chaffing about Polonius's corpse, the straitjacketing of Ophelia in a padded cell—but one Branagh touch seems just plain misreading. Claudius (in Act III, Scene 1) says he has "closely sent for Hamlet" so that the prince can meet Ophelia while Claudius and Polonius are hidden and watching. They do hide, Hamlet enters, finds the chamber empty though he has been sent for, muses aloud while waiting ("To be or not to be"). Then Ophelia enters— the girl who, for days, has been forbidden to see him. And it was the king who summoned him here. Surely, in simple reason, Hamlet must be suspicious that this is a set-up from the moment she appears. Instead, Branagh plays it merely petulantly until, after the nunnery speech, he hears a noise behind the door and the deception dawns on him. Branagh's treatment not only makes Hamlet less acute than we are, it takes the bite out of "Are you honest?"

Interpretations and innovations have different weights in a Shakespeare film from such matters in a theater production. When I saw Ingmar Bergman's production of *Hamlet,* with his sluttish Ophelia wandering through scenes in which Shakespeare forgot to include her, I was relieved that Bergman had not filmed it. Branagh's film, warts and all, will be with us for some time to come.

On the whole, this is good news. Though his *Henry V* and *Much Ado About Nothing* were closer to perfection, *Hamlet* is more difficult in every way. Flaws, problems, bumps, yes; but the film surpasses them finally through Branagh's talent and the talents of his colleagues. And, not to be slighted, there is Branagh's infectious joy—the right word even for *Hamlet*—in doing Shakespeare.

RUSSELL JACKSON [B. 1949]

A FILM DIARY OF THE SHOOTING
OF KENNETH BRANAGH'S HAMLET   [1996]

WEDNESDAY 3 JANUARY REHEARSALS BEGIN

First morning in Shepperton. This may be one of the major British studios but it's not, on first sight, impressive. Located in a semi-suburban hinterland southwest of London, it seems at first like an industrial estate, a jumble of sheds, hangars, work-shops, and what look like builders' yards, with a mansion trapped in the middle of it all like a genteel hostage from Edwardian England....

We're in the elegant boardroom of the old house, round a long green-baize covered table. First session is with Derek Jacobi (Claudius) and Julie Christie (Gertrude), plus Ken, Orlando Seale (his "acting double"), Annie Wotton (Script Supervisor), Simon Mosley (First A.D.), and Hugh Cruttwell.

Ken distributes phials [vials] of a herbal "Rescue Remedy" (only half a joke, admitting nervous apprehension). Everyone has read the screenplay, and the ac-tors have already had some discussion of their roles with Ken, but these days of rehearsal before we begin shooting will give everyone time for reappraisal, adjust-ments, and (most important) finding out how the story will be told by *this* company of actors, in *these* circumstances. We won't start with a read-through; better to edge toward the play. We discuss royal families (including the current one), privacy, politics, and draw toward a reading of the scenes when Claudius and Gertrude are together. There's talk about the issue of complicity between them (not at all, so far as murder is concerned) and the "essential" Claudius, which she took (and part of him still takes) as loving, kind, a "good" man. Derek goes along with this, though he and Hugh Cruttwell remind us of Hamlet's very different point of view. Gertrude and Claudius feel responsible for Hamlet but Claudius has another agenda she knows nothing about—concerning the potential threat posed by her son.

After lunch the Polonius family join us, with Horatio. By now we feel able to discuss frankly and simply (and off the record) our own experiences of family, be-reavement, grief. (This is not just to canvass ideas about the emotions of the play to draw on them in performance: it also establishes common ground among us.) Then we try to imagine an "ideal" family, successful and well-balanced according to cur-rent middle-class notions, professional but not competitive, materially well-off but not showy—which (we agree) turns out quite repulsive. Then on to the Polonius family.

5   Polonius (Richard Briers) was promoted by new king. Laertes (Michael Maloney) is in Paris getting the gentlemanly accomplishments (N.B. not at Wittenberg). Ophelia (Kate Winslet) and Hamlet have been having an affair (yes, they have been to bed to-gether, because we want this relationship to be as serious as possible) since the death of Hamlet senior. (Effect of a surge of feeling in time of bereavement and crisis?)

THURSDAY 4–MONDAY 8 JANUARY

We work through scenes, trying various approaches, finding snags, problems, opportunities. Ophelia's motivations in returning Hamlet's love tokens are con-sidered: she is going further than Polonius suggested in any instructions we have heard, and whatever her father and the king expect from this confrontation, she has her own agenda (perhaps to find out why Hamlet is behaving this way to her, to put him on the spot?). The kinder and more circumspect Polonius seems, the harder it will be for her to betray him—hence her lying to Hamlet ("Where's your father?—At home, my lord"). In "To be or not to be" Ken wants to show Hamlet alone with his mirror image(s) in the vast space of the mirrored hall. He has to be careful not to give the soliloquy an energy or momentum that it does not need— those qualities are coming soon enough in what follows when he encounters Ophelia. Ken steers Derek toward seeming even more vulnerable as Claudius, "quietly anxious" about Hamlet after the "nunnery" scene, rarely openly angry, even when Rosencrantz and Guildenstern have screwed up. So, when he does flare up, becomes desperate, it will be more shocking.

On 8 January we go over each actor's list of their character's priorities. Claudius has specific aims: inspiring confidence and trust in himself; loving Gertrude; making Hamlet look indulgent and neurotic (and thus defusing him); creating a new, strong, triumphalist Denmark (a military regime). Gertrude's aims are more general: decorum, sense of behaving properly in public; *noblesse oblige,* etiquette; sense of culture, confidence; loving Hamlet. Old Hamlet (Brian Blessed) points out that when he was alive he never let Claudius see how little he mattered—there has to be an underlying bitterness in what Claudius has done to get the crown as well as intense love for Gertrude. We consider different ways of showing these relationships in a short flashback—perhaps Old Hamlet and his son playing chess while Gertrude and Claudius watch, or some other activity (perhaps outdoors) that will focus their various feelings for each other.

> From *Hamlet.* Screenplay and Introduction by
> Kenneth Branagh. Film diary by Russell Jackson.

Exploring the Literature of Innocence and Experience: Options for Making Connections, Building Arguments, and Using Research

 MAKING CONNECTIONS

1. Consider the ways in which personal experiences have influenced your life. Do any of the stories, poems, plays, or essays in this section remind you of your own experiences or the circumstances of your life? Choose one or more of these works, and write a response essay that compares your experience or circumstances with those in the literature.

2. Our personal experiences can affect how we see the world and the formation of our values. These values can strongly influence our response to literature. We may agree or disagree with what an author says or what characters say or do. So, too, this literature may influence us and help to form our ideas about innocence and experience. Write an essay about the ways in which one or more works in this section helped you learn something about innocence and experience.

MAKING AN ARGUMENT

1. Over two thousand years ago, Plato wrote in the *Symposium,* "The life which is unexamined is not worth living." Do you agree? Consider this quote, and write an essay about the value of examining or reflecting on a personal experience in one or more works in this section.

2. Oscar Wilde has written that "...it is well to remember from time to time that nothing worth knowing can be taught." Do you agree?

   Write about this quote as it applies to the experience of a character in one or more works in this section.

3. Choose a quote (or quotes) in the introduction to this section, Innocence and Experience, and pair it (or them) with one of the longer pieces in this section that either supports or argues against it. For example, La Rochefoucauld's maxim, "The mind is always the dupe of the heart," might be compared to James Joyce's "Araby." Or Huxley's comment that "Experience is not what happens to you; it is what you do with what happens to you" might be compared with Liliana Heker's "The Stolen Party."

Using Research

Toni Cade Bambara's "The Lesson," Shakespeare's *Hamlet,* and David Sedaris's "The Learning Curve" all have something to say about innocence and experience. However insightful each of these pieces is by itself, expanding our exploration of literature by seeking, using, and citing relevant secondary sources can add support and credibility to our writing.

1. Research has shown that boys and girls react differently to youthful experiences and mature at a different rate. Pick out one work about male experience and one work about female experience, and write about the differences. Support your conclusion with secondary source evidence from research in the field of developmental psychology or a related field.

2. James Joyce's short story "Araby," A. E. Housman's poem "When I Was One and Twenty," and Judith Ortiz Cofer's essay "I Fell in Love, or My Hormones Awakened" are about unrequited young love. Compare the three pieces, and cite secondary sources from research done on the impact of unrequited young love to support your views.

3. Read William Blake's poems "The Chimney Sweeper" in both the *Songs of Innocence* and *Songs of Experience* versions. Which do you think is accurate and why? Broaden your view by reading Blake's "London." Explore the historical context of the poems by doing research on life in London in the late eighteenth century and the role of chimney sweepers. Integrate what you find into your essay, and cite this secondary source research to support your interpretations of the poems.

Writing About Connections Across Themes

Most of the literature in the text has been organized into theme sections, but good literature is much too complex to be reduced to a single broad theme. Many of the works included under Innocence and Experience could just as easily fit under other themes—and in many cases works arranged in other themes or chapters could fit here as well.

Choose one or more of the following works from earlier chapters or other themes and consider how they can be linked to Innocence and Experience—and how this combination of the work with more than one theme provides additional insight into the literature and fresh topics for writing.

From Chapter 1
"Advice to My Son"—p. 9
"Zimmer in Grade School"—p. 11
"Those Winter Sundays"—p. 13
"Barbie Doll"—p. 14
"Ballad of Birmingham"—p. 17
From Chapter 2
"Incident"—p. 24
"Eleven"—p. 26
"Salvation"—p. 32
From Chapter 3
"The Story of an Hour"—p. 71
"The Road Not Taken"—p. 82
"When I Heard the Learn'd Astronomer"—p. 89
From Chapter 5
"Eveline"—p. 201
From Family and Friends
"Sonny's Blues"—p. 218
"The Red Convertible"—p. 241
"Reunion"—p. 254
"The Road"—p. 257
A Raisin in the Sun—p. 310
From Women and Men
"The Yellow Wallpaper"—p. 676
"The Horse Dealer's Daughter"—p. 693
"The Day It Happened"—p. 716
"The Nymph's Reply to the Shepherd"—p. 720
"Woman"—p. 729
"The Wedding Couple"—p. 733
"How to Watch Your Brother Die"—p. 736
"What Lips My Lips Have Kissed, and Where, and Why"—p. 739
Trifles—p. 770
"A Jury of Her Peers"—p. 780
A Doll's House—p. 803

Collaboration: Writing and Revising with Your Peers

In addition to applying your own values and standards to writing about the literature in this section, you may find it beneficial to share and discuss your work with classmates. Getting feedback from others can help you generate and clarify your ideas and revise and edit your writing more effectively. For details, see pages 397–398.

A Writing/Research Portfolio Option

A portfolio is a collection of your work, related materials, and commentary about your work collected over time. Gathering materials in a portfolio will provide you with resources for research and development. See page 398 for details.

CASE STUDY IN AESTHETIC CONTEXT

Poetry and Painting

The purpose of this Case Study is to provide you with an opportunity to compare two forms of art, painting and poetry. Long before the advent of writing, people recorded their innermost feelings and impulses in images painted on cave walls. In fact, a number of cave paintings found in South Africa are nearly thirty thousand years old. Throughout history, artists have celebrated great writing by sculpting, painting, and drawing their responses to literature. The work of Homer, Shakespeare, Dickens, Joyce, and many other writers has inspired sculpture, painting, and illustration. Art inspires art. Conversely then, it's not surprising that poems are inspired by great paintings. Viewed and read together, the eight paintings that follow and the poems written in response to them invite comparisons and connections—not only with each other, but with your own experience of the subject they address.

In one way or another, these paintings and poems have something to say about many different themes and are not limited to time and place. Like the brief quotations that open the thematic units, these paintings and poems are a dialogue across history. W. H. Auden's modern poem "Musée des Beaux Arts" responds to Brueghel's sixteenth-century *Landscape with the Fall of Icarus,* itself a response to ancient Greek mythology. And Alan Devenish's "Icarus Again" is a 1999 poem written in response to the ancient myth, the paintings and poems it has inspired over the ages, and the tragedies of modern life. Both Lun-Yi Tsai's painting *Disbelief* and Lucille Clifton's "tuesday 9/11/01" are contemporary responses to the same horrific event. Edward Hopper's painting *Nighthawks* and the poem it prompts, Samuel Yellen's "Nighthawks," are both modern pieces; van Gogh's nineteenth-century *Starry Night* evokes Anne Sexton's twentieth-century "The Starry Night"; Jan Vermeer's *The Loveletter* speaks across three hundred years to Sandra Nelson, who answers with her poem "When a Woman Holds a Letter." The painter of *Dance,* Henri Matisse, produced his painting more than eighty years before the poet Natalie Safir interprets it in "Matisse's Dance." Cathy Song's poem "Beauty and Sadness" is inspired by Kitagawa Utamaro's eighteenth-century painting *Two Women Dressing Their Hair*. Adrienne Rich had not been born when Edwin Romanzo Elmer painted his *Mourning Picture* in memory of his young daughter Effie. Yet Rich's response to the painting, "Mourning Picture," brings Effie back to life as the mournful speaker of the poem.

Whatever they hold in common, each painting and poem is an individual work. So before you read the poems, look at each of the paintings separately and write your own response. On the next page are prompts and questions that may help you organize your responses.

641

FIRST RESPONSES: PAINTING AND POETRY

1. Before you read its accompanying poem, write your own response to each of the paintings.

   - As you look at the painting, write down what strikes you first. How does it make you feel? What do you like most about it? Do you find anything disturbing?
   - Do you sense a prevailing mood or tone? How do the colors affect you?

2. When you finish recording your responses to the painting, read the companion poem.

   - Compare your response to the painting with the poet's response. How are they similar? How are they different?
   - Has the poet mentioned anything that is not included in your response? Have you raised issues that the poet has not?

3. Compare and contrast the poem with the painting.

   - Are the details of each the same? What details are contained in the poem that are not in the painting? What details are in the painting but not in the poem?
   - Do the painting and the poem seem to be saying the same thing? If not, how do they differ? Which do you prefer?
   - Has reading the poem revised your response to the painting? If so, how?

Following the paintings and poems in the glossy insert is the process (p. 659) and product (p. 662) of a Student's Comparison and Contrast Essay and questions for Making Connections and Making an Argument on page 666 that build on the prompts above. You may find the student model and the questions useful for writing essays about the poems and paintings in this section.

Making Connections with Painting and Poetry

Pieter Brueghel the Elder (Dutch, 1520–1569). *Landscape with the Fall of Icarus.*
Ca. 1558. Musée Royaux des Beaux-Arts, Brussels, Belgium. Photo: Scala/Art
Resource, NY.

W. H. AUDEN [1907–1973]

MUSÉE DES BEAUX ARTS   [1940]

About suffering they were never wrong,
The Old Masters: how well they understood
Its human position; how it takes place
While someone else is eating or opening a window or just walking dully along;
How, when the aged are reverently, passionately waiting   5
For the miraculous birth, there always must be
Children who did not specially want it to happen, skating
On a pond at the edge of the wood:
They never forgot
That even the dreadful martyrdom must run its course   10
Anyhow in a corner, some untidy spot
Where the dogs go on with their doggy life and the torturer's horse
Scratches its innocent behind on a tree.

In Brueghel's *Icarus,* for instance: how everything turns away
Quite leisurely from the disaster; the ploughman may   15
Have heard the splash, the forsaken cry,
But for him it was not an important failure; the sun shone
As it had to on the white legs disappearing into the green
Water; and the expensive delicate ship that must have seen
Something amazing, a boy falling out of the sky,   20
Had somewhere to get to and sailed calmly on.

ALAN DEVENISH [B. 1947]

ICARUS AGAIN   [1999]

You'd think we'd have enough of falling
since that sunny day high off the coast of Crete. Air disasters
appalling and impersonal. The bomber's hate
made potent with a bit of plastic and some altitude. Spacecrafts
with schoolteachers aboard—exploding over and over   5
again. The parents aghast at the pure Icarian sky of Florida
suddenly emptied of their child.

What is myth if not an early version of what's been happening
all along? (The arrogance of flight brought down
by faulty gaskets.)   10

As Auden would have it: the way we plow through life
head bent to the furrow while tragedy falls from the sky.

Bruegel shows only the legs—flailing and white—scissoring
into a pitiless green sea.

Williams treats a distant casualty in his clinical   15
little sketch. (Did the astronauts feel their fall
or breathe instantly the killing fumes?)

Matisse plays it another way. It's color—Icarus' love
for color and who can blame him? His poor heart
waxing red as he falls through blue and what might be   20
a scatter of sunbursts or a vision of war—the enemy
aces sighting Icarus in their crosshairs over France.

In Ovid the line that never fails to move me is
And he saw the wings on the waves . . .

The way it comes to the father. His lofty design reduced to this   25
little detritus as he hovers in the left-hand corner of the myth
grieving wingbeats wrinkling the surface of the sea.

Even in bad prints of the Bruegel I can't help feeling sorry
for this kid. And dismay at our constant clumsiness. Our light
heart pulling us down. Love itself believing against all gravity   30
that what we say is what is bound to happen. How foolish to trust
our waxen wings and how foolish not to.

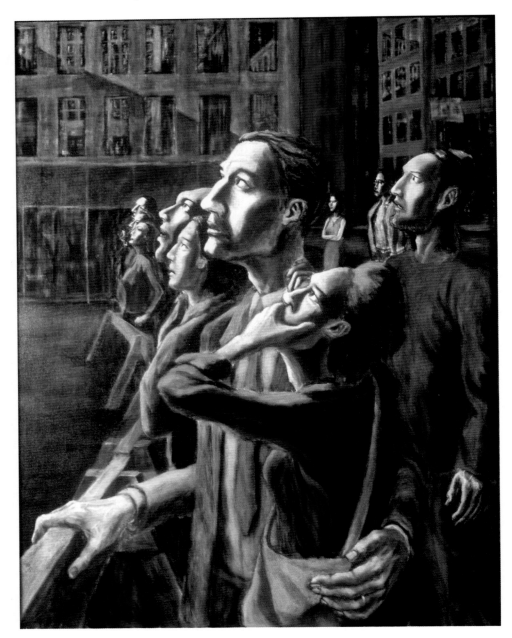

Lun-Yi Tsai, *Disbelief.* 2002. Oil on linen, 66 − 50 inches. Collection of the artist.

LUCILLE CLIFTON [B. 1936]

TUESDAY *9/11/01*   [2004]

thunder and lightning and our world
is another place   no day
will ever be the same   no blood

they know this storm in otherwheres
israel   ireland   palestine   5
but God has blessed America
we sing

and God has blessed America
to learn that no one   is exempt
the world is one   all fear   10
is one   all life   all death
all one

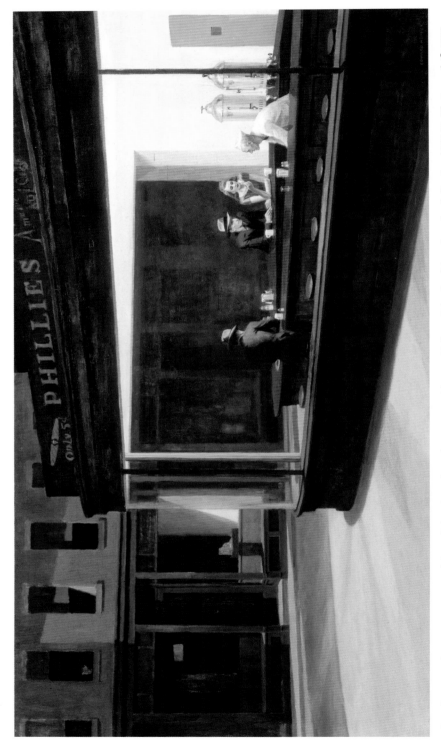

Edward Hopper (American, 1882–1967), *Nighthawks*. 1942. Oil on canvas, 84.1 – 152.4 cm. Friends of American Art Collection 1942.51. Photograph © 2009, The Art Institute of Chicago. All rights reserved.

SAMUEL YELLEN [B. 1906]

NIGHTHAWKS   [1951]

The place is the corner of Empty and Bleak,
The time is night's most desolate hour,
The scene is Al's Coffee Cup or the Hamburger Tower,
The persons in this drama do not speak.

We who peer through that curve of plate glass   5
Count three nighthawks seated there—patrons of life:
The counterman will be with you in a jiff,
The thick white mugs were never meant for demitasse.

The single man whose hunched back we see
Once put a gun to his head in Russian roulette,   10
Whirled the chamber, pulled the trigger, won the bet,
And now lives out his *x* years' guarantee.

And facing us, the two central characters
Have finished their coffee, and have lit
A contemplative cigarette;   15
His hand lies close, but not touching hers.

Not long ago together in a darkened room,
Mouth burned mouth, flesh beat and ground
On ravaged flesh, and yet they found
No local habitation and no name.   20

Oh, are we not lucky to be none of these!
We can look on with complacent eye:
Our satisfactions satisfy,
Our pleasures, our pleasures please.

Vincent van Gogh (Dutch, 1853–1890.) *Starry Night*. 1889. Oil on canvas. 29 − 36¼" (73.7 − 92.1 cm). The Museum of Modern Art, New York. Acquired through the Lillie P. Bliss Bequest (472.1941). Photo: The Museum of Modern Art/Licensed by SCALA/Art Resource, NY.

ANNE SEXTON [1928–1975]

THE STARRY NIGHT   [1961]

That does not keep me from having a terrible need of—shall I say the word—
religion. Then I go out at night to paint the stars.
   —Vincent van Gogh in a letter to his brother

The town does not exist
except where one black-haired tree slips
up like a drowned woman into the hot sky.
The town is silent. The night boils with eleven stars
Oh starry starry night! This is how   5
I want to die.

It moves. They are all alive.
Even the moon bulges in its orange irons
to push children, like a god, from its eye.
The old unseen serpent swallows up the stars.   10
Oh starry starry night! This is how
I want to die:

into that rushing beast of the night,
sucked up by that great dragon, to split
from my life with no flag,   15
no belly,
no cry.

Henri Matisse (French, 1869–1954). *Dance (first version)*. Paris, March 1909. Oil on canvas 8' 6½" − 12' 9½" (259.7 − 390.1 cm). Gift of Nelson A. Rockefeller in honor of Alfred H. Barr Jr. Digital Image © The Museum of Modern Art/Licensed by SCALA/Art Resource, NY. © 2009 Succession H. Matisse, Paris/Artists Rights Society (ARS), New York.

NATALIE SAFIR [B. 1935]

MATISSE'S DANCE   [1990]

A break in the circle dance of naked women,
dropped stitch between the hands
of the slender figure stretching too hard
to reach her joyful sisters.

Spirals of glee sail from the arms   5
of the tallest woman. She pulls
the circle around with her fire.
What has she found that she doesn't
keep losing, her torso
a green-burning torch?   10

Grass mounds curve ripely beneath
two others who dance beyond the blue.
Breasts swell and multiply and
rhythms rise to a gallop.

Hurry, frightened one and grab on—before   15
the stitch is forever lost, before the dance
unravels and a black sun swirls from that space.

Kitagawa Utamaro (1753–1806). *Two Women Dressing Their Hair.*
1774–1775. New York Public Library/Art Resource, NY.

CATHY SONG [B. 1952]

(See biography on p. 274.)

BEAUTY AND SADNESS   [1983]

for Kitagawa Utamaro

He drew hundreds of women
in studies unfolding
like flowers from a fan.
Teahouse waitresses, actresses,
geishas, courtesans and maids.   5

They arranged themselves
before this quick, nimble man
whose invisible presence
one feels in these prints
is as delicate   10
as the skinlike paper
he used to transfer
and retain their fleeting loveliness.

    Crouching like cats,
they purred amid the layers of kimono   15
swirling around them
as though they were bathing
in a mountain pool with irises
growing in the silken sunlit water.
Or poised like porcelain vases,   20
slender, erect and tall; their heavy
brocaded hair was piled high
with sandalwood combs and blossom sprigs
poking out like antennae.
They resembled beautiful iridescent insects,   25
creatures from a floating world.

    Utamaro absorbed these women of Edo
in their moments of melancholy
He captured the wisp of shadows,
the half-draped body   30
emerging from a bath; whatever
skin was exposed
was powdered white as snow.
A private space disclosed.   35
Portraying another girl
catching a glimpse of her own vulnerable
face in the mirror, he transposed
the trembling plum lips
like a drop of blood
soaking up the white expanse of paper.   40

    At times, indifferent to his inconsolable
eye, the women drifted
through the soft gray feathered light,
maintaining stillness, the moments in between.   45
Like the dusty ash-winged moths
that cling to the screens in summer
and that the Japanese venerate
as ancestors reincarnated;
Utamaro graced these women with immortality

in the thousand sheaves of prints   50
fluttering into the reverent hands of keepers:
the dwarfed and bespectacled painter
holding up to a square of sunlight
what he had carried home beneath his coat
one afternoon in winter.   55

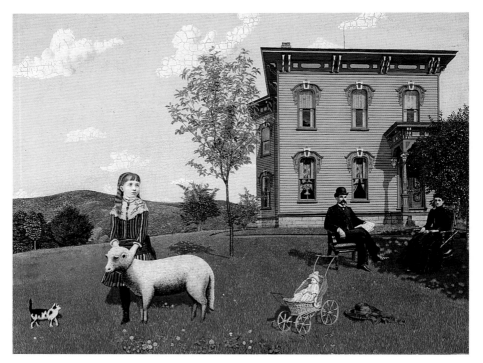

Edwin Romanzo Elmer (1850–1923). *Mourning Picture*. 1890. Oil on canvas, $27^{15}/_{16}$ − 36 in.
(70.9 − 91.4 cm). Smith College Museum of Art, Northampton, Massachusetts. Purchased 1953.

ADRIENNE RICH [B. 1929]

MOURNING PICTURE [1965]

The picture was painted by Edwin Romanzo Elmer (1850–1923) as a memorial to his daughter Effie. In the poem, it is the dead girl who speaks.

They have carried the mahogany chair and the cane rocker
out under the lilac bush,
and my father and mother darkly sit there, in black clothes.
Our clapboard house stands fast on its hill,
my doll lies in her wicker pram   5
gazing at western Massachusetts.
This was our world,
I could remake each shaft of grass
feeling its rasp on my fingers,
draw out the map of every lilac leaf   10
or the net of veins on my father's
grief-tranced hand.

Out of my head, half-bursting,
still filling, the dream condenses—
shadows, crystals, ceilings, meadows, globes of dew.   15
Under the dull green of the lilacs, out in the light
carving each spoke of the pram, the turned porch-pillars,
under high early-summer clouds,
I am Effie, visible and invisible,
remembering and remembered.   20

They will move from the house,
give the toys and pets away.
Mute and rigid with loss my mother
will ride the train to Baptist Corner,
the silk-spool will run bare.   25
I tell you, the thread that bound us lies
faint as a web in the dew.
Should I make you, world, again,
could I give back the leaf its skeleton, the air
its early-summer cloud, the house   30
its noonday presence, shadowless,
and leave *this* out? I am Effie, you were my dream.

Jan Vermeer (Dutch, 1632–1675). *The Loveletter.* c. 1670. Oil on canvas 44 − 38.5 cm. © Rijksmuseum, Amsterdam.

SANDRA NELSON [B. 1951]

WHEN A WOMAN HOLDS A LETTER   [1993]

It is always from a man. Jan Vermeer
knows this as he paints the dark
note in Clarissa's right hand;
her left strangling the fretted neck coming
from the pear-shaped body of his   5
mandolin. Her upturned eyes may be tied
to a ferris wheel of sparrows' biting love.
Or she may feel the heavy curve of his instrument
against her stomach and her eyes
instinctively flip up to heaven to see   10
if anyone is watching. I am
probably wrong. There *is* another woman
behind her (a washer-woman whose head
is wrapped in a wimple to keep out the dirt).
Perhaps it is to her that Clarissa's eyes roll.   15

A Student's Comparison and Contrast Essay: Process and Product

On the following pages, we follow Barbara Pfister's process as she generates ideas for her comparison and contrast essay about Vincent van Gogh's *Starry Night* and Anne Sexton's poem. At the core of this process are journal responses and semantic maps. By completing her written response and semantic map after viewing the painting—before she reads Sexton's poem—she comes up with her own interpretation of the painting. When she finally reads Sexton's poem, she has two sources to compare it with, the painting and her own interpretation—giving her a base from which to respond to the poem—and enriching the content of her subsequent essay.

Barbara Pfister's Semantic Map in Response to van Gogh's painting Starry Night

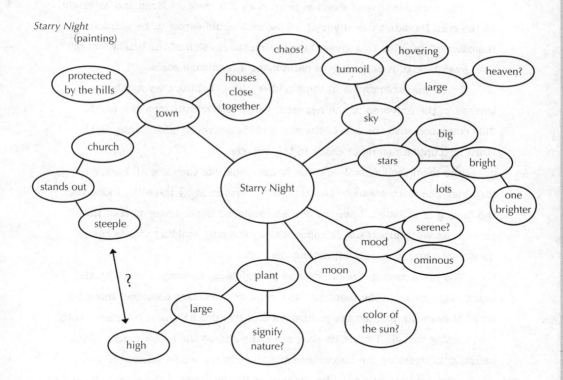

Starry Night
(painting)

Barbara's Journal Response to van Gogh's Painting Starry Night

> When I first looked at this painting, the overall impression I got was ominous and quiet, but not gloomy. The feeling was of both foreboding and powerful beauty at the same time.

I liked the short brushstrokes he used to paint this scene. They give the feeling of separate and distinct pieces that together make up the whole. The colors in the picture depict a night sky, but at the same time appear as vivid as day.

The sky takes up a major portion of the painting and it stands out quite vividly. I love the way van Gogh painted the stars. They appear to be very large and bright, not little pinpoints in the sky as we usually see them. Their size and brightness stress their importance in the picture. I think he is symbolizing the greatness of heaven or the universe. There is one star that is especially bright in the lower part of the sky, and I feel this must mean something but I'm not sure exactly what.

The crescent-shaped moon is painted as if it were as large and as bright as the sun. He didn't use silver or white, as I would depict it; he painted it the color of the sun. This gives the painting the illusion of the brightness of day, even though it is actually a painting of a nighttime scene.

I find the large swirls in the sky disturbing. I think they symbolize turmoil in the universe or the heavens, which is hovering over the earth. This combined with the size of the sky and its heavenly inhabitants, the stars, prompts a feeling of chaos in the universe.

The town seems small and the houses look like they are all huddled together. The town seems to be sheltered or protected by the hills. I also get the feeling of isolation. I see the church, centered in the lower part of the picture, as very important. It appears to be the only building that is really discernible, and it stands out among the rest.

The plant seen in the foreground is very large in comparison with the rest of the objects in the painting. This must be important because I think he could have easily painted the picture without it. I don't think it interferes with the painting though. I think its size, spanning almost the entire height of the painting, is stressing the importance of nature in the whole scheme of life.

After contemplating the importance or the meaning of the plant, I looked at the town and the church again. Maybe it is symbolic that the plant reaches all the way to the sky, signifying the relationship between nature and the heavens. The plant also seems to spear right through the swirling turmoil in the night. The steeple of the church, in comparison, barely reaches the horizon. I wonder if this is intentional and therefore, symbolic, or merely a coincidence.

I can summarize my feelings in a few different ways. The colors he used seem to imply that the heavens at night are as bright and clear as day, and perhaps that is how our understanding of the universe should be. With reference to the plant and the church, another idea is that people can only make a small attempt to understand the heavens or the universe, while nature is at one with the universe.

Barbara's Semantic Map in Response to Anne Sexton's poem "The Starry Night"

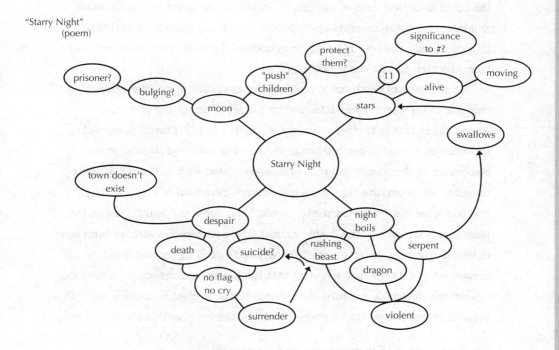

Barbara's Journal Response to Anne Sexton's poem "The Starry Night"

My initial reaction after reading this poem was one of despair and gloom. It projects an overall feeling of death or possibly suicide. The wording used throughout the poem is very vivid and somewhat violent in nature.

When the poet starts off the poem with the line "The town does not exist" (1), I got the impression of a dream, which led me to an initially pleasant feeling that would not last long as I read further. In examining the first three lines together, I feel the speaker is saying the town only exists in the eyes of death--the drowned woman. Is the poet questioning our view of reality? Maybe we can only see the truth of the universe in death.

I liked the description of the stars "boiling" in the sky. It created a very vivid picture in my mind. The way the poet gives the stars and the moon life is wonderful, saying the stars are alive and moving. Personalizing the moon was a bit confusing at first. I can remember as a child hearing the usual fairy tales of "the man in the moon." The image of the moon given in the poem was initially very different from my childhood memory. The description in the poem is at first kind of violent, when saying the moon wants "to push children, like a god, from its eye" (9). On examining these lines further though, I think the poet is trying to symbolize the moon protecting children from the turmoil and chaos above.

The theme of death, most probably suicide I feel, is steadily present throughout the poem. I was intrigued by the repetition of the lines "Oh starry night! This is how / I want to die" (5, 6; 11, 12). I feel this carried the common thread of death through the poem to the third stanza, which elaborated on that death and the feelings associated with it. From beginning to end in the poem, the sky or the heavens are described in a violent way. The poet uses the words "serpent," "beast," and "dragon," which creates the illusion of a dangerous and deadly animal. The poet depicts death as surrender to that threatening creature when she writes "sucked up by that great dragon..." (14). I find it interesting that the last three lines show no struggle against the menacing creature she described. This is what makes me think this poem is probably a view of suicide, describing someone lacking the will to live.

A Student Essay—Comparison and Contrast

Barbara Pfister

Dr. Madden

English 102

February 9, 20XX

Quiet Contemplation or Silent Desperation?

Examining art in the written word or in a painting can be a very personal experience. We bring our own, sometimes very different, responses and interpretations to each work that we study or explore. As there seems to be no one correct interpretation, I find that keeping an open mind and looking at others' views may open up new avenues of thought.

I examined my responses to both Vincent van Gogh's *Starry Night* and the poem "The Starry Night" written by Anne Sexton. I found a few similar ideas, and some very interesting differences. It is apparent that the poet had a very different response to the painting than I did.

When I first looked at the painting, the overall impression I got was ominous and quiet, but not gloomy. There was a feeling of both foreboding and powerful beauty at the same time. The short brushstrokes he used to paint the scene gave the feeling of separate and distinct pieces that together make up the whole. My initial reaction after reading the poem was one of despair and gloom. It projected an overall feeling of death or possibly suicide. The wording used throughout the poem is very vivid and seemed somewhat violent in nature.

The colors I see in the picture depict a night sky, but at the same time they appear as vivid as day. The sky, taking up a major portion of the painting, stands out quite vividly. I love the way van Gogh painted the stars. They appear to be very large and bright, not little pinpoints in the sky as we usually see them. In the poem, however, I found the description of the stars "boiling" in the sky captivating, but different from my reaction. It created a very vivid picture in my mind, and I liked the way the poet gave the stars life, saying they are alive and moving. Similar to the poet's description of the stars, I found the large swirls in the sky of the painting somewhat disturbing. I think they symbolize turmoil in the universe or the heavens, and that discord is hovering over the earth. This combined with the size of the sky and its heavenly dwellers, the stars, prompts a feeling of chaos in the universe.

The crescent-shaped moon in the painting is as large and as bright as the sun. Van Gogh didn't use silver or white, as I would portray it; he painted it the color of the sun. Anne Sexton's personalization of the moon was a bit confusing for me at first. I can remember as a child hearing the usual fairy tales of "the man in the moon." The image of the moon given in the poem was initially very different from my amiable childhood memory. The description in the poem is at first rather violent, when declaring that the moon wants "to push children, like a god, from its eye" (9). On examining these lines further though, I think the poet is trying to symbolize the moon protecting children from the turmoil and chaos above.

The town, as it is portrayed in the painting, seems small and the houses look like they are all huddled together. The town seems to be sheltered or protected by the hills, but this also hints at an uneasy feeling of isolation. The church was not mentioned at all in the poem. I see the church, centered in the lower part of the picture, as being very symbolic. It appears to be the only building that is really discernible; it stands out among the rest.

When Sexton started the poem with the line "The town does not exist" (1), I got the initially pleasant impression of a dream, which would not last long as I read further. The poet describes the plant shown in the painting as a "drowned woman." In examining the first three lines of the poem together, I feel the speaker is saying the town only exists in the eyes of death, the drowned woman. Is the poet questioning our view of reality? Perhaps we can see the reality of the universe only in the act of death.

I had a very different impression when contemplating the plant in the painting. It is very large in comparison with the rest of the objects pictured. This must be significant because I think he could have easily painted the picture without it, if he felt it was in the way. I don't think it interferes with the painting though. I think its size, spanning almost the entire height of the painting, is stressing the importance of nature in the whole scheme of life. This is very different from the poet's interpretation of the meaning of the plant.

After contemplating the significance of the plant, I looked at the town and the church again. Maybe it is symbolic that the plant reaches all the way to the sky, signifying the relationship between nature and the heavens. The plant also seems to spear right through the swirling turmoil in the night. The steeple of the church, in comparison, barely reaches the horizon. I wonder if this is intentional, and therefore very symbolic, or merely a coincidence.

The theme of death, most probably suicide I feel, is steadily present throughout the poem. I was intrigued by the repetition of the lines "Oh starry night! This is how / I want to die" (5, 6; 11,12). I feel this carried the common thread of death through the poem to the third stanza, which elaborated on that death and the feelings associated with it. From beginning to end in the poem, the sky or the heavens are described in a violent way, much different than the contemplative way I interpreted them. The poet uses the words "serpent," "beast," and "dragon," which creates the illusion of a dangerous and deadly animal. The poet depicts death as surrender to that threatening creature when she writes, "sucked up by that great dragon ..." (14). I found it interesting that the last three lines show no struggle against the menacing creature that she described. This apathy is what makes me think this poem is probably a view of suicide, describing someone lacking the will to live. There is a silent desperation in the poem. This is strikingly different from the impression the painting left in my mind.

My overall feeling of the painting is more of a quiet contemplation about the relationship between mankind and the universe. The colors van Gogh used seem to imply that the heavens at night are as bright and clear as day, and perhaps that is how our understanding of the universe should be. When looking at the symbolism of the plant and the church, another notion is that people can only make a small attempt to understand the heavens or the universe, as symbolized by the church's barely reaching the horizon. The plant, representing nature, is at one with the universe as it breaks through and spans the turmoil seen in the heavens.

If our understanding of the universe is as shallow as van Gogh has pictured it, perhaps that is the same desperation that Anne Sexton sees in the painting. This may explain the futility of life she described in her poem. From a broader perspective, these two different interpretations may be more alike than they seem.

[New Page]

Works Cited

Madden, Frank, ed. *Exploring Literature*. 5th ed. New York: Longman, 2012. Print.

Sexton, Anne. "The Starry Night." Madden 651.

van Gogh, Vincent. *Starry Night*. Madden 650.

EXPLORING POETRY AND PAINTING: OPTIONS FOR MAKING CONNECTIONS, BUILDING ARGUMENTS, AND USING RESEARCH

MAKING CONNECTIONS

1. Choose a painting and write a response to your viewing. Go back and view the painting again. Write another response. Compare your first response with your second response. Did your re-viewing change your response? If so, how?

2. Do any of the poems or paintings in this section remind you of your own experiences or circumstances in your life? If so, choose one or more of these works, and write a response essay that compares your experiences or circumstances with those in the poem and/or painting.

3. Many factors, including personal experiences, influence our perspective and can strongly influence our response to poems and paintings. Conversely, the way we are affected by a poem or painting may change our perspective. Write an essay about the way in which one or more poems and/or paintings in this section gave you a new insight and influenced your thinking.

MAKING AN ARGUMENT

1. Interpreting a painting, like interpreting a poem, requires attention to details. Choose one of the paintings in this section, and write an interpretive essay. Analyze the "text" of the painting the way you would a literary text. Identify the visual elements of the painting that support your interpretation.

2. Choose a painting and a poem, and write an essay that compares the poet's response to the painting with your own. Cite the text of the poem and the details of the painting for support.

3. Pick a poem that agrees with your view of a painting in this section, and write an argument that supports the poet's interpretation. Cite the text of the poem as well as details in the painting to support your argument.

4. Choose a painting, a poem, and another work of literature in the text that seem to treat the same theme, and write a thematic critical essay. In addition to writing about the three works, explore the theme and state why—and in what ways—the painting and literature exemplify the theme so well.

Using Research

Expanding our exploration of poems and paintings to include the context in which these works were produced can be an enriching and enlightening experience. Choose a painting and one or more poems in this section, and write a research essay that includes secondary source material about the historical, social, or political background of the works.

Women & Men

Women & Men
A DIALOGUE ACROSS HISTORY

The gate of the subtle and profound female / Is the root of Heaven and Earth. / It is continuous, and seems to be always existing. / Use it and you will never wear out.
 —Lao-tzu, *Tao te Ching*, c. 550 BCE

A woman is always a fickle, unstable thing.
 —Vergil, *Eclogues*, 37 BCE

The education of women should always be relative to that of men. To please, to be useful to us, to make us love and esteem them, to educate us when young, to take care of us when grown up; to advise, to console us, to render our lives easy and agreeable. These are the duties of women at all times, and what they should be taught in their infancy.
 —Jean Jacques Rousseau, *Emile*, 1762

It would be an endless task to trace the variety of meannesses, cares, and sorrows into which women are plunged by the prevailing opinion that they were created rather to feel than reason, and that all power they obtain must be obtained by their charms and weakness.
 —Mary Wollstonecraft, *A Vindication of the Rights of Women*, 1792

We hold these truths to be self-evident, that all men and women are created equal.
 —Elizabeth Cady Stanton, *Declaration of Sentiments*, 1848

With women the heart argues, not the mind.
 —Matthew Arnold, *Merope*, 1858

The great question . . . which I have not been able to answer, despite my thirty years of research into the feminine soul, is "What does a woman want?"
 —Sigmund Freud, 1930

The usual masculine disillusionment is discovering that a woman has a brain.
 —Margaret Mitchell, *Gone with the Wind*, 1936

We know of no culture that has said articulately, that there is no difference between men and women except in the way they contribute to the creation of the next generation.
    —Margaret Mead, *Male and Female*, 1948

This has always been a man's world, and none of the reasons hitherto brought forward in explanation of this fact has seemed adequate.
    —Simone de Beauvoir, *The Second Sex*, 1949

A girl should not expect special privileges because of her sex, but neither should she "adjust" to prejudice and discrimination. She must learn to compete . . . not as a woman, but as a human being.
    —Betty Friedan, *The Feminine Mystique*, 1963

If women had wives to keep house for them, to stay home with vomiting children, to get the car fixed, fight with the painters, run to the supermarket, reconcile the bank statements, listen to everyone's problems, cater the dinner parties, and nourish the spirit each night, just imagine the possibilities for expansion—the number of books that would be written, companies started, professorships filled, political offices that would be held, by women.
    —Gail Sheehy, *Passages*, 1976

Depriving millions of gay American adults the marriages of their choice, and the rights that flow from marriage, denies equal protection of the law. They, their families and friends, together with fair-minded people everywhere, should demand an end to this monstrous injustice.
    —Thomas Stoddard, *Gay Marriages: Make Them Legal*, 1988

We have defective mythologies that ignore masculine depth of feeling, assign men a place in the sky instead of earth, and teach obedience to the wrong powers . . . .
    —Robert Bly, *Iron John*, 1990

We all want, above all, to be heard—but not merely to be heard. We want to be understood—heard for what we think we are saying, for what we know we meant. With increased understanding of the ways women and men use language should come a decrease in the frequency of the complaint, You just don't understand.
    —Deborah Tannen, *You Just Don't Understand*, 1990

I'm tough, I'm ambitious, and I know exactly what I want. If that makes me a bitch, okay.
    —Madonna, 1992

[Feminism is] a socialist, anti-family, political movement that encourages women to leave their husbands, kill their children, practice witchcraft, destroy capitalism and become lesbians.
    —Pat Robertson, 1992

WOMEN AND MEN: EXPLORING YOUR OWN VALUES AND BELIEFS

"Can't live with them, can't live without them." We've heard this statement directed at both men and women. What is more compelling, more passionate, or more divisive than a debate about women and men? It's a debate that has been going on since humans have existed. Beyond our reproductive functions, are there significant differences between men and women? Are we intellectually and emotionally different? Should there be a different role for each gender?

Throughout most of history, women have been treated as inferior to men. It is only within the past two hundred years or so that women have had a voice loud enough to be acknowledged. While Elizabeth Cady Stanton's statement of 150 years ago "We hold these truths to be self-evident, that all *men and women* are created equal" may seem "self-evident" to us today, it has been less than a hundred years since women have even had the right to vote in this country. Although it is still not clear that women have been given equal opportunity in all areas, it is obvious how far women have come. Many men, however, now find themselves confused, frustrated, and even "bashed" by the emergence of women and the blurring of gender roles. If women's roles have been redefined, what about the roles of men?

Your gender may influence your aspirations or the expectations others have for you, the encouragement you receive for education and career goals, marriage and family, even your involvement in sports. It probably influences the formation of your values. And it certainly influences your view of the opposite sex. As a preparation for reading the literature in this section, you may find it helpful to think about your own values and beliefs about gender.

READING AND WRITING ABOUT WOMEN AND MEN

Exploring your beliefs and values and connecting your experience with what you read is an important first step toward our ultimate goal—an appreciation of literature and the ability to think and write critically about it. Critical analysis will require rereading and reflection, writing and revising, gathering evidence, and constructing a solid argument to support your responses.

At least one aspect of the many stories, poems, plays, and essays that follow is the way that gender determines how men and women define themselves and each other—and the impact that has on their relationships: a demented lover in Robert Browning's poem "Porphyria's Lover," a woman's discovery that her marriage has kept her a child in Henrik Ibsen's drama, *A Doll's House,* and Bruno Bettelheim's essay on the psychological meaning of the Cinderella fairy tale. The brief quotes that open this section also give you some idea of the number of compelling ethical, political, and social arguments connected to gender. Equal rights and opportunity, intellectual equality, stereotyping, bigotry, arrogance, and styles of communication head a long list of concerns. Any of these or other related issues might provide a fine topic for building an argument and writing an essay.

♦ FICTION ♦

ROBERT OLEN BUTLER [B. 1945]

Son of a theater professor, Butler began his writing career as a playwriting major at the University of Iowa, where he received an M.A. in 1969. Upon graduation, he was drafted to serve in Vietnam, an experience that has influenced much of his later writing. "Jealous Husband Returns in Form of Parrot" originally appeared in Tabloid Dreams, *(1996). A Pulitzer Prize winner (1993), Butler's latest collection of short fiction,* Intercourse, *was published in 2008. His latest novel,* Hell, *was published in 2009.*

JEALOUS HUSBAND RETURNS IN FORM OF PARROT   [1995]

I never can quite say as much as I know. I look at other parrots and I wonder if it's the same for them, if somebody is trapped in each of them paying some kind of price for living their life in a certain way. For instance, "Hello," I say, and I'm sitting on a perch in a pet store in Houston and what I'm really thinking is Holy shit. It's you. And what's happened is I'm looking at my wife.

"Hello," she says, and she comes over to me and I can't believe how beautiful she is. Those great brown eyes, almost as dark as the center of mine. And her nose— I don't remember her for her nose but its beauty is clear to me now. Her nose is a little too long, but it's redeemed by the faint hook to it.

She scratches the back of my neck.

Her touch makes my tail flare. I feel the stretch and rustle of me back there. I bend my head to her and she whispers, "Pretty bird."

5   For a moment I think she knows it's me. But she doesn't, of course. I say "Hello" again and I will eventually pick up "pretty bird." I can tell that as soon as she says it, but for now I can only give her another hello. Her fingertips move through my feathers and she seems to know about birds. She knows that to pet a bird you don't smooth his feathers down, you ruffle them.

But of course she did that in my human life, as well. It's all the same for her. Not that I was complaining, even to myself, at that moment in the pet shop when she found me like I presume she was supposed to. She said it again, "Pretty bird," and this brain that works like it does now could feel that tiny little voice of mine ready to shape itself around these sounds. But before I could get them out of my beak there was this guy at my wife's shoulder and all my feathers went slick flat like to make me small enough not to be seen and I backed away. The pupils of my eyes pinned and dilated and pinned again.

He circled around her. A guy that looked like a meat packer, big in the chest and thick with hair, the kind of guy that I always sensed her eyes moving to when I was alive. I had a bare chest and I'd look for little black hairs on the sheets when I'd come home on a day with the whiff of somebody else in the air. She was still in the same goddam rut.

A "hello" wouldn't do and I'd recently learned "good night" but it was the wrong suggestion altogether, so I said nothing and the guy circled her and he was looking at me with a smug little smile and I fluffed up all my feathers, made myself about twice as big, so big he'd see he couldn't mess with me. I waited for him to draw close enough for me to take off the tip of his finger.

But she intervened. Those nut-brown eyes were before me and she said, "I want him."

10   And that's how I ended up in my own house once again. She bought me a large black wrought-iron cage, very large, convinced by some young guy who clerked in the bird department and who took her aside and made his voice go much too soft when he was doing the selling job. The meat packer didn't like it. I didn't either. I'd missed a lot of chances to take a bite out of this clerk in my stay at the shop and I regretted that suddenly.

But I got my giant cage and I guess I'm happy enough about that. I can pace as much as I want. I can hang upside down. It's full of bird toys. That dangling thing over there with knots and strips of rawhide and a bell at the bottom needs a good thrashing a couple of times a day and I'm the bird to do it. I look at the very dangle of it and the thing is rough, the rawhide and the knotted rope, and I get this restlessness back in my tail, a burning thrashing feeling, and it's like all the times when I was sure there was a man naked with my wife. Then I go to this thing that feels so familiar and I bite and bite and it's very good.

I could have used the thing the last day I went out of this house as a man. I'd found the address of the new guy at my wife's office. He'd been there a month in the shipping department and three times she'd mentioned him. She didn't even have to work with him and three times I heard about him, just dropped into the conversation. "Oh," she'd say when a car commercial came on the television, "that car there is like the one the new man in shipping owns. Just like it." Hey, I'm not stupid. She said another thing about him and then another and right after the third one I locked myself in the bathroom because I couldn't rage about this anymore. I felt like a damn fool whenever I actually said anything about this kind of feeling and she looked at me like she could start hating me real easy and so I was working on saying nothing, even if it meant locking myself up. My goal was to hold my tongue about half the time. That would be a good start.

But this guy from shipping. I found out his name and his address and it was one of her typical Saturday afternoons of vague shopping. So I went to his house, and his car that was just like the commercial was outside. Nobody was around in the neighborhood and there was this big tree in the back of the house going up to a second-floor window that was making funny little sounds. I went up. The shade was drawn but not quite all the way. I was holding on to a limb with arms and legs wrapped around it like it was her in those times when I could forget the others for a little while. But the crack in the shade was just out of view and I crawled on along till there was no limb left and I fell on my head. Thinking about that now, my wings flap and I feel myself lift up and it all seems so avoidable. Though I know I'm different now. I'm a bird.

Except I'm not. That's what's confusing. It's like those times when she would tell me she loved me and I actually believed her and maybe it was true and we clung to each other in bed and at times like that I was different. I was the man in her life. I was whole with her. Except even at that moment, holding her sweetly, there was this other creature inside me who knew a lot more about it and couldn't quite put all the evidence together to speak.

15   My cage sits in the den. My pool table is gone and the cage is sitting in that space and if I come all the way down to one end of my perch I can see through the door and down the back hallway to the master bedroom. When she keeps the bedroom door open I can see the space at the foot of the bed but not the bed itself. That I can sense to the left, just out of sight. I watch the men go in and I hear the sounds but I can't quite see. And they drive me crazy.

I flap my wings and I squawk and I fluff up and I slick down and I throw seed and I attack that dangly toy as if it was the guy's balls, but it does no good. It never did any good in the other life either, the thrashing around I did by myself. In that other life I'd have given anything to be standing in this den with her doing this thing with some other guy just down the hall and all I had to do was walk down there and turn the corner and she couldn't deny it anymore.

But now all I can do is try to let it go. I sidestep down to the opposite end of the cage and I look out the big sliding glass doors to the back yard. It's a pretty yard. There are great placid maple trees with good places to roost. There's a blue sky that plucks at the feathers on my chest. There are clouds. Other birds. Fly away. I could just fly away.

I tried once and I learned a lesson. She forgot and left the door to my cage open and I climbed beak and foot, beak and foot, along the bars and curled around to stretch sideways out the door and the vast scene of peace was there at the other end of the room. I flew.

And a pain flared through my head and I fell straight down and the room whirled around and the only good thing was she held me. She put her hands under my wings and lifted me and clutched me to her breast and I wish there hadn't been bees in my head at the time so I could have enjoyed that, but she put me back in the cage and wept awhile. That touched me, her tears. And I looked back to the wall of sky and trees. There was something invisible there between me and that dream of peace. I remembered, eventually, about glass, and I knew I'd been lucky, I knew that for the little fragile-boned skull I was doing all this thinking in, it meant death.

20   She wept that day but by the night she had another man. A guy with a thick Georgia truck-stop accent and pale white skin and an Adam's apple big as my seed ball. This guy has been around for a few weeks and he makes a whooping sound down the hallway, just out of my sight. At times like that I want to fly against the bars of the cage, but I don't. I have to remember how the world has changed.

She's single now, of course. Her husband, the man that I was, is dead to her. She does not understand all that is behind my "hello." I know many words, for a parrot. I am a yellow-nape Amazon, a handsome bird, I think, green with a splash of yellow at the back of my neck. I talk pretty well, but none of my words are adequate. I can't make her understand.

And what would I say if I could? I was jealous in life. I admit it. I would admit it to her. But it was because of my connection to her. I would explain that. When we held each other, I had no past at all, no present but her body, no future but to lie there and not let her go. I was an egg hatched beneath her crouching body, I entered as a chick into her wet sky of a body, and all that I wished was to sit on her shoulder and fluff my feathers and lay my head against her cheek, my neck exposed to her hand. And so the glances that I could see in her troubled me deeply, the movement of her eyes in public to other men, the laughs sent across a room, the tracking of her mind behind her blank eyes, pursuing images of others, her distraction even in our bed, the ghosts that were there of men who'd touched her, perhaps even that very day. I was not part of all those other men who were part of her. I didn't want to connect to all that. It was only her that I would fluff for but these others were there also and I couldn't put them aside. I sensed them inside her and so they were inside me. If I had the words, these are the things I would say.

But half an hour ago there was a moment that thrilled me. A word, a word we all knew in the pet shop, was just the right word after all. This guy with his cowboy belt buckle and rattlesnake boots and his pasty face and his twanging words of love trailed after my wife through the den, past my cage, and I said, "Cracker." He even flipped his head back a little at this in surprise. He'd been called that before to his face, I realized. I said it again, "Cracker." But to him I was a bird and he let it pass. "Cracker," I said. "Hello, cracker." That was even better. They were out of sight through the hall doorway and I hustled along the perch and I caught a glimpse of them before they made the turn to the bed and I said, "Hello, cracker," and he shot me one last glance.

It made me hopeful. I eased away from that end of the cage, moved toward the scene of peace beyond the far wall. The sky is chalky blue today, blue like the brow of the blue-front Amazon who was on the perch next to me for about a week at the store. She was very sweet, but I watched her carefully for a day or two when she first came in. And it wasn't long before she nuzzled up to a cockatoo named Gordo and I knew she'd break my heart. But her color now in the sky is sweet, really. I left all those feelings behind me when my wife showed up. I am a faithful man, for all my suspicions. Too faithful, maybe. I am ready to give too much and maybe that's the problem.

25   The whooping began down the hall and I focussed on a tree out there. A crow flapped down, his mouth open, his throat throbbing, though I could not hear his sound. I was feeling very odd. At least I'd made my point to the guy in the other room. "Pretty bird," I said, referring to myself. She called me "pretty bird" and I believed her and I told myself again, "Pretty bird."

But then something new happened, something very difficult for me. She appeared in the den naked. I have not seen her naked since I fell from the tree and had no wings to fly. She always had a certain tidiness in things. She was naked in the bedroom, clothed in the den. But now she appears from the hallway and I look at her and she is still slim and she is beautiful, I think—at least I clearly remember that as her husband I found her beautiful in this state. Now, though, she seems too naked. Plucked. I find that a sad thing. I am sorry for her and she goes by me and she disappears into the kitchen. I want to pluck some of my own feathers, the feathers from my chest, and give them to her. I love her more in that moment, seeing her terrible nakedness, than I ever have before.

And since I've had success in the last few minutes with words, when she comes back I am moved to speak. "Hello," I say, meaning. You are still connected to me, I still want only you. "Hello," I say again. Please listen to this tiny heart that beats fast at all times for you.

And she does indeed stop and she comes to me and bends to me. "Pretty bird," I say and I am saying, You are beautiful, my wife, and your beauty cries out for protection. "Pretty." I want to cover you with my own nakedness. "Bad bird," I say. If there are others in your life, even in your mind, then there is nothing I can do. "Bad." Your nakedness is touched from inside by the others. "Open," I say. How can we be whole together if you are not empty in the place that I am to fill?

She smiles at this and she opens the door to my cage. "Up," I say, meaning, Is there no place for me in this world where I can be free of this terrible sense of others?

30 She reaches in now and offers her hand and I climb onto it and I tremble and she says, "Poor baby."

"Poor baby," I say. You have yearned for wholeness too and somehow I failed you. I was not enough. "Bad bird," I say. I'm sorry.

And then the cracker comes around the corner. He wears only his rattlesnake boots. I take one look at his miserable, featherless body and shake my head. We keep our sexual parts hidden, we parrots, and this man is a pitiful sight. "Peanut," I say. I presume that my wife simply has not noticed. But that's foolish, of course. This is, in fact, what she wants. Not me. And she scrapes me off her hand onto the open cage door and she turns her naked back to me and embraces this man and they laugh and stagger in their embrace around the corner.

For a moment I still think I've been eloquent. What I've said only needs repeating for it to have its transforming effect. "Hello," I say. "Hello. Pretty bird. Pretty. Bad bird. Bad. Open. Up. Poor baby. Bad bird." And I am beginning to hear myself as I really sound to her. "Peanut." I can never say what is in my heart to her. Never.

I stand on my cage door now and my wings stir. I look at the corner to the hallway and down at the end the whooping has begun again. I can fly there and think of things to do about all this.

35 But I do not. I turn instead and I look at the trees moving just beyond the other end of the room. I look at the sky the color of the brow of a blue-front Amazon. A shadow of birds spanks across the lawn. And I spread my wings. I will fly now. Even though I know there is something between me and that place where I can be free of all these feelings, I will fly. I will throw myself there again and again. Pretty bird. Bad bird. Good night.

MAKING CONNECTIONS

1. In his human life, what do you think the narrator's relationship with his wife was like? Explain.

2. Describe the husband's life as a parrot. How would this story be different if the narrator had returned as a dog? A cat? A goldfish?

3. What is the role of communication in the story? Describe the husband's communication skills as a human and as a parrot.

4. Do you think the wife was unfaithful to her husband? Use evidence from the text to support your answer.

5. How does the narrator's transformation into a parrot relate to his past marriage, his character or personality, his desires, etc.?

MAKING AN ARGUMENT

1. Communication seems to be a source of difficulties in both this story and
    Bobbie Ann Mason's "Shiloh" (p. 705). But Mason's and Butler's writing
    styles are quite different. Write an essay that analyzes the style of each
    piece, and compare their effectiveness in delivering the theme. What is
    the theme of each story? What does each say about communication?
    Cite examples from both texts to support your views.

CHARLOTTE PERKINS GILMAN [1860–1935]

*Charlotte Perkins Gilman was born in Hartford, Connecticut.
Because her father, the writer Frederick Beecher Perkins,
abandoned the family when she was only an infant, she
was often left in the company of relatives, who included
Harriet Beecher Stowe, the author of* Uncle Tom's Cabin,
*and the feminist activists Isabella Beecher Hooker and
Catherine Beecher. These women instilled in Gilman the
ideas of equality and independence, which formed the ba-*
*sis for the political activism that made her famous later in life. Though she wrote
numerous works about the conditions of women, her reputation as a writer of
literature rests almost solely on her short story "The Yellow Wallpaper," which
adds a feminist twist to the psychological horror story pioneered by Edgar Allan
Poe. The story, written in 1892, was based on her own experiences. During her
unhappy first marriage, Gilman suffered a severe depression following the birth
of her daughter. A noted doctor of the time prescribed a regimen of bed rest and
minimal intellectual stimulation. Her condition only worsened. Eventually she
rebelled, and, taking responsibility for her own cure, separated from her husband
and moved to California. In 1900, she married again, this time happily to her
cousin George Houghton Gilman. She remained active politically until she took
her own life in 1935, after fighting a losing battle with breast cancer.*

THE YELLOW WALLPAPER   [1892]

It is very seldom that mere ordinary people like John and myself secure ancestral
halls for the summer.

A colonial mansion, a hereditary estate, I would say a haunted house and reach
the height of romantic felicity—but that would be asking too much of fate!

Still I will proudly declare that there is something queer about it.

Else, why should it be let so cheaply? And why have stood so long untenanted?

5   John laughs at me, of course, but one expects that.

John is practical in the extreme. He has no patience with faith, an intense horror
of superstition, and he scoffs openly at any talk of things not to be felt and seen and
put down in figures.

John is a physician, and *perhaps*—(I would not say it to a living soul, of course,
but this is dead paper and a great relief to my mind)—*perhaps* that is one reason I do
not get well faster.

You see, he does not believe I am sick! And what can one do?

If a physician of high standing, and one's own husband, assures friends and relatives that there is really nothing the matter with one but temporary nervous depression—a slight hysterical tendency—what is one to do?

10   My brother is also a physician, and also of high standing, and he says the same thing.

So I take phosphates or phosphites—whichever it is—and tonics, and air and exercise, and journeys, and am absolutely forbidden to "work" until I am well again.

Personally, I disagree with their ideas.

Personally, I believe that congenial work, with excitement and change, would do me good.

But what is one to do?

15   I did write for a while in spite of them: but it *does* exhaust me a good deal—having to be so sly about it, or else meet with heavy opposition.

I sometimes fancy that in my condition, if I had less opposition and more society and stimulus—but John says the very worst thing I can do is to think about my condition, and I confess it always makes me feel bad.

So I will let it alone and talk about the house.

The most beautiful place! It is quite alone, standing well back from the road, quite three miles from the village. It makes me think of English places that you read about, for there are hedges and walls and gates that lock, and lots of separate little houses for the gardeners and people.

There is a *delicious* garden! I never saw such a garden—large and shady, full of box-bordered paths, and lined with long grape-covered arbors with seats under them.

20   There were greenhouses, but they are all broken now.

There was some legal trouble, I believe, something about the heirs and co-heirs; anyhow, the place has been empty for years.

That spoils my ghostliness, I am afraid, but I don't care—there is something strange about the house—I can feel it.

I even said so to John one moonlight evening, but he said what I felt was a draught, and shut the window.

I get unreasonably angry with John sometimes. I'm sure I never used to be so sensitive. I think it is due to this nervous condition.

25   But John says if I feel so I shall neglect proper self-control; so I take pains to control myself—before him, at least, and that makes me very tired.

I don't like our room a bit. I wanted one downstairs that opened onto the piazza and had roses all over the window, and such pretty old-fashioned chintz hangings! But John would not hear of it.

He said there was only one window and not room for two beds, and no near room for him if he took another.

He is very careful and loving, and hardly lets me stir without special direction.

I have a schedule prescription for each hour in the day; he takes all care from me, and so I feel basely ungrateful not to value it more.

30   He said he came here solely on my account, that I was to have perfect rest and all the air I could get. "Your exercise depends on your strength, my dear," said he,

"and your food somewhat on your appetite; but air you can absorb all the time." So we took the nursery at the top of the house.

It is a big, airy room, the whole floor nearly, with windows that look all ways, and air and sunshine galore. It was nursery first, and then playroom and gymnasium, I should judge, for the windows are barred for little children, and there are rings and things in the walls.

The paint and paper look as if a boys' school had used it. It is stripped off—the paper—in great patches all around the head of my bed, about as far as I can reach, and in a great place on the other side of the room low down. I never saw a worse paper in my life. One of those sprawling, flamboyant patterns committing every artistic sin.

It is dull enough to confuse the eye in following, pronounced enough to constantly irritate and provoke study, and when you follow the lame uncertain curves for a little distance they suddenly commit suicide—plunge off at outrageous angles, destroy themselves in unheard-of contradictions.

The color is repellent, almost revolting: a smouldering unclean yellow, strangely faded by the slow-turning sunlight. It is a dull yet lurid orange in some places, a sickly sulphur tint in others.

35 No wonder the children hated it! I should hate it myself if I had to live in this room long.

There comes John, and I must put this away—he hates to have me write a word.

We have been here two weeks, and I haven't felt like writing before, since that first day.

I am sitting by the window now, up in this atrocious nursery, and there is nothing to hinder my writing as much as I please, save lack of strength.

John is away all day, and even some nights when his cases are serious.

40 I am glad my case is not serious!

But these nervous troubles are dreadfully depressing.

John does not know how much I really suffer. He knows there is no reason to suffer, and that satisfies him.

Of course it is only nervousness. It does weigh on me so not to do my duty in any way!

I meant to be such a help to John, such a real rest and comfort, and here I am a comparative burden already!

45 Nobody would believe what an effort it is to do what little I am able—to dress and entertain, and order things.

It is fortunate Mary is so good with the baby. Such a dear baby!

And yet I *cannot* be with him, it makes me so nervous.

I suppose John never was nervous in his life. He laughs at me so about this wallpaper!

At first he meant to repaper the room, but afterward he said that I was letting it get the better of me, and that nothing was worse for a nervous patient than to give way to such fancies.

50 He said that after the wallpaper was changed it would be the heavy bedstead, and then the barred windows, and then that gate at the head of the stairs, and so on.

"You know the place is doing you good," he said, "and really, dear, I don't care to renovate the house just for a three months' rental."

"Then do let us go downstairs," I said, "there are such pretty rooms there."

Then he took me in his arms and called me a blessed little goose, and said he would go down to the cellar, if I wished, and have it whitewashed into the bargain.

But he is right enough about the beds and windows and things.

55 It is as airy and comfortable a room as anyone need wish, and, of course, I would not be so silly as to make him uncomfortable just for a whim.

I'm really getting quite fond of the big room, all but that horrid paper.

Out of one window I can see the garden—those mysterious deep-shaded arbors, the riotous old-fashioned flowers, and bushes and gnarly trees.

Out of another I get a lovely view of the bay and a little private wharf belonging to the estate. There is a beautiful shaded lane that runs down there from the house. I always fancy I see people walking in these numerous paths and arbors, but John has cautioned me not to give way to fancy in the least. He says that with my imaginative power and habit of story-making, a nervous weakness like mine is sure to lead to all manner of excited fancies, and that I ought to use my will and good sense to check the tendency. So I try.

I think sometimes that if I were only well enough to write a little it would relieve the press of ideas and rest me.

60 But I find I get pretty tired when I try.

It is so discouraging not to have any advice and companionship about my work. When I get really well, John says we will ask Cousin Henry and Julia down for a long visit; but he says he would as soon put fireworks in my pillowcase as to let me have those stimulating people about now.

I wish I could get well faster.

But I must not think about that. This paper looks to me as if it *knew* what a vicious influence it had!

There is a recurrent spot where the pattern lolls like a broken neck and two bulbous eyes stare at you upside down.

65 I get positively angry with the impertinence of it and the everlastingness. Up and down and sideways they crawl, and those absurd, unblinking eyes are everywhere. There is one place where two breadths didn't match, and the eyes go all up and down the line, one a little higher than the other.

I never saw so much expression in an inanimate thing before, and we all know how much expression they have! I used to lie awake as a child and get more entertainment and terror out of blank walls and plain furniture than most children could find in a toystore.

I remember what a kindly wink the knobs of our big, old bureau used to have, and there was one chair that always seemed like a strong friend.

I used to feel that if any of the other things looked too fierce I could always hop into that chair and be safe.

The furniture in this room is no worse than inharmonious, however, for we had to bring it all from downstairs. I suppose when this was used as a playroom they had to take the nursery things out, and no wonder! I never saw such ravages as the children have made here.

70   The wallpaper, as I said before, is torn off in spots, and it sticketh closer than a brother—they must have had perseverance as well as hatred.

Then the floor is scratched and gouged and splintered, the plaster itself is dug out here and there, and this great heavy bed which is all we found in the room, looks as if it had been through the wars.

But I don't mind it a bit—only the paper.

There comes John's sister. Such a dear girl as she is, and so careful of me! I must not let her find me writing.

She is a perfect and enthusiastic housekeeper, and hopes for no better profession. I verily believe she thinks it is the writing which made me sick!

75   But I can write when she is out, and see her a long way off from these windows.

There is one that commands the road, a lovely shaded winding road, and one that just looks off over the country. A lovely country, too, full of great elms and velvet meadows.

This wallpaper has a kind of sub-pattern in a different shade, a particularly irritating one, for you can only see it in certain lights, and not clearly then.

But in the places where it isn't faded and where the sun is just so—I can see a strange, provoking, formless sort of figure that seems to skulk about behind that silly and conspicuous front design.

There's sister on the stairs!

80   Well, the Fourth of July is over! The people are all gone and I am tired out. John thought it might do me good to see a little company, so we just had Mother and Nellie and the children down for a week.

Of course I didn't do a thing. Jennie sees to everything now.

But it tired me all the same.

John says if I don't pick up faster he shall send me to Weir Mitchell[1] in the fall.

But I don't want to go there at all. I had a friend who was in his hands once, and she says he is just like John and my brother, only more so!

85   Besides, it is such an undertaking to go so far.

I don't feel as if it was worth while to turn my hand over for anything, and I'm getting dreadfully fretful and querulous.

I cry at nothing, and cry most of the time.

Of course I don't when John is here, or anybody else, but when I am alone.

And I am alone a good deal just now. John is kept in town very often by serious cases, and Jennie is good and lets me alone when I want her to.

90   So I walk a little in the garden or down that lovely lane, sit on the porch under the roses, and lie down up here a good deal.

I'm getting really fond of the room in spite of the wallpaper. Perhaps *because* of the wallpaper.

It dwells in my mind so!

I lie here on this great immovable bed—it is nailed down, I believe—and follow that pattern about by the hour. It is as good as gymnastics, I assure you. I start, we'll say, at the bottom, down in the corner over there where it has not been

---

[1]**Weir Mitchell** a physician known for his "rest cure" for psychoneuroses

touched, and I determine for the thousandth time that I *will* follow that pointless pattern to some sort of a conclusion.

I know a little of the principle of design, and I know this thing was not arranged on any laws of radiation, or alternation, or repetition, or symmetry, or anything else that I ever heard of.

95   It is repeated, of course, by the breadths, but not otherwise.

Looked at in one way each breadth stands alone; the bloated curves and flourishes—a kind of "debased Romanesque" with delirium tremens go waddling up and down in isolated columns of fatuity.

But, on the other hand, they connect diagonally, and the sprawling outlines run off in great slanting waves of optic horror, like a lot of wallowing sea-weeds in full chase.

The whole thing goes horizontally, too, at least it seems so, and I exhaust myself in trying to distinguish the order of its going in that direction.

They have used a horizontal breadth for a frieze, and that adds wonderfully to the confusion.

100   There is one end of the room where it is almost intact, and there, when the crosslights fade and the low sun shines directly upon it, I can almost fancy radiation after all—the interminable grotesque seems to form around a common center and rush off in headlong plunges of equal distraction.

It makes me tired to follow it. I will take a nap, I guess.

I don't know why I should write this.

I don't want to.

I don't feel able.

105   And I know John would think it absurd. But I *must* say what I feel and think in some way—it is such a relief.

But the effort is getting to be greater than the relief!

Half the time now I am awfully lazy, and lie down ever so much. John says I mustn't lose my strength, and has me take cod liver oil and lots of tonics and things, to say nothing of ale and wine and rare meat.

Dear John! He loves me very dearly, and hates to have me sick. I tried to have a real earnest reasonable talk with him the other day, and tell him how I wish he would let me go and make a visit to Cousin Henry and Julia.

But he said I wasn't able to go, nor able to stand it after I got there: and I did not make out a very good case for myself, for I was crying before I had finished.

110   It is getting to be a great effort for me to think straight. Just this nervous weakness, I suppose.

And dear John gathered me up in his arms, and just carried me upstairs and laid me on the bed, and sat by me and read to me till it tired my head.

He said I was his darling and his comfort and all he had, and that I must take care of myself for his sake, and keep well.

He says no one but myself can help me out of it, that I must use my will and self-control and not let any silly fancies run away with me.

There's one comfort—the baby is well and happy, and does not have to occupy this nursery with the horrid wallpaper.

115   If we had not used it, that blessed child would have! What a fortunate escape! Why, I wouldn't have a child of mine, an impressionable little thing, live in such a room for worlds.

I never thought of it before, but it is lucky that John kept me here after all. I can stand it so much easier than a baby, you see.

Of course I never mention it to them any more—I am too wise—but I keep watch for it all the same.

There are things in that paper that nobody knows but me, or ever will.

Behind that outside pattern the dim shapes get clearer every day.

120   It is always the same shape, only very numerous.

And it is like a woman stooping down and creeping about behind that pattern. I don't like it a bit. I wonder—I begin to think—I wish John would take me away from here!

It is so hard to talk with John about my case, because he is so wise, and because he loves me so.

But I tried last night.

It was moonlight. The moon shines in all around just as the sun does.

125   I hate to see it sometimes, it creeps so slowly, and always comes in by one window or another.

John was asleep and I hated to waken him, so I kept still and watched the moonlight on that undulating wallpaper till I felt creepy.

The faint figure behind seemed to shake the pattern, just as if she wanted to get out.

I got up softly and went to feel and see if the paper *did* move, and when I came back John was awake.

"What is it, little girl?" he said. "Don't go walking about like that—you'll get cold."

130   I thought it was a good time to talk, so I told him that I really was not gaining here, and that I wished he would take me away.

"Why darling!" said he, "our lease will be up in three weeks, and I can't see how to leave before."

"The repairs are not done at home, and I cannot possibly leave town just now. Of course if you were in any danger, I could and would, but you really are better, dear, whether you can see it or not. I am a doctor, dear, and I know. You are gaining flesh and color, your appetite is better, I feel really much easier about you."

"I don't weigh a bit more," said I, "nor as much; and my appetite may be better in the evening when you are here but it is worse in the morning when you are away!"

"Bless her little heart!" said he with a big hug. "She shall be as sick as she pleases! But now let's improve the shining hours by going to sleep, and talk about it in the morning!"

135   "And you won't go away?" I asked gloomily.

"Why, how can I, dear? It is only three weeks more and then we will take a nice little trip of a few days while Jennie is getting the house ready. Really, dear, you are better!"

"Better in body perhaps—" I began, and stopped short, for he sat up straight and looked at me with such a stern, reproachful look that I could not say another word.

"My darling," said he, "I beg of you, for my sake and for our child's sake, as well as for your own, that you will never for one instant let that idea enter your mind! There is nothing so dangerous, so fascinating, to a temperament like yours. It is a false and foolish fancy. Can you not trust me as a physician when I tell you so?"

So of course I said no more on that score, and we went to sleep before long. He thought I was asleep first, but I wasn't and lay there for hours trying to decide whether that front pattern and the back pattern really did move together or separately.

140   On a pattern like this, by daylight, there is a lack of sequence, a defiance of law, that is a constant irritant to a normal mind.

The color is hideous enough, and unreliable enough, and infuriating enough, but the pattern is torturing.

You think you have mastered it, but just as you get well under way in following, it turns a back-somersault and there you are. It slaps you in the face, knocks you down, and tramples upon you. It is like a bad dream.

The outside pattern is a florid arabesque, reminding one of a fungus. If you can imagine a toadstool in joints, an interminable string of toadstools, budding and sprouting in endless convolutions—why, that is something like it.

That is, sometimes!

145   There is one marked peculiarity about this paper, a thing nobody seems to notice but myself, and that is that it changes as the light changes.

When the sun shoots in through the east window—I always watch for that first long, straight ray—it changes so quickly that I never can quite believe it.

That is why I watch it always.

By moonlight—the moon shines in all night when there is a moon—I wouldn't know it was the same paper.

At night in any kind of light, in twilight, candlelight, lamplight, and worst of all by moonlight, it becomes bars! The outside pattern, I mean, and the woman behind it is as plain as can be.

150   I didn't realize for a long time what the thing was that showed behind, that dim sub-pattern, but now I am quite sure it is a woman.

By daylight she is subdued, quiet. I fancy it is the pattern that keeps her so still. It is so puzzling. It keeps me quiet by the hour.

I lie down ever so much now. John says it is good for me, and to sleep all I can. Indeed he started the habit by making me lie down for an hour after each meal.

It is a very bad habit, I am convinced, for you see, I don't sleep.

155   And that cultivates deceit, for I don't tell them I'm awake—oh, no!

The fact is I am getting a little afraid of John.

He seems very queer sometimes, and even Jennie has an inexplicable look.

It strikes me occasionally, just as a scientific hypothesis, that perhaps it is the paper!

I have watched John when he did not know I was looking, and come into the room suddenly on the most innocent excuses, and I've caught him several times *looking at the paper!* And Jennie too. I caught Jennie with her hand on it once.

160   She didn't know I was in the room, and when I asked her in a quiet, a very quiet voice, with the most restrained manner possible, what she was doing with

the paper, she turned around as if she had been caught stealing, and looked quite angry—asked me why I should frighten her so!

Then she said that the paper stained everything it touched, that she had found yellow smooches on all my clothes and John's, and she wished we would be more careful!

Did not that sound innocent? But I know she was studying that pattern, and I am determined that nobody shall find it out but myself!

Life is very much more exciting now than it used to be. You see I have something more to expect, to look forward to, to watch. I really do eat better, and am more quiet than I was.

John is so pleased to see me improve! He laughed a little the other day, and said I seemed to be flourishing in spite of my wallpaper.

165　　I turned it off with a laugh. I had no intention of telling him it was *because* of the wallpaper—he would make fun of me. He might even want to take me away.

I don't want to leave now until I have found it out. There is a week more, and I think that will be enough.

I'm feeling so much better!

I don't sleep much at night, for it is so interesting to watch developments, but I sleep a good deal during the daytime.

In the daytime it is tiresome and perplexing.

170　　There are always new shoots on the fungus, and new shades of yellow all over it. I cannot keep count of them, though I have tried conscientiously.

It is the strangest yellow, that wallpaper! It makes me think of all the yellow things I ever saw—not beautiful ones like buttercups, but old foul, bad yellow things.

But there is something else about that paper—the smell! I noticed it the moment we came into the room, but with so much air and sun it was not bad. Now we have had a week of fog and rain, and whether the windows are open or not, the smell is here.

It creeps all over the house.

I find it hovering in the dining-room, skulking in the parlor, hiding in the hall, lying in wait for me on the stairs.

175　　It gets into my hair.

Even when I go to ride, if I turn my head suddenly and surprise it—there is that smell!

Such a peculiar odor, too! I have spent hours in trying to analyze it, to find what it smelled like.

It is not bad—at first—and very gentle, but quite the subtlest, most enduring odor I ever met.

In this damp weather it is awful, I wake up in the night and find it hanging over me.

180　　It used to disturb me at first. I thought seriously of burning the house—to reach the smell.

But now I am used to it. The only thing I can think of that it is like is the *color* of the paper! A yellow smell.

There is a very funny mark on this wall, low down, near the mopboard. A streak that runs round the room. It goes behind every piece of furniture, except the bed, a long, straight, even *smooch,* as if it had been rubbed over and over.

I wonder how it was done and who did it, and what they did it for. Round and round and round—round and round and round—it makes me dizzy!

I really have discovered something at last.

185 Through watching so much at night, when it changes so, I have finally found out. The front pattern *does* move—and no wonder! The woman behind shakes it!

Sometimes I think there are a great many women behind, and sometimes only one, and she crawls around fast, and her crawling shakes it all over.

Then in the very bright spots she keeps still, and in the very shady spots she just takes hold of the bars and shakes them hard.

And she is all the time trying to climb through. But nobody could climb through that pattern—it strangles so: I think that is why it has so many heads.

190 They get through, and then the pattern strangles them off and turns them upside down, and makes their eyes white!

If those heads were covered or taken off it would not be half so bad.

I think that woman gets out in the daytime!

And I'll tell you why—privately—I've seen her!

I can see her out of every one of my windows!

195 It is the same woman, I know, for she is always creeping, and most women do not creep by daylight.

I see her in that long shaded lane, creeping up and down. I see her in those dark grape arbors, creeping all around the garden.

I see her on that long road under the trees, creeping along, and when a carriage comes she hides under the blackberry vines.

I don't blame her a bit. It must be very humiliating to be caught creeping by daylight!

I always lock the door when I creep by daylight. I can't do it at night, for I know John would suspect something at once.

200 And John is so queer now, that I don't want to irritate him. I wish he would take another room! Besides, I don't want anybody to get that woman out at night but myself.

I often wonder if I could see her out of all the windows at once.

But, turn as fast as I can, I can only see out of one at one time.

And though I always see her, she *may* be able to creep faster than I can turn! I have watched her sometimes away off in the open country, creeping as fast as a cloud shadow in a wind.

If only that top pattern could be gotten off from the under one! I mean to try it, little by little.

205 I have found out another funny thing, but I shan't tell it this time! It does not do to trust people too much.

There are only two more days to get this paper off, and I believe John is beginning to notice. I don't like the look in his eyes.

And I heard him ask Jennie a lot of professional questions about me. She had a very good report to give.

She said I slept a good deal in the daytime.

John knows I don't sleep very well at night, for all I'm so quiet!

210 He asked me all sorts of questions, too, and pretended to be very loving and kind.

As if I couldn't see through him!

Still, I don't wonder he acts so, sleeping under this paper for three months.

It only interests me, but I feel sure John and Jennie are affected by it.

Hurrah! This is the last day, but it is enough. John is to stay in town over night, and won't be out until this evening.

215 Jennie wanted to sleep with me—the sly thing; but I told her I should undoubtedly rest better for a night all alone.

That was clever, for really I wasn't alone a bit! As soon as it was moonlight and that poor thing began to crawl and shake the pattern, I got up and ran to help her.

I pulled and she shook. I shook and she pulled, and before morning we had peeled off yards of that paper.

A strip about as high as my head and half around the room.

And then when the sun came and that awful pattern began to laugh at me, I declared I would finish it today!

220 We go away tomorrow, and they are moving all my furniture down again to leave things as they were before.

Jennie looked at the wall in amazement, but I told her merrily that I did it out of pure spite at the vicious thing.

She laughed and said she wouldn't mind doing it herself, but I must not get tired.

How she betrayed herself that time!

But I am here, and no person touches this paper but Me—not *alive!*

225 She tried to get me out of the room—it was too patent! But I said it was so quiet and empty and clean now that I believed I would lie down again and sleep all I could, and not to wake me even for dinner—I would call when I woke.

So now she is gone, and the servants are gone, and the things are gone, and there is nothing left but that great bedstead nailed down, with the canvas mattress we found on it.

We shall sleep downstairs tonight, and take the boat home tomorrow.

I quite enjoy the room, now it is bare again.

How those children did tear about here!

230 This bedstead is fairly gnawed!

But I must get to work.

I have locked the door and thrown the key down into the front path.

I don't want to go out, and I don't want to have anybody come in, till John comes.

I want to astonish him.

235 I've got a rope up here that even Jennie did not find. If that woman does get out, and tries to get away, I can tie her!

But I forgot I could not reach far without anything to stand on!

This bed will *not* move!

I tried to lift and push it until I was lame, and then I got so angry I bit off a little piece at one corner—but it hurt my teeth.

Then I peeled off all the paper I could reach standing on the floor. It sticks horribly and the pattern just enjoys it! All those strangled heads and bulbous eyes and waddling fungus growths just shriek with derision!

240   I am getting angry enough to do something desperate. To jump out of the window would be admirable exercise, but the bars are too strong even to try.

Besides I wouldn't do it. Of course not. I know well enough that a step like that is improper and might be misconstrued.

I don't like to *look* out of the windows even—there are so many of those creeping women, and they creep so fast.

I wonder if they all come out of that wallpaper as I did?

But I am securely fastened now by my well-hidden rope—you don't get *me* out in the road there!

245   I suppose I shall have to get back behind the pattern when it comes night, and that is hard!

It is so pleasant to be out in this great room and creep around as I please!

I don't want to go outside. I won't, even if Jennie asks me to.

For outside you have to creep on the ground, and everything is green instead of yellow.

But here I can creep smoothly on the floor, and my shoulder just fits in that long smooch around the wall, so I cannot lose my way.

250   Why, there's John at the door!

It is no use, young man, you can't open it!

How he does call and pound!

Now he's crying to Jennie for an axe.

It would be a shame to break down that beautiful door!

255   "John, dear!" said I in the gentlest voice, "The key is down by the front steps, under a plantain leaf!"

That silenced him for a few moments.

Then he said, very quietly indeed, "Open the door, my darling!"

"I can't," said I. "The key is down by the front door under a plantain leaf!" And then I said it again, several times, very gently and slowly, and said it so often that he had to go and see, and he got it of course, and came in. He stopped short by the door.

"What is the matter?" he cried. "For God's sake, what are you doing!"

260   I kept on creeping just the same, but I looked at him over my shoulder.

"I've got out at last," said I, "in spite of you and Jane. And I've pulled off most of the paper, so you can't put me back!"

Now why should that man have fainted? But he did, and right across my path by the wall, so that I had to creep over him every time!

MAKING CONNECTIONS

1. The narrator is the main character in the story. To what extent does this influence what you are told in this story? Can you describe the narrator? Do you think she is reliable? Explain.

2. Describe her relationship with her husband, John. What is he like? How does he treat her?

3. What kind of illness does the narrator say she has? What does her physician-husband prescribe as a cure? Do you think it's an appropriate cure? Why or why not?

4. In what way is the yellow wallpaper symbolic in this story? To what extent does the narrator's description of it change as the story progresses? Do you see any other symbols in the story?

5. Who is the woman in the wallpaper? What connection does she have to the narrator? To what extent is the yellow wallpaper an appropriate metaphor in this story? Would another color make a difference?

6. To what extent does the narrator change as the story progresses? What are the indications of that in the story? Near the end of the story, the narrator says, "I've got out at last." Has she? Explain.

7. How are gender roles depicted in this story?

MAKING AN ARGUMENT

1. Gilman indicated that this story was written in response to a "rest cure" she was given for her own severe, multi-year bout of depression—a rest cure that prohibited her from writing and limited her to "two hours intellectual life a day." She said that this advice nearly drove her insane, and it was only by returning to her writing that she was able to recover. In the light of this information—and what you know of attitudes toward women when the story was published in 1892—write an interpretation of the story. Cite the text of the story and its historical context for support.

ERNEST HEMINGWAY [1899–1961]

Ernest Hemingway was born in Oak Park, Illinois, and began his writing career as a newspaper reporter, where he claimed to have learned the fundamentals of writing: short sentences, short first paragraphs, vigorous English, and smoothness. He was an active participant in World War I, the Spanish Civil War, and World War II, and often used his personal experiences as the source of his work. His writing includes A Farewell to Arms *(1929),* For Whom the Bell Tolls *(1940), and* The Old Man and the Sea *(1952). He was a Pulitzer Prize winner and received the Nobel Prize for literature in 1954. His direct, spare writing style, exemplified in the short story below, was a major influence on many writers in the twentieth century.*

HILLS LIKE WHITE ELEPHANTS

[1927]

The hills across the valley of the Ebro were long and white. On this side there was no shade and no trees and the station was between two lines of rails in the sun. Close against the side of the station there was the warm shadow of the building and a curtain, made of strings of bamboo beads, hung across the open door into the bar, to keep out flies. The American and the girl with him sat at a table in the shade, outside the building. It was very hot and the express from Barcelona would come in forty minutes. It stopped at this junction for two minutes and went on to Madrid.

"What should we drink?" the girl asked. She had taken off her hat and put it on the table.

"It's pretty hot," the man said.

"Let's drink beer."

5   "Dos cervezas," the man said into the curtain.

"Big ones?" a woman asked from the doorway.

"Yes. Two big ones."

The woman brought two glasses of beer and two felt pads. She put the felt pads and the beer glasses on the table and looked at the man and the girl. The girl was looking off at the line of hills. They were white in the sun and the country was brown and dry.

"They look like white elephants," she said.

10   "I've never seen one," the man drank his beer.

"No, you wouldn't have."

"I might have," the man said. "Just because you say I wouldn't have doesn't prove anything."

The girl looked at the bead curtain. "They've painted something on it," she said. "What does it say?"

"Anis del Toro. It's a drink."

15   "Could we try it?"

The man called "Listen" through the curtain. The woman came out from the bar.

"Four reales."

"We want two Anis del Toro."

"With water?"

20   "Do you want it with water?"

"I don't know," the girl said. "Is it good with water?"

"It's all right."

"You want them with water?" asked the woman.

"Yes, with water."

25   "It tastes like licorice," the girl said and put the glass down.

"That's the way with everything."

"Yes," said the girl. "Everything tastes of licorice. Especially all the things you've waited so long for, like absinthe."

"Oh, cut it out."

"You started it," the girl said. "I was being amused. I was having a fine time."

30   "Well, let's try and have a fine time."

"All right. I was trying. I said the mountains looked like white elephants. Wasn't that bright?"

"That was bright."

"I wanted to try this new drink. That's all we do, isn't it—look at things and try new drinks?"

"I guess so."

35   The girl looked across at the hills.

"They're lovely hills," she said. "They don't really look like white elephants. I just meant the coloring of their skin through the trees."

"Should we have another drink?"

"All right."

The warm wind blew the bead curtain against the table.

"The beer's nice and cool," the man said.

"It's lovely," the girl said.

"It's really an awfully simple operation, Jig," the man said. "It's not really an operation at all."

The girl looked at the ground the table legs rested on.

"I know you wouldn't mind it, Jig. It's really not anything. It's just to let the air in."

The girl did not say anything.

"I'll go with you and I'll stay with you all the time. They just let the air in and then it's all perfectly natural."

"Then what will we do afterward?"

"We'll be fine afterward. Just like we were before."

"What makes you think so?"

"That's the only thing that bothers us. It's the only thing that's made us unhappy."

The girl looked at the bead curtain, put her hand out and took hold of two of the strings of beads.

"And you think then we'll be all right and be happy."

"I know we will. You don't have to be afraid. I've known lots of people that have done it."

"So have I," said the girl. "And afterward they were all so happy."

"Well," the man said, "if you don't want to you don't have to. I wouldn't have you do it if you didn't want to. But I know it's perfectly simple."

"And you really want to?"

"I think it's the best thing to do. But I don't want you to do it if you don't really want to."

"And if I do it you'll be happy and things will be like they were and you'll love me?"

"I love you now. You know I love you."

"I know. But if I do it, then it will be nice again if I say things are like white elephants, and you'll like it?"

"I'll love it. I love it now but I just can't think about it. You know how I get when I worry."

"If I do it you won't ever worry?"

"I won't worry about that because it's perfectly simple."

"Then I'll do it. Because I don't care about me."

"What do you mean?"

"I don't care about me."

"Well, I care about you."

"Oh, yes. But I don't care about me. And I'll do it and then everything will be fine."

"I don't want you to do it if you feel that way."

The girl stood up and walked to the end of the station. Across, on the other side, were fields of grain and trees along the banks of the Ebro. Far away, beyond the river, were mountains. The shadow of a cloud moved across the field of grain and she saw the river through the trees.

"And we could have all this," she said. "And we could have everything and every day we make it more impossible."

"What did you say?"

"I said we could have everything."

"We can have everything."

75   "No, we can't."

"We can have the whole world."

"No, we can't."

"We can go everywhere."

"No, we can't. It isn't ours any more."

80   "It's ours."

"No, it isn't. And once they take it away, you never get it back."

"But they haven't taken it away."

"We'll wait and see."

"Come on back in the shade," he said. "You mustn't feel that way."

85   "I don't feel any way," the girl said. "I just know things."

"I don't want you to do anything that you don't want to do—"

"Nor that isn't good for me," she said. "I know. Could we have another beer?"

"All right. But you've got to realize—"

"I realize," the girl said. "Can't we maybe stop talking?"

90   They sat down at the table and the girl looked across at the hills on the dry side of the valley and the man looked at her and at the table.

"You've got to realize," he said, "that I don't want you to do it if you don't want to. I'm perfectly willing to go through with it if it means anything to you."

"Doesn't it mean anything to you? We could get along."

"Of course it does. But I don't want anybody but you. I don't want any one else. And I know it's perfectly simple."

"Yes, you know it's perfectly simple."

95   "It's all right for you to say that, but I do know it."

"Would you do something for me now?"

"I'd do anything for you."

"Would you please please please please please please please stop talking?"

He did not say anything but looked at the bags against the wall of the station. There were labels on them from all the hotels where they had spent nights.

100   "But I don't want you to," he said, "I don't care anything about it."

"I'll scream," the girl said.

The woman came out through the curtains with two glasses of beer and put them down on the damp felt pads. "The train comes in five minutes," she said.

"What did she say?" asked the girl.

"That the train is coming in five minutes."

105   The girl smiled brightly at the woman, to thank her.

"I'd better take the bags over to the other side of the station," the man said. She smiled at him.

"All right. Then come back and we'll finish the beer."

He picked up the two heavy bags and carried them around the station to the other tracks. He looked up the tracks but could not see the train. Coming back, he walked through the barroom, where people waiting for the train were drinking. He drank an Anis at the bar and looked at the people. They were all waiting reasonably for the train. He went out through the bead curtain. She was sitting at the table and smiled at him.

"Do you feel better?" he asked.

110 "I feel fine," she said. "There's nothing wrong with me. I feel fine."

MAKING CONNECTIONS

1. What are the man and woman discussing? Do you have strong feelings about this topic? If so, how does that influence your response? If you were placed in this situation, what would you say or do?

2. From what narrative perspective or point of view is the story told? What difference does it make to the story and how does it affect your response?

3. How old are the man and the woman? Have they known each other long? Are there differences in their levels of life experience? How did they meet? What kind of past relationship has led up to their present situation? What details in the story support your description of the couple?

4. What is a "white elephant"? What is significant in the woman's initial comparison of the hills to white elephants? To what extent are her later thoughts revealed through her comment that they "don't really look like white elephants. I just meant the coloring of their skin through the trees"?

5. Some researchers have suggested that men and women talk to each other with different intentions. Do you see any indication of this in the story? How are you affected by the language of the conversation?

MAKING AN ARGUMENT

1. What does the conversation between the man and the woman tell you about these characters and their relationship? Do they both want the same thing? Why do they place so much emphasis on having "a fine time"? How do you think they would define "a fine time"? Do you think "fine times" are enough to keep them together? Write an essay that analyzes these characters and this relationship—and its future. Cite the text of the story for support.

D. H. LAWRENCE [1885–1930]

D[avid] H[erbert] Lawrence was born in Nottinghamshire, England. In the largely autobiographical novel, Sons and Lovers *(1913), Lawrence wrote about his difficult childhood as the son of a coarse (and often drunken) coal miner and an overprotective and demanding mother. After earning a teaching degree while on a scholarship at Nottingham University College in 1908, Lawrence taught school while he worked on his first novel,* The White Peacock *(1911), and published his first poems and short stories in* The English Review. *In 1912, he quit teaching after meeting and falling in love with Frieda von Richthofen, the sister of the German flying ace, the Red Baron. They were married in 1914, following her divorce. In 1915, Lawrence published his novel,* The Rainbow, *a story of three generations of a family in Nottinghamshire. Like much of his following work, the novel was extremely controversial for its frank depiction of sexual relationships and was banned by the English courts. Lawrence spent the rest of his life in self-imposed exile with his wife, traveling around the world. Though he wrote numerous novels, poems, and essays, many critics consider Lawrence's best work to be his short stories.*

THE HORSE DEALER'S DAUGHTER   [1922]

"Well, Mabel, and what are you going to do with yourself?" asked Joe, with foolish flippancy. He felt quite safe himself. Without listening for an answer, he turned aside, worked a grain of tobacco to the tip of his tongue and spat it out. He did not care about anything, since he felt safe himself.

The three brothers and the sister sat round the desolate breakfast table, attempting some sort of desultory consultation. The morning's post had given the final tap to the family fortune, and all was over. The dreary dining room itself, with its heavy mahogany furniture, looked as if it were waiting to be done away with.

But the consultation amounted to nothing. There was a strange air of ineffectuality about the three men, as they sprawled at table, smoking and reflecting vaguely on their own condition. The girl was alone, a rather short, sullen-looking young woman of twenty-seven. She did not share the same life as her brothers. She would have been good-looking, save for the impassive fixity of her face, "bull-dog," as her brothers called it.

There was a confused tramping of horses' feet outside. The three men all sprawled round in their chairs to watch. Beyond the dark hollybushes that separated the strip of lawn from the highroad, they could see a cavalcade of shire horses swinging out of their own yard, being taken for exercise. This was the last time. These were the last horses that would go through their hands. The young men watched with critical, callous looks. They were all frightened at the collapse of their lives, and the sense of disaster in which they were involved left them no inner freedom.

5   Yet they were three fine, well-set fellows enough. Joe, the eldest, was a man of thirty-three, broad and handsome in a hot, flushed way. His face was red, he twisted his black moustache over a thick finger, his eyes were shallow and restless. He had a sensual way of uncovering his teeth when he laughed, and his bearing was stupid. Now he watched the horses with a glazed look of helplessness in his eyes, a certain stupor of downfall.

The great draught-horses swung past. They were tied head to tail, four of them, and they heaved along to where a lane branched off from the highroad, planting their great hoofs floutingly in the fine black mud, swinging their great rounded haunches sumptuously, and trotting a few sudden steps as they were led into the lane, round the corner. Every movement showed a massive, slumbrous strength, and a stupidity which held them in subjection. The groom at the head looked back, jerking the leading rope. And the cavalcade moved out of sight up the lane, the tail of the last horse, bobbed up tight and stiff, held out taut from the swinging great haunches as they rocked behind the hedges in a motion like sleep.

Joe watched with glazed hopeless eyes. The horses were almost like his own body to him. He felt he was done for now. Luckily he was engaged to a woman as old as himself, and therefore her father, who was steward of a neighboring estate, would provide him with a job. He would marry and go into harness. His life was over, he would be a subject animal now.

He turned uneasily aside, the retreating steps of the horses echoing in his ears. Then, with foolish restlessness, he reached for the scraps of bacon-rind from the plates, and making a faint whistling sound, flung them to the terrier that lay against the fender. He watched the dog swallow them, and waited till the creature looked into his eyes. Then a faint grin came on his face, and in a high, foolish voice he said:

"You won't get much more bacon, shall you, you little bitch?"

10   The dog faintly and dismally wagged its tail, then lowered its haunches, circled round, and lay down again.

There was another helpless silence at the table. Joe sprawled uneasily in his seat, not willing to go till the family conclave was dissolved. Fred Henry, the second brother, was erect, clean-limbed, alert. He had watched the passing of the horses with more sangfroid. If he was an animal, like Joe, he was an animal which controls, not one which is controlled. He was master of any horse, and he carried himself with a well-tempered air of mastery. But he was not master of the situations of life. He pushed his coarse brown moustache upwards, off his lip, and glanced irritably at his sister, who sat impassive and inscrutable.

"You'll go and stop with Lucy for a bit, shan't you?" he asked. The girl did not answer.

"I don't see what else you can do," persisted Fred Henry.

"Go as a skivvy," Joe interpolated laconically.

15   The girl did not move a muscle.

"If I was her, I should go in for training for a nurse," said Malcolm, the youngest of them all. He was the baby of the family, a young man of twenty-two, with a fresh, jaunty *museau*.[1]

But Mabel did not take any notice of him. They had talked at her and round her for so many years, that she hardly heard them at all.

The marble clock on the mantelpiece softly chimed the half-hour, the dog rose uneasily from the hearthrug and looked at the party at the breakfast table. But still they sat on in ineffectual conclave.

"Oh, all right," said Joe suddenly, apropos of nothing. "I'll get a move on."

20   He pushed back his chair, straddled his knees with a downward jerk, to get them free, in horsey fashion, and went to the fire. Still he did not go out of the room; he was curious to know what the others would do or say. He began to charge his pipe, looking down at the dog and saying, in a high, affected voice:

"Going wi' me? Going wi' me are ter? Tha'rt goin' further than tha counts on just now, dost hear?"

---

[1]*museau* muzzle or snout; slang for "face"

The dog faintly wagged its tail, the man stuck out his jaw and covered his pipe with his hands, and puffed intently, losing himself in the tobacco, looking down all the while at the dog with an absent brown eye. The dog looked at him in mournful distrust. Joe stood with his knees stuck out, in real horsey fashion.

"Have you had a letter from Lucy?" Fred Henry asked of his sister.

"Last week," came the neutral reply.

"And what does she say?"

There was no answer.

"Does she *ask* you to go and stop there?" persisted Fred Henry.

"She says I can if I like."

"Well, then, you'd better. Tell her you'll come on Monday."

This was received in silence.

"That's what you'll do then, is it?" said Fred Henry, in some exasperation.

But she made no answer. There was a silence of futility and irritation in the room. Malcolm grinned fatuously.

"You'll have to make up your mind between now and next Wednesday," said Joe loudly, "or else find yourself lodgings on the kurbstone."

The face of the young woman darkened, but she sat on immutable.

"Here's Jack Fergusson!" exclaimed Malcolm, who was looking aimlessly out of the window.

"Where?" exclaimed Joe, loudly.

"Just gone past."

"Coming in?"

Malcolm craned his neck to see the gate.

"Yes," he said.

There was a silence. Mabel sat on like one condemned, at the head of the table. Then a whistle was heard from the kitchen. The dog got up and barked sharply. Joe opened the door and shouted:

"Come on."

After a moment a young man entered. He was muffled up in overcoat and a purple woolen scarf, and his tweed cap, which he did not remove, was pulled down on his head. He was of medium height, his face was rather long and pale, his eyes looked tired.

"Hello, Jack! Well, Jack!" exclaimed Malcolm and Joe. Fred Henry merely said, "Jack."

"What's doing?" asked the newcomer, evidently addressing Fred Henry.

"Same. We've got to be out by Wednesday. Got a cold?"

"I have—got it bad, too."

"Why don't you stop in?"

"*Me* stop in? When I can't stand on my legs, perhaps I shall have a chance." The young man spoke huskily. He had a slight Scotch accent.

"It's a knock-out, isn't it," said Joe, boisterously, "if a doctor goes round croaking with a cold. Looks bad for the patients, doesn't it?"

The young doctor looked at him slowly.

"Anything the matter with *you,* then?" he asked sarcastically.

"Not as I know of. Damn your eyes. I hope not. Why?"

"I thought you were very concerned about the patients, wondered if you might be one yourself."

55   "Damn it, no, I've never been patient to no flaming doctor, and hope I never shall be," returned Joe.

At this point Mabel rose from the table, and they all seemed to become aware of her existence. She began putting the dishes together. The young doctor looked at her, but did not address her. He had not greeted her. She went out of the room with the tray, her face impassive and unchanged.

"When are you off then, all of you?" asked the doctor.

"I'm catching the eleven-forty," replied Malcolm. "Are you goin down wi' th' trap, Joe?"

"Yes, I've told you I am going down wi' th' trap, haven't I?"

60   "We'd better be getting her in then. So long, Jack, if I don't see you before I go," said Malcolm, shaking hands.

He went out, followed by Joe, who seemed to have his tail between his legs.

"Well, this is the devil's own," exclaimed the doctor, when he was left alone with Fred Henry. "Going before Wednesday, are you?"

"That's the orders," replied the other.

65   "Where, to Northampton?"

"That's it."

"The devil!" exclaimed Fergusson, with quiet chagrin.

And there was silence between the two.

"All settled up, are you?" asked Fergusson.

"About."

70   There was another pause.

"Well, I shall miss yer, Freddy, boy," said the young doctor.

"And I shall miss thee, Jack," returned the other.

"Miss you like hell," mused the doctor.

Fred Henry turned aside. There was nothing to say. Mabel came in again, to finish clearing the table.

75   "What are *you* going to do, then, Miss Pervin?" asked Fergusson. "Going to your sister's, are you?"

Mabel looked at him with her steady, dangerous eyes, that always made him uncomfortable, unsettling his superficial ease.

"No," she said.

"Well, what in the name of fortune are *you* going to do? Say what you mean to do," cried Fred Henry, with futile intensity.

But she only averted her head, and continued her work. She folded the white table-cloth, and put on the chenile cloth.

80   "The sulkiest bitch that ever trod!" muttered her brother.

But she finished her task with perfectly impassive face, the young doctor watching her interestedly all the while. Then she went out.

Fred Henry stared after her, clenching his lips, his blue eyes fixing in sharp antagonism, as he made a grimace of sour exasperation.

"You could bray her into bits, and that's all you'd get out of her," he said in a small, narrowed tone.

The doctor smiled faintly.

85 "What's she *going* to do, then?" he asked.

"Strike me if I know!" returned the other.

There was a pause. Then the doctor stirred.

"I'll be seeing you to-night, shall I?" he said to his friend.

"Ay—where's it to be? Are we going over to Jessdale?"

90 "I don't know. I've got such a cold on me. I'll come round to the Moon and Stars, anyway."

"Let Lizzie and May miss their night for once, eh?"

"That's it—if I feel as I do now."

"All's one—"

The two young men went through the passage and down to the back door together. The house was large, but it was servantless now, and desolate. At the back was a small bricked house-yard, and beyond that a big square, graveled fine and red, and having stables on two sides. Sloping, dank, winter-dark fields stretched away on the open sides.

95 But the stables were empty. Joseph Pervin, the father of the family, had been a man of no education, who had become a fairly large horse dealer. The stables had been full of horses, there was a great turmoil and come-and-go of horses and of dealers and grooms. Then the kitchen was full of servants. But of late things had declined. The old man had married a second time, to retrieve his fortunes. Now he was dead and everything was gone to the dogs, there was nothing but debt and threatening.

For months, Mabel had been servantless in the big house, keeping the home together in penury for her ineffectual brothers. She had kept house for ten years. But previously it was with unstinted means. Then, however brutal and coarse everything was, the sense of money had kept her proud, confident. The men might be foul-mouthed, the women in the kitchen might have bad reputations, her brothers might have illegitimate children. But so long as there was money, the girl felt herself established, and brutally proud, reserved.

No company came to the house, save dealers and coarse men. Mabel had no associates of her own sex, after her sister went away. But she did not mind. She went regularly to church, she attended to her father. And she lived in the memory of her mother, who had died when she was fourteen, and whom she had loved. She had loved her father, too, in a different way, depending upon him, and feeling secure in him, until at the age of fifty-four he married again. And then she had set hard against him. Now he had died and left them all hopelessly in debt.

She had suffered badly during the period of poverty. Nothing, however, could shake the curious sullen, animal pride that dominated each member of the family. Now, for Mabel, the end had come. Still she would not cast about her. She would follow her own way just the same. She would always hold the keys of her own situation. Mindless and persistent, she endured from day to day. Why should she think? Why should she answer anybody? It was enough that this was the end, and there was no way out. She need not pass any more darkly along the main street of the small town, avoiding every eye. She need not demean herself any more, going into the shops and buying the cheapest food. This was at an end. She thought of nobody, not even of herself. Mindless and persistent, she seemed in a sort of ecstasy to be coming nearer to her fulfillment, her own glorification, approaching her dead mother, who was glorified.

In the afternoon she took a little bag, with shears and sponge and a small scrubbing brush, and went out. It was a gray, wintry day, with saddened, dark green fields and an atmosphere blackened by the smoke of foundries not far off. She went quickly, darkly along the causeway, heeding nobody, through the town to the churchyard.

100   There she always felt secure, as if no one could see her, although as a matter of fact she was exposed to the stare of every one who passed along under the churchyard wall. Nevertheless, once under the shadow of the great looming church, among the graves, she felt immune from the world, reserved within the thick churchyard wall as in another country.

Carefully she clipped the grass from the grave, and arranged the pinky white, small chrysanthemums in the tin cross. When this was done, she took an empty jar from a neighboring grave, brought water, and carefully, most scrupulously sponged the marble head-stone and the coping-stone.

It gave her sincere satisfaction to do this. She felt in immediate contact with the world of her mother. She took minute pains, went through the park in a state bordering on pure happiness, as if in performing this task she came into a subtle, intimate connection with her mother. For the life she followed here in the world was far less real than the world of death she inherited from her mother.

The doctor's house was just by the church. Fergusson, being a mere hired assistant, was slave to the country-side. As he hurried now to attend to the out-patients in the surgery, glancing across the graveyard with his quick eyes, he saw the girl at her task at the grave. She seemed so intent and remote, it was like looking into another world. Some mystical element was touched in him. He slowed down as he walked, watching her as if spellbound.

She lifted her eyes, feeling him looking. Their eyes met. And each looked away again at once, each feeling, in some way, found out by the other. He lifted his cap and passed on down the road. There remained distinct in his consciousness, like a vision, the memory of her face, lifted from the tombstone in the churchyard, and looking at him with slow, large, portentous eyes. It *was* portentous, her face. It seemed to mesmerize him. There was a heavy power in her eyes which laid hold of his whole being, as if he had drunk some powerful drug. He had been feeling weak and done before. Now the life came back into him, he felt delivered from his own fretted, daily self.

105   He finished his duties at the surgery as quickly as might be, hastily filling up the bottles of the waiting people with cheap drugs. Then, in perpetual haste, he set off again to visit several cases in another part of his round, before tea-time. At all times he preferred to walk if he could, but particularly when he was not well. He fancied the motion restored him.

The afternoon was falling. It was gray, deadened, and wintry, with a slow, moist, heavy coldness sinking in and deadening all the faculties. But why should he think or notice? He hastily climbed the hill and turned across the dark green fields, following the black cindertrack. In the distance, across a shallow dip in the country, the small town was clustered like smouldering ash, a tower, a spire, a heap of low, raw, extinct houses. And on the nearest fringe of the town, sloping into the dip, was Oldmeadow, the Pervins's house. He could see the stables and the outbuildings distinctly, as they lay towards him on the slope. Well, he would not go there many more times! Another resource would be lost to him, another place gone: the only company he cared for in the alien, ugly little town he was losing. Nothing but work, drudgery, constant hastening from dwelling to dwelling among the colliers and the ironworkers. It wore him out, but at the same time he had a craving for it. It was a stimulant to him to be in the homes of the working people, moving as it were through the innermost body of their life. His nerves were excited and gratified. He could come so near, into the very lives of the rough, inarticulate, powerfully emotional men and women. He grumbled, he said he hated the hellish hole. But as a matter of fact it excited him, the contact with the rough, strongly-feeling people was a stimulant applied direct to his nerves.

Below Oldmeadow, in the green, shallow, soddened hollow of fields, lay a square, deep pond. Roving across the landscape, the doctor's quick eye detected a figure in black passing through the gate of the field, down towards the pond. He looked again. It would be Mabel Pervin. His mind suddenly became alive and attentive.

Why was she going down there? He pulled up on the path on the slope above, and stood staring. He could just make sure of the small black figure moving in the hollow of the failing day. He seemed to see her in the midst of such obscurity, that he was like a clairvoyant, seeing rather with the mind's eye than with ordinary sight. Yet he could see her positively enough, while he kept his eye attentive. He felt, if he looked away from her, in the thick, ugly falling dusk, he would lose her altogether.

He followed her minutely as she moved, direct and intent, like something transmitted rather than stirring in voluntary activity, straight down the field towards the pond. There she stood on the bank for a moment. She never raised her head. Then she waded slowly into the water.

110　　He stood motionless as the small black figure walked slowly and deliberately towards the center of the pond, very slowly, gradually moving deeper into the motionless water, and still moving forward as the water got up to her breast. Then he could see her no more in the dusk of the dead afternoon.

"There!" he exclaimed. "Would you believe it?"

And he hastened straight down, running over the wet soddened fields, pushing through the hedges, down into the depression of callous wintry obscurity. It took him several minutes to come to the pond. He stood on the bank, breathing heavily. He could see nothing. His eyes seemed to penetrate the dead water. Yes, perhaps that was the dark shadow of her black clothing beneath the surface of the water.

He slowly ventured into the pond. The bottom was deep, soft clay, he sank in, and the water clasped dead cold round his legs. As he stirred he could smell the cold, rotten clay that fouled up into the water. It was objectionable in his lungs. Still, repelled and yet not heeding, he moved deeper into the pond. The cold water rose over his thighs, over his loins, upon his abdomen. The lower part of his body was all sunk in the hideous cold element. And the bottom was so deeply soft and uncertain he was afraid of pitching with his mouth underneath. He could not swim, and was afraid.

He crouched a little, spreading his hands under the water and moving them round, trying to feel for her. The dead cold pond swayed upon his chest. He moved again, a little deeper, and again, with his hands underneath, he felt all around under the water. And he touched her clothing. But it evaded his fingers. He made a desperate effort to grasp it.

115   And so doing he lost his balance and went under, horribly, suffocating in the foul earthy water, struggling madly for a few moments. At last, after what seemed an eternity, he got his footing, rose again into the air and looked around. He gasped, and knew he was in the world. Then he looked at the water. She had risen near him. He grasped her clothing, and drawing her nearer, turned to take his way to land again.

He went very slowly, carefully, absorbed in the slow progress. He rose higher, climbing out of the pond. The water was now only about his legs: he was thankful, full of relief to be out of the clutches of the pond. He lifted her and staggered on to the bank, out of the horror of wet, gray clay.

He laid her down on the bank. She was quite unconscious and running with water. He made the water come from her mouth, he worked to restore her. He did not have to work very long before he could feel the breathing begin again in her: she was breathing naturally. He worked a little longer. He could feel her live beneath his hands: she was coming back. He wiped her face, wrapped her in his overcoat, looked round into the dim, dark gray world, then lifted her and staggered down the bank and across the fields.

It seemed an unthinkably long way, and his burden so heavy he felt he would never get to the house. But at last he was in the stable-yard, and then in the house-yard. He opened the door and went into the house. In the kitchen he laid her down on the hearthrug, and called. The house was empty. But the fire was burning in the grate.

Then again he kneeled to attend to her. She was breathing regularly, her eyes were wide open and as if conscious, but there seemed something missing in her look. She was conscious in herself, but unconscious of her surroundings.

120   He ran upstairs, took blankets from a bed, and put them before the fire to warm. Then he removed her saturated, earthy-smelling clothing, rubbed her dry with a towel, and wrapped her naked in the blankets. Then he went into the dining-room, to look for spirits. There was a little whisky. He drank a gulp himself, and put some into her mouth.

The effect was instantaneous. She looked full into his face, as if she had been seeing him for some time, and yet had only just become conscious of him.

"Dr. Fergusson?" she said.

"What?" he answered.

He was divesting himself of his coat, intending to find some dry clothing upstairs. He could not bear the smell of the dead, clayey water, and he was mortally afraid of his own health.

125   "What did I do?" she asked.

"Walked into the pond," he replied. He had begun to shudder like one sick, and could hardly attend to her. Her eyes remained full on him, he seemed to be going dark in his mind, looking back at her helplessly. The shuddering became quieter in him, his life came back in him, dark and unknowing, but strong again.

"Was I out of my mind?" she asked, while her eyes were fixed on him all the time.

"Maybe, for the moment," he replied. He felt quiet, because his strength came back. The strange fretful strain had left him.

"Am I out of my mind now?" she asked.

130 "Are you?" he reflected a moment. "No." he answered truthfully. "I don't see that you are." He turned his face aside. He was afraid now, because he felt dazed, and felt dimly that her power was stronger than his, in this issue. And she continued to look at him fixedly all the time. "Can you tell me where I shall find some dry things to put on?" he asked.

"Did you dive into the pond for me?" she asked.

"No," he answered. "I walked in. But I went in overhead as well."

There was silence for a moment. He hesitated. He very much wanted to go upstairs to get into dry clothing. But there was another desire in him. And she seemed to hold him. His will seemed to have gone to sleep, and left him, standing there slack before her. But he felt warm inside himself. He did not shudder at all, though his clothes were sodden on him.

"Why did you?" she asked.

135 "Because I didn't want you to do such a foolish thing," he said.

"It wasn't foolish," she said, still gazing at him as she lay on the floor, with a sofa cushion under her head. "It was the right thing to do. *I* knew best, then."

"I'll go and shift these wet things," he said. But still he had not the power to move out of her presence, until she sent him. It was as if she had the life of his body in her hands, and he could not extricate himself. Or perhaps he did not want to.

Suddenly she sat up. Then she became aware of her own immediate condition. She felt the blankets about her, she knew her own limbs.

For a moment it seemed as if her reason were going. She looked round, with wild eye, as if seeking something. He stood still with fear. She saw her clothing lying scattered.

140 "Who undressed me?" she asked, her eyes resting full and inevitable on his face.

"I did," he replied, "to bring you round."

For some moments she sat and gazed at him awfully, her lips parted.

"Do you love me, then?" she asked.

He only stood and stared at her, fascinated. His soul seemed to melt.

145 She shuffled forward on her knees, and put her arms round him, round his legs, as he stood there, pressing her breasts against his knees and thighs, clutching him with strange, convulsive certainty, pressing his thighs against her, drawing him to her face, her throat, as she looked up at him with flaring, humble eyes of transfiguration, triumphant in first possession.

"You love me," she murmured, in strange transport, yearning and triumphant and confident. "You love me. I know you love me, I know."

And she was passionately kissing his knees, through the wet clothing, passionately and indiscriminately kissing his knees, his legs, as if unaware of everything.

He looked down at the tangled wet hair, the wild, bare, animal shoulders. He was amazed, bewildered, and afraid. He had never thought of loving her. He had never wanted to love her. When he rescued her and restored her, he was a doctor, and she was a patient. He had had no single personal thought of her. Nay, this introduction of the personal element was very distasteful to him, a violation of his professional honor. It was horrible to have her there embracing his knees. It was horrible. He revolted from it, violently. And yet—and yet—he had not the power to break away.

She looked at him again, with the same supplication of powerful love, and that same transcendent, frightening light of triumph. In view of the delicate flame which seemed to come from her face like a light, he was powerless. And yet he had never intended to love her. He had never intended. And something stubborn in him could not give way.

150   "You love me," she repeated, in a murmur of deep, rhapsodic assurance. "You love me."

Her hands were drawing him, drawing him down to her. He was afraid, even a little horrified. For he had, really, no intention of loving her. Yet her hands were drawing him towards her. He put out his hand quickly to steady himself, and grasped her bare shoulder. A flame seemed to burn the hand that grasped her soft shoulder. He had no intention of loving her: his whole will was against his yielding. It was horrible. And yet wonderful was the touch of her shoulders, beautiful the shining of her face. Was she perhaps mad? He had a horror of yielding to her. Yet something in him ached also.

He had been staring away at the door, away from her. But his hand remained on her shoulder. She had gone suddenly very still. He looked down at her. Her eyes were now wide with fear, with doubt, the light was dying from her face, a shadow of terrible grayness was returning. He could not bear the touch of her eyes' question upon him, and the look of death behind the question.

With an inward groan he gave way, and let his heart yield towards her. A sudden gentle smile came on his face. And her eyes, which never left his face, slowly, slowly filled with tears. He watched the strange water rise in her eyes, like some slow fountain coming up. And his heart seemed to burn and melt away in his breast.

He could not bear to look at her any more. He dropped on his knees and caught her head with his arms and pressed her face against his throat. She was very still. His heart, which seemed to have broken, was burning with a kind of agony in his breast. And he felt her slow, hot tears wetting his throat. But he could not move.

155   He felt the hot tears wet his neck and the hollows of his neck, and he remained motionless, suspended through one of man's eternities. Only now it had become indispensable to him to have her face pressed close to him; he could never let her go again. He could never let her head go away from the close clutch of his arm. He wanted to remain like that for ever, with his heart hurting him in a pain that was also life to him. Without knowing, he was looking down on her damp, soft brown hair.

Then, as it were suddenly, he smelt the horrid stagnant smell of that water. And at the same moment she drew away from him and looked at him. Her eyes were wistful and unfathomable. He was afraid of them, and he fell to kissing her, not knowing what he was doing. He wanted her eyes not to have that terrible, wistful, unfathomable look.

When she turned her face to him again, a faint delicate flush was glowing, and there was again dawning that terrible shining of joy in her eyes, which really terrified him, and yet which he now wanted to see, because he feared the look of doubt still more.

"You love me?" she said, rather faltering.

"Yes." The word cost him a painful effort. Not because it wasn't true. But because it was too newly true, the *saying* seemed to tear open again his newly torn heart. And he hardly wanted it to be true, even now.

160   She lifted her face to him, and he bent forward and kissed her on the mouth, gently, with the one kiss that is an eternal pledge. And as he kissed her his heart strained again in his breast. He never intended to love her. But now it was over. He had crossed over the gulf to her, and all that he had left behind had shriveled and become void.

After the kiss, her eyes again slowly filled with tears. She sat still, away from him, with her face drooped aside, and her hands folded in her lap. The tears fell very slowly. There was complete silence. He too sat there motionless and silent on the hearthrug. The strange pain of his heart that was broken seemed to consume him. That he should love her? That this was love! That he should be ripped open in this way! Him, a doctor! How they would all jeer if they knew! It was agony to him to think they might know.

In the curious naked pain of the thought he looked again to her. She was sitting there drooped into a muse. He saw a tear fall, and his heart flared hot. He saw for the first time that one of her shoulders was quite uncovered, one arm bare, he could see one of her small breasts; dimly, because it had become almost dark in the room.

"Why are you crying?" he asked, in an altered voice.

She looked up at him, and behind her tears the consciousness of her situation for the first time brought a dark look of shame to her eyes.

165   "I'm not crying, really," she said, watching him half frightened.

He reached his hand, and softly closed it on her bare arm.

"I love you! I love you!" he said in a soft, low vibrating voice, unlike himself.

She shrank, and dropped her head. The soft, penetrating grip of his hand on her arm distressed her. She looked up at him.

"I want to go," she said. "I want to go and get you some dry things."

170   "Why?" he said. "I'm all right."

"But I want to go," she said. "And I want you to change your things."

He released her arm, and she wrapped herself in the blanket, looking at him rather frightened. And still she did not rise.

"Kiss me," she said wistfully.

He kissed her, but briefly, half in anger.

175   Then, after a second, she rose nervously, all mixed up in the blanket. He watched her in her confusion, as she tried to extricate herself and wrap herself up so that she could walk. He watched her relentlessly, as she knew. And as she went, the blanket trailing, and as he saw a glimpse of her feet and her white leg, he tried to remember her as she was when he had wrapped her in the blanket. But then he didn't want to remember, because she had been nothing to him then,

and his nature revolted from remembering her as she was when she was nothing to him.

A tumbling, muffled noise from within the dark house startled him. Then he heard her voice:—"There are clothes." He rose and went to the foot of the stairs, and gathered up the garments she had thrown down. Then he came back to the fire, to rub himself down and dress. He grinned at his own appearance when he had finished.

The fire was sinking, so he put on coal. The house was now quite dark, save for the light of a street-lamp that shone in faintly from beyond the holly trees. He lit the gas with matches he found on the mantelpiece. Then he emptied the pockets of his own clothes, and threw all his wet things in a heap into the scullery. After which he gathered up her sodden clothes, gently, and put them in a separate heap on the copper-top in the scullery.

It was six o'clock on the clock. His own watch had stopped. He ought to go back to the surgery. He waited, and still she did not come down. So he went to the foot of the stairs and called:

"I shall have to go."

180   Almost immediately he heard her coming down. She had on her best dress of black voile, and her hair was tidy, but still damp. She looked at him—and in spite of herself, smiled.

"I don't like you in those clothes," she said.

"Do I look a sight?" he answered.

They were shy of one another.

"I'll make you some tea," she said.

185   "No, I must go."

"Must you?" And she looked at him again with the wide, strained, doubtful eyes. And again, from the pain of his breast, he knew how he loved her. He went and bent to kiss her, gently, passionately, with his heart's painful kiss.

"And my hair smells so horrible," she murmured in distraction. "And I'm so awful, I'm so awful! Oh, no, I'm too awful." And she broke into bitter, heart-broken sobbing. "You can't want to love me, I'm horrible."

"Don't be silly, don't be silly," he said, trying to comfort her, kissing her, holding her in his arms. "I want you, I want to marry you, we're going to be married, quickly, quickly—tomorrow if I can."

But she only sobbed terribly, and cried:

190   "I feel awful. I feel awful. I feel I'm horrible to you."

"No, I want you, I want you," was all he answered, blindly, with that terrible intonation which frightened her almost more than her horror lest he should *not* want her.

MAKING CONNECTIONS

1. In what way is the setting of the story a factor? How would you describe the surroundings and their effect on Mabel and Fergusson?

2. Describe Mabel. What is her everyday existence like? How has she been treated by her father and brothers? In what ways does she differ from them?

3. Describe Fergusson. What is his everyday existence like?
4. Pick out the images, emotions, and language that are used to describe love in this story.
5. At the end of the story Fergusson cries out, "I want you, I want you." Why does he seem to want Mabel so much? Do you think they are really in love? Explain.

MAKING AN ARGUMENT

1. To what extent are the "earthy" setting and the hard life of the characters important factors in this story? Write about the internal and external conflict in this story and its relationship to setting and characterization. Cite the text of the story for support.

BOBBIE ANN MASON [B. 1940]

Bobbie Ann Mason grew up in rural Kentucky on a dairy farm. An excellent student, Mason was encouraged in her studies by her parents, who never finished high school. She attended college at the University of Kentucky, where she majored in journalism, and later earned an M.A. from the State University of New York at Binghamton, and a Ph.D. from the University of Connecticut. Her first collection of short stories, Shiloh and Other Stories *(1982), was enormously well received, winning the Ernest Hemingway Foundation Award in 1982 for the year's most distinguished work of fiction. Her 1985 novel,* In Country, *was made into a film. A collection of stories,* Zigzagging Down a Wild Trail, *appeared in 2001, and her latest book,* Nancy Culpepper, *was published in 2006. Mason has described her work, which is usually set in the South and filled with popular culture references, as "southern Gothic going to the supermarket."*

SHILOH   [1982]

Leroy Moffitt's wife, Norma Jean, is working on her pectorals. She lifts three-pound dumbbells to warm up, then progresses to a twenty-pound barbell. Standing with her legs apart, she reminds Leroy of Wonder Woman.

"I'd give anything if I could just get these muscles to where they're real hard," says Norma Jean. "Feel this arm. It's not as hard as the other one."

"That's 'cause you're right-handed," says Leroy, dodging as she swings the barbell in an arc.

"Do you think so?"

"Sure."

5   Leroy is a truckdriver. He injured his leg in a highway accident four months ago, and his physical therapy, which involves weights and a pulley, prompted Norma Jean to try building herself up. Now she is attending a body-building class. Leroy has been collecting temporary disability since his tractor-trailer jackknifed in

Missouri, badly twisting his left leg in its socket. He has a steel pin in his hip. He will probably not be able to drive his rig again. It sits in the backyard, like a gigantic bird that has flown home to roost. Leroy has been home in Kentucky for three months, and his leg is almost healed, but the accident frightened him and he does not want to drive any more long hauls. He is not sure what to do next. In the meantime, he makes things from craft kits. He started by building a miniature log cabin from notched Popsicle sticks. He varnished it and placed it on the TV set, where it remains. It reminds him of a rustic Nativity scene. Then he tried string art (sailing ships on black velvet), a macramé owl kit, a snap-together B-17 Flying Fortress, and a lamp made out of a model truck, with a light fixture screwed in the top of the cab. At first the kits were diversions, something to kill time, but now he is thinking about building a full-scale log house from a kit. It would be considerably cheaper than building a regular house, and besides, Leroy has grown to appreciate how things are put together. He has begun to realize that in all the years he was on the road he never took time to examine anything. He was always flying past scenery.

"They won't let you build a log cabin in any of the new subdivisions," Norma Jean tells him.

"They will if I tell them it's for you," he says, teasing her. Ever since they were married, he has promised Norma Jean he would build her a new home one day. They have always rented, and the house they live in is small and nondescript. It does not even feel like a home, Leroy realizes now.

Norma Jean works at the Rexall drugstore, and she has acquired an amazing amount of information about cosmetics. When she explains to Leroy the three stages of complexion care, involving creams, toners, and moisturizers, he thinks happily of other petroleum products—axle grease, diesel fuel. This is a connection between him and Norma Jean. Since he has been home, he has felt unusually tender about his wife and guilty over his long absences. But he can't tell what she feels about him. Norma Jean has never complained about his traveling; she has never made hurt remarks, like calling his truck a "widow-maker." He is reasonably certain she has been faithful to him, but he wishes she would celebrate his permanent homecoming more happily. Norma Jean is often startled to find Leroy at home, and he thinks she seems a little disappointed about it. Perhaps he reminds her too much of the early days of their marriage, before he went on the road. They had a child who died as an infant, years ago. They never speak about their memories of Randy, which have almost faded, but now that Leroy is home all the time, they sometimes feel awkward around each other, and Leroy wonders if one of them should mention the child. He has the feeling that they are waking up out of a dream together—that they must create a new marriage, start afresh. They are lucky they are still married. Leroy has read that for most people losing a child destroys the marriage—or else he heard this on *Donahue*. He can't always remember where he learns things anymore.

10   At Christmas, Leroy bought an electric organ for Norma Jean. She used to play the piano when she was in high school. "It don't leave you," she told him once. "It's like riding a bicycle."

The new instrument had so many keys and buttons that she was bewildered by it at first. She touched the keys tentatively, pushed some buttons, then pecked out "Chopsticks." It came out in an amplified fox-trot rhythm, with marimba sounds.

"It's an orchestra!" she cried.

The organ had a pecan-look finish and eighteen preset chords, with optional flute, violin, trumpet, clarinet, and banjo accompaniments. Norma Jean mastered the organ almost immediately. At first she played Christmas songs. Then she bought *The Sixties Songbook* and learned every tune in it, adding variations to each with the rows of brightly colored buttons.

"I didn't like these old songs back then," she said. "But I have this crazy feeling I missed something."

15   "You didn't miss a thing," said Leroy.

Leroy likes to lie on the couch and smoke a joint and listen to Norma Jean play "Can't Take My Eyes Off You" and "I'll Be Back." He is back again. After fifteen years on the road, he is finally settling down with the woman he loves. She is still pretty. Her skin is flawless. Her frosted curls resemble pencil trimmings.

Now that Leroy has come home to stay, he notices how much the town has changed. Subdivisions are spreading across western Kentucky like an oil slick. The sign at the edge of town says "Pop: 11,500"—only seven hundred more than it said twenty years before. Leroy can't figure out who is living in all the new houses. The farmers who used to gather around the courthouse square on Saturday afternoons to play checkers and spit tobacco juice have gone. It has been years since Leroy has thought about the farmers, and they have disappeared without his noticing.

Leroy meets a kid named Stevie Hamilton in the parking lot at the new shopping center. While they pretend to be strangers meeting over a stalled car, Stevie tosses an ounce of marijuana under the front seat of Leroy's car. Stevie is wearing orange jogging shoes and a T-shirt that says CHATTAHOOCHEE SUPER-RAT. His father is a prominent doctor who lives in one of the expensive subdivisions in a new white-columned brick house that looks like a funeral parlor. In the phone book under his name there is a separate number, with the listing "Teenagers."

"Where do you get this stuff?" asks Leroy. "From your pappy?"

20   "That's for me to know and you to find out," Stevie says. He is slit-eyed and skinny.

"What else you got?"

"What you interested in?"

"Nothing special. Just wondered."

Leroy used to take speed on the road. Now he has to go slowly. He needs to be mellow. He leans back against the car and says, "I'm aiming to build me a log house, soon as I get time. My wife, though, I don't think she likes the idea."

25   "Well, let me know when you want me again," Stevie says. He has a cigarette in his cupped palm, as though sheltering it from the wind. He takes a long drag, then stomps it on the asphalt and slouches away.

Stevie's father was two years ahead of Leroy in high school. Leroy is thirty-four. He married Norma Jean when they were both eighteen, and their child Randy was born a few months later, but he died at the age of four months and three days. He would be about Stevie's age now. Norma Jean and Leroy were at the drive-in, watching a double feature (*Dr. Strangelove* and *Lover Come Back*), and the baby was sleeping in the back seat. When the first movie ended, the baby was dead.

It was the sudden infant death syndrome. Leroy remembers handing Randy to a nurse at the emergency room, as though he were offering her a large doll as a present. A dead baby feels like a sack of flour. "It just happens sometimes," said the doctor, in what Leroy always recalls as a nonchalant tone. Leroy can hardly remember the child anymore, but he still sees vividly a scene from *Dr. Strangelove* in which the President of the United States was talking in a folksy voice on the hot line to the Soviet premier about the bomber accidentally headed toward Russia. He was in the War Room, and the world map was lit up. Leroy remembers Norma Jean standing catatonically beside him in the hospital and himself thinking: Who is this strange girl? He had forgotten who she was. Now scientists are saying that crib death is caused by a virus. Nobody knows anything, Leroy thinks. The answers are always changing.

When Leroy gets home from the shopping center, Norma Jean's mother, Mabel Beasley, is there. Until this year. Leroy has not realized how much time she spends with Norma Jean. When she visits, she inspects the closets and then the plants, informing Norma Jean when a plant is droopy or yellow. Mabel calls the plants "flowers," although there are never any blooms. She also notices if Norma Jean's laundry is piling up. Mabel is a short, overweight woman whose tight, brown-dyed curls look more like a wig than the actual wig she sometimes wears. Today she has brought Norma Jean an off-white dust ruffle she made for the bed; Mabel works in a custom-upholstery shop.

"This is the tenth one I made this year," Mabel says. "I got started and couldn't stop."

"It's real pretty," says Norma Jean.

30   "Now we can hide things under the bed," says Leroy, who gets along with his mother-in-law primarily by joking with her. Mabel has never really forgiven him for disgracing her by getting Norma Jean pregnant. When the baby died, she said that fate was mocking her.

"What's that thing?" Mabel says to Leroy in a loud voice, pointing to a tangle of yarn on a piece of canvas.

Leroy holds it up for Mabel to see. "It's my needlepoint," he explains. "This is a *Star Trek* pillow cover."

"That's what a woman would do," says Mabel. "Great day in the morning!"

"All the big football players on TV do it," he says.

35   "Why, Leroy, you're always trying to fool me. I don't believe you for one minute. You don't know what to do with yourself—that's the whole trouble. Sewing!"

"I'm aiming to build us a log house," says Leroy. "Soon as my plans come."

"Like *heck* you are," says Norma Jean. She takes Leroy's needlepoint and shoves it into a drawer. "You have to find a job first. Nobody can afford to build now anyway."

Mabel straightens her girdle and says, "I still think before you get tied down y'all ought to take a little run to Shiloh."

"One of these days, Mama," Norma Jean says impatiently.

40   Mabel is talking about Shiloh, Tennessee. For the past few years, she has been urging Leroy and Norma Jean to visit the Civil War battleground there. Mabel went there on her honeymoon—the only real trip she ever took. Her husband died of a perforated

ulcer when Norma Jean was ten, but Mabel, who was accepted into the United Daughters of the Confederacy in 1975, is still preoccupied with going back to Shiloh.

"I've been to kingdom come and back in that truck out yonder," Leroy says to Mabel, "but we never yet set foot in that battleground. Ain't that something? How did I miss it?"

"It's not even that far," Mabel says.

After Mabel leaves, Norma Jean reads to Leroy from a list she has made. "Things you could do," she announces. "You could get a job as a guard at Union Carbide, where they'd let you set on a stool. You could get on at the lumberyard. You could do a little carpenter work, if you want to build so bad. You could—"

"I can't do something where I'd have to stand up all day."

45   "You ought to try standing up all day behind a cosmetics counter. It's amazing that I have strong feet, coming from two parents that never had strong feet at all." At the moment Norma Jean is holding on to the kitchen counter, raising her knees one at a time as she talks. She is wearing two-pound ankle weights.

"Don't worry," says Leroy. "I'll do something."

"You could truck calves to slaughter for somebody. You wouldn't have to drive any big old truck for that."

"I'm going to build you this house," says Leroy. "I want to make you a real home."

"I don't want to live in any log cabin."

50   "It's not a cabin. It's a house."

"I don't care. It looks like a cabin."

"You and me together could lift those logs. It's just like lifting weights."

Norma Jean doesn't answer. Under her breath, she is counting. Now she is marching through the kitchen. She is doing goose steps.

Before his accident, when Leroy came home he used to stay in the house with Norma Jean, watching TV in bed and playing cards. She would cook fried chicken, picnic ham, chocolate pie—all his favorites. Now he is home alone much of the time. In the mornings, Norma Jean disappears, leaving a cooling place in the bed. She eats a cereal called Body Buddies, and she leaves the bowl on the table, with the soggy tan balls floating in a milk puddle. He sees things about Norma Jean that he never realized before. When she chops onions, she stares off into a corner, as if she can't bear to look. She puts on her house slippers almost precisely at nine o'clock every evening and nudges her jogging shoes under the couch. She saves bread heels for the birds. Leroy watches the birds at the feeder. He notices the peculiar way goldfinches fly past the window. They close their wings, then fall, then spread their wings to catch and lift themselves. He wonders if they close their eyes when they fall. Norma Jean closes her eyes when they are in bed. She wants the lights turned out. Even then, he is sure she closes her eyes.

55   He goes for long drives around town. He tends to drive a car rather carelessly. Power steering and an automatic shift make a car feel so small and inconsequential that his body is hardly involved in the driving process. His injured leg stretches out comfortably. Once or twice he has almost hit something, but even the prospect of an accident seems minor in a car. He cruises the new subdivisions, feeling like a

criminal rehearsing for a robbery. Norma Jean is probably right about a log house being inappropriate here in the new subdivision. All the houses look grand and complicated. They depress him.

One day when Leroy comes home from a drive he finds Norma Jean in tears. She is in the kitchen making a potato and mushroom-soup casserole, with grated cheese topping. She is crying because her mother caught her smoking.

"I didn't hear her coming. I was standing here puffing away pretty as you please," Norma Jean says, wiping her eyes.

"I knew it would happen sooner or later," says Leroy, putting his arm around her.

"She don't know the meaning of the word 'knock,'" says Norma Jean. "It's a wonder she hadn't caught me years ago."

60   "Think of it this way," Leroy says. "What if she caught me with a joint?"

"You better not let her!" Norma Jean shrieks. "I'm warning you, Leroy Moffitt!"

"I'm just kidding. Here, play me a tune. That'll help you relax."

Norma Jean puts the casserole in the oven and sets the timer. Then she plays a ragtime tune, with horns and banjo, as Leroy lights up a joint and lies on the couch, laughing to himself about Mabel's catching him at it. He thinks of Stevie Hamilton—a doctor's son pushing grass. Everything is funny. The whole town seems crazy and small. He is reminded of Virgil Mathis, a boastful policeman Leroy used to shoot pool with. Virgil recently led a drug bust in a back room at a bowling alley, where he seized ten thousand dollars worth of marijuana. The newspaper had a picture of him holding up the bags of grass and grinning widely. Right now, Leroy can imagine Virgil breaking down the door and arresting him with a lungful of smoke. Virgil would probably have been alerted to the scene because of all the racket Norma Jean is making. Now she sounds like a hard-rock band. Norma Jean is terrific. When she switches to a Latin-rhythm version of "Sunshine Superman," Leroy hums along. Norma Jean's foot goes up and down, up and down.

"Well, what do you think?" Leroy says, when Norma Jean pauses to search through her music.

65   "What do I think about what?"

His mind has gone blank. Then he says, "I'll sell my rig and build us a house." That wasn't what he wanted to say. He wanted to know what she thought—what she *really* thought—about them.

"Don't start in on that again," says Norma Jean. She begins playing "Who'll Be the Next in Line?"

Leroy used to tell hitchhikers his whole life story—about his travels, his hometown, the baby. He would end with a question: "Well, what do you think?" It was just a rhetorical question. In time, he had the feeling that he'd been telling the same story over and over to the same hitchhikers. He quit talking to hitch-hikers when he realized how his voice sounded—whining and self-pitying, like some teenage-tragedy song. Now Leroy has the sudden impulse to tell Norma Jean about himself, as if he had just met her. They have known each other so long they have forgotten a lot about each other. They could become reacquainted. But when the oven timer goes off and she runs to the kitchen, he forgets why he wants to do this.

The next day, Mabel drops by. It is Saturday and Norma Jean is cleaning. Leroy is studying the plans of his log house, which have finally come in the mail. He has them spread out on the table—big sheets of stiff blue paper, with diagrams and numbers printed in white. While Norma Jean runs the vacuum, Mabel drinks coffee. She sets her coffee cup on a blueprint.

70   "I'm just waiting for time to pass," she says to Leroy, drumming her fingers on the table.

As soon as Norma Jean switches off the vacuum, Mabel says in a loud voice. "Did you hear about the datsun dog that killed the baby?"

Norma Jean says, "The word is 'dachshund.'"

"They put the dog on trial. It chewed the baby's legs off. The mother was in the next room all the time." She raises her voice. "They thought it was neglect."

Norma Jean is holding her ears. Leroy manages to open the refrigerator and get some Diet Pepsi to offer Mabel. Mabel still has some coffee and she waves away the Pepsi.

75   "Datsuns are like that," Mabel says. "They're jealous dogs. They'll tear a place to pieces if you don't keep an eye on them."

"You better watch out what you're saying, Mabel," says Leroy.

"Well, facts is facts."

Leroy looks out the window at his rig. It is like a huge piece of furniture gathering dust in the backyard. Pretty soon it will be an antique. He hears the vacuum cleaner. Norma Jean seems to be cleaning the living room rug again.

Later, she says to Leroy. "She just said that about the baby because she caught me smoking. She's trying to pay me back."

80   "What are you talking about?" Leroy says, nervously shuffling blueprints.

"You know good and well," Norma Jean says. She is sitting in a kitchen chair with her feet up and her arms wrapped around her knees. She looks small and helpless. She says, "The very idea, her bringing up a subject like that! Saying it was neglect."

"She didn't mean that," Leroy says.

"She might not have *thought* she meant it. She always says things like that. You don't know how she goes on."

"But she didn't really mean it. She was just talking."

85   Leroy opens a king-sized bottle of beer and pours it into two glasses, dividing it carefully. He hands a glass to Norma Jean and she takes it from him mechanically. For a long time, they sit by the kitchen window watching the birds at the feeder.

Something is happening. Norma Jean is going to night school. She has graduated from her six-week body-building course, and now she is taking an adult-education course in composition at Paducah Community College. She spends her evenings outlining paragraphs.

"First, you have a topic sentence," she explains to Leroy. "Then you divide it up. Your secondary topic has to be connected to your primary topic."

To Leroy, this sounds intimidating. "I never was any good in English," he says.

"It makes a lot of sense."

90   "What are you doing this for, anyhow?"

She shrugs. "It's something to do." She stands up and lifts her dumbbells a few times.

"Driving a rig, nobody cared about my English."

"I'm not criticizing your English."

Norma Jean used to say, "If I lose ten minutes' sleep, I just drag all day." Now she stays up late, writing compositions. She got a B on her first paper—a how-to theme on soup-based casseroles. Recently Norma Jean has been cooking unusual foods—tacos, lasagna, Bombay chicken. She doesn't play the organ anymore, though her second paper was called "Why Music Is Important to Me." She sits at the kitchen table, concentrating on her outlines, while Leroy plays with his log house plans, practicing with a set of Lincoln Logs. The thought of getting a truckload of notched, numbered logs scares him, and he wants to be prepared. As he and Norma Jean work together at the kitchen table, Leroy has the hopeful thought that they are sharing something, but he knows he is a fool to think this. Norma Jean is miles away. He knows he is going to lose her. Like Mabel, he is just waiting for time to pass.

95 One day, Mabel is there before Norma Jean gets home from work, and Leroy finds himself confiding in her. Mabel, he realizes, must know Norma Jean better than he does.

"I don't know what's got into that girl," Mabel says. "She used to go to bed with the chickens. Now you say she's up all hours. Plus her a-smoking. I like to died."

"I want to make her this beautiful home," Leroy says, indicating the Lincoln Logs. "I don't think she even wants it. Maybe she was happier with me gone."

"She don't know what to make of you, coming home like this."

"Is that it?"

100 Mabel takes the roof off his Lincoln Log cabin. "You couldn't get *me* in a log cabin," she says. "I was raised in one. It's no picnic, let me tell you."

"They're different now," says Leroy.

"I tell you what," Mabel says, smiling oddly at Leroy.

"What?"

"Take her on down to Shiloh. Y'all need to get out together, stir a little. Her brain's all balled up over them books."

105 Leroy can see traces of Norma Jean's features in her mother's face. Mabel's worn face has the texture of crinkled cotton, but suddenly she looks pretty. It occurs to Leroy that Mabel has been hinting all along that she wants them to take her with them to Shiloh.

"Let's all go to Shiloh," he says. "You and me and her. Come Sunday."

Mabel throws up her hand in protest. "Oh, no, not me. Young folks want to be by theirselves."

When Norma Jean comes in with groceries, Leroy says excitedly, "Your mama here's been dying to go to Shiloh for thirty-five years. It's about time we went, don't you think?"

"I'm not going to butt in on anybody's second honeymoon," Mabel says.

110 "Who's going on a honeymoon, for Christ's sake?" Norma Jean says loudly.

"I never raised no daughter of mine to talk that-a-way," Mabel says.

"You ain't seen nothing yet," says Norma Jean. She starts putting away boxes and cans, slamming cabinet doors.

"There's a log cabin at Shiloh," Mabel says. "It was there during the battle. There's bullet holes in it."

"When are you going to *shut up* about Shiloh, Mama?" asks Norma Jean.

115   "I always thought Shiloh was the prettiest place, so full of history," Mabel goes on. "I just hoped y'all could see it once before I die, so you could tell me about it." Later, she whispers to Leroy, "You do what I said. A little change is what she needs."

"Your name means 'the king,'" Norma Jean says to Leroy that evening. He is trying to get her to go to Shiloh, and she is reading a book about another century.

"Well, I reckon I ought to be right proud."

"I guess so."

"Am I still king around here?"

120   Norma Jean flexes her biceps and feels them for hardness. "I'm not fooling around with anybody, if that's what you mean," she says.

"Would you tell me if you were?"

"I don't know."

"What does your name mean?"

"It was Marilyn Monroe's real name."

125   "No kidding!"

"Norma comes from the Normans. They were invaders," she says. She closes her book and looks hard at Leroy. "I'll go to Shiloh with you if you'll stop staring at me."

On Sunday, Norma Jean packs a picnic and they go to Shiloh. To Leroy's relief Mabel says she does not want to come with them. Norma Jean drives, and Leroy, sitting beside her, feels like some boring hitchhiker she has picked up. He tries some conversation, but she answers him in monosyllables. At Shiloh, she drives aimlessly through the park, past bluffs and trails and steep ravines. Shiloh is an immense place, and Leroy cannot see it as a battleground. It is not what he expected. He thought it would look like a golf course. Monuments are everywhere, showing through the thick clusters of trees. Norma Jean passes the log cabin Mabel mentioned. It is surrounded by tourists looking for bullet holes.

"That's not the kind of log house I've got in mind," says Leroy apologetically.

"I know *that*."

130   "This is a pretty place. Your mama was right."

"It's O.K.," says Norma Jean. "Well, we've seen it. I hope she's satisfied."

They burst out laughing together.

At the park museum, a movie on Shiloh is shown every half hour, but they decide that they don't want to see it. They buy a souvenir Confederate flag for Mabel, and then they find a picnic spot near the cemetery. Norma Jean has brought a picnic cooler, with pimento sandwiches, soft drinks, and Yodels. Leroy eats a sandwich and then smokes a joint, hiding it behind the picnic cooler. Norma Jean has quit smoking altogether. She is picking cake crumbs from the cellophane wrapper, like a fussy bird.

Leroy says, "So the boys in gray ended up in Corinth. The Union soldiers zapped 'em finally. April 7, 1862."

135   They both know that he doesn't know any history. He is just talking about some of the historical plaques they have read. He feels awkward, like a boy on a date with an older girl. They are still just making conversation.

"Corinth is where Mama eloped to," says Norma Jean.

They sit in silence and stare at the cemetery for the Union dead and, beyond, at a tall cluster of trees. Campers are parked nearby, bumper to bumper, and small children in bright clothing are cavorting and squealing. Norma Jean wads up the cake wrapper and squeezes it tightly in her hand. Without looking at Leroy, she says, "I want to leave you."

Leroy takes a bottle of Coke out of the cooler and flips off the cap. He holds the bottle poised near his mouth but cannot remember to take a drink. Finally he says, "No, you don't."

"Yes, I do."

140   "I won't let you."

"You can't stop me."

"Don't do me that way."

Leroy knows Norma Jean will have her own way. "Didn't I promise to be home from now on?" he says.

"In some ways, a woman prefers a man who wanders," says Norma Jean. "That sounds crazy, I know."

145   "You're not crazy."

Leroy remembers to drink from his Coke. Then he says, "Yes, you *are* crazy. You and me could start all over again. Right back at the beginning."

"We *have* started all over again," says Norma Jean. "And this is how it turned out."

"What did I do wrong?"

"Nothing."

150   "Is this one of those women's lib things?" Leroy asks.

"Don't be funny."

The cemetery, a green slope dotted with white markers, looks like a subdivision site. Leroy is trying to comprehend that his marriage is breaking up, but for some reason he is wondering about white slabs in a graveyard.

"Everything was fine till Mama caught me smoking," says Norma Jean, standing up. "That set something off."

"What are you talking about?"

155   "She won't leave me alone—*you* won't leave me alone." Norma Jean seems to be crying, but she is looking away from him. "I feel eighteen again. I can't face that all over again." She starts walking away. "No, it *wasn't* fine. I don't know what I'm saying. Forget it."

Leroy takes a lungful of smoke and closes his eyes as Norma Jean's words sink in. He tries to focus on the fact that thirty-five hundred soldiers died on the grounds around him. He can only think of that war as a board game with plastic soldiers. Leroy almost smiles, as he compares the Confederates' daring attack on the Union camps and Virgil Mathis's raid on the bowling alley. General Grant, drunk and furious, shoved the Southerners back to Corinth, where Mabel and Jet Beasley were married years later, when Mabel was still thin and good-looking. The next day, Mabel and Jet visited the battleground, and then Norma Jean was born, and then she married Leroy and they had a baby, which they lost, and now Leroy and Norma Jean are here at the same battleground. Leroy knows he is leaving out a lot. He is leaving out the insides of history. History was always just names and dates to him. It occurs to him that building a house of logs is similarly empty—too simple. And the real inner workings of a marriage, like most of history, have escaped him. Now he sees that building a log house is the dumbest idea he could have had. It was clumsy of him to think Norma Jean would want a log house. It was a crazy idea. He'll have to think of something else, quickly. He will wad the blueprints into tight balls and fling them into the lake. Then he'll get moving again. He opens his eyes. Norma Jean has moved away and is walking through the cemetery, following a serpentine brick path.

Leroy gets up to follow his wife, but his good leg is asleep and his bad leg still hurts him. Norma Jean is far away, walking rapidly toward the bluff by the river, and he tries to hobble toward her. Some children run past him, screaming noisily. Norma Jean has reached the bluff, and she is looking out over the Tennessee River. Now she turns toward Leroy and waves her arms. Is she beckoning to him? She seems to be doing an exercise for her chest muscles. The sky is unusually pale—the color of the dust ruffle Mabel made for their bed.

MAKING CONNECTIONS

1. To what extent does your own background or experience influence your response to this story? Have you ever had the experience of "growing away" from someone? Explain.
2. The two main characters, Leroy and Norma Jean, seem to change as the story progresses. What do you think is happening to each of them? To their relationship?
3. Norma Jean and Leroy don't seem to have much to say to each other. Why? Are there times when you expect them to say more? What do you think remains unsaid?
4. Shiloh was the site of a major Civil War battle won by Union forces. Do you think this is an appropriate setting for this story? Explain.

MAKING AN ARGUMENT

1. It's clear that Norma Jean has changed in ways that make it very difficult for her to stay with Leroy. If you were a marriage counselor, and Norma Jean and Leroy came to you for help, what would you suggest to them? Would you suggest they stay together? Do you think this relationship should be saved? Write an argument for or against the continuance of this marriage. Cite the text of the story for evidence to support your view.

ROSARIO MORALES [B. 1930]

With her daughter Aurora Levins Morales, Rosario Morales coauthored Getting Home Alive, *a collection of poetry and prose published in 1986 and described by one critic as the most important book to come out of the Puerto Rican diaspora in a generation. It is considered a landmark in U.S.–Puerto Rican literature. "The Day It Happened" was published in* Callaloo.

THE DAY IT HAPPENED   [1992]

The day it happened I was washing my hair. I had long hair then that went half-way down my back and I washed it once a week and rinsed it with lemon juice "to bring out the blond highlights" Mami said. Then I'd set it into pincurls that took an age to do because there was so much to wind around and around my finger. But if Mami was in a good mood, and she looked like she might be that day, she curled the back for me. I usually did all this on Saturday so I would look great for church on Sunday, and for a date Saturday night if I ever had one. ¡ojala!

Naturally the moment when it all began I was rinsing the big soapy mess. Nosy Maria was leaning out the window drying her dark red fingernails in the breeze when Josie stepped out of our apartment house doorway with a suitcase in her hand. Maria sucked in her breath so hard the sound brought my mother who took one look, crossed herself, or so Maria says, and started praying. Someone needed to pray for Josie. It was five o'clock and Ramón was due home any minute.

I wouldn't have known anything about any of this if Olga next door hadn't rung our doorbell and banged on the door just when Mami was too deep in prayer to hear and Maria was leaning out over the sill with her eyes bugging out. I cursed, very quietly of course, because if Mami or Papi heard me curse I'd get a slap across my face. I wrapped my sopping head in a towel and opened the door to Olga's "Oh my goodness, oh my dear. Oh honey, did you see? Look out the window this minute. I wouldn't have believed it if I hadn't seen it with my own two eyes. That poor little kid. I hate to think..." and on and on as we crossed the apartment to look out on the street.

Little Mikey from across the way was telling the rest of the kids how he'd found a taxi for Josie the minute he'd hit Southern Boulevard and how he'd hailed it and how the driver had let him ride back to Brook Street in the front seat—even though all of them had seen him arrive and step out with his back stiff with pride. Meantime Josie was back down in the street with Doña Toña from across the hall and Betty Murphy upstairs right behind her, all of them loaded down with two lamps, a typewriter and a big box of books. Doña Toña was muttering something we couldn't hear up here on the second story but it was probably either the prayer I was hearing on my right or the "...hurry oh hurry oh God he'll be here any minute are you mad girl, are you mad" that came at me from the left.

5   It was hard not to be scared as well as glad that Josie was packing up and leaving Ramón. They'd been married only six months but already they were in a pattern, like the Garcias down the block who did everything the same way on the same day, all year. Ramón worked late till seven every week day and five on Saturday. When he arrived he expected a good dinner to be on the table at the right temperature exactly five minutes after he walked in the door. He yelled if she didn't get it right and sometimes even if she did.

Saturday evening they went out to a party or the bar down the avenue, both of them dressed up and Ramón looking proud and cheerful for a change. Josie always looked great. She's so cute. Small and plump with long lashes on her dark eyes and, get this, naturally curly hair. She smiled a lot when she was happy but she hadn't been happy much lately and not at all since she got pregnant. I wasn't supposed to know this. God, I was almost thirteen! But Maria, who was fourteen and a half and thought she was twenty, listened in on conversations in the living room by opening the door a sliver and she told me all about it.

Saturday nights there was sure to be a fight. Either it was that Josie was "no fun, a man can't be a man with such a wet rag around." Or it was that Josie was "a tramp. Why else was that guy staring at you, eating you up with his eyes?" The first time it happened, soon after they moved in, it woke me up from a deep sleep and I was so scared I crept into Maria's bed. I'd never heard such yelling in my life. When my parents fight it's during the day and in angry whispers. It sounds like a snake convention in my parents' bedroom. That's bad enough. Maria and I get real nervous and nothing's right until they make up and talk in normal voices again. But Ramón could be heard right through the floor at two in the morning. And then he took to throwing things and then he started hitting her. The first time that happened Josie didn't go to morning mass at St. Francis and Mami went down to her apartment to see if she was sick or something. Josie came to the door with a big bruise on her face. After that Mami went to fetch her every Sunday and stayed with her if she was too ashamed to go to church.

After she found out she was pregnant Josie had talked it over with Doña Toña and Doña Toña had talked it over with Mami and by and by we all knew she was scared he would hurt the little baby growing inside of her and worried about the child growing up with Ramón for a father. He expected too much of everyone and little kids hurt so when a parent thinks whatever they do is all wrong. Ha! Tell that to Mami and Papi, will you.

I don't think there was anyone in the neighborhood on Ramón's side not even Joe who liked to bully his wife and daughters but didn't realize he did or Tito who talked all the time about "wearing the pants in this family." Ramón was too much, even for them. Josie was so clearly a fine person, a quiet homebody, a sweetypie. Ramón was out of his mind, that's what most of us thought. I mean you had to be to be so regularly mean to a person who adored you. And she did, at least at first. You could see it in the way she looked at him, boasted about his strength, his good job, his brains. The way she excused his temper. "He can't help himself. He doesn't mean it."

10   And now she was packed up and sitting in the taxi. Waiting for him to come home, I guess. That was too much for Mami and she scooted out the door with

Olga, Maria, Papi, no less, and me right behind her with that soaked blue towel wrapped sloppily around my head. "Ai Mamita! Jesus, Maria y José. Jesus Maria y José," came faintly up the stairs in the front of the hurrying line. I knew Mami and I knew she meant to stand in front of Josie to protect her from that bully and, sure as shooting, Papi was going to protect Mami who was going so fast in her house slippers she almost fell down except that Olga gripped her hard and kept her upright.

When we streamed out the door into the small crowd that had gathered by now it was to see Ramón coming down the street with a sour look on his face. He looked up once or twice but mostly just stared at his feet as he strode up the block. He swept past us and almost into the house the way he did when he came home weary from the shipyard and the long ride home. He would have missed seeing Josie for sure, as I was praying he would, except that she called to him.

"Ramón," she said in her soft voice, stepping out of the taxi. "Ramón." He looked up and around then, took in the crowd, the taxi with a tall lamp lying on the back seat and Josie in her good suit. He stood looking at all this and especially at Josie for a long time. When he spoke it was only to Josie, as if we weren't there at all. He had to clear his throat to say "Josie?"

I was totally surprised and confused. He sounded so small, you know. So uncertain. It was Josie looked tall now and hard. If I hadn't known what I knew I would've said Josie was the bully in the family. She looked him straight in the eye and said stiffly, as if they were lines someone had given her to memorize, "I warned you. I said I would leave if you ever hit me again. I am not safe with you. Our child is not safe with you. I'm going now. I left arroz con pollo on the stove and the electric bill on the table." He didn't answer so she turned to hug Doña Toña and Mami before sitting herself back down. It was then that Ramón acted. Before I could blink he'd hurled himself at her, thrown himself on his knees and gripped her around her stockinged legs. No ! No te vayas. Tu no comprendes. Eres muy joven para comprender. Tu no puedes dejarme asi. Estamos casados para la vida. Te amo para siempre, para siempre. Josita, mi amor, no te vayas. Si te vas me mato. Te lo juro. No te puedes ir. No te puedes ir..." and on and on in a hoarse voice while Josie stood there frozen, fear on her face. There was no sound but Maria whispering occasional translations into Olga's impatient ear "Don't go." "You're too young to understand." "We're married for life." "I'll love you always." "I'll kill myself, I swear it."

It went on forever, Josie standing there, Ramón kneeling, all of us listening, tears running down my face, Josie's face, Mami's face. It was Olga who ended it, who walked up to Ramón, knelt down beside him, put an arm around him, and started talking, telling him Josie was a mother now and had to think about what was best for her baby, that it was his baby too, that he had to let her go now so she could bear a baby healthy in body and soul, that she knew he loved Josie, that his love would let him do what was best for them all. He was crying now, arguing with her while he slowly let go while he said he never could let her go that she was his whole life, that he would die without her, while Josie kissed Toña quickly on the cheek and climbed in next to the taxi driver who sat there looking the way I probably looked, dazed, like he'd stumbled into a movie screen and couldn't get out. She had to tell him to drive off.

◣ MAKING CONNECTIONS

1. Who is the narrator? How does her point of view influence your response to the story?
2. Describe Ramón. Why is Josie leaving him? Why is Josie upset that she is pregnant?
3. Why does Ramón sound so small when he realizes Josie is leaving? Do you believe what he says in response? Explain.
4. Do you think Josie will eventually take Ramón back? Do you think she should? Why or why not?
5. How are gender roles depicted in this story?
6. Compare Josie with Nora Helmer in *A Doll's House* (p. 803). Do you think she is more or less justified in leaving her husband than Nora? Explain.

◣ MAKING AN ARGUMENT

1. Research the subject of spousal abuse. Based on what you learn, write an argument for or against Josie giving Ramón another chance. Cite what you've learned through your research as well as the story to support your position.

◆ POETRY ◆

CONNECTING THROUGH COMPARISON: BE MY LOVE

The three poems that follow address a subtheme of this section: proposals of love. Each proposes a different view of love: Marlowe's shepherd idealizes his love, but Raleigh's nymph is skeptical and resists. Marvell's speaker qualifies his love as imperfect but nonetheless real in an imperfect world. Read and discussed together, they invite comparison and connections—not only with each other, but with similar experiences of your own.

CHRISTOPHER MARLOWE [1564–1593]

Christopher Marlowe was a contemporary of Shakespeare and one of the most successful playwrights and poets of the Elizabethan era, but his career was cut short when he was murdered in a tavern brawl. His major plays include Tamburlaine the Great *(1587),* Dr. Faustus *(1588), and* Edward II *(1592).*

THE PASSIONATE SHEPHERD TO HIS LOVE   [1599]

Come live with me and be my love
And we will all the pleasures prove
That valleys, groves, hills, and fields
Woods, or steepy mountain yields.

And we will sit upon the rocks, 5
Seeing the shepherds feed their flocks,
By shallow rivers to whose falls
Melodious birds sing madrigals.

And I will make thee beds of roses
And a thousand fragrant posies, 10
A cap of flowers, and a kirtle°
Embroidered with leaves of myrtle;

A gown made of the finest wool
Which from our pretty lambs we pull;
Fair lined slippers for the cold, 15
With buckles of the purest gold;

A belt of straw and ivy buds,
With coral clasps and amber studs:
And if these pleasures may thee move
Come live with me and be my love. 20

The shepherds' swains° shall dance and sing
For thy delight each May morning:
If these delights thy mind may move
Then live with me and be my love.

WALTER RALEIGH [1552–1618]

Walter Raleigh is best known as an adventurer, explorer, and adviser to Queen Elizabeth I. He organized expeditions to North America, founded a settlement in Virginia, and introduced tobacco to Europe. Involved in political intrigue for much of his career, he was imprisoned for thirteen years in the Tower of London and was eventually executed by James I. "The Nymph's Reply to the Shepherd" was written in response to Christopher Marlowe's "The Passionate Shepherd to His Love."

THE NYMPH'S REPLY TO THE SHEPHERD [1600]

If all the world were young,
And truth in every shepherd's tongue,
These pretty pleasures might me move
To live with thee and be thy love.

Time drives the flocks from field to fold 5
When rivers rage and rocks grow cold,

11 kirtle a long gown   **21 swains** boy servants

And Philomel° becometh dumb;
The rest complains of cares to come.

The flowers do fade, and wanton fields
To wayward winter reckoning yields; 10
A honey tongue, a heart of gall,
Is fancy's spring, but sorrow's fall.

Thy gowns, thy shoes, thy bed of roses,
Thy cap, thy kirtle,° and thy posies
Soon break, soon winter, soon forgotten— 15
In folly ripe, in season rotten.

Thy belt of straw and ivy buds,
Thy coral clasps and amber studs,
All these in me no means can move
To come to thee and be thy love. 20

But could youth last and love still breed,
Had joys no date nor age no need,
Then these delights my mind might move
To come with thee and be thy love.

ANDREW MARVELL [1621–1678]

Andrew Marvell was born in the town of Hull, England, and attended Cambridge University, graduating in 1638. During the English civil war, he held posts as a tutor in the family of an important general on the Parliamentary side and as a secretary to the poet Milton. During the war, in 1659, Marvell was elected to Parliament and served, even after the Restoration, as a well-regarded member until his death. Marvell, who was known during his lifetime only for the few satires he published, was recognized as an important lyric poet after his death, when his Miscellaneous Poems *were published in 1681. "To His Coy Mistress" is widely considered one of the greatest English love poems.*

TO HIS COY MISTRESS [1641]

Had we but world enough, and time,
This coyness, lady, were no crime.
We would sit down, and think which way
To walk, and pass our long love's day.
Thou by the Indian Ganges' side 5

7 Philomel nightingale bird　**14 kirtle** a long gown

Shoudst rubies find: I by the tide
Of Humber° would complain. I would
Love you ten years before the flood,
And you should, if you please, refuse
Till the conversion of the Jews.°   10
My vegetable love° should grow
Vaster than empires and more slow;
An hundred years should go to praise
Thine eyes, and on thy forehead gaze;
Two hundred to adore each breast,   15
But thirty thousand to the rest;
An age at least to every part,
And the last age should show your heart.
For, lady, you deserve this state,
Nor would I love at lower rate.   20
    But at my back I always hear
Time's winged chariot hurrying near;
And yonder all before us lie
Deserts of vast eternity.
Thy beauty shall no more be found;   25
Nor, in thy marble vault, shall sound
My echoing song, then worms shall try
That long-preserved virginity,
And your quaint honor turn to dust,
And into ashes all my lust: 30
The grave's a fine and private place,
But none, I think, do there embrace.
    Now therefore, while the youthful hue
Sits on thy skin like morning dew
And while thy willing soul transpires°   35
At every pore with instant fires,
Now let us sport us while we may,
And now, like amorous birds of prey,
Rather at once our time devour
Than languish in his slow-chapped° power.   40
Let us roll all our strength and all
Our sweetness up into one ball,
And tear our pleasures with rough strife
Through the iron gates of life:
Thus, though we cannot make our sun   45
Stand still, yet we will make him run.

---

7 Humber the river that runs through Marvell's native town, Hull   **10 the conversion of the Jews** supposedly to occur at the end of time   **11 vegetable love** growing slowly   **35 transpires** breathes   **40 slow-chapped** devouring slowly

MAKING CONNECTIONS

1. In "The Passionate Shepherd to His Love," what does the shepherd want? What does he offer?
2. Do you think he is being realistic? Explain.
3. Do you agree with "The Nymph's Reply to the Shepherd"? Explain.
4. Why doesn't the speaker give the shepherd what he wants? How does her vision of reality differ from his? What reality does she recognize that he does not?
5. What does the speaker in "To His Coy Mistress" want? Why does he think he should have it?
6. "To His Coy Mistress" is divided into three parts. Discuss the content of each section and describe how the speaker builds his argument.
7. What images does the speaker use to dramatize his points?

MAKING AN ARGUMENT

1. Do you find Marvell's argument in "To His Coy Mistress" sincere and convincing? How do you imagine the speaker in "The Nymph's Reply to the Shepherd" might respond to the speaker in "To His Coy Mistress"? Take a position for or against Marvell's poem, and write an essay that supports your view. Cite the text of the poems for support.

MAYA ANGELOU [B. 1928]

Maya Angelou was born Marguerite Johnson in St. Louis, Missouri, and lived with her grandmother in Stamps, Arkansas. She studied music, dance, and drama, and also became a writer. She became very involved in the black civil rights movement, and from 1963 to 1966, she lived in Ghana. Angelou is known for her many volumes of auto-biographical novels, the first of which is I Know Why the Caged Bird Sings *(1969). Her six works of poetry are* Just Give Me a Cool Drink of Water 'Fore I Die *(1971),* Oh Pray My Wings Are Gonna Fit Me Well *(1975),* And Still I Rise *(1978),* Shaker, Why Don't You Sing? *(1983),* Now Sheba Sings the Song *(1987), and* I Shall Not Be Moved *(1990). She read her poem* "On the Pulse of Morning" *at the inauguration ceremony for President Bill Clinton in 1990. In the same year, a collection of Angelou's essays,* Wouldn't Take Nothing for My Journey, *was published. She teaches at Wake Forest University, and in 2002, she published her autobiography,* A Song Flung Up to Heaven. *Her latest books are* Letter to My Daughter *(2008) and a recipe book,* Great Food, All Day Long *(2010).*

PHENOMENAL WOMAN   [1978]

Pretty women wonder where my secret lies.
I'm not cute or built to suit a fashion model's size
But when I start to tell them,

They think I'm telling lies.
I say,
It's in the reach of my arms,
The span of my hips,
The stride of my step,
The curl of my lips.
I'm a woman
Phenomenally.
Phenomenal woman,
That's me.

I walk into a room
Just as cool as you please,
And to a man,
The fellows stand or
Fall down on their knees.
Then they swarm around me,
A hive of honey bees.
I say,
It's the fire in my eyes,
And the flash of my teeth,
The swing in my waist,
And the joy in my feet.
I'm a woman
Phenomenally.
Phenomenal woman,
That's me.

Men themselves have wondered
What they see in me.
They try so much
But they can't touch
My inner mystery.
When I try to show them
They say they still can't see.
I say,
It's in the arch of my back,
The sun of my smile,
The ride of my breasts,
The grace of my style.
I'm a woman
Phenomenally.
Phenomenal woman,
That's me.

Now you understand
Just why my head's not bowed.
I don't shout or jump about

5

10

15

20

25

30

35

40

45

Or have to talk real loud.
When you see me passing   50
It ought to make you proud.
I say,
It's in the click of my heels,
The bend of my hair,
The palm of my hand,   55
The need for my care.
'Cause I'm a woman
Phenomenally.
Phenomenal woman,
That's me.   60

MAKING CONNECTIONS

1. What is so "phenomenal" about the speaker? What lines in the poem indicate that?
2. Do you think the speaker in this poem thinks "too much" of herself? Explain.

MAKING AN ARGUMENT

1. Write a comparison of this poem with "Barbie Doll" on page 14. To what extent do you think the "girlchild" of that poem might have become a phenomenal woman? Cite the text of both poems for support.

MARGARET ATWOOD [B. 1939]

(See biography on p. 278.)

YOU FIT INTO ME   [1971]

you fit into me
like a hook into an eye

a fish hook
an open eye

MAKING CONNECTIONS

1. The "hook" and the "eye" combo is the simile here. Is there more than one definition of a hook and an eye? Explain. Given the type of hook and type of eye in the second stanza, how would you describe the attitude of the speaker toward this relationship?
2. The first stanza introduces the second. The second is an abrupt shift. Is this combination effective? Explain.

MAKING AN ARGUMENT

1. Interpret the "hook" and "eye" combo in the poem, and write about how the simile applies to relationships in other works of literature in this section ("The Day It Happened" on p. 716, "Shiloh" on p. 705, "The Proposal" on p. 759, or others). Cite the text of the literature for support.

ELIZABETH BARRETT BROWNING [1806–1861]

Elizabeth Barrett Browning was born in Durham, England, the oldest of eleven children, and at fifteen, suffered a spinal injury that left her partially paralyzed. In 1845, she met Robert Browning and the two fell in love. They were forced to elope, however, because of her extremely possessive father. A very popular poet during her lifetime, she published many volumes of poetry, including her most famous collection, Sonnets from the Portuguese, *love poems written to her husband. "How Do I Love Thee?" is one of the sonnets in this collection.*

HOW DO I LOVE THEE? [1850]

How do I love thee? Let me count the ways.
I love thee to the depth and breadth and height
My soul can reach, when feeling out of sight
For the ends of being and ideal grace.
I love thee to the level of every day's   5
Most quiet need, by sun and candle-light.
I love thee freely, as men strive for right.
I love thee purely, as they turn from praise.
I love thee with the passion put to use
In my old griefs, and with my childhood's faith.   10
I love thee with a love I seemed to lose
With my lost saints. I love thee with the breath,
Smiles, tears, of all my life; and, if God choose,
I shall but love thee better after death.

MAKING CONNECTIONS

1. The sentiments expressed in this poem are very idealistic. Do you think the depth of love described in this poem is possible? Is the poem too sentimental? Explain.
2. This poem is written in answer to the question it poses: "How Do I Love Thee?" With specific reference to the text of the poem, pick out passages and discuss the effectiveness of the speaker's language as she answers that question.

MAKING AN ARGUMENT

1. Both this poem and Edna St. Vincent Millay's "Love Is Not All" (p. 739) are
    love sonnets. But what they say about love—and how they say it—differ in
    many ways. Which do you prefer and why? Write an essay that compares
    and contrasts the two poems. Consider both content and form, and cite the
    text of both poems for support.

ROBERT BROWNING [1812–1889]

The son of a banker, Robert Browning was born in a sub-
urb of London and first learned the joy of reading in his
father's vast library. He published his first collection of
poems, Pauline, *in 1833, and over the next thirty years*
followed it with numerous other volumes, which, though
they contained some of his greatest works, were finan-
cially unsuccessful. In 1846, in one of the most famous
matches in literary history, he married the celebrated poet
Elizabeth Barrett, who wrote the sonnet that begins "How Do I Love Thee?" (see
p. 726) to him. Because of her ill health and to escape her overbearing father,
the couple moved to Italy. After her death in 1861, he returned to England and
wrote The Ring and the Book *(1868–1869), a long narrative poem about a*
famous seventeenth-century murder case. The poem was Browning's first major
success and brought him the wide recognition and respect that had thus far
eluded him. Many of his best regarded poems, including "Porphyria's Lover,"
take the form of dramatic monologues, in which the poet creates a character
who reveals himself or herself while delivering an extended speech, often to a
silent listener.

PORPHYRIA'S LOVER   [1834]

The rain set early in tonight,
   The sullen wind was soon awake,
It tore the elm-tops down for spite,
   And did its worst to vex the lake:
I listened with heart fit to break.   5
   When glided in Porphyria; straight
She shut the cold out and the storm,
   And kneeled and made the cheerless grate
Blaze up, and all the cottage warm;
   Which done, she rose, and from her form   10
Withdrew the dripping cloak and shawl,
   And laid her soiled gloves by, untied
Her hat and let the damp hair fall,
   And, last, she sat down by my side

And called me. When no voice replied,   15
   She put my arm about her waist,
And made her smooth white shoulder bare,
   And all her yellow hair displaced,
And, stooping, made my cheek lie there,
   And spread, o'er all, her yellow hair,   20
Murmuring how she loved me—she
   Too weak, for all her heart's endeavor,
To set its struggling passion free
   From pride, and vainer ties dissever,
And give herself to me forever.   25
   But passion sometimes would prevail,
Nor could tonight's gay feast restrain
   A sudden thought of one so pale
For love of her, and all in vain:
   So, she was come through wind and rain.   30
Be sure I looked up at her eyes
   Happy and proud; at last I knew
Porphyria worshiped me: surprise
   Made my heart swell, and still it grew
While I debated what to do.   35
   That moment she was mine, mine, fair,
Perfectly pure and good: I found
   A thing to do, and all her hair
In one long yellow string I wound
   Three times her little throat around,   40
And strangled her. No pain felt she;
   I am quite sure she felt no pain.
As a shut bud that holds a bee,
   I warily opened her lids: again
Laughed the blue eyes without a stain.   45
   And I untightened next the tress
About her neck; her cheek once more
   Blushed bright beneath my burning kiss:
I propped her head up as before,
   Only, this time my shoulder bore   50
Her head, which droops upon it still:
   The smiling rosy little head,
So glad it has its utmost will,
   That all it scorned at once is fled,
And I, its love, am gained instead!   55
   Porphyria's love: she guessed not how
Her darling one wish would be heard.
   And thus we sit together now,
And all night long we have not stirred,
   And yet God has not said a word!   60

MAKING CONNECTIONS

1. What details set the mood early in the poem?
2. Paraphrase the speaker's argument. According to him, why is it appropriate to strangle Porphyria? Interpret the last line of the poem. Is the speaker showing consciousness of guilt?
3. Compare the love described in this poem with that described in Elizabeth Barrett Browning's "How Do I Love Thee?" (p. 726).
4. Compare the speaker in this poem with Emily in Faulkner's "A Rose for Emily" (p. 907).

MAKING AN ARGUMENT

1. This poem is a dramatic monologue told from the speaker's point of view. What difference does that make? Imagine that you are a newspaper reporter or a police officer investigating the case. How would you describe this scene? Based on your interpretation of the poem, write a history of the speaker and his relationship with Porphyria. Cite the text of the poem for support.

NIKKI GIOVANNI [B. 1943]

One of the most prominent poets to emerge from the black literary movement of the 1960s, Nikki Giovanni was born in Knoxville, Tennessee. Her father was a probation officer, and her mother a social worker. Growing up, she was particularly close to her maternal grandmother and spent summers with her in Knoxville even after her family moved to Cincinnati, Ohio. It was while she was at Fisk University in Nashville that she grew politically aware, serving in Fisk's chapter of the SNCC (Student Non-Violent Coordinating Committee), which promoted the concept of "black power" in confronting the social and economic problems of the time. Her first books of poetry, Black Feeling and Black Talk *(1968),* Black Judgment *(1968), and* Re: Creation *(1970), were enormously successful and brought her much acclaim. A vibrant personality, she has toured the United States giving lectures and reading her poetry, and has recorded numerous albums of her poetry, including* Truth Is on Its Way, *which was the best-selling spoken-word album of 1971. Though her recent work is more introspective and less political, she remains deeply committed to the transforming power of poetry. She has said: "If everybody became a poet, the world would be so much better." Her latest book of poetry,* Acolytes, *was published in 2007. She is a University Distinguished Professor at Virginia Polytechnic Institute and State University.*

WOMAN   [1978]

she wanted to be a blade
of grass amid the fields
but he wouldn't agree
to be the dandelion

she wanted to be a robin singing   5
through the leaves
but he refused to be
her tree

she spun herself into a web
and looking for a place to rest   10
turned to him
but he stood straight
declining to be her corner

she tried to be a book
but he wouldn't read   15

she turned herself into a bulb
but he wouldn't let her grow

she decided to become
a woman
and though he still refused   20
to be a man
she decided it was all
right.

MAKING CONNECTIONS

1. When we "personify" objects or animals, we give them human characteristics. Where does this reversal of personification occur in the poem and how does it affect you?

2. Compare this poem to "Barbie Doll" (p. 14), "Phenomenal Woman" (p. 723), or "Ella, in a Square Apron, Along Highway 80" (p. 732).

MAKING AN ARGUMENT

1. Identify each of the metaphors for the woman and the man, and write about the kind of relationship they create. Would it have been better if he was the things she wanted him to be—or not? Take a position and cite the text of the poem to support your view.

SHARON OLDS [B. 1942]

(See biography on p. 285.)

RITE OF PASSAGE   [1984]

As the guests arrive at my son's party
they gather in the living room—
short men, men in first grade
with smooth jaws and chins.
Hands in pockets, they stand around   5

jostling, jockeying for place, small fights
breaking out and calming. One says to another
How old are you? Six. I'm seven. So?
They eye each other, seeing themselves
tiny in each other's pupils. They clear their   10
throats a lot, a room of small bankers,
they fold their arms and frown. *I could beat you
up*, a seven says to a six,
the dark cake, round and heavy as a
turret, behind them on the table. My son,   15
freckles like specks of nutmeg on his cheeks,
chest narrow as the balsa keel of a
model boat, long hands
cool and thin as the day they guided him
out of me, speaks up as a host   20
for the sake of the group.

We could easily kill a two-year-old,
he says in a clear voice. The other
men agree, they clear their throats
like Generals, they relax and get down to   25
playing war, celebrating my son's life.

MAKING CONNECTIONS

1. "We could easily kill a two-year old," says the speaker's son. What was
    your reaction when you read that? Is her son evil? Explain.
2. After her son makes his comment (above), the speaker says "The other
    men agree." Why does she refer to them as "men"? Are they men? Explain.
3. At the end the speaker says they are "celebrating my son's life." Why does
    she say that rather than "celebrating his birthday"?

MAKING AN ARGUMENT

1. Do you think this kind of discussion would occur at a boy's birthday party?
    Would it occur at a girl's birthday party? Do boys and girls have different
    attitudes toward violence? Take a position on this issue and support that
    position from the text of this poem and secondary sources.

JUDY GRAHN [B. 1940]

*Judy Grahn was born in Chicago, Illinois. Her father worked
as a cook, and her mother was a photographer's assistant. In
her twenties, Grahn worked in a series of odd jobs, including
short-order cook, artist's model, and nurse's aide before starting the Women's Press Collective with artist Wendy Cadden
in Oakland, California, in 1969. In the 1980s, although she
was already a well-established poet, she returned to school at
San Francisco State University and earned a B.A. degree. She*

currently teaches in the New College of California in San Francisco, where she helped create the Gay and Lesbian Studies department. Her publications include The Work of a Common Woman: The Collected Poetry of Judy Grahn, 1964–1977 *(1978),* The Queen of Wands *(1982), and a collection of nonfiction,* Blood and Bread and Roses *(1986).*

ELLA, IN A SQUARE APRON, ALONG HIGHWAY 80 [1971]

She's a copperheaded waitress,
tired and sharp-worded, she hides
her bad brown tooth behind a wicked
smile, and flicks her ass
out of habit, to fend off the pass   5
that passes for affection.
She keeps her mind the way men
keep a knife—keen to strip the game
down to her size. She has a thin spine,
swallows her eggs cold, and tells lies.   10
She slaps a wet rag at the truck drivers
if they should complain. She understands
the necessity for pain, turns away
the smaller tips, out of pride, and
keeps a flask under the counter. Once,   15
she shot a lover who misused her child.
Before she got out of jail, the courts had pounced
and given the child away. Like some isolated lake,
her flat blue eyes take care of their own stark
bottoms. Her hands are nervous, curled, ready   20
to scrape.
The common woman is as common
as a rattlesnake.

MAKING CONNECTIONS

1. Who is Ella? What words or phrases in the poem help you to see her?
2. What does the speaker mean by "The common woman is as common / as a rattlesnake"? How has the speaker in the poem defined "common"? Can you think of people in your own experience that this definition of "common" might be applied to? Explain.

MAKING AN ARGUMENT

1. Write a comparison of the character description in this poem with those in "Barbie Doll" (p. 14), "Phenomenal Woman" (p. 723), and "Woman" (p. 729). Analyze the language used to create the images in the texts of each poem to support your view.

DONALD HALL [B. 1928]

Donald Hall began to pursue writing during adolescence. At just sixteen years old, he attended the Bread Loaf Writers Conference and published his first work. Hall studied at Harvard, Oxford, and Stanford before accepting a faculty position at the University of Michigan, where he met and married fellow poet Jane Kenyon. Early in 1994, Kenyon was diagnosed with leukemia, which took her life just fifteen months later. Kenyon's sickness and death became the subject of much of Hall's subsequent poetry. "The Wedding Couple" originally appeared in Hall's 1996 book, This Old Life. *His latest book,* White Apples and the Taste of Stones: Selected Poems 1946–2006, *was published in 2006.*

THE WEDDING COUPLE   [1996]

Fifteen years ago his heart
infarcted and he stopped smoking.
   At eighty he trembled
like a birch but remained vigorous
   and acute.   5
      When they married,
fifty years ago, I was twelve.
   I observed the white lace
veil, the mumbling preacher, and the flowers
   of parlor silence   10
and ordinary absurdity; but
   I thought I stood outside
the parlor.
      For two years she dwindled
   by small strokes   15
into a mannequin—speechless almost, almost
   unmoving, eyes open
and blinking, fitful in perception
   but a mannequin that suffered
shame when it stained the bed sheet.   20
   Slowly, shaking with purpose,
he carried her to the bathroom,
   undressed and washed her,
dressed her in clean clothes, and carried her back
   to CNN and bed. "All   25
you need is love," sang John and Paul:
   He touched her shoulder: her eyes
caressed him like a bride's bold eyes.

MAKING CONNECTIONS

1. Who is the speaker in this poem? What do we know about his relationship to the other characters?
2. Did your reading of the brief biography that precedes this poem illuminate the poem's tone?
3. Prepare a brief paraphrase of this poem that focuses on the timeline. How does time move in the poem? What effect is created by this nonlinear use of time?
4. Have you ever had to watch a loved one's health fade? To what extent does this experience (or lack thereof) influence your response to this poem?

MAKING AN ARGUMENT

1. Michael Lassell's poem "How to Watch Your Brother Die" (p. 736) also deals with the sickness and death of a lover. Write an essay that compares the use of tone and imagery in the two poems. Cite the text of both poems for support.

Essex Hemphill [1957–1995]

The primary focus of Essex Hemphill's writing is the difficult plight of black gay men, and his books include a collection of writings by black gay men, Brother to Brother *(1991). The poem below is taken from his book,* Ceremonies: Prose and Poetry *(1992). Hemphill died of AIDS-related illness at the age of thirty-eight.*

Commitments   (1992)

I will always be there
When the silence is exhumed.
When the photographs are examined
I will be pictured smiling
among siblings, parents,   5
nieces and nephews.

In the background of the photographs
the hazy smoke of barbecue,
a checkered red-and-white tablecloth
laden with blackened chicken,   10
glistening ribs, paper plates,
bottles of beer, and pop.

In the photos
the smallest children
are held by their parents.   15
My arms are empty, or around

the shoulders of unsuspecting aunts
expecting to throw rice at me someday.

Or picture tinsel, candles,
ornamented, imitation trees,   20
or another table, this one
set for Thanksgiving,
a turkey steaming the lens.

My arms are empty
in those photos, too,   25
so empty they would break around a lover.

I am always there
for critical emergencies,
graduations,
the middle of the night.   30

I am the invisible son.
In the family photos
nothing appears out of character.
I smile as I serve my duty.

 ## MAKING CONNECTIONS

1. What does the speaker mean by "I will always be there"? In what way will
   he always be there?
2. The speaker says that his arms are around "the shoulders of unsuspecting
   aunts." What are they unsuspecting of?
3. To what extent is the speaker the "invisible son"? How can he be invisible
   if he's in the photographs?

MAKING AN ARGUMENT

1. How does the narrative perspective in this poem compare with that in "How
   to Watch Your Brother Die" on page 736? Who are the speakers in each
   poem—and what difference does it make? Write a comparative essay about
   the two poems that includes the relationship between narrative perspective
   and theme. Cite the text of each poem for support.

MICHAEL LASSELL [B. 1947]

*Michael Lassell is the author of six books of poetry, fiction,
and nonfiction, including* A Flame for the Touch That
Matters *(1998) and* Decade Dance *(1990), which won a
Lambda Literary Award. He is also the editor of five books,
including (with Elena Georgiou)* The World in Us: Lesbian
and Gay Poetry of the Next Wave *(2000) and* Elton John and
Tim Rice's Aida: The Making of a Broadway Show *(2000).*

He holds degrees from Colgate University, California Institute of the Arts, and Yale, and lives in New York City, where he is the features editor of Metropolitan Home *magazine. His most recent book,* Disney on Broadway, *was published in 2002. His latest book is about architecture and design,* Making It Modern *(2009).*

HOW TO WATCH YOUR BROTHER DIE   [1990]

for Carl Morse

When the call comes, be calm.
Say to your wife, "My brother is dying. I have to fly
to California."
Try not to be shocked that he already looks like
a cadaver.   5
Say to the young man sitting by your brother's side,
"I'm his brother."
Try not to be shocked when the young man says,
"I'm his lover. Thanks for coming."

Listen to the doctor with a steel face on.   10
Sign the necessary forms.
Tell the doctor you will take care of everything.
Wonder why doctors are so remote.

Watch the lover's eyes as they stare into
your brother's eyes as they stare into   15
space.
Wonder what they see there.
Remember the time he was jealous and
opened your eyebrow with a sharp stick.
Forgive him out loud   20
even if he can't
understand you.
Realize the scar will be
all that's left of him.

Over coffee in the hospital cafeteria   25
say to the lover, "You're an extremely good-looking
young man."
Hear him say,
"I never thought I was good enough looking to
deserve your brother."   30

Watch the tears well up in his eyes. Say,
"I'm sorry, I don't know what it means to be
the lover of another man."
Hear him say,
"It's just like a wife, only the commitment is   35

deeper because the odds against you are so much
greater."
Say nothing, but
take his hand like a brother's.

Drive to Mexico for unproved drugs that might   40
help him live longer.
Explain what they are to the border guard.
Fill with rage when he informs you,
"You can't bring those across."

Begin to grow loud.   45
Feel the lover's hand on your arm
restraining you. See in the guard's eye
how much a man can hate another man.
Say to the lover, "How can you stand it?"
Hear him say, "You get used to it."   50
Think of one of your children getting used to
another man's hatred.

Call your wife on the telephone. Tell her,
"He hasn't much time.
I'll be home soon." Before you hang up, say,   55
"How could anyone's commitment be deeper than
a husband and wife?" Hear her say,
"Please. I don't want to know all the details."

When he slips into an irrevocable coma,
hold his lover in your arms while he sobs,   60
no longer strong. Wonder how much longer
you will be able to be strong.
Feel how it feels to hold a man in your arms
whose arms are used to holding men.
Offer God anything to bring your brother back.   65
Know you have nothing God could possibly want.
Curse God, but do not
abandon Him.

Stare at the face of the funeral director
when he tells you he will not   70
embalm the body for fear of
contamination. Let him see in your eyes
how much a man can hate another man.

Stand beside a casket covered in flowers,
white flowers. Say,   75
"Thank you for coming," to each of several
hundred men
who file past in tears, some of them

holding hands. Know that your brother's life
was not what you imagined. Overhear two   80
mourners say, "I wonder who'll be next?" and
"I don't care anymore,
as long as it isn't you."

Arrange to take an early flight home,
his lover will drive you to the airport.   85
When your flight is announced say,
awkwardly, "If I can do anything, please
let me know." Do not flinch when he says,
"Forgive yourself for not wanting to know him
after he told you. He did."   90
Stop and let it soak in. Say,
"He forgave me, or he knew himself?"
"Both," the lover will say, not knowing what else
to do. Hold him like a brother while he
kisses you on the cheek. Think that   95
you haven't been kissed by a man since
your father died. Think,
"This is no moment not to be strong."

Fly first class and drink Scotch. Stroke
your split eyebrow with a finger and   100
think of your brother alive. Smile
at the memory and think
how your children will feel in your arms,
warm and friendly and without challenge.

MAKING CONNECTIONS

1. What do you think of the title of the poem? Is this how to watch your
    brother die? Explain.
2. Who is the "you" to whom the speaker addresses himself?
3. What does the speaker mean by "See in the guard's eye / how much a man
    can hate another man"? What other images of love or hate can you find in
    the poem?
4. The poem concludes with "think / how your children will feel in your arms, /
    warm and friendly and without challenge." Is this a fitting conclusion? Explain.

MAKING AN ARGUMENT

1. The author of this poem is gay, but the speaker in the poem is hetero-
    sexual and is not always comfortable with what he encounters. What kind
    of impact does this speaker have on the content of the poem? To what
    extent would this be a different poem if the speaker were gay? Write
    about the effectiveness of narration in this poem. Cite the text of the
    poem for support.

◼ EDNA ST. VINCENT MILLAY [1892–1950]

Edna St. Vincent Millay was born in Rockland, Maine, and began writing poetry as a child. After graduating from Vassar College in 1917, she moved to New York City, where she quickly became a noted figure in the bustling arts scene of Greenwich Village. She published her first book of poetry, the acclaimed Renascence and Other Poems, *that same year. In 1923, she won the Pulitzer Prize for* The Harp Weaver and Other Poems. *Her later poetry, which became increasingly political, never received the same acclaim as her early work, and, after 1940, when she suffered a nervous breakdown, she wrote very little. She died in 1950, feeling that she had been largely forgotten. After her death, the publication of her collected poems in 1956 restored her position as one of the most accomplished poets of the century.*

WHAT LIPS MY LIPS HAVE KISSED, AND WHERE, AND WHY   [1923]

What lips my lips have kissed, and where, and why,
I have forgotten, and what arms have lain
Under my head till morning; but the rain
Is full of ghosts tonight, that tap and sigh
Upon the glass and listen for reply,   5
And in my heart there stirs a quiet pain
For unremembered lads that not again
Will turn to me at midnight with a cry.
Thus in the winter stands the lonely tree,
Nor knows what birds have vanished one by one,   10
Yet knows its boughs more silent than before:
I cannot say what loves have come and gone,
I only know that summer sang in me
A little while, that in me sings no more.

LOVE IS NOT ALL   [1931]

Love is not all; it is not meat nor drink
Nor slumber nor a roof against the rain;
Nor yet a floating spar to men that sink
And rise and sink and rise and sink again;
Love cannot fill the thickened lung with breath,   5
Nor clean the blood, nor set the fractured bone;
Yet many a man is making friends with death
Even as I speak, for lack of love alone.
It well may be that in a difficult hour,
Pinned down by pain and moaning for release   10
Or nagged by want past resolution's power,
I might be driven to sell your love for peace,
Or trade the memory of this night for food.
It well may be. I do not think I would.

MAKING CONNECTIONS

1. How would you respond to the title "What Lips My Lips Have Kissed, and Where, and Why"?
2. What do you think the speaker means when she says, "I only know that summer sang in me / A little while, that in me sings no more"?
3. What role does irony play in "Love Is Not All"?

MAKING AN ARGUMENT

1. Write a comparison of Millay's sonnet "Love Is Not All" with Shakespeare's "Sonnet 29" (p. 87). Include an analysis of structure, rhyme, rhythm, and imagery—and their effectiveness in conveying the content of each poem.

SHARON OLDS [B. 1942]

(See biography on p. 285.)

SEX WITHOUT LOVE

[1984]

How do they do it, the ones who make love
without love? Beautiful as dancers,
gliding over each other like ice-skaters
over the ice, fingers hooked
inside each other's bodies, faces   5
red as steak, wine, wet as the
children at birth whose mothers are going to
give them away. How do they come to the
come to the come to the God come to the
still waters, and not love   10
the one who came there with them, light
rising slowly as steam off their joined
skin? These are the true religious,
the purists, the pros, the ones who will not
accept a false Messiah, love the   15
priest instead of the God. They do not
mistake the lover for their own pleasure,
they are like great runners, they know they are alone
with the road surface, the cold, the wind,
the fit of their shoes, their over-all cardio-
vascular health—just factors; like the partner   20
in the bed, and not the truth, which is the
single body alone in the universe
against its own best time.

MAKING CONNECTIONS

1. What is the tone of this poem? How would you characterize the speaker's attitude?
2. In what way do the lovers glide "over each other like ice-skaters / over the ice"?
3. What is the purpose of the stammered "come to the" in lines 8 and 9?
4. We are regularly bombarded by popular media, especially through advertising, with "sex without love." Do you see this as a problem? Does it matter? Explain.

MAKING AN ARGUMENT

1. What is the "truth" referred to at the end of the poem? How would you describe it in your own words? Identify and write about the images in this poem, what you think they mean, and the way that these images "add up" to the "truth" of this poem. Cite the text of the poem for support.

OCTAVIO PAZ [1914–1998]

Octavio Paz was born into a politically active family in Mexico City during the early stages of the Mexican Revolution. His grandfather fought for Benito Juarez, and Paz was forced to temporarily flee to the United States after the assassination of Emiliano Zapata, a leading figure in the Mexican Revolution. Later in life, Paz took a diplomatic position with the Mexican government that included posts in both France and India, but he retired in 1968 to protest the Mexican government's repres-
sion of student demonstrations. In addition to collections of poetry, Paz was an essayist. He received the Nobel Prize for literature in 1990. He is the first Mexican author to have received this honor.

TWO BODIES   [1984]

Two bodies face to face
are at times two waves
and night is an ocean.

Two bodies face to face
are at times two stones   5
and night a desert.

Two bodies face to face
are at times two roots
laced into night.

Two bodies face to face   10
are at times two knives
and night strikes sparks.

Two bodies face to face
are two stars falling
in an empty sky.   15

MAKING CONNECTIONS

1. What is the effect of the repetition of the first line? Does it mean the same
   thing in each stanza?
2. What is the relationship between night and the two bodies in each stanza?
   Is this relationship consistent throughout? Or different each time?
3. What is the effect of the shift in the final paragraph?

MAKING AN ARGUMENT

1. What is the relationship between the stanzas? Are the two bodies the same
   throughout? Write an explication of this poem that supports your interpretation. Carefully cite the text of the poem for support.

SYLVIA PLATH   [1932–1963]

*Encouraged by her mother, Sylvia Plath began writing poetry
as a precocious child in Boston, publishing her first poem in
the* Boston Traveller *when she was only eight years old. That
same year her father died, an event that haunted her for the
rest of her life. Like the protagonist in her autobiographical
novel,* The Bell Jar *(1963), she was a star student at Smith
College, became a guest editor of a fashion magazine, and
moved for a short time to New York City. When she returned
home, she suffered the first of her serious mental breakdowns and attempted suicide.
She was institutionalized for over a year and received electric shock treatments.
When she returned to Smith, she again excelled, winning a Fulbright scholarship to
England after her final year. While studying at Cambridge, she met and fell in love
with the English poet Ted Hughes. Married in 1956, the couple eventually settled in
the English countryside and produced two children. The marriage was a difficult
one, and the couple separated in 1962. Once again Plath entered a severe depression, committing suicide in 1963. Her greatest work dates to the tortured final years
of her life, when she was able to channel her energies into highly personal, ironic,
and often terrifying poems. Her* Collected Poems, *edited by Ted Hughes, appeared in
1981 and was awarded the Pulitzer Prize.*

MIRROR   [1963]

I am silver and exact. I have no preconceptions.
Whatever I see I swallow immediately
Just as it is, unmisted by love or dislike.
I am not cruel, only truthful—
The eye of a little god, four-cornered.   5
Most of the time I meditate on the opposite wall.

It is pink, with speckles. I have looked at it so long
I think it is a part of my heart. But it flickers.
Faces and darkness separate us over and over.

Now I am a lake. A woman bends over me.   10
Searching my reaches for what she really is.
Then she turns to those liars, the candles or the moon.
I see her back, and reflect it faithfully.
She rewards me with tears and an agitation of hands.
I am important to her. She comes and goes.   15
Each morning it is her face that replaces the darkness.
In me she has drowned a young girl, and in me an old woman
Rises toward her day after day, like a terrible fish.

MAKING CONNECTIONS

1. Discuss the personification of the mirror in the poem. The mirror has a
    voice. How does the mirror describe itself? Cite lines from the text of the
    poem to support your response.
2. To what extent is the mirror honest? In what way are "the candles or the
    moon" liars? What rises toward her "like a terrible fish"?

MAKING AN ARGUMENT

1. To what extent do the mirror and the lake help the woman discover who she
    is? In what way do they interfere with her self-discovery? Are the mirror and
    the lake responsible for what she sees? Write about the woman in this poem.
    What do you think her problem is? Compare her to characters in other poems
    in this section. Cite the text of this poem and/or other poems for support.

CONNECTING THROUGH COMPARISON AND PARODY:
SHALL I COMPARE THEE?

The three poems that follow address a subtheme of this section: the adequacy—
or inadequacy—of language to describe a lover. Shakespeare's speaker in "Sonnet 18"
seems to believe that nature falls short of his love as a source of comparison; whereas
the speaker in "Sonnet 130" believes that nature as a source exaggerates his love's
qualities. Finally, Howard Moss, "goofs" on the whole business of love sonnets through
parody. Read and discussed together, they invite comparisons and connections—not
only with each other, but with similar experiences of your own.

WILLIAM SHAKESPEARE   [1564–1616]

(See biography on p. 495.)

SHALL I COMPARE THEE TO A SUMMER'S DAY? (SONNET 18)   [1609]

Shall I compare thee to a summer's day?
Thou art more lovely and more temperate:
Rough winds do shake the darling buds of May,

And summer's lease hath all too short a date;
Sometime too hot the eye of heaven shines,   5
And often is his gold complexion dimm'd;
And every fair from fair sometime declines,
By chance or nature's changing course untrimm'd;
But thy eternal summer shall not fade
Nor lose possession of that fair thou ow'st;   10
Nor shall Death brag thou wand'rest in his shade,
When in eternal lines to time thou grow'st;
So long as men can breathe or eyes can see,
So long lives this, and this gives life to thee.

MY MISTRESS' EYES ARE NOTHING LIKE THE SUN (SONNET 130)   [1609]

My mistress' eyes are nothing like the sun;
Coral is far more red than her lips' red;
If snow be white, why then her breasts are dun;
If hairs be wires, black wires grow on her head.
I have seen roses damasked,° red and white,   5
But no such roses see I in her cheeks;
And in some perfumes is there more delight
Than in the breath that from my mistress reeks.°
I love to hear her speak, yet well I know
That music hath a far more pleasing sound;   10
I grant I never saw a goddess go;°
My mistress, when she walks, treads on the ground.
And yet, by heaven, I think my love as rare
As any she belied with false compare.

HOWARD MOSS [1922–1987]

Howard Moss was a poet, critic, and dramatist, and in 1971, he received the National Book Award for poetry for his Selected Poems. *He was the poetry editor for* The New Yorker *magazine for more than thirty years.*

SHALL I COMPARE THEE TO A SUMMER'S DAY?   [1976]

Who says you're like one of the dog days?
You're nicer. And better.
Even in May, the weather can be gray,

---

5 damasked of mingled red and white   **8 reeks** (in Shakespeare's time) to emit vapour
11 go walk

And a summer sub-let doesn't last forever.
Sometimes the sun's too hot;   5
Sometimes it is not.
Who can stay young forever?
People break their necks or just drop dead!
But you? Never!
If there's just one condensed reader left   10
Who can figure out the abridged alphabet,
After you're dead and gone,
In this poem you'll live on!

MAKING CONNECTIONS

1. In "Sonnet 18," do you think the speaker should compare his beloved to a summer's day? Why or why not?
2. In many of Shakespeare's sonnets, a dilemma is presented in the first eight lines—a turning point and solution in the next six. To what extent is that the case here?
3. The poem by Howard Moss is a parody of Shakespeare's "Sonnet 18." Define "parody" and explain how it works in this case.
4. Compare and contrast both of these poems with "My Mistress' Eyes Are Nothing Like the Sun."
5. According to the speaker in "Sonnet 130," his mistress's eyes, lips, breasts, hair, cheeks, breath, voice, and walk don't stand up to nature very well. Do you think he is insulting her? Explain. In what way do the last two lines reverse the first twelve?

MAKING AN ARGUMENT

1. To what extent are these sonnets about the limitations of language rather than love? Write a comparison of the three poems that focuses on the use of language and its inability to capture and convey the qualities of the beloved. Cite all three poems to support your view.
2. Compare the Moss parody of Shakespeare's sonnet with Christopher Durang's parody (*For Whom the Southern Belle Tolls*) of *The Glass Menagerie* on p. 966. Cite the texts for support.

CONNECTING AND COMPARING ACROSS GENRES: CINDERELLA

The fairy tale, the poem, and the essay that follow present a subtheme of this section: the Grimm fairy tale, Cinderella, and what they mean. Have the modern references and explanations in the Anne Sexton poem and Bruno Bettelheim essay accounted for everything that is in the fairy tale? Read and discussed together, they invite comparisons and connections—not only with each other, but with your own experience of this classic tale.

Jacob Ludwig Karl Grimm [1785–1863]
and Wilhelm Karl Grimm [1786–1859]

The Brothers Grimm are best known today for their collection of children's tales known popularly as Grimm's fairy tales, though during their lifetimes they were both renowned as scholars of the German language. They derived most of the fairy tales in their volume not from written sources, but by interviewing German peasants.

CINDERELLA   [1812]

Translated by Margaret Hunt and James Stern

The wife of a rich man fell sick, and as she felt that her end was drawing near, she called her only daughter to her bedside and said: "Dear child, be good and pious, and then the good God will always protect you, and I will look down on you from heaven and be near you." Thereupon she closed her eyes and departed. Every day the maiden went out to her mother's grave and wept, and she remained pious and good. When winter came the snow spread a white sheet over the grave, and by the time the spring sun had drawn it off again, the man had taken another wife.

The woman had brought with her into the house two daughters, who were beautiful and fair of face, but vile and black of heart. Now began a bad time for the poor step-child. "Is the stupid goose to sit in the parlor with us?" they said. "He who wants to eat bread must earn it; out with the kitchen-wench." They took her pretty clothes away from her, put an old grey bedgown on her, and gave her wooden shoes. "Just look at the proud princess, how decked out she is!" they cried, and laughed, and led her into the kitchen. There she had to do hard work from morning till night, get up before daybreak, carry water, light fires, cook and wash. Besides this, the sisters did her every imaginable injury—they mocked her and emptied her peas and lentils into the ashes, so that she was forced to sit and pick them out again. In the evening when she had worked till she was weary she had no bed to go to, but had to sleep by the hearth in the cinders. And as on that account she always looked dusty and dirty, they called her Cinderella.

It happened that the father was once going to the fair, and he asked his two step-daughters what he should bring back for them. "Beautiful dresses," said one, "pearls and jewels," said the second. "And you, Cinderella," said he, "what will you have?" "Father, break off for me the first branch which knocks against your hat on your way home." So he bought beautiful dresses, pearls and jewels for his two step-daughters, and on his way home, as he was riding through a green thicket, a hazel twig brushed against him and knocked off his hat. Then he broke off the branch and took it with him. When he reached home he gave his step-daughters the things which they had wished for, and to Cinderella he gave the branch from the hazel bush. Cinderella thanked him, went to her mother's grave and planted the branch on it, and wept so much that the tears fell down on it and watered it. And it grew and became a handsome tree. Thrice a day Cinderella went and sat beneath it, and wept and prayed, and a little white bird always came on the tree, and if Cinderella expressed a wish, the bird threw down to her what she had wished for.

It happened, however, that the King gave orders for a festival which was to last three days, and to which all the beautiful young girls in the county were invited, in order that his son might choose himself a bride. When the two step-sisters heard that they too were to appear among the number, they were delighted, called Cinderella and said: "Comb our hair for us, brush our shoes and fasten our buckles, for we are going to the wedding at the King's palace." Cinderella obeyed, but wept, because she too would have liked to go with them to the dance, and begged her step-mother to allow her to do so. "You go, Cinderella!" said she; "covered in dust and dirt as you are, and would go to the festival? You have no clothes and shoes, and yet would dance!" As, however, Cinderella went on asking, the step-mother said at last: "I have emptied a dish of lentils into the ashes for you, if you have picked them out again in two hours, you shall go with us." The maiden went through the backdoor into the garden, and called: "You tame pigeons, you turtle-doves, and all you birds beneath the sky, come and help me to pick

> The good into the pot,
> The bad into the crop."

5   Then two white pigeons came in by the kitchen-window, and afterwards the turtle-doves, and at last all the birds beneath the sky, came whirring and crowding in, and alighted amongst the ashes. And the pigeons nodded with their heads and began pick, pick, pick, pick, and the rest began also pick, pick, pick, pick, and gathered all the good grains into the dish. Hardly had one hour passed before they had finished, and all flew out again. Then the girl took the dish to her step-mother, and was glad, and believed that now she would be allowed to go with them to the festival. But the step-mother said: "No, Cinderella, you have no clothes and you cannot dance; you would only be laughed at." And as Cinderella wept at this, the step-mother said: "If you can pick two dishes of lentils out of the ashes for me in one hour, you shall go with us." And she thought to herself: "That she most certainly cannot do again." When the step-mother had emptied the two dishes of lentils amongst the ashes, the maiden went through the back-door into the garden and cried: "You tame pigeons, you turtle-doves, and all you birds beneath the sky, come and help me to pick

> The good into the pot,
> The bad into the crop."

Then two white pigeons came in by the kitchen-window, and afterwards the turtle-doves, and at length all the birds beneath the sky, came whirring and crowding in, and alighted amongst the ashes. And the doves nodded with their heads and began pick, pick, pick, pick, and the others began also pick, pick, pick, pick, and gathered all the good seeds into the dishes, and before half an hour was over they had already finished, and all flew out again. Then the maiden carried the dishes to the step-mother and was delighted, and believed that she might now go with them to the festival. But the step-mother said: "All this will not help; you cannot go with us, for you have no clothes and cannot dance; we should be ashamed of you!" On this she turned her back on Cinderella, and hurried away with her two proud daughters.

As no one was now at home, Cinderella went to her mother's grave beneath the hazel tree, and cried:

> "Shiver and quiver, little tree,
> Silver and gold throw down over me."

Then the bird threw a gold and silver dress down to her, and slippers embroidered with silk and silver. She put on the dress with all speed, and went to the festival. Her step-sisters and the step-mother however did not know her, and thought she must be a foreign princess, for she looked so beautiful in the golden dress. They never once thought of Cinderella, and believed that she was sitting at home in the dirt, picking lentils out of the ashes. The prince approached her, took her by the hand and danced with her. He would dance with no other maiden, and never let loose of her hand, and if any one else came to invite her, he said: "This is my partner."

She danced till it was evening, and then she wanted to go home. But the King's son said: "I will go with you and bear you company," for he wished to see to whom the beautiful maiden belonged. She escaped from him, however, and sprang into the pigeon-house. The King's son waited until her father came, and then he told him that the unknown maiden had leapt into the pigeon-house. The old man thought: "Can it be Cinderella?" and they had to bring him an axe and a pickaxe that he might hew the pigeon-house to pieces, but no one was inside it. And when they got home Cinderella lay in her dirty clothes among the ashes, and a dim little oil-lamp was burning on the mantle-piece, for Cinderella had jumped quickly down from the back of the pigeon-house and had run to the little hazel-tree, and there she had taken off her beautiful clothes and laid them on the grave, and the bird had taken them away again, and then she had seated herself in the kitchen amongst the ashes in her grey gown.

10   Next day when the festival began afresh, and her parents and the step-sisters had gone once more, Cinderella went to the hazel-tree and said:

> "Shiver and quiver, little tree,
> Silver and gold throw down over me."

Then the bird threw down a much more beautiful dress than on the preceding day. And when Cinderella appeared at the festival in this dress, every one was astonished at her beauty. The King's son had waited until she came, and instantly took her by the hand and danced with no one but her. When others came and invited her he said: "This is my partner." When evening came she wished to leave, and the King's son followed her and wanted to see into which house she went. But she sprang away from him, and into the garden behind the house. Therein stood a beautiful tall tree on which hung the most magnificent pears. She clambered so nimbly between the branches like a squirrel that the King's son did not know where she was gone. He waited until her father came, and said to him: "The unknown maiden has escaped from me, and I believe she has climbed up the pear-tree." The father thought: "Can it be Cinderella?" and had an axe brought and cut the tree down, but no one was on it. And when they got into the kitchen, Cinderella lay there among the ashes, as usual, for she had jumped down on the other side of the tree, had taken the beautiful dress to the bird on the little hazel-tree, and put on her grey gown.

On the third day, when the parents and sisters had gone away, Cinderella went once more to her mother's grave and said to the little tree:

> "Shiver and quiver, little tree,
> Silver and gold throw down over me."

And now the bird threw down to her a dress which was more splendid and magnificent than any she had yet had, and the slippers were golden. And when she went to the festival in the dress, no one knew how to speak for astonishment. The King's son danced with her only, and if any one invited her to dance, he said: "This is my partner."

When evening came, Cinderella wished to leave, and the King's son was anxious to go with her, but she escaped from him so quickly that he could not follow her. The King's son, however, had employed a ruse, and had caused the whole staircase to be smeared with pitch, and there, when she ran down, had the maiden's left slipper remained stuck. The King's son picked it up, and it was small and dainty, and all golden. Next morning, he went with it to the father, and said to him: "No one shall be my wife but she whose foot this golden slipper fits." Then were the two sisters glad, for they had pretty feet. The eldest went with the shoe into her room and wanted to try it on, and her mother stood by. But she could not get her big toe into it, and the shoe was too small for her. Then her mother gave her a knife and said: "Cut the toe off; when you are Queen you will no more need to go on foot." The maiden cut the toe off, forced the foot into the shoe, swallowed the pain, and went out to the King's son. Then he took her on his horse as his bride and rode away with her. They were obliged, however, to pass the grave, and there, on the hazel-tree, the two little pigeons sat on it and cried:

> "Turn and peep, turn and peep,
> There's blood within the shoe,
> The shoe it is too small for her,
> The true bride waits for you."

15   Then he looked at her foot and saw how the blood was trickling from it. He turned his horse round and took the false bride home again, and said she was not the true one, and that the other sister was to put the shoe on. Then this one went into her chamber and got her toes safely into the shoe, but her heel was too large. So her mother gave her a knife and said: "Cut a bit off your heel; when you are Queen you will have no more need to go on foot." The maiden cut a bit off her heel, forced her foot into the shoe, swallowed the pain, and went out to the King's son. He took her on his horse as his bride, and rode away with her, but when they passed by the hazel-tree, the two little pigeons sat on it and cried:

> "Turn and peep, turn and peep,
> There's blood within the shoe,
> The shoe it is too small for her,
> The true bride waits for you."

He looked down at her foot and saw how the blood was running out of her shoe, and how it had stained her white stocking quite red. Then he turned his horse and took the false bride home again. "This also is not the right one," said he, "have you no other daughter?" "No," said the man, "there is still a little stunted kitchen-wench which my late wife left behind her, but she cannot possibly be the bride." The King's son said he was to send her up to him; but the mother answered: "Oh no, she is much too dirty, she cannot show herself!" But he absolutely insisted on it, and Cinderella had to be called. She first washed her hands and face clean, and then went and bowed down before the King's son, who gave her the golden shoe. Then she seated herself on a stool, drew her foot out of the heavy wooden shoe, and put it into the slipper, which fitted like a glove. And when she rose up and the King's son looked at her face he recognized the beautiful maiden who had danced with him and cried: "That is the true bride!" The step-mother and the two sisters were horrified and became pale with rage; he, however, took Cinderella on his horse and rode away with her. As they passed by the hazel tree, the two white doves cried:

> "Turn and peep, turn and peep,
> No blood is in the shoe,
> The shoe is not too small for her,
> The true bride rides with you,"

and when they had cried that, the two came flying down and placed themselves on Cinderella's shoulders, one on the right, the other on the left, and remained sitting there.

When the wedding with the King's son was to be celebrated, the two false sisters came and wanted to get into favor with Cinderella and share her good fortune. When the betrothed couple went to church, the elder was at the right side and the younger at the left, and the pigeons pecked out one eye from each of them. Afterwards as they came back, the elder was at the left, and the younger at the right, and then the pigeons pecked out the other eye from each. And thus, for their wickedness and falsehood, they were punished with blindness all their days.

🔲 **ANNE SEXTON** [1928–1974]

(See biography on p. 474.)

CINERELLA

CINDERELLA   [1970]

You always read about it:
the plumber with twelve children
who wins the Irish Sweepstakes.
From toilets to riches.
That story.   5

Or the nursemaid,
some luscious sweet from Denmark
who captures the oldest son's heart.
From diapers to Dior.
That story.   10

Or a milkman who serves the wealthy,
eggs, cream, butter, yogurt, milk,
the white truck like an ambulance
who goes into real estate
and makes a pile.   15
From homogenized to martinis at lunch.

Or the charwoman
who is on the bus when it cracks up
and collects enough from the insurance.
From mops to Bonwit Teller.   20
That story.

Once
the wife of a rich man was on her deathbed
and she said to her daughter Cinderella:
Be devout. Be good. Then I will smile   25
down from heaven in the seam of a cloud.
The man took another wife who had
two daughters, pretty enough
but with hearts like blackjacks.
Cinderella was their maid.   30
She slept on the sooty hearth each night
and walked around looking like Al Jolson.
Her father brought presents home from town,
jewels and gowns for the other women
but the twig of a tree for Cinderella.   35
She planted that twig on her mother's grave
and it grew to a tree where a white dove sat.
Whenever she wished for anything the dove
would drop it like an egg upon the ground.
The bird is important, my dears, so heed him.   40

Next came the ball, as you all know.
It was a marriage market.
The prince was looking for a wife.
All but Cinderella were preparing
and gussying up for the big event.   45
Cinderella begged to go too.
Her stepmother threw a dish of lentils
into the cinders and said: Pick them
up in an hour and you shall go.
The white dove brought all his friends;   50
all the warm wings of the fatherland came,
and picked up the lentils in a jiffy.
No, Cinderella, said the stepmother,
you have no clothes and cannot dance.
That's the way with stepmothers.   55

Cinderella went to the tree at the grave
and cried forth like a gospel singer:
Mama! Mama! My turtledove,
send me to the prince's ball!
The bird dropped down a golden dress   60
and delicate little gold slippers.
Rather a large package for a simple bird.
So she went. Which is no surprise.
Her stepmother and sisters didn't
recognize her without her cinder face   65
and the prince took her hand on the spot
and danced with no other the whole day.

As nightfall came she thought she'd better
get home. The prince walked her home
and she disappeared into the pigeon house   70
and although the prince took an axe and broke
it open she was gone. Back to her cinders.
These events repeated themselves for three days.
However on the third day the prince
covered the palace steps with cobbler's wax   75
and Cinderella's gold shoe stuck upon it.
Now he would find whom the shoe fit
and find his strange dancing girl for keeps.
He went to their house and the two sisters
were delighted because they had lovely feet.   80
The eldest went into a room to try the slipper on
but her big toe got in the way so she simply
sliced it off and put on the slipper;
The prince rode away with her until the white dove
told him to look at the blood pouring forth.   85
That is the way with amputations.
They don't just heal up like a wish.
The other sister cut off her heel
but the blood told as blood will.
The prince was getting tired.   90

He began to feel like a shoe salesman.
But he gave it one last try.
This time Cinderella fit into the shoe
like a love letter into its envelope.

At the wedding ceremony   95
the two sisters came to curry favor
and the white dove pecked their eyes out.
Two hollow spots were left
like soup spoons.

Cinderella and the prince   100
lived, they say, happily ever after,
like two dolls in a museum case
never bothered by diapers or dust,
never arguing over the timing of an egg,
never telling the same story twice,   105
never getting a middle-aged spread,
their darling smiles pasted on for eternity
Regular Bobbsey Twins.
That story.

BRUNO BETTELHEIM [1903–1996]

Austrian-born psychologist, educator, and author Bruno
Bettelheim came to the United States in 1939, after surviving
a series of German concentration camps. He wrote about his
experience in the widely read and enormously influential
Individual and Mass Behavior in Extreme Situations *(1943).*
Once in America, Bettelheim established himself as an expert
on the psychology of children, publishing works such as Love
Is Not Enough *(1950),* The Children of the Dream *(1969),*
A Home for the Heart *(1974), and* Surviving and Other Essays *(1979). "Cinderella"*
is taken from The Uses of Enchantment *(1976), in which Bettelheim discusses the*
psychosocial importance of fairy tales.

CINDERELLA   [1976]

By all accounts, "Cinderella" is the best-known fairy tale, and probably also the
best-liked. It is quite an old story; when first written down in China during the
ninth century A.D., it already had a history. The unrivaled tiny foot size as a mark
of extraordinary virtue, distinction, and beauty, and the slipper made of precious
material are facets which point to an Eastern, if not necessarily Chinese, origin. The
modern hearer does not connect sexual attractiveness and beauty in general with
extreme smallness of the foot, as the ancient Chinese did, in accordance with their
practice of binding women's feet.

"Cinderella," as we know it, is experienced as a story about the agonies and
hopes which form the essential content of sibling rivalry; and about the degraded
heroine winning out over her siblings who abused her. Long before Perrault gave
"Cinderella" the form in which it is now widely known, "having to live among the
ashes" was a symbol of being debased in comparison to one's siblings, irrespective
of sex. In Germany, for example, there were stories in which such an ash-boy later
becomes king, which parallels Cinderella's fate. "Aschenputtel" is the title of the
Brothers Grimm's version of the tale. The term originally designated a lowly, dirty
kitchenmaid who must tend to the fireplace ashes.

There are many examples in the German language of how being forced to dwell
among the ashes was a symbol not just of degradation, but also of sibling rivalry, and

of the sibling who finally surpasses the brother or brothers who have debased him. Martin Luther[1] in his *Table Talks* speaks about Cain as the God-forsaken evildoer who is powerful, while pious Abel is forced to be his ash-brother (*Aschebrüdel*), a mere nothing, subject to Cain; in one of Luther's sermons he says that Esau was forced into the role of Jacob's ash-brother. Cain and Abel, Jacob and Esau are Biblical examples of one brother being suppressed or destroyed by the other.

The fairy tale replaces sibling relations with relations between step-siblings—perhaps a device to explain and make acceptable an animosity which one wishes would not exist among true siblings. Although sibling rivalry is universal and "natural" in the sense that it is the negative consequence of being a sibling, this same relation also generates equally as much positive feeling between siblings, highlighted in fairy tales such as "Brother and Sister."

5   No other fairy tale renders so well as the "Cinderella" stories the inner experiences of the young child in the throes of sibling rivalry, when he feels hopelessly outclassed by his brothers and sisters. Cinderella is pushed down and degraded by her stepsisters; her interests are sacrificed to theirs by her (step)mother; she is expected to do the dirtiest work and although she performs it well, she receives no credit for it; only more is demanded of her. This is how the child feels when devastated by the miseries of sibling rivalry. Exaggerated though Cinderella's tribulations and degradations may seem to the adult, the child carried away by sibling rivalry feels, "That's me; that's how they mistreat me, or would want to; that's how little they think of me." And there are moments—often long time periods—when for inner reasons a child feels this way even when his position among his siblings may seem to give him no cause for it.

When a story corresponds to how the child feels deep down—as no realistic narrative is likely to do—it attains an emotional quality of "truth" for the child. The events of "Cinderella" offer him vivid images that give body to his overwhelming but nevertheless often vague and nondescript emotions; so these episodes seem more convincing to him than his life experiences.

The term "sibling rivalry" refers to a most complex constellation of feelings and their causes. With extremely rare exceptions, the emotions aroused in the person subject to sibling rivalry are far out of proportion to what his real situation with his sisters and brothers would justify, seen objectively. While all children at times suffer greatly from sibling rivalry, parents seldom sacrifice one of the children to the others, nor do they condone the other children's persecuting one of them. Difficult as objective judgments are for the young child—nearly impossible when his emotions are aroused—even he in his more rational moments "knows" that he is not treated as badly as Cinderella. But the child often feels mistreated, despite all his "knowledge" to the contrary. That is why he believes in the inherent truth of "Cinderella," and then he also comes to believe in her eventual deliverance and victory. From her triumph he gains the exaggerated hopes for his future which he needs to counteract the extreme misery he experiences when ravaged by sibling rivalry.

[1]**Martin Luther** (1483–1546) German leader of the Protestant Reformation and Lutheranism

Despite the name "sibling rivalry," this miserable passion has only incidentally to do with a child's actual brothers and sisters. The real source of it is the child's feelings about his parents. When a child's older brother or sister is more competent than he, this arouses only temporary feelings of jealousy. Another child being given special attention becomes an insult only if the child fears that, in contrast, he is thought little of by his parents, or feels rejected by them. It is because of such an anxiety that one or all of a child's sisters or brothers may become a thorn in his flesh. Fearing that in comparison to them he cannot win his parents' love and esteem is what inflames sibling rivalry. This is indicated in stories by the fact that it matters little whether the siblings actually possess greater competence. The Biblical story of Joseph tells that it is jealousy of parental affection lavished on him which accounts for the destructive behavior of his brothers. Unlike Cinderella's, Joseph's parent does not participate in degrading him, and, on the contrary, prefers him to his other children. But Joseph, like Cinderella, is turned into a slave, and, like her, he miraculously escapes and ends by surpassing his siblings.

Telling a child who is devastated by sibling rivalry that he will grow up to do as well as his brothers and sisters offers little relief from his present feelings of dejection. Much as he would like to trust our assurances, most of the time he cannot. A child can see things only with subjective eyes, and comparing himself on this basis to his siblings, he has no confidence that he, on his own, will someday be able to fare as well as they. If he could believe more in himself, he would not feel destroyed by his siblings no matter what they might do to him, since then he could trust that time would bring about a desired reversal of fortune. But since the child cannot, on his own, look forward with confidence to some future day when things will turn out all right for him, he can gain relief only through fantasies of glory—a domination over his siblings—which he hopes will become reality through some fortunate event.

10   Whatever our position within the family, at certain times in our lives we are beset by sibling rivalry in some form or other. Even an only child feels that other children have some great advantages over him, and this makes him intensely jealous. Further, he may suffer from the anxious thought that if he did have a sibling, his parents would prefer this other child to him. "Cinderella" is a fairy tale which makes nearly as strong an appeal to boys as to girls, since children of both sexes suffer equally from sibling rivalry, and have the same desire to be rescued from their lowly position and surpass those who seem superior to them.

On the surface, "Cinderella" is as deceptively simple as the story of Little Red Riding Hood, with which it shares greatest popularity. "Cinderella" tells about the agonies of sibling rivalry, of wishes coming true, of the humble being elevated, of true merit being recognized even when hidden under rags, of virtue rewarded and evil punished—a straightforward story. But under this overt content is concealed a welter of complex and largely unconscious material, which details of the story allude to just enough to set our unconscious associations going. This makes a contrast between surface simplicity and underlying complexity which arouses deep interest in the story and explains its appeal to the millions over centuries. To begin gaining an understanding of these hidden meanings, we have to penetrate behind the obvious sources of sibling rivalry discussed so far.

As mentioned before, if the child could only believe that it is the infirmities of his age which account for his lowly position, he would not have to suffer so wretchedly from sibling rivalry, because he could trust the future to right matters. When he thinks that his degradation is deserved, he feels his plight is utterly hopeless. Djuna Barnes's perceptive statement about fairy tales—that the child knows something about them which he cannot tell (such as that he likes the idea of Little Red Riding Hood and the wolf being in bed together)—could be extended by dividing fairy tales into two groups: one group where the child responds only unconsciously to the inherent truth of the story and thus cannot tell about it; and another large number of tales where the child preconsciously or even consciously knows what the "truth" of the story consists of and thus could tell about it, but does not want to let on that he knows. Some aspects of "Cinderella" fall into the latter category. Many children believe that Cinderella probably deserves her fate at the beginning of the story, as they feel they would, too; but they don't want anyone to know it. Despite this, she is worthy at the end to be exalted, as the child hopes he will be too, irrespective of his earlier shortcomings.

Every child believes at some period of his life—and this is not only at rare moments—that because of his secret wishes, if not also his clandestine actions, he deserves to be degraded, banned from the presence of others, relegated to a netherworld of smut. He fears this may be so, irrespective of how fortunate his situation may be in reality. He hates and fears those others—such as his siblings—whom he believes to be entirely free of similar evilness, and he fears that they or his parents will discover what he is really like, and then demean him as Cinderella was by her family. Because he wants others—most of all, his parents—to believe in his innocence, he is delighted that "everybody" believes in Cinderella's. This is one of the great attractions of this fairy tale. Since people give credence to Cinderella's goodness, they will also believe in his, so the child hopes. And "Cinderella" nourishes this hope, which is one reason it is such a delightful story.

Another aspect which holds large appeal for the child is the vileness of the stepmother and stepsisters. Whatever the shortcomings of a child may be in his own eyes, these pale into insignificance when compared to the stepsisters' and stepmother's falsehood and nastiness. Further, what these stepsisters do to Cinderella justifies whatever nasty thoughts one may have about one's siblings: they are so vile that anything one may wish would happen to them is more than justified. Compared to their behavior, Cinderella is indeed innocent. So the child, on hearing her story, feels he need not feel guilty about his angry thoughts.

15   On a very different level—and reality considerations coexist easily with fantastic exaggerations in the child's mind—as badly as one's parents or siblings seem to treat one, and much as one thinks one suffers because of it, all this is nothing compared to Cinderella's fate. Her story reminds the child at the same time how lucky he is, and how much worse things could be. (Any anxiety about the latter possibility is relieved, as always in fairy tales, by the happy ending.)

The behavior of a five-and-a-half-year-old girl, as reported by her father, may illustrate how easily a child may feel that she is a "Cinderella." This little girl had a younger sister of whom she was very jealous. The girl was very fond of "Cinderella," since the story offered her material with which to act out her feelings, and because without the story's imagery she would have been hard pressed to comprehend and express them. This little girl had used to dress very neatly and liked pretty clothes, but she became unkempt and dirty. One day when she was asked to fetch some salt, she said as she was doing so, "Why do you treat me like Cinderella?"

Almost speechless, her mother asked her, "Why do you think I treat you like Cinderella?"

"Because you make me do all the hardest work in the house!" was the little girl's answer. Having thus drawn her parents into her fantasies, she acted them out more openly, pretending to sweep up all the dirt, etc. She went even further, playing that she prepared her little sister for the ball. But she went the "Cinderella" story one better, based on her unconscious understanding of the contradictory emotions fused into the "Cinderella" role, because at another moment she told her mother and sister, "You shouldn't be jealous of me just because I am the most beautiful in the family."

This shows that behind the surface humility of Cinderella lies the conviction of her superiority to mother and sisters, as if she would think: "You can make me do all the dirty work, and I pretend that I am dirty, but within me I know that you treat me this way because you are jealous of me because I am so much better than you." This conviction is supported by the story's ending, which assures every "Cinderella" that eventually she will be discovered by her prince.

20   Why does the child believe deep within himself that Cinderella deserves her dejected state? This question takes us back to the child's state of mind at the end of the oedipal period. Before he is caught in oedipal entanglements, the child is convinced that he is lovable, and loved, if all is well within his family relationships. Psychoanalysis describes this stage of complete satisfaction with oneself as "primary narcissism." During this period the child feels certain that he is the center of the universe, so there is no reason to be jealous of anybody.

The oedipal disappointments which come at the end of this developmental stage cast deep shadows of doubt on the child's sense of his worthiness. He feels that if he were really as deserving of love as he had thought, then his parents would never be critical of him or disappoint him. The only explanation for parental criticism the child can think of is that there must be some serious flaw in him which accounts for what he experiences as rejection. If his desires remain unsatisfied and his parents disappoint him, there must be something wrong with him or his desires, or both. He cannot yet accept that reasons other than those residing within him could have an impact on his fate. In his oedipal jealousy, wanting to get rid of the parent of the same sex had seemed the most natural thing in the world, but now the child realizes that he cannot have his own way, and that maybe this is so because the desire was wrong. He is no longer so sure that he is preferred to his siblings, and he begins to suspect that this may be due to the fact that *they* are free of any bad thoughts or wrongdoing such as his.

All this happens as the child is gradually subjected to ever more critical attitudes as he is being socialized. He is asked to behave in ways which run counter to his natural desires, and he resents this. Still he must obey, which makes him very angry. This anger is directed against those who make demands, most likely his parents; and this is another reason to wish to get rid of them, and still another reason to feel guilty about such wishes. This is why the child also feels that he deserves to be chastised for his feelings, a punishment he believes he can escape only if nobody learns what he is thinking when he is angry. The feeling of being unworthy to be loved by his parents at a time when his desire for their love is very strong leads to the fear of rejection, even when in reality there is none. This rejection fear compounds the anxiety that others are preferred and also may be preferable—the root of sibling rivalry.

MAKING CONNECTIONS

1. Did you find anything different about the Grimm brothers' fairy tale of Cinderella than the one you are used to reading or viewing?
2. How are you affected by the harsh punishment that Cinderella's stepsisters receive? Do you think they deserve it?
3. Do these gruesome details change the impact of the story? Why do you think they have been removed in the modern version of this fairy tale?
4. Compare Anne Sexton's poem of "Cinderella" with the Grimm brothers' version.
5. Who is the speaker in the poem's version? How does the speaker's "voice" differ from that of the narrator in the Grimm version? What words or phrases exemplify that difference? How are you affected by the repetition of the phrase "That story"?
6. The last stanza of Sexton's poem is a variation on the usual ending of a fairy tale. What is its tone? To what extent does it emphasize the tone of the entire poem?
7. Bettelheim argues that children without siblings—as well as older siblings—respond to the Cinderella story in the same way that younger siblings do. Explain his argument. Do you find it convincing? Or do you think that if "Cinderella" is about sibling rivalry, then younger siblings, older siblings, and "only" children would respond to the story in different ways?
8. Do you think that boys respond to Cinderella's plight in the same way that girls do? Why or why not?
9. Do you think Bettelheim's interpretation of the Cinderella tale pertains to the Sexton poem as well? Why or why not? Does Sexton seem to think that the tale is about sibling rivalry?

MAKING AN ARGUMENT

1. Write an argument that agrees or disagrees with Bettelheim's essay that "Cinderella" is a tale "about the agonies and hopes which form the essential content of sibling rivalry." If you disagree, then what do you think the tale is about and why? Cite the text of both "Cinderella" and Bettelheim's essay for support.

✦ DRAMA ✦

ANTON CHEKHOV [1860–1904]

One of the first practitioners of the modern short story and the modern play, Anton Pavlovich Chekhov was born in the town of Taganrog, near the Black Sea in Russia. His grandfather was a serf who bought his family's freedom. Chekhov attended the University of Moscow on a scholarship, eventually earning a degree in medicine. In an effort to support himself and his impoverished family during this period, Chekhov began writing short pieces, first sketches and jokes, and later short stories for newspapers and journals. By 1886, Chekhov had gained enough recognition to make writing his chief interest and occupation. His long association with the famed Moscow Arts Theater began with its acclaimed production of The Seagull *in 1898 (which had had a disastrous premiere two years earlier in St. Petersburg), and continued with productions of his greatest plays,* The Three Sisters, Uncle Vanya, *and* The Cherry Orchard. *In his later years, which were plagued by ill health, Chekhov married Olga Knipper, a star of the theater company. He died in 1904 of tuberculosis. Unlike much of his work, which is set against a mood of pervading sadness,* The Proposal *is a comedy. Like his other work, however, it is an insightful look at human nature.*

THE PROPOSAL   [1889]

Translated by Paul Schmidt

CHARACTERS
STEPÁN STEPÁNICH CHUBUKÓV, *a landowner*
NATÁLIA STEPÁNOVNA [NATÁSHA], *his daughter*
IVÁN VASSÍLIEVICH LÓMOV, *their neighbor*

The action takes place in CHUBUKÓV's *farmhouse.*
A room in CHUBUKÓV's *farmhouse. Enter* LÓMOV, *wearing a tailcoat and white gloves.* CHUBUKÓV *goes to meet him.*

CHUBUKÓV: By God, if it isn't my old friend Iván Vassílievich! Glad to see you, boy, glad to see you. [*Shakes his hand*] This is certainly a surprise, and that's a fact. How are you doing?
LÓMOV: Oh, thanks a lot. And how are you? Doing, I mean?
CHUBUKÓV: We get by, my boy, we get by. Glad to know you think of us occasionally and all the rest of it. Have a seat, boy, be my guest, glad you're here, and that's a fact. Don't want to forget your old friends and neighbors, you know. But why so formal, boy? What's the occasion? You're all dressed up and everything—you on your way to a party, or what?

LÓMOV: No, I only came to see you, Stepán Stepánich.

5   CHUBUKÓV: But why the fancy clothes, boy? You look like you're still celebrating New Year's Eve!

LÓMOV: Well, I'll tell you. [*Takes his arm*] You see, Stepán Stepánich, I hope I'm not disturbing you, but I came to ask you a little favor. This isn't the first time I've, uh, had occasion, as they say, to ask you for help, and I want you to know that I really admire you when I do it.... Er, what I mean is... Look, you have to excuse me, Stepán Stepánich, this is making me very nervous. I'll just take a little drink of water, if it's all right with you. [*Takes a drink of water*]

CHUBUKÓV [*Aside*]:   He wants me to lend him some money. I won't. [*To him*] So! What exactly are you here for, hm? A big strong boy like you.

LÓMOV: You see, I really have the greatest respect for you, Stepán Respéctovich—excuse me, I mean Stepán Excúsemevich. What I mean is—I'm really nervous, as you can plainly see.... Well, what it all comes down to is this: you're the only person who can give me what I want and I know I don't deserve it of course that goes without saying and I haven't any real right to it either—

CHUBUKÓV: Now, my boy, you don't have to beat about the bush with me. Speak right up. What do you want?

10   LÓMOV: All right, I will. I will. Well, what I came for is, I came to ask for the hand of your daughter Natásha.

CHUBUKÓV [*Overjoyed*]:   Oh, mama! Iván Vassílievich, say it again! I don't think I caught that last part!

LÓMOV: I came to ask—

CHUBUKÓV: Lover boy! Buddy boy! I can't tell you how happy I am and everything. And that's a fact. And all the rest of it. [*Gives him a bear hug*] I've always hoped this would happen. It's a longtime dream come true. [*Sheds a tear*] I have always loved you, boy, just like you were my own son, and you know it. God bless you both and all the rest of it. This is a dream come true. But why am I standing here like a big dummy? Happiness has got my tongue, that's what's happened, happiness has got my tongue. Oh, from the bottom of my heart... You wait right here, I'll go get Natásha and whatever.

LÓMOV [*Intense concern*]:   What do you think, Stepán Stepánich? Do you think she'll say yes?

15   CHUBUKÓV: Big, good-looking fellow like you—how could she help herself? Of course she'll say yes, and that's a fact. She's like a cat in heat. And all the rest of it. Don't go away, I'll be right back. [*Exit.*]

LÓMOV: It must be cold in here. I'm starting to shiver, just like I was going to take an exam. The main thing is, you have to make up your mind. You just keep thinking about it, you argue back and forth and talk a lot and wait for the ideal woman or for true love, you'll never get married. Brr... it's cold in here. Natásha is a very good housekeeper, she's kind of good-looking, she's been to school... What more do I need? I'm starting to get that hum in my ears again; it must be my nerves. [*Drinks some water*] And I can't just *not* get married. First of all, I'm already thirty-five, and that's about what they call the turning point. Second of all, I have to start leading a regular, normal life. There's something wrong with my heart—I've got a *murmur;* I'm always nervous as a tick, and the least little thing can drive me crazy. Like right now, for instance. My lips are starting to shudder, and this little whatsit keeps twitching in my right eyelid. But the worst thing about me is sleep. I mean, I don. I go to bed, and as soon as I start falling asleep, all of a sudden something in my left side goes *drrrk!* and it pounds right up into my shoulder and my head.... I jump out of bed like crazy and walk around for a while and then I lie down again and as soon as I start falling asleep all of a sudden something in my left side goes *drrrk!* And that happens twenty times a night—

[*Enter* NATÁSHA.]

NATÁSHA: Oh, it's you. It's just you, and Papa said go take a look in the other room, somebody wants to sell you something. Oh, well. How are you anyway?

LÓMOV: How do you do, Natásha?

NATÁSHA: You'll have to excuse me, I'm still in my apron. We were shelling peas. How come you haven't been by to see us for so long? Sit down.... [*They both sit.*] You feel like something to eat?

20   LÓMOV: No, thanks. I ate already.

NATÁSHA: You smoke? Go ahead if you want to; here's some matches. Beautiful day today, isn't it? And yesterday it was raining so hard the men in the hay-fields couldn't do a thing. How many stacks you people got cut so far? You know what happened to me? I got so carried away I had them cut the whole meadow, and now I'm sorry I did—the hay's going to rot. Oh, my! Look at you! What've you got on those fancy clothes for? Well, if you aren't some-thing! You going to a party, or what? You know, you're looking kind of cute these days.... Anyway, what are you all dressed up for?

LÓMOV [*A bit nervous*]:   Well, you see, Natásha...well, the fact is I decided to come ask you to...to listen to what I have to say. Of course, you'll probably be sort of surprised and maybe get mad, but I...[*Aside*] It's awful cold in here.

NATÁSHA: So...so what did you come for, huh? [*Pause*] Huh?

LÓMOV: I'll try to make this brief. Now, Natásha, you know, we've known each other for a long time, ever since we were children, and I've had the pleasure of knowing your entire family. My poor dead aunt and her husband—as you know, I inherited my land from them—they always had the greatest respect for your father and your poor dead mother. The Lómovs and the Chubukóvs have always been on very friendly terms, almost like we were related. And besides—well, you already know this—and besides, your land and mine are right next door to each other. Take my Meadowland, for instance. It lies right alongside of your birch grove.

25   NATÁSHA: Excuse me. I don't mean to interrupt you, but I think you said "my Meadowland." Are you saying that Meadowland belongs to you?

LÓMOV: Well, yes; as a matter of fact, I am.

NATÁSHA: Well, I never! Meadowland belongs to us, not you!

LÓMOV: No, Natásha. Meadowland is mine.

NATÁSHA: Well, that's news to me. Since when is it yours?

30 LÓMOV: What do you mean, since when? I'm talking about the little pasture they
call Meadowland, the one that makes a wedge between your birch grove and
Burnt Swamp.

NATÁSHA: Yes, I know the one you mean. But it's ours.

LÓMOV: Natásha, I think you're making a mistake. That field belongs to me.

NATÁSHA: Iván Vassílich, do you realize what you're saying? And just how long has
it belonged to you?

LÓMOV: What do you mean, how long? As far as I know, it's always been mine.

35 NATÁSHA: Now wait just a minute. Excuse me, but—

LÓMOV: It's all very clearly marked on the deeds, Natásha. Now, it's true there
was some argument about it back a ways, but nowadays everybody knows it
belongs to me. So there's no use arguing about it. You see, what happened
was, my aunt's grandmother let your grandfather's tenants have that field free
of charge for an indefinite time in exchange for their making bricks for her.
So your grandfather's people used that land for free for about forty years and
they started to think it was theirs, but then, when it turned out what the real
situation was—

NATÁSHA: My grandfather and my great-grandfather both always said that the land
went as far as Burnt Swamp, which means Meadowland belongs to us. So
what's the point of arguing about it? I think you're just being rude.

LÓMOV: I can show you the papers, Natálya Stepánovna!

NATÁSHA: Oh, you're just teasing! You're trying to pull my leg! This is all a big
joke, isn't it? We've owned that land for going on three hundred years, and all
of a sudden you say it doesn't belong to us. Excuse me, Iván Vassílich, excuse
me, but I can't believe you said that. And believe me, I don't care one bit
about that old meadow: it's only twenty acres, it's not worth three hundred
rubles, even, but that's not the point. It's the injustice of it that hurts. And I
don't care what anybody says—injustice is something I just can't put up with.

40 LÓMOV: But you didn't listen to what I was saying! Please! Your grandfather's tenants, as I was trying very politely to point out to you, made bricks for my
aunt's grandmother. Now, my aunt's grandmother just wanted to make things
easier and—

NATÁSHA: Grandmother, grandfather, father—what difference does it all make?
The field belongs to us, and that's that.

LÓMOV: That field belongs to me!

NATÁSHA: That field belongs to us! You can go on about your grandmother until
you're blue in the face, you can wear fifteen fancy coats—it still belongs to
us! It's ours, ours, ours! I don't want anything that belongs to you, but I do
want to keep what's my own, thank you very much!

LÓMOV: Natálya Stepánovna, I don't care about that field either; I don't need that
field; I'm talking about the principle of the thing. If you want the field, you
can have it. I'll give it to you.

45 NATÁSHA: If there's any giving to be done, I'll do it! That field belongs to me! Iván
Vassílich, I have never gone through anything this crazy in all my life! Up till
now I've always thought of you as a good neighbor, a real friend—last year

we even lent you our threshing machine, which meant that we were threshing *our* wheat in November—and now all of a sudden you start treating us like Gypsies. *You'll* give *me* my own field? Excuse me, but that is a pretty unneighborly thing to do. In fact, in my opinion, it's downright insulting!

LÓMOV: So in your opinion I'm some kind of claim jumper, you mean? Look, lady, I have never tried to take anybody else's land, and I'm not going to let anybody try to tell me I did, not even you. [*Runs to the table and takes a drink of water*] Meadowland is mine!

NATÁSHA: You lie! It's ours!

LÓMOV: It's mine!

NATÁSHA: You lie! I'll show you! I'll send my mowers out there today!

50 LÓMOV: You'll what!

NATÁSHA: I said I'll have my mowers out there today, and they'll hay that field flat!

LÓMOV: You do, and I'll break their necks!

NATÁSHA: You wouldn't dare!

LÓMOV [*Clutches his chest*]:   Meadowland is mine! You understand? Mine!

55 NATÁSHA: Please don't shout. You can scream and carry on all you want in your own house, but as long as you're in mine, try to behave like a gentleman.

LÓMOV: I tell you, if I didn't have these murmurs, these awful pains, these veins throbbing in my temples, I wouldn't be talking like this. [*Shouts*] Meadowland is mine!

NATÁSHA: Ours!

LÓMOV: Mine!

NATÁSHA: Ours!

60 LÓMOV: Mine!

[*Enter* CHUBUKÓV.]

CHUBUKÓV: What's going on? What are you both yelling for?

NATÁSHA: Papa, will you please explain to this gentleman just who owns Meadowland, him or us?

CHUBUKÓV: Lover boy, Meadowland belongs to us.

LÓMOV: I beg your pardon, Stepán Stepánich, how can it belong to you? Think what you're saying! My aunt's grandmother let your grandfather's people have that land to use free of charge, temporarily, and they used that land for forty years and started thinking it was theirs, but it turned out what the problem was—

65 CHUBUKÓV: Allow me, sweetheart. You're forgetting that the reason those people didn't pay your granny and all the rest of it was because there was *already* a real problem about just who *did* own the meadow. And everything. But nowadays every dog in the village knows it belongs to us, and that's a fact. I don't think you've ever seen the survey map—

LÓMOV: Look, I can prove to you that Meadowland belongs to me!

CHUBUKÓV: No you can't, lover boy.

LÓMOV: I can too!

CHUBUKÓV: Oh, for crying out loud! What are you shouting for? You can't prove anything by shouting, and that's a fact. Look, I am not interested in taking any of your land, and neither am I interested in giving away any of my own. Why should I? And if it comes down to it, lover boy, if you want to make a case out of this, or anything like that, I'd just as soon give it to the peasants as give it to you. So there!

70   LÓMOV: You're not making any sense. What gives you the right to give away someone else's land?

CHUBUKÓV: I'll be the judge of whether I have the right or not! The fact is, boy, I am not used to being talked to in that tone of voice and all the rest of it. I am twice your age, boy, and I'll ask you to talk to me without getting so excited and whatever.

LÓMOV: No! You think I'm just stupid, and you're making fun of me! You stand there and tell me my own land belongs to you, and then you expect me to be calm about it and talk as if nothing had happened! That's not the way good neighbors behave, Stepán Stepánich! You are not a neighbor, you are a *usurper!*

CHUBUKÓV: I'm a *what?* What did you call me?

NATÁSHA: Papa, you send our mowers out to Meadowland right this very minute!

75   CHUBUKÓV: You, boy! What did you just call me?

NATÁSHA: Meadowland belongs to us, and I'll never give it up—never, never, never!

LÓMOV: We'll see about that! I'll take you to court, and then we'll see who it belongs to!

CHUBUKÓV: To court! Well, you just go right ahead, boy, you take us to court! I dare you! Oh, now I get it, you were just waiting for a chance to take us to court and all the rest of it! And whatever! It's inbred, isn't it? Your whole family was like that—they couldn't wait to start suing. They were always in court! And that's a fact!

LÓMOV: You leave my family out of this! The Lómovs were all decent, law-abiding citizens, every one of them, not like some people I could name, who were arrested for embezzlement—your uncle, for instance!

80   CHUBUKÓV: Every single one of the Lómovs was crazy! All of them!

NATÁSHA: All of them! Every single one!

CHUBUKÓV: Your uncle was a falling-down drunk, and that's a fact! And your aunt, the youngest one, she used to run around with an architect! An architect! And that's a fact!

LÓMOV: And your mother was a hunchback! [*Clutches his chest*] Oh, my God, I've got a pain in my side... my head's beginning to pound! Oh, my God, give me some water!

CHUBUKÓV: And your father was a gambler and a glutton!

85   NATÁSHA: And your aunt was a tattletale; she was the worst gossip in town!

LÓMOV: My left leg is paralyzed.... And you're a sneak! Oh, my heart! And everybody knows that during the elections, you people... I've got spots in front of my eyes.... Where's my hat?

NATÁSHA: You're low! And lousy! And cheap!

CHUBUKÓV: You are a lowdown two-faced snake in the grass, and that's a fact! An absolute fact!

LÓMOV: Here's my hat! My heart! How do I get out of here... where's the door? I think I'm dying... I can't move my leg. [*Heads for the door*]

90   CHUBUKÓV [*Following him*]:   And don't you ever set foot in this house again!

NATÁSHA: And you just take us to court! Go ahead, see what happens!

[*Exit* LÓMOV, *staggering.*]

CHUBUKÓV [*Walks up and down in agitation*]:   He can go to hell!

NATÁSHA: What a creep! See if I ever trust a neighbor again after this!

CHUBUKÓV: Crook!

95   NATÁSHA: Creep! He takes over somebody else's land and then has the nerve to threaten them!

CHUBUKÓV: And would you believe that wig-worm, that chicken-brain, had the nerve to come here and propose? Hah? He proposed!

NATÁSHA: He proposed what?

CHUBUKÓV: What? He came here to propose to you!

NATÁSHA: To propose? To me? Why didn't you tell me that before!

100   CHUBUKÓV: That's why he was all dressed up in that stupid coat! What a silly sausage!

NATÁSHA: Me? He came to propose to me? Oh, my God, my God! [*Collapses into a chair and wails*] Oh, make him come back! Make him come back! Oh, please, make him come back! [*She has hysterics*]

CHUBUKÓV: What's the matter? What's the matter with you? [*Smacks his head*] Oh, my God, what have I done! I ought to shoot myself! I ought to be hanged! I ought to be tortured to death!

NATÁSHA: I think I'm going to die! Make him come back!

CHUBUKÓV: All right! Just stop screaming! Please! [*Runs out*]

105   NATÁSHA [*Alone, wailing*]:   What have we done? Oh, make him come back! Make him come back!

CHUBUKÓV [*Reenters*]:   He's coming, he's coming back and everything, goddamn it! You talk to him yourself this time; I can't.... And that's a fact!

NATÁSHA [*Wailing*]:   Make him come back!

CHUBUKÓV: I just told you, he *is* coming back. Oh, God almighty, what an ungrateful assignment, being the father of a grown-up girl! I'll slit my throat, I swear I'll slit my throat! We yell at the man, we insult him, we chase him away...and it's all your fault. It's your fault!

NATÁSHA: No, it's your fault!

110   CHUBUKÓV: All right, I'm sorry, it's my fault. Or whatever. [LÓMOV *appears in the doorway.*] This time you do the talking yourself! [*Exit.*]

LÓMOV [*Entering, exhausted*]:   I'm having a heart murmur, it's awful, my leg is paralyzed...my left side is going *drrrk!*

NATÁSHA: You'll have to excuse us, Iván Vassílich—we got a little bit carried away.... Anyway, I just remembered, Meadowland belongs to you after all.

LÓMOV: There's something wrong with my heart—it's beating too loud.... Meadowland is mine? These little whatsits are twitching in both my eyelids....

NATÁSHA: It's your—Meadowland is all yours. Here, sit down. [*They both sit.*] We made a mistake.

115 LÓMOV: It was always just the principle of the thing. I don't care about the land,
but I do care about the principle of the thing.

NATÁSHA: I know, the principle of the thing.... Why don't we talk about something else?

LÓMOV: And besides, I really can prove it. My aunt's grandmother let your grandfather's tenants have that field—

NATÁSHA: That's enough! I think we should change the subject. [*Aside*] I don't
know where to start.... [*To* LÓMOV] How's the hunting? Are you going hunting anytime soon?

LÓMOV: Oh, yes, geese and grouse hunting, Natásha, geese and grouse. I was
thinking of going after the harvest is in. Oh, by the way, did I tell you? The
worst thing happened to me! You know my old hound Guesser? Well, he
went lame on me.

120 NATÁSHA: Oh, that's terrible! What happened?

LÓMOV: I don't know; he must have dislocated his hip, or maybe he got into a
fight with some other dogs and got bit. [*Sighs*] And he was the best hound
dog, not to mention how much he cost. I got him from Mirónov, and I paid
a hundred and twenty-five for him.

NATÁSHA [*Beat*]:   Iván Vassílich, you paid too much.

LÓMOV [*Beat*]:   I thought I got him pretty cheap. He's a real good dog.

NATÁSHA: Papa paid only eighty-five for his hound dog Messer, and Messer is a lot
better than your old Guesser!

125 LÓMOV: Messer is better than Guesser? What do you mean? [*Laughs*] Messer is better
than Guesser!

NATÁSHA: Of course he's better! I mean, he's not full grown yet, he's still a pup,
but when it comes to a bark and a bite, nobody has a better dog.

LÓMOV: Excuse me, Natásha, but I think you're forgetting something. He's got
an underslung jaw, and a dog with an underslung jaw can never be a good
retriever.

NATÁSHA: An underslung jaw? That's the first I ever heard of it!

LÓMOV: I'm telling you, his lower jaw is shorter than his upper.

130 NATÁSHA: What did you do, measure it?

LÓMOV: Of course I measured it! I grant you he's not so bad on point, but you tell
him to go fetch, and he can barely—

NATÁSHA: In the first place, our Messer is a purebred from a very good line—
he's the son of Pusher and Pisser, so that limp-foot mutt of yours couldn't
touch him for breeding. Besides which, your dog is old and ratty and full
of fleas—

LÓMOV: He may be old, but I wouldn't take five of your Messers for him. How can
you even say that? Guesser is a real hound, and that Messer is a joke, he's not
even worth worrying about. Every old fart in the country's got a dog just like
your Messer—there's a mess of them everywhere you look! You paid twenty
rubles, you paid too much!

NATÁSHA: Iván Vassílich, for some reason you are being perverse on purpose.
First you think Meadowlands belongs to you, now you think Guesser is
better than Messer. I don't think much of a man who doesn't say what he

knows to be a fact. You know perfectly well that Messer is a hundred times better than that...that dumb Guesser of yours. So why do you keep saying the opposite?

135 LÓMOV: You must think I'm either blind or stupid! Can't you understand that your Messer has an underslung jaw!

NATÁSHA: It's not true!

LÓMOV: He has an underslung jaw!

NATÁSHA [*Shouting*]:   It's not true!

LÓMOV: What are you shouting for?

140 NATÁSHA: What are you lying for? I can't stand any more of this. You ought to be getting ready to put your old Guesser out of his misery, and here you are comparing him to our Messer!

LÓMOV: You'll have to excuse me, I can't go on with this conversation. I'm having a heart murmur.

NATÁSHA: This just goes to prove what I've always known: the hunters who talk the most are the ones who know the least.

LÓMOV: Will you please do me a favor and just shut up.... My heart is starting to pound.... [*Shouts*] Shut up!

NATÁSHA: I will not shut up until you admit that Messer is a hundred times better than Guesser!

145 LÓMOV: He's a hundred times worse! I hope he croaks, your Messer.... My head... my eyes...my shoulders...

NATÁSHA: And your dumb old Guesser doesn't need to croak—he's dead already!

LÓMOV: Shut up! [*Starts to cry*] I'm having a heart attack!

NATÁSHA: I will not shut up!

[*Enter* CHUBUKÓV.]

CHUBUKÓV: Now what's the matter?

150 NATÁSHA: Papa, will you please tell us frankly, on your honor, who's a better dog: Guesser or Messer?

LÓMOV: Stepán Stepánich, I just want to know one thing: does your Messer have an underslung jaw or doesn't he? Yes or no?

CHUBUKÓV: Well? So what if he does? What difference does it make? Anyway, there isn't a better dog in the whole county, and that's a fact.

LÓMOV: But you don't think my Guesser is better? On your honor!

CHUBUKÓV: Now, loverboy, don't get all upset; just wait a minute. Please. Your Guesser has his good points and whatever. He's a thoroughbred, got a good stance, nice round hindquarters, all the rest of it. But that dog, if you really want to know, boy, has got two vital defects: he's old and he's got a short bite.

155 LÓMOV: You'll have to excuse me, I'm having another heart murmur. Let's just look at the facts, shall we? All I'd like you to do is just think back to that time at the field trials when my Guesser kept up with the count's dog Fresser. They were going ear to ear, and your Messer was a whole half mile behind.

CHUBUKÓV: He was behind because one of the count's men whopped him with his whip!

LÓMOV: That's not the point! All the other dogs were after the fox, and your Messer was chasing a sheep!

CHUBUKÓV: That's not true! Now listen, boy, I have a very quick temper, as you very well know, and that's a fact, so I think we should keep this discussion very short. He whopped him because none of the rest of you can stand watching other people's dogs perform! You're all rotten with envy! Even you, buddy boy, even you! The fact is, all somebody has to do is point out that somebody's dog is better than your Guesser, and right away you start in with this and that and all the rest of it. I happen to remember exactly what happened!

LÓMOV: And I remember too!

160 CHUBUKÓV [*Mimics him*]:   "And I remember too!" What do you remember?

LÓMOV: My heart murmur...My leg is paralyzed...I can't move...

NATÁSHA [*Mimics him*]:   "My heart murmur!" What kind of hunter are you? You'd do better in the kitchen catching cockroaches instead of out hunting foxes! A heart murmur!

CHUBUKÓV: She's right—what kind of hunter are you? You and your heart murmur should stay home instead of galloping cross-country, and that's a fact. You say you like to hunt; all you really want to do is ride around arguing and interfering with other people's dogs and whatever. You are *not,* and that's a fact, a hunter.

LÓMOV: And what makes you think you're a hunter? The only reason you go hunting is so you can get in good with the count! My heart! You're a sneak!

165 CHUBUKÓV: I'm a what? A sneak! [*Shouts*] Shut up!

LÓMOV: A sneak!

CHUBUKÓV: You young whippersnapper! You puppy!

LÓMOV: You rat! You rickety old rat!

CHUBUKÓV: You shut up, or I'll give you a tailful of buckshot! You snoop!

170 LÓMOV: Everybody knows your poor dead wife—oh, my heart!—used to beat you. My legs...my head...I see spots...I'm going to faint, I'm going to faint!

CHUBUKÓV: And everyone knows your housekeeper has you tied to her apron strings!

LÓMOV: Wait wait wait...here it comes! A heart attack! My shoulder just came undone—where's my shoulder? I'm going to die! [*Collapses into a chair*] Get a doctor! [*Faints*]

CHUBUKÓV: Whippersnapper! Milk sucker! Snoop! You make me sick! [*Drinks some water*] Sick!

NATÁSHA: What kind of a hunter are you? You can't even ride a horse! [*To* CHUBUKÓV] Papa! What's the matter with him? Papa! Look at him, Papa! [*Screeching*] Iván Vassílich! He's dead!

175 CHUBUKÓV: I'm sick! I can't breathe...give me some air!

NATÁSHA: He's dead! [*Shakes* LÓMOV's *shoulders*] Iván Vassílich! Iván Vassílich! What have we done? He's dead! [*Collapses into the other chair*] Get a doctor! Get a doctor! [*She has hysterics*]

CHUBUKÓV: Oh, now what? What's the matter with you?

NATÁSHA [*Wailing*]:   He's dead! He's dead!

CHUBUKÓV: Who's dead? [*Looks at* LÓMOV] Oh, my God, he *is* dead! Oh, my God! Get some water! Get a doctor! [*Puts glass to* LÓMOV'*s mouth*] Here, drink this.... He's not drinking it.... That means he's really dead...and every-thing! Oh, what a mess! I'll kill myself! I'll kill myself! Why did I wait so long to kill myself? What am I waiting for right now? Give me a knife! Lend me a gun! [LÓMOV *stirs*] I think he's going to live! Here, drink some water. That's the way.

180 LÓMOV: Spots...everything is all spots...it's all cloudy.... Where am I?

CHUBUKÓV: Just get married as soon as you can and then get out of here! She says yes! [*Joins* LÓMOV'*s and* NATÁSHA'*s hands*] She says yes and all the rest of it. I give you both my blessing and whatever. Only please just leave me in peace!

LÓMOV: Huh? Wha'? [*Starts to get up*] Who?

CHUBUKÓV: She says yes! All right? Go ahead and kiss her.... And then get the hell out of here!

NATÁSHA [*Moaning*]:   He's alive.... Yes, yes, I say yes....

185 CHUBUKÓV: Go ahead, give him a kiss.

LÓMOV: Huh? Who? [NATÁSHA *kisses him.*] Oh, that's very nice.... Excuse me, but what's happening? Oh, yes, I remember now.... My heart...those spots.... I'm so happy, Natásha! [*Kisses her hand*] My leg is still paralyzed....

NATÁSHA: I'm...I'm very happy too.

CHUBUKÓV: And I'm getting a weight off my shoulders. Oof!

NATÁSHA: But all the same—you can admit it now, can't you?—Messer is better than Guesser.

190 LÓMOV: He's worse!

NATÁSHA: He's better!

CHUBUKÓV: And they lived happily ever after! Bring on the champagne!

LÓMOV: He's worse!

NATÁSHA: Better! Better! Better!

195 CHUBUKÓV [*Tries to make himself heard*]:   Champagne! Bring on the champagne!

Curtain.

MAKING CONNECTIONS

1. It doesn't take long in this comedy to identify the basic personality traits of Natásha and Lómov. To what extent does their relationship remind you of relationships you know?

2. All of the characters in this play seem to have the same objective in mind. Why is it so hard, then, for them to reach it? Given their reactions to each other, why do they want this marriage to happen?

3. This play is a comedy. What makes it funny? Does Chekhov make any serious points about human nature here? Explain.

4. Is this a good match? Can you predict what this relationship will be like in five years? Explain.

MAKING AN ARGUMENT

1. Opposites attract. Or do they? They do in this play, but do they in real life? And do opposites make a good long-term relationship? Using your own knowledge, this play, and other literature that you have read, write an argument one way or the other. Cite the text of your sources for support.

CONNECTING AND COMPARING ACROSS GENRES: FICTION AND DRAMA

The two works that follow address a subtheme of this section: comparing fiction and drama. Susan Glaspell tells the same story in two different genres: a one-act play, *Trifles*, and a short story, "A Jury of Her Peers." Written by one author, they give us a unique glimpse into the creative process of Susan Glaspell and the differences between drama and prose fiction. Read and discussed together, they invite connections and comparisons.

SUSAN GLASPELL [1882–1948]

Susan Keating Glaspell was born in Davenport, Iowa, and attended Drake University. After working for a time as a reporter, she decided to devote herself to writing fiction, publishing two well-regarded novels, Glory of the Conquered *(1909) and* The Visioning *(1911). In 1913, she married George Cram Cook, a stage director. Together, they moved to Provincetown, Massachusetts, and founded the Provincetown Players, one of the first influential noncommercial theaters* in the country. The theater provided an artistic home to many illustrious writers of the time, including Edna St. Vincent Millay and Eugene O'Neill. Glaspell wrote a number of plays for the Players, often with feminist themes. In her later years she wrote, among other works, a biography of her husband,* The Road to the Temple *(1927), and* Alison's House, *which won the Pulitzer Prize in 1930. In the original Provincetown Players production of her best-known play,* Trifles *(1916), Susan Glaspell took the role of Mrs. Hale. The short story, "A Jury of Her Peers," was published in 1917.*

TRIFLES   [1916]

SCENE: *The kitchen in the now abandoned farmhouse of* JOHN WRIGHT, *a gloomy kitchen, and left without having been put in order—unwashed pans under the sink, a loaf of bread outside the breadbox, a dish towel on the table—other signs of incompleted work. At the rear the outer door opens, and the* SHERIFF *comes in, followed by the* COUNTY ATTORNEY *and* HALE: *The* SHERIFF *and* HALE *are men in middle life, the* COUNTY ATTORNEY *is a young man; all are much bundled up and go at once to the stove. They are followed by the two women—the* SHERIFF'S *wife,* MRS. PETERS, *first; she is a slight wiry woman, a thin nervous face.* MRS. HALE *is larger and would ordinarily be called more comfortable looking, but she is disturbed now and looks fearfully about as she enters. The women have come in slowly and stand close together near the door.*

COUNTY ATTORNEY [*at the stove rubbing his hands*]:   This feels good. Come up to the fire, ladies.

MRS. PETERS [*after taking a step forward*]:   I'm not—cold.

SHERIFF [*unbuttoning his overcoat and stepping away from the stove as if to the beginning of official business*]:   Now, Mr. Hale, before we move things about, you explain to Mr. Henderson just what you saw when you came here yesterday morning.

COUNTY ATTORNEY [*crossing down to left of the table*]:   By the way, has anything been moved? Are things just as you left them yesterday?

5   SHERIFF [*looking about*]:   It's just the same. When it dropped below zero last night, I thought I'd better send Frank out this morning to make a fire for us—[*sits right of center table*] no use getting pneumonia with a big case on, but I told him not to touch anything except the stove—and you know Frank.

COUNTY ATTORNEY: Somebody should have been left here yesterday.

SHERIFF: Oh—yesterday. When I had to send Frank to Morris Center for that man who went crazy—I want you to know I had my hands full yesterday. I knew you could get back from Omaha by today, and as long as I went over everything here myself—

COUNTY ATTORNEY: Well, Mr. Hale, tell just what happened when you came here yesterday morning.

HALE [*crossing down to above table*]:   Harry and I had started to town with a load of potatoes. We came along the road from my place and as I got here, I said, "I'm going to see if I can't get John Wright to go in with me on a party telephone." I spoke to Wright about it once before and he put me off, saying folks talked too much anyway, and all he asked was peace and quiet—I guess you know about how much he talked himself; but I thought maybe if I went to the house and talked about it before his wife, though I said to Harry that I didn't know as what his wife wanted made much difference to John—

10 COUNTY ATTORNEY: Let's talk about that later, Mr. Hale. I do want to talk about that, but tell now just what happened when you got to the house.

HALE: I didn't hear or see anything; I knocked at the door, and still it was all quiet inside. I knew they must be up, it was past eight o'clock. So I knocked again, and I thought I heard somebody say, "Come in." I wasn't sure, I'm not sure yet, but I opened the door—this door [*indicating the door by which the two women are still standing*] and there in that rocker—[*pointing to it*] sat Mrs. Wright.

[*They all look at the rocker.*]

COUNTY ATTORNEY: What—was she doing?

HALE: She was rockin' back and forth. She had her apron in her hand and was kind of—pleating it.

COUNTY ATTORNEY: And how did she—look?

15 HALE: Well, she looked queer.

COUNTY ATTORNEY: How do you mean—queer?

HALE: Well, as if she didn't know what she was going to do next. And kind of done up.

COUNTY ATTORNEY: How did she seem to feel about your coming?

HALE: Why, I don't think she minded—one way or other. She didn't pay much attention. I said, "How do, Mrs. Wright, it's cold, ain't it?" And she said, "Is it?"—and went on kind of pleating at her apron. Well, I was surprised; she didn't ask me to come up to the stove, or to set down, but just sat there, not even looking at me, so I said, "I want to see John." And then she—laughed. I guess you would call it a laugh. I thought of Harry and the team outside, so I said a little sharp: "Can't I see John?" "No," she says, kind o' dull like. "Ain't he home?" says I. "Yes," says she, "he's home." "Then why can't I see him?" I asked her, out of patience. "'Cause he's dead," says she. "*Dead?*" says I. She just nodded her head, not getting a bit excited, but rockin' back and forth. "Why—where is he?" says I, not knowing what to say. She just pointed upstairs—like that [*himself pointing to the room above*]. I got up, with the idea of going up there. I walked from there to here—then I says, "Why, what did he die of?" "He died of a rope around his neck," says she, and just went on pleatin' at her apron. Well, I went out and called Harry. I thought I might help. We went upstairs, and there he was lyin'—

20   COUNTY ATTORNEY: I think I'd rather have you go into that upstairs, where you can point it all out. Just go on now with the rest of the story.

HALE: Well, my first thought was to get that rope off. I looked…[*stops, his face twitches.*]…but Harry, he went up to him, and he said, "No, he's dead all right, and we'd better not touch anything." So we went back downstairs. She was still sitting that same way. "Has anybody been notified?" I asked. "No," says she, unconcerned. "Who did this, Mrs. Wright?" said Harry. He said it businesslike—and she stopped pleatin' of her apron. "I don't know," she says. "You don't *know?*" says Harry. "No," says she, "Weren't you sleepin' in the bed with him?" says Harry. "Yes," says she, "but I was on the inside." "Somebody slipped a rope round his neck and strangled him, and you didn't wake up?" says Harry. "I didn't wake up," she said after him. We must 'a looked as if we didn't see how that could be, for after a minute she said, "I sleep sound." Harry was going to ask her more questions but I said maybe we ought to let her tell her story first to the coroner, or the Sheriff, so Harry went fast as he could to Rivers' place, where there's a telephone.

COUNTY ATTORNEY: And what did Mrs. Wright do when she knew that you had gone for the coroner?

HALE: She moved from that chair to this one over here [*pointing to a small chair in the corner*] and just sat there with her hands held together and looking down. I got a feeling that I ought to make some conversation, so I said I had come in to see if John wanted to put in a telephone, and at that she started to laugh, and then she stopped and looked at me—scared. [*The* COUNTY ATTORNEY, *who has had his notebook out, makes a note.*] I dunno, maybe it wasn't scared. I wouldn't like to say it was. Soon Harry got back, and then Dr. Lloyd came, and you, Mr. Peters, and so I guess that's all I know that you don't.

COUNTY ATTORNEY [*looking around*]:   I guess we'll go upstairs first—and then out to the barn and around there. [*to the* SHERIFF] You're convinced that there was nothing important here—nothing that would point to any motive?

25   SHERIFF: Nothing here but kitchen things.

[*The* COUNTY ATTORNEY, *after again looking around the kitchen, opens the door of a cupboard closet. He gets up on a chair and looks on a shelf. Pulls his hand away, sticky.*]

COUNTY ATTORNEY: Here's a nice mess.

[*The women draw nearer.*]

MRS. PETERS [*to the other woman*]:   Oh, her fruit; it did freeze. [*to the* COUNTY ATTORNEY] She worried about that when it turned so cold. She said the fire'd go out and her jars would break.

SHERIFF: Well, can you beat the women! Held for murder and worryin' about her preserves.

COUNTY ATTORNEY: I guess before we're through she may have something more serious than preserves to worry about.

30   HALE: Well, women are used to worrying over trifles.

[*The two women move a little closer together.*]

COUNTY ATTORNEY [*with the gallantry of a young politician*]:   And yet, for all their worries, what would we do without the ladies? [*The women do not unbend. He goes to the sink, takes a dipperful of water from the pail and pouring it into a basin, washes his hands. Starts to wipe them on the roller towel, turns it for a cleaner place.*] Dirty towels! [*kicks his foot against the pans under the sink.*] Not much of a housekeeper, would you say: ladies?

MRS. HALE [*stiffly*]:   There's a great deal of work to be done on a farm.

COUNTY ATTORNEY: To be sure. And yet [*with a little bow to her*] I know there are some Dickson county farmhouses which do not have such roller towels.

[*He gives it a pull to expose its full length again.*]

MRS. HALE: Those towels get dirty awful quick. Men's hands aren't always as clean as they might be.

35   COUNTY ATTORNEY: Ah, loyal to your sex, I see. But you and Mrs. Wright were neighbors. I suppose you were friends, too.

MRS. HALE [*shaking her head*]:   I've not seen much of her of late years. I've not been in this house—it's more than a year.

COUNTY ATTORNEY: And why was that? You didn't like her?

MRS. HALE: I liked her all well enough. Farmers' wives have their hands full, Mr. Henderson. And then—

COUNTY ATTORNEY: Yes—?

40   MRS. HALE [*looking about*]:   It never seemed a very cheerful place.

COUNTY ATTORNEY: No—it's not cheerful. I shouldn't say she had the homemaking instinct.

MRS. HALE: Well, I don't know as Wright had, either.

COUNTY ATTORNEY: You mean that they didn't get on very well?

MRS. HALE: No, I don't mean anything. But I don't think a place'd be any cheerfuler for John Wright's being in it.

45   COUNTY ATTORNEY: I'd like to talk more of that a little later. I want to get the lay of things upstairs now.

[*He goes to the left, where three steps lead to a stair door.*]

SHERIFF: I suppose anything Mrs. Peters does'll be all right. She was to take in some clothes for her, you know, and a few little things. We left in such a hurry yesterday.

COUNTY ATTORNEY: Yes, but I would like to see what you take, Mrs. Peters, and keep an eye out for anything that might be of use to us.

MRS. PETERS: Yes, Mr. Henderson.

[*The women listen to the men's steps on the stairs, then look about the kitchen.*]

MRS. HALE: I'd hate to have men coming into my kitchen, snooping around and criticizing.

[*She arranges the pans under the sink which the* COUNTY ATTORNEY *had shoved out of place.*]

50   MRS. PETERS: Of course it's no more than their duty.

MRS. HALE: Duty's all right, but I guess that deputy Sheriff that came out to make the fire might have got a little of this on. [*gives the roller towel a pull*] Wish I'd thought of that sooner. Seems mean to talk about her for not having things slicked up when she had to come away in such a hurry.

MRS. PETERS [*who has gone to a small table in the left rear corner of the room, and lifted one end of a towel that covers a pan*]:   She had bread set.

[*Stands still.*]

MRS. HALE [*Eyes fixed on a loaf of bread beside the breadbox, which is on a low shelf at the other side of the room, moves slowly toward it.*]:   She was going to put this in there. [*Picks up loaf, then abruptly drops it. In a manner of returning to familiar things.*] It's a shame about her fruit. I wonder if it's all gone. [*gets up on the chair and looks.*] I think there's some here that's all right, Mrs. Peters. Yes—here; [*holding it toward the window*] this is cherries, too. [*looking again*] I declare I believe that's the only one. [*Gets down, bottle in her hand. Goes to the sink and wipes it off on the outside.*] She'll feel awful bad after all her hard work in the hot weather. I remember the afternoon I put up my cherries last summer.

[*She puts the bottle on the big kitchen table, center of the room. With a sigh, is about to sit down in the rocking-chair. Before she is seated realizes what chair it is; with a slow look at it, steps back. The chair which she has touched rocks back and forth.*]

MRS. PETERS: Well, I must get those things from the front room closet. [*She goes to the door at the right, but after looking into the other room, steps back.*] You coming with me, Mrs. Hale? You could help me carry them.

[*They go into the other room; reappear,* MRS. PETERS *carrying a dress and skirt,* MRS. HALE *following with a pair of shoes.*]

55   MRS. PETERS: My, it's cold in there.

[*She puts the clothes on the big table, and hurries to the stove.*]

MRS. HALE [*examining the skirt*]:   Wright was close. I think maybe that's why she kept so much to herself. She didn't even belong to the Ladies Aid. I suppose she felt she couldn't do her part, and then you don't enjoy things when you feel shabby. She used to wear pretty clothes and be lively, when she was Minnie

Foster, one of the town girls singing in the choir. But that—oh, that was thirty years ago. This all you was to take in?

MRS. PETERS: She said she wanted an apron. Funny thing to want, for there isn't much to get you dirty in jail, goodness knows. But I suppose just to make her feel more natural. She said they was in the top drawer in this cupboard. Yes, here. And then her little shawl that always hung behind the door. [*opens stair door and looks*] Yes, here it is.

[*Quickly shuts door leading upstairs.*]

MRS. HALE [*abruptly moving toward her*]: Mrs. Peters?

MRS. PETERS: Yes, Mrs. Hale?

60 MRS. HALE: Do you think she did it?

MRS. PETERS [*in a frightened voice*]: Oh, I don't know.

MRS. HALE: Well, I don't think she did. Asking for an apron and her little shawl. Worrying about her fruit.

MRS. PETERS [*starts to speak, glances up, where footsteps are heard in the room above. In a low voice*]: Mr. Peters says it looks bad for her. Mr. Henderson is awful sarcastic in speech and he'll make fun of her sayin' she didn't wake up.

MRS. HALE: Well, I guess John Wright didn't wake when they was slipping that rope under his neck.

65 MRS. PETERS: No, it's strange. It must have been done awful crafty and still. They say it was such a—funny way to kill a man, rigging it all up like that.

MRS. HALE: That's just what Mr. Hale said. There was a gun in the house. He says that's what he can't understand.

MRS. PETERS: Mr. Henderson said coming out that what was needed for the case was a motive; something to show anger, or—sudden feeling.

MRS. HALE [*who is standing by the table*]: Well, I don't see any signs of anger around here. [*She puts her hand on the dish towel which lies on the table, stands looking down at the table, one half of which is clean, the other half messy.*] It's wiped to here. [*Makes a move as if to finish work, then turns and looks at loaf of bread outside the breadbox. Drops towel. In that voice of coming back to familiar things.*] Wonder how they are finding things upstairs? I hope she had it a little more red-up up there. You know, it seems kind of sneaking. Locking her up in town and then coming out here and trying to get her own house to turn against her!

MRS. PETERS: But, Mrs. Hale, the law is the law.

70 MRS. HALE: I s'pose 'tis. [*unbuttoning her coat*] Better loosen up your things, Mrs. Peters. You won't feel them when you go out.

[MRS. PETERS *takes off her fur tippet, goes to hang it on hook at the back of room, stands looking at the under part of the small corner table.*]

MRS. PETERS: She was piecing a quilt.

[*She brings the large sewing basket and they look at the bright pieces.*]

MRS. HALE: It's log cabin pattern. Pretty, isn't it? I wonder if she was goin' to quilt or just knot it?

[*Footsteps have been heard coming down the stairs. The* SHERIFF *enters, followed by* HALE *and the* COUNTY ATTORNEY.]

SHERIFF: They wonder if she was going to quilt it or just knot it.

[*The men laugh; the women look abashed.*]

COUNTY ATTORNEY [*rubbing his hands over the stove*]:   Frank's fire didn't do much up there, did it? Well, let's go out to the barn and get that cleared up.

[*The men go outside.*]

75   MRS. HALE [*resentfully*]:   I don't know as there's anything so strange, our takin' up our time with little things while we're waiting for them to get the evidence. [*She sits down at the big table, smoothing out a block with decision.*] I don't see as it's anything to laugh about.

MRS. PETERS [*apologetically*]:   Of course they've got awful important things on their minds.

[*Pulls up a chair and joins* MRS. HALE *at the table.*]

MRS. HALE [*examining another block*]:   Mrs. Peters, look at this one. Here, this is the one she was working on, and look at the sewing! All the rest of it has been so nice and even. And look at this! It's all over the place! Why, it looks as if she didn't know what she was about!

[*After she has said this, they look at each other, then start to glance back at the door. After an instant* MRS. HALE *has pulled at a knot and ripped the sewing.*]

MRS. PETERS: Oh, what are you doing, Mrs. Hale?

MRS. HALE [*mildly*]:   Just pulling out a stitch or two that's not sewed very good. [*threading a needle*] Bad sewing always made me fidgety.

80   MRS. PETERS [*nervously*]:   I don't think we ought to touch things.

MRS. HALE: I'll just finish up this end. [*suddenly stopping and leaning forward*] MRS. PETERS?

MRS. PETERS: Yes, Mrs. Hale?

MRS. HALE: What do you suppose she was so nervous about?

MRS. PETERS: Oh—I don't know. I don't know as she was nervous. I sometimes sew awful queer when I'm just tired. [MRS. HALE *starts to say something, looks at* MRS. PETERS, *then goes on sewing.*] Well, I must get these things wrapped up. They may be through sooner than we think. [*putting apron and other things together*] I wonder where I can find a piece of paper, and string.

85   MRS. HALE: In that cupboard, maybe.

MRS. PETERS [*looking in cupboard*]:   Why, here's a birdcage. [*holds it up*] Did she have a bird, Mrs. Hale?

MRS. HALE: Why, I don't know whether she did or not—I've not been here for so long. There was a man around last year selling canaries cheap, but I don't know as she took one; maybe she did. She used to sing real pretty herself.

MRS. PETERS [*glancing around*]:   Seems funny to think of a bird here. But she must have had one, or why should she have a cage? I wonder what happened to it.

MRS. HALE: I s'pose maybe the cat got it.

90   MRS. PETERS: No, she didn't have a cat. She's got that feeling some people have about cats—being afraid of them. My cat got in her room, and she was real upset and asked me to take it out.

MRS. HALE: My sister Bessie was like that. Queer, ain't it?

MRS. PETERS [*examining the cage*]:   Why, look at this door. It's broke. One hinge is pulled apart.

MRS. HALE [*looking, too*]:   Looks as if someone must have been rough with it.

MRS. PETERS: Why, yes.

[*She brings the cage forward and puts it on the table.*]

95   MRS. HALE: I wish if they're going to find any evidence they'd be about it. I don't like this place.

MRS. PETERS: But I'm awful glad you came with me, Mrs. Hale. It would be lonesome for me sitting here alone.

MRS. HALE: It would, wouldn't it? [*dropping her sewing*] But I tell you what I do wish, Mrs. Peters. I wish I had come over sometimes when *she* was here. I—[*looking around the room*]—wish I had.

MRS. PETERS: But of course you were awful busy, Mrs. Hale—your house and your children.

MRS. HALE: I could've come. I stayed away because it weren't cheerful—and that's why I ought to have come. I—I've never liked this place. Maybe because it's down in a hollow and you don't see the road. I dunno what it is, but it's a lonesome place and always was. I wish I had come over to see Minnie Foster sometimes. I can see now—

[*Shakes her head.*]

100   MRS. PETERS: Well, you mustn't reproach yourself, Mrs. Hale. Somehow we just don't see how it is with other folks until—something comes up.

MRS. HALE: Not having children makes less work—but it makes a quiet house, and Wright out to work all day, and no company when he did come in. Did you know John Wright, Mrs. Peters?

MRS. PETERS: Not to know him; I've seen him in town. They say he was a good man.

MRS. HALE: Yes—good; he didn't drink, and kept his word as well as most, I guess, and paid his debts. But he was a hard man, Mrs. Peters. Just to pass the time of day with him—[*shivers*] Like a raw wind that gets to the bone. [*pauses, her eye falling on the cage*] I should think she would 'a wanted a bird. But what do you suppose went with it?

MRS. PETERS: I don't know, unless it got sick and died.

[*She reaches over and swings the broken door, swings it again; both women watch it.*]

105   MRS. HALE: You weren't raised round here, were you? [MRS. PETERS *shakes her head.*] You didn't know—her?

MRS. PETERS: Not till they brought her yesterday.

MRS. HALE: She—come to think of it, she was kind of like a bird herself—real sweet and pretty, but kind of timid and—fluttery. How—she—did—change. [*silence; then as if struck by a happy thought and relieved to get back to everyday things.*] Tell you what, Mrs. Peters; why don't you take the quilt in with you? It might take up her mind.

MRS. PETERS: Why, I think that's a real nice idea, Mrs. Hale. There couldn't possibly be any objection to it, could there? Now, just what would I take? I wonder if her patches are in here—and her things.

[*They look in the sewing basket.*]

MRS. HALE: Here's some red. I expect this has got sewing things in it [*brings out a fancy box*] What a pretty box. Looks like something somebody would give you. Maybe her scissors are in here. [*Opens box. Suddenly puts her hand to her nose.*] Why—[MRS. PETERS *bends nearer, then turns her face away.*] There's something wrapped up in this piece of silk.

110   MRS. PETERS: Why, this isn't her scissors.

MRS. HALE [*lifting the silk*]:   Oh, Mrs. Peters—it's—

[MRS. PETERS *bends closer.*]

MRS. PETERS: It's the bird.

MRS. HALE [*jumping up*]:   But, Mrs. Peters—look at it. Its neck! Look at its neck! It's all—other side *to*.

MRS. PETERS: Somebody—wrung—its neck.

[*Their eyes meet. A look of growing comprehension, of horror. Steps are heard outside.* MRS. HALE *slips box under quilt pieces, and sinks into her chair. Enter* SHERIFF *and* COUNTY ATTORNEY. MRS. PETERS *rises.*]

115   COUNTY ATTORNEY: [*as one turning from serious things to little pleasantries*] Well, ladies, have you decided whether she was going to quilt it or knot it?

MRS. PETERS: We think she was going to—knot it.

COUNTY ATTORNEY: Well, that's interesting, I'm sure. [*seeing the birdcage*] Has the bird flown?

MRS. HALE [*putting more quilt pieces over the box*]:   We think the—cat got it.

COUNTY ATTORNEY [*preoccupied*]:   Is there a cat?

[MRS. HALE *glances in a quick covert way at* MRS. PETERS.]

120   MRS. PETERS: Well, not *now*. They're superstitious, you know. They leave.

COUNTY ATTORNEY [*to* SHERIFF PETERS, *continuing an interrupted conversation*]:   No sign at all of anyone having come from the outside. Their own rope. Now let's go up again and go over it piece by piece. [*They start upstairs.*] It would have to have been someone who knew just the—

[MRS. PETERS *sits down. The two women sit there not looking at one another, but as if peering into something and at the same time holding back. When they talk now it is the manner of feeling their way over strange ground, as if afraid of what they are saying, but as if they cannot help saying it.*]

MRS. HALE: She liked the bird. She was going to bury it in that pretty box.

MRS. PETERS [*in a whisper*]:   When I was a girl—my kitten—there was a boy took a hatchet, and before my eyes—and before I could get there—[*covers her face an instant*] If they hadn't held me back, I would have—[*catches herself, looks upstairs where steps are heard, falters weakly*]—hurt him.

MRS. HALE [*with a slow look around her*]:   I wonder how it would seem never to have had any children around. [*pause*] No, Wright wouldn't like the bird—a thing that sang. She used to sing. He killed that, too.

125   MRS. PETERS [*moving uneasily*]:   We don't know who killed the bird.

MRS. HALE: I knew John Wright.

MRS. PETERS: It was an awful thing was done in this house that night, Mrs. Hale. Killing a man while he slept, slipping a rope around his neck that choked the life out of him.

MRS. HALE: His neck. Choked the life out of him.

[*Her hand goes out and rests on the birdcage.*]

MRS. PETERS: [*with a rising voice*] We don't know who killed him. We don't know.

130   MRS. HALE [*her own feeling not interrupted*]:   If there'd been years and years of nothing, then a bird to sing to you, it would be awful—still, after the bird was still.

MRS. PETERS [*something within her speaking*]:   I know what stillness is. When we homesteaded in Dakota, and my first baby died—after he was two years old, and me with no other then—

MRS. HALE: [*moving*] How soon do you suppose they'll be through, looking for evidence?

MRS. PETERS: I know what stillness is. [*pulling herself back*—] The law has got to punish crime, Mrs. Hale.

MRS. HALE [*not as if answering that*]:   I wish you'd seen Minnie Foster when she wore a white dress with blue ribbons and stood up there in the choir and sang. [*a look around the room*] Oh, I *wish* I'd come over here once in a while! That was a crime! That was a crime! Who's going to punish that?

135   MRS. PETERS [*looking upstairs*]:   We mustn't—take on.

MRS. HALE: I might have known she needed help! I know how things can be—for women. I tell you, it's queer, Mrs. Peters. We live close together and we live far apart. We all go through the same things—it's all just a different kind of the same thing. [*brushes her eyes, noticing the bottle of fruit, reaches out for it*] If I was you, I wouldn't tell her her fruit was gone. Tell her it ain't. Tell her it's all right. Take this in to prove it to her. She—she may never know whether it was broke or not.

MRS. PETERS [*Takes the bottle, looks about for something to wrap it in; takes petticoat from the clothes brought from the other room, very nervously begins winding this around the bottle. In a false voice.*]:   My, it's a good thing the men couldn't hear us. Wouldn't they just laugh! Getting all stirred up over a little thing like a—dead canary. As if that could have anything to do with—with— wouldn't they *laugh!*

[*The men are heard coming downstairs.*]

MRS. HALE [*under her breath*]:   Maybe they would—maybe they wouldn't.

COUNTY ATTORNEY: No, Peters, it's all perfectly clear except a reason for doing it. But you know juries when it comes to women. If there was some definite thing. Something to show—something to make a story about—a thing that would connect up with this strange way of doing it—

[*The women's eyes meet for an instant. Enter* HALE *from outer door.*]

140   HALE: Well, I've got the team around. Pretty cold out there.

COUNTY ATTORNEY: I'm going to stay here awhile by myself. [*to the* SHERIFF] You can send Frank out for me, can't you? I want to go over everything. I'm not satisfied that we can't do better.

SHERIFF: Do you want to see what Mrs. Peters is going to take in? [*The* LAWYER *goes to the table, picks up the apron, laughs.*]

COUNTY ATTORNEY: Oh, I guess they're not very dangerous things the ladies have picked up. [*Moves a few things about, disturbing the quilt pieces which cover the box. Steps back.*] No, Mrs. Peters doesn't need supervising. For that matter, a Sheriff's wife is married to the law. Ever think of it that way, Mrs. Peters?

MRS. PETERS: Not—just that way.

145   SHERIFF [*chuckling*]:   Married to the law. [*moves down right door to the other room*] I just want you to come in here a minute, George. We ought to take a look at these windows.

COUNTY ATTORNEY [*scoffingly*]:   Oh windows!

SHERIFF: We'll be right out, Mr. Hale. [HALE *goes outside. The* SHERIFF *follows the* COUNTY ATTORNEY *into the other room. Then* MRS. HALE *rises, hands tight together, looking intensely at* MRS. PETERS, *whose eyes take a slow turn, finally meeting* MRS. HALE's. *A moment* MRS. HALE *holds her, then her own eyes point the way to where the box is concealed. Suddenly* MRS. PETERS *throws back quilt pieces and tries to put the box in the bag she is carrying. It is too big. She opens box, starts to take the bird out, cannot touch it, goes to pieces, stands there helpless. Sound of a knob turning in the other room.* MRS. HALE *snatches the box and puts it in the pocket of her big coat. Enter* COUNTY ATTORNEY *and* SHERIFF.]

COUNTY ATTORNEY [*crosses to up left door facetiously*]:   Well, Henry, at least we found out that she was not going to quilt it. She was going to—what is it you call it, ladies?

MRS. HALE [*standing center below table facing front, her hand against her pocket*]: We call it—knot it, Mr. Henderson.

Curtain

A JURY OF HER PEERS: A SHORT STORY   [1917]

When Martha Hale opened the storm-door and got a cut of the north wind, she ran back for her big woolen scarf. As she hurriedly wound that round her head her eye made a scandalized sweep of her kitchen. It was no ordinary thing that called her away—it was probably farther from ordinary than anything that had ever happened in Dickson County. But what her eye took in was that her kitchen was in no shape for leaving: her bread all ready for mixing, half the flour sifted and half unsifted.

She hated to see things half done; but she had been at that when the team from town stopped to get Mr. Hale, and then the sheriff came running in to say his wife wished Mrs. Hale would come too—adding, with a grin, that he guessed she was getting scarey and wanted another woman along. So she had dropped everything right where it was.

"Martha!" now came her husband's impatient voice. "Don't keep folks waiting out here in the cold."

She again opened the storm-door, and this time joined the three men and the one woman waiting for her in the big two-seated buggy.

5   After she had the robes tucked around her she took another look at the woman who sat beside her on the back seat. She had met Mrs. Peters the year before at the county fair, and the thing she remembered about her was that she didn't seem like a sheriff's wife. She was small and thin and didn't have a strong voice. Mrs. Gorman, sheriff's wife before Gorman went out and Peters came in, had a voice that somehow seemed to be backing up the law with every word. But if Mrs. Peters didn't look like a sheriff's wife, Peters made it up in looking like a sheriff. He was to a dot the kind of man who could get himself elected sheriff—a heavy man with a big voice, who was particularly genial with the law-abiding, as if to make it plain that he knew the difference between criminals and non-criminals. And right there it came into Mrs. Hale's mind, with a stab, that this man who was so pleasant and lively with all of them was going to the Wrights' now as a sheriff.

"The country's not very pleasant this time of year," Mrs. Peters at last ventured, as if she felt they ought to be talking as well as the men.

Mrs. Hale scarcely finished her reply, for they had gone up a little hill and could see the Wright place now, and seeing it did not make her feel like talking. It looked very lonesome this cold March morning. It had always been a lonesome-looking place. It was down in a hollow, and the poplar trees around it were lonesome-looking trees. The men were looking at it and talking about what had happened. The county attorney was bending to one side of the buggy, and kept looking steadily at the place as they drew up to it.

"I'm glad you came with me," Mrs. Peters said nervously, as the two women were about to follow the men in through the kitchen door.

Even after she had her foot on the door-step, her hand on the knob, Martha Hale had a moment of feeling she could not cross that threshold. And the reason it seemed she couldn't cross it now was simply because she hadn't crossed it before. Time and time again it had been in her mind, "I ought to go over and see Minnie Foster"—she still thought of her as Minnie Foster, though for twenty years she had been Mrs. Wright. And then there was always something to do and Minnie Foster would go from her mind. But *now* she could come.

10   The men went over to the stove. The women stood close together by the door. Young Henderson, the county attorney, turned around and said, "Come up to the fire, ladies."

Mrs. Peters took a step forward, then stopped. "I'm not—cold," she said.

And so the two women stood by the door, at first not even so much as looking around the kitchen.

The men talked for a minute about what a good thing it was, the sheriff had sent his deputy out that morning to make a fire for them, and then Sheriff Peters stepped back from the stove, unbuttoned his outer coat, and leaned his hands on the kitchen table in a way that seemed to mark the beginning of official business. "Now, Mr. Hale," he said in a sort of semi-official voice, "before we move things about, you tell Mr. Henderson just what it was you saw when you came here yesterday morning."

The county attorney was looking around the kitchen.

15   "By the way," he said, "has anything been moved?" He turned to the sheriff. "Are things just as you left them yesterday?"

Peters looked from cupboard to sink; from that to a small worn rocker a little to one side of the kitchen table.

"It's just the same."

"Somebody should have been left here yesterday," said the county attorney.

"Oh—yesterday," returned the sheriff, with a little gesture as of yesterday having been more than he could bear to think of. "When I had to send Frank to Morris Center for that man who went crazy—let me tell you. I had my hands full yesterday. I knew you could get back from Omaha by today, George, and as long as I went over everything here myself—"

20   "Well, Mr. Hale," said the county attorney, in a way of letting what was past and gone go, "tell just what happened when you came here yesterday morning."

Mrs. Hale, still leaning against the door, had that sinking feeling of the mother whose child is about to speak a piece. Lewis often wandered along and got things mixed up in a story. She hoped he would tell this straight and plain, and not say unnecessary things that would just make things harder for Minnie Foster. He didn't begin at once, and she noticed that he looked queer—as if standing in that kitchen and having to tell what he had seen there yesterday morning made him almost sick.

"Yes, Mr. Hale?" the county attorney reminded.

"Harry and I had started to town with a load of potatoes," Mrs. Hale's husband began.

Harry was Mrs. Hale's oldest boy. He wasn't with them now, for the very good reason that those potatoes never got to town yesterday and he was taking them this morning, so he hadn't been home when the sheriff stopped to say he wanted Mr. Hale to come over to the Wright place and tell the county attorney his story there, where he could point it all out. With all Mrs. Hale's other emotions came the fear now that maybe Harry wasn't dressed warm enough—they hadn't any of them realized how that north wind did bite.

25   "We come along this road," Hale was going on, with a motion of his hand to the road over which they had just come, "and as we got in sight of the house I says to Harry, 'I'm goin' to see if I can't get John Wright to take a telephone.' You see," he explained to Henderson, "unless I can get somebody to go in with me they won't come out this branch road except for a price *I* can't pay. I'd spoke to Wright about it once before; but he put me off, saying folks talked too much anyway, and all he asked was peace and quiet—guess you know about how much he talked himself. But I thought maybe if I went to the house and talked about it before his wife, and said all the women-folks liked the telephones, and that in this lonesome stretch of road it would be a good thing—well, I said to Harry that that was what I was going to say—though I said at the same time that I didn't know as what his wife wanted made much difference to John—"

Now there he was!—saying things he didn't need to say. Mrs. Hale tried to catch her husband's eye, but fortunately the county attorney interrupted with:

"Let's talk about that a little later, Mr. Hale. I do want to talk about that, but I'm anxious now to get along to just what happened when you got here."

When he began this time, it was very deliberately and carefully:

"I didn't see or hear anything. I knocked at the door. And still it was all quiet inside. I knew they must be up—it was past eight o'clock. So I knocked again, louder, and I thought I heard somebody say, 'Come in.' I wasn't sure—I'm not sure yet. But I opened the door—this door," jerking a hand toward the door by which the two women stood, "and there, in that rocker"—pointing to it—"sat Mrs. Wright."

30   Everyone in the kitchen looked at the rocker. It came into Mrs. Hale's mind that that rocker didn't look in the least like Minnie Foster—the Minnie Foster of twenty years before. It was a dingy red, with wooden rungs up the back, and the middle rung was gone, and the chair sagged to one side.

"How did she—look?" the county attorney was inquiring.

"Well," said Hale, "she looked—queer."

"How do you mean—queer?"

As he asked it he took out a note-book and pencil. Mrs. Hale did not like the sight of that pencil. She kept her eye fixed on her husband, as if to keep him from saying unnecessary things that would go into that note-book and make trouble.

35   Hale did speak guardedly, as if the pencil had affected him too.

"Well, as if she didn't know what she was going to do next. And kind of—done up."

"How did she seem to feel about your coming?"

"Why, I don't think she minded—one way or other. She didn't pay much attention. I said, 'Ho' do, Mrs. Wright? It's cold, ain't it?' And she said, 'Is it?'—and went on pleatin' at her apron.

"Well, I was surprised. She didn't ask me to come up to the stove, or to sit down, but just set there, not even lookin' at me. And so I said: 'I want to see John.'

40   "And then she—laughed. I guess you would call it a laugh.

"I thought of Harry and the team outside, so I said, a little sharp, 'Can I see John?' 'No,' says she—kind of dull like. 'Ain't he home?' says I. Then she looked at me. 'Yes,' says she, 'he's home.' 'Then why can't I see him?' I asked her, out of patience with her now. 'Cause he's dead' says she, just as quiet and dull—and fell to pleatin' her apron. 'Dead?' says I, like you do when you can't take in what you've heard.

"She just nodded her head, not getting a bit excited, but rockin' back and forth.

"'Why—where is he?' says I, not knowing *what* to say.

"She just pointed upstairs—like this"—pointing to the room above.

45   "I got up, with the idea of going up there myself. By this time I—didn't know what to do. I walked from there to here; then I says: 'Why, what did he die of?'

"'He died of a rope around his neck,' says she; and just went on pleatin' at her apron."

Hale stopped speaking, and stood staring at the rocker, as if he were still seeing the woman who had sat there the morning before. Nobody spoke; it was as if every one were seeing the woman who had sat there the morning before.

"And what did you do then?" the county attorney at last broke the silence.

"I went out and called Harry. I thought I might—need help. I got Harry in, and we went upstairs." His voice fell almost to a whisper. "There he was—lying over the—"

50   "I think I'd rather have you go into that upstairs," the county attorney interrupted, "where you can point it all out. Just go on now with the rest of the story."

"Well, my first thought was to get that rope off. It looked—"

He stopped, his face twitching.

"But Harry, he went up to him, and he said, 'No, he's dead all right, and we'd better not touch anything.' So we went downstairs.

"She was still sitting that same way. 'Has anybody been notified?' I asked. 'No,' says she, unconcerned.

55   "'Who did this, Mrs. Wright?' said Harry. He said it businesslike, and she stopped pleatin' at her apron. 'I don't know,' she says. 'You don't *know?*' says Harry. 'Weren't you sleepin' in the bed with him?' 'Yes,' says she, 'but I was on the inside.' 'Somebody slipped a rope round his neck and strangled him, and you didn't wake up?' says Harry. 'I didn't wake up,' she said after him.

"We may have looked as if we didn't see how that could be, for after a minute she said, 'I sleep sound.'

"Harry was going to ask her more questions, but I said maybe that weren't our business; maybe we ought to let her tell her story first to the coroner or the sheriff. So Harry went fast as he could over to High Road—the Rivers' place, where there's a telephone."

"And what did she do when she knew you had gone for the coroner?" The attorney got his pencil in his hand all ready for writing.

"She moved from that chair to this one over here"—Hale pointed to a small chair in the corner—"and just sat there with her hands held together and looking down. I got a feeling that I ought to make some conversation, so I said I had come in to see if John wanted to put in a telephone; and at that she started to laugh, and then she stopped and looked at me—scared."

60   At the sound of a moving pencil the man who was telling the story looked up.

"I dunno—maybe it wasn't scared," he hastened: "I wouldn't like to say it was. Soon Harry got back, and then Dr. Lloyd came, and you, Mr. Peters, and so I guess that's all I know that you don't."

He said that last with relief, and moved a little, as if relaxing. Everyone moved a little. The county attorney walked toward the stair door.

"I guess we'll go upstairs first—then out to the barn and around there."

He paused and looked around the kitchen.

65   "You're convinced there was nothing important here?" he asked the sheriff. "Nothing that would—point to any motive?"

The sheriff too looked all around, as if to re-convince himself.

"Nothing here but kitchen things," he said, with a little laugh for the insignificance of kitchen things.

The county attorney was looking at the cupboard—a peculiar, ungainly structure, half closet and half cupboard, the upper part of it being built in the wall, and the lower part just the old-fashioned kitchen cupboard. As if its queerness attracted him, he got a chair and opened the upper part and looked in. After a moment he drew his hand away sticky.

"Here's a nice mess," he said resentfully.

70   The two women had drawn nearer, and now the sheriff's wife spoke.

"Oh—her fruit," she said, looking to Mrs. Hale for sympathetic understanding. She turned back to the county attorney and explained: "She worried about that when it turned so cold last night. She said the fire would go out and her jars might burst."

Mrs. Peters' husband broke into a laugh.

"Well, can you beat the women! Held for murder, and worrying about her preserves!"

The young attorney set his lips.

75   "I guess before we're through with her she may have something more serious than preserves to worry about."

"Oh, well," said Mrs. Hale's husband, with good-natured superiority, "women are used to worrying over trifles."

The two women moved a little closer together. Neither of them spoke. The county attorney seemed suddenly to remember his manners—and think of his future.

"And yet," said he, with the gallantry of a young politician, "for all their worries, what would we do without the ladies?"

The women did not speak, did not unbend. He went to the sink and began washing his hands. He turned to wipe them on the roller towel—whirled it for a cleaner place.

80   "Dirty towels! Not much of a housekeeper, would you say, ladies?"

He kicked his foot against some dirty pans under the sink.

"There's a great deal of work to be done on a farm," said Mrs. Hale stiffly.

"To be sure. And yet"—with a little bow to her—"I know there are some Dickson County farm-houses that do not have such roller towels." He gave it a pull to expose its full length again.

"Those towels get dirty awful quick. Men's hands aren't always as clean as they might be."

85   "Ah, loyal to your sex, I see," he laughed. He stopped and gave her a keen look. "But you and Mrs. Wright were neighbors. I suppose you were friends, too."

Martha Hale shook her head.

"I've seen little enough of her of late years. I've not been in this house—it's more than a year."

"And why was that? You didn't like her?"

"I liked her well enough," she replied with spirit. "Farmers' wives have their hands full, Mr. Henderson. And then"—She looked around the kitchen.

90   "Yes?" he encouraged.

"It never seemed a very cheerful place," said she, more to herself than to him.

"No," he agreed; "I don't think anyone would call it cheerful. I shouldn't say she had the home-making instinct."

"Well, I don't know as Wright had, either," she muttered.

"You mean they didn't get on very well?" he was quick to ask.

95   "No; I don't mean anything," she answered, with decision. As she turned a little away from him, she added: "But I don't think a place would be any the cheerfuler for John Wright's bein' in it."

"I'd like to talk to you about that a little later, Mrs. Hale," he said. "I'm anxious to get the lay of things upstairs now."

He moved toward the stair door, followed by the two men.

"I suppose anything Mrs. Peters does'll be all right?" the sheriff inquired. "She was to take in some clothes for her, you know—and a few little things. We left in such a hurry yesterday."

The county attorney looked at the two women they were leaving alone there among the kitchen things.

100 "Yes—Mrs. Peters," he said, his glance resting on the woman who was not Mrs. Peters, the big farmer woman who stood behind the sheriff's wife. "Of course Mrs. Peters is one of us," he said, in a manner of entrusting responsibility. "And keep your eye out, Mrs. Peters, for anything that might be of use. No telling; you women might come upon a clue to the motive—and that's the thing we need."

Mr. Hale rubbed his face after the fashion of a show man getting ready for a pleasantry.

"But would the women know a clue if they did come upon it?" he said; and, having delivered himself of this, he followed the others through the stair door.

The women stood motionless and silent, listening to the footsteps, first upon the stairs, then in the room above them.

Then, as if releasing herself from something strange, Mrs. Hale began to arrange the dirty pans under the sink, which the county attorney's disdainful push of the foot had deranged.

105 "I'd hate to have men comin' into my kitchen," she said testily—"snoopin' round and criticizin'."

"Of course it's no more than their duty," said the sheriff's wife, in her manner of timid acquiescence.

"Duty's all right," replied Mrs. Hale bluffly; "but I guess that deputy sheriff that come out to make the fire might have got a little of this on." She gave the roller towel a pull. "Wish I'd thought of that sooner! Seems mean to talk about her for not having things slicked up, when she had to come away in such a hurry."

She looked around the kitchen. Certainly it was not "slicked up." Her eye was held by a bucket of sugar on a low shelf. The cover was off the wooden bucket, and beside it was a paper bag—half full.

Mrs. Hale moved toward it.

110 "She was putting this in there," she said to herself—slowly.

She thought of the flour in her kitchen at home—half sifted, half not sifted. She had been interrupted, and had left things half done. What had interrupted Minnie Foster? Why had that work been left half done? She made a move as if to finish it,—unfinished things always bothered her,—and then she glanced around and saw that Mrs. Peters was watching her—and she didn't want Mrs. Peters to get that feeling she had got of work begun and then—for some reason—not finished.

"It's a shame about her fruit," she said, and walked toward the cupboard that the county attorney had opened, and got on the chair, murmuring: "I wonder if it's all gone."

It was a sorry enough looking sight, but "Here's one that's all right," she said at last. She held it toward the light. "This is cherries, too." She looked again. "I declare I believe that's the only one."

With a sigh, she got down from the chair, went to the sink, and wiped off the bottle.

115 "She'll feel awful bad, after all her hard work in the hot weather. I remember the afternoon I put up my cherries last summer."

She set the bottle on the table, and, with another sigh, started to sit down in the rocker. But she did not sit down. Something kept her from sitting down in that chair. She straightened—stepped back, and, half turned away, stood looking at it, seeing the woman who had sat there "pleatin' at her apron."

The thin voice of the sheriff's wife broke in upon her: "I must be getting those things from the front-room closet." She opened the door into the other room, started in, stepped back. "You coming with me, Mrs. Hale?" she asked nervously. "You—you could help me get them."

They were soon back—the stark coldness of that shut-up room was not a thing to linger in.

"My!" said Mrs. Peters, dropping the things on the table and hurrying to the stove.

120   Mrs. Hale stood examining the clothes the woman who was being detained in town had said she wanted.

"Wright was close!" she exclaimed, holding up a shabby black skirt that bore the marks of much making over. "I think maybe that's why she kept so much to herself. I s'pose she felt she couldn't do her part; and then, you don't enjoy things when you feel shabby. She used to wear pretty clothes and be lively—when she was Minnie Foster, one of the town girls, singing in the choir. But that—oh, that was twenty years ago."

With a carefulness in which there was something tender, she folded the shabby clothes and piled them at one corner of the table. She looked up at Mrs. Peters, and there was something in the other woman's look that irritated her.

"She don't care," she said to herself. "Much difference it makes to her whether Minnie Foster had pretty clothes when she was a girl."

Then she looked again, and she wasn't so sure; in fact, she hadn't at any time been perfectly sure about Mrs. Peters. She had that shrinking manner, and yet her eyes looked as if they could see a long way into things.

125   "This all you was to take in?" asked Mrs. Hale.

"No," said the sheriff's wife; "she said she wanted an apron. Funny thing to want," she ventured in her nervous little way, "for there's not much to get you dirty in jail, goodness knows. But I suppose just to make her feel more natural. If you're used to wearing an apron—. She said they were in the bottom drawer of this cupboard. Yes—here they are. And then her little shawl that always hung on the stair door."

She took the small gray shawl from behind the door leading upstairs, and stood a minute looking at it.

Suddenly Mrs. Hale took a quick step toward the other woman.

"Mrs. Peters!"

130   "Yes, Mrs. Hale?"

"Do you think she—did it?"

A frightened look blurred the other things in Mrs. Peters' eyes.

"Oh, I don't know," she said, in a voice that seemed to shrink away from the subject.

"Well, I don't think she did," affirmed Mrs. Hale stoutly. "Asking for an apron, and her little shawl. Worryin' about her fruit."

135   "Mr. Peters says—" Footsteps were heard in the room above; she stopped, looked up, then went on in a lowered voice: "Mr. Peters says—it looks bad for her.

Mr. Henderson is awful sarcastic in speech, and he's going to make fun of her saying she didn't—wake up."

For a moment Mrs. Hale had no answer. Then, "Well, I guess John Wright didn't wake up—when they was slippin' that rope under his neck," she muttered.

"No, it's *strange*," breathed Mrs. Peters. "They think it was such a—funny way to kill a man."

She began to laugh; at sound of the laugh, abruptly stopped.

"That's just what Mr. Hale said," said Mrs. Hale, in a resolutely natural voice. "There was a gun in the house. He says that's what he can't understand."

140   "Mr. Henderson said, coming out, that what was needed for the case was a motive. Something to show anger—or sudden feeling."

"Well, I don't see any signs of anger around here," said Mrs. Hale, "I don't—"

She stopped. It was as if her mind tripped on something. Her eye was caught by a dish-towel in the middle of the kitchen table. Slowly she moved toward the table. One half of it was wiped clean, the other half messy. Her eyes made a slow, almost unwilling turn to the bucket of sugar and the half empty bag beside it. Things begun—and not finished.

After a moment she stepped back, and said, in that manner of releasing herself:

"Wonder how they're finding things upstairs? I hope she had it a little more red up up there. You know,"—she paused, and feeling gathered,—"it seems kind of *sneaking*: locking her up in town and coming out here to get her own house to turn against her!"

145   "But, Mrs. Hale," said the sheriff's wife, "the law is the law."

"I s'pose 'tis," answered Mrs. Hale shortly.

She turned to the stove, saying something about that fire not being much to brag of. She worked with it a minute, and when she straightened up she said aggressively:

"The law is the law—and a bad stove is a bad stove. How'd you like to cook on this?"—pointing with the poker to the broken lining. She opened the oven door and started to express her opinion of the oven; but she was swept into her own thoughts, thinking of what it would mean, year after year, to have that stove to wrestle with. The thought of Minnie Foster trying to bake in that oven—and the thought of her never going over to see Minnie Foster—.

She was startled by hearing Mrs. Peters say: "A person gets discouraged—and loses heart."

150   The sheriff's wife had looked from the stove to the sink—to the pail of water which had been carried in from outside. The two women stood there silent, above them the footsteps of the men who were looking for evidence against the woman who had worked in that kitchen. That look of seeing into things, of seeing through a thing to something else, was in the eyes of the sheriff's wife now. When Mrs. Hale next spoke to her, it was gently:

"Better loosen up your things, Mrs. Peters. We'll not feel them when we go out."

Mrs. Peters went to the back of the room to hang up the fur tippet she was wearing. A moment later she exclaimed, "Why, she was piecing a quilt," and held up a large sewing basket piled high with quilt pieces.

Mrs. Hale spread some of the blocks on the table.

"It's log-cabin pattern," she said, putting several of them together, "Pretty, isn't it?"

155   They were so engaged with the quilt that they did not hear the footsteps on the stairs. Just as the stair door opened Mrs. Hale was saying:

"Do you suppose she was going to quilt it or just knot it?"

The sheriff threw up his hands.

"They wonder whether she was going to quilt it or just knot it!"

There was a laugh for the ways of women, a warming of hands over the stove, and then the county attorney said briskly:

160   "Well, let's go right out to the barn and get that cleared up."

"I don't see as there's anything so strange," Mrs. Hale said resentfully, after the outside door had closed on the three men—"our taking up our time with little things while we're waiting for them to get the evidence. I don't see as it's anything to laugh about."

"Of course they've got awful important things on their minds," said the sheriff's wife apologetically.

They returned to an inspection of the blocks for the quilt. Mrs. Hale was look-ing at the fine, even sewing, and preoccupied with thoughts of the woman who had done that sewing, when she heard the sheriff's wife say, in a queer tone:

"Why, look at this one."

165   She turned to take the block held out to her.

"The sewing," said Mrs. Peters, in a troubled way, "All the rest of them have been so nice and even—but—this one. Why, it looks as if she didn't know what she was about!"

Their eyes met—something flashed to life, passed between them; then, as if with an effort, they seemed to pull away from each other. A moment Mrs. Hale sat there, her hands folded over that sewing which was so unlike all the rest of the sewing. Then she had pulled a knot and drawn the threads.

"Oh, what are you doing, Mrs. Hale?" asked the sheriff's wife, startled.

"Just pulling out a stitch or two that's not sewed very good," said Mrs. Hale mildly.

170   "I don't think we ought to touch things," Mrs. Peters said, a little helplessly.

"I'd just finish up this end," answered Mrs. Hale, still in that mild, matter-of-fact fashion.

She threaded a needle and started to replace bad sewing with good. For a little while she sewed in silence. Then, in that thin, timid voice, she heard:

"Mrs. Hale!"

"Yes, Mrs. Peters?"

175   "What do you suppose she was so—nervous about?"

"Oh, *I* don't know," said Mrs. Hale, as if dismissing a thing not important enough to spend much time on. "I don't know as she was—nervous. I sew awful queer sometimes when I'm just tired."

She cut a thread, and out of the corner of her eye looked up at Mrs. Peters. The small, lean face of the sheriff's wife seemed to have tightened up. Her eyes had that look of peering into something. But next moment she moved, and said in her thin, indecisive way:

"Well, I must get those clothes wrapped. They may be through sooner than we think. I wonder where I could find a piece of paper—and string."

"In that cupboard, maybe," suggested Mrs. Hale, after a glance around.

180   One piece of the crazy sewing remained unripped. Mrs. Peters' back turned, Martha Hale now scrutinized that piece, compared it with the dainty, accurate sewing of the other blocks. The difference was startling. Holding this block made her feel queer, as if the distracted thoughts of the woman who had perhaps turned to it to try and quiet herself were communicating themselves to her.

Mrs. Peters' voice roused her.

"Here's a bird-cage," she said. "Did she have a bird, Mrs. Hale?"

"Why, I don't know whether she did or not." She turned to look at the cage Mrs. Peters was holding up. "I've not been here in so long." She sighed. "There was a man round last year selling canaries cheap—but I don't know as she took one. Maybe she did. She used to sing real pretty herself."

Mrs. Peters looked around the kitchen.

185   "Seems kind of funny to think of a bird here." She half laughed—an attempt to put up a barrier. "But she must have had one—or why would she have a cage? I wonder what happened to it."

"I suppose maybe the cat got it," suggested Mrs. Hale, resuming her sewing.

"No; she didn't have a cat. She's got that feeling some people have about cats— being afraid of them. When they brought her to our house yesterday, my cat got in the room, and she was real upset and asked me to take it out."

"My sister Bessie was like that," laughed Mrs. Hale.

The sheriff's wife did not reply. The silence made Mrs. Hale turn round. Mrs. Peters was examining the bird-cage.

190   "Look at this door," she said slowly. "It's broke. One hinge has been pulled apart."

Mrs. Hale came nearer.

"Looks as if someone must have been—rough with it."

Again their eyes met—startled, questioning, apprehensive. For a moment neither spoke nor stirred. Then Mrs. Hale, turning away, said brusquely:

"If they're going to find any evidence, I wish they'd be about it. I don't like this place."

195   "But I'm awful glad you came with me, Mrs. Hale." Mrs. Peters put the bird-cage on the table and sat down. "It would be lonesome for me—sitting here alone."

"Yes, it would, wouldn't it?" agreed Mrs. Hale, a certain determined naturalness in her voice. She had picked up the sewing, but now it dropped in her lap, and she murmured in a different voice: "But I tell you what I *do* wish, Mrs. Peters. I wish I had come over sometimes when she was here. I wish—I had."

"But of course you were awful busy, Mrs. Hale. Your house—and your children."

"I could've come," retorted Mrs. Hale shortly. "I stayed away because it weren't cheerful—and that's why I ought to have come. I"—she looked around—"I've never liked this place. Maybe because it's down in a hollow and you don't see the road. I don't know what it is, but it's a lonesome place, and always was. I wish I had come over to see Minnie Foster sometimes. I can see now—" She did not put it into words.

"Well, you mustn't reproach yourself," counseled Mrs. Peters. "Somehow, we just don't see how it is with other folks till—something comes up."

200 "Not having children makes less work," mused Mrs. Hale, after a silence, "but it makes a quiet house—and Wright out to work all day—and no company when he did come in. Did you know John Wright, Mrs. Peters?"

"Not to know him. I've seen him in town. They say he was a good man."

"Yes—good," conceded John Wright's neighbor grimly. "He didn't drink, and kept his word as well as most, I guess, and paid his debts. But he was a hard man, Mrs. Peters. Just to pass the time of day with him—." She stopped, shivered a little. "Like a raw wind that gets to the bone." Her eye fell upon the cage on the table before her, and she added, almost bitterly: "I should think she would've wanted a bird!"

Suddenly she leaned forward, looking intently at the cage. "But what do you s'pose went wrong with it?"

"I don't know," returned Mrs. Peters; "unless it got sick and died."

205 But after she said it she reached over and swung the broken door. Both women watched it as if somehow held by it.

"You didn't know—her?" Mrs. Hale asked, a gentler note in her voice.

"Not till they brought her yesterday," said the sheriff's wife.

"She—come to think of it, she was kind of like a bird herself. Real sweet and pretty, but kind of timid and—fluttery. How—she—did—change."

That held her for a long time. Finally, as if struck with a happy thought and relieved to get back to everyday things, she exclaimed:

210 "Tell you what, Mrs. Peters, why don't you take the quilt in with you? It might take up her mind."

"Why, I think that's a real nice idea, Mrs. Hale," agreed the sheriff's wife, as if she too were glad to come into the atmosphere of a simple kindness. "There couldn't possibly be any objection to that, could there? Now, just what will I take? I wonder if her patches are in here—and her things?"

They turned to the sewing basket.

"Here's some red," said Mrs. Hale, bringing out a roll of cloth. Underneath that was a box. "Here, maybe her scissors are in here—and her things." She held it up. "What a pretty box! I'll warrant that was something she had a long time ago—when she was a girl."

She held it in her hand a moment; then, with a little sigh, opened it.

215 Instantly her hand went to her nose.

"Why—!"

Mrs. Peters drew nearer—then turned away.

"There's something wrapped up in this piece of silk," faltered Mrs. Hale.

"This isn't her scissors," said Mrs. Peters, in a shrinking voice.

220 Her hand not steady, Mrs. Hale raised the piece of silk. "Oh, Mrs. Peters!" she cried. "It's—"

Mrs. Peters bent closer.

"It's the bird," she whispered.

"But, Mrs. Peters!" cried Mrs. Hale. "*Look* at it! Its *neck*—look at its neck! It's all—other side *to*."

She held the box away from her.

225   The sheriff's wife again bent closer.

"Somebody wrung its neck," said she, in a voice that was slow and deep.

And then again the eyes of the two women met—this time clung together in a look of dawning comprehension, of growing horror. Mrs. Peters looked from the dead bird to the broken door of the cage. Again their eyes met. And just then there was a sound at the outside door.

Mrs. Hale slipped the box under the quilt pieces in the basket, and sank into the chair before it. Mrs. Peters stood holding to the table. The county attorney and the sheriff came in from outside.

"Well, ladies," said the county attorney, as one turning from serious things to little pleasantries, "have you decided whether she was going to quilt it or knot it?"

230   "We think," began the sheriff's wife in a flurried voice, "that she was going to—knot it."

He was too preoccupied to notice the change that came in her voice on that last.

"Well, that's very interesting, I'm sure," he said tolerantly. He caught sight of the bird-cage. "Has the bird flown?"

"We think the cat got it," said Mrs. Hale in a voice curiously even.

He was walking up and down, as if thinking something out.

235   "Is there a cat?" he asked absently.

Mrs. Hale shot a look up at the sheriff's wife.

"Well, not *now*," said Mrs. Peters. "They're superstitious, you know; they leave."

She sank into her chair.

The county attorney did not heed her. "No sign at all of anyone having come in from the outside," he said to Peters, in the manner of continuing an interrupted conversation. "Their own rope. Now let's go upstairs again and go over it, piece by piece. It would have to have been someone who knew just the—"

240   The stair door closed behind them and their voices were lost.

The two women sat motionless, not looking at each other, but as if peering into something and at the same time holding back. When they spoke now it was as if they were afraid of what they were saying, but as if they could not help saying it.

"She liked the bird," said Martha Hale, low and slowly. "She was going to bury it in that pretty box."

"When I was a girl," said Mrs. Peters, under her breath, "my kitten—there was a boy took a hatchet, and before my eyes—before I could get there—" She covered her face an instant. "If they hadn't held me back I would have"—she caught herself, looked upstairs where footsteps were heard, and finished weakly—"hurt him."

Then they sat without speaking or moving.

245   "I wonder how it would seem," Mrs. Hale at last began, as if feeling her way over strange ground—"never to have had any children around?" Her eyes made a slow sweep of the kitchen, as if seeing what that kitchen had meant through all the years. "No, Wright wouldn't like the bird," she said after that—"a thing that sang. She used to sing. He killed that too." Her voice tightened.

Mrs. Peters moved uneasily.

"Of course we don't know who killed the bird."

"I knew John Wright," was Mrs. Hale's answer.

"It was an awful thing was done in this house that night, Mrs. Hale," said the sheriff's wife. "Killing a man while he slept—slipping a thing round his neck that choked the life out of him."

250   Mrs. Hale's hand went out to the bird-cage.

"His neck. Choked the life out of him."

"We don't *know* who killed him," whispered Mrs. Peters wildly. "We don't *know*."

Mrs. Hale had not moved. "If there had been years and years of—nothing, then a bird to sing to you, it would be awful—still—after the bird was still."

It was as if something within her not herself had spoken, and it found in Mrs. Peters something she did not know as herself.

255   "I know what stillness is," she said, in a queer, monotonous voice. "When we homesteaded in Dakota, and my first baby died—after he was two years old—and me with no other then—"

Mrs. Hale stirred.

"How soon do you suppose they'll be through looking for the evidence?"

"I know what stillness is," repeated Mrs. Peters, in just that same way. Then she too pulled back. "The law has got to punish crime, Mrs. Hale," she said in her tight little way.

"I wish you'd seen Minnie Foster," was the answer, "when she wore a white dress with blue ribbons, and stood up there in the choir and sang."

260   The picture of that girl, the fact that she had lived neighbor to that girl for twenty years, and had let her die for lack of life, was suddenly more than she could bear.

"Oh, I *wish* I'd come over here once in a while!" she cried. "That was a crime! That was a crime. Who's going to punish that?"

"We mustn't take on," said Mrs. Peters, with a frightened look toward the stairs.

"I might 'a' *known* she needed help! I tell you, it's *queer,* Mrs. Peters. We live close together, and we live far apart. We all go through the same things—it's all just a different kind of the same thing! If it weren't—why do you and I *understand?* Why do we *know*—what we know this minute?"

She dashed her hand across her eyes. Then, seeing the jar of fruit on the table she reached for it and choked out:

265   "If I was you I wouldn't *tell* her her fruit was gone! Tell her it *ain't*. Tell her it's all right—all of it. Here—take this in to prove it to her! She—she may never know whether it was broke or not."

She turned away.

Mrs. Peters reached out for the bottle of fruit as if she were glad to take it—as if touching a familiar thing, having something to do, could keep her from something else. She got up, looked about for something to wrap the fruit in, took a petticoat from the pile of clothes she had brought from the front room, and nervously started winding that round the bottle.

"My!" she began, in a high, false voice, "it's a good thing the men couldn't hear us! Getting all stirred up over a little thing like a—dead canary." She hurried over that. "As if that could have anything to do with—with—My, wouldn't they *laugh?*"

Footsteps were heard on the stairs.

270   "Maybe they would," muttered Mrs. Hale—"maybe they wouldn't."

"No, Peters," said the county attorney incisively; "it's all perfectly clear, except the reason for doing it. But you know juries when it comes to women. If there was some definite thing—something to show. Something to make a story about. A thing that would connect up with this clumsy way of doing it."

In a covert way Mrs. Hale looked at Mrs. Peters. Mrs. Peters was looking at her. Quickly they looked away from each other. The outer door opened and Mr. Hale came in.

"I've got the team round now," he said. "Pretty cold out there."

"I'm going to stay here awhile by myself," the county attorney suddenly announced. "You can send Frank out for me, can't you?" he asked the sheriff. "I want to go over everything. I'm not satisfied we can't do better."

275   Again, for one brief moment, the two women's eyes found one another.

The sheriff came up to the table.

"Did you want to see what Mrs. Peters was going to take in?"

The county attorney picked up the apron. He laughed.

"Oh, I guess they're not very dangerous things the ladies have picked out."

280   Mrs. Hale's hand was on the sewing basket in which the box was concealed. She felt that she ought to take her hand off the basket. She did not seem able to. He picked up one of the quilt blocks which she had piled on to cover the box. Her eyes felt like fire. She had a feeling that if he took up the basket she would snatch it from him.

But he did not take it up. With another little laugh, he turned away, saying:

"No; Mrs. Peters doesn't need supervising. For that matter, a sheriff's wife is married to the law. Ever think of it that way, Mrs. Peters?"

Mrs. Peters was standing beside the table. Mrs. Hale shot a look up at her; but she could not see her face. Mrs. Peters had turned away. When she spoke, her voice was muffled.

"Not—just that way," she said.

285   "Married to the law!" chuckled Mrs. Peters' husband. He moved toward the door into the front room, and said to the county attorney:

"I just want you to come in here a minute, George. We ought to take a look at these windows."

"Oh—windows," said the county attorney scoffingly.

"We'll be right out, Mr. Hale," said the sheriff to the farmer, who was still waiting by the door.

Hale went to look after the horses. The sheriff followed the county attorney into the other room. Again—for one final moment—the two women were alone in that kitchen.

290   Martha Hale sprang up, her hands tight together, looking at that other woman, with whom it rested. At first she could not see her eyes, for the sheriff's wife had not turned back, since she turned away at that suggestion of being married to the

law. But now Mrs. Hale made her turn back. Her eyes made her turn back. Slowly, unwillingly, Mrs. Peters turned her head until her eyes met the eyes of the other woman. There was a moment when they held each other in a steady, burning look in which there was no evasion or flinching. Then Martha Hale's eyes pointed the way to the basket in which was hidden the thing that would make certain the conviction of the other woman—that woman who was not there and yet who had been there with them all through the hour.

For a moment Mrs. Peters did not move. And then she did it. With a rush forward, she threw back the quilt pieces, got the box, tried to put it in her handbag. It was too big. Desperately she opened it, started to take the bird out. But there she broke—she could not touch the bird. She stood there helpless, foolish.

There was the sound of a knob turning in the inner door. Martha Hale snatched the box from the sheriff's wife, and got it in the pocket of her big coat just as the sheriff and the county attorney came back into the kitchen.

"Well, Henry," said the county attorney facetiously, "at least we found out that she was not going to quilt it. She was going to—what is it you call it, ladies?"

Mrs. Hale's hand was against the pocket of her coat.

295   "We call it—knot it, Mr. Henderson."

MAKING CONNECTIONS— "A JURY OF HER PEERS" AND *TRIFLES*

1. Which title do you prefer, "A Jury of Her Peers" or *Trifles*? Which one conveys more of the complexities of the conflict? The short story was published a year after the play. Does it show? Explain.
2. In many ways, the central characters of the short story and the play are John Wright and his wife, neither of whom appear in the story or onstage. What is the effect of learning about them through other characters? How would this story and play be different if they included the scenes leading up to the death of John Wright?
3. Why don't Mrs. Peters and Mrs. Hale reveal the evidence they discover? Do they think it would help or hinder Mrs. Wright's case?
4. If all the evidence were to come to light, do you think that it would matter whether or not Mrs. Wright were tried by a jury composed of all women versus a jury composed of all men? Explain.
5. Given the attitudes of the men, how would you describe the values of this culture? What are these women supposed to know? What do they really know?

MAKING AN ARGUMENT

1. Which form, fiction or drama, do you prefer as the vehicle for this story? Why? What does one have that the other lacks? Do you think either could have been written more effectively? Analyze the effectiveness of each, and write an argument in favor of one form or the other. Cite the text of both play and story to support your view.

◆ ESSAYS ◆

STEVEN DOLOFF [B. 1948]

*Steven Doloff is a professor of English at the Pratt Insti-
tute in New York. He has published essays on topics of
contemporary culture in many scholarly and general-
interest publications, including* The New York Times,
Newsday, *and* The Chronicle of Higher Education. *The
following essay was originally printed in* The Washington
Post *in 1983.*

THE OPPOSITE SEX   [1983]

For just one day, imagine yourself a boy (wow!). A girl (ugh).

Having seen Dustin Hoffman's female impersonation in the movie, "Tootsie," I decided to give myself some reading over the Christmas recess by assigning in-class essays
to my English composition students on how each would spend a day as a member
of his or her respective opposite sex. From four classes I received approximately
100 essays. The sample, perhaps like the movie, proved both entertaining and
annoying in its predictability.

The female students, as a group, took to the subject immediately and with
obvious gusto, while the male students tended to wait a while (in several cases half
the period), in something of a daze, before starting. The activities hypothetically
engaged in by the women, whose ages averaged about 20, generally reflected two
areas: envy of men's physical and social privileges, and curiosity regarding men's
true feelings concerning women.

In their essays, women jauntily went places *alone*, and sometimes stayed out *all
night*. They threw their clothes on the floor and left dishes in the sink. They hung out
on the street and sweated happily in a variety of sports from football to weightlifting.

More than a third of them went out to cruise for dates. Appointing themselves
in brand names of men's clothing and dousing themselves in men's cologne I
have never heard of (I was instructed to read Gentleman's Quarterly magazine),
they deliberately and aggressively accosted women, *many* women, on the street,
in discos, in supermarkets. Others sought out the proverbial locker room for the
kinds of bull sessions they hoped would reveal the real nitty-gritty masculine mind
at work (on the subject of women).

5   At least two female students in each class spent chunks of their essays under
the sheets with imaginary girlfriends, wives or strangers, finding out with a kind of
scientific zeal what sex is like as a man.

Some, but not all of the women ended their essays with a formal, almost oblig-
atory sounding statement of preference to be a female, and of gratitude in returning
to their correct gender after a day as Mr. Hyde.

The male students, after their initial paralysis wore off, did not write as much
as the females. They seemed envious of very little that was female, and curious

about nothing. Three or four spent their day as women frantically seeking medical help to turn back into men more quickly. Those who accepted the assignment more seriously, if unenthusiastically, either stayed home and apathetically checked off a list of domestic chores or, more evasively, went off to work in an office and engaged in totally asexual business office routines.

A small percentage of the men ventured into the more feminine pursuits of putting on makeup and going to the beauty parlor. They agreed looking good was important.

If they stayed home as housewives, when their hypothetical husbands returned from work they ate dinner, watched some television and then went right to sleep. If they were businesswomen, they came directly home after work, ate some dinner, watched TV and went right to sleep. A handful actually went out on dates, had dinner in the most expensive restaurants they could cajole their escorts into taking them to, and then, after being taken home, very politely slammed the doors in their escorts' faces and went right to sleep. Not one male student let anybody lay a finger on him/her.

10   Finally, the sense of heartfelt relief at the end of the male students' essays, underscored by the much-repeated fervent anticipation of masculinity returning with the dawn, seemed equivalent to that of jumping up after having been forced to sit on a lit stove.

Granted, my flimsy statistical sample is nothing to go to the Ford Foundation with for research money. But on the other hand, do I really need to prove that young people even now are still burdened with sexist stereotypes and sexist self-images not nearly as vestigial as we would like to think? (One male student rhetorically crumpled up his paper after 10 minutes and growled. "You can't make me write this!") What does that imply about the rest of us? What would you do as a member of the opposite sex for a day? This last question is your essay assignment.

MAKING CONNECTIONS

1. This article was written in 1983. Do you think the results would differ if one hundred college students were assigned the essay now? If you believe that they would differ, explain what these differences would be. If you believe that they would not, explain why not.
2. Write the essay that Doloff assigns. Analyze how your essay confirms or differs from Doloff's study.
3. Why do the male students in Doloff's assignment have more trouble than the female students getting started on their essays?

MAKING AN ARGUMENT

1. In today's world, is it easier to be male or female? Using this essay—and at least one other source from this section—write an essay that defends your view. Cite the texts of the works you chose for support.

VIRGINIA WOOLF [1882–1941]

Virginia Woolf was born in London, England. Her father, Leslie Stephen, was a prominent scholar, and through him Woolf was introduced to many of the leading lights of the Victorian age. Unlike her brothers, who were sent to college, she was educated at home in her father's massive library. After his death, she and her sister, Vanessa Bell, moved to London, where they became the center of the so-called "Bloomsbury Group," informal gatherings of the era's most important intellectuals, including E. M. Forster and John Maynard Keynes. Throughout her life, Woolf was acutely aware of what she felt was the inferior status accorded her as a woman, and this theme runs throughout much of her work. A pioneer in the technique of "stream of consciousness," she is best known for her experimental novels, including Mrs. Dalloway *(1925),* To the Lighthouse *(1927),* Orlando *(1928), and* The Waves *(1931). After suffering a series of nervous breakdowns during which she feared she was going insane, Woolf committed suicide in 1941. "If Shakespeare Had a Sister" is taken from her 1929 classic feminist work,* A Room of One's Own.

IF SHAKESPEARE HAD A SISTER   [1929]

It would have been impossible, completely and entirely, for any woman to have written the plays of Shakespeare in the age of Shakespeare. Let me imagine, since facts are so hard to come by, what would have happened had Shakespeare had a wonderfully gifted sister, called Judith, let us say. Shakespeare himself went, very probably—his mother was an heiress—to the grammar school, where he may have learnt Latin—Ovid, Virgil and Horace—and the elements of grammar and logic. He was, it is well known, a wild boy who poached rabbits, perhaps shot a deer, and had, rather sooner than he should have done, to marry a woman in the neighborhood, who bore him a child rather quicker than was right. That escapade sent him to seek his fortune in London. He had, it seemed, a taste for the theatre; he began by holding horses at the stage door. Very soon he got work in the theatre, became a successful actor, and lived at the hub of the universe, meeting everybody, knowing everybody, practicing his art on the boards, exercising his wits in the streets, and even getting access to the palace of the queen. Meanwhile his extraordinarily gifted sister, let us suppose, remained at home. She was as adventurous, as imaginative, as agog to see the world as he was. But she was not sent to school. She had no chance of learning grammar and logic, let alone of reading Horace and Virgil. She picked up a book now and then, one of her brother's perhaps, and read a few pages. But then her parents came in and told her to mend the stockings or mind the stew and not moon about with books and papers. They would have spoken sharply but kindly, for they were substantial people who knew the conditions of life for a woman and loved their daughter—indeed, more likely than not she was the apple of her father's eye.

Perhaps she scribbled some pages up in an apple loft on the sly, but was careful to hide them or set fire to them. Soon, however, before she was out of her teens, she was to be betrothed to the son of a neighboring woolstapler. She cried out that marriage was hateful to her, and for that she was severely beaten by her father. Then he ceased to scold her. He begged her instead not to hurt him, not to shame him in this matter of her marriage. He would give her a chain of beads or a fine petticoat, he said; and there were tears in his eyes. How could she disobey him? How could she break his heart? The force of her own gift alone drove her to it. She made up a small parcel of her belongings, let herself down by a rope one summer's night and took the road to London. She was not seventeen. The birds that sang in the hedge were not more musical than she was. She had the quickest fancy, a gift like her brother's, for the tune of words. Like him, she had a taste for the theatre. She stood at the stage door; she wanted to act, she said. Men laughed in her face. The manager—a fat, loose-lipped man—guffawed. He bellowed something about poodles dancing and women acting—no woman, he said, could possibly be an actress. He hinted—you can imagine what. She could get no training in her craft. Could she even seek her dinner in a tavern or roam the streets at midnight? Yet her genius was for fiction and lusted to feed abundantly upon the lives of men and women and the study of their ways. At last—for she was very young, oddly like Shakespeare the poet in her face, with the same grey eyes and rounded brows—at last Nick Greene the actor-manager took pity on her; she found herself with child by that gentleman and so—who shall measure the heat and violence of the poet's heart when caught and tangled in a woman's body?—killed herself one winter's night and lies buried at some cross-roads where the omnibuses now stop outside the Elephant and Castle.

That, more or less, is how the story would run, I think, if a woman in Shakespeare's day had had Shakespeare's genius. But for my part, I agree with the deceased bishop, if such he was—it is unthinkable that any woman in Shakespeare's day should have had Shakespeare's genius. For genius like Shakespeare's is not born among labouring, uneducated, servile people. It was not born in England among the Saxons and the Britons. It is not born today among the working classes. How, then, could it have been born among women whose work began, according to Professor Trevelyan, almost before they were out of the nursery, who were forced to it by their parents and held to it by all the power of law and custom? Yet genius of a sort must have existed among women as it must have existed among the working classes. Now and again an Emily Brontë or a Robert Burns blazes out and proves its presence. But certainly it never got itself on to paper. When, however, one reads of a witch being ducked, of a woman possessed by devils, of a wise woman selling herbs, or even of a very remarkable man who had a mother, then I think we are on the track of a lost novelist, a suppressed poet, of some mute and inglorious Jane Austen, some Emily Brontë who dashed her brains out on the moor or mopped and mowed about the highways crazed with the torture that her gift had put her to. Indeed, I would venture to guess that Anon, who wrote so many poems without signing them, was often a woman.

MAKING CONNECTIONS

1. Why does Woolf create a sister for Shakespeare? What basic point is she trying to make?
2. In what ways does she indicate that Judith would have been deprived of the opportunities that William had?

MAKING AN ARGUMENT

1. If Shakespeare were alive today and had a sister, she could do whatever she wanted to. Or could she? Write an argument that agrees or disagrees with the proposition "Women today have equal opportunity to become or to do whatever their potential will allow." Cite evidence from your own knowledge and/or literature in this section or elsewhere to support your views.

CASE STUDY IN HISTORICAL CONTEXT

Women in Culture and History

The purpose of this case study is to provide you with material for a self-contained research unit. As outlined in Chapter 5, one popular area of literary research is inquiry into the social, historical, or cultural background of a work. The materials that follow contain a primary source—the play *A Doll's House*—and a number of secondary sources—a brief biography, the playwright's comments, a changed ending for one production, letters and articles that reflect the attitudes of that period, and an essay describing the plight of women over the last millennium. By themselves, or in combination with other sources, they provide a good resource for a research essay. The best literature has a universal, timeless quality. It speaks to us across time and culture and appeals to our humanity. Being aware of the historical and cultural context from which literature springs can enrich our understanding of it and lead to greater insight.

A number of the stories and plays in this section depict the lives of women in the late nineteenth and early twentieth centuries. Their actions and reactions are strongly motivated by the cultural imperatives of their time. Though we still struggle with issues of social justice at the beginning of the twenty-first century, it is impossible for us to fully appreciate the impact of these imperatives on people who lived in those times. But a look at some sample letters, notes, newspaper columns, and excerpts from speeches and essays—the historical and cultural artifacts—may give us a better feel for the assumptions about women that dominated that era.

With the exception of our final essay, "The Rest of the Story," published by Natalie Zemon Davis and Jill Ker Conway in 1999, all of the selections that follow are more than a century old. The letters of John and Abigail Adams are more than two hundred years old and seem to draw the battle lines for the prolonged struggle for women's rights that followed. On the eve of one rebellion, Abigail Adams forecasts another if the men creating the new "code of laws" are not "more generous and favorable" to women than their ancestors have been. In its own way, each of the other selections acts for or against that rebellion. A German husband's letter to his uncooperative wife illustrates the righteousness and arrogance of the male role in marriage. Having severed one bond of slavery herself, Sojourner

Truth encourages and inspires women to overcome another in her speech to a women's rights meeting in Ohio.

Adding to their other pieces in this section, Henrik Ibsen and Charlotte Perkins Stetson (Gilman) show us their views of women's rights from another angle. Ibsen's "notes" for the play *A Doll's House,* a changed ending he wrote reluctantly for a German production of the play, and his speech to the Norwegian League for Women's Rights inject some interesting complications into our understanding of his intentions. Charlotte Perkins Stetson (Gilman), writing in a very different voice than the speaker in her short story "The Yellow Wallpaper," makes her case for women's rights in an excerpt from her scholarly essay "Women and Economics."

Elizabeth Cady Stanton writes about the compelling need for women to be given their "birthright of self-sovereignty." And in the latest of the nineteenth-century pieces, two journalists, Wilbur Fisk Tillet and Dorothy Dix, assess the progress made by women in the nineteenth century. Tillet believes much progress has been made—as long as women don't develop masculine qualities and wander outside the home. Dix, a pioneer advice-to-women columnist for a New Orleans newspaper, *The Daily Picayune,* is a bit more feisty and realistic with her assessment.

At the end of the nineteenth century, 134 years after Abigail Adams's letter, it's clear that her prophesied rebellion was still going strong. It's sobering to realize, however, that twenty more years would pass before women even had the right to vote.

In addition to the pieces that follow the play, you may inform your response further by reading Virginia Woolf's twentieth-century essay "If Shakespeare Had a Sister" on page 798. This essay complements and supports similar concerns expressed so long ago.

HENRIK IBSEN [1828–1906]

Henrik Ibsen was born in the seaport town of Skien, Norway. When he was still a child, his father, once a prosperous businessman, lost his fortune, and the family was reduced to poverty. As a teenager, Ibsen was apprenticed to a pharmacist and briefly studied medicine, but soon found himself employed as a stage manager in a small regional theater. He turned to writing historical plays and enjoyed some success. Moving to the capital city of Christiania (now Oslo), Ibsen managed the Norwegian Theater. When the theater failed in 1864, due in part to lack of government support, a disillusioned Ibsen left Norway and spent over twenty years living in continental Europe. His greatest plays, including A Doll's House, Ghosts, An Enemy of the People, The Wild Duck, *and* Hedda Gabler, *date to this period. These highly realistic plays revolutionized modern drama by wedding characters of psychological depth to thoughtful plots concerning the age's most pressing social problems. His later plays,* John Gabriel Borkman *(1896) and* When We Dead Awaken *(1899), which he wrote after his triumphant return to Norway in 1891, were heavily symbolic and poetic.*

A Doll's House[1]

[1879]

Translated by R. Farquharson Sharp

CHARACTERS

TORVALD HELMER, A LAWYER AND BANK MANAGER
NORA, HIS WIFE
DOCTOR RANK
MRS. CHRISTINE LINDE
NILS KROGSTAD, A LAWYER AND BANK CLERK
IVAR, BOB, AND EMMY, THE HELMERS' THREE YOUNG CHILDREN
ANNE, THEIR NURSE
HELEN, A HOUSEMAID
A PORTER

The action takes place in HELMER'S *apartment.*

ACT 1

SCENE. *A room furnished comfortably and tastefully, but not extravagantly. At the back, a door to the right leads to the entrance hall, another to the left leads to* HELMER'S *study. Between the doors stands a piano. In the middle of the left-hand wall is a door, and beyond it a window. Near the window are a round table, armchairs and a small sofa. In the right-hand wall, at the farther end, another door; and on the same side, nearer the footlights, a stove, two easy chairs and a rocking-chair; between the stove and the door, a small table. Engravings on the walls; a cabinet with china and other small objects; a small book case with well-bound books. The floors are carpeted, and a fire burns in the stove. It is winter.*

A bell rings in the hall; shortly afterwards the door is heard to open. Enter NORA, *humming a tune and in high spirits. She is in outdoor dress and carries a number of parcels; these she lays on the table to the right. She leaves the outer door open after her, and through it is seen a* PORTER *who is carrying a Christmas Tree and a basket, which he gives to the* MAID *who has opened the door.*

NORA: Hide the Christmas Tree carefully, Helen. Be sure the children do not see it till this evening, when it is dressed. [*to the* PORTER, *taking out her purse.*] How much?

PORTER: Sixpence.

NORA: There is a shilling. No, keep the change. [*The* PORTER *thanks her, and goes out. Nora shuts the door. She is laughing to herself, as she takes off her hat and coat. She takes a packet of macaroons from her pocket and eats one or two; then goes cautiously to her husband's door and listens.*] Yes, he is in.

[*Still humming, she goes to the table on the right.*]

---

[1]Originally translated from the Norwegian "Et Dukkehjem" as "A Dollhouse."

HELMER: [*calls out from his room*] Is that my little lark twittering out there?

5   NORA: [*busy opening some of the parcels*] Yes, it is!

HELMER: Is my little squirrel bustling about?

NORA: Yes!

HELMER: When did my squirrel come home?

NORA: Just now. [*puts the bag of macaroons into her pocket and wipes her mouth.*] Come in here, Torvald, and see what I have bought.

10   HELMER: Don't disturb me. [*A little later, he opens the door and looks into the room, pen in hand.*] Bought, did you say? All these things? Has my little spendthrift been wasting money again?

NORA: Yes, but, Torvald, this year we really can let ourselves go a little. This is the first Christmas that we have not needed to economise.

HELMER: Still, you know, we can't spend money recklessly.

NORA: Yes, Torvald, we may be a wee bit more reckless now, mayn't we? Just a tiny wee bit! You are going to have a big salary and earn lots and lots of money.

HELMER: Yes, after the New Year; but then it will be a whole quarter before the salary is due.

15   NORA: Pooh! we can borrow till then.

HELMER: Nora! [*goes up to her and takes her playfully by the ear.*] The same little featherhead! Suppose, now, that I borrowed fifty pounds to-day, and you spent it all in the Christmas week, and then on New Year's Eve a slate fell on my head and killed me, and—

NORA: [*putting her hands over his mouth*] Oh! don't say such horrid things.

HELMER: Still, suppose that happened—what then?

NORA: If that were to happen, I don't suppose I should care whether I owed money or not.

20   HELMER: Yes, but what about the people who had lent it?

NORA: They? Who would bother about them? I should not know who they were.

HELMER: That is like a woman! But seriously, Nora, you know what I think about that. No debt, no borrowing. There can be no freedom or beauty about a home life that depends on borrowing and debt. We two have kept bravely on the straight road so far, and we will go on the same way for the short time longer that there need be any struggle.

NORA: [*moving towards the stove*] As you please, Torvald.

HELMER: [*following her*] Come, come, my little skylark must not droop her wings. What is this! Is my little squirrel out of temper? [*taking out his purse.*] Nora, what do you think I have got here?

25   NORA: [*turning around quickly*] Money!

HELMER: There you are. [*gives her some money*] Do you think I don't know what a lot is wanted[2] for housekeeping at Christmas-time?

NORA: [*counting*] Ten shillings—a pound—two pounds! Thank you, thank you, Torvald; that will keep me going for a long time.

HELMER: Indeed it must.

---

[2]**what a lot is wanted** how much is needed

NORA: Yes, yes, it will. But come here and let me show you what I have bought. And all so cheap! Look, here is a new suit for Ivar, and a sword; and a horse and a trumpet for Bob; and a doll and dolly's bedstead for Emmy—they are very plain, but anyway she will soon break them in pieces. And here are dress-lengths and handkerchiefs for the maids; old Anne ought really to have something better.

30   HELMER: And what is in this parcel?

NORA: [*crying out*] No, no! you mustn't see that till this evening.

HELMER: Very well. But now tell me, you extravagant little person, what would you like for yourself?

NORA: For myself? Oh, I am sure I don't want anything.

HELMER: Yes, but you must. Tell me something reasonable that you would particularly like to have.

35   NORA: No, I really can't think of anything—unless, Torvald—

HELMER: Well?

NORA: [*playing with his coat buttons, and without raising her eyes to his*] If you really want to give me something, you might—you might—

HELMER: Well, out with it!

NORA: [*speaking quickly*] You might give me money, Torvald. Only just as much as you can afford; and then one of these days I will buy something with it.

40   HELMER: But, Nora—

NORA: Oh, do! dear Torvald; please, please do! Then I will wrap it up in beautiful gilt paper and hang it on the Christmas Tree. Wouldn't that be fun?

HELMER: What are little people called that are always wasting money?

NORA: Spendthrifts—I know. Let us do as you suggest, Torvald, and then I shall have time to think what I am most in want of. That is a very sensible plan, isn't it?

HELMER: [*smiling*] Indeed it is—that is to say, if you were really to save out of the money I give you, and then really buy something for yourself. But if you spend it all on the housekeeping and any number of unnecessary things, then I merely have to pay up again.

45   NORA: Oh but, Torvald—

HELMER: You can't deny it, my dear little Nora. [*puts his arm round her waist*] It's a sweet little spendthrift, but she uses up a deal of money. One would hardly believe how expensive such little persons are!

NORA: It's a shame to say that. I do really save all I can.

HELMER: [*laughing*] That's very true—all you can. But you can't save anything!

NORA: [*smiling quietly and happily*] You haven't any idea how many expenses we skylarks and squirrels have, Torvald.

50   HELMER: You are an odd little soul. Very like your father. You always find some new way of wheedling money out of me, and, as soon as you have got it, it seems to melt in your hands. You never know where it has gone. Still, one must take you as you are. It is in the blood; for indeed it is true that you can inherit these things, Nora.

NORA: Ah, I wish I had inherited many of papa's qualities.

HELMER: And I would not wish you to be anything but just what you are, my sweet little skylark. But, do you know, it strikes me that you are looking rather—what shall I say—rather uneasy to-day?

NORA: Do I?

HELMER: You do, really. Look straight at me.

55   NORA: [*looks at him*] Well?

HELMER: [*wagging his finger at her*] Hasn't Miss Sweet-Tooth been breaking rules
in town to-day?

NORA: No; what makes you think that?

HELMER: Hasn't she paid a visit to the confectioner's?

NORA: No, I assure you, Torvald—

60   HELMER: Not been nibbling sweets?

NORA: No, certainly not.

HELMER: Not even taken a bite at a macaroon or two?

NORA: No, Torvald, I assure you really—

HELMER: There, there, of course I was only joking.

65   NORA: [*going to the table on the right*] I should not think of going against your
wishes.

HELMER: No, I am sure of that! besides, you gave me your word—[*going up to her*]
Keep your little Christmas secrets to yourself, my darling. They will all be
revealed to-night when the Christmas Tree is lit, no doubt.

NORA: Did you remember to invite Doctor Rank?

HELMER: No. But there is no need; as a matter of course he will come to dinner
with us. However, I will ask him when he comes in this morning. I have
ordered some good wine. Nora, you can't think how I am looking forward
to this evening.

NORA: So am I! And how the children will enjoy themselves, Torvald!

70   HELMER: It is splendid to feel that one has a perfectly safe appointment, and a big
enough income. It's delightful to think of, isn't it?

NORA: It's wonderful!

HELMER: Do you remember last Christmas? For a full three weeks beforehand you
shut yourself up every evening till long after midnight, making ornaments for
the Christmas Tree and all the other fine things that were to be a surprise to
us. It was the dullest three weeks I ever spent!

NORA: I didn't find it dull.

HELMER: [*smiling*] But there was precious little result, Nora.

75   NORA: Oh, you shouldn't tease me about that again. How could I help the cat's
going in and tearing everything to pieces?

HELMER: Of course you couldn't, poor little girl. You had the best of intentions to
please us all, and that's the main thing. But it is a good thing that our hard
times are over.

NORA: Yes, it is really wonderful.

HELMER: This time I needn't sit here and be dull all alone, and you needn't ruin
your dear eyes and your pretty little hands—

NORA: [*clapping her hands*] No, Torvald, I needn't any longer, need I! It's wonderfully lovely to hear you say so! [*taking his arm*] Now I will tell you how I have
been thinking we ought to arrange things, Torvald. As soon as Christmas is
over—[*A bell rings in the hall.*] There's the bell. [*She tidies the room a little.*]
There's someone at the door. What a nuisance!

80　HELMER:　If it is a caller, remember I am not at home.

　　MAID:　[*in the doorway*] A lady to see you, ma'am—a stranger.

　　NORA:　Ask her to come in.

　　MAID:　[*to* HELMER] The doctor came at the same time, sir.

　　HELMER:　Did he go straight into my room?

85　MAID:　Yes sir.

[HELMER *goes into his room. The* MAID *ushers in* MRS. LINDE, *who is in travelling dress, and shuts the door.*]

MRS. LINDE:　[*in a dejected and timid voice*] How do you do, Nora?

NORA:　[*doubtfully*] How do you do—

MRS. LINDE:　You don't recognise me, I suppose.

NORA:　No, I don't know—yes, to be sure, I seem to—[*suddenly*] Yes! Christine! Is it really you?

90　MRS. LINDE:　Yes, it is I.

NORA:　Christine! To think of my not recognising you! And yet how could I—[*in a gentle voice*] How you have altered, Christine!

MRS. LINDE:　Yes, I have indeed. In nine, ten long years—

NORA:　Is it so long since we met? I suppose it is. The last eight years have been a happy time for me, I can tell you. And so now you have come into the town, and have taken this long journey in winter—that was plucky of you.

MRS. LINDE:　I arrived by steamer this morning.

95　NORA:　To have some fun at Christmas-time, of course. How delightful! We will have such fun together! But take off your things. You are not cold, I hope. [*helps her*] Now we will sit down by the stove, and be cosy. No, take this arm-chair; I will sit here in the rocking-chair. [*takes her hands*] Now you look like your old self again; it was only the first moment—You are a little paler, Christine, and perhaps a little thinner.

MRS. LINDE:　And much, much older, Nora.

NORA:　Perhaps a little older; very, very little; certainly not much. [*stops suddenly and speaks seriously*] What a thoughtless creature I am, chattering away like this. My poor, dear Christine, do forgive me.

MRS. LINDE:　What do you mean, Nora?

NORA:　[*gently*] Poor Christine, you are a widow.

100　MRS. LINDE:　Yes; it is three years ago now.

NORA:　Yes, I knew; I saw it in the papers. I assure you, Christine, I meant ever so often to write to you at the time, but I always put it off and something always prevented me.

MRS. LINDE:　I quite understand, dear.

NORA:　It was very bad of me, Christine. Poor thing, how you must have suffered. And he left you nothing?

MRS. LINDE:　No.

105　NORA:　And no children?

MRS. LINDE:　No.

NORA:　Nothing at all, then?

MRS. LINDE:　Not even any sorrow or grief to live upon.

NORA: [*looking incredulously at her*] But, Christine, is that possible?

110 MRS. LINDE: [*smiles sadly and strokes her hair*] It sometimes happens, Nora.

NORA: So you are quite alone. How dreadfully sad that must be. I have three lovely children. You can't see them just now, for they are out with their nurse. But now you must tell me all about it.

MRS. LINDE: No, no; I want to hear you.

NORA: No, you must begin. I mustn't be selfish to-day; to-day I must only think of your affairs. But there is one thing I must tell you. Do you know we have just had a great piece of good luck?

MRS. LINDE: No, what is it?

115 NORA: Just fancy, my husband has been made manager of the Bank!

MRS. LINDE: Your husband? What good luck!

NORA: Yes, tremendous! A barrister's[3] profession is such an uncertain thing, especially if he won't undertake unsavoury cases; and naturally Torvald has never been willing to do that, and I quite agree with him. You may imagine how pleased we are! He is to take up his work in the Bank at the New Year, and then he will have a big salary and lots of commissions. For the future we can live quite differently—we can do just as we like. I feel so relieved and so happy, Christine! It will be splendid to have heaps of money and not need to have any anxiety, won't it?

MRS. LINDE: Yes, anyhow I think it would be delightful to have what one needs.

NORA: No, not only what one needs, but heaps and heaps of money.

120 MRS. LINDE: [*smiling*] Nora, Nora haven't you learnt sense yet? In our schooldays you were a great spendthrift.

NORA: [*laughing*] Yes, that is what Torvald says now. [*wags her finger at her*] But "Nora, Nora" is not so silly as you think. We have not been in a position for me to waste money. We have both had to work.

MRS. LINDE: You too?

NORA: Yes; odds and ends, needlework, crochet-work, embroidery, and that kind of thing. [*dropping her voice*] And other things as well. You know Torvald left his office when we were married? There was no prospect of promotion there, and he had to try and earn more than before. But during the first year he overworked himself dreadfully. You see, he had to make money every way he could, and he worked early and late; but he couldn't stand it, and fell dreadfully ill, and the doctors said it was necessary for him to go south.

MRS. LINDE: You spent a whole year in Italy didn't you?

125 NORA: Yes. It was no easy matter to get away, I can tell you. It was just as Ivar was born; but naturally we had to go. It was a wonderfully beautiful journey, and it saved Torvald's life. But it cost a tremendous lot of money, Christine.

MRS. LINDE: So I should think.

NORA: It cost about two hundred and fifty pounds. That's a lot, isn't it?

MRS. LINDE: Yes, and in emergencies like that it is lucky to have the money.

NORA: I ought to tell you that we had it from papa.

130 MRS. LINDE: Oh, I see. It was just about that time that he died, wasn't it?

---

[3]**barrister's** lawyer's

NORA: Yes; and, just think of it, I couldn't go and nurse him. I was expecting little Ivar's birth every day and I had my poor sick Torvald to look after. My dear, kind father—I never saw him again, Christine. That was the saddest time I have known since our marriage.

MRS. LINDE: I know how fond you were of him. And then you went off to Italy?

NORA: Yes; you see we had money then, and the doctors insisted on our going, so we started a month later.

MRS. LINDE: And your husband came back quite well?

135 NORA: As sound as a bell!

MRS. LINDE: But—the doctor?

NORA: What doctor?

MRS. LINDE: I thought your maid said the gentleman who arrived here just as I did was the doctor?

NORA: Yes, that was Doctor Rank, but he doesn't come here professionally. He is our greatest friend, and comes in at least once every day. No, Torvald has not had an hour's illness since then, and our children are strong and healthy and so am I. [*jumps up and claps her hands*] Christine! Christine! it's good to be alive and happy!—But how horrid of me; I am talking of nothing but my own affairs. [*sits on a stool near her, and rests her arms on her knees*] You mustn't be angry with me. Tell me, is it really true that you did not love your husband? Why did you marry him?

140 MRS. LINDE: My mother was alive then, and was bedridden and helpless, and I had to provide for my two younger brothers; so I did not think I was justified in refusing his offer.

NORA: No, perhaps you were quite right. He was rich at that time, then?

MRS. LINDE: I believe he was quite well off. But his business was a precarious one; and, when he died, it all went to pieces and there was nothing left.

NORA: And then?—

MRS. LINDE: Well, I had to turn my hand to anything I could find—first a small shop, then a small school, and so on. The last three years have seemed like one long working-day, with no rest. Now it is at an end, Nora. My poor mother needs me no more, for she is gone; and the boys do not need me either; they have got situations and can shift for themselves.

145 NORA: What a relief you must feel it—

MRS. LINDE: No, indeed; I only feel my life unspeakably empty. No one to live for any more. [*gets up restlessly*] That was why I could not stand the life in my little backwater any longer. I hope it may be easier here to find something which will busy me and occupy my thoughts. If only I could have the good luck to get some regular work—office work of some kind—

NORA: But, Christine, that is so frightfully tiring, and you look tired out now. You had far better go away to some watering-place.

MRS. LINDE: [*walking to the window*] I have no father to give me money for a journey, Nora.

NORA: [*rising*] Oh, don't be angry with me.

150 MRS. LINDE: [*going up to her*] It is you that must not be angry with me, dear. The worst of a position like mine is that it makes one so bitter. No one to work

for, and yet obliged to be always on the look-out for chances. One must live, and so one becomes selfish. When you told me of the happy turn your fortunes have taken—you will hardly believe it—I was delighted not so much on your account as on my own.

NORA: How do you mean?—Oh, I understand. You mean that perhaps Torvald could get you something to do.

MRS. LINDE: Yes, that was what I was thinking of.

NORA: He must, Christine. Just leave it to me; I will broach the subject very cleverly— I will think of something that will please him very much. It will make me so happy to be of some use to you.

MRS. LINDE: How kind you are, Nora, to be so anxious to help me! It is doubly kind in you, for you know so little of the burdens and troubles of life.

155 NORA: I—? I know so little of them?

MRS. LINDE: [*smiling*] My dear! Small household cares and that sort of thing!—You are a child, Nora.

NORA: [*tosses her head and crosses the stage*] You ought not to be so superior.

MRS. LINDE: No?

NORA: You are just like the others. They all think that I am incapable of anything really serious—

160 MRS. LINDE: Come, come—

NORA: —that I have gone through nothing in this world of cares.

MRS. LINDE: But, my dear Nora, you have just told me all your troubles.

NORA: Pooh!—those were trifles. [*lowering her voice*] I have not told you the important thing.

MRS. LINDE: The important thing? What do you mean?

165 NORA: You look down upon me altogether, Christine—but you ought not to. You are proud, aren't you, of having worked so hard and so long for your mother?

MRS. LINDE: Indeed, I don't look down on any one. But it is true that I am both proud and glad to think that I was privileged to make the end of my mother's life almost free from care.

NORA: And you are proud to think of what you have done for your brothers.

MRS. LINDE: I think I have the right to be.

NORA: I think so, too. But now, listen to this; I too have something to be proud of and glad of.

170 MRS. LINDE: I have no doubt you have. But what do you refer to?

NORA: Speak low. Suppose Torvald were to hear! He mustn't on any account—no one in the world must know, Christine, except you.

MRS. LINDE: But what is it?

NORA: Come here [*pulls her down on the sofa beside her*] Now I will show you that I too have something to be proud and glad of. It was I who saved Torvald's life.

MRS. LINDE: "Saved"? How?

175 NORA: I told you about our trip to Italy. Torvald would never have recovered if he had not gone there—

MRS. LINDE: Yes, but your father gave you the necessary funds.

NORA: [*smiling*] Yes, that is what Torvald and all the others think, but—

MRS. LINDE: But—

NORA: Papa didn't give us a shilling. It was I who procured the money.

180 MRS. LINDE: You? All that large sum?

NORA: Two hundred and fifty pounds. What do you think of that?

MRS. LINDE: But, Nora, how could you possibly do it? Did you win a prize in the Lottery?

NORA: [*contemptuously*] In the Lottery? There would have been no credit in that.

MRS. LINDE: But where did you get it from, then?

185 NORA: [*humming and smiling with an air of mystery*] Hm, hm! Aha!

MRS. LINDE: Because you couldn't have borrowed it.

NORA: Couldn't I? Why not?

MRS. LINDE: No, a wife cannot borrow without her husband's consent.

NORA: [*tossing her head*] Oh, if it is a wife who has any head for business—a wife who has the wit to be a little bit clever—

190 MRS. LINDE: I don't understand it at all, Nora.

NORA: There is no need you should. I never said I had borrowed the money. I may have got it some other way. [*lies back on the sofa*] Perhaps I got it from some other admirer. When anyone is as attractive as I am—

MRS. LINDE: You are a mad creature.

NORA: Now, you know you're full of curiosity, Christine.

MRS. LINDE: Listen to me, Nora dear. Haven't you been a little bit imprudent?

195 NORA: [*sits up straight*] Is it imprudent to save your husband's life?

MRS. LINDE: It seems to me imprudent, without his knowledge, to—

NORA: But it was absolutely necessary that he should not know! My goodness, can't you understand that? It was necessary he should have no idea what a dangerous condition he was in. It was to me that the doctors came and said that his life was in danger, and that the only thing to save him was to live in the south. Do you suppose I didn't try, first of all, to get what I wanted as if it were for myself? I told him how much I should love to travel abroad like other young wives; I tried tears and entreaties with him; I told him that he ought to remember the condition I was in, and that he ought to be kind and indulgent to me; I even hinted that he might raise a loan. That nearly made him angry, Christine. He said I was thoughtless, and that it was his duty as my husband not to indulge me in my whims and caprices—as I believe he called them. Very well I thought, you must be saved—and that was how I came to devise a way out of the difficulty—

MRS. LINDE: And did your husband never get to know from your father that the money had not come from him?

NORA: No, never. Papa died just at that time. I had meant to let him into the secret and beg him never to reveal it. But he was so ill then—alas, there never was any need to tell him.

200 MRS. LINDE: And since then have you never told your secret to your husband?

NORA: Good Heavens, no! How could you think so? A man who has such strong opinions about these things! And besides, how painful and humiliating it would be for Torvald, with his manly independence, to know that he owed me anything! It would upset our mutual relations altogether; our beautiful happy home would no longer be what it is now.

MRS. LINDE: Do you mean never to tell him about it?

NORA: [*meditatively, and with a half smile*] Yes—some day, perhaps, after many years, when I am no longer as nice-looking as I am now. Don't laugh at me! I mean of course, when Torvald is no longer as devoted to me as he is now; when my dancing and dressing-up and reciting have palled on him; then it may be a good thing to have something in reserve—[*breaking off*] What nonsense! That time will never come. Now, what do you think of my great secret, Christine? Do you still think I am of no use? I can tell you, too, that this affair has caused me a lot of worry. It has been by no means easy for me to meet my engagements punctually. I may tell you that there is something that is called, in business, quarterly interest, and another thing called payment in instalments, and it is always so dreadfully difficult to manage them. I have had to save a little here and there, where I could, you understand. I have not been able to put aside much from my housekeeping money, for Torvald must have a good table. I couldn't let my children be shabbily dressed; I have felt obliged to use up all he gave me for them, the sweet little darlings!

MRS. LINDE: So it has all had to come out of your own necessaries of life, poor Nora?

205 NORA: Of course. Besides, I was the one responsible for it. Whenever Torvald has given me the money for new dresses and such things, I have never spent more than half of it; I have always bought the simplest and cheapest things. Thank Heaven, any clothes look well on me, and so Torvald has never noticed it. But it was often very hard on me, Christine—because it is delightful to be really well dressed, isn't it?

MRS. LINDE: Quite so.

NORA: Well, then I have found other ways of earning money. Last winter I was lucky enough to get a lot of copying to do; so I locked myself up and sat writing every evening until quite late at night. Many a time I was desperately tired; but all the same it was a tremendous pleasure to sit there working and earning money. It was like being a man.

MRS. LINDE: How much have you been able to pay off in that way?

NORA: I can't tell you exactly. You see, it is very difficult to keep an account of a business matter of that kind. I only know that I have paid every penny that I could scrape together. Many a time I was at my wit's end. [*smiles*] Then I used to sit here and imagine that a rich old gentleman had fallen in love with me—

210 MRS. LINDE: What! Who was it?

NORA: Be quiet!—that he had died; and that when his will was opened it contained, written in big letters, the instruction: "The lovely Mrs. Nora Helmer is to have all I possess paid over to her at once in cash."

MRS. LINDE: But, my dear Nora—who could the man be?

NORA: Good gracious, can't you understand? There was no old gentleman at all; it was only something that I used to sit here and imagine, when I couldn't think of any way of procuring money. But it's all the same now; the tiresome old person can stay where he is, as far as I am concerned; I don't care about him or his will either, for I am free from care now. [*jumps up*] My goodness, it's delightful to think of, Christine! Free from care! To be able to be free from care, quite free from care; to be able to play and romp with the children; to be able to keep the house beautifully and have everything just as Torvald likes it! And, think of it, soon the spring will come and the big blue sky! Perhaps we shall be able to take a little trip—perhaps I shall see the sea again! Oh, it's a wonderful thing to be alive and be happy. [*A bell is heard in the hall.*]

MRS. LINDE: [*rising*] There is the bell; perhaps I had better go.

215   NORA: No, don't go; no one will come in here; it is sure to be for Torvald.

SERVANT: [*at the hall door*] Excuse me, ma'am—there is a gentleman to see the master, and as the doctor is with him—

NORA: Who is it?

KROGSTAD: [*at the door*] It is I, Mrs. Helmer. [*MRS. LINDE starts, trembles, and turns to the window.*]

NORA: [*takes a step towards him, and speaks in a strained, low voice*] You? What is it? What do you want to see my husband about?

220   KROGSTAD: Bank business—in a way. I have a small post in the Bank, and I hear your husband is to be our chief now—

NORA: Then it is—

KROGSTAD: Nothing but dry business matters, Mrs. Helmer; absolutely nothing else.

NORA: Be so good as to go into the study, then. [*She bows indifferently to him and shuts the door into the hall; then comes back and makes up the fire in the stove.*]

MRS. LINDE: Nora—who was that man?

225   NORA: A lawyer, of the name of Krogstad.

MRS. LINDE: Then it really was he.

NORA: Do you know the man?

MRS. LINDE: I used to—many years ago. At one time he was a solicitor's clerk in our town.

NORA: Yes, he was.

230   MRS. LINDE: He is greatly altered.

NORA: He made a very unhappy marriage.

MRS. LINDE: He is a widower now, isn't he?

NORA: With several children. There now, it is burning up.

[*Shuts the door of the stove and moves the rocking-chair aside.*]

MRS. LINDE: They say he carries on various kinds of business.

235   NORA: Really! Perhaps he does; I don't know anything about it. But don't let us think of business; it is so tiresome.

DOCTOR RANK: [*comes out of HELMER's study. Before he shuts the door he calls to him.*] No, my dear fellow, I won't disturb you; I would rather go in to your wife for a little while. [*shuts the door and sees MRS. LINDE*] I beg your pardon; I am afraid I am disturbing you too.

NORA: No, not at all. [*introducing him*] Doctor Rank, Mrs. Linde.

RANK: I have often heard Mrs. Linde's name mentioned here. I think I passed you on the stairs when I arrived, Mrs. Linde?

MRS. LINDE: Yes, I go up very slowly; I can't manage stairs well.

240   RANK: Ah! some slight internal weakness?

MRS. LINDE: No, the fact is I have been overworking myself.

RANK: Nothing more than that? Then I suppose you have come to town to amuse yourself with our entertainments?

MRS. LINDE: I have come to look for work.

RANK: Is that a good cure for overwork?

245 MRS. LINDE: One must live, Doctor Rank.

RANK: Yes, the general opinion seems to be that it is necessary.

NORA: Look here, Doctor Rank—you know you want to live.

RANK: Certainly. However wretched I may feel, I want to prolong the agony as long as possible. All my patients are like that. And so are those who are morally diseased; one of them, and a bad case too, is at this very moment with Helmer—

MRS. LINDE: [*sadly*] Ah!

250 NORA: Whom do you mean?

RANK: A lawyer of the name of Krogstad, a fellow you don't know at all. He suffers from a diseased moral character, Mrs. Helmer; but even he began talking of its being highly important that he should live.

NORA: Did he? What did he want to speak to Torvald about?

RANK: I have no idea; I only heard that it was something about the Bank.

NORA: I didn't know this—what's his name—Krogstad had anything to do with the Bank.

255 RANK: Yes, he has some sort of appointment there. [*to* MRS. LINDE] I don't know whether you find also in your part of the world that there are certain people who go zealously snuffing about to smell out moral corruption, and, as soon as they have found some, put the person concerned into some lucrative position where they can keep their eye on him. Healthy natures are left out in the cold.

MRS. LINDE: Still I think the sick are those who most need taking care of.

RANK: [*shrugging his shoulders*] Yes, there you are. That is the sentiment that is turning Society into a sickhouse.

[NORA, *who has been absorbed in her thoughts, breaks out into smothered laughter and claps her hands.*]

RANK: Why do you laugh at that? Have you any notion what Society really is?

NORA: What do I care about tiresome Society? I am laughing at something quite different, something extremely amusing. Tell me, Doctor Rank, are all the people who are employed in the Bank dependent on Torvald now?

260 RANK: Is that what you find so extremely amusing?

NORA: [*smiling and humming*] That's my affair! [*walking about the room*] It's perfectly glorious to think that we have—that Torvald has so much power over so many people. [*takes the packet from her pocket*] Doctor Rank, what do you say to a macaroon?

RANK: What, macaroons? I thought they were forbidden here.

NORA: Yes, but these are some Christine gave me.

MRS. LINDE: What! I?—

265 NORA: Oh, well, don't be alarmed! You couldn't know that Torvald had forbidden them. I must tell you that he is afraid they will spoil my teeth. But, bah!—once

in a way—That's so, isn't it, Doctor Rank? By your leave? [*puts a macaroon into his mouth*] You must have one too, Christine. And I shall have one, just a little one—or at most two. [*walking about*] I am tremendously happy. There is just one thing in the world now that I should dearly love to do.

RANK: Well, what is that?

NORA: It's something I should dearly love to say, if Torvald could hear me.

RANK: Well, why can't you say it?

NORA: No, I daren't; it's so shocking.

270 MRS. LINDE: Shocking?

RANK: Well, I should not advise you to say it. Still, with us you might. What is it you would so much like to say if Torvald could hear you?

NORA: I should just love to say—Well, I'm damned!

RANK: Are you mad?

MRS. LINDE: Nora, dear—!

275 RANK: Say it, here he is!

NORA: [*hiding the packet*] Hush! Hush! Hush!

[*HELMER comes out of his room, with his coat over his arm and his hat in his hands.*]

NORA: Well, Torvald dear, have you got rid of him?

HELMER: Yes, he has just gone.

NORA: Let me introduce you—this is Christine, who has come to town.

280 HELMER: Christine—? Excuse me, but I don't know—

NORA: Mrs. Linde, dear; Christine Linde.

HELMER: Of course. A school friend of my wife's, I presume?

MRS. LINDE: Yes, we have known each other since then.

NORA: And just think, she has taken a long journey in order to see you.

285 HELMER: What do you mean?

MRS. LINDE: No, really, I—

NORA: Christine is tremendously clever at book-keeping, and she is frightfully anxious to work under some clever man, so as to perfect herself—

HELMER: Very sensible, Mrs. Linde.

NORA: And when she heard you had been appointed manager of the Bank—the news was telegraphed, you know—she travelled here as quick as she could. Torvald, I am sure you will be able to do something for Christine, for my sake, won't you?

290 HELMER: Well, it is not altogether impossible. I presume you are a widow, Mrs. Linde?

MRS. LINDE: Yes.

HELMER: And have had some experience of book-keeping?

MRS. LINDE: Yes, a fair amount.

HELMER: Ah! well, it's very likely I may be able to find something for you—

295 NORA: [*clapping her hands*] What did I tell you? What did I tell you?

HELMER: You have just come at a fortunate moment, Mrs. Linde.

MRS. LINDE: How am I to thank you?

HELMER: There is no need. [*puts on his coat*] But to-day you must excuse me—

RANK: Wait a minute; I will come with you.

[*Brings his fur coat from the hall and warms it at the fire.*]

300 NORA: Don't be long away, Torvald dear.

HELMER: About an hour, not more.

NORA: Are you going too, Christine?

MRS. LINDE: [*putting on her cloak*] Yes, I must go and look for a room.

HELMER: Oh, well then, we can walk down the street together.

305 NORA: [*helping her*] What a pity it is we are so short of space here: I am afraid it is impossible for us—

MRS. LINDE: Please don't think of it! Good-bye, Nora dear, and many thanks.

NORA: Good-bye for the present. Of course you will come back this evening. And you too, Dr. Rank. What do you say? If you are well enough? Oh, you must be! Wrap yourself up well.

[*They go to the door all talking together. Children's voices are heard on the staircase.*]

NORA: There they are. There they are! [*She runs to open the door. The NURSE comes in with the children.*] Come in! Come in! [*stoops and kisses them*] Oh, you sweet blessings! Look at them, Christine! Aren't they darlings?

RANK: Don't let us stand here in the draught.

310 HELMER: Come along, Mrs. Linde; the place will only be bearable for a mother now!

[*RANK, HELMER and MRS. LINDE go downstairs. The NURSE comes forward with the children; NORA shuts the hall door.*]

NORA: How fresh and well you look! Such red cheeks!—like apples and roses. [*The children all talk at once while she speaks to them.*] Have you had great fun? That's splendid! What, you pulled both Emmy and Bob along on the sledge?—both at once?—that was good. You are a clever boy, Ivar. Let me take her for a little, Anne. My sweet little baby doll! [*takes the baby from the MAID and dances it up and down*] Yes, yes, mother will dance with Bob too. What! Have you been snowballing? I wish I had been there too! No, no, I will take their things off, Anne; please let me do it, it is such fun. Go in now, you look half frozen. There is some coffee for you on the stove.

[*The NURSE goes into the room on the left. NORA takes off the children's things and throws them about, while they all talk to her at once.*]

NORA: Really! Did a big dog run after you? But it didn't bite you? No, dogs don't bite nice little dolly children. You mustn't look at the parcels, Ivar. What are they? Ah, I daresay you would like to know. No, no—it's something nasty! Come, let us have a game! What shall we play at? Hide and Seek? Yes, we'll play Hide and Seek. Bob shall hide first. Must I hide? Very well, I'll hide first.

[*She and the children laugh and shout, and romp in and out of the room; at last NORA hides under the table, the children rush in and look for her, but do not see her; they hear her smothered laughter, run to the table, lift up the cloth and find her. Shouts of laughter. She crawls forward and pretends to frighten them. Fresh laughter. Meanwhile there has been a knock at the hall door, but none of them has noticed it. The door is half opened, and KROGSTAD appears. He waits a little; the game goes on.*]

KROGSTAD: Excuse me, Mrs. Helmer.

NORA: [*with a stifled cry, turns round and gets up on to her knees*] Ah! what do you want?

315 KROGSTAD: Excuse me, the outer door was ajar; I suppose someone forgot to shut it.

NORA: [*rising*] My husband is out, Mr. Krogstad.

KROGSTAD: I know that.

NORA: What do you want here, then?

KROGSTAD: A word with you.

320 NORA: With me?—[*to the children, gently*] Go in to nurse. What? No, the strange man won't do mother any harm. When he has gone we will have another game. [*She takes the children into the room on the left, and shuts the door after them.*] You want to speak to me?

KROGSTAD: Yes, I do.

NORA: To-day? It is not the first of the month yet.

KROGSTAD: No, it is Christmas Eve, and it will depend on yourself what sort of a Christmas you will spend.

NORA: What do you want? To-day it is absolutely impossible for me—

325 KROGSTAD: We won't talk about that till later on. This is something different. I presume you can give me a moment?

NORA: Yes—yes, I can—although—

KROGSTAD: Good. I was in Olsen's Restaurant and saw your husband going down the street—

NORA: Yes?

KROGSTAD: With a lady.

330 NORA: What then?

KROGSTAD: May I make so bold as to ask if it was a Mrs. Linde?

NORA: It was.

KROGSTAD: Just arrived in town?

NORA: Yes, to-day.

335 KROGSTAD: She is a great friend of yours, isn't she?

NORA: She is. But I don't see—

KROGSTAD: I knew her too, once upon a time.

NORA: I am aware of that.

KROGSTAD: Are you? So you know all about it; I thought as much. Then I can ask you, without beating about the bush—is Mrs. Linde to have an appointment in the Bank?

340 NORA: What right have you to question me, Mr. Krogstad?—You, one of my husband's subordinates! But since you ask, you shall know. Yes, Mrs. Linde is to have an appointment. And it was I who pleaded her cause, Mr. Krogstad, let me tell you that.

KROGSTAD: I was right in what I thought, then.

NORA: [*walking up and down the stage*] Sometimes one has a tiny little bit of influence, I should hope. Because one is a woman, it does not necessarily follow that—. When anyone is in a subordinate position, Mr. Krogstad, they should really be careful to avoid offending anyone who—who—

KROGSTAD: Who has influence?

NORA: Exactly.

345 KROGSTAD: [*changing his tone*] Mrs. Helmer, you will be so good as to use your influence on my behalf.

NORA: What? What do you mean?

KROGSTAD: You will be so kind as to see that I am allowed to keep my subordinate position in the Bank.

NORA: What do you mean by that? Who proposes to take your post away from you?

KROGSTAD: Oh, there is no necessity to keep up the pretence of ignorance. I can quite understand that your friend is not very anxious to expose herself to the chance of rubbing shoulders with me; and I quite understand, too, whom I have to thank for being turned out.

350 NORA: But I assure you—

KROGSTAD: Very likely; but, to come to the point, the time has come when I should advise you to use your influence to prevent that.

NORA: But, Mr. Krogstad, I *have* no influence.

KROGSTAD: Haven't you? I thought you said yourself just now—

NORA: Naturally I did not mean you to put that construction on it. I! What should make you think I have any influence of that kind with my husband?

355 KROGSTAD: Oh, I have known your husband from our student days. I don't suppose he is any more unassailable than other husbands.

NORA: If you speak slightingly of my husband, I shall turn you out of the house.

KROGSTAD: You are bold, Mrs. Helmer.

NORA: I am not afraid of you any longer. As soon as the New Year comes, I shall in a very short time be free of the whole thing.

KROGSTAD: [*controlling himself*] Listen to me, Mrs. Helmer. If necessary, I am prepared to fight for my small post in the Bank as if I were fighting for my life.

360 NORA: So it seems.

KROGSTAD: It is not only for the sake of the money; indeed, that weighs least with me in the matter. There is another reason—well, I may as well tell you. My position is this. I daresay you know, like everybody else, that once, many years ago, I was guilty of an indiscretion.

NORA: I think I have heard something of the kind.

KROGSTAD: The matter never came into court; but every way seemed to be closed to me after that. So I took to the business that you know of. I had to do something; and, honestly, I don't think I've been one of the worst. But now I must cut myself free from all that. My sons are growing up; for their sake I must try and win back as much respect as I can in the town. This post in the Bank was like the first step up for me—and now your husband is going to kick me downstairs again into the mud.

NORA: But you must believe me, Mr. Krogstad; it is not in my power to help you at all.

365 KROGSTAD: Then it is because you haven't the will; but I have means to compel you.

NORA: You don't mean that you will tell my husband that I owe you money?

KROGSTAD: Hm!—suppose I were to tell him?

NORA: It would be perfectly infamous of you. [*sobbing*] To think of his learning my secret, which has been my joy and pride, in such an ugly, clumsy way—that he should learn it from you! And it would put me in a horribly disagreeable position—

KROGSTAD: Only disagreeable?

370   NORA: [*impetuously*] Well, do it, then!—and it will be the worse for you. My husband will see for himself what a blackguard[4] you are, and you certainly won't keep your post then.

KROGSTAD: I asked you if it was only a disagreeable scene at home that you were afraid of?

NORA: If my husband does get to know of it, of course he will at once pay you what is still owing, and we shall have nothing more to do with you.

KROGSTAD: [*coming a step nearer*] Listen to me, Mrs. Helmer. Either you have a very bad memory or you know very little of business. I shall be obliged to remind you of a few details.

NORA: What do you mean?

375   KROGSTAD: When your husband was ill, you came to me to borrow two hundred and fifty pounds.

NORA: I didn't know any one else to go to.

KROGSTAD: I promised to get you that amount—

NORA: Yes, and you did so.

KROGSTAD: I promised to get you that amount, on certain conditions. Your mind was so taken up with your husband's illness, and you were so anxious to get the money for your journey, that you seem to have paid no attention to the conditions of our bargain. Therefore it will not be amiss if I remind you of them. Now, I promised to get the money on the security of a bond which I drew up.

380   NORA: Yes, and which I signed.

KROGSTAD: Good. But below your signature there were a few lines constituting your father a surety for the money; those lines your father should have signed.

NORA: Should? He did sign them.

KROGSTAD: I had left the date blank; that is to say your father should himself have inserted the date on which he signed the paper. Do you remember that?

NORA: Yes, I think I remember—

385   KROGSTAD: Then I gave you the bond to send by post to your father. Is that not so?

NORA: Yes.

KROGSTAD: And you naturally did so at once, because five or six days afterwards you brought me the bond with your father's signature. And then I gave you the money.

NORA: Well, haven't I been paying it off regularly?

KROGSTAD: Fairly so, yes. But—to come back to the matter in hand—that must have been a very trying time for you, Mrs. Helmer?

390   NORA: It was, indeed.

KROGSTAD: Your father was very ill, wasn't he?

NORA: He was very near his end.

KROGSTAD: And died soon afterwards?

NORA: Yes.

[4]**blackguard** scoundrel

395 KROGSTAD: Tell me, Mrs. Helmer, can you by any chance remember what day your
         father died?—on what day of the month, I mean.
NORA: Papa died on the 29th of September.
KROGSTAD: That is correct; I have ascertained it for myself. And, as that is so, there
         is a discrepancy [*taking a paper from his pocket*] which I cannot account for.
NORA: What discrepancy? I don't know—
KROGSTAD: The discrepancy consists, Mrs. Helmer, in the fact that your father
         signed this bond three days after his death.
400 NORA: What do you mean? I don't understand—
KROGSTAD: Your father died on the 29th of September. But, look here; your father
         has dated his signature the 2nd of October. It is a discrepancy, isn't it? [*NORA
         is silent.*] Can you explain it to me? [*NORA is still silent.*] It is a remarkable
         thing, too, that the words "2nd of October," as well as the year, are not
         written in your father's handwriting but in one that I think I know. Well, of
         course it can be explained; your father may have forgotten to date his signa-
         ture, and someone else may have dated it haphazard before they knew of his
         death. There is no harm in that. It all depends on the signature of the name;
         and *that* is genuine, I suppose, Mrs. Helmer? It was your father himself who
         signed his name here?
NORA: [*after a short pause, throws her head up and looks defiantly at him*] No, it
         was not. It was I that wrote papa's name.
KROGSTAD: Are you aware that is a dangerous confession?
NORA: In what way? You shall have your money soon.
405 KROGSTAD: Let me ask you a question; why did you not send the paper to your
         father?
NORA: It was impossible; papa was so ill. If I had asked him for his signature, I
         should have had to tell him what the money was to be used for; and when he
         was so ill himself I couldn't tell him that my husband's life was in danger—it
         was impossible.
KROGSTAD: It would have been better for you if you had given up your trip abroad.
NORA: No, that was impossible. That trip was to save my husband's life; I couldn't
         give that up.
KROGSTAD: But did it never occur to you that you were committing a fraud on me?
410 NORA: I couldn't take that into account; I didn't trouble myself about you at all. I
         couldn't bear you, because you put so many heartless difficulties in my way,
         although you knew what a dangerous condition my husband was in.
KROGSTAD: Mrs. Helmer, you evidently do not realise clearly what it is that you
         have been guilty of. But I can assure you that my one false step, which lost
         me all my reputation, was nothing more or nothing worse than what you
         have done.
NORA: You? Do you ask me to believe that you were brave enough to run a risk
         to save your wife's life?
KROGSTAD: The law cares nothing about motives.
NORA: Then it must be a very foolish law.
415 KROGSTAD: Foolish or not, it is the law by which you will be judged, if I produce
         this paper in court.

NORA: I don't believe it. Is a daughter not to be allowed to spare her dying father anxiety and care? Is a wife not to be allowed to save her husband's life? I don't know much about law; but I am certain that there must be laws permitting such things as that. Have you no knowledge of such laws—you who are a lawyer? You must be a very poor lawyer, Mr. Krogstad.

KROGSTAD: Maybe. But matters of business—such business as you and I have had together—do you think I don't understand that? Very well. Do as you please. But let me tell you this—if I lose my position a second time, you shall lose yours with me.

[*He bows, and goes out through the hall.*]

NORA: [*appears buried in thought for a short time, then tosses her head*] Nonsense! Trying to frighten me like that!—I am not so silly as he thinks. [*begins to busy herself putting the children's things in order*] And yet—? No, it's impossible! I did it for love's sake.

THE CHILDREN: [*in the doorway on the left*] Mother, the stranger man has gone out through the gate.

420   NORA: Yes, dears, I know. But, don't tell anyone about the stranger man. Do you hear? Not even papa.

CHILDREN: No, mother; but will you come and play again?

NORA: No, no—not now.

CHILDREN: But, mother, you promised us.

NORA: Yes, but I can't now. Run away in; I have such a lot to do. Run away in, my sweet little darlings. [*She gets them into the room by degrees and shuts the door on them; then sits down on the sofa, takes up a piece of needlework and sews a few stitches, but soon stops.*] No! [*throws down the work, gets up, goes to the hall door and calls out*] Helen! bring the Tree in. [*goes to the table on the left, opens a drawer, and stops again*] No, no! it is quite impossible!

425   MAID: [*coming in with the Tree*] Where shall I put it, ma'am?

NORA: Here, in the middle of the floor.

MAID: Shall I get you anything else?

NORA: No, thank you. I have all I want.

[*Exit* MAID.]

NORA: [*begins dressing the tree*] A candle here—and flowers here—. The horrible man! It's all nonsense—there's nothing wrong. The Tree shall be splendid! I will do everything I can think of to please you, Torvald!—I will sing for you, dance for you—[HELMER *comes in with some papers under his arm*] Oh! are you back already?

430   HELMER: Yes. Has anyone been here?

NORA: Here? No.

HELMER: That is strange. I saw Krogstad going out of the gate.

NORA: Did you? Oh yes, I forgot, Krogstad was here for a moment.

HELMER: Nora, I can see from your manner that he has been here begging you to say a good word for him.

435   NORA: Yes.

HELMER: And you were to appear to do it of your own accord; you were to conceal from me the fact of his having been here; didn't he beg that of you too?

NORA: Yes, Torvald, but—

HELMER: Nora, Nora, and you would be a party to that sort of thing? To have any talk with a man like that, and give him any sort of promise? And to tell me a lie into the bargain?

NORA: A lie—?

440   HELMER: Didn't you tell me no one had been here? [*shakes his finger at her*] My little song-bird must never do that again. A song-bird must have a clean beak to chirp with—no false notes! [*puts his arm round her waist*] That is so, isn't it? Yes, I am sure it is. [*lets her go*] We will say no more about it. [*sits down by the stove*] How warm and snug it is here!

[*Turns over his papers.*]

NORA: [*after a short pause, during which she busies herself with the Christmas Tree*] Torvald!

HELMER: Yes.

NORA: I am looking forward tremendously to the fancy dress ball at the Stenborgs' the day after to-morrow.

HELMER: And I am tremendously curious to see what you are going to surprise me with.

445   NORA: It was very silly of me to want to do that.

HELMER: What do you mean?

NORA: I can't hit upon anything that will do; everything I think of seems so silly and insignificant.

HELMER: Does my little Nora acknowledge that at last?

NORA: [*standing behind his chair with her arms on the back of it*] Are you very busy, Torvald?

450   HELMER: Well—

NORA: What are all those papers?

HELMER: Bank business.

NORA: Already?

HELMER: I have got authority from the retiring manager to undertake the necessary changes in the staff and in the rearrangement of the work; and I must make use of the Christmas week for that, so as to have everything in order for the new year.

455   NORA: Then that was why this poor Krogstad—

HELMER: Hm!

NORA: [*leans against the back of his chair and strokes his hair*] If you hadn't been so busy I should have asked you a tremendously big favour, Torvald.

HELMER: What is that? Tell me.

NORA: There is no one has such good taste as you. And I do so want to look nice at the fancy-dress ball. Torvald, couldn't you take me in hand and decide what I shall go as, and what sort of a dress I shall wear?

460   HELMER: Aha! so my obstinate little woman is obliged to get someone to come to her rescue?

NORA: Yes, Torvald, I can't get along a bit without your help.

HELMER: Very well, I will think it over, we shall manage to hit upon something.

NORA: That is nice of you. [*Goes to the Christmas Tree. A short pause.*] How pretty the red flowers look—. But, tell me, was it really something very bad that this Krogstad was guilty of?

HELMER: He forged someone's name. Have you any idea what that means?

465 NORA: Isn't it possible that he was driven to do it by necessity?

HELMER: Yes; or, as in so many cases, by imprudence. I am not so heartless as to condemn a man altogether because of a single false step of that kind.

NORA: No you wouldn't, would you, Torvald?

HELMER: Many a man has been able to retrieve his character, if he has openly confessed his fault and taken his punishment.

NORA: Punishment—?

470 HELMER: But Krogstad did nothing of that sort; he got himself out of it by a cunning trick, and that is why he has gone under altogether.

NORA: But do you think it would—?

HELMER: Just think how a guilty man like that has to lie and play the hypocrite with everyone, how he has to wear a mask in the presence of those near and dear to him, even before his own wife and children. And about the children— that is the most terrible part of it all, Nora.

NORA: How?

HELMER: Because such an atmosphere of lies infects and poisons the whole life of a home. Each breath the children take in such a house is full of the germs of evil.

475 NORA: [*coming nearer him*] Are you sure of that?

HELMER: My dear, I have often seen it in the course of my life as a lawyer. Almost everyone who has gone to the bad early in life has had a deceitful mother.

NORA: Why do you only say—mother?

HELMER: It seems most commonly to be the mother's influence, though naturally a bad father's would have the same result. Every lawyer is familiar with the fact. This Krogstad, now, has been persistently poisoning his own children with lies and dissimulation; that is why I say he has lost all moral character. [*holds out his hands to her*] That is why my sweet little Nora must promise me not to plead his cause. Give me your hand on it. Come, come, what is this? Give me your hand. There now, that's settled. I assure you it would be quite impossible for me to work with him; I literally feel physically ill when I am in the company of such people.

NORA: [*takes her hand out of his and goes to the opposite side of the Christmas Tree*] How hot it is in here; and I have such a lot to do.

480 HELMER: [*getting up and putting his papers in order*] Yes, and I must try and read through some of these before dinner; and I must think about your costume, too. And it is just possible I may have something ready in gold paper to hang up on the Tree. [*Puts his hand on her head.*] My precious little singing-bird!

[*He goes into his room and shuts the door after him.*]

NORA: [*after a pause, whispers*] No, no—it isn't true. It's impossible; it must be impossible.

[*The* NURSE *opens the door on the left.*]

NURSE: The little ones are begging so hard to be allowed to come in to mamma.
NORA: No, no, no! Don't let them come in to me! You stay with them, Anne.
NURSE: Very well, ma'am.

[*Shuts the door.*]

485   NORA: [*pale with terror*] Deprave my little children? Poison my home? [*a short
    pause. Then she tosses her head.*] It's not true. It can't possibly be true.

ACT 2

THE SAME SCENE. *The Christmas Tree is in the corner by the piano, stripped of its ornaments and with burnt-down candle-ends on its dishevelled branches.* NORA's *cloak
and hat are lying on the sofa. She is alone in the room, walking about uneasily. She
stops by the sofa and takes up her cloak.*

NORA: [*drops the cloak*] Someone is coming now! [*goes to the door and listens*]
    No—it is no one. Of course, no one will come to-day, Christmas Day—nor
    tomorrow either. But, perhaps—[*opens the door and looks out*] No, nothing in
    the letter-box; it is quite empty. [*comes forward*] What rubbish! of course he
    can't be in earnest about it. Such a thing couldn't happen; it is impossible—
    I have three little children.

[*Enter the* NURSE *from the room on the left, carrying a big cardboard box.*]

NURSE: At last I have found the box with the fancy dress.
NORA: Thanks; put it on the table.
NURSE: [*doing so*] But it is very much in want of mending.
5   NORA: I should like to tear it into a hundred thousand pieces.
NURSE: What an idea! It can easily be put in order—just a little patience.
NORA: Yes, I will go and get Mrs. Linde to come and help me with it.
NURSE: What, out again? In this horrible weather? You will catch cold, ma'am, and
    make yourself ill.
NORA: Well, worse than that might happen. How are the children?
10   NURSE: The poor little souls are playing with their Christmas presents, but—
NORA: Do they ask much for me?
NURSE: You see, they are so accustomed to have their mamma with them.
NORA: Yes, but, nurse, I shall not be able to be so much with them now as I was
    before.
NURSE: Oh well, young children easily get accustomed to anything.
15   NORA: Do you think so? Do you think they would forget their mother if she went
    away altogether?
NURSE: Good heavens!—went away altogether?
NORA: Nurse, I want you to tell me something I have often wondered about—how
    could you have the heart to put your own child out among strangers?
NURSE: I was obliged to, if I wanted to be little Nora's nurse.
NORA: Yes, but how could you be willing to do it?

20   NURSE: What, when I was going to get such a good place by it? A poor girl who
has got into trouble should be glad to. Besides, that wicked man didn't do a
single thing for me.

NORA: But I suppose your daughter has quite forgotten you.

NURSE: No, indeed she hasn't. She wrote to me when she was confirmed, and
when she was married.

NORA: [*putting her arms round her neck*] Dear old Anne, you were a good mother
to me when I was little.

NURSE: Little Nora, poor dear, had no other mother but me.

25   NORA: And if my little ones had no other mother, I am sure you would—What
nonsense I am talking! [*opens the box*] Go in to them. Now I must—. You will
see tomorrow how charming I shall look.

NURSE: I am sure there will be no one at the ball so charming as you, ma'am.

[*Goes into the room on the left.*]

NORA: [*begins to unpack the box, but soon pushes it away from her*] If only I dared
go out. If only no one would come. If only I could be sure nothing would
happen here in the meantime. Stuff and nonsense! No one will come. Only I
mustn't think about it. I will brush my muff. What, lovely gloves! Out of my
thoughts, out of my thoughts! One, two, three, four, five, six—[*Screams.*] Ah!
there is someone coming—

[*Makes a movement towards the door, but stands irresolute.*]

[*Enter MRS. LINDE from the hall, where she has taken off her cloak and hat.*]

NORA: Oh, it's you, Christine. There is no one else out there, is there? How good
of you to come!

MRS. LINDE: I heard you were up asking for me.

30   NORA: Yes, I was passing by. As a matter of fact, it is something you could help
me with. Let us sit down here on the sofa. Look here. To-morrow evening
there is to be a fancy-dress ball at the Stenborgs', who live about us; and Torvald wants me to go as a Neapolitan fishergirl, and dance the Tarantella that
I learnt at Capri.

MRS. LINDE: I see; you are going to keep up the character.[1]

NORA: Yes, Torvald wants me to. Look, here is the dress; Torvald had it made for
me there, but now it is all so torn, and I haven't any idea—

MRS. LINDE: We will easily put that right. It is only some of the trimming come
unsewn here and there. Needle and thread? Now then, that's all we want.

NORA: It *is* nice of you.

35   MRS. LINDE: [*sewing*] So you are going to be dressed up to-morrow, Nora. I will
tell you what—I shall come in for a moment and see you in your fine feathers. But I have completely forgotten to thank you for a delightful evening
yesterday.

---

[1]**keep up the character** wear the same costume

NORA: [*gets up, and crosses the stage*] Well I don't think yesterday was as pleasant as usual. You ought to have come to town a little earlier, Christine. Certainly Torvald does understand how to make a house dainty and attractive.

MRS. LINDE: And so do you, it seems to me; you are not your father's daughter for nothing. But tell me, is Doctor Rank always as depressed as he was yesterday?

NORA: No; yesterday it was very noticeable. I must tell you that he suffers from a very dangerous disease. He has consumption of the spine, poor creature. His father was a horrible man who committed all sorts of excesses; and that is why his son was sickly from childhood, do you understand?

MRS. LINDE: [*dropping her sewing*] But, my dearest Nora, how do you know anything about such things?

40 NORA: [*walking about*] Pooh! When you have three children, you get visits now and then from—from married women, who know something of medical matters, and they talk about one thing and another.

MRS. LINDE: [*goes on sewing. A short silence*] Does Doctor Rank come here every day?

NORA: Every day regularly. He is Torvald's most intimate friend, and a great friend of mine too. He is just like one of the family.

MRS. LINDE: But tell me this—is he perfectly sincere? I mean, isn't he the kind of man that is very anxious to make himself agreeable?

NORA: Not in the least. What makes you think that?

45 MRS. LINDE: When you introduced him to me yesterday, he declared he had often heard my name mentioned in this house; but afterwards I noticed that your husband hadn't the slightest idea who I was. So how could Doctor Rank—?

NORA: That is quite right, Christine. Torvald is so absurdly fond of me that he wants me absolutely to himself, as he says. At first he used to seem almost jealous if I mentioned any of the dear folk at home, so naturally I gave up doing so. But I often talk about such things with Doctor Rank, because he likes hearing about them.

MRS. LINDE: Listen to me, Nora. You are still very like a child in many things, and I am older than you in many ways and have a little more experience. Let me tell you this—you ought to make an end of it with Doctor Rank.

NORA: What ought I to make an end of?

MRS. LINDE: Of two things, I think. Yesterday you talked some nonsense about a rich admirer who was to leave you money—

50 NORA: An admirer who doesn't exist, unfortunately! But what then?

MRS. LINDE: Is Doctor Rank a man of means?

NORA: Yes, he is.

MRS. LINDE: And has no one to provide for?

NORA: No, no one; but—

55 MRS. LINDE: And comes here every day?

NORA: Yes, I told you so.

MRS. LINDE: But how can this well-bred man be so tactless?

NORA: I don't understand you at all.

MRS. LINDE: Don't prevaricate, Nora. Do you suppose I don't guess who lent you the two hundred and fifty pounds?

60 NORA: Are you out of your senses? How can you think of such a thing! A friend of ours, who comes here every day! Do you realise what a horribly painful position that would be?

MRS. LINDE: Then it really isn't he?

NORA: No, certainly not. It would never have entered into my head for a moment. Besides, he had no money to lend then; he came into his money afterwards.

MRS. LINDE: Well, I think that was lucky for you, my dear Nora.

NORA: No, it would never have come into my head to ask Doctor Rank. Although I am quite sure that if I had asked him—

65 MRS. LINDE: But of course you won't.

NORA: Of course not. I have no reason to think it could possibly be necessary. But I am quite sure that if I told Doctor Rank—

MRS. LINDE: Behind your husband's back?

NORA: I *must* make an end of it with the other one, and that will be behind his back too. I *must* make an end of it with him.

MRS. LINDE: Yes, that is what I told you yesterday, but—

70 NORA: [*walking up and down*] A man can put a thing like that straight much easier than a woman—

MRS. LINDE: One's husband, yes.

NORA: Nonsense! [*standing still*] When you pay off a debt you get your bond back, don't you?

MRS. LINDE: Yes, as a matter of course.

NORA: And can tear it into a hundred thousand pieces, and burn it up—the nasty dirty paper!

75 MRS. LINDE: [*looks hard at her, lays down her sewing and gets up slowly*] Nora, you are concealing something from me.

NORA: Do I look as if I were?

MRS. LINDE: Something has happened to you since yesterday morning. Nora, what is it?

NORA: [*going nearer to her*] Christine! [*listens*] Hush! there's Torvald come home. Do you mind going in to the children for the present? Torvald can't bear to see dressmaking going on. Let Anne help you.

MRS. LINDE: [*gathering some of the things together*] Certainly—but I am not going away from here till we have had it out with one another.

[*She goes into the room on the left, as* HELMER *comes in from the hall.*]

80 NORA: [*going up to* HELMER] I have wanted you so much, Torvald dear.

HELMER: Was that the dressmaker?

NORA: No, it was Christine; she is helping me to put my dress in order. You will see I shall look quite smart.

HELMER: Wasn't that a happy thought of mine, now?

NORA: Splendid! But don't you think it is nice of me, too, to do as you wish?

85 HELMER: Nice?—because you do as your husband wishes? Well, well, you little rogue, I am sure you did not mean it in that way. But I am not going to disturb you; you will want to try on your dress, I expect.

NORA: I suppose you are going to work.

HELMER: Yes. [*shows her a bundle of papers*] Look at that. I have just been to the
    bank. [*Turns to go into his room.*]

NORA: Torvald.

HELMER: Yes.

90 NORA: If your little squirrel were to ask you for something very, very prettily—?

HELMER: What then?

NORA: Would you do it?

HELMER: I should like to hear what it is, first.

NORA: Your squirrel would run about and do all her tricks if you would be nice,
    and do what she wants.

95 HELMER: Speak plainly.

NORA: Your skylark would chirp about in every room, with her song rising and
    falling—

HELMER: Well, my skylark does that anyhow.

NORA: I would play the fairy and dance for you in the moonlight, Torvald.

HELMER: Nora—you surely don't mean that request you made of me this morning?

100 NORA: [*going near him*] Yes, Torvald, I beg you so earnestly—

HELMER: Have you really the courage to open up that question again?

NORA: Yes, dear, you *must* do as I ask; you *must* let Krogstad keep his post in
    the Bank.

HELMER: My dear Nora, it is his post that I have arranged Mrs. Linde shall have.

NORA: Yes, you have been awfully kind about that; but you could just as well
    dismiss some other clerk instead of Krogstad.

105 HELMER: This is simply incredible obstinacy! Because you chose to give him a
    thoughtless promise that you would speak for him, I am expected to—

NORA: That isn't the reason, Torvald. It is for your own sake. This fellow writes in
    the most scurrilous newspapers; you have told me so yourself. He can do you
    an unspeakable amount of harm. I am frightened to death of him—

HELMER: Ah, I understand; it is recollections of the past that scare you.

NORA: What do you mean?

HELMER: Naturally you are thinking of your father.

110 NORA: Yes—yes, of course. Just recall to your mind what these malicious creatures
    wrote in the papers about papa, and how horribly they slandered him. I be-
    lieve they would have procured his dismissal if the Department had not sent
    you over to inquire into it, and if you had not been so kindly disposed and
    helpful to him.

HELMER: My little Nora, there is an important difference between your father and
    me. Your father's reputation as a public official was not above suspicion.
    Mine is, and I hope it will continue to be so, as long as I hold my office.

NORA: You never can tell what mischief these men may contrive. We ought to be so
    well off, so snug and happy here in our peaceful home, and have no cares—
    you and I and the children, Torvald! That is why I beg you so earnestly—

HELMER: And it is just by interceding for him that you make it impossible for me to
    keep him. It is already known at the Bank that I mean to dismiss Krogstad. Is
    it to get about now that the new manager has changed his mind at his wife's
    bidding—

NORA: And what if it did?

115 HELMER: Of course!—if only this obstinate little person can get her way! Do you suppose I am going to make myself ridiculous before my whole staff, to let people think that I am a man to be swayed by all sorts of outside influence? I should very soon feel the consequences of it, I can tell you! And besides, there is one thing that makes it quite impossible for me to have Krogstad in the Bank as long as I am manager.

NORA: Whatever is that?

HELMER: His moral failings I might perhaps have overlooked, if necessary—

NORA: Yes, you could—couldn't you?

HELMER: And I hear he is a good worker, too. But I knew him when we were boys. It was one of those rash friendships that so often prove an incubus in after life.[2] I may as well tell you plainly, we were once on very intimate terms with one another. But this tactless fellow lays no restraint on himself when other people are present. On the contrary, he thinks it gives him the right to adopt a familiar tone with me, and every minute it is "I say, Helmer, old fellow!" and that sort of thing. I assure you it is extremely painful for me. He would make my position in the Bank intolerable.

120 NORA: Torvald, I don't believe you mean that.

HELMER: Don't you? Why not?

NORA: Because it is such a narrow-minded way of looking at things.

HELMER: What are you saying? Narrow-minded? Do you think I am narrow-minded?

NORA: No, just the opposite, dear—and it is exactly for that reason.

125 HELMER: It's the same thing. You say my point of view is narrow-minded, so I must be so too. Narrow-minded! Very well—I must put an end to this. [*Goes to the hall-door and calls.*] Helen!

NORA: What are you going to do?

HELMER: [*looking among his papers*] Settle it. [*Enter MAID.*] Look here; take this letter and go downstairs with it at once. Find a messenger and tell him to deliver it, and be quick. The address is on it, and here is the money.

MAID: Very well, sir.

[*Exits with the letter.*]

HELMER: [*putting his papers together*] Now then, little Miss Obstinate.

130 NORA: [*breathlessly*] Torvald—what was that letter?

HELMER: Krogstad's dismissal.

NORA: Call her back, Torvald! There is still time. Oh Torvald, call her back! Do it for my sake—for your own sake—for the children's sake! Do you hear me, Torvald? Call her back!! You don't know what that letter can bring upon us.

HELMER: It's too late.

NORA: Yes, it's too late.

135 HELMER: My dear Nora, I can forgive the anxiety you are in, although really it is an insult to me. It is, indeed. Isn't it an insult to think that I should be afraid of a starving quill-driver's vengeance? But I forgive you nevertheless, because

---

[2]**incubus in after life** burden in later life

it is such eloquent witness to your great love for me. [*takes her in his arms*] And that is as it should be, my own darling Nora. Come what will, you may be sure I shall have both courage and strength if they be needed. You will see I am man enough to take everything upon myself.

NORA: [*in a horror-stricken voice*] What do you mean by that?

HELMER: Everything, I say—

NORA: [*recovering herself*] You will never have to do that.

HELMER: That's right. Well, we will share it, Nora, as man and wife should. That is how it shall be. [*caressing her*] Are you content now? There! there!—not these frightened dove's eyes! The whole thing is only the wildest fancy!—Now, you must go and play through the Tarantella and practise with your tambourine. I shall go into the inner office and shut the door, and I shall hear nothing; you can make as much noise as you please. [*turns back at the door*] And when Rank comes, tell him where he will find me.

[*Nods to her, takes his papers and goes into his room, and shuts the door after him*]

140 NORA: [*bewildered with anxiety, stands as if rooted to the spot, and whispers*] He is capable of doing it. He will do it. He will do it in spite of everything.—No, not that! Never, never! Anything rather than that! Oh, for some help, some way out of it! [*The door-bell rings.*] Doctor Rank! Anything rather than that— anything, whatever it is!

[*She puts her hands over her face, pulls herself together, goes to the door and opens it. RANK is standing without, hanging up his coat. During the following dialogue it begins to grow dark.*]

NORA: Good-day, Doctor Rank. I knew your ring. But you mustn't go in to Torvald now; I think he is busy with something.

RANK: And you?

NORA: [*brings him in and shuts the door after him*] Oh, you know very well I always have time for you.

RANK: Thank you. I shall make use of as much of it as I can.

145 NORA: What do you mean by that? As much of it as you can?

RANK: Well, does that alarm you?

NORA: It was such a strange way of putting it. Is anything likely to happen?

RANK: Nothing but what I have long been prepared for. But I certainly didn't expect it to happen so soon.

NORA: [*gripping him by the arm*] What have you found out? Doctor Rank, you must tell me.

150 RANK: [*sitting down by the stove*] It is all up with me. And it can't be helped.

NORA: [*with a sigh of relief*] Is it about yourself?

RANK: Who else? It is no use lying to one's self. I am the most wretched of all my patients, Mrs. Helmer. Lately I have been taking stock of my internal economy. Bankrupt! Probably within a month I shall lie rotting in the churchyard.

NORA: What an ugly thing to say!

RANK: The thing itself is cursedly ugly, and the worst of it is that I shall have to face so much more that is ugly before that. I shall only make one more examination of myself; when I have done that, I shall know pretty certainly when it will be that the horrors of dissolution will begin. There is something I want to tell you. Helmer's refined nature gives him an unconquerable disgust at everything that is ugly; I won't have him in my sick-room.

155 NORA: Oh, but, Doctor Rank—

RANK: I won't have him there. Not on any account. I bar my door to him. As soon as I am quite certain that the worst has come, I shall send you my card with a black cross on it, and then you will know that the loathsome end has begun.

NORA: You are quite absurd to-day. And I wanted you so much to be in a really good humour.

RANK: With death stalking beside me?—To have to pay this penalty for another man's sin! Is there any justice in that? And in every single family, in one way or another, some such inexorable retribution is being exacted—

NORA: [*putting her hands over her ears*] Rubbish! Do talk of something cheerful.

160 RANK: Oh, it's a mere laughing matter, the whole thing. My poor innocent spine has to suffer for my father's youthful amusements.

NORA: [*sitting at the table on the left*] I suppose you mean that he was too partial to asparagus and pâté de foie gras, don't you.

RANK: Yes, and to truffles.

NORA: Truffles, yes. And oysters too, I suppose?

RANK: Oysters, of course, that goes without saying.

165 NORA: And heaps of port and champagne. It is sad that all these nice things should take their revenge on our bones.

RANK: Especially that they should revenge themselves on the unlucky bones of those who have not had the satisfaction of enjoying them.

NORA: Yes, that's the saddest part of it all.

RANK: [*with a searching look at her*] Hm!—

NORA: [*after a short pause*] Why did you smile?

170 RANK: No, it was you that laughed.

NORA: No, it was you that smiled, Doctor Rank!

RANK: [*rising*] You are a greater rascal than I thought.

NORA: I am in a silly mood to-day.

RANK: So it seems.

175 NORA: [*putting her hands on his shoulders*] Dear, dear Doctor Rank, death mustn't take you away from Torvald and me.

RANK: It is a loss you would easily recover from. Those who are gone are soon forgotten.

NORA: [*looking at him anxiously*] Do you believe that?

RANK: People form new ties, and then—

NORA: Who will form new ties?

180 RANK: Both you and Helmer, when I am gone. You yourself are already on the high road to it, I think. What did that Mrs. Linde want here last night?

NORA: Oho!—you don't mean to say you are jealous of poor Christine?

RANK: Yes, I am. She will be my successor in this house. When I am done for, this woman will—

NORA: Hush! don't speak so loud. She is in that room.

RANK: To-day again. There, you see.

185 NORA: She has only come to sew my dress for me. Bless my soul, how unreasonable you are! [*sits down on the sofa*] Be nice now, Doctor Rank, and tomorrow
you will see how beautifully I shall dance, and you can imagine I am doing
it all for you—and for Torvald too, of course. [*takes various things out of the
box*] Doctor Rank, come and sit down here, and I will show you something.

RANK: [*sitting down*] What is it?

NORA: Just look at those!

RANK: Silk stockings.

NORA: Flesh-coloured. Aren't they lovely? It is so dark here now, but to-morrow—.
No, no, no! you must only look at the feet. Oh well, you may have leave to
look at the legs too.

190 RANK: Hm!—

NORA: Why are you looking so critical? Don't you think they will fit me?

RANK: I have no means of forming an opinion about that.

NORA: [*looks at him for a moment*] For shame! [*hits him lightly on the ear with the
stockings*] That's to punish you. [*folds them up again*]

RANK: And what other nice things am I to be allowed to see?

195 NORA: Not a single thing more, for being so naughty. [*She looks among the things,
humming to herself.*]

RANK: [*after a short silence*] When I am sitting here, talking to you as intimately as
this, I cannot imagine for a moment what would have become of me if I had
never come into this house.

NORA: [*smiling*] I believe you do feel thoroughly at home with us.

RANK: [*in a lower voice, looking straight in front of him*] And to be obliged to
leave it all—

NORA: Nonsense, you are not going to leave it.

200 RANK: [*as before*] And not be able to leave behind one the slightest token of one's
gratitude, scarcely even a fleeting regret—nothing but an empty place which
the first comer can fill as well as any other.

NORA: And if I asked you now for a—? No!

RANK: For what?

NORA: For a big proof of your friendship—

RANK: Yes, yes!

205 NORA: I mean a tremendously big favour—

RANK: Would you really make me so happy for once?

NORA: Ah, but you don't know what it is yet.

RANK: No—but tell me.

NORA: I really can't, Doctor Rank. It is something out of all reason; it means advice,
and help, and a favour—

210 RANK: The bigger a thing it is the better. I can't conceive what it is you mean. Do
tell me. Haven't I your confidence?

NORA: More than anyone else. I know you are my truest and best friend, and so
I will tell you what it is. Well, Doctor Rank, it is something you must help
me to prevent. You know how devotedly, how inexpressibly deeply Torvald
loves me; he would never for a moment hesitate to give his life for me.

RANK: [*leaning towards her*] Nora—do you think he is the only one—?

NORA: [*with a slight start*] The only one—?

RANK: The only one who would gladly give his life for your sake.

215 NORA: [*sadly*] Is that it?

RANK: I was determined you should know it before I went away, and there will never be a better opportunity than this. Now you know it, Nora. And now you know, too, that you can trust me as you would trust no one else.

NORA: [*rises, deliberately and quietly*] Let me pass.

RANK: [*makes room for her to pass him, but sits still*] Nora!

NORA: [*at the hall door*] Helen, bring in the lamp. [*goes over to the stove*] Dear Doctor Rank, that was really horrid of you.

220 RANK: To have loved you as much as anyone else does? Was that horrid?

NORA: No, but to go and tell me so. There was really no need—

RANK: What do you mean? Did you know—? [*MAID enters with lamp, puts it down on the table, and goes out.*] Nora—Mrs. Helmer—tell me, had you any idea of this?

NORA: Oh, how do I know whether I had or whether I hadn't? I really can't tell you—To think you could be so clumsy, Doctor Rank! We were getting on so nicely.

RANK: Well, at all events you know now that you can command me, body and soul. So won't you speak out?

225 NORA: [*looking at him*] After what happened?

RANK: I beg you to let me know what it is.

NORA: I can't tell you anything now.

RANK: Yes, yes. You mustn't punish me in that way. Let me have permission to do for you whatever a man may do.

NORA: You can do nothing for me now. Besides, I really don't need any help at all. You will find that the whole thing is merely fancy on my part. It really is so—of course it is! [*Sits down in the rocking-chair, and looks at him with a smile*] You are a nice sort of man, Doctor Rank!—don't you feel ashamed of yourself, now the lamp has come?

230 RANK: Not a bit. But perhaps I had better go—for ever?

NORA: No, indeed, you shall not. Of course you must come here just as before. You know very well Torvald can't do without you.

RANK: Yes, but you?

NORA: Oh, I am always tremendously pleased when you come.

RANK: It is just that, that put me on the wrong track. You are a riddle to me. I have often thought that you would almost as soon be in my company as in Helmer's.

235 NORA: Yes—you see there are some people one loves best, and others whom one would almost always rather have as companions.

RANK: Yes, there is something in that.

NORA: When I was at home, of course I loved papa best. But I always thought it tremendous fun if I could steal down into the maid's room, because they never moralised at all, and talked to each other about such entertaining things.

RANK: I see—it is *their* place I have taken.

NORA: [*jumping up and going to him*] Oh, dear, nice Doctor Rank, I never meant
that at all. But surely you can understand that being with Torvald is a little
like being with papa—

[*Enter* MAID *from the hall.*]

240 MAID: If you please, ma'am. [*whispers and hands her a card*]

NORA: [*glancing at the card*] Oh! [*puts it in her pocket*]

RANK: Is there anything wrong?

NORA: No, no, not in the least. It is only something—it is my new dress—

RANK: What? Your dress is lying there.

245 NORA: Oh, yes, that one; but this is another. I ordered it. Torvald mustn't know
about it—

RANK: Oho! Then that was the great secret.

NORA: Of course. Just go in to him; he is sitting in the inner room. Keep him as
long as—

RANK: Make your mind easy; I won't let him escape. [*goes into* HELMER'S *room*]

NORA: [*to the* MAID] And he is standing waiting in the kitchen?

250 MAID: Yes; he came up the back stairs.

NORA: But didn't you tell him no one was in?

MAID: Yes, but it was no good.

NORA: He won't go away?

MAID: No; he says he won't until he has seen you, ma'am.

255 NORA: Well, let him come in—but quietly. Helen, you mustn't say anything about
it to anyone. It is a surprise for my husband.

MAID: Yes, ma'am, I quite understand.   [*Exit.*]

NORA: This dreadful thing is going to happen! It will happen in spite of me! No,
no, no, it can't happen—it shan't happen!

[*She bolts the door of* HELMER'S *room. The* MAID *opens the hall door for* KROGSTAD *and
shuts it after him. He is wearing a fur coat, high boots and a fur cap.*]

NORA: [*advancing towards him*] Speak low—my husband is at home.

KROGSTAD: No matter about that.

260 NORA: What do you want of me?

KROGSTAD: An explanation of something.

NORA: Make haste then. What is it?

KROGSTAD: You know, I suppose, that I have got my dismissal.

NORA: I couldn't prevent it, Mr. Krogstad. I fought as hard as I could on your side,
but it was no good.

265 KROGSTAD: Does your husband love you so little, then? He knows that what I can
expose you to, and yet he ventures—

NORA: How can you suppose that he has any knowledge of the sort?

KROGSTAD: I didn't suppose so at all. It would not be the least like our dear Torvald
Helmer to show so much courage—

NORA: Mr. Krogstad, a little respect for my husband, please.

KROGSTAD: Certainly—all the respect he deserves. But since you have kept the
matter so carefully to yourself, I make bold to suppose that you have a little
clearer idea, than you had yesterday, of what it actually is that you have done?

270 NORA: More than you could ever teach me.

KROGSTAD: Yes, such a bad lawyer as I am.

NORA: What is it you want of me?

KROGSTAD: Only to see how you were, Mrs. Helmer. I have been thinking about you all day long. A mere cashier, a quill-driver,[3] a—well, a man like me— even he has a little of what is called feeling, you know.

NORA: Show it, then; think of my little children.

275 KROGSTAD: Have you and your husband thought of mine? But never mind about that. I only wanted to tell you that you need not take this matter too seriously. In the first place there will be no accusation made on my part.

NORA: No, of course not; I was sure of that.

KROGSTAD: The whole thing can be arranged amicably; there is no reason why anyone should know anything about it. It will remain a secret between us three.

NORA: My husband must never get to know anything about it.

KROGSTAD: How will you be able to prevent it? Am I to understand that you can pay the balance that is owing?

280 NORA: No, not just at present.

KROGSTAD: Or perhaps that you have some expedient for raising the money soon?

NORA: No expedient that I mean to make use of.

KROGSTAD: Well, in any case, it would have been of no use to you now. If you stood there with ever so much money in your hand, I would never part with your bond.

NORA: Tell me what purpose you mean to put it to.

285 KROGSTAD: I shall only preserve it—keep it in my possession. No one who is not concerned in the matter shall have the slightest hint of it. So that if the thought of it has driven you to any desperate resolution—

NORA: It has.

KROGSTAD: If you had it in your mind to run away from your home—

NORA: I had.

KROGSTAD: Or even something worse—

290 NORA: How could you know that?

KROGSTAD: Give up the idea.

NORA: How did you know I had thought of *that*?

KROGSTAD: Most of us think of that at first. I did, too—but I hadn't the courage.

NORA: [*faintly*] No more had I.

295 KROGSTAD: [*in a tone of relief*] No, that's it, isn't it—you hadn't the courage either?

NORA: No, I haven't—I haven't.

KROGSTAD: Besides, it would have been a great piece of folly. Once the first storm at home is over—. I have a letter for your husband in my pocket.

NORA: Telling him everything?

KROGSTAD: In as lenient a manner as I possibly could.

300 NORA: [*quickly*] He mustn't get the letter. Tear it up. I will find some means of getting money.

---

[3]**quill-driver** pen-pusher

KROGSTAD: Excuse me, Mrs. Helmer, but I think I told you just now—

NORA: I am not speaking of what I owe you. Tell me what sum you are asking my husband for, and I will get the money.

KROGSTAD: I am not asking your husband for a penny.

NORA: What do you want, then?

305 KROGSTAD: I will tell you. I want to rehabilitate myself, Mrs. Helmer; I want to get on; and in that your husband must help me. For the last year and a half I have not had a hand in anything dishonourable, and all that time I have been struggling in most restricted circumstances. I was content to work my way up step by step. Now I am turned out, and I am not going to be satisfied with merely being taken into favour again. I want to get on, I tell you. I want to get into the Bank again, in a higher position. Your husband must make a place for me—

NORA: That he will never do!

KROGSTAD: He will; I know him; he dare not protest. And as soon as I am in there again with him, then you will see! Within a year I shall be the manager's right hand. It will be Nils Krogstad and not Torvald Helmer who manages the Bank.

NORA: That's a thing you will never see!

KROGSTAD: Do you mean that you will—?

310 NORA: I have courage enough for it now.

KROGSTAD: Oh, you can't frighten me. A fine, spoilt lady like you—

NORA: You will see, you will see.

KROGSTAD: Under the ice, perhaps? Down into the cold, coal-black water? And then, in the spring, to float up to the surface, all horrible and unrecognisable, with your hair fallen out—

NORA: You can't frighten me.

315 KROGSTAD: Nor you me. People don't do such things, Mrs. Helmer. Besides, what use would it be? I should have him completely in my power all the same.

NORA: Afterwards? When I am no longer—

KROGSTAD: Have you forgotten that it is I who have the keeping of your reputation? [NORA *stands speechlessly looking at him.*] Well, now, I have warned you. Do not do anything foolish. When Helmer has had my letter, I shall expect a message from him. And be sure you remember that it is your husband himself who has forced me into such ways as this again. I will never forgive him for that. Good-bye, Mrs. Helmer.

[*Exit through the hall.*]

NORA: [*goes to the hall door, opens it slightly and listens*] He is going. He is not putting the letter in the box. Oh no, no! that's impossible! [*opens the door by degrees*] What is that? He is standing outside. He is not going downstairs. Is he hesitating? Can he—

[*A letter drops into the box; then* KROGSTAD'S *footsteps are heard, till they die away as he goes downstairs.* NORA *utters a stifled cry and runs across the room to the table by the sofa. A short pause.*]

NORA: In the letter-box. [*steals across to the hall door*] There it lies—Torvald, Torvald, there is no hope for us now!

[MRS. LINDE *comes in from the room on the left, carrying the dress.*]

320 MRS. LINDE: There, I can't see anything more to mend now. Would you like to try it on—?

NORA: [*in a hoarse whisper*] Christine, come here.

MRS. LINDE: [*throwing the dress down on the sofa*] What is the matter with you? You look so agitated!

NORA: Come here. Do you see that letter? There, look—you can see it through the glass in the letter-box.

MRS. LINDE: Yes, I see it.

325 NORA: That letter is from Krogstad.

MRS. LINDE: Nora—it was Krogstad who lent you the money!

NORA: Yes, and now Torvald will know all about it.

MRS. LINDE: Believe me, Nora, that's the best thing for both of you.

NORA: You don't know all. I forged a name.

330 MRS. LINDE: Good heavens—!

NORA: I only want to say this to you, Christine—you must be my witness.

MRS. LINDE: Your witness? What do you mean? What am I to—?

NORA: If I should go out of my mind—and it might easily happen—

MRS. LINDE: Nora!

335 NORA: Or if anything else should happen to me—anything, for instance, that might prevent my being here—

MRS. LINDE: Nora! Nora! you are quite out of your mind.

NORA: And if it should happen that there were someone who wanted to take all the responsibility, all the blame, you understand—

MRS. LINDE: Yes, yes—but how can you suppose—?

NORA: Then you must be my witness, that it is not true, Christine. I am not out of my mind at all; I am in my right senses now, and I tell you no one else has known anything about it; I, and I alone, did the whole thing. Remember that.

340 MRS. LINDE: I will, indeed. But I don't understand all this.

NORA: How should you understand it? A wonderful thing is going to happen.

MRS. LINDE: A wonderful thing?

NORA: Yes, a wonderful thing!—But it is so terrible, Christine; it *mustn't* happen, not for all the world.

MRS. LINDE: I will go at once and see Krogstad.

345 NORA: Don't go to him; he will do you some harm.

MRS. LINDE: There was a time when he would gladly do anything for my sake.

NORA: He?

MRS. LINDE: Where does he live?

NORA: How should I know—? Yes [*feeling in her pocket*] here is his card. But the letter, the letter—!

350 HELMER: [*calls from his room, knocking at the door*] Nora!

NORA: [*cries out anxiously*] Oh, what's that? What do you want?

HELMER: Don't be so frightened. We are not coming in; you have locked the door. Are you trying on your dress?

NORA: Yes, that's it. I look so nice, Torvald.

MRS. LINDE: [*who has read the card*] I see he lives at the corner here.

355 NORA: Yes, but it's no use. It is hopeless. The letter is lying there in the box.

MRS. LINDE: And your husband keeps the key?

NORA: Yes, always.

MRS. LINDE: Krogstad must ask for his letter back unread, he must find some pretence—

NORA: But it is just at this time that Torvald generally—

360 MRS. LINDE: You must delay him. Go in to him in the meantime. I will come back as soon as I can.

[She goes out hurriedly through the hall door.]

NORA: *[goes to HELMER's door, opens it and peeps in]* Torvald!

HELMER: *[from the inner room]* Well? May I venture at last to come into my own room again? Come along, Rank, now you will see—*[halting in the doorway]* But what is this?

NORA: What is what, dear?

HELMER: Rank led me to expect a splendid transformation.

365 RANK: *[in the doorway]* I understood so, but evidently I was mistaken.

NORA: Yes, nobody is to have the chance of admiring me in my dress until tomorrow.

HELMER: But, my dear Nora, you look so worn out. Have you been practising too much?

NORA: No, I have not practised at all.

HELMER: But you will need to—

370 NORA: Yes, indeed I shall, Torvald. But I can't get on a bit without you to help me; I have absolutely forgotten the whole thing.

HELMER: Oh, we will soon work it up again.

NORA: Yes, help me, Torvald. Promise that you will! I am so nervous about it—all the people—. You must give yourself up to me entirely this evening. Not the tiniest bit of business—you mustn't even take a pen in your hand. Will you promise, Torvald dear?

HELMER: I promise. This evening I will be wholly and absolutely at your service, you helpless little mortal. Ah, by the way, first of all I will just—

[Goes towards the hall door]

NORA: What are you going to do there?

375 HELMER: Only see if any letters have come.

NORA: No, no! don't do that, Torvald!

HELMER: Why not?

NORA: Torvald, please don't. There is nothing there.

HELMER: Well, let me look. *[Turns to go to the letter-box. NORA, at the piano, plays the first bars of the Tarantella. HELMER stops in the doorway.]* Aha!

380 NORA: I can't dance to-morrow if I don't practise with you.

HELMER: *[going up to her]* Are you really so afraid of it, dear.

NORA: Yes, so dreadfully afraid of it. Let me practise at once; there is time now, before we go to dinner. Sit down and play for me, Torvald dear; criticise me, and correct me as you play.

HELMER: With great pleasure, if you wish me to.

[Sits down at the piano.]

NORA: [*takes out of the box a tambourine and a long variegated shawl. She hastily drapes the shawl round her. Then she springs to the front of the stage and calls out.*] Now play for me! I am going to dance!

[*HELMER plays and NORA dances. RANK stands by the piano behind HELMER and looks on.*]

385   HELMER: [*as he plays*] Slower, slower!

NORA: I can't do it any other way.

HELMER: Not so violently, Nora!

NORA: This is the way.

HELMER: [*stops playing*] No, no—that is not a bit right.

390   NORA: [*laughing and swinging the tambourine*] Didn't I tell you so?

RANK: Let me play for her.

HELMER: [*getting up*] Yes, do. I can correct her better then.

[*RANK sits down at the piano and plays. NORA dances more and more wildly. HELMER has taken up a position beside the stove, and during her dance gives her frequent instructions. She does not seem to hear him; her hair comes down and falls over her shoulders; she pays no attention to it, but goes on dancing. Enter MRS. LINDE.*]

MRS. LINDE: [*standing as if spell-bound in the doorway*] Oh!—

NORA: [*as she dances*] Such fun, Christine!

395   HELMER: My dear darling Nora, you are dancing as if your life depended on it.

NORA: So it does.

HELMER: Stop, Rank; this is sheer madness. Stop, I tell you! [*RANK stops playing, and NORA suddenly stands still. HELMER goes up to her.*] I could never have believed it. You have forgotten everything I taught you.

NORA: [*throwing away the tambourine*] There, you see.

HELMER: You will want a lot of coaching.

400   NORA: Yes, you see how much I need it. You must coach me up to the last minute. Promise me that, Torvald!

HELMER: You can depend on me.

NORA: You must not think of anything but me, either to-day or to-morrow; you mustn't open a single letter—not even open the letter-box—

HELMER: Ah, you are still afraid of that fellow—

NORA: Yes, indeed I am.

405   HELMER: Nora, I can tell from your looks that there is a letter from him lying there.

NORA: I don't know; I think there is; but you must not read anything of that kind now. Nothing horrid must come between us till this is all over.

RANK: [*whispers to HELMER*] You mustn't contradict her.

HELMER: [*taking her in his arms*] The child shall have her way. But to-morrow night, after you have danced—

NORA: Then you will be free.

[*MAID appears in the doorway to the right.*]

410   MAID: Dinner is served, ma'am.

NORA: We will have champagne, Helen.

MAID: Very good, ma'am.

[*Exit.*]

HELMER: Hullo!—are we going to have a banquet?

NORA: Yes, a champagne banquet till the small hours. [*calls out*] And a few macaroons, Helen—lots, just for once!

415 HELMER: Come, come, don't be so wild and nervous. Be my own little skylark, as
you used.

NORA: Yes, dear, I will. But go in now and you too, Doctor Rank. Christine, you
must help me to do up my hair.

RANK: [*whispers to* HELMER *as they go out*] I suppose there is nothing—she is not
expecting anything?

HELMER: Far from it, my dear fellow; it is simply nothing more than this childish
nervousness I was telling you of.

[*They go into the right-hand room.*]

NORA: Well!

420 MRS. LINDE: Gone out of town.

NORA: I could tell from your face.

MRS. LINDE: He is coming home to-morrow evening. I wrote a note for him.

NORA: You should have let it alone; you must prevent nothing. After all, it is
splendid to be waiting for a wonderful thing to happen.

MRS. LINDE: What is it that you are waiting for?

425 NORA: Oh, you wouldn't understand. Go in to them, I will come in a moment.
[MRS. LINDE *goes into the dining-room.* NORA *stands still for a little while, as if
to compose herself. Then she looks at her watch.*] Five o'clock. Seven hours
till midnight; and then four-and-twenty hours till the next midnight. Then the
Tarantella will be over. Twenty-four and seven? Thirty-one hours to live.

HELMER: [*from the doorway on the right*] Where's my little skylark?

NORA: [*going to him with her arms outstretched*] Here she is!

ACT 3

THE SAME SCENE. *The table has been placed in the middle of the stage, with chairs
round it. A lamp is burning on the table. The door into the hall stands open. Dance
music is heard in the room above.* MRS. LINDE *is sitting at the table idly turning over
the leaves of a book; she tries to read, but does not seem able to collect her thoughts.
Every now and then she listens intently for a sound at the outer door.*

MRS. LINDE: [*looking at her watch*] Not yet—and the time is nearly up. If only he
does not—. [*listens again*] Ah, there he is. [*Goes into the hall and opens the
outer door carefully. Light footsteps are heard on the stairs. She whispers.*]
Come in. There is no one here.

KROGSTAD: [*in the doorway*] I found a note from you at home. What does this
mean?

MRS. LINDE: It is absolutely necessary that I should have a talk with you.

KROGSTAD: Really? And is it absolutely necessary that it should be here?

5 MRS. LINDE: It is impossible where I live; there is no private entrance to my rooms.
Come in; we are quite alone. The maid is asleep, and the Helmers are at the
dance upstairs.

KROGSTAD: [*coming into the room*] Are the Helmers really at a dance to-night?

MRS. LINDE: Yes, why not?

KROGSTAD: Certainly—why not?

MRS. LINDE: Now, Nils, let us have a talk.

10   KROGSTAD: Can we two have anything to talk about?

MRS. LINDE: We have a great deal to talk about.

KROGSTAD: I shouldn't have thought so.

MRS. LINDE: No, you have never properly understood me.

KROGSTAD: Was there anything else to understand except what was obvious to all the world—a heartless woman jilts a man when a more lucrative chance turns up?

15   MRS. LINDE: Do you believe I am as absolutely heartless as all that? And do you believe that I did it with a light heart?

KROGSTAD: Didn't you?

MRS. LINDE: Nils, did you really think that?

KROGSTAD: If it were as you say, why did you write to me as you did at the time?

MRS. LINDE: I could do nothing else. As I had to break with you, it was my duty to put an end to all that you felt for me.

20   KROGSTAD: [*wringing his hands*] So that was it, and all this—only for the sake of money!

MRS. LINDE: You must not forget that I had a helpless mother and two little brothers. We couldn't wait for you, Nils; your prospects seemed hopeless then.

KROGSTAD: That may be so, but you had no right to throw me over for any one else's sake.

MRS. LINDE: Indeed I don't know. Many a time did I ask myself if I had the right to do it.

KROGSTAD: [*more gently*] When I lost you, it was as if all the solid ground went from under my feet. Look at me now—I am a shipwrecked man clinging to a bit of wreckage.

25   MRS. LINDE: But help may be near.

KROGSTAD: It *was* near; but then you came and stood in my way.

MRS. LINDE: Unintentionally, Nils. It was only to-day that I learnt it was your place I was going to take in the Bank.

KROGSTAD: I believe you, if you say so. But now that you know it, are you not going to give it up to me?

MRS. LINDE: No, because that would not benefit you in the least.

30   KROGSTAD: Oh, benefit, benefit—I would have done it whether or no.

MRS. LINDE: I have learnt to act prudently. Life, and hard, bitter necessity have taught me that.

KROGSTAD: And life has taught me not to believe in fine speeches.

MRS. LINDE: Then life has taught you something very reasonable. But deeds you must believe in?

KROGSTAD: What do you mean by that?

35   MRS. LINDE: You said you were like a shipwrecked man clinging to some wreckage.

KROGSTAD: I had good reason to say so.

MRS. LINDE: Well, I am like a shipwrecked woman clinging to some wreckage—no one to mourn for, no one to care for.

KROGSTAD: It was your own choice.

MRS. LINDE: There was no other choice—then.

40   KROGSTAD: Well, what now?

MRS. LINDE: Nils, how would it be if we two shipwrecked people could join forces?

KROGSTAD: What are you saying?

MRS. LINDE: Two on the same piece of wreckage would stand a better chance than each on their own.

KROGSTAD: Christine!

45   MRS. LINDE: What do you suppose brought me to town?

KROGSTAD: Do you mean that you gave me a thought?

MRS. LINDE: I could not endure life without work. All my life, as long as I can remember, I have worked, and it has been my greatest and only pleasure. But now I am quite alone in the world—my life is so dreadfully empty and I feel so forsaken. There is not the least pleasure in working for one's self. Nils, give me someone and something to work for.

KROGSTAD: I don't trust that. It is nothing but a woman's overstrained sense of generosity that prompts you to make such an offer of yourself.

MRS. LINDE: Have you ever noticed anything of the sort in me?

50   KROGSTAD: Could you really do it? Tell me—do you know all about my past life?

MRS. LINDE: Yes.

KROGSTAD: And do you know what they think of me here?

MRS. LINDE: You seemed to me to imply that with me you might have been quite another man.

KROGSTAD: I am certain of it.

55   MRS. LINDE: Is it too late now?

KROGSTAD: Christine, are you saying this deliberately? Yes, I am sure you are. I see it in your face. Have you really the courage, then—?

MRS. LINDE: I want to be a mother to someone, and your children need a mother. We two need each other. Nils, I have faith in your real character—I can dare anything together with you.

KROGSTAD: [*grasps her hands*] Thanks, thanks, Christine! Now I shall find a way to clear myself in the eyes of the world. Ah, but I forgot—

MRS. LINDE: [*listening*] Hush! The Tarantella! Go, go!

60   KROGSTAD: Why? What is it?

MRS. LINDE: Do you hear them up there? When that is over, we may expect them back.

KROGSTAD: Yes, yes—I will go. But it is all no use. Of course you are not aware what steps I have taken in the matter of the Helmers.

MRS. LINDE: Yes. I know all about that.

KROGSTAD: And in spite of that have you the courage to—?

65   MRS. LINDE: I understand very well to what lengths a man like you might be driven by despair.

KROGSTAD: If I could only undo what I have done!

MRS. LINDE: You can. Your letter is lying in the letter-box now.

KROGSTAD: Are you sure of that?

MRS. LINDE: Quite sure, but—

70   KROGSTAD: [*with a searching look at her*] Is that what it all means?—that you want to save your friend at any cost? Tell me frankly. Is that it?

MRS. LINDE: Nils, a woman who has once sold herself for another's sake, doesn't do it a second time.

KROGSTAD: I will ask for my letter back.

MRS. LINDE: No, no.

KROGSTAD: Yes, of course I will. I will wait here till Helmer comes; I will tell him he must give me my letter back—that it only concerns my dismissal—that he is not to read it—

75   MRS. LINDE: No, Nils, you must not recall your letter.

KROGSTAD: But, tell me, wasn't it for that very purpose that you asked me to meet you here?

MRS. LINDE: In my first moment of fright, it was. But twenty-four hours have elapsed since then, and in that time I have witnessed incredible things in this house. Helmer must know all about it. This unhappy secret must be disclosed; they must have a complete understanding between them, which is impossible with all this concealment and falsehood going on.

KROGSTAD: Very well, if you will take the responsibility. But there is one thing I can do in any case, and I shall do it at once.

MRS. LINDE: [*listening*] You must be quick and go! The dance is over; we are not safe a moment longer.

80   KROGSTAD: I will wait for you below.

MRS. LINDE: Yes, do. You must see me back to my door.

KROGSTAD: I have never had such an amazing piece of good fortune in my life.

[*Goes out through the outer door. The door between the room and the hall remains open.*]

MRS. LINDE: [*tidying up the room and laying her hat and cloak ready*] What a difference! what a difference! Someone to work for and live for—a home to bring comfort into. That I will do, indeed. I wish they would be quick and come—[*listens*] Ah, there they are now. I must put on my things.

[*Takes up her hat and cloak. HELMER's and NORA's voices are heard outside; a key is turned, and HELMER brings NORA almost by force into the hall. She is in an Italian costume with a large black shawl round her; he is in evening dress and a black domino which is flying open.*]

NORA: [*hanging back in the doorway, and struggling with him*] No, no, no!—don't take me in. I want to go upstairs again; I don't want to leave so early.

85   HELMER: But, my dearest Nora—

NORA: Please, Torvald dear—please, *please*—only an hour more.

HELMER: Not a single minute, my sweet Nora. You know that was our agreement. Come along into the room; you are catching cold standing there.

[*He brings her gently into the room, in spite of her resistance.*]

MRS. LINDE: Good evening.

NORA: Christine!

90   HELMER: You here, so late, Mrs. Linde?

MRS. LINDE: Yes, you must excuse me; I was so anxious to see Nora in her dress.

NORA: Have you been sitting here waiting for me?

MRS. LINDE: Yes, unfortunately I came too late, you had already gone upstairs; and I thought I couldn't go away without having seen you.

HELMER: [*taking off NORA'S shawl*] Yes, take a good look at her. I think she is worth looking at. Isn't she charming, Mrs. Linde?

95 MRS. LINDE: Yes, indeed she is.

HELMER: Doesn't she look remarkably pretty? Everyone thought so at the dance. But she is terribly self-willed, this sweet little person. What are we to do with her? You will hardly believe that I had almost to bring her away by force.

NORA: Torvald, you will repent not having let me stay, even if it were only for half an hour.

HELMER: Listen to her, Mrs. Linde! She had danced her Tarantella, and it had been a tremendous success, as it deserved—although possibly the performance was a trifle too realistic—a little more so, I mean, than was strictly compatible with the limitations of art. But never mind about that! The chief thing is, she had made a success—she had made a tremendous success. Do you think I was going to let her remain there after that, and spoil the effect? No indeed! I took my charming little Capri maiden—my capricious little Capri maiden, I should say—on my arm; took one quick turn round the room; a curtsey on either side, and, as they say in novels, the beautiful apparition disappeared. An exit ought always to be effective, Mrs. Linde; but that is what I cannot make Nora understand. Pooh! this room is hot. [*throws his domino on a chair and opens the door of his room*] Hullo! it's all dark in here. Oh, of course— excuse me—.

[*He goes in and lights some candles.*]

NORA: [*in a hurried and breathless whisper*] Well?

100 MRS. LINDE: [*in a low voice*] I have had a talk with him.

NORA: Yes, and—

MRS. LINDE: Nora, you must tell your husband all about it.

NORA: [*in an expressionless voice*] I knew it.

MRS. LINDE: You have nothing to be afraid of as far as Krogstad is concerned; but you must tell him.

105 NORA: I won't tell him.

MRS. LINDE: Then the letter will.

NORA: Thank you, Christine. Now I know what I must do. Hush—!

HELMER: [*coming in again*] Well, Mrs. Linde, have you admired her?

MRS. LINDE: Yes, and now I will say good-night.

110 HELMER: What already? Is this yours, this knitting?

MRS. LINDE: [*taking it*] Yes, thank you, I had very nearly forgotten it.

HELMER: So you knit?

MRS. LINDE: Of course.

HELMER: Do you know, you ought to embroider.

115 MRS. LINDE: Really? Why?

HELMER: Yes, it's far more becoming. Let me show you. You hold the embroidery thus in your left hand, and use the needle with the right—like this—with a long, easy sweep. Do you see?

MRS. LINDE: Yes, perhaps—

HELMER: But in the case of knitting—that can never be anything but ungraceful; look here—the arms close together, the knitting-needles going up and down—it has a sort of Chinese effect—. That was really excellent champagne they gave us.

MRS. LINDE: Well,—good-night, Nora, and don't be self-willed any more.

120   HELMER: That's right, Mrs. Linde.

MRS. LINDE: Good-night, Mr. Helmer.

HELMER: [*accompanying her to the door*] Good-night, good-night. I hope you will get home all right. I should be very happy to—but you haven't any great distance to go. Good-night, good-night. [*She goes out; he shuts the door after her, and comes in again.*] Ah!—at last we have got rid of her. She is a frightful bore, that woman.

NORA: Aren't you very tired, Torvald?

HELMER: No, not in the least.

125   NORA: Nor sleepy?

HELMER: Not a bit. On the contrary, I feel extraordinarily lively. And you?—you really look both tired and sleepy.

NORA: Yes, I am very tired. I want to go to sleep at once.

HELMER: There, you see it was quite right of me not to let you stay there any longer.

NORA: Everything you do is quite right, Torvald.

130   HELMER: [*kissing her on the forehead*] Now my little skylark is speaking reasonably. Did you notice what good spirits Rank was in this evening?

NORA: Really? Was he? I didn't speak to him at all.

HELMER: And I very little, but I have not for a long time seen him in such good form. [*looks for a while at her and then goes nearer to her*] It is delightful to be at home by ourselves again, to be all alone with you—you fascinating, charming little darling!

NORA: Don't look at me like that, Torvald.

HELMER: Why shouldn't I look at my dearest treasure?—at all the beauty that is mine, all my very own?

135   NORA: [*going to the other side of the table*] You mustn't say things like that to me to-night.

HELMER: [*following her*] You have still got the Tarantella in your blood, I see. And it makes you more captivating than ever. Listen—the guests are beginning to go now. [*in a lower voice*] Nora—soon the whole house will be quiet.

NORA: Yes, I hope so.

HELMER: Yes, my own darling Nora. Do you know, when I am out at a party with you like this, why I speak so little to you, keep away from you, and only send a stolen glance in your direction now and then?—do you know why I do that? It is because I make believe to myself that we are secretly in love, and you are my secretly promised bride, and that no one suspects there is anything between us.

NORA: Yes, yes—I know very well your thoughts are with me all the time.

140 HELMER: And when we are leaving, and I am putting the shawl over your beautiful young shoulders—on your lovely neck—then I imagine that you are my young bride and that we have just come from the wedding, and I am bringing you for the first time into our home—to be alone with you for the first time—quite alone with my shy little darling! All this evening I have longed for nothing but you. When I watched the seductive figures of the Tarantella, my blood was on fire; I could endure it no longer, and that was why I brought you down so early—

NORA: Go away, Torvald! You must let me go. I won't—

HELMER: What's that? You're joking, my little Nora! You won't—you won't? Am I not your husband—?

[*A knock is heard at the outer door.*]

NORA: [*starting*] Did you hear—?

HELMER: [*going into the hall*] Who is it?

145 RANK: [*outside*] It is I. May I come in for a moment?

HELMER: [*in a fretful whisper*] Oh, what does he want now? [*aloud*] Wait a minute! [*unlocks the door*] Come, that's kind of you not to pass by our door.

RANK: I thought I heard your voice, and felt as if I should like to look in. [*with a swift glance round*] Ah, yes!—these dear familiar rooms. You are very happy and cosy in here, you two.

HELMER: It seems to me that you looked after yourself pretty well upstairs too.

RANK: Excellently. Why shouldn't I? Why shouldn't one enjoy everything in this world?—at any rate as much as one can, and as long as one can. The wine was capital—

150 HELMER: Especially the champagne.

RANK: So you noticed that too? It is almost incredible how much I managed to put away!

NORA: Torvald drank a great deal of champagne tonight, too.

RANK: Did he?

NORA: Yes, and he is always in such good spirits afterwards.

155 RANK: Well, why should one not enjoy a merry evening after a well-spent day?

HELMER: Well spent? I am afraid I can't take credit for that.

RANK: [*clapping him on the back*] But I can, you know!

NORA: Doctor Rank, you must have been occupied with some scientific investigation to-day.

RANK: Exactly.

160 HELMER: Just listen!—little Nora talking about scientific investigations!

NORA: And may I congratulate you on the result?

RANK: Indeed you may.

NORA: Was it favourable, then?

RANK: The best possible, for both doctor and patient—certainty.

165 NORA: [*quickly and searchingly*] Certainty?

RANK: Absolute certainty. So wasn't I entitled to make a merry evening of it after that?

NORA: Yes, you certainly were, Doctor Rank.

HELMER: I think so too, so long as you don't have to pay for it in the morning.

RANK: Oh well, one can't have anything in this life without paying for it.

170 NORA: Doctor Rank—are you fond of fancy-dress balls?

RANK: Yes, if there is a fine lot of pretty costumes.

NORA: Tell me—what shall we two wear at the next?

HELMER: Little featherbrain!—are you thinking of the next already?

RANK: We two? Yes, I can tell you. You shall go as a good fairy—

175 HELMER: Yes, but what do you suggest as an appropriate costume for that?

RANK: Let your wife go dressed just as she is in everyday life.

HELMER: That was really very prettily turned. But can't you tell us what you will be?

RANK: Yes, my dear friend, I have quite made up my mind about that.

HELMER: Well?

180 RANK: At the next fancy dress ball I shall be invisible.

HELMER: That's a good joke!

RANK: There is a big black hat—have you never heard of hats that make you invisible? If you put one on, no one can see you.

HELMER: [*suppressing a smile*] Yes, you are quite right.

RANK: But I am clean forgetting what I came for. Helmer, give me a cigar—one of the dark Havanas.

185 HELMER: With the greatest pleasure. [*offers him his case*]

RANK: [*takes a cigar and cuts off the end*] Thanks.

NORA: [*striking a match*] Let me give you a light.

RANK: Thank you. [*She holds the match for him to light his cigar.*] And now good-bye!

HELMER: Good-bye, good-bye, dear old man!

190 NORA: Sleep well, Doctor Rank.

RANK: Thank you for that wish.

NORA: Wish me the same.

RANK: You? Well, if you want me to: sleep well! And thanks for the light.

[*He nods to them both and goes out.*]

HELMER: [*in a subdued voice*] He has drunk more than he ought.

195 NORA: [*absently*] Maybe. [HELMER *takes a bunch of keys out of his pocket and goes into the hall.*] Torvald! What are you going to do there?

HELMER: Empty the letter-box; it is quite full; there will be no room to put the newspaper in tomorrow morning.

NORA: Are you going to work to-night?

HELMER: You know quite well I'm not. What is this? Some one has been at the lock.

NORA: At the lock—?

200 HELMER: Yes, someone has. What can it mean? I should never have thought the maid—. Here is a broken hairpin. Nora, it is one of yours.

NORA: [*quickly*] Then it must have been the children—

HELMER: Then you must get them out of those ways. There, at last I have got it open. [*Takes out the contents of the letter-box, and calls to the kitchen.*] Helen!—Helen, put out the light over the front door. [*Goes back into the room and shuts the door into the hall. He holds out his hand full of letters.*] Look at that—look what a heap of them there are. [*turning them over*] What on earth is that?

NORA: [*at the window*] The letter—No! Torvald, no!

HELMER: Two cards—of Rank's.

205   NORA: Of Doctor Rank's?

HELMER: [*looking at them*] Doctor Rank. They were on the top. He must have put them in when he went out.

NORA: Is there anything written on them?

HELMER: There is a black cross over the name. Look there—what an uncomfortable idea! It looks as if he were announcing his own death.

NORA: It is just what he is doing.

210   HELMER: What? Do you know anything about it? Has he said anything to you?

NORA: Yes. He told me that when the cards came it would be his leave-taking from us. He means to shut himself up and die.

HELMER: My poor old friend. Certainly I knew we should not have him very long with us. But so soon! And so he hides himself away like a wounded animal.

NORA: If it has to happen, it is best it should be without a word—don't you think so, Torvald?

HELMER: [*walking up and down*] He had so grown into our lives. I can't think of him as having gone out of them. He, with his sufferings and his loneliness, was like a cloudy background to our sunlit happiness. Well, perhaps it is best so. For him, anyway. [*standing still*] And perhaps for us too, Nora. We two are thrown quite upon each other now. [*puts his arms round her*] My darling wife, I don't feel as if I could hold you tight enough. Do you know, Nora, I have often wished that you might be threatened by some great danger, so that I might risk my life's blood, and everything, for your sake.

215   NORA: [*disengages herself, and says firmly and decidedly*] Now you must read your letters, Torvald.

HELMER: No, no; not to-night. I want to be with you, my darling wife.

NORA: With the thought of your friend's death—

HELMER: You are right, it has affected us both. Something ugly has come between us—the thought of the horrors of death. We must try and rid our minds of that. Until then—we will each go to our own room.

NORA: [*hanging on his neck*] Good-night, Torvald—Good-night!

220   HELMER: [*kissing her on the forehead.*] Good-night, my little singing-bird. Sleep sound, Nora. Now I will read my letters through.

[*He takes his letters and goes into his room, shutting the door after him.*]

NORA: [*gropes distractedly about, seizes* HELMER'S *domino, throws it round her, while she says in quick, hoarse, spasmodic whispers*] Never to see him again. Never! Never! [*puts her shawl over her head*] Never to see my children again either—never again. Never! Never!—Ah! the icy, black water—the unfathomable depths—If only it were over! He has got it now—now he is reading it. Good-by, Torvald and my children!

[*She is about to rush out through the hall, when* HELMER *opens his door hurriedly and stands with an open letter in his hand.*]

HELMER: Nora!

NORA: Ah!—

HELMER: What is this? Do you know what is in this letter?

225 NORA: Yes, I know. Let me go! Let me get out!

HELMER: [*holding her back*] Where are you going?

NORA: [*trying to get free*] You shan't save me, Torvald!

HELMER: [*reeling*] True? Is this true, that I read here? Horrible! No, no—it is impossible that it can be true.

NORA: It is true. I have loved you above everything else in the world.

230 HELMER: Oh, don't let us have any silly excuses.

NORA: [*taking a step towards him*] Torvald—!

HELMER: Miserable creature—what have you done?

NORA: Let me go. You shall not suffer for my sake. You shall not take it upon yourself.

HELMER: No tragedy airs, please. [*locks the hall door*] Here you shall stay and give me an explanation. Do you understand what you have done? Answer me? Do you understand what you have done?

235 NORA: [*looks steadily at him and says with a growing look of coldness in her face*] Yes, now I am beginning to understand thoroughly.

HELMER: [*walking about the room*] What a horrible awakening! All these eight years—she who was my joy and pride—a hypocrite, a liar—worse, worse— a criminal! The unutterable ugliness of it all! For shame! For shame! [*NORA is silent and looks steadily at him. He stops in front of her.*] I ought to have suspected that something of the sort would happen. I ought to have foreseen it. All your father's want of principle—be silent!—all your father's want of principle has come out in you. No religion, no morality, no sense of duty—. How I am punished for having winked at what he did! I did it for your sake, and this is how you repay me.

NORA: Yes, that's just it.

HELMER: Now you have destroyed all my happiness. You have ruined all my future. It is horrible to think of! I am in the power of an unscrupulous man; he can do what he likes with me, ask anything he likes of me, give me any orders he pleases—I dare not refuse. And I must sink to such miserable depths because of a thoughtless woman!

NORA: When I am out of the way, you will be free.

240 HELMER: No fine speeches, please. Your father had always plenty of those ready, too. What good would it be to me if you were out of the way, as you say? Not the slightest. He can make the affair known everywhere; and if he does, I may be falsely suspected of having been a party to your criminal action. Very likely people will think I was behind it all—that it was I who prompted you! And I have to thank you for all this—you whom I have cherished during the whole of our married life. Do you understand now what it is you have done for me?

NORA: [*coldly and quietly*] Yes.

HELMER: It is so incredible that I can't take it in. But we must come to some understanding. Take off that shawl. Take it off, I tell you. I must try and appease him some way or another. The matter must be hushed up at any cost. And as for you and me, it must appear as if everything between us were just as before—but naturally only in the eyes of the world. You will still remain in my house, that is a matter of course. But I shall not allow you to bring up the children; I dare not trust them to you. To think that I should be obliged to say so to one whom I have loved so dearly, and whom I still—. No, that is all over. From this moment happiness is not the question; all that concerns us is to save the remains, the fragments, the appearance—

[*A ring is heard at the front-door bell.*]

HELMER: [*with a start*] What is that? So late! Can the worst—? Can he—? Hide yourself, Nora. Say you are ill.

[NORA *stands motionless.* HELMER *goes and unlocks the hall door.*]

MAID: [*half-dressed, comes to the door*] A letter for the mistress.

245 HELMER: Give it to me. [*takes the letter, and shuts the door*] Yes, it is from him. You shall not have it; I will read it myself.

NORA: Yes, read it.

HELMER: [*standing by the lamp*] I scarcely have the courage to do it. It may mean ruin for both of us. No, I must know. [*tears open the letter, runs his eye over a few lines, looks at a paper enclosed and gives a shout of joy*] Nora! [*She looks at him questioningly.*] Nora!—No, I must read it once again—. Yes, it is true! I am saved! Nora, I am saved!

NORA: And I?

HELMER: You too, of course; we are both saved, both you and I. Look, he sends you your bond back. He says he regrets and repents—that a happy change in his life—never mind what he says! We are saved, Nora! No one can do anything to you. Oh, Nora, Nora!—no, first I must destroy these hateful things. Let me see—. [*takes a look at the bond*] No, no, I won't look at it. The whole thing shall be nothing but a bad dream to me. [*tears up the bond and both letters, throws them all into the stove, and watches them burn*] There—now it doesn't exist any longer. He says that since Christmas Eve you—. These must have been three dreadful days for you, Nora.

250 NORA: I have fought a hard fight these three days.

HELMER: And suffered agonies, and seen no way out but—. No, we won't call any of the horrors to mind. We will only shout with joy, and keep saying "It's all over! It's all over!" Listen to me, Nora. You don't seem to realise that it is all over. What is this?—such a cold, set face! My poor little Nora, I quite understand; you don't feel as if you could believe that I have forgiven you. But it is true, Nora, I swear it; I have forgiven you everything. I know that what you did, you did out of love for me.

NORA: That is true.

HELMER: You have loved me as a wife ought to love her husband. Only you had not sufficient knowledge to judge of the means you used. But do you suppose you are any the less dear to me, because you don't understand how to act on your own responsibility? No, no; only lean on me; I will advise you and direct you. I should not be a man if this womanly helplessness did not just give you a double attractiveness in my eyes. You must not think any more about the hard things I said in my first moment of consternation, when I thought everything was going to overwhelm me. I have forgiven you, Nora; I swear to you I have forgiven you.

NORA: Thank you for your forgiveness.

[*She goes out through the door to the right.*]

255   HELMER: No, don't go—. [*looks in*] What are you doing in there?

NORA: [*from within*] Taking off my fancy dress.

HELMER: [*standing at the open door*] Yes, do. Try and calm yourself, and make your mind easy again, my frightened little singing-bird. Be at rest, and feel secure; I have broad wings to shelter you under. [*walks up and down by the door*] How warm and cosy our home is, Nora. Here is shelter for you; here I will protect you like a hunted dove that I have saved from a hawk's claws. I will bring peace to your poor beating heart. It will come, little by little, Nora, believe me. Tomorrow morning you will look upon it all quite differently; soon everything will be just as it was before. Very soon you won't need me to assure you that I have forgiven you; you will yourself feel the certainty that I have done so. Can you suppose I should ever think of such a thing as repudiating you, or even reproaching you? You have no idea what a true man's heart is like, Nora. There is something so indescribably sweet and satisfying, to a man, in the knowledge that he has forgiven his wife—forgiven her freely, and with all his heart. It seems as if that had made her, as it were, doubly his own; he has given her a new life, so to speak; and she has in a way become both wife and child to him. So you shall be for me after this, my little scared, helpless darling. Have no anxiety about anything, Nora; only be frank and open with me, and I will serve as will and conscience both to you—. What is this? Not gone to bed? Have you changed your things?

NORA: [*in everyday dress*] Yes, Torvald, I have changed my things now.

HELMER: But what for?—so late as this.

260   NORA: I shall not sleep to-night.

HELMER: But, my dear Nora—

NORA: [*looking at her watch*] It is not so very late. Sit down here, Torvald. You and I have much to say to one another.

[*She sits down at one side of the table.*]

HELMER: Nora—what is this?—this cold, set face?

NORA: Sit down. it will take some time; I have a lot to talk over with you.

265   HELMER: [*sits down at the opposite side of the table*] You alarm me, Nora!—and don't understand you.

NORA: No, that is just it. You don't understand me, and I have never understo you either—before to-night. No, you mustn't interrupt me. You must sim listen to what I say. Torvald, this is a settling of accounts.

HELMER: What do you mean by that?

NORA: [*after a short silence*] Isn't there one thing that strikes you as strange i sitting here like this?

HELMER: What is that?

270 NORA: We have been married now eight years. Does it not occur to you that this is the first time we two, you and I, husband and wife, have had a serious conversation?

HELMER: What do you mean by serious?

NORA: In all these eight years—longer than that—from the very beginning of our acquaintance, we have never exchanged a word on any serious subject.

HELMER: Was it likely that I would be continually and for ever telling you about worries that you could not help me to bear?

NORA: I am not speaking about business matters. I say that we have never sat down in earnest together to try and get at the bottom of anything.

275 HELMER: But, dearest Nora, would it have been any good to you?

NORA: That is just it; you have never understood me. I have been greatly wronged, Torvald—first by papa and then by you.

HELMER: What! By us two—by us two, who have loved you better than anyone else in the world?

NORA: [*shaking her head*] You have never loved me. You have only thought it pleasant to be in love with me.

HELMER: Nora, what do I hear you saying?

280 NORA: It is perfectly true, Torvald. When I was at home with papa, he told me his opinion about everything, and so I had the same opinions; and if I differed from him I concealed the fact, because he would not have liked it. He called me his doll-child, and he played with me just as I used to play with my dolls. And when I came to live with you—

HELMER: What sort of an expression is that to use about our marriage?

NORA: [*undisturbed*] I mean that I was simply transferred from papa's hands into yours. You arranged everything according to your own taste, and so I got the same tastes as you—or else I pretended to, I am really not quite sure which— I think sometimes the one and sometimes the other. When I look back on it, it seems to me as if I had been living here like a poor woman—just from hand to mouth. I have existed merely to perform tricks for you, Torvald. But you would have it so. You and papa have committed a great sin against me. It is your fault that I have made nothing of my life.

    How unreasonable and how ungrateful you are, Nora! Have you not been happy here?

    I have never been happy. I thought I was, but it has never really been so.

   —not happy!

    ...ly merry. And you have always been so kind to me. But our home has been nothing but a playroom. I have been your doll-wife, just as at home I was papa's doll-child; and here the children have been my dolls. I thought it great fun when you played with me, just as they thought it great fun when I played with them. That is what our marriage has been, Torvald.

    ...ome truth in what you say—exaggerated and strained as your view of it is. But for the future it shall be different. Playtime shall be over, and lesson-time shall begin.

    Mine, or the children's?

    ...d the children's, my darling Nora.

...an to educate me into being a proper wife

for you.

290 NORA: Alas, Torvald, you are not ... bring up the children?

HELMER: And you can say...

NORA: And I—how am ...elf a little while ago—that you dare not trust me to

HELMER: Nora!

NORA: ...ger! Why do you pay any heed to that?

HELMER: Didn't ...perfectly right. I am not fit for the task. There is another

NORA: ...ke first. I must try and educate myself—you are not the bring... that. I must do that for myself. And that is why I am going

295 HELMER: ...w.

NORA: ...up] What do you say?

...d quite alone, if I am to understand myself and everything about ...r that reason that I cannot remain with you any longer.

... Nora!

...going away from here now, at once. I am sure Christine will take me ...the night—

...ou are out of your mind! I won't allow it! I forbid you!

...t is no use forbidding me anything any longer. I will take with me what belongs to myself. I will take nothing from you, either now or later.

HELMER: What sort of madness is this!

NORA: To-morrow I shall go home—I mean, to my old home. It will be easiest for me to find something to do there.

305 HELMER: You blind, foolish woman!

NORA: I must try and get some sense, Torvald.

HELMER: To desert your home, your husband and your children! And you don't consider what people will say!

NORA: I cannot consider that at all. I only know that it is necessary for me.

HELMER: It's shocking. This is how you would neglect your most sacred duties.

310 NORA: What do you consider my most sacred duties?

HELMER: Do I need to tell you that? Are they not your duties to your husband and your children?

NORA: I have other duties just as sacred.

HELMER: That you have not. What duties could those be?

NORA: Duties to myself.

315 HELMER: Before all else, you are a wife and a mother.

NORA: I don't believe that any longer. I believe that before all else I am a reasonable human being, just as you are—or, at all events, that I must try and become one. I know quite well, Torvald, that most people would think you right, and that views of that kind are to be found in books; but I can no longer content myself with what most people say, or with what is found in books. I must think over things for myself and get to understand them.

HELMER: Can you not understand your place in your own home? Have you not a reliable guide in such matters as that?—have you no religion?

NORA: I am afraid, Torvald, I do not exactly know what religion is.

HELMER: What are you saying?

320 NORA: I know nothing but what the clergyman

He told us that religion was this, and that,

from all this, and am alone, I will look into tha~

the clergyman said is true, or at all events if it is

HELMER: This is unheard of in a girl of your age! But i~

aright, let me try and awaken your conscience. I su~

moral sense? Or—answer me—am I to think you have ~

NORA: I assure you, Torvald, that is not an easy question to ans~

know. The thing perplexes me altogether. I only know that ~

at it in quite a different light. I am learning, too, that the law is ~

thing from what I supposed; but I find it impossible to convince ~

the law is right. According to it a woman has no right to spare her o~

father, or to save her husband's life. I can't believe that.

HELMER: You talk like a child. You don't understand the conditions of the wo~

in which you live.

NORA: No, I don't. But now I am going to try. I am going to see if I can make out

who is right, the world or I.

325 HELMER: You are ill, Nora; you are delirious; I almost think you are out of your

mind.

NORA: I have never felt my mind so clear and certain as to-night.

HELMER: And is it with a clear and certain mind that you forsake your husband

and your children?

NORA: Yes, it is.

HELMER: Then there is only one possible explanation.

330 NORA: What is that?

HELMER: You do not love me any more.

NORA: No, that is just it.

HELMER: Nora!—and you can say that?

NORA: It gives me great pain, Torvald, for you have always been so kind to me,

but I cannot help it. I do not love you any more.

335 HELMER: [*regaining his composure*] Is that a clear and certain conviction too?

NORA: Yes, absolutely clear and certain. That is the reason why I will not stay here

any longer.

HELMER: And can you tell me what I have done to forfeit your love?

NORA: Yes, indeed I can. It was to-night, when the wonderful thing did not happen;

then I saw you were not the man I had thought you.

HELMER: Explain yourself better—I don't understand you.

340 NORA: I have waited so patiently for eight years; for, goodness knows, I knew

very well that wonderful things don't happen every day. Then this horrible

misfortune came upon me; and then I felt quite certain that the wonder-

ful thing was going to happen at last. When Krogstad's letter was lying out

there, never for a moment did I imagine that you would consent to accept

this man's conditions. I was so absolutely certain that you would say to him:

Publish the thing to the whole world. And when that was done—

HELMER: Yes, what then?—when I had exposed my wife to shame and disgrace?

NORA: When that was done, I was so absolutely certain, you would come forward and take everything upon yourself, and say: I am the guilty one.

HELMER: Nora—!

NORA: You mean that I would never have accepted such a sacrifice on your part? No, of course not. But what would my assurances have been worth against yours? That was the wonderful thing which I hoped for and feared; and it was to prevent that, that I wanted to kill myself.

345 HELMER: I would gladly work night and day for you, Nora—bear sorrow and want for your sake. But no man would sacrifice his honour for the one he loves.

NORA: It is a thing hundreds of thousands of women have done.

HELMER: Oh, you think and talk like a heedless child.

NORA: Maybe. But you neither think nor talk like the man I could bind myself to. As soon as your fear was over—and it was not fear for what threatened me, but for what might happen to you—when the whole thing was past, as far as you were concerned it was exactly as if nothing at all had happened. Exactly as before, I was your little skylark, your doll, which you would in future treat with doubly gentle care, because it was so brittle and fragile. [*getting up*] Torvald—it was then it dawned upon me that for eight years I had been living here with a strange man, and had borne him three children—. Oh, I can't bear to think of it! I could tear myself into little bits!

HELMER: [*sadly*] I see, I see. An Abyss has opened between us—there is no denying it. But, Nora, would it not be possible to fill it up?

350 NORA: As I am now, I am no wife for you.

HELMER: I have it in me to become a different man.

NORA: Perhaps—if your doll is taken away from you.

HELMER: But to part!—to part from you! No, no, Nora, I can't understand that idea.

NORA: [*going out to the right*] That makes it all the more certain that it must be done.

[*She comes back with her cloak and hat and a small bag which she puts on a chair by the table.*]

355 HELMER: Nora, Nora, not now! Wait till to-morrow.

NORA: [*putting on her cloak*] I cannot spend the night in a strange man's room.

HELMER: But can't we live here like brother and sister—?

NORA: [*putting on her hat*] You know very well that would not last long. [*puts the shawl round her*] Good-bye, Torvald. I won't see the little ones. I know they are in better hands than mine. As I am now, I can be of no use to them.

HELMER: But some day, Nora—some day?

360 NORA: How can I tell? I have no idea what is going to become of me.

HELMER: But you are my wife, whatever becomes of you.

NORA: Listen, Torvald. I have heard that when a wife deserts her husband's house, as I am doing now, he is legally freed from all obligations towards her. In any case I set you free from all your obligations. You are not to feel yourself bound in the slightest way, any more than I shall. There must be perfect freedom on both sides. See here is your ring back. Give me mine.

HELMER: That too?

NORA: That too.

365 HELMER: Here it is.

NORA: That's right. Now it is all over. I have put the keys here. The maids know all about everything in the house—better than I do. To-morrow, after I have left her, Christine will come here and pack up my own things that I brought with me from home. I will have them sent after me.

HELMER: All over! All over!—Nora, shall you never think of me again?

NORA: I know I shall often think of you and the children and this house.

HELMER: May I write to you, Nora?

370 NORA: No—never. You must not do that.

HELMER: But at least let me send you—

NORA: Nothing—nothing—

HELMER: Let me help you if you are in want.

NORA: No. I can receive nothing from a stranger.

375 HELMER: Nora—can I never be anything more than a stranger to you?

NORA: [*taking her bag*] Ah, Torvald, the most wonderful thing of all would have to happen.

HELMER: Tell me what that would be!

NORA: Both you and I would have to be so changed that—. Oh, Torvald, I don't believe any longer in wonderful things happening.

HELMER: But I will believe in it. Tell me? So changed that—?

380 NORA: That our life together would be a real wedlock. Good-bye.

[*She goes out through the hall.*]

HELMER: [*sinks down on a chair at the door and buries his face in his hands*] Nora! Nora! [*looks round, and rises*] Empty. She is gone. [*A hope flashes across his mind.*] The most wonderful thing of all—?

[*The sound of a door slamming is heard from below.*]

MAKING CONNECTIONS

1. To what extent was your response to this play influenced by your own background or experience?

2. What kind of relationship do the Helmers have? In what way do their conversations early in the play tell us almost everything there is to know about their relationship?

3. To what extent is Nora a victim of society? Of Torvald? Of herself?

4. Who is Mrs. Linde and how does she differ from Nora?

5. What is your response to Krogstad? To what extent is he a victim of society?

6. Consider the kinds of statements that are made about marriage by the past experience of supporting characters (Mrs. Linde, Krogstad, Anne) in this play.

7. What kind of relationship do Krogstad and Mrs. Linde have? Compare it to the Helmers' relationship.

8. What is the role of Dr. Rank in the play? To what extent does he know Nora better than Torvald? Why is Nora so upset when he confesses his love for her?

9. What is the theme of the play? What objects or actions in the play seem symbolic of the play's theme?
10. Is the play still relevant? Are there relationships like this today? Explain.
11. What conventions of society are being criticized in the play? Consider Ibsen's statements on page 861. What is your response to his views in light of your response to the play?

MAKING AN ARGUMENT

1. How do you feel about Nora leaving Torvald and their children at the end of the play? Do you think she has a choice? Consider Ibsen's changed ending on page 861. Which ending do you prefer? Write an argument for or against Nora's action at the end of the play. Cite the text of the play for support.
2. Many women today still feel the frustrations of Nora Helmer. For them, the world still seems made for men. The specific conditions of Nora's problem are out of date, but *A Doll's House* remains the classic statement of the problem. With this in mind, bring Ibsen's play into the twenty-first century and write about Nora's situation now. In addition to your own experience, consider examples from other literature, television, and movies.

THE ADAMS LETTERS [1776]

From Abigail to John
Braintree
March 31, 1776

 —I long to hear that you have declared an independancy (sic)—and by the way in the new Code of Laws which I suppose it will be necessary for you to make I desire you would Remember the Ladies and be more generous and favorable to them than your ancestors. Do not put such unlimited powers into the hands of the Husbands. Remember all Men would be tyrants if they could. If perticular (sic) care and attention is not paid to the Laidies (sic) we are determined to foment a Rebellion, and will not hold ourselves bound by any Laws in which we have no voice, or Representation.

 That your Sex are Naturally Tyrannical is a Truth so thoroughly established as to admit of no dispute, but such of you as wish to be happy willingly give up the harsh title of Master for the more tender and endearing one of Friend. Why then, not put it out of power of the vicious and the Lawless to use us with cruelty and indignity with impunity. Men of Sense in all Ages abhor those customs which treat us only as the vassals of your Sex. Regard us then as Beings placed by providence under your protection and in imitation of the Supreem (sic) Being make use of that power only for our happiness.

From John to Abigail
April 14, 1776

 As to your extraordinary Code of Laws, I cannot but laugh. We have been told that our Struggle has loosened the bands of Government everywhere. The Children and Apprentices were disobedient—that schools and Colledges (sic) were grown turbulent—that Indians slighted their Guardians and Negroes grew insolent to their Masters. But your Letter was the first Intimation that another Tribe more numerous and powerfull (sic) than all the rest were grown discontented.—This is rather too coarse a Compliment but you are so saucy, I won't blot it out.

Depend upon it, We know better than to repeal our Masculine systems. Altho (sic) they are in full Force, you know they are little more than Theory. We dare not exert our Power in its full Latitude. We are obliged to go fair, and softly, and in Practice you know We are the subjects. We have only the Name of Masters, and rather than give this, which would compleatly (sic) subject us to the Despotism of the Peticoat, I hope General Washington, and all our Brave Heroes would fight.

A Husband's Letter to His Wife [1844]

June 23, 1844
Dear Wife,

You have sinned greatly—and maybe I too; but this much is certain: Adam sinned after Eve had already sinned. So it is with us; you, alone, carry the guilt of all the misfortune which, however, I helped to enlarge later by my behavior. Listen now, since I still believe certain things to be necessary in order that we may have a peaceful life. If we want not only to be content for a day but forever, you will have to follow my wishes. So examine yourself and determine if you are strong enough to conquer your false ambitions and your stubbornness to submit to all the conditions, the fulfillment of which I cannot ignore. Every sensible person will tell you that all I ask of you is what is easily understood. If you insist on remaining stubborn, then do not return to my house, for you will never be happy with me; your husband, children, and the entire city threaten indifference or even contempt.

But if you decide to act *sensibly and correctly, that is justly and kindly,* then be certain that many in the world will envy you.

I am including here the paper which I read to you in front of the rabbi; ask anyone in your residence if the wishes expressed by me are not quite reasonable, and are of a kind to which every wife can agree for the welfare of domestic happiness. In any case, act in a way you think best.

When you decide to return, write to tell me on which day and hour you depart from Berlin and give me your itinerary whether by way of Kuestrin and Pinne or by way of Wollstein. I will then meet you at Wollstein or Pinne. I expect you will bring Solomon with you.

5   Don't travel unprepared. If you need money, ask your father.

May God enlighten your heart and mind.

I remain your so far unhappy, [Marcus]

Greetings to my parents, brothers, and sisters; also your brother. Show them what you wish, this letter, the enclosure, whatever you want. The children are fortunately healthy,

If you want to return with joy and peace, write me by return mail. In that case, I would rather send you a carriage. Maybe Madam Fraenkel will come along....

(*Enclosure*)

My wife promises—for which every wife is obligated to her husband—to follow my wishes in everything and to strictly obey my orders. It is already self-evident that our marital relations have often been disturbed by the fact that my wife does not follow my wishes but believes herself to be entitled to act on her own, even if this is totally against my orders. In order not to have to remind my wife every second what my wishes are regarding homemaking and public conduct—wishes which I have often expressed—I want to make here a few rules which shall serve as a code of conduct. A home is best run if the work for each hour is planned ahead of time, if possible.

10   Servants get up no later than 5:00 A.M. in summer and 6:00 A.M. in winter, the children an hour later. The cook prepares breakfast. The nursemaid puts out clothes for every child, prepares water and sponge, cleans the combs, etc. The cook should stay in the kitchen unless there is time to clean the rooms. At least once a week the rooms should be cleaned whenever possible, but not all on the same day.

Every Wednesday, the people in the house should do a laundry. Every last Wednesday in the month, there shall be a large laundry with an outside washerwoman. At least every Monday, the seamstress shall come into the house to fix what is necessary.

Every Thursday or Friday, bread is baked for the week; I think it is best to buy grain and have it ground, but to knead it at home.

Every Friday special bread (Barches) should be bought for the evening meal.

The kitchen list will be prepared and discussed every Thursday evening, jointly, by me and my wife; but my wish is to be decisive.

15   After this, provisions are to be bought every Friday at the market. For this purpose, my wife, herself, will go to the market on Fridays, accompanied by a servant; she can substitute a special woman who does errands (*Faktorfrau*) if she wishes, but not a servant.

All expenditures have to be written down daily and punctually.

The children receive a bath every Thursday evening. The children's clothes must be kept in a specially appointed chest, with a separate compartment for each child with the child's name upon it. The boys' suits and girls' dresses are to be kept separately. To keep used laundry, there must be a hamper easily accessible. Equally important is the food storage box in which provisions are kept in order, locked and safe from vermin.

The kitchen should be kept in order. Once a week all woodwork and copper must be scoured. The lights and lamps have to be cleaned daily. Toward servants, one has to be strict and just. Therefore, one should not call them names which aren't suitable for a decent wife. One should give them enough nourishing food. Disobedience and obstinacy are to be referred to me.

My wife will never make visits in my absence. However, she should visit the synagogue every Saturday—at least once a month; also she should go for a walk with the children at least once a week.

SOJOURNER TRUTH

AIN'T I A WOMAN   [1851]

This impromptu speech given by Sojourner Truth, a freed slave, was recorded with her own commentary by Frances Gage at a woman's rights convention in Ohio.

"WALL, CHILERN, WHAR DAR IS SO MUCH racket dar must be somethin' out o' kilter. I tink dat 'twixt de niggers of de Souf and de womin at de Norf, all talkin' 'bout rights, de white men will be in a fix pretty soon. But what's all dis here talkin' 'bout?

"Dat man ober dar say dat womin needs to be helped into carriages, and lifted ober ditches, and to hab de best place everywhar. Nobody eber helps me into carriages, or ober mud puddles, or gibs me any best place!" And raising herself to her full height, and her voice to a pitch like rolling thunder, she asked, "And an't I a woman? Look at me! Look at my arm! (and she bared her right arm to the shoulder, showing her tremendous muscular power). I have ploughed, and planted, and gathered into barns, and no man could head me! And an't I a woman? I could work as much and eat as much as a man—when I could get it—and bear de lash as well! And an't I a woman? I have borne thirteen chilern, and seen 'em mos' all sold off to slavery, and when I cried out with my mother's grief, none but Jesus heard me! And an't I a woman?

"Den dey talks 'bout dis ting in de head; what dis dey call it?" ("Intellect," whispered someone near.) "Dat's it, honey. What's dat got to do wid womin's rights or nigger's rights? If my cup won't hold but a pint, and yourn holds a quart, wouldn't ye be mean not to let me have my little half-measure full?" And she pointed her significant finger, and sent a keen glance at the minister who had made the argument. The cheering was long and loud.

"Den dat little man in black dar, he say women can't have as much rights as men, 'cause Christ wan't a woman! Whar did your Christ come from?" Rolling thunder couldn't have stilled that crowd, as did those deep, wonderful tones, as she stood there with outstretched arms and eyes of fire. Raising her voice still louder, she repeated, "Whar did your Christ come from? From God and a, woman! Man had nothin' to do wid Him." Oh, what a rebuke that was to that little man.

5   Turning again to another objector, she took up the defense of Mother Eve. I cannot follow her through it all. It was pointed, and witty, and solemn; eliciting at almost every sentence deafening applause; and she ended by asserting: "If de fust woman God ever made was strong enough to turn de world upside down all alone, dese women togedder (and she glanced her eye over the platform) ought to be able to turn it back, and get it right side up again! And now dey is asking to do it, de men better let 'em." Long-continued cheering greeted this. "'Bleeged to ye for hearin' on me, and now ole Sojourner han't got nothin' more to say."

Amid roars of applause, she returned to her corner, leaving more than one of us with streaming eyes, and hearts beating with gratitude. She had taken us up in her strong arms and carried us safely over the slough of difficulty turning the whole tide in our favor. I have never in my life seen anything like the magical influence that subdued the mobbish spirit of the day, and turned the sneers and jeers of an excited crowd into notes of respect and admiration. Hundreds rushed up to shake hands with her, and congratulate the glorious old mother, and bid her God-speed on her mission of "testifyin' agin concerning the wickedness of this 'ere people."

⬛ HENRIK IBSEN

NOTES FOR THE MODERN TRAGEDY   [1878]

There are two kinds of spiritual law, two kinds of conscience, one in man and another, altogether different, in woman. They do not understand each other; but in practical life the woman is judged by man's law, as though she were not a woman but a man.

The wife in the play ends by having no idea of what is right or wrong; natural feeling on the one hand and belief in authority on the other have altogether bewildered her.

A woman cannot be herself in the society of the present day, which is an exclusively masculine society, with laws framed by men and with a judicial system that judges feminine conduct from a masculine point of view.

She has committed forgery, and she is proud of it; for she did it out of love for her husband, to save his life. But this husband with his commonplace principles of honor is on the side of the law and looks at the question from the masculine point of view.

5   Spiritual conflicts. Oppressed and bewildered by the belief in authority, she loses faith in her moral right and ability to bring up her children. Bitterness. A mother in modern society, like certain insects who go away and die when she has done her duty in the propagation of the race. Love of life, of home, of husband and children and family. Now and then a womanly shaking off of her thoughts. Sudden return of anxiety and terror. She must bear it all alone. The catastrophe approaches, inexorably, inevitably. Despair, conflict, and destruction.

THE CHANGED ENDING OF A DOLL'S HOUSE *FOR A GERMAN*
PRODUCTION   [1880]

NORA: ...Where we could make a real marriage out of our lives together. Goodbye.
      [*Begins to go.*]
HELMER: Go then! [*Seizes her arm.*] But first you shall see your children for the
      last time!
NORA: Let me go! I will not see them! I cannot!
HELMER [*draws her over to the door, left*]:   You shall see them. [*Opens the door and
      says softly.*] Look, there they are asleep, peaceful and carefree. Tomorrow,
      when they wake up and call for their mother, they will be—motherless.
NORA [*trembling*]:   Motherless...!
HELMER: As you once were.
NORA: Motherless! [*Struggles with herself, lets her traveling bag fall, and says.*] Oh,
      this is a sin against myself, but I cannot leave them. [*Half sinks down by
      the door.*]
HELMER [*joyfully, but softly*]:   Nora!

[*The Curtain Falls.*]

SPEECH AT THE BANQUET OF THE NORWEGIAN LEAGUE
FOR WOMEN'S RIGHTS   [1898]

Christiania, May 26, 1898

I am not a member of the Women's Rights League. Whatever I have written has been without any conscious thought of making propaganda. I have been more the poet and less the social philosopher than people generally seem inclined to believe. I thank you for the toast, but must disclaim the honor of having consciously worked for the women's rights movement. I am not even quite clear as to just what this women's rights movement really is. To me it has seemed a problem of mankind in general. And if you read my books carefully you will understand this. True enough, it is desirable to solve the woman problem, along with all the others; but that has not been the whole purpose. My task has been the *description of humanity*. To be sure, whenever such a description is felt to be reasonably true, the reader will read his own feelings and sentiments into the work of the poet. These are then attributed to the poet; but incorrectly so. Every reader remolds the work beautifully and neatly, each according to his own personality. Not only those who write but also those who read are poets. They are collaborators. They are often more poetical than the poet himself.

ELIZABETH CADY STANTON

EXCERPT FROM "THE SOLITUDE OF SELF"   [1892]

The strongest reason for giving woman all the opportunities for higher education, for the full development of her faculties, her forces of mind and body; for giving her the most enlarged freedom of thought and action; a complete emancipation from all forms of bondage, of custom, dependence, superstition; from all the crippling influences of fear—is the solitude and personal responsibility of her own individual life. The strongest reason why we ask for woman a voice in the government under which she lives; in the religion she is asked to believe; equality in social life, where she is the chief factor; a place in the trades and professions, where she may earn her bread, is because of her birthright to self-sovereignty; because, as an individual, she must rely on herself. No matter how much women prefer to lean, to be protected and supported, nor how much men desire to have them do so, they must make the voyage of life alone, and for safety in an emergency, they must know something of the laws of navigation. To guide our own craft, we must be captain, pilot, engineer; with chart and compass to stand at the wheel; to watch the winds and waves, and know when to take in the sail, and to read the signs in the firmament over all. It matters not whether the solitary voyager is man or woman; nature, having endowed them equally, leaves them to their own skill and judgment in the hour of danger, and, if not equal to the occasion, alike they perish.

To appreciate the importance of fitting every human soul for independent action, think for a moment of the immeasurable solitude of self. We come into the world alone, unlike all who have gone before us, we leave it alone, under circumstances peculiar to ourselves. No mortal ever has been, no mortal ever will be like the soul just launched on the sea of life. There can never again be just such a combination of prenatal influences; never again just such environments as make up the infancy, youth and manhood of this one. Nature never repeats herself, and the possibilities of one human soul will never be found in another. No one has ever found two blades of ribbon grass alike, and no one will ever find two human beings alike. Seeing, then, that what must be the infinite diversity in human character, we can in a measure appreciate the loss to a nation when any class of the people is uneducated and unrepresented in the government.

WILBUR FISK TILLETT

EXCERPT FROM "SOUTHERN WOMANHOOD" [1891]

The growing respectability of self-support in woman is everywhere recognized as one of the healthiest signs of the times. The number of vocations open to women is constantly on the increase. Some modes of self-support are, and always will be, socially more respectable than others. In the report for 1888 of the Commissioner of Labor concerning the number and condition of working-women in the large cities is the following concerning Charleston, South Carolina:

> In no other Southern city has the exclusion of women from business been so rigid and the tradition that respectability is forfeited by manual labor so influential and powerful. Proud and well-born women have practised great self-denial at ill-paid conventional pursuits in preference to independence in untrodden paths. The embargo against self-support, however, has to some extent been lifted, and were there a larger number of remunerative occupations open to women, the rush to avail of them would show how ineffectual the old traditions have become.

A similar report of 1890 would show rapid changes and advances in public sentiment concerning the respectability of self-support in women, and would reveal that the "embargo" had, in most parts of the South at least, been entirely removed.

If we look at the South as a whole, and not at individual portions of it, it is unquestionably true that the great changes which the past thirty years have witnessed have wrought most favorably upon the intellectual life of Southern womanhood. The conditions under which Southern women now live are far more favorable for developing literary women than those existing in the days of slavery. In 1869 a volume was published by Mr. James Wood Davidson entitled "The Living Writers of the South," in which 241 writers are noticed, of which number 75 are women and 166 are men. Of the 241 named, 40 had written only for newspapers and magazines, while 201 had published one or more volumes, aggregating 739 in all. Although this book was published only four years after the close of the war, it was even then true that from two thirds to three fourths of the volumes mentioned in it as having been published by women—not to speak of the others—had been written and published after the opening of the war. They had been called forth by the war and the trying experiences following it. Whether the changed conditions under which we live have anything to do with it, it is nevertheless certainly true that there have been more literary women developed in the South in the thirty years since the war than in all our previous history.

It is Victor Hugo who has called this "the century of woman." It is certainly an age that has witnessed great changes in the life, education, and labor of women everywhere; and these changes have all been in the direction of enlarging the sphere of woman's activities, increasing her liberties, and opening up possibilities to her life hitherto restricted to man. It is a movement limited to no land and to no race. So far as this movement may have any tendency to take woman out of her true place in the home, to give her man's work to do and to develop masculine qualities in her, it finds no sympathy in the South. The Southern woman loves the retirement of home, and shrinks from everything that would tend to bring her into the public gaze.

DOROTHY DIX

THE AMERICAN WIFE
[1898]

It always seems to the American woman that the wives of other countries, who are held up for her admiration and imitation, have rather the easiest time of it. It would be comparatively simple to make yourself a decorative object to adorn a man's house, if that were all that was expected of you. It would be simple enough to accomplish marvels of cooking and housekeeping if that were the chief end of life. It is when one attempts to combine the useful and the ornamental—to be a Dresden statuette in the parlor and a reliable range in the kitchen—that the situation becomes trying, and calls for genuine ability. Yet this is what we expect of the average American wife, merely as a matter of course. She must be a paragon of domesticity, an ornament in society, a wonder in finance and a light in the literary circle to which she belongs.

In our curious social system, many things are left to her that the men attend to in other countries. For one thing, her husband expects her to assume all authority and management of the home and family. He doesn't want to be bothered about it. When he makes the money he feels he has done his whole duty, and he leaves the rest to her. When he comes home, tired out, after a day's work, he wants to rest, to read his paper, to think out some scheme in which he is interested. If his wife has any idea of leaning on his superior judgment and asking his advice about domestic problems she is very soon undeceived. "Great Scotts, Mary," is the impatient reply, "can't you manage your own affairs? I haven't got time to see about it. Settle it yourself."

It is the same way about the children. The American father is generally a devoted parent, but he wants his wife to do the managing and disciplining. In the brief hours he is at home, the little ones are his playthings, and he spoils them, and indulges them with a happy sense that he has no responsibility about it and that their mother will have to do the subsequent disciplining. She is responsible for their mental and physical well-being. She decides on the schools, and what they shall study, what colleges they shall attend, and all the rest of it. The average American John has a well-founded belief that his Mary is the smartest woman in the world, and knows what she is about, and so, at last, when she announces that the children need to go to Europe to study this or that, he consents through mere force of habit. He is so much in the way of letting her decide things it doesn't occur to him he could raise a dissenting voice.

To her, too, he leaves the matter of society. She dominates it, and runs it, and an American married man's social position depends entirely on his wife. If she is ambitious he climbs meekly up the social ladder in her wake; if she is not ambitious, they sit comfortably and contentedly down on the lower rungs, and stay there. He feels that he would be a bungler in the game of society, and he simply backs her hand for all it is worth. He pays for the house in the fashionable neighborhood of her choice, and for her entertainments, but he leaves all the rest to "mother and the girls." They must attend to the intricate social machinery, that he admits is a necessity, and is perfectly willing to support with anything but his own presence.

WOMEN AND SUICIDE   [1899]

The claim recently put boldly forth by a distinguished lawyer that a person has a right to die, when by means of disease or misfortune life becomes a burden, has provoked renewed discussion of the suicide question, and it is interesting, in this connection, to note that by far the larger number of suicides are among men. Women seldom take their own lives, and so we have the curious and contradictory spectacle of the sex that is universally accounted the braver and stronger, flinging themselves out of the world to avoid its troubles, while the weaklings patiently bear theirs on to the bitter end.

Nothing is more common than for the man who has speculated with other people's money and lost, and so brought ruin and disgrace on his family, to commit suicide. In fact, after reading of the trusted cashier going wrong, in one column, we almost expect to read in the next that he shot himself. No thought apparently comes to him of having any duty to stay and help lift the misery he brought on innocent people. In times of great financial stress, when a rich man has everything swept away, he, too, often solves the question of the future for himself by suicide, leaving his wife and little children to face a situation for which they are wholly unprepared. You never hear of a woman committing suicide and leaving her little children to the cruel mercies of the world, because she has lost her property. Instead, she feels more than ever that they need her care, and her help, and that she would be incapable of the unmentionable baseness of deserting them in such a crisis.

Yet if suicide is ever justifiable, it is for woman far more than men. She is always handicapped in the race of life. Sometimes with bodily infirmities, sometimes with mental idiosyncrasies, always by lack of training and business experience. Hard as poverty is for a man, it is harder still for a woman. Desperate as the struggle for existence is for him, it is still more desperate for her, limited by narrower opportunities, and rewarded with lesser pay. Terrible as are the tortures suffered by many a poor wretch, they are no worse than the life-long martyrdom that many a woman endures with never a thought of doing anything but bearing them with Christian fortitude and resignation until God's own hand sets her free.

There are many reasons why this state of affairs should exist. Woman's whole life is one long lesson in patience and submission. She must always give in. Men feel that they are born to command, to force circumstances to their will, and when circumstances can no longer be forced or bent, and they must yield to untoward fate, too many yield to the desire to avoid the misery they see before them by sneaking out of life. It is always a coward's deed. The babe salutes life with a wail, and the dying man takes leave of it with a groan. Between there is no time that has not its own troubles, and cares, and sorrows, and it is our part to bear them with courage, and it should be part of our pride in our sex that so many women sustain this brave attitude towards life under circumstances that might well tempt them to play the coward's part.

CHARLOTTE PERKINS STETSON (GILMAN)

EXCERPT FROM "WOMEN AND ECONOMICS"   [1899]

Worse than the check set upon the physical activities of women has been the restriction of their power to think and judge for themselves. The extended use of the human will and its decisions is conditioned upon free, voluntary action. In her rudimentary position, woman was denied the physical freedom which underlies all knowledge, she was denied the mental freedom which is the path to further wisdom, she was denied the moral freedom of being mistress of her own action and of learning by the merciful law of consequences what was right and what was wrong; and she has remained, perforce, undeveloped in the larger judgment of ethics.

Her moral sense is large enough, morbidly large, because in this tutelage she is always being praised or blamed for her conduct. She lives in a forcing-bed of sensitiveness to moral distinctions, but the broad judgment that alone can guide and govern this sensitiveness she has not. Her contribution to moral progress has added to the anguish of the world the fierce sense of sin and shame, the desperate desire to do right, the fear of wrong; without giving it the essential help of a practical wisdom and a regulated will. Inheriting with each generation the accumulating forces of our social nature, set back in each generation by the conditions of the primitive human female, women have become vividly self-conscious centres of moral impulse, but poor guides as to the conduct which alone can make that impulse useful and build the habit of morality into the constitution of the race.

Recognizing her intense feeling on moral lines, and seeing in her the rigidly preserved virtues of faith, submission, and self-sacrifice,—qualities which in the Dark Ages were held to be the first of virtues,—we have agreed of late years to call woman the moral superior of man. But the ceaseless growth of human life, social life, has developed in him new virtues, later, higher, more needful; and the moral nature of woman, as maintained in this rudimentary stage by her economic dependence, is a continual check to the progress of the human soul. The main feature of her life—the restriction of her range of duty to the love and service of her own immediate family— acts upon us continually as a retarding influence, hindering the expansion of the spirit of social love and service on which our very lives depend. It keeps the moral standard of the patriarchal era still before us, and blinds our eyes to the full duty of man.

An intense self-consciousness, born of the ceaseless contact of close personal relation; an inordinate self-interest, bred by the constant personal attention and service of this relation; a feverish, torturing, moral sensitiveness, without the width and clarity of vision of a full-grown moral sense; a thwarted will, used to meek surrender, cunning evasion, or futile rebellion; a childish, wavering, short-range judgment, handicapped by emotion; a measureless devotion to one's own sex relatives, and a maternal passion swollen with the full strength of the great social heart, but denied social expression,—such psychic qualities as these, born in us all, are the inevitable result of the sexuo-economic relation.

5   It is not alone upon woman, and, through her, upon the race, that the ill-effects may be observed. Man, as master, has suffered from his position also. The lust for power and conquest, natural to the male of any species, has been fostered in him to an enormous degree by this cheap and easy lordship. His dominance is not that of one chosen as best fitted to rule or of one ruling by successful competition with "foemen worthy of his steel"; but it is a sovereignty based on the accident of sex, and holding over such helpless and inferior dependants as could not question or oppose. The easy superiority that needs no striving to maintain it; the temptation to cruelty always begotten by irresponsible power; the pride and self-will which surely accompany it,—these qualities have been bred into the souls of men by their side of the relation. When man's place was maintained by brute force, it made him more brutal: when his place was maintained by purchase, by the power of economic necessity, then he grew into the merciless use of such power as distinguishes him to-day.

Yet here, as in the other evil results of the sexuo-economic relation, we can see the accompanying good that made the condition necessary in its time; and we can follow the beautiful results of our present changes with comforting assurance. A healthy, normal moral sense will be ours, freed from its exaggerations and contradictions; and, with that clear perception, we shall no longer conceive of the ethical process as something outside of and against nature, but as the most natural thing in the world.

Where now we strive and agonize after impossible virtues, we shall then grow naturally and easily into those very qualities; and we shall not even think of them as especially commendable. Where our progress hitherto has been warped and hindered by the retarding influence of surviving rudimentary forces, it will flow on smoothly and rapidly when both men and women stand equal in economic relation. When the mother of the race is free, we shall have a better world, by the easy right of birth and by the calm, slow, friendly forces of social evolution.

NATALIE ZEMON DAVIS AND JILL KER CONWAY

THE REST OF THE STORY   [1999]

For all their drama and insight, traditional histories of the last thousand years fall short. Written mostly by men, they introduced women into the standard parade of wars, revolutions, monarchs and parliaments only at moments like their ascension to inherited thrones or religious authority. In the nineteenth century, most male historians compounded the problem by making women's history sound as though women had only then begun making headway.

Women's history has more to it than that. Women have always questioned their subordination and often found ways around it. Further, some institutions important in the lives of women that seem timeless, like monogamous marriage, are in fact rooted in the last thousand years; some ostensibly modern movements reach far back in time. Indeed, many turning points on the thousand-year time line of women's history are little known or little understood. The following brief account of that history describes the rest of the story.

Who Says Men Are Closer to God?

Are women and men more alike than they are different? And where they are different, are women inferior or superior? Such questions have been debated since biblical times, and especially in the years after 1000. Some medieval theologians— male, that is—taught that woman was not created in God's image. But that could not be true, abbesses and nuns objected, for they had felt Christ's "imprint of resemblance" on them. Hildegard of Bingen, a nun in the Rhineland in the twelfth century, insisted that women's "weakness" did not refer to spiritual capacities. A woman could mortify the flesh and draw close to God as well as any man.

Such women accepted the general view that the universe was organized into realms of higher and lower: angels over humans, humans over animals, nobles over commoners, soul over body. But when it came to men over women, women balked. Christine de Pizan, poet and moralist at the French court, said in her "Book of the City of Ladies" of 1405 that God had created men and women with equal potential. If men had stronger bodies, women had freer and sharper minds, if they were just educated. Against the old medical idea that women had a hungry womb—that is, a sexual appetite less controllable than men's—Christine countered that women were by nature virtuous and modest.

5   The hottest debates about male-female relations in medieval Europe turned on celibacy. In the tenth and eleventh centuries, many priests were married, and their wives had access to the sacred. In a turning point in women's history, the eleventh-century reforms of Pope Gregory VII did away with clerical marriage in the Roman Church. These reforms inaugurated ten centuries in which sexually active males—and all women—were forbidden to perform important liturgical functions. A spiritual demotion it may have been, but it also confirmed an ideal of the celibate life, leaving nuns like Hildegard of Bingen scope for high ascetic devotions.

One Man, One Wife

The church put all its force behind insisting on monogamous, permanent marriage. An important step was declaring the full doctrine of marriage as a religious sacrament in 1215. Getting the doctrine accepted by lay people was another matter. Among the landed classes, men lived with concubines instead of, or along with, wives and cast their women aside at will. Only when the great families decided that the church's rule would help keep feudal property together did they go along.

Then in the sixteenth century, the Protestant Reformation did away with marriage as a religious sacrament and allowed for divorce. Yet it legitimated marriage all the more by allowing clergymen to wed and doing away with celibate nunneries and monasteries. In Europe, prostitution was made illegal in both Catholic and Protestant cities. It was still practiced, of course, as was concubinage, especially between European settlers in America and their female slaves. But monogamous marriage remained the triumphant cultural ideal.

According to religious teaching and secular law, the wife was "subject" to her husband, and her property was under his control. He was to rule her justly and not be cruel. Moderate beating was permissible, though some Protestant pastors preached against using it at all, and Ashkenazic rabbis disagreed about whether it was grounds for divorce. Divorce was not an easy out: a single woman with children could scarcely survive. Marriage was a frame that most women accepted, hoping for affectionate unions. What we today would call lesbian couples lived as married partners in the seventeenth and eighteenth centuries, one cross-dressing as a man. Protofeminists chronicled abuses in marriage, but did not reject the notion of "subjection" outright until the eighteenth century. A seventeenth-century male feminist said that wives should defer to their husbands not because the men were truly superior, but to keep the peace.

Nine Babies, Three Adults
More worrisome to women than subjection was procreation. For most of the millennium, the pattern was many births, many deaths. Given the poor food and poor health, it was not always easy to get and stay pregnant. Many infants, even among the wealthy, died at birth. In seventeenth-century France, a long-lived peasant mother might bring nine children to term; half might survive till age five, and she could rejoice if two or three reached adulthood. Under these circumstances, the local midwife was consulted much more often for medicines to conceive than for those to abort. Only in the late seventeenth century, when a better food supply in Western Europe allowed more children to survive, did couples start to limit the number of their children.

10   The model of man over woman had some effect in every sphere, forcing women to find means to cope or resist. Female wage earners were paid less than men; the women improvised new ways to stitch, smuggle, peddle or beg. Male surgeons began to deliver babies in the wealthy families in the seventeenth century; midwives defended their female turf in the village, claiming their dexterous hands would do better than the surgeon's forceps.

Does "Man" Include Woman?
Since the days of Hildegard of Bingen, women had tried for a larger role in religion. The witchcraft prosecutions that swept Europe and then New England in the fifteenth through seventeenth centuries threatened that initiative: among the many thousands executed, women outnumbered men everywhere, at least four to one. To rulers and churchmen seeking control, the sorceress with her pact with the devil was the symbol of secret revolt. Out of jealousy, infertile village women even accused other women. Meanwhile, during the Counter Reformation, energetic women founded teaching orders that brought instruction to many girls other than nuns; contemplative orders were reformed by leaders like Teresa of Avila. Her

autobiography, a profound account of a woman's interior and mystical life, was read as eagerly as Augustine's "Confessions."

Jewish women followed their own leader in the women's gallery of the synagogue; one Yiddish prayer visualized women studying Torah in Paradise. Protestant women expanded their Bible reading, but it was especially radical sects like the Quakers who challenged the limits on women. Margaret Fell wrote her 1666 tract, "Women's Speaking Justified," against Paul's admonition that women should keep silent in church. Women "led by the Spirit of God" could preach "Christ in the Male and Female is one."

For centuries, women had been queens, some of whom, like Elizabeth I of England, sustained authority by combining "masculine" and "feminine" styles of rulership. But no woman served in the law courts or chancelleries of late medieval and early modern monarchies. If a woman wanted to fight in the royal army, she had to do so disguised as a man. Joan of Arc, openly leading soldiers into battle to save France, was an exception in her day—and she ended up burned at the stake.

Most political action of women was taken informally through conversations and coquetry at court and as sponsors of the salons that arose in many cities in the seventeenth century. More open influence came about through increased literacy and printing. By the eighteenth century, women of diverse views were contributing to the abundant pamphlet literature on public affairs. The English historian Catharine Sawbridge Macaulay published tracts defending authors' copyright, frequently elected parliaments and the rights of the American colonies. As for the illiterate women of the lower classes in England, France and the Netherlands, their only lever of protest was joining in street riots.

15   All these forms of political action came together in the French Revolution, and some new ones were added as women made public political speeches and joined the army openly. The new philosophy of rational natural rights placed all men on an equal footing in regard to citizenship and the law. But did "men" include women? The French playwright Olympe de Gouges insisted that it did in her "Declaration of the Rights of Woman," in 1791, as did Mary Wollstonecraft the following year in "A Vindication of the Rights of Woman." Others did not want women to have so much of a share in political life. Men of the revolution said that women should stay home and rear their sons to be good citizens. Even evangelical women encouraged their sisters to seek reform through religion and leave matters of state to men. It would be the new American republic where the issues of women's status would play out most vigorously over the next century.

"The Slavery of Marriage"

When enlightenment ideas came to America, the debate about women's rights found a new context, since the most powerful form of social hierarchy there was not gender but race. And the American Constitution, by dispensing with hereditary rank and monarchical institutions, immediately granted women a new role: teaching republican values to young Americans. The new republic opened many avenues to women: social, economic, political, educational and religious. Evangelical Christianity made the home, not the church, the site of religious instruction.

As women increasingly assumed this responsibility, they also began teaching outside the home and stressed the need for women's schools. In the first half of the nineteenth century, Emma Willard's Troy Female Seminary and Catharine Beecher's Hartford Female Seminary became thriving institutions, followed by Mary Lyon's Mount Holyoke Female Seminary. By midcentury, it was clear that tax revenues should be spent to educate girls as well as boys, at least in New York and New England. By the 1870s, many public universities admitted women, and elite women's colleges like Smith and Wellesley were established. In 1894, feminist donors to Johns Hopkins Medical School used their gifts to compel the admission of women.

Still, far into the first half of the twentieth century, many professional schools continued to bar women, and when they were admitted, discrimination drove them to lower-status professional fields. Female doctors were steered toward public health, lawyers to social work, language scholars to library cataloguing, scientists to high-school teaching.

Within the white middle-class family, education and religious responsibility for children improved women's status through the nineteenth century. By the 1830s, magazines analyzing life from a woman's point of view began to flourish in North America. In Europe, female writers of philosophical insight, from George Eliot to Virginia Woolf in the early twentieth century and on up to Simone de Beauvoir, steadily clarified women's issues. But mostly, wives were still considered their husbands' subordinates.

20   American feminists wishing to convey their critique of marriage often did so through the lens of slavery, the most volatile public issue of the mid- and late nineteenth century. "The investigation of the rights of the slave has led me to a better understanding of my own," wrote Angelina Grimké, a Southern abolitionist. "I have found the Anti-Slavery cause to be the high school of morals in our land. Now if rights are founded in the nature of our moral being, then the mere circumstance of sex does not give to man higher rights and responsibilities than to woman."

Though they didn't participate in elections, American women believed that they had access to the political system through the right to petition Congress. But as the conflict over abolition escalated, it became clear that women's petitions were not being heard. The right to vote was moved to the top of the list. Female reformers like Elizabeth Cady Stanton and Anna Howard Shaw combined spellbinding oratory with noisy street politics. Stanton was well known, for instance, for her lecture The Slavery of Marriage. The argument for suffrage then became more expedient: white women's votes would balance those of newly enfranchised black males and immigrants. The majority that ratified the nineteenth Amendment in 1920 was built on these racist grounds.

New Experts in Mothering: Men

Meanwhile, biological science was replacing theology as the language for discussing the differences between women and men. The popularity of Darwinian thought and the discovery of the endocrine system anchored the discussion firmly in science. Nor were such discussions purely theoretical, for by the 1920s women and men began to inhabit the same workplace. Even so, the young women taking clerical jobs in corporate offices were considered little threat, for it was thought that their hormones would drive them to maternity and service rather than wealth and power.

The new economic forces at work in America radically altered the role of women as workers, mothers and wives. Industrialization had created jobs for women in factories and textile mills in the mid-1800s. At the same time, the fruits of industrialization produced clothing and foods—gave middle-class mothers a new role: manager of household consumption. But many female responsibilities were subject to male guidance at the turn of the century. In the new field of child studies, male experts like G. Stanley Hall even tried to make mothering a science.

Isolation made mothers willing recipients of such expertise. The middle class had begun its flight from the city in the mid-nineteenth century, and by its close servants were being replaced by new labor-saving household equipment. So suburban women were alone with their children. Whereas in the eighteenth century the family was a partnership for spouses and children, the twentieth-century family became based on intimacy. Greater life expectancy meant that marriages lasted longer, well past a woman's childbearing years. As infant mortality declined, the family became more child-centered, and private insurance and pensions, as well as governmental assistance, made older parents less dependent on working children.

25   The emotional tone of marriages also changed with the rise of the corporation and the profession. Increasingly, the vocations of middle-class men excluded their families. This prompted a movement for more accessible divorce, along with longer marriages, increased mobility and the growing ideal of emotional and sexual fulfillment between spouses.

Not-So-Equal Rights

Sigmund Freud and other pioneers of psychology profoundly affected the status of women by arguing that an acceptance of gender difference was a prerequisite for mental health. From the 1920s through the 1970s, women with political, scientific or intellectual interests were stigmatized as neurotic, while men involved in the more feminine realms like the arts were considered less than fully male. The family dynamic laid out by Freud, based on latent erotic attachments, encouraged sons to overcome their mother complexes by becoming strong and independent. Daughters, meanwhile, were encouraged to replace their love for their fathers by finding a male romantic partner rather than by developing an independent self. In time, however, feminist interpretations of difference developed. In the 1970s, Nancy Chodorow reworked Freud's Oedipal system to point out that the strongest erotic gratification a female infant receives comes from a same-sex relationship with her mother, raising questions about the inevitability of female dependence on males.

In the political sphere, meanwhile, female voting didn't change party power structures, and women began developing parallel institutions like the National Woman's Party, in 1916. Its 1923 drive for an equal rights amendment failed, just as its successor failed in the 1970s, partly because Americans, including women, remained resistant to the idea of a woman as President. Once again, feminists created parallel structures to support female candidates, like Emily's List (Early Money Is Like Yeast). Where once the rare women elected to public office were typically the widows of male officeholders, the election of women became unremarkable, though even now they comprise only a fraction of Congress and high state officials.

In the 1960s, feminists began to focus on changing the composition of high-status professions. Once access to graduate education was won, feminist scholars pushed to change patterns of research and teaching so that women were no longer regarded as a failed model of the male norm, but as a norm themselves. In so doing, they helped ignite the culture wars of the 1980s and 90s. And by the end of the 90s, women constituted 60 percent of college graduates. Even so, on leaving school they still face the continuing reality of the glass ceiling.

Inflation, rising economic expectations and women's quest for professional equality after World War II produced the reinvention of the nanny—a movement promptly challenged by the argument that only birth mothers could care effectively for their children. A successful dual-track life as mother and professional, therefore, required heroic energy or a flouting of this conventional wisdom. Two careers within one family often meant a commuter marriage, which may have seemed new but which echoed the old aristocratic pattern: spouses parted by attendance at court and by journeys to distant estates or remote colonies. But now there is a big difference: a woman's property and income do not necessarily belong to her husband.

30   While feminist interpretations of gender difference gained favor in the 1970s, and while lesbian feminists argued in the 1980s for difference with a difference, claiming the superiority of same-sex relationships, a strong backlash arose in conservative quarters. This was marked not only by a denigration of feminism but also by an elevation of macho versions of male power and fresh assertions of difference. Such arguments were once again located in theology by Christian, Jewish and Islamic fundamentalists. Meanwhile, new debates about gender difference emerged in brain research. While female and male synapses might fire the same way, doubters insisted that there must surely be a difference in the circuitry. Questions about differences in wiring are a new form of debate that goes back to the medieval question about whether women have souls.

The New Terrain

So what has happened to women over the past thousand years? Western women and their children have made astonishing gains in health and life expectancy, though most of their non-Western sisters have not yet shared those benefits. The scope of women's work has expanded vastly, much of it paying well enough so that women with children can survive. Women in the West have secured access to education beyond the wildest dreams of their medieval counterparts. Women's athletic prowess has captured public imagination, and a female general is no longer a novelty.

But what of the mixed outcomes? Feminist spirituality today provides a powerful leaven within some Christian, Jewish and Islamic communities, but others still forbid female participation, and the loss of the institutional structure once provided by female religious orders has shrunk the territory controlled by women. The reduced number of women's colleges has had a similar effect. Women's reproductive lives, though, are now managed by technologies subject to male control. The ability to detect the sex of a fetus can result in higher abortion rates for female infants, whereas in medieval society the girl babies at least had a chance to be born. Sexual freedoms have enlarged the sphere of pleasure, but with them have come unresolved problems about sexual behavior.

What will be the new terrain for addressing the issues of likeness and difference? What new strategies will women develop to dismantle exclusively male hierarchies? The cognitive sciences will most likely inherit the role of theology in arguing about differences between male and female. Still, the global rise of religious fundamentalism will counter women's efforts to secure equal footing. And among women worldwide there will remain stark differences about how to achieve a better life.

But argument—and laughter—about the relationship between women and men will never end. Our physical bodies are cultural texts that are constantly revised, and no single formulation of the relationship between the sexes can last.

ONE PLAY: THREE TYPES OF ESSAYS

The purpose of the student essays that follow, each written in response to *A Doll's House*, is to demonstrate three different approaches to writing about the same work of literature: a personal response essay, a critical/argumentative essay, and a research essay. Though these essays have different objectives—a personal essay shares, an argumentative essay proves a thesis, a research essay expands the writer's support base to include secondary sources—they have one very important thing in common: each of them brings evidence, details, and illustrations from the text of the play for support and clarification.

A Student's Personal Response Essay

In the response essay that follows, Trisa Hayes describes her personal response to Henrik Ibsen's *A Doll's House* and Kate Chopin's "The Story of an Hour." In contrast to the plight of the women in these works, her thesis describes how grateful she is for the encouragement her parents and others gave her to be independent when she was growing up. She realizes, moreover, that she would not have had this opportunity had it not been for the women of previous centuries who fought so hard for women's rights. It is a personal response essay because Trisa does not intend to analyze the works or try to "prove" an interpretation. Her intention is to share her response—what these works have meant to her—and provide details and illustrations to clarify and support her thesis.

Trisa Hayes

Dr. Madden

English 102

December 20, 20XX

The Age of Living Dolls

When I was a little girl, I desperately wanted a dollhouse. After my persistent begging, whining, and promise making, my parents finally gave in and bought me one. I spent hours playing with my doll, the new house, and all its tiny furniture. I loved it simply because I had sole control over all aspects of my doll's life: when she would eat, where she would shop, what she would wear, what time she would go to bed. These were things my parents had control over in my life.

Playing with my doll was fun until the newness wore off; after that I only played with her when I was bored. The rest of the time she just sat in her house, lifeless and waiting patiently for the next string of activities I would plan for her.

Over the years my parents and others encouraged me to make my own decisions no matter how big they were, and having the freedom to do so is something I'll never take for granted again. After reading Henrik Ibsen's *A Doll's House* and Kate Chopin's "The Story of an Hour," I saw what life could be like through the eyes of women who are treated like dolls. These stories are an illustration of women's roles and the dilemmas women faced in society during the nineteenth century.

The protagonist in *A Doll's House* is Nora, a simple housewife who is treated like a five-year-old by her husband, Torvald. It appears at first that the only thing Nora is capable of is mirroring what her husband wishes to see in her. Because he expects her to be like a pet, she flutters and twitters about the room like a helpless bird, or she takes on the characteristics of a small woodland creature that relies entirely on a much larger beast for its safety. As I continued to read about her incomprehensible submissiveness, I found myself getting angrier and angrier. First she hides her macaroons because Torvald doesn't want her to have sweets. Then there's my favorite example: Nora tells Torvald, "Everything you do is quite right, Torvald" (845). Her spineless actions are infuriating.

Torvald's overwhelming male chauvinistic attitude only intensified my frustrations. When Nora approaches him on Krogstad's behalf, Torvald insists he will have to replace him and gives this revealing excuse: "Is it to get about now that the new manager has changed his mind at his wife's bidding..." (828). And when Nora tells him he is always right, he responds, "Now my little skylark is speaking reasonably" (845).

But this is 1879, and Nora and Torvald are only filling the female/male roles that were socially acceptable at that time. It is a man's world, with only male views and male rules. What gives men the right to tell women how to behave? Nothing. They are just the physically stronger of the two sexes.

As Charlotte Perkins Stetson says in "Women and Economics," published in 1899, a man's role in relation to women is "a sovereignty based on the accident of sex" (867). But Nora is growing tired of being treated like mindless property and snaps to Mrs. Linde, "You are just like the others. They all think that I am incapable of anything really serious..." (810).

When Torvald opens Krogstad's letter, she is so terrified of him, she wants to escape from the house before he has a chance to confront her. He grabs her arm and declares with great despair and rage, "And I must sink to such miserable depths because of a thoughtless woman" (849). This is hardly a way for him to show his gratitude to the woman who saved his life. As soon as Torvald receives the next letter and returned IOU from Krogstad, he cries "I am saved!" (850) and digs himself into a deeper hole in Nora's eyes when he adds, "There is something so indescribably sweet and satisfying, to a man, in the knowledge that he has forgiven his wife...It seems as if that had made her, as it were, doubly his own; he has given her a new life, so to speak; and she has in a way become both wife and child to him" (851). Torvald's response has provided Nora with a revelation about Torvald and about herself. She begins to discover how very little she knows about herself and the world around her. She isn't even aware of her own interests because she has always been so eager to please her husband.

His unsavory responses present her with a new dilemma. Should she abandon her family and comfortable home for a sense of self-worth? Or should she stay and sacrifice any future prospects of happiness? I can't imagine being forced to believe that it's a woman's duty to maintain a man's happiness even if she must sacrifice her own. Furthermore, Nora had to consider how others would treat her if she left, for back then women absolutely, positively did not go against the grain of society's expectations unless they were fully prepared to endure vicious slurs and be shunned by respected members of the community, lifelong friends, and in some instances even their own families.

Then, with a mature demeanor, Nora sits down with her husband to have a serious discussion for the first time. The tide of power shifts as she reveals her observations of their life together. She explains to him how both he and her father have treated her like a doll, and that now she is certain of what she needs to do. She announces to Torvald that she is leaving him. He is dumbfounded but attempts to reason with her by reminding her of her "sacred duty" to him and their children, but she unleashes her pent up feelings on him: "I can no longer content myself with what most people say, or with what is found in books. I must think over things for myself and get to understand them" (853). "I am going to see if I can make out who is right, the world or I" (854). And she leaves to try to discover the choices and opportunities for those who are not confined to a child's boundaries.

Kate Chopin, who was born in 1851 and died in 1904, probably witnessed such struggles firsthand. The signs of her times are expressed through her writing, specifically through "The Story of an Hour." It's evident that throughout history many women have walked in Nora's shoes, thus the fight for the right to vote. But most women of her time didn't dare acknowledge the slightest dissatisfaction with their roles as wives and mothers, much less have the courage to leave. "The Story of an Hour" is the story of such a woman.

Her story is that of a woman who has just found out that her husband has died in a railroad disaster. At first she is in shock, void of all emotion. And then without warning she begins to cry hysterically. After her sister Josephine succeeds in calming her somewhat, she retreats to the solitude of her room to collect her thoughts. Then, after a sincere struggle to maintain the specific emotions that society expects her to have over the loss of her husband, she finally succumbs to her true feelings by uttering softly to herself, "Free, free, free!" (71).

Her sister, out of concern, begs her to open the door. She "breathed a quick prayer that life might be long. It was only yesterday she had thought with a shudder that life might be long" (72). Then, almost in a tranquil state, she rises to let Josephine in and agrees to accompany her downstairs. But as they descend, the front door unlocks and in walks her husband, completely unscathed and very much alive. She instantly dies of a heart attack at the sight of her husband. The doctors say she died from a "joy that kills" (72), but nothing could be further from the truth. She and Nora, though worlds apart in some ways, share a common bond. They both have a burning desire to be free, to break the mold of their doll-like lives.

It's frightening to read about all the stifling rules and regulations women had to follow back then. Just thinking about it makes me claustrophobic. The sad part is that there are still an astounding number of women in our country who are forced to obey each and every command given to them by their husbands, no matter how humiliating or dehumanizing. The ability to think as an individual is gradually stripped and they become more and more lifeless, mindless dolls every day.

I am deeply grateful to the women who believed that they deserved more in life than that. Because of these two stories, I have a new respect for and understanding of the women who lived in the nineteenth century, a time I think of as "the age of the living dolls." For without these pioneering women who struggled through and endured many hardships to obtain basic human rights, life for women now would only be something to be endured and not enjoyed.

[New Page]

Works Cited

Chopin, Kate. "The Story of an Hour." Madden 71–72.

Ibsen, Henrik. *A Doll's House.* Madden 803–56.

Madden, Frank, ed. *Exploring Literature.* 5th ed. New York: Longman, 2012. Print.

Stetson (Gilman), Charlotte Perkins. Excerpt from "Women and Economics." Madden 866–67.

A Student's Argumentative Essay

In the argumentative essay that follows, Kathryn Pagano writes about Henrik Ibsen's *A Doll's House* and claims that Ibsen's play not only exposes the way that sexist views affected women during the late nineteenth and early twentieth century but inspired important changes in the perception of gender roles. It is a argumentative essay because Kathryn intends to "prove" her interpretation by analyzing the play within its historical and social context.

Kathryn Pagano

Professor Frank Madden

Composition and Literature 2

Spring 20XX

Women Then and Now

Over time, significant changes have altered the world in which we live today. Specifically, the views and role of women have dramatically changed since the late nineteenth and early twentieth centuries. Henrik Ibsen's classic play, *A Doll's House*, is a remarkable drama that illustrates the imbalance between the sexes during that time. It is difficult to comprehend the vast progress that has been made, but taking a glimpse into the past allows us to value and appreciate the opportunities available to women in the present. *A Doll's House* provides that glimpse and is a prime example of how sexist views affected women during the late nineteenth and early twentieth century.

History shows that, "Women were long considered naturally weaker than men, squeamish, and unable to perform work requiring muscular or intellectual development" (Women's History, "The Weaker Sex?"). In the past, it was understood that the role of a female was to take care of the home, children, and her husband. It is apparent that women were not entitled to their own opinions and were treated with disregard. Men, on the other hand, were viewed as strong and intellectually superior and took care of the more important obligations of life.

A Doll's House centers on Nora Helmer, the wife of Torvald Helmer. Throughout the play, it is evident that Nora is oblivious to the real world and that she is completely dependent on her husband. She makes it her priority to make her husband happy at all times, even if it means sacrificing her own happiness. Luckily, at the end of the play, Nora has an epiphany and finally realizes that, female or not, she has the right to have a voice of her own.

Ibsen opens the play by introducing the Helmers and the setting of the play, the Christmas holiday season. From the beginning of the first act, Nora is belittled by her husband. When she comes home from doing some holiday shopping, he welcomes her with his pet names for her, "Is my little squirrel bustling about?" (Ibsen, *A Doll's House*, 804). These degrading little names symbolize Nora's lack of importance and her helplessness.

"During the early history of the United States, a man virtually owned his wife and children as he did his material possessions" (Women's History, "The Legal Status of Women"). Torvald is extremely controlling over his wife. He takes pleasure in offering his advice about money and debt. The "all knowing" Torvald tells his wife that she needs to watch her spending habits, sarcastically calling her his "little spendthrift." Torvald, like the rest of society at the time, views men to be all knowing and believes that women are incapable of understanding money, due to their gender. He lectures Nora on how he hates debts and how a home that owes money is not beautiful because it is not free. Ironically, when Nora shows a bit of sadness, Torvald reciprocates by giving her money. Torvald expresses his concern for her foolish spending, but then hands over money, as though he were giving an allowance to a child.

As if Torvald didn't have enough of a hold on Nora already, he even prohibits her from eating sweets. Nora feels the need to hide her purchase of macaroons in order to keep it a secret from her husband. It is obvious that Nora takes a back seat to her husband. He states that while Nora made ornaments the previous Christmas, he was bored. He even makes the remark, "This time I needn't sit here and be dull all alone, and you needn't ruin your dear eyes and pretty hands" (Ibsen, *A Doll's House*, 806). To Torvald, Nora's job is to look pretty and tend to his needs. Instead of trying to be her own person, Nora makes sure she satisfies her husband, even agreeing to his requests, "As you please, Torvald" (Ibsen, *A Doll's House*, 804).

As the story progresses, the reader becomes aware of the potentially life-changing sacrifice that Nora makes in an attempt to save her husband's life. During a needy and vulnerable time, Nora forges her father's signature in an attempt to obtain a loan from Mr. Krogstad. To Nora, she is not committing a crime, instead she is acting like any loving wife would. Unfortunately, when Torvald learns the truth, he doesn't view Nora's behavior as she does. Instead of understanding the reasons behind Nora's actions, he becomes infuriated and thinks only of himself, "Now you have destroyed all my happiness. You have ruined all my future. It is horrible to think of!" (Ibsen, *A Doll's House*, 849).

Once Torvald realizes that Krogstad no longer wishes to expose the truth, his feelings toward Nora completely change. While he was once upset and intolerant, he is now subdued and comforting. He says that everything is okay and that he forgives Nora, since she only acted out of love. As was common among men during this time, Torvald acted selfishly and condescendingly towards his wife. Unfortunately for him, Nora had come to know the truth about her relationship with Torvald. She was going to give him the biggest surprise of them all.

Unlike many women during this time, Nora decides to have a talk with Torvald and share her true feelings. During the first and only serious talk that she and her husband have, Nora tells her husband that she feels as though he treats her like a doll. She lets Torvald know that she no longer is willing to be the person that he can form and treat as he pleased. Nora tells

Torvald that she no longer loves him and that she knows that he couldn't possibly love her. As expected, Torvald makes it known to Nora where her place is, at home with her children and her husband. Torvald forbids Nora to leave the family, telling her that she is "delirious" and acting like a child.

Nora feels that leaving her family will offer her the opportunity to explore and understand who she truly is. For the first time in her life, Nora is taking a stand and following through with what she believes in. She no longer is thinking of her obligations as a wife, but as an individual who deserves the same rights as any man. It is refreshing to know that Nora has come to realize that there is more to life than the one she has at home with her husband. Nora's goal and intentions throughout the play remain honorable.

Ibsen's *A Doll's House* does not end in a typical manner. For its time, it goes against the norm of society by showing a female take a strong stance against her husband. A housewife leaving her family in an attempt to gain personal happiness is not only looked upon as selfish, but also as completely obscene. It is for this reason that Ibsen, reluctantly, agreed to write a different ending for a German production of the play.

In the revised ending of the play, Nora does not leave her family. Torvald forces his wife to see the children before she walks out on them, "Look, there they are asleep, peaceful and carefree. Tomorrow, when they wake up and call for their mother, they will be motherless" (Ibsen, "A Changed Ending of *A Doll's House* for a German Production," 861). The guilt is too much for Nora to bear so she gives in to Torvald. Her decision to stay and give up her own contentment is a dramatically different ending from the one Ibsen intended. Clearly there were audiences that were not very pleased with the original ending and felt the need for a more "realistic" finale. Fortunately the original ending was restored, and Nora leaves Torvald.

Women have often faced discrimination simply due to their gender. In the past, women were looked down upon if they worked in a career that was not considered gender appropriate. The early nineteenth century marked a period when "women were excluded from the professions, except for writing and teaching" (Women's History, "Women at Work"). In addition to these limitations, women struggled for a long time just to gain the right to vote. On August 26, 1920, with the help of Elizabeth Cady Stanton and

Susan B. Anthony, the nineteenth amendment finally allowed women the right to vote. As Stanton once stated,

> "The strongest reason...for the full development of her faculties, her forces of mind and body; for giving her the most enlarged freedom of thought and action; a complete emancipation from all forms of bondage, of custom, dependence, superstition; from all the crippling influences of fear—is the solitude and personal responsibility of her own individual life" (Stanton 862).

It is apparent that through the ages women have had to fight hard for justice. It is also understandable why Ibsen's original ending is controversial. Ibsen's play perfectly depicts the disparity between males and females in the past. However, credit should be given to the author himself, who took an extraordinary risk when he wrote the play. Not only did he allow Nora to be seen as a strong female in the end, but he also understood the need for Torvald's "skylark" to be set free.

[New Page]

Works Cited

Ibsen, Henrik. *A Doll's House*. Madden 803–56.

Ibsen, Henrik. "The Changed Ending of *A Doll's House* for a German Production." Madden 861.

Madden, Frank, ed. *Exploring Literature*. 5th ed. New York: Longman, 2012. Print.

Stanton, Elizabeth. Excerpt from "The Solitude of Self." Madden 862–63.

"Women's History in America: Presented by Women's International Center." Excerpted from *Compton's Interactive Encyclopedia*. Compton's NewMedia, Inc. 1994. Web. April 17, 2010. http://www.wic.org/misc/history.htm.

"Women's Suffrage in the United States." Wikipedia: The Free Encyclopedia. Web. April 16, 2010. http://en.wikipedia.org/wiki/Women's_suffrage_in_the_United_States.

A Student's Research Essay

In the research essay that follows, James Militana writes about Henrik Ibsen's *A Doll's House* and claims that Ibsen did not set out to write a play about women's rights but rather a play that criticized society as a whole. James intends to prove that

Ibsen's play is less about Ibsen's attitude toward women than about society's attitude toward women. It is a research essay because he relies on secondary sources to prove his point. His research is based on "a need to know." That need takes him well beyond the text of the play and requires the kind of sources that only research can provide.

James Militana

Professor Madden

Composition and Literature 2

March 14, 20XX

On Her Own

Henrik Ibsen scrutinizes the institution of marriage and the role of women in the early nineteenth century in his play *A Doll's House*. The play does not sugarcoat marriage and presents it in a sentimental fashion. Instead Ibsen sheds light on the reality of how men and women of the time interacted and how women were often confined by marriage. Yet Ibsen did not set out to make a statement about women's rights, rather his cause was to highlight the failing of society as a whole. *A Doll's House* was less about Ibsen's attitude toward women and more about society's attitude toward women. Despite his intended goal, the reception of Ibsen's message and the response to it did effect change for women. His message resonated at the play's inception in 1879 and is still relevant today.

Henrik Ibsen believed in human rights and the idea of self-transformation, which parallels the redefinition of Norway itself, upon being freed from four centuries of Danish rule in 1814. Issues involving freedom were important in the minds of Norwegians and this was reflected in Ibsen's play. In 1879, women were restricted and a wife was not legally permitted to borrow money without her husband's consent. Poverty had forced women into the workplace. But many of the protections provided to women were aimed at the lower class and employment opportunities for women were limited to low-paying domestic jobs, secretarial work, or teaching. Middle-class women witnessed few of these advantages. Indeed the institution of marriage restricted the freedom of these middle-class women. Professor Brian Downs notes that "the disagreement on which the drama of *A Doll's House* is built accordingly is not so much that between a wife and a husband as one between a woman and the society in which she lives, the society which imposes its laws upon her" (Lyons 122). Ibsen examines this phenomenon and centers his play on this theme.

Set at Christmas time just before the New Year, the play introduces Nora and Torvald Helmer and their relationship is quickly understood. Torvald treats Nora as if she is one of the children, calling her his "little squirrel" (Ibsen 804) and his "sweet little skylark" (Ibsen 805). In addition, he is quite condescending to her and chastises her for making purchases, telling her that she is a "spendthrift" who has "been wasting money again" (Ibsen 804). He clearly controls every aspect of her life, even controlling what she eats, forbidding her to eat macaroons. Nora, on the other hand, is very proud of Torvald's recent promotion to Bank Manager, and is happy that they will now be financially set. Nora seems content to follow his orders and does exactly as he asks. Lest the reader think that this marriage is an anomaly due to their personalities, Ibsen provides another view of marriage when Nora's friend Mrs. Linde comes to visit. Mrs. Linde admits her marriage was not based on love, but rather the fact that her husband, now dead, was able to provide for her sick mother and her two younger brothers.

Mrs. Linde's visit also provides an opportunity to expose a depth in Nora previously unseen. Linde indicates that with her husband dead, she is bereft of money. When she looks down her nose at Nora for never having had to struggle, Nora reveals that when Torvald was ill and needed to go to Italy to convalesce, she had arranged for a loan that now she scrimps to pay, all without Torvald's knowledge. Nora is seen as more than just a pretty woman when she acknowledges that "it was a tremendous pleasure to sit there working and earning money. It was like being a man" (Ibsen 812.) But her good decision is questioned when the man who loaned her the money divulges that he knows she forged her father's signature on the document. Nora's innocence is evident because she sees no wrongdoing in her actions; she was merely intent on helping her husband get better. Ibsen alluded to this disparity in his notes on *A Doll's House:* "There are two kinds of spiritual law, two kinds of conscience, one in man and another, altogether different in woman. They do not understand each other; but in practical life the woman is judged by man's law, as though she were not a woman but a man" (Weigand 69).

Tension mounts as the Christmas tree which Nora had decorated for the family now stands stripped of its ornaments, symbolic of what is to come: Nora being stripped of her secret. Torvald's personality is solidified as he states that "almost everyone who has gone to the bad early in life has had a deceitful mother" (Ibsen 823). This reveals his true feeling about women and foreshadows how he will behave if Nora's secret comes out. Torvald explodes as Nora pleads again for him to reconsider giving Krogstad a job. He admits that the real reason he won't hire Krogstad is because he doesn't show Torvald the respect he demands. Clearly his social standing is paramount. Krogstad returns and threatens to blackmail Nora by letting Torvald know about the loan and the forged documents. He drops a letter in the mailbox for which only Torvald has the key. Torvald has such total control over the house that only he can check the mail. Nora distracts him from checking the mail by insisting that he rehearse the tarantella, which she is to dance at the party. Once again he derides her, saying that she has "forgotten everything I taught you" (Ibsen 839). The disparity of their relationship is clear as Nora does not feel that she can tell him the truth. There is no equality in the marriage: it is as if she reports to him. Ibsen makes a point about society at that time and what it expected of women. Nora was meant to be subservient to her husband—she is not much more than a plaything for Torvald. Ibsen shines a spotlight on the problems that he sees as inherent in marriage at that time.

Act 3 brings a dramatic end to *A Doll's House* and Ibsen succeeds in highlighting how limited women's freedom was in the 1800s, with most of their lives directed by others, as Nora's was by Torvald. Mrs. Linde and Krogstad realize they still care for each other and decide to get married. Krogstad is transformed from an angry, vindictive man to a gentler, reasonable man. Clearly he has been misjudged by society based on his previous actions. When Linde says she knows that he is a better man than his actions have shown, he decides to retrieve his letter to Torvald. But in an interesting switch, Linde tells him that he shouldn't take back the letter. "This unhappy secret must be disclosed; they must have a complete understanding between them" (Ibsen 843). Linde has seen the relationship between Nora and Torvald and realizes what Nora does not, that they are not like a husband and wife; they are more like a father and child. With secrets between them, they will never change.

Nora and Torvald return home with Nora resisting, wanting to stay longer at the party. But the time of reckoning has arrived and Torvald goes out to get the mail. Nora is nervous knowing that Krogstad's letter is in the mailbox. In an ironic statement Torvald says that he wishes Nora "might be threatened by some great danger, so that I might risk my life's blood, and everything, for your sake" (Ibsen 848). However, when he reads Krogstad's letter he erupts in anger calling her a "hypocrite, a liar - worse, worse - a criminal" (Ibsen 849). He doesn't "risk his life's blood" (Ibsen 848)—he is too concerned about how it will look to others. He doesn't seem to care that Nora did it to help him. Instead he turns on her and says that she can stay in "[his] house" (Ibsen 850) but she will not be allowed to bring up the children. Even in his anger he is concerned about appearances and says that "it must appear as if everything between us was just as before" (Ibsen 849). The doorbell rings, and a second letter from Krogstad arrives with the bond and a letter of regret. Now that his reputation is saved, Torvald is ecstatic and forgives Nora and says he will "advise and direct" (Ibsen 850) her due to her "womanly helplessness" (Ibsen 850).

Yet his forgiveness cannot undo the "the distorted mask of fury and aversion that he turned upon her after opening Krogstad's fatal letter. It was the face of a strange man with whom she had been living" (Downs 129). Nora changes out of her party dress and sits down at the table. Her demeanor makes it apparent to Torvald that something has changed. She tells him that she is tired of being treated like a toy, a plaything, a doll. She had left her father's house for Torvald without ever having been able to stand on her own. She announces that she is leaving Torvald; he is not the man she thought he was. Torvald forbids her to leave, but he can no longer forbid her to do anything; she is in control of her life now. When Torvald says she has a duty to him and the children, she says she has a duty first to herself. Ibsen elevates Nora with the slam of the door on her departure. It is a particularly brave and dangerous act, as divorce was socially stigmatized, and Torvald's objection would make Nora's alienation from society even greater. As a forerunner of the feminist movement, she would be completely alone in trying to establish a new life for herself.

Reaction to the play *A Doll's House* aroused a veritable furor. Professor Errol Durbach notes that "heated debate, difference of opinion in domestic parlors, and endless talk were the dominant responses to Ibsen's play" (Durbach 13). For some, it was interpreted as a shockingly immoral attack on the sanctity of marriage and an obscene denial of a wife's primary duty to her husband and children. Yet critics like Joan Templeton are quick to point out that Ibsen was not commenting on marriage but rather on "the conflict between love and law, between heart and head, between feminine and masculine" (Templeton 35). Stella Adler confirms that "he is not anxious to solve a play about a man and a woman. He is out to resolve the problem of Man and Woman, the problem of Man and Society" (Adler 50).

And while Ibsen did not see himself as a supporter of women's rights, per se, others have a different interpretation. Professor Weigand addressed the issue of intent: "Ibsen was an ardent champion of woman's rights before and after writing *A Doll's House*. Apostle of freedom and individualism as he was, Ibsen felt that organized society was trying to keep woman in a state of virtual slavery. His indignation over this state of affairs fathered the plot of *A Doll's House*" (Weigand 74). Professor Katharine M. Rogers concurs that "Ibsen had an unusually enlightened attitude toward women and was seriously concerned with women's rights rather than merely using them as a timely theme for *A Doll's House*" (Mitchell 112). Certainly Ibsen's actions show him to be sympathetic to women and their struggle for freedom as he supported "a bill to assure married women control of their own property" and "his impassioned efforts toward giving women equal membership privileges in the Scandinavian Society in Rome" (Mitchell 115). Change was evidenced for women: in 1882, women obtained inheritance rights and were successful in petitioning for the right to a university education and in 1888, married women in Norway were finally given control over their own money.

Ibsen celebrates people breaking free from the restrictions of society and trying to establish their own individuality and freedom. Ibsen's focus on real life issues has given his work continued relevance and timelessness. *A Doll's House* is almost predictive in its rendering of the helpless position of married women in the nineteenth century. Feminism today stresses the issues of equality and freedom, along with other issues essential to women, but the need for feminine independence and individuality has never been more originally and compellingly dramatized than in *A Doll's House*. Author Elaine Hoffman Baruch asserts that "from a feminist point of view, Nora is the new adventurer, a mythic hero for women to emulate... There is no aspect of the contemporary women's movement that Ibsen doesn't anticipate and comment on. In this sense, he may rightly be termed a seer" (Mitchell 32). Without a doubt, Ibsen was a visionary who contributed significantly to the change of social attitudes and demonstrated the power of the stage in motivating social conduct.

[New Page]

Works Cited

Adler, Stella. *Stella Adler on Ibsen, Strindberg, and Chekhov.* Ed. Barry Paris. New York: Knopf, 1999. Print.

Downs, Brian W. *A Study of Six Plays by Ibsen.* Cambridge, England: University, 1950. Print.

Durbach, Errol. *A Doll's House: Ibsen's Myth of Transformation.* Boston: Twayne, 1991. Print.

Ibsen, Henrik. *A Doll's House. Exploring Literature.* Ed. Frank Madden. 5th ed. New York: Longman, 2012. 803–56. Print.

Lyons, Charles R. *Critical Essays on Henrik Ibsen.* Boston, Mass.: G.K. Hall, 1987. Print.

Mitchell, Hayley R. *Readings on A Doll's House.* San Diego, CA: Greenhaven, 1999. Print.

Templeton, Joan. "*The Doll House* Backlash: Criticism, Feminism, and Ibsen." *PMLA*, Vol. 104, No. 1 (Jan., 1989), pp. 28–40. JSTOR. Web. 5 May 2010.

Weigand, Hermann John. *The Modern Ibsen: A Reconsideration.* New York: H. Holt and Company, 1925. Print.

EXPLORING THE LITERATURE OF WOMEN AND MEN: OPTIONS FOR MAKING CONNECTIONS, BUILDING ARGUMENTS, AND USING RESEARCH

MAKING CONNECTIONS

1. Consider the ways your gender or the gender of those you know has affected your life. Do any of the stories, poems, plays, or essays in this section remind you of your own experiences or the circumstances of your life? Choose one or more of these works, and write a response essay that compares your experience or circumstances with those in the literature.

2. Our own values about gender can affect how we see the world and strongly influence our response to literature. We may agree or disagree with what an author says or what characters say or do. So too, literature may influence us and the formation of our values about gender. Write an essay about the ways in which one or more works in this section either provoked a moral judgment on your part or helped you learn something.

MAKING AN ARGUMENT

1. Over two hundred years ago, Mary Wollstonecraft in *A Vindication of the Rights of Women* wrote: "It would be an endless task to trace the variety of meannesses, cares, and sorrows into which women are plunged by the prevailing opinion that they were created rather to feel than reason, and that all power they obtain must be obtained by their charms and weakness." Consider this quote, and write an essay about how this kind of stereotyping has influenced the way women are treated or how they behave in one or more works in this section.

2. In the best-selling book *Iron John,* Robert Bly wrote: "We have defective mythologies that ignore masculine depth of feeling, assign men a place in the sky instead of earth, teach obedience to the wrong powers, and entangle men and women in systems of industrial domination." Write about this quote as it applies to the roles of men in one or more works in this section.

3. Choose a quote (or quotes) in the introduction to this section, Women and Men (pp. 668–669), and pair it (or them) with one of the longer pieces in this section that either supports it or argues against it. For example, pair Rousseau's quote about the education (training) of women with Virginia Woolf's essay "If Shakespeare Had a Sister," which argues against it. On the other hand, if you choose Gail Sheehy's quote about the plight of the modern married woman, you might choose the Woolf essay to exemplify and support the point Sheehy is making.

   Write an essay comparing or contrasting the quote (or quotes) you chose from the introduction with the story, poem, play, or essay you chose to support or argue against it.

Using Research

Andrew Marvell's poem "To His Coy Mistress," Henrik Ibsen's play *A Doll's House,* and Virginia Woolf's essay "If Shakespeare Had a Sister" all have something important to say about gender and relationships. However insightful each of these pieces is by itself, expanding our exploration of this literature by seeking, using, and citing relevant secondary sources can add support and credibility to our writing.

1. Do you think women and men experience love differently? Research suggests that we do. Pick out a work or works in this section, and write about the differences between male and female experiences of love as depicted in the literature. Support your conclusions with secondary source research.

2. In an influential work, *The Second Sex*, published in 1949, Simone de Beauvoir wrote: "This has always been a man's world, and none of the reasons hitherto brought forward in explanation of this fact has seemed adequate." A look at some of the literature in this section seems to bear this out. But it has been more than sixty years since this work was published. Have things changed? With reference to literature in this section and secondary sources, make a case for or against the notion that it's still a man's world.

3. As reflected in the works in this section, consider the different attitudes toward gender that have prevailed at different times over the last four hundred years. Write about those differences and refer to secondary source material—in this text and from other sources—to support your views.

Writing About Connections Across Themes

Most of the literature in the text has been organized into theme sections, but good literature is much too complex to be reduced to a single broad theme. Many of the works included under Women and Men could just as easily fit under other themes—and in many cases works arranged in other themes could fit here as well.

Choose one or more of the following works from earlier chapters or other themes, and consider how they can be linked to Women and Men—and how this combination of the work with more than one theme provides additional insight into the literature and fresh topics for writing.

Collaboration: Writing and Revising with Your Peers

In addition to applying your own values and standards to writing about the literature in this section, you may find it beneficial to share and discuss your work with classmates. Getting feedback from others can help you generate and clarify your ideas and revise and edit your writing more effectively. For details, see pages 397–398.

A Writing/Research Portfolio Option

A portfolio is a collection of your work, related materials, and commentary about your work collected over time. Gathering materials in a portfolio will provide you with resources for research and development. See page 398 for details.

Culture & Identity

Culture & Identity
A DIALOGUE ACROSS HISTORY

Better one's own duty, [though] imperfect, / Than another's duty well performed.
> —from the *Bhagavad Gita,* c. 250 BCE–250 CE

Man is born a barbarian, and only raises himself above the beast by culture.
> —Baltasar Gracian, *The Art of Worldly Wisdom,* 1647

The great law of culture is: Let each become all that he was created capable of being.
> —Thomas Carlyle, *Critical Essays,* 1827

Instead of boiling up individuals into the species, I would draw a chalk line round every individuality, and preach to it to keep within that, and preserve and cultivate its identity.
> —Jane Welsh Carlyle, letter, 1845

If a man does not keep pace with his companions, perhaps it is because he hears a different drummer. Let him step to the music which he hears, however measured or far away.
> —Henry David Thoreau, *Walden,* 1854

It is not the consciousness of men that determines their existence, but on the contrary it is their social existence that determines their consciousness.
> —Karl Marx, *Critique of Political Economy,* 1859

I'm Nobody! Who are you? / Are you—Nobody—too?
> —Emily Dickinson, c. 1861

When I found that I had crossed that line [during her first escape from slavery], I looked at my hands to see if I was the same person. There was such a glory over everything.
> —Harriet Tubman, her biography, 1868

Knowledge of [another] culture should sharpen our ability to scrutinize more steadily, to appreciate more lovingly, our own.
> —Margaret Mead, *Coming of Age in Somoa,* 1928

The most powerful obstacle to culture ... is the tendency to aggression, [which is] an innate, independent, instinctual disposition in man.
　　—Sigmund Freud, *Civilization and Its Discontents*, 1930

From the moment of his birth the customs into which [an individual] is born shape his experience and behavior. By the time he can talk, he is the little creature of his culture.
　　—Ruth Benedict, *Patterns of Culture*, 1934

I wouldn't want to belong to any club that would accept me as a member.
　　—Groucho Marx, c. 1935

Men can starve from a lack of self-realization as much as ... from a lack of bread.
　　—Richard Wright, *Native Son*, 1940

It is thus with most of us; we are what other people say we are. We know ourselves chiefly by hearsay.
　　—Eric Hoffer, *The Passionate State of Mind*, 1954

We become what we are only by the radical and profound rejection of what others have said about us.
　　—Jean Paul Sartre, preface to Frantz Fanon's *Wretched of the Earth*, 1961

I have a dream that one day on the red hills of Georgia the sons of former slaves and the sons of former slaveowners will be able to sit down together at the table of brotherhood.
　　—Martin Luther King, Jr., speech, 1963

[Culture] is a product of man: he projects himself into it, he recognizes himself in it; that critical mirror alone offers him his image.
　　—Jean Paul Sartre, *The Words*, 1964

No matter what our achievements might be, we think well of ourselves only in rare moments. We need people to bear witness against our inner judge, who keeps book on our shortcomings and transgressions. We need people to convince us that we are not as bad as we think we are.
　　—Eric Hoffer, 1954

I began to feel oddly detached. I was "there"; but I was also looking at myself being there. . . . I had learned much about the ways actors worked ... the small signs and tags that they offered to display emotions they might not feel. [And] I began to feel that I was performing my life instead of living it.
　　—Pete Hamill, *A Drinking Life*, 1994

I suppose I have a highly developed capacity for self-delusion, so it's no problem for me to believe that I'm somebody else.
　　—Daniel Day-Lewis, actor

CULTURE AND IDENTITY: EXPLORING YOUR OWN VALUES AND BELIEFS

What comes to mind when you hear the word *culture*? In everyday conversation, this word is often used to evaluate people rather than to identify their background. So it's common to hear people depicted as "cultured" as being praised for their good taste, aesthetic appreciation, behavior, or character. But our use of the term *culture* here, as reflected in the quotes on the previous pages and in the literature that follows, is based on a more formal definition. For our purposes, *culture* represents the shared attitudes, the values, or the behavioral patterns of a social or ethnic group.

Culture and identity are closely related. Cultural values and institutions play a big part in shaping who we are. Our ethnicity, families, geographic location, religious background, economic resources, education, and other factors influence how we see the world. But are we who we are exclusively because of our cultural backgrounds? Or are we who we are ultimately because of conscious choices we make as individuals? Are we responsible only to ourselves for our actions, or do we have an added responsibility to others in society?

The elusive answers to these questions are at the heart of our search for identity. Whether we seek our personal identity by marching to the beat of Thoreau's "different drummer," celebrate our common humanity at Martin Luther King, Jr.'s "table of brotherhood," or recognize in ourselves the cultural traditions and values we carry with us, we spend much of our lives finding our place in the world and our sense of who we are.

How we respond to literature, too, is often influenced by our sense of cultural and personal identity—how we see ourselves, our backgrounds, and our circumstances reflected in what we read. As a preparation for reading the literature in this section, you may find it helpful to think about your own beliefs about culture and identity.

READING AND WRITING ABOUT CULTURE AND IDENTITY

Exploring your beliefs and values and connecting your experience with what you read is an important first step toward our ultimate goal—an appreciation of literature and the ability to think and write critically about it. Critical analysis will require rereading and reflection, writing and revising, gathering evidence, and constructing a solid argument to support your responses.

At least one aspect of the many stories, poems, plays, and essays in this section is about the impact that culture and identity have on the characters: W. H. Auden's satirical tribute to an "identityless" hero in his poem "The Unknown Citizen"; the struggle of migrant farm workers in Luis Valdez's play *Los Vendidos*; and Frederick Douglass's valiant efforts to educate himself in the hostile atmosphere of slavery in the essay, "Learning to Read and Write." The brief quotes that open this section also give you some idea of the number of compelling ethical, political, and social arguments that are connected to culture and identity. Civil rights, equal opportunity, stereotyping, bigotry, oppression, social pressure and individual conscience, community and anonymity, and responsibility and self-realization head a long list of concerns. Any of these or other related issues might provide a fine topic for building an argument and writing an essay.

♦ FICTION ♦

JOSÉ ARMAS [B. 1944]

José Armas is deeply commited to the Latino community in New Mexico and beyond and is best known for his weekly column in the Albuquerque Journal *that focuses on Latino issues. In addition to other awards, Armas has received a National Endowment of the Arts fellowship for his writing.*

EL TONTO DEL BARRIO   [1982]

Romero Estrada was called "El Cotoro"[1] because he was always whistling and singing. He made nice music even though his songs were spontaneous compositions made up of words with sounds that he liked but which seldom made any sense. But that didn't seem to bother either Romero or anyone else in the Golden Heights Centro where he lived. Not even the kids made fun of him. It just was not permitted.

Romero had a ritual that he followed almost every day. After breakfast he would get his broom and go up and down the main street of the Golden Heights Centro whistling and singing and sweeping the sidewalks for all the businesses. He would sweep in front of the Tortillería America, the XXX Liquor Store, the Tres Milpas Bar run by Tino Gabaldon, Barelas' Barber Shop, the used furniture store owned by Goldstein, El Centro Market of the Avila family, the Model Cities Office, and Lourdes Printing Store. Then, in the afternoons, he would come back and sit in Barelas' Barber Shop and spend the day looking at magazines and watching and waving to the passing people as he sang and composed his songs without a care in the world.

When business was slow, Barelas would let him sit in the barber's chair. Romero loved it. It was a routine that Romero kept every day except Sundays and Mondays when Barelas' Barber Shop was closed. After a period of years, people in the barrio got used to seeing Romero do his little task of sweeping the sidewalks and sitting in Barelas' Barber Shop. If he didn't show up one day someone assumed the responsibility to go to his house to see if he was ill. People would stop to say hello to Romero on the street and although he never initiated a conversation while he was sober, he always smiled and responded cheerfully to everyone. People passing the barber shop in the afternoons made it a point to wave even though they couldn't see him; they knew he was in there and was expecting some salutation.

When he was feeling real good, Romero would sweep in front of the houses on both sides of the block also. He took his job seriously and took great care to sweep cleanly, between the cracks and even between the sides of the buildings. The dirt and small scraps went into the gutter. The bottles and bigger pieces of litter were put carefully in cardboard boxes, ready for the garbage man.

[1]**El Cotoro** parrot

5   If he did it the way he wanted, the work took him the whole morning. And always cheerful—always with some song.

Only once did someone call attention to his work. Frank Avila told him in jest that Romero had forgotten to pick up an empty bottle of wine from his door. Romero was so offended and made such a commotion that it got around very quickly that no one should criticize his work. There was, in fact, no reason to.

Although it had been long acknowledged that Romero was a little "touched," he fit very well into the community. He was a respected citizen.

He could be found at the Tres Milpas Bar drinking his occasional beer in the evenings. Romero had a rivalry going with the Ranchera songs on the jukebox. He would try to outsing the songs using the same melody but inserting his own selection of random words. Sometimes, like all people, he would "bust out" and get drunk.

One could always tell when Romero was getting drunk because he would begin telling everyone that he loved them.

10   "I looov youuu," he would sing to someone and offer to compose them a song.

"Ta bueno, Romero. Ta bueno, ya bete,"[2] they would tell him.

Sometimes when he got too drunk he would crap in his pants and then Tino would make him go home.

Romero received some money from Social Security but it wasn't much. None of the merchants gave him any credit because he would always forget to pay his bills. He didn't do it on purpose, he just forgot and spent his money on something else. So instead, the businessmen preferred to do little things for him occasionally. Barelas would trim his hair when things were slow. The Tortillería America would give him menudo and fresh-made tortillas at noon when he was finished with his sweeping. El Centro Market would give him the overripe fruit and broken boxes of food that no one else would buy. Although it was unspoken and unwritten, there was an agreement that existed between Romero and the Golden Heights Centro. Romero kept the sidewalks clean and the barrio looked after him. It was a contract that worked well for a long time.

Then, when Seferino, Barelas' oldest son, graduated from high school he went to work in the barber shop for the summer. Seferino was a conscientious and sensitive young man and it wasn't long before he took notice of Romero and came to feel sorry for him.

15   One day when Romero was in the shop Seferino decided to act.

"Mira, Romero. Yo te doy 50 centavos por cada dia que me barres la banqueta.[3] Fifty cents for every day you sweep the sidewalk for us. Qué te parece?"[4]

Romero thought about it carefully.

"Hecho![5] Done!" he exclaimed. He started for home right away to get his broom.

"Why did you do that for, m'ijo?"[6] asked Barelas.

---

[2]**Ta bueno, Romero. Ta bueno, ya bete** It's OK, Romero. It's OK.
[3]**Mira…banqueta** Look Romero, I will give you 50 cents for each day that you sweep my sidewalk.
[4]**Qué te parece** Does that seem OK to you?
[5]**Hecho** Done
[6]**m'ijo** abbreviation for "my son"

20   "It don't seem right, Dad, The man works and no one pays him for his work. Everyone should get paid for what they do."

"He don't need no pay. Romero has everything he needs."

"It's not the same, Dad. How would you like to do what he does and be treated the same way? It's degrading the way he has to go around getting scraps and handouts."

"I'm not Romero. Besides you don't know about these things, m'ijo. Romero would be unhappy if his schedule was upset. Right now everyone likes him and takes care of him. He sweeps the sidewalks because he wants something to do, not because he wants money."

"I'll pay him out of my money, don't worry about it then."

25   "The money is not the point. The point is that money will not help Romero. Don't you understand that?"

"Look, Dad. Just put yourself in his place. Would you do it? Would you cut hair for nothing?"

Barelas just knew his son was putting something over on him but he didn't know how to answer. It seemed to make sense the way Seferino explained it. But it still went against his "instinct." On the other hand, Seferino had gone and finished high school. He must know something. There were few kids who had finished high school in the barrio, and fewer who had gone to college. Barelas knew them all. He noted (with some pride) that Seferino was going to be enrolled at Harvard University this year. That must count for something, he thought. Barelas himself had never gone to school. So maybe his son had something there. On the other hand…it upset Barelas that he wasn't able to get Seferino to see the issue. How can we be so far apart on something so simple, he thought. But he decided not to say anything else about it.

Romero came back right away and swept the front of Barelas' shop again and put what little dirt he found into the curb. He swept up the gutter, put the trash in a shoe box and threw it in a garbage can.

Seferino watched with pride as Romero went about his job and when he was finished he went outside and shook Romero's hand. Seferino told him he had done a good job. Romero beamed.

30   Manolo was coming into the shop to get his hair cut as Seferino was giving Romero his wages. He noticed Romero with his broom.

"What's going on?" he asked. Barelas shrugged his shoulders. "Qué tiene Romero?[7] Is he sick or something?"

"No, he's not sick," explained Seferino, who had now come inside. He told Manolo the story.

"We're going to make Romero a businessman," said Seferino. "Do you realize how much money Romero would make if everyone paid him just fifty cents a day. Like my dad says, 'Everyone should be able to keep his dignity, no matter how poor.' And he does a job, you know."

"Well, it makes sense," said Manolo.

[7]**Qué tiene Romero?** What's with Romero?

35   "Hey. Maybe I'll ask people to do that," said Seferino. "That way the poor old man could make a decent wage. Do you want to help, Manolo? You can go with me to ask people to pay him."

"Well," said Manolo as he glanced at Barelas, "I'm not too good at asking people for money."

This did not discourage Seferino. He went out and contacted all the businesses on his own, but no one else wanted to contribute. This didn't discourage Seferino either. He went on giving Romero fifty cents a day.

After a while, Seferino heard that Romero had asked for credit at the grocery store. "See, Dad. What did I tell you? Things are getting better for him already. He's becoming his own man. And look. It's only been a couple of weeks." Barelas did not reply.

But then the next week Romero did not show up to sweep any sidewalks. He was around but he didn't do any work for anybody the entire week. He walked around Golden Heights Centro in his best gray work pants and his slouch hat, looking important and making it a point to walk right past the barber shop every little while.

40   Of course, the people in the Golden Heights Centro noticed the change immediately, and since they saw Romero in the street, they knew he wasn't ill. But the change was clearly disturbing the community. They discussed him in the Tortillería America where people got together for coffee, and at the Tres Milpas Bar. Everywhere the topic of conversation was the great change that had come over Romero. Only Barelas did not talk about it.

The following week Romero came into the barber shop and asked to talk with Seferino in private. Barelas knew immediately something was wrong. Romero never initiated a conversation unless he was drunk.

They went into the back room where Barelas could not hear and then Romero informed Seferino, "I want a raise."

"What? What do you mean, a raise? You haven't been around for a week. You only worked a few weeks and now you want a raise?" Seferino was clearly angry but Romero was calm and insistent.

Romero correctly pointed out that he had been sweeping the sidewalks for a long time. Even before Seferino finished high school.

45   "I deserve a raise," he repeated after an eloquent presentation.

Seferino looked coldly at Romero. It was clearly a stand-off.

Then Seferino said, "Look, maybe we should forget the whole thing. I was just trying to help you out and look at what you do."

Romero held his ground. "I helped you out too. No one told me to do it and I did it anyway. I helped you many years."

"Well, let's forget about the whole thing then," said Seferino.

50   "I quit then," said Romero.

"Quit?" exclaimed Seferino as he laughed at Romero.

"Quit! I quit!" said Romero as he walked out the front of the shop past Barelas who was cutting a customer's hair.

Seferino came out shaking his head and laughing.

"Can you imagine that old guy?"

55   Barelas did not seem too amused. He felt he could have predicted that something bad like this would happen.

Romero began sweeping the sidewalks again the next day with the exception that when he came to the barber shop he would go around it and continue sweeping the rest of the sidewalks. He did this for the rest of the week. And the following Tuesday he began sweeping the sidewalk all the way up to the shop and then pushing the trash to the sidewalk in front of the barber shop. Romero then stopped coming to the barber shop in the afternoon.

The barrio buzzed with fact and rumor about Romero. Tino commented that Romero was not singing anymore. Even if someone offered to buy him a beer he wouldn't sing. Frank Avila said the neighbors were complaining because he was leaving his TV on loud the whole day and night. He still greeted people but seldom smiled. He had run up a big bill at the liquor store and when the manager stopped his credit, he caught Romero stealing bottles of whiskey. He was also getting careless about his dress. He didn't shave and clean like he used to. Women complained that he walked around in soiled pants, that he smelled bad. Even one of the little kids complained that Romero had kicked his puppy, but that seemed hard to believe.

Barelas felt terrible. He felt responsible. But he couldn't convince Seferino that what he had done was wrong. Barelas himself stopped going to the Tres Milpas Bar after work to avoid hearing about Romero. Once he came across Romero on the street and Barelas said hello but with a sense of guilt. Romero responded, avoiding Barelas' eyes and moving past him awkwardly and quickly. Romero's behavior continued to get erratic and some people started talking about having Romero committed.

"You can't do that," said Barelas when he was presented with a petition.

60   "He's flipped," said Tino, who made up part of the delegation circulating the petition. "No one likes Romero more than I do, you know that Barelas."

"But he's really crazy," said Frank Avila.

"He was crazy before. No one noticed," pleaded Barelas.

"But it was a crazy we could depend on. Now he just wants to sit on the curb and pull up the women's skirts. It's terrible. The women are going crazy. He's also running into the street stopping traffic. You see how he is. What choice do we have?"

"It's for his own good," put in one of the workers from the Model Cities Office. Barelas dismissed them as outsiders. Seferino was there and wanted to say something but a look from Barelas stopped him.

65   "We just can't do that," insisted Barelas. "Let's wait. Maybe he's just going through a cycle. Look. We've had a full moon recently, qué no? That must be it. You know how the moon affects people in his condition."

"I don't know," said Tino. "What if he hurts ... "

"He's not going to hurt anyone," cut in Barelas.

"No, Barelas. I was going to say, what if he hurts himself. He has no one at home. I'd say, let him come home with me for a while but you know how stubborn he is. You can't even talk to him any more."

"He gives everyone the finger when they try to pull him out of the traffic," said Frank Avila. "The cops have missed him, but it won't be long before they see him doing some of his antics and arrest him. Then what? Then the poor guy is in real trouble."

70   "Well, look," said Barelas. "How many names you got on the list?"

Tino responded slowly, "Well, we sort of wanted you to start off the list."

"Let's wait a while longer," said Barelas. "I just know that Romero will come around. Let's wait just a while, okay?"

No one had the heart to fight the issue and so they postponed the petition.

There was no dramatic change in Romero even though the full moon had completed its cycle. Still, no one initiated the petition again and then in the middle of August Seferino left for Cambridge to look for housing and to register early for school. Suddenly everything began to change again. One day Romero began sweeping the entire sidewalk again. His spirits began to pick up and his strange antics began to disappear.

75   At the Tortillería America the original committee met for coffee and the talk turned to Romero.

"He's going to be all right now," said a jubilant Barelas. "I guarantee it."

"Well, don't hold your breath yet," said Tino. "The full moon is coming up again."

"Yeah," said Frank Avila dejectedly.

When the next full moon was in force the group was together again drinking coffee and Tino asked, "Well, how's Romero doing?"

80   Barelas smiled and said, "Well. Singing songs like crazy."

MAKING CONNECTIONS

1. Why does Romero change after receiving money for his work? Why does he change back after Seferino leaves for college?
2. Is Romero crazy? If not, how would you characterize him? Use examples from the text to back up your view.
3. What is it that Barelas understands about Romero that Seferino cannot? How does Barelas know that Seferino's idea will backfire?
4. The title roughly translates to "The Neighborhood Idiot." Is Romero "El Tonto del Barrio"? Are there any other characters that the title could describe?

MAKING AN ARGUMENT

1. Seferino states, "Everyone should get paid for what they do." Despite the consequences in the story, do you agree that Romero should have been paid? Is there any way that Seferino's plan to turn Romero into a business-man could have worked? Write an argument for or against paying Romero, using evidence from the text to support your claims.

KATE CHOPIN [1851–1904]

Kate Chopin was born in St. Louis, Missouri. Her father, an Irish immigrant, became a successful businessman. Her mother was a prominent member of the French-Creole community and traveled in exclusive social circles. Chopin attended Catholic school, was much admired for her beauty and wit, and, at nineteen, married Creole cotton broker Oscar Chopin. The couple settled first in New Orleans and, following the collapse of Oscar's business, moved to his family's planta-
tions in Natchitoches Parish. Following his unexpected death in 1883, at a doctor's suggestion, Chopin began writing. Her stories, which are set among the Creole people of the Louisiana bayou, were collected and published in two anthologies, Bayou Folk *(1894) and* A Night in Arcadie *(1897). Her greatest work, the novel* The Awakening *(1899), which tells the story of an extramarital affair, was denounced as obscene and was largely ignored until it was reevaluated by critics, beginning in the 1930s, who praised it for its emotional honesty and beautiful prose.*

DÉSIRÉE'S BABY   [1892]

As the day was pleasant, Madame Valmondé drove over to L'Abri to see Désirée and the baby.

It made her laugh to think of Désirée with a baby. Why, it seemed but yesterday that Désirée was little more than a baby herself; when Monsieur in riding through the gateway of Valmondé had found her lying asleep in the shadow of the big stone pillar.

The little one awoke in his arms and began to cry for "Dada." That was as much as she could do or say. Some people thought she might have strayed there of her own accord, for she was of the toddling age. The prevailing belief was that she had been purposely left by a party of Texans, whose canvas-covered wagon, late in the day, had crossed the ferry that Coton Maïs kept, just below the plantation. In time Madame Valmondé abandoned every speculation but the one that Désirée had been sent to her by a beneficent Providence to be the child of her affection, seeing that she was without child of the flesh. For the girl grew to be beautiful and gentle, affectionate and sincere—the idol of Valmondé.

It was no wonder, when she stood one day against the stone pillar in whose shadow she had lain asleep, eighteen years before, that Armand Aubigny riding by and seeing her there, had fallen in love with her. That was the way all the Aubignys fell in love, as if struck by a pistol shot. The wonder was that he had not loved her before; for he had known her since his father brought him home from Paris, a boy of eight, after his mother died there. The passion that awoke in him that day, when he saw her at the gate, swept along like an avalanche, or like a prairie fire, or like anything that drives headlong over all obstacles.

5   Monsieur Valmondé grew practical and wanted things well considered: that is, the girl's obscure origin. Armand looked into her eyes and did not care. He was reminded that she was nameless. What did it matter about a name when he could

give her one of the oldest and proudest in Louisiana? He ordered the *corbeille* from Paris, and contained himself with what patience he could until it arrived; then they were married.

Madame Valmondé had not seen Désirée and the baby for four weeks. When she reached L'Abri she shuddered at the first sight of it, as she always did. It was a sad looking place, which for many years had not known the gentle presence of a mistress, old Monsieur Aubigny having married and buried his wife in France, and she having loved her own land too well ever to leave it. The roof came down steep and black like a cowl, reaching out beyond the wide galleries that encircled the yellow stuccoed house. Big, solemn oaks grew close to it, and their thick-leaved, far-reaching branches shadowed it like a pall. Young Aubigny's rule was a strict one, too, and under it his Negroes had forgotten how to be gay, as they had been during the old master's easy-going and indulgent lifetime.

The young mother was recovering slowly, and lay full length, in her soft white muslins and laces, upon a couch. The baby was beside her, upon her arm, where it had fallen asleep, at her breast. The yellow nurse woman sat beside a window fanning herself.

Madame Valmondé bent her portly figure over Désirée and kissed her, holding her an instant tenderly in her arms. Then she turned to the child.

"This is not the baby!" she exclaimed, in startled tones. French was the language spoken at Valmondé in those days.

10   "I knew you would be astonished," laughed Désirée, "at the way he has grown. The little *cochon de lait!* Look at his legs, mamma, and his hands and fingernails, —real finger-nails. Zandrine had to cut them this morning. Isn't is true, Zandrine?"

The woman bowed her turbaned head majestically, "Maïs si, Madame."

"And the way he cries," went on Désirée, "is deafening. Armand heard him the other day as far away as La Blanche's cabin."

Madame Valmondé had never removed her eyes from the child. She lifted it and walked with it over to the window that was lightest. She scanned the baby narrowly, then looked as searchingly at Zandrine, whose face was turned to gaze across the fields.

"Yes, the child has grown, has changed," said Madame Valmondé, slowly, as she replaced it beside its mother. "What does Armand say?"

15   Désirée's face became suffused with a glow that was happiness itself.

"Oh, Armand is the proudest father in the parish, I believe, chiefly because it is a boy to bear his name; though he says not,—that he would have loved a girl as well. But I know it isn't true. I know he says that to please me. And mamma," she added, drawing Madame Valmondé's head down to her, and speaking in a whisper, "he hasn't punished one of them—not one of them—since the baby is born. Even Négrillon, who pretended to have burnt his leg that he might rest from work—he only laughed and said Négrillon was a great scamp. Oh, mamma, I'm so happy; it frightens me."

What Désirée said was true. Marriage, and later the birth of his son, had softened Armand Aubigny's imperious and exacting nature greatly. This was what made the gentle Désirée so happy, for she loved him desperately. When he frowned she trembled, but loved him. When he smiled, she asked no greater blessing of God.

But Armand's dark, handsome face had not often been disfigured by frowns since the day he fell in love with her.

When the baby was about three months old, Désirée awoke one day to the conviction that there was something in the air menacing her peace. It was at first too subtle to grasp. It had only been a disquieting suggestion; an air of mystery among the blacks; unexpected visits from far-off neighbors who could hardly account for their coming. Then a strange, an awful change in her husband's manner, which she dared not ask him to explain. When he spoke to her, it was with averted eyes, from which the old love-light seemed to have gone out. He absented himself from home; and when there, avoided her presence and that of her child, without excuse. And the very spirit of Satan seemed suddenly to take hold of him in his dealings with the slaves. Désirée was miserable enough to die.

She sat in her room, one hot afternoon, in her *peignoir*, listlessly drawing through her fingers the strands of her long, silky brown hair that hung about her shoulders. The baby, half naked, lay asleep upon her own great mahogany bed, that was like a sumptuous throne, with its satin lined halfcanopy. One of LaBlanche's little quadroon boys—half naked too—stood fanning the child slowly with a fan of peacock feathers. Désirée's eyes had been fixed absently and sadly upon the baby, while she was striving to penetrate the threatening mist that she felt closing about her. She looked from her child to the boy who stood beside him, and back again; over and over. "Ah!" It was a cry that she could not help, which she was not conscious of having uttered. The blood turned like ice in her veins, and a clammy moisture gathered upon her face.

20   She tried to speak to the little quadroon boy; but no sound would come, at first. When he heard his name uttered, he looked up, and his mistress was pointing to the door. He laid aside the great, soft fan, and obediently stole away, over the polished floor, on his bare tiptoes.

She stayed motionless, with gaze riveted upon her child, and her face the picture of fright.

Presently her husband entered the room, and without noticing her, went to a table and began to search among some papers which covered it.

"Armand," she called to him, in a voice which must have stabbed him, if he was human. But he did not notice. "Armand," she said again. Then she rose and tottered toward him. "Armand," she panted once more, clutching his arm, "look at our child. What does it mean? Tell me."

He coldly but gently loosened her fingers from about his arm and thrust the hand away from him. "Tell me what it means!" she cried despairingly.

25   "It means," he answered lightly, "that the child is not white; it means that you are not white."

A quick conception of all that this accusation meant for her nerved her with unwonted courage to deny it. "It is a lie; it is not true, I am white! Look at my hair, it is brown; and my eyes are gray. Armand, you know they are gray. And my skin is fair," seizing his wrist. "Look at my hand; whiter than yours, Armand," she laughed hysterically.

"As white as LaBlanche's," he returned cruelly; and went away leaving her alone with their child.

When she could hold a pen in her hand, she sent a despairing letter to Madame Valmondé.

"My mother, they tell me I am not white. Armand has told me I am not white. For God's sake tell them it is not true. You must know it is not true. I shall die. I must die. I cannot be so unhappy, and live."

30   The answer that came was as brief.

"My own Désirée: Come home to Valmondé; back to your mother who loves you. Come with your child."

When the letter reached Désirée she went with it to her husband's study, and laid it open upon the desk before which he sat. She was like a stone image: silent, white, motionless after she placed it there.

In silence he ran his cold eyes over the written words. He said nothing.

"Shall I go, Armand?" she asked in tones sharp with agonized suspense.

35   "Yes, go."

"Do you want me to go?"

"Yes, I want you to go."

He thought Almighty God had dealt cruelly and unjustly with him; and felt, somehow, that he was paying Him back in kind when he stabbed thus into his wife's soul. Moreover he no longer loved her, because of the unconscious injury she had brought upon his home and his name.

She turned away like one stunned by a blow, and walked slowly towards the door, hoping he would call her back.

40   "Good-by, Armand," she moaned.

He did not answer her. That was his last blow at fate.

Désirée went in search of her child. Zandrine was pacing the somber gallery with it. She took the little one from the nurse's arms with no word of explanation, and descending the steps, walked away, under the live-oak branches.

It was an October afternoon; the sun was just sinking. Out in the still fields the Negroes were picking cotton.

Désirée had not changed the thin white garment nor the slippers which she wore. Her hair was uncovered and the sun's rays brought a golden gleam from its brown meshes. She did not take the broad, beaten road which led to the far-off plantation of Valmondé. She walked across a deserted field, where the stubble bruised her tender feet, so delicately shod, and tore her thin gown to shreds.

45   She disappeared among the reeds and willows that grew thick along the banks of the deep, sluggish bayou; and she did not come back again.

Some weeks later there was a curious scene enacted at L'Abri. In the center of the smoothly swept back yard was a great bonfire. Armand Aubigny sat in the wide hallway that commanded a view of the spectacle; and it was he who dealt out to a half dozen Negroes the material which kept this fire ablaze.

A graceful cradle of willow, with all its dainty furbishings, was laid upon the pyre, which had already been fed with the richness of a priceless *layette*. Then there were silk gowns, and velvet and satin ones added to these; laces, too, and embroideries; bonnets and gloves, for the *corbeille* had been of rare quality.

The last thing to go was a tiny bundle of letters; innocent little scribblings that Désirée had sent to him during the days of their espousal. There was the remnant of one back in the drawer from which he took them. But it was not Désirée's; it was part of an old letter from his mother to his father. He read it. She was thanking God for the blessing of her husband's love:—

"But, above all," she wrote, "night and day, I thank the good God for having arranged our lives that our dear Armand will never know that his mother, who adores him, belongs to the race that is cursed with the brand of slavery."

MAKING CONNECTIONS

1. What causes Armand's change in attitude toward Désirée? To what extent does the prevailing culture influence his attitude? Why does what he thinks he's discovered about Désirée matter so much to him?
2. What happens to Désirée and the baby? What evidence in the text of the story indicates that?
3. What does Armand discover about himself as he destroys all traces of Désirée? Do you think he will be as tough on himself as he was on Désirée? Do you think he should be? What do you think he will do?
4. How does the author mislead us into thinking that Désirée is responsible for the mixed race of the child?

MAKING AN ARGUMENT

1. This story is a good example of situational irony. What is ironic about this story? Do you think it's credible that events would come together like this? Using this story—and at least one other story in this section—write about the impact of irony in literature. Cite the texts of the stories for support.

WILLIAM FAULKNER [1897–1962]

William Faulkner was born into a genteel Southern family and was raised in Oxford, Mississippi, where he attended the University of Mississippi. Following World War I, during which he served in the Canadian air force, he settled in Oxford, Mississippi, and worked for a time in the post office until he was forced to resign—he was lax in his duties and often became absorbed in writing or reading. By 1930 he had published a book of verse and a number of novels, including two of his greatest, The Sound and The Fury *(1929) and* As I Lay Dying *(1930), but he did not reach a wide readership until the publication of the novel* Sanctuary, *in 1931. Fifteen of his novels, as well as many of his short stories, are set in fictional Yoknapatawpha County, Mississippi, and concern themselves with the interconnected fortunes of a group of families of different social classes from the Civil War to modern times. Other major works include* Light in August *(1932),* Absalom! Absalom! *(1936),* The Hamlet *(1940), and* Collected Stories *(1950). Faulkner was awarded the Nobel Prize in 1950. When asked about his inspiration for "A Rose*

for Emily," which originally appeared in These Thirteen *(1931), a collection of short stories, Faulkner said: "That came from a picture of the strand of hair on the pillow. It was a ghost story, simply a picture of a strand of hair on the pillow in the abandoned house."*

A ROSE FOR EMILY

[1931]

I

When Miss Emily Grierson died, our whole town went to her funeral: the men through a sort of respectful affection for a fallen monument, the women mostly out of curiosity to see the inside of her house, which no one save an old manservant—a combined gardener and cook—had seen in at least ten years.

It was a big, squarish frame house that had once been white, decorated with cupolas and spires and scrolled balconies in the heavily lightsome style of the seventies, set on what had once been our most select street. But garages and cotton gins had encroached and obliterated even the august names of that neighborhood; only Miss Emily's house was left, lifting its stubborn and coquettish decay above the cotton wagons and the gasoline pumps—an eyesore among eyesores. And now Miss Emily had gone to join the representatives of those august names where they lay in the cedar-bemused cemetery among the ranked and anonymous graves of Union and Confederate soldiers who fell at the battle of Jefferson.

Alive, Miss Emily had been a tradition, a duty, and a care; a sort of hereditary obligation upon the town, dating from that day in 1894 when Colonel Sartoris, the mayor—he who fathered the edict that no Negro woman should appear on the streets without an apron—remitted her taxes, the dispensation dating from the death of her father on into perpetuity. Not that Miss Emily would have accepted charity. Colonel Sartoris invented an involved tale to the effect that Miss Emily's father had loaned money to the town, which the town, as a matter of business, preferred this way of repaying. Only a man of Colonel Sartoris' generation and thought could have invented it, and only a woman could have believed it.

When the next generation, with its more modern ideas, became mayors and aldermen, this arrangement created some little dissatisfaction. On the first of the year they mailed her a tax notice. February came, and there was no reply. They wrote her a formal letter, asking her to call at the sheriff's office at her convenience. A week later the mayor wrote her himself, offering to call or to send his car for her, and received in reply a note on paper of an archaic shape, in a thin, flowing calligraphy in faded ink, to the effect that she no longer went out at all. The tax notice was also enclosed, without comment.

5   They called a special meeting of the Board of Aldermen. A deputation waited upon her, knocked at the door through which no visitor had passed since she ceased giving china-painting lessons eight or ten years earlier. They were admitted by the old Negro into a dim hall from which a staircase mounted into still more shadow. It smelled of dust and disuse—a close, dank smell. The Negro led them into the parlor. It was furnished in heavy, leather-covered furniture. When the Negro opened the blinds of one window, they could see that the leather was cracked; and when they sat down, a faint dust rose sluggishly about their thighs,

spinning with slow motes in the single sunray. On a tarnished gilt easel before the fireplace stood a crayon portrait of Miss Emily's father.

They rose when she entered—a small, fat woman in black, with a thin gold chain descending to her waist and vanishing into her belt, leaning on an ebony cane with a tarnished gold head. Her skeleton was small and spare; perhaps that was why what would have been merely plumpness in another was obesity in her. She looked bloated, like a body long submerged in motionless water, and of that pallid hue. Her eyes, lost in the fatty ridges of her face, looked like two small pieces of coal pressed into a lump of dough as they moved from one face to another while the visitors stated their errand.

She did not ask them to sit. She just stood in the door and listened quietly until the spokesman came to a stumbling halt. Then they could hear the invisible watch ticking at the end of the gold chain.

Her voice was dry and cold. "I have no taxes in Jefferson. Colonel Sartoris explained it to me. Perhaps one of you can gain access to the city records and satisfy yourselves."

"But we have. We are the city authorities, Miss Emily. Didn't you get a notice from the sheriff, signed by him?"

10   "I received a paper, yes," Miss Emily said. "Perhaps he considers himself the sheriff.... I have no taxes in Jefferson."

"But there is nothing on the books to show that, you see. We must go by the—"

"See Colonel Sartoris. I have no taxes in Jefferson."

"But, Miss Emily—"

"See Colonel Sartoris." (Colonel Sartoris had been dead almost ten years.) "I have no taxes in Jefferson. Tobe!" The Negro appeared. "Show these gentlemen out."

II

15   So she vanquished them, horse and foot, just as she had vanquished their fathers thirty years before about the smell. That was two years after her father's death and a short time after her sweetheart—the one we believed would marry her—had deserted her. After her father's death she went out very little; after her sweetheart went away, people hardly saw her at all. A few of the ladies had the temerity to call, but were not received, and the only sign of life about the place was the Negro man—a young man then—going in and out with a market basket.

"Just as if a man—any man—could keep a kitchen properly," the ladies said; so they were not surprised when the smell developed. It was another link between the gross, teeming world and the high and mighty Griersons.

A neighbor, a woman, complained to the mayor, Judge Stevens, eighty years old.

"But what will you have me do about it, madam?" he said.

"Why, send her word to stop it," the woman said. "Isn't there a law?"

20   "I'm sure that won't be necessary," Judge Stevens said. "It's probably just a snake or a rat that nigger of hers killed in the yard. I'll speak to him about it."

The next day he received two more complaints, one from a man who came in diffident deprecation. "We really must do something about it, Judge, I'd be the last one in the world to bother Miss Emily, but we've got to do something." That night the Board of Aldermen met—three gray-beards and one younger man, a member of the rising generation.

"It's simple enough," he said. "Send her word to have her place cleaned up. Give her a certain time to do it in, and if she don't..."

"Dammit, sir," Judge Stevens said, "will you accuse a lady to her face of smelling bad?"

So the next night, after midnight, four men crossed Miss Emily's lawn and slunk about the house like burglars, sniffing along the base of the brickwork and at the cellar openings while one of them performed a regular sowing motion with his hand out of a sack slung from his shoulder. They broke open the cellar door and sprinkled lime there, and in all the outbuildings. As they recrossed the lawn, a window that had been dark was lighted and Miss Emily sat in it, the light behind her, and her upright torso motionless as that of an idol. They crept quietly across the lawn and into the shadow of the locusts that lined the street. After a week or two the smell went away.

25   That was when people had begun to feel really sorry for her. People in our town remembering how old lady Wyatt, her great-aunt, had gone completely crazy at last, believed that the Griersons held themselves a little too high for what they really were. None of the young men were quite good enough for Miss Emily and such. We had long thought of them as a tableau; Miss Emily a slender figure in white in the background, her father a spraddled silhouette in the foreground, his back to her and clutching a horsewhip, the two of them framed by the backflung front door. So when she got to be thirty and was still single, we were not pleased exactly, but vindicated; even with insanity in the family she wouldn't have turned down all of her chances if they had really materialized.

When her father died, it got about that the house was all that was left to her; and in a way, people were glad. At last they could pity Miss Emily. Being left alone, and a pauper, she had become humanized. Now she too would know the old thrill and the old despair of a penny more or less.

The day after his death all the ladies prepared to call at the house and offer condolence and aid, as is our custom. Miss Emily met them at the door, dressed as usual and with no trace of grief on her face. She told them that her father was not dead. She did that for three days, with the ministers calling on her, and the doctors, trying to persuade her to let them dispose of the body. Just as they were about to resort to law and force, she broke down, and they buried her father quickly.

We did not say she was crazy then. We believed she had to do that. We remembered all the young men her father had driven away, and we knew that with nothing left, she would have to cling to that which had robbed her, as people will.

III

She was sick for a long time. When we saw her again, her hair was cut short, making her look like a girl, with a vague resemblance to those angels in colored church windows—sort of tragic and serene.

30   The town had just let the contracts for paving the sidewalks, and in the summer after her father's death they began to work. The construction company came

with niggers and mules and machinery, and a foreman named Homer Barron, a Yankee—a big, dark, ready man, with a big voice and eyes lighter than his face. The little boys would follow in groups to hear him cuss the niggers, and the niggers singing in time to the rise and fall of picks. Pretty soon he knew everybody in town. Whenever you heard a lot of laughing anywhere about the square, Homer Barron would be in the center of the group. Presently we began to see him and Miss Emily on Sunday afternoons driving in the yellow-wheeled buggy and the matched team of bays from the livery stable.

At first we were glad that Miss Emily would have an interest, because the ladies all said, "Of course a Grierson would not think seriously of a Northerner, a day laborer." But there were still others, older people, who said that even grief could not cause a real lady to forget *noblesse oblige*—without calling it *noblesse oblige*. They just said, "Poor Emily. Her kinsfolk should come to her." She had some kin in Alabama; but years ago her father had fallen out with them over the estate of old lady Wyatt, the crazy woman, and there was no communication between the two families. They had not even been represented at the funeral.

And as soon as the old people said, "Poor Emily," the whispering began. "Do you suppose it's really so?" they said to one another. "Of course it is. What else could...." This behind their hands; rustling of craned silk and satin behind jalousies closed upon the sun of Sunday afternoon as the thin, swift clop-clop-clop of the matched team passed: "Poor Emily."

She carried her head high enough—even when we believed that she was fallen. It was as if she demanded more than ever the recognition of her dignity as the last Grierson; as if it had wanted that touch of earthiness to reaffirm her imperviousness. Like when she bought the rat poison, the arsenic. That was over a year after they had begun to say "Poor Emily," and while the two female cousins were visiting her.

"I want some poison," she said to the druggist. She was over thirty then, still a slight woman, though thinner than usual, with cold, haughty black eyes in a face the flesh of which was strained across the temples and about the eyesockets as you imagine a lighthouse-keeper's face ought to look. "I want some poison," she said.

35   "Yes, Miss Emily. What kind? For rats and such? I'd recom—"

"I want the best you have. I don't care what kind."

The druggist named several. "They'll kill anything up to an elephant. But what you want is—"

"Arsenic." Miss Emily said. "Is that a good one?"

"Is...arsenic? Yes ma'am. But what you want—"

40   "I want arsenic."

The druggist looked down at her. She looked back at him, erect, her face like a strained flag. "Why, of course," the druggist said. "If that's what you want. But the law requires you to tell what you are going to use it for."

Miss Emily just stared at him, her head tilted back in order to look him eye for eye, until he looked away and went and got the arsenic and wrapped it up. The Negro delivery boy brought her the package; the druggist didn't come back. When she opened the package at home there was written on the box, under the skull and bones: "For rats."

IV

So the next day we all said, "She will kill herself"; and we said it would be the best thing. When she had first begun to be seen with Homer Barron, we had said, "She will marry him." Then we said, "She will persuade him yet," because Homer himself had remarked—he liked men, and it was known that he drank with the younger men in the Elks' Club—that he was not a marrying man. Later we said, "Poor Emily," behind the jalousies as they passed on Sunday afternoon in the glittering buggy, Miss Emily with her head high and Homer Barron with his hat cocked and a cigar in his teeth, reins and whip in a yellow glove.

Then some of the ladies began to say that it was a disgrace to the town and a bad example to the young people. The men did not want to interfere, but at last the ladies forced the Baptist minister—Miss Emily's people were Episcopal—to call upon her. He would never divulge what happened during that interview, but he refused to go back again. The next Sunday they again drove about the streets, and the following day the minister's wife wrote to Miss Emily's relations in Alabama.

45   So she had blood-kin under her roof again and we sat back to watch developments. At first nothing happened. Then we were sure that they were to be married. We learned that Miss Emily had been to the jeweler's and ordered a man's toilet set in silver, with the letters H.B. on each piece. Two days later we learned that she had bought a complete outfit of men's clothing, including a nightshirt, and we said, "They are married." We were really glad. We were glad because the two female cousins were even more Grierson than Miss Emily had ever been.

So we were surprised when Homer Barron—the streets had been finished some time since—was gone. We were a little disappointed that there was not a public blowing-off, but we believed that he had gone on to prepare for Miss Emily's coming, or to give her a chance to get rid of the cousins. (By that time it was a cabal, and we were all Miss Emily's allies to help circumvent the cousins.) Sure enough, after another week they departed. And, as we had expected all along, within three days Homer Barron was back in town. A neighbor saw the Negro man admit him at the kitchen door at dusk one evening.

And that was the last we saw of Homer Barron. And of Miss Emily for some time. The Negro man went in and out with the market basket, but the front door remained closed. Now and then we would see her at a window for a moment, as the men did that night when they sprinkled the lime, but for almost six months she did not appear on the streets. Then we knew that this was to be expected too; as if that quality of her father which had thwarted her woman's life so many times had been too virulent and too furious to die.

When we next saw Miss Emily, she had grown fat and her hair was turning gray. During the next few years it grew grayer and grayer until it attained an even pepper-and-salt iron-gray, when it ceased turning. Up to the day of her death at seventy-four it was still that vigorous iron-gray, like the hair of an active man.

From that time on her front door remained closed, save for a period of six or seven years, when she was about forty, during which she gave lessons in china-painting. She fitted up a studio in one of the downstairs rooms, where the daughters and granddaughters of Colonel Sartoris' contemporaries were sent to her with the same regularity and in the same spirit that they were sent on Sundays with a twenty-five cent piece for the collection plate. Meanwhile her taxes had been remitted.

50   Then the newer generation became the backbone and the spirit of the town, and the painting pupils grew up and fell away and did not send their children to her with boxes of color and tedious brushes and pictures cut from the ladies' magazines. The front door closed upon the last one and remained closed for good. When the town got free postal delivery, Miss Emily alone refused to let them fasten the metal numbers above her door and attach a mailbox to it. She would not listen to them.

Daily, monthly, yearly we watched the Negro grow grayer and more stooped, going in and out with the market basket. Each December we sent her a tax notice, which would be returned by the post office a week later, unclaimed. Now and then we could see her in one of the downstairs windows—she had evidently shut up the top floor of the house—like the carven torso of an idol in a niche, looking or not looking at us, we could never tell which. Thus she passed from generation to generation—dear, inescapable, impervious, tranquil, and perverse.

And so she died. Fell ill in the house filled with dust and shadows, with only a doddering Negro man to wait on her. We did not even know she was sick; we had long since given up trying to get any information from the Negro. He talked to no one, probably not even to her, for his voice had grown harsh and rusty, as if from disuse.

She died in one of the downstairs rooms, in a heavy walnut bed with a curtain, her gray head propped on a pillow yellow and moldy with age and lack of sunlight.

V

The Negro met the first of the ladies at the front door and let them in, with their hushed, sibilant voices and their quick, curious glances, and then he disappeared. He walked right through the house and out the back and was not seen again.

55   The two female cousins came at once. They held the funeral on the second day, with the town coming to look at Miss Emily beneath a mass of bought flowers, with the crayon face of her father musing profoundly above the bier and the ladies sibilant and macabre; and the very old men—some in their brushed Confederate uniforms—on the porch and the lawn, talking of Miss Emily as if she had been a contemporary of theirs, believing that they had danced with her and courted her perhaps, confusing time with its mathematical progression, as the old do, to whom all the past is not a diminishing road, but, instead, a huge meadow which no winter ever quite touches, divided from them now by the narrow bottleneck of the most recent decade of years.

Already we knew that there was one room in that region above stairs which no one had seen in forty years, and which would have to be forced. They waited until Miss Emily was decently in the ground before they opened it.

The violence of breaking down the door seemed to fill this room with pervading dust. A thin, acrid pall as of the tomb seemed to lie everywhere upon this room decked and furnished as for a bridal: upon the valance curtains of faded rose color, upon the rose-shaded lights, upon the dressing table, upon the delicate array of crystal and the man's toilet things backed with tarnished silver, silver so tarnished that the monogram was obscured. Among them lay a collar and tie, as if they had just been removed, which, lifted, left upon the surface a pale crescent in the dust. Upon a chair hung the suit, carefully folded; beneath it the two mute shoes and the discarded socks.

The man himself lay in the bed.

For a long while we just stood there, looking down at the profound and flesh-less grin. The body had apparently once lain in the attitude of an embrace, but now the long sleep that outlasts love, that conquers even the grimace of love, had cuckolded him. What was left of him, rotted beneath what was left of the nightshirt, had become inextricable from the bed in which he lay; and upon him and upon the pillow beside him lay that even coating of the patient and biding dust.

60   Then we noticed that in the second pillow was the indentation of a head. One of us lifted something from it, and leaning forward, that faint and invisible dust dry and acrid in the nostrils, we saw a long strand of iron-gray hair.

MAKING CONNECTIONS

1. Who is the narrator? How does the narrator's unusual point of view (third person but from the perspective of "we") influence what you know in the story? What difference does it make that the story is told in flash-backs instead of from beginning to end? What is the narrator's attitude toward Emily?
2. How do you feel about Emily Grierson? What is her conflict?
3. Who is Homer Barron? How does his characterization differ from Emily's?
4. At the end of the story, what is the significance of the iron-gray strand of hair on the second pillow? Are there indications earlier in the story that foreshadow this outcome?
5. Why is Emily such a formidable force in the town? Why does she seem to get away with so much?
6. To what extent is this a story about change—or the inability to change?

MAKING AN ARGUMENT

1. The culture of the setting (the town, the era, Mississippi) is essential to this story. Write an argument that demonstrates the strong relationship between culture/setting and the characterization and conflict in this story. Cite the text of the story (and other stories if appropriate) for support.

JAMAICA KINCAID [B. 1949]

Jamaica Kincaid, whose given name was Elaine Potter Rich-ardson, was born in St. John's Antigua, an island in the West Indies. She left the rural island when she was seven-teen and went to New York City to work as an au pair. She studied photography at the New School in New York and attended Franconia College in New Hampshire. Much of her work is drawn from her own experiences, both as a child in Antigua and as an immigrant in the United States. Her works include a collection of short stories, At the Bottom of

the River *(1983); two novels,* Annie John *(1985) and* Lucy *(1990); and a book of
essays,* A Small Place *(1988). Her most recent book,* Among Flowers: A Walk in the
Himalaya *was published in 2005. She currently divides her time between New York
City, where she has worked for many years as a staff writer for* The New Yorker,
and Bennington College in Vermont, where she is a lecturer.

GIRL   [1978]

Wash the white clothes on Monday and put them on the stone heap; wash the color
clothes on Tuesday and put them on the clothes-line to dry; don't walk barehead
in the hot sun; cook pumpkin fritters in very hot sweet oil; soak your little clothes
right after you take them off; when buying cotton to make yourself a nice blouse,
be sure that it doesn't have gum on it, because that way it won't hold up well after
a wash; soak salt fish overnight before you cook it; is it true that you sing benna in
Sunday school? always eat your food in such a way that it won't turn someone else's
stomach; on Sundays try to walk like a lady and not like the slut you are so bent
on becoming; don't sing benna in Sunday school; you mustn't speak to wharf-rat
boys, not even to give directions; don't eat fruits on the street—flies will follow you;
but I don't sing benna on Sundays at all and never in Sunday school; this is how
to sew on a button; this is how to make a buttonhole for the button you have just
sewed on; this is how to hem a dress when you see the hem coming down and so
to prevent yourself from looking like the slut I know you are so bent on becoming;
this is how you iron your father's khaki shirt so that it doesn't have a crease; this is
how you iron your fathers' khaki pants so that they don't have a crease; this is how
you grow okra—far from the house, because okra tree harbors red ants; when you
are growing dasheen, make sure it gets plenty of water or else it makes your throat
itch when you are eating it; this is how you sweep a corner; this is how you sweep
a whole house; this is how you sweep a yard; this is how you smile to someone
you donlike too much; this is how you smile at someone you don't like at all; this is
how you smile to someone you like completely; this is how you set a table for tea;
this is how you set a table for dinner; this is how you set a table for dinner with an
important guest; this is how you set a table for lunch; this is how you set a table for
breakfast; this is how to behave in the presence of men who don't know you very
well, and this way they won't recognize immediately the slut I have warned you
against becoming; be sure to wash every day, even if it is with your own spit; don't
squat down to play marbles—you are not a boy, you know; don't pick people's
flowers—you might catch something; don't throw stones at blackbirds, because it
might not be a blackbird at all; this is how to make a bread pudding; this is how to
make doukona; this is how to make pepper pot; this is how to make a good medicine for a cold; this is how to make a good medicine to throw away a child before
it even becomes a child; this is how to catch a fish; this is how to throw back a fish
you don't like, and that way something bad won't fall on you; this is how to bully
a man; this is how a man bullies you; this is how to love a man, and if this doesn't
work there other ways, and if they don't work don't feel too bad about giving
up; this is how to spit up in the air if you feel like it, and this is how to move quick
so that it doesn't fall on you; this is how to make ends meet; always squeeze bread

to make sure it's fresh; *but what if the baker won't let me feel the bread?* you mean to say that after all you are really going to be the kind of woman who the baker won't let near the bread?

MAKING CONNECTIONS

1. Describe the point of view and voice in this story. Who is the narrator? What effect does the nonstop advice—in a nonstop sentence—have on you?
2. Who is making the italicized comments? What difference do they make to you?
3. How would you describe this relationship?

MAKING AN ARGUMENT

1. Given the nature of the language, this seems to be a story from the author's native culture, but to what extent is this a cross-cultural comment on the relationship between mothers and daughters in general? Pick out the elements of this monologue that reveal the mother and daughter, and write an argument that shows how it might apply to your own—or any other—culture.

THOMAS KING [B. 1943]

Thomas King was born in Sacramento, California, and moved to Canada in 1980. He is a novelist and broadcaster who often writes about Canada's First Nations and is an outspoken advocate for First Nations causes. His ancestry is Cherokee, German, and Greek. His work includes Medicine River *(1990),* A Coyote Columbus Story *(1992),* Green Grass, Running Water *(1993),* Coyotes Sing to the Moon *(1998),* Truth and Bright Water *(1999), and* Dreadful Water Shows Up *(2002). His latest book is a work of juvenile fiction,* A Coyote Columbus Story *(2007). He lives in Guelph, Ontario, is an English professor at the University of Guelph, and is the creator of* Dead Dog Cafe, *a CBC Radio One series.*

BORDERS   [1993]

When I was twelve, maybe thirteen, my mother announced that we were going to go to Salt Lake City to visit my sister who had left the reserve, moved across the line, and found a job. Laetitia had not left home with my mother's blessing, but over time my mother had come to be proud of the fact that Laetitia had done all of this on her own.

"She did real good," my mother would say.

Then there were the fine points to Laetitia's going. She had not, as my mother liked to tell Mrs. Manyfingers, gone floating after some man like a balloon on a string. She hadn't snuck out of the house, either, and gone to Vancouver or Edmonton or Toronto to chase rainbows down alleys. And she hadn't been pregnant.

"She did real good."

5   I was seven or eight when Laetitia left home. She was seventeen. Our father was from Rocky Boy on the American side.

"Dad's American," Laetitia told my mother, "so I can go and come as I please."

"Send us a postcard."

Laetitia packed her things, and we headed for the border. Just outside of Milk River, Laetitia told us to watch for the water tower.

"Over the next rise. It's the first thing you see."

10   "We got a water tower on the reserve," my mother said.

"There's a big one in Lethbridge, too."

"You'll be able to see the tops of the flagpoles, too. That's where the border is."

When we got to Coutts, my mother stopped at the convenience store and bought her and Laetitia a cup of coffee. I got an Orange Crush.

"This is real lousy coffee."

15   "You're just angry because I want to see the world."

"It's the water. From here on down, they got lousy water."

"I can catch the bus from Sweetgrass. You don't have to lift a finger."

"You're going to have to buy your water in bottles if you want good coffee."

There was an old wooden building about a block away, with a tall sign in the yard that said "Museum." Most of the roof had been blown away. Mom told me to go and see when the place was open. There were boards over the windows and doors. You could tell that the place was closed, and I told Mom so, but she said to go and check anyway. Mom and Laetitia stayed by the car. Neither one of them moved. I sat down on the steps of the museum and watched them, and I don't know that they ever said anything to each other. Finally, Laetitia got her bag out of the trunk and gave Mom a hug.

20   I wandered back to the car. The wind had come up, and it blew Laetitia's hair across her face. Mom reached out and pulled the strands out of Laetitia's eyes, and Laetitia let her.

"You can still see the mountain from here," my mother told Laetitia in Blackfoot.

"Lots of mountains in Salt Lake," Laetitia told her in English.

"The place is closed," I said. "Just like I told you."

Laetitia tucked her hair into her jacket and dragged her bag down the road to the brick building with the American flag flapping on a pole. When she got to where the guards were waiting, she turned, put the bag down, and waved to us. We waved back. Then my mother turned the car around, and we came home.

25   We got postcards from Laetitia regular, and, if she wasn't spreading jelly on the truth, she was happy. She found a good job and rented an apartment with a pool.

"And she can't even swim," my mother told Mrs. Manyfingers.

Most of the postcards said we should come down and see the city, but whenever I mentioned this, my mother would stiffen up.

So I was surprised when she bought two new tires for the car and put on her blue dress with the green and yellow flowers. I had to dress up, too, for my mother did not want us crossing the border looking like Americans. We made sandwiches and put them in a big box with pop and potato chips and some apples and bananas and a big jar of water.

"But we can stop at one of those restaurants, too, right?"

30   "We maybe should take some blankets in case you get sleepy."

"But we can stop at one of those restaurants, too, right?"

The border was actually two towns, though neither one was big enough to amount to anything. Coutts was on the Canadian side and consisted of the convenience store and gas station, the museum that was closed and boarded up, and a motel. Sweetgrass was on the American side, but all you could see was an overpass that arched across the highway and disappeared into the prairies. Just hearing the names of these towns, you would expect that Sweetgrass, which is a nice name and sounds like it is related to other places such as Medicine Hat and Moose Jaw and Kicking Horse Pass, would be on the Canadian side, and that Coutts, which sounds abrupt and rude, would be on the American side. But this was not the case.

Between the two borders was a duty-free shop where you could buy cigarettes and liquor and flags. Stuff like that.

We left the reserve in the morning and drove until we got to Coutts.

35   "Last time we stopped here," my mother said, "you had an Orange Crush. You remember that?"

"Sure," I said. "That was when Laetitia took off."

"You want another Orange Crush?"

"That means we're not going to stop at a restaurant, right?"

My mother got a coffee at the convenience store, and we stood around and watched the prairies move in the sunlight. Then we climbed back in the car. My mother straightened the dress across her thighs, leaned against the wheel, and drove all the way to the border in first gear, slowly, as if she were trying to see through a bad storm or riding high on black ice.

40   The border guard was an old guy. As he walked to the car, he swayed from side to side, his feet set wide apart, the holster on his hip pitching up and down. He leaned into the window, looked into the back seat, and looked at my mother and me.

"Morning, ma'am."

"Good morning."

"Where you heading?"

"Salt Lake City."

45   "Purpose of your visit?"

"Visit my daughter."

"Citizenship?"

"Blackfoot," my mother told him.

"Ma'am?"

50   "Blackfoot," my mother repeated.

"Canadian?"

"Blackfoot."

It would have been easier if my mother had just said "Canadian" and been done with it, but I could see she wasn't going to do that. The guard wasn't angry or anything. He smiled and looked towards the building. Then he turned back and nodded.

"Morning, ma'am."

55   "Good morning."

"Any firearms or tobacco?"

"No."

"Citizenship?"

"Blackfoot."

60   He told us to sit in the car and wait, and we did. In about five minutes, another guard came out with the first man. They were talking as they came, both men swaying back and forth like two cowboys headed for a bar or a gunfight.

"Morning, ma'am."

"Good morning."

"Cecil tells me you and the boy are Blackfoot."

"That's right."

65   "Now, I know that we got Blackfeet on the American side and the Canadians got Blackfeet on their side. Just so we can keep our records straight, what side do you come from?"

I knew exactly what my mother was going to say, and I could have told them if they had asked me.

"Canadian side or American side?" asked the guard.

"Blackfoot side," she said.

It didn't take them long to lose their sense of humor, I can tell you that. The one guard stopped smiling altogether and told us to park our car at the side of the building and come in.

70   We sat on a wood bench for about an hour before anyone came over to talk to us. This time it was a woman. She had a gun, too.

"Hi," she said. "I'm Inspector Pratt. I understand there is a little misunderstanding."

"I'm going to visit my daughter in Salt Lake City," my mother told her. "We don't have any guns or beer."

"It's a legal technicality, that's all."

"My daughter's Blackfoot, too."

75   The woman opened a briefcase and took out a couple of forms and began to write on one of them. "Everyone who crosses our border has to declare their citizenship. Even Americans. It helps us keep track of the visitors we get from the various countries."

She went on like that for maybe fifteen minutes, and a lot of the stuff she told us was interesting.

"I can understand how you feel about having to tell us your citizenship, and here's what I'll do. You tell me, and I won't put it down on the form. No-one will know but you and me."

Her gun was silver. There were several chips in the wood handle and the name "Stella" was scratched into the metal butt.

We were in the border office for about four hours, and we talked to almost everyone there. One of the men bought me a Coke. My mother brought a couple of sandwiches in from the car. I offered part of mine to Stella, but she said she wasn't hungry.

80   I told Stella that we were Blackfoot and Canadian, but she said that that didn't count because I was a minor. In the end, she told us that if my mother didn't declare her citizenship, we would have to go back to where we came from. My mother stood up and thanked Stella for her time. Then we got back in the car and drove to the Canadian border, which was only about a hundred yards away.

I was disappointed. I hadn't seen Laetitia for a long time, and I had never been to Salt Lake City. When she was still at home, Laetitia would go on and on about Salt Lake City. She had never been there, but her boyfriend Lester Tallbull had spent a year in Salt Lake at a technical school.

"It's a great place," Lester would say. "Nothing but blondes in the whole state."

Whenever he said that, Laetitia would slug him on his shoulder hard enough to make him flinch. He had some brochures on Salt Lake and some maps, and every so often the two of them would spread them out on the table.

"That's the temple. It's right downtown. You got to have a pass to get in."

85 "Charlotte says anyone can go in and look around."

"When was Charlotte in Salt Lake? Just when the hell was Charlotte in Salt Lake?"

"Last year."

"This is Liberty Park. It's got a zoo. There's good skiing in the mountains."

"Got all the skiing we can use," my mother would say. "People come from all over the world to ski at Banff. Cardston's got a temple, if you like those kinds of things."

90 "Oh, this one is real big," Lester would say. "They got armed guards and everything."

"Not what Charlotte says."

"What does she know?"

Lester and Laetitia broke up, but I guess the idea of Salt Lake stuck in her mind.

The Canadian border guard was a young woman, and she seemed happy to see us. "Hi," she said. "You folks sure have a great day for a trip. Where are you coming from?"

95 "Standoff."

"Is that in Montana?"

"No."

"Where are you going?"

"Standoff."

100 The woman's name was Carol and I don't guess she was any older than Laetitia. "Wow, you both Canadians?"

"Blackfoot."

"Really? I have a friend I went to school with who is Blackfoot. Do you know Mike Harley?"

"No."

"He went to school in Lethbridge, but he's really from Browning."

105 It was a nice conversation and there were no cars behind us, so there was no rush.

"You're not bringing any liquor back, are you?"

"No."

"Any cigarettes or plants or stuff like that?"

"No."

110 "Citizenship?"

"Blackfoot."

"I know," said the woman, "and I'd be proud of being Blackfoot if I were Blackfoot. But you have to be American or Canadian."

When Laetitia and Lester broke up, Lester took his brochures and maps with him, so Laetitia wrote to someone in Salt Lake City, and, about a month later, she got a big envelope of stuff. We sat at the table and opened up all the brochures, and Laetitia read each one out loud.

"Salt Lake City is the gateway to some of the world's most magnificent skiing.

115   "Salt Lake City is the home of one of the newest professional basketball franchises, the Utah Jazz.

"The Great Salt Lake is one of the natural wonders of the world."

It was kind of exciting seeing all those color brochures on the table and listening to Laetitia read all about how Salt Lake City was one of the best places in the entire world.

"That Salt Lake City place sounds too good to be true," my mother told her.

"It has everything."

120   "We got everything right here."

"It's boring here."

"People in Salt Lake City are probably sending away for brochures of Calgary and Lethbridge and Pincher Creek right now."

In the end, my mother would say that maybe Laetitia should go to Salt Lake City, and Laetitia would say that maybe she would.

We parked the car to the side of the building and Carol led us into a small room on the second floor. I found a comfortable spot on the couch and flipped through some back issues of *Saturday Night* and *Alberta Report*.

125   When I woke up, my mother was just coming out of another office. She didn't say a word to me. I followed her down the stairs and out to the car. I thought we were going home, but she turned the car around and drove back towards the American border, which made me think we were going to visit Laetitia in Salt Lake City after all. Instead she pulled into the parking lot of the duty-free store and stopped.

"We going to see Laetitia?"

"No."

"We going home?"

Pride is a good thing to have, you know. Laetitia had a lot of pride, and so did my mother. I figured that someday, I'd have it, too.

130   "So where are we going?"

Most of that day, we wandered around the duty-free store, which wasn't very large. The manager had a name tag with a tiny American flag on one side and a tiny Canadian flag on the other. His name was Mel. Towards evening, he began suggesting that we should be on our way. I told him we had nowhere to go, that neither the Americans nor the Canadians would let us in. He laughed at that and told us that we should buy something or leave.

The car was not very comfortable, but we did have all that food and it was April, so even if it did snow as it sometimes does on the prairies, we wouldn't freeze. The next morning my mother drove to the American border.

It was a different guard this time, but the questions were the same. We didn't spend as much time in the office as we had the day before. By noon, we were back at the Canadian border. By two we were back in the duty-free shop parking lot.

The second night in the car was not as much fun as the first, but my mother seemed in good spirits, and, all in all, it was as much an adventure as an inconvenience. There wasn't much food left and that was a problem, but we had lots of water as there was a faucet at the side of the duty-free shop.

135   One Sunday, Laetitia and I were watching television. Mom was over at Mrs. Manyfingers's. Right in the middle of the program, Laetitia turned off the set and said she was going to Salt Lake City, that life around here was too boring. I had wanted to see the rest of the program and really didn't care if Laetitia went to Salt Lake City or not. When Mom got home, I told her what Laetitia had said.

What surprised me was how angry Laetitia got when she found out that I had told Mom.

"You got a big mouth."

"That's what you said."

"What I said is none of your business."

140   "I didn't say anything."

"Well, I'm going for sure, now."

That weekend, Laetitia packed her bags, and we drove her to the border.

Mel turned out to be friendly. When he closed up for the night and found us still parked in the lot, he came over and asked us if our car was broken down or something. My mother thanked him for his concern and told him that we were fine, that things would get straightened out in the morning.

"You're kidding," said Mel. "You'd think they could handle the simple things."

145   "We got some apples and a banana," I said, "but we're all out of ham sandwiches."

"You know, you read about these things, but you just don't believe it. You just don't believe it."

"Hamburgers would be even better because they got more stuff for energy."

My mother slept in the back seat. I slept in the front because I was smaller and could lie under the steering wheel. Late that night, I heard my mother open the car door. I found her sitting on her blanket leaning against the bumper of the car.

"You see all those stars," she said. "When I was a little girl, my grandmother used to take me and my sisters out on the prairies and tell us stories about all the stars."

150   "Do you think Mel is going to bring us any hamburgers?"

"Every one of those stars has a story. You see that bunch of stars over there that look like a fish?"

"He didn't say no."

"Coyote went fishing, one day. That's how it all started." We sat out under the stars that night, and my mother told me all sorts of stories. She was serious about it, too. She'd tell them slow, repeating parts as she went, as if she expected me to remember each one.

Early the next morning, the television vans began to arrive, and guys in suits and women in dresses came trotting over to us, dragging microphones and cameras and lights behind them. One of the vans had a table set up with orange juice and sandwiches and fruit. It was for the crew, but when I told them we hadn't eaten for a while, a really skinny blonde woman told us we could eat as much as we wanted.

155   They mostly talked to my mother. Every so often one of the reporters would come over and ask me questions about how it felt to be an Indian without a country. I told them we had a nice house on the reserve and that my cousins had a couple of horses we rode when we went fishing. Some of the television people went over to the American border, and then they went to the Canadian border.

Around noon, a good-looking guy in a dark blue suit and an orange tie with little ducks on it drove up in a fancy car. He talked to my mother for a while, and, after they were done talking, my mother called me over, and we got into our car. Just as my mother started the engine, Mel came over and gave us a bag of peanut brittle and told us that justice was a damn hard thing to get, but that we shouldn't give up.

I would have preferred lemon drops, but it was nice of Mel anyway.

"Where are we going now?"

"Going to visit Laetitia."

160   The guard who came out to our car was all smiles. The television lights were so bright they hurt my eyes, and, if you tried to look through the windshield in certain directions, you couldn't see a thing.

"Morning, ma'am."

"Good morning."

"Where you heading?"

"Salt Lake City."

165   "Purpose of your visit?"

"Visit my daughter."

"Any tobacco, liquor, or firearms?"

"Don't smoke."

"Any plants or fruit?"

170   "Not any more."

"Citizenship?"

"Blackfoot."

The guard rocked back on his heels and jammed his thumbs into his gun belt. "Thank you," he said, his fingers patting the butt of the revolver. "Have a pleasant trip."

My mother rolled the car forward, and the television people had to scramble out of the way. They ran alongside the car as we pulled away from the border, and, when they couldn't run any farther, they stood in the middle of the highway and waved and waved and waved.

175   We got to Salt Lake City the next day. Laetitia was happy to see us, and, that first night, she took us out to a restaurant that made really good soups. The list of pies took up a whole page. I had cherry. Mom had chocolate. Laetitia said that she saw us on television the night before and, during the meal, she had us tell her the story over and over again.

Laetitia took us everywhere. We went to a fancy ski resort. We went to the temple. We got to go shopping in a couple of large malls, but they weren't as large as the one in Edmonton, and Mom said so.

After a week or so, I got bored and wasn't at all sad when my mother said we should be heading back home. Laetitia wanted us to stay longer, but Mom said no, that she had things to do back home and that, next time, Laetitia should come up and visit. Laetitia said she was thinking about moving back, and Mom told her to do as she pleased, and Laetitia said that she would.

On the way home, we stopped at the duty-free shop, and my mother gave Mel a green hat that said "Salt Lake" across the front. Mel was a funny guy. He took the hat and blew his nose and told my mother that she was an inspiration to us all. He gave us some more peanut brittle and came out into the parking lot and waved at us all the way to the Canadian border.

It was almost evening when we left Coutts. I watched the border through the rear window until all you could see were the tops of the flagpoles and the blue water tower, and then they rolled over a hill and disappeared.

MAKING CONNECTIONS

1. Why do you think the story moves back and forth between the border scenes and the talk about Salt Lake City? Discuss the relationship between the structure of the story and its content.

2. What happens at the end of the story? Why are they finally allowed to cross the border? Why does Mel say the narrator's mother is "an inspiration to us all"? Is she? Explain.

3. Compare this story to Gloria Anzaldúa's "To Live in the Borderlands Means You" on page 948.

MAKING AN ARGUMENT

1. When asked about her citizenship, the narrator's mother insists on identifying the two of them as "Blackfoot." Why? Given all the trouble it seems to cause, would it have been better if she had simply said "Canadian"? Write an argument that agrees or disagrees with her refusal to declare her citizenship. Cite the text of the story for support.

GABRIEL GARCÍA MÁRQUEZ [B. 1928]

Gabriel García Márquez was born in Aracataca, Colombia, and is one of South America's most heralded writers. Typical of his fiction, including "The Handsomest Drowned Man in the World," is the mingling of realistic fiction and magical or fantastic elements. The author of several novels and collections of stories, including the internationally best-selling One Hundred Years of Solitude *(1967) and* Love in the Time of Cholera *(1986), he was awarded the Nobel Prize for literature in 1982. His latest book,* Memories of My Melancholy Whores, *was published in 2004.*

THE HANDSOMEST DROWNED MAN IN THE WORLD [1970]

A TALE FOR CHILDREN, TRANSLATED BY GREGORY RABASSA

The first children who saw the dark and slinky bulge approaching through the sea let themselves think it was an empty ship. Then they saw it had no flags or masts and they thought it was a whale. But when it washed up on the beach, they removed the clumps of seaweed, the jellyfish tentacles, and the remains of fish and flotsam, and only then did they see that it was a drowned man.

They had been playing with him all afternoon, burying him in the sand and digging him up again, when someone chanced to see them and spread the alarm in the village. The men who carried him to the nearest house noticed that he weighed more than any dead man they had ever known, almost as much as a horse, and they said to each other that maybe he'd been floating too long and the water had got into his bones. When they laid him on the floor they said he'd been taller than all the other men because there was barely enough room for him in the house, but they thought that maybe the ability to keep on growing after death was part of the nature of certain drowned men. He had the smell of the sea about him and only his shape gave one to suppose that it was the corpse of a human being, because the skin was covered with a crust of mud and scales.

They did not even have to clean off his face to know that the dead man was a stranger. The village was made up of only twenty-odd wooden houses that had stone courtyards with no flowers and which were spread about on the end of a desertlike cape. There was so little land that mothers always went about with the fear that the wind would carry off their children and the few dead that the years had caused among them had to be thrown off the cliffs. But the sea was calm and bountiful and all the men fit into seven boats. So when they found the drowned man they simply had to look at one another to see that they were all there. That night they did not go out to work at sea. While the men went to find out if anyone was missing in neighboring villages, the women stayed behind to care for the drowned man. They took the mud off with grass swabs, they removed the underwater stones entangled in his hair, and they scraped the crust off with tools used for scaling fish. As they were doing that they noticed that the vegetation on him came from faraway oceans and deep water and that his clothes were in tatters, as if he had sailed through labyrinths of coral. They noticed too that he bore his death with pride, for he did not have the lonely look of other drowned men who came out of the sea or that haggard, needy look of men who drowned in rivers. But only when they finished cleaning him off did they become aware of the kind of man he was and it left them breathless. Not only was he the tallest, strongest, most virile, and best built man they had ever seen, but even though they were looking at him there was no room for him in their imagination.

They could not find a bed in the village large enough to lay him on nor was there a table solid enough to use for his wake. The tallest men's holiday pants would not fit him, nor the fattest ones' Sunday shirts, nor the shoes of the one with the biggest feet. Fascinated by his huge size and his beauty, the women then decided to make him some pants from a large piece of sail and a shirt from some bridal brabant linen so that he could continue through his death with dignity. As they sewed, sitting in a circle and gazing at the corpse between stitches, it seemed to them that the wind had never been so steady nor the sea so restless as on that night and they supposed that the change had something to do with the dead man. They thought that if that magnificent man had lived in the village, his house would have had the widest doors, the highest ceiling, and the strongest floor, his bedstead would have been made from a midship frame held together by iron bolts, and his wife would have been the happiest woman. They thought that he would have had so much authority that he could have drawn fish out of the sea simply by calling their names and that he would have put so much work into his land that springs would have burst forth from among the rocks so that he would have been able to plant flowers on the cliffs. They secretly compared him to their own men, thinking that for all their lives theirs were incapable of doing what he could do in one night, and they ended up dismissing them deep in their hearts as the weakest, meanest, and most useless creatures on earth. They were wandering through the maze of fantasy when the oldest woman, who as the oldest had looked upon the drowned man with more compassion than passion, sighed:

5   "He has the face of someone called Esteban."

It was true. Most of them had only to take another look at him to see that he could not have any other name. The more stubborn among them, who were the youngest, still lived for a few hours with the illusion that when they put his clothes on and he lay among the flowers in patent leather shoes his name might be Lautaro. But it was a vain illusion. There had not been enough canvas, the poorly cut and worse sewn pants were too tight, and the hidden strength of his heart popped the buttons on his shirt. After midnight the whistling of the wind died down and the sea fell into its Wednesday drowsiness. The silence put an end to any last doubts: he was Esteban. The women who had dressed him, who had combed his hair, had cut his nails and shaved him were unable to hold back a shudder of pity when they had to resign themselves to his being dragged along the ground. It was then that they understood how unhappy he must have been with that huge body since it bothered him even after death. They could see him in life, condemned to going through doors sideways, cracking his head on crossbeams, remaining on his feet during visits, not knowing what to do with his soft, pink, sea lion hands while the lady of the house looked for her most resistant chair and begged him, frightened to death, sit here, Esteban, please, and he, leaning against the wall, smiling, don't bother, ma'am, I'm fine where I am, his heels raw and his back roasted from having done the same thing so many times whenever he paid a visit, don't bother, ma'am, I'm fine where I am, just to avoid the embarrassment of breaking up the chair, and never knowing perhaps that the ones who said don't go, Esteban, at least wait till the coffee's ready, were the ones who later on would whisper the big boob finally left, how nice, the handsome fool has gone. That was what the women were thinking beside the body a little before dawn. Later, when they covered his face with a handkerchief so that the light would not bother him, he looked so forever dead, so defenseless, so much like their men that the first furrows of tears opened in their hearts. It was one of the younger ones who began the weeping. The others, coming to, went from sighs to wails, and the more they sobbed the more they felt like weeping, because the drowned man was becoming all the more Esteban for them, and so they wept so much, for he was the most destitute, most peaceful, and most obliging man on earth, poor Esteban. So when the men returned with the news that the drowned man was not from the neighboring villages either, the women felt an opening of jubilation in the midst of their tears.

"Praise the Lord," they sighed, "he's ours!"

The men thought the fuss was only womanish frivolity. Fatigued because of the difficult nighttime inquiries, all they wanted was to get rid of the bother of the newcomer once and for all before the sun grew strong on that arid, windless day. They improvised a litter with the remains of foremasts and gaffs, tying it together with rigging so that it would bear the weight of the body until they reached the cliffs. They wanted to tie the anchor from a cargo ship to him so that he would sink easily into the deepest waves, where fish are blind and divers die of nostalgia, and bad currents would not bring him back to shore, as had happened with other bodies. But the more they hurried, the more the women thought of ways to waste time. They walked about like startled hens, pecking with the sea charms on their breasts, some interfering on one side to put a scapular of the good wind on the drowned man, some on the other side to put a wrist compass on him, and after a great deal of *get away from there, woman, stay out of the way, look, you almost made me fall on top of the dead man,* the men began to feel mistrust in their livers and started grumbling about why so many main-altar decorations for a stranger, because no matter how many nails and holy-water jars he had on him, the sharks would chew him all the same, but the women kept piling on their junk relics, running back and forth, stumbling, while they released in sighs what they did not in tears, so that the men finally exploded with *since when has there ever been such a fuss over a drifting corpse, a drowned nobody, a piece of cold Wednesday meat.* One of the women, mortified by so much lack of care, then removed the handkerchief from the dead man's face and the men were left breathless too.

He was Esteban. It was not necessary to repeat it for them to recognize him. If they had been told Sir Walter Raleigh, even they might have been impressed with his gringo accent, the macaw on his shoulder, his cannibal-killing blunderbuss, but there could be only one Esteban in the world and there he was, stretched out like a sperm whale, shoeless, wearing the pants of an undersized child, and with those stony nails that had to be cut with a knife. They only had to take the handkerchief off his face to see that he was ashamed, that it was not his fault that he was so big or so heavy or so handsome, and if he had known that this was going to happen, he would have looked for a more discreet place to drown in, seriously, I even would have tied the anchor off a galleon around my neck and staggered off a cliff like someone who doesn't like things in order not to be upsetting people now with this Wednesday dead body, as you people say, in order not to be bothering anyone with this filthy piece of cold meat that doesn't have anything to do with me. There was so much truth in his manner that even the most mistrustful men, the ones who felt the bitterness of endless nights at sea fearing that their women would tire of dreaming about them and begin to dream of drowned men, even they and others who were harder still shuddered in the marrow of their bones at Esteban's sincerity.

10   That was how they came to hold the most splendid funeral they could conceive of for an abandoned drowned man. Some women who had gone to get

flowers in the neighboring villages returned with other women who could not believe what they had been told, and those women went back for more flowers when they saw the dead man, and they brought more and more until there were so many flowers and so many people that it was hard to walk about. At the final moment it pained them to return him to the waters as an orphan and they chose a father and mother from among the best people, and aunts and uncles and cousins, so that through him all the inhabitants of the village became kinsmen. Some sailors who heard weeping from a distance went off course and people heard of one who had himself tied to the mainmast, remembering ancient fables about sirens. While they fought for the privilege of carrying him on their shoulders along the steep escarpment by the cliffs, men and women became aware for the first time of the desolation of their streets, the dryness of their courtyards, the narrowness of their dreams as they faced the splendor and beauty of their drowned man. They let him go without an anchor so that he could come back if he wished and whenever he wished, and they all held their breath for the fraction of centuries the body took to fall into the abyss. They did not need to look at one another to realize that they were no longer all present, that they would never be. But they also knew that everything would be different from then on, that their houses would have wider doors, higher ceilings, and stronger floors so that Esteban's memory could go everywhere without bumping into beams and so that no one in the future would dare whisper the big boob finally died, too bad, the handsome fool has finally died, because they were going to paint their house fronts gay colors to make Esteban's memory eternal and they were going to break their backs digging for springs among the stones and planting flowers on the cliffs so that in future years at dawn the passengers on great liners would awaken, suffocated by the smell of gardens on the high seas, and the captain would have to come down from the bridge in his dress uniform, with his astrolabe, his pole star, and his row of war medals and, pointing to the promontory of roses on the horizon, he would say in fourteen languages, look there, where the wind is so peaceful now that it's gone to sleep beneath the beds, over there, where the sun's so bright that the sunflowers don't know which way to turn, yes, that's Esteban's village.

MAKING CONNECTIONS

1. Why do the villagers care for the drowned man? How does he bring about such a change in the village?
2. How do you think the villagers would have treated the drowned man if his appearance had not been so striking?
3. Why do the villagers invent a history for the drowned man? Why do they name him and claim him as their own?
4. What is the significance of the subtitle "A Tale for Children"? Is this a tale for children? Why did the author choose to label it this way?
5. How does the drowned man's identity take shape as the story continues? In what ways does it develop throughout the story?
6. What is the effect of the shift in narration in the second-to-last paragraph?

MAKING AN ARGUMENT

1. This story comes from a literary tradition called "magical realism"—fiction that blends realistic or ordinary details and events with those that are magical or fantastic. Identify those elements in the story that you consider to be fantastic and/or satirical, and write about their effectiveness in conveying the theme of the story. Cite the text of the story for support.

TAHIRA NAQVI [B. 1945]

Originally from Lahore, Pakistan, Tahira Naqvi is now settled in the United States with her family. She has taught English and Urdu Literature at Western Connecticut State University, SUNY Westchester Community College, and Columbia University. She currently teaches in the Department of Middle Eastern and Islamic Studies at New York University. In addition, she is a writer of English fiction and a translator of Urdu. Her own short fiction has been widely anthologized, and a first collection of short stories, titled Attar of Roses and Other Stories of Pakistan, *appeared in 1997. A second collection,* Dying in a Strange Country, *was published in 2001. She recently completed her first novel.*

BRAVE WE ARE   [2001]

"Mom, Ammi," he asks, the little boy Kasim who is my son, who has near-black eyes and whose buck teeth give him a Bugs Bunny look when his mouth is open, as it is now, in query. "What does hybrid mean?"

"Hybrid?" I'm watching the water in the pot very closely; the tiny bubbles quivering restlessly on its surface indicate it's about to come to boil. Poised over the pot, clutching a batch of straw-colored Prince spaghetti, is my hand, suspended, warm from the steam and waiting for the moment when the bubbles will suddenly and turbulently come to life.

I'm not fussy about brands, especially where spaghetti is concerned (it's all pasta, after all), but I wish there was one which would fit snugly at the outset into my largest pot. As things stand now, the strands bend uncomfortably, contort, embroiling themselves in something of a struggle within the confines of the pot once they've been dropped into the boiling water. Some day of course, I will have a pot large enough to accommodate all possible lengths and varieties.

"Yeah, hybrid. Do you know what it means?"

5   The note of restive insistence in his voice compels me to tear my gaze away from the water. Kasim's face looks darker now than when he left for school this morning. Perhaps running up the steep driveway with the March wind lashing against his lean nine-year-old frame has forced the blood to rush to his face. Flushed, his face reminds me he's still only a child, 'only ten, just a baby,' as my mother often says when I sometimes take him to task in her presence, arguing with him as if he were a man behaving like a child.

A new spelling word? Such a difficult word for a fourth-grader. "Are you studying plants?"

"No, but can you tell me what it means?" Impatient, so impatient, so like the water that's hissing and tumbling in the pot, demanding immediate attention. He slides against the kitchen counter and hums, his fingers beating an indecipherable rhythm on the Formica, his eyes raised above mine, below mine, behind me, to the window outside which white, lavender and gray have mingled to become a muddied brown. Just as he reaches for the cookie jar I quickly throw in the spaghetti.

"Well, that's a hard word. Let me see." Helplessly I watch as he breaks off a Stella Doro biscuit in his mouth and crumbs disperse in a steady fall-out, over the counter, on the kitchen tile, some getting caught in his blue-and-green striped sweater, like flies in a spider's web. "It's a sort of mixture, a combination of different sorts of things," I say wisely, with the absolute knowledge that 'things' is susceptible to misinterpretation. I rack my brain for a good example. If I don't hurry up with one he's going to move away with the notion that his mother doesn't know what hybrid means.

"You mean if you mix orange juice with lemonade it's going to become hybrid juice?" The idea has proved ticklish, he smiles, crumbs from the Stella Doro dangling on the sides of his face; they obviously don't bother him as much as they bother me. I lean forward and rub a hand around his mouth just as he lunges toward the cookie jar again. He squirms and recoils at the touch of my ministering hand. Another biscuit is retrieved. I turn down the heat under the spaghetti to medium and start chopping onions.

10   Today I'm making spaghetti the way my mother makes it in Lahore, like pulao, the way I used to make it after I got married and was just learning to cook for a husband who had selective tastes in food. That was about the only thing I could make then so I worked hard to embellish and innovate. There, we call it noodles, although it's unmistakably spaghetti, with no tomato sauce or meatballs in or anywhere near it, no cheese either, and no one has heard of mozzarella or romano. The idea of cheese with our recipe would surprise the people in Lahore; even the ones with the most adventurous palates will cringe.

"Well, that too." And why not? My eyes smart from the sharpness of the onions, tears fill my eyes and spill over my cheeks. I turn away from the chopping board. "The word is used when you breed two different kinds of plants or animals, it's called cross-breeding." I snaffle. This gets harder. I know his knowledge of breeding is limited and 'cross' isn't going to help at all.

"What's cross-whatyoumaycallit?"

An example. One that will put the seal on hybrid forever. So he can boast his mother knows everything.

I wipe my watering eyes with a paper napkin and turn to the onions again. These, chopped thinly, are for the ground beef which will be cooked with small green peas, cubed potatoes and cut-leaf spinach and will be spiced with coriander, garlic, cumin, a touch of turmeric and half-inch long bristly strands of fresh ginger root. I'll throw the beef into the spaghetti when it's done and my husband and I alone will eat what I make. My children like spaghetti the way it should be, the way it is, in America.

15   Moisture runs down my cheeks and my eyes smart. I place the knife down on the chopping board, tear out another sheet from the roll of Bounty towels on my right and rub my eyes and nose with it, my attention driven to the stark, brown limbs of trees outside as I wipe my face. The kitchen window that I now face as I do innumerable times during the day, faithfully reflects the movements of time and seasons of the small town in Connecticut where we live, compelling the spirit to buoyancy or, when the tones on its canvas are achromatous and dark, to melancholy, to sadness. Today, the sun is visible again and the white of the snow is distinguishable from the lavender of the bare, thin, stalky birches, unhealthy because we haven't tended them well. Sharply the sun cuts shadows on the clean, uncluttered snow.

Why does snow in February always remind me of February in Lahore? Incongruent, disparate, the seasons have so little in common. March is spring, grass so thick your foot settles into it, roses that bloom firm, their curves fleshy, the colors like undisturbed paint on an artist's palette, the air timberous, weaving in and out of swishing tree branches with *the sar, sar, sar* of a string instrument. Why do I turn to Eileen, my cleaning lady, and say, "Eileen do you know it's spring in Lahore?" She looks up from the pot she's scrubbing in the kitchen sink with a good-humored smile. "No kidding? Really?" she asks, as if she didn't already know, as if she hadn't already heard it from me before.

An example, yes. "Now take an apple. A farmer can cross-breed a Macintosh apple with a Golden Yellow and get something which is a little bit like both. That will be a hybrid apple." I look closely at the boy's face for some signs of comprehension.

"You mean the apple's going to have a new name, like Macintosh Yellow?" he asks, his forehead creased thoughtfully.

"Yes." Relieved, I return to the onions, making a mental note to check the spaghetti soon, which, languorously swelled now, will have to be taken off from the stove and drained.

20   "But what about animals? You said there's *crosswhatyoumaycallit* in animals too." He sprawls against the counter, up and down, right and left, like a gymnast.

"Yes there is. A cow from one family may be bred with a steer from another family and they'll end up with a calf that's a bit like the two of them." I wash my hands and he skips on the floor, dance-like steps, his arms raised.

"But man's an animal too, teacher says. Do people also cross...*umm*...breed?"

He's humming again. I know the tune now: *"Suzie Q/ Suzie Q/ I love you/ O Suzie Q!"* It's from a song on his older brother Haider's tape, a catchy tune, sort of stays with you and you can't stop humming it. Both Haider and my younger son, Asghar, were amused when I showed an interest in the song. What do I know about music, their kind of music? Once, nearly two years ago, I tried to bribe Haider to memorize a ghazal by the poet Ghalib. The greatest Urdu poet of the subcontinent, I said passionately, the most complex. Egged on by the fifty dollars I was offering, he mastered the first verse by listening to a tape of ghazals sung by Mehdi Hasan.

> *Yeh naa thi hamari qismet ke visal-e-yaar ho*
> *Agar aurjeete rehte yehi intizar hota*

> It was not fated that I should meet my beloved,
> Life will merely prolong the waiting

Then, unable to sustain his interest, despite the now a thirty-dollar verse rate, Haider abandoned the project.

25   "The words are too hard," he complained when I protested, somewhat angrily. "The music's easy, but I can't keep up with the lyrics."

And I would have given him the money too. Actually I had decided to give him all of it after he had moved on to the second verse.

"Does that mean Mary is also hybrid?" Kasim's voice crashes into my thoughts of Suzie Q with a loud boom.

I lower the heat under the spaghetti—so what if it's a bit overdone. The yellow-white strands jump at each other in frantic embraces, hurried, as if there's no time to be lost.

"Mary? What are you talking about?" I know exactly what he's talking about. His vagueness passes through the sieve in my head and comes out as clarity. I fill in any blanks, uncannily, never ceasing to be surprised at the way this peculiar magic works.

30   "You know, Mary Khan, Dr. Khan's daughter? She's in my class Mom, you know her."

Yes, I know Mary well. Her full name is Marium. Her father, Amjad Khan and my husband, Ali, were together in the same medical school in Lahore, they graduated the same year, they completed residencies together at the same hospital in New York, where Amjad met and married Helen, a nurse. Helen is English. She's a few years older than I, very tall, almost a half-inch taller than Amjad, and has sleek, golden hair. We're good friends, Helen and I, and at least once a week we meet for lunch at a restaurant, an activity we decided to call 'sampling restaurants for later.' Over salmon lasagna or papadi chat and dosa or tandoori chicken she'll tell me how difficult Amjad is when it comes to their children, how upset he is that their son has taken it upon himself to date without his father's consent or approval. I'll shake my head and try to explain that Amjad might have dated *her,* but like a good Muslim father, he can't accept that his son can have girlfriends. "Wait till Mary is older," I say with my hand on Helen's arm, "the Muslim father in him will drop all his masks." Together we do what most women do quite unabashedly: spend a great deal of time talking about husbands.

When Mary was born Amjad said, "We're going to call her Marium, it's a name everyone knows." Familiar and convenient is what he meant, since it's tri-religious. That doesn't sound right, but if we can say bisexual, surely we can say tri-religious, too. Why not? After all Islam, Christianity and Judaism all profess a claim to this name. However, before the child was quite one 'Marium' was shortened permanently to Mary.

Kasim is at the breakfast table now, some of his earlier energy dissipated. A small piece of biscuit lies forlornly before him on the table and he fusses with it slowly, obviously unwilling to pop the last bit in his mouth, content just to play with it.

"You know, her mother's English and her father's Pakistani like Dad, and she's got blue eyes and black hair."

35   "Yes, she does have lovely blue eyes and they look so pretty with her dark hair." I grapple with something to blunt the sharpness of his next question which I anticipate and I know I cannot repel.

"Well, then she's hybrid too, isn't she?" He's looking straight at me. His eyes are bright with the defiance of someone who knows he's scored a point.

Brave we are, we who answer questions that spill forth artlessly from the mouths of nine-year-old purists, questions that can neither be waved nor dismissed with flippant ambiguity. Vigilant and alert, we must be ready with our answers.

"Technically speaking she is, I mean, wait, you can say she is." I lift a hand and stop him before he says more. "But we don't use the word for people." The firmness in my voice sounds forced. "Don't say anything to her, okay?"

"Why? Is it a swear?"

40   "No!" I hasten with denial. "Of course not. It's just a word we don't use for people, that's all. Understand?"

"But what do you call them then?" He persists. "Mary's like the apple, isn't she? Isn't she? Her name's Mary Khan, isn't it?"

"Yes, Kas, it is. But there's nothing wrong with that name, a name's a name." Kasim looks contemplative. I know he's saying to himself, *Mom doesn't really know, but Mary's a hybrid, she's got blue eyes and black hair.*

"She's a person Kasim, not an apple. Anyway, you didn't tell me where you heard that word. Is it on your spelling list for this week?"

"No, Mrs. Davis was reading us something about plants in the *Weekly Reader.* It's not homework." He shrugs, abandons the Stella Doro and humming, leaves the kitchen.

45   "Get to homework now," I call after him, wondering if there's an equivalent of 'hybrid' in Urdu, a whole word, not one or two strung together in a phrase to mean the same thing. Offhand I can't think of one.

Without meaning to I throw in some oregano into the boiling spaghetti. I shouldn't have done that. How's oregano going to taste in the company of coriander and cumin? Well, no matter, it's too late anyway.

After I've drained the spaghetti I will take some out for the meat mixture, saving the rest for my children. Then I'll add to our portion, my husband's and mine, the beef and vegetable mixture and turn everything over ever so gently, making sure that the spaghetti isn't squelched. The strands must remain smooth, elusive, separate.

MAKING CONNECTIONS

1. In giving her explanation, what is the narrator's conflict? What is she concerned about? Should she be? Would you be in this circumstance? Explain.
2. Describe the "voice" of the narrator. How has she "shown" what is told? What details in the story help to give you a picture of the setting and the difficulty of the situation?

MAKING AN ARGUMENT

1. To what extent is the meal the narrator is preparing a metaphor for what she is explaining? What does she mean in the last line of the story by "The strands must remain smooth, elusive, separate"? Do you agree? Interpret the theme of the story and take a position on the closing metaphor. Cite the text of the story for support.

ALICE WALKER [B. 1944]

*Alice Walker was one of eight children born in rural Geor-
gia to sharecropper parents and was particularly close to
her mother. Walker first attended Spelman College, and then
transferred to Sarah Lawrence, where she earned a B.A. in
1965. In 1967, she married a white civil rights lawyer (they
have since divorced), and the couple settled in Jackson, Mississippi, where they were the first legally married interracial
couple in the city. The following year, while she was teaching*
at Jackson State University, she published the first of her seven volumes of concise
and unsentimental verse, Once. *Though she first attracted national attention with
her edition of* I Love Myself When I Am Laughing *(1979), an anthology of essays
about Zora Neale Hurston, it was her novel* The Color Purple, *the story of a black
woman's struggle in the early twentieth century, that made her the literary equivalent of a superstar. Her other novels include* The Temple of My Familiar *(1989) and*
Possessing the Secret of Joy *(1992). Her most recent book is a collection of poems,*
Hard Times Require Furious Dancing, *which was published in 2010. Walker currently resides in southern California.*

EVERYDAY USE   [1973]

For Your Grandmama

I will wait for her in the yard that Maggie and I made so clean and wavy yesterday
afternoon. A yard like this is more comfortable than most people know. It is not just
a yard. It is like an extended living room. When the hard clay is swept clean as a
floor and the fine sand around the edges lined with tiny, irregular grooves anyone
can come and sit and look up into the elm tree and wait for the breezes that never
come inside the house.

Maggie will be nervous until after her sister goes: she will stand hopelessly in
corners homely and ashamed of the burn scars down her arms and legs, eyeing her
sister with a mixture of envy and awe. She thinks her sister has held life always in
the palm of one hand, that "no" is a word the world never learned to say to her.

You've no doubt seen those TV shows where the child who has "made it" is
confronted, as a surprise, by her own mother and father, tottering in weakly from
backstage. (A pleasant surprise, of course: What would they do if parent and child
came on the show only to curse out and insult each other?) On TV mother and child
embrace and smile into each other's faces. Sometimes the mother and father weep,
the child wraps them in her arms and leans across the table to tell how she would
not have made it without their help. I have seen these programs.

Sometimes I dream a dream in which Dee and I are suddenly brought together
on a TV program of this sort. Out of a dark and soft-seated limousine I am ushered
into a bright room filled with many people. There I meet a smiling, gray, sporty
man like Johnny Carson who shakes my hand and tells me what a fine girl I have.
Then we are on the stage and Dee is embracing me with tears in her eyes. She

pins on my dress a large orchid, even though she has told me once that she thinks orchids are tacky flowers.

5   In real life I am a large, big-boned woman with rough, man-working hands. In the winter I wear flannel nightgowns to bed and overalls during the day. I can kill and clean a hog as mercilessly as a man. My fat keeps me hot in zero weather. I can work outside all day, breaking ice to get water for washing; I can eat pork liver cooked over the open fire minutes after it comes steaming from the hog. One winter I knocked a bull calf straight in the brain between the eyes with a sledge hammer and had the meat hung up to chill before nightfall. But of course all this does not show on television.⟨I am the way my daughter would want me to be: a hundred pounds lighter, my skin like an uncooked barley pancake. My hair glistens in the hot bright lights. Johnny Carson has much to do to keep up with my quick and witty tongue.⟩

But that is a mistake. I know even before I wake up. Who ever knew a Johnson with a quick tongue? Who can even imagine me looking a strange white man in the eye? It seems to me I have talked to them always with one foot raised in flight, with my head turned in whichever way is farthest from them. Dee, though. She would always look anyone in the eye. Hesitation was no part of her nature.

"How do I look, Mama?" Maggie says, showing just enough of her thin body enveloped in pink skirt and red blouse for me to know she's there, almost hidden by the door.

"Come out into the yard," I say.

Have you ever seen a lame animal, perhaps a dog run over by some careless person rich enough to own a car, sidle up to someone who is ignorant enough to be kind to him? That is the way my Maggie walks. She has been like this, chin on chest, eyes on ground, feet in shuffle, ever since the fire that burned the other house to the ground.

10   Dee is lighter than Maggie, with nicer hair and a fuller figure. She's a woman now, though sometimes I forget. How long ago was it that the other house burned? Ten, twelve years? Sometimes I can still hear the flames and feel Maggie's arms sticking to me, her hair smoking and her dress falling off her in little black papery flakes. Her eyes seemed stretched open, blazed open by the flames reflected in them. And Dee. I see her standing off under the sweet gum tree she used to dig gum out of, a look of concentration on her face as she watched the last dingy gray board of the house fall in toward the red-hot brick chimney. Why don't you do a dance around the ashes? I'd wanted to ask her. She had hated the house that much.

I used to think she hated Maggie, too. But that was before we raised the money, the church and me, to send her to Augusta to school⟨She used to read to us without pity; forcing words, lies, other folks' habits, whole lives upon us two, sitting trapped and ignorant underneath her voice. She washed us in a river of make-believe, burned us with a lot of knowledge we didn't necessarily need to know. Pressed us to her with the serious way she read, to shove us away at just the moment, like dimwits, we seemed about to understand.⟩

Dee wanted nice things. A yellow organdy dress to wear to her graduation from high school; black pumps to match a green suit she'd made from an old suit somebody gave me. She was determined to stare down any disaster in her efforts. Her eyelids would not flicker for minutes at a time. Often I fought off the temptation to shake her. At sixteen she had a style of her own: and knew what style was.

(I never had an education myself. After second grade the school was closed down. Don't ask me why: in 1927 colored asked fewer questions than they do now.) Sometimes Maggie reads to me. She stumbles along good-naturedly but can't see well. She knows she is not bright. Like good looks and money, quickness passed her by. She will marry John Thomas (who has mossy teeth in an earnest face) and then I'll be free to sit here and I guess just sing church songs to myself. Although I never was a good singer. Never could carry a tune. I was always better at a man's job. I used to love to milk till I was hooked in the side in '49. Cows are soothing and slow and don't bother you, unless you try to milk them the wrong way.

I have deliberately turned my back on the house. It is three rooms, just like the one that burned, except the roof is tin; they don't make shingle roofs any more. There are no real windows, just some holes cut in the sides, like the portholes in a ship, but not round and not square, with rawhide holding the shutters up on the outside. This house is in a pasture, too, like the other one. No doubt when Dee sees it she will want to tear it down. She wrote me once that no matter where we "choose" to live, she will manage to come see us. But she will never bring her friends. Maggie and I thought about this and Maggie asked me, "Mama, when did Dee ever *have* any friends?"

15   She had a few. Furtive boys in pink shirts hanging about on washday after school. Nervous girls who never laughed. Impressed with her they worshiped the well-turned phrase, the cute shape, the scalding humor that erupted like bubbles in lye. She read to them.

When she was courting Jimmy T she didn't have much time to pay to us, but turned all her faultfinding power on him. *He flew* to marry a cheap gal from a family of ignorant flashy people. She hardly had time to recompose herself.

When she comes I will meet—but there they are!

Maggie attempts to make a dash for the house, in her shuffling way, but I stay her with my hand. "Come back here," I say. And she stops and tries to dig a well in the sand with her toe.

It is hard to see them clearly through the strong sun. But even the first glimpse of leg out of the car tells me it is Dee. Her feet were always neat-looking, as if God himself had shaped them with a certain style. From the other side of the car comes a short, stocky man. Hair is all over his head a foot long and hanging from his chin like a kinky mule tail. I hear Maggie suck in her breath. "Uhnnnh," is what it sounds like. Like when you see the wriggling end of a snake just in front of your foot on the road. "Uhnnnh."

20   Dee next. A dress down to the ground, in this hot weather. A dress so loud it hurts my eyes. There are yellows and oranges enough to throw back the light of the sun. *I* feel my whole face warming from the heat waves it throws out. Earrings, too, gold and hanging down to her shoulders. Bracelets dangling and making noises when she moves her arm up to shake the folds of the dress out of her armpits. The dress is loose and flows, and as she walks closer, I like it. I hear Maggie go

"Uhnnnh" again. It is her sister's hair. It stands straight up like the wool on a sheep. It is black as night and around the edges are two long pigtails that rope about like small lizards disappearing behind her ears.

"Wa-su-zo-Tean-o!" she says, coming on in that gliding way the dress makes her move. The short stocky fellow with the hair to his navel is all grinning and he follows up with "Asalamalakim, my mother and sister!" He moves to hug Maggie but she falls back, right up against the back of my chair. I feel her trembling there and when I look up I see the perspiration falling off her chin.

"Don't get up," says Dee. Since I am stout it takes something of a push. You can see me trying to move a second or two before I make it. She turns, showing white heels through her sandals, and goes back to the car. Out she peeks next with a Polaroid. She stoops down quickly and lines up picture after picture of me sitting there in front of the house with Maggie cowering behind me. She never takes a shot without making sure the house is included. When a cow comes nibbling around the edge of the yard she snaps it and me and Maggie *and* the house. Then she puts the Polaroid in the back seat of the car, and comes up and kisses me on the forehead.

Meanwhile Asalamalakim is going through the motions with Maggie's hand. Maggie's hand is as limp as a fish, and probably as cold, despite the sweat, and she keeps trying to pull it back. It looks like Asalamalakim wants to shake hands but wants to do it fancy. Or maybe he don't know how people shake hands. Anyhow, he soon gives up on Maggie.

"Well," I say. "Dee."

25   "No, Mama," she says. "Not Dee, Wangero Leewanika Kemanjo!"

"What happened to 'Dee'?" I wanted to know.

"She's dead," Wangero said. "I couldn't bear it any longer being named after the people who oppress me."

"You know as well as me you was named after your aunt Dicie," I said. Dicie is my sister. She named Dee. We called her "Big Dee" after Dee was born.

"But who was *she* named after?" asked Wangero.

30   "I guess after Grandma Dee," I said.

"And who was she named after?" asked Wangero.

"Her mother," I said, and saw Wangero was getting tired. "That's about as far back as I can trace it," I said. Though, in fact, I probably could have carried it back beyond the Civil War through the branches.

"Well," said Asalamalakim, "there you are."

"Uhnnnh," I heard Maggie say.

35   "There I was not," I said, "before 'Dicie' cropped up in our family, so why should I try to trace it that far back?"

He just stood there grinning, looking down on me like somebody inspecting a Model A car. Every once in a while he and Wangero sent eye signals over my head.

"How do you pronounce this name?" I asked.

"You don't have to call me by it if you don't want to," said Wangero.

"Why shouldn't I?" I asked. "If that's what you want us to call you, we'll call you."

40   "I know it might sound awkward at first," said Wangero.

"I'll get used to it," I said. "Ream it out again."

Well, soon we got the name out of the way. Asalamalakim had a name twice as long and three times as hard. After I tripped over it two or three times he told me to just call him Hakim-a-barber. I wanted to ask him was he a barber, but I didn't really think he was, so I didn't ask.

"You must belong to those beef-cattle peoples down the road," I said. They said "Asalamalakim" when they met you, too, but they didn't shake hands. Always too busy: feeding the cattle, fixing the fences, putting up saltlick shelters, throwing down hay. When the white folks poisoned some of the herd the men stayed up all night with rifles in their hands. I walked a mile and a half just to see the sight.

Hakim-a-barber said, "I accept some of their doctrines, but farming and raising cattle is not my style." (They didn't tell me, and I didn't ask, whether Wangero [Dee] had really gone and married him.)

45   We sat down to eat and right away he said he didn't eat collards and pork was unclean. Wangero, though, went on through the chitlins and corn bread, the greens and everything else. She talked a blue streak over the sweet potatoes. Everything delighted her. Even the fact that we still used the benches her daddy made for the table when we couldn't afford to buy chairs.

"Oh, Mama!" she cried. Then turned to Hakim-a-barber. "I never knew how lovely these benches are. You can feel the rump prints," she said, running her hands underneath her and along the bench. Then she gave a sigh and her hand closed over Grandma Dee's butter dish. "That's it!" she said. "I knew there was something I wanted to ask you if I could have." She jumped up from the table and went over in the corner where the churn stood, the milk in it clabber by now. She looked at the churn and looked at it.

"This churn top is what I need," she said. "Didn't Uncle Buddy whittle it out of a tree you all used to have?"

"Yes," I said.

"Uh huh," she said happily. "And I want the dasher, too."

50   "Uncle Buddy whittle that, too?" asked the barber.

Dee (Wangero) looked up at me.

"Aunt Dee's first husband whittled the dash," said Maggie so low you almost couldn't hear her. "His name was Henry, but they called him Stash."

"Maggie's brain is like an elephant's," Wangero said, laughing. "I can use the churn top as a centerpiece for the alcove table," she said, sliding a plate over the churn, "and I'll think of something artistic to do with the dasher."

When she finished wrapping the dasher the handle stuck out. I took it for a moment in my hands. You didn't even have to look close to see where hands pushing the dasher up and down to make butter had left a kind of sink in the wood. In fact, there were a lot of small sinks; you could see where thumbs and fingers had sunk into the wood. It was beautiful light yellow wood, from a tree that grew in the yard where Big Dee and Stash had lived.

55   After dinner Dee (Wangero) went to the trunk at the foot of my bed and started rifling through it. Maggie hung back in the kitchen over the dishpan. Out came Wangero with two quilts. They had been pieced by Grandma Dee and then Big Dee and me had hung them on the quilt frames on the front porch and quilted them. One was in the Lone Star pattern. The other was Walk Around the Mountain.

In both of them were scraps of dresses Grandma Dee had worn fifty and more years ago. Bits and pieces of Grandpa Jarrell's Paisley shirts. And one teeny faded blue piece, about the size of a penny matchbox, that was from Great Grandpa Ezra's uniform that he wore in the Civil War.

"Mama," Wangero said sweet as a bird. "Can I have these old quilts?"

I heard something fall in the kitchen, and a minute later the kitchen door slammed.

"Why don't you take one or two of the others?" I asked. "These old things was just done by me and Big Dee from some tops your grandma pieced before she died."

"No," said Wangero. "I don't want those. They are stitched around the border by machine."

60 "That'll make them last better," I said.

"That's not the point," said Wangero. "These are all pieces of dresses Grandma used to wear. She did all this stitching by hand. Imagine!" She held the quilts securely in her arms, stroking them.

"Some of the pieces, like those lavender ones, come from old clothes her mother handed down to her," I said, moving up to touch the quilts. Dee (Wangero) moved back just enough so that I couldn't reach the quilts. They already belonged to her.

"Imagine!" she breathed again, clutching them closely to her bosom.

"The truth is," I said, "I promised to give them quilts to Maggie, for when she marries John Thomas."

65 She gasped like a bee had stung her.

"Maggie can't appreciate these quilts!" she said. "She'd probably be backward enough to put them to everyday use."

"I reckon she would," I said. "God knows I been saving 'em for long enough with nobody using 'em. I hope she will!" I didn't want to bring up how I had offered Dee (Wangero) a quilt when she went away to college. Then she had told me they were old-fashioned, out of style.

"But they're *priceless!*" she was saying now, furiously; for she has a temper. "Maggie would put them on the bed and in five years they'd be in rags. Less than that!"

"She can always make some more," I said. "Maggie knows how to quilt."

70 Dee (Wangero) looked at me with hatred. "You just will not understand. The point is these quilts, *these* quilts!"

"Well," I said, stumped. "What would *you* do with them?"

"Hang them," she said. As if that was the only thing you *could* do with quilts.

Maggie by now was standing in the door. I could almost hear the sound her feet made as they scraped over each other.

"She can have them, Mama," she said, like somebody used to never winning anything, or having anything reserved for her. "I can 'member Grandma Dee without the quilts."

75 I looked at her hard. She had filled her bottom lip with checkerbeny snuff and it gave her face a kind of dopey, hangdog look. It was Grandma Dee and Big Dee who taught her how to quilt herself. She stood there with her scarred hands

hidden in the folds of her skirt. She looked at her sister with something like fear but she wasn't mad at her. This was Maggie's portion. This was the way she knew God to work.

When I looked at her like that something hit me in the top of my head and ran down to the soles of my feet, just like when I'm in church and the spirit of God touches me and I get happy and shout. I did something I never had done before: hugged Maggie to me, then dragged her on into the room, snatched the quilts out of Miss Wangero's hands and dumped them into Maggie's lap. Maggie just sat there on my bed with her mouth open.

"Take one or two of the others," I said to Dee.

But she turned without a word and went out to Hakim-a-barber.

"You just don't understand," she said, as Maggie and I came out to the car.

80   "What don't I understand?" I wanted to know.

"Your heritage," she said. And then she turned to Maggie, kissed her, and said, "You ought to try to make something of yourself, too, Maggie. It's really a new day for us. But from the way you and Mama still live you'd never know it."

She put on some sunglasses that hid everything above the tip of her nose and her chin.

Maggie smiled; maybe at the sunglasses. But a real smile, not scared. After we watched the car dust settle I asked Maggie to bring me a dip of snuff. And then the two of us sat there just enjoying, until it was time to go in the house and go to bed.

MAKING CONNECTIONS

1. This story is told from Mama's point of view. In what way does that affect how and what you are told? If the story were told from Dee's point of view, how would it differ? Cite some examples from the text.

2. The setting of "Everyday Use" seems to mean something different to each of the characters. What does it mean to Mama? To Dee? To Maggie?

3. How does Maggie's character change in the course of the story? What do you think prompts this change?

4. If you were in Dee's situation, would you have acted differently? Would you have seen the quilt as a valuable artifact or something to be used every day? Explain.

5. Is the title of the story appropriate? How so? How would you define *everyday use*?

MAKING AN ARGUMENT

1. Consider the different views of cultural identity represented by Mama and Dee. Mama sees her cultural identity expressed personally and locally, whereas Dee sees it expressed more impersonally and globally. Is one more important than the other? Take a position on this issue and write an essay that argues for one position or the other (or both). Cite the text of the story for support.

◆ POETRY ◆

CONNECTING THROUGH COMPARISON: THE MASK WE WEAR

The three poems that follow address a subtheme of this section: the mask we wear. The idea of hiding or running away from one's identity has been a common theme in much modern literature. Read and discussed together, these poems invite comparisons and connections—not only with each other, but with your own experience of being afraid to be yourself.

W. H. AUDEN   [1907–1973]

W[ystan] H[ugh] Auden was born in York, England, and educated at Oxford University. Like many intellectuals of his generation, his left-wing politics led him to serve on the loyalist side of the Spanish Civil War, but Auden quickly became disillusioned after witnessing the destruction and looting of Roman Catholic churches and returned to England. He immigrated to America in 1939, becoming a citizen in 1946. In 1947, he coined the term "the Age of Anxiety" in a long poem of the same name, which has since served as a shorthand term for the intellectual mood of the mid-twentieth century. His early work is characterized by his sharp wit and facility with elaborate verse forms. His later work, influenced by his reawakening interest in Christianity, became increasingly religious in tone.

THE UNKNOWN CITIZEN   [1940]

To
SOCIAL SECURITY ACCOUNT NUMBER 067-01-9818
THIS MARBLE MONUMENT IS ERECTED BY THE STATE

He was found by the Bureau of Statistics to be
One against whom there was no official complaint,
And all the reports on his conduct agree
That, in the modern sense of an old-fashioned word, he was a saint,
For in everything he did he served the Greater Community.   5
Except for the war, till the day he retired
He worked in one factory and never got fired,
But satisfied his employers, Fudge Motors, Inc.,
Yet was neither a scab nor odd in his views,
For his Union reports that he paid his dues   10
(Our report on his Union says it was sound),
And our Social Psychology workers found
He was popular with his mates and liked a drink.
The Press are convinced that he bought a paper every day,
And that his reactions to advertisements were normal in every way.   15

Policies taken out in his name prove that he was fully insured,
And a certificate shows that he was once in hospital but left it cured.
Both *Producer's Research* and *High Grade Living* declare
He was fully sensible to the advantages of the Installment Plan,
And had everything necessary to the Modern Man—   20
A victrola, a radio, a car, and a frigidaire.
Our investigators into Public Opinion are content
That he held the proper opinions for the time of year;
When there was peace, he was for peace; when there was war, he went.
He was married and added five children to the population,   25
Which, our eugenist says, was the right number for a parent of his generation,
And our teachers report that he never interfered with their education.
Was he free? Was he happy? The question is absurd;
Had anything been wrong, we should certainly have heard.

PAUL LAURENCE DUNBAR [1872–1906]

Paul Laurence Dunbar was born and raised in Dayton, Ohio. Both of his parents had been slaves. Dunbar excelled in high school, where he was the only African American in his class, and served both as the class president and class poet. While in high school, he worked as an editor at the Dayton Tattler, *a short-lived newspaper for blacks. His widowed mother's financial situation ruled out college, and, unable to find a position as a writer because of his race, he was forced to find work at a number of jobs (including one as an elevator operator) that allowed him the leisure to continue writing and publishing poems. By 1892, he had earned enough recognition that he could pursue a literary career. He wrote prolifically but was plagued by ill health. In 1906, at the age of thirty-three, he died of tuberculosis. Though he is best known for his poems, which were the first to incorporate African American speech, Dunbar published numerous novels, short stories, and essays.*

WE WEAR THE MASK   [1895]

We wear the mask that grins and lies,
It hides our cheeks and shades our eyes—
This debt we pay to human guile;
With torn and bleeding hearts we smile,
And mouth with myriad subtleties.   5

Why should the world be over-wise,
In counting all our tears and sighs?
Nay, let them only see us, while
   We wear the mask.

We smile, but, O great Christ, our cries   10
To thee from tortured souls arise.

We sing, but oh the clay is vile
Beneath our feet, and long the mile;
But let the world dream otherwise,
    We wear the mask!   15

T. S. ELIOT [1888–1965]

*Born to a wealthy family in St. Louis, Missouri, T[homas]
S[tearns] Eliot attended Harvard University, where he studied literature as an undergraduate, and, as a graduate
student, Sanskrit and philosophy. After further studies at
the Sorbonne and Oxford University, he settled in England
in 1915, taking a job first at an insurance company and
later in publishing, becoming a British citizen in 1926.
Eliot, with his first volume of poetry,* Prufrock and Other
Observations *(1917), and the 1922 publication of* The Waste Land, *transformed
the landscape of modern poetry, shattering literary conventions in order to give
voice to what he felt was the spiritual emptiness of the modern world. An influential
critic, he also wrote verse plays, including* Murder in the Cathedral *(1935) and* The
Cocktail Party *(1949). He was awarded the Nobel Prize in 1948. Recent biographies
of Eliot have not always treated him kindly, and there is much scholarly debate on
the extent and importance of his anti-Semitism. Nevertheless, Eliot remains perhaps
the most influential poet of the twentieth century.*

THE LOVE SONG OF J. ALFRED PRUFROCK   [1917]

*S'io credessi che mia risposta fosse
A persona che mai tornasse al mondo,
Questa fiamma staria senza più scosse.
Ma per ciò che giammai di questo fondo
Non tornò vivo alcun, s'i'odo il vero,
Senza tema d'infamia ti rispondo.°*   5

Let us go then, you and I,
When the evening is spread out against the sky
Like a patient etherised upon a table;
Let us go, through certain half-deserted streets,   10
The muttering retreats
Of restless nights in one-night cheap hotels
And sawdust restaurants with oyster-shells:
Streets that follow like a tedious argument

6 The statement introducing the confession of the poet Guido da Montefeltro in Dante's
Inferno (1321), canto xxcii, 61–66. "If I thought I was speaking to someone who would
go back to, the world, this flame would shake no more. But since nobody has ever gone
back alive from this place, if what I hear is true, I answer you without fear of infamy."

Of insidious intent   15
To lead you to an overwhelming question…
Oh, do not ask, "What is it?"
Let us go and make our visit.

In the room the women come and go
Talking of Michelangelo.°   20

The yellow fog that rubs its back upon the window-panes,
The yellow smoke that rubs its muzzle on the window-panes,
Licked its tongue into the corners of the evening,
Lingered upon the pools that stand in drains,
Let fall upon its back the soot that falls from chimneys,   25
Slipped by the terrace, made a sudden leap,
And seeing that it was a soft October night,
Curled once about the house, and fell asleep.

And indeed there will be time
For the yellow smoke that slides along the street   30
Rubbing its back upon the window-panes;
There will be time, there will be time
To prepare a face to meet the faces that you meet;
There will be time to murder and create,
And time for all the works and days° of hands   35
That lift and drop a question on your plate;
Time for you and time for me,
And time yet for a hundred indecisions,
And for a hundred visions and revisions,
Before the taking of a toast and tea.   40

In the room the women come and go
Talking of Michelangelo.

And indeed there will be time
To wonder, "Do I dare?" and, "Do I dare?"
Time to turn back and descend the stair,   45
With a bald spot in the middle of my hair—
[They will say: "How his hair is growing thin!"]
My morning coat, my collar mounting firmly to the chin,
My necktie rich and modest, but asserted by a simple pin—
[They will say: "But how his arms and legs are thin!"]   50
Do I dare
Disturb the universe?
In a minute there is time
For decisions and revisions which a minute will reverse.

20 Michelangelo (1474–1564) the most famous artist of the Italian Renaissance   **35 works
and days** possibly an allusion to *Works and Days*, a poem giving practical advice on farming
by the Greek poet Hesiod (eighth century BCE)

For I have known them all already, known them all—   55
Have known the evenings, mornings, afternoons,
I have measured out my life with coffee spoons;
I know the voices dying with a dying fall
Beneath the music from a farther room.
    So how should I presume?   60

And I have known the eyes already, known them all—
The eyes that fix you in a formulated phrase,
And when I am formulated, sprawling on a pin,
When I am pinned and wriggling on the wall,
Then how should I begin   65
To spit out all the butt-ends of my days and ways?
    And how should I presume?

And I have known the arms already, known them all—
Arms that are braceleted and white and bare
[But in the lamplight, downed with light brown hair!°]   70
Is it perfume from a dress
That makes me so digress?
Arms that lie along a table, or wrap about a shawl.
    And should I then presume?
    And how should I begin?   75

              .....

Shall I say, I have gone at dusk through narrow streets
And watched the smoke that rises from the pipes
Of lonely men in shirt-sleeves, leaning out of windows?...

I should have been a pair of ragged claws
Scuttling across the floors of silent seas.   80

And the afternoon, the evening, sleeps so peacefully!
Smoothed by long fingers,
Asleep...tired...or it malingers,
Stretched on the floor, here beside you and me.
Should I, after tea and cakes and ices,   85
Have the strength to force the moment to its crisis?
But though I have wept and fasted, wept and prayed,
Though I have seen my head [grown slightly bald] brought in upon a platter,°
I am no prophet—and here's no great matter;
I have seen the moment of my greatness flicker,   90
And I have seen the eternal Footman hold my coat, and snicker,
And in short, I was afraid.

70 see Shakespeare's *Twelfth Night* (1623), Act I, scene I, 1–4   **88** an allusion to John the
Baptist, the New Testament prophet whose head was presented to Queen Herodias on a
charger, Matthew 14:3–11

And would it have been worth it, after all,
After the cups, the marmalade, the tea,
Among the porcelain, among some talk of you and me,   95
Would it have been worth while,
To have bitten off the matter with a smile,
To have squeezed the universe into a ball°
To roll it toward some overwhelming question,
To say: "I am Lazarus,° come from the dead.   100
Come back to tell you all, I shall tell you all"—
If one, settling a pillow by her head,
    Should say: "That is not what I meant at all.
    That is not it, at all."

And would it have been worth it, after all,   105
Would it have been worth while,
After the sunsets and the dooryards and the sprinkled streets,
After the novels, after the teacups, after the skirts that trail along the floor—
And this, and so much more?—
It is impossible to say just what I mean!   110
But as if a magic lantern threw the nerves in patterns on a screen:
Would it have been worth while
If one, settling a pillow or throwing off a shawl,
And turning toward the window, should say:
    "That is not it at all,   115
    That is not what I meant, at all."
          .....

No! I am not Prince Hamlet, nor was meant to be;
Am an attendant lord, one that will do
To swell a progress, start a scene or two,
Advise the prince; no doubt, an easy tool,   120
Deferential, glad to be of use,
Politic, cautious, and meticulous;
Full of high sentence, but a bit obtuse;
At times, indeed, almost ridiculous—
Almost, at times, the Fool.   125

I grow old... I grow old...
I shall wear the bottoms of my trousers rolled.

Shall I part my hair behind? Do I dare to eat a peach?
I shall wear white flannel trousers, and walk upon the beach.
I have heard the mermaids singing, each to each.   130

98 see Andrew Marvell's "To His Coy Mistress," lines 41–42, pages 721–722.   **100 Lazarus**
the man raised by Jesus from the dead, John 11:1–44 (see also Luke 16:19–31)

I do not think that they will sing to me.

I have seen them riding seaward on the waves
Combing the white hair of the waves blown back
When the wind blows the water white and black.

We have lingered in the chambers of the sea   135
By sea-girls wreathed with seaweed red and brown
Till human voices wake us, and we drown.

MAKING CONNECTIONS

1. What is the tone of "The Unknown Citizen"? What lines in the poem indicate this?
2. This poem was written in 1940, so a few of the unknown citizen's possessions are not state-of-the-art and need to be updated to present-day equivalents. What do our possessions say about us and about our culture?
3. Based on what is said about him, who is "the Unknown Citizen"? Was he "free"? Was he "happy"? Are these questions absurd?
4. In "We Wear the Mask," who is the "we" the speaker refers to?
5. What does the "mask" look like? What are the different forms it takes?
6. To what extent does Dunbar's background and the year in which the poem was published amplify its content?
7. What is the tone of "The Love Song of J. Alfred Prufrock"? How does the language in the poem convey that tone? Is this a love song, as the title indicates?
8. Who is J. Alfred Prufrock? What is his world like? He says, "I have measured out my life with coffee spoons." What do you think he means? Find other images in the poem that convey his self-image.
9. What does he mean when he says, "Do I dare / Disturb the universe?" What is he afraid of?
10. Do you ever feel that you have "To prepare a face to meet the faces that you meet"? If so, to what extent does that help you understand J. Alfred Prufrock—and this poem?
11. Compare and contrast the three poems. Compare them to "Zimmer in Grade School" on page 11.

MAKING AN ARGUMENT

1. To what extent do the "masks" we wear result from the cultural imperatives that surround us and form our identities? Write an essay that identifies these cultural pressures and indicates how they "form" the subjects in these three poems—and us. Cite the text of the poems for support.

SHERMAN ALEXIE [B. 1966]

Sherman Alexie achieved the goal of having ten books of poetry and fiction published before he turned thirty. His very first book, The Business of Fancydancing *(1992), was chosen as a* New York Times *Notable Book of the Year and reviewer James R. Kincaid wrote: "Mr. Alexie's is one of the major lyric voices of our time." The film* Smoke Signals, *for which he wrote a script adapted from one of the short stories in his book,* The Lone Ranger and Tonto Fistfight in Heaven *(1993), won rave reviews and large audiences. In 2002, he made his directorial debut with the film of* The Business of Fancydancing. *His most recent book,* War Dances, *which includes poetry and short fiction, was published in 2010.*

Alexie's poems and stories have appeared widely, and he has read from his work in virtually every state as well as in several European countries. Among many awards, he has won a Lila Wallace Reader's Digest *Writer's Award, an American Book Award, and a Creative Writing Fellowship from the National Endowment for the Arts.*

An enrolled Spokane/Coeur d'Alene Indian, Alexie was born on the Spokane reservation in Wellpinit, Washington, in 1966. He is very active in the American Indian community and frequently gives workshops. He lives in Seattle with his wife and son.

EVOLUTION   [1992]

Buffalo Bill opens a pawn shop on the reservation
right across the border from the liquor store
and he stays open 24 hours a day, 7 days a week

and the Indians come running in with jewelry
television sets, a VCR, a full-length beaded buckskin outfit   5

it took Inez Muse 12 years to finish. Buffalo Bill
takes everything the Indians have to offer, keeps it
all catalogued and filed in a storage room. The Indians
pawn their hands, saving the thumbs for last, they pawn

their skeletons, falling endlessly from the skin   10
and when the last Indian has pawned everything
but his heart, Buffalo Bill takes that for twenty bucks

closes up the pawn shop, paints a new sign over the old
calls his venture THE MUSEUM OF NATIVE AMERICAN CULTURES
charges the Indians five bucks a head to enter.   15

MAKING CONNECTIONS

1. Who is Buffalo Bill? How does the speaker feel about Buffalo Bill?
2. What is the significance of the title? How does it relate to the poem?

MAKING AN ARGUMENT

1. "Buffalo" Bill Cody gained notoriety in the late 1800s when he was under contract to kill as many buffalo as possible for the railroad companies that were encountering difficulties laying tracks across the country. Later, Buffalo Bill gained international fame with his Wild West Shows. Do an Internet search to learn more about Buffalo Bill. Write an essay that argues why Alexie chose Buffalo Bill for his poem and how he uses him symbolically. Support your view with citations from the poem and from your research.

GLORIA ANZALDÚA [1942–2004]

Gloria Anzaldúa was born in southern Texas of Mexican, Native American, and Anglo ancestry. Her mixed background served as the major influence on her writing. She taught at the University of Texas at Austin, San Francisco State University, the University of California at Santa Cruz, and Vermont College. Her last book is entitled This Bridge We Call Home: Radical Visions for Transformation *(2002). "To Live in the Borderlands Means You" is taken from her critically acclaimed book* Borderlands / LaFrontera: The New Mestiza *(1987).*

TO LIVE IN THE BORDERLANDS MEANS YOU

[1987]

[To live in the Borderlands means you]
are neither *hispana india negra española*
ni gabacha,° eres mestiza, mulata, half-breed
caught in the crossfire between camps
while carrying all five races on your back   5
not knowing which side to turn to, run from;

To live in the Borderlands means knowing
    that the *india* in you,
    betrayed for 500 years,
    is no longer speaking to you,   10
    that *mexicanas* call you *rajetas,°*
    that denying the Anglo inside you
    is as bad as having denied
    the Indian or Black;

Cuando vives en la frontera
    people walk through you, the wind steals your voice,   15
    you're a *burra, buey,* scapegoat,
    forerunner of a new race,
    half and half—both woman and man, neither—
    a new gender;

                                                                        20

3 gabacha a white woman   **11 rajetas** "split"

To live in the Borderlands means to
    put *chile* in the borscht,
    eat whole wheat *tortillas,*
    speak Tex-Mex with a Brooklyn accent;
    be stopped by *la migra* at the border checkpoints;   25

Living in the Borderlands means you fight hard to
    resist the gold elixir beckoning from the bottle,
    the pull of the gun barrel,
    the rope crushing the hollow of your throat;

In the Borderlands   30
    you are the battleground
    where enemies are kin to each other;
    you are at home, a stranger,
    the border disputes have been settled
    the volley of shots have shattered the truce   35
    you are wounded, lost in action
    dead, fighting back;

To live in the Borderlands means
    the mill with the razor white teeth wants to shred off
    your olive-red skin, crush out the kernel, your heart   40
    pound you pinch you roll you out
    smelling like white bread but dead;

To survive the Borderlands
    you must live *sin fronteras*
    be a crossroads.   45

MAKING CONNECTIONS

1. What are the "Borderlands"? Is this solely a geographical location? To what extent do you, your family, or your friends live in the Borderlands?
2. How are you affected by the mixture of English and Spanish words in the text of the poem? To what extent is this mixture especially appropriate in this poem?
3. In the last stanza, what does the speaker mean by "To survive the Borderlands / you must.../ be a crossroads"?

MAKING AN ARGUMENT

1. Both the speaker in this poem and the narrator of the short story "Borders" on page 915 see themselves culturally "on the border"—in a location and a dominant culture physically, but not ethnically or emotionally. Write a comparison of the two pieces and address the issue of cultural identification. Cite the text of both pieces for support.

ELIZABETH BISHOP [1911–1979]

Elizabeth Bishop was born in Worcester, Massachusetts. Her father died when she was still an infant, and her mother suffered a serious mental breakdown and was institutionalized. Bishop was raised first by her mother's family in Nova Scotia, and then, when she was six, by her father's parents, who lived in Worcester. Sickly and shy, she spent most of her childhood immersed in books before attending boarding school during her teens. While at Vassar College, her poetry attracted the attention of a librarian, who introduced Bishop to the poet Marianne Moore. Moore became Bishop's mentor, and her influence can be seen in Bishop's early work. Following graduation, Bishop lived in Key West for nine years, and then moved to Brazil, where she lived for almost twenty years. Returning to the United States in 1966, she held positions at the University of Washington and the Massachusetts Institute of Technology before settling at Harvard University, where she was teaching when she died. Her collections of poetry include North and South *(1946),* A Cold Spring *(winner of the Pulitzer Prize in 1956),* Complete Poems *(winner of the National Book Award in 1970), and* Geography III *(1977). She was also a respected travel writer, publishing numerous volumes, including* Questions of Travel *(1965) and* Brazil *(1967). Considered a "poet's poet," Bishop's poems are characterized by a spare style and a distinctive, ironic voice.*

IN THE WAITING ROOM   [1976]

In Worcester, Massachusetts,
I went with Aunt Consuelo
to keep her dentist's appointment
and sat and waited for her
in the dentist's waiting room.   5
It was winter. It got dark
early. The waiting room
was full of grown-up people,
arctics and overcoats,
lamps and magazines.   10
My aunt was inside
what seemed like a long time
and while I waited I read
the *National Geographic*
(I could read) and carefully   15
studied the photographs:
the inside of a volcano,
black, and full of ashes;
then it was spilling over
in rivulets of fire.   20
Osa and Martin Johnson

dressed in riding breeches,
laced boots, and pith helmets.
A dead man slung on a pole
—"Long Pig," the caption said.   25
Babies with pointed heads
wound round and round with string;
black, naked women with necks
wound round and round with wire
like the necks of light bulbs.   30
Their breasts were horrifying.
I read it right straight through.
I was too shy to stop.
And then I looked at the cover
the yellow margins, the date.   35
Suddenly, from inside,
came an *oh!* of pain
—Aunt Consuelo's voice—
not very loud or long.

I wasn't at all surprised;   40
even then I knew she was
a foolish, timid woman.
I might have been embarrassed,
but wasn't. What took me
completely by surprise   45
was that it was *me:*
my voice, in my mouth.
Without thinking at all
I was my foolish aunt,
I—we—were falling, falling,   50
our eyes glued to the cover
of the *National Geographic,*
February, 1918.

I said to myself: three days
and you'll be seven years old   55
I was saying it to stop
the sensation of falling off
the round, turning world
into cold, blue-black space.
But I felt: you are an *I,*   60
you are an *Elizabeth,*
you are one of *them.*
Why should you be one, too?
I scarcely dared to look
to see what it was I was.   65
I gave a sidelong glance

—I couldn't look any higher—
at shadowy gray knees,
trousers and skirts and boots
and different pairs of hands   70
lying under the lamps.
I knew that nothing stranger
had ever happened, that nothing
stranger could ever happen.

Why should I be my aunt,   75
or me, or anyone?
What similarities—
boots, hands, the family voice
I felt in my throat, or even
the *National Geographic*   80
and those awful hanging breasts—
held us all together
or made us all just one?
How—I didn't know any
word for it—how "unlikely" ...   85
How had I come to be here,
like them, and overhear
a cry of pain that could have
got loud and worse but hadn't?
The waiting room was bright   90
and too hot. It was sliding
beneath a big black wave,
another, and another.

Then I was back in it.
The War was on. Outside,   95
in Worcester, Massachusetts,
were night and slush and cold,
and it was still the fifth
of February, 1918.

MAKING CONNECTIONS

1. Who is the speaker? How old is she? Does it matter? Explain.
2. What does the sound of Aunt Consuelo's voice reveal to her?
3. What do you think the speaker means by "But I felt: you are an *I*, / you are
   an *Elizabeth*, / you are one of *them*"? Have you ever had a similar experience? Explain.
4. In the last stanza, she says, "Then I was back in it." Where has she been?
   What is she "back in"?

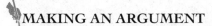

MAKING AN ARGUMENT

1. Write about the way the narrator is experiencing a revelation about her identity that can't be explained in rational terms but is compelling and quite real in her mind and emotions. Cite the text for items that seem to prompt the narrator's reactions.

GWENDOLYN BROOKS [1917–2000]

Born in Topeka, Kansas, Gwendolyn Brooks was raised on the South Side of Chicago. She graduated from Wilson Junior College in 1936, and married in 1939. Though Brooks began writing poetry as a child, she did not find her vocation until she entered a poetry workshop at a local community arts center in the early 1940s. Influenced by Langston Hughes and other poets of the Harlem Renaissance, Brooks attempted to wed the familiar idiom and rhythms of the colloquial speech of Chicago's South Side to the traditional poetic forms she encountered in the workshop. Her first collection of poetry, A Street in Bronzeville, *appeared in 1945. In 1949, with the publication of* Annie Allen, *she became the first African American woman awarded the Pulitzer Prize. After attending a conference of African American writers at Fisk University in 1967, Brooks became convinced that "black poets should write as blacks, about blacks, and address themselves to blacks." As a result, she became a devoted teacher of writing, particularly in the African American community, and abandoned her New York publisher in favor of small African American presses. In addition to numerous volumes of poetry, she published children's books; a novel,* Maud Martha *(1953); and an autobiography,* Report from Part I *(1972). She received over fifty honorary degrees.*

WE REAL COOL

[1960]

The Pool Players.
Seven at the Golden Shovel.

We real cool. We
Left school. We

Lurk late. We   5
Strike straight. We

Sing sin. We
Thin gin. We

Jazz June. We
Die soon.   10

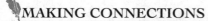

MAKING CONNECTIONS

1. Who is the speaker in this poem?
2. No sentence in the poem is more than three words long, and almost every line ends with the same word. What does that diction say about the speaker in the poem?
3. Were you surprised by the last line? Explain.

MAKING AN ARGUMENT

1. This is a very brief poem that makes a strong statement about culture, society, and individual responsibility. What is its point? Write about the effectiveness of the "we" speaker and the relationship between rhyme and rhythm in conveying the poem's theme. Cite the text of the poem for support.

E. E. CUMMINGS [1894–1962]

E[dwin] E[stlin] Cummings was born in Cambridge, Massachusetts. He began writing poetry as a child, and claimed that he wrote at least one poem a day between the ages of eight and twenty-two. He attended Harvard University, earning a B.A. in 1915 and an M.A. in 1916. During World War I, he served as an ambulance driver and was confined for a time in a French internment camp for what proved to be a mistaken suspicion of treason. In 1922, he wrote of these experiences in his novel The Enormous Room, *which proved to be a great critical success. In the 1920s, he published the collections of poetry—including* & *(1925),* XLI Poems *(1925), and* is 5 *(1926)—that would establish him as America's foremost avant-garde poet. His* Complete Poems: 1910 to 1962 *was published in 1980. Though his poems employ slang, dialect, and all kinds of typographical games, they are often much more accessible than they immediately appear.*

ANYONE LIVED IN A PRETTY HOW TOWN   [1940]

anyone lived in a pretty how town
(with up so floating many bells down)
spring summer autumn winter
he sang his didn't he danced his did.

Women and men (both little and small)   5
cared for anyone not at all
they sowed their isn't they reaped their same
sun moon stars rain

children guessed (but only a few
and down they forgot as up they grew   10
autumn winter spring summer)
that noone loved him more by more

when by now and tree by leaf
she laughed his joy she cried his grief,
bird by snow and stir by still   15
anyone's any was all to her

someones married their everyones
laughed their cryings and did their dance
(sleep wake hope and then) they
said their nevers they slept their dream   20

stars rain sun moon
(and only the snow can begin to explain
how children are apt to forget to remember
with up so floating many bells down)

one day anyone died i guess   25
(and noone stooped to kiss his face)
busy folk buried them side by side
little by little and was by was

all by all and deep by deep
and more by more they dream their sleep   30
noone and anyone earth by april
wish by spirit and if by yes.

Women and men (both dong and ding)
summer autumn winter spring
reaped their sowing and went their came   35
sun moon stars rain

 ## MAKING CONNECTIONS

1. Who is "anyone"?
2. How was your reading affected by the unusual style of the writing? Pick out some lines and describe what you think they mean.

MAKING AN ARGUMENT

1. What do you think the poem means? Why do you think Cummings wrote the poem in this unusual style? Does it help to convey its meaning? Do you think he should have written it in a more conventional form? Write an analysis of this poem, and take a position in favor of or against the author's writing style. Cite the text of the poem for support.

MARTIN ESPADA [B. 1957]

Martin Espada was born in Brooklyn, New York, of Puerto Rican ancestry. He has received many awards, including two National Endowment for the Arts fellowships, a PEN/Revson fellowship, and the Paterson Poetry Prize for Rebellion in the Circle of a Lover's Hands *(1990). His latest book of poems,* The Trouble Ball, *was published in 2011. He worked as a tenant lawyer for six years, often defending the civil rights of immigrants. He is currently a Professor of English at the University of Massachusetts at Amherst.*

COCA-COLA AND COCO FRÍO   [1993]

On his first visit to Puerto Rico,
island of family folklore,
the fat boy wandered
from table to table
with his mouth open.   5
At every table, some great-aunt
would steer him with cool spotted hands
to a glass of Coca-Cola.
One even sang to him, in all the English
she could remember, a Coca-Cola jingle   10
from the forties. He drank obediently, though
he was bored with this potion, familiar
from soda fountains in Brooklyn.
Then, at a roadside stand off the beach, the fat boy
opened his mouth to coco frío, a coconut   15
chilled, then scalped by a machete
so that a straw could inhale the clear milk.
The boy tilted the green shell overhead
and drooled coconut milk down his chin;
suddenly, Puerto Rico was not Coca-Cola   20
or Brooklyn, and neither was he.

For years afterward, the boy marveled at an island
where the people drank Coca-Cola
and sang jingles from World War II
in a language they did not speak,   25
while so many coconuts in the trees
sagged heavy with milk, swollen
and unsuckled.

MAKING CONNECTIONS

1. In Espada's poem, why do the boy's relatives keep pushing him toward Coca-Cola? What does Coca-Cola symbolize for them? What does it symbolize for the boy?

2. How does the taste of coco frío change the boy's perception of Puerto Rico? Does the experience change the boy?
3. Think about your own experiences that have brought you in contact with new cultures, whether it be traveling across the globe or just going to dinner at a friend's house. Do you like to experience new cultures? Why or why not?

MAKING AN ARGUMENT

1. Many are concerned that in our increasingly global world, local cultures will be stamped out as mass-produced products and outside media come in. How is this issue reflected in "Coca-Cola and Coco Frío"? Can you think of any examples of your local culture disappearing? Is this new global, uniform culture a positive or negative change? Write an essay that takes a positive or negative position on globalization, using citations from the poem and your personal experiences as support.

CONNECTING THROUGH COMPARISON: IMMIGRATION

The three poems that follow address a subtheme of this section: immigration. Most Americans are immigrants or descendants of immigrants. The following poems explore the immigrant experience from different cultural backgrounds, different times, different levels of acceptance—allowing each its own perspective. Read and discussed together, they invite comparisons and connections—not only with each other, but with your own experience.

EMMA LAZARUS [1849–1887]

Emma Lazarus is best known for the following sonnet, "The New Colossus," which was written in 1883 as a donation to an auction that raised money to build the pedestal on which the Statue of Liberty stands. In 1903, the poem was engraved onto a bronze plaque and placed inside the base of the statue.

THE NEW COLOSSUS   [1888]

Not like the brazen giant of Greek fame,
With conquering limbs astride from land to land;
Here at our sea-washed, sunset gates shall stand
A mighty woman with a torch, whose flame
Is the imprisoned lightning, and her name   5
Mother of Exiles. From her beacon-hand
Glows world-wide welcome; her mild eyes command
The air-bridged harbor that twin cities frame.
"Keep, ancient lands, your storied pomp!" cries she

With silent lips. "Give me your tired, your poor,   10
Your huddled masses yearning to breathe free,
The wretched refuse of your teeming shore.
Send these, the homeless, tempest-tost to me,
I lift my lamp beside the golden door!"

SHIRLEY GEOK-LIN LIM [B. 1944]

*Born and raised in Malaysia, Shirley Geok-lin Lim was
attracted to writing at an early age, publishing her first
poem at the age of ten. She received a scholarship that
allowed her to attend the University of Malaya, and later
a Fulbright scholarship for graduate study at Brandeis
University. A diverse writer, Lim publishes across many
genres, including poetry, fiction, memoir, and criticism.
Currently, Lim is a Professor in the English Department at
the University of California, Santa Barbara.*

LEARNING TO LOVE AMERICA   [1998]

because it has no pure products

because the Pacific Ocean sweeps along the coastline
because the water of the ocean is cold
and because land is better than ocean

because I say we rather than they   5

because I live in California
I have eaten fresh artichokes
and jacarandas bloom in April and May

because my senses have caught up with my body
my breath with the air it swallows   10
my hunger with my mouth

because I walk barefoot in my house

because I have nursed my son at my breast
because he is a strong American boy
because I have seen his eyes redden when he is asked who he is   15
because he answers I don't know

because to have a son is to have a country

because my son will bury me here
because countries are in our blood and we bleed them

because it is late and too late to change my mind   20
because it is time.

PAT MORA [B. 1942]

Pat Mora was born in El Paso, Texas. Her father was an ophthalmologist and her mother a homemaker. Mora earned her B.A. from Texas Western College in 1963 and an M.A. in 1967 from the University of Texas at El Paso. She taught for many years at both the high school and university levels, but now she devotes herself completely to her poetry. Chants, *her first volume of verse, was published in 1984, and she has since published three additional collec-*
tions: Borders *(1986),* Communion *(1991), and* Holy Water *(1995). Her latest publication is a collection of poems about love,* Dizzy in Your Eyes *(2010). "For a variety of complex reasons," she told* Contemporary Authors, *"anthologized American literature does not reflect the ethnic diversity of the United States. I write, in part, because Hispanic perspectives need to be part of our literary heritage; I want to be part of that validation process. I also write because I am fascinated by the pleasure and power of words."*

IMMIGRANTS [1986]

wrap their babies in the American flag,
feed them mashed hot dogs and apple pie,
name them Bill and Daisy,
buy them blonde dolls that blink blue
eyes or a football and tiny cleats   5
before the baby can even walk,
speak to them in thick English,
    hallo, babee, hallo,
whisper in Spanish or Polish
when the babies sleep, whisper   10
in a dark parent bed, that dark
parent fear, "Will they like
our boy, our girl, our fine american
boy, our fine american girl?"

MAKING CONNECTIONS

1. What is "The New Colossus" describing?
2. What is the poet's opinion of America in "The New Colossus"?
3. Can we infer anything about how the poet feels about immigrants in "The New Colossus"? What?
4. What does the title "Learning to love America" suggest about the speaker's attitude toward living in America?
5. What is the tone of "Learning to love America"? How does the speaker convey this tone?

6. Does the speaker in "Learning to love America" learn to love America? Why or why not?
7. Discuss the different voices represented in "Immigrants." How many are there? What do they represent?
8. To whom is the speaker saying, "wrap their babies in the American flag"?
9. What does she mean by "that dark / parent fear"?
10. Examine the picture of the Statue of Liberty that accompanies these poems. What feelings does it stir in you? What feelings do you think it would stir for the three poets?

MAKING AN ARGUMENT

1. "The New Colossus" was written in 1888. Does its view of America and its attitudes toward immigration still resonate? Immigration is a hot-button issue in today's America. How has the issue evolved since the publication of "The New Colossus"? Write an essay where you explore this issue, using citations from "The New Colossus" for support.
2. In both "Immigrants" and "Learning to love America," the speakers mention the issue of the cultural identity of the first generation born in America. Compare these attitudes with the reality of Richard Rodriguez's experience in "Workers" (p. 1041). Write an essay that compares these attitudes, citing examples from the texts for support.
3. Do you think America is a "melting pot"? Do you think it should be? Compare this poem to the short stories "Two Kinds" on page 264 and "Brave We Are" on page 928, and write about the different issues that are raised in each selection. Cite the texts of all three for support.

JOHN UPDIKE [B. 1932]

(See biography on pp. 455–456.)

EX-BASKETBALL PLAYER   [1958]

Pearl Avenue runs past the high-school lot,
Bends with the trolley tracks, and stops, cut off
Before it has a chance to go two blocks,
At Colonel McComsky Plaza. Berth's Garage
Is on the corner facing west, and there,   5
Most days, you'll find Flick Webb, who helps Berth out.

Flick stands tall among the idiot pumps—
Five on a side, the old bubble-head° style,
Their rubber elbows hanging loose and low.
One's nostrils are two S's, and his eyes   10
An E and O.° And one is squat, without
A head at all—more of a football type.

Once Flick played for the high-school team, the Wizards.
He was good: in fact, the best. In '46
He bucketed three hundred ninety points,   15
A county record still. The ball loved Flick.
I saw him rack up thirty-eight or forty
In one home game. His hands were like wild birds.

He never learned a trade, he just sells gas,
Checks oil, and changes flats. Once in a while,   20
As a gag, he dribbles an inner tube,
But most of us remember anyway.
His hands are fine and nervous on the lug wrench.
It makes no difference to the lug wrench, though.

Off work, he hangs around Mae's luncheonette.   25
Grease-gray and kind of coiled, he plays pinball,
Smokes those thin cigars, nurses lemon phosphates.
Flick seldom says a word to Mae, just nods
Beyond her face toward bright applauding tiers
Of Necco Wafers, Nibs, and Juju Beads.   30

MAKING CONNECTIONS

1. Describe Flick Webb. To what extent do the images in the poem bring him to life? Give some examples.
2. Who is the speaker in the poem? What point of view does he represent? If Flick were the speaker in the poem, how do you think it would change?
3. Discuss the structure of the poem. To what extent do each of the five stanzas represent a different aspect of Flick's life?

8 bubble head Gasoline pumps from this era had rounded tops.   **11 ESSO** brand of gasoline (now called Exxon)

MAKING AN ARGUMENT

1. Write a comparison of this poem with A. E. Housman's "To an Athlete Dying Young" on page 1180. Cite the text of both poems for support.

WILLIAM CARLOS WILLIAMS [1883–1961]

William Carlos Williams was born in Rutherford, New Jersey. While attending high school in New York City, where he focused most of his energies on math and science, he first discovered his love for writing poetry. He skipped a traditional college education at his parents' insistence and went directly to medical school at the University of Pennsylvania. While completing his studies, he came into contact with Ezra Pound, then a graduate student, who would become his lifelong friend and critic, and Hilda Doolitle (the poet H.D.). Pound and H.D. introduced Williams to the imagist movement, which rejected rigid and ordered poetry in favor of simple phrases and an embrace of the ordinary. Over the next forty years, though he practiced medicine full time, Williams wrote volumes of poetry, often finding inspiration in the stories of his patients, jotting poems on prescription pads or between appointments turning to a typewriter he kept in his office. His publications include Collected Poems *(1934);* Later Collected Poems *(1950); a five-volume poem about a nearby city in New Jersey,* Paterson *(1946–1958); a collection of experimental plays,* Many Loves and Other Plays *(1961); a series of novels; and numerous short stories and essays. His final book of poems,* Pictures from Brueghel and Other Poems, *was awarded the Pulitzer Prize in 1963. With his innovative use of free verse, his embrace of American speech, and his insistence on the importance of the commonplace, Williams profoundly influenced the course of American poetry.*

AT THE BALL GAME   [1923]

The crowd at the ball game
is moved uniformly

by a spirit of uselessness
which delights them—

all the exciting detail   5
of the chase

and the escape, the error
the flash of genius—

all to no end save beauty
the eternal—   10

So in detail they, the crowd,
are beautiful

for this
to be warned against

saluted and defied—   15
It is alive, venomous

it smiles grimly
its words cut—

The flashy female with her
mother, gets it—   20

The Jew gets it straight—it
is deadly, terrifying—

It is the Inquisition, the
Revolution

It is the beauty itself   25
that lives

day by day in them
idly—

This is
the power of their faces   30

It is summer, it is the solstice
the crowd is

cheering, the crowd is laughing
in detail

permanently, seriously   35
without thought

MAKING CONNECTIONS

1. The setting of this poem is a baseball game. Is this a poem about baseball?
   Explain.
2. What do you think the references to "the flashy female," "the Jew," "the
   Inquisition," and "the Revolution" mean?
3. What does the speaker mean by "the crowd is laughing / in detail / permanently, seriously / without thought"? Who is the crowd?

MAKING AN ARGUMENT

1. What is the place of crowds in our contemporary culture? Do you think
   they are as dangerous as Williams's poem implies? Identify the points that
   Williams makes in his poem, and write about the impact that crowds and
   "crowd mentalities" have on cultural and political aspects of our society.
   Cite the text of the poem for support.

WILLIAM BUTLER YEATS   [1865–1939]

Considered one of the greatest poets of the twentieth century, William Butler Yeats was born in Dublin, Ireland. Follow- ing in the footsteps of his father, a well-known painter, Yeats studied art for a time in Dublin and London, but gradually turned his focus to writing. While still a young man, Yeats became politically active in the movement for an indepen- dent Ireland. In 1899, he was an instrumental figure in the formation of the Irish National Theatre (now the Abbey Theatre), writing a number of verse plays for the theater and encouraging other important playwrights, including John Millington Synge, to do likewise. He served as a senator in the newly established Irish Free State from 1922 to 1928. In 1923, he became the first Irishman awarded the Nobel Prize. Though he wrote poetry filled with the sights, sounds, and folklore of his native land throughout his life, much of his greatest work dates to his final years, when he combined his Irish perspective with a deeply felt spiritual sense and symbolic system. "The Lake Isle of Innisfree" was writ- ten in 1893 and, like much of Yeats's early poetry, is deeply Romantic in its outlook.

THE LAKE ISLE OF INNISFREE   [1893]

I will arise and go now, and go to Innisfree,
And a small cabin build there, of clay and wattles° made:
Nine bean-rows will I have there, a hive for the honey-bee,
And live alone in the bee-loud glade.

And I shall have some peace there, for peace comes dropping slow,   5
Dropping from the veils of the morning to where the cricket sings;
There midnight's all a glimmer, and noon a purple glow,
And evening full of the linnet's wings.

I will arise and go now, for always night and day
I hear lake water lapping with low sounds by the shore;   10
While I stand on the roadway, or on the pavements gray,
I hear it in the deep heart's core.

WHEN YOU ARE OLD   [1893]

When you are old and grey and full of sleep,
And nodding by the fire, take down this book,
And slowly read, and dream of the soft look
Your eyes had once, and of their shadows deep;

How many loved your moments of glad grace,   5
And loved your beauty with love false or true,
But one man loved the pilgrim soul in you,
And loved the sorrows of your changing face;

2 wattles twigs woven together

And bending down beside the glowing bars,
Murmur, a little sadly, how Love fled   10
And paced upon the mountains overhead
And hid his face amid a crowd of stars.

MAKING CONNECTIONS

1. List the parts of Yeats's refuge at Innisfree. Identify the qualities that make each of them a contributing factor to the whole of his ideal escape there.
2. In what way does the (ABAB) rhyme scheme of "The Lake Isle of Innisfree" and the (ABBA) rhyme scheme of "When You Are Old" affect your response to the content of each poem?
3. What does the speaker in "The Lake Isle of Innisfree" mean by "I hear it in the deep heart's core"? Does the speaker in "When You Are Old" hear it in the deep heart's core as well? Explain.
4. Both "The Lake Isle of Innisfree" and "When You Are Old" were written early in Yeats's career and are considered works of Romanticism, a perspective that emphasizes emotion, imagination, and subjectivity over logic and objectivity. Identify and compare the elements of Romanticism in each poem.

MAKING AN ARGUMENT

1. Yeats was a student living in the city of London when he wrote "The Lake Isle of Innisfree." To what extent do you think that might have influenced the ideal nature of his images? Write a comparison of this poem with "A Man Said to the Universe" (p. 1172). Which view of nature do you prefer? Cite the text of both poems for support.

◆ D R A M A ◆

CONNECTING THROUGH COMPARISON: MODERN REALISM AND PARODY

The two plays that follow, Tennessee Williams' *The Glass Menagerie* and Christopher Durang's *For Whom the Southern Belle Tolls*, describe a dysfunctional family with a controlling mother who seems stuck in time, but in fact, the Durang play is a parody of the Williams play. Read and discussed together, they invite comparisons and connections.

TENNESSEE WILLIAMS [1911–1983]

Tennessee Williams was born in Columbus, Mississippi, and moved with his family to St. Louis, Missouri, when he was twelve. The troubled family of The Glass Menagerie *resembles Williams's own—his mother was a faded south-ern beauty, his sister suffered from intense shyness, and Williams himself, a frustrated writer, worked at a series of low-paying, unsatisfying jobs. After years of struggling, The*

Glass Menagerie *opened on Broadway to tremendous acclaim in 1945, and Williams was instantly established as an important new voice in the theater. Lonely women inhabiting a world of dreams, much like Amanda in* The Glass Menagerie, *are central figures in many of his greatest plays, including* A Streetcar Named Desire, *which won the Pulitzer Prize in 1947, and* Summer and Smoke *(1948). His other major works include the Pulitzer Prize–winning* Cat on a Hot Tin Roof *(1955),* The Rose Tattoo *(1951),* Orpheus Descending *(1957),* Sweet Bird of Youth *(1959), and* The Night of the Iguana *(1961). Though he continued to write until his death, his later plays were less successful. Nevertheless, Williams remains one of the giants of twentieth-century drama.*

THE GLASS MENAGERIE [1945]

CHARACTERS

AMANDA WINGFIELD, *the mother. A little woman of great but confused vitality clinging frantically to another time and place. Her characterization must be carefully created, not copied from type. She is not paranoiac, but her life is paranoia. There is much to admire in* AMANDA, *and as much to love and pity as there is to laugh at. Certainly she has endurance and a kind of heroism, and though her foolishness makes her unwittingly cruel at times, there is tenderness in her slight person.*

LAURA WINGFIELD, *her daughter.* AMANDA, *having failed to establish contact with reality, continues to live vitally in her illusions, but Laura's situation is even graver. A childhood illness has left her crippled, one leg slightly shorter than the other, and held in a brace. This defect need not be more than suggested on the stage. Stemming from this,* LAURA'S *separation increases till she is like a piece of her own glass collection, too exquisitely fragile to move from the shelf.*

TOM WINGFIELD, *her son. And the narrator of the play. A poet with a job in a warehouse. His nature is not remorseless, but to escape from a trap he has to act without pity.*

JIM O'CONNOR, *the gentleman caller. A nice, ordinary, young man.*

SCENE: *An alley in St. Louis.*
PART I: *Preparation for a Gentleman Caller.*
PART II: *The Gentleman Calls.*
TIME: *Now and the Past.*

SCENE 1

The Wingfield apartment is in the rear of the building, one of those vast hive-like conglomerations of cellular living-units that flower as warty growths in over-crowded urban centers of lower middle-class population and are symptomatic of the impulse of this largest and fundamentally enslaved section of American society to avoid fluidity and differentiation and to exist and function as one interfused mass of automatism.

The apartment faces an alley and is entered by a fire escape, a structure whose name is a touch of accidental poetic truth, for all of these huge buildings are always burning with the slow and implacable fires of human desperation. The fire escape is included in the set—that is, the landing of it and steps descending from it.

The scene is memory and is therefore nonrealistic. Memory takes a lot of poetic license. It omits some details; others are exaggerated, according to the emotional value of the articles it touches, for memory is seated predominantly in the heart. The interior is therefore rather dim and poetic.

At the rise of the curtain, the audience is faced with the dark, grim rear wall of the Wingfield tenement. This building, which runs parallel to the footlights, is flanked on both sides by dark, narrow alleys which run into murky canyons of tangled clotheslines, garbage cans and the sinister latticework of neighboring fire escapes. It is up and down these side alleys that exterior entrances and exits are made, during the play. At the end of TOM'S *opening commentary, the dark tenement wall slowly reveals (by means of a transparency) the interior of the ground floor Wingfield apartment.*

Downstage is the living room, which also serves as a sleeping room for LAURA, *the sofa unfolding to make her bed. Upstage, center, and divided by a wide arch or second proscenium with transparent faded portieres (or second curtain), is the dining room. In an old-fashioned what-not in the living room are seen scores of transparent glass animals. A blown-up photograph of the father hangs on the wall of the living room, facing the audience, to the left of the archway. It is the face of a very handsome young man in a doughboy's First World War cap. He is gallantly smiling, ineluctably smiling, as if to say, "I will be smiling forever."*

The audience hears and sees the opening scene in the dining room through both the transparent fourth wall of the building and the transparent gauze portieres of the dining room arch. It is during this revealing scene that the fourth wall slowly ascends, out of sight. This transparent exterior wall is not brought down again until the very end of the play, during TOM'S *final speech.*

The narrator is an undisguised convention of the play. He takes whatever license with dramatic convention as is convenient to his purposes.

TOM *enters dressed as a merchant sailor from alley, stage left, and strolls across the front of the stage to the fire escape. There he stops and lights a cigarette. He addresses the audience.*

TOM: Yes, I have tricks in my pocket, I have things up my sleeve. But I am the opposite of a stage magician. He gives you illusion that has the appearance of truth. I give you truth in the pleasant disguise of illusion. To begin with, I turn back time. I reverse it to that quaint period, the thirties, when the huge middle class of America was matriculating in a school for the blind. Their eyes had failed them, or they had failed their eyes, and so they were having their fingers pressed forcibly down on the fiery Braille alphabet of a dissolving economy. In Spain there was revolution. Here there was only shouting and confusion. In Spain there was Guernica. Here there were disturbances of labor, sometimes pretty violent, in otherwise peaceful cities such as Chicago, Cleveland, Saint Louis.... This is the social background of the play.

[*Music.*]

The play is memory.

Being a memory play, it is dimly lighted, it is sentimental, it is not realistic. In memory everything seems to happen to music. That explains the fiddle in the wings. I am the narrator of the play, and also a character in it. The other characters are my mother, Amanda, my sister, Laura, and a gentleman caller who appears in the final scenes. He is the most realistic character in the play, being an emissary from a world of reality that we were somehow set apart from. But since I have a poet's weakness for symbols, I am using this character also as a symbol; he is the long delayed but always expected something that we live for. There is a fifth character in the play who doesn't appear except in this larger-than-life photograph over the mantel. This is our father who left us a long time ago. He was a telephone man who fell in love with long distances; he gave up his job with the telephone company and skipped the light fantastic out of town.... The last we heard of him was a picture postcard from Mazatlan, on the Pacific coast of Mexico, containing a message of two words—"Hello—Goodbye!" and no address. I think the rest of the play will explain itself....

AMANDA'S *voice becomes audible through the portieres.*

[*Legend on screen: "Où Sont les Neiges."*[1]]

He divides the portieres and enters the upstage area.

AMANDA *and* LAURA *are seated at a drop-leaf table. Eating is indicated by gestures without food or utensils.* AMANDA *faces the audience.* TOM *and* LAURA *are seated in profile.*

The interior has lit up softly and through the scrim we see AMANDA *and* LAURA *seated at the table in the upstage area.*

AMANDA [*calling*]:   Tom?
TOM: Yes, Mother.
AMANDA: We can't say grace until you come to the table!
TOM: Coming, Mother. [*He bows slightly and withdraws, reappearing a few moments later in his place at the table.*]
AMANDA [*to her son*]:   Honey, don't *push* with your *fingers*. If you have to push with something, the thing to push with is a crust of bread. And chew—chew! Animals have sections in their stomachs which enable them to digest food without mastication, but human beings are supposed to chew their food before they swallow it down. Eat food leisurely, son, and really enjoy it. A well-cooked meal has lots of delicate flavors that have to be held in the mouth for appreciation. So chew your food and give your salivary glands a chance to function!

TOM *deliberately lays his imaginary fork down and pushes his chair back from the table.*

TOM: I haven't enjoyed one bite of this dinner because of your constant directions on how to eat it. It's you that makes me rush through meals with your hawk-like attention to every bite I take. Sickening—spoils my appetite—all this discussion of animals' secretion—salivary glands—mastication!

[1]**Où Sont les Neiges [d'antan]** "Where are the snows of yesteryear?" A quotation from the French poet Francois Villon to be projected on a screen at the back of the stage.

AMANDA [*lightly*]:   Temperament like a Metropolitan star! [*He rises and crosses downstage.*] You're not excused from the table.

TOM: I am getting a cigarette.

AMANDA: You smoke too much.

LAURA *rises.*

LAURA: I'll bring in the blanc mange.

He remains standing with his cigarette by the portieres during the following.

AMANDA [*rising*]:   No, sister, no, sister—you be the lady this time and I'll be the darky.

LAURA: I'm already up.

AMANDA: Resume your seat, little sister—I want you to stay fresh and pretty—for gentlemen callers!

LAURA: I'm not expecting any gentlemen callers.

AMANDA [*crossing out to kitchenette. Airily*]:   Sometimes they come when they are least expected! Why, I remember one Sunday afternoon in Blue Mountain— [*enters kitchenette.*]

TOM: I know what's coming!

LAURA: Yes. But let her tell it.

TOM: Again?

LAURA: She loves to tell it.

AMANDA *returns with bowl of dessert.*

AMANDA: One Sunday afternoon in Blue Mountain—your mother received—*seventeen*—gentlemen callers! Why, sometimes there weren't chairs enough to accommodate them all. We had to send the nigger over to bring in folding chairs from the parish house.

TOM [*remaining at portieres*]:   How did you entertain those gentlemen callers?

AMANDA: I understood the art of conversation!

TOM: I bet you could talk.

AMANDA: Girls in those days *knew* how to talk, I can tell you.

TOM: Yes?

[*Image:* AMANDA *as a girl on a porch greeting callers.*]

AMANDA: They knew how to entertain their gentlemen callers. It wasn't enough for a girl to be possessed of a pretty face and a graceful figure—although I wasn't slighted in either respect. She also needed to have a nimble wit and a tongue to meet all occasions.

TOM: What did you talk about?

AMANDA: Things of importance going on in the world! Never anything coarse or common or vulgar. [*She addresses* TOM *as though he were seated in the vacant chair at the table though he remains by portieres. He plays this scene as though he held the book.*] My callers were gentlemen—all! Among my callers were some of the most prominent young planters of the Mississippi Delta—planters and sons of planters!

TOM *motions for music and a spot of light on* AMANDA. *Her eyes lift, her face glows, her voice becomes rich and elegiac.*

[*Screen legend: "Où Sont les Neiges."*]

>   There was young Champ Laughlin who later became vice president of the Delta Planters Bank. Hadley Stevenson who was drowned in Moon Lake and left his widow one hundred and fifty thousand in Government bonds. There were the Cutrere brothers, Wesley and Bates. Bates was one of my bright particular beaux! He got in a quarrel with that wild Wainright boy. They shot it out on the floor of Moon Lake Casino. Bates was shot through the stomach. Died in the ambulance on his way to Memphis. His widow was also well-provided for, came into eight or ten thousand acres, that's all. She married him on the rebound—never loved her—carried my picture on him the night he died! And there was that boy that every girl in Delta had set her cap for! That beautiful, brilliant young Fitzhugh boy from Green County!

TOM: What did he leave his widow?

AMANDA: He never married! Gracious, you talk as though all of my old admirers had turned up their toes to the daisies!

TOM: Isn't this the first you mentioned that still survives?

AMANDA: That Fitzhugh boy went North and made a fortune—came to be known as the Wolf of Wall Street! He had the Midas touch, whatever he touched turned to gold! And I could have been Mrs. Duncan J. Fitzhugh, mind you! But—I picked your *father!*

LAURA [*rising*]:   Mother, let me clear the table.

AMANDA: No dear, you go in front and study your typewriter chart. Or practice your shorthand a little. Stay fresh and pretty—It's almost time for our gentlemen callers to start arriving. [*She flounces girlishly toward the kitchenette.*] How many do you suppose we're going to entertain this afternoon?

TOM *throws down the paper and jumps up with a groan.*

LAURA [*alone in the dining room*]:   I don't believe we're going to receive any, Mother.

AMANDA [*reappearing, airily*]:   What? No one—not one? You must be joking! [LAURA *nervously echoes her laugh. She slips in a fugitive manner through the half-open portieres and draws them gently behind her. A shaft of very clear light is thrown on her face against the faded tapestry of the curtains.*] [*Music: "The Glass Menagerie" under faintly.*] [*lightly.*] Not one gentleman caller? It can't be true! There must be a flood, there must have been a tornado!

LAURA: It isn't a flood, it's not a tornado, Mother. I'm just not popular like you were in Blue Mountain.... [TOM *utters another groan.* LAURA *glances at him with a faint, apologetic smile. Her voice catching a little.*] Mother's afraid I'm going to be an old maid.

[*The scene dims out with "The Glass Menagerie" music.*]

SCENE 2

"LAURA, *Haven't You Ever Liked Some Boy?"*

On the dark stage the screen is lighted with the image of blue roses. Gradually LAURA's *figure becomes apparent and the screen goes out. The music subsides.*

LAURA *is seated in the delicate ivory chair at the small clawfoot table.*

She wears a dress of soft violet material for a kimono—her hair tied back from her forehead with a ribbon.

She is washing and polishing her collection of glass.

AMANDA *appears on the fire-escape steps. At the sound of her ascent, Laura catches her breath, thrusts the bowl of ornaments away and seats herself stiffly before the diagram of the typewriter keyboard as though it held her spellbound. Something has happened to* AMANDA. *It is written in her face as she climbs to the landing: a look that is grim and hopeless and a little absurd.*

She has on one of those cheap or imitation velvety-looking cloth coats with imitation fur collar. Her hat is five or six years old, one of those dreadful cloche hats that were worn in the late twenties, and she is clasping an enormous black patent-leather pocketbook with nickel clasp and initials. This is her full-dress outfit, the one she usually wears to the D.A.R.

Before entering she looks through the door.

She purses her lips, opens her eyes wide, rolls them upward and shakes her head.

Then she slowly lets herself in the door. Seeing her mother's expression LAURA *touches her lips with a nervous gesture.*

LAURA: Hello, Mother, I was—[*She makes a nervous gesture toward the chart on the wall.* AMANDA *leans against the shut door and stares at* LAURA *with a martyred look.*]

AMANDA: Deception? Deception? [*She slowly removes her hat and gloves, continuing the swift suffering stare. She lets the hat and gloves fall on the floor—a bit of acting.*]

LAURA [*shakily*]:   How was the D.A.R. meeting? [AMANDA *slowly opens her purse and removes a dainty white handkerchief which she shakes out delicately and delicately touches to her lips and nostrils.*] Didn't you go to the D.A.R. meeting, Mother?

AMANDA [*faintly, almost inaudibly*]:   —No.—No. [*then more forcibly.*] I did not have the strength—to go to the D.A.R. In fact, I did not have the courage! I wanted to find a hole in the ground and hide myself in it forever! [*She crosses slowly to the wall and removes the diagram of the typewriter keyboard. She holds it in front of her for a second, staring at it sweetly and sorrowfully—then bites her lips and tears it in two pieces.*]

LAURA [*faintly*]:   Why did you do that, Mother? [AMANDA *repeats the same procedure with the chart of the Gregg alphabet.*] Why are you—

AMANDA: Why? Why? How old are you, Laura?

LAURA: Mother, you know my age.

AMANDA: I thought that you were an adult; it seems that I was mistaken. [*She crosses slowly to the sofa and sinks down and stares at* LAURA.]

LAURA: Please don't stare at me, Mother.

AMANDA *closes her eyes and lowers her head. Count ten.*

AMANDA: What are we going to do, what is going to become of us, what is the future?

Count ten.

LAURA: Has something happened, Mother? [AMANDA *draws a long breath and takes out the handkerchief again. Dabbing process.*] Mother, has—something happened?

AMANDA: I'll be all right in a minute. I'm just bewildered—[*count five*]—by life....

LAURA: Mother, I wish that you would tell me what's happened.

AMANDA: As you know, I was supposed to be inducted into my office at the D.A.R. this afternoon. [*Image: A swarm of typewriters.*] But I stopped off at Rubicam's Business College to speak to your teachers about your having a cold and ask them what progress they thought you were making down there.

LAURA: Oh....

AMANDA: I went to the typing instructor and introduced myself as your mother. She didn't know who you were. Wingfield, she said. We don't have any such student enrolled at the school! I assured her she did, that you had been going to classes since early in January. "I wonder," she said, "if you could be talking about that terribly shy little girl who dropped out of school after only a few days' atten- dance?" "No," I said, "Laura, my daughter, has been going to school every day for the past six weeks!" "Excuse me," she said. She took the attendance book out and there was your name, unmistakably printed, and all the dates you were absent until they decided that you had dropped out of school. I still said, "No, there must have been some mistake! There must have been some mix-up in the records!" And she said, "No—I remember her perfectly now. Her hand shook so that she couldn't hit the right keys! The first time we gave a speed-test, she broke down completely—was sick at the stomach and almost had to be carried into the wash-room! After that morning she never showed up any more. We phoned the house but never got any answer"—while I was working at Famous and Barr, I suppose, demonstrating those—Oh! I felt so weak I could barely keep on my feet. I had to sit down while they got me a glass of water! Fifty dollars tuition, all of our plans—my hopes and ambitions for you—just gone up the spout, just gone up the spout like that. [LAURA *draws a long breath and gets awkwardly to her feet. She crosses to the victrola and winds it up.*] What are you doing?

LAURA: Oh! [*She releases the handle and returns to her seat.*]

AMANDA: Laura, where have you been going when you've gone out pretending that you were going to business college?

LAURA: I've just been going out walking.

AMANDA: That's not true.

LAURA: It is. I just went walking.

AMANDA: Walking? Walking? In winter? Deliberately courting pneumonia in that light coat? Where did you walk to, Laura?

LAURA: It was the lesser of two evils, Mother. [*Image: Winter scene in park.*] I couldn't go back up. I—threw up—on the floor!

AMANDA: From half past seven till after five every day you mean to tell me you walked around in the park, because you wanted to make me think that you were still going to Rubicam's Business College?

LAURA: It wasn't as bad as it sounds. I went inside places to get warmed up.

AMANDA: Inside where?

LAURA: I went in the art museum and the bird-houses at the zoo. I visited the penguins every day! Sometimes I did without lunch and went to the movies. Lately I've been spending most of my afternoons in the Jewel box, that big glass house where they raise the tropical flowers.

AMANDA: You did all this to deceive me, just for the deception? [LAURA *looks down*.] Why?

LAURA: Mother, when you're disappointed, you get that awful suffering look on your face, like the picture of Jesus' mother in the museum!

AMANDA: Hush!

LAURA: I couldn't face it.

Pause. A whisper of strings.

[*Legend: "The Crust of Humility."*]

AMANDA: [*hopelessly fingering the huge pocketbook*] So what are we going to do the rest of our lives? Stay home and watch the parades go by? Amuse ourselves with the glass menagerie, darling? Eternally play those worn-out phonograph records your father left as a painful reminder of him? We won't have a business career—we've given that up because it gave us nervous indigestion! [*laughs wearily*.] What is there left but dependency all our lives? I know so well what becomes of unmarried women who aren't prepared to occupy a position. I've seen such pitiful cases in the South—barely tolerated spinsters living upon the grudging patronage of sister's husband or brother's wife!—stuck away in some little mousetrap of a room—encouraged by one in-law to visit another—little birdlike women without any nest—eating the crust of humility all their life! Is that the future that we've mapped out for ourselves? I swear it's the only alternative I can think of! It isn't a very pleasant alternative, is it? Of course—some girls *do marry*. [LAURA *twists her hands nervously*.] Haven't you ever liked some boy?

LAURA: Yes. I liked one once. [*rises*.] I came across his picture a while ago.

AMANDA: [*with some interest*] He gave you his picture?

LAURA: No, it's in the year-book.

AMANDA [*disappointed*]:   Oh—a high-school boy.

[*Screen Image: JIM as a high-school hero bearing a silver cup.*]

LAURA: Yes. His name was Jim. [LAURA *lifts the heavy annual from the clawfoot table*.] Here he is in *The Pirates of Penzance*.

AMANDA [*absently*]:   The what?

LAURA: The operetta the senior class put on. He had a wonderful voice and we sat across the aisle from each other Mondays, Wednesdays and Fridays in the Aud. Here he is with the silver cup for debating! See his grin?

AMANDA [*absently*]:   He must have had a jolly disposition.

LAURA: He used to call me—Blue Roses.

[*Image: Blue roses.*]

AMANDA: Why did he call you such a name as that?

LAURA: When I had that attack of pleurosis—he asked me what was the matter when I came back. I said pleurosis—he thought that I said Blue Roses! So that's what he always called me after that. Whenever he saw me, he'd holler, "Hello, Blue Roses!" I didn't care for the girl that he went out with. Emily Meisenbach. Emily was the best-dressed girl at Soldan. She never struck me, though, as being sincere.... It says in the Personal Section—they're engaged. That's—six years ago! They must be married by now.

AMANDA: Girls that aren't cut out for business careers usually wind up married to some nice man. [*gets up with a spark of revival.*] Sister, that's what you'll do!

LAURA *utters a startled, doubtful laugh. She reaches quickly for a piece of glass.*

LAURA: But, Mother—

AMANDA: Yes? [*crossing to photograph.*]

LAURA [*in a tone of frightened apology*]: I'm—crippled!

[*Image: Screen.*]

AMANDA: Nonsense! Laura, I've told you never, never to use that word. Why, you're not crippled, you just have a little defect—hardly noticeable, even! When people have some slight disadvantage like that, they cultivate other things to make up for it—develop charm—and vivacity—and—*charm!* That's all you have to do! [*She turns again to the photograph.*] One thing your father had plenty of—was charm!

TOM *motions to the fiddle in the wings.*

[*The scene fades out with music.*]

SCENE 3

[*Legend on screen: "After the Fiasco—"*]

TOM *speaks from the fire escape landing.*

TOM: After the fiasco at Rubicam's Business College, the idea of getting a gentleman caller for Laura began to play a more important part in Mother's calculations. It became an obsession. Like some archetype of the universal unconscious, the image of the gentleman caller haunted our small apartment.... [*Image: Young man at door with flowers.*] An evening at home rarely passed without some allusion to this image, this specter, this hope.... Even when he wasn't mentioned, his presence hung in Mother's preoccupied look and in my sister's frightened, apologetic manner—hung like a sentence passed upon the Wingfields! Mother was a woman of action as well as words. She began to take logical steps in the planned direction. Late that winter and in the early spring—realizing that extra money would be needed to properly feather the nest and plume the bird—she conducted a vigorous campaign on the telephone, roping in subscribers to one of those magazines for matrons called *The Homemaker's Companion,* the type of journal that features the serialized sublimations of ladies of letters who think in terms of delicate cuplike breasts, slim, tapering waists, rich, creamy thighs, eyes like wood smoke in autumn, fingers that soothe and caress like strains of music, bodies as powerful as Etruscan sculpture.

[*Screen image: Glamour magazine cover.*]

AMANDA *enters with phone on long extension cord. She is spotted in the dim stage.*

AMANDA: Ida Scott? This is Amanda Wingfield! We *missed* you at the D.A.R. last Monday! I said to myself: She's probably suffering with that sinus condition! How is that sinus condition? Horrors! Heaven have mercy!—You're a Christian martyr, yes, that's what you are, a Christian martyr! Well, I just now happened to notice that your subscription to the *Companion*'s about to expire! Yes, it expires with the next issue, honey!—just when that wonderful new serial by Bessie Mae Hopper is getting off to such an exciting start. Oh, honey, it's something that you can't miss! You remember how *Gone with the Wind* took everybody by storm? You simply couldn't go out if you hadn't read it. All everybody *talked* was Scarlett O'Hara. Well, this is a book that critics already compare to *Gone with the Wind.* It's the *Gone with the Wind* of the post–World War generation!—What?—Burning?—Oh, honey, don't let them burn, go take a look in the oven and I'll hold the wire! Heavens—I think she's hung up!

[*Dim out.*]

[*Legend on screen: "You Think I'm in Love with Continental Shoemakers?"*]

Before the stage is lighted, the violent voices of TOM *and* AMANDA *are heard. They are quarreling behind the portieres. In front of them stands* LAURA *with clenched hands and panicky expression.*

A clear pool of light on her figure throughout this scene.

TOM: What in Christ's name am I—
AMANDA [*shrilly*]:   Don't you use that—
TOM: Supposed to do!
AMANDA: Expression! Not in my—
TOM: Ohhh!
AMANDA: Presence! Have you gone out of your senses?
TOM: I have, that's true, *driven* out!
AMANDA: What is the matter with you, you—big—big—IDIOT!
TOM: Look—I've got *no thing,* no single thing—
AMANDA: Lower your voice!
TOM: In my life here that I can call my OWN! Everything is—
AMANDA: Stop that shouting!
TOM: Yesterday you confiscated my books! You had the nerve to—
AMANDA: I took that horrible novel back to the library—yes! That hideous book by that insane Mr. Lawrence. [TOM *laughs wildly.*] I cannot control the output of diseased minds or people who cater to them—[Tom laughs still more wildly.] BUT I WON'T ALLOW SUCH FILTH BROUGHT INTO MY HOUSE! No, no, no, no, no!
TOM: House, house! Who pays rent on it, who makes a slave of himself to—
AMANDA [*fairly screeching*]:   Don't you DARE to—

TOM: No, no, *I* mustn't say things! *I've* got to just—

AMANDA: Let me tell you—

TOM: I don't want to hear any more! [*He tears the portieres open. The upstage area is lit with a turgid smoky red glow.*]

AMANDA'S *hair is in metal curlers and she wears a very old bathrobe, much too large for her slight figure, a relic of the faithless Mr. Wingfield.*

An upright typewriter and a wild disarray of manuscripts are on the dropleaf table. The quarrel was probably precipitated by AMANDA'S *interruption of his creative labor. A chair lying overthrown on the floor.*

Their gesticulating shadows are cast on the ceiling by the fiery glow.

AMANDA: You *will* hear more, you—

TOM: No, I won't hear more, I'm going out!

AMANDA: You come right back in—

TOM: Out, out, out! Because I'm—

AMANDA: Come back here, Tom Wingfield! I'm not through talking to you!

TOM: Oh, go—

LAURA [*desperately*]:   Tom!

AMANDA: You're going to listen, and no more insolence from you! I'm at the end of my patience! [*He comes back toward her.*]

TOM: What do you think I'm at? Aren't I supposed to have any patience to reach the end of, Mother? I know, I know. It seems unimportant to you, what I'm *doing*—what I *want* to do—having a little *difference* between them! You don't think that—

AMANDA: I think you've been doing things that you're ashamed of. That's why you act like this. I don't believe that you go every night to the movies. Nobody goes to the movies night after night. Nobody in their right minds goes to the movies as often as you pretend to. People don't go to the movies at nearly midnight, and movies don't let out at two A.M. Come in stumbling. Muttering to yourself like a maniac! You get three hours' sleep and then go to work. Oh, I can picture the way you're doing down there. Moping, doping, because you're in no condition.

TOM [*wildly*]:   No, I'm in no condition!

AMANDA: What right have you got to jeopardize your job? Jeopardize the security of us all? How do you think we'd manage if you were—

TOM: Listen! You think I'm crazy *about* the *warehouse*? [*He bends fiercely toward her slight figure.*] You think I'm in love with the Continental Shoemakers? You think I want to spend fifty-five *years* down there in that—*celotex interior!* with—*fluorescent—tubes!* Look! I'd rather somebody picked up a crowbar and battered out my brains—than go back mornings! I *go!* Every time you come in yelling that God damn "*Rise and Shine!*" "*Rise and Shine!*" I say to myself "How *lucky dead* people are!" But I get up. I *go!* For sixty-five dollars a month I give up all that I dream of doing and being *ever!* And you say self—*self's* all I ever think of. Why, listen, if self is what I thought of, Mother, I'd be where he is—GONE! [*pointing to father's picture.*] As far as the system of transportation reaches! [*He starts past her. She grabs his arm.*] Don't grab at me, Mother!

AMANDA: Where are you going?

TOM: I'm going to the *movies!*

AMANDA: I don't believe that lie!

TOM [*Crouching toward her, overtowering her tiny figure. She backs away, gasping*]:   I'm going to opium dens! Yes, opium dens, dens of vice and criminals' hangouts, Mother. I've joined the Hogan gang, I'm a hired assassin, I carry a tommy-gun in a violin case! I run a string of cathouses in the valley! They call me Killer, Killer Wingfield, I'm leading a double-life, a simple, honest warehouse worker by day, by night a dynamic *czar* of the *underworld, Mother.* I go to gambling casinos, I spin away fortunes on the roulette table! I wear a patch over one eye and a false mustache, sometimes I put on green whiskers. On those occasions they call me—*El Diablo!* Oh, I could tell you things to make you sleepless! My enemies plan to dynamite this place. They're going to blow us all sky high some night! I'll be glad, very happy, and so will you! You'll go up, up on a broomstick, over Blue Mountain with seventeen gentlemen callers! You ugly—babbling old—*witch*....

[*He goes through a series of violent, clumsy movements, seizing his overcoat, lunging to the door, pulling it fiercely open. The women watch him, aghast. His arm catches in the sleeve of the coat as he struggles to pull it on. For a moment he is pinioned by the bulky garment. With an outraged groan he tears the coat off again, splitting the shoulders of it and hurls it across the room. It strikes against the shelf of* LAURA's *glass collection, there is a tinkle of shattering glass.* LAURA *cries out as if wounded.*]

[*Music legend: "The Glass Menagerie."*]

LAURA [*shrilly*]:   My glass!—menagerie.... [*She covers her face and turns away.*]

But AMANDA *is still stunned and stupefied by the "ugly witch" so that she barely notices this occurrence. Now she recovers her speech.*

AMANDA [*in an awful voice*]:   I won't speak to you—until you apologize!

[*She crosses through portieres and draws them together behind her.* TOM *is left with* LAURA. LAURA *clings weakly to the mantel with her face averted.* TOM *stares at her stupidly for a moment. Then he crosses to shelf. Drops, awkwardly to his knees to collect the fallen glass, glancing at* LAURA *as if he would speak but couldn't.*]

"The Glass Menagerie" steals in as

[*The scene dims out.*]

SCENE 4

The interior is dark. Faint light in the alley.

A deep-voiced bell in a church is tolling the hour of five as the scene commences.

TOM *appears at the top of the alley. After each solemn boom of the bell in the tower, he shakes a little noise-maker or rattle as if to express the tiny spasm of man in contrast to the sustained power and dignity of the Almighty. This and the unsteadiness of his advance make it evident that he has been drinking.*

As he climbs the few steps to the fire-escape landing light steals up inside. LAURA *appears in nightdress, observing* TOM's *empty bed in the front room.*

TOM *fishes in his pockets for the door key, removing a motley assortment of articles in the search, including a perfect shower of movie ticket stubs and an empty bottle. At last he finds the key, but just as he is about to insert it, it slips from his fingers. He strikes a match and crouches below the door.*

TOM [*bitterly*]:   One crack—and it falls through!

LAURA *opens the door.*

LAURA: Tom! Tom, what are you doing?

TOM: Looking for a door key.

LAURA: Where have you been all this time?

TOM: I have been to the movies.

LAURA: All this time at the movies?

TOM: There was a very long program. There was a Garbo picture and a Mickey Mouse and a travelogue and a newsreel and a preview of coming attractions. And there was an organ solo and a collection for the milk fund—simultaneously—which ended up in a terrible fight between a fat lady and an usher!

LAURA [*innocently*]:   Did you have to stay through everything?

TOM: Of course! And, oh, I forgot! There was a big stage show! The headliner on this stage show was Malvolio the Magician. He performed wonderful tricks, many of them, such as pouring water back and forth between pitchers. First it turned to wine and then it turned to beer and then it turned to whiskey. I know it was whiskey it finally turned into because he needed somebody to come up out of the audience to help him, and I came up—both shows! It was Kentucky Straight Bourbon. A very generous fellow, he gave souvenirs. [*He pulls from his back pocket a shimmering rainbow-colored scarf.*] He gave me this. This is his magic scarf. You can have it, Laura. You wave it over a canary cage and you get a bowl of goldfish. You wave it over the goldfish bowl and they fly away canaries.... But the wonderfullest trick of all was the coffin trick. We nailed him into a coffin and he got out of the coffin without removing one nail. [*He has come inside.*] There is a trick that would come in handy for me—get me out of this two-by-four situation! [*flops onto bed and starts removing shoes.*]

LAURA: Tom—Shhh!

TOM: What you shushing me for?

LAURA: You'll wake up Mother.

TOM: Goody, goody! Pay 'er back for all those "Rise an' shines." [*lies down, groaning.*] You know it don't take much intelligence to get yourself into a nailed-up coffin, Laura. But who in hell ever got himself out of one without removing one nail?

As if in answer, the father's grinning photograph lights up.

[*Scene dims out.*]

Immediately following: The church bell is heard striking six. At the sixth stroke the alarm clock goes off in AMANDA's *room, and after a few moments we hear her calling: "Rise and shine! Rise and shine! Laura, go tell your brother to rise and shine!"*

TOM [*sitting up slowly*]:   I'll rise—but I won't shine. *The light increases.*

AMANDA: Laura, tell your brother his coffee is ready.

LAURA *slips into front room.*

LAURA: Tom! it's nearly seven. Don't make Mother nervous. [*He stares at her stupidly. Beseechingly.*] Tom, speak to Mother this morning. Make up with her,
apologize, speak to her!

TOM: She won't to me. It's her that started not speaking.

LAURA: If you just say you're sorry she'll start speaking.

TOM: Her not speaking—is that such a tragedy?

LAURA: Please—please!

AMANDA [*calling from kitchenette*]:   Laura, are you going to do what I asked you to
do, or do I have to get dressed and go out myself?

LAURA: Going, going—soon as I get on my coat! [*She pulls on a shapeless felt hat
with nervous, jerky movement, pleadingly glancing at* TOM. *Rushes awkwardly for coat. The coat is one of* AMANDA'S, *inaccurately made-over, the sleeves too
short for* LAURA.] Butter and what else?

AMANDA [*entering upstage*]:   Just butter. Tell them to charge it.

LAURA: Mother, they make such faces when I do that.

AMANDA: Sticks and stones may break my bones, but the expression on Mr. Garfinkel's face won't harm us! Tell your brother his coffee is getting cold.

LAURA [*at door*]:   Do what I asked you, will you, will you, Tom?

He looks sullenly away.

AMANDA: Laura, go now or just don't go at all!

LAURA [*rushing out*]:   Going—going! [*A second later she cries out.* TOM *springs
up and crosses to the door.* AMANDA *rushes anxiously in.* TOM *opens the
door.*]

TOM: Laura?

LAURA: I'm all right. I slipped, but I'm all right.

AMANDA [*peering anxiously after her*]:   If anyone breaks a leg on those fire escape
steps, the landlord ought to be sued for every cent he possesses!

[*She shuts door. Remembers she isn't speaking and returns to other room.*]

As TOM *enters listlessly for his coffee, she turns her back to him and stands rigidly
facing the window on the gloomy gray vault of the areaway. Its light on her face with
its aged but childish features is cruelly sharp, satirical as a Daumier[2] print.*

[*Music Under: "Ave Maria."*]

TOM *glances sheepishly but sullenly at her averted figure and slumps at the table.
The coffee is scalding hot; he sips it and gasps and spits it back in the cup. At his
gasp,* AMANDA *catches her breath and half turns. Then catches herself and turns
back to window.*

---

[2]**Honoré Daumier** (1808–1879) French caricaturist, painter, and sculptor who was
known for the lithographs he created to mock middle-class society.

TOM *blows on his coffee, glancing sidewise at his mother. She clears her throat.* TOM *clears his. He starts to rise. Sinks back down again, scratches his head, clears his throat again.* AMANDA *coughs.* TOM *raises his cup in both hands to blow on it, his eyes staring over the rim of it at his mother for several moments. Then he slowly sets the cup down and awkwardly and hesitantly rises from the chair.*

TOM [*hoarsely*]:   Mother. I—I apologize. Mother. [AMANDA *draws a quick, shuddering breath. Her face works grotesquely. She breaks into childlike tears.*] I'm sorry for what I said, for everything that I said, I didn't mean it.

AMANDA [*sobbingly*]:   My devotion has made me a witch and so I make myself hateful to my children!

TOM: No you *don't.*

AMANDA: I worry so much, don't sleep, it makes me nervous!

TOM [*gently*]:   I understand that.

AMANDA: I've had to put up a solitary battle all these years. But you're my right-hand bower! Don't fall down, don't fail!

TOM [*gently*]:   I try, Mother.

AMANDA [*with great enthusiasm*]:   Try and you will SUCCEED! [*The notion makes her breathless.*] Why, you—you're just *full* of natural endowments! Both of my children—they're *unusual* children! Don't you think I know it? I'm so—proud! Happy and—feel I've—so much to be thankful for but—promise me one thing, son!

TOM: What, Mother?

AMANDA: Promise, son, you'll—never be a drunkard!

TOM [*turns to her grinning*]:   I will never be a drunkard, Mother.

AMANDA: That's what frightened me so, that you'd be drinking! Eat a bowl of Purina!

TOM: Just coffee, Mother.

AMANDA: Shredded wheat biscuit?

TOM: No. No, Mother, just coffee.

AMANDA: You can't put in a day's work on an empty stomach. You've got ten minutes—don't gulp! Drinking too-hot liquids makes cancer of the stomach.... Put cream in.

TOM: No, thank you.

AMANDA: To cool it.

TOM: No! No, thank you, I want it black.

AMANDA: I know, but it's not good for you. We have to do all that we can to build ourselves up. In these trying times we live in, all that we have to cling to is—each other.... That's why it's so important to—Tom, I—I sent out your sister so I could discuss something with you. If you hadn't spoken I would have spoken to you. [*sits down.*]

TOM [*gently*]:   What is it, Mother, that you want to discuss?

AMANDA: Laura!

TOM *puts his cup down slowly.*

[*Legend on screen: "Laura."*]

[*Music: "The Glass Menagerie."*]

TOM: —Oh.—Laura...

AMANDA [*touching his sleeve*]:   You know how Laura is. So quiet but—still water runs deep! She notices things and I think she—broods about them. [TOM *looks up*.] A few days ago I came in and she was crying.

TOM: What about?

AMANDA: You.

TOM: Me?

AMANDA: She has an idea that you're not happy here.

TOM: What gave her that idea?

AMANDA: What gives her any idea? However, you do act strangely. I—I'm not criticizing, understand *that!* I know your ambitions do not lie in the warehouse, that like everybody in the whole wide world—you've had to—make sacrifices, but—Tom—Tom—life's not easy, it calls for—Spartan endurance! There's so many things in my heart that I cannot describe to you! I've never told you but I—*loved* your father....

TOM [*gently*]:   I know that, Mother.

AMANDA: And you—when I see you taking after his ways! Staying out late—and—well, you *had* been drinking the night you were in that—terrifying condition! Laura says that you hate the apartment and that you go out nights to get away from it! Is that true, Tom?

TOM: No. You say there's so much in your heart that you can't describe to me. That's true of me, too. There's so much in my heart that I can't describe to *you!* So let's respect each other's—

AMANDA: But, why—*why,* Tom—are you always so *restless?* Where do you go to, nights?

TOM: I—go to the movies.

AMANDA: Why do you go to the movies so much, Tom?

TOM: I go to the movies because—I like adventure. Adventure is something I don't have much of at work, so I go to the movies.

AMANDA: But, Tom, you go to the movies *entirely* too *much!*

TOM: I like a lot of adventure.

AMANDA *looks baffled, then hurt. As the familiar inquisition resumes he becomes hard and impatient again.* AMANDA *slips back into her querulous attitude toward him.*

[*Image on screen: Sailing vessel with Jolly Roger.*]

AMANDA: Most young men find adventure in their careers.

TOM: Then most young men are not employed in a warehouse.

AMANDA: The world is full of young men employed in warehouses and offices and factories.

TOM: Do all of them find adventure in their careers?

AMANDA: They do or they do without it! Not everybody has a craze for adventure.

TOM: Man is by instinct a lover, a hunter, a fighter, and none of those instincts are given much play at the warehouse!

AMANDA: Man is by instinct! Don't quote instinct to me! Instinct is something that people have got away from! It belongs to animals! Christian adults don't want it!

TOM: What do Christian adults want, then, Mother?

AMANDA: Superior things! Things of the mind and the spirit! Only animals have to satisfy instincts! Surely your aims are somewhat higher than theirs! Than monkeys—pigs—

TOM: I reckon they're not.

AMANDA: You're joking. However, that isn't what I wanted to discuss.

TOM [*rising*]:   I haven't much time.

AMANDA [*pushing his shoulders*]:   Sit down.

TOM: You want me to punch in red at the warehouse, Mother?

AMANDA: You have five minutes. I want to talk about Laura.

[*Legend: "Plans and Provisions."*]

TOM: All right! What about Laura?

AMANDA: We have to be making plans and provisions for her. She's older than you, two years, and nothing has happened. She just drifts along doing nothing. It frightens me terribly how she just drifts along.

TOM: I guess she's the type that people call home girls.

AMANDA: There's no such type, and if there is, it's a pity! That is unless the home is hers, with a husband!

TOM: What?

AMANDA: Oh, I can see the handwriting on the wall as plain as I see the nose in the front of my face! It's terrifying! More and more you remind me of your father! He was out all hours without explanation—Then *left! Goodbye!* And me with the bag to hold. I saw that letter you got from the merchant marine. I know what you're dreaming of. I'm not standing here blindfolded. Very well, then. Then *do* it! But not till there's somebody to take your place.

TOM: What do you mean?

AMANDA: I mean that as soon as Laura has got somebody to take care of her, married, a home of her own, independent—why, then you'll be free to go wherever you please, on land, on sea, whichever way the wind blows! But until that time you've got to look out for your sister. I don't say me because I'm old and don't matter! I say for your sister because she's young and dependent. I put her in business college—a dismal failure! Frightened her so it made her sick to her stomach. I took her over to the Young People's League at the church. Another fiasco. She spoke to nobody, nobody spoke to her. Now all she does is fool with those pieces of glass and play those worn-out records. What kind of a life is that for a girl to lead!

TOM: What can I do about it?

AMANDA: Overcome selfishness! Self, self, self is all that you ever think of! [TOM *springs up and crosses to get his coat. It is ugly and bulky. He pulls on a cap with earmuffs.*] Where is your muffler? Put your wool muffler on! [*He snatches it angrily from the closet and tosses it around his neck and pulls both ends tight.*] Tom! I haven't said what I had in mind to ask you.

TOM: I'm too late to—

AMANDA [*catching his arms—very importunately. Then shyly*]:   Down at the warehouse, aren't there some—nice young men?

TOM: No!

AMANDA: There must be—*some.*

TOM: Mother—

Gesture.

AMANDA: Find out one that's clean-living—doesn't drink and—ask him out for sister!

TOM: What?

AMANDA: For *sister!* To *meet!* Get *acquainted!*

TOM [*stamping to door*]:   Oh, my *go-osh!*

AMANDA: Will you? [*He opens door. Imploringly.*] Will you? [*He starts down*] Will
  you? Will you, dear?

TOM [*calling back*]:   Yes!

AMANDA *closes the door hesitantly and with a troubled but faintly hopeful expression.*

[*Screen image: Glamour magazine cover.*]

Spot AMANDA *at phone.*

AMANDA: Ella Cartwright? This is Amanda Wingfield! How are you, honey? How
  is that kidney condition? [*count five.*] Horrors! [*count five.*] You're a Christian martyr, yes, honey, that's what you are, a Christian martyr! Well, I just
  happened to notice in my little red book that your subscription to the *Companion* has just run out! I knew that you wouldn't want to miss out on the
  wonderful serial starting in this new issue. It's by Bessie Mae Hopper, the first
  thing she's written since *Honeymoon for Three.* Wasn't that a strange and interesting story? Well, this one is even lovelier, I believe. It has a sophisticated
  society background. It's all about the horsey set on Long Island!

[*Fade out.*]

SCENE 5

[*Legend on screen: "Annunciation."*] *Fade with music.*

*It is early dusk of a spring evening. Supper has just been finished at the Wingfield
apartment.* AMANDA *and* LAURA *in light colored dresses are removing dishes from the
table, in the upstage area, which is shadowy, their movements formalized almost as
a dance or ritual, their moving forms as pale and silent as moths.*

TOM, *in white shirt and trousers, rises from the table and crosses toward the fire
escape.*

AMANDA [*as he passes her*]:   Son, will you do me a favor?

TOM: What?

AMANDA: Comb your hair! You look so pretty when your hair is combed! [TOM
  slouches on sofa with evening paper. Enormous caption: "Franco Triumphs."]
  There is only one respect in which I would like you to emulate your father.

TOM: What respect is that?

AMANDA: The care he always took of his appearance. He never allowed himself to look untidy. [*He throws down the paper and crosses to fire escape.*] Where are you going?

TOM: I'm going out to smoke.

AMANDA: You smoke too much. A pack a day at fifteen cents a pack. How much would that amount to in a month? Thirty times fifteen is how much, Tom? Figure it out and you will be astounded at what you could save. Enough to give you a night-school course in accounting at Washington U! Just think what a wonderful thing that would be for you, son!

TOM *is unmoved by the thought.*

TOM: I'd rather smoke. [*He steps out on landing, letting the screen door slam.*]

AMANDA [*sharply*]:   I know! That's the tragedy of it.... [*Alone, she turns to look at her husband's picture.*]

[*Dance music: "All the World Is Waiting for the Sunrise!"*]

TOM [*to the audience*]:   Across the alley from us was the Paradise Dance Hall. On evenings in spring the windows and doors were open and the music came outdoors. Sometimes the lights were turned out except for a large glass sphere that hung from the ceiling. It would turn slowly about and filter the dusk with delicate rainbow colors. Then the orchestra played a waltz or a tango, something that had a slow and sensuous rhythm. Couples would come outside, to the relative privacy of the alley. You could see them kissing behind ash pits and telephone poles. This was the compensation for lives that passed like mine, without any change or adventure. Adventure and change were imminent in this year. They were waiting around the corner for all these kids. Suspended in the mist over Berchtesgaden,[3] caught in the folds of Chamberlain's[4] umbrella—In Spain there was Guernica! But here there was only hot swing music and liquor, dance halls, bars, and movies, and sex that hung in the gloom like a chandelier and flooded the world with brief, deceptive rainbows.... All the world was waiting for bombardments!

AMANDA *turns from the picture and comes outside.*

AMANDA [*sighing*]:   A fire escape landing's a poor excuse for a porch. [*She spreads a newspaper on a step and sits down, gracefully and demurely as if she were settling into a swing on a Mississippi veranda.*] What are you looking at?

TOM: The moon.

AMANDA: Is there a moon this evening?

TOM: It's rising over Garfinkel's Delicatessen.

AMANDA: So it is! A little silver slipper of a moon. Have you made a wish on it yet?

TOM: Um-hum.

---

[3]**Berchtesgaden** A resort town in Bavaria, Germany, where Hitler met with the leaders of the Third Reich to plan strategy.   [4]**Neville Chamberlain** (1869–1940) British prime minister who believed that Hitler could be appeased, a policy that many thought led to World War II.

AMANDA: What did you wish for?

TOM: That's a secret.

AMANDA: A secret, huh? Well, I won't tell mine either. I will be just as mysterious as you.

TOM: I bet I can guess what yours is.

AMANDA: Is my head so transparent?

TOM: You're not a sphinx.

AMANDA: No, I don't have secrets. I'll tell you what I wished for on the moon. Success and happiness for my precious children! I wish for that whenever there's a moon, and when there isn't a moon, I wish for it, too.

TOM: I thought perhaps you wished for a gentleman caller.

AMANDA: Why do you say that?

TOM: Don't you remember asking me to fetch one?

AMANDA: I remember suggesting that it would be nice for your sister if you brought some nice young man from the warehouse. I think I've made that suggestion more than once.

TOM: Yes, you have made it repeatedly.

AMANDA: Well?

TOM: We are going to have one.

AMANDA: What?

TOM: A gentleman caller!

[*The Annunciation Is Celebrated with Music.*]

AMANDA *rises.*

[*Image on screen: Caller with bouquet.*]

AMANDA: You mean you have asked some nice young man to come over?

TOM: Yep. I've asked him to dinner.

AMANDA: You really did?

TOM: I did!

AMANDA: You did, and did he—*accept?*

TOM: He did!

AMANDA: Well, well—well, well! That's—lovely!

TOM: I thought that you would be pleased.

AMANDA: It's definite, then?

TOM: Very definite.

AMANDA: Soon?

TOM: Very soon.

AMANDA: For heaven's sake, stop putting on and tell me some things, will you?

TOM: What things do you want me to tell you?

AMANDA: Naturally I would like to know when he's *coming!*

TOM: He's coming tomorrow.

AMANDA: *Tomorrow?*

TOM: Yep. Tomorrow.

AMANDA: But, Tom!

TOM: Yes, Mother?

AMANDA: Tomorrow gives me no time!

TOM: Time for what?

AMANDA: Preparations! Why didn't you phone me at once, as soon as you asked him, the minute that he accepted? Then, don't you see, I could have been getting ready!

TOM: You don't have to make any fuss.

AMANDA: Oh, Tom, Tom, Tom, of course I have to make a fuss! I want things nice, not sloppy! Not thrown together. I'll certainly have to do some fast thinking, won't I?

TOM: I don't see why you have to think at all.

AMANDA: You just don't know. We can't have a gentleman caller in a pigsty! All my wedding silver has to be polished, the monogrammed table linen ought to be laundered! The windows have to be washed and fresh curtains put up. And how about clothes? We have to *wear* something, don't we?

TOM: Mother, this boy is no one to make a fuss over!

AMANDA: Do you realize he's the first young man we've introduced to your sister? It's terrible, dreadful, disgraceful that poor little sister has never received a single gentleman caller! Tom, come inside! [*She opens the screen door.*]

TOM: What for?

AMANDA: I want to ask you some things.

TOM: If you're going to make such a fuss, I'll call it off, I'll tell him not to come.

AMANDA: You certainly won't do anything of the kind. Nothing offends people worse than broken engagements. It simply means I'll have to work like a Turk! We won't be brilliant, but we'll pass inspection. Come on inside. [TOM *follows, groaning.*] Sit down.

TOM: Any particular place you would like me to sit?

AMANDA: Thank heavens I've got that new sofa! I'm also making payments on a floor lamp I'll have sent out! And put the chintz covers on, they'll brighten things up! Of course I'd hoped to have these walls repapered.... What is the young man's name?

TOM: His name is O'Connor.

AMANDA: That, of course, means fish—tomorrow is Friday! I'll have that salmon loaf—with Durkee's dressing! What does he do? He works at the warehouse?

TOM: Of course! How else would I—

AMANDA: Tom, he—doesn't drink?

TOM: Why do you ask me that?

AMANDA: Your father *did*!

TOM: Don't get started on that!

AMANDA: He *does* drink, then?

TOM: Not that I know of!

AMANDA: Make sure, be certain! The last thing I want for my daughter's a boy who drinks!

TOM: Aren't you being a little premature? Mr. O'Connor has not yet appeared on the scene!

AMANDA: But will tomorrow. To meet your sister, and what do I know about his character? Nothing! Old maids are better off than wives of drunkards!

TOM: Oh, my God!

AMANDA: Be still!

TOM [*leaning forward to whisper*]: Lots of fellows meet girls whom they don't marry!

AMANDA: Oh, talk sensibly, Tom—and don't be sarcastic! [*She has gotten a hairbrush.*]

TOM: What are you doing?

AMANDA: I'm brushing that cowlick down! What is this young man's position at the warehouse?

TOM [*submitting grimly to the brush and the interrogation*]: This young man's position is that of a shipping clerk, Mother.

AMANDA: Sounds to me like a fairly responsible job, the sort of a job *you* would be in if you just had more *get-up*. What is his salary? Have you got any idea?

TOM: I would judge it to be approximately eighty-five dollars a month.

AMANDA: Well—not princely, but—

TOM: Twenty more than I make.

AMANDA: Yes, how well I know! But for a family man, eighty-five dollars a month is not much more than you can just get by on....

TOM: Yes, but Mr. O'Connor is not a family man.

AMANDA: He might be, mightn't he? Some time in the future?

TOM: I see. Plans and provisions.

AMANDA: You are the only young man that I know of who ignores the fact that the future becomes the present, the present the past, and the past turns into everlasting regret if you don't plan for it!

TOM: I will think that over and see what I can make of it.

AMANDA: Don't be supercilious with your mother! Tell me some more about this— what do you call him?

TOM: James D. O'Connor. The D. is for Delaney.

AMANDA: Irish on *both* sides! *Gracious!* And doesn't drink?

TOM: Shall I call him up and ask him right this minute?

AMANDA: The only way to find out about those things is to make discreet inquiries at the proper moment. When I was a girl in Blue Mountain and it was suspected that a young man drank, the girl whose attentions he had been receiving, if any girl *was,* would sometimes speak to the minister of his church, or rather her father would if her father was living, and sort of feel him out on the young man's character. That is the way such things are discreetly handled to keep a young woman from making a tragic mistake!

TOM: Then how did you happen to make a tragic mistake?

AMANDA: That innocent look of your father's had everyone fooled! He *smiled*—the world was *enchanted!* No girl can do worse than put herself at the mercy of a handsome appearance! I hope that Mr. O'Connor is not too good-looking.

TOM: No, he's not too good-looking. He's covered with freckles and hasn't too much of a nose.

AMANDA: He's not right-down homely, though?

TOM: Not right-down homely. Just medium homely, I'd say.

AMANDA: Character's what to look for in a man.

TOM: That's what I've always said, Mother.

AMANDA: You've never said anything of the kind and I suspect you would never give it a thought.

TOM: Don't be suspicious of me.

AMANDA: At least I hope he's the type that's up and coming.

TOM: I think he really goes in for self-improvement.

AMANDA: What reason have you to think so?

TOM: He goes to night school.

AMANDA [*beaming*]: Splendid! What does he do, I mean study?

TOM: Radio engineering and public speaking!

AMANDA: Then he has visions of being advanced in the world! Any young man who studies public speaking is aiming to have an executive job some day! And radio engineering? A thing for the future! Both of these facts are very illuminating. Those are the sort of things that a mother should know concerning any young man who comes to call on her daughter. Seriously or—not.

TOM: One little warning. He doesn't know about Laura. I didn't let on that we had dark ulterior motives. I just said, why don't you come have dinner with us? He said okay and that was the whole conversation.

AMANDA: I bet it was! You're eloquent as an oyster. However, he'll know about Laura when he gets here. When he sees how lovely and sweet and pretty she is, he'll thank his lucky stars he was asked to dinner.

TOM: Mother, you mustn't expect too much of Laura.

AMANDA: What do you mean?

TOM: Laura seems all those things to you and me because she's ours and we love her. We don't even notice she's crippled any more.

AMANDA: Don't say crippled! You know that I never allow that word to be used!

TOM: But face facts, Mother. She is and—that's not all—

AMANDA: What do you mean "not all"?

TOM: Laura is very different from other girls.

AMANDA: I think the difference is all to her advantage.

TOM: Not quite all—in the eyes of others—strangers—she's terribly shy and lives in a world of her own and those things make her seem a little peculiar to people outside the house.

AMANDA: Don't say peculiar.

TOM: Face the facts. She is.

[*The dance-hall music changes to a tango that has a minor and somewhat ominous tone.*]

AMANDA: In what way is she peculiar—may I ask?

TOM [*gently*]: She lives in a world of her own—a world of—little glass ornaments, Mother.... [*Gets up.* AMANDA *remains holding brush, looking at him, troubled.*] She plays old phonograph records and—that's about all—[*He glances at himself in the mirror and crosses to door.*]

AMANDA [*sharply*]: Where are you going?

TOM: I'm going to the movies. [*out screen door.*]

AMANDA: Not to the movies, every night to the movies! [*follows quickly to screen door.*] I don't believe you always go to the movies! [*He is gone.* AMANDA *looks worriedly after him for a moment. Then vitality and optimism return and she turns from the door. Crossing to portieres.*] Laura! Laura! [LAURA *answers from kitchenette.*]

LAURA: Yes, Mother.

AMANDA: Let those dishes go and come in front! [LAURA *appears with dish towel. Gaily.*] Laura, come here and make a wish on the moon!

LAURA [*entering*]:   Moon—moon?

AMANDA: A little silver slipper of a moon. Look over your left shoulder, Laura, and make a wish! [LAURA *looks faintly puzzled as if called out of sleep.* AMANDA *seizes her shoulders and turns her at an angle by the door.*] Now! Now, darling, *wish!*

LAURA: What shall I wish for, Mother?

AMANDA [*her voice trembling and her eyes suddenly filling with tears*]:   Happiness! Good fortune!

The violin rises and the stage dims out.

SCENE 6

[*Image: High school hero.*]

TOM: And so the following evening I brought Jim home to dinner. I had known Jim slightly in high school. In high school Jim was a hero. He had tremendous Irish good nature and vitality with the scrubbed and polished look of white chinaware. He seemed to move in a continual spotlight. He was a star in basketball, captain of the debating club, president of the senior class and the glee club and he sang the male lead in the annual light operas. He was always running or bounding, never just walking. He seemed always at the point of defeating the law of gravity. He was shooting with such velocity through his adolescence that you would logically expect him to arrive at nothing short of the White House by the time he was thirty. But Jim apparently ran into more interference after his graduation from Soldan. His speed had definitely slowed. Six years after he left high school he was holding a job that wasn't much better than mine.

[*Image: Clerk.*]

He was the only one at the warehouse with whom I was on friendly terms. I was valuable to him as someone who could remember his former glory, who had seen him win basketball games and the silver cup in debating. He knew of my secret practice of retiring to a cabinet of the washroom to work on poems when business was slack in the warehouse. He called me Shakespeare. And while the other boys in the warehouse regarded me with suspicious hostility, Jim took a humorous attitude toward me. Gradually his attitude affected the others, their hostility wore off and they also began to smile at me as people smile at an oddly fashioned dog who trots across their path at some distance.

I knew that Jim and Laura had known each other at Soldan, and I had heard Laura speak admiringly of his voice. I didn't know if Jim remembered her or not. In high school Laura had been as unobtrusive as Jim had been astonishing. If he did remember Laura, it was not as my sister, for when I asked him to dinner, he grinned and said, "You know, Shakespeare, I never thought of you as having folks!"

He was about to discover that I did....

[*Light upstage*]

[*Legend on screen: "The Accent of a Coming Foot."*]

Friday evening. It is about five o'clock of a late spring evening which comes "scattering poems in the sky."

A delicate lemony light is in the Wingfield apartment.

AMANDA *has worked like a Turk in preparation for the gentleman caller. The results are astonishing. The new floor lamp with its rose-silk shade is in place, a colored paper lantern conceals the broken light fixture in the ceiling, new billowing white curtains are at the windows, chintz covers are on chairs and sofa, a pair of new sofa pillows make their initial appearance.*

Open boxes and tissue paper are scattered on the floor.

LAURA *stands in the middle with lifted arms while* AMANDA *crouches before her, adjusting the hem of the new dress, devout and ritualistic. The dress is colored and designed by memory. The arrangement of* LAURA'S *hair is changed; it is softer and more becoming. A fragile, unearthly prettiness has come out in* LAURA: *she is like a piece of translucent glass touched by light, given a momentary radiance, not actual, not lasting.*

AMANDA [*impatiently*]: Why are you trembling?

LAURA: Mother, you've made me so nervous!

AMANDA: How have I made you nervous?

LAURA: By all this fuss! You make it seem so important!

AMANDA: I don't understand you, Laura. You couldn't be satisfied with just sitting home, and yet whenever I try to arrange something for you, you seem to resist it. [*She gets up.*] Now take a look at yourself. No, wait! Wait just a moment—I have an idea!

LAURA: What is it now?

AMANDA *produces two powder puffs which she wraps in handkerchiefs and stuffs in* LAURA'S *bosom.*

LAURA: Mother, what are you doing?

MANDA: They call them "Gay Deceivers!"

URA: I won't wear them!

NDA: You will!

ʌ: Why should I?

ʌ: Because, to be painfully honest, your chest is flat.

You make it seem like we were setting a trap.

AMANDA: All pretty girls are a trap, a pretty trap, and men expect them to be. [*Legend: "A Pretty Trap."*] Now look at yourself, young lady. This is the prettiest you will ever be! I've got to fix myself now! You're going to be surprised by your mother's appearance! [*She crosses through portieres, humming gaily.*]

LAURA *moves slowly to the long mirror and stares solemnly at herself.*

A wind blows the white curtains inward in a slow, graceful motion and with a faint sorrowful sighing.

AMANDA [*off stage*]:   It isn't dark enough yet. [*She turns slowly before the mirror with a troubled look.*]

[*Legend on screen: "This Is My Sister: Celebrate Her with Strings!" Music.*]

AMANDA [*laughing, off*]:   I'm going to show you something. I'm going to make a spectacular appearance!
LAURA: What is it, Mother?
AMANDA: Possess your soul in patience—you will see! Something I've resurrected from that old trunk! Styles haven't changed so terribly much after all.... [*She parts the portieres.*] Now just look at your mother! [*She wears a girlish frock of yellowed voile with a blue silk sash. She carries a bunch of jonquils—the legend of her youth is nearly revived. Feverishly.*] This is the dress in which I led the cotillion. Won the cakewalk twice at Sunset Hill, wore one spring to the governor's ball in Jackson! See how I sashayed around the ballroom, Laura? [*She raises her skirt and does a mincing step around the room.*] I wore it on Sundays for my gentlemen callers! I had it on the day I met your father—I had malaria fever all that spring. The change of climate from East Tennessee to the Delta—weakened resistance—I had a little temperature all the time—not enough to be serious—just enough to make me restless and giddy! Invitations poured in—parties all over the Delta!—"Stay in bed," said Mother, "you have fever!"—but I just wouldn't.—I took quinine but kept on going, going!—Evenings, dances!—Afternoons, long, long rides! Picnics—lovely!—So lovely, that country in May.—All lacy with dogwood, literally flooded with jonquils!—That was the spring I had the craze for jonquils. Jonquils became an absolute obsession. Mother said, "Honey, there's no more room for jonquils." And still I kept bringing in more jonquils. Whenever, wherever I saw them, I'd say, "Stop! Stop! I see jonquils!" I made the young men help me gather the jonquils! It was a joke, Amanda and her jonquils! Finally there were no more vases to hold them, every available space was filled with jonquils. No vases to hold them? All right, I'll hold them myself! And then I—[*She stops in front of the picture. Music.*] met your father! Malaria fever and jonquils and then—this—boy.... [*She switches on the rose-colored lamp.*] I hope they get here before it starts to rain. [*She crosses upstage and places the jonquils in bowl on table.*] I gave your brother a little extra change so he and Mr. O'Connor could take the service car home.
LAURA [*with altered look*]:   What did you say his name was?
AMANDA: O'Connor.

LAURA: What is his first name?

AMANDA: I don't remember. Oh, yes, I do. It was—Jim!

LAURA *sways slightly and catches hold of a chair.*

[*Legend on screen: "Not Jim!"*]

LAURA [*faintly*]:   Not—Jim!

AMANDA: Yes, that was it, it was Jim! I've never known a Jim that wasn't nice!

[*Music: Ominous.*]

LAURA: Are you sure his name is Jim O'Connor?

AMANDA: Yes. Why?

LAURA: Is he the one that Tom used to know in high school?

AMANDA: He didn't say so. I think he just got to know him at the warehouse.

LAURA: There was a Jim O'Connor we both knew in high school—[*Then, with effort.*] If
      that is the one that Tom is bringing to dinner—you'll have to excuse me, I won't
      come to the table.

AMANDA: What sort of nonsense is this?

LAURA: You asked me once if I'd ever liked a boy. Don't you remember I showed
      you this boy's picture?

AMANDA: You mean the boy you showed me in the year book?

LAURA: Yes, that boy.

AMANDA: Laura, Laura, were you in love with that boy?

LAURA: I don't know, Mother. All I know is I couldn't sit at the table if it was him!

AMANDA: It won't be him! It isn't the least bit likely. But whether it is or not, you
      will come to the table. You will not be excused.

LAURA: I'll have to be, Mother.

AMANDA: I don't intend to humor your silliness, Laura. I've had too much from
      you and your brother, both! So just sit down and compose yourself till they
      come. Tom has forgotten his key so you'll have to let them in, when they
      arrive.

LAURA [*panicky*]:   Oh, Mother—*you* answer the door!

AMANDA [*lightly*]:   I'll be in the kitchen—busy!

LAURA: Oh, Mother, please answer the door, don't make me do it!

AMANDA [*crossing into kitchenette*]:   I've got to fix the dressing for the salmon. Fuss,
      fuss—silliness!—over a gentleman caller!

Door swings shut. LAURA *is left alone.*

[*Legend: "Terror!"*]

*She utters a low moan and turns off the lamp—sits stiffly on the edge of the sofa,
knotting her fingers together.*

[*Legend on screen: "The Opening of a Door!"*]

TOM *and* JIM *appear on the fire escape steps and climb to landing. Hearing their
approach,* LAURA *rises with a panicky gesture. She retreats to the portieres.*

The doorbell. LAURA *catches her breath and touches her throat. Low drums.*

AMANDA [*calling*]:   Laura, sweetheart! The door!

LAURA *stares at it without moving.*

JIM: I think we just beat the rain.

TOM: Uh-huh. [*He rings again, nervously.* JIM *whistles and fishes for a cigarette.*]

AMANDA [*very, very gaily*]:   Laura, that is your brother and Mr. O'Connor! Will you let them in, darling?

LAURA *crosses toward kitchenette door.*

LAURA [*breathlessly*]:   Mother—you go to the door!

AMANDA *steps out of kitchenette and stares furiously at* LAURA: *She points imperiously at the door.*

LAURA: Please, please!

AMANDA [*in a fierce whisper*]:   What is the matter with you, you silly thing?

LAURA [*desperately*]:   Please, you answer it, *please!*

AMANDA: I told you I wasn't going to humor you, Laura. Why have you chosen this moment to lose your mind?

LAURA: Please, please, please, you go!

AMANDA: You'll have to go to the door because I can't!

LAURA [*despairingly*]:   I can't either!

AMANDA: Why?

LAURA: I'm *sick!*

AMANDA: I'm sick, too—of your nonsense! Why can't you and your brother be normal people? Fantastic whims and behavior! [TOM *gives a long ring.*] Preposterous goings on! Can you give me one reason—[*calls out lyrically.*] COMING! JUST ONE SECOND!—why should you be afraid to open a door? Now you answer it, Laura!

LAURA: Oh, oh, oh… [*She returns through the portieres. Darts to the victrola and winds it frantically and turns it on.*]

AMANDA: Laura Wingfield, you march right to that door!

LAURA: Yes—yes, Mother!

A faraway, scratchy rendition of "Dardanella" softens the air and gives her strength to move through it. She slips to the door and draws it cautiously open. TOM *enters with caller,* JIM O'CONNOR.

TOM: Laura, this is Jim. Jim, this is my sister, Laura.

JIM [*stepping inside*]:   I didn't know that Shakespeare had a sister!

LAURA [*retreating stiff and trembling from the door*]:   How—how do you do?

JIM [*heartily extending his hand*]:   Okay!

LAURA *touches it hesitantly with hers.*

JIM: Your hand's *cold,* Laura!

LAURA: Yes, well—I've been playing the victrola.…

JIM: Must have been playing classical music on it! You ought to play a little hot swing music to warm you up!

LAURA: Excuse me—I haven't finished playing the victrola.…

She turns awkwardly and hurries into the front room. She pauses a second by the victrola. Then catches her breath and darts through the portieres like a frightened deer.

JIM [*grinning*]:   What was the matter?

TOM: Oh—with Laura? Laura is—terribly shy.

JIM: Shy, huh? It's unusual to meet a shy girl nowadays. I don't believe you ever mentioned you had a sister.

TOM: Well, now you know. I have one. Here is the *Post Dispatch*. You want a piece of it?

JIM: Uh-huh.

TOM: What piece? The comics?

JIM: Sports! [*glances at it*] Ole Dizzy Dean is on his bad behavior.

TOM [*disinterest*]:   Yeah? [*lights cigarette and crosses back to fire escape door.*]

JIM: Where are *you* going?

TOM: I'm going out on the terrace.

JIM [*goes after him*]:   You know, Shakespeare—I'm going to sell you a bill of goods!

TOM: What goods?

JIM: A course I'm taking.

TOM: Huh?

JIM: In public speaking! You and me, we're not the warehouse type.

TOM: Thanks—that's good news. But what has public speaking got to do with it?

JIM: It fits you for—executive positions!

TOM: Awww.

JIM: I tell you it's done a helluva lot for me.

[*Image: Executive at desk.*]

TOM: In what respect?

JIM: In every! Ask yourself what is the difference between you an' me and men in the office down front? Brains?—No!—Ability?—No! Then what? Just one little thing—

TOM: What is that one little thing?

JIM: Primarily it amounts to—social poise! Being able to square up to people and hold your own on any social level!

AMANDA [*off stage*]:   Tom?

TOM: Yes, Mother?

AMANDA: Is that you and Mr. O'Connor?

TOM: Yes, Mother.

AMANDA: Well, you just make yourselves comfortable in there.

TOM: Yes, Mother.

AMANDA: Ask Mr. O'Connor if he would like to wash his hands.

JIM: Aw—no—no—thank you—I took care of that at the warehouse. Tom—

TOM: Yes?

JIM: Mr. Mendoza was speaking to me about you.

TOM: Favorably?

JIM: What do you think?

TOM: Well—

JIM: You're going to be out of a job if you don't wake up.

TOM: I am waking up—

JIM: You show no signs.

TOM: The signs are interior.

[*Image on screen: The sailing vessel with Jolly Roger again.*]

TOM: I'm planning to change. [*He leans over the rail speaking with quiet exhilaration. The incandescent marquees and signs of the first-run movie houses light his face from across the alley. He looks like a voyager.*] I'm right at the point of committing myself to a future that doesn't include the warehouse and Mr. Mendoza or even a night-school course in public speaking.

JIM: What are you gassing about?

TOM: I'm tired of the movies.

JIM: Movies!

TOM: Yes, movies! Look at them—[*a wave toward the marvels of Grand Avenue.*] All of those glamorous people—having adventures—hogging it all, gobbling the whole thing up! You know what happens? People go to the *movies* instead of *moving!* Hollywood characters are supposed to have all the adventures for everybody in America, while everybody in America sits in a dark room and watches them have them! Yes, until there's a war. That's when adventure becomes available to the masses! *Everyone's* dish, not only Gable's! Then the people in the dark room come out of the dark room to have some adventures themselves—Goody, goody—It's our turn now, to go to the South Sea Island—to make a safari—to be exotic, far off—But I'm not patient. I don't want to wait till then. I'm tired of the movies and I am *about to move!*

JIM [*incredulously*]:   Move?

TOM: Yes.

JIM: When?

TOM: Soon!

JIM: Where? Where?

Theme three music Seems to Answer the Question, while TOM *thinks it over. He searches among his pockets.*

TOM: I'm starting to boil inside. I know I seem dreamy, but inside—well, I'm boiling! Whenever I pick up a shoe, I shudder a little thinking how short life is and what I am doing!—Whatever that means. I know it doesn't mean shoes—except as something to wear on a traveler's feet [*finds paper.*] Look—

JIM: What?

TOM: I'm a member.

JIM [*reading*]:   The Union of Merchant Seamen.

TOM: I paid my dues this month, instead of the light bill.

JIM: You will regret it when they turn the lights off.

TOM: I won't be here.

JIM: How about your mother?

TOM: I'm like my father. The bastard son of a bastard! See how he grins? And he's been absent going on sixteen years!

JIM: You're just talking, you drip. How does your mother feel about it?

TOM: Shhh—Here comes Mother! Mother is not acquainted with my plans!

AMANDA [*enters portieres*]:   Where are you all?

TOM: On the terrace, Mother.

They start inside. She advances to them. TOM *is distinctly shocked at her appearance. Even* JIM *blinks a little. He is making his first contact with girlish Southern vivacity and in spite of the night-school course in public speaking is somewhat thrown off the beam by the unexpected outlay of social charm.*

Certain responses are attempted by JIM *but are swept aside by* AMANDA'S *gay laughter and chatter.* TOM *is embarrassed but after the first shock* JIM *reacts very warmly. Grins and chuckles, is altogether won over.*

[*Image:* AMANDA *as a girl.*]

AMANDA [*coyly smiling, shaking her girlish ringlets*]:   Well, well, well, so this is Mr. O'Connor. Introductions entirely unnecessary. I've heard so much about you from my boy. I finally said to him, Tom—good gracious!—why don't you bring this paragon to supper? I'd like to meet this nice young man at the warehouse!—Instead of just hearing him sing your praises so much! I don't know why my son is so standoffish—that's not Southern behavior! Let's sit down and—I think we could stand a little more air in here! Tom, leave the door open. I felt a nice fresh breeze a moment ago. Where has it gone? Mmm, so warm already! And not quite summer, even. We're going to burn up when summer really gets started. However, we're having—we're having a very light supper. I think light things are better fo' this time of year. The same as light clothes are. Light clothes an' light food are what warm weather calls fo'. You know our blood gets so thick during th' winter—it takes a while fo' us to *adjust* ou'selves—when the season changes.... It's come so quick this year, I wasn't prepared. All of a sudden—heavens! Already summer!—I ran to the trunk an' pulled out this light dress—Terribly old! Historical almost! But feels so good—so good an' co-ol, y'know....

TOM: Mother—

AMANDA: Yes, honey?

TOM: How about—supper?

AMANDA: Honey, you go ask Sister if supper is ready! You know that Sister is in full charge of supper! Tell her you hungry boys are waiting for it. [*to* JIM] Have you met Laura?

JIM: She—

AMANDA: Let you in? Oh, good, you've met already! It's rare for a girl as sweet an' pretty as Laura to be domestic! But Laura is, thank heavens, not only pretty but also very domestic. I'm not at all. I never was a bit. I never could make a thing but angel-food cake. Well, in the South we had so many servants. Gone, gone, gone. All vestiges of gracious living! Gone completely! I wasn't prepared for what the future brought me. All of my gentlemen callers were sons of planters and so of course I assumed that I would be married to one and raise my family on a large piece of land with plenty of servants. But man proposes—and woman accepts the proposal!—To vary that old, old saying a little bit—I married no planter! I married a man who worked for the telephone company!—that gallantly smiling gentleman over there! [*points to the picture.*] A telephone man who—fell in love with long distance!—Now he travels and I don't even know where!—But what am I going on for about my—tribulations! Tell me yours—I hope you don't have any! Tom?

TOM [*returning*]: Yes, Mother?

AMANDA: Is supper nearly ready?

TOM: It looks to me like supper is on the table.

AMANDA: Let me look—[*She rises prettily and looks through portieres.*] Oh, lovely— But where is Sister?

TOM: Laura is not feeling well and she says that she thinks she'd better not come to the table.

AMANDA: What?—Nonsense!—Laura? Oh, Laura!

LAURA [*off stage, faintly*]: Yes, Mother.

AMANDA: You really must come to the table. We won't be seated until you come to the table! Come in, Mr. O'Connor. You sit over there and I'll—Laura? Laura Wingfield! You're keeping us waiting, honey! We can't say grace until you come to the table!

The back door is pushed weakly open and LAURA *comes in. She is obviously quite faint, her lips trembling, her eyes wide and staring. She moves unsteadily toward the table.*

[*Legend: "Terror!"*]

Outside a summer storm is coming abruptly. The white curtains billow inward at the windows and there is a sorrowful murmur and deep blue dusk.

LAURA *suddenly stumbles—She catches a chair with a faint moan.*

TOM: Laura!

AMANDA: Laura! [*There is a clap of thunder.*] [*Legend: "Ah!"*] [*despairingly.*] Why, Laura, you are sick, darling! Tom, help your sister into the living room, dear! Sit in the living room, Laura—rest on the sofa. Well! [*to the gentleman caller.*] Standing over the hot stove made her ill!—I told her that it was just too warm this evening, but—[TOM *comes back in.* LAURA *is on the sofa.*] Is Laura all right now?

TOM: Yes.

AMANDA: What *is* that? Rain? A nice cool rain has come up! [*She gives the gentleman caller a frightened look.*] I think we may—have grace—now…[Tom *looks at her stupidly.*] Tom, honey—you say grace!

TOM: Oh … "For these and all thy mercies—" [*They bow their heads.* AMANDA *stealing a nervous glance at* JIM. *In the living room* LAURA, *stretched on the sofa, clenches her hand to her lips, to hold back a shuddering sob.*] God's Holy Name be praised—

[*The scene dims out.*]

SCENE 7

A Souvenir

Half an hour later. Dinner is just being finished in the upstage area which is concealed by the drawn portieres.

As the curtain rises LAURA *is still huddled upon the sofa, her feet drawn under her, her head resting on a pale blue pillow, her eyes wide and mysteriously watchful. The new floor lamp with its shade of rose-colored silk gives a soft, becoming light to her face, bringing out the fragile, unearthly prettiness which usually escapes attention. There is a steady murmur of rain, but it is slackening and stops soon after the scene begins; the air outside becomes pale and luminous as the moon breaks out.*

A moment after the curtain rises, the lights in both rooms flicker and go out.

JIM: Hey, there, Mr. Light Bulb!

AMANDA *laughs nervously.*

[*Legend: "Suspension of a Public Service."*]

AMANDA: Where was Moses when the lights went out? Ha-ha. Do you know the answer to that one, Mr. O'Connor?

JIM: No, Ma'am, what's the answer?

AMANDA: In the dark! [JIM *laughs appreciatively.*] Everybody sit still. I'll light the candles. Isn't it lucky we have them on the table? Where's a match? Which of you gentlemen can provide a match?

JIM: Here.

AMANDA: Thank you, sir.

JIM: Not at all, Ma'am!

AMANDA: I guess the fuse has burnt out. Mr. O'Connor, can you tell a burnt-out fuse? I know I can't and Tom is a total loss when it comes to mechanics. [*Sound: Getting up: Voices recede a little to kitchenette.*] Oh, be careful you don't bump into something. We don't want our gentleman caller to break his neck. Now wouldn't that be a fine howdy-do?

JIM: Ha-ha! Where is the fuse box?

AMANDA: Right here next to the stove. Can you see anything?

JIM: Just a minute.

AMANDA: Isn't electricity a mysterious thing? Wasn't it Benjamin Franklin who tied a key to a kite? We live in such a mysterious universe, don't we? Some people say that science clears up all the mysteries for us. In my opinion it only creates more! Have you found it yet?

JIM: No, Ma'am. All these fuses look okay to me.

AMANDA: Tom!

TOM: Yes, Mother?

AMANDA: That light bill I gave you several days ago. The one I told you we got the notices about?

TOM: Oh.—Yeah.

[*Legend: "Ha!"*]

AMANDA: You didn't neglect to pay it by any chance?

TOM: Why, I—

AMANDA: Didn't! I might have known it!

JIM: Shakespeare probably wrote a poem on that light bill, Mrs. Wingfield.

AMANDA: I might have known better than to trust him with it! There's such a high price for negligence in this world!

JIM: Maybe the poem will win a ten-dollar prize.

AMANDA: We'll just have to spend the remainder of the evening in the nineteenth century, before Mr. Edison made the Mazda[5] lamp!

JIM: Candlelight is my favorite kind of light.

AMANDA: That shows you're romantic! But that's no excuse for Tom. Well, we got through dinner. Very considerate of them to let us get through dinner before they plunged us into everlasting darkness, wasn't it, Mr. O'Connor?

JIM: Ha-ha!

AMANDA: Tom, as a penalty for your carelessness you can help me with the dishes.

JIM: Let me give you a hand.

AMANDA: Indeed you will not!

JIM: I ought to be good for something.

AMANDA: Good for something? [*Her tone is rhapsodic.*] *You?* Why, Mr. O'Connor, nobody, *nobody's* given me this much entertainment in years—as you have!

JIM: Aw, now, Mrs. Wingfield!

AMANDA: I'm not exaggerating, not one bit! But Sister is all by her lonesome. You go keep her company in the parlor! I'll give you this lovely old candelabrum that used to be on the altar at the church of the Heavenly Rest. It was melted a little out of shape when the church burnt down. Lightning struck it one spring. Gypsy Jones was holding a revival at the time and he intimated that the church was destroyed because the Episcopalians gave card parties.

JIM: Ha-ha.

AMANDA: And how about coaxing Sister to drink a little wine? I think it would be good for her! Can you carry both at once?

JIM: Sure. I'm Superman!

AMANDA: Now, Thomas, get into this apron!

The door of kitchenette swings closed on AMANDA's *gay laughter; the flickering light approaches the portieres.*

LAURA *sits up nervously as he enters. Her speech at first is low and breathless from the almost intolerable strain of being alone with a stranger.*

[*Legend: "I Don't Suppose You Remember Me at All!"*]

In her first speeches in this scene, before JIM's *warmth overcomes her paralyzing shyness,* LAURA's *voice is thin and breathless as though she has run up a steep flight of stairs.*

JIM's *attitude is gently humorous. In playing this scene it should be stressed that while the incident is apparently unimportant, it is to* LAURA *the climax of her secret life.*

---

[5]**Mazda lamp** electric lamp

Jim: Hello, there, Laura.

Laura [*faintly*]:   Hello. [*She clears her throat.*]

Jim: How are you feeling now? Better?

Laura: Yes. Yes, thank you.

Jim: This is for you. A little dandelion wine. [*He extends it toward her with extravagant gallantry.*]

Laura: Thank you.

Jim: Drink it—but don't get drunk! [*He laughs heartily.* Laura *takes the glass uncertainly; laughs shyly.*] Where shall I set the candles?

Laura: Oh—oh, anywhere...

Jim: How about here on the floor? Any objections?

Laura: No.

Jim: I'll spread a newspaper under to catch the drippings. I like to sit on the floor. Mind if I do?

Laura: Oh, no.

Jim: Give me a pillow?

Laura: What?

Jim: A pillow!

Laura: Oh... [*hands him one quickly.*]

Jim: How about you? Don't you like to sit on the floor?

Laura: Oh—yes.

Jim: Why don't you, then?

Laura: I—will.

Jim: Take a pillow! [Laura *does. Sits on the other side of the candelabrum.* Jim *crosses his legs and smiles engagingly at her.*] I can't hardly see you sitting way over there.

Laura: I can—see you.

Jim: I know, but that's not fair, I'm in the limelight. [Laura *moves her pillow closer.*] Good! Now I can see you! Comfortable?

Laura: Yes.

Jim: So am I. Comfortable as a cow. Will you have some gum?

Laura: No, thank you.

Jim: I think that I will indulge, with your permission [*musingly unwraps it and holds it up.*] Think of the fortune made by the guy that invented the first piece of chewing gum. Amazing, huh? The Wrigley Building is one of the sights of Chicago.—I saw it summer before last when I went up to the Century of Progress. Did you take in the Century of Progress?

Laura: No, I didn't.

Jim: Well, it was quite a wonderful exposition. What impressed me most was the Hall of Science. Gives you an idea of what the future will be in America, even more wonderful than the present time is! [*Pause. Smiling at her.*] Your brother tells me you're shy. Is that right, Laura?

Laura: I—don't know.

Jim: I judge you to be an old-fashioned type of girl. Well, I think that's a pretty good type to be. Hope you don't think I'm being too personal—do you?

LAURA [*hastily, out of embarrassment*]:   I believe I *will* take a piece of gum, if you—don't mind. [*clearing her throat.*] Mr. O'Connor, have you—kept up with your singing?

JIM: Singing? Me?

LAURA: Yes. I remember what a beautiful voice you had.

JIM: When did you hear me sing?

[*Voice offstage in the pause*]

VOICE [*offstage*]:   O blow, ye winds, heigh-ho.
    A-roving I will go!
    I'm off to my love
    With a boxing glove—
    Ten thousand miles away!

JIM: You say you've heard me sing?

LAURA: Oh, yes! Yes, very often... I—don't suppose you remember me—at all?

JIM [*smiling doubtfully*]:   You know I have an idea I've seen you before. I had that idea soon as you opened the door. It seemed almost like I was about to remember your name. But the name that I started to call you—wasn't a name! And so I stopped myself before I said it.

LAURA: Wasn't it—Blue Roses?

JIM [*springs up, grinning*]:   Blue Roses! My gosh, yes—Blue Roses! That's what I had on my tongue when you opened the door! Isn't it funny what tricks your memory plays? I didn't connect you with the high school somehow or other. But that's where it was; it was high school. I didn't even know you were Shakespeare's sister! Gosh, I'm sorry.

LAURA: I didn't expect you to. You—barely knew me!

JIM: But we did have a speaking acquaintance, huh?

LAURA: Yes, we—spoke to each other.

JIM: When did you recognize me?

LAURA: Oh, right away!

JIM: Soon as I came in the door?

LAURA: When I heard your name I thought it was probably you. I knew that Tom used to know you a little in high school. So when you came in the door—Well, then I was—sure.

JIM: Why didn't you *say* something, then?

LAURA [*breathlessly*]:   I didn't know what to say, I was—too surprised!

JIM: For goodness' sakes! You know, this sure is funny!

LAURA: Yes! Yes, isn't it, though....

JIM: Didn't we have a class in something together?

LAURA: Yes, we did.

JIM: What class was that?

LAURA: It was—singing—Chorus!

JIM: Aw!

LAURA: I sat across the aisle from you in the Aud.

JIM: Aw.

LAURA: Mondays, Wednesdays, and Fridays.

JIM: Now I remember—you always came in late.

LAURA: Yes, it was so hard for me, getting upstairs. I had a brace on my leg—it clumped so loud!

JIM: I never heard any clumping.

LAURA [*wincing at the recollection*]:   To me it sounded like—thunder!

JIM: Well, well, well. I never even noticed.

LAURA: And everybody was seated before I came in. I had to walk in front of all those people. My seat was in the back row. I had to go clumping all the way up the aisle with everyone watching!

JIM: You shouldn't have been self-conscious.

LAURA: I know, but I was. It was always such a relief when the singing started.

JIM: Aw, yes, I've placed you now! I used to call you Blue Roses. How was it that I got started calling you that?

LAURA: I was out of school a little while with pleurosis. When I came back you asked me what was the matter. I said I had pleurosis—you thought I said Blue Roses. That's what you always called me after that!

JIM: I hope you didn't mind.

LAURA: Oh, no—I liked it. You see, I wasn't acquainted with many—people....

JIM: As I remember you sort of stuck by yourself.

LAURA: I—I—never had much luck at—making friends.

JIM: I don't see why you wouldn't.

LAURA: Well, I—started out badly.

JIM: You mean being—

LAURA: Yes, it sort of—stood between me—

JIM: You shouldn't have let it!

LAURA: I know, but it did, and—

JIM: You were shy with people!

LAURA: I tried not to be but never could—

JIM: Overcome it?

LAURA: No, I—I never could!

JIM: I guess being shy is something you have to work out of kind of gradually.

LAURA [*sorrowfully*]:   Yes—I guess it—

JIM: Takes time!

LAURA: Yes—

JIM: People are not so dreadful when you know them. That's what you have to remember! And everybody has problems, not just you, but practically everybody has got some problems. You think of yourself as having the only problems, as being the only one who is disappointed. But just look around you and you will see lots of people as disappointed as you are. For instance, I hoped when I was going to high school that I would be further along at this time, six years later, than I am now—You remember that wonderful write-up I had in *The Torch?*

LAURA: Yes! [*She rises and crosses to table.*]

JIM: It said I was bound to succeed in anything I went into! [LAURA *returns with the annual.*] Holy Jeez! *The Torch!* [*He accepts it reverently. They smile across it with mutual wonder.* LAURA *crouches beside him and they begin to turn through it.* LAURA'S *shyness is dissolving in his warmth.*]

LAURA: Here you are in *Pirates of Penzance!*

JIM [*wistfully*]:   I sang the baritone lead in that operetta.

LAURA [*rapidly*]:   So—*beautifully!*

JIM [*protesting*]:   Aw—

LAURA: Yes, yes—beautifully—beautifully!

JIM: You heard me?

LAURA: All three times!

JIM: No!

LAURA: Yes!

JIM: All three performances?

LAURA [*looking down*]:   Yes.

JIM: Why?

LAURA: I—wanted to ask you to—autograph my program.

JIM: Why didn't you ask me to?

LAURA: You were always surrounded by your own friends so much that I never had a chance to.

JIM: You should have just—

LAURA: Well, I—thought you might think I was—

JIM: Thought I might think you was—what?

LAURA: Oh—

JIM [*with reflective relish*]:   I was beleaguered by females in those days.

LAURA: You were terribly popular!

JIM: Yeah—

LAURA: You had such a—friendly way—

JIM: I was spoiled in high school.

LAURA: Everybody—liked you!

JIM: Including you?

LAURA: I—yes, I—I did, too—[*She gently closes the book in her lap.*]

JIM: Well, well, well!—Give me that program, Laura. [*She hands it to him. He signs it with a flourish.*] There you are—better late than never!

LAURA: Oh, I—what a—surprise!

JIM: My signature isn't worth very much right now. But some day—maybe—it will increase in value! Being disappointed is one thing and being discouraged is something else. I am disappointed but I'm not discouraged. I'm twenty-three years old. How old are you?

LAURA: I'll be twenty-four in June.

JIM: That's not old age!

LAURA: No, but—

JIM: You finished high school?

LAURA [*with difficulty*]:   I didn't go back.

JIM: You mean you dropped out?

LAURA: I made bad grades in my final examinations. [*She rises and replaces the book and the program. Her voice strained.*] How is—Emily Meisenbach getting along?

JIM: Oh, that kraut-head!

LAURA: Why do you call her that?

JIM: That's what she was.

LAURA: You're not still—going with her?

JIM: I never see her.

LAURA: It said in the Personal Section that you were—engaged!

JIM: I know, but I wasn't impressed by that—propaganda!

LAURA: It wasn't—the truth?

JIM: Only in Emily's optimistic opinion!

LAURA: Oh—

[*Legend: "What Have You Done Since High School?"*]

JIM *lights a cigarette and leans indolently back on his elbows smiling at* LAURA *with a warmth and charm which light her inwardly with altar candles. She remains by the table and turns in her hands a piece of glass to cover her tumult.*

JIM [*after several reflective puffs on a cigarette*]: What have you done since high school? [*She seems not to hear him.*] Huh? [LAURA *looks up.*] I said what have you done since high school, Laura?

LAURA: Nothing much.

JIM: You must have been doing something these six long years.

LAURA: Yes.

JIM: Well, then, such as what?

LAURA: I took a business course at business college—

JIM: How did that work out?

LAURA: Well, not very—well—I had to drop out, it gave me—indigestion—

JIM *laughs gently.*

JIM: What are you doing now?

LAURA: I don't do anything—much. Oh, please don't think I sit around doing nothing! My glass collection takes up a good deal of my time. Glass is something you have to take good care of.

JIM: What did you say—about glass?

LAURA: Collection I said—I have one—[*She clears her throat and turns away again, acutely shy.*]

JIM [*abruptly*]: You know what I judge to be the trouble with you? Inferiority complex! Know what that is? That's what they call it when someone low rates himself! I understand it because I had it, too. Although my case was not so aggravated as yours seems to be. I had it until I took up public speaking, developed my voice, and learned that I had an aptitude for science. Before that time I never thought of myself as being outstanding in any way whatsoever! Now I've never made a regular study of it, but I have a friend who says I can analyze people better than doctors that make a profession of it. I don't claim that to be necessarily true, but I can sure guess a person's psychology, Laura! [*takes out his gum.*] Excuse me, Laura. I always take it out when the flavor is gone. I'll use this scrap of paper to wrap it in. I know how it is to get it stuck on a shoe. Yep—that's what I judge to be your principal trouble. A lack of confidence in yourself as a person. You don't have the proper amount of faith in yourself. I'm basing that fact on a number of your remarks and also on certain observations I've made. For instance that clumping you thought was so awful in high school. You say that you even dreaded to walk into class. You see what you did? You dropped out of school, you gave up an education because of a clump, which as far as I know was practically nonexistent! A little physical defect is what you have. Hardly noticeable even! Magnified thousands of times by imagination! You know what my strong advice to you is? Think of yourself as *superior* in some way!

LAURA: In what way would I think?

JIM: Why, man alive, Laura! Just look about you a little. What do you see? A world full of common people! All of 'em born and all of 'em going to die! Which of them has one-tenth of your good points! Or mine! Or anyone else's, as far as that goes—Gosh! Everybody excels in some one thing. Some in many! [*unconsciously glances at himself in the mirror.*] All you've got to do is discover in *what!* Take me, for instance. [*He adjusts his tie at the mirror.*] My interest happens to lie in electro-dynamics. I'm taking a course in radio engineering at night school, Laura, on top of a fairly responsible job at the warehouse. I'm taking that course and studying public speaking.

LAURA: Ohhhh.

JIM: Because I believe in the future of television! [*turning back to her.*] I wish to be ready to go up right along with it. Therefore I'm planning to get in on the ground floor. In fact, I've already made the right connections and all that remains is for the industry itself to get under way! Full steam—[*His eyes are starry.*] *Knowledge*—Zzzzzp! *Money*—Zzzzzzp!—*Power!* That's the cycle democracy is built on! [*His attitude is convincingly dynamic.* LAURA *stares at him, even her shyness eclipsed in her absolute wonder. He suddenly grins.*] I guess you think I think a lot of myself!

LAURA: No-o-o-o, I—

JIM: Now how about you? Isn't there something you take more interest in than anything else?

LAURA: Well, I do—as I said—have my—glass collection—

A peal of girlish laughter from the kitchen.

JIM: I'm not right sure I know what you're talking about. What kind of glass is it?

LAURA: Little articles of it, they're ornaments mostly! Most of them are little animals made out of glass, the tiniest little animals in the world. Mother calls them a glass menagerie! Here's an example of one, if you'd like to see it! This one is one of the oldest. It's nearly thirteen. [*He stretches out his hand.*] [*Music: "The Glass Menagerie."*] Oh, be careful—if you breathe, it breaks!

JIM: I'd better not take it. I'm pretty clumsy with things.

LAURA: Go on, I trust you with him! [*places it in his palm.*] There now—you're holding him gently! Hold him over the light, he loves the light! You see how the light shines through him?

JIM: It sure does shine!

LAURA: I shouldn't be partial, but he is my favorite one.

JIM: What kind of a thing is this one supposed to be?

LAURA: Haven't you noticed the single horn on his forehead?

JIM: A unicorn, huh?

LAURA: Mmm-hmmm!

JIM: Unicorns, aren't they extinct in the modern world?

LAURA: I know!

JIM: Poor little fellow, he must feel sort of lonesome.

LAURA [*smiling*]:   Well, if he does he doesn't complain about it. He stays on a shelf with some horses that don't have horns and all of them seem to get along nicely together.

JIM: How do you know?

LAURA [*lightly*]:   I haven't heard any arguments among them!

JIM [*grinning*]:   No arguments, huh? Well, that's a pretty good sign! Where shall I set him?

LAURA: Put him on the table. They all like a change of scenery once in a while!

JIM [*stretching*]:   Well, well, well, well—Look how big my shadow is when I stretch!

LAURA: Oh, oh, yes—it stretches across the ceiling!

JIM [*crossing to door*]:   I think it's stopped raining. [*opens fire escape door.*] Where does the music come from?

LAURA: From the Paradise Dance Hall across the alley.

JIM: How about cutting the rug a little, Miss Wingfield?

LAURA: Oh, I—

JIM: Or is your program filled up? Let me have a look at it. [*grasps imaginary card.*] Why, every dance is taken! I'll just have to scratch some out. [*Waltz music: "La Golondrina."*] Ahhh, a waltz! [*He executes some sweeping turns by himself then holds his arms toward* LAURA.]

LAURA [*breathlessly*]:   I—can't dance!

JIM: There you go, that inferiority stuff!

LAURA: I've never danced in my life!

JIM: Come on, try!

LAURA: Oh, but I'd step on you!

JIM: I'm not made out of glass.

LAURA: How—how—how do we start?

JIM: Just leave it to me. You hold your arms out a little.

LAURA: Like this?

JIM: A little bit higher. Right. Now don't tighten up, that's the main thing about it—relax.

LAURA [*laughing breathlessly*]:   It's hard not to.

JIM: Okay.

LAURA: I'm afraid you can't budge me.

JIM: What do you bet I can't? [*He swings her into motion.*]

LAURA: Goodness, yes, you can!

JIM: Let yourself go, now, Laura, just let yourself go.

LAURA: I'm—

JIM: Come on!

LAURA: Trying?

JIM: Not so stiff—Easy does it!

LAURA: I know but I'm—

JIM: Loosen th' backbone! There now, that's a lot better.

LAURA: Am I?

JIM: Lots, lots better! [*He moves her about the room in a clumsy waltz.*]

LAURA: Oh, my!

JIM: Ha-ha!

LAURA: Goodness, yes you can!

JIM: Ha-ha-ha! [*They suddenly bump into the table.* JIM *stops.*] What did we hit on?

LAURA: Table.

JIM: Did something fall off it? I think—

LAURA: Yes.

JIM: I hope that it wasn't the little glass horse with the horn!

LAURA: Yes.

JIM: Aw, aw, aw. Is it broken?

LAURA: Now it is just like all the other horses.

JIM: It's lost its—

LAURA: Horn! It doesn't matter. Maybe it's a blessing in disguise.

JIM: You'll never forgive me. I bet that that was your favorite piece of glass.

LAURA: I don't have favorites much. It's no tragedy, Freckles. Glass breaks so easily. No matter how careful you are. The traffic jars the shelves and things fall
off them.

JIM: Still I'm awfully sorry that I was the cause.

LAURA [*smiling*]:   I'll just imagine he had an operation. The horn was removed to
make him feel less—freakish! [*They both laugh.*] Now he will feel more at
home with the other horses, the ones that don't have horns…

JIM: Ha-ha, that's very funny! [*suddenly serious.*] I'm glad to see that you have a
sense of humor. You know—you're—well—very different! Surprisingly different from anyone else I know! [*His voice becomes soft and hesitant with a
genuine feeling.*] Do you mind me telling you that? [LAURA *is abashed beyond
speech.*] You make me feel sort of—I don't know how to put it! I'm usually
pretty good at expressing things, but—This is something that I don't know
how to say! [LAURA *touches her throat and clears it—turns the broken unicorn in her hands.*] [*even softer*] Has anyone ever told you that you were
pretty? [*Pause: Music.*] [LAURA *looks up slowly, with wonder, and shakes her
head.*] Well, you are! In a very different way from anyone else. And all the
nicer because of the difference, too. [*His voice becomes low and husky.* LAURA
turns away, nearly faint with the novelty of her emotions.] I wish that you
were my sister. I'd teach you to have some confidence in yourself. The different people are not like other people, but being different is nothing to be
ashamed of. Because other people are not such wonderful people. They're
one hundred times one thousand. You're one times one! They walk all over
the earth. You just stay here. They're common as—weeds, but—you—well,
you're—*Blue Roses!*

[*Image on screen: Blue Roses.*]

[*Music changes.*]

LAURA: But blue is wrong for—roses...

JIM: It's right for you—You're—pretty!

LAURA: In what respect am I pretty?

JIM: In all respects—believe me! Your eyes—your hair—are pretty! Your hands are pretty! [*He catches hold of her hand.*] You think I'm making this up because I'm invited to dinner and have to be nice. Oh, I could do that! I could put on an act for you, Laura, and say lots of things without being very sincere. But this time I am. I'm talking to you sincerely. I happened to notice you had this inferiority complex that keeps you from feeling comfortable with people. Somebody needs to build your confidence up and make you proud instead of shy and turning away and—blushing—Somebody ought to—ought to—kiss you, Laura! [*His hand slips slowly up her arm to her shoulder.*] [*Music Swells Tumultuously.*] [*He suddenly turns her about and kisses her on the lips. When he releases her* LAURA *sinks on the sofa with a bright, dazed look.* JIM *backs away and fishes in his pocket for a cigarette.*] [*Legend on screen: "Souvenir."*] Stumble-john! [*He lights the cigarette, avoiding her look. There is a peal of girlish laughter from* AMANDA *in the kitchen.* LAURA *slowly raises and opens her hand. It still contains the little broken glass animal. She looks at it with a tender, bewildered expression.*] Stumble-john! I shouldn't have done that—That was way off the beam. You don't smoke, do you? [*She looks up, smiling, not hearing the question. He sits beside her a little gingerly. She looks at him speechlessly—waiting. He coughs decorously and moves a little farther aside as he considers the situation and senses her feelings, dimly, with perturbation. Gently.*] Would you—care for a—mint? [*She doesn't seem to hear him but her look grows brighter even.*] Peppermint—Life Saver? My pocket's a regular drug store—wherever I go... [*He pops a mint in his mouth. Then gulps and decides to make a clean breast of it. He speaks slowly and gingerly.*] Laura, you know, if I had a sister like you, I'd do the same thing as Tom. I'd bring out fellows—introduce her to them. The right type of boys of a type to—appreciate her. Only—well—he made a mistake about me. Maybe I've got no call to be saying this. That may not have been the idea in having me over. But what if it was? There's nothing wrong about that. The only trouble is that in my case—I'm not in a situation to—do the right thing. I can't take down your number and say I'll phone. I can't call up next week and—ask for a date. I thought I had better explain the situation in case you misunderstood it and—hurt your feelings.... [*Pause. Slowly, very slowly,* LAURA'S *look changes, her eyes returning slowly from his to the ornament in her palm.*]

AMANDA *utters another gay laugh in the kitchen.*

LAURA [*faintly*]:   You—won't—call again?

JIM: No, Laura, I can't. [*He rises from the sofa.*] As I was just explaining, I've—got strings on me, Laura, I've—been going steady! I go out all the time with a girl named Betty. She's a home-girl like you, and Catholic, and Irish, and in a great many ways we—get along fine. I met her last summer on a moonlight boat trip up the river to Alton, on the Majestic. Well—right away from the start it was—love! [*Legend: Love!*] [LAURA *sways slightly forward and grips the arm of the sofa. He fails to notice, now enrapt in his own comfortable being.*]

Being in love has made a new man of me! [*Leaning stiffly forward, clutching the arm of the sofa,* LAURA *struggles visibly with her storm. But* JIM *is oblivious, she is a long way off.*] The power of love is really pretty tremendous! Love is something that—changes the whole world, Laura! [*The storm abates a little and* LAURA *leans back. He notices her again.*] It happened that Betty's aunt took sick, she got a wire and had to go to Centralia. So Tom—when he asked me to dinner—I naturally just accepted the invitation, not knowing that you—that he—that I—[*He stops awkwardly.*] Huh—I'm a stumble-john! [*He flops back on the sofa. The holy candles in the altar of* LAURA's *face have been snuffed out! There is a look of almost infinite desolation.* JIM *glances at her uneasily.*] I wish that you would—say something. [*She bites her lip which was trembling and then bravely smiles. She opens her hand again on the broken glass ornament. Then she gently takes his hand and raises it level with her own. She carefully places the unicorn in the palm of his hand, then pushes his fingers closed upon it.*] What are you—doing that for? You want me to have him?—Laura? [*She nods.*] What for?

LAURA: A—souvenir...

She rises unsteadily and crouches beside the victrola to wind it up.

[*Legend on screen: "Things Have a Way of Turning Out So Badly."*]

[*Or image: "Gentleman Caller Waving Goodbye!—Gaily."*]

At this moment AMANDA *rushes brightly back in the front room. She bears a pitcher of fruit punch in an old-fashioned cut-glass pitcher and a plate of macaroons. The plate has a gold border and poppies painted on it.*

AMANDA: Well, well, well! Isn't the air delightful after the shower? I've made you children a little liquid refreshment. [*turns gaily to the gentleman caller.*] Jim, do you know that song about lemonade?

"Lemonade, lemonade
Made in the shade and stirred with a spade—
Good enough for any old maid!"

JIM [*uneasily*]:   Ha-ha! No—I never heard it.

AMANDA: Why, Laura! You look so serious!

JIM: We were having a serious conversation.

AMANDA: Good! Now you're better acquainted!

JIM [*uncertainly*]:   Ha-ha! Yes.

AMANDA: You modern young people are much more serious-minded than my generation. I was so gay as a girl!

JIM: You haven't changed, Mrs. Wingfield.

AMANDA: Tonight I'm rejuvenated! The gaiety of the occasion, Mr. O'Connor! [*She tosses her head with a peal of laughter. Spills lemonade.*] Oooo! I'm baptizing myself!

JIM: Here—let me—

AMANDA [*setting the pitcher down*]:   There now. I discovered we had some maraschino cherries. I dumped them in, juice and all!

JIM: You shouldn't have gone to that trouble, Mrs. Wingfield.

AMANDA: Trouble, trouble? Why it was loads of fun! Didn't you hear me cutting up in the kitchen? I bet your ears were burning! I told Tom how outdone with him I was for keeping you to himself so long a time! He should have brought you over much, much sooner! Well, now that you've found your way, I want you to be a very frequent caller! Not just occasional but all the time. Oh, we're going to have a lot of gay times together! I see them coming! Mmm, just breathe that air! So fresh, and the moon's so pretty! I'll skip back out—I know where my place is when young folks are having a—serious conversation!

JIM: Oh, don't go out, Mrs. Wingfield. The fact of the matter is I've got to be going.

AMANDA: Going, now? You're joking! Why, it's only the shank of the evening, Mr. O'Connor!

JIM: Well, you know how it is.

AMANDA: You mean you're a young workingman and have to keep workingmen's hours. We'll let you off early tonight. But only on the condition that next time you stay later. What's the best night for you? Isn't Saturday night the best night for you workingmen?

JIM: I have a couple of time clocks to punch, Mrs. Wingfield. One at morning, another one at night!

AMANDA: My, but you *are* ambitious! You work at night, too?

JIM: No, Ma'am, not work but—Betty! [*He crosses deliberately to pick up his hat. The band at the Paradise Dance Hall goes into a tender waltz.*]

AMANDA: Betty? Betty? Who's—Betty! [*There is an ominous cracking sound in the sky.*]

JIM: Oh, just a girl. The girl I go steady with! [*He smiles charmingly. The sky falls.*]

[*Legend: "The Sky Falls."*]

AMANDA [*a long-drawn exhalation*]:   Ohhh … Is it a serious romance, Mr. O'Connor?

JIM: We're going to be married the second Sunday in June.

AMANDA: Ohhhh—how nice! Tom didn't mention that you were engaged to be married.

JIM: The cat's not out of the bag at the warehouse yet. You know how they are. They call you Romeo and stuff like that. [*He stops at the oval mirror to put on his hat. He carefully shapes the brim and the crown to give a discreetly dashing effect.*] It's been a wonderful evening, Mrs. Wingfield. I guess this is what they mean by Southern hospitality.

AMANDA: It really wasn't anything at all.

JIM: I hope it don't seem like I'm rushing off. But I promised Betty I'd pick her up at the Wabash depot, an' by the time I get my jalopy down there her train'll be in. Some women are pretty upset if you keep 'em waiting.

AMANDA: Yes, I know—The tyranny of women! [*extends her hand.*] Goodbye, Mr. O'Connor. I wish you luck—and happiness—and success! All three of them, and so does Laura!—Don't you, Laura?

LAURA: Yes!

JIM [*taking her hand*]:   Goodbye, Laura. I'm certainly going to treasure that souvenir. And don't you forget the good advice I gave you. [*raises his voice to a cheery shout.*] So long, Shakespeare! Thanks again, ladies—good night!

He grins and ducks jauntily out.

Still bravely grimacing, AMANDA *closes the door on the gentleman caller. Then she turns back to the room with a puzzled expression. She and* LAURA *don't dare to face each other.* LAURA *crouches beside the victrola to wind it.*

AMANDA [*faintly*]:   Things have a way of turning out so badly. I don't believe that I would play the victrola. Well, well—well—Our gentleman caller was engaged to be married! Tom!

TOM [*from back*]:   Yes, Mother?

AMANDA: Come in here a minute. I want to tell you something awfully funny.

TOM [*enters with macaroon and a glass of lemonade*]:   Has the gentleman caller gotten away already?

AMANDA: The gentleman caller has made an early departure. What a wonderful joke you played on us!

TOM: How do you mean?

AMANDA: You didn't mention that he was engaged to be married.

TOM: Jim? Engaged?

AMANDA: That's what he just informed us.

TOM: I'll be jiggered! I didn't know about that.

AMANDA: That seems very peculiar.

TOM: What's peculiar about it?

AMANDA: Didn't you call him your best friend down at the warehouse?

TOM: He is, but how did I know?

AMANDA: It seems extremely peculiar that you wouldn't know your best friend was going to be married!

TOM: The warehouse is where I work, not where I know things about people!

AMANDA: You don't know things anywhere! You live in a dream; you manufacture illusions! [*He crosses to door.*] Where are you going?

TOM: I'm going to the movies.

AMANDA: That's right, now that you've had us make such fools of ourselves. The effort, the preparations, all the expense! The new floor lamp, the rug, the clothes for Laura! All for what? To entertain some other girl's fiancé! Go to the movies, go! Don't think about us, a mother deserted, an unmarried sister who's crippled and has no job! Don't let anything interfere with your selfish pleasure! Just go, go, go—to the movies!

TOM: All right, I will! The more you shout about my selfishness to me the quicker I'll go, and I won't go to the movies!

AMANDA: Go, then! Then go to the moon—you selfish dreamer!

TOM *smashes his glass on the floor. He plunges out on the fire escape, slamming the door.* LAURA *screams—cut by door.*

Dance-hall music up. TOM *goes to the rail and grips it desperately, lifting his face in the chill white moonlight penetrating the narrow abyss of the alley.*

[*Legend on screen:* "And So Good-bye..."]

TOM'S *closing speech is timed with the interior pantomime. The interior scene is played as though viewed through sound-proof glass.* AMANDA *appears to be making a comforting speech to* LAURA *who is huddled upon the sofa. Now that we cannot hear the mother's speech, her silliness is gone and she has dignity and tragic beauty.* LAURA'S *dark hair hides her face until at the end of the speech she lifts it to smile at her mother.* AMANDA'S *gestures are slow and graceful, almost dancelike, as she comforts the daughter. At the end of her speech she glances a moment at the father's picture—then withdraws through the portieres. At close of* TOM'S *speech,* LAURA *blows out the candles, ending the play.*

TOM: I didn't go to the moon, I went much further—for time is the longest distance between two places—Not long after that I was fired for writing a poem on the lid of a shoe box. I left Saint Louis. I descended the steps of this fire-escape for a last time and followed, from then on, in my father's footsteps, attempting to find in motion what was lost in space—I traveled around a great deal. The cities swept about me like dead leaves, leaves that were brightly colored but torn away from the branches. I would have stopped, but I was pursued by something. It always came upon me unawares, taking me altogether by surprise. Perhaps it was a familiar bit of music. Perhaps it was only a piece of transparent glass. Perhaps I am walking along a street at night, in some strange city, before I have found companions. I pass the lighted window of a shop where perfume is sold. The window is filled with pieces of colored glass, tiny transparent bottles in delicate colors, like bits of a shattered rainbow. Then all at once my sister touches my shoulder. I turn around and look into her eyes... Oh, Laura, Laura, I tried to leave you behind me, but I am more faithful than I intended to be! I reach for a cigarette, I cross the street, I run into the movies or a bar, I buy a drink, I speak to the nearest stranger— anything that can blow your candles out! [LAURA *bends over the candles.*]—for nowadays the world is lit by lightning! Blow out your candles, Laura—and so goodbye...

She blows the candles out.

[*The scene dissolves.*]

CHRISTOPHER DURANG [B. 1949]

Christopher Durang graduated from Harvard University and the Yale School of Drama. He is best known for his popular play, Sr. Mary Ignatius Explains It All for You *(1980), for which he won an Obie Award. He has taught playwriting at Yale and The Juilliard School.*

FOR WHOM THE SOUTHERN BELLE TOLLS   [1994]

CHARACTERS
AMANDA, *the mother*
LAWRENCE, *the son*
TOM, *the other son*
GINNY

Lights up on a fussy living room setting. Enter Amanda, the Southern belle mother.

AMANDA:　Rise and shine! Rise and shine! [*Calls off.*] Lawrence, honey, come on out here and let me have a look at you!

Enter Lawrence, who limps across the room. He is very sensitive, and is wearing what are clearly his dress clothes. Amanda fiddles with his bow tie and stands back to admire him.

AMANDA:　Lawrence, honey, you look lovely.

LAWRENCE:　No, I don't mama. I have a pimple on the back of my neck.

AMANDA:　Don't say the word "pimple," honey, it's common. Now your brother Tom is bringing home a girl from the warehouse for you to meet, and I want you to make a good impression, honey.

5　LAWRENCE:　It upsets my stomach to meet people, mama.

AMANDA:　Oh, Lawrence honey, you're so sensitive it makes me want to hit you.

LAWRENCE:　I don't need to meet people, mama. I'm happy just by myself, playing with my collection of glass cocktail stirrers.

Lawrence limps over to a table on top of which sits a glass jar filled with glass swizzle sticks.

AMANDA:　Lawrence, you are a caution. Only retarded people and alcoholics are interested in glass cocktail stirrers.

LAWRENCE [*picking up some of them*]:　Each one of them has a special name, mama. This one is called Stringbean because it's long and thin; and this one is called Stringbean because it's long and thin; and this one is called Blue because it's blue.

10　AMANDA:　All my children have such imagination, why was I so blessed? Oh. Lawrence, honey, how are you going to get on in the world if you just stay home all day, year after year, playing with your collection of glass cocktail stirrers?

LAWRENCE:　I don't like the world, mama, I like it here in this room.

AMANDA:　I know you do, Lawrence honey, that's part of your charm. Some days. But, honey, what about making a living?

LAWRENCE:　I can't work, mama. I'm crippled. [*He limps over to the couch and sits.*]

AMANDA:　There is nothing wrong with your leg, Lawrence honey, all the doctors have told you that. This limping thing is an affectation.

15　LAWRENCE:　I only know how I feel, mama.

AMANDA:　Oh, if only I had connections in the Mafia, I'd have someone come and break both your legs.

LAWRENCE:　Don't try to make me laugh, mama. You know I have asthma.

AMANDA:　Your asthma, your leg, your eczema. You're just a mess, Lawrence.

LAWRENCE:　I have scabs from the itching, mama.

20　AMANDA:　That's lovely, Lawrence. You must tell us more over dinner.

LAWRENCE:　Alright.

AMANDA:　That was a joke, Lawrence.

LAWRENCE:　Don't try to make me laugh, mama. My asthma.

AMANDA:　Now, Lawrence, I don't want you talking about your ailments to the feminine caller your brother Tom is bringing home from the warehouse, honey.

No nice-bred young lady likes to hear a young man discussing his eczema, Lawrence.

25 LAWRENCE: What else can I talk about, mama?

AMANDA: Talk about the weather. Or Red China.

LAWRENCE: Or my collection of glass cocktail stirrers?

AMANDA: I suppose so, honey, if the conversation comes to some godawful stand-still. Otherwise, I'd shut up about it. Conversation is an art, Lawrence. Back at Blue Mountain, when I had seventeen gentlemen callers, I was able to converse with charm and vivacity for six hours without stop and never once mention eczema or bone cancer or vivisection. Try to emulate me, Lawrence, honey. Charm and vivacity. And charm. And vivacity. And charm.

LAWRENCE: Well, I'll try, but I doubt it.

30 AMANDA: Me too, honey. But we'll go through the motions anyway, won't we?

LAWRENCE: I don't know if I want to meet some girl who works in a warehouse, mama.

AMANDA: Your brother Tom says she's a lovely girl with a nice personality. And where else does he meet girls except the few who work at the warehouse? He only seems to meet men at the movies. Your brother goes to the movies entirely too much. I must speak to him about it.

LAWRENCE: It's unfeminine for a girl to work at a warehouse.

AMANDA: Lawrence, honey, if you can't go out the door without getting an upset stomach or an attack of vertigo, then we got to find some nice girl who's will-ing to support you. Otherwise, how am I ever going to get you out of this house and off my hands?

35 LAWRENCE: Why do you want to be rid of me, mama?

AMANDA: I suppose it's unmotherly of me, dear, but you really get on my nerves. Limping around the apartment, pretending to have asthma. If only some nice girl would marry you and I knew you were taken care of, then I'd feel free to start to live again. I'd join Parents Without Partners. I'd go to dinner dances, I'd have a life again. Rather than just watch you mope about this stupid apart-ment. I'm not bitter, dear, it's just that I hate my life.

LAWRENCE: I understand, mama.

AMANDA: Do you, dear? Oh, you're cute. Oh listen, I think I hear them.

TOM [*from offstage*]:   Mother, I forgot my key.

40 LAWRENCE: I'll be in the other room. [*Starts to limp away.*]

AMANDA: I want you to let them in, Lawrence.

LAWRENCE: Oh, I couldn't mama. She'd see I limp.

AMANDA: Then don't limp, damn it.

TOM [*from off*]:   Mother, are you there?

45 AMANDA: Just a minute, Tom, honey. Now, Lawrence, you march over to that door or I'm going to break all your swizzle sticks.

LAWRENCE: Mama. I can't.

AMANDA: Lawrence, you're a grown boy. Now you answer that door like any nor-mal person.

LAWRENCE: I can't.

TOM: Mother. I'm going to break the door down in a minute.

50 AMANDA: Just be patient, Tom. Now you're causing a scene, Lawrence. I want you to answer that door.

LAWRENCE: My eczema itches.

AMANDA: I'll itch it for you in a second, Lawrence.

TOM: Alright, I'm breaking it down.

Sound of door breaking down. Enter Tom and Ginny Bennett, a vivacious girl dressed in factory clothes.

AMANDA: Oh, Tom, you got in.

55 TOM: Why must we go through this every night? You know the stupid fuck won't open the door, so why don't you let him alone about it? [*To Ginny.*] My kid brother has a thing about answering doors. He thinks people will notice his limp and his asthma and his eczema.

LAWRENCE: Excuse me. I think I hear someone calling me in the other room. [*Limps off, calls to imaginary person.*] Coming!

AMANDA: Now see what you've done. He's probably going to refuse to come to the table due to your insensitivity. Oh, was any woman as cursed as I? With one son who's too sensitive and another one who's this big ox. I'm sorry, how rude of me. I'm Amanda Wingvalley. You must be Virginia Bennett from the warehouse. Tom has spoken so much about you I feel you're almost one of the family, preferably a daughter-in-law. Welcome, Virginia.

GINNY [*speaking very loudly*]:   Call me Ginny or Gin. But just don't call me late for dinner! [*Roars with laughter.*]

AMANDA: Oh, how amusing. [*Whispers to Tom.*] Why is she shouting? Is she deaf?

60 GINNY: You're asking why I am speaking loudly. It's so that I can be heard! I am taking a course in public speaking, and so far we've covered organizing your thoughts and speaking good and loud so the people in the back of the room can hear you.

AMANDA: Public speaking. How impressive. You must be interested in improving yourself.

GINNY [*truly not having heard*]:   What?

AMANDA [*loudly*]:   YOU MUST BE INTERESTED IN IMPROVING YOURSELF.

GINNY [*loudly and happily*]:   YES I AM!

65 TOM: When's dinner? I want to get this over with fast if everyone's going to shout all evening.

GINNY: What?

AMANDA [*to Ginny*]:   Dinner is almost ready, Ginny.

GINNY: Who's Freddy?

AMANDA: Oh, Lord. No, dear. DINNER IS READY.

70 GINNY: Oh good. I'm as hungry as a bear! [*Growls enthusiastically.*]

AMANDA: You must be very popular at the warehouse, Ginny.

GINNY: No popsicle for me, ma'am, although I will take you up on some gin.

AMANDA [*confused*]:   What?

GINNY [*loudly*]   I WOULD LIKE SOME GIN.

75 AMANDA: Well, fine. I think I'd like to get drunk too. Tom, why don't you go and make two Southern ladies some nice summer gin and tonics? And see if your sister would like a lemonade.

TOM: Sister?

AMANDA: I'm sorry, did I say sister? I meant brother.

TOM [*calling as he exits*]:   Hey, four eyes, you wanna lemonade?

AMANDA: Tom's so amusing. He calls Lawrence four eyes even though he doesn't wear glasses.

80 GINNY: And does Lawrence wear glasses?

AMANDA [*confused*]:   What?

GINNY: You said Tom called Lawrence four eyes even though he doesn't wear glasses, and I wondered if Lawrence wore glasses. Because that would, you see, explain it.

AMANDA [*looks at her with despair*]:   Ah. I don't know. I'll have to ask Lawrence someday. Speaking of Lawrence, let me go check on the supper and see if I can convince him to come out here and make conversation with you.

GINNY: No, thank you, ma'am, I'll just have the gin.

85 AMANDA: What?

GINNY: What?

AMANDA: Never mind. I'll be back. Or with luck I won't.

Amanda exits. Ginny looks around uncomfortably, and crosses to the table with the collection of glass cocktail stirrers.

GINNY: They must drink a lot here.

Enter Tom with a glass of gin for Ginny.

TOM: Here's some gin for Ginny.

90 GINNY: What?

TOM: Here's your poison.

GINNY: No, thanks, I'll just wait here.

TOM: Have you ever thought all that loud machinery at the warehouse may be affecting your hearing?

GINNY: Scenery? You mean, like trees? Yeah, I like trees.

95 TOM: I like trees, too.

AMANDA [*from offstage*]:   Now you get out of that bed this minute. Lawrence Wing-valley, or I'm going to give that overbearing girl your entire collection of glass gobbledygook—is that clear?

Amanda pushes in Lawrence, who is wearing a nightshirt.

AMANDA: I believe Lawrence would like to visit with you, Ginny.

GINNY [*shows her drink*]:   Tom brought me my drink already, thank you, Mrs. Wingvalley.

AMANDA: You know a hearing aid isn't really all that expensive, dear, you might look into that.

100 GINNY: No, if I have the gin, I don't really want any Gatorade. Never liked the stuff anyway. But you feel free.

AMANDA: Thank you, dear. I will. Come. Tom, come to the kitchen and help me prepare the dinner. And we'll let the two young people converse. Remember, Lawrence. Charm and vivacity.

TOM: I hope this dinner won't take long, mother. I don't want to get to the movies too late.

AMANDA: Oh shut up about the movies.

Amanda and Tom exit. Lawrence stands still, uncomfortable. Ginny looks at him pleasantly. Silence for a while.

GINNY: Hi.

105   LAWRENCE: Hi. [*Pause.*] I'd gone to bed.

GINNY: I never eat bread. It's too fattening. I have to watch my figure if I want to get ahead in the world. Why are you wearing that nightshirt?

LAWRENCE: I'd gone to bed. I wasn't feeling well. My leg hurts and I have a headache, and I have palpitations of the heart.

GINNY: I don't know. Hum a few bars, and I'll see.

LAWRENCE: We've met before, you know.

110   GINNY: I've never seen snow. Is it exciting?

LAWRENCE: We were in high school together. You were voted Girl Most Likely To Succeed. We sat next to one another in glee club.

GINNY: I'm sorry, I really can't hear you. You're talking to softly.

LAWRENCE [*louder*]:   You used to call me BLUE ROSES.

GINNY: Blue Roses? Oh yes, I remember, sort of. Why did I do that?

115   LAWRENCE: I had been absent from school for several months, and when I came back, you asked me where I'd been, and I said I'd been sick with viral pneumonia, but you thought I said "blue roses."

GINNY: I didn't get much of that, but I remember you now. You used to make a spectacle of yourself every day in glee class, clumping up the aisle with this great big noisy leg brace on your leg. God, you made a racket.

LAWRENCE: I was always so afraid people were looking at me, and pointing. But then eventually mama wouldn't let me wear the leg brace anymore. She gave it to the Salvation Army.

GINNY: I've never been in the army. How long were you in for?

LAWRENCE: I've never been in the army. I have asthma.

120   GINNY: You do? May I see it?

LAWRENCE [*confused*]:   See it?

GINNY: Well, sure, unless you don't want to.

LAWRENCE: Maybe you want to see my collection of glass cocktail stirrers. [*He limps to the table, and limps back to her, holding his collection.*]

LAWRENCE [*holds up a stick*]:   I call this one Stringbean, because it's long and thin.

125   GINNY: Thank you. [*Puts it in her glass and stirs it.*]

LAWRENCE [*fairly appalled*]:   They're not for use. [*Takes it back from her.*] They're a collection.

GINNY: Well, I guess I stirred it enough.

LAWRENCE: They're my favorite thing in the world. [*Holds up another one.*] I call this one Q-tip, because I realized it looks like a Q-tip, except it's made out of glass and doesn't have little cotton swabs at the end of it. [*She looks blank.*] Q-TIPS.

GINNY: Really? [*She takes it and puts it in her ear.*]

130 LAWRENCE: No! Don't put it in your ear. [*Take it back.*] Now it's disgusting.

GINNY: Well, I didn't think it was a Q-tip, but that's what you said it was.

LAWRENCE: I call it that. I think I'm going to throw it out now. [*Holds up another one.*] I call this one Pinocchio because if you hold it perpendicular to your nose it makes your nose look long. [*He holds it to his nose.*]

GINNY: Uh huh.

LAWRENCE: And I call this one Henry Kissinger, because he wears glasses and it's made of glass.

135 GINNY: Uh huh. [*Takes it and stirs her drink.*]

LAWRENCE: No! They're just for looking, not for stirring. Mama, she's making a mess with my collection.

AMANDA [*from off*]:   Oh shut up about your collection, honey, you're probably driving the poor girl bananas.

GINNY: No bananas, thank you! My nutritionist says I should avoid potassium. You know what I take your trouble to be, Lawrence?

LAWRENCE: Mama says I'm retarded.

140 GINNY: I know you're tired, I figured that's why you put on the nightshirt, but this won't take long. I judge you to be lacking in self-confidence. Am I right?

LAWRENCE: Well, I am afraid of people and things, and I have a lot of ailments.

GINNY: But that makes you special, Lawrence.

LAWRENCE: What does?

GINNY: I don't know. Whatever you said. And that's why you should present yourself with more confidence. Throw back your shoulders, and say, "HI! HOW YA DOIN'?" Now you try it.

145 LAWRENCE [*unenthusiastically, softly*]:   Hello, How are you?

GINNY [*looking at watch, in response to his supposed question*]:   I don't know, it's about 8:30, but this won't take long and then you can go to bed. Alright, now try it. [*Booming.*] "HI! HOW YA DOIN'?"

LAWRENCE: Hi. How ya doin'?

GINNY: Now swagger a bit. [*Kinda butch.*] HI. HOW YA DOIN'?

LAWRENCE [*imitates her fairly successfully*]:   HI. HOW YA DOIN'?

150 GINNY: Good, Lawrence. That's much better. Again.

Amanda and Tom enter from behind them and watch this.

GINNY [*continued*]:   HI! HOW YA DOIN'?

LAWRENCE: HI! HOW YA DOIN'?

GINNY: THE BRAVES PLAYED A HELLUVA GAME, DON'TCHA THINK?

LAWRENCE: THE BRAVES PLAYED A HELLUVA GAME, DON'TCHA THINK?

155 AMANDA: Oh God I feel sorry for their children. Is this the only girl who works at the warehouse, Tom?

GINNY: HI, MRS. WINGVALLEY. YOUR SON LAWRENCE AND I ARE GETTING ON JUST FINE. AREN'T WE, LAWRENCE?

AMANDA: Please, no need to shout, I'm not deaf, even if you are.

GINNY: What?

AMANDA: I'm glad you like Lawrence.

160 GINNY: What?

AMANDA: I'M GLAD YOU LIKE LAWRENCE.

GINNY: What?

AMANDA: WHY DON'T YOU MARRY LAWRENCE?

GINNY [*looks shocked; has heard this*]:   Oh.

165   LAWRENCE: Oh, mama.

GINNY: Oh dear, I see. So that's why Shakespeare asked me here.

AMANDA [*to Tom*]:   Shakespeare?

TOM: The first day of work she asked my name, and I said Tom Wingvalley, and she thought I said Shakespeare.

GINNY: Oh dear, Mrs. Wingvalley, if I had a young brother as nice and as special as Lawrence, I'd invite girls from the warehouse home to meet him too.

170   AMANDA: I'm sure I don't know what you mean.

GINNY: And you're probably hoping I'll say that I'll call again.

AMANDA: Really, we haven't even had dinner yet. Tom, shouldn't you be checkin' on the roast pigs feet?

TOM: I guess so. If anything interesting happens, call me. [*Exits.*]

GINNY: But I'm afraid I won't be calling on Lawrence again.

175   LAWRENCE: This is so embarrassing. I told you I wanted to stay in my room.

AMANDA: Hush up, Lawrence.

GINNY: But, Lawrence, I don't want you to think that I won't be calling because I don't like you. I do like you.

LAWRENCE: You do?

GINNY: Sure. I like everybody. But I got two time clocks to punch, Mrs. Wingvalley. One at the warehouse, and one at night.

180   AMANDA: At night? You have a second job? That is ambitious.

GINNY: Not a second job, ma'am. Betty.

AMANDA: Pardon?

GINNY: Now who's deaf, eh what? Betty. I'm involved with a girl named Betty. We've been going together for about a year. We're saving money so that we can buy a farmhouse and a tractor together. So you [*to Lawrence*] can see why I can't visit your son, though I wish I could. No hard feelings, Lawrence. You're a good kid.

LAWRENCE [*offers her another swizzle stick*]:   I want you to keep this. It's my very favorite one. I call it Thermometer because it looks like a thermometer.

185   GINNY: You want me to have this?

LAWRENCE: Yes, as a souvenir.

GINNY [*offended*]:   Well, there's no need to call me a queer. Fuck you and your stupid swizzle sticks. [*Throws the offered gift upstage.*]

LAWRENCE: [*very upset*] You've broken it!

GINNY: What?

190   LAWRENCE: You've broken it. YOU'VE BROKEN IT.

GINNY: So I've broken it. Big fuckin' deal. You have twenty more of them here.

AMANDA: Well, I'm so sorry you have to be going.

GINNY: What?

AMANDA: Hadn't you better be going?

195   GINNY: What?

AMANDA: Go away!

GINNY: Well I guess I can tell when I'm not wanted. I guess I'll go now.

AMANDA: You and Betty must come over some evening. Preferably when we're out.

GINNY: I wasn't shouting. [*Calls off.*] So long, Shakespeare. See you at the ware-house. [*To Lawrence.*] So long, Lawrence. I hope your rash gets better.

200 LAWRENCE [*saddened, holding the broken swizzle stick*]: You broke Thermometer.

GINNY: What?

LAWRENCE: YOU BROKE THERMOMETER!

GINNY: Well, what was a thermometer doing in with the swizzle sticks anyway?

LAWRENCE: Its name was Thermometer, you nitwit!

205 AMANDA: Let it go, Lawrence. There'll be other swizzle sticks. Good-bye, Virginia.

GINNY: I sure am hungry. Any chance I might be able to take a sandwich with me?

AMANDA: Certainly you can shake hands with me, if that will make you happy.

GINNY: I said I'm hungry.

AMANDA: Really, dear? What part of Hungary are you from?

210 GINNY: Oh never mind. I guess I'll go.

AMANDA: That's right. You have two time clocks. It must be getting near to when you punch in Betty.

GINNY: Well, so long, everybody. I had a nice time. [*Exits.*]

AMANDA: Tom, come in here please. Lawrence, I don't believe I would play the victrola right now.

LAWRENCE: What victrola?

215 AMANDA: Any victrola.

Enter Tom.

TOM: Yes, mother? Where's Ginny?

AMANDA: The feminine caller made a hasty departure.

TOM: Old four eyes bored her to death, huh?

LAWRENCE: Oh, drop dead.

220 TOM: We should have you institutionalized.

AMANDA: That's the first helpful thing you've said all evening, but first things first. You played a little joke on us, Tom.

TOM: What are you talking about?

AMANDA: You didn't mention that your friend is already spoken for.

TOM: Really? I didn't even think she liked men.

225 AMANDA: Yes, well. It seems odd that you know so little about a person you see every day at the warehouse.

TOM: The warehouse is where I work, not where I know things about people.

AMANDA: The disgrace. The expense of the pigs feet, a new tie for Lawrence. And you—bringing a lesbian into this house. We haven't had a lesbian in this house since your grandmother died, and now you have the audacity to bring in that...that...

LAWRENCE: Dyke.

AMANDA: Thank you, Lawrence. That overbearing, booming-voiced bull dyke. Into a Christian home.

230 TOM: Oh look, who cares? No one in their right mind would marry four eyes here.

AMANDA: You have no Christian charity, or filial devotion, or fraternal affection.

TOM: I don't want to listen to this. I'm going to the movies.

AMANDA: You go to the movies to excess, Tom. It isn't healthy.

LAWRENCE: While you're out, could you stop at the liquor store and get me some more cocktail stirrers? She broke Thermometer, and she put Q-tip in her ear.

235 AMANDA: Listen to your brother, Tom. He's pathetic. How are we going to support ourselves once you go? And I know you want to leave. I've seen the brochure for the merchant marines in your underwear drawer. And the application to the Air Force. And your letter of inquiry to the Ballet Trockadero. So I'm not unaware of what you're thinking. But don't leave us until you fulfill your duties here. Tom. Help brother find a wife, or a job, or a doctor. Or consider euthanasia. But don't leave me here all alone, saddled with him.

LAWRENCE: Mama, don't you like me?

AMANDA: Of course, dear. I'm just making jokes.

LAWRENCE: Be careful of my asthma.

AMANDA: I'll try. dear. Now why don't you hold your breath in case you get a case of terminal hiccups?

240 LAWRENCE: Alright. [*Holds his breath.*]

TOM: I'm leaving.

AMANDA: Where are you going?

TOM: I'm going to the movies.

AMANDA: I don't believe you go to the movies. What did you see last night?

245 TOM: Hyapatia Lee in "Beaver City."

AMANDA: And the night before that?

TOM: I don't remember. "Humpy Busboys" or something.

AMANDA: Humpy what?

TOM: Nothing. Leave me alone.

250 AMANDA: These are not mainstream movies, Tom. Why can't you see a normal movie like "The Philadelphia Story." Or "The Bitter Tea of General Yen"?

TOM: Those movies were made in the 1930s.

AMANDA: They're still good today.

TOM: I don't want to have this conversation. I'm going to the movies.

AMANDA: That's right, go to the movies! Don't think about us, a mother alone, an unmarried brother who thinks he's crippled, and has no job. Stop holding your breath, Lawrence, mama was kidding. [*Back to Tom.*] Don't let anything interfere with your selfish pleasure. Go see your pornographic trash that's worse than anything Mr. D. H. Lawrence ever envisioned. Just go, go, go—to the movies!

255 TOM: Alright, I will! And the more you shout about my selfishness and my taste in movies the quicker I'll go, and I won't just go to the movies!

AMANDA: Go then! Go to the moon—you selfish dreamer!

Tom exits.

AMANDA [*continued*]: Oh Lawrence, honey, what's to become of us?

LAWRENCE: Tom forgot his newspaper, mama.

AMANDA: He forgot a lot more than that, Lawrence honey. He forgot his mama and brother.

Amanda and Lawrence stay in place. Tom enters down right and stands apart from them in a spot. He speaks to the audience.

260 TOM: I didn't go to the moon. I went to the movies. In Amsterdam. A long, lonely trip working my way on a freighter. They had good movies in Amsterdam. They weren't in English, but I didn't really care. And as for my mother and brother—well. I was adopted anyway. So I didn't miss them.

Or at least so I thought. For something pursued me. It always came upon me unawares, it always caught me by surprise. Sometimes it would be a swizzle stick in someone's vodka glass, or sometimes it would just be a jar of pigs feet. But then all of a sudden my brother touches my shoulder, and my mother puts her hands around my neck, and everywhere I look I am reminded of them. And in all the bars I go to there are those damn swizzle sticks everywhere. I find myself thinking of my brother Lawrence. And of his collection of glass. And of my mother. I begin to think that their story would maybe make a good novel, or even a play. A mother's hopes, a brother's dreams. Pathos, humor, even tragedy. But then I lose interest. I really haven't the energy. So I'll leave them both, dimly lit, in my memory. For nowadays the world is lit by lightning, and when we get those colored lights going, it feels like I'm on LSD. Or some other drug. Or maybe it's the trick of memory, and the fact that life is very, very sad. Play with your cocktail stirrers, Lawrence. And so, good-bye.

AMANDA [*calling over in Tom's direction*]:   Tom, I hear you out on the porch talking. Who are you talking to?

TOM: No one, mother. I'm just on my way to the movies.

AMANDA: Well, try not to be too late, you have to work early at the warehouse tomorrow. And please don't bring home any visitors from the movies. I'm not up to it after that awful girl. Besides, if some sailor misses his boat, that's no reason you have to put him up in your room. You're too big-hearted, son.

TOM: Yes, mother. See you later. [*Exits.*]

265 LAWRENCE: Look at the light through the glass, mama. [*Looks through a swizzle stick.*] Isn't it amazin'?

AMANDA: Yes, I guess it is, Lawrence. Oh, but both my children are weird. What have I done, O Lord, to deserve them?

LAWRENCE: Just lucky, mama.

AMANDA: Don't make jokes, Lawrence. Your asthma. Your eczema. My life.

LAWRENCE: Don't be sad, mama. We have each other for company and amusement.

270 AMANDA: That's right. It's always darkest before the dawn. Or right before a typhoon sweeps up and kills everybody.

LAWRENCE: Oh, poor mama, let me try to cheer you up with my collection. Is that a good idea?

AMANDA: It's just great. Lawrence. Thank you.

LAWRENCE: I call this one Daffodil, because its yellow, and daffodils are yellow.

AMANDA: Uh huh.

275 LAWRENCE [*holds up another one*]:   And I call this one Curtain Rod because it reminds me of a curtain rod.

AMANDA: Uh huh.

LAWRENCE: And I call this one Ocean, because it's blue, and the ocean is…

AMANDA: I THOUGHT YOU CALLED THE BLUE ONE BLUE, YOU IDIOT CHILD! DO I HAVE TO LISTEN TO THIS PATHETIC PRATTLING THE REST OF MY LIFE??? CAN'T YOU AT LEAST BE CONSISTENT???

LAWRENCE [*pause, hurt*]: No, I guess I can't.

280 AMANDA: Well, try, can't you? [*Silence.*] I'm sorry, Lawrence. I'm a little short-tempered today.

LAWRENCE: That's alright.

Silence.

AMANDA [*trying to make up*]: Do you have any other swizzle sticks with names, Lawrence?

LAWRENCE: Yes, I do. [*Holds one up.*] I call this one "Mama." [*He throws it over his shoulder onto the floor.*]

AMANDA: Well, that's lovely, Lawrence, thank you.

285 LAWRENCE: I guess I can be a little short-tempered too.

AMANDA: Yes, well, whatever. I think we won't kill each other this evening, alright?

LAWRENCE: Alright.

AMANDA: I'll just distract myself from my rage and despair, and read about other people's rage and despair in the newspaper, shall I? [*Picks up Tom's newspaper.*] Your brother has the worst reading and viewing taste of any living creature. This is just a piece of filth. [*Reads.*] Man Has Sex With Chicken, Then Makes Casserole. [*Closes the paper.*] Disgusting. Oh, Lawrence honey, look—it's the Evening Star. [*She holds the paper out in front of them.*] Let's make a wish on it, honey, shall we?

LAWRENCE: Alright, mama.

Amanda holds up the newspaper, and she and Lawrence close their eyes and make a wish.

290 AMANDA: What did you wish for, darlin'?

LAWRENCE: More swizzle sticks.

AMANDA: You're so predictable, Lawrence. It's part of your charm, I guess.

LAWRENCE: What did you wish for, mama?

AMANDA: The same thing, honey. Maybe just a little happiness, too, but mostly just some more swizzle sticks.

Sad music. Amanda and Lawrence look up at the Evening Star. Fade to black.

MAKING CONNECTIONS

1. Who is the central character in *The Glass Menagerie*? What criteria do you use to make your determination?

2. A central issue in *The Glass Menagerie* is whether Tom will obey his mother's wishes and stay in St. Louis with her and his sister. Yet when Tom addresses us at the start of the play, he wears a merchant marine uniform, signaling that he will not choose to remain at home. Does this visual clue influence your understanding of Tom as the play develops? Instead of suspense as to whether Tom will obey his mother's wishes, what effect does this create?

3. It is presented as a fact that Laura is the recluse of the family. Yet neither Amanda nor Tom has many friends and acquaintances. How has Laura garnered the reputation of "recluse"? Is it fair? Explain.

4. Which Wingfield changes the most over the course of the play? Which one changes the least?

5. Over and over, Jim tells Laura what he would do if she were his sister. Is this an indictment of Tom as a brother? Do you think Tom does his duty by his family?

6. As Laura reveals herself to Jim, does he react in the way you expect him to? Do his reactions to Laura change what you think of Amanda and Tom?

7. In what ways is Jim different from the Wingfields? Why is Laura able to give Jim the broken horse? Do you see this as an unselfish act or as an exchange for something she has received from him? Explain.

8. Why does Tom leave home? Is either Amanda or Laura responsible? Could they have done anything to make him stay?

9. Do you think *The Glass Menagerie* is an appropriate title for this play? Explain.

10. Compare the sibling relationship in *The Glass Menagerie* with those in the stories "Sonny's Blues" (p. 218) or "The Red Convertible" (p. 241).

11. Christopher Durang's *For Whom the Southern Belle Tolls* is a making fun of *The Glass Menagerie*. Did you laugh when you read the Durang play? Do you think you would have found it funny if you were not familiar with the Williams play? Explain.

12. How are the objects and characters in Williams's play transformed into something quite different? Is Durang being insensitive when he takes such a serious subject and spoofs it?

MAKING AN ARGUMENT

1. Plays are meant to be seen more than read. Nevertheless, Williams provides detailed and vivid descriptions of the setting, characters, and stage action. Carefully reread his descriptions of the three Wingfields at the start of the play, and write an essay about characterization in the play. Could you learn this much about each character solely by reading the scenes that follow? Does the play deliver the characters that Williams promises? Cite the text of the play to support your view.

2. Is this also true of the Durang play? In what way would it be more effective to read it than see it on the stage.

3. Compare Durang's parody of *The Glass Menagerie* with Howard Moss's parody of Shakespeare's Sonnet 18 on page 743.

CONNECTING THROUGH COMPARISON: POLITICAL SATIRE ACROSS TIME AND GENRE

The two works that follow, Jonathan Swift's "A Modest Proposal" and Luis Valdez's "Los Vendidos," employ satire to protest the bad treatment and terrrible living conditions of the poor. Though the subject of Swift's essay is the Irish of the eighteenth century and of Valdez's play, Mexican-Americans of the twentieth century, they are similar. Both intend to make political and moral points in order to change the conditions and the behavior of those who have the power to make these changes. Read and discussed together, they invite comparisons and connections.

JONATHAN SWIFT [1667–1745]

Jonathan Swift was born to English parents in Ireland and attended Trinity College in Dublin. Forced to flee Ireland during the period of turmoil that followed the abdication of James II, Swift lived ten years in the household of a wealthy relative, where he spent his time reading and where he first discovered his talent as a writer of satire. After many years of indecision, Swift decided on a career in the Church of England, which in turn led to his involvement in politics, where he was an active member of the Tory party. In 1713, he reluctantly returned to Ireland following his appointment as dean of St. Patrick's Cathedral in Dublin and eventually became a fervent Irish patriot in the struggle for Irish independence. Swift wrote "A Modest Proposal" (1729), widely considered the greatest satire produced in English, in response to his disgust with the heartless policies of the English government toward the poor in Ireland.

A MODEST PROPOSAL   [1729]

For preventing the Children of Poor People in Ireland from Being a Burden to Their Parents or Country, and for Making Them Beneficial to the Public

It is a melancholy object to those who walk through this great town or travel in the country, when they see the streets, the roads and cabindoors crowded with beggars of the female sex, followed by three, four, or six children, all in rags, and importuning every passenger for an alms. These mothers, instead of being able to work for their honest livelihood, are forced to employ all their time in strolling to beg sustenance for their helpless infants: who as they grow up either turn thieves for want of work, or leave their dear native country to fight for the pretender in Spain, or sell themselves to the Barbadoes.

I think it is agreed by all parties that this prodigious number of children in the arms, or on the backs, or at the heels of their mothers, and frequently of their fathers, is in the present deplorable state of the kingdom a very great additional grievance; and, therefore, whoever could find out a fair, cheap, and easy method of making these children sound, and useful members of the commonwealth, would deserve so well of the public as to have his statue set up for a preserver of the nation.

But my intention is very far from being confined to provide only for the children of professed beggars; it is of a much greater extent, and shall take in the whole number of infants at a certain age who are born of parents in effect as little able to support them as those who demand our charity in the streets.

As to my own part, having turned my thoughts for many years upon this important subject, and maturely weighed the several schemes of other projectors,[1] I have always found them grossly mistaken in their computation. It is true a child just dropped from its dam may be supported by her milk for a solar year, with little other nourishment; at most not above the value of 2s,[2] which the mother may certainly get, or the value in scraps, by her lawful occupation of begging; and it is exactly at one year old that I propose to provide for them in such a manner as, instead of being a charge upon their parents or the parish, or wanting food and raiment for the rest of their lives, they shall on the contrary contribute to the feeding, and partly to the clothing of many thousands.

5   There is likewise another great advantage in my scheme, that it will prevent those voluntary abortions, and that horrid practice of women murdering their bastard children, alas! too frequent among us! sacrificing the poor innocent babes I doubt more to avoid the expense than the shame, which would move tears and pity in the most savage and inhuman breast.

The number of souls in this kingdom being usually reckoned one million and a half, of these I calculate there may be about 200,000 couples whose wives are breeders; from which number I subtract 30,000 couples who are able to maintain their own children (although I apprehend there cannot be so many, under the present distresses of the kingdom); but this being granted, there will remain 170,000 breeders. I again subtract 50,000 for those women who miscarry, or whose children die by accident or disease within the year. There only remain 120,000 children of poor parents annually born. The question therefore is, how this number shall be reared and provided for, which, as I have already said, under the present situation of affairs, is utterly impossible by all the methods hitherto proposed. For we can neither employ them in handicraft or agriculture; we neither build houses (I mean in the country) nor cultivate land; they can very seldom pick up a livelihood by stealing, until they arrive at six years old, except where they are of towardly parts; although I confess they learn the rudiments much earlier; during which time they can, however, be properly looked upon only as probationers; as I have been informed by a principal gentleman in the County of Cavan, who protested to me that he never knew above one or two instances under the age of six, even in a part of the kingdom so renowned for the quickest proficiency in that art.

I am assured by our merchants, that a boy or a girl before twelve years old is no saleable commodity; and even when they come to this age they will not yield above or 3£[3] or 3£. 2s. 6d.[4] at most on the exchange; which cannot turn to account either to the parents or the kingdom, the charge of nutriment and rags having been at least four times that value.

I shall now therefore humbly propose my own thoughts, which I hope will not be liable to the least objection.

I have been assured by a very knowing American of my acquaintance in London, that a young healthy child well nursed is at a year old a most delicious, nourishing, and wholesome food, whether stewed, roasted, baked, or boiled; and I make no doubt that it will equally serve in a fricassee, or a ragout.

---

[1]**projectors** planners   [2]**2s** two shillings   [3]**3£** three pounds   [4]**6d** six pence

10   I do therefore humbly offer it to public consideration that of the 120,000 children already computed, 20,000 may be reserved for breed, whereof only one-fourth part to be males; which is more than we allow to sheep, black-cattle, or swine; and my reason is, that these children are seldom the fruits of marriage, a circumstance not much regarded by our savages; therefore one male will be sufficient to serve four females. That the remaining 100,000 may, at a year old, be offered in sale to the persons of quality and fortune through the kingdom, always advising the mother to let them suck plentifully in the last month, so as to render them plump and fat for a good table. A child will make two dishes at an entertainment for friends; and when the family dines alone, the fore or hind quarter will make a reasonable dish, and seasoned with a little pepper or salt will be very good boiled on the fourth day, especially in winter.

I have reckoned upon a medium that a child just born will weigh 12 pounds, and in a solar year, if tolerably nursed, increaseth to 28 pounds.

I grant this food will be somewhat dear, and therefore very proper for landlords, who, as they have already devoured most of the parents, seem to have the best title to the children.

Infant's flesh will be in season throughout the year, but more plentiful in March, and a little before and after: for we are told by a grave author, an eminent French physician, that fish being a prolific diet, there are more children born in Roman Catholic countries about nine months after Lent than at any other season; therefore, reckoning a year after Lent, the markets will be more glutted than usual, because the number of popish infants is at least three to one in this kingdom: and therefore it will have one other collateral advantage, by lessening the number of papists among us.

I have already computed the charge of nursing a beggar's child (in which list I reckon all cottagers, laborers, and four-fifths of the farmers) to be about 2s per annum, rags included; and I believe no gentleman would repine to give 10s for the carcass of a good fat child, which, as I have said, will make four dishes of excellent nutritive meat, when he hath only some particular friend or his own family to dine with him. Thus the squire will learn to be a good landlord, and grow popular among his tenants; the mother will have 8s net profit, and be fit for work until she produces another child.

15   Those who are more thrifty (as I must confess the times require) may flay the carcass; the skin of which artificially dressed, will make admirable gloves for ladies, and summer boots for fine gentlemen.

As to our city of Dublin, shambles[5] may be appointed for this purpose in the most convenient parts of it, and butchers we may be assured will not be wanting: although I rather recommend buying the children alive, and dressing them hot from the knife as we do roasting pigs.

A very worthy person, a true lover of his country, and whose virtues I highly esteem, was lately pleased in discoursing on this matter to offer a refinement upon my scheme. He said that many gentlemen of this kingdom, having of late destroyed their deer, he conceived that the want of venison might be well supplied by the

---

[5]**shambles** slaughterhouses

bodies of young lads and maidens, not exceeding fourteen years of age nor under twelve; so great a number of both sexes in every county being now ready to starve for want of work and service; and these to be disposed of by their parents, if alive, or otherwise by their nearest relations. But with due deference to so excellent a friend and so deserving a patriot, I cannot be altogether in his sentiments; for as to the males, my American acquaintance assured me from frequent experience that their flesh was generally tough and lean, like that of our schoolboys by continual exercise, and their taste disagreeable; and to fatten them would not answer the charge. Then as to the females, it would, I think with humble submission be a loss to the public, because they soon would become breeders themselves: and besides, it is not improbable that some scrupulous people might be apt to censure such a practice (although indeed very unjustly), as a little bordering upon cruelty; which, I confess, hath always been with me the strongest objection against any project, how well soever intended.

But in order to justify my friend, he confessed that this expedient was put into his head by the famous Psalmanazar,[6] a native of the island Formosa, who came from thence to London above twenty years ago; and in conversation told my friend that in his country when any young person happened to be put to death, the execu-tioner sold the carcass to persons of quality as a prime dainty; and that in his time the body of a plump girl of fifteen, who was crucified for an attempt to poison the emperor, was sold to his imperial majesty's prime minister of state, and other great mandarins of the court, in joints from the gibbet, at 400 crowns. Neither indeed can I deny, that if the same use were made of several plump young girls in this town, who without one single groat to their fortunes cannot stir abroad without a chair, and appear at the playhouse and assemblies in foreign fineries which they never will pay for, the kingdom would not be the worse.

Some persons of a desponding spirit are in great concern about the vast num-ber of poor people, who are aged, diseased, or maimed, and I have been desired to employ my thoughts what course may be taken to ease the nation of so grievous an encumbrance. But I am not in the least pain upon that matter, because it is very well known that they are every day dying and rotting by cold and famine, and filth and vermin, as fast as can be reasonably expected. And as to the younger laborers, they are now in as hopeful a condition: they cannot get work, and consequently pine away from want of nourishment, to a degree that if at any time they are acci-dentally hired to common labor, they have not strength to perform it; and thus the country and themselves are delivered from the evils to come.

20   I have too long digressed, and therefore shall return to my subject. I think the advantages by the proposal which I have made are obvious and many, as well as of the highest importance.

For first, as I have already observed, it would greatly lessen the number of papists, with whom we are yearly overrun, being the principal breeders of the nation; as well as our most dangerous enemies; and who stay at home on purpose to

---

[6]**Psalmanazar** George Psalmanazar (c. 1679–1763) wrote *An Historical and Geographical Description of Formosa* (1704). He had never been to Formosa and his book was quickly discovered to be fraudulent.

deliver the kingdom to the Pretender, hoping to take their advantage by the absence of so many good Protestants, who have chosen rather to leave their country than stay at home and pay tithes against their conscience to an Episcopal curate.

Secondly, The poorer tenants will have something valuable of their own, which by law may be made liable to distress and help to pay their landlord's rent, their corn and cattle being already seized, and money a thing unknown.

Thirdly, Whereas the maintenance of 100,000 children from two years old and upwards, cannot be computed at less than 10s. a-piece per annum, the nation's stock will be thereby increased £ 50,000 per annum, besides the profit of a new dish introduced to the tables of all gentlemen of fortune in the kingdom who have any refinement in taste. And the money will circulate among ourselves, the goods being entirely of our own growth and manufacture.

Fourthly, The constant breeders beside the gain of 8s sterling per annum by the sale of their children, will be rid of the charge of maintaining them after the first year.

25   Fifthly, This food would likewise bring great custom to taverns, where the vintners will certainly be so prudent as to procure the best receipts for dressing it to perfection, and consequently have their houses frequented by all the fine gentlemen, who justly value themselves upon their knowledge in good eating; and a skilful cook, who understands how to oblige his guests, will contrive to make it as expensive as they please.

Sixthly, This would be a great inducement to marriage, which all wise nations have either encouraged by rewards or enforced by laws and penalties. It would increase the care and tenderness of mothers towards their children, when they were sure of a settlement for life to the poor babes, provided in some sort by the public, to their annual profit instead of expense. We should soon see an honest emulation among the married women, which of them could bring the fattest child to the market. Men would become as fond of their wives during the time of their pregnancy as they are now of their mares in foal, their cows in calf, or sows when they are ready to farrow; nor offer to beat or kick them (as it is too frequent a practice) for fear of a miscarriage.

Many other advantages might be enumerated. For instance, the addition of some thousand carcasses in our exportation of barreled beef, the propagation of swine's flesh, and improvement in the art of making good bacon, so much wanted among us by the great destruction of pigs, too frequent at our tables, which are no way comparable in taste or magnificence to a well-grown, fat, yearling child, which roasted whole will make a considerable figure at a lord mayor's feast or any other public entertainment. But this and many others I omit, being studious of brevity.

Supposing that 1,000 families in this city would be constant customers for infants' flesh, besides others who might have it at merry-meetings, particularly weddings and christenings, I compute that Dublin would take off annually about 20,000 carcasses; and the rest of the kingdom (where probably they will be sold somewhat cheaper) the remaining 80,000.

I can think of no one objection that will possibly be raised against this proposal, unless it should be urged that the number of people will be thereby much lessened in the kingdom. This I freely own, and it was indeed one principal design in offering it to the world. I desire the reader will observe, that

I calculate my remedy for this one individual kingdom of Ireland and for no other that ever was, is, or I think ever can be upon earth. Therefore let no man talk to me of other expedients: of taxing our absentees at 5s. a pound: of using neither clothes, nor household furniture except what is of our own growth and manufacture: of utterly rejecting the materials and instruments that promote foreign luxury: of curing the expensiveness of pride, vanity, idleness, and gaming in our women: of introducing a vein of parsimony, prudence, and temperance: of learning to love our country, in the want of which we differ even from Laplanders and the inhabitants of Topinamboo: of quitting our animosities and factions, nor act any longer like the Jews, who were murdering one another at the very moment their city was taken: of being a little cautious not to sell our country and conscience for nothing: of teaching landlords to have at least one degree of mercy towards their tenants: lastly, of putting a spirit of honesty, industry, and skill into our shopkeepers; who, if a resolution could now be taken to buy only our native goods, would immediately unite to cheat and exact upon us in the price, the measure, and the goodness, nor could ever yet be brought to make one fair proposal of just dealing, though often and earnestly invited to it.

30   Therefore I repeat, let no man talk to me of these and the like expedients, till he hath at least a glimpse of hope that there will ever be some hearty and sincere attempt to put them in practice.

But as to myself, having been wearied out for many years with offering vain, idle, visionary thoughts, and at length utterly despairing of success, I fortunately fell upon this proposal; which, as it is wholly new, so it has something solid and real, of no expense and little trouble, full in our own power, and whereby we can incur no danger in disobliging England. For this kind of commodity will not bear exportation, the flesh being of too tender a consistence to admit a long continuance in salt, although perhaps I could name a country which would be glad to eat up our whole nation without it.

After all, I am not so violently bent upon my own opinion as to reject any offer proposed by wise men, which shall be found equally innocent, cheap, easy, and effectual. But before something of that kind shall be advanced in contradiction to my scheme, and offering a better, I desire the author or authors will be pleased maturely to consider two points. First, as things now stand, how they will be able to find food and raiment for 100,000 useless mouths and backs. And secondly, there being a round million of creatures in human figure throughout this kingdom, whose whole subsistence put into a common stock would leave them in debt 2,000,000£ sterling, adding those who are beggars by profession to the bulk of farmers, cottagers, and laborers with their wives and children who are beggars in effect; I desire those politicians who dislike my overture, and may perhaps be so bold to attempt an answer, that they will first ask the parents of these mortals, whether they would not at this day think it a great happiness to have been sold for food at a year old in the manner I prescribe, and thereby have avoided such a perpetual scene of misfortunes as they have since gone through, by the oppression of landlords, the impossibility of paying rent without money or trade, the want of common sustenance, with neither house nor clothes to cover them from the inclemencies of weather, and the most inevitable prospect of entailing the like or greater miseries upon their breed for ever.

I profess in the sincerity of my heart; that I have not the least personal interest in endeavoring to promote this necessary work, having no other motive than the public good of my country, by advancing our trade, providing for infants, relieving the poor, and giving some pleasure to the rich. I have no children by which I can propose to get a single penny; the youngest being nine years old, and my wife past child-bearing.

LUIS VALDEZ [B. 1940]

Playwright and filmmaker Luis Valdez was born in Delano, California, to farm worker parents. In 1964, after graduating from San Jose State University, where he first began writing and directing plays, Valdez joined the United Farm Workers Union, staging improvisations and short scenes meant to educate union members, who were mostly migrant workers, about labor issues. These experiences resulted in his founding of the El Teatro Campesino, a theater company devoted to exploring aspects of the Chicano experience. The company, which over the years has earned an enviable reputation in the theater world, has remained Valdez's artistic home throughout his career. In addition to his work in the theater, Valdez has written and directed a number of films, most notably La Bamba *(1987), the story of the Chicano pop musician Ritchie Valens. His latest work,* Mummified Deer, *was published in 2005.* Los Vendidos, *one of his first efforts at playwriting, was written in 1967. The title can be translated as "The Sellouts."*

LOS VENDIDOS   [1967]

CHARACTERS
HONEST SANCHO
SECRETARY
FARM WORKER
JOHNNY
REVOLUCIONARIO
MEXICAN-AMERICAN

SCENE: *Honest Sancho's Used Mexican Lot and Mexican Curio Shop. Three models are on display in Honest Sancho's shop: to the right, there is a* REVOLUCIONARIO, *complete with sombrero, carrilleras and carabina. At center, on the floor, there is the* FARM WORKER, *under a broad straw sombrero. At stage left is the* PACHUCO, *filero in hand.* HONEST SANCHO *is moving among his models, dusting them off and preparing for another day of business.*

SANCHO: *Bueno, bueno, mis monos, vamos a ver a quien vendemos ahora, ¿no?*
                [to audience] ¡Quihubo! I'm Honest Sancho and this is my shop. *Antes fui
                contratista pero ahora logré tener mi negocito.* All I need now is a customer.
                [A bell rings offstage.] Ay, a customer!
SECRETARY *[entering]:*   Good morning, I'm Miss Jiménez from—

SANCHO: *¡Ah, una chicana!* Welcome, welcome *Señorita* Jiménez.

SECRETARY [*Anglo pronunciation*]:   JIM-enez.

SANCHO: *¿Qué?*

SECRETARY: My name is Miss JIM-enez. Don't you speak English? What's wrong with you?

SANCHO: Oh, nothing, Señorita JIM-enez. I'm here to help you.

SECRETARY: That's better. As I was starting to say, I'm a secretary from Governor Reagan's office, and we're looking for a Mexican type for the administration.

SANCHO: Well, you come to the right place, lady. This is Honest Sancho's Used Mexican Lot, and we got all types here. Any particular type you want?

SECRETARY: Yes, we were looking for somebody suave—

SANCHO: Suave.

SECRETARY: Debonair.

SANCHO: *De buen aire.*

SECRETARY: Dark.

SANCHO: *Prieto.*

SECRETARY: But of course not too dark.

SANCHO: *No muy prieto.*

SECRETARY: Perhaps, beige.

SANCHO: Beige, just the tone. *Así como cafecito con leche, ¿no?*

SECRETARY: One more thing. He must be hardworking.

SANCHO: That could only be one model. Step right over here to the center of the shop, lady. [*They cross to the* FARM WORKER.] This is our standard farm worker model. As you can see, in the words of our beloved Senator George Murphy, he is "built close to the ground." Also take special notice of his four-ply Good-year *huaraches,* made from the rain tire. This wide-brimmed sombrero is an extra added feature—keeps off the sun, rain, and dust.

SECRETARY: Yes, it does look durable.

SANCHO: And our farm worker model is friendly. *Muy amable.* Watch. [*snaps his fingers*]

FARM WORKER [*lifts up head*]:   *Buenos días, señorita.* [*His head drops.*]

SECRETARY: My, he's friendly.

SANCHO: Didn't I tell you? Loves his *patrones!* But his most attractive feature is that he's hard working. Let me show you. [*Snaps fingers.* FARM WORKER *stands.*]

FARM WORKER: *¡El jale!* [*He begins to work.*]

SANCHO: As you can see, he is cutting grapes.

SECRETARY: Oh, I wouldn't know.

SANCHO: He also picks cotton. [*Snap.* FARM WORKER *begins to pick cotton.*]

SECRETARY: Versatile isn't he?

SANCHO: He also picks melons. [*Snap.* FARM WORKER *picks melons.*] That's his slow speed for late in the season. Here's his fast speed. [*Snap.* FARM WORKER *picks faster.*]

SECRETARY: *¡Chihuahua!* … I mean, goodness, he sure is a hard worker.

SANCHO [*pulls the* FARM WORKER *to his feet*]:   And that isn't the half of it. Do you see these little holes on his arms that appear to be pores? During those hot slug-gish days in the field, when the vines or the branches get so entangled, it's almost impossible to move; these holes emit a certain grease that allow our model to slip and slide right through the crop with no trouble at all.

SECRETARY: Wonderful. But is he economical?

SANCHO: Economical? *Señorita,* you are looking at the Volkswagen of Mexicans. Pennies a day is all it takes. One plate of beans and tortillas will keep him going all day. That, and chile. Plenty of chile. *Chile jalapeños, chile verde, chile colorado.* But, of course, if you do give him chile [*Snap.* FARM WORKER *turns left face. Snap.* FARM WORKER *bends over.*] then you have to change his oil filter once a week.

SECRETARY: What about storage?

SANCHO: No problem. You know these new farm labor camps our Honorable Governor Reagan has built out by Parlier or Raisin City? They were designed with our model in mind. Five, six, seven, even ten in one of those shacks will give you no trouble at all. You can also put him in old barns, old cars, river banks. You can even leave him out in the field overnight with no worry!

SECRETARY: Remarkable.

SANCHO: And here's an added feature: Every year at the end of the season, this model goes back to Mexico and doesn't return, automatically, until next spring.

SECRETARY: How about that. But tell me: does he speak English?

SANCHO: Another outstanding feature is that last year this model was programmed to go out on STRIKE! [*Snap.*]

FARM WORKER: ¡HUELGA! ¡HUELGA! *Hermanos, sálganse de esos files.* [*Snap. He stops.*]

SECRETARY: No! Oh no, we can't strike in the state capitol.

SANCHO: Well, he also scabs. [*Snap.*]

FARM WORKER: *Me vendo barato, ¿y qué?* [*Snap.*]

SECRETARY: That's much better, but you didn't answer my question. Does he speak English?

SANCHO: *Bueno...no, pero* he has other—

SECRETARY: No.

SANCHO: Other features.

SECRETARY: NO! He just won't do!

SANCHO: Okay, okay *pues.* We have other models.

SECRETARY: I hope so. What we need is something a little more sophisticated.

SANCHO: Sophisti—*¿qué?*

SECRETARY: An urban model.

SANCHO: Ah, from the city! Step right back. Over here in this corner of the shop is exactly what you're looking for. Introducing our new 1969 JOHNNY PACHUCO model! This is our fast-back model. Streamlined. Built for speed, low-riding, city life. Take a look at some of these features. Mag shoes, dual exhausts, green chartreuse paint-job, dark-tint windshield, a little poof on top. Let me just turn him on. [*Snap.* JOHNNY *walks to stage center with a pachuco bounce.*]

SECRETARY: What was that?

SANCHO: That, *señorita,* was the Chicano shuffle.

SECRETARY: Okay, what does he do?

SANCHO: Anything and everything necessary for city life. For instance, survival: He knife fights. [*Snap.* JOHNNY *pulls out switchblade and swings at* SECRETARY.]

[SECRETARY *screams.*]

SANCHO: He dances. [*Snap.*]

JOHNNY [*singing*]:   "Angel Baby, my Angel Baby…" [*Snap.*]

SANCHO: And here's a feature no city model can be without. He gets arrested, but not without resisting, of course. [*Snap.*]

JOHNNY: *¡En la madre, la placa!* I didn't do it! I didn't do it! [JOHNNY *turns and stands up against an imaginary wall, legs spread out, arms behind his back.*]

SECRETARY: Oh no, we can't have arrests! We must maintain law and order.

SANCHO: But he's bilingual!

SECRETARY: Bilingual?

SANCHO: *Simón que yes.* He speaks English! Johnny, give us some English. [*Snap.*]

JOHNNY [*comes downstage*]:   Fuck you!

SECRETARY [*gasps*]:   Oh! I've never been so insulted in my whole life!

SANCHO: Well, he learned it in your school.

SECRETARY: I don't care where he learned it.

SANCHO: But he's economical!

SECRETARY: Economical?

SANCHO: Nickels and dimes. You can keep Johnny running on hamburgers, Taco Bell tacos, Lucky Lager beer, Thunderbird wine, *yesca*—

SECRETARY: *Yesca?*

SANCHO: *Mota.*

SECRETARY: *Mota?*

SANCHO: *Leños… Marijuana.* [*Snap;* JOHNNY *inhales on an imaginary joint.*]

SECRETARY: That's against the law!

JOHNNY [*big smile, holding his breath*]:   Yeah.

SANCHO: He also sniffs glue. [*Snap.* JOHNNY *inhales glue, big smile.*]

JOHNNY: That's too much man, *ése.*

SECRETARY: No, Mr. Sancho, I don't think this—

SANCHO: Wait a minute, he has other qualities I know you'll love. For example, an inferiority complex. [*Snap.*]

JOHNNY [*to* SANCHO]:   You think you're better than me, huh *ése?* [*Swings switchblade.*]

SANCHO: He can also be beaten and he bruises, cut him and he bleeds; kick him and he—[*He beats, bruises and kicks* PACHUCO.] would you like to try it?

SECRETARY: Oh, I couldn't.

SANCHO: Be my guest. He's a great scapegoat.

SECRETARY: No, really.

SANCHO: Please.

SECRETARY: Well, all right. Just once. [*She kicks* PACHUCO.] Oh, he's so soft.

SANCHO: Wasn't that good? Try again.

SECRETARY [*kicks* PACHUCO]:   Oh, he's so wonderful! [*She kicks him again.*]

SANCHO: Okay, that's enough, lady. You ruin the merchandise. Yes, our Johnny Pachuco model can give you many hours of pleasure. Why, the L.A.P.D. just bought twenty of these to train their rookie cops on. And talk about maintenance. Señorita, you are looking at an entirely self-supporting machine. You're never going to find our Johnny Pachuco model on the relief rolls. No, sir, this model knows how to liberate.

SECRETARY: Liberate?

SANCHO: He steals. [*Snap.* JOHNNY *rushes the* SECRETARY *and steals her purse.*]

JOHNNY: *¡Dame esa bolsa, vieja!* [*He grabs the purse and runs. Snap by* SANCHO: *He stops.*]

[SECRETARY *runs after* JOHNNY *and grabs purse away from him, kicking him as she goes.*]

SECRETARY: No, no, no! We can't have any *more* thieves in the state administration. Put him back.

SANCHO: Okay, we still got other models. Come on, Johnny, we'll sell you to some old lady.

[SANCHO *takes* JOHNNY *back to his place.*]

SECRETARY: Mr. Sancho, I don't think you quite understand what we need. What we need is something that will attract the women voters. Something more traditional, more romantic.

SANCHO: Ah, a lover. [*He smiles meaningfully.*] Step right over here, *señorita.* Introducing our standard Revolucionario and/or Early California Bandit type. As you can see he is well built, sturdy, durable. This is the International Harvester of Mexicans.

SECRETARY: What does he do?

SANCHO: You name it, he does it. He rides horses, stays in the mountains, crosses deserts, plains, rivers, leads revolutions, follows revolutions, kills, can be killed, serves as a martyr, hero, movie star—did I say movie star? Did you ever see *Viva Zapata? Viva Villa? Villa Rides? Pancho Villa Returns? Pancho Villa Goes Back? Pancho Villa Meets Abbott and Costello*—

SECRETARY: I've never seen any of those.

SANCHO: Well, he was in all of them. Listen to this. [*Snap.*]

REVOLUCIONARIO: [*scream*] *¡VIVA VILLAAAAA!*

SECRETARY: That's awfully loud.

SANCHO: He has a volume control. [*He adjusts volume. Snap.*]

REVOLUCIONARIO [*mousey voice*]:   *¡Viva Villa!*

SECRETARY: That's better.

SANCHO: And even if you didn't see him in the movies, perhaps you saw him on TV. He makes commercials. [*Snap.*]

REVOLUCIONARIO: Is there a Frito Bandito in your house?

SECRETARY: Oh yes, I've seen that one!

SANCHO: Another feature about this one is that he is economical. He runs on raw horsemeat and tequila!

SECRETARY: Isn't that rather savage?

SANCHO: *Al contrario,* it makes him a lover. [*Snap.*]

REVOLUCIONARIO: [*to* SECRETARY] *¡Ay, mamasota, cochota, ven pa'ca!* [*He grabs* SECRETARY *and folds her back—Latin-lover style.*]

SANCHO [*Snap.* REVOLUCIONARIO *goes back upright.*]:   Now wasn't that nice?

SECRETARY: Well, it was rather nice.

SANCHO: And finally, there is one outstanding feature about this model I KNOW the ladies are going to love: He's a GENUINE antique! He was made in Mexico in 1910!

SECRETARY: Made in Mexico?

SANCHO: That's right. Once in Tijuana, twice in Guadalajara, three times in Cuernavaca.

SECRETARY: Mr. Sancho, I thought he was an American product.

SANCHO: No, but—

SECRETARY: No, I'm sorry. We can't buy anything but American-made products. He just won't do.

SANCHO: But he's an antique!

SECRETARY: I don't care. You still don't understand what we need. It's true we need Mexican models such as these, but it's more important that he be *American*.

SANCHO: American?

SECRETARY: That's right, and judging from what you've shown me, I don't think you have what we want. Well, my lunch hour's almost over, I better—

SANCHO: Wait a minute! Mexican but American?

SECRETARY: That's correct.

SANCHO: Mexican but... [*a sudden flash*.] AMERICAN! Yeah, I think we've got exactly what you want. He just came in today! Give me a minute. [*He exits. Talks from backstage*.] Here he is in the shop. Let me just get some papers off. There. Introducing our new 1970 Mexican-American! Ta-ra-ra-ra-ra-ra-RA-RAAA!

[SANCHO *brings out the* MEXICAN-AMERICAN *model, a clean-shaven middle-class type in a business suit, with glasses*.]

SECRETARY [*impressed*]: Where have you been hiding this one?

SANCHO: He just came in this morning. Ain't he a beauty? Feast your eyes on him! Sturdy US STEEL frame, streamlined, modern. As a matter of fact, he is built exactly like our Anglo models except that he comes in a variety of darker shades: naugahyde, leather, or leatherette.

SECRETARY: Naugahyde.

SANCHO: Well, we'll just write that down. Yes, *señorita*, this model represents the apex of American engineering! He is bilingual, college educated, ambitious! Say the word "acculturate" and he accelerates. He is intelligent, well-mannered, clean—did I say clean? [*Snap*. MEXICAN-AMERICAN *raises his arm*.] Smell.

SECRETARY [*smells*]: Old Sobaco, my favorite.

SANCHO [*Snap*. MEXICAN-AMERICAN *turns toward* SANCHO]: Eric! [*to* SECRETARY] We call him Eric García. [*to* ERIC] I want you to meet Miss JIM-enez, Eric.

MEXICAN-AMERICAN: Miss JIM-enez, I am delighted to make your acquaintance. [*He kisses her hand*.]

SECRETARY: Oh, my, how charming!

SANCHO: Did you feel the suction? He has seven especially engineered suction cups right behind his lips. He's a charmer all right!

SECRETARY: How about boards? Does he function on boards?

SANCHO: You name them, he is on them. Parole boards, draft boards, school boards, taco quality control boards, surf boards, two-by-fours.

SECRETARY: Does he function in politics?

SANCHO: *Señorita,* you are looking at a political MACHINE. Have you ever heard of the OEO, EOC, COD, WAR ON POVERTY? That's our model! Not only that, he makes political speeches.

SECRETARY: May I hear one?

SANCHO: With pleasure. [*Snap.*] Eric, give us a speech.

MEXICAN-AMERICAN: Mr. Congressman, Mr. Chairman, members of the board, honored guests, ladies and gentlemen. [SANCHO *and* SECRETARY *applaud.*] Please, please. I come before you as a Mexican-American to tell you about the problems of the Mexican. The problems of the Mexican stem from one thing and one thing alone: He's stupid. He's uneducated. He needs to stay in school. He needs to be ambitious, forward-looking, harder-working. He needs to think American, American, American, AMERICAN, AMERICAN, AMERICAN. GOD BLESS AMERICA! GOD BLESS AMERICA! GOD BLESS AMERICA!! [*He goes out of control.*]

[SANCHO *snaps frantically and the* MEXICAN-AMERICAN *finally slumps forward, bending at the waist.*]

SECRETARY: Oh my, he's patriotic too!

SANCHO: *Sí, señorita,* he loves his country. Let me just make a little adjustment here. [*Stands* MEXICAN-AMERICAN *up.*]

SECRETARY: What about upkeep? Is he economical?

SANCHO: Well, no, I won't lie to you. The Mexican-American costs a little bit more, but you get what you pay for. He's worth every extra cent. You can keep him running on dry Martinis, Langendorf bread.

SECRETARY: Apple pie?

SANCHO: Only Mom's. Of course, he's also programmed to eat Mexican food on ceremonial functions, but I must warn you: an overdose of beans will plug up his exhaust.

SECRETARY: Fine! There's just one more question: HOW MUCH DO YOU WANT FOR HIM?

SANCHO: Well, I tell you what I'm gonna do. Today and today only, because you've been so sweet, I'm gonna let you steal this model from me! I'm gonna let you drive him off the lot for the simple price of—let's see taxes and license included—$15,000.

SECRETARY: Fifteen thousand DOLLARS? For a MEXICAN!

SANCHO: Mexican? What are you talking, lady? This is a Mexican-AMERICAN! We had to melt down two *pachucos,* a farm worker and three *gabachos* to make this model! You want quality, but you gotta pay for it! This is no cheap run-about. He's got class!

SECRETARY: Okay, I'll take him.

SANCHO: You will?

SECRETARY: Here's your money.

SANCHO: You mind if I count it?

SECRETARY: Go right ahead.

SANCHO: Well, you'll get your pink slip in the mail. Oh, do you want me to wrap him up for you? We have a box in the back.

SECRETARY: No, thank you. The governor is having a luncheon this afternoon, and
we need a brown face in the crowd. How do I drive him?

SANCHO: Just snap your fingers. He'll do anything you want.

[SECRETARY *snaps.* MEXICAN-AMERICAN *steps forward.*]

MEXICAN-AMERICAN: RAZA QUERIDA, ¡VAMOS LEVANTANDO ARMAS PARA LIBERA-
NOS DE ESTOS DESGRACIADOS GABACHOS QUE NOS EXPLOTAN¡ VAMOS.

SECRETARY: What did he say?

SANCHO: Something about lifting arms, killing white people, etc.

SECRETARY: But he's not supposed to say that!

SANCHO: Look, lady, don't blame me for bugs from the factory. He's your Mexican-
American; you bought him, now drive him off the lot!

SECRETARY: But he's broken!

SANCHO: Try snapping another finger.

[SECRETARY *snaps.* MEXICAN-AMERICAN *comes to life again.*]

MEXICAN-AMERICAN: ¡ESTA GRAN HUMANIDAD HA DICHO BASTA! ¡Y SE HA
PUESTO EN MARCHA! ¡BASTA! ¡BASTA! ¡VIVA LA RAZA! ¡VIVA LA CAUSA!
¡VIVA LA HUELGA! ¡VIVAN LOS BROWN BERETS! ¡VIVAN LOS ESTUDI-
ANTES! ¡CHICANO POWER!

[*The* MEXICAN-AMERICAN *turns toward the* SECRETARY, *who gasps and backs up. He
keeps turning toward the* PACHUCO, FARM WORKER, *and* REVOLUCIONARIO, *snapping his
fingers and turning each of them on, one by one.*]

PACHUCO [*Snap. To* SECRETARY]:   I'm going to get you, baby! *¡Viva La Raza!*

FARM WORKER [*Snap. To* SECRETARY]:   *¡Viva la huelga! ¡Viva la Huelga! ¡VIVA LA
HUELGA!*

REVOLUCIONARIO [*Snap. To* SECRETARY]:   *¡Viva la revolución! ¡VIVA LA REVOLUCIÓN!*

[*The three models join together and advance toward the* SECRETARY, *who backs up
and runs out of the shop screaming.* SANCHO *is at the other end of the shop holding
his money in his hand. All freeze. After a few seconds of silence, the* PACHUCO *moves
and stretches, shaking his arms and loosening up. The* FARM WORKER *and* REVOLUCIO-
NARIO *do the same.* SANCHO *stays where he is, frozen to his spot.*]

JOHNNY: Man, that was a long one, *ése.* [*Others agree with him.*]

FARM WORKER: How did we do?

JOHNNY: Perty good, look at all that *lana,* man! [*He goes over to* SANCHO *and
removes the money from his hand.* SANCHO *stays where he is.*]

REVOLUCIONARIO: *En la madre,* look at all the money.

JOHNNY: We keep this up, we're going to be rich.

FARM WORKER: They think we're machines.

REVOLUCIONARIO: *Burros.*

JOHNNY: Puppets.

MEXICAN-AMERICAN: The only thing I don't like is—how come I always got to play the
goddamn Mexican-American?

JOHNNY: That's what you get for finishing high school.

FARM WORKER: How about our wages, *ése?*

JOHNNY: Here it comes right now. Three-thousand dollars for you, three-thousand dollars for you, three-thousand dollars for you, and three-thousand dollars for me. The rest we put back into the business.

MEXICAN-AMERICAN: Too much, man. Heh, where you *vatos* going tonight?

FARM WORKER: I'm going over to Concha's. There's a party.

JOHNNY: Wait a minute, *vatos.* What about our salesman? I think he needs an oil job.

REVOLUCIONARIO: Leave him to me.

[*The* PACHUCO, FARM WORKER, *and* MEXICAN-AMERICAN *exit, talking loudly about their plans for the night. The* REVOLUCIONARIO *goes over to* SANCHO, *removes his derby hat and cigar, lifts him up and throws him over his shoulder.* SANCHO *hangs loose, lifeless.*]

REVOLUCIONARIO [*to audience*]:   He's the best model we got! *¡Ajua! [Exit.]*

MAKING CONNECTIONS

1. Both the Swift essay and the Valdez play are satires. How do you know? What words or phrases or exaggerations indicate this?

2. How would you characterize *Los Vendidos*? Is it surrealistic? Political? A parable? Does it have a moral? If so, what is it?

3. What do you think is the significance of the different ways Sancho and the Secretary pronounce "Jimenez"? What do we learn about the Secretary through her pronunciation of her name?

4. How are the Farm Worker, Johnny, and the Revolucionario different? Why does the Secretary reject each?

5. What happens at the end of the play? Why are the four "models" ultimately more real than Sancho?

6. If Swift doesn't really mean the exaggerated things he proposes in his essay, why do you think he proposes them? Identify the issues that Swift raises, and write an essay that translates his exaggerated propositions into the steps toward social justice he implies should be taken. Cite the text of the essay for support.

MAKING AN ARGUMENT

1. Immigrants in our culture are treated differently than the rest of society. Or are they? Take a position on this statement, and write about the ways that *Los Vendidos* reveals the problem—or not. Cite the text of the play and other sources in this book for support.

Stereotypes:

- What do you know, what have you experienced about stereotypes?
- What groups (ethnic, religious, cultural, sexual) do you belong to?
- Are any of these groups stereotyped? What is the basis for this stereotyping?

- Have you been stereotyped? If so, what effect has it had on you—emotionally, psychologically, socially, professionally, etc.?
- Have you stereotyped a group or its apparent members? Who? How?

Los Vendidos:

- How are Mexican stereotypes "employed" in this play? How do the various characters embody common social, cultural, political stereotypes of Mexicans (and possibly other Latin American people)?
- How do the stereotyped characters address prejudice, cultural assimilation, political power, human rights, or other issues?
- Who is your favorite character? Why?
- (How) do these stereotypes relate to current realities such as "illegal aliens," undocumented immigrants, American identity, etc.?

"A Modest Proposal":

- How do you understand Swift's proposal? What's his purpose?
- What's the author's method in making his argument?
- Cite a passage in the essay that gets your attention, impresses, disturbs, interests, or even confuses you? What about it does so?
- What "voice," tone, or attitude do you hear in the writing?

Los Vendidos or "A Modest Proposal":

- What's the role of humor in these works? How do the authors bring humor to serious issues like social justice, prejudice, poverty, or political oppression? Why would they do so?

◆ ESSAYS ◆

CONNECTING THROUGH COMPARISON: WORK AND IDENTITY

The two pieces that follow address a subtheme of this section: work and identity. Read and discussed together, they invite comparisons and connections—not only with each other, but with your own sense of work and your own identity.

RICHARD RODRIGUEZ [B. 1944]

Richard Rodriguez was born in San Francisco, the son of Mexican immigrants. He received a Ph.D. in English Renaissance Literature from the University of California at Berkeley. His essays have appeared in a variety of publications, and he has published several books, including Hunger of Memory *(1981),* The Ethics of Change *(1992),* Days of Obligation *(1993), and his latest,* Next of Kin *(2009).*

He is a contributing editor to Harper's Magazine *and* U.S. News *and* World Report, *and a lecturer, freelance writer, educational consultant, and frequent contributor to the* Lehrer News Hour *on public television. He lives in San Francisco.*

WORKERS   [1982]

It was at Stanford, one day near the end of my senior year, that a friend told me about a summer construction job he knew was available. I was quickly alert. Desire uncoiled within me. My friend said that he knew I had been looking for summer employment. He knew I needed some money. Almost apologetically he explained: It was something I probably wouldn't be interested in, but a friend of his, a contractor, needed someone for the summer to do menial jobs. There would be lots of shoveling and raking and sweeping. Nothing too hard. But nothing more interesting either. Still, the pay would be good. Did I want it? Or did I know someone who did?

I did. Yes, I said, surprised to hear myself say it.

In the weeks following, friends cautioned that I had no idea how hard physical labor really is. ("You only *think* you know what it is like to shovel for eight hours straight.") Their objections seemed to me challenges. They resolved the issue. I became happy with my plan. I decided, however, not to tell my parents. I wouldn't tell my mother because I could guess her worried reaction. I would tell my father only after the summer was over, when I could announce that, after all, I did know what "real work" is like.

The day I met the contractor (a Princeton graduate, it turned out), he asked me whether I had done any physical labor before. "In high school, during the summer," I lied. And although he seemed to regard me with skepticism, he decided to give me a try. Several days later, expectant, I arrived at my first construction site. I would take off my shirt to the sun. And at last grasp desired sensation. No longer afraid. At last become like a *bracero*.[1] "We need those tree stumps out of here by tomorrow," the contractor said. I started to work.

5   I labored with excitement that first morning—and all the days after. The work was harder than I could have expected. But it was never as tedious as my friends had warned me it would be. There was too much physical pleasure in the labor. Especially early in the day, I would be most alert to the sensations of movement and straining. Beginning around seven each morning (when the air was still damp but the scent of weeds and dry earth anticipated the heat of the sun), I would feel my body resist the first thrusts of the shovel. My arms, tightened by sleep, would gradually loosen; after only several minutes, sweat would gather in beads on my forehead and then—a short while later—I would feel my chest silky with sweat in the breeze. I would return to my work. A nervous spark of pain would fly up my arm and settle to burn like an ember in the thick of my shoulder. An hour, two passed. Three. My whole body would assume regular movements; my shoveling would be described by identical, even movements. Even later in the day, my enthusiasm for primitive sensation would survive the heat and the dust and the insects pricking my back. I would strain wildly for sensation as the day came to a close. At

[1]**bracero** laborer

three-thirty, quitting time, I would stand upright and slowly let my head fall back, luxuriating in the feeling of tightness relieved.

Some of the men working nearby would watch me and laugh. Two or three of the older men took the trouble to teach me the right way to use a pick, the correct way to shovel. "You're doing it wrong, too fucking hard," one man scolded. Then proceeded to show me—what persons who work with their bodies all their lives quickly learn—the most economical way to use one's body in labor.

"Don't make your back do so much work," he instructed. I stood impatiently listening, half listening, vaguely watching, then noticed his work-thickened fingers clutching the shovel. I was annoyed. I wanted to tell him that I enjoyed shoveling the wrong way. And I didn't want to learn the right way. I wasn't afraid of back pain. I liked the way my body felt sore at the end of the day.

I was about to, but, as it turned out, I didn't say a thing. Rather it was at that moment I realized that I was fooling myself if I expected a few weeks of labor to gain me admission to the world of the laborer. I would not learn in three months what my father had meant by "real work." I was not bound to this job; I could imagine its rapid conclusion. For me the sensations of exertion and fatigue could be savored. For my father or uncle, working at comparable jobs when they were my age, such sensations were to be feared. Fatigue took a different toll on their bodies—and minds.

It was, I know, a simple insight. But it was with this realization that I took my first step that summer toward realizing something even more important about the "worker." In the company of carpenters, electricians, plumbers, and painters at lunch, I would often sit quietly, observant. I was not shy in such company. I felt easy, pleased by the knowledge that I was casually accepted, my presence taken for granted by men (exotics) who worked with their hands. Some days the younger men would talk and talk about sex, and they would howl at women who drove by in cars. Other days the talk at lunchtime was subdued; men gathered in separate groups. It depended on who was around. There were rough, good-natured workers. Others were quiet. The more I remember that summer, the more I realize that there was no single *type* of worker. I am embarrassed to say I had not expected such diversity. I certainly had not expected to meet, for example, a plumber who was an abstract painter in his off hours and admired the work of Mark Rothko. Nor did I expect to meet so many workers with college diplomas. (They were the ones who were not surprised that I intended to enter graduate school in the fall.) I suppose what I really want to say here is painfully obvious, but I must say it nevertheless: The men of that summer were middle-class Americans. They certainly didn't constitute an oppressed society. Carefully completing their work sheets; talking about the fortunes of local football teams; planning Las Vegas vacations; comparing the gas mileage of various makes of campers—they were not *los pobres*[2] my mother had spoken about.

10   On two occasions, the contractor hired a group of Mexican aliens. They were employed to cut down some trees and haul off debris. In all, there were six men of varying age. The youngest in his late twenties; the oldest (his father?) perhaps sixty

---

[2]**los pobres** the poor

years old. They came and they left in a single old truck. Anonymous men. They were never introduced to the other men at the site. Immediately upon their arrival, they would follow the contractor's directions, start working—rarely resting—seemingly driven by a fatalistic sense that work which had to be done was best done as quickly as possible.

I watched them sometimes. Perhaps they watched me. The only time I saw them pay me much notice was one day at lunchtime when I was laughing with the other men. The Mexicans sat apart when they ate, just as they worked by themselves. Quiet. I rarely heard them say much to each other. All I could hear were their voices calling out sharply to one another, giving directions. Otherwise, when they stood briefly resting, they talked among themselves in voices too hard to overhear.

The contractor knew enough Spanish, and the Mexicans—or at least the oldest of them, their spokesman—seemed to know enough English to communicate. But because I was around, the contractor decided one day to make me his translator. (He assumed I could speak Spanish.) I did what I was told. Shyly I went over to tell the Mexicans that the *patrón*[3] wanted them to do something else before they left for the day. As I started to speak, I was afraid with my old fear that I would be unable to pronounce the Spanish words. But it was a simple instruction I had to convey. I could say it in phrases.

The dark sweating faces turned toward me as I spoke. They stopped their work to hear me. Each nodded in response. I stood there. I wanted to say something more. But what could I say in Spanish, even if I could have pronounced the words right? Perhaps I just wanted to engage them in small talk, to be assured of their confidence, our familiarity. I thought for a moment to ask them where in Mexico they were from. Something like that. And maybe I wanted to tell them (a lie, if need be) that my parents were from the same part of Mexico.

I stood there.

15   Their faces watched me. The eyes of the man directly in front of me moved slowly over my shoulder, and I turned to follow his glance toward *el patrón* some distance away. For a moment I felt swept up by that glance into the Mexicans' company. But then I heard one of them returning to work. And then the others went back to work. I left them without saying anything more.

When they had finished, the contractor went over to pay them in cash. (He later told me that he paid them collectively—"for the job," though he wouldn't tell me their wages. He said something quickly about the good rate of exchange "in their own country"). I can still hear the loudly confident voice he used with the Mexicans. It was the sound of the *gringo*[4] I had heard as a very young boy. And I can still hear the quiet, indistinct sounds of the Mexican, the oldest, who replied. At hearing that voice I was sad for the Mexicans. Depressed by their vulnerability. Angry at myself. The adventure of the summer seemed suddenly ludicrous. I would not shorten the distance I felt from *los pobres* with a few weeks of physical labor. I would not become like them. They were different from me....

[3]**patrón** boss   [4]**gringo** Yankee

That summer I worked in the sun may have made me physically indistinguishable from the Mexicans working nearby. (My skin was actually darker because, unlike them, I worked without wearing a shirt. By late August my hands were probably as tough as theirs.) But I was not one of *los pobres*. What made me different from them was an attitude of *mind*, my imagination of myself....

In the end, my father was right—though perhaps he did not know how right or why—to say that I would never know what real work is. I will never know what he felt at his last factory job. If tomorrow I worked at some kind of factory, it would go differently for me. My long education would favor me. I could act as a public person—able to defend my interests, to unionize, to petition, to speak up—to challenge and demand. (I will never know what real work is.) I will never know what the Mexicans knew, gathering their shovels and ladders and saws.

Their silence stays with me now. The wages those Mexicans received for their labor were only a measure of their disadvantaged condition. Their silence is more telling. They lack a public identity. They remain profoundly alien. Persons apart. People lacking a union obviously, people without grounds. They depend upon the relative good will or fairness of their employers each day. For such people, lacking a better alternative, it is not such an unreasonable risk.

20   Their silence stays with me. I have taken these many words to describe its impact. Only: the quiet. Something uncanny about it. Its compliance. Vulnerability. Pathos. As I heard their truck rumbling away, I shuddered, my face mirrored with sweat. I had finally come face to face with *los pobres*.

MARGE PIERCY [B. 1936]

Born in Detroit, Michigan, to a working-class family, Marge Piercy attended the University of Michigan (B.A., 1957) and Northwestern University (M.A., 1958). Piercy began writing poems as a result of her involvement in the antiwar movement of the 1960s. In 1969, in reaction to what she considered the misogyny of many activists, she changed her focus to the growing women's movement. She has published many volumes of poetry, beginning with Breaking Camp *in 1968, and many novels.* City of Darkness, City of Light: A Novel *appeared in 1996, and her latest collection of poems,* The Hunger Moon, *was published in 2011. Much of her work is political, and she has expressed a desire for her writing to be "useful." She has written: "To find ourselves spoken for in art gives dignity to our pain, our anger, our lust, our losses. We can hear what we hope for and what we most fear in the small release of cadenced utterance."*

TO BE OF USE   [1973]

The people I love the best
jump into work head first
without dallying in the shallows
and swim off with sure strokes almost out of sight.

They seem to become natives of that element,   5
the black sleek heads of seals
bouncing like half-submerged balls.

I love people who harness themselves, an ox to a heavy cart,
who pull like water buffalo, with massive patience,
who strain in the mud and the muck to move things forward,   10
who do what has to be done, again and again.

I want to be with people who submerge
in the task, who go into the fields to harvest
and work in a row and pass the bags along,
who are not parlor generals and field deserters   15
but move in common rhythm
when the food must come in or the fire be put out.

The work of the world is common as mud,
Botched, it smears the hands, crumbles to dust.
But the thing worth doing well done   20
has a shape that satisfies, clean and evident.
Greek amphoras for wine or oil,
Hopi vases that held corn, are put in museums
but you know they were made to be used.
The pitcher cries for water to carry   25
and a person for work that is real.

MAKING CONNECTIONS

1. What is the tone of the Rodriguez essay? Do you think the narrator sees himself as better than the workers he describes? Explain.
2. What does the writer mean by "Their objections seemed to me challenges"?
3. To what extent have you experienced hard, physical labor? Does your experience of it match the writer's? Could you say, "I liked the way my body felt sore at the end of the day"? Explain.
4. The writer says, "I would not learn in three months what my father had meant by 'real work.'" Explain.
5. With reference to the Mexican workers, the writer says, "What made me different from them was an attitude of *mind,* my imagination of myself...." What does he mean?
6. In what way has the author/narrator "grown" from the experience he describes here? What do you think he wants us to understand from his essay?
7. Do you agree with the premise of Piercy's poem—that it's important "to be of use"? Why?
8. The speaker says that Greek amphoras and Hopi vases "are put in museums/but you know they were made to be used." What does she mean?

MAKING AN ARGUMENT

1. How important is usefulness in our culture? We live in a culture where people often identify themselves by what they do for a living. But how do we get our identities from our work? Both Rodriguez and Piercy address this issue, but seem to approach it from different directions. Write a comparison of "Workers" and "To Be of Use" and how each addresses the issue of identity and work. Cite the text of both for support.

FREDERICK DOUGLASS [1818–1895]

Frederick Douglass was born a slave on a plantation in Maryland. His father was probably a white overseer. After being separated from his mother at the age of eight, Douglass worked first in the household of a wealthy family and then as a field hand, where he suffered brutal beatings. In 1838, when he was twenty-one, Douglass escaped to the North. Fearful because of his fugitive slave status, Douglass nevertheless attracted public notice after delivering a powerful antislavery speech at an abolitionist convention in Nantucket, and he was subsequently asked to become a full-time speaker on behalf of the Massachusetts Anti-Slavery Society. In 1845, he published his harrowing and inspiring Narrative of the Life of Frederick Douglass, an American Slave, *which he later revised and titled the* Life and Times of Frederick Douglass. *The book made him famous and, consequently, more at risk. He moved to England, where he lectured extensively, eventually earning enough money to buy his freedom and return to the United States. A tireless advocate for the rights of African Americans and women, he spent the rest of life in the public eye, holding a number of governmental and political positions and publishing his own newspaper,* The North Star.

LEARNING TO READ AND WRITE   [1845]

I lived in Master Hugh's family about seven years. During this time, I succeeded in learning to read and write. In accomplishing this, I was compelled to resort to various stratagems. I had no regular teacher. My mistress, who had kindly commenced to instruct me, had, in compliance with the advice and direction of her husband, not only ceased to instruct, but had set her face against my being instructed by any one else. It is due, however, to my mistress to say of her, that she did not adopt this course of treatment immediately. She at first lacked the depravity indispensable to shutting me up in mental darkness. It was at least necessary for her to have some training in the exercise of irresponsible power, to make her equal to the task of treating me as though I were a brute.

My mistress was, as I have said, a kind and tender-hearted woman; and in the simplicity of her soul she commenced, when I first went to live with her, to treat me as she supposed one human being ought to treat another. In entering upon the duties of a slaveholder, she did not seem to perceive that I sustained to her the relation of a mere chattel, and that for her to treat me as a human being was not only wrong, but dangerously so. Slavery proved as injurious to her as it did to me. When I went there, she was a pious, warm, and tender-hearted woman. There was no sorrow or suffering for which she had not a tear. She had bread for the hungry, clothes for the naked, and comfort for every mourner that came within her reach. Slavery soon proved its ability to divest her of these heavenly qualities. Under its influence, the tender heart became stone, and the lamblike disposition gave way to one of tiger-like fierceness. The first step in her downward course was in her ceasing to instruct me. She now commenced to practice her husband's precepts. She finally became even more violent in her opposition than her husband himself. She was not satisfied with simply doing as well as he had commanded; she seemed anxious to do better. Nothing seemed to make her more angry than to see me with a newspaper. She seemed to think that here lay the danger. I have had her rush at me with a face made all up of fury, and snatch from me a newspaper, in a manner that fully revealed her apprehension. She was an apt woman; and a little experience soon demonstrated, to her satisfaction, that education and slavery were incompatible with each other.

From this time I was most narrowly watched. If I was in a separate room any considerable length of time, I was sure to be suspected of having a book, and was at once called to give an account of myself. All this, however, was too late. The first step had been taken. Mistress, in teaching me the alphabet, had given me the *inch*, and no precaution could prevent me from taking the *ell*.

The plan which I adopted, and the one by which I was most successful, was that of making friends of all the little white boys whom I met in the street. As many of these as I could, I converted into teachers. With their kindly aid, obtained at different times and in different places, I finally succeeded in learning to read. When I was sent on errands, I always took my book with me, and by going one part of my errand quickly, I found time to get a lesson before my return. I used also to carry bread with me, enough of which was always in the house, and to which I was always welcome; for I was much better off in this regard than many of the poor white children in our neighborhood. This bread I used to bestow upon the hungry little urchins, who, in return, would give me that more valuable bread of knowledge. I am strongly tempted to give the names of two or three of those little boys, as a testimonial of the gratitude and affection I bear them; but prudence forbids; not that it would injure me, but it might embarrass them; for it is almost an unpardonable offence to teach slaves to read in this Christian country. It is enough to say of the dear little fellows, that they lived on Philpot Street, very near Durgin and Bailey's ship-yard. I used to talk this matter of slavery over with them. I would sometimes say to them, I wished I could be as free as they would be when they got to be men. "You will be free as soon as you are twenty-one, *but I am a slave for life!* Have not I as good a right to be free as you have?" These words used to trouble them; they would express for me the liveliest sympathy, and console me with the hope that something would occur by which I might be free.

5   I was now about twelve years old, and the thought of being *a slave for life* began to bear heavily upon my heart. Just about this time, I got hold of a book entitled "The Columbian Orator." Every opportunity I got, I used to read this book.

Among much of other interesting matter, I found in it a dialogue between a master and his slave. The slave was represented as having run away from his master three times. The dialogue represented the conversation which took place between them, when the slave was retaken the third time. In this dialogue, the whole argument in behalf of slavery was brought forward by the master, all of which was disposed of by the slave. The slave was made to say some very smart as well as impressive things in reply to his master—things which had the desired though unexpected effect; for the conversation resulted in the voluntary emancipation of the slave on the part of the master.

In the same book, I met with one of Sheridan's mighty speeches on and in behalf of Catholic emancipation. These were choice documents to me. I read them over and over again with unabated interest. They gave tongue to interesting thoughts of my own soul, which had frequently flashed through my mind, and died away for want of utterance. The moral which I gained from the dialogue was the power of truth over the conscience of even a slaveholder. What I got from Sheridan was a bold denunciation of slavery, and a powerful vindication of human rights. The reading of these documents enabled me to utter my thoughts, and to meet the arguments brought forward to sustain slavery; but while they relieved me of one difficulty, they brought on another even more painful than the one of which I was relieved. The more I read, the more I was led to abhor and detest my enslavers. I could regard them in no other light than a band of successful robbers, who had left their homes, and gone to Africa, and stolen us from our homes, and in a strange land reduced us to slavery. I loathed them as being the meanest as well as the most wicked of men. As I read and contemplated the subject, behold! that very discontentment which Master Hugh had predicted would follow my learning to read had already come, to torment and sting my soul to unutterable anguish. As I writhed under it, I would at times feel that learning to read had been a curse rather than a blessing. It had given me a view of my wretched condition, without the remedy. It opened my eyes to the horrible pit, but to no ladder upon which to get out. In moments of agony, I envied my fellow-slaves for their stupidity. I have often wished myself a beast. I preferred the condition of the meanest reptile to my own. Any thing, no matter what, to get rid of thinking! It was this everlasting thinking of my condition that tormented me. There was no getting rid of it. It was pressed upon me by every object within sight or hearing, animate or inanimate. The silver trump of freedom had roused my soul to eternal wakefulness. Freedom now appeared, to disappear no more forever. It was heard in every sound, and seen in every thing. It was ever present to torment me with a sense of my wretched condition. I saw nothing without seeing it, I heard nothing without hearing it, and felt nothing without feeling it. It looked from every star, it smiled in every calm, breathed in every wind, and moved in every storm.

I often found myself regretting my own existence, and wishing myself dead; and but for the hope of being free, I have no doubt but that I should have killed myself, or done something for which I should have been killed. While in this state of mind, I was eager to hear any one speak of slavery. I was a ready listener. Every little while, I could hear something about the abolitionists. It was some time before I found what the word meant. It was always used in such connections as to make it an interesting word to me. If a slave ran away and succeeded in getting clear, or if a slave killed his master, set fire to a barn, or did any thing very wrong in the mind of a slaveholder, it was spoken of as the fruit of *abolition*. Hearing the word in this connection very often, I set about learning what it meant. The dictionary afforded me little or no help. I found it was "the act of abolishing"; but then I did not know what was to be abolished. Here I was perplexed. I did not dare to ask any one about its meaning, for I was satisfied that it was something they wanted me to know very little about. After a patient waiting, I got one of our city papers, containing an account of the number of petitions from the north, praying for the abolition of slavery in the District of Columbia, and of the slave trade between the States. From this time I understood the words *abolition* and *abolitionist,* and always drew near when that word was spoken, expecting to hear something of importance to myself and fellow-slaves. The light broke in upon me by degrees. I went one day down on the wharf of Mr. Waters; and seeing two Irishmen unloading a scow of stone, I went, unasked, and helped them. When we had finished, one of them came to me and asked me if I were a slave. I told him I was. He asked, "Are ye a slave for life?" I told him that I was. The good Irishman seemed to be deeply affected by the statement. He said to the other that it was a pity so fine a little fellow as myself should be a slave for life. He said it was a shame to hold me. They both advised me to run away to the north; that I should find friends there, and that I should be free. I pretended not to be interested in what they said, and treated them as if I did not understand them; for I feared they might be treacherous. White men have been known to encourage slaves to escape, and then, to get the reward, catch them and return them to their masters. I was afraid that these seemingly good men might use me so; but I nevertheless remembered their advice, and from that time I resolved to run away. I looked forward to a time at which it would be safe for me to escape. I was too young to think of doing so immediately; besides, I wished to learn how to write, as I might have occasion to write my own pass. I consoled myself with the hope that I should one day find a good chance. Meanwhile, I would learn to write.

The idea as to how I might learn to write was suggested to me by being in Durgin and Bailey's ship-yard, and frequently seeing the ship carpenters, after hewing, and getting a piece of timber ready to use, write on the timber the name of that part of the ship for which it was intended. When a piece of timber was intended for the larboard side, it would be marked thus—"L." When a piece was for the starboard side, it would be marked thus—"S." A piece for the larboard side forward, would be marked thus—"L. F." When a piece was for starboard side forward, it would be marked thus—"S. F." For larboard aft, it would be marked thus—"L. A." For starboard aft, it would be marked thus—"S. A." I soon learned the names of these letters, and for what they were intended when placed upon a piece of timber in the ship-yard. I immediately commenced copying them, and in a short time was able to make the four letters named. After that, when I met with any boy who I knew could write, I would tell him I could write as well as he. The next word would be, "I don't believe you. Let me see you try it." I would then make the letters which I had been so fortunate as to learn, and ask him to beat that. In this way I got a good many lessons in writing, which it is quite possible I should never have gotten in any other way. During this time, my copy-book was the board fence, brick wall, and pavement; my pen and ink was a lump of chalk. With these, I learned mainly how to write. I then commenced and continued copying the Italics in Webster's Spelling Book, until I could make them all without looking on the book. By this time, my little Master Thomas had gone to school, and learned how to write, and had written over a number of copy-books. These had been brought home, and shown to some of our near neighbors, and then laid aside. My mistress used to go to class meeting at the Wilk Street meetinghouse every Monday afternoon, and leave me to take care of the house. When left thus, I used to spend the time in writing in the spaces left in Master Thomas's copy-book, copying what he had written. I continued to do this until I could write a hand very similar to that of Master Thomas. Thus, after a long, tedious effort for years, I finally succeeded in learning how to write.

MAKING CONNECTIONS

1. Imagine yourself in Frederick Douglass's position as a slave. Would you run away as he did or would you accept your plight? Explain. Imagine yourself as a person who was in a position to help a runaway slave. How would you respond?
2. Why does Master Hugh's wife change her mind about helping Douglass to read and write?
3. What similarities does Douglass find between his own situation and the struggle for Catholic emancipation in Ireland? What does he learn from *The Columbian Orator*?
4. In what way is Douglass's learning to read and write a powerful statement against the evil of slavery?

MAKING AN ARGUMENT

1. Of all the things he could be taught, why are reading and writing the most important skill for Douglass to learn? Write about the importance of reading and writing for him as well as for anyone who wants to be successful in contemporary society. Cite the text of the essay for support.

MARTIN LUTHER KING, JR. [1929–1968]

Martin Luther King, Jr., was born in Atlanta, Georgia. His father was a minister, and his mother, a teacher. He received a B.A. from Morehouse College in 1951, a Ph.D. from Boston University in 1955, and a D.D. from the Chicago Theological Seminary in 1957. King embraced the teachings of Indian leader Mahatma Gandhi, who preached nonviolence as a route to social reform. In 1955 and 1956, applying Gandhi's teaching, King became a national celebrity after organiz-ing a successful boycott of Montgomery, Alabama's, segregated bus system. In the following years, King moved to the forefront of the movement to dismantle all forms

*of segregation in the United States, organizing the march on Washington in 1963
and challenging the voting laws in Selma, Alabama, in 1965. In 1964, he became
the youngest man ever to win the Nobel Peace Prize. During his lifetime his publications included* Stride Toward Freedom: The Montgomery Story *(1958),* Why We
Can't Wait *(1964), and his famous open letter in which he defended his nonviolent
philosophy,* Letter from Birmingham City Jail *(1963), written while he was imprisoned for organizing protests. King was assassinated on April 4, 1968. "I Have a
Dream" was delivered on August 28, 1963, to an audience of over 250,000 who had
gathered at the Lincoln Memorial as part of the march on Washington.*

I HAVE A DREAM   [1963]

Five score years ago, a great American, in whose symbolic shadow we stand, signed
the Emancipation Proclamation. This momentous decree came as a great beacon
light of hope to millions of Negro slaves who had been seared in the flames of
withering injustice. It came as a joyous daybreak to end the long night of captivity.

But one hundred years later, we must face the tragic fact that the Negro is still
not free. One hundred years later, the life of the Negro is still sadly crippled by the
manacles of segregation and the chains of discrimination. One hundred years later,
the Negro lives on a lonely island of poverty in the midst of a vast ocean of material
prosperity. One hundred years later, the Negro is still languishing in the corners of
American society and finds himself an exile in his own land. So we have come here
today to dramatize an appalling condition.

In a sense we have come to our nation's Capitol to cash a check. When the
architects of our republic wrote the magnificent words of the Constitution and the
Declaration of Independence, they were signing a promissory note to which every
American was to fall heir. This note was a promise that all men would be guaranteed the unalienable rights of life, liberty, and the pursuit of happiness.

It is obvious today that America has defaulted on this promissory note insofar
as her citizens of color are concerned. Instead of honoring this sacred obligation,
America has given the Negro people a bad check; a check which has come back
marked "insufficient funds." But we refuse to believe that the bank of justice is
bankrupt. We refuse to believe that there are insufficient funds in the great vaults
of opportunity of this nation. So we have come to cash this check—a check that
will give us upon demand the riches of freedom and the security of justice. We have
also come to this hallowed spot to remind America of the fierce urgency of *now.*
This is no time to engage in the luxury of cooling off or to take the tranquilizing
drug of gradualism. *Now* is the time to make real the promises of Democracy. *Now*
is the time to rise from the dark and desolate valley of segregation to the sunlit path
of racial justice. *Now* is the time to open the doors of opportunity to all of God's
children. *Now* is the time to lift our nation from the quicksands of racial injustice to
the solid rock of brotherhood.

5   It would be fatal for the nation to overlook the urgency of the moment and
to underestimate the determination of the Negro. This sweltering summer of the
Negro's legitimate discontent will not pass until there is an invigorating autumn of
freedom and equality. 1963 is not an end, but a beginning. Those who hope that the

Negro needed to blow off steam and will now be content will have a rude awakening if the nation returns to business as usual. There will be neither rest nor tranquility in America until the Negro is granted his citizenship rights. The whirlwinds of revolt will continue to shake the foundations of our nation until the bright day of justice emerges.

But there is something I must say to my people who stand on the warm threshold which leads into the palace of justice. In the process of gaining our rightful place we must not be guilty of wrongful deeds. Let us not seek to satisfy our thirst for freedom by drinking from the cup of bitterness and hatred. We must forever conduct our struggle on the high plane of dignity and discipline. We must not allow our creative protest to degenerate into physical violence. Again and again we must rise to the majestic heights of meeting physical force with soul force. The marvelous new militancy which has engulfed the Negro community must not lead us to a distrust of all white people, for many of our white brothers, as evidenced by their presence here today, have come to realize that their destiny is tied up with our destiny and their freedom is inextricably bound to our freedom. We cannot walk alone.

And as we walk, we must make the pledge that we shall march ahead. We cannot turn back. There are those who are asking the devotees of civil rights, "When will you be satisfied?" We can never be satisfied as long as the Negro is the victim of the unspeakable horrors of police brutality. We can never be satisfied as long as our bodies, heavy with the fatigue of travel, cannot gain lodging in the motels of the highways and the hotels of the cities. We cannot be satisfied as long as the Negro's basic mobility is from a smaller ghetto to a larger one. We can never be satisfied as long as a Negro in Mississippi cannot vote and a Negro in New York believes he has nothing for which to vote. No, no, we are not satisfied, and we will not be satisfied until justice rolls down like waters and righteousness like a mighty stream.

I am not unmindful that some of you have come here out of great trials and tribulations. Some of you have come fresh from narrow jail cells. Some of you have come from areas where your quest for freedom left you battered by the storms of persecution and staggered by the winds of policy brutality. You have been the veterans of creative suffering. Continue to work with the faith that unearned suffering is redemptive.

Go back to Mississippi, go back to Alabama, go back to South Carolina, go back to Georgia, go back to Louisiana, go back to the slums and ghettoes of our northern cities, knowing that somehow this situation can and will be changed. Let us not wallow in the valley of despair.

10   I say to you today, my friends, that in spite of the difficulties and frustrations of the moment I still have a dream. It is a dream deeply rooted in the American dream.

I have a dream that one day this nation will rise up and live out the true meaning of its creed: "We hold these truths to be self-evident; that all men are created equal."

I have a dream that one day on the red hills of Georgia the sons of former slaves and the sons of former slaveowners will be able to sit down together at the table of brotherhood.

I have a dream that the state of Mississippi, a desert state sweltering with the heat of injustice and oppression, will be transformed into an oasis of freedom and justice.

I have a dream that my four little children will one day live in a nation where they will not be judged by the color of their skin but by the content of their character.

15   I have a dream today.

I have a dream that the state of Alabama, whose governor's lips are presently dripping with the words of interposition and nullification, will be transformed into a situation where little black boys and black girls will be able to join hands with little white boys and white girls and walk together as sisters and brothers.

I have a dream today.

I have a dream that one day every valley shall be exalted, every hill and mountain shall be made low, the rough places will be made plain, and the crooked places will be made straight, and the glory of the Lord shall be revealed, and all flesh shall see it together.

This is our hope. This is the faith with which I return to the South. With this faith we will be able to hew out of the mountain of despair a stone of hope. With this faith we will be able to transform the jangling discords of our nation into a beautiful symphony of brotherhood. With this faith we will be able to work together, to pray together, to struggle together, to go to jail together, to stand up for freedom together, knowing that we will be free one day.

20   This will be the day when all of God's children will be able to sing with new meaning.

> My country, tis of thee
> Sweet land of liberty,
>   Of thee I sing:
> Land where my fathers died,
> Land of the pilgrims' pride,
> From every mountainside
>   Let freedom ring.

And if America is to be a great nation this must become true. So let freedom ring from the prodigious hilltops of New Hampshire. Let freedom ring from the mighty mountains of New York. Let freedom ring from the heightening Alleghenies of Pennsylvania!

Let freedom ring from the snowcapped Rockies of Colorado!

Let freedom ring from the curvaceous peaks of California!

But not only that; let freedom ring from Stone Mountain of Georgia!

25   Let freedom ring from Lookout Mountain of Tennessee!

Let freedom ring from every hill and molehill of Mississippi. From every mountainside, let freedom ring.

When we let freedom ring, when we let it ring from every village and every hamlet, from every state and every city, we will be able to speed up that day when all of God's children, black men and white men, Jews and Gentiles, Protestants and Catholics, will be able to join hands and sing in the words of the old Negro spiritual, "Free at last! Free at last! Thank God almighty, we are free at last!"

MAKING CONNECTIONS

1. What is the dream of Martin Luther King, Jr.?
2. He says his dream is derived from the "American Dream." What is the American Dream?
3. What does he mean by "This will be the day when all of God's children will be able to sing with new meaning 'My country, tis of thee / Sweet land of liberty'"?
4. What is the tone of this essay? Who is the intended audience? What is its objective?

MAKING AN ARGUMENT

1. This is both an inspirational speech and an effective essay. Analyze the style, structure, and use of figurative language—especially the imagery—in the essay, and write about its effectiveness. Cite the text of the essay for support.

HENRY DAVID THOREAU [1817–1862]

Henry David Thoreau was born and raised in Concord, Massachusetts, to a hardworking but poor family. As a child, he worked at home in a so-called "family-circle" factory making pencils. Determined to get an education, he worked his way through Harvard, and afterward, held a series of posts as a teacher. Beginning in 1843, while working as a handyman at the house of the poet and philosopher Ralph Waldo Emerson, Thoreau became a part of the Transcen-
dentalist movement—an influential circle of American writers and thinkers who believed that the earth was a microcosm of the entire universe, and that the human soul was the same as that of the "Over-Soul." From 1845 to 1847, on land owned by Emerson, Thoreau lived in a cabin he built on Walden Pond in an effort to "front only the essential facts of life." He later edited the journal he kept during this period—Thoreau kept a journal his entire life—and in 1854 published it as Walden: or, Life in the Woods, *which, though it attracted little notice during his lifetime, has become one of the most influential books in American literature. After Thoreau returned to the world, he worked for a time in his family's pencil business, and later traveled to Canada, Maine, Minnesota, Cape Cod, and New York. Politically active (as in the excerpt below from his famous tract "Civil Disobedience," an explanation of his refusal to pay a poll tax while at Walden), he spoke publicly on many issues, most notably against the Fugitive Slave Law. He died in 1862 of tuberculosis, following a trip to Minnesota.*

FROM *CIVIL DISOBEDIENCE*   [1849]

How can a man be satisfied to entertain an opinion merely, and enjoy *it?* Is there any enjoyment in it, if his opinion is that he is aggrieved? If you are cheated out of a single dollar by your neighbor, you do not rest satisfied with knowing that you are cheated, or with saying that you are cheated, or even with petitioning him to pay you your due; but you take effectual steps at once to obtain the full amount, and see that you are never cheated again. Action from principle, the perception and the performance of right, changes things and relations; it is essentially revolutionary, and does not consist wholly with anything which was. It not only divides states and churches, it divides families; ay, it divides the *individual,* separating the diabolical in him from the divine.

Unjust laws exist: shall we be content to obey them, or shall we endeavor to amend them, and obey them until we have succeeded, or shall we transgress them at once? Men generally, under such a government as this, think that they ought to wait until they have persuaded the majority to alter them. They think that, if they should resist, the remedy would be worse than the evil. But it is the fault of the government itself that the remedy *is* worse than the evil. *It* makes it worse. Why is it not more apt to anticipate and provide for reform? Why does it not cherish its wise minority? Why does it cry and resist before it is hurt? Why does it not encourage its citizens to be on the alert to point out its faults and *do* better than it would have them? Why does it always crucify Christ, and excommunicate Copernicus and Luther, and pronounce Washington and Franklin rebels?

. . . . .

I meet this American government, or its representative, the state government, directly, and face to face, once a year—no more—in the person of its tax-gatherer; this is the only mode in which a man situated as I am necessarily meets it; and it then says distinctly, Recognize me; and the simplest, most effectual, and, in the present posture of affairs, the indispensablest mode of treating with it on this head, of expressing your little satisfaction with and love for it, is to deny it then. My civil neighbor, the tax-gatherer, is the very man I have to deal with,—for it is, after all, with men and not with parchment that I quarrel,—and he has voluntarily chosen to be an agent of the government. How shall he ever know well what he is and does as an officer of the government, or as a man, until he is obliged to consider whether he shall treat me, his neighbor, for whom he has respect, as a neighbor and well-disposed man, or as a maniac and disturber of the peace, and see if he can get over this obstruction to his neighborliness without a ruder and more impetuous thought or speech corresponding with his action. I know this well, that if one thousand, if one hundred, if ten men whom I could name,—if ten *honest* men only,—ay, if *one* HONEST man, in this State of Massachusetts, *ceasing to hold slaves,* were actually to withdraw from this co-partnership, and be locked up in the county jail therefore, it would be the abolition of slavery in America. For it matters not how small the beginning may seem to be: what is once well done is done forever. But we love better to talk about it: that we say is our mission. Reform keeps many scores of newspapers in its service, but not one man. If my esteemed neighbor, the State's ambassador, who will devote his days to the settlement of the question of human rights in the Council Chamber, instead of being threatened with the prisons of Carolina, were to sit down the prisoner of Massachusetts, that State which is so anxious to foist the sin of slavery upon her sister,—though at present she can discover only an act of inhospitality to be the ground of a quarrel with her,—the Legislature would not wholly waive the subject the following winter.

Under a government which imprisons any unjustly, the true place for a just man is also a prison. The proper place to-day, the only place which Massachusetts has provided for her freer and less desponding spirits, is in her prisons, to be put out and locked out of the State by her own act, as they have already put themselves out by their principles. It is there that the fugitive slave, and the Mexican prisoner on parole, and the Indian come to plead the wrongs of his race should find them; on that separate, but more free and honorable ground, where the State places those who are not *with* her, but *against* her,—the only house in a slave State in which a free man can abide with honor. If any think that their influence would be lost there, and their voices no longer afflict the ear of the State, that they would not be as an enemy within its walls, they do not know by how much truth is stronger than error, nor how much more eloquently and effectively he can combat injustice who has experienced a little in his own person. Cast your whole vote, not a strip of paper merely, but your whole influence. A minority is powerless while it conforms to the majority; it is not even a minority then; but it is irresistible when it clogs by its whole weight. If the alternative is to keep all just men in prison, or give up war and slavery, the State will not hesitate which to choose. If a thousand men were not to pay their tax bills this year, that would not be a violent and bloody measure, as it would be to pay them, and enable the State to commit violence and shed innocent blood. This is, in fact, the definition of a peaceable revolution, if any such is possible. If the tax-gatherer, or any other public officer, asks me, as one has done, "But what shall I do?" my answer is, "If you really wish to do anything, resign your office." When the subject has refused allegiance, and the officer has resigned his office, then the revolution is accomplished. But even suppose blood should flow. Is there not a sort of blood shed when the conscience is wounded? Through this wound a man's real manhood and immortality flow out, and he bleeds to an everlasting death. I see this blood flowing now....

MAKING CONNECTIONS

1. Do you think it's ever permissible to break the law? Explain.
2. How well does Thoreau make his point? What are the major reasons he gives to justify these "disobedient" actions?

MAKING AN ARGUMENT

1. Compare this essay to Sophocles's *Antigonê* on page 113 and/or Plato's "The Allegory of the Cave" on page 1235. Cite the texts of each for support.

CASE STUDY IN CULTURAL CONTEXT

Writers of the Harlem Renaissance

The purpose of this Case Study is to provide you with historical and cultural material for a self-contained research unit on the writers of the Harlem Renaissance. It contains a small sample of the many works of poetry, fiction, and essays produced during a period of extraordinary creativity. Literature was only one aspect of an artistic explosion that included music, dance, painting, and sculpture.

What forces and circumstances came together to create this artistic and cultural renaissance? Perhaps the most important factor was the great migration of African Americans to the North following the end of post–Civil War Reconstruction in the South. Oppressive, legal segregation was endorsed by rulings of the U.S. Supreme Court. An official attitude and attendant actions that treated African Americans as less than human and unprotected before the law—including widespread lynchings—made it impossible for many African Americans to remain in the South. Though there is not universal agreement about how long this renaissance lasted or even its location in Harlem, New York City in the 1920s were essential to its flowering. Chicago, Philadelphia, and Cleveland were among other destinations favored by oppressed southern blacks, but New York City, the largest, most sophisticated, and diverse city in the country, was the most popular destination. And the timing was right. Real estate investment and speculation in Harlem created an overabundance of middle-class housing. Facing economic ruin, landlords were willing to break the color barrier and offer fashionable housing to all classes of blacks now migrating to the city, including leading artists, musicians, and writers. Harlem quickly became the strongest magnet for and primary producer of African American art, culture, and politics in the country.

The essays, poems, and fiction that follow are only a tiny sampling of what was produced by the writers of this period. Though their work is not included, W. E. B. Dubois, James Weldon Johnson, Arthur Schomburg, Marcus Garvey, Nella Larsen, Arna Bontemps, Sterling Brown, Wallace Thurman, Rudolph Fisher, Angela Weld Grimké, Helene Johnson, and others made important contributions to or had a significant influence on the work produced during this period. The work that follows represents a range of what was produced by these writers. It begins with Alain Locke's "The New Negro," a declaration of a new era and a call to break the stereotypes of African Americans long fostered in this country, and it ends with a retrospective on Zora Neale Hurston by Alice Walker. In between, much of the work represented is by Langston Hughes and Zora Neale Hurston, who are, perhaps, the two most prominent writers of this era. For the sake of comparison, two of Hughes's works written later in his career, the short story "One Friday Morning" and the poem "Theme for English B," are also included.

ALAIN LOCKE [1886–1954]

Alain Locke grew up in Philadelphia and graduated magna cum laude from Harvard University. He was the first African American to be a Rhodes Scholar and earned a degree from Oxford University in 1911. When he returned to the United States, he taught at Howard University, where he eventually became chair of the philosophy department. In addition to publishing a substantial body of his own work, he was an influential booster of the Harlem Renaissance and mentor for many of its artists, including Langston Hughes, Zora Neale Hurston, and Claude McKay.

THE NEW NEGRO   [1925]

In the last decade something beyond the watch and guard of statistics has happened in the life of the American Negro and the three norns[1] who have traditionally presided over the Negro problem have a changeling in their laps. The Sociologist, the Philanthropist, the Race-leader are not unaware of the New Negro, but they are at a loss to account for him. He simply cannot be swathed in their formulae. For the younger generation is vibrant with a new psychology; the new spirit is awake in the masses, and under the wary eyes of the professional observers is transforming what has been a perennial problem into the progressive phases of contemporary Negro life.

   Could such a metamorphosis have taken place as suddenly as it has appeared to? The answer is no; not because the New Negro is not here, but because the Old Negro had long become more of a myth than a man. The Old Negro, we must remember, was a creature of moral debate and historical controversy. His has been a stock figure perpetuated as an historical fiction partly in innocent sentimentalism, partly in deliberate reactionism. The Negro himself has contributed his share to this through a sort of protective social mimicry forced upon him by the adverse circumstances of dependence. So for generations in the mind of America, the Negro has been more of a formula than a human being—a something to be argued about, condemned or defended, to be "kept down," or "in his place," or "helped up," to be worried with or worried over, harassed or patronized, a social bogey or a social burden. The thinking Negro even has been induced to share this same general attitude, to focus his attention on controversial issues, to see himself in the distorted perspective of a social problem. His shadow, so to speak, has been more real to him than his personality. Through having had to appeal from the unjust stereotypes of his oppressors and traducers to those of his liberators, friends and benefactors he has had to subscribe to the traditional positions from which his

[1]**three norns** the three fates of Norse mythology

case has been viewed. Little true social or self-understanding has or could come from such a situation.

But while the minds of most of us, black and white, have thus burrowed in the trenches of the Civil War and Reconstruction, the actual march of development has simply flanked these positions, necessitating a sudden reorientation of view. We have not been watching in the right direction; set North and South on a sectional axis, we have not noticed the East till the sun has us blinking.

Recall how suddenly the Negro spirituals revealed themselves; suppressed for generations under the stereotypes of Wesleyan hymn[2] harmony, secretive, half-ashamed, until the courage of being natural brought them out—and behold, there was folk-music. Similarly, the mind of the Negro seems suddenly to have slipped from under the tyranny of social intimidation and to be shaking off the psychology of imitation and implied inferiority. By shedding the old chrysalis of the Negro problem we are achieving something like a spiritual emancipation. Until recently, lacking self-understanding, we have been almost as much of a problem to ourselves as we still are to others. But the decade[3] that found us with a problem has left us with only a task. The multitude perhaps feels as yet only a strange relief and a new vague urge, but the thinking few know that in the reaction the vital inner grip of prejudice has been broken.

5   With this renewed self-respect and self-dependence, the life of the Negro community is bound to enter a new dynamic phase, the buoyancy from within compensating for whatever pressure there may be of conditions from without. The migrant masses, shifting from countryside to city, hurdle several generations of experience at a leap, but more important, the same thing happens spiritually in the life-attitudes and self-expression of the Young Negro, in his poetry, his art, his education and his new outlook, with the additional advantage, of course, of the poise and greater certainty of knowing what it is all about. From this comes the promise and warrant of a new leadership. As one of them[4] has discerningly put it:

> We have tomorrow
> Bright before us
> Like a flame.
>
> Yesterday, a night-gone thing
> A sun-down name.
>
> And dawn today
> Broad arch above the road we came.
> We march!

This is what, even more than any "most creditable record of fifty years of freedom," requires that the Negro of today be seen through other than the dusty spectacles of past controversy. The day of "aunties," "uncles" and "mammies" is equally gone. Uncle Tom and Sambo have passed on, and even the "Colonel" and "George"[5] play barnstorm

---

[2]**Wesleyan hymn** after Charles Wesley (1707–1788), English hymnist and brother of John Wesley, founder of Methodism   [3]**decade** the 1920s   [4]**one of them** Langston Hughes (1902–1967). The following lines are from "Youth."   [5]**the "Colonel" and "George"** typical forms of interracial address during slavery and segregation

roles from which they escape with relief when the public spotlight is off. The popular melodrama has about played itself out, and it is time to scrap the fictions, garret the bogeys and settle down to a realistic facing of the facts.

First we must observe some of the changes which since the traditional lines of opinion were drawn have rendered these quite obsolete. A main change has been, of course, that shifting of the Negro population which has made the Negro problem no longer exclusively or even predominantly Southern. Why should our minds remain sectionalized, when the problem itself no longer is? Then the trend of migration has not only been toward the North and the Central Midwest, but city-ward and to the great centers of industry—the problems of adjustment are new, practical, local and not peculiarly racial. Rather they are an integral part of the large industrial and social problems of our present-day democracy. And finally, with the Negro rapidly in process of class differentiation, if it ever was warrantable to regard and treat the Negro *en masse* it is becoming with every day less possible, more unjust and more ridiculous.

In the very process of being transplanted, the Negro is becoming transformed.

The tide of the Negro migration, northward and city-ward, is not to be fully explained as a blind flood started by the demands of war industry coupled with the shutting off of foreign migration, or by the pressure of poor crops coupled with increased social terrorism in certain sections of the South and Southwest. Neither labor demand, the bollweevil[6] nor the Ku Klux Klan is a basic factor, however contributory any or all of them may have been. The wash and rush of this human tide on the beach line of the northern city centers is to be explained primarily in terms of a new vision of opportunity, of social and economic freedom, of a spirit to seize, even in the face of an extortionate and heavy toll, a chance for the improvement of conditions. With each successive wave of it, the movement of the Negro becomes more and more a mass movement toward the larger and the more democratic chance—in the Negro's case a deliberate flight not only from countryside to city, but from medieval America to modern.

10   Take Harlem as an instance of this. Here in Manhattan is not merely the largest Negro community in the world, but the first concentration in history of so many diverse elements of Negro life. It has attracted the African, the West Indian, the Negro American; has brought together the Negro of the North and the Negro of the South; the man from the city and man from the town and village; the peasant, the student, the business man, the professional man, artist, poet, musician, adventurer and worker, preacher and criminal, exploiter and social outcast. Each group has come with its own separate motives and for its own special ends, but their greatest experience has been the finding of one another. Proscription and prejudice have thrown these dissimilar elements into a common area of contact and interaction. Within this area, race sympathy and unity have determined a further fusing of sentiment and experience. So what began in terms of segregation becomes more and more, as its elements mix and react, the laboratory of a great race-welding. Hitherto, it must be admitted that American Negroes have been race more in name than in fact, or to be exact, more in sentiment than in experience. The chief bond

[6]**bollweevil** a snout beetle notorious for destroying cotton crops

between them has been that of a common condition rather than a common consciousness; a problem in common rather than a life in common. In Harlem, Negro life is seizing upon its first chances for group expression and self-determination. It is—or promises at least to be—a race capital. That is why our comparison is taken with those nascent centers of folk-expression and self-determination which are playing a creative part in the world today. Without pretense to their political significance, Harlem has the same role to play for the New Negro as Dublin has had for the New Ireland or Prague for the New Czechoslovakia.

Harlem, I grant you, isn't typical—but it is significant, it is prophetic. No sane observer, however sympathetic to the new trend, would contend that the great masses are articulate as yet, but they stir, they move, they are more than physically restless. The challenge of the new intellectuals among them is clear enough—the "race radicals" and realists who have broken with the old epoch of philanthropic guidance, sentimental appeal and protest. But are we after all only reading into the stirrings of a sleeping giant the dreams of an agitator? The answer is in the migrating peasant. It is the "man farthest down" who is most active in getting up. One of the most characteristic symptoms of this is the professional man, himself migrating to recapture his constituency after a vain effort to maintain in some Southern corner what for years back seemed an established living and clientele. The clergyman following his errant flock, the physician or lawyer trailing his clients, supply the true clues. In a real sense it is the rank and file who are leading, and the leaders who are following. A transformed and transforming psychology permeates the masses.

When the racial leaders of twenty years ago spoke of developing race-pride and stimulating race-consciousness, and of the desirability of race solidarity, they could not in any accurate degree have anticipated the abrupt feeling that has surged up and now pervades the awakened centers. Some of the recognized Negro leaders and a powerful section of white opinion identified with "race work" of the older order have indeed attempted to discount this feeling as a "passing phase," an attack of "race nerves" so to speak, an "aftermath of the war," and the like. It has not abated, however, if we are to gauge by the present tone and temper of the Negro press, or by the shift in popular support from the officially recognized and orthodox spokesmen to those of the independent, popular, and often radical type who are unmistakable symptoms of a new order. It is a social disservice to blunt the fact that the Negro of the Northern centers has reached a stage where tutelage, even of the most interested and well-intentioned sort, must give place to new relationships, where positive self-direction must be reckoned with in ever increasing measure. The American mind must reckon with a fundamentally changed Negro.

The Negro too, for his part, has idols of the tribe to smash. If on the one hand the white man has erred in making the Negro appear to be that which would excuse or extenuate his treatment of him, the Negro, in turn, has too often unnecessarily excused himself because of the way he has been treated. The intelligent Negro of today is resolved not to make discrimination an extenuation for his shortcomings in performance, individual or collective; he is trying to hold himself at par, neither inflated by sentimental allowances nor depreciated by current social discounts. For this he must know himself and be known for precisely what he is, and for that reason he welcomes the new scientific rather than the old sentimental interest. Sentimental interest in the Negro has ebbed. We used to lament this as the falling off of our friends; now we rejoice and pray to be delivered both from self-pity and condescension. The mind of each radical group has had a bitter weaning, apathy or hatred on one side matching disillusionment or resentment on the other; but they face each other today with the possibility at least of entirely new mutual attitudes.

It does not follow that if the Negro were better known, he would be better liked or better treated. But mutual understanding is basic for any subsequent cooperation and adjustment. The effort toward this will at least have the effect of remedying in large part what has been the most unsatisfactory feature of our present stage of race relationships in America, namely the fact that the more intelligent and representative elements of the two race groups have at so many points got quite out of vital touch with one another.

15   The fiction is that the life of the races is separate, and increasingly so. The fact is that they have touched too closely at the unfavorable and too lightly at the favorable levels.

While inter-racial councils have sprung up in the South, drawing on forward elements of both races, in the Northern cities manual laborers may brush elbows in their everyday work, but the community and business leaders have experienced no such interplay or far too little of it. These segments must achieve contact or the race situation in America becomes desperate. Fortunately this is happening. There is a growing realization that in social effort the cooperative basis must supplant long-distance philanthropy, and that the only safeguard for mass relations in the future must be provided in the carefully maintained contacts of the enlightened minorities of both race groups. In the intellectual realm a renewed and keen curiosity is replacing the recent apathy; the Negro is being carefully studied, not just talked about and discussed. In art and letters, instead of being wholly caricatured, he is being seriously portrayed and painted.

To all of this the New Negro is keenly responsive as an augury of a new democracy in American culture. He is contributing his share to the new social understanding. But the desire to be understood would never in itself have been sufficient to have opened so completely the protectively closed portals of the thinking Negro's mind. There is still too much possibility of being snubbed or patronized for that. It was rather the necessity for fuller, truer self-expression, the realization of the unwisdom of allowing social discrimination to segregate him mentally, and a counter-attitude to cramp and fetter his own living—and so the "spite-wall" that the intellectuals built over the "color-line" has happily been taken down. Much of this reopening of intellectual contacts has centered in New York and has been richly fruitful not merely in the enlarging of personal experience, but in the definite enrichment of American art and letters and in the classifying of our common vision of the social tasks ahead.

The particular significance in the re-establishment of contact between the more advanced and representative classes is that it promises to offset some of the unfavorable reactions of the past, or at least to re-surface race contacts somewhat for the future. Subtly the conditions that are molding a New Negro are molding a new American attitude.

However, this new phase of things is delicate; it will call for less charity but more justice; less help, but infinitely closer understanding. This is indeed a critical stage of race relationships because of the likelihood, if the new temper is not understood, of engendering sharp group antagonism and a second crop of more calculated prejudice. In some quarters, it has already done so. Having weaned the Negro, public opinion cannot continue to paternalize. The Negro today is inevitably moving forward under the control largely of his own objectives. What are these objectives? Those of his outer life are happily already well and finally formulated, for they are none other than the ideals of American institutions and democracy. Those of his inner life are yet in process of formation, for the new psychology at present is more of a consensus of feeling than of opinion, of attitude rather than of program. Still some points seem to have crystallized.

20   Up to the present one may adequately describe the Negro's "inner objectives" as an attempt to repair a damaged group psychology and reshape a warped social perspective. Their realization has required a new mentality for the American Negro. And as it matures we begin to see its effects; at first, negative, iconoclastic, and then positive and constructive. In this new group psychology we note the lapse of sentimental appeal, then the development of a more positive self-respect and self-reliance; the repudiation of social dependence, and then the gradual recovery from hyper-sensitiveness and "touchy" nerves, the repudiation of the double standard of judgment with its special philanthropic allowances and then the sturdier desire for objective and scientific appraisal; and finally the rise from social disillusionment to race pride, from the sense of social debt to the responsibilities of social contribution, and offsetting the necessary working and common-sense acceptance of restricted conditions, the belief in ultimate esteem and recognition. Therefore the Negro today wishes to be known for what he is, even in his faults and shortcomings, and scorns a craven and precarious survival at the price of seeming to be what he is not. He resents being spoken of as a social ward or minor, even by his own, and to being regarded a chronic patient for the sociological clinic, the sick man of American Democracy. For the same reasons, he himself is through with those social nostrums and panaceas, the so-called "solutions" of his "problem," with which he and the country have been so liberally dosed in the past. Religion, freedom, education, money—in turn, he has ardently hoped for and peculiarly trusted these things; he still believes in them, but not in blind trust that they alone will solve his life-problem.

Each generation, however, will have its creed, and that of the present is the belief in the efficacy of collective effort, in race cooperation. This deep feeling of race is at present the mainspring of Negro life. It seems to be the outcome of the reaction to proscription and prejudice; an attempt, fairly successful on the whole, to convert a defensive into an offensive position, a handicap into an incentive. It is radical in tone, but not in purpose and only the most stupid forms of opposition, misunderstanding or persecution could make it otherwise. Of course, the thinking Negro has shifted a little toward the left with the world-trend, and there is an increasing group who affiliate with radical and liberal movements. But fundamentally for the present the Negro is radical on race matters, conservative on others, in other words, a "forced radical," a social protestant rather than a genuine radical. Yet under further pressure and injustice iconoclastic thought and motives will inevitably increase. Harlem's quixotic radicalisms call for their ounce of democracy today lest tomorrow they be beyond cure.

The Negro mind reaches out as yet to nothing but American wants, American ideas. But this forced attempt to build his Americanism on race values is a unique social experiment, and its ultimate success is impossible except through the fullest sharing of American culture and institutions. There should be no delusion about this. American nerves in sections unstrung with race hysteria are often fed the opiate that the trend of Negro advance is wholly separatist, and that the effect of its operation will be to encyst the Negro as a benign foreign body in the body politic. This cannot be—even if it were desirable. The racialism of the Negro is no limitation or reservation with respect to American life; it is only a constructive effort to build the obstructions in the stream of his progress into an efficient dam of social energy and power. Democracy itself is obstructed and stagnated to the extent that any of its channels are closed. Indeed they cannot be selectively closed. So the choice is not between one way for the Negro and another way for the rest, but between American institutions frustrated on the one hand and American ideals progressively fulfilled and realized on the other.

There is, of course, a warrantably comfortable feeling in being on the right side of the country's professed ideals. We realize that we cannot be undone without America's undoing. It is within the gamut of this attitude that the thinking Negro faces America, but with variations of mood that are if anything more significant than the attitude itself. Sometimes we have it taken with the defiant ironic challenge of McKay:[7]

> Mine is the future grinding down to-day
> Like a great landslip moving to the sea,
> Bearing its freight of debris far away
> Where the green hungry waters restlessly
> Heave mammoth pyramids, and break and roar
> Their eerie challenge to the crumbling shore.

Sometimes, perhaps more frequently as yet, it is taken in the fervent and almost filial appeal and counsel of Weldon Johnson's:[8]

> O Southland, dear Southland!
> Then why do you still cling
> To an idle age and a musty page,
> To a dead and useless thing?

But between defiance and appeal, midway almost between cynicism and hope, the prevailing mind stands in the mood of the same author's *To America*,[9] an attitude of sober query and stoical challenge:

> How would you have us, as we are?
>   Or sinking 'neath the load we bear,
> Our eyes fixed forward on a star,
>   Or gazing empty at despair?

---

[7]**McKay** Claude McKay (1889–1948). Harlem Renaissance poet   [8]**Weldon Johnson's** from *O Southland!* (1907)   [9]***To America*** published in 1917

> Rising or falling? Men or things?
>   With dragging pace or footsteps fleet?
> Strong, willing sinews in your wings,
>   Or tightening chains about your feet?

More and more, however, an intelligent realization of the great discrepancy between the American social creed and the American social practice forces upon the
Negro the taking of the moral advantage that is his. Only the steadying and sobering
effect of a truly characteristic gentleness of spirit prevents the rapid rise of a definite
cynicism and counter-hate and a defiant superiority feeling. Human as this reaction
would be, the majority still deprecate its advent, and would gladly see it forestalled
by the speedy amelioration of its causes. We wish our race pride to be a healthier,
more positive achievement than a feeling based upon a realization of the shortcomings of others. But all paths toward the attainment of a sound social attitude have
been difficult; only a relatively few enlightened minds have been able as the phrase
puts it "to rise above" prejudice. The ordinary man has had until recently only a
hard choice between the alternatives of supine and humiliating submission and
stimulating but hurtful counter-prejudice. Fortunately from some inner, desperate
resourcefulness has recently sprung up the simple expedient of fighting prejudice
by mental passive resistance, in other words by trying to ignore it. For the few, this
manna may perhaps be effective, but the masses cannot thrive upon it.

25   Fortunately there are constructive channels opening out into which the balked
social feelings of the American Negro can flow freely.

Without them there would be much more pressure and danger than there is.
These compensating interests are racial but in a new and enlarged way. One is the
consciousness of acting as the advance-guard of the African peoples in their contact
with Twentieth Century civilization; the other, the sense of mission of rehabilitating
the race in world esteem from that loss of prestige for which the fate and conditions
of slavery have so largely been responsible. Harlem, as we shall see, is the center of
both these movements; she is the home of the Negro's "Zionism."[10] The pulse of the
Negro world has begun to beat in Harlem. A Negro newspaper carrying news material in English, French and Spanish, gathered from all quarters of America, the West
Indies and Africa has maintained itself in Harlem for over five years. Two important magazines,[11] both edited from New York, maintain their news and circulation
consistently on a cosmopolitan scale. Under American auspices and backing, three
pan-African congresses have been held abroad for the discussion of common interests, colonial questions and the future cooperative development of Africa. In terms
of the race question as a world problem, the Negro mind has leapt, so to speak,
upon the parapets of prejudice and extended its cramped horizons. In so doing it
has linked up with the growing group consciousness of the dark-peoples and is
gradually learning their common interests. As one of our writers has recently put it:
"It is imperative that we understand the white world in its relations to the non-white
world." As with the Jew, persecution is making the Negro international.

---

[10]**"Zionism"** an international movement aimed at securing a homeland for the Jewish
people   [11]**magazines** probably *Opportunity* and the *Crisis*

As a world phenomenon this wider race consciousness is a different thing from the much asserted rising tide of color. Its inevitable causes are not of our making. The consequences are not necessarily damaging to the best interests of civilization. Whether it actually brings into being new Armadas[12] of conflict or argosies[13] of cultural exchange and enlightenment can only be decided by the attitude of the dominant races in an era of critical change. With the American Negro, his new internationalism is primarily an effort to recapture contact with the scattered peoples of African derivation. Garveyism[14] may be a transient, if spectacular, phenomenon, but the possible role of the American Negro in the future development of Africa is one of the most constructive and universally helpful missions that any modern people can lay claim to.

Constructive participation in such causes cannot help giving the Negro valuable group incentives, as well as increased prestige at home and abroad. Our greatest rehabilitation may possibly come through such channels, but for the present, more immediate hope rests in the revaluation by white and black alike of the Negro in terms of his artistic endowments and cultural contributions, past and prospective. It must be increasingly recognized that the Negro has already made very substantial contributions, not only in his folk-art, music especially, which has always found appreciation, but in larger, though humbler and less acknowledged ways. For generations the Negro has been the peasant matrix of that section of America which has most undervalued him, and here he has contributed not only materially in labor and in social patience, but spiritually as well. The South has unconsciously absorbed the gift of his folk-temperament. In less than half a generation it will be easier to recognize this, but the fact remains that a leaven of humor, sentiment, imagination and tropic nonchalance has gone into the making of the South from a humble, unacknowledged source. A second crop of the Negro's gifts promises still more largely. He now becomes a conscious contributor and lays aside the status of a beneficiary and ward for that of a collaborator and participant in American civilization. The great social gain in this is the releasing of our talented group from the arid fields of controversy and debate to the productive fields of creative expression. The especially cultural recognition they win should in him prove the key to that revaluation of the Negro which must precede or accompany any considerable further betterment of race relationships. But whatever the general effect, the present generation will have added the motives of self-expression and spiritual development to the old and still unfinished task of making material headway and progress. No one who understandingly faces the situation with its substantial accomplishment or views the new scene with its still more abundant promise can be entirely without hope. And certainly, if in our lifetime the Negro should not be able to celebrate his full initiation into American democracy, he can at least, on the warrant of these things, celebrate the attainment of a significant and satisfying new phase of group development, and with it a spiritual Coming of Age.

---

[12]**Armadas** fleets of warships   [13]**argosies** merchant ships   [14]**Garveyism** the Back to Africa movement of Marcus Garvey (1887–1940)

Archibald J. Motley, Jr. (American, 1891–1981). *Blues.* 1929. Chicago Historical Society.

⬛ LANGSTON HUGHES [1902–1967]

One of the most important figures of the Harlem Renais-
sance, Langston Hughes was born in Joplin, Missouri, and
graduated from Lincoln University in Pennsylvania. As a
young man, he traveled the world as a merchant seaman,
visiting Africa and living for a time in Paris and Rome.
A poet, writer of fiction, playwright, lyricist, editor, critic,
and essayist, Hughes published two volumes of autobio-
graphy, The Big Sea *(1940) and* I Wonder as I Wander
(1956). Hughes's work, which is filled with the sounds and music of the African
American experience, has influenced generations of American writers.

FROM *THE BIG SEA*   [1940]

I was there. I had a swell time while it lasted. But I thought it wouldn't last long. (I remember the vogue for things Russian, the season the Chauve-Souris first came to town.) For how could a large and enthusiastic number of people be crazy about Negroes forever? But some Harlemites thought the millennium had come. They thought the race problem had at last been solved through Art plus Gladys Bently. They were sure the New Negro would lead a new life from then on in green pastures of tolerance created by Countee Cullen, Ethel Waters, Claude McKay, Duke Ellington, Bojangles, and Alain Locke.

I don't know what made any Negroes think that—except that they were mostly intellectuals doing the thinking. The ordinary Negroes hadn't heard of the Negro Renaissance. And if they had, it hadn't raised their wages any. As for all those white folks in the speakeasies and night clubs of Harlem—well, maybe a colored man could find *some* place to have a drink that the tourists hadn't yet discovered.

Then it was that house-rent parties began to flourish—and not always to raise the rent either. But, as often as not, to have a get-together of one's own, where you could do the black-bottom with no stranger behind you trying to do it, too. Non-theatrical, non-intellectual Harlem was an unwilling victim of its own vogue. It didn't like to be stared at by white folks. But perhaps the downtowners never knew this—for the cabaret owners, the entertainers, and the speakeasy proprietors treated them fine—as long as they paid.

The Saturday night rent parties that I attended were often more amusing than any night club, in small apartments where God knows who lived—because the guests seldom did—but where the piano would often be augmented by a guitar, or an odd cornet, or somebody with a pair of drums walking in off the street. And where awful bootleg whiskey and good fried fish or steaming chitterling were sold at very low prices. And the dancing and singing and impromptu entertaining went on until dawn came in at the window.

5   These parties, often termed whist parties or dances, were usually announced by brightly colored cards stuck in the grille of apartment house elevators. Some of the cards were highly entertaining in themselves:

We got yellow girls, we've got black and tan
Will you have a good time? - YEAH MAN !

A Social Whist Party
—GIVEN BY—
MARY WINSTON

147 West 145th Street   Apt.5

SATURDAY EVE., MARCH 19th, 1932

GOOD MUSIC   REFRESHMENTS

H U R R A Y

COME AND SEE WHAT IS IN STORE FOR YOU AT THE

TEA CUP PARTY

GIVEN BY MRS. VANDERBILT SMITH

at 409 EDGECOMBE AVENUE
NEW YORK CITY
Apartment 10 - A

on Thursday evening, January 23rd, 1930
at 8:30 P. M.

ORIENTAL – GYPSY – SOUTHERN MAMMY – STARLIGHT
and other readers will be present

Music and Talent   —   —   Refreshments Served

Ribbons-Maws and Tretters A Specialty.

Fall in line, and watch your step, For there'll be
Lots of Browns with plenty of Pep At

A Social Whist Party

Given by

Lucille & Minnie

149 West 117th Street, N. Y. Gr. floor, W,

Saturday Evening, Nov. 2nd 1929

Refreshments Just It   Music Won't Quit

If Sweet Mamma is running wild, and you are looking
for a Do-right child, just come around and
linger awhile at a

SOCIAL WHIST PARTY

GIVEN BY

PINKNEY & EPPS

260 West 129th Street   Apartment 10

SATURDAY EVENING, JUNE 9, 1928

GOOD MUSIC   REFRESHMENTS

Railroad Men's Ball

AT CANDY'S PLACE

FRIDAY, SATURDAY & SUNDAY,

April 29-30, May 1, 1927

Black Wax, says change your mind and say they
do and he will give you a hearing, while MEAT
HOUSE SLIM, laying in the bin
killing all good men.

L. A. VAUGH, *President*

OH BOY   OH JOY

The Eleven Brown Skins

of the

Evening Shadow Social Club

are giving their

Second Annual St. Valentine Dance

Saturday evening, Feb. 18th, 1928

At 129 West 136th Street, New York City

Good Music   Refreshments Served

Subscription   25 Cents

---

*Some wear pajamas, some wear pants, what does it matter
just so you can dance, at*

A Social Whist Party

GIVEN BY

MR. & MRS. BROWN

AT 258 W. 115TH STREET, APT. 9

SATURDAY EVE., SEPT. 14, 1929

The music is sweet and everything good to eat!

Almost every Saturday night when I was in Harlem I went to a house-rent party. I wrote lots of poems about house-rent parties, and ate thereat many a fried fish and pig's foot—with liquid refreshments on the side. I met ladies' maids and truck drivers, laundry workers and shoe shine boys, seamstresses and porters. I can still hear their laughter in my ears, hear the soft slow music, and feel the floor shaking as the dancers danced.

THE NEGRO ARTIST AND THE RACIAL MOUNTAIN   [1926]

One of the most promising of the young Negro poets said to me once, "I want to be a poet—not a Negro poet," meaning, I believe, "I want to write like a white poet"; meaning subconsciously, "I would like to be a white poet"; meaning behind that, "I would like to be white." And I was sorry the young man said that, for no great poet has ever been afraid of being himself. And I doubted then that, with his desire to run away spiritually from his race, this boy would ever be a great poet. But this is the mountain standing in the way of any true Negro art in America—this urge within the race toward whiteness, the desire to pour racial individuality into the mold of American standardization, and to be as little Negro and as much American as possible.

But let us look at the immediate background of this young poet. His family is of what I suppose one would call the Negro middle class: people who are by no means rich yet never uncomfortable nor hungry—smug, contented, respectable folk, members of the Baptist church. The father goes to work every morning. He is a chief steward at a large white club. The mother sometimes does fancy sewing or supervises parties for the rich families of the town. The children go to a mixed school. In the home they read white papers and magazines. And the mother often says, "Don't be like niggers" when the children are bad. A frequent phrase from the father is, "Look how well a white man does things." And so the word white comes to be unconsciously a symbol of all virtues. It holds for the children beauty, morality, and money. The whisper of "I want to be white" runs silently through their minds. This young poet's home is, I believe, a fairly typical home of the colored middle class. One sees immediately how difficult it would be for an artist born in such a home to interest himself in interpreting the beauty of his own people. He is never taught to see that beauty. He is taught rather not to see it, or if he does, to be ashamed of it when it is not according to Caucasian patterns.

For racial culture the home of a self-styled "high-class" Negro has nothing better to offer. Instead there will perhaps be more aping of things white than in a less cultured or less wealthy home. The father is perhaps a doctor, lawyer, landowner, or politician. The mother may be a social worker, or a teacher, or she may do nothing and have a maid. Father is often dark but he has usually married the lightest woman he could find. The family attends a fashionable church where few really colored faces are to be found. And they themselves draw a color line. In the North they go to white theaters and white movies. And in the South they have at least two cars and house "like white folks." Nordic manners, Nordic faces, Nordic hair, Nordic art (if any), and an Episcopal heaven. A very high mountain indeed for the would-be racial artist to climb in order to discover himself and his people.

But then there are the low-down folks, the so-called common element, and they are the majority—may the Lord be praised! The people who have their hip of gin on Saturday nights and are not too important to themselves or the community, or too well fed, or too learned to watch the lazy world go round. They live on Seventh Street in Washington or State Street in Chicago and they do not particularly care whether they are like white folks or anybody else. Their joy runs, bang! into ecstasy. Their religion soars to a shout. Work maybe a little today, rest a little tomorrow. Play awhile. Sing awhile. O, let's dance! These common people are not afraid of spirituals, as for a long time their more intellectual brethren were, and jazz is their child. They furnish a wealth of colorful, distinctive material for any artist because they still hold their own individuality in the face of American standardizations. And perhaps these common people will give to the world its truly great Negro artist, the one who is not afraid to be himself. Whereas the better-class Negro would tell the artist what to do, the people at least let him alone when he does appear. And they are not ashamed of him—if they know he exists at all. And they accept what beauty is their own without question.

5   Certainly there is, for the American Negro artists who can escape the restrictions the more advanced among his own group would put upon him, a great field of unused material ready for his art. Without going outside his race, and even among the better classes with their "white" culture and conscious American manners, but still Negro enough to be different, there is sufficient matter to furnish a black artist with a lifetime of creative work. And when he chooses to touch on the relations between Negroes and whites in this country with their innumerable overtones and undertones surely, and especially for literature and the drama, there is an inexhaustible supply of themes at hand. To these the Negro artist can give his racial individuality, his heritage of rhythm and warmth, and his incongruous humor that so often, as in the Blues, becomes ironic laughter mixed with tears. But let us look again at the mountain.

A prominent Negro clubwoman in Philadelphia paid eleven dollars to hear Raquel Meller sing Andalusian[1] popular songs. But she told me a few weeks before she would not think of going to hear "that woman," Clara Smith,[2] a great black artist, sing Negro folksongs. And many an upper-class Negro church, even now, would not dream of employing a spiritual in its services. The drab melodies in white folks' hymnbooks are much to be preferred. "We want to worship the Lord correctly and quietly. We don't believe in 'shouting.' Let's be dull like the Nordics," they say, in effect.

The road for the serious black artist, then, who would produce a racial art is most certainly rocky and the mountain is high. Until recently he received almost no encouragement for his work from either white or colored people. The fine novels of Chesnutt[3] go out of print with neither race noticing their passing. The quaint charm and humor of Dunbar's[4] dialect verse brought to him, in his day, largely the

---

[1]**Andalusian** from a region of Spain   [2]**Clara Smith** major blues singer (1885–1935)
[3]**Chesnutt** Charles Chesnutt (1858–1932), author of three novels, *The House behind the Cedars* (1900), *The Marrow of Tradition* (1901), and *The Colonel's Dream* (1905); a biography of Frederick Douglass; and two short story collections, *The Conjure Woman* (1899) and *The Wife of His Youth and Other Stories of the Color Line* (1899)   [4]**Dunbar's** Paul Laurence Dunbar (1872–1906), poet and author of the novel *Sport of the Gods* (1907)

same kind of encouragement one would give a sideshow freak (A colored man writing poetry! How odd!) or a clown (How amusing!).

The present vogue in things Negro, although it may do as much harm as good for the budding colored artist, has at least done this: it has brought him forcibly to the attention of his own people among whom for so long, unless the other race had noticed him beforehand, he was a prophet with little honor. I understand that Charles Gilpin[5] acted for years in Negro theaters without any special acclaim from his own, but when Broadway gave him eight curtain calls, Negroes, too, began to beat a tin pan in his honor. I know a young colored writer, a manual worker by day, who had been writing well for the colored magazines for some years, but it was not until he recently broke into the white publications and his first book was accepted by a prominent New York publisher that the "best" Negroes in his city took the trouble to discover that he lived there. Then almost immediately they decided to give a grand dinner for him. But the society ladies were careful to whisper to his mother that perhaps she'd better not come. They were not sure she would have an evening gown.[6]

The Negro artist works against an undertow of sharp criticism and misunderstanding from his own group and unintentional bribes from the whites. "Oh, be respectable, write about nice people, show how good we are," say the Negroes. "Be stereotyped, don't go too far, don't shatter our illusions about you, don't amuse us too seriously. We will pay you," say the whites. Both would have told Jean Toomer not to write *Cane*.[7] The colored people did not praise it. The white people did not buy it. Most of the colored people who did read *Cane* hate it. They are afraid of it. Although the critics gave it good reviews the public remained indifferent. Yet (excepting the work of Du Bois[8]) *Cane* contains the finest prose written by a Negro in America. And like the singing of Robeson,[9] it is truly racial.

10   But in spite of the Nordicized Negro intelligentsia and the desires of some white editors we have an honest American Negro literature already with us. Now I await the rise of the Negro theater. Our folk music, having achieved world-wide fame, offers itself to the genius of the great individual American composer who is to come. And within the next decade I expect to see the work of a growing school of colored artists who paint and model the beauty of dark faces and create with new technique the expressions of their own soul-world. And the Negro dancers who will dance like flames and the singers who will continue to carry our songs to all who listen—they will be with us in even greater numbers tomorrow.

Most of my own poems are racial in theme and treatment, derived from the life I know. In many of them I try to grasp and hold some of the meanings and rhythms of jazz. I am as sincere as I know how to be in these poems and yet after every

[5]**Charles Gilpin** American actor (1878–1930)   [6]This incident, which happened to Hughes himself in 1925, is related in his autobiography *The Big Sea* (1940).   [7]*Cane* a 1923 collection of short stories and poetry about the rural South and the urban North   [8]**Du Bois** W. E. B. Du Bois (1868–1963) helped found the NAACP and edited its journal, *Crisis,* from 1910 to 1934; he is best known for *The Souls of Black Folk* (1903).   [9]**Robeson** Paul Robeson (1898–1976), actor and singer.

reading I answer questions like these from my own people: Do you think Negroes should always write about Negroes? I wish you wouldn't read some of your poems to white folks. How do you find anything interesting in a place like a cabaret? Why do you write about black people? You aren't black. What makes you do so many jazz poems?

But jazz to me is one of the inherent expressions of Negro life in America; the eternal tom-tom beating in the Negro soul—the tom-tom of revolt against weariness in a white world, a world of subway trains, and work, work, work; the tom-tom of joy and laughter, and pain swallowed in a smile. Yet the Philadelphia clubwoman is ashamed to say that her race created it and she does not like me to write about it. The old subconscious "white is best" runs through her mind. Years of study under white teachers, a lifetime of white books, pictures, and papers, and white manners, morals, and Puritan standards made her dislike the spirituals. And now she turns up her nose at jazz and all its manifestations—likewise almost everything else distinctly racial. She doesn't care for the Winold Reiss[10] portraits of Negroes because they are "too Negro." She does not want a true picture of herself from anybody. She wants the artist to flatter her, to make the white world believe that all Negroes are as smug and as near white in soul as she wants to be. But, to my mind, it is the duty of the younger Negro artist, if he accepts any duties at all from outsiders, to change through the force of his art that old whispering "I want to be white," hidden in the aspirations of his people, to "Why should I want to be white? I am a Negro—and beautiful."

So I am ashamed for the black poet who says, "I want to be a poet, not a Negro poet," as though his own racial world were not as interesting as any other world. I am ashamed, too, for the colored artist who runs from the painting of Negro faces to the painting of sunsets after the manner of the academicians because he fears the strange un-whiteness of his own features. An artist must be free to choose what he does, certainly, but he must also never be afraid to do what he might choose.

Let the blare of Negro jazz bands and the bellowing voice of Bessie Smith singing Blues penetrate the closed ears of the colored near-intellectuals until they listen and perhaps understand. Let Paul Robeson singing "Water Boy," and Rudolph Fisher writing about the streets of Harlem, and Jean Toomer holding the heart of Georgia in his hands, and Aaron Douglas drawing strange black fantasies cause the smug Negro middle class to turn from their white, respectable, ordinary books and papers to catch a glimmer of their own beauty. We younger Negro artists who create now intend to express our individual dark-skinned selves without fear or shame. If white people are pleased we are glad. If they are not, it doesn't matter. We know we are beautiful. And ugly too. The tom-tom cries and the tom-tom laughs. If colored people are pleased we are glad. If they are not, their displeasure doesn't matter either. We build our temples for tomorrow, strong as we know how, and we stand on top of the mountain, free within ourselves.

---

[10]**Winold Reiss** portrait painter (1886–1953)

THE NEGRO SPEAKS OF RIVERS° [1921]

I've known rivers:
I've known rivers ancient as the world and older than the
       Flow of human blood in human veins.

My soul has grown deep like the rivers.

I bathed in the Euphrates when dawns were young.   5
I built my hut near the Congo and it lulled me to sleep.
I looked upon the Nile and raised the Pyramids above it.
I heard the singing of the Mississippi when Abe Lincoln went down
      To New Orleans, and I've seen its muddy bosom turn all golden
       in the sunset.   10

I've known rivers:
Ancient, dusky rivers.

My soul has grown deep like the rivers.

I, TOO [1925]

I, too, sing America.

I am the darker brother.
They send me to eat in the kitchen
When company comes,
But I laugh,   5
And eat well,
And grow strong.

Tomorrow,
I'll sit at the table
When company comes.   10
Nobody'll dare
Say to me,
"Eat in the kitchen,"
Then.

Besides,   15
They'll see how beautiful I am
And be ashamed—
I, too, am America.

THE WEARY BLUES [1926]

    Droning a drowsy syncopated tune,
Rocking back and forth to a mellow croon,
    I heard a Negro play.
    Down on Lenox Avenue the other night

For commentary on this poem, see page 1096.

By the pale dull pallor of an old gas light   5
   He did a lazy sway....
   He did a lazy sway....
To the tune o' those Weary Blues.
With his ebony hands on each ivory key
He made that poor piano moan with melody.   10
    O Blues!
Swaying to and fro on his rickety stool
He played that sad raggy tune like a musical fool.
    Sweet Blues!
Coming from a black man's soul.   15
    O Blues!
In a deep song voice with a melancholy tone
I heard that Negro sing, that old piano moan—
"Ain't got nobody in all this world,
   Ain't got nobody but ma self.   20
   I's gwine to quit ma frownin'
   And put ma troubles on the shelf."
Thump, thump, thump, went his foot on the floor.
He played a few chords then he sang some more
   "I got the Weary Blues   25
   And I can't be satisfied.
   Got the Weary Blues
   And can't be satisfied—
   I ain't happy no mo'
   And I wish that I had died."   30
And far into the night he crooned that tune.
The stars went out and so did the moon.
The singer stopped playing and went to bed
While the Weary Blues echoed through his head.
He slept like a rock or a man that's dead.   35

ONE FRIDAY MORNING   [1939]

The thrilling news did not come directly to Nancy Lee, but it came in little indirections that finally added themselves up to one tremendous fact: she had won the prize! But being a calm and quiet young lady, she did not say anything, although the whole high school buzzed with rumors, guesses, reportedly authentic announcements on the part of students who had no right to be making announcements at all—since no student really knew yet who had won this year's art scholarship.

But Nancy Lee's drawing was so good, her lines so sure, her colors so bright and harmonious, that certainly no other student in the senior art class at George Washington High was thought to have very much of a chance. Yet you never could tell. Last year nobody had expected Joe Williams to win the Artist Club scholarship with that funny modernistic water color he had done of the high-level bridge. In fact, it was hard to make out there was a bridge until you had looked at the picture a long time. Still, Joe Williams got the prize, was feted by the community's leading painters, club women, and society folks at a big banquet at the Park-Rose Hotel, and was now an award student at the Art School—the city's only art school.

Nancy Lee Johnson was a colored girl, a few years out of the South. But seldom did her high-school classmates think of her as colored. She was smart, pretty, and brown, and fitted in well with the life of the school. She stood high in scholarship, played a swell game of basketball, had taken part in the senior musical in a soft, velvety voice, and had never seemed to intrude or stand out, except in pleasant ways, so it was seldom even mentioned—her color.

Nancy Lee sometimes forgot she was colored herself. She liked her classmates and her school. Particularly she liked her art teacher, Miss Dietrich, the tall red-haired woman who taught her law and order in doing things; and the beauty of working step by step until a job is done; a picture finished; a design created; or a block print carved out of nothing but an idea and a smooth square of linoleum, inked, proofs made, and finally put down on paper—clean, sharp, beautiful, individual, unlike any other in the world, thus making the paper have a meaning nobody else could give it except Nancy Lee. That was the wonderful thing about true creation. You made something nobody else on earth could make but you.

5   Miss Dietrich was the kind of teacher who brought out the best in her students—but their own best, not anybody else's copied best. For anybody else's best, great though it might be, even Michelangelo's, wasn't enough to please Miss Dietrich, dealing with the creative impulses of young men and women living in an American city in the Middle West, and being American.

Nancy Lee was proud of being American, a Negro American with blood out of Africa a long time ago, too many generations back to count. But her parents had taught her the beauties of Africa, its strength, its songs, its mighty rivers, its early smelting of iron, its building of the pyramids, and its ancient and important civilizations. And Miss Dietrich had discovered for her the sharp and humorous lines of African sculpture, Benin, Congo, Makonde. Nancy Lee's father was a mail carrier, her mother a social worker in a city settlement house. Both parents had been to Negro colleges in the South. And her mother had gotten a further degree in social work from a Northern university. Her parents were, like most Americans, simple, ordinary people who had worked hard and steadily for their education. Now they were trying to make it easier for Nancy Lee to achieve learning than it had been for them. They would be very happy when they heard of the award to their daughter—yet Nancy did not tell them. To surprise them would be better. Besides, there had been a promise.

Casually, one day, Miss Dietrich asked Nancy Lee what color frame she thought would be best on her picture. That had been the first inkling.

"Blue," Nancy Lee said. Although the picture had been entered in the Artist Club contest a month ago, Nancy Lee did not hesitate in her choice of a color for the possible frame, since she could still see her picture clearly in her mind's eye for that picture waiting for the blue frame had come out of her soul, her own life, and had bloomed into miraculous being with Miss Dietrich's help. It was, she knew, the best water color she had painted in her four years as a high-school art student, and she was glad she had made something Miss Dietrich liked well enough to permit her to enter in the contest before she graduated.

It was not a modernistic picture in the sense that you had to look at it a long time to understand what it meant. It was just a simple scene in the city park on a spring day, with the trees still leaflessly lacy against the sky, the new grass fresh and green, a flag on a tall pole in the center, children playing, and an old Negro woman sitting on a bench with her head turned. A lot for one picture, to be sure, but it was not there in heavy and final detail like a calendar. Its charm was that everything was light and airy, happy like spring, with a lot of blue sky, paper-white clouds, and air showing through. You could tell that the old Negro woman was looking at the flag, and that the flag was proud in the spring breeze, and that the breeze helped to make the children's dresses billow as they played.

10   Miss Dietrich had taught Nancy Lee how to paint spring, people, and a breeze on what was only a plain white piece of paper from the supply closet. But Miss Dietrich had not said make it like any other spring-people-breeze ever seen before. She let it remain Nancy Lee's own. That is how the old Negro woman happened to be there looking at the flag—for in her mind the flag, the spring, and the woman formed a kind of triangle holding a dream Nancy Lee wanted to express. White stars on a blue field, spring, children, ever-growing life, and an old woman. Would the judges at the Artist Club like it?

One wet, rainy April afternoon Miss O'Shay, the girls' vice-principal, sent for Nancy Lee to stop by her office as school closed. Pupils without umbrellas or raincoats were clustered in doorways, hoping to make it home between showers. Outside the skies were gray. Nancy Lee's thoughts were suddenly gray, too.

She did not think she had done anything wrong, yet that tight little knot came in her throat just the same as she approached Miss O'Shay's door. Perhaps she had banged her locker too often and too hard. Perhaps the note in French she had written to Sallie halfway across the study hall just for fun had never gotten to Sallie but into Miss O'Shay's hands instead. Or maybe she was failing in some subject and wouldn't be allowed to graduate. Chemistry! A pang went through the pit of her stomach. She knocked on Miss O'Shay's door. That familiarly solid and competent voice said, "Come in."

Miss O'Shay had a way of making you feel welcome, even if you came to be expelled.

"Sit down, Nancy Lee Johnson," said Miss O'Shay. "I have something to tell you." Nancy Lee sat down. "But I must ask you to promise not to tell anyone yet."

15   "I won't, Miss O'Shay," Nancy Lee said, wondering what on earth the principal had to say to her.

"You are about to graduate," Miss O'Shay said. "And we shall miss you. You have been an excellent student, Nancy, and you will not be without honors on the senior list, as I am sure you know."

At that point there was a light knock on the door. Miss O'Shay called out, "Come in," and Miss Dietrich entered. "May I be a part of this, too?" she asked, tall and smiling.

"Of course," Miss O'Shay said. "I was just telling Nancy Lee what we thought of her. But I hadn't gotten around to giving her the news. Perhaps, Miss Dietrich, you'd like to tell her yourself."

Miss Dietrich was always direct. "Nancy Lee," she said, "your picture has won the Artist Club scholarship."

20   The slender brown girl's eyes widened, her heart thumped, then her throat tightened again. She tried to smile, but instead tears came to her eyes.

"Dear Nancy Lee," Miss O'Shay said, "we are so happy for you." The elderly white woman took her hand and shook it warmly while Miss Dietrich beamed with pride.

Nancy Lee must have danced all the way home. She never remembered quite how she got there through the rain. She hoped she had been dignified. But certainly she hadn't stopped to tell anybody her secret on the way. Raindrops, smiles, and tears mingled on her brown cheeks. She hoped her mother hadn't yet gotten home and that the house was empty. She wanted to have time to calm down and look natural before she had to see anyone. She didn't want to be bursting with excitement—having a secret to contain.

Miss O'Shay's calling her to the office had been in the nature of a preparation and a warning. The kind, elderly vice-principal said she did not believe in catching young ladies unawares, even with honors, so she wished her to know about the coming award. In making acceptance speeches she wanted her to be calm, prepared, not nervous, overcome, and frightened. So Nancy Lee was asked to think what she would say when the scholarship was conferred upon her a few days hence, both at the Friday morning high-school assembly hour, when the announcement would be made, and at the evening banquet of the Artist Club. Nancy Lee promised the vice-principal to think calmly about what she would say.

Miss Dietrich had then asked for some facts about her parents, her background, and her life, since such material would probably be desired for the papers. Nancy Lee had told her how, six years before, they had come up from the Deep South, her father having been successful in achieving a transfer from the one post office to another, a thing he had long sought in order to give Nancy Lee a chance to go to school in the North. Now they lived in a modest Negro neighborhood, went to see the best plays when they came to town, and had been saving to send Nancy Lee to art school, in case she were permitted to enter. But the scholarship would help a great deal, for they were not rich people.

25   "Now Mother can have a new coat next winter," Nancy Lee thought, "because my tuition will all be covered for the first year. And once in art school, there are other scholarships I can win."

Dreams began to dance through her head, plans and ambitions, beauties she would create for herself, her parents, and the Negro people—for Nancy Lee possessed a deep and reverent race pride. She could see the old woman in her picture (really her grandmother in the South) lifting her head to the bright stars on the flag in the distance. A Negro in America! Often hurt, discriminated against, sometimes lynched—but always there were the stars on the blue body of the flag. Was there any other flag in the world that had so many stars? Nancy Lee thought deeply, but she could remember none in all the encyclopedias or geographies she had ever looked into.

"Hitch your wagon to a star," Nancy Lee thought, dancing home in the rain. "Who were our flag-makers?"

Friday morning came, the morning when the world would know—her high-school world, the newspaper world, her mother and dad. Dad could not be there at the assembly to hear the announcement, nor see her prize picture displayed on the stage, nor to listen to Nancy Lee's little speech of acceptance, but Mother would be able to come, although Mother was much puzzled as to why Nancy Lee was so insistent she be at school on that particular Friday morning.

When something is happening, something new and fine, something that will change your very life, it is hard to go to sleep at night for thinking about it, and hard to keep your heart from pounding, or a strange little knot of joy from gathering in your throat. Nancy Lee had taken her bath, brushed her hair until it glowed, and had gone to bed thinking about the next day, the big day, when before three thousand students, she would be the one student honored, her painting the one painting to be acclaimed as the best of the year from all the art classes of the city. Her short speech of gratitude was ready. She went over it in her mind, not word for word (because she didn't want it to sound as if she had learned it by heart), but she let the thoughts flow simply and sincerely through her consciousness many times.

30   When the president of the Artist Club presented her with the medal and scroll of the scholarship award, she would say:

"Judges and members of the Artist Club, I want to thank you for this award that means so much to me personally and through me to my people, the colored people of this city, who, sometimes, are discouraged and bewildered, thinking that color and poverty are against them. I accept this award with gratitude and pride, not for myself alone, but for my race that believes in American opportunity and American fairness—and the bright stars in our flag. I thank Miss Dietrich and the teachers who made it possible for me to have the knowledge and training that lie behind this honor you have conferred upon my painting. When I came here from the South a few years ago, I was not sure how you would receive me. You received me well. You have given me a chance and helped me along the road I wanted to follow. I suppose the judges know that every week here at assembly the students of this school pledge allegiance to the flag. I shall try to be worthy of that pledge, and of the help and friendship and understanding of my fellow citizens of whatever race or creed, and of our American dream of 'Liberty and justice for all!'"

That would be her response before the students in the morning. How proud and happy the Negro pupils would be, perhaps almost as proud as they were of the one colored star on the football team. Her mother would probably cry with happiness. Thus Nancy Lee went to sleep dreaming of a wonderful tomorrow.

The bright sunlight of an April morning woke her. There was breakfast with her parents—their half-amused and puzzled faces across the table, wondering what could be this secret that made her eyes so bright. The swift walk to school; the clock in the tower almost nine; hundreds of pupils streaming into the long, rambling old building that was the city's largest high school; the sudden quiet of the homeroom after the bell rang; then the teacher opening her record book to call the roll. But just before she began, she looked across the room until her eyes located Nancy Lee.

"Nancy," she said, "Miss O'Shay would like to see you in her office, please."

35   Nancy Lee rose and went out while the names were being called and the word *present* added its period to each name. Perhaps, Nancy Lee thought, the reporters

from the papers had already come. Maybe they wanted to take her picture before assembly, which wasn't until ten o'clock. (Last year they had had the photograph of the winner of the award in the morning papers as soon as the announcement had been made.)

Nancy Lee knocked at Miss O'Shay's door.

"Come in."

The vice-principal stood at her desk. There was no one else in the room. It was very quiet.

"Sit down, Nancy Lee," she said. Miss O'Shay did not smile. There was a long pause. The seconds went by slowly. "I do not know how to tell you what I have to say," the elderly woman began, her eyes on the papers on her desk. "I am indignant and ashamed for myself and for this city." Then she lifted her eyes and looked at Nancy Lee in the near blue dress, sitting there before her. "You are not to receive the scholarship this morning."

40   Outside in the hall the electric bells announcing the first period rang, loud and interminably long. Miss O'Shay remained silent. To the brown girl here in the chair, the room grew suddenly smaller, smaller, smaller, and there was no air. She could not speak.

Miss O'Shay said, "When the committee learned that you were colored, they changed their plans."

Still Nancy Lee said nothing, for there was no air to give breath to her lungs.

"Here is the letter from the committee, Nancy Lee." Miss O'Shay picked it up and read the final paragraph to her.

"'It seems to us wiser to arbitrarily rotate the award among the various high schools of the city from now on. And especially in this case since the student chosen happens to be colored, a circumstance which unfortunately, had we known, might have prevented this embarrassment. But there have never been any Negro students in the local art school, and the presence of one there might create difficulties for all concerned. We have high regard for the quality of Nancy Lee Johnson's talent, but we do not feel it would be fair to honor it with the Artist Club award.'" Miss O'Shay paused. She put the letter down.

45   "Nancy Lee, I am very sorry to have to give you this message."

"But my speech," Nancy Lee said, "was about...." The words stuck in her throat. "...about America...."

Miss O'Shay had risen; she turned her back and stood looking out the window at the spring tulips in the school yard.

"I thought, since the award would be made at assembly right after our oath of allegiance," the words rumbled almost hysterically from Nancy Lee's throat now, "I would put part of the flag salute in my speech. You know, Miss O'Shay, that part about 'liberty and justice for all.'"

"I know," said Miss O'Shay, slowly facing the room again. "But America is only what we who believe in it make it. I am Irish. You may not know, Nancy Lee, but years ago we were called the dirty Irish, and mobs rioted against us in the big cities, and we were invited to go back where we came from. But we didn't go. And we didn't give up, because we believed in the American dream, and in our power to make that dream come true. Difficulties, yes. Mountains to climb, yes.

Discouragements to face, yes. Democracy to make, yes. That is it, Nancy Lee! We still have in this world of ours democracy to *make*. You and I, Nancy Lee. But the premise and the base are here, the lines of the Declaration of Independence and the words of Lincoln are here, and the stars in our flag. Those who deny you this scholarship do not know the meaning of those stars, but it's up to us to make them know. As a teacher in the public schools of this city, I myself will go before the school board and ask them to remove from our system the offer of any prizes or awards denied to any student because of race or color."

50   Suddenly Miss O'Shay stopped speaking. Her clear, clear blue eyes looked into those of the girl before her. The woman's eyes were full of strength and courage. "Lift up your head, Nancy Lee, and smile at me."

Miss O'Shay stood against the open window with the green lawn and the tulips beyond, the sunlight tangled in her gray hair, her voice an electric flow of strength to the hurt spirit of Nancy Lee. The Abolitionists who believed in freedom when there was slavery must have been like that. The first white teachers who went into the Deep South to teach the freed slaves must have been like that. All those who stand against ignorance, narrowness, hate, and mud on stars must be like that.

Nancy Lee lifted her head and smiled. The bell for assembly rang. She went through the long hall filled with students, toward the auditorium.

"There will be other awards," Nancy Lee thought. "There are schools in other cities. This won't keep me down. But when I'm a woman, I'll fight to see that these things don't happen to other girls as this has happened to me. And men and women like Miss O'Shay will help me."

She took her seat among the seniors. The doors of the auditorium closed. As the principal came onto the platform, the students rose and turned their eyes to the flag on the stage.

55   One hand went to the heart, the other outstretched toward the flag. Three thousand voices spoke. Among them was the voice of a dark girl whose cheeks were suddenly wet with tears, "...one nation indivisible, with liberty and justice for all."

"That is the land we must make," she thought.

THEME FOR ENGLISH B   [1951]

The instructor said,

Go home and write
A page tonight.

And let that page come out of you—
Then, it will be true.   5

I wonder if it's that simple?

I am twenty-two, colored, born in Winston-Salem.
I went to school there, then Durham, then here
To this college on the hill above Harlem.
I am the only colored student in my class.   10

The steps from the hill lead down to Harlem,
Through a park, then I cross St. Nicholas,
Eighth Avenue, Seventh, and I come to the Y,
The Harlem Branch Y, where I take the elevator
Up to my room, sit down, and write this page: 15

It's not easy to know what is true for you or me
At twenty-two, my age. But I guess I'm what
I feel and see and hear. Harlem, I hear you:
Hear you, hear me—we two—you, me talk on this page.
(I hear New York, too.) Me—who?   20

Well, I like to eat, sleep, drink, and be in love.
I like to work, read, learn, and understand life.
I like a pipe for a Christmas present,
Or records—Bessie, bop, or Bach.

I guess being colored doesn't make me not like   25
The same things other folks like who are other races.
So will my page be colored that I write?
Being me, it will not be white.
But it will be
A part of you, instructor.   30
You are white—
Yet a part of me, as I am part of you.
That's American.
Sometimes perhaps you don't want to be a part of me.
Nor do I often want to be a part of you.   35
But we are, that's true!
As I learn from you,
I guess you learn from me—
Although you're older—and white—
And somewhat more free.   40

This is my page for English B.

CLAUDE McKAY [1889–1948]

*Claude McKay was born to peasant farmers in Sunny Ville,
Jamaica. He won an award for his first volume of poetry,*
Songs of Jamaica, *published in London in 1912. The award
money allowed McKay to travel to the United States, where
he studied for a time at the Tuskegee Institute and at Kansas
State University before settling in New York City. Energized
by the racism he encountered, McKay continued to write
poetry, much of it political, as he became active in a num-*

*ber of social causes. McKay became one of the leading features of the Harlem
Renaissance.* Home to Harlem, *his 1928 novel about a black soldier's return home*

following World War I, was a tremendous commercial success. His other works include two novels, Banjo: A Story Without a Plot *(1929) and* Banana Bottom *(1933); and an autobiography,* A Long Way from Home *(1937).*

AMERICA
[1921]

Although she feeds me bread of bitterness,
And sinks into my throat her tiger's tooth,
Stealing my breath of life, I will confess
I love this cultured hell that tests my youth!
Her vigor flows like tides into my blood,   5
Giving me strength erect against her hate.
Her bigness sweeps my being like a flood.
Yet as a rebel fronts a king in state,
I stand within her walls with not a shred
Of terror, malice, not a word of jeer.   10
Darkly I gaze into the days ahead,
And see her might and granite wonders there,
Beneath the touch of Time's unerring hand,
Like priceless treasures sinking in the sand.

GWENDOLYN B. BENNETT [1902–1981]

Gwendolyn Bennett was born in Giddings, Texas, studied Fine Arts at Columbia University and the Pratt Institute, and taught art at Howard University in Washington, D.C. In addition to her poetry, she published illustrations in the prominent journals Opportunity *and* Crisis. *Her poetry (including "Heritage," below) expresses an appreciation of the beauty of her African descent and a sadness in response to the ways in which it had been defiled.*

HERITAGE
[1923]

I want to see the slim palm-trees,
Pulling at the clouds
With little pointed fingers....

I want to see lithe Negro girls,
Etched dark against the sky   5
While sunset lingers.

I want to hear the silent sands,
Singing to the moon
Before the Sphinx-still face....

I want to hear the chanting
Around a heathen fire   10
Of a strange black race.

I want to breathe the Lotus flow'r,
Sighing to the stars
With tendrils drinking at the Nile....   15

I want to feel the surging
Of my sad people's soul
Hidden by a minstrel-smile.

JEAN TOOMER [1894–1967]

One of the important figures of the Harlem Renaissance, Jean Toomer was born in Washington, D.C. Toomer, who was of mixed racial heritage, was raised in the house of his grandfather, who had been governor of Louisiana during Reconstruction. In 1921, Toomer held a position for a few months as principal of a technical institute in Sparta, Georgia, traveling to the Deep South for the first time in his life. The experience inspired him to write his great masterpiece, Cane *(1923), an experimental novel made up of the poems, songs, and stories he encountered among the African Americans of the region. The novel established Toomer's reputation, and throughout the twenties his work appeared in many of the leading African American and avant-garde journals of the day. He was largely forgotten until the republication of* Cane *in 1969 reawakened interest in his life and works.*

REAPERS   [1923]

Black reapers with the sound of steel on stones
Are sharpening scythes. I see them place the hones
In their hip-pockets as a thing that's done,
And start their silent swinging, one by one.
Black horses drive a mower through the weeds,   5
And there, a field rat, started squealing bleeds,
His belly close to ground. I see the blade,
Blood-stained, continue cutting weeds and shade.

COUNTEE CULLEN [1903–1946]

Countee Cullen was adopted by a Methodist minister and spent his childhood years living in Harlem. He attended New York University and Harvard. While a college student, he published his first poetry and soon became identified with the black writers of the Harlem Renaissance period. His works of poetry include Color *(1925),* Copper Sun *(1927), and* The Black Christ *(1929); and other works include a novel,* One Way to Heaven *(1932), and a collection of poems,* Medea *(1935). On* These I Stand, *a collection of his favorite poems, was published the year after he died. Another of his poems, "Incident," published in 1925, appears on page 24 of this text.*

YET DO I MARVEL   [1925]

I doubt not God is good, well-meaning, kind,
And did He stoop to quibble could tell why
The little buried mole continues blind,
Why flesh that mirrors Him must some day die,
Make plain the reason tortured Tantalus   5
Is baited by the fickle fruit, declare
If merely brute caprice dooms Sisyphus
To struggle up a never-ending stair.
Inscrutable His ways are, and immune
To catechism by a mind too strewn   10
With petty cares to slightly understand
What awful brain compels His awful hand.
Yet do I marvel at this curious thing;
To make a poet black, and bid him sing!

FROM THE DARK TOWER   [1927]

(To Charles S. Johnson)

We shall not always plant while others reap
The golden increment of bursting fruit,
Not always countenance, abject and mute,
That lesser men should hold their brothers cheap;
Not everlastingly while others sleep   5
Shall we beguile their limbs with mellow flute,
Not always bend to some more subtle brute;
We were not made eternally to weep.

The night whose sable breast relieves the stark,
White stars is no less lovely being dark,   10
And there are buds that cannot bloom at all
In light, but crumple, piteous, and fall;
So in the dark we hide the heart that bleeds,
And wait, and tend our agonizing seeds.

ANNE SPENCER [1882–1975]

*Born Anne Bethel Bannister, Anne Spencer graduated from
the Virginia Seminary in 1899. She was an avid gardener
and taught in a public school in West Virginia. She did
not publish her first poem until 1920, when James Weldon
Johnson, noted editor and writer, encouraged her to submit
it to Crisis, an important journal of the time. Most of her
poetry is more concerned with gender than with race, and
fewer than thirty of her poems were published during her
lifetime. After she died, her home and garden in Lynchburg, Virginia, were given
the status of historic landmark.*

LADY, LADY   [1925]

Lady, Lady, I saw your face,
Dark as night withholding a star …
The chisel fell, or it might have been
You had borne so long the yoke of men.

Lady, Lady, I saw your hands,   5
Twisted, awry, like crumpled roots,
Bleached poor white in a sudsy tub,
Wrinkled and drawn from your rub-a-dub.

Lady, Lady, I saw your heart,
And altared there in its darksome place   10
Were the tongues of flame the ancients knew,
Where the good God sits to spangle through.

GEORGIA DOUGLAS JOHNSON [1886–1966]

*Considered the most popular female poet of the Harlem
Renaissance, Georgia Douglas Johnson never actually lived
in Harlem. She grew up in Rome, Georgia, and Atlanta. She
taught in Marietta, Georgia, and was an assistant school
principal in Atlanta. While many of her poems and short
stories address the issue of race and race relations, it's clear
that her favorite topic was the role of love in the lives of
women. The following poem was set to music and became a
very popular song of the late 1920s.*

I WANT TO DIE WHILE YOU LOVE ME   [1927]

I want to die while you love me,
    While yet you hold me fair,
While laughter lies upon my lips
    And lights are in my hair.

I want to die while you love me,   5
    And bear to that still bed,
Your kisses turbulent, unspent,
    To warm me when I'm dead.

I want to die while you love me,
    Oh, who would care to live   10
Till love has nothing more to ask
    And nothing more to give!

I want to die while you love me
    And never, never see
The glory of this perfect day   15
    Grow dim or cease to be.

▥ ZORA NEALE HURSTON [1891–1960]

Zora Neale Hurston was born and spent her early childhood in Eatonville, Florida. When her mother died in 1912, she spent the rest of her years growing up being moved from one relative to another. In 1925, she moved to New York City and became a prominent member of the Harlem Renaissance. A distinguishing feature of her work is that her characters speak in the black country dialect of her native Florida. Her best-known novel is Their Eyes Were Watching God *(1937).*

SWEAT   [1926]

I

It was eleven o'clock of a Spring night in Florida. It was Sunday. Any other night, Delia Jones would have been in bed for two hours by this time. But she was a wash-woman, and Monday morning meant a great deal to her. So she collected the soiled clothes on Saturday when she returned the clean things. Sunday night after church, she sorted and put the white things to soak. It saved her almost a half-day's start. A great hamper in the bedroom held the clothes that she brought home. It was so much neater than a number of bundles lying around.

She squatted on the kitchen floor beside the great pile of clothes, sorting them into small heaps according to color, and humming a song in a mournful key, but wondering through it all where Sykes, her husband, had gone with her horse and buckboard.

Just then something long, round, limp, and black fell upon her shoulders and slithered to the floor beside her. A great terror took hold of her. It softened her knees and dried her mouth so that it was a full minute before she could cry out or move. Then she saw that it was the big bull whip her husband liked to carry when he drove.

She lifted her eyes to the door and saw him standing there bent over with laughter at her fright. She screamed at him.

5   "Sykes, what you throw dat whip on me like dat? You know it would skeer me—looks just like a snake, an' you knows how skeered Ah is of snakes."

"Course Ah knowed it! That's how come Ah done it." He slapped his leg with his hand and almost rolled on the ground in his mirth. "If you such a big fool dat you got to have a fit over a earth worm or a string, Ah don't keer how bad Ah skeer you."

"You ain't got no business doing it. Gawd knows it's a sin. Some day Ah'm gointuh drop dead from some of yo' foolishness. 'Nother thing, where you been wid mah rig? Ah feeds dat pony. He ain't fuh you to be drivin' wid no bull whip."

"You sho' is one aggravatin' nigger woman!" he declared and stepped into the room. She resumed her work and did not answer him at once. "Ah done tole you time and again to keep them white folks' clothes outa dis house."

He picked up the whip and glared at her. Delia went on with her work. She went out into the yard and returned with a galvanized tub and set it on the wash-bench. She saw that Sykes had kicked all of the clothes together again, and now stood in her way truculently, his whole manner hoping, *praying,* for an argument. But she walked calmly around him and commenced to re-sort the things.

10   "Next time, Ah'm gointer kick 'em outdoors," he threatened as he struck a match along the leg of his corduroy breeches.

Delia never looked up from her work, and her thin, stooped shoulders sagged further.

"Ah ain't for no fuss t'night, Sykes. Ah just come from taking sacrament at the church house."

He snorted scornfully. "Yeah, you just come from de church house on a Sunday night, but heah you is gone to work on them clothes. You ain't nothing but a hypocrite. One of them amen-corner Christians—sing, whoop, and shout, then come home and wash white folks' clothes on the Sabbath."

He stepped roughly upon the whitest pile of things, kicking them helter-skelter as he crossed the room. His wife gave a little scream of dismay, and quickly gathered them together again.

15   "Sykes, you quit grindin' dirt into these clothes! How can Ah git through by Sat'day if Ah don't start on Sunday?"

"Ah don't keer if you never git through. Anyhow, Ah done promised Gawd and a couple of other men, Ah ain't gointer have it in mah house. Don't gimme no lip neither, else Ah'll throw 'em out and put mah fist up side yo' head to boot."

Delia's habitual meekness seemed to slip from her shoulders like a blown scarf. She was on her feet; her poor little body, her bare knuckly hands bravely defying the strapping hulk before her.

"Looka heah, Sykes, you done gone too fur. Ah been married to you fur fifteen years, and Ah been takin' in washin' fur fifteen years. Sweat, sweat, sweat! Work and sweat, cry and sweat, pray and sweat!"

"What's that got to do with me?" he asked brutally.

20   "What's it got to do with you, Sykes? Mah tub of suds is filled yo' belly with vittles more times than yo' hands is filled it. Mah sweat is done paid for this house and Ah reckon Ah kin keep on sweatin' in it."

She seized the iron skillet from the stove and struck a defensive pose, which act surprised him greatly, coming from her. It cowed him and he did not strike her as he usually did.

"Naw you won't," she panted, "that ole snaggle-toothed black woman you runnin' with ain't comin' heah to pile up on *mah* sweat and blood. You ain't paid for nothin' on this place, and Ah'm gointer stay right heah till Ah'm toted out foot foremost."

"Well, you better quit gittin' me riled up, else they'll be totin' you out sooner than you expect. Ah'm so tired of you Ah don't know whut to do. Gawd! How Ah hates skinny wimmen!"

A little awed by this new Delia, he sidled out of the door and slammed the back gate after him. He did not say where he had gone, but she knew too well. She knew very well that he would not return until nearly daybreak also. Her work over, she went on to bed but not to sleep at once. Things had come to a pretty pass!

25   She lay awake, gazing upon the debris that cluttered their matrimonial trail. Not an image left standing along the way. Anything like flowers had long ago been

drowned in the salty stream that had been pressed from her heart. Her tears, her sweat, her blood. She had brought love to the union and he had brought a longing after the flesh. Two months after the wedding, he had given her the first brutal beating. She had the memory of his numerous trips to Orlando with all of his wages when he had returned to her penniless, even before the first year had passed. She was young and soft then, but now she thought of her knotty, muscled limbs, her harsh knuckly hands, and drew herself up into an unhappy little ball in the middle of the big feather bed. Too late now to hope for love, even if it were not Bertha it would be someone else. This case differed from the others only in that she was bolder than the others. Too late for everything except her little home. She had built it for her old days, and planted one by one the trees and flowers there. It was lovely to her, lovely.

Somehow, before sleep came, she found herself saying aloud: "Oh well, whatever goes over the Devil's back, is got to come under his belly. Sometime or ruther, Sykes, like everybody else, is gointer reap his sowing." After that she was able to build a spiritual earthworks against her husband. His shells could no longer reach her. AMEN. She went to sleep and slept until he announced his presence in bed by kicking her feet and rudely snatching the covers away.

"Gimme some kivah heah, an' git yo' damn foots over on yo' own side! Ah oughter mash you in yo' mouf fuh drawing dat skillet on me."

Delia went clear to the rail without answering him. A triumphant indifference to all that he was or did.

II

The week was full of work for Delia as all other weeks, and Saturday found her behind her little pony, collecting and delivering clothes.

30   It was a hot, hot day near the end of July. The village men on Joe Clarke's porch even chewed cane listlessly. They did not hurl the cane-knots as usual. They let them dribble over the edge of the porch. Even conversation had collapsed under the heat.

"Heah come Delia Jones," Jim Merchant said, as the shaggy pony came 'round the bend of the road toward them. The rusty buckboard was heaped with baskets of crisp, clean laundry.

"Yep," Joe Lindsay agreed. "Hot or col', rain or shine, jes'ez reg'lar ez de weeks roll roun' Delia carries 'em an' fetches 'em on Sat'day."

"She better if she wanter eat," said Moss. "Syke Jones ain't wuth de shot an' powder hit would tek tuh kill 'em. Not to *huh* he ain't."

"He sho' ain't," Walter Thomas chimed in. "It's too bad, too, cause she wuz a right pretty li'l trick when he got huh. Ah'd uh mah'ied huh mahself if he hadnter beat me to it."

35   Delia nodded briefly at the men as she drove past.

"Too much knockin' will ruin *any* 'oman. He done beat huh 'nough tuh kill three women, let 'lone change they looks," said Elijah Moseley. "How Syke kin stommuck dat big black greasy Mogul he's layin' roun' wid, gits me. Ah swear dat eight-rock couldn't kiss a sardine can Ah done thowed out de back do' 'way las' yeah."

"Aw, she's fat, thass how come. He's allus been crazy 'bout fat women," put in Merchant. "He'd a' been tied up wid one long time ago if he could a' found one tuh have him. Did Ah tell yuh 'bout him come sidlin' roun' *mah* wife—bringin' her a basket uh peecans outa his yard fuh a present? Yessir, mah wife! She tol' him tuh take 'em right straight back home, 'cause Delia works so hard ovah dat washtub she reckon everything on de place taste lak sweat an' soapsuds. Ah jus' wisht Ah'd a' caught 'im 'roun' dere! Ah'd a' made his hips ketch on fiah down dat shell road."

"Ah know he done it, too. Ah sees 'im grinnin' at every 'oman dat passes," Walter Thomas said. "But even so, he useter eat some mighty big hunks uh humble pie tuh git dat li'l 'oman he got. She wuz ez pretty ez a speckled pup! Dat wuz fifteen years ago. He useter be so skeered uh losin' huh, she could make him do some parts of a husband's duty. Dey never wuz de same in de mind."

"There oughter be a law about him," said Lindsay. "He ain't fit tuh carry guts tuh a bear."

40   Clarke spoke for the first time. "Tain't no law on earth dat kin make a man be decent if it ain't in 'im. There's plenty men dat takes a wife lak dey do a joint uh sugar-cane. It's round, juicy, an' sweet when dey gits it. But dey squeeze an' grind, squeeze an' grind an' wring tell dey wring every drop uh pleasure dat's in 'em out. When dey's satisfied dat dey is wrung dry, dey treates 'em jes' lak dey do a cane-chew. Dey thows 'em away. Dey knows whut dey is doin' while dey is at it, an' hates theirselves fuh it but they keeps on hangin' after huh tell she's empty. Den dey hates huh fuh bein' a cane-chew an' in de way."

"We oughter take Syke an' dat stray 'oman uh his'n down in Lake Howell swamp an' lay on de rawhide till they cain't say Lawd a' mussy. He allus wuz uh ovahbearin niggah, but since dat white 'oman from up north done teached 'im how to run a automobile, he done got too beggety to live—an' we oughter kill 'im," Old Man Anderson advised.

A grunt of approval went around the porch. But the heat was melting their civic virtue and Elijah Moseley began to bait Joe Clarke.

"Come on, Joe, git a melon outa dere an' slice it up for yo' customers. We'se all sufferin' wid de heat. De bear's done got *me!*"

"Thass right, Joe, a watermelon is jes' whut Ah needs tuh cure de eppizudicks," Walter Thomas joined forces with Moseley. "Come on dere, Joe. We all is steady customers an' you ain't set us up in a long ime. Ah chooses dat long, bow-legged Floridy favorite."

45   "A god, an' be dough. You all gimme twenty cents and slice away," Clarke retorted. "Ah needs a col' slice m'self. Heah, everybody chip in. Ah'll lend y'all mah meat knife."

The money was all quickly subscribed and the huge melon brought forth. At that moment, Sykes and Bertha arrived. A determined silence fell on the porch and the melon was put away again.

Merchant snapped down the blade of his jacknife and moved toward the store door.

"Come on in, Joe, an' gimme a slab uh sow belly an' uh pound uh coffee— almost fuhgot 'twas Sat'day. Got to git on home." Most of the men left also.

Just then Delia drive past on her way home, as Sykes was ordering magnificently for Bertha. It pleased him for Delia to see.

50 "Git whutsoever yo' heart desires, Honey. Wait a minute, Joe. Give huh two bottles uh strawberry soda-water, uh quart parched ground-peas, an' a block uh chewin' gum."

With all this they left the store, with Sykes reminding Bertha that this was his town and she could have it if she wanted it.

The men returned soon after they left, and held their watermelon feast.

"Where did Syke Jones git da 'oman from nohow?" Lindsay asked.

"Ovah Apopka. Guess dey musta been cleanin' out de town when she lef'. She don't look lak a thing but a hunk uh liver wid hair on it."

55 "Well, she sho' kin squall," Dave Carter contributed. "When she gits ready tuh laff, she jes' opens huh mouf an' latches it back tuh de las' notch. No ole granpa alligator down in Lake Bell ain't go nothin' on huh."

III

Bertha had been in town three months now. Sykes was still paying her room-rent at Della Lewis'—the only house in town that would have taken her in. Sykes took her frequently to Winter Park to "stomps." He still assured her that he was the swellest man in the state.

"Sho' you kin have dat li'l ole house soon's Ah git dat 'oman outa dere. Everything b'longs tuh me an' you sho' kin have it. Ah sho 'bominates uh skinny 'oman. Lawdy, you sho' is got one portly shape on you! You kin git *anything* you wants. Dis is *mah* town an' you sho' kin have it."

Delia's work-worn knees crawled over the earth in Gethsemane[1] and up the rocks of Calvary many, many times during these months. She avoided the villagers and meeting places in her efforts to be blind and deaf. But Bertha nullified this to a degree, by coming to Delia's house to call Sykes out to her at the gate.

Delia and Sykes fought all the time now with no peaceful interludes. They slept and ate in silence. Two or three times Delia had attempted a timid friendliness, but she was repulsed each time. It was plain that the breaches must remain agape.

60 The sun had burned July to August. The heat streamed down like a million hot arrows, smiting all things living upon the earth. Grass withered, leaves browned, snakes went blind in shedding, and men and dogs went mad. Dog days!

Delia came home one day and found Sykes there before her. She wondered, but started to go on into the house without speaking, even though he was standing at the kitchen door and she must either stoop under his arm or ask him to move. He made no room for her. She noticed a soap box beside the steps, but paid no particular attention to it, knowing that he must have brought it there. As she was stooping to pass under his outstretched arm, he suddenly pushed her backward, laughingly.

"Look in de box dere Delia, Ah done brung yuh somethin'!"

She nearly fell upon the box in her stumbling, and when she saw what it held, she all but fainted outright.

[1]**Gethsemane** a reference to the garden where Jesus was betrayed (in the Gospels) before being tried and crucified on Calvary or Golgotha, the "hill of skulls."

"Syke! Syke, mah Gawd! You take dat rattlesnake 'way from heah! You *gottuh*. Oh, Jesus, have mussy!"

65   "Ah ain't got tuh do nuthin' uh de kin'—fact is Ah ain't got tuh do nothin' but die. Tain't no use uh you puttin' on airs makin' out lak you skeered uh dat snake—he's gointer stay right heah tell he die. He wouldn't bite me cause Ah knows how tuh handle 'im. Nohow he wouldn't risk breakin' out his fangs 'gin *yo* skinny laigs."

"Naw, now Syke, don't keep dat thing 'round tryin' tuh skeer me tuh death. You knows Ah'm even feared uh earth worms. Thass de biggest snake Ah evah did se. Kill 'im Syke, please."

"Doan ast me tuh do nothin' fuh yuh. Goin' 'round tryin' tuh be so damn aster-perious. Naw, Ah ain't gonna kill it. Ah think uh damn sight mo' uh him dan you! Dat's a nice snake an' anybody doan lak 'im kin jes' hit de grit."

The village soon heard that Sykes had the snake, and came to see and ask questions.

"How de hen-fire did you ketch dat six-foot rattler, Syke?" Thomas asked.

70   "He's full uh frogs so he cain't hardly move, thass how Ah eased up on 'm. But Ah'm a snake charmer an' knows how to handle 'em. Shux, dat ain't nothin'. Ah could ketch one eve'y day if Ah so wanted tuh."

"What he needs is a heavy hick'ry club leaned real heavy on his head. Dat's de bes' way tuh charm a rattlesnake."

"Naw, Walt, y'all jes' don't understand dese diamon' backs lak Ah do," said Sykes in a superior tone of voice.

The village agreed with Walter, but the snake stayed on. His box remained by the kitchen door with its screen wire covering. Two or three days later it had digested its meal of frogs and literally came to life. It rattled at every movement in the kitchen or the yard. One day as Delia came down the kitchen steps she saw his chalky-white fangs curved like scimitars hung in the wire meshes. This time she did not run away with averted eyes as usual. She stood for a long time in the doorway in a red fury that grew bloodier for every second that she regarded the creature that was her torment.

That night she broached the subject as soon as Sykes sat down to the table.

75   "Syke, Ah wants you tuh take dat snake 'way fum heah. You done starved me an' Ah put up widcher, you done beat me an Ah took dat, but you don kilt all mah insides bringin' dat varmint heah."

Sykes poured out a saucer full of coffee and drank it deliberately before he answered her.

"A whole lot Ah keer 'bout how you feels inside uh out. Dat snake ain't goin' no damn wheah till Ah gits ready fuh 'im tuh go. So fur as beatin' is concerned, yuh ain't took near all dat you gointer take ef yuh stay 'round *me*."

Delia pushed back her plate and got up from the table. "Ah hates you, Sykes," she said calmly. "Ah hates you tuh de same degree dat Ah useter love yuh. Ah done took an' took till mah belly is full up tuh mah neck. Dat's de reason Ah got mah letter fum de church an' moved mah membership tuh Woodbridge—so Ah don't haftuh take no sacrament wid yuh. Ah don't wantuh see yuh 'round me atall. Lay 'round wid dat 'oman all yuh wants tuh, but gwan 'way from me an' mah house. Ah hates yuh lak uh suck-egg dog."

Sykes almost let the huge wad of corn bread and collard greens he was chewing fall out of his mouth in amazement. He had a hard time whipping himself up to the proper fury to try to answer Delia.

80   "Well, Ah'm glad you does hate me. Ah'm sho' tiahed uh you hangin' ontuh me. Ah don't want yuh. Look at yuh stringey old neck! Yo' rawbony laigs an' arms is enough tuh cut uh man tuh death. You looks jes' lak de devvul's doll-baby tuh *me*. You cain't hate me no worse dan Ah hates you. Ah been hatin' *you* fuh years."

"Yo' ole black hide don't look lak nothin' tuh me, but uh passle uh wrinkled up rubber, wid yo' big ole yeahs flappin' on each side lak uh paih uh buzzard wings. Don't think Ah'm gointuh be run 'way fum mah house neither. Ah'm goin' tuh de white folks 'bout *you*, mah young man, de very nex' time you lay yo' han's on me. Mah cup is done run ovah." Delia said this with no signs of fear and Sykes departed from the house, threatening her, but made not the slightest move to carry out any of them.

That night he did not return at all, and the next day being Sunday, Delia was glad she did not have to quarrel before she hitched up her pony and drove the four miles to Woodbridge.

She stayed to the night service—"love feast"—which was very warm and full of spirit. In the emotional winds her domestic trials were borne far and wide so that she sang as she drove homeward,

> *Jurden water, black an' col*
> *Chills de body, not de soul*
> *An 'Ah wantah cross Jurden in uh calm time.*

She came from the barn to the kitchen door and stopped.

"Whut's de mattah, ol' Satan, you ain't kicken' up yo' racket?" She addressed the snake's box. Complete silence. She went on into the house with a new hope in its birth struggles. Perhaps her threat to go to the white folks had frightened Sykes! Perhaps he was sorry! Fifteen years of misery and suppression had brought Delia to the place where she would hope *anything* that looked towards a way over or through her wall of inhibitions.

85   She felt in the match-safe behind the stove at once for a match. There was only one there.

"Dat niggah wouldn't fetch nothin' heah tuh save his rotten neck, but he kin run thew whut Ah brings quick enough. Now he done toted off nigh on tuh haff un box uh matches. He done had dat 'oman heah in mah house, too."

Nobody but a woman could tell how she knew this even before she struck the match. But she did and it put her into a new fury.

Presently she brought in the tubs to put the white things to soak. This time she decided she need not bring the hamper out of the bedroom; she would go in there and do the sorting. She picked up the pot-bellied lamp and went in. The room was small and the hamper stood hard by the foot of the white iron bed. She could sit and reach through the bedposts—resting as she worked.

"*Ah wantah cross Jurden in uh calm time.*" She was singing again. The mood of the "love feast," had returned. She threw back the lid of the basket almost gaily. Then, moved by both horror and terror, she sprang back toward the door. *There lay the snake in the basket!* He moved sluggishly at first, but even as she turned round and round, jumped up and down in insanity of fear, he began to stir vigorously. She saw him pouring his awful beauty from the basket upon the bed, then she seized the lamp and ran as fast as she could to the kitchen. The wind from the open door blew out the light and the darkness added to her terror. She sped to the darkness of the yard, slamming the door after her before she thought to set down the lamp. She did not feel safe even on the ground, so she climbed up in the hay barn.

90   There for an hour or more she lay sprawled upon the hay a gibbering wreck.

Finally she grew quiet, and after that came coherent thought. With this stalked through her a cold, bloody rage. Hours of this. A period of introspection, a space of retrospection, then a mixture of both. Out of this an awful calm.

"Well, Ah done de bes' Ah could. If things ain't right, Gawd knows tain't mah fault."

She went to sleep—a twitch sleep—and woke up to a faint gray sky. There was a loud hollow sound below. She peered out. Sykes was at the woodpile, demolishing a wire-covered box.

He hurried to the kitchen door, but hung outside there some minutes before he entered, and stood some minutes more inside before he closed it after him.

95   The gray in the sky was spreading. Delia descended without fear now, and crouched beneath the low bedroom window. The drawn shade shut out the dawn, shut in the night. But the thin walls held back no sound.

"Dat ol' scratch is woke up now!" She mused at the tremendous whirr inside, which every woodsman knows, is one of the sound illusions. The rattle is a ventriloquist. His whirr sounds to the right, to the left, straight ahead, behind, close under foot—everywhere but where it is. Woe to him who guesses wrong unless he is prepared to hold up his end of the argument! Sometimes he strikes without rattling at all.

Inside, Sykes heard nothing until he knocked a pot lid off the stove while trying to reach the match-safe in the dark. He had emptied his pockets at Bertha's.

The snake seemed to wake up under the stove and Sykes made a quick leap into the bedroom. In spite of the gin he had had, his head was clearing now.

"Mah Gawd!" he chattered, "ef Ah could on'y strack uh light!"

100   The rattling ceased for a moment as he stood paralyzed. He waited. It seemed that the snake waited also.

"Oh, fuh de light! Ah thought he'd be too sick"—Sykes was muttering to himself when the whirr began again, closer, right underfoot this time. Long before this, Sykes' ability to think had been flattened down to primitive instinct and he leaped—onto the bed.

Outside Delia heard a cry that might have come from a maddened chimpanzee, a stricken gorilla. All the terror, all the horror, all the rage that man possibly could express, without a recognizable human sound.

A tremendous stir inside there, another series of animal screams, the intermittent whirr of the reptile. The shade torn violently down from the window, letting in the red dawn, a huge brown hand seizing the window stick, great dull blows upon the wooden floor punctuating the gibberish of sound long after the rattle of the snake had abruptly subsided. All this Delia could see and hear from her place beneath the window, and it made her ill. She crept over to the four o'clocks and stretched herself on the cool earth to recover.

She lay there. "Delia, Delia!" She could hear Sykes calling in a most despairing tone as one who expected no answer. The sun crept on up, and he called. Delia could not move—her legs had gone flabby. She never moved, he called, and the sun kept rising.

105   "Mah Gawd!" she heard him moan, "Mah Gawd fum Heben!" She heard him stumbling about and got up from her flower-bed. The sun was growing warm. As she approached the door she heard him call out hopefully, "Delia, is dat you Ah hear?"

She saw him on his hands and knees as soon as she reached the door. He crept an inch or two toward her—all that he was able, and she saw his horribly swollen neck and his one open eye shining with hope. A surge of pity too strong to support her bore her away from that eye that must, could not, fail to see the tubs. He would see the lamp. Orlando with its doctors was too far. She could scarcely reach the chinaberry tree, where she waited in the growing heat while inside she knew the cold river was creeping up and up to extinguish that eye which must know by now that she knew.

COMMENTARY ON "THE NEGRO SPEAKS OF RIVERS"

LANGSTON HUGHES   [1940]

The one of my poems that has perhaps been most often reprinted in anthologies, was written on the train during this trip to Mexico when I was feeling very bad. It's called "The Negro Speaks of Rivers" and was written just outside St. Louis, as the train rolled toward Texas.

It came about in this way. All day on the train I had been thinking about my father and his strange dislike of his own people. I don't understand it, because I was a Negro, and I like Negroes very much. One of the happiest jobs I had ever had was during my freshman year in high school, when I worked behind the soda fountain for a Mrs. Kitzmiller, who ran a refreshment parlor on Central Avenue in the heart of the colored neighborhood. People just up from the South used to come in for ice cream and sodas and watermelon. And I never tired of hearing them talk, listening to the thunderclaps of their laughter, to their troubles, to their discussions of the war and the men who had gone to Europe from the Jim Crow South, their complaints over the high rent and the long overtime hours that brought what seemed like big checks, until the weekly bills were paid. They seemed to me like the gayest and the bravest people possible—these Negroes from the southern ghettos—facing tremendous odds, working and laughing and trying to get somewhere in the world.

I had been in to dinner early that afternoon on the train. Now it was just sunset, and we crossed the Mississippi, slowly, over a long bridge. I looked out the window of the Pullman at the great muddy river flowing down toward the heart of the South, and I began to think what that river, the old Mississippi, had meant to Negroes in the past—how to be sold down the river was the worst fate that could overtake a slave in times of bondage. Then I remembered reading how Abraham Lincoln had made a trip down the Mississippi on a raft to New Orleans, and how he had seen slavery at its worst, and had decided within himself that it should be removed from American life. Then I began to think about other rivers in our past— the Congo, and the Niger, and the Nile in Africa—and the thought came to me; "I've known rivers," and I put it down on the back of an envelope I had in my pocket, and within the space of ten or fifteen minutes, as the train gathered speed in the dusk, I had written this poem, which I called "The Negro Speaks of Rivers":

> I've known rivers:
> I've known rivers ancient as the world and older than
>   the flow of human blood in human veins.
>
> My soul has grown deep like the rivers.
>
> I bathed in the Euphrates when dawns were young.
> I built my hut near the Congo and it lulled me to sleep.
> I looked upon the Nile and raised the pyramids above it.
> I heard the singing of the Mississippi when Abe Lincoln
>   went down to New Orleans, and I've seen its muddy
>   bosom turn all golden in the sunset.
>
> I've known rivers:
> Ancient, dusky rivers.
>
> My soul has grown deep like the rivers.

No doubt I changed a few words the next day, or maybe crossed out a line or two. But there are seldom many changes in my poems, once they're down. Generally, the first two or three lines come to me from something I'm thinking about, or looking at, or doing, and the rest of the poem (if there is to be a poem) flows from those first few lines, usually right away. If there is a chance to put the poem down then, I write it down. If not, I try to remember it until I get to a pencil and paper; for poems are like rainbows: they escape you quickly.

JESSIE FAUSET   [1926]

Very perfect is the memory of my first literary acquaintance with Langston Hughes. In the unforgettable days when we were publishing *The Brownies' Book* we had already appreciated a charming fragile conceit which read:

> Out of the dust of dreams,
> Fairies weave their garments;
> Out of the purple and rose of old memories,
> They make purple wings.
> No wonder we find them such marvelous things.

Then one day came "The Negro Speaks of Rivers." I took the beautiful dignified creation to Dr. Du Bois and said: "What colored person is there, do you suppose, in the United States who writes like that and yet is unknown to us?" And I wrote and found him to be a Cleveland high school graduate who had just gone to live in

Mexico. Already he had begun to assume that remote, so elusive quality which permeates most of his work. Before long we had the pleasure of seeing the work of the boy, whom we had sponsored, copied and recopied in journals far and wide. "The Negro Speaks of Rivers" even appeared in translation in a paper printed in Germany.

ONWUCHEKWA JEMIE   [1973]

"The Negro Speaks of Rivers" is perhaps the most profound of these poems of heritage and strength. Composed when Hughes was a mere 17 years old, and dedicated to W. E. B. Du Bois, it is a sonorous evocation of transcendent essences so ancient as to appear timeless, predating human existence, longer than human memory. The rivers are part of God's body, and participate in his immortality. They are the earthly analogues of eternity: deep, continuous, mysterious. They are named in the order of their association with black history. The black man has drunk of their life-giving essences, and thereby borrowed their immortality. He and the rivers have become one. The magical transformation of the Mississippi from mud to gold by the sun's radiance is mirrored in the transformation of slaves into free men by Lincoln's Proclamation (and, in Hughes' poems, the transformation of shabby cabarets into gorgeous palaces, dancing girls into queens and priestesses by the spell of black music). As the rivers deepen with time, so does the black man's soul; as their waters ceaselessly flow, so will the black soul endure. The black man has seen the rise and fall of civilizations from the earliest times, seen the beauty and death-changes of the world over the thousands of years, and will survive even this America. The poem's meaning is related to Zora Neale Hurston's judgment of the mythic High John de Conquer, whom she held as a symbol of the triumphant spirit of black America: that John was of the "Be" class. "*Be* here when the ruthless man comes, and *be* here when he is gone." In a time and place where black life is held cheap and the days of black men appear to be numbered, the poem is a majestic reminder of the strength and fullness of history, of the source of that life which transcends even ceaseless labor and burning crosses.

R. BAXTER MILLER   [1989]

"Rivers" presents the narrator's skill in retracing known civilization back to the source in East Africa. Within thirteen lines and five stanzas, through the suggestion of wisdom by anagoge, we re-project ourselves into aboriginal consciousness. Then the speaker affirms the spirit distilled from human history, ranging from 3000 B.C. through the mid-nineteenth century to the author himself at the brink of the Harlem Renaissance. The powerful repeated "I've known rivers. / Ancient, dusky rivers" closes the human narrative in nearly a circle, for the verse has turned itself subtly from an external focus to a unified and internal one: "My soul has grown deep like the rivers." Except for the physical and spiritual dimensions, the subjective "I" and the "river" read the same.

When the Euphrates flows from eastern Turkey southeast and southwest into the Tigris, it recalls the rise as well as the fall of the Roman Empire. For over two thousand years the water helped delimit that domain. Less so did the Congo, which south of the Sahara demarcates the natural boundaries between white and Black Africa. The latter empties into the Atlantic Ocean; the Nile flows northward from Uganda into the Mediterranean; in the United States the Mississippi River flows southeast from north central Minnesota to the Gulf of Mexico. Whether north or south, east or west, "River" signifies the fertility as well as the dissemination of life in concentric half-circles. The liquid, as the externalized form of the contemplative imagination, has both depth and flow. "The Negro Speaks of Rivers" reclaims the origins in Africa of both physical and spiritual humanity.

ALICE WALKER   [1979]

ZORA NEALE HURSTON: A CAUTIONARY TALE AND A PARTISAN VIEW

During the early and middle years of her career Zora was a cultural revolutionary simply because she was always herself. Her work, so vigorous among the rather pallid productions of many of her contemporaries, comes from the essence of black folk life. During her later life she became frightened of the life she had always dared bravely before. Her work too became reactionary, static, shockingly misguided and timid. (This is especially true of her last novel, *Seraphs on the Sewannee,* which is not even about black people, which is no crime, but *is* about white people for whom it is impossible to care, which is.)

A series of misfortunes battered Zora's spirit and her health. And she was broke. *Being broke made all the difference.*

Without money of one's own in a capitalist society, there is no such thing as independence. This is one of the clearest lessons of Zora's life, and why I consider the telling of her life "a cautionary tale." We must learn from it what we can.

5   Without money, an illness, even a simple one, can undermine the will. Without money, getting into a hospital is problematic and getting out without money to pay for the treatment is nearly impossible. Without money, one becomes dependent on other people, who are likely to be—even in their kindness—erratic in their support and despotic in their expectations of return. Zora was forced to rely, like Tennessee Williams's Blanche, "on the kindness of strangers." Can anything be more dangerous, if the strangers are forever in control? Zora, who worked so hard, was never able to make a living from her work.

She did not complain about not having money. She was not the type. (Several months ago I received a long letter from one of Zora's nieces, a bright ten-year-old, who explained to me that her aunt was so proud that the only way the family could guess she was ill or without funds was by realizing they had no idea where she was. Therefore, none of the family attended either Zora's sickbed or her funeral.) Those of us who have had "grants and fellowships from 'white folks'" know this aid is extended in precisely the way welfare is extended in Mississippi. One is asked, *curtly,* more often than not: How much do you need *just to survive?* Then one is—if fortunate—given a third of that. What is amazing is that Zora, who became an orphan at nine, a runaway at fourteen, a maid and manicurist (because of necessity and not from love of the work) before she was twenty—with one dress—managed to become Zora Neale Hurston, author and anthropologist, at all.

For me, the most unfortunate thing Zora ever wrote is her autobiography. After the first several chapters, it rings false. One begins to hear the voice of someone whose life required the assistance of too many transitory "friends." A Taoist proverb states that *to act sincerely with the insincere is dangerous.* (A mistake blacks as a group have tended to make in America.) And so we have Zora sincerely offering gratitude and kind words to people one knows she could not have respected. But this unctuousness, so out of character for Zora, is also a result of dependency, a sign of her powerlessness, her inability to pay back her debts with anything but words. They must have been bitter ones for her. In her dependency, it should be remembered, Zora was not alone—because it is quite true that America does not support or honor us as human beings, let alone as blacks, women, and artists. We have taken help where it was offered because we are committed to what we do and to the survival of our work. Zora was committed to the survival of her people's cultural heritage as well.

In my mind, Zora Neale Hurston, Billie Holiday, and Bessie Smith form a sort of unholy trinity. Zora *belongs* in the tradition of black women singers, rather than among "the literati," at least to me. There were the extreme highs and lows of her life, her undaunted pursuit of adventure, passionate emotional and sexual experience, and her love of freedom. Like Billie and Bessie she followed her own road, believed in her own gods, pursued her own dreams, and refused to separate herself from "common" people. It would have been nice if the three of them had had one another to turn to, in times of need. I close my eyes and imagine them: Bessie would be in charge of all the money; Zora would keep Billie's masochistic tendencies in check and prevent her from singing embarrassing anything-for-a-man songs, thereby preventing Billie's heroin addiction. In return, Billie could be, along with Bessie, the family that Zora felt she never had.

We are a people. A people do not throw their geniuses away. And if they are thrown away, it is our duty *as artists and as witnesses for the future* to collect them again for the sake of our children, and, if necessary, bone by bone.

A Student's Argumentative Essay

In the argumentative essay that follows, William Winters shows how two poems, "Incident" by Countee Cullen and Langston Hughes's "Theme for English B," exemplify the criteria set forth in Hughes's essay "The Negro Artist and the Racial Mountain." His thesis is that while each poem is thematically different, "both [according to the criteria in Hughes's essay] have a strong sense of the 'innumerable overtones and undertones' in relations between the races." It is an argumentative essay because the student writer is not simply indicating his personal experience of these poems, but also is interpreting them within the larger context of artistic or literary theory.

William Winters

Dr. Madden

English 102

November 16, 20XX

<h2 style="text-align:center">The Racial Mountain</h2>

In his essay "The Negro Artist and the Racial Mountain," Langston Hughes insists that the black artist can find "a lifetime of creative work" without going outside his own race (1072). He asserts further that race "relations between Negroes and whites...with their innumerable overtones and undertones" provide an "inexhaustible supply of themes" (1072). Two poems about race relations, Countee Cullen's "Incident" and Hughes's own poem "Theme for English B," provide us with examples of Hughes's view. Each has a different theme and both have a strong sense of the "innumerable overtones and undertones" in relations between the races.

When someone passes judgment on someone else based on that person's race or ethnicity, we call it racism. Most of us have been fortunate enough not to be the subject of racist remarks. We never thought about what it would be like to have someone direct racist comments at us. Even though we cannot understand how it feels to be a victim of racism unless we experience it in real life, these two poems give us a small taste of it. Though the poems were written twenty-six years apart, and they address different aspects of being black in a white society, each continues to have a strong impact.

Countee Cullen's "Incident" is short, simple, and to the point, and though the young boy has only visited Baltimore for a short time, racism is branded into his mind forever. Here we have an innocent eight-year-old child whose heart and head are "filled with glee" (2) because he is excited about visiting the city of Baltimore. The child sees another boy and smiles at him. The boy then points to him and calls the child a "nigger." When the speaker describes this happening, I could feel the child's heart sink. And my heart sank, too. The child must have felt he was not wanted in this new place. Countee Cullen does an excellent job of letting the reader see the world through the child's eyes.

Racism is not something we are born with. Instead, it is something we learn from others. The child in the poem did not judge the other boy by the color of his skin. When the child smiled at him, the color of the boy's skin did not even cross his young mind. However, the young bigot has now made the child aware that people feel strongly about the color of his skin. That bigoted child was not born a racist. He learned to hate from others. This brief, simple poem is very powerful and says a lot with a few words.

Langston Hughes's "Theme for English B" also deals with the topic of racism. It gets its message across very well, too, but in a slightly different way. Unlike "Incident," it does not put us in the shoes of the main character. It feels more like having a conversation with the speaker in the poem. He seems more like a friend, and as he continues to speak we identify and sympathize with him. The message we get from this poem is that people are generally the same, but the color of their skin can separate them.

The main character is very aware of his ethnicity. He describes himself as "twenty-two, colored, born in Winston-Salem" (7). He also tells us that he is the only "colored" student in his class. This contrasts with the poem "Incident," in which the speaker, who is only eight years old, has not yet learned to see the world in black and white. The speaker says he likes to "eat, sleep, drink, and be in love" (21). He also tells us of other "normal" things that he likes. He does this to show that his interests are the same as white people's. Some people might be surprised by this!

He continues, however, by saying, "So will my page be colored that I write? / Being me, it will not be white" (27–28). Here he is telling us that even though he enjoys many of the same things that white people enjoy, his paper will be different because he is black. For him, this is an excellent segue into another thought: "Sometimes perhaps you don't want to be a part of me. / Nor do I often want to be a part of you" (34–35). Here, too, he indicates that though we share the same humanity, there are things that make us different. Our ethnic backgrounds, where we grew up, our families, our individual personalities make us different. But this difference is good. It is not something negative. It is good for all of us to have pride in our backgrounds. It gives us the opportunity to learn something from each other. As the speaker in the poem says, "That's American" (33). It is the abuse of these differences that separates ethnicity from racism.

We are all different. We come from different races, cultures, classes, and families. These differences, however, are good. They make us unique and give us something to have pride in. Much too often our ethnicity is looked upon as something negative and this results in racism. Unlike our ethnicity, racism is not something we are born with, but something we learn from others and from living our lives. Racism is not logical; it is stupid. How can we dislike someone just because of the color of his or her skin? Yes, there are evil people in all races, yet there are good people, too.

In "The Negro Artist and the Racial Mountain," Langston Hughes suggests that race relations are very complex and that there is more than enough material here for black artists to write about. The poems "Incident" and "Theme for English B" are strong reflections of this belief.

[New Page]

Works Cited

Cullen, Countee. "Incident." Madden 24.

Hughes, Langston. "The Negro Artist and the Racial Mountain." Madden 1071–74.

———. "Theme for English B." Madden 1082–83.

Madden, Frank, ed. *Exploring Literature*. 5th ed. New York: Longman, 2012.

EXPLORING THE LITERATURE OF CULTURE AND IDENTITY: OPTIONS FOR MAKING CONNECTIONS, BUILDING ARGUMENTS, AND USING RESEARCH

MAKING CONNECTIONS

1. Consider the ways in which your culture and identity have affected your life. Do any of the stories, poems, plays, or essays in this section remind you of your own experiences or the circumstances in your life? Choose one or more of these works, and write a response essay that compares your experience or circumstances with those in the literature.

2. Where we grow up, the society or culture we grow up in, and similar factors can influence how we see the world and our response to literature. Based on these values, we may agree or disagree with what an author says or what characters say or do. So, too, the ideas expressed about culture and identity in literature may influence us and the formation of our values. Write an essay about the ways in which one or more works in this section either provoked a moral judgment on your part or helped you learn something.

MAKING AN ARGUMENT

1. In her book *Patterns of Culture,* anthropologist Ruth Benedict wrote, "From the moment of his birth the customs into which [an individual] is born shape his experience and behavior. By the time he can talk, he is the little creature of his culture." Consider this quote, and write an essay about how an author or a character in one or more works in this section is influenced by his or her culture.

2. In his 1859 book, *Critique of Political Economy,* political and economic philosopher Karl Marx wrote, "It is not the consciousness of men that determines their existence, but on the contrary it is their social existence that determines their consciousness." Write about this quote as it affects the way a character or an author in one or more works in this section sees the world.

3. Choose a quote (or quotes) from the introduction to this section, Culture and Identity (pp. 892–1106), and pair it (or them) with one of the longer pieces in this section that either supports it or argues against it. For example, Thoreau's statement from *Walden,* "If a man does not keep pace with his companions,...Let him step to the music which he hears, however measured or far away," might be paired with the excerpt from his essay "Civil Disobedience." If you choose Karl Marx's statement about social existence determining consciousness, you might choose Luis Valdez's *Los Vendidos* to support it. Write an essay that compares or contrasts a quote (or quotes) from the introduction with a story, poem, play, or essay that supports or argues against it.

Using Research

William Faulkner's story "A Rose for Emily," Shirley Geok-lin Lim's "Learning to love America," Luis Valdez's play *Los Vendidos,* and Martin Luther King, Jr.'s "I Have a Dream" all have something important to say about the impact of culture and identity. Each of these works, however, springs from a very different historical, social, or political context. Expanding our exploration of literature to include the context in which these works were produced can be an enriching and enlightening experience.

1. Choose one or more of these or other works in this section, and write a research essay that includes secondary source material about the historical, social, or political background of the literature. However insightful each of these pieces is by itself, expanding our exploration of this literature by seeking, using, and citing relevant secondary sources can add support and credibility to our writing.

2. Do you think different ethnic groups in previous centuries experienced immigration differently? Are immigrants today less welcome than they were a hundred or 150 years ago? Using literature in this section and relevant primary and secondary source materials to support your views, compare the immigration experiences of different ethnic groups in comparison to each other today and in comparison to a century ago.

3. Though not one of the best poems in this anthology, Emma Lazarus's poem "The New Colossus" (written in 1888) is engraved on the pedestal of the Statue of Liberty and seems to represent an ideal of America's welcome to the world's immigrants. Read the poem and research its background. Where did this poem come from and why is it engraved on the statue? Did this poem accurately represent the attitude of most citizens of this country in 1888? Does it represent the prevailing attitude today? Citing relevant historical and contemporary sources, write a research essay that takes a position one way or the other.

Writing About Connections Across Themes

Most of the literature in the text has been organized into theme sections, but good literature is much too complex to be reduced to a single, broad theme. Many of the works included under Culture and Identity could just as easily fit under other themes—and in many cases works arranged in other themes could fit here as well.

Choose one or more of the following works from earlier chapters or other themes, and consider how they can be linked to Culture and Identity—and how combining works with more than one theme provides additional insight into the literature and fresh topics for writing.

From Chapter 1
 "Zimmer in Grade School"—p. 11
 "Barbie Doll"—p. 14
 "Ballad of Birmingham"—p. 17
From Chapter 2
 "Incident"—p. 24
 "Eleven"—p. 26
 "Mothers"—p. 31
 "Salvation"—p. 32
From Chapter 5
 "Eveline"—p. 201
From Family and Friends
 "Sonny's Blues"—p. 218
 "The Red Convertible"—p. 241
 "Marriage Is a Private Affair"—p. 249
 "The Road"—p. 257
 "For My Father"—p. 272
 "Digging"—p. 281
From Innocence and Experience
 "The Stolen Party"—p. 403
 "Snow"—p. 412
 "The Lesson"—p. 414
 "Battle Royal"—p. 421
 "Pain for a Daughter"—p. 474
From Women and Men
 "Shiloh"—p. 705

Collaboration: Writing and Revising with Your Peers

In addition to applying your own values and standards to writing about the literature in this section, you may find it beneficial to share and discuss your work with classmates. Getting feedback from others can help you generate and clarify your ideas and revise and edit your writing more effectively. For details, see pages 397–398.

A Writing/Research Portfolio Option

A portfolio is a collection of your work, related materials, and commentary about your work collected over time. Gathering materials in a portfolio will provide you with resources for research and development. See page 398 for details.

Faith & Doubt

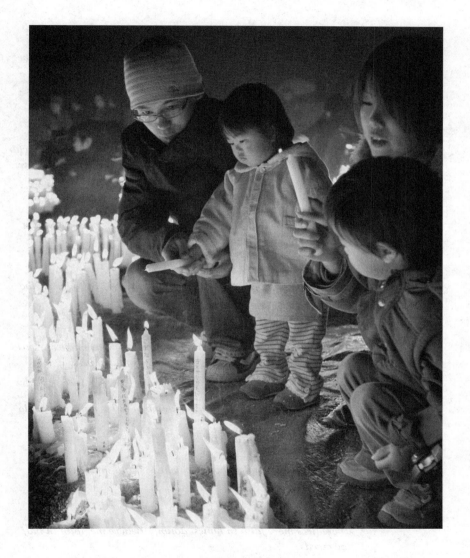

Faith & Doubt

A DIALOGUE ACROSS HISTORY

All men know the utility of useful things; but they do not know the utility of futility.
— Chuang-tzu, 369–286 BCE

The business of the samurai consists in reflecting on his own station in life, in discharging loyal service to his master if he has one, in deepening his fidelity in associations with friends, and with due consideration of his own position, in devoting himself to duty above all.
— Yamaga Soko, c. 1650

Men never do evil so completely and cheerfully as when they do it from religious conviction.
— Blaise Pascal, *Pensées*, 1670

In the Affairs of this World, Men are saved not by Faith but by the want of it.
— Benjamin Franklin, *Poor Richard's Almanac*, 1757

Morality is not properly the doctrine of how we may make ourselves happy, but how we make ourselves worthy of happiness.
— Immanuel Kant, 1788

The only thing necessary for the triumph of evil is for good men to do nothing.
— Edmund Burke, c. 1800

Life can only be understood backwards; but it must be lived forwards.
— Søren Kierkegaard, c. 1850

There lives more faith in honest doubt, / Believe me, than in half the creeds.
— Alfred Lord Tennyson, "In Memoriam," 1850

The mass of men lead lives of quiet desperation.
— Henry David Thoreau, *Walden*, 1854

The essence of religion consists solely in the question, "Why do I live and what is my relation to the infinite universe around me?"
  —Leo Tolstoy, c. 1878

So long as man remains free he strives for nothing so incessantly and so painfully as to find someone to worship.
  —Fedor Dostoevski, *The Brothers Karamazov,* 1879

Like all weak men he laid an exaggerated stress on not changing one's mind.
  —Somerset Maugham, *Of Human Bondage,* 1915

A life without religion is a life without principles, and a life without principles is like a ship without a rudder.
  —Mahatma Gandhi, *Autobiography,* 1924

The certainties of one age are the problems of the next.
  —R. H. Tawney, *Religion and the Rise of Capitalism,* 1926

Truth has no special time of its own. Its hour is now—always.
  —Albert Schweitzer, *Out of My Life and Thought,* 1949

Liberty is the possibility of doubting, the possibility of making a mistake, the possibility of searching and experimenting, the possibility of saying "No" to any authority—literary, artistic, philosophic, religious, social, and even political.
  —Ignazio Silone, essay in *The God That Failed,* 1950

I cannot and will not cut my conscience to fit this year's fashions.
  —Lillian Hellman, letter, 1952

Doubt isn't the opposite of faith; it is an element of faith.
  —Paul Tillich, 1886–1965

We are born into a world where alienation awaits us.
  —R. D. Laing, *The Politics of Experience,* 1967

We all want to know why. Man is the asking animal. And while the finding, the belief that we have found the Answer, can separate us and make us forget our humanity, it is the seeking that continues to bring us together, that makes and keeps us human.
  —Daniel Boorstin, *The Seekers,* 1998

FAITH AND DOUBT: EXPLORING YOUR OWN VALUES AND BELIEFS

We all want something to believe in—something to give our lives meaning. But we seek and act out our beliefs in many different ways. Many people join communities that share a common religious, ethical, ethnic, or political belief. Others see individual conscience as the most important guide for their beliefs and actions.

In what way do your values and beliefs influence how you see the world? Do religious, ethical, ethnic, or cultural values form the core of those beliefs? If you are deeply religious, that's probably at the heart of almost everything you value. If you are not religious, the nature of your experiences, the values you grew up with, influential people in your life, what you read, or other factors may strongly influence your perspective.

The *certainty* of your beliefs, however, may be challenged by almost everything you experience. What part does *doubt* about religion and other beliefs play in your life? In what way have events in your life or in the world—9/11, Hurricane Katrina, the Haiti earthquake, the tsunami and nuclear disaster in Japan—or the literature you've read challenged what you believe in? Before you respond to the literature in this section, you may want to think about your own beliefs and/or doubts and how they affect your point of view.

READING AND WRITING ABOUT FAITH AND DOUBT

Exploring your beliefs and values and connecting your experience with what you read is an important first step toward our ultimate goal—an appreciation of literature and the ability to think and write critically about it. Critical analysis will require rereading and reflection, writing and revising, gathering evidence, and constructing a solid argument to support your responses.

At least one aspect of the many stories, poems, plays, and essays in this section is concerned with the conflict of faith and doubt: from young soldiers struggling to stay connected with life back home in the midst of the horror and absurdity of war in Tim O'Brien's story "The Things They Carried," to the seeming randomness of fate in Thomas Hardy's poem "Hap." The brief quotes that open this section and the photo of the mother and children in Japan, lighting candles for the victims of the tsunami, also give you some idea of the number of compelling ethical, political, and social arguments that are connected to faith and doubt. Religion, conscience, self-reflection, self-interest, and emotion versus intellect head a long list of concerns. Any of these or other related issues might provide a fine topic for building an argument and writing an essay.

◆ FICTION ◆

RAYMOND CARVER [1938–1988]

Raymond Carver was born in Clatskanie, Oregon, and raised in Yakima, Washington. After working at a series of low-paying jobs, he entered Humboldt State University in 1963, where he first began to write poetry and short stories, and then went on to earn an M.F.A. from the University of Iowa in 1966. Usually set among working-class people, his stories, like "Cathedral," often hinge on moments of sudden insight. His collections include Put Yourself in My Shoes *(1974),* Will You Please Be Quiet, Please? *(1976),* What We Talk About When We Talk About Love *(1981),* Cathedral *(1983), and* Where I'm Calling From: New and Collected Stories *(1988). His stories inspired* Short Cuts, *the critically acclaimed 1993 film directed by Robert Altman. Carver died of lung cancer in 1988. Unlike many writers who came of age in the 1970s, Carver did not see the writing of fiction as a political act: "It just has to be there for the pleasure we take in doing it, and the different kind of pleasure that's taken in reading something that's durable and made to last, as well as beautiful in and of itself. Something that throws off these sparks—a persistent and steady glow, however dim."*

CATHEDRAL   [1984]

This blind man, an old friend of my wife's, he was on his way to spend the night. His wife had died. So he was visiting the dead wife's relatives in Connecticut. He called my wife from his in-laws'. Arrangements were made. He would come by train, a five-hour trip, and my wife would meet him at the station. She hadn't seen him since she worked for him one summer in Seattle ten years ago. But she and the blind man had kept in touch. They made tapes and mailed them back and forth. I wasn't enthusiastic about his visit. He was no one I knew. And his being blind bothered me. My idea of blindness came from the movies. In the movies, the blind moved slowly and never laughed. Sometimes they were led by seeing-eye dogs. A blind man in my house was not something I looked forward to.

That summer in Seattle she had needed a job. She didn't have any money. The man she was going to marry at the end of the summer was in officers' training school. He didn't have any money, either. But she was in love with the guy, and he was in love with her, etc. She'd seen something in the paper: HELP WANTED—*Reading to Blind Man,* and a telephone number. She phoned and went over, was hired on the spot. She'd worked with this blind man all summer. She read stuff to him, case studies, reports, that sort of thing. She helped him organize his little office in the county social-service department. They'd become good friends, my wife and the blind man. How do I know these things? She told me. And she told me something else. On her last day in the office, the blind man asked if he could touch her face. She agreed to this. She told me he touched his fingers to every part of her face, her nose—even her neck! She never forgot it. She even tried to write a poem about it.

She was always trying to write a poem. She wrote a poem or two every year, usually after something really important had happened to her.

When we first started going out together, she showed me the poem. In the poem, she recalled his fingers and the way they had moved around over her face. In the poem, she talked about what she had felt at the time, about what went through her mind when the blind man touched her nose and lips. I can remember I didn't think much of the poem. Of course, I didn't tell her that. Maybe I just don't understand poetry. I admit it's not the first thing I reach for when I pick up something to read.

Anyway, this man who'd first enjoyed her favors, the officer-to-be, he'd been her childhood sweetheart. So okay. I'm saying that at the end of the summer she let the blind man run his hands over her face, said goodbye to him, married her childhood etc., who was now a commissioned officer, and she moved away from Seattle. But they'd kept in touch, she and the blind man. She made the first contact after a year or so. She called him up one night from an Air Force base in Alabama. She wanted to talk. They talked. He asked her to send him a tape and tell him about her life. She did this. She sent the tape. On the tape, she told the blind man about her husband and about their life together in the military. She told the blind man she loved her husband but she didn't like it where they lived and she didn't like it that he was part of the military-industrial thing. She told the blind man she'd written a poem and he was in it. She told him that she was writing a poem about what it was like to be an Air Force officer's wife. The poem wasn't finished yet. She was still writing it. The blind man made a tape. He sent her the tape. She made a tape. This went on for years. My wife's officer was posted to one base and then another. She sent tapes from Moody AFB, McGuire, McConnell, and finally Travis, near Sacramento, where one night she got to feeling lonely and cut off from people she kept losing in that moving-around life. She got to feeling she couldn't go it another step. She went in and swallowed all the pills and capsules in the medicine chest and washed them down with a bottle of gin. Then she got into a hot bath and passed out.

5   But instead of dying, she got sick. She threw up. Her officer—why should he have a name? he was the childhood sweetheart, and what more does he want?—came home from somewhere, found her, and called the ambulance. In time, she put it all on a tape and sent the tape to the blind man. Over the years, she put all kinds of stuff on tapes and sent the tapes off lickety-split. Next to writing a poem every year, I think it was her chief means of recreation. On one tape, she told the blind man she'd decided to live away from her officer for a time. On another tape, she told him about her divorce. She and I began going out, and of course she told her blind man about it. She told him everything, or so it seemed to me. Once she asked me if I'd like to hear the latest tape from the blind man. This was a year ago. I was on the tape, she said. So I said okay, I'd listen to it. I got us drinks and we settled down in the living room. We made ready to listen. First she inserted the tape into the player and adjusted a couple of dials. Then she pushed a lever. The tape squeaked and someone began to talk in this loud voice. She lowered the volume. After a few minutes of harmless chitchat, I heard my own name in the mouth of this stranger, this blind man I didn't even know! And then this: "From all you've said about him, I can only conclude—" But we were interrupted, a knock at the door, something, and we didn't ever get back to the tape. Maybe it was just as well. I'd heard all I wanted to.

Now this same blind man was coming to sleep in my house.

"Maybe I could take him bowling," I said to my wife. She was at the draining board doing scalloped potatoes. She put down the knife she was using and turned around.

"If you love me," she said, "you can do this for me. If you don't love me, okay. But if you had a friend, any friend, and the friend came to visit, I'd make him feel comfortable." She wiped her hands with the dish towel.

"I don't have any blind friends," I said.

10   "You don't have *any* friends," she said. "Period. Besides," she said, "goddamn it, his wife's just died! Don't you understand that? The man's lost his wife!"

I didn't answer. She'd told me a little about the blind man's wife. Her name was Beulah. Beulah! That's a name for a colored woman.

"Was his wife a Negro?" I asked.

"Are you crazy?" my wife said. "Have you just flipped or something?" She picked up a potato. I saw it hit the floor, then roll under the stove. "What's wrong with you?" she said. "Are you drunk?"

"I'm just asking," I said.

15   Right then my wife filled me in with more detail than I cared to know. I made a drink and sat at the kitchen table to listen. Pieces of the story began to fall into place.

Beulah had gone to work for the blind man the summer after my wife had stopped working for him. Pretty soon Beulah and the blind man had themselves a church wedding. It was a little wedding—who'd want to go to such a wedding in the first place?—just the two of them, plus the minister and the minister's wife. But it was a church wedding just the same. It was what Beulah had wanted, he'd said. But even then Beulah must have been carrying the cancer in her glands. After they had been inseparable for eight years—my wife's word, *inseparable*—Beulah's health went into rapid decline. She died in a Seattle hospital room, the blind man sitting beside the bed and holding on to her hand. They'd married, lived and worked together, slept together—had sex, sure—and then the blind man had to bury her. All this without his having ever seen what the goddamned woman looked like. It was beyond my understanding. Hearing this, I felt sorry for the blind man for a little bit. And then I found myself thinking what a pitiful life this woman must have led. Imagine a woman who could never see herself as she was seen in the eyes of her loved one. A woman who could go on day after day and never receive the smallest compliment from her beloved. A woman whose husband could never read the expression on her face, be it misery or something better. Someone who could wear makeup or not—what difference to him? She could, if she wanted, wear green eye-shadow around one eye, a straight pin in her nostril, yellow slacks and purple shoes, no matter. And then to slip off into death, the blind man's hand on her hand, his blind eyes streaming tears—I'm imagining now—her last thought maybe this: that he never even knew what she looked like, and she on an express to the grave. Robert was left with a small insurance policy and half of a twenty-peso Mexican coin. The other half of the coin went into the box with her. Pathetic.

So when the time rolled around, my wife went to the depot to pick him up. With nothing to do but wait—sure, I blamed him for that—I was having a drink and watching the TV when I heard the car pull into the drive. I got up from the sofa with my drink and went to the window to have a look.

I saw my wife laughing as she parked the car. I saw her get out of the car and shut the door. She was still wearing a smile. Just amazing. She went around to the other side of the car to where the blind man was already starting to get out. This blind man, feature this, he was wearing a full beard! A beard on a blind man! Too much, I say. The blind man reached into the back seat and dragged out a suitcase. My wife took his arm, shut the car door, and, talking all the way, moved him down the drive and then up the steps to the front porch. I turned off the TV. I finished my drink, rinsed the glass, dried my hands. Then I went to the door.

My wife said, "I want you to meet Robert. Robert, this is my husband. I've told you all about him." She was beaming. She had this blind man by his coat sleeve.

20   The blind man let go of his suitcase and up came his hand.

I took it. He squeezed hard, held my hand, and then he let it go.

"I feel like we've already met," he boomed.

"Likewise," I said. I didn't know what else to say. Then I said, "Welcome. I've heard a lot about you." We began to move then, a little group, from the porch into the living room, my wife guiding him by the arm. The blind man was carrying his suitcase in his other hand. My wife said things like, "To your left here, Robert. That's right. Now watch it, there's a chair. That's it. Sit down right here. This is the sofa. We just bought this sofa two weeks ago."

I started to say something about the old sofa. I'd liked that old sofa. But I didn't say anything. Then I wanted to say something else, small-talk, about the scenic ride along the Hudson. How going *to* New York, you should sit on the right-hand side of the train, and coming *from* New York, the left-hand side.

25   "Did you have a good train ride?" I said. "Which side of the train did you sit on, by the way?"

"What a question, which side!" my wife said. "What's it matter which side?" she said.

"I just asked," I said.

"Right side," the blind man said. "I hadn't been on a train in nearly forty years. Not since I was a kid. With my folks. That's been a long time. I'd nearly forgotten the sensation. I have winter in my beard now," he said. "So I've been told, anyway. Do I look distinguished, my dear?" the blind man said to my wife.

"You look distinguished, Robert," she said. "Robert," she said. "Robert, it's just so good to see you."

30   My wife finally took her eyes off the blind man and looked at me. I had the feeling she didn't like what she saw. I shrugged.

I've never met, or personally known, anyone who was blind. This blind man was late forties, a heavy-set, balding man with stooped shoulders, as if he carried a great weight there. He wore brown slacks, brown shoes, a light-brown shirt, a tie, a sports coat. Spiffy. He also had this full beard. But he didn't use a cane and he didn't wear dark glasses. I'd always thought dark glasses were a must for the blind. Fact was, I wished he had a pair. At first glance, his eyes looked like anyone else's eyes. But if you looked close, there was something different about them. Too much white in the iris, for one thing, and the pupils seemed to move around in the sockets without his knowing it or being able to stop it. Creepy. As I stared at his face, I saw the left pupil turn in toward his nose while the other made an effort to keep in one place. But it was only an effort, for that eye was on the roam without his knowing it or wanting it to be.

I said, "Let me get you a drink. What's your pleasure? We have a little of everything. It's one of our pastimes."

"Bub. I'm a Scotch man myself," he said fast enough in this big voice.

"Right," I said. Bub! "Sure you are. I knew it."

35   He let his fingers touch his suitcase, which was sitting alongside the sofa. He was taking his bearings. I didn't blame him for that.

"I'll move that up to your room," my wife said.

"No, that's fine," the blind man said loudly. "It can go up when I go up."

"A little water with the Scotch?" I said.

"Very little," he said.

40   "I knew it." I said.

He said, "Just a tad. The Irish actor, Barry Fitzgerald? I'm like that fellow. When I drink water, Fitzgerald said, I drink water. When I drink whiskey, I drink whiskey." My wife laughed. The blind man brought his hand up under his beard. He lifted his beard slowly and let it drop.

I did the drinks, three big glasses of Scotch with a splash of water in each. Then we made ourselves comfortable and talked about Robert's travels. First the long flight from the West Coast to Connecticut, we covered that. Then from Connecticut up here by train. We had another drink concerning that leg of the trip.

I remembered having read somewhere that the blind didn't smoke because, as speculation had it, they couldn't see the smoke they exhaled. I thought I knew that much and that much only about blind people. But this blind man smoked his cigarette down to the nubbin and then lit another one. This blind man filled his ashtray and my wife emptied it.

When we sat down at the table for dinner, we had another drink. My wife heaped Robert's plate with cube steak, scalloped potatoes, green beans. I buttered him up two slices of bread. I said, "Here's bread and butter for you." I swallowed some of my drink. "Now let us pray," I said, and the blind man lowered his head. My wife looked at me, her mouth agape. "Pray the phone won't ring and the food doesn't get cold," I said.

45   We dug in. We ate everything there was to eat on the table. We ate like there was no tomorrow. We didn't talk. We ate. We scarfed. We grazed that table. We were into serious eating. The blind man had right away located his foods, he knew just where everything was on his plate. I watched with admiration as he used his knife and fork on the meat. He'd cut two pieces of meat, fork the meat into his mouth and then go all out for the scalloped potatoes, the beans next, and then he'd tear off a hunk of buttered bread and eat that. He'd follow this up with a big drink of milk. It didn't seem to bother him to use his fingers once in a while, either.

We finished everything, including half a strawberry pie. For a few moments, we sat as if stunned. Sweat beaded on our faces. Finally, we got up from the table and left the dirty plates. We didn't look back. We took ourselves into the living room and sank into our places again. Robert and my wife sat on the sofa. I took the big chair. We had us two or three more drinks while they talked about the major things that had come to pass for them in the past ten years. For the most part, I just listened. Now and then I joined in. I didn't want him to think I'd left the room, and I didn't want her to think I was feeling left out. They talked of things that had happened to them—to them—these past ten years. I waited in vain to hear my name on my wife's sweet lips: "And then my dear husband came into my life"—something like that. But I heard nothing of the sort. More talk of Robert. Robert had done a little of everything, it seemed, a regular blind jack-of-all-trades. But most recently he and his wife had had an Amway distributorship, from which, I gathered, they'd earned their living, such as it was. The blind man was also a ham radio operator. He talked in his loud voice about conversations he'd had with fellow operators in Guam, in the Philippines, in Alaska, and even in Tahiti. He said he'd have a lot of friends there if he ever wanted to go visit those places. From time to time, he'd turn his blind face toward me, put his hand under his beard, ask me something. How long had I been in my present position? (Three years.) Did I like my work? (I didn't.) Was I going to stay with it? (What were the options?) Finally, when I thought he was beginning to run down, I got up and turned on the TV.

My wife looked at me with irritation. She was heading toward a boil. Then she looked at the blind man and said, "Robert, do you have a TV?"

The blind man said, "My dear, I have two TVs. I have a color set and a black-and-white thing, an old relic. It's funny, but if I turn the TV on, and I'm always turning it on, I turn on the color set. It's funny, don't you think?"

I didn't know what to say to that. I had absolutely nothing to say to that. No opinion. So I watched the news program and tried to listen to what the announcer was saying.

50   "This is a color TV," the blind man said. "Don't ask me how, but I can tell."

"We traded up a while ago," I said.

The blind man had another taste of his drink. He lifted his beard, sniffed it, and let it fall. He leaned forward on the sofa. He positioned his ashtray on the coffee table, then put the lighter to his cigarette. He leaned back on the sofa and crossed his legs at the ankles.

My wife covered her mouth, and then she yawned. She stretched. She said. "I think I'll go upstairs and put on my robe. I think I'll change into something else. Robert, you make yourself comfortable," she said.

"I'm comfortable," the blind man said.

55   "I want you to feel comfortable in this house," she said.

"I am comfortable," the blind man said.

After she'd left the room, he and I listened to the weather report and then to the sports roundup. By that time, she'd been gone so long I didn't know if she was going to come back. I thought she might have gone to bed. I wished she'd come back downstairs. I didn't want to be left alone with a blind man. I asked him if he wanted another drink, and he said sure. Then I asked if he wanted to smoke some dope with me. I said I'd just rolled a number. I hadn't, but I planned to do so in about two shakes. "I'll try some with you," he said.

"Damn right," I said. "That's the stuff."

I got our drinks and sat down on the sofa with him. Then I roll us two fat numbers. I lit one and passed it. I brought it to his fingers. He took it and inhaled.

60   "Hold it as long as you can," I said. I could tell he didn't know the first thing.

My wife came back downstairs wearing her pink robe and her pink slippers.

"What do I smell?" she said.

"We thought we'd have us some cannabis," I said.

My wife gave me a savage look. Then she looked at the blind man and said, "Robert, I didn't know you smoked."

65   He said, "I do now, my dear. There's a first time for everything. But I don't feel anything yet."

"This stuff is pretty mellow," I said. "This stuff is mild. It's dope you can reason with," I said. "It doesn't mess you up."

"Not much it doesn't, bub," he said, and laughed.

My wife sat on the sofa between the blind man and me. I passed her the number. She took it and toked and then passed it back to me. "Which way is this going?" she said. Then she said, "I shouldn't be smoking this. I can hardly keep my eyes open as it is. That dinner did me in. I shouldn't have eaten so much."

"It was the strawberry pie," the blind man said. "That's what did it," he said, and he laughed his big laugh. Then he shook his head.

70   "There's more strawberry pie," I said.

"Do you want some more, Robert?" my wife said.

"Maybe in a little while," he said.

We gave our attention to the TV. My wife yawned again. She said, "Your bed is made up when you feel like going to bed, Robert. I know you must have had a long day. When you're ready to go to bed, say so." She pulled his arm. "Robert?"

He came to and said, "I've had a real nice time. This beats tapes, doesn't it?"

75   I said, "Coming at you," and I put the number between his fingers. He inhaled, held the smoke, and then let it go. It was like he'd been doing it since he was nine years old.

"Thanks, bub," he said. "But I think this is all for me. I think I'm beginning to feel it," he said. He held the burning roach out for my wife.

"Same here," she said. "Ditto. Me, too." She took the roach and passed it to me. "I may just sit here for a while between you two guys with my eyes closed. But don't let me bother you, okay? Either one of you. If it bothers you, say so. Otherwise, I may just sit here with my eyes closed until you're ready to go to bed," she said. "Your bed's made up, Robert, when you're ready. It's right next to our room at the top of the stairs. We'll show you up when you're ready. You wake me up now, you guys, if I fall asleep." She said that and then she closed her eyes and went to sleep.

The news program ended. I got up and changed the channel. I sat back down on the sofa. I wished my wife hadn't pooped out. Her head lay across the back of the sofa, her mouth open. She'd turned so that her robe had slipped away from her legs, exposing a juicy thigh. I reached to draw her robe back over her, and it was then that I glanced at the blind man. What the hell! I flipped the robe open again.

"You say when you want some strawberry pie," I said.

80   "I will," he said.

I said, "Are you tired? Do you want me to take you up to your bed? Are you ready to hit the hay?"

"Not yet," he said. "No, I'll stay up with you, bub. If that's all right. I'll stay up until you're ready to turn in. We haven't had a chance to talk. Know what I mean? I feel like me and her monopolized the evening." He lifted his beard and he let it fall. He picked up his cigarettes and his lighter.

"That's all right," I said. Then I said, "I'm glad for the company."

And I guess I was. Every night I smoked dope and stayed up as long as I could before I fell asleep. My wife and I hardly ever went to bed at the same time. When

I did go to sleep, I had these dreams. Sometimes I'd wake up from one of them, my heart going crazy.

85 Something about the church and the Middle Ages was on the TV. Not your run-of-the-mill TV fare. I wanted to watch something else. I turned to the other channels. But there was nothing on them, either. So I turned back to the first channel and apologized.

"Bub, it's all right," the blind man said. "It's fine with me. Whatever you want to watch is okay. I'm always learning something. Learning never ends. It won't hurt me to learn something tonight. I got ears," he said.

We didn't say anything for a time. He was leaning forward with his head turned at me, his right ear aimed in the direction of the set. Very disconcerting. Now and then his eyelids drooped and then they snapped open again. Now and then he put his fingers into his beard and tugged, like he was thinking about something he was hearing on the television.

On the screen, a group of men wearing cowls was being set upon and tormented by men dressed in skeleton costumes and men dressed as devils. The men dressed as devils wore devil masks, horns, and long tails. This pageant was part of a procession. The Englishman who was narrating the thing said it took place in Spain once a year. I tried to explain to the blind man what was happening.

"Skeletons," he said. "I know about skeletons," he said, and he nodded.

90 The TV showed this one cathedral. Then there was a long, slow look at another one. Finally, the picture switched to the famous one in Paris, with its flying buttresses and its spires reaching up to the clouds. The camera pulled away to show the whole of the cathedral rising above the skyline.

There were times when the Englishman who was telling the thing would shut up, would simply let the camera move around over the cathedrals. Or else the camera would tour the countryside, men in fields walking behind oxen. I waited as long as I could. Then I felt I had to say something. I said, "They're showing the outside of this cathedral now. Gargoyles. Little statues carved to look like monsters. Now I guess they're in Italy. Yeah, they're in Italy. There's paintings on the walls of this one church."

"Are those fresco paintings, bub?" he asked, and he sipped from his drink.

I reached for my glass. But it was empty. I tried to remember what I could remember. "You're asking me are those frescoes?" I said. "That's a good question. I don't know."

The camera moved to a cathedral outside Lisbon. The differences in the Portuguese cathedral compared with the French and Italian were not that great. But they were there. Mostly the interior stuff. Then something occurred to me, and I said, "Something has occurred to me. Do you have any idea what a cathedral is? What they look like, that is? Do you follow me? If somebody says cathedral to you, do you have any notion what they're talking about? Do you know the difference between that and a Baptist church, say?"

95 He let the smoke dribble from his mouth. "I know they took hundreds of workers fifty or a thousand years to build," he said. "I just heard the man say that, of course. I know generations of the same families worked on a cathedral. I heard him say that, too. The men who began their life's work on them, they never lived

to see the completion of their work. In that wise, bub, they're no different from the rest of us, right?" He laughed. Then his eyelids drooped again. His head nodded. He seemed to be snoozing. Maybe he was imagining himself in Portugal. The TV was showing another cathedral now. This one was in Germany. The Englishman's voice droned on. "Cathedrals," the blind man said. He sat up and rolled his head back and forth. "If you want the truth, bub, that's about all I know. What I just said. What I heard him say. But maybe you could describe one to me? I wish you'd do it. I'd like that. If you want to know, I really don't have a good idea."

I stared hard at the shot of the cathedral on the TV. How could I even begin to describe it? But say my life depended on it. Say my life was being threatened by an insane guy who said I had to do it or else.

I stared some more at the cathedral before the picture flipped off into the countryside. There was no use. I turned to the blind man and said, "To begin with, they're very tall." I was looking around the room for clues. "They reach way up. Up and up. Toward the sky. They're so big, some of them, they have to have these supports. To help hold them up, so to speak. These supports are called buttresses. They remind me of viaducts, for some reason. But maybe you don't know viaducts, either? Sometimes the cathedrals have devils and such carved into the front. Sometimes lords and ladies. Don't ask me why this is," I said.

He was nodding. The whole upper part of his body seemed to be moving back and forth.

"I'm not doing so good, am I?" I said.

100   He stopped nodding and leaned forward on the edge of the sofa. As he listened to me, he was running his fingers through his beard. I wasn't getting through to him, I could see that. But he waited for me to go on just the same. He nodded, like he was trying to encourage me. I tried to think what else to say. "They're really big," I said. "They're massive. They're built of stone. Marble, too, sometimes. In those olden days, when they built cathedrals, men wanted to be close to God. In those olden days, God was an important part of everyone's life. You could tell this from their cathedral-building. I'm sorry," I said, "but it looks like that's the best I can do for you. I'm just no good at it."

"That's all right, bub," the blind man said. "Hey, listen. I hope you don't mind my asking you. Can I ask you something? Let me ask you a simple question, yes or no. I'm just curious and there's no offense. You're my host. But let me ask if you are in any way religious? You don't mind my asking?"

I shook my head. He couldn't see that, though. A wink is the same as a nod to a blind man. "I guess I don't believe in it. In anything. Sometimes it's hard. You know what I'm saying?"

"Sure, I do," he said.

"Right," I said.

105   The Englishman was still holding forth. My wife sighed in her sleep. She drew a long breath and went on with her sleeping.

"You'll have to forgive me," I said. "But I can't tell you what a cathedral looks like. It just isn't in me to do it. I can't do any more than I've done."

The blind man sat very still, his head down, as he listened to me.

I said, "The truth is, cathedrals don't mean anything special to me. Nothing. Cathedrals. They're something to look at on late-night TV. That's all they are."

It was then that the blind man cleared his throat. He brought something up. He took a handkerchief from his back pocket. Then he said, "I get it, bub. It's okay. It happens. Don't worry about it," he said. "Hey, listen to me. Will you do me a favor? I got an idea. Why don't you find us some heavy paper? And a pen. We'll do something. We'll draw one together. Get us a pen and some heavy paper. Go on, bub, get the stuff," he said.

110   So I went upstairs. My legs felt like they didn't have any strength in them. They felt like they did after I'd done some running. In my wife's room, I looked around. I found some ballpoints in a little basket on her table. And then I tried to think where to look for the kind of paper he was talking about.

Downstairs, in the kitchen, I found a shopping bag with onion skins in the bottom of the bag. I emptied the bag and shook it. I brought it into the living room and sat down with it near his legs. I moved some things, smoothed the wrinkles from the bag, spread it out on the coffee table.

The blind man got down from the sofa and sat next to me on the carpet.

He ran his fingers over the paper. He went up and down the sides of the paper. The edges, even the edges. He fingered the corners.

"All right," he said. "All right, let's do her."

115   He found my hand, the hand with the pen. He closed his hand over my hand. "Go ahead, bub, draw," he said. "Draw. You'll see. I'll follow along with you. It'll be okay. Just begin now like I'm telling you. You'll see. Draw," the blind man said.

So I began. First I drew a box that looked like a house. It could have been the house I lived in. Then I put a roof on it. At either end of the roof, I drew spires. Crazy.

"Swell," he said. "Terrific. You're doing fine," he said. "Never thought anything like this could happen in your lifetime, did you, bub? Well, it's a strange life, we all know that. Go on now. Keep it up."

I put in windows with arches. I drew flying buttresses. I hung great doors. I couldn't stop. The TV station went off the air. I put down the pen and closed and opened my fingers. The blind man felt around over the paper. He moved the tips of his fingers over the paper, all over what I had drawn, and he nodded.

"Doing fine," the blind man said.

120   I took up the pen again, and he found my hand. I kept at it. I'm no artist. But I kept drawing just the same.

My wife opened up her eyes and gazed at us. She sat up on the sofa, her robe hanging open. She said, "What are you doing? Tell me, I want to know."

I didn't answer her.

The blind man said, "We're drawing a cathedral. Me and him are working on it. Press hard," he said to me. "That's right. That's good," he said. "Sure. You got it, bub, I can tell. You didn't think you could. But you can, can't you? You're cooking with gas now. You know what I'm saying? We're going to really have us something here in a minute. How's the old arm?" he said. "Put some people in there now. What's a cathedral without people?"

125   My wife said, "What's going on? Robert, what are you doing? What's going on?"
       "It's all right," he said to her. "Close your eyes now," the blind man said to me.
       I did it. I closed them just like he said.
       "Are they closed?" he said. "Don't fudge."
       "They're closed," I said.
       "Keep them that way," he said. "Don't stop now. Draw."

130   So we kept on with it. His fingers rode my fingers as my hand went over the paper. It was like nothing else in my life up to now.
       Then he said, "I think that's it. I think you got it," he said. "Take a look. What do you think?"
       But I had my eyes closed. I thought I'd keep them that way for a little longer. I thought it was something I ought to do.
       "Well?" he said. "Are you looking?"
       My eyes were still closed. I was in my house. I knew that. But I didn't feel like I was inside anything.

135   "It's really something," I said.

MAKING CONNECTIONS

1. Why does the narrator consistently refer to Robert as "the blind man"? Why doesn't he use his name?
2. The narrator states, "A blind man in my house was not something I looked forward to." What does the narrator have against blind people? Or do you think he objects to something specific about Robert? If so, what might that be?
3. How does the wife's relationship with her husband differ from her relationship with Robert? It there anything that Robert offers her that her husband doesn't?
4. Are there things you need to see to understand? What do you think contributes more to understanding: seeing or experiencing? Explain.
5. Does Robert learn what a cathedral is in this story? Prior to their drawing together, does the narrator know much more about cathedrals than Robert does? What does the narrator learn to "see"?

MAKING AN ARGUMENT

1. The narrator of this story is not a particularly sympathetic character. Write about the effectiveness of the narration and the narrator's development as he moves toward his—"It's really something"—realization at the end of the story. To what extent would a more sympathetic narrator work just as well—or better? Cite the text of the story for support.
2. Write an essay that compares the marriage in this story with Leroy and Norma's marriage in Bobbie Ann Mason's "Shiloh" on page 705. Cite the text of both stories for support.

NATHANIEL HAWTHORNE [1804–1864]

Nathaniel Hawthorne was born in Salem, Massachusetts to a once-influential Puritan family. Two of his ancestors had served as judges: one in the persecution of Quakers, the other in the Salem witch trials. His father, a ship's captain, died when Hawthorne was four, and his mother, after moving the family back to her parents' house, became a recluse, emerging from her room only for meals. Following an injury that left him lame, Hawthorne was educated mostly at home.

After attending Bowdoin College in Maine, he returned home to live with his sisters and mother, where he began writing and publishing stories. In 1828, he published a little-read novel about his college experiences, Fanshawe. *His next publication,* Twice-Told Tales *(1837)—a collection of stories—fared better. After his marriage in 1842 and the birth of a daughter, Hawthorne wrote less, working as a customs inspector at various times to support his young family. In 1849, following the death of his mother, Hawthorne moved back to Salem, where he wrote his masterpiece,* The Scarlet Letter. *The book was an enormous critical and financial success, as was his next novel,* The House of the Seven Gables *(1851). Hawthorne was then financially able to devote himself fully to his writing. Later in his life, following the election of his college friend Franklin Pierce to the presidency, Hawthorne served as American consul at Liverpool from 1853 to 1857, and then remained in Europe until 1860, where he wrote his final novel,* The Marble Faun *(1860). He died in Concord, Massachusetts, in 1864.*

YOUNG GOODMAN BROWN   [1828]

Young Goodman Brown came forth at sunset into the street at Salem village; but put his head back, after crossing the threshold, to exchange a parting kiss with his young wife. And Faith, as the wife was aptly named, thrust her own pretty head into the street, letting the wind play with the pink ribbons of her cap while she called to Goodman Brown.

"Dearest heart," whispered she, softly and rather sadly, when her lips were close to his ear, "prithee put off your journey until sunrise and sleep in your own bed to-night. A lone woman is troubled with such dreams and such thoughts that she's afeared of herself sometimes. Pray tarry with me this night, dear husband, of all nights in the year."

"My love and my Faith," replied young Goodman Brown, "of all nights in the year, this one night must I tarry away from thee. My journey, as thou callest it, forth and back again, must needs be done 'twixt now and sunrise. What, my sweet, pretty wife, dost thou doubt me already, and we but three months married?"

"Then God bless you!" said Faith, with the pink ribbons; "and may you find all well when you come back."

5   "Amen!" cried Goodman Brown. "Say thy prayers, dear Faith, and go to bed at dusk, and no harm will come to thee."

So they parted; and the young man pursued his way until, being about to turn the corner by the meeting-house, he looked back and saw the head of Faith still peeping after him with a melancholy air, in spite of her pink ribbons.

"Poor little Faith!" thought he, for his heart smote him. "What a wretch am I to leave her on such an errand! She talks of dreams, too. Methought as she spoke there was trouble in her face, as if a dream had warned her what work is to be done to-night. But no, no; 'twould kill her to think it. Well, she's a blessed angel on earth; and after this one night I'll cling to her skirts and follow her to heaven."

With this excellent resolve for the future, Goodman Brown felt himself justified in making more haste on his present evil purpose. He had taken a dreary road, darkened by all the gloomiest trees of the forest, which barely stood aside to let the narrow path creep through, and closed immediately behind. It was all as lonely as could be; and there is this peculiarity in such a solitude, that the traveler knows not who may be concealed by the innumerable trunks and the thick boughs overhead; so that with lonely footsteps he may yet be passing through an unseen multitude.

"There may be a devilish Indian behind every tree," said Goodman Brown to himself; and he glanced fearfully behind him as he added, "What if the devil himself should be at my very elbow!"

10   His head being turned back, he passed a crook of the road, and, looking forward again, beheld the figure of a man, in grave and decent attire, seated at the foot of an old tree. He arose at Goodman Brown's approach and walked onward side by side with him.

"You are late, Goodman Brown," said he. "The clock of the Old South was striking as I came through Boston, and that is full fifteen minutes agone."

"Faith kept me back a while," replied the young man, with a tremor in his voice, caused by the sudden appearance of his companion, though not wholly unexpected.

It was now deep dusk in the forest, and deepest in that part of it where these two were journeying. As nearly as could be discerned, the second traveller was about fifty years old, apparently in the same rank of life as Goodman Brown, and bearing a considerable resemblance to him, though perhaps more in expression than features. Still they might have been taken for father and son. And yet, though the elder person was as simply clad as the younger, and as simple in manner too, he had an indescribable air of one who knew the world, and who would not have felt abashed at the governor's dinner table or in King William's court, were it possible that his affairs should call him thither. But the only thing about him that could be fixed upon as remarkable was his staff, which bore the likeness of a great black snake, so curiously wrought that it might almost be seen to twist and wriggle itself like a living serpent. This, of course, must have been an ocular deception, assisted by the uncertain light.

"Come, Goodman Brown," cried his fellow-traveller, "this is a dull pace for the beginning of a journey. Take my staff, if you are so soon weary."

15   "Friend," said the other, exchanging his slow pace for a full stop, "Having kept covenant by meeting thee here, it is my purpose now to return whence I came. I have scruples touching the matter thou wot'st of."

"Sayest thou so?" replied he of the serpent, smiling apart. "Let us walk on, nevertheless, reasoning as we go; and if I convince thee not thou shalt turn back. We are but a little way in the forest yet."

"Too far! too far!" exclaimed the goodman, unconsciously resuming his walk. "My father never went into the woods on such an errand, nor his father before him. We have been a race of honest men and good Christians since the days of the martyrs; and shall I be the first of the name of Brown that ever took this path and kept"—

"Such company, thou wouldst say," observed the elder person, interpreting his pause. "Well said, Goodman Brown! I have been as well acquainted with your family as with ever a one among the Puritans; and that's no trifle to say. I helped your grandfather, the constable, when he lashed the Quaker woman so smartly through the streets of Salem: and it was I that brought your father a pitch-pine knot, kindled at my own hearth, to set fire to an Indian village, in King Philip's war. They were my good friends, both; and many a pleasant walk have we had along this path, and returned merrily after midnight. I would fain be friends with you for their sake."

"If it be as thou sayest," replied Goodman Brown, "I marvel they never spoke of these matters: or, verily, I marvel not, seeing that the least rumor of the sort would have driven them from New England. We are a people of prayer, and good works to boot, and abide no such wickedness."

20   "Wickedness or not," said the traveller with the twisted staff, "I have a very general acquaintance here in New England. The deacons of many a church have drunk the communion wine with me; the selectmen of divers towns make me their chairman; and a majority of the Great and General Court are firm supporters of my interest. The governor and I, too—But these are state secrets."

"Can this be so?" cried Goodman Brown, with a stare of amazement at his undisturbed companion. "Howbeit, I have nothing to do with the governor and council; they have their own ways, and are no rule for a simple husbandman like me. But, were I to go on with thee, how should I meet the eye of that good old man, our minister, at Salem village? Oh, his voice would make me tremble both Sabbath day and lecture day."

Thus far the elder traveller had listened with due gravity; but now burst into a fit of irrepressible mirth, shaking himself so violently that his snake-like staff actually seemed to wriggle in sympathy.

"Ha! ha! ha!" shouted he again and again; then composing himself, "Well, go on, Goodman Brown, go on; but, prithee, don't kill me with laughing."

"Well, then, to end the matter at once," said Goodman Brown, considerably nettled, "there is my wife, Faith. It would break her dear little heart; and I'd rather break my own."

25   "Nay, if that be the case," answered the other, "e'en go thy ways, Goodman Brown. I would not for twenty old women like the one hobbling before us that Faith should come to any harm."

As he spoke he pointed his staff at a female figure on the path, in whom Goodman Brown recognized a very pious and exemplary dame, who had taught him his catechism in youth, and was still his moral and spiritual adviser, jointly with the minister and Deacon Gookin.

"A marvel, truly, that Goody Cloyse should be so far in the wilderness at nightfall," said he. "But with your leave, friend, I shall take a cut through the woods until we have left this Christian woman behind. Being a stranger to you, she might ask whom I was consorting with and whither I was going."

"Be it so," said his fellow-traveller. "Betake you the woods, and let me keep the path."

Accordingly the young man turned aside, but took care to watch his companion, who advanced softly along the road until he had come within a staff's length of the old dame. She, meanwhile, was making the best of her way, with singular speed for so aged a woman, and mumbling some indistinct words—a prayer, doubtless—as she went. The traveller put forth his staff and touched her withered neck with what seemed the serpent's tail.

30   "The devil!" screamed the pious old lady.

"Then Goody Cloyse knows her old friend?" observed the traveller, confronting her and leaning on his writhing stick.

"Ah, forsooth, and is it your worship indeed?" cried the good dame. "Yea, truly is it, and in the very image of my old gossip, Goodman Brown, the grandfather of the silly fellow that now is. But—would your worship believe it?—my broomstick hath strangely disappeared, stolen, as I suspect, by that unhanged witch, Goody Cory, and that, too, when I was all anointed with the juice of smallage, and cinquefoil, and wolf's bane—"

"Mingled with fine wheat and the fat of a new-born babe," said the shape of old Goodman Brown.

"Ah, your worship knows the recipe," cried the old lady, cackling aloud. "So, as I was saying, being all ready for the meeting, and no horse to ride on, I made up my mind to foot it; for they tell me there is a nice young man to be taken into communion to-night. But now your good worship will lend me your arm, and we shall be there in a twinkling."

35   "That can hardly be," answered her friend. "I may not spare you my arm, Goody Cloyse; but here is my staff, if you will."

So saying, he threw it down at her feet, where, perhaps, it assumed life, being one of the rods which its owner had formerly lent to the Egyptian magi. Of this fact, however, Goodman Brown could not take cognizance. He had cast up his eyes in astonishment, and, looking down again, beheld neither Goody Cloyse nor the serpentine staff, but his fellow-traveller alone, who waited for him as calmly as if nothing had happened.

"That old woman taught me my catechism," said the young man; and there was a world of meaning in this simple comment.

They continued to walk onward, while the elder traveller exhorted his companion to make good speed and persevere in the path, discoursing so aptly that his arguments seemed rather to spring up in the bosom of his auditor than to be suggested by himself. As they went, he plucked a branch of maple to serve for a walking stick, and began to strip it of the twigs and the little boughs, which were wet with evening dew. The moment his fingers touched them they became strangely withered and dried up as with a week's sunshine. Thus the pair proceeded, at a good free pace, until suddenly, in a gloomy hollow of the road,

Goodman Brown sat himself down on the stump of a tree and refused to go any farther.

"Friend," said he, stubbornly, "my mind is made up. Not another step will I budge on this errand. What if a wretched old woman do choose to go to the devil when I thought she was going to heaven: is that any reason why I should quit my dear Faith and go after her?"

40   "You will think better of this by and by," said his acquaintance, composedly. "Sit here and rest yourself a while; and when you feel like moving again, there is my staff to help you along."

Without more words, he threw his companion the maple stick, and was as speedily out of sight as if he had vanished into the deepening gloom. The young man sat a few moments by the roadside, applauding himself greatly, and thinking with how clear a conscience he should meet the minister in his morning walk, nor shrink from the eye of good old Deacon Gookin. And what calm sleep would be his that very night, which was to have been spent so wickedly, but so purely and sweetly now, in the arms of Faith! Amidst these pleasant and praiseworthy meditations, Goodman Brown heard the tramp of horses along the road, and deemed it advisable to conceal himself within the verge of the forest, conscious of the guilty purpose that had brought him thither, though now so happily turned from it.

On came the hoof tramps and the voices of the riders, two grave old voices, conversing soberly as they drew near. These mingled sounds appeared to pass along the road, within a few yards of the young man's hiding-place; but, owing doubtless to the depth of the gloom at that particular spot, neither the travellers nor their steeds were visible. Though their figures brushed the small boughs by the wayside, it could not be seen that they intercepted, even for a moment, the faint gleam from the strip of bright sky athwart which they must have passed. Goodman Brown alternately crouched and stood on tiptoe, pulling aside the branches and thrusting forth his head as far as he durst without discerning so much as a shadow. It vexed him the more, because he could have sworn, were such a thing possible, that he recognized the voices of the minister and Deacon Gookin, jogging along quietly, as they were wont to do, when bound to some ordination or ecclesiastical council. While yet within hearing, one of the riders stopped to pluck a switch.

"Of the two, reverend sir," said the voice like the deacon's, "I had rather miss an ordination dinner than to-night's meeting. They tell me that some of our community are to be here from Falmouth and beyond, and others from Connecticut and Rhode Island, besides several of the Indian powwows, who, after their fashion, know almost as much deviltry as the best of us. Moreover, there is a goodly young woman to be taken into communion."

"Mighty well, Deacon Gookin!" replied the solemn old tones of the minister. "Spur up, or we shall be late. Nothing can be done, you know, until I get on the ground."

45   The hoofs clattered again; and the voices, talking so strangely in the empty air, passed on through the forest, where no church had ever been gathered or solitary Christian prayed. Whither, then, could these holy men be journeying so deep into the heathen wilderness? Young Goodman Brown caught hold of a tree for support, being ready to sink down on the ground, faint and overburdened with the heavy

sickness of his heart. He looked up to the sky, doubting whether there really was a heaven above him. Yet there was the blue arch, and the stars brightening in it.

"With heaven above and Faith below, I will yet stand firm against the devil!" cried Goodman Brown.

While he still gazed upward into the deep arch of the firmament and had lifted his hands to pray, a cloud, though no wind was stirring, hurried across the zenith and hid the brightening stars. The blue sky was still visible, except directly overhead, where this black mass of cloud was sweeping swiftly northward. Aloft in the air, as if from the depths of the cloud, came a confused and doubtful sound of voices. Once the listener fancied that he could distinguish the accents of towns-people of his own, men and women, both pious and ungodly, many of whom he had met at the communion table, and had seen others rioting at the tavern. The next moment, so indistinct were the sounds, he doubted whether he had heard aught but the murmur of the old forest, whispering without a wind. Then came a stronger swell of those familiar tones, heard daily in the sunshine at Salem village, but never until now from a cloud of night. There was one voice, of a young woman, uttering lamentations, yet with an uncertain sorrow, and entreating for some favor, which, perhaps, it would grieve her to obtain; and all the unseen multitude, both saints and sinners, seemed to encourage her onward.

"Faith!" shouted Goodman Brown, in a voice of agony and desperation; and the echoes of the forest mocked him, crying, "Faith! Faith!" as if bewildered wretches were seeking her all through the wilderness.

The cry of grief, rage, and terror was yet piercing the night, when the unhappy husband held his breath for a response. There was a scream, drowned immediately in a louder murmur of voices, fading into far-off laughter, as the dark cloud swept away, leaving the clear and silent sky above Goodman Brown. But something fluttered lightly down through the air and caught on the branch of a tree. The young man seized it, and beheld a pink ribbon.

50   "My Faith is gone!" cried he, after one stupefied moment. "There is no good on earth; and sin is but a name. Come, devil; for to thee is this world given."

And, maddened with despair, so that he laughed loud and long, did Goodman Brown grasp his staff and set forth again, at such a rate that he seemed to fly along the forest path rather than to walk or run. The road grew wilder and drearier and more faintly traced, and vanished at length, leaving him in the heart of the dark wilderness, still rushing onward with the instinct that guides mortal man to evil. The whole forest was peopled with frightful sounds—the creaking of the trees, the howling of wild beasts, and the yell of Indians; while sometimes the wind tolled like a distant church bell, and sometimes gave a broad roar around the traveller, as if all Nature were laughing him to scorn. But he was himself the chief horror of the scene, and shrank not from its other horrors.

"Ha! ha! ha!" roared Goodman Brown when the wind laughed at him. "Let us hear which will laugh loudest. Think not to frighten me with your deviltry. Come witch, come wizard, come Indian powwow, come devil himself, and here comes Goodman Brown. You may as well fear him as he fear you."

In truth, all through the haunted forest there could be nothing more frightful than the figure of Goodman Brown. On he flew among the black pines, brandishing his staff with frenzied gestures, now giving vent to an inspiration of horrid blasphemy, and now shouting forth such laughter as set all the echoes of the forest laughing like demons around him. The fiend in his own shape is less hideous than when he rages in the breast of man. Thus sped the demoniac on his course, until, quivering among the trees, he saw a red light before him, as when the felled trunks and branches of a clearing have been set on fire, and throw up their lurid blaze against the sky, at the hour of midnight. He paused, in a lull of the tempest that had driven him onward, and heard the swell of what seemed a hymn, rolling solemnly from a distance with the weight of many voices. He knew the tune; it was a familiar one in the choir of the village meeting-house. The verse died heavily away, and was lengthened by a chorus, not of human voices, but of all the sounds of the benighted wilderness pealing in awful harmony together. Goodman Brown cried out, and his cry was lost to his own ear by its unison with the cry of the desert.

In the interval of silence he stole forward until the light glared full upon his eyes. At one extremity of an open space, hemmed in by the dark wall of the forest, arose a rock, bearing some rude, natural resemblance either to an altar or a pulpit, and surrounded by four blazing pines, their tops aflame, their stems untouched, like candles at an evening meeting. The mass of foliage that had overgrown the summit of the rock was all on fire, blazing high into the night and fitfully illuminating the whole field. Each pendent twig and leafy festoon was in a blaze. As the red light arose and fell, a numerous congregation alternately shone forth, then disappeared in shadow, and again grew, as it were, out of the darkness, peopling the heart of the solitary woods at once.

55   "A grave and dark-clad company," quoth Goodman Brown.

In truth they were such. Among them, quivering to and fro between gloom and splendor, appeared faces that would be seen next day at the council board of the province, and others which, Sabbath after Sabbath, looked devoutly heavenward, and benignantly over the crowded pews, from the holiest pulpits in the land. Some affirm that the lady of the governor was there. At least there were high dames well known to her, and wives of honored husbands, and widows, a great multitude, and ancient maidens, all of excellent repute, and fair young girls, who trembled lest their mothers should espy them. Either the sudden gleams of light flashing over the obscure field bedazzled Goodman Brown, or he recognized a score of the church members of Salem village famous for their especial sanctity. Good old Deacon Gookin had arrived, and waited at the skirts of that venerable saint, his revered pastor. But, irreverently consorting with these grave, reputable, and pious people, these elders of the church, these chaste dames and dewy virgins, there were men of dissolute lives and women of spotted fame, wretches given over to all mean and filthy vice, and suspected even of horrid crimes. It was strange to see that the good shrank not from the wicked, nor were the sinners abashed by the saints. Scattered also among their pale-faced enemies were the Indian priests, or powwows, who had often scared their native forest with more hideous incantations than any known to English witchcraft.

"But where is Faith?" thought Goodman Brown; and, as hope came into his heart, he trembled.

Another verse of the hymn arose, a slow and mournful strain, such as the pious love, but joined to words which expressed all that our nature can conceive of sin, and darkly hinted at far more. Unfathomable to mere mortals is the lore of fiends. Verse after verse was sung; and still the chorus of the desert swelled between like the deepest tone of a mighty organ; and with the final peal of that dreadful anthem there came a sound, as if the roaring wind, the rushing streams, the howling beasts, and every other voice of the unconcerted wilderness were mingling and according with the voice of guilty man in homage to the prince of all. The four blazing pines threw up a loftier flame, and obscurely discovered shapes and visages of horror on the smoke wreaths above the impious assembly. At the same moment the fire on the rock shot redly forth and formed a glowing arch above its base, where now appeared a figure. With reverence be it spoken, the figure bore no slight similitude, both in garb and manner, to some grave divine of the New England churches.

"Bring forth the converts!" cried a voice that echoed through the field and rolled into the forest.

60   At the word, Goodman Brown stepped forth from the shadow of the trees and approached the congregation, with whom he felt a loathful brotherhood by the sympathy of all that was wicked in his heart. He could have well-nigh sworn that the shape of his own dead father beckoned him to advance, looking downward from a smoke wreath, while a woman, with dim features of despair, threw out her hand to warn him back. Was it his mother? But he had no power to retreat one step, nor to resist, even in thought, when the minister and good old Deacon Gookin seized his arms and led him to the blazing rock. Thither came also the slender form of a veiled female, led between Goody Cloyse, that pious teacher of the catechism, and Martha Carrier, who had received the devil's promise to be queen of hell. A rampant hag was she. And there stood the proselytes beneath the canopy of fire.

"Welcome, my children," said the dark figure, "to the communion of your race. Ye have found thus young your nature and your destiny. My children, look behind you!"

They turned; and flashing forth, as it were, in a sheet of flame, the fiend worshippers were seen; the smile of welcome gleamed darkly on every visage.

"There," resumed the sable form, "are all whom ye have reverenced from youth. Ye deemed them holier than yourselves and shrank from your own sin, contrasting it with their lives of righteousness and prayerful aspirations heavenward. Yet here are they all in my worshipping assembly. This night it shall be granted you to know their secret deeds: how hoary-bearded elders of the church have whispered wanton words to the young maids of their households; how many a woman, eager for widows' weeds, has given her husband a drink at bedtime and let him sleep his last sleep in her bosom; how beardless youths have made haste to inherit their fathers' wealth; and how fair damsels—blush not, sweet ones—have dug little graves in the garden, and bidden me, the sole guest, to an infant's funeral. By the sympathy of your human hearts for sin ye shall scent out all the places—whether in church, bedchamber, street, field, or forest—where crime has been committed, and shall exult to behold the whole earth one stain of guilt, one mighty blood spot. Far more than this! It shall be yours to penetrate, in every bosom, the deep mystery of sin, the fountain of all wicked arts, and which inexhaustibly supplies more evil impulses than human power—than my power at its utmost—can make manifest in deeds. And now, my children, look upon each other."

They did so; and, by the blaze of the hell-kindled torches, the wretched man beheld his Faith, and the wife her husband, trembling before that unhallowed altar.

65   "Lo, there ye stand, my children," said the figure, in a deep and solemn tone, almost sad with its despairing awfulness, as if his once angelic nature could yet mourn for our miserable race. "Depending upon one another's hearts, ye had still hoped that virtue were not all a dream. Now are ye undeceived. Evil is the nature of mankind. Evil must be your only happiness. Welcome again, my children, to the communion of your race."

"Welcome," repeated the fiend worshippers, in one cry of despair and triumph.

And there they stood, the only pair, as it seemed, who were yet hesitating on the verge of wickedness in this dark world. A basin was hollowed, naturally, in the rock. Did it contain water, reddened by the lurid light? or was it blood? or, perchance, a liquid flame? Herein did the shape of evil dip his hand and prepare to lay the mark of baptism upon their foreheads, that they might be partakers of the mystery of sin, more conscious of the secret guilt of others, both in deed and thought, than they could now be of their own. The husband cast one look at his pale wife, and Faith at him. What polluted wretches would the next glance show them to each other, shuddering alike at what they disclosed and what they saw!

"Faith! Faith!" cried the husband, "look up to heaven, and resist the wicked one."

Whether Faith obeyed he knew not. Hardly had he spoken when he found himself amid calm night and solitude, listening to a roar of the wind which died heavily away through the forest. He staggered against the rock, and felt it chill and damp; while a hanging twig, that had been all on fire, besprinkled his cheek with the coldest dew.

70   The next morning young Goodman Brown came slowly into the street of Salem village, staring around him like a bewildered man. The good old minister was taking a walk along the graveyard to get an appetite for breakfast and meditate his sermon, and bestowed a blessing, as he passed, on Goodman Brown. He shrank from the venerable saint as if to avoid an anathema. Old Deacon Gookin was at domestic worship, and the holy words of his prayer were heard through the open window. "What God doth the wizard pray to?" quoth Goodman Brown. Goody Cloyse, that excellent old Christian, stood in the early sunshine at her own lattice, catechizing a little girl who had brought her a pint of morning's milk. Goodman Brown snatched away the child as from the grasp of the fiend himself. Turning the corner by the meeting-house, he spied the head of Faith, with the pink ribbons, gazing anxiously forth, and bursting into such joy at sight of him that she skipped along the street and almost kissed her husband before the whole village. But Goodman Brown looked sternly and sadly into her face, and passed on without a greeting.

Had Goodman Brown fallen asleep in the forest and only dreamed a wild dream of a witch-meeting?

Be it so if you will; but alas! it was a dream of evil omen for young Goodman Brown. A stern, a sad, a darkly meditative, a distrustful, if not a desperate man did he become from the night of that fearful dream. On the Sabbath day, when the congregation were singing a holy psalm, he could not listen because an anthem of sin rushed loudly upon his ear and drowned all the blessed strain. When the minister spoke from the pulpit with power and fervid eloquence, and, with his hand on the open Bible, of the sacred truths of our religion, and of saint-like lives and triumphant deaths, and of future bliss or misery unutterable, then did Goodman Brown turn pale, dreading lest the roof should thunder down upon the gray blasphemer and his hearers. Often, awaking suddenly at midnight, he shrank from the bosom of Faith; and at morning or eventide, when the family knelt down at prayer, he scowled and muttered to himself, and gazed sternly at his wife, and turned away. And when he had lived long, and was borne to his grave a hoary corpse, followed by Faith, an aged woman, and children and grandchildren, a goodly procession, besides neighbors not a few, they carved no hopeful verse upon his tombstone, for his dying hour was gloom.

MAKING CONNECTIONS

1. What is the significance of the names in this story? For example, is Faith aptly named? Explain.
2. In what way does the setting of this story, Puritan New England, influence your response?
3. Why do you suppose the stranger in the woods looks like Goodman Brown himself?
4. This is a story about good and evil. How are they defined here? In what way is this story about human nature? How would you interpret the story's theme?

MAKING AN ARGUMENT

1. Do you think Brown's experience was real or a dream? Write an argument that supports one or the other position. Be sure to account for all the evidence in the text (not just the evidence that supports your view), and cite the text of the story for support.

TIM O'BRIEN [B. 1946]

Tim O'Brien was born in Austin, Minnesota. He was draft- ed immediately after he graduated from Macalester College in 1968 and served in the infantry for two years during the Vietnam War. He has since published four novels and a book of anecdotes, all based on his war experiences. He told an interviewer in Publishers Weekly *that for him, writing "requires a sense of passion, and my passion as a human being and as a writer intersect in Vietnam, not in the physi- cal stuff but in the issue of Vietnam—of courage, rectitude, enlightenment, holi- ness, trying to do the right thing in the world." The following story is taken from his collection* The Things They Carried *(1990), narrated by a character named "Tim O'Brien." His novel* In the Lake of the Woods *was named by* Time *magazine as the best novel of 1994. His most recent novel is* July, July *(2002). He is current- ly a visiting professor at Southwest Texas State University where he teaches in the Creative Writing Program.*

THE THINGS THEY CARRIED [1990]

First Lieutenant Jimmy Cross carried letters from a girl named Martha, a junior at Mount Sebastian College in New Jersey. They were not love letters, but Lieutenant Cross was hoping, so he kept them folded in plastic at the bottom of his rucksack. In the late afternoon, after a day's march, he would dig his foxhole, wash his hands under a canteen, unwrap the letters, hold them with the tips of his fingers, and spend the last hour of light pretending. He would imagine romantic camping trips into the White Mountains in New Hampshire. He would sometimes taste the envelope flaps, knowing her tongue had been there. More than anything, he wanted Martha to love him as he loved her, but the letters were mostly chatty, elusive on the matter of love. She was a virgin, he was almost sure. She was an English major at Mount Sebastian, and she wrote beautifully about her professors and roommates and midterm exams, about her respect for Chaucer and her great affection for Virginia Woolf. She often quoted lines of poetry; she never mentioned the war, except to say, Jimmy, take care of yourself. The letters weighed ten ounces. They were signed "Love, Martha," but Lieutenant Cross understood that Love was only a way of signing and did not mean what he sometimes pretended it meant. At dusk, he would carefully return the letters to his rucksack. Slowly, a bit distracted, he would get up and move among his men, checking the perimeter, then at full dark he would return to his hold and watch the night and wonder if Martha was a virgin.

The things they carried were largely determined by necessity. Among the necessities or near-necessities were P-38 can openers, pocket knives, heat tabs, wristwatches, dog tags, mosquito repellent, chewing gum, candy, cigarettes, salt tablets, packets of Kool-Aid, lighters, matches, sewing kits, Military Payment Certificates, C rations, and two or three canteens of water. Together, these items weighed between fifteen and twenty pounds, depending upon a man's habits or rate of metabolism. Henry Dobbins, who was a big man, carried extra rations; he was especially fond of canned peaches in heavy syrup over pound cake. Dave Jensen, who practiced field hygiene, carried a toothbrush, dental floss, and several hotel-sized bars of soap he'd stolen on R&R[1] in Sydney, Australia. Ted Lavender, who was scared, carried tranquilizers until he was shot in the head outside the village of Than Khe in mid-April. By necessity, and because it was SOP,[2] they all carried steel helmets that weighed 5 pounds including the liner and camouflage cover. They carried the standard fatigue jackets and trousers. Very few carried underwear. On their feet they carried jungle boots—2.1 pounds—and Dave Jensen carried three pairs of socks and a can of Dr. Scholl's foot powder as a precaution against trench foot. Until he was shot, Ted Lavender carried six or seven ounces of premium dope, which for him was a necessity. Mitchell Sanders, the RTO,[3] carried condoms. Norman Bowker carried a diary. Rat Kiley carried comic books. Kiowa, a devout Baptist, carried an illustrated New Testament that had been presented to him by his father, who taught Sunday school in Oklahoma City, Oklahoma. As a hedge against bad times, however, Kiowa also

---

[1]**R&R** the military abbreviation for "rest and rehabilitation," a brief vacation from active service   [2]**SOP** standard operating procedure   [3]**RTO** Radio and Telephone Operator

carried his grandmother's distrust of the white man, his grandfather's old hunting hatchet. Necessity dictated. Because the land was mined and booby-trapped, it was SOP for each man to carry a steel-centered, nylon-covered flak jacket, which weighed 6.7 pounds, but which on hot days seemed much heavier. Because you could die so quickly, each man carried at least one large compress bandage, usually in the helmet band for easy access. Because the nights were cold, and because the monsoons were wet, each carried a green plastic poncho that could be used as a raincoat or ground sheet or makeshift tent. With its quilted liner, the poncho weighed almost two pounds, but it was worth every ounce. In April, for instance, when Ted Lavender was shot, they used his poncho to wrap him up, then to carry him across the paddy, then to lift him into the chopper that took him away.

They were called legs or grunts.

To carry something was to "hump" it, as when Lieutenant Jimmy Cross humped his love for Martha up the hills and through the swamps. In its intransitive form, "to hump" meant "to walk," or "to march," but it implied burdens far beyond the intransitive.

5   Almost everyone humped photographs. In his wallet, Lieutenant Cross carried two photographs of Martha. The first was a Kodacolor snapshot signed "Love," though he knew better. She stood against a brick wall. Her eyes were gray and neutral, her lips slightly open as she stared straight-on at the camera. At night, sometimes, Lieutenant Cross wondered who had taken the picture, because he knew she had boyfriends, because he loved her so much, and because he could see the shadow of the picture taker spreading out against the brick wall. The second photograph had been clipped from the 1968 Mount Sebastian yearbook. It was an action shot—women's volleyball—and Martha was bent horizontal to the floor, reaching, the palms of her hands in sharp focus, the tongue taut, the expression frank and competitive. There was no visible sweat. She wore white gym shorts. Her legs, he thought, were almost certainly the legs of a virgin, dry and without hair, the left knee cocked and carrying her entire weight, which was just over one hundred pounds. Lieutenant Cross remembered touching that left knee. A dark theater, he remembered, and the movie was *Bonnie and Clyde,* and Martha wore a tweed skirt, and during the final scene, when he touched her knee, she turned and looked at him in a sad, sober way that made him pull his hand back, but he would always remember the feel of the tweed skirt and the knee beneath it and the sound of the gunfire that killed Bonnie and Clyde, how embarrassing it was, how slow and oppressive. He remembered kissing her good night at the dorm door. Right then, he thought, he should've done something brave. He should've carried her up the stairs to her room and tied her to the bed and touched that left knee all night long. He should've risked it. Whenever he looked at the photographs, he thought of new things he should've done.

What they carried was partly a function of rank, partly of field specialty.

As a first lieutenant and platoon leader, Jimmy Cross carried a compass, maps, code books, binoculars, and a .45-caliber pistol that weighted 2.9 pounds fully loaded. He carried a strobe light and the responsibility for the lives of his men.

As an RTO, Mitchell Sanders carried the PRC-25 radio, a killer, 26 pounds with its battery.

As a medic, Rat Kiley carried a canvas satchel filled with morphine and plasma and malaria tablets and surgical tape and comic books and all the things a medic must carry, including M&M's[4] for especially bad wounds, for a total weight of nearly 20 pounds.

10   As a big man, therefore a machine gunner, Henry Dobbins carried the M-60, which weighed 23 pounds unloaded, but which was almost always loaded. In addition, Dobbins carried between 10 and 15 pounds of ammunition draped in belts across his chest and shoulders.

As PFCs or Spec 4s, most of them were common grunts and carried the standard M-16 gas-operated assault rifle. The weapon weighed 7.5 pounds unloaded, 8.2 pounds with its full 20-round magazine. Depending on numerous factors, such as topography and psychology, the riflemen carried anywhere from 12 to 20 magazines, usually in cloth bandoliers, adding on another 8.4 pounds at minimum, 14 pounds as maximum. When it was available, they also carried M-16 maintenance gear—rods and steel brushes and swabs and tubes of LSA oil—all of which weighed about a pound. Among the grunts, some carried the M-79 grenade launcher, 5.9 pounds unloaded, a reasonably light weapon except for the ammunition, which was heavy. A single round weighed 10 ounces. The typical load was 25 rounds. But Ted Lavender, who was scared, carried 34 pounds when he was shot and killed outside Than Khe, and he went down under an exceptional burden, more than 20 pounds of ammunition, plus the flak jacket and helmet and rations and water and toilet paper and tranquilizers and all the rest, plus the unweighed fear. He was dead weight. There was no twitching or flopping. Kiowa, who saw it happen, said it was like watching a rock fall, or a big sandbag or something—just boom, then down—not like the movies where the dead guy rolls around and does fancy spins and goes ass over teakettle—not like that, Kiowa said the poor bastard just flat-fuck fell. Boom. Down. Nothing else. It was a bright morning in mid-April. Lieutenant Cross felt the pain. He blamed himself. They stripped off Lavendar's canteens and ammo, all the heavy things, and Rat Kiley said the obvious, the guy's dead, and Mitchell Sanders used his radio to report one U.S. KIA[5] and to request a chopper. Then they wrapped Lavender in his poncho. They carried him out to a dry paddy, established security, and sat smoking the dead man's dope until the chopper came. Lieutenant Cross kept to himself. He pictured Martha's smooth young face, thinking he loved her more than anything, more than his men, and now Ted Lavender was dead because he loved her so much and could not stop thinking about her. When the dustoff arrived, they carried Lavender aboard. Afterward they burned Than Khe. They marched until dusk, then dug their holes, and that night Kiowa kept explaining how you had to be there, how fast it was, how the poor guy just dropped like so much concrete. Boom-down, he said. Like cement.

In addition to the three standard weapons—the M-60, M-16, and M-79—they carried whatever presented itself, or whatever seemed appropriate as a means of

---

[4]**M&M's** comic slang for medical supplies   [5]**KIA** killed in action

killing or staying alive. They carried catch-as-catch-can. At various times, in various situations, they carried M-14s and CAR-15s and Swedish Ks and grease guns and captured AK-47s and Chi-Coms and RPGs and Simonov carbines and black market Uzis and .38-caliber Smith & Wesson handguns and 66 mm LAWs and shotguns and silencers and blackjacks and bayonets and C-4 plastic explosives. Lee Strunk carried a slingshot; a weapon of last resort, he called it. Mitchell Sanders carried brass knuckles. Kiowa carried his grandfather's feathered hatchet. Every third or fourth man carried a Claymore antipersonnel mine—3.5 pounds with its firing device. They all carried fragmentation grenades—14 ounces each. They all carried at least one M-18 colored smoke grenade—24 ounces. Some carried CS or tear gas grenades. Some carried white phosphorus grenades. They carried all they could bear, and then some, including a silent awe for the terrible power of the things they carried.

In the first week of April, before Lavendar died, Lieutenant Jimmy Cross received a good-luck charm from Martha. It was a simple pebble, an ounce at most. Smooth to the touch, it was a milky white color with flecks of orange and violet, oval-shaped, like a miniature egg. In the accompanying letter, Martha wrote that she had found the pebble on the Jersey shoreline, precisely where the land touched water at high tide, where things came together but also separated. It was this separate-but-together quality, she wrote, that had inspired her to pick up the pebble and to carry it in her breast pocket for several days, where it seemed worthless, and then to send it through the mail, by air, as a token of her truest feeling for him. Lieutenant Cross found this romantic. But he wondered what her truest feelings were, exactly, and what she meant by separate-but-together. He wondered how the tides and waves had come into play on that afternoon along the Jersey shoreline when Martha saw the pebble and bent down to rescue it from geology. He imagined bare feet. Martha was a poet, with the poet's sensibilities, and her feet would be brown and bare, the toenails unpainted, the eyes chilly and somber like the ocean in March, and though it was painful, he wondered who had been with her that afternoon. He imagined a pair of shadows moving along the strip of sand where things came together but also separated. It was phantom jealousy, he knew, but he couldn't help himself. He loved her so much. On the march, through the hot days of early April, he carried the pebble in his mouth, turning it with his tongue, tasting sea salt and moisture. His mind wandered. He had difficulty keeping his attention on the war. On occasion he would yell at his men to spread out the column, to keep their eyes open, but then he would slip away into daydreams, just pretending, walking barefoot along the Jersey shore, with Martha, carrying nothing. He would feel himself rising. Sun and waves and gentle winds, all love and lightness.

What they carried varied by mission.

15   When a mission took them to the mountains, they carried mosquito netting, machetes, canvas tarps, and extra bug juice.

If a mission seemed especially hazardous, or if it involved a place they knew to be bad, they carried everything they could. In certain heavily mined AOs,[6] where

---

[6]**AOs** areas of operation

the land was dense with Toe Poppers and Bouncing Betties, they took turns humping a 28-pound mine detector. With its headphones and big sensing plate, the equipment was a stress on the lower back and shoulders, awkward to handle, often useless because of the shrapnel in the earth, but they carried it anyway, partly for safety, partly for the illusion of safety.

On ambush, or other night missions, they carried peculiar little odds and ends. Kiowa always took along his New Testament and a pair of moccasins for silence. Dave Jensen carried night-sight vitamins high in carotene. Lee Strunk carried his slingshot; ammo, he claimed, would never be a problem. Rat Kiley carried brandy and M&M's candy. Until he was shot, Ted Lavender carried the starlight scope, which weighed 6.3 pounds with its aluminum carrying case. Henry Dobbins carried his girlfriend's pantyhose wrapped around his neck as a comforter. They all carried ghosts. When dark came, they would move out single file across the meadows and paddies to their ambush coordinates, where they would quietly set up the Claymores and lie down and spend the night waiting.

Other missions were more complicated and required special equipment. In mid-April, it was their mission to search out and destroy the elaborate tunnel complexes in the Than Khe area south of Chu Lai. To blow the tunnels, they carried one-pound blocks of pentrite high explosives, four blocks to a man, 68 pounds in all. They carried wiring, detonators, and battery-powered clackers. Dave Jensen carried earplugs. Most often, before blowing the tunnels, they were ordered by higher command to search them, which was considered bad news, but by and large they just shrugged and carried out orders. Because he was a big man, Henry Dobbins was excused from tunnel duty. The others would draw numbers. Before Lavender died there were 17 men in the platoon, and whoever drew the number 17 would strip off his gear and crawl in head first with a flashlight and Lieutenant Cross's .45-caliber pistol. The rest of them would fan out as security. They would sit down or kneel, not facing the hole, listening to the ground beneath them, imagining cobwebs and ghosts, whatever was down there—the tunnel walls squeezing in—how the flashlight seemed impossibly heavy in the hand and how it was tunnel vision in the very strictest sense, compression in all ways, even time, and how you had to wiggle in—ass and elbows—a swallowed-up feeling—and how you found yourself worrying about odd things—will your flashlight go dead? Do rats carry rabies? If you screamed, how far would the sound carry? Would your buddies hear it? Would they have the courage to drag you out? In some respects, though not many, the waiting was worse than the tunnel itself. Imagination was a killer.

On April 16, when Lee Strunk drew the number seventeen, he laughed and muttered something and went down quickly. The morning was hot and very still. Not good, Kiowa said. He looked at the tunnel opening, then out across a dry paddy toward the village of Than Khe. Nothing moved. No clouds or birds or people. As they waited, the men smoked and drank Kool-Aid, not talking much, feeling sympathy for Lee Strunk but also feeling the luck of the draw. You win some, you lose some, said Mitchell Sanders, and sometimes you settle for a rain check. It was a tired line and no one laughed.

20   Henry Dobbins ate a tropical chocolate bar. Ted Lavender popped a tranquilizer and went off to pee.

After five minutes, Lieutenant Jimmy Cross moved to the tunnel, leaned down, and examined the darkness. Trouble, he thought—a cave-in maybe. And then suddenly, without willing it, he was thinking about Martha. The stresses and fractures, the quick collapse, the two of them buried alive under all that weight. Dense, crushing love. Kneeling, watching the hole, he tried to concentrate on Lee Strunk and the war, all the dangers, but his love was too much for him, he felt paralyzed, he wanted to sleep inside her lungs and breathe her blood and be smothered. He wanted her to be a virgin and not a virgin, all at once. He wanted to know her. Intimate secrets— why poetry? Why so sad? Why that grayness in her eyes? Why so alone? Not lonely, just alone—riding her bike across campus or sitting off by herself in the cafeteria. Even dancing, she danced alone—and it was the aloneness that filled him with love. He remembered telling her that one evening. How she nodded and looked away. And how, later, when he kissed her, she received the kiss without returning it, her eyes wide open, not afraid, not a virgin's eyes, just flat and uninvolved.

Lieutenant Cross gazed at the tunnel. But he was not there. He was buried with Martha under the white sand at the Jersey shore. They were pressed together, and the pebble in his mouth was her tongue. He was smiling. Vaguely, he was aware of how quiet the day was, the sullen paddies, yet he could not bring himself to worry about matters of security. He was beyond that. He was just a kid at war, in love. He was twenty-two years old. He couldn't help it.

A few moments later Lee Strunk crawled out of the tunnel. He came up grinning, filthy but alive. Lieutenant Cross nodded and closed his eyes while the others clapped Strunk on the back and made jokes about rising from the dead.

Worms, Rat Kiley said. Right out of the grave. Fuckin' zombie.

25   The men laughed. They all felt great relief.

Spook city, said Mitchell Sanders.

Lee Strunk made a funny ghost sound, a kind of moaning, yet very happy, and right then, when Strunk made that high happy moaning sound, when he went Ahhooooo, right then Ted Lavender was shot in the head on his way back from peeing. He lay with his mouth open. The teeth were broken. There was a swollen black bruise under his left eye. The cheekbone was gone. Oh shit, Rat Kiley said, the guy's dead. The guy's dead, he kept saying, which seemed profound—the guy's dead. I mean really.

The things they carried were determined to some extent by superstition. Lieutenant Cross carried his good-luck pebble. Dave Jensen carried a rabbit's foot. Norman Bowker, otherwise a very gentle person, carried a thumb that had been presented to him as a gift by Mitchell Sanders. The thumb was dark brown, rubbery to the touch, and weighed four ounces at most. It had been cut from a VC corpse, a boy of fifteen or sixteen. They'd found him at the bottom of an irrigation ditch, badly burned, flies in his mouth and eyes. The boy wore black shorts and sandals. At the time of his death he had been carrying a pouch of rice, a rifle, and three magazines of ammunition.

You want my opinion, Mitchell Sanders said, there's a definite moral here.

30   He put his hand on the dead boy's wrist. He was quiet for a time, as if counting a pulse, then he patted the stomach, almost affectionately, and used Kiowa's hunting hatchet to remove the thumb.

Henry Dobbins asked what the moral was.

Moral?

You know. Moral.

Sanders wrapped the thumb in toilet paper and handed it across to Norman Bowker. There was no blood. Smiling, he kicked the boy's head, watched the flies scatter, and said, It's like with that old TV show—Paladin. Have gun, will travel.

35   Henry Dobbins thought about it.

Yeah, well, he finally said. I don't see no moral.

There it is, man.

Fuck off.

They carried USO stationery and pencils and pens. They carried Sterno, safety pins, trip flares, signal flares, spools of wire, razor blades, chewing tobacco, liberated joss sticks and statuettes of the smiling Buddha, candles, grease pencils, *The Stars and Stripes,* fingernail clippers, Psy Ops leaflets, bush hats, bolos, and much more. Twice a week, when the resupply choppers came in, they carried hot chow in green Mermite cans and large canvas bags filled with iced beer and soda pop. They carried plastic water containers, each with a two-gallon capacity. Mitchell Sanders carried a set of starched tiger fatigues for special occasions. Henry Dobbins carried Black Flag insecticide. Dave Jensen carried empty sandbags that could be filled at night for added protection. Lee Strunk carried tanning lotion. Some things they carried in common. Taking turns, they carried the big PRC-77 scrambler radio, which weighed thirty pounds with its battery. They shared the weight of memory. They took up what others could no longer bear. Often, they carried each other, the wounded or weak. They carried infections. They carried chess sets, basketballs, Vietnamese-English dictionaries, insignia of rank, Bronze Stars and Purple Hearts, plastic cards imprinted with the Code of Conduct. They carried diseases, among them malaria and dysentery. They carried lice and ringworm and leeches and paddy algae and various rots and molds. They carried the land itself—Vietnam, the place, the soil—a powdery orange-red dust that covered their boots and fatigues and faces. They carried the sky. The whole atmosphere, they carried it, the humidity, the monsoons, the stink of fungus and decay, all of it, they carried gravity. They moved like mules. By daylight they took sniper fire, at night they were mortared, but it was not battle, it was just the endless march, village to village, without purpose, nothing won or lost. They marched for the sake of the march. They plodded along slowly, dumbly, leaning forward against the heat, unthinking, all blood and bone, simple grunts, soldiering with their legs, toiling up the hills and down into the paddies and across the rivers and up again and down, just humping, one step and then the next and then another, but no volition, no will, because it was automatic, it was anatomy, and the war was entirely a matter of posture and carriage, the hump was everything, a kind of inertia, a kind of emptiness, a dullness of desire and intellect and conscience and hope and human sensibility. Their principles were in their feet. Their calculations were biological. They had no sense of strategy or mission. They searched the villages without knowing what to look for, not caring, kicking over jars of rice, frisking children and old men, blowing tunnels, sometimes setting fires and sometimes not, then forming up and moving on to the next village, then other villages, where it would always be the same. They carried their own lives. The pressures were enormous. In the heat of early afternoon, they would remove their helmets and flak jackets, walking bare, which was dangerous but which helped ease the strain. They would often discard things along the route of march. Purely for comfort, they would throw away rations, blow their Claymores and grenades, no matter, because by nightfall the resupply choppers would arrive with more of the same, then a day or two later still more, fresh watermelons and crates of ammunition and sunglasses and woolen sweaters—the resources were stunning—sparklers for the Fourth of July, colored eggs for Easter. It was the great American war chest—the fruits of science, the smokestacks, the canneries, the arsenals at Hartford, the Minnesota forests, the machine shops, the vast fields of corn and wheat—they carried like freight trains; they carried it on their backs and shoulders—and for all the ambiguities of Vietnam, all the mysteries and unknowns, there was at least the single abiding certainty that they would never be at a loss for things to carry.

40   After the chopper took Lavender away, Lieutenant Jimmy Cross led his men into the village of Than Khe. They burned everything. They shot chickens and dogs, they trashed the village well, they called in artillery and watched the wreckage, then they marched for several hours through the hot afternoon, and then at dusk, while Kiowa explained how Lavender died, Lieutenant Cross found himself trembling.

He tried not to cry. With his entrenching tool, which weighed five pounds, he began digging a hole in the earth.

He felt shame. He hated himself. He had loved Martha more than his men, and as a consequence Lavender was now dead, and this was something he would have to carry like a stone in his stomach for the rest of the war.

All he could do was dig. He used his entrenching tool like an ax, slashing, feeling both love and hate, and then later, when it was full dark, he sat at the bottom of his foxhole and wept. It went on for a long while. In part, he was grieving for Ted Lavender, but mostly it was for Martha, and for himself, because she belonged to another world, which was not quite real, and because she was a junior at Mount Sebastian College in New Jersey, a poet and a virgin and uninvolved, and because he realized she did not love him and never would.

Like cement, Kiowa whispered in the dark. I swear to God—boom-down. Not a word.

45   I've heard this, said Norman Bowker.

A pisser, you know? Still zipping himself up. Zapped while zipping.

All right, fine. That's enough.

Yeah, but you had to see it, the guy just—

I heard, man. Cement. So why not shut the fuck *up*?

50   Kiowa shook his head sadly and glanced over at the hole where Lieutenant Jimmy Cross sat watching the night. The air was thick and wet. A warm dense fog had settled over the paddies and there was the stillness that precedes rain.

After a time Kiowa sighed.

One thing for sure, he said. The lieutenant's in some deep hurt. I mean that crying jag—the way he was carrying on—it wasn't fake or anything, it was real heavy-duty hurt. The man cares.

Sure, Norman Bowker said.

Say what you want, the man does care.

55   We all got problems.

Not Lavender.

No, I guess not, Bowker said. Do me a favor, though.

Shut up?

That's a smart Indian. Shut up.

60   Shrugging, Kiowa pulled off his boots. He wanted to say more, just to lighten up his sleep, but instead he opened his New Testament and arranged it beneath his head as a pillow. The fog made things seem hollow and unattached. He tried not to think about Ted Lavender, but then he was thinking how fast it was, no drama, down and dead, and how it was hard to feel anything except surprise. It seemed un-Christian. He wished he could find some great sadness, or even anger, but the emotion wasn't there and he couldn't make it happen. Mostly he felt pleased to be alive. He liked the smell of the New Testament under his cheek, the leather and ink and paper and glue, whatever the chemicals were. He liked hearing the sounds of night. Even his fatigue, it felt fine, the stiff muscles and the prickly awareness of his own body, a floating feeling. He enjoyed not being dead. Lying there, Kiowa admired Lieutenant Jimmy Cross's capacity for grief. He wanted to share the man's pain, he wanted to care as Jimmy Cross cared. And yet when he closed his eyes, all he could think was Boom-down, and all he could feel was the pleasure of having his boots off and the fog curling in around him and the damp soil and the Bible smells and the plush comfort of night.

After a moment Norman Bowker sat up in the dark.

What the hell, he said. You want to talk, *talk*. Tell it to me.

Forget it.

No, man, go on. One thing I hate, it's a silent Indian.

65   For the most part they carried themselves with poise, a kind of dignity. Now and then, however, there were times of panic, when they squealed or wanted to squeal but couldn't, when they twitched and made moaning sounds and covered their heads and said Dear Jesus and flopped around on the earth and fired their weapons blindly and cringed and sobbed and begged for the noise to stop and went wild and made stupid promises to themselves and to God and to their mothers and fathers, hoping not to die. In different ways, it happened to all of them. Afterward, when the firing ended, they would blink and peek up. They would touch their bodies, feeling shame, then quickly hiding it. They would force themselves to stand. As if in slow motion, frame by frame, the world would take on the old logic—absolute silence, then the wind, then sunlight, then voices. It was the burden of being alive. Awkwardly, the men would reassemble themselves, first in private, then in groups, becoming soldiers again. They would repair the leaks in their eyes. They would check for casualties, call in dustoffs, light cigarettes, try to smile, clear their throats and spit and begin cleaning their weapons. After a time

someone would shake his head and say, No lie, I almost shit my pants, and someone else would laugh, which meant it was bad, yes, but the guy had obviously
not shit his pants, it wasn't that bad, and in any case nobody would ever do such
a thing and then go ahead and talk about it. They would squint into the dense,
oppressive sunlight. For a few moments, perhaps, they would fall silent, lighting
a joint and tracking its passage from man to man, inhaling, holding in the humiliation. Scary stuff, one of them might say. But then someone else would grin or flick
his eyebrows and say, Roger-dodger, almost cut me a new asshole, *almost*.

There were numerous such poses. Some carried themselves with a sort of wistful
resignation, others with pride or stiff soldierly discipline or good humor or macho
zeal. They were afraid of dying but they were even more afraid to show it.

They found jokes to tell.

They used a hard vocabulary to contain the terrible softness. *Greased* they'd
say. *Offed, lit up, zapped while zipping*. It wasn't cruelty, just stage presence. They
were actors. When someone died, it wasn't quite dying, because in a curious way it
seemed scripted, and because they had their lines mostly memorized, irony mixed
with tragedy, and because they called it by other names, as if to encyst and destroy
the reality of death itself. They kicked corpses. They cut off thumbs. They talked
grunt lingo. They told stories about Ted Lavender's supply of tranquilizers, how the
poor guy didn't feel a thing, how incredibly tranquil he was.

There's a moral here, said Mitchell Sanders.

70   They were waiting for Lavender's chopper, smoking the dead man's dope.

The moral's pretty obvious, Sanders said, and winked. Stay away from drugs.
No joke, they'll ruin your day every time.

Cute, said Henry Dobbins.

Mind blower, get it? Talk about wiggy. Nothing left, just blood and brains.

They made themselves laugh.

75   There it is, they'd say. Over and over—there it is, my friend, there it is—as if
the repetition itself were an act of poise, a balance between crazy and almost crazy,
knowing without going, there it is, which meant be cool, let it ride, because Oh
yeah, man, you can't change what can't be changed, there it is, there it absolutely
and positively and fucking well *is*.

They were tough.

They carried all the emotional baggage of men who might die. Grief, terror,
love, longing—these were intangibles, but the intangibles had their own mass
and specific gravity, they had tangible weight. They carried shameful memories.
They carried the common secret of cowardice barely restrained, the instinct to
run or freeze or hide, and in many respects this was the heaviest burden of all,
for it could never be put down, it required perfect balance and perfect posture.
They carried their reputations. They carried the soldier's greatest fear, which was
the fear of blushing. Men killed, and died, because they were embarrassed not
to. It was what had brought them to the war in the first place, nothing positive,
no dreams of glory or honor, just to avoid the blush of dishonor. They died so
as not to die of embarrassment. They crawled into tunnels and walked point and
advanced under fire. Each morning, despite the unknowns, they made their legs
move. They endured. They kept humping. They did not submit to the obvious

alternative, which was simply to close the eyes and fall. So easy, really. Go limp and tumble to the ground and let the muscles unwind and not speak and not budge until your buddies picked you up and lifted you into the chopper that would roar and dip its nose and carry you off to the world. A mere matter of falling, yet no one ever fell. It was not courage, exactly; the object was not valor. Rather, they were too frightened to be cowards.

By and large they carried these things inside, maintaining the masks of composure. They sneered at sick call. They spoke bitterly about guys who had found release by shooting off their own toes or fingers. Pussies, they'd say. Candyasses. It was fierce, mocking talk, with only a trace of envy or awe, but even so, the image played itself out behind their eyes.

They imagined the muzzle against flesh. So easy: squeeze the trigger and blow away a toe. They imagined it. They imagined the quick, sweet pain, then the evacuation to Japan, then a hospital with warm beds and cute geisha nurses.

80   And they dreamed of freedom birds.

At night, on guard, staring into the dark, they were carried away by jumbo jets. They felt the rush of takeoff. *Gone!* they yelled. And then velocity—wings and engines—a smiling stewardess—but it was more than a plane, it was a real bird, a big sleek silver bird with feathers and talons and high screeching. They were flying. The weights fell off, there was nothing to bear. They laughed and held on tight, feeling the cold slap of wind and altitude, soaring, thinking *It's over, I'm gone!*—they were naked, they were light and free—it was all lightness, bright and fast and buoyant, light as light, a helium buzz in the brain, a giddy bubbling in the lungs as they were taken up over the clouds and the war, beyond duty, beyond gravity and mortification and global entanglements—*Sin loi!*[7] they yelled, *I'm sorry, mother-fuckers, but I'm out of it, I'm goofed, I'm on a space cruise, I'm gone!*—and it was a restful, unencumbered sensation, just riding the light waves, sailing that big silver freedom bird over the mountains and oceans, over America, over the farms and great sleeping cities and cemeteries and highways and the golden arches of McDonald's. It was flight, a kind of fleeing, a kind of falling, falling higher and higher, spinning off the edge of the earth and beyond the sun and through the vast, silent vacuum where there were no burdens and where everything weighed exactly nothing—*Gone!* They screamed, *I'm sorry but I'm gone!*—and so at night, not quite dreaming, they gave themselves over to lightness, they were carried, so they were purely borne.

On the morning after Ted Lavender died, First Lieutenant Jimmy Cross crouched at the bottom of his foxhole and burned Martha's letters. Then he burned the two photographs. There was a steady rain falling, which made it difficult, but he used heat tabs and Sterno to build a small fire, screening it with his body, holding the photographs over the tight blue flame with the tips of his fingers.

He realized it was only a gesture. Stupid, he thought. Sentimental, too, but mostly just stupid.

Lavender was dead. You couldn't burn the blame.

[7]***Sin loi!*** Vietnamese for "sorry"

85   Besides, the letters were in his head. And even now, without photographs, Lieutenant Cross could see Martha playing volleyball in her white gym shorts and yellow T-shirt. He could see her moving in the rain.

When the fire died out, Lieutenant Cross pulled his poncho over his shoulders and ate breakfast from a can.

There was no great mystery, he decided.

In those burned letters Martha had never mentioned the war, except to say, Jimmy, take care of yourself. She wasn't involved. She signed the letters Love, but it wasn't love, and all the fine lines and technicalities did not matter. Virginity was no longer an issue. He hated her. Yes, he did. He hated her. Love, too, but it was a hard, hating kind of love.

The morning came up wet and blurry. Everything seemed part of everything else, the fog and Martha and the deepening rain.

90   He was a soldier, after all.

Half smiling, Lieutenant Jimmy Cross took out his maps. He shook his head hard, as if to clear it, then bent forward and began planning the day's march. In ten minutes, or maybe twenty, he would rouse the men and they would pack up and head west, where the maps showed the country to be green and inviting. They would do what they had always done. The rain might add some weight, but otherwise it would be one more day layered upon all the other days.

He was realistic about it. There was that new hardness in his stomach. He loved her but he hated her.

No more fantasies, he told himself.

Henceforth, when he thought about Martha, it would be only to think that she belonged elsewhere. He would shut down the daydreams. This was not Mount Sebastian, it was another world, where there were no pretty poems or midterm exams, a place where men died because of carelessness and gross stupidity. Kiowa was right. Boom-down, and you were dead, never partly dead.

95   Briefly, in the rain, Lieutenant Cross saw Martha's gray eyes gazing back at him.

He understood.

It was very sad, he thought. The things men carried inside. The things men did or felt they had to do.

He almost nodded at her, but didn't.

Instead he went back to his maps. He was now determined to perform his duties firmly and without negligence. It wouldn't help Lavender, he knew that, but from this point on he would comport himself as a soldier. He would dispose of his good-luck pebble. Swallow it, maybe, or use Lee Strunk's slingshot, or just drop it along the trail. On the march he would impose strict field discipline. He would be careful to send out flank security, to prevent straggling or bunching up, to keep his troops moving at the proper pace and at the proper interval. He would insist on clean weapons. He would confiscate the remainder of Lavender's dope. Later in the day, perhaps, he would call the men together and speak to them plainly. He would accept the blame for what had happened to Ted Lavender. He would be a man about it. He would look them in the eyes, keeping his chin level, and he would issue the new SOPs in a calm, impersonal tone of voice, a lieutenant's voice, leaving no room for argument or discussion. Commencing immediately, he'd tell them, they would no longer abandon equipment along the route of march. They would police up their acts. They would get their shit together, and keep it together, and maintain it neatly and in good working order.

100   He would not tolerate laxity. He would show strength, distancing himself.

Among the men there would be grumbling, of course, and maybe worse, because their days would seem longer and their loads heavier, but Lieutenant Jimmy Cross reminded himself that his obligation was not to be loved but to lead. He would dispense with love; it was not now a factor. And if anyone quarreled or complained, he would simply tighten his lips and arrange his shoulders in the correct command posture. He might give a curt little nod. Or he might not. He might just shrug and say, Carry on, then they would saddle up and form into a column and move out toward the villages of Than Khe.

MAKING CONNECTIONS

1. Describe Jimmy Cross. What do you know about him? How does he change?
2. How are you affected by the setting? What brings the setting to life?
3. Why is Lavender's death referred to so often in the story? Kiowa believes that Cross is crying over Lavender's death. Do you agree? Is there any other reason he might be crying? Explain.
4. Why does Jimmy Cross burn Martha's letters?
5. Why is the list of what they carried repeated so often in the story?
6. Do you carry things that indicate something important about you—or your current situation? Explain.

MAKING AN ARGUMENT

1. In addition to the physical things they carried, the narrator says, "They carried all the emotional baggage of men who might die." Using this story and poems you've selected from the subtheme Connecting Through Comparison: The Impact of War that begins on page 1173, write an essay about the "emotional baggage" of war. Cite the text of the story and the selected poems to support your view.

FLANNERY O'CONNOR [1925–1964]

Flannery O'Connor was born in Savannah, Georgia, and at the age of twelve moved with her family to nearby Milledgeville. After graduating from Women's College of Georgia, O'Connor attended the University of Iowa, earning an M.F.A. in 1947. Following graduation, she stayed for a short time at Yaddo, a prestigious writer's colony in Saratoga Springs, New York, and then with friends in New York City and Connecticut. In 1950, after she was diagnosed with lupus, an incurable de-generative disease, she returned to Milledgeville, where she spent the rest of her life.

O'Connor was a devout Roman Catholic. A profound faith permeates her work, which, with its blend of grotesque characterizations and religious faith, is often characterized as Southern gothic. About her stories she wrote: "My subject in fiction is the action of grace in a territory held largely by the devil."

A GOOD MAN IS HARD TO FIND   [1955]

The grandmother didn't want to go to Florida. She wanted to visit some of her connections in east Tennessee and she was seizing at every chance to change Bailey's mind. Bailey was the son she lived with, her only boy. He was sitting on the edge of his chair at the table, bent over the orange sports section of the *Journal.* "Now look here, Bailey," she said, "see here, read this," and she stood with one hand on her thin hip and the other rattling the newspaper at his bald head. "Here this fellow that calls himself The Misfit is aloose from the Federal Pen and headed toward Florida and you read here what it says he did to these people. Just you read it. I wouldn't take my children in any direction with a criminal like that aloose in it. I couldn't answer to my conscience if I did."

Bailey didn't look up from his reading so she wheeled around then and faced the children's mother, a young woman in slacks, whose face was as broad and innocent as a cabbage and was tied around with a green head-kerchief that had two points on the top like a rabbit's ears. She was sitting on the sofa, feeding the baby his apricots out of a jar. "The children have been to Florida before," the old lady said. "You all ought to take them somewhere else for a change so they would see different parts of the world and be broad. They never have been to east Tennessee."

The children's mother didn't seem to hear her but the eight-year-old boy, John Wesley, a stocky child with glasses, said, "If you don't want to go to Florida, why dontcha stay at home?" He and the little girl, June Star, were reading the funny papers on the floor.

"She wouldn't stay at home to be queen for a day," June Star said without raising her yellow head.

5   "Yes and what would you do if this fellow, The Misfit, caught you?" the grandmother asked.

"I'd smack his face," John Wesley said.

"She wouldn't stay at home for a million bucks," June Star said. "Afraid she'd miss something. She has to go everywhere we go."

"All right, Miss," the grandmother said. "Just remember that the next time you want me to curl your hair."

June Star said her hair was naturally curly.

10   The next morning the grandmother was the first one in the car, ready to go. She had her big black valise that looked like the head of a hippopotamus in one corner, and underneath it she was hiding a basket with Pitty Sing, the cat, in it. She didn't intend for the cat to be left alone in the house for three days because he would miss her too much and she was afraid he might brush against one of the gas burners and accidentally asphyxiate himself. Her son, Bailey, didn't like to arrive at a motel with a cat.

She sat in the middle of the back seat with John Wesley and June Star on either side of her. Bailey and the children's mother and the baby sat in front and they left Atlanta at eight forty-five with the mileage on the car at 55890. The grandmother wrote this down because she thought it would be interesting to say how many miles they had been when they got back. It took them twenty minutes to reach the outskirts of the city.

The old lady settled herself comfortably, removing her white cotton gloves and putting them up with her purse on the shelf in front of the back window. The children's mother still had on slacks and still had her head tied up in a green kerchief, but the grandmother had on a navy blue straw sailor hat with a bunch of white violets on the brim and a navy blue dress with a small white dot in the print. Her collars and cuffs were white organdy trimmed with lace and at her neckline she had pinned a purple spray of cloth violets containing a sachet. In case of an accident, anyone seeing her dead on the highway would know at once that she was a lady.

She said she thought it was going to be a good day for driving, neither too hot nor too cold, and she cautioned Bailey that the speed limit was fifty-five miles an hour and that the patrolmen hid themselves behind billboards and small clumps of trees and sped out after you before you had a chance to slow down. She pointed out interesting details of the scenery: Stone Mountain; the blue granite that in some places came up to both sides of the highway; the brilliant red clay banks slightly streaked with purple; and the various crops that made rows of green lace-work on the ground. The trees were full of silver-white sunlight and the meanest of them sparkled. The children were reading comic magazines and their mother had gone back to sleep.

"Let's go through Georgia fast so we won't have to look at it much," John Wesley said.

15   "If I were a little boy," said the grandmother, "I wouldn't talk about my native state that way. Tennessee has the mountains and Georgia has the hills."

"Tennessee is just a hillbilly dumping ground," John Wesley said, "and Georgia is a lousy state too."

"You said it," June Star said.

"In my time," said the grandmother, folding her thin veined fingers, "children were more respectful of their native states and their parents and everything else. People did right then. Oh look at the cute little pickaninny!" she said and pointed to a Negro child standing in the door of a shack. "Wouldn't that make a picture, now?" she asked and they all turned and looked at the little Negro out of the back window. He waved.

"He didn't have any britches on," June Star said.

20   "He probably didn't have any," the grandmother explained. "Little niggers in the country don't have things like we do. If I could paint, I'd paint that picture," she said.

The children exchanged comic books.

The grandmother offered to hold the baby and the children's mother passed him over the front seat to her. She set him on her knee and bounced him and told him about the things they were passing. She rolled her eyes and screwed up her mouth and stuck her leathery thin face into his smooth bland one. Occasionally he gave her a faraway smile. They passed a large cotton field with five or six graves fenced in the middle of it, like a small island. "Look at the graveyard!" the grandmother said, pointing it out. "That was the old family burying ground. That belonged to the plantation."

"Where's the plantation?" John Wesley asked.

"Gone With the Wind," said the grandmother. "Ha. Ha."

25   When the children finished all the comic books they had brought, they opened the lunch and ate it. The grandmother ate a peanut butter sandwich and an olive and would not let the children throw the box and the paper napkins out the window. When there was nothing else to do they played a game by choosing a cloud and making the other two guess what shape it suggested. John Wesley took one of the shape of a cow and June Star guessed a cow and John Wesley said, no, an automobile, and June Star said he didn't play fair, and they began to slap each other over the grandmother.

The grandmother said she would tell them a story if they would keep quiet. When she told a story, she rolled her eyes and waved her head and was very dramatic. She said once when she was a maiden lady she had been courted by a Mr. Edgar Atkins Teagarden from Jasper, Georgia. She said he was a very good-looking man and a gentleman and that he brought her a watermelon every Saturday afternoon with his initials cut in it, E. A. T. Well, one Saturday, she said, Mr. Teagarden brought the watermelon and there was nobody at home and he left it on the front porch and returned in his buggy to Jasper, but she never got the watermelon, she said, because a nigger boy ate it when he saw the initials, E. A. T.! This story tickled John Wesley's funny bone and he giggled and giggled but June Star didn't think it was any good. She said she wouldn't marry a man that just brought her a watermelon on Saturday. The grandmother said she would have done well to marry Mr. Teagarden because he was a gentleman and had bought Coca-Cola stock when it first came out and that he had died only a few years ago, a very wealthy man.

They stopped at The Tower for barbecued sandwiches. The Tower was a part stucco and part wood filling station and dance hall set in a clearing outside of Timothy. A fat man named Red Sammy Butts ran it and there were signs stuck here and there on the building and for miles up and down the highway saying, TRY RED SAMMY'S FAMOUS BARBECUE. NONE LIKE FAMOUS RED SAMMY'S! RED SAM! THE FAT BOY WITH THE HAPPY LAUGH! A VETERAN! RED SAMMY'S YOUR MAN!

Red Sammy was lying on the bare ground outside The Tower with his head under a truck while a gray monkey about a foot high, chained to a small chinaberry tree, chattered nearby. The monkey sprang back into the tree and got on the highest limb as soon as he saw the children jump out of the car and run toward him.

Inside, The Tower was a long dark room with a counter at one end and tables at the other and dancing space in the middle. They sat down at a board table next to the nickelodeon and Red Sam's wife, a tall burnt-brown woman with hair and eyes lighter than her skin, came and took their order. The children's mother put a dime in the machine and played "The Tennessee Waltz," and the grandmother said that tune always made her want to dance. She asked Bailey if he would like to dance but he only glared at her. He didn't have a naturally sunny disposition

like she did and trips made him nervous. The grandmother's brown eyes were very
bright. She swayed her head from side to side and pretended she was dancing in
her chair. June Star said play something she could tap to so the children's mother
put in another dime and played a fast number and June Star stepped out onto the
dance floor and did her tap routine.

30   "Ain't she cute?" Red Sam's wife said, leaning over the counter. "Would you like
to come be my little girl?"

"No I certainly wouldn't," June Star said. "I wouldn't live in a broken-down
place like this for a million bucks!" and she ran back to the table.

"Ain't she cute?" the woman repeated, stretching her mouth politely.

"Aren't you ashamed?" hissed the grandmother.

Red Sam came in and told his wife to quit lounging on the counter and hurry
up with these people's order. His khaki trousers reached just to his hip bones and
his stomach hung over them like a sack of meal swaying under his shirt. He came
over and sat down at a table nearby and let out a combination sigh and yodel. "You
can't win," he said. "You can't win," and he wiped his sweating red face off with a
gray handkerchief. "These days you don't know who to trust," he said. "Ain't that
the truth?"

35   "People are certainly not nice like they used to be," said the grandmother.

"Two fellers come in here last week," Red Sammy said, "driving a Chrysler. It
was a old beat-up car but it was a good one and these boys looked all right to me.
Said they worked at the mill and you know I let them fellers charge the gas they
bought? Now why did I do that?"

"Because you're a good man!" the grandmother said at once.

"Yes'm, I suppose so," Red Sam said as if he were struck with this answer.

His wife brought the orders, carrying the five plates all at once without a tray,
two in each hand and one balanced on her arm. "It isn't a soul in this green world
of God's that you can trust," she said. "And I don't count nobody out of that, not
nobody," she repeated, looking at Red Sammy.

40   "Did you read about that criminal, The Misfit, that's escaped?" asked the
grandmother.

"I wouldn't be a bit surprised if he didn't attact this place right here," said the
woman. "If he hears about it being here, I wouldn't be none surprised to see him.
If he hears it's two cent in the cash register, I wouldn't be a tall surprised if he…"

"That'll do," Red Sam said. "Go bring these people their Co'-Colas," and the
woman went off to get the rest of the order.

"A good man is hard to find," Red Sammy said. "Everything is getting terrible.
I remember the day you could go off and leave your screen door unlatched. Not
no more."

He and the grandmother discussed better times. The old lady said that in her
opinion Europe was entirely to blame for the way things were now. She said the
way Europe acted you would think we were made of money and Red Sam said it
was no use talking about it, she was exactly right. The children ran outside into the
white sunlight and looked at the monkey in the lacy chinaberry tree. He was busy
catching fleas on himself and biting each one carefully between his teeth as if it
were a delicacy.

45   They drove off again into the hot afternoon. The grandmother took cat naps and woke up every few minutes with her own snoring. Outside of Toombsboro she woke up and recalled an old plantation that she had visited in this neighborhood once when she was a young lady. She said the house had six white columns across the front and that there was an avenue of oaks leading up to it and two little wooden trellis arbors on either side in front where you sat down with your suitor after a stroll in the garden. She recalled exactly which road to turn off to get to it. She knew that Bailey would not be willing to lose any time looking at an old house, but the more she talked about it, the more she wanted to see it once again and find out if the little twin arbors were still standing. "There was a secret panel in this house," she said craftily, not telling the truth but wishing that she were, "and the story went that all the family silver was hidden in it when Sherman came through but it was never found…"

       "Hey!" John Wesley said. "Let's go see it! We'll find it! We'll poke all the woodwork and find it! Who lives there? Where do you turn off at? Hey Pop, can't we turn off there?"

       "We never have seen a house with a secret panel!" June Star shrieked. "Let's go to the house with the secret panel! Hey Pop, can't we go see the house with the secret panel!"

       "It's not far from here, I know," the grandmother said. "It wouldn't take over twenty minutes."

       Bailey was looking straight ahead. His jaw was as rigid as a horseshoe. "No," he said.

50   The children began to yell and scream that they wanted to see the house with the secret panel. John Wesley kicked the back of the front seat and June Star hung over her mother's shoulder and whined desperately into her ear that they never had any fun even on their vacation, that they could never do what THEY wanted to do. The baby began to scream and John Wesley kicked the back of the seat so hard that his father could feel the blows in his kidney.

       "All right!" he shouted and drew the car to a stop at the side of the road. "Will you all shut up? Will you all just shut up for one second? If you don't shut up, we won't go anywhere."

       "It would be very educational for them," the grandmother murmured.

       "All right," Bailey said, "but get this: this is the only time we're going to stop for anything like this. This is the one and only time."

       "The dirt road that you have to turn down is about a mile back," the grandmother directed. "I marked it when we passed."

55   "A dirt road," Bailey groaned.

       After they had turned around and were headed toward the dirt road, the grandmother recalled other points about the house, the beautiful glass over the front doorway and the candle-lamp in the hall. John Wesley said that the secret panel was probably in the fireplace.

       "You can't go inside this house," Bailey said. "You don't know who lives there."

       "While you all talk to the people in front, I'll run around behind and get in a window," John Wesley suggested.

       "We'll all stay in the car," his mother said.

60   They turned onto the dirt road and the car raced roughly along in a swirl of pink dust. The grandmother recalled the times when there were no paved roads and thirty miles was a day's journey. The dirt road was hilly and there were sudden washes in it and sharp curves on dangerous embankments. All at once they would be on a hill, looking down over the blue tops of trees for miles around, then the next minute, they would be in a red depression with the dust-coated trees looking down on them.

"This place had better turn up in a minute," Bailey said, "or I'm going to turn around."

The road looked as if no one had traveled on it in months.

"It's not much farther," the grandmother said and just as she said it, a horrible thought came to her. The thought was so embarrassing that she turned red in the face and her eyes dilated and her feet jumped up, upsetting her valise in the corner. The instant the valise moved, the newspaper top she had over the basket under it rose with a snarl and Pitty Sing, the cat, sprang onto Bailey's shoulder.

The children were thrown to the floor and their mother, clutching the baby, was thrown out the door onto the ground; the old lady was thrown into the front seat. The car turned over once and landed right-side-up in a gulch off the side of the road. Bailey remained in the driver's seat with the cat—gray-striped with a broad white face and an orange nose—clinging to his neck like a caterpillar.

65   As soon as the children saw they could move their arms and legs, they scrambled out of the car, shouting, "We've had an ACCIDENT!" The grandmother was curled up under the dashboard, hoping she was injured so that Bailey's wrath would not come down on her all at once. The horrible thought she had had before the accident was that the house she had remembered so vividly was not in Georgia but in Tennessee.

Bailey removed the cat from his neck with both hands and flung it out the window against the side of a pine tree. Then he got out of the car and started looking for the children's mother. She was sitting against the side of the red gutted ditch, holding the screaming baby, but she only had a cut down her face and a broken shoulder. "We've had an ACCIDENT!" the children screamed in a frenzy of delight.

"But nobody's killed," June Star said with disappointment as the grandmother limped out of the car, her hat still pinned to her head but the broken front brim standing up at a jaunty angle and the violet spray hanging off the side. They all sat down in the ditch, except the children, to recover from the shock. They were all shaking.

"Maybe a car will come along," said the children's mother hoarsely.

"I believe I have injured an organ," said the grandmother, pressing her side, but no one answered her. Bailey's teeth were clattering. He had on a yellow sport shirt with bright blue parrots designed in it and his face was as yellow as the shirt. The grandmother decided that she would not mention that the house was in Tennessee.

70   The road was about ten feet above and they could see only the tops of the trees on the other side of it. Behind the ditch they were sitting in there were more woods, tall and dark and deep. In a few minutes they saw a car some distance away on top of a hill, coming slowly as if the occupants were watching them. The grandmother stood up and waved both arms dramatically to attract their attention.

The car continued to come on slowly, disappeared around a bend and appeared again, moving even slower, on top of the hill they had gone over. It was a big black battered hearse-like automobile. There were three men in it.

It came to a stop just over them and for some minutes, the driver looked down with a steady expressionless gaze to where they were sitting, and didn't speak. Then he turned his head and muttered something to the other two and they got out. One was a fat boy in black trousers and a red sweat shirt with a silver stallion embossed on the front of it. He moved around on the right side of them and stood staring, his mouth partly open in a kind of loose grin. The other had on khaki pants and a blue striped coat and a gray hat pulled down very low, hiding most of his face. He came around slowly on the left side. Neither spoke.

The driver got out of the car and stood by the side of it, looking down at them. He was an older man than the other two. His hair was just beginning to gray and he wore silver-rimmed spectacles that gave him a scholarly look. He had a long creased face and didn't have on any shirt or undershirt. He had on blue jeans that were too tight for him and was holding a black hat and a gun. The two boys also had guns.

"We've had an ACCIDENT!" the children screamed.

The grandmother had the peculiar feeling that the bespectacled man was someone she knew. His face was as familiar to her as if she had known him all her life but she could not recall who he was. He moved away from the car and began to come down the embankment, placing his feet carefully so that he wouldn't slip. He had on tan and white shoes and no socks, and his ankles were red and thin. "Good afternoon," he said. "I see you all had you a little spill."

75   "We turned over twice!" said the grandmother.

"Oncet," he corrected. "We seen it happen. Try their car and see will it run, Hiram," he said quietly to the boy with the gray hat.

"What you got that gun for?" John Wesley asked. "Whatcha gonna do with that gun?"

"Lady," the man said to the children's mother, "would you mind calling them children to sit down by you? Children make me nervous. I want all you to sit down right together there where you're at."

"What are you telling US what to do for?" June Star asked.

80   Behind them the line of woods gaped like a dark open mouth. "Come here," said their mother.

"Look here now," Bailey began suddenly, "we're in a predicament! We're in..."

The grandmother shrieked. She scrambled to her feet and stood staring. "You're The Misfit!" she said. "I recognized you at once!"

"Yes'm," the man said, smiling slightly as if he were pleased in spite of himself to be known, "but it would have been better for all of you, lady, if you hadn't of reckernized me."

Bailey turned his head sharply and said something to his mother that shocked even the children. The old lady began to cry and The Misfit reddened.

85   "Lady," he said, "don't you get upset. Sometimes a man says things he don't mean. I don't reckon he meant to talk to you thataway."

"You wouldn't shoot a lady, would you?" the grandmother said and removed a clean handkerchief from her cuff and began to slap at her eyes with it.

The Misfit pointed the toe of his shoe into the ground and made a little hole and then covered it up again. "I would hate to have to," he said.

"Listen," the grandmother almost screamed, "I know you're a good man. You don't look a bit like you have common blood. I know you must come from nice people!"

"Yes mam," he said, "finest people in the world." When he smiled he showed a row of strong white teeth. "God never made a finer woman than my mother and my daddy's heart was pure gold," he said. The boy with the red sweat shirt had come around behind them and was standing with his gun at his hip. The Misfit squatted down on the ground. "Watch them children, Bobby Lee," he said. "You know they make me nervous." He looked at the six of them huddled together in front of him and he seemed to be embarrassed as if he couldn't think of anything to say. "Ain't a cloud in the sky," he remarked, looking up at it. "Don't see no sun but don't see no cloud neither."

90 "Yes, it's a beautiful day," said the grandmother. "Listen," she said, "you shouldn't call yourself The Misfit because I know you're a good man at heart. I can just look at you and tell."

"Hush!" Bailey yelled. "Hush! Everybody shut up and let me handle this!" He was squatting in the position of a runner about to sprint forward but he didn't move.

"I pre-chate that, lady," The Misfit said and drew a little circle in the ground with the butt of his gun.

"It'll take a half a hour to fix this here car," Hiram called, looking over the raised hood of it.

"Well, first you and Bobby Lee get him and that little boy to step over yonder with you," The Misfit said, pointing to Bailey and John Wesley. "The boys want to ast you something," he said to Bailey. "Would you mind stepping back in them woods there with them?"

95 "Listen," Bailey began, "we're in a terrible predicament! Nobody realizes what this is," his voice cracked. His eyes were as blue and intense as the parrots in his shirt and he remained perfectly still.

The grandmother reached up to adjust her hat brim as if she were going to the woods with him but it came off in her hand. She stood staring at it and after a second she let it fall on the ground. Hiram pulled Bailey up by the arm as if he were assisting an old man. John Wesley caught hold of his father's hand and Bobby Lee followed. They went off toward the woods and just as they reached the dark edge, Bailey turned and supporting himself against a gray naked pine trunk, he shouted, "I'll be back in a minute, Mamma, wait on me!"

"Come back this instant!" his mother shrilled but they all disappeared into the woods.

"Bailey Boy!" the grandmother called in a tragic voice but she found she was looking at The Misfit squatting on the ground in front of her. "I just know you're a good man," she said desperately. "You're not a bit common!"

"Nome, I ain't a good man," The Misfit said after a second as if he had considered her statement carefully, "but I ain't the worst in the world neither. My daddy said I was a different breed of dog from my brothers and sisters. 'You know,' Daddy said, 'it's some that can live their whole life out without asking about it and it's others has to know why it is, and this boy is one of the latters. He's going to be into everything!'" He put on his black hat and looked up suddenly and then away deep into the woods as if he were embarrassed again. "I'm sorry I don't have on a shirt before you ladies," he said, hunching his shoulders slightly. "We buried our clothes that we had on when we escaped and we're just making do until we can get better. We borrowed these from some folks we met," he explained.

100   "That's perfectly all right," the grandmother said. "Maybe Bailey has an extra shirt in his suitcase."

"I'll look and see terrectly," The Misfit said.

"Where are they taking him?" the children's mother screamed.

"Daddy was a card himself," The Misfit said. "You couldn't put anything over on him. He never got in trouble with the Authorities though. Just had the knack of handling them."

"You could be honest too if you'd only try," said the grandmother. "Think how wonderful it would be to settle down and live a comfortable life and not have to think about somebody chasing you all the time."

105   The Misfit kept scratching in the ground with the butt of his gun as if he were thinking about it. "Yes'm, somebody is always after you," he murmured.

The grandmother noticed how thin his shoulder blades were just behind his hat because she was standing up looking down on him. "Do you ever pray?" she asked.

He shook his head. All she saw was the black hat wiggle between his shoulder blades. "Nome," he said.

There was a pistol shot from the woods, followed closely by another. Then silence. The old lady's head jerked around. She could hear the wind move through the tree tops like a long satisfied insuck of breath. "Bailey Boy!" she called.

"I was a gospel singer for a while," The Misfit said. "I been most everything. Been in the arm service, both land and sea, at home and abroad, been twice married, been an undertaker, been with the railroads, plowed Mother Earth, been in a tornado, seen a man burnt alive oncet," and looked up at the children's mother and the little girl who were sitting close together, their faces white and their eyes glassy; "I even seen a woman flogged," he said.

110   "Pray, pray," the grandmother began, "pray, pray..."

"I never was a bad boy that I remember of," The Misfit said in an almost dreamy voice, "but somewheres along the line I done something wrong and got sent to the penitentiary. I was buried alive," and he looked up and held her attention to him by a steady stare.

"That's when you should have started to pray," she said. "What did you do to get sent to the penitentiary that first time?"

"Turn to the right, it was a wall," The Misfit said, looking up again at the cloudless sky. "Turn to the left, it was a wall. Look up it was a ceiling, look down it was a floor. I forget what I done, lady. I set there and set there, trying to remember what it was I done and I ain't recalled it to this day. Oncet in a while, I would think it was coming to me, but it never come."

"Maybe they put you in by mistake," the old lady said vaguely.

115   "Nome," he said. "It wasn't no mistake. They had the papers on me."

"You must have stolen something," she said.

The Misfit sneered slightly. "Nobody had nothing I wanted," he said. "It was a head-doctor at the penitentiary said what I had done was kill my daddy but I know that for a lie. My daddy died in nineteen ought nineteen of the epidemic flu and I never had a thing to do with it. He was buried in the Mount Hopewell Baptist churchyard and you can go there and see for yourself."

"If you would pray," the old lady said, "Jesus would help you."

"That's right," The Misfit said.

120   "Well then, why don't you pray?" she asked trembling with delight suddenly.

"I don't want no hep," he said. "I'm doing all right by myself."

Bobby Lee and Hiram came ambling back from the woods. Bobby Lee was dragging a yellow shirt with bright blue parrots in it.

"Throw me that shirt, Bobby Lee," The Misfit said. The shirt came flying at him and landed on his shoulder and he put it on. The grandmother couldn't name what the shirt reminded her of. "No, lady," The Misfit said while he was buttoning it up, "I found out the crime don't matter. You can do one thing or you can do another, kill a man or take a tire off his car, because sooner or later you're going to forget what it was you done and just be punished for it."

The children's mother had begun to make heaving noises as if she couldn't get her breath. "Lady," he asked, "would you and that little girl like to step off yonder with Bobby Lee and Hiram and join your husband?"

125   "Yes, thank you," the mother said faintly. Her left arm dangled helplessly and she was holding the baby, who had gone to sleep, in the other. "Hep that lady up, Hiram," The Misfit said as she struggled to climb out of the ditch, "and Bobby Lee, you hold onto that little girl's hand."

"I don't want to hold hands with him," June Star said. "He reminds me of a pig."

The fat boy blushed and laughed and caught her by the arm and pulled her off into the woods after Hiram and her mother.

Alone with The Misfit, the grandmother found that she had lost her voice. There was not a cloud in the sky nor any sun. There was nothing around her but woods. She wanted to tell him that he must pray. She opened and closed her mouth several times before anything came out. Finally she found herself saying, "Jesus, Jesus," meaning, Jesus will help you, but the way she was saying it, it sounded as if she might be cursing.

"Yes'm," The Misfit said as if he agreed. "Jesus thrown everything off balance. It was the same case with Him as with me except He hadn't committed any crime and they could prove I had committed one because they had the papers on me. Of course," he said, "they never shown me my papers. That's why I sign myself now. I said long ago, you get you a signature and sign everything you do and keep a copy of it. Then you'll know what you done and you can hold up the crime to the punishment and see do they match and in the end you'll have something to prove you ain't been treated right. I call myself The Misfit," he said, "because I can't make what all I done wrong fit what all I gone through in punishment."

130   There was a piercing scream from the woods, followed closely by a pistol report. "Does it seem right to you, lady, that one is punished a heap and another ain't punished at all?"

"Jesus!" the old lady cried. "You've got good blood! I know you wouldn't shoot a lady! I know you come from nice people! Pray! Jesus, you ought not to shoot a lady. I'll give you all the money I've got!"

"Lady," The Misfit said, looking beyond her far into the woods, "there never was a body that give the undertaker a tip."

There were two more pistol reports and the grandmother raised her head like a parched old turkey hen crying for water and called, "Bailey Boy, Bailey Boy!" as if her heart would break.

"Jesus was the only One that ever raised the dead," The Misfit continued, "and He shouldn't have done it. He thrown everything off balance. If He did what He said, then it's nothing for you to do but throw away everything and follow Him, and if He didn't, then it's nothing for you to do but enjoy the few minutes you got left the best way you can—by killing somebody or burning down his house or doing some other meanness to him. No pleasure but meanness," he said and his voice had become almost a snarl.

135   "Maybe He didn't raise the dead," the old lady mumbled, not knowing what she was saying and feeling so dizzy that she sank down in the ditch with her legs twisted under her.

"I wasn't there so I can't say He didn't," The Misfit said. "I wisht I had of been there," he said, hitting the ground with his fist. "It ain't right I wasn't there be-cause if I had of been there I would of known. Listen lady," he said in a high voice, "if I had of been there I would of known and I wouldn't be like I am now." His voice seemed about to crack and the grandmother's head cleared for an instant. She saw the man's face twisted close to her own as if he were going to cry and she murmured, "Why you're one of my babies. You're one of my own children!" She reached out and touched him on the shoulder. The Misfit sprang back as if a snake had bitten him and shot her three times through the chest. Then he put his gun down on the ground and took off his glasses and began to clean them.

Hiram and Bobby Lee returned from the woods and stood over the ditch, looking down at the grandmother who half sat and half lay in a puddle of blood with her legs crossed under her like a child's and her face smiling up at the cloudless sky.

Without his glasses, The Misfit's eyes were red-rimmed and pale and defense-less looking. "Take her off and throw her where you thrown the others," he said, picking up the cat that was rubbing itself against his leg.

"She was a talker, wasn't she?" Bobby Lee said, sliding down the ditch with a yodel.

140   "She would have been a good woman," The Misfit said, "if it had been some-body there to shoot her every minute of her life."

"Some fun!" Bobby Lee said.

"Shut up, Bobby Lee," The Misfit said. "It's no real pleasure in life."

MAKING CONNECTIONS

1. What is the point of the long introductory section, where we are introduced to the grandmother and her family before and during the early stages of the trip? Would the story be better if it began with a brief introduction and then the accident? Explain.

2. The Misfit says of Jesus, "He thrown everything off balance." Why does he say that, and what do you think he is making reference to? Support your comments with reference to details in the story.

3. This is a nightmarish story filled with sudden violence and cold-blooded killing. But is there a spiritual element to this story? Why do you think The Misfit reacts so violently to the grandmother's comment "Why you're one of my babies. You're one of my own children"?

4. To what extent is the grandmother heroic in the story? What does The Misfit mean when he says, "She would have been a good woman if it had been somebody there to shoot her every minute of her life"?

MAKING AN ARGUMENT

1. Flannery O'Connor has written that "Much of my fiction takes its character from a reasonable use of the unreasonable." To what extent is that the case in "A Good Man Is Hard to Find"? Write an essay that shows how this story exemplifies a "reasonable use of the unreasonable." Cite the text of this story (and if appropriate, other O'Connor stories you have read) for support.

♦ **POETRY** ♦

CONNECTING THROUGH COMPARISON: FACING OUR OWN MORTALITY

Though we understand that death is inevitable, facing our own deaths or the deaths of those we care about is perhaps the most difficult thing we have to experience. Donne's "Death, Be Not Proud," Keats's "When I Have Fears That I May Cease to Be," and Oliver's "When Death Comes" explore what it means to face mortality. Read and discussed together, they invite comparisons and connections—not only with each other, but with your own experience of facing death.

MLL JOHN DONNE [1572–1631]

John Donne was born into a Roman Catholic family and attended Oxford and Cambridge. As a young man, in response to the rabid anti-Catholic sentiments of Elizabethan England, he abandoned his faith and determined to make his way in the court of Queen Elizabeth I using his charm, learning, and poetic abilities. In 1601, he destroyed his chances for serious advancement by secretly marrying

Ann More, the niece of Sir Thomas Egerton, his employer. Donne then struggled to make ends meet, publishing treatises and poetry only occasionally. In 1615, after years of resistance, he converted to Anglicanism and became a priest. Renowned for his preaching, Donne was considered one of the greatest preachers of the age. In 1621, he was appointed Dean of St. Paul's Cathedral, a post he held until his death. His poetry, most of which was published posthumously, is usually divided into two periods: his love poetry is said to date from the beginning of his career, while his religious poems are said to date from his later years. The greatest of the so-called metaphysical school of poets, Donne's poetry is remarkable for its elaborate conceits (extended metaphors), unconventional imagery, and highly compressed meanings.

DEATH, BE NOT PROUD [1633]

Death, be not proud, though some have called thee
Mighty and dreadful, for thou art not so;
For those whom thou think'st thou dost overthrow
Die not, poor Death, nor yet canst thou kill me.
From rest and sleep, which but thy pictures be, 5
Much pleasure, then from thee much more must flow,
And soonest our best men with thee do go,
Rest of their bones, and soul's delivery.
Thou art slave to fate, chance, kings, and desperate men,
And dost with poison, war, and sickness dwell, 10
And poppy or charms can make us sleep as well,
And better than thy stroke; why swell'st thou then?
One short sleep past, we wake eternally
And death shall be no more; Death, thou shalt die.

JOHN KEATS [1795–1821]

John Keats was born in London and abandoned a medical career for writing when a number of his poems were published. His work is characterized by a passionate concern with the relationship between beauty and truth and emotion and knowledge. He died of tuberculosis at the age of twenty-six.

WHEN I HAVE FEARS THAT I MAY CEASE TO BE [1818]

When I have fears that I may cease to be
    Before my pen has gleaned my teeming brain,
Before high-piled books, in charact'ry,
    Hold like rich garners the full-ripened grain;
When I behold, upon the night's starred face, 5
    Huge cloudy symbols of a high romance,

And think that I may never live to trace
    Their shadows, with the magic hand of chance;
And when I feel, fair creature of an hour,
    That I shall never look upon thee more,   10
Never have relish in the fairy power
    Of unreflecting love—then on the shore
Of the wide world I stand alone, and think
    Till love and fame to nothingness do sink.

MARY OLIVER   [B. 1935]

Mary Oliver's style is regarded for its use of images from the natural world. She is the recipient of many poetry awards, including the National Book Award for Poetry, the Pulitzer Prize for Poetry, the Lannan Literary Award for Poetry, and the Shelley Memorial Award. "When Death Comes" was originally published in her New and Selected Poems *(1992). Her most recent book of poems is* Evidence *(2009). She currently resides in Provincetown, Massachusetts, on Cape Cod.*

WHEN DEATH COMES   [1992]

When death comes
like the hungry bear in autumn;
when death comes and takes all the bright coins from his purse

to buy me, and snaps the purse shut;
when death comes   5
like the measle-pox;

when death comes
like an iceberg between the shoulder blades,

I want to step through the door full of curiosity, wondering:
what is it going to be like, that cottage of darkness?   10

And therefore I look upon everything
as a brotherhood and a sisterhood,
and I look upon time as no more than an idea,
and I consider eternity as another possibility,

and I think of each life as a flower, as common   15
as a field daisy, and as singular,

and each name a comfortable music in the mouth,
tending, as all music does, toward silence,

and each body a lion of courage, and something
precious to the earth.   20

When it's over, I want to say: all my life
I was a bride married to amazement.
I was the bridegroom, taking the world into my arms.

When it's over, I don't want to wonder
if I have made of my life something particular, and real.   25
I don't want to find myself sighing and frightened,
or full of argument.

I don't want to end up simply having visited this world.

MAKING CONNECTIONS

1. Why do you think the speaker in "Death, Be Not Proud" suggests that Death is proud? Do you agree? Explain.
2. The speaker concludes, "Death, thou shalt die." What is the speaker's reasoning to support this? Do you agree? Explain.
3. Compare this poem to John Keats's "When I Have Fears That I May Cease to Be."
4. Do you ever have fears that you may cease to be? If so, how do those fears affect your response to Keats's poem?
5. Keats was only twenty-three years old when he wrote this poem—and died at twenty-six—so young death turned out to be a reality for him. What is the speaker especially anxious about? To what extent is this surprising for a poet? If Keats had lived much longer and had been older when he wrote this poem, do you think the speaker's anxieties might have been different? Explain.
6. What is the speaker's attitude toward death in "When Death Comes"? Toward life?
7. In "When Death Comes," the poet uses several metaphors to describe death. Choose one and write a brief essay analyzing this image and how it is used.

MAKING AN ARGUMENT

1. "Death, Be Not Proud" is a poem about death, but the speaker's intended audience, the structure, the tone, and other factors in the poems differ from the others in this subtopic. Choose another poem and write an essay that compares and contrasts the two. Cite the text of both poems for support.
2. Write a comparison of John Keats's poem with John Donne's "Death, Be Not Proud." Cite the text of the poems to support your views.
3. In the final stanza of "When Death Comes," the speaker repeatedly tells us what she does not want. Write an essay that argues your interpretation of what she does want. How does this compare to what the speaker in "When I Have Fears That I May Cease to Be" wants? Use citations from both poems for support.

CONNECTING THROUGH COMPARISON: NATURE AND HUMANITY

The poems that follow literally and metaphorically explore the relationship between nature and humanity. Are we alienated from nature? Are we just another species struggling to survive in an indifferent natural world? Or does our self-surpassing consciousness and spiritually give us a special responsibility for the natural environment that we exploit? Read and discussed together, these poems invite comparisons and connections—not only with each other, but with your own experience of nature.

MATTHEW ARNOLD [1822–1888]

*Poet and critic Matthew Arnold was born in Laleham, a
tiny village along the Thames in England. Arnold attended
Oxford University, where he spent as much time roaming the
countryside and writing poems as he did on his formal studies. After working for a time for a member of Parliament,
Arnold secured a post as an inspector of schools in 1851, a
position he held for most of his life. In addition, he served as
a professor of poetry at Oxford for ten years, beginning in
1857. In his old age, Arnold embarked on two lecture tours of the United States in
1883 and 1886. He died suddenly in 1888, shortly after returning from his second
trip. An acclaimed literary critic and poet, Arnold strongly believed that the primary purpose of literature was a moral one—that it should "animate and ennoble"
its readers. His first collection of poetry,* The Strayed Reveler and Other Poems, *was published in 1849 and was followed by six others, including* Poems, Second
Series *(1855), in which "Dover Beach" first appeared. His works of literary criticism
include two volumes of* Essays in Criticism *(1865 and 1888),* Literature and Dogma
(1873), and The Study of Poetry *(1880), in which he argued that "most of what now
passes for religion and philosophy will be replaced by poetry."*

DOVER BEACH

[1867]

The sea is calm tonight.
The tide is full, the moon lies fair
Upon the straits; on the French coast the light
Gleams and is gone; the cliffs of England stand,
Glimm'ering and vast, out in the tranquil bay.   5
Come to the window, sweet is the night-air!
Only, from the long line of spray
Where the sea meets the moon-blanched land,
Listen! you hear the grating roar
Of pebbles which the waves draw back, and fling,   10
At their return, up the high strand,
Begin, and cease, and then again begin,
With tremulous cadence slow, and bring
The eternal note of sadness in.

Sophocles long ago   15
Heard it on the Aegean, and it brought
Into his mind the turbid ebb and flow
Of human misery; we
Find also in the sound a thought,
Hearing it by this distant northern sea.   20

The Sea of Faith
Was once, too, at the full, and round earth's shore
Lay like the folds of a bright girdle furled.
But now I only hear
Its melancholy, long, withdrawing roar,   25
Retreating, to the breath
Of the night-wind, down the vast edges drear
And naked shingles' of the world.

Ah, love, let us be true
To one another! for the world, which seems   30
To lie before us like a land of dreams,
So various, so beautiful, so new,
Hath really neither joy, nor love, nor light,
Nor certitude, nor peace, nor help for pain—,
And we are here as on a darkling plain   35
Swept with confused alarms of struggle and flight,
Where ignorant armies clash by night.

ROBERT BRIDGES   [1844–1930]

*Robert Bridges was born the son of a prosperous landowner
and took his degree at Corpus Christi College, Oxford, where
he made friends with Gerard Manley Hopkins. He was a
medical student at St. Bartholomew's Hospital, London, and
practiced medicine until 1881, when illness forced his
retirement. For the rest of his life he dedicated himself to his
writing. In 1913, he was named Poet Laureate of England.*

LONDON SNOW   [1880]

When men were all asleep the snow came flying,
In large white flakes falling on the city brown,
Stealthily and perpetually settling and loosely lying,
    Hushing the latest traffic of the drowsy town;
Deadening, muffling, stifling its murmurs failing;   5
Lazily and incessantly floating down and down;
    Silently sifting and veiling road, roof and railing;

Hiding difference, making unevenness even,
Into angles and crevices softly drifting and sailing.
    All night it fell, and when full inches seven   10
It lay in the depth of its uncompacted lightness,
The clouds blew off from a high and frosty heaven;
    And all woke earlier for the unaccustomed brightness
Of the winter dawning, the strange unheavenly glare:
The eye marvelled—marvelled at the dazzling whiteness;   15
    The ear hearkened to the stillness of the solemn air;
No sound of wheel rumbling nor of foot falling,
And the busy morning cries came thin and spare.
    Then boys I heard, as they went to school, calling;
They gathered up the crystal manna to freeze   20
Their tongues with tasting, their hands with snowballing;
    Or rioted in a drift, plunging up to the knees;
Or peering up from under the white-mossed wonder,
"O look at the trees!" they cried. "O look at the trees!"
    With lessened load, a few carts creak and blunder,   25
Following along the white deserted way,
A country company long dispersed asunder:
    When, now, already the sun, in pale display
Standing by Paul's high dome, spread forth below
His sparkling beams, and awoke the stir of the day.   30
    For now doors open, and war is waged with the snow;
And trains of sombre men, past tale of number,
Tread long brown paths, as toward their toil they go:
    But even for them awhile no cares encumber
Their minds diverted; the daily word is unspoken,   35
The daily thoughts of labour and sorrow slumber
At the sight of the beauty that greets them, for the charm they
    have broken.

ROBERT FROST   [1874–1963]

(See biography on p. 279.)

FIRE AND ICE   [1923]

Some say the world will end in fire,
Some say in ice.
From what I've tasted of desire
I hold with those who favor fire.
But if I had to perish twice,   5
I think I know enough of hate
To say that for destruction ice
Is also great
And would suffice.

GALWAY KINNELL [B. 1927]

Born and raised in Providence, Rhode Island, Galway Kinnell first became interested in poetry while attending Wilbraham Academy, a prep school in Massachusetts. He attended college at Princeton University (where his roommate was the poet W. S. Merwin) and later earned an M.A. from the University of Rochester. His first collection of poems, What a Kingdom It Was, *was published in 1960, and* Imperfect Thirst *appeared in 1994. His latest collection is titled* Strong Is Your Hold *(2006). A dedicated teacher as well as a poet, Kinnell has taught at numerous universities and held writing workshops throughout the world. He currently divides his time between Vermont and New York City, where he is a professor at New York University. His intensely personal poetry often explores the darkest aspects of human consciousness. In a 1989 interview with* Contemporary Authors, *Kinnell described the ideal reader: "As far as the person who buys and reads your poems is concerned, every living reader is an ideal reader. Anybody who recognizes the poem and puts something of his or her own experience into it is the ideal reader. The less than ideal reader is the one who reads without engagement: very often the critic."*

SAINT FRANCIS AND THE SOW   [1980]

The bud
stands for all things
even for those things that don't flower,
for everything flowers, from within, of self-blessing;
though sometimes it is necessary   5
to reteach a thing its loveliness,
to put a hand on its brow
of the flower
and retell it in words and in touch
it is lovely   10
until it flowers again from within of self-blessing;
as Saint Francis
put his hand on the creased forehead
of the sow, and told her in words and in touch
blessings of earth on the sow, and the sow   15
began remembering all down her thick length
from the earthen snout all the way
through the fodder and slops to the spiritual curl of the tail,
from the hard spininess spiked out from the spine
down through the great broken heart   20
to the sheer blue milken dreaminess spurting and shuddering
from the fourteen teats into the fourteen mouths sucking and
    blowing beneath them:
the long, perfect loveliness of sow.

WILLIAM STAFFORD [1914–1992]

William Stafford grew up in Kansas, earned a Ph.D. from Iowa State University, and for many years taught at Lewis and Clark College in Portland, Oregon. The rural regions he lived in are central to his poetry; he spent much of his time hunting, camping, and fishing, and he often wrote about the relationship between humans and animals. His collection of poems Traveling through the Dark, *from which the poem below is taken, received the National Book Award in 1963.*

TRAVELING THROUGH THE DARK   [1960]

Traveling through the dark I found a deer
dead on the edge of the Wilson River road.
It is usually best to roll them into the canyon:
that road is narrow; to swerve might make more dead.

By glow of the taillight I stumbled back of the car   5
and stood by the heap, a doe, a recent killing;
she had stiffened already, almost cold.
I dragged her off; she was large in the belly.

My fingers touching her side brought me the reason—
her side was warm; her fawn lay there waiting,   10
alive, still, never to be born.
Beside that mountain road I hesitated.

The car aimed ahead its lowered parking lights;
under the hood purred the steady engine.
I stood in the glare of the warm exhaust turning red;   15
around our group I could hear the wilderness listen.
I thought hard for us all—my only swerving—
then pushed her over the edge into the river.

WALT WHITMAN [1819–1892]

(See biography on p. 476.)

SONG OF MYSELF 6   [1855]

A child said *What is the grass?* fetching it to me with full hands;
How could I answer the child? I do not know what it is any more than he.

I guess it must be the flag of my disposition, out of hopeful green stuff woven.

Or I guess it is the handkerchief of the Lord,
A scented gift and remembrancer designedly dropped,   5
Bearing the owner's name someway in the corners, that we may see and remark,
   and say *Whose?*

Or I guess the grass is itself a child, the produced babe of the vegetation.

Or I guess it is a uniform hieroglyphic,
And it means, Sprouting alike in broad zones and narrow zones,
Growing among black folks as among white,   10
Kanuck, Tuckahoe, Congressman, Cuff, I give them the same,
     I receive them the same.

And now it seems to me the beautiful uncut hair of graves.

Tenderly will I use you curling grass,
It may be you transpire from the breasts of young men,
It may be if I had known them I would have loved them,   15
It may be you are from old people, or from offspring taken soon out of their
     mothers' laps,
And here you are the mothers' laps.

This grass is very dark to be from the white heads of old mothers,
Darker than the colorless beards of old men,
Dark to come from under the faint red roofs of mouths.   20
O I perceive after all so many uttering tongues,
And I perceive they do not come from the roofs of mouths for nothing.

I wish I could translate the hints about the dead young men and women,
And the hints about old men and mothers, and the offspring taken soon out of
     their laps.

What do you think has become of the young and old men?   25
And what do you think has become of the women and children?

They are alive and well somewhere,
The smallest sprout shows there is really no death,
And if ever there was it led forward life, and does not wait at the end to arrest it,
And ceased the moment life appeared.   30

All goes onward and outward, nothing collapses,
And to die is different from what anyone supposed, and luckier.

MAKING CONNECTIONS

1. What is the speaker's attitude toward nature in "Dover Beach"? How do you
   think the speaker formed his impression of nature? To what extent is an
   answer suggested in the poem?
2. In the final image of "Dover Beach," the speaker says, "we are here as on a
   darkling plain / Swept with confused alarms of struggle and flight, / Where
   ignorant armies clash by night." What do you think he means?
3. To what extent does your own experience of snow affect your response to
   "London Snow"?
4. In "London Snow," the speaker says, "For now doors open, and war is waged
   with the snow." Pick out phrases in the poem that describe "the charm they
   have broken."

5. What do you think fire and ice symbolize in Frost's "Fire and Ice"?

6. How are you affected by the rhyme scheme in "Fire and Ice"? In what way does it serve as a vehicle for the poem's meaning? In particular, consider the conclusion of "Fire and Ice" and how the word "suffice" as a rhyme for "ice" affects the meaning of the poem.

7. What is a sow? Do you think a sow is an appropriate subject for a poem? Explain.

8. To what extent is it "necessary / to reteach a thing its loveliness"? Why is it "necessary," and how can you do it?

9. According to the speaker the sow has a "broken heart." Why? What do you think he means?

10. Do you think "Traveling through the Dark" is an appropriate title for that poem? Explain.

11. What does the speaker of "Traveling through the Dark" mean when he says, "I thought hard for us all—my only swerving"?

12. Why does he roll the dead deer into the canyon? Does the pregnancy make any difference? Do you think it should? Explain.

13. Who is the speaker in "Song of Myself"? How does he experience the world? Do you experience the world this way? Explain.

14. What do you think the speaker of "Song of Myself" means by "to die is different from what anyone supposed, and luckier"? Does the rest of this poem support that? Explain.

MAKING AN ARGUMENT

1. In the Dialogue Across History that opens this theme, Tennyson is quoted: "There lives more faith in honest doubt, / Believe me, than in half the creeds." Arnold's poem seems to express this "honest doubt." Write about the effectiveness of the imagery in the poem in conveying this theme. Cite the text of the poem for support.

2. Both "London Snow" and "Dover Beach" were written well over a century ago, but their images are still very much alive. Write about the language and poetic devices in these poems, their effect on you, and their effectiveness in re-creating this scene. Cite the texts of the poems to support your view.

3. Write a comparison of "Fire and Ice" with other Frost poems in this text— "Out, Out…" on page 480 and "Mending Wall" on page 280. Is there a similar philosophy expressed in all three? If not, how do they differ? Cite the text of all three for support.

4. Write a comparison of "St. Francis and the Sow" with the excerpt from Walt Whitman's "Song of Myself 6" or other poems in this text where relearning "loveliness" is "necessary." Cite the texts of the poems to support your views.

5. "Traveling through the Dark" has especially vivid details of the scene and the speaker's car. Identify the images in the poem, and write about the way

they create the moment of choice and the burden for the speaker. Cite the text of the poem to support your views.

6. Write a comparison of Whitman's view of death with the views expressed in "Death, Be Not Proud" on page 1157, "When I Have Fears That I May Cease to Be" on page 1157, or "Brilliance" on page 1178. Cite the texts of the poems to support your view.

CONNECTING THROUGH COMPARISON: SEPTEMBER 11, 2001

The three poems that follow address a subtheme of this section: September 11, 2001. A date that seems long ago now, the horror, the grief, the courage, the loss is brought back to life as we read these three poignant poems. Read and discussed together, they invite comparisons and connections—not only with each other, but with your own experience of the events of that day.

DEBORAH GARRISON   [B. 1965]

Deborah Garrison was born in Ann Arbor, Michigan, and has a degree in Creative Writing from Brown University. She is a senior nonfiction editor at The New Yorker, *where she has worked since 1986. In 1998, she published a collection of poems,* A Working Girl Can't Win and Other Poems. *Her latest collection is* The Second Child *(2007). She lives in Montclair, New Jersey, with her husband and daughter.*

I SAW YOU WALKING   [2001]

I saw you walking through Newark Penn Station
in your shoes of white ash. At the corner
of my nervous glance your dazed passage
first forced me away, tracing the crescent
berth you'd give a drunk, a lurcher, nuzzling   5
all comers with ill will and his stench, but
not this one, not today: one shirt arm's sheared
clean from the shoulder, the whole bare limb
wet with muscle and shining dimly pink,
the other full-sheathed in cotton, Brooks Bros.   10
type, the cuff yet buttoned at the wrist, a
parody of careful dress, preparedness—
so you had not rolled up your sleeves yet this
morning when your suit jacket (here are
the pants, dark gray, with subtle stripe, as worn   15
by men like you on ordinary days)
and briefcase (you've none, reverse commuter
come from the pit with nothing to carry
but your life) were torn from you, as your life

was not. Your face itself seemed to be walking,   20
leading your body north, though the age
of the face, blank and ashen, passing forth
and away from me, was unclear, the sandy
crown of hair powdered white like your feet, but
underneath not yet gray-forty-seven?   25
forty-eight? the age of someone's father—
and I trembled for your luck, for your broad,
dusted back, half shirted, walking away;
I should have dropped to my knees to thank God
you were alive, o my God, in whom I don't believe.   30

BRIAN DOYLE [B. 1941]

Brian Doyle is the editor of Portland Magazine *at the
University of Portland in Oregon. He is the author of three
collections of essays:* Credo *(1999),* Saints Passionate &
Peculiar *(2002), and (with his father, Jim Doyle)* Two Voices *(1996). Doyle's essays have been reprinted in the* Best
American Essays *anthologies for 1998 and 1999. The prose
poem "Leap" was included in a PBS television special about
the impact of September 11 called "Faith and Doubt." His
latest collection of poems,* Epiphanies and Elegies, *was published in 2007.*

LEAP   [2002]

A couple leaped from the south tower, hand in hand. They reached for each other
and their hands met and they jumped.

Jennifer Brickhouse saw them falling, hand in hand.

Many people jumped. Perhaps hundreds. No one knows. They struck the pavement
with such force that there was a pink mist in the air.

The mayor reported the mist.

5   A kindergarten boy who saw people falling in flames told his teacher that the
birds were on fire. She ran with him on her shoulders out of the ashes.

Tiffany Keeling saw fireballs falling that she later realized were people. Jennifer
Griffin saw people falling and wept as she told the story. Niko Winstral saw people free-falling backwards with their hands out, like they were parachuting. Joe
Duncan on his roof on Duane Street looked up and saw people jumping. Henry
Weintraub saw people "leaping as they flew out." John Carson saw six people
fall, "falling over themselves, falling, they were somersaulting." Steve Miller saw
people jumping from a thousand feet in the air. Kirk Kjeldsen saw people flailing on the way down, people lining up and jumping, "too many people falling."
Jane Tedder saw people leaping and the sight haunts her at night. Steve Tamas

counted fourteen people jumping and then he stopped counting. Stuart DeHann saw one woman's dress billowing as she fell, and he saw a shirtless man falling end over end, and he too saw the couple leaping hand in hand.

Several pedestrians were killed by people falling from the sky. A fireman was killed by a body falling from the sky.

But he reached for her hand and she reached for his hand and they leaped out the window holding hands.

I try to whisper prayers for the sudden dead and the harrowed families of the dead and the screaming souls of the murderers but I keep coming back to his hand and her hand nestled in each other with such extraordinary ordinary succinct ancient naked stunning perfect simple ferocious love.

10 Their hands reaching and joining are the most powerful prayer I can imagine, the most eloquent, the most graceful. It is everything that we are capable of against horror and loss and death. It is what makes me believe that we are not craven fools and charlatans to believe in God, to believe that human beings have greatness and holiness within them like seeds that open only under great fires, to believe that some unimaginable essence of who we are persists past the dissolution of what we were, to believe against such evil hourly evidence that love is why we are here.

No one knows who they were: husband and wife, lovers, dear friends, colleagues, strangers thrown together at the window there at the lip of hell. Maybe they didn't even reach for each other consciously, maybe it was instinctive, a reflex, as they both decided at the same time to take two running steps and jump out the shattered window, but they did reach for each other, and they held on tight, and leaped, and fell endlessly into the smoking canyon, at two hundred miles an hour, falling so far and so fast that they would have blacked out before they hit the pavement near Liberty Street so hard that there was a pink mist in the air.

Jennifer Brickhouse saw them holding hands, and Stuart DeHann saw them holding hands, and I hold onto that.

BILLY COLLINS [B. 1941]

Billy Collins is the author of six books of poetry, and his work has appeared in a variety of publications, including Po-etry, American Poetry Review, American Scholar, Harper's, Paris Review, and The New Yorker. He has received fellow-ships from the National Endowment for the Arts and the Guggenheim Foundation, and in 1992, he was chosen to serve as "Literary Lion" by The New York Public Library. He teaches at Lehman College, of the City University of New York, and lives in Somers, New York. In 2000, he was named U.S. Poet Laureate. His latest book of poems is Ballistics (2008). *The poem below was read before Congress at its joint session in New York City on September 6, 2002.*

THE NAMES   [2002]

Yesterday, I lay awake in the palm of the night.
A fine rain stole in, unhelped by any breeze,
And when I saw the silver glaze on the windows,
I started with A, with Ackerman, as it happened,
Then Baxter and Calabro,   5
Davis and Eberling, names falling into place
As droplets fell through the dark.

Names printed on the ceiling of the night.
Names slipping around a watery bend.
Twenty-six willows on the banks of a stream.   10

In the morning, I walked out barefoot
Among thousands of flowers
Heavy with dew like the eyes of tears,
And each had a name—
Fiori inscribed on a yellow petal   15
Then Gonzalez and Han, Ishikawa and Jenkins.

Names written in the air
And stitched into the cloth of the day.
A name under a photograph taped to a mailbox.
Monogram on a torn shirt,   20
I see you spelled out on storefront windows
And on the bright unfurled awnings of this city.
I say the syllables as I turn a corner—
Kelly and Lee,
Medina, Nardella, and O'Connor.   25

When I peer into the woods,
I see a thick tangle where letters are hidden
As in a puzzle concocted for children.
Parker and Quigley in the twigs of an ash,
Rizzo, Schubert, Torres, and Upton,   30
Secrets in the boughs of an ancient maple.

Names written in the pale sky.
Names rising in the updraft amid buildings.
Names silent in stone
Or cried out behind a door.   35
Names blown over the earth and out to sea.

In the evening—weakening light, the last swallows.
A boy on a lake lifts his oars.

A woman by a window puts a match to a candle,
And the names are outlined on the rose clouds—   40
Vanacore and Wallace,
(let X stand, if it can, for the ones unfound)
Then Young and Ziminsky, the final jolt of Z.

Names etched on the head of a pin.
One name spanning a bridge, another undergoing a tunnel.   45
A blue name needled into the skin.
Names of citizens, workers, mothers and fathers,
The bright-eyed daughter, the quick son.
Alphabet of names in green rows in a field.
Names in the small tracks of birds.   50
Names lifted from a hat
Or balanced on the tip of the tongue.
Names wheeled into the dim warehouse of memory.
So many names, there is barely room on the walls of the heart.

MAKING CONNECTIONS

1. All three poems are about the horrific events of September 11, 2001, but their narrative perspectives are quite different. Compare and contrast each speaker's point of view in these poems and how you were affected by each.
2. The speaker in "Leap" is describing one of the most horrible aspects of the World Trade Center disaster—people jumping from the buildings. But is the tone of this prose poem negative? Explain.
3. These poems are very graphic in their use of imagery. Which images were you most affected by? Why?

MAKING AN ARGUMENT

1. Written at different times after September 11, 2001, each of these poems seems to have a different purpose in mind. Identify what you believe is the purpose of each poem, and write an essay that supports your view. Compare the poems, and cite the text of each poem for support.

CONNECTING THROUGH COMPARISON: BELIEF IN A SUPREME BEING

Religion and the existence of God or a Supreme Being is a topic of great importance for people and cultures throughout the world. It can be a source of great comfort and meaning or a source of exclusion and hatred. The poems that follow address a subtheme of belief in a Supreme Being. Read and discussed together, they invite comparisons and connections—not only with each other, but with your own experience with this topic.

STEPHEN CRANE [1871–1900]

Stephen Crane was the youngest of fourteen children born to a Methodist minister in Newark, New Jersey. After briefly attending LaFayette College and Syracuse University, Crane moved to New York City to work as a freelance journalist. He lived an often impoverished existence and came to know life in the slums firsthand. These experiences inspired his first novel, Maggie, a Girl of the Streets *(1893), which he published at his own expense under a pseudonym. The novel impressed members of New York's literary elite and set the stage for the publication of his second novel,* The Red Badge of Courage *(1895). In 1895, Crane also published a book of short poems,* The Black Riders. *In 1899,* Other Lines *and another collection of poems,* War Is Kind, *would prove influential after his death. Crane died of tuberculosis when he was only twenty-eight.*

A MAN SAID TO THE UNIVERSE [1899]

A man said to the universe:
"Sir, I exist!"
"However," replied the universe,
"The fact has not created in me
A sense of obligation."   5

THOMAS HARDY [1840–1928]

Thomas Hardy was born near Dorchester in southwestern England. Apprenticed to an architect at the age of fifteen, Hardy received very little formal schooling outside the local schools he attended as a boy, but improved himself by reading in his spare time. Unhappy as an architect, he began writing fiction and poetry and, though his first novel was not a success, the success of his second, Under the Greenwood Tree *(1872), allowed him to devote himself to a literary career. Hardy followed this with a string of eleven remarkable novels set in his native Dorchester (called Wessex in the novels), including* Far from the Madding Crowd *(1874),* The Return of the Native *(1879),* The Mayor of Casterbridge *(1887), and* Tess of the D'Urbervilles *(1891). These often bleak novels share a common theme—that human destiny is controlled not by human will but by forces beyond humankind's control. Disillusioned after the hostile reception to* Jude the Obscure *(1895), considered by many modern critics to be his greatest work, Hardy turned to writing highly original poetry that often explored the same themes as his novels. His* Collected Poems *was published in 1931.*

HAP

[1898]

If but some vengeful god would call to me
From up the sky, and laugh: "Thou suffering thing,
Know that thy sorrow is my ecstasy
That thy love's loss is my hate's profiting!"

Then I would bear it, clench myself and die,   5
Steeled by the sense of ire unmerited;
Half-eased in that a Powerfuller than I
Had willed and meted me the tears I shed.

But not so. How arrives it joy lies slain,
And why unblooms the best hope ever sown?   10
Crass Casualty obstructs the sun and rain,
And dicing Time for gladness casts a moan....
These purblind Doomsters had as readily strown
Blisses about my pilgrimage as pain.

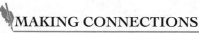

MAKING CONNECTIONS

1. In "A Man Said to the Universe," what do you think the man expects from
   the universe?
2. Why does he say, "I exist"? Are you surprised by the universe's response?
   Explain.
3. Does it make sense to you that the speaker of "Hap" would prefer to be
   doomed by an evil force rather than by blind chance? Explain.
4. Compare Hardy's poem with Crane's.

MAKING AN ARGUMENT

1. Using either or both of these poems, write a comparison with Matthew
   Arnold's "Dover Beach" on page 1160.
2. The attitude of the speaker in "Hap" is very pessimistic. He does not specify
   a particular event that caused him to feel this way, but we can imagine, have
   heard about, or have experienced the kinds of events that might have made
   him feel this way. What is your response to what he says? Write an essay that
   agrees or disagrees with the speaker's conclusion in the poem. Cite the text
   of the poem and your own knowledge and/or experience for support.

CONNECTING THROUGH COMPARISON: THE IMPACT OF WAR

The four poems that follow address a subtheme of this section: the impact of war.
Though we have advanced dramatically and tragically in our ability to kill on a
massive scale, we have advanced very little in our ability to stop the carnage of war.
The chronology of the poems that follow, from the Boer War in South Africa through

the world wars and Vietnam, represents a brief history of the modern world. Read and discussed together, these poems invite comparisons and connections—with each other and with your own experience of and reactions to the subject of war.

THOMAS HARDY [1840–1928]

(See biography on p. 1172.)

THE MAN HE KILLED [1902]

Had he and I but met
By some old ancient inn,
We should have sat us down to wet
Right many a nipperkin!

But ranged as infantry,   5
And staring face to face,
I shot at him as he at me,
And killed him in his place.

I shot him dead because—
Because he was my foe.   10
Just so: my foe of course he was;
That's clear enough; although

He thought he'd list, perhaps,
Off-hand like—just as I—
Was out of work—had sold his traps—   15
No other reason why.

Yes; quaint and curious war is!
You shoot a fellow down
You'd treat, if met where any bar is,
Or help to half-a-crown.   20

WILFRED OWEN [1893–1918]

Born in the Shropshire region of England, Wilfred Owen spent two years studying to be a clergyman before becoming disillusioned with the Anglican church. In 1914, World War I broke out. Owen spent a year debating whether or not his Christian beliefs allowed him to fight. In 1915, he decided to enlist. He became a commander, and in 1916, was stationed with the Lancashire Fusiliers in the trenches in France. In 1917, Owen suffered a nervous breakdown and was sent to an army hospital in Scotland to recover. He spent fourteen months at the hospital, where, befriended by the poet Siegfried Sassoon, he turned to writing poetry. Shipped back to the front, he was killed in action at Sambre Canal, France, only one week before the end of the war. Only four of Owen's poems were published during his lifetime. The rest were collected

and published by Sassoon in 1920. Sassoon said of Owen: "My trench sketches were like rockets, set up to illuminate the darkness…. It was Owen who revealed how, out of realistic horror and scorn, poetry might be made." The last two lines (and title) of "Dulce et Decorum Est" are taken from an ode by Horace, a great Roman poet. They mean: "It is sweet and fitting to die for one's country."

DULCE ET DECORUM EST   [1918]

Bent double, like old beggars under sacks,
Knock-kneed, coughing like hags, we cursed through sludge,
Till on the haunting flares we turned our backs
And towards our distant rest began to trudge.
Men marched asleep. Many had lost their boots   5
But limped on, blood-shod. All went lame; all blind;
Drunk with fatigue; deaf even to the hoots
Of tired, outstripped Five-Nines that dropped behind.

Gas! gas! Quick, boys!—An ecstasy of fumbling,
Fitting the clumsy helmets just in time;   10
But someone still was yelling out and stumbling
And flound'ring like a man in fire or lime…
Dim, through the misty panes and thick green light,
As under a green sea, I saw him drowning.
In all my dreams, before my helpless sight,   15
He plunges at me, guttering, choking, drowning.

If in some smothering dreams you too could pace
Behind the wagon that we flung him in,
And watch the white eyes writhing in his face,
His hanging face, like a devil's sick of sin;   20
If you could hear, at every jolt, the blood
Come gargling from the froth-corrupted lungs,
Obscene as cancer, bitter as the cud
Of vile, incurable sores on innocent tongues,—
My friend, you would not tell with such high zest   25
To children ardent for some desperate glory.
The old Lie: *Dulce et decorum est*
Pro patria mori.

CARL SANDBURG   [1878–1967]

Born in Galesburg, Illinois, to Swedish-immigrant parents, Carl Sandburg quit school at thirteen and worked for a number of years at a series of low-paying jobs, even spending time as a hobo riding trains around the Midwest. Following his service in the army during the Spanish-American War (1898), Sandburg returned to Galesburg and worked his way through Lombard (now Knox) College. He left without a

degree but with a sense that he wanted to be a poet, publishing his first (and largely forgotten) collection of poetry, In Reckless Ecstasy, *in 1904. For the next four years, Sandburg again worked at a number of odd jobs, until he married and eventually settled into a job as a reporter for the* Chicago Daily News. *In 1916, he published* Chicago Poems *and soon became one of the leading members of the Chicago Group, which included such famous writers as Theodore Dreiser, Ben Hecht, and Edgar Lee Masters. Beginning in the 1920s, Sandburg began touring the country with his guitar and giving readings of his poetry, a practice he continued until he died. In addition to his numerous volumes of free verse poems, Sandburg published a monumental six-volume biography of Abraham Lincoln, one of his personal heroes, that won the Pulitzer Prize for history in 1940.*

GRASS   [1918]

Pile the bodies high at Austerlitz and Waterloo.
Shovel them under and let me work—
    I am the grass; I cover all.
And pile them high at Gettysburg
And pile them high at Ypres and Verdun   5
Shovel them under and let me work.
Two years, ten years, and passengers ask the conductor:
    What place is this?
    Where are we now?

    I am the grass.   10
    Let me work.

YUSEF KOMUNYAKAA [B. 1947]

Yusef Komunyakaa was born in Bogalusa, Louisiana, and served in the Vietnam War. His volumes of poetry include Copacetic *(1984),* I Apologize for the Eyes in My Head *(1986), and* Neon Vernacular, *which won the Pulitzer Prize in 1994. His latest book of poems is* Warhorses *(2008). "Facing It," a poem about the Vietnam Memorial in Washington, D.C., is taken from* Dien Cai Dau *(1988). He teaches at New York University.*

FACING IT   [1988]

My black face fades,
hiding inside the black granite.
I said I wouldn't,
dammit: No tears.
I'm stone. I'm flesh.   5
My clouded reflection eyes me

like a bird of prey, the profile of night
slanted against morning. I turn
this way—the stone lets me go.
I turn that way—I'm inside   10
the Vietnam Veterans Memorial
again, depending on the light
to make a difference.
I go down the 58,022 names,
half-expecting to find   15
my own in letters like smoke.
I touch the name Andrew Johnson;
I see the booby trap's white flash.
Names shimmer on a woman's blouse
but when she walks away   20
the names stay on the wall.
Brushstrokes flash, a red bird's
wings cutting across my stare.
The sky. A plane in the sky.
A white vet's image floats   25
closer to me, then his pale eyes
look through mine. I'm a window.
He's lost his right arm
inside the stone. In the black mirror
a woman's trying to erase names: 30
No, she's brushing a boy's hair.

MAKING CONNECTIONS

1. Who is the speaker in the "The Man He Killed"? What does his diction tell you about him?
2. What do you think he concludes? To what extent do you agree?
3. In *"Dulce et Decorum Est"* when the speaker says at the beginning of the last stanza, "If in some smothering dreams you too could pace," "you" seems to refer to us—the readers. What does he assume about "us"? What does he assume might change our view?
4. Why does he call the Latin saying that is the title of this poem "The old Lie"?
5. In "Grass," what do "Austerlitz," "Waterloo," "Gettysburg," "Ypres," and "Verdun" refer to?
6. Why would the passengers ask the conductor, "What place is this?" Does it matter? Explain.
7. Who is the speaker in "Facing It"? What is the speaker's point of view?
8. How many different things does he see reflected in the wall? In what way is it fitting that he mistakes the woman's brushing the boy's hair as trying to erase names?
9. Compare any of these poems to Stephen Crane's "War Is Kind" on page 77.

MAKING AN ARGUMENT

1. Except for *"Dulce et Decorum Est,"* all of these poems are removed from the "heat" of battle itself. The speakers are remembering or grieving sad news. But all of them, like the speaker in the Owen poem, seem to state explicitly or implicitly some doubt about the wisdom and necessity of war. Do you agree? Write an essay about the theme of "doubt" as exemplified by the poems in this section. Cite the texts of the poems for support.

CONNECTING THROUGH COMPARISON: RESPONDING TO THE DEATHS OF OTHERS

One of our most poignant experiences can be the death of someone we know. If we are close to the deceased, that loss can be devastating, but even if we do not know the person well, we are often reminded of our own mortality. The poems that follow address a subtheme of faith and doubt: the deaths of others. Read and discussed together, they invite comparisons and connections—not only with each other, but with your own experience with this topic.

MARK DOTY [B. 1953]

Mark Doty is the author of several collections of poems including Atlantis *(1995);* Turtle, Swan *(1987);* Bethlehem in Broad Daylight *(1991); and* My Alexandria *(1993), which won the National Book Critics Circle Award, the* Los Angeles Times *Book Award, the T. S. Eliot Award, and the National Poetry Series Award, and was a finalist for the National Book Award. Doty has also been the recipient of grants from the National Endowment for the Arts and the Guggenheim Foundation. His latest collection of poems,* Fire to Fire, *was published in 2008. He lives in Provincetown, Massachusetts.*

BRILLIANCE   [1993]

Maggie's taking care of a man
who's dying; he's attended to everything,
said goodbye to his parents,

paid off his credit card.
She says *Why don't you just*   5
run it up to the limit?

but he wants everything
squared away, no balance owed,
though he misses the pets

he's already found a home for   10
—he can't be around dogs or cats,
too much risk. He says,

I can't have anything.
She says, *A bowl of goldfish?*
He says he doesn't want to start   15

with anything and then describes
the kind he'd maybe like,
how their tails would fan

to a gold flaring. They talk
about hot jewel tones,   20
gold lacquer, say maybe

they'll go pick some out
though he can't go much of anywhere and then
abruptly he says *I can't love*

anything I can't finish.   25
He says it like he's had enough
of the whole scintillant world,

though what he means is
he'll never be satisfied and therefore
has established this discipline,   30

a kind of severe rehearsal.
That's where they leave it,
him looking out the window,

her knitting as she does because
she needs to do something.   35
Later he leaves a message:

Yes to the bowl of goldfish.
Meaning: let me go, if I have to,
in brilliance. In a story I read,

a Zen master who'd perfected   40
his detachment from the things of the world
remembered, at the moment of dying,

a deer he used to feed in the park,
and wondered who might care for it,
and at that instant was reborn   45

in the stunned flesh of a fawn.
So, Maggie's friend—
is he going out

into the last loved object
of his attention?   50
Fanning the veined translucence

of an opulent tail,
undulant in some uncapturable curve,
is he bronze chrysanthemums,

copper leaf, hurried darting,   55
doubloons, icon-colored fins
troubling the water?

A. E. HOUSMAN [1859–1934]

(See biography on p. 470.)

TO AN ATHLETE DYING YOUNG   [1896]

The time you won your town the race
We chaired you through the market-place;
Man and boy stood cheering by,
And home we brought you shoulder-high.

To-day, the road all runners come,   5
Shoulder-high we bring you home,
And set you at your threshold down,
Townsman of a stiller town.

Smart lad, to slip betimes away
From fields where glory does not stay   10
And early though the laurel grows
It withers quicker than the rose.

Eyes the shady night has shut
Cannot see the record cut,
And silence sounds no worse than cheers   15
After earth has stopped the ears:

Now you will not swell the rout
Of lads that wore their honours out,
Runners whom renown outran
And the name died before the man.   20

So set, before its echoes fade,
The fleet foot on the sill of shade,
And hold to the low lintel up
The still-defended challenge-cup.

And round that early-laurelled head   25
Will flock to gaze the strengthless dead
And find unwithered on its curls
The garland briefer than a girl's.

PABLO NERUDA   [1904–1973]

A revered and influential poet, Pablo Neruda was born in Chile, where he remained politically active until his death. His poetry often mixes his views on political oppression with passionate lyrics about romantic love. His many works include Twenty Love Poems and a Song of Despair *(1924) and* Memorial of Isla Negra *(1964). He was awarded the Nobel Prize for literature in 1971.*

THE DEAD WOMAN   [1972]

Translated by Donald Walsh

If suddenly you do not exist,
if suddenly you are not living,
I shall go on living.

I do not dare,
I do not dare to write it,   5
if you die.

I shall go on living.

Because where a man has no voice,
there, my voice.

Where blacks are beaten,   10
I can not be dead.
When my brothers go to jail
I shall go with them.

When victory,
not my victory   15
but the great victory
arrives,
even though I am mute I must speak:
I shall see it come even though I am blind.

No, forgive me.   20
If you are not living,
if you, beloved, my love,
if you
have died,
all the leaves will fall on my breast,   25
it will rain upon my soul night and day,
the snow will burn my heart,
I shall walk with cold and fire and death and snow,
my feet will want to march toward where you sleep,
but   30

I shall go on living,
because you wanted me to be, above all things,
untamable,
and, love, because you know that I am not just one man
but all men.   35

DYLAN THOMAS [1914–1953]

*Dylan Thomas was born in Swansea, Wales, a region of
Great Britain with its own linguistic and cultural heritage.
Though he began publishing his work when he was only
twenty, Thomas struggled throughout his life to make ends
meet, first as a reporter in London, and later, when he was
better established, by writing screenplays and short stories
from his home in Wales. Beginning in the late 1940s,
Thomas became internationally famous for his poetry*
*readings both in person and on the radio, making numerous recordings and
touring in both England and the United States. In 1953, Thomas, who was well
known for his drinking, died following a drinking binge in New York City. The
influence of the Welsh language can be clearly felt throughout his works, particularly in his remarkable radio play* Under Milk Wood *(1954), which depicts a day
in the life of the inhabitants of a Welsh village.*

DO NOT GO GENTLE INTO THAT GOOD NIGHT   [1952]

Do not go gentle into that good night,
Old age should burn and rave at close of day;
Rage, rage against the dying of the light.

Though wise men at their end know dark is right,
Because their words had forked no lightning they   5
Do not go gentle into that good night.

Good men, the last wave by, crying how bright
Their frail deeds might have danced in a green bay,
Rage, rage against the dying of the light.

Wild men who caught and sang the sun in flight,   10
And learn, too late, they grieved it on its way,
Do not go gentle into that good night.

Grave men, near death, who see with blinding sight
Blind eyes could blaze like meteors and be gay,
Rage, rage against the dying of the light.   15

And you, my father, there on the sad height,
Curse, bless, me now with your fierce tears, I pray.
Do not go gentle into that good night.
Rage, rage against the dying of the light.

MAKING CONNECTIONS

1. Have you ever thought about the potential death of a loved one? Did it make you feel that you wouldn't be able to go on living? Or does the thought make you feel more resolved to make the most of your life? Explain.
2. Why do you think the dying man in "Brilliance" wants a bowl of goldfish? What would you want in the same situation?
3. To what extent is "Brilliance" an appropriate title for this poem?
4. Who is the "you" addressed by the speaker in "To an Athlete Dying Young"? Both the first and second stanzas make reference to carrying the subject "shoulder-high." What does the term mean in each stanza? In what way is it ironic?
5. Dying young is not a pleasant prospect. But what does the speaker mean by "Now you will not swell the rout / Of lads that wore their honours out"? Is there a positive side to dying young? Explain.
6. Write a paraphrase of "The Dead Woman." What is the speaker saying about the impact of his beloved's death on his life?
7. Neruda wrote "The Dead Woman" at the age of sixty-eight, approximately one year before his own death. Do you think that his advancing age had an impact on his attitude toward death in this poem?
8. Who is the speaker in "Do Not Go Gentle into That Good Night"? To what extent do you think that influences his attitude toward this death?
9. Were you surprised by the advice of Thomas's poem? Why?
10. If "wise men…know dark is right," why do you think the speaker wants his father to rage against it?
11. Thomas's poem is a villanelle (see p. 1304). How does the form of the poem support its content?

MAKING AN ARGUMENT

1. In the biography on page 1181 you read that Neruda's work is character-ized by a melding of "his views on political oppression with passionate lyrics about romantic love." Write an essay that explores how "The Dead Woman" exemplifies this stylistic tendency. Be sure to cite the text of the poem for support.
2. The poem "Brilliance" begins with a man who is dying and ends with an image of a goldfish darting through the water. Write about the structure of the poem and its images and how they convey its content. Cite the text of the poem for support.
3. Write an essay that compares and contrasts "To an Athlete Dying Young" with "Out, Out…" on page 480. Cite the text of both poems for support.
4. Dylan Thomas's "Do Not Go Gentle into That Good Night" and John Donne's "Death, Be Not Proud" seem to have different attitudes toward death. Identify the theme of each poem, and write an essay that takes a position in favor of one view or the other. Cite the text of both poems for support.

◆ DRAMA ◆

DAVID MAMET [B. 1947]

David Mamet was born in Chicago and has written over twenty plays. He is best known for plays like American Buffalo *(1975), which won the New York Drama Critics Circle Award, and* Glengarry Glen Ross *(1984), for which he was awarded a Pulitzer Prize. He has also written several successful screenplays including* The Verdict *(1982), which received an Academy Award nomination, and* The Untouchables *(1987). He has both written and directed a number of movies, including* House of Games *(1987),* Homicide *(1991), the film version of* Oleanna *(1994),* The Spanish Prisoner *(1997),* State and Main *(1991), and* Heist *(2001). His latest play is a comic farce called* November *(2011).*

OLEANNA [1994]

"to be in *Oleanna*
    That's where I would rather be.
    Than be bound in Norway
    And drag the chains of slavery."
                  —folk song

CHARACTERS

CAROL, *a woman of twenty*
JOHN, *a man in his forties*
The play takes place in John's office.

ONE

JOHN *is talking on the phone.* CAROL *is seated across the desk from him.*

JOHN: [*on the phone*] And what about the land. [*Pause*] The land. And what about the land? [*Pause*] What about it? [*Pause*] No. I don't understand. Well, yes, I'm I'm…no, I'm *sure* it's signif…I'm sure it's significant. [*Pause*] Because it's significant to mmmmmm…did you call Jerry? [*Pause*] Because…no, no, no, no. What did they say…? Did you speak to the *real* estate…where *is* she…? Well, well, all right. Where are her notes? Where are the notes we took with her. [*Pause*] I thought you were? No. No, I'm sorry, I didn't mean that, I just thought that I saw you, when we were there…what…? I thought I saw you with a *pencil.* WHY NOW? is what I'm say…well, that's why I say "call Jerry." Well, I can't right now, be…no, I *didn't* schedule any…Grace: I *didn't*…I'm well aware…Look: Look. Did you call Jerry? Will you call Jerry…? Because I can't now. I'll be there, I'm sure I'll be there in fifteen, in twenty. I intend to. No, we aren't *going* to lose the, we aren't *going* to lose the house. Look: Look, I'm not minimizing it. The "easement." Did she say "easement"? [*Pause*] What did she *say;* is it a "term of art," are we *bound* by it…I'm sorry…[*Pause*] are:

we: yes. *Bound* by...Look: [*He checks his watch.*] before the other side *goes home,* all right? "a term of art." Because: that's right [*Pause*] The yard for the boy. Well, that's the whole...Look: I'm going to meet you there...[*He checks his watch.*] Is the realtor there? All right, tell her to show you the basement again. Look at the *this* because...Bec...I'm leaving in, I'm leaving in ten or fifteen...Yes. No, no, I'll meet you at the new...That's a good. If he thinks it's necc...you tell Jerry to meet...All right? We *aren't* going to lose the deposit. All right? I'm sure it's going to be...[*Pause*] I hope so. [*Pause*] I love you, too. [*Pause*] I love you, too. As soon as...I will.

    [*He hangs up.*] [*He bends over the desk and makes a note.*] [*He looks up.*] [*To* CAROL:] I'm sorry...

CAROL: [*Pause*] What is a "term of art"?

JOHN: [*Pause*] I'm sorry...?

CAROL: [*Pause*] What is a "term of art"?

JOHN: Is that what you want to talk about?

CAROL: ...to talk about...?

JOHN: Let's take the mysticism out of it, shall we? Carol? [*Pause*] Don't you think? I'll tell you: when you have some "thing." Which must be broached. [*Pause*] Don't you think...? [*Pause*]

CAROL: ...don't I think...?

JOHN: Mmm?

CAROL: ...did I...?

JOHN: ...what?

CAROL: Did...did I...did I say something wr...

JOHN: [*Pause*] No. I'm sorry. No. You're right. I'm very sorry. I'm somewhat rushed. As you see. I'm sorry. You're right. [*Pause*] What is a "term of art"? It seems to mean a *term,* which has come, through its use, to mean something *more specific* than the words would, to someone *not acquainted* with them...indicate. That, I believe, is what a "term of art," would mean. [*Pause*]

CAROL: You don't know what it means...?

JOHN: I'm not sure that I know what it means. It's one of those things, perhaps you've had them, that, you look them up, or have someone explain them to you, and you say "aha," and, you immediately *forget* what...

CAROL: You don't do that.

JOHN: ...I...?

CAROL: You don't do...

JOHN: ...I don't, what...?

CAROL: ...for...

JOHN: ...I don't for...

CAROL: ...no...

JOHN: ...forget things? Everybody does that.

CAROL: No, they don't.

JOHN: They don't...

CAROL: No.

JOHN: [*Pause*] No. Everybody does that.

CAROL: Why would they do that...?

JOHN: Because. I don't know. Because it doesn't interest them.

CAROL: No.

JOHN: I think so, though. [*Pause*] I'm sorry that I was distracted.

CAROL: You don't have to say that to me.

JOHN: You paid me the compliment, or the "obeisance"—all right—of coming in here…All right. *Carol.* I find that I am at a *standstill.* I find that I…

CAROL: …what…

JOHN: …one moment. In regard to your…to your…

CAROL: Oh, oh. You're buying a new house!

JOHN: No, let's get on with it.

CAROL: "get on"? [*Pause*]

JOHN: I know how…*believe* me. I know how…potentially *humiliating* these…I have no desire to…I have no desire other than to help you. But [*He picks up some papers on his desk.*] I won't even say "but." I'll say that as I go back over the…

CAROL: I'm just, I'm just trying to…

JOHN: …no, it will not do.

CAROL: …what? What will…?

JOHN: No. I see, I see what you, it…[*He gestures to the papers.*] but your work…

CAROL: I'm just: I sit in class I…[*She holds up her notebook.*] I take notes…

JOHN: [*simultaneously with* "notes"] Yes. I understand. What I am trying to *tell* you is that some, some basic…

CAROL: …I…

JOHN: …one moment: some basic missed communi…

CAROL: I'm doing what I'm told. I bought your book, I read your…

JOHN: No, I'm sure you…

CAROL: No, no, no. I'm doing what I'm told. It's *difficult* for me. It's *difficult*…

JOHN: …but…

CAROL: I don't…lots of the *language*…

JOHN: …please…

CAROL: The *language,* the "things" that you say…

JOHN: I'm sorry. No. I don't think that that's true.

CAROL: It *is* true. I…

JOHN: I think…

CAROL: It *is* true.

JOHN: …I…

CAROL: Why would I…?

JOHN: I'll tell you why: you're an incredibly bright girl.

CAROL: …I…

JOHN: You're an incredibly…you have no problem with the…Who's kidding who?

CAROL: …I…

JOHN: No. No. I'll tell you why. I'll tell…I think you're *angry,* I…

CAROL: …why would I…

JOHN: …wait one moment. I…

CAROL: It *is* true. I have *problems*…

JOHN: …every…

CAROL: ...I come from a different *social*...

JOHN: ...ev...

CAROL: a different economic...

JOHN: ...Look:

CAROL: No. I: when I *came* to this school:

JOHN: Yes. Quite...[*Pause*]

CAROL: ...does that mean nothing...?

JOHN: ...but look: look...

CAROL: ...I...

JOHN: [*Picks up paper.*] Here: Please: Sit down. [*Pause*] Sit down. [*Reads from her paper.*] "I think that the ideas contained in this work express the author's feelings in a way that he intended, based on his results." What can that mean? Do you see? What...

CAROL: I, the best that I...

JOHN: I'm saying, that perhaps this course...

CAROL: No, no, no, you can't, you can't...I have to...

JOHN: ...how...

CAROL: ...I have to pass it...

JOHN: Carol, I.

CAROL: I *have* to pass this course, I...

JOHN: Well.

CAROL: ...don't you...

JOHN: Either the...

CAROL: ...I...

JOHN: ...either the, I...either the *criteria* for judging progress in the class are...

CAROL: No, no, no, no, I have to pass it.

JOHN: Now, look: I'm a human being, I...

CAROL: I did what you told me. I did, I did everything that, I read your *book,* you told me to buy your book and read it. Everything you *say* I...[*She gestures to her notebook.*] [*The phone rings.*] I do....Ev...

JOHN: ...look:

CAROL: ...everything I'm told...

JOHN: Look. Look. I'm not your *father.* [*Pause*]

CAROL: What?

JOHN: I'm.

CAROL: Did I say you were my father?

JOHN: ...no...

CAROL: Why did you say that...?

JOHN: I...

CAROL: ...why...?

JOHN: ...in class I...[*He picks up the phone.*] [*Into phone:*] Hello. I can't talk now. Jerry? Yes? I underst...I can't talk now. I know...I know...Jerry. I can't *talk* now. Yes, I. Call me back in...Thank you. [*He hangs up.*] [*To* CAROL:] What do you want me to do? We are two people, all right? Both of whom have subscribed to...

CAROL: No, no...

JOHN: …certain arbitrary…

CAROL: No. You have to help me.

JOHN: Certain institutional…you tell me what you want me to do.…You tell me what you want me to…

CAROL: How can I go back and tell them the *grades* that I…

JOHN: …what can I do…?

CAROL: *Teach* me. *Teach* me,

JOHN: …I'm trying to teach you.

CAROL: I read your book. I read it. I don't under…

JOHN: …you don't understand it.

CAROL: No.

JOHN: Well, perhaps it's not well *written*…

CAROL: [*simultaneously with* "written"] No. No. No. I want to *understand* it.

JOHN: What don't you understand? [*Pause*]

CAROL: *Any* of it. What you're trying to say. When you talk about…

JOHN: …yes…? [*She consults her notes.*]

CAROL: "Virtual warehousing of the young"…

JOHN: "Virtual warehousing of the young." If we artificially prolong adolescence…

CAROL: …and about "The Curse of Modern Education."

JOHN: …well…

CAROL: I don't…

JOHN: Look. It's just a *course,* it's just a *book,* it's just a…

CAROL: No. No. There are *people* out there. People who came *here*. To know something they didn't *know*. Who *came* here. To be *helped*. To be *helped*. So someone would *help* them. To *do* something. To *know* something. To get, what do they say? "To get on in the world." How can I do that if I don't, if I fail? But I don't *understand*. I don't *understand*. I don't understand what anything means…and I walk around. From morning 'til night: with this one thought in my head. I'm *stupid*.

JOHN: No one thinks you're stupid.

CAROL: No? What am I…?

JOHN: I…

CAROL: …what am I, then?

JOHN: I think you're angry. Many people are. I have a *telephone* call that I have to make. And an *appointment,* which is rather *pressing;* though I sympathize with your concerns, and though I wish I had the time, this was not a previously scheduled meeting and I…

CAROL: …you think I'm nothing…

JOHN: …have an appointment with a *realtor,* and with my wife and…

CAROL: You think that I'm stupid.

JOHN: No. I certainly don't.

CAROL: You said it.

JOHN: No. I did not.

CAROL: You did.

JOHN: When?

CAROL: …you…

JOHN: No. I never did, or never would say that to a student, and…

CAROL: You said, "What can that mean?" [*Pause*] "What can that mean?"…[*Pause*]

JOHN: …and what did that mean to you…?

CAROL: That meant I'm stupid. And I'll never learn. That's what that meant. And you're right.

JOHN: …I…

CAROL: But then. But then, what am I doing here…?

JOHN: …if you thought that I…

CAROL: …when nobody wants me, and…

JOHN: …if you interpreted…

CAROL: Nobody *tells* me anything. And I *sit* there…in the *corner.* In the *back.* And everybody's talking about "this" all the time. And "concepts," and "precepts" and, and, and, and, and, WHAT IN THE WORLD ARE YOU *TALKING* ABOUT? And I read your book. And they said, "Fine, go in that class." Because you talked about responsibility to the young. I DON'T KNOW WHAT IT MEANS AND I'M *FAILING*…

JOHN: May…

CAROL: No, you're right. "Oh, hell." I failed. Flunk me out of it. It's garbage. Everything I do. "The ideas contained in this work express the author's feelings." That's right. That's right. I know I'm stupid. I know what I am. [*Pause*] I know what I am, Professor. You don't have to tell me. [*Pause*] It's pathetic. Isn't it?

JOHN: …Aha…[*Pause*] Sit down. Sit down. Please. [*Pause*] Please sit down.

CAROL: Why?

JOHN: I want to talk to you.

CAROL: Why?

JOHN: Just sit down. [*Pause*] Please. Sit down. Will you, please…? [*Pause. She does so.*] Thank you.

CAROL: What?

JOHN: I want to tell you something.

CAROL: [*Pause*] What?

JOHN: Well, I know what you're talking about.

CAROL: No. You don't.

JOHN: I think I do. [*Pause*]

CAROL: How can you?

JOHN: I'll tell you a story about myself. [*Pause*] Do you mind? [*Pause*] I was raised to think myself stupid. That's what I want to tell you. [*Pause*]

CAROL: What do you mean?

JOHN: Just what I said. I was brought up, and my earliest, and most persistent memories are of being told that I was stupid. "You have such *intelligence.* Why must you behave so *stupidly?*" Or, "Can't you *understand?* Can't you *understand?*" And I could *not* understand. I could *not* understand.

CAROL: What?

JOHN: The simplest problem. Was beyond me. It was a mystery.

CAROL: What was a mystery?

JOHN: How people learn. How *I* could learn. Which is what I've been speaking of in class. And of *course* you can't hear it. Carol. Of *course* you can't. [*Pause*] I used to speak of "real people," and wonder what the *real* people did. The *real* people. Who were they? *They* were the people other than myself. The *good* people. The *capable* people. The people who could do the things, *I* could not do: learn, study, retain...all that *garbage*—which is what I have been talking of in class, and that's *exactly* what I have been talking of—If you are told...Listen to this. If the young child is told he cannot understand. Then he takes it as a *description* of himself. What am I? I am *that which cannot understand* And I saw you out there, when we were speaking of the concepts of...

CAROL: I can't understand any of them.

JOHN: Well, then, that's *my* fault. That's not your fault. And that is not verbiage. That's what I firmly hold to be the truth. And I am sorry, and I owe you an apology.

CAROL: Why?

JOHN: And I suppose that I have had some *things* on my mind...We're buying a *house,* and...

CAROL: People said that you were stupid...?

JOHN: Yes.

CAROL: When?

JOHN: I'll tell you when. Through my life. In my childhood; and, perhaps, they stopped. But I heard them continue.

CAROL: And what did they say?

JOHN: They said I was incompetent. Do you see? And when I'm tested the, the, the *feelings* of my youth about the *very subject of learning* come up. And I...I become, I feel "unworthy," and "unprepared."...

CAROL: ...yes.

JOHN: ...eh?

CAROL: ...yes.

JOHN: And I feel that I must fail. [*Pause*]

CAROL: ...but then you *do* fail. [*Pause*] You have to. [*Pause*] Don't you?

JOHN: A *pilot.* Flying a plane. The pilot is flying the plane. He thinks: Oh, my *God,* my mind's been drifting! Oh, my God! What kind of a cursed imbecile am I, that I, with this so precious cargo of *Life* in my charge, would allow my attention to wander. Why was I born? How deluded are those who put their trust in me,... et cetera, so on, and he crashes the plane.

CAROL: [*Pause*] He could just...

JOHN: That's right.

CAROL: He could say:

JOHN: My attention *wandered* for a moment...

CAROL: ...uh huh...

JOHN: I had a *thought* I did not like...but now:

CAROL: ...but now it's...

JOHN: That's what I'm telling you. It's time to put my attention...see: it is not: this is what I learned. It is Not Magic. Yes. Yes. *You.* You are going to be frightened. When faced with what may or may not be but which you are going to perceive as a test. You will become frightened. And you will say: "I am incapable of..." and everything *in* you will think these two things. "I must. But I can't." And you will think: Why was I born to be the laughing-stock of a world in which everyone is better than I? In which I am entitled to nothing. Where I cannot learn. [*Pause*]

CAROL: Is that...[*Pause*] Is that what I have...?

JOHN: Well. I don't know if I'd put it that way. Listen: I'm talking to you as I'd talk to my son. Because that's what I'd like him to have that I never had. I'm talking to you the way I wish that someone had talked to me. I don't know how to do it, other than to be *personal*,...but...

CAROL: Why would you want to be personal with me?

JOHN: Well, you see? That's what I'm saying. We can only interpret the behavior of others through the screen we...[*The phone rings.*] Through...[*To phone:*] Hello...? [*To* CAROL:] Through the screen we create. [*To phone:*] Hello. [*To* CAROL:] Excuse me a moment. [*To phone:*] Hello? No, I can't talk nnn... I know I did. In a few...I'm...is he coming to the...yes. I talked to him. We'll meet you at the...No, because I'm with a *student*. It's going to be fff...This is important, too. I'm with a *student,* Jerry's going to...Listen: the sooner I get off, the sooner I'll be down, all right. I love you. Listen, listen, I said. "I love you," it's going to work *out* with the, because I feel that it is, I'll be right down. All right? Well, then it's going to take as long as it takes. [*He hangs up.*] [*To* CAROL:] I'm sorry.

CAROL: What was that?

JOHN: There are some problems, as there usually are, about the final agreements for the new house.

CAROL: You're buying a new house.

JOHN: That's right.

CAROL: Because of your promotion.

JOHN: Well, I suppose that that's right.

CAROL: Why did you stay here with me?

JOHN: Stay here.

CAROL: Yes. When you should have gone.

JOHN: Because I like you.

CAROL: You like me.

JOHN: Yes.

CAROL: Why?

JOHN: Why? Well? Perhaps we're similar. [*Pause*] Yes. [*Pause*]

CAROL: You said "everyone has problems."

JOHN: Everyone has problems.

CAROL: Do they?

JOHN: Certainly.

CAROL: You do?

JOHN: Yes.

CAROL: What are they?

JOHN: Well. [*Pause*] Well, you're perfectly right. [*Pause*] If we're going to take off the Artificial *Stricture,* of "Teacher," and "Student," why should *my* problems be any more a mystery than your own? Of *course* I have problems. As you saw.

CAROL: ...with what?

JOHN: With my *wife*…with *work*…

CAROL: With work?

JOHN: Yes. And, and, perhaps my problems are, do you see? *Similar* to yours.

CAROL: Would you tell me?

JOHN: All right. [*Pause*] I came *late* to teaching. And I found it Artificial. The notion of "I know and you do not"; and I saw an *exploitation* in the education process. I told you. I hated school, I hated teachers. I hated everyone who was in the position of a "boss" because I *knew*—I didn't *think,* mind you, I *knew I* was going to fail. Because I was a fuckup. I was just no goddamned good. When I…late in life…[*Pause*] When I *got out from under*…when I worked my way out of the need to fail. When I…

CAROL: How do you do that? [*Pause*]

JOHN: You have to look at what you are, and what you feel, and how you act. And, finally, you have to look at how you act. And say: If that's what I *did,* that must be how I think of myself.

CAROL: I don't understand.

JOHN: If I fail all the time, it must be that I think of myself as a failure. If I do not want to think of myself as a failure, perhaps I should begin by *succeeding* now and again. Look. The tests, you see, which you encounter, in school, in college, in life, were designed, in the most part, for idiots. *By* idiots. There is no need to fail at them. They are not a test of your worth. They are a test of your ability to retain and spout back misinformation. Of *course* you fail them. They're *nonsense.* And I…

CAROL: …no…

JOHN: Yes. They're *garbage.* They're a *joke.* Look at me. Look at me. The Tenure Committee. The Tenure Committee. Come to judge me. The Bad Tenure Committee.

The "Test." Do you see? They put me to the test. Why, they had people voting on me I wouldn't employ to wax my car. And yet, I go before the Great Tenure Committee, and I have an urge, to *vomit,* to, to, to puke my *badness* on the table, to show them: "I'm no good. Why would you pick *me?*"

CAROL: They granted you tenure.

JOHN: Oh no, they announced it, but they haven't *signed.* Do you see? "At any moment…"

CAROL: …mmm…

JOHN: "They might not *sign*"…I might not…the *house* might not go through…Eh? Eh? They'll find out my "dark secret." [*Pause*]

CAROL: …what is it…?

JOHN: There *isn't* one. But *they* will find an index of my badness…

CAROL: Index?

JOHN: A "…pointer." A "Pointer." You see? Do you see? I *understand* you. I. Know. That. Feeling. Am I entitled to my job, and my nice *home,* and my *wife,* and my *family,* and so on. This is what I'm saying: That theory of education which, that *theory:*

CAROL: I…I…[*Pause*]

JOHN: What?

CAROL: I...

JOHN: What?

CAROL: I want to know about my grade. [*Long pause*]

JOHN: Of course you do.

CAROL: Is that bad?

JOHN: No.

CAROL: Is it bad that I asked you that?

JOHN: No.

CAROL: Did I upset you?

JOHN: No. And I apologize. Of *course* you want to know about your grade. And, of course, you can't concentrate on anyth...[*The telephone starts to ring.*] Wait a moment.

CAROL: I should go.

JOHN: I'll make you a deal.

CAROL: No; you have to...

JOHN: Let it ring. I'll make you a deal. You stay here. We'll start the whole course over. I'm going to say it was not you, it was I who was not paying attention. We'll start the whole course over. Your grade is an "A." Your final grade is an "A." [*The phone stops ringing.*]

CAROL: But the class is only half over...

JOHN: [*simultaneously with* "over"] Your grade for the whole term is an "A." If you will come back and meet with me. A few more times. Your grade's an "A." Forget about the paper. You didn't like it, you didn't like writing it. It's not important. What's important is that I awake your interest, if I can, and that I answer your questions. Let's start over. [*Pause*]

CAROL: Over. With what?

JOHN: Say this is the beginning.

CAROL: The beginning.

JOHN: Yes.

CAROL: Of what?

JOHN: Of the class.

CAROL: But we can't start over.

JOHN: I say we can. [*Pause*] I say we can.

CAROL: But I don't believe it.

JOHN: Yes, I know that. But it's true. What is The Class but you and me? [*Pause*]

CAROL: There are rules.

JOHN: Well. We'll break them.

CAROL: How can we?

JOHN: We won't tell anybody.

CAROL: Is that all right?

JOHN: I say that it's fine.

CAROL: Why would you do this for me?

JOHN: I like you. Is that so difficult for you to...

CAROL: Um...

JOHN: There's no one here but you and me. [*Pause*]

CAROL: All right. I did not understand. When you referred...

JOHN: All right, yes?

CAROL: When you referred to hazing.

JOHN: Hazing.

CAROL: You wrote, in your book. About the comparative…the comparative…[*She checks her notes.*]

JOHN: Are you checking your notes…?

CAROL: Yes.

JOHN: Tell me in your own…

CAROL: I want to make sure that I have it right.

JOHN: No. Of course. You want to be exact.

CAROL: I want to know everything that went on.

JOHN: …that's good.

CAROL: …so I…

JOHN: That's very good. But I was suggesting, many times, that that which we wish to retain is retained oftentimes, I think, *better* with less expenditure of effort.

CAROL: [*Of notes*] Here it is: you wrote of *hazing*.

JOHN: …that's correct. Now: I said "hazing." It means ritualized annoyance. We shove this book at you, we say read it. Now, you say you've read it? I think that you're *lying*. I'll *grill* you, and when I find you've lied, you'll be disgraced, and your life will be ruined. It's a sick game. Why do we do it? Does it educate? In no sense. Well, then, what is higher education? It is something-other-than-useful.

CAROL: What is "something-other-than-useful?"

JOHN: It has become a ritual, it has become an article of faith. That all must be subjected to, or to put it differently, that all are entitled to Higher Education. And my point…

CAROL: You disagree with that?

JOHN: Well, let's address that. What do you think?

CAROL: I don't know.

JOHN: What do you think, though? [*Pause*]

CAROL: I don't know.

JOHN: I spoke of it in class. Do you remember my example?

CAROL: Justice.

JOHN: Yes. Can you repeat it to me? [*She looks down at her notebook.*] Without your notes? I ask you as a favor to me, so that I can see if my idea was interesting.

CAROL: You said "justice"…

JOHN: Yes?

CAROL: …that all are entitled…[*Pause*] I…I…I…

JOHN: Yes. To a speedy trial. To a fair trial. But they needn't be given a trial *at all* unless they stand accused. Eh? Justice is their right, should they choose to avail themselves of it, they should have a fair trial. It does not follow, of necessity, a person's life is incomplete without a trial in it. Do you see?

        My point is a confusion between equity and *utility* arose. So we confound the *usefulness* of higher education with our, granted, right to equal access to the same. We, in effect, create a *prejudice* toward it, completely independent of…

CAROL: …that it is prejudice that we should go to school?

JOHN: Exactly. [*Pause*]

CAROL: How can you say that? How...

JOHN: Good. Good. *Good*. That's right! Speak up! What is a prejudice? An unrea-
soned belief. We are all subject to it. None of us is not. When it is threatened, or
opposed, we feel anger, and feel, do we not? As you do now. Do you not? Good.

CAROL: ...but how can you...

JOHN: ...let us examine. Good.

CAROL: How...

JOHN: Good. Good. When...

CAROL: I'M SPEAKING...[*Pause*]

JOHN: I'm sorry.

CAROL: How can you...

JOHN: ...I beg your pardon.

CAROL: That's all right.

JOHN: I beg your pardon.

CAROL: That's all right.

JOHN: I'm sorry I interrupted you.

CAROL: That's all right.

JOHN: You were saying?

CAROL: I was saying...I was saying...[*She checks her notes.*] How can you say in a
class. Say in a college class, that college education is prejudice?

JOHN: I said that our predilection for it...

CAROL: Predilection...

JOHN: ...you know what that means.

CAROL: Does it mean "liking"?

JOHN: Yes.

CAROL: But how can you say that? That College...

JOHN: ...that's my *job,* don't you know.

CAROL: What is?

JOHN: To provoke you.

CAROL: No.

JOHN: Oh. Yes, though.

CAROL: To provoke me?

JOHN: That's right.

CAROL: To make me mad?

JOHN: That's right. To force you...

CAROL: ...to make me mad is your job?

JOHN: To force you to...listen: [*Pause*] Ah. [*Pause*] When I was young somebody
told me, are you ready, the rich copulate less often than the poor. But
when they do, they take more of their clothes off. Years. Years, mind you,
I would compare experiences of my own to this dictum, saying, aha, this
fits the norm, or ah, this is a variation from it. What did it mean? Nothing.
It was some jerk thing, some school kid told me that took up room inside
my head. [*Pause*]

Somebody told *you,* and you hold it as an article of faith, that higher education
is an unassailable good. This notion is so dear to you that when I question it
you become angry. Good. Good, I say. Are not those the very things which we

should question? I say college education, since the war, has become so a matter of course, and such a fashionable necessity, for those either of or aspiring
to the new vast middle class, that we *espouse* it, as a matter of right, and have
ceased to ask, "What is it good for?" [*Pause*]

What might be some reasons for pursuit of higher education?
One: A love of learning.
Two: The wish for mastery of a skill.
Three: For economic betterment.
[*Stops. Makes a note.*]

CAROL: I'm keeping you.

JOHN: One moment. I have to make a note…

CAROL: It's something that I said?

JOHN: No, we're buying a house.

CAROL: You're buying the new house.

JOHN: To go with the tenure. That's right. Nice *house,* close to the *private*
school…[*He continues making his note.*]…We were talking of economic *bet-*
terment [CAROL *writes in her notebook.*]…I was thinking of the School Tax.
[*He continues writing.*] [*To himself:*]…*where is it written* that I have to send
my child to public school.…Is it a law that I have to improve the City Schools
at the expense of my own interest? And, is this not simply *The White Man's*
Burden? Good. And [*Looks up to* CAROL]…does this interest you?

CAROL: No. I'm taking notes…

JOHN: You don't have to take notes, you know, you can just listen.

CAROL: I want to make sure I remember it. [*Pause*]

JOHN: I'm not lecturing you, I'm just trying to tell you some things I think.

CAROL: What do you think?

JOHN: Should all kids go to college? *Why…*

CAROL: [*Pause*] To learn.

JOHN: But if he does not learn.

CAROL: If the child does not learn?

JOHN: Then why is he in college? Because he was told it was his "right"?

CAROL: Some might find college instructive.

JOHN: I would hope so.

CAROL: But how do they feel? Being told they are wasting their time?

JOHN: I don't think I'm telling them that.

CAROL: You said that education was "prolonged and systematic hazing."

JOHN: Yes. It can be so.

CAROL: …if education is so *bad,* why do you do it?

JOHN: I do it because I love it. [*Pause*] Let's.…I suggest you look at the demo-
graphics, wage-earning capacity, college- and non-college-educated men and
women, 1855 to 1980, and let's see if we can wring some worth from the
statistics. Eh? And…

CAROL: No.

JOHN: What?

CAROL: I can't understand them.

JOHN: …you…?

CAROL: …the "charts." The *Concepts,* the…

JOHN: "Charts" are simply…

CAROL: When I leave here…

JOHN: Charts, do you see…

CAROL: No, I can't….

JOHN: You can, though.

CAROL: NO, NO—I DON'T UNDERSTAND. DO YOU SEE??? I DON'T *UNDERSTAND*…

JOHN: What?

CAROL: *Any* of it. *Any* of it. I'm *smiling* in class, I'm *smiling,* the whole time. What are you *talking* about? What is everyone *talking* about? I don't *understand.* I don't know what it *means.* I don't know what it means to *be* here…you tell me I'm intelligent, and then you tell me I should not be *here,* what do you *want* with me? What does it *mean?* Who should I *listen* to…I…
[*He goes over to her and puts his arm around her shoulder.*]
NO! [*She walks away from him.*]

JOHN: Sshhhh.

CAROL: No, I don't under…

JOHN: Sshhhhh.

CAROL: I don't know what you're *saying*…

JOHN: Sshhhhh. It's all right.

CAROL: …I have to…

JOHN: Sshhhhh. Sshhhhh. Let it go a moment. [*Pause*] Sshhhhh…let it go. [*Pause*] Just let it go. [*Pause*] Just let it go. It's all right. [*Pause*] Sshhhhh. [*Pause*] I understand…[*Pause*] What do you feel?

CAROL: I feel bad.

JOHN: I know. It's all right.

CAROL: I…[*Pause*]

JOHN: What?

CAROL: I…

JOHN: What? Tell me.

CAROL: I don't understand you.

JOHN: I know. It's all right.

CAROL: I…

JOHN: What? [*Pause*] What? *Tell* me.

CAROL: I can't tell you.

JOHN: No, you must.

CAROL: I can't.

JOHN: No. Tell me. [*Pause*]

CAROL: I'm bad. [*Pause*] Oh, God. [*Pause*]

JOHN: It's all right.

CAROL: I'm…

JOHN: It's all right.

CAROL: I can't talk about this.

JOHN: It's all right. Tell me.

CAROL: Why do you want to know this?

JOHN: I don't want to know. I want to know whatever you…

CAROL: I always…

JOHN: …good…

CAROL: I always…all my life…I have never told anyone this…

JOHN: Yes. Go on. [*Pause*] Go on.

CAROL: All of my life…[*The phone rings.*] [*Pause.* JOHN *goes to the phone and picks it up.*]

JOHN: [*into phone*] I can't talk now. [*Pause*] What? [*Pause*] Hmm. [*Pause*] All right, I…I. Can't. Talk. Now. No, no, no, I *Know* I did, but….What? Hello. What? She *what?* She *can't,* she said the agreement is void? How, how is the agreement *void? That's Our House.*

I have the *paper;* when we come down, next week, with the payment, and the paper, that house is…wait, wait, wait, wait, wait, wait, wait: Did Jerry…is Jerry there? [*Pause*] Is *she* there…? Does she have a *lawyer*…? How the *hell,* how the *Hell.* That is…it's a question, you said, of the *easement.* I don't underst…it's not the *whole agreement.* It's just the *easement,* why would she? Put, put, put, *Jerry* on. [*Pause*] Jer, *Jerry:* What the *Hell*…that's my *house.* That's…Well, I'm no, no, no, I'm *not* coming ddd…List, *Listen, screw* her. You *tell* her. You, listen: I want you to take *Grace,* you take Grace, and get out of that house. You *leave* her there. Her and her lawyer, and you *tell* them, we'll see them in court next…no. No. Leave her there, leave her to *stew* in it: You tell her, we're *getting* that house, and we are going to…No. I'm *not* coming down. I'll be damned if I'll sit in the same rrr…the next, you tell her the next time I *see* her is in court…I…[*Pause*] What? [*Pause*] What? I don't understand. [*Pause*] Well, what about the house? [*Pause*] There isn't any problem with the hhh…[*Pause*] No, no, no, that's all right. All ri…All right…[*Pause*] Of course. Tha…Thank you. No, I will. Right away. [*He hangs up.*] [*Pause*]

CAROL: What is it? [*Pause*]

JOHN: It's a surprise party.

CAROL: It is.

JOHN: Yes.

CAROL: A party for you.

JOHN: Yes.

CAROL: Is it your birthday?

JOHN: No.

CAROL: What is it?

JOHN: The tenure announcement.

CAROL: The tenure announcement.

JOHN: They're throwing a party for us in our new house.

CAROL: Your new house.

JOHN: The house that we're buying.

CAROL: You have to go.

JOHN: It seems that I do.

CAROL: [*Pause*] They're proud of you.

JOHN: Well, there are those who would say it's a form of aggression.

CAROL: What is?

JOHN: A surprise.

TWO

JOHN *and* CAROL *seated across the desk from each other.*

JOHN: You see, [*pause*] I love to teach. And flatter myself I am *skilled* at it. And I love the, the aspect of *Performance*. I think I must confess that.

When I found I loved to teach I swore that I would not become that cold, rigid automaton of an instructor which I had encountered as a child.

Now, I was not unconscious that it was given me to err upon the other side. And, so, I asked and *ask* myself if I engaged in heterodoxy, I will not say "gratuitously" for I do not care to posit orthodoxy as a given good—but, "to the detriment of, of my students." [*Pause*]

As I said. When the possibility of tenure opened, and, of course, I'd long pursued it, I was, of course *happy,* and *covetous* of it. I asked myself if I was wrong to covet it. And thought about it long, and, I hope, truthfully, and saw in myself several things in, I think, no particular order. [*Pause*]

That I *would* pursue it. That I *desired* it, that I was not pure of longing for security, and that that, perhaps, was not reprehensible in me. That I had duties *beyond* the school, and that my duty to my home, for instance, was, or should be, if it were not, of an equal weight. That tenure, and security, and yes, and *comfort,* were not, of themselves, to be scorned; and were even worthy of honorable pursuit. And that it was given. Here, in this place, which I enjoy, and in which I find comfort, to assure myself of—as far as it rests in The Material—a continuation of that joy and comfort. In exchange for what? Teaching? Which I love.

What was the price of this security? To obtain *tenure*. Which tenure the committee is in the process of granting me. And on the basis of which I contracted to purchase a house. Now, as you don't have your own family, at this point, you may not know what that means. But to me it is important. A home. A Good Home. To raise my family. Now: The Tenure Committee will meet. This is the process, and a *good* process. Under which the school has functioned for quite a long time. They will meet, and hear your complaint—which you have the right to make; and they will dismiss it. They will *dismiss* your complaint; and, in the intervening period, I will lose my house. I will not be able to close on my house. I will lose my *deposit,* and the home I'd picked out for my wife and son will go by the boards. Now: I see I have angered you. I understand your anger at teachers. I was angry with mine. I felt hurt and humiliated by them. Which is one of the reasons that I went into education.

CAROL: What do you want of me?

JOHN: [*Pause*] I was hurt. When I received the report. Of the tenure committee. I was shocked. And I was hurt. No, I don't mean to subject you to my weak sensibilities. All right. Finally, I didn't understand. Then I thought: is it not always at those points at which we reckon ourselves unassailable that we are most vulnerable and…[*Pause*] Yes. All right. You find me pedantic. Yes. I am. By nature, by *birth,* by profession. I don't know…I'm always looking for a *paradigm* for…

CAROL: I don't know what a paradigm is.

JOHN: It's a model.

CAROL: Then why can't you use that word? [*Pause*]

JOHN: If it is important to you. Yes, all right. I was looking for a model. To continue: I feel that one point.

CAROL: I...

JOHN: One second...upon which I am unassailable is my unflinching concern for my students' dignity. I asked you here to...in the spirit of *investigation,* to ask you...to ask...[*Pause*] What have I done to you? [*Pause*] And, and, I suppose, how can I make amends. Can we not settle this now? It's pointless, really, and I want to know.

CAROL: What you can do to force me to retract?

JOHN: That is not what I meant at all.

CAROL: To bribe me, to convince me...

JOHN: ...No.

CAROL: To retract...

JOHN: That is not what I meant at all. I think that you know it is not.

CAROL: That is not what I know. I *wish* I...

JOHN: I do not want to...you wish what?

CAROL: No, you said what amends can you make. To force me to retract.

JOHN: That is not what I said.

CAROL: I have my notes.

JOHN: Look. Look. The Stoics say...

CAROL: The Stoics?

JOHN: The Stoical Philosophers say if you remove the phrase "I have been injured," you have removed the injury. Now: Think: I know that you're upset. Just tell me. Literally. Literally: what wrong have I done you?

CAROL: Whatever you have done to me—to the extent that you've done it to *me,* do you know, rather than to me as a *student,* and, so, to the student body, is contained in my report. To the tenure committee.

JOHN: Well, all right. [*Pause*] Let's see. [*He reads.*] I find that I am sexist. That I am *elitist.* I'm not sure I know what that means, other than it's a derogatory word, meaning "bad." That I...That I insist on wasting time, in nonprescribed, in self-aggrandizing and theatrical *diversions* from the prescribed *text*...that these have taken both sexist and pornographic forms...here we find listed...[*Pause*]. Here we find listed...instances "...closeted with a student"..."Told a rambling, sexually explicit story, in which the frequency and attitudes of fornication of the poor and rich are, it would seem, the central point...moved to *embrace* said student and...all part of a pattern..." [*Pause*]

[*He reads.*] That I used the phrase "The White Man's Burden"...that I told you how I'd asked you to my room because I quote like you. [*Pause*]

[*He reads.*] "He said he 'liked' me. That he 'liked being with me.' He'd let me write my examination paper over, if I could come back oftener to see him in his office." [*Pause*] [*To* CAROL:] It's *ludicrous.* Don't you know that? It's not *necessary.* It's going to *humiliate* you, and it's going to cost me my *house,* and...

CAROL: It's "*ludicrous...*"?

JOHN picks up the report and reads again.

JOHN: "He told me he had problems with his wife; and that he wanted to take off the artificial stricture of Teacher and Student. He put his arm around me..."

CAROL: Do you deny it? Can you deny it...? Do you see? [*Pause*] Don't you see? You don't see, do you?

JOHN: I don't see...

CAROL: You think, you think you can deny that these things happened; or, if they *did,* if they *did,* that they meant what you *said* they meant. Don't you see? You drag me in here, you drag us, to listen to you "go on"; and "go on" about this, or that, or we don't "express" ourselves very well. We don't say what we mean. Don't we? Don't we? We *do* say what we mean. And you say that "I don't understand you...." Then *you*...[*Points.*]

JOHN: "Consult the Report"?

CAROL: ...that's right.

JOHN: You see. You see. Can't you....You see what I'm saying? Can't you tell me in your own words?

CAROL: Those are my own words. [*Pause*]

JOHN: [*He reads.*] "He told me that if I would stay alone with him in his office, he would change my grade to an A." [*To* CAROL:] What have I done to you? Oh. My God, are you so hurt?

CAROL: What I "feel" is irrelevant. [*Pause*]

JOHN: Do you know that I tried to help you?

CAROL: What I know I have reported.

JOHN: I would like to help you now. I would. Before this escalates.

CAROL: [*simultaneously with* "escalates"] You see. I don't think that I need your help. I don't think I need anything you have.

JOHN: I feel...

CAROL: I don't *care* what you feel. Do you see? DO YOU SEE? You can't *do* that anymore. You. Do. Not. Have. The. Power. Did you misuse it? *Someone* did. Are you part of that group? *Yes. Yes.* You Are. You've *done* these things. And to say, and to say, "Oh. Let me help you with your problem..."

JOHN: Yes. I understand. I understand. You're *hurt.* You're *angry.* Yes. I think your *anger* is *betraying* you. Down a path which helps no one.

CAROL: I don't *care* what you think.

JOHN: You don't? [*Pause*] But you talk of *rights.* Don't you see? *I* have rights too. Do you see? I have a *house*...part of the *real* world; and The Tenure Committee, Good Men and True...

CAROL: ...Professor...

JOHN: ...Please: *Also* part of that world: you understand? This is my *life.* I'm not a *bogeyman.* I don't "stand" for something, I...

CAROL: ...Professor...

JOHN: ...I...

CAROL: Professor. I came here as a *favor.* At your personal request. Perhaps I should not have done so. But I did. On my behalf, and on behalf of my group. And you speak of the tenure committee, one of whose members is a woman, as you know. And though you might call it Good Fun, or An Historical Phrase, or An Oversight, or, All of the Above, to refer to the committee as Good Men and True, it is a demeaning remark. It is a sexist remark, and to overlook it is to countenance continuation of that method of thought. It's a remark…

JOHN: OH COME ON. Come on.…Sufficient to deprive a family of…

CAROL: Sufficient? Sufficient? Sufficient? Yes. It is a *fact*…and that story, which I quote, is *vile* and *classist,* and *manipulative* and *pornographic.* It…

JOHN: …it's pornographic…?

CAROL: What gives you the *right.* Yes. To speak to a *woman* in your private…Yes. Yes. I'm sorry. I'm sorry. You feel yourself empowered…you say so yourself. To *strut.* To *posture.* To "perform." To "Call me in here…" Eh? You say that higher education is a joke. And treat it as such, you *treat* it as such. And *confess* to a taste to play the *Patriarch* in your class. To grant *this*: To deny *that*: To embrace your students.

JOHN: How can you assert. How can you stand there and…

CAROL: How can you *deny* it. You did it to me. *Here.* You *did.*… You *confess.* You love the Power. To *deviate.* To *invent,* to transgress…to *transgress* whatever norms have been established for us. And you think it's charming to "question" in yourself this taste to mock and destroy. But you should question it. Professor. And you pick those things which you feel *advance* you: publication, *tenure,* and the steps to get them you call "harmless rituals." And you perform those steps. Although you say it is hypocrisy. But to the aspirations of your students. Of *hardworking students,* who come here, who *slave* to come here—you have no idea what it cost me to come to this school—you *mock* us. You call education "hazing," and from your so-protected, so-elitist seat you hold our confusion as a *joke,* and our hopes and efforts with it. Then you sit there and say "what have I done?" And ask me to understand that *you* have aspirations too. But I tell you. I tell you. That you are vile. And that you are exploitative. And if you possess one ounce of that inner honesty you describe in your book, you can look in yourself and see those things that I see. And you can find revulsion equal to my own. Good day. [*She prepares to leave the room.*]

JOHN: Wait a second, will you, just one moment. [*Pause*] Nice day today.

CAROL: What?

JOHN: You said "Good day." *I* think that it is a nice day today.

CAROL: *Is* it?

JOHN: Yes, I think it is.

CAROL: And why is that important?

JOHN: Because it is the essence of all human communication. I say something conventional, you respond, and the information we exchange is not about the "weather," but that we both agree to converse. In effect, we agree that we are both human. [*Pause*]

I'm not a…"exploiter," and you're not a…"deranged," what? *Revolutionary*… that we may, that we may have…positions, and that we may have…desires, which are in *conflict,* but that we're just human. [*Pause*] That means that sometimes we're *imperfect.* [*Pause*] Often we're in conflict…[*Pause*] *Much* of what we do, you're right, in the name of "principles" is *self-serving*...much of what we do is *conventional.* [*Pause*] You're right. [*Pause*] You said you came in the class because you wanted to learn about *education.* I don't know that I can teach you about education. But I know that I can tell you what I *think* about education, and then *you* decide. And you don't have to fight with me. *I'm* not the subject. [*Pause*] And where I'm *wrong*...perhaps it's not your job to "fix" me. I don't want to fix *you.* I would like to tell you what I *think,* because that *is* my job, conventional as it is, and flawed as I may be. And then, if you can show me some better *form,* then we can proceed from there. But, just like "nice day, isn't it...?" I don't think we can proceed until we accept that each of us is human. [*Pause*] And we still can have difficulties. We *will* have them...that's all right too. [*Pause*] Now:

CAROL: ...wait...

JOHN: Yes. I want to hear it.

CAROL: ...the...

JOHN: Yes. Tell me frankly.

CAROL: ...my position...

JOHN: I want to hear it. In your own words. What you want. And what you feel.

CAROL: ...I...

JOHN: ...yes...

CAROL: My Group.

JOHN: Your "Group"...? [*Pause*]

CAROL: The people I've been talking to...

JOHN: There's no shame in that. Everybody needs advisers. Everyone needs to expose themselves. To various points of view. It's not wrong. It's essential. Good. Good. Now: You and I...[*The phone rings.*]

You and I...

[*He hesitates for a moment, and then picks it up.*] [*Into phone*] Hello. [*Pause*] Um...no, I know they do. [*Pause*] I know she does. Tell her that I...can I call you back?...Then tell her that I think it's going to be fine. [*Pause*] Tell her just, just hold on, I'll...can I get back to you?...Well...no, no, no, we're *taking* the house...we're...no, no, nn...no, she will nnn, it's not a *question* of refunding the dep...no...it's not a *question* of the deposit...will you call Jerry? Babe, baby, will you just call Jerry? Tell him, nnn...tell him they, well, they're to keep the deposit, because the deal, be...because the deal is going to go *through*...because I know...be...will you please? Just *trust* me. Be...well, I'm dealing with the complaint. Yes. Right *Now.* Which is why I...yes, no, no, it's really, I can't *talk* about it now. Call Jerry, and I can't talk now. Ff...fine. Gg...good-bye. [*Hangs up.*] [*Pause*] I'm sorry we were interrupted.

CAROL: No...

JOHN: I...I was saying:

CAROL: You said that we should agree to talk about my complaint.

JOHN: That's correct.

CAROL: But we *are* talking about it.

JOHN: Well, that's correct too. You see? This is the *gist* of education.

CAROL: No, no. I mean, we're talking about it at the Tenure Committee Hearing. [*Pause*]

JOHN: Yes, but I'm saying: we can talk about it *now,* as easily as…

CAROL: No. I think that we should stick to the process…

JOHN: …wait a…

CAROL: …the "conventional" process. As you said. [*She gets up.*] And you're right, I'm sorry if I was, um, if I was "discourteous" to you. You're right.

JOHN: Wait, wait a…

CAROL: I really should go.

JOHN: Now, look, granted. I have an interest. In the status quo. All right? Everyone does. But what I'm saying is that the *committee*…

CAROL: Professor, you're right. Just don't impinge on me. We'll take our differences, and…

JOHN: You're going to make a…look, look, look, you're going to…

CAROL: I shouldn't have come here. They told me…

JOHN: One moment. No. No. There are *norms,* here, and there's no reason. Look: I'm trying to *save* you…

CAROL: No one *asked* you to…you're trying to save *me?* Do me the courtesy to…

JOHN: I *am* doing you the courtesy. I'm talking *straight* to you. We can settle this *now.* And I want you to sit *down* and…

CAROL: You must excuse me…[*She starts to leave the room.*]

JOHN: Sit down, it seems we each have a ….Wait one moment. Wait one moment… just do me the courtesy to…

He restrains her from leaving.

CAROL: LET ME GO.

JOHN: I have no desire to *hold* you, I just want to *talk* to you…

CAROL: LET ME GO. LET ME GO. WOULD SOMEBODY *HELP* ME? WOULD SOMEBODY *HELP* ME PLEASE…?

THREE

At rise, CAROL *and* JOHN *are seated.*

JOHN: I have asked you here. [*Pause*] I have asked you here against, against my…

CAROL: I was most surprised you asked me.

JOHN: …against my better *judgment,* against…

CAROL: I was most surprised…

JOHN: …against the…yes. I'm sure.

CAROL: …If you would like me to leave, I'll leave. I'll go right now…[*She rises.*]

JOHN: Let us begin *correctly,* may we? I feel…

CAROL: That is what I wished to do. That's why I came here, but now…

JOHN: …I feel…

CAROL: But now perhaps you'd like me to leave…

JOHN: I don't want you to leave. I asked you to come…

CAROL: I didn't have to come here.

JOHN: No. [*Pause*] Thank you.

CAROL: All right. [*Pause*] [*She sits down.*]

JOHN: Although I feel that it *profits,* it would *profit* you something, to…

CAROL: …what I…

JOHN: If you would hear me out, if you would hear me out.

CAROL: I came here to, the court officers told me not to come.

JOHN: …the "court" officers…?

CAROL: I was shocked that you asked.

JOHN: …wait…

CAROL: Yes. But I did *not* come here to hear what it "profits" me.

JOHN: The "court" officers…

CAROL: …no, no, perhaps I should leave…[*She gets up.*]

JOHN: Wait.

CAROL: No. I shouldn't have…

JOHN: …wait. Wait. Wait a moment.

CAROL: Yes? What is it you want? [*Pause*] What is it you want?

JOHN: I'd like you to stay.

CAROL: You want me to stay.

JOHN: Yes.

CAROL: You do.

JOHN: Yes. [*Pause*] Yes. I would like to have you hear me out. If you would. [*Pause*] Would you please? If you would do that I would be in your debt. [*Pause*] [*She sits.*] Thank you. [*Pause*]

CAROL: What is it you wish to tell me?

JOHN: All right. I cannot…[*Pause*] I cannot help but feel you are owed an apology. [*Pause*] [*Of papers in his hands*] I have read. [*Pause*] And reread these accusations.

CAROL: What "accusations"?

JOHN: The, the tenure comm…what other accusations…?

CAROL: The tenure committee…?

JOHN: Yes.

CAROL: Excuse me, but those are not accusations. They have been *proved.* They are facts.

JOHN: …I…

CAROL: No. Those are not "accusations."

JOHN: …those?

CAROL: …the committee [*The phone starts to ring.*] the committee has…

JOHN: …All right…

CAROL: …those are not accusations. The Tenure Committee.

JOHN: ALL RIGHT. ALL RIGHT. ALL RIGHT. [*He picks up the phone.*] Hello! Yes. No. I'm here. Tell Mister…No, I can't talk to him now…I'm sure he has, but I'm fff…I know…No, I have no time t…tell Mister…tell Mist…tell Jerry that I'm *fine* and that I'll call him right aw…[*Pause*] My wife…Yes. I'm sure she has. Yes, thank you. Yes, I'll call her too. I cannot talk to you now. [*He hangs up.*] [*Pause*] All right. It was good of you to come Thank you. I have studied. I have spent some time studying the indictment.

CAROL: You will have to explain that word to me.

JOHN: An "indictment"...

CAROL: Yes.

JOHN: Is a "bill of particulars." A...

CAROL: All right. Yes.

JOHN: In which is alleged...

CAROL: No. I cannot allow that. I cannot allow that. Nothing is alleged. Everything is proved...

JOHN: Please, wait a sec...

CAROL: I cannot *come* to allow...

JOHN: If I may...If I may, from whatever you feel is "established," by...

CAROL: The issue here is not what I "feel." It is not my "feelings," but the feelings of women. And men. Your superiors, who've been "polled," do you see? To whom *evidence* has been presented, who have *ruled*, do you see? Who have weighed the testimony and the evidence, and have *ruled*, do you see? That you are *negligent*. That you are *guilty*, that you are found *wanting*, and in *error*; and are *not*, for the reasons so-told, to be given tenure. That you are to be disciplined. For facts. For *facts*. Not "alleged," what is the word? But *proved*. Do you see? *By your own actions*.

That is what the tenure committee has said. That is what my lawyer said. For what you did in class. For what you did *in this office*.

JOHN: They're going to discharge me.

CAROL: As full well they should. You don't understand? You're angry? What has *led* you to this place? Not your sex. Not your race. Not your class. YOUR OWN ACTIONS. And you're *angry*. You *ask* me here. What *do* you want? You want to "charm" me. You want to "convince" me. You want me to recant. I will *not* recant. Why should I...? What I say is right. You tell me, you are going to tell me that you have a wife and child. You are going to say that you have a career and that you've worked for twenty years for this. Do you know what you've *worked* for? *Power*. For *power*. Do you understand? And you sit there, and you tell me *stories*. About your *house*, about all the private *schools*, and about *privilege*, and how you are entitled. To *buy*, to *spend*, to *mock*, to *summon*. All your stories: All your silly weak *guilt*, it's all about *privilege*; and you won't know it. Don't you see? You worked twenty years for the right to *insult* me. And you feel entitled to be *paid* for it. Your Home. Your Wife...Your sweet "deposit" on your house...

JOHN: Don't you have feelings?

CAROL: That's my point. You see? Don't you have feelings? Your final argument. What is it that has no feelings. *Animals*. I don't take your side, you question if I'm Human.

JOHN: Don't you have feelings?

CAROL: I have a responsibility. I...

JOHN: ...to...?

CAROL: To? This institution. To the *students*. To my *group*.

JOHN: ...your "group."...

CAROL: Because I speak, yes, not for myself. But for the group; for those who suffer what I suffer. On behalf of whom, even if I, were, inclined, to what, forgive? Forget? What? Overlook your...

JOHN: …my behavior?

CAROL: …it would be wrong.

JOHN: Even if you were inclined to "forgive" me.

CAROL: It would be wrong.

JOHN: And what would transpire.

CAROL: Transpire?

JOHN: Yes.

CAROL: "Happen?"

JOHN: Yes.

CAROL: Then *say* it. For Christ's sake. Who the *hell* do you think that you are? You want a post. You want unlimited power. To do and to say what you want. As it pleases you—Testing, Questioning, Flirting…

JOHN: I never…

CAROL: Excuse me, one moment, will you?

[*She reads from her notes.*]

The twelfth: "Have a good day, dear."

The fifteenth: "Now, don't *you* look fetching…"

April seventeenth: "If you girls would come over here…" I saw you. I saw you, Professor. For two semesters sit there, stand there and exploit our, as you thought, "paternal prerogative," and what is that but rape, I swear to God. You asked me in here to explain something to me, as a child, that I did not understand. But I came to explain something to you. You Are Not God. You ask me why I came? I came here to instruct you.

[*She produces his book.*]

And your book? You think you're going to show me some "light"? You "*maverick.*" Outside of tradition. No, no, [*She reads from the book's liner notes.*] "*of* that fine tradition of *inquiry.* Of Polite *skepticism*"…and you say you believe in free intellectual discourse. YOU BELIEVE IN NOTHING. YOU BELIEVE IN NOTHING AT ALL.

JOHN: I believe in freedom of thought.

CAROL: Isn't that fine. *Do* you?

JOHN: Yes. I do.

CAROL: Then why do you question, for one moment, the committee's decision refusing your tenure? Why do you question your suspension? You believe in what *you call* freedom of thought. Then, fine. *You* believe in freedom-of-thought *and* a home, and, *and* prerogatives for your kid, *and* tenure. And I'm going to tell you. You believe *not* in "freedom of thought," but in an elitist in, in a protected hierarchy which rewards you. And for whom you are the clown. And you mock and exploit the system which pays your rent. You're wrong. I'm not wrong. You're wrong. You think that I'm full of hatred. I know what you think I am.

JOHN: Do you?

CAROL: You think I'm a, of course I do. You think I am a frightened, repressed, confused, I don't know, abandoned young thing of some doubtful sexuality, who wants, power and revenge. [*Pause*] *Don't* you? [*Pause*]

JOHN: Yes. I do. [*Pause*]

CAROL: Isn't that better? And I feel that that is the first moment which you've treated me with respect. For you told me the truth. [*Pause*] I did not come here,
as you are assured, to gloat. Why would I want to gloat? I've profited nothing
from your, your, as you say, your "misfortune." I came here, as you did me the
honor to *ask* me here, I came here to *tell* you something.

[*Pause*] That I think...that I think you've been wrong. That I think you've
been terribly wrong. Do you hate me now? [*Pause*]

JOHN: Yes.

CAROL: Why do you hate me? Because you think me wrong? No. Because I have,
you think, *power* over you. Listen to me. Listen to me, Professor. [*Pause*] It is
the power that you hate. So deeply that, that any atmosphere of free discussion is impossible. It's not "unlikely." It's *impossible*. Isn't it?

JOHN: Yes.

CAROL: *Isn't* it...?

JOHN: Yes. I suppose.

CAROL: Now. The thing which you find so cruel is the self-same process of
selection I, and my group, go through *every day of our lives*. In admittance
to school. In our tests, in our class rankings....Is it unfair? I can't tell you.
But, if it is fair. Or even if it is "unfortunate but necessary" for us, then, by
God, so must it be for you. [*Pause*] You write of your "responsibility to the
young." Treat us with respect, and that will *show* you your responsibility.
You write that education is just hazing. [*Pause*] But we worked to get to this
school.

[*Pause*] And some of us. [*Pause*] Overcame prejudices. Economic, sexual, you
cannot begin to imagine. And endured humiliations I *pray* that you and those
you love never will encounter. [*Pause*] To gain admittance here. To pursue
that same dream of security *you* pursue. We, who, who are, at any moment,
in danger of being deprived of it. By...

JOHN: ...by...?

CAROL: By the administration. By the teachers. By *you*. By, say, one low grade,
that keeps us out of graduate school; by one, say, one capricious or inventive
answer on our parts, which, perhaps, you don't find amusing. Now you *know*,
do you see? What it is to be subject to that power. [*Pause*]

JOHN: I don't understand. [*Pause*]

CAROL: My charges are not trivial. You see that in the haste, I think, with which
they were accepted. A *joke* you have told, with a sexist tinge. The language
you use, a verbal or physical caress, yes, yes, I know, you say that it is meaningless. I understand. I differ from you. To lay a hand on someone's shoulder.

JOHN: It was devoid of sexual content.

CAROL: I say it was not. I SAY IT WAS NOT. Don't you begin to *see*...? Don't you
begin to understand? IT'S NOT FOR YOU TO SAY.

JOHN: I take your point, and I see there is much good in what you refer to.

CAROL: ...do you think so...?

JOHN: ...but, and this is not to say that I cannot change, in those things in which
I am deficient...But, the...

CAROL: Do you hold yourself harmless from the charges of sexual exploitativeness...?
[*Pause*]

JOHN: Well, I...I...I...You know I, as I said, I...think I am not too old to *learn*,
and I *can* learn, I...

CAROL: Do you hold yourself innocent of the charge of...

JOHN: ...wait, wait, wait...All right, let's go back to...

CAROL: YOU FOOL. Who do you think I am? To come here and be taken in by a
smile. You little yapping fool. You think I want "revenge." I don't want revenge.
I WANT UNDERSTANDING.

JOHN: ...*do* you?

CAROL: I do. [*Pause*]

JOHN: What's the use. It's over.

CAROL: Is it? What is?

JOHN: My job.

CAROL: Oh. Your job. That's what you want to talk about. [*Pause*] [*She starts to
leave the room. She steps and turns back to him.*] All right. [*Pause*] What if it
were possible that my Group withdraws its complaint. [*Pause*]

JOHN: What?

CAROL: That's right. [*Pause*]

JOHN: Why.

CAROL: Well, let's say as an act of friendship.

JOHN: An act of friendship.

CAROL: Yes. [*Pause*]

JOHN: In exchange for what.

CAROL: Yes. But I don't think, "exchange." Not "in exchange." For what do we derive
from it? [*Pause*]

JOHN: "Derive."

CAROL: Yes.

JOHN: [*Pause*] Nothing. [*Pause*]

CAROL: That's right. We derive nothing. [*Pause*] Do you see that?

JOHN: Yes.

CAROL: That is a little word, Professor. "Yes." "I see that." But you will.

JOHN: And you might speak to the committee...?

CAROL: To the committee?

JOHN: Yes.

CAROL: Well. Of course. That's on your mind. We might.

JOHN: "If" what?

CAROL: "Given" what. Perhaps. I think that that is more friendly.

JOHN: GIVEN WHAT?

CAROL: And, believe me, I understand your rage. It is not that I don't feel it. But
I do not see that it is deserved, so I do not resent it....All right. I have a list.

JOHN: ...a list.

CAROL: Here is a list of books, which we...

JOHN: ...a list of books...?

CAROL: That's right. Which we find questionable.

JOHN: What?

CAROL: Is this so bizarre...?

JOHN: I can't believe...

CAROL: It's not necessary you believe it.

JOHN: Academic freedom...

CAROL: Someone chooses the books. If you can choose them, others can. What are you, "God"?

JOHN: ...no, no, the "dangerous."...

CAROL: You have an agenda, we have an agenda. I am not interested in your feelings or your motivation, but your actions. If you would like me to speak to the Tenure Committee, here is my list. You are a Free Person, you decide. [*Pause*]

JOHN: Give me the list. [*She does so. He reads.*]

CAROL: I think you'll find...

JOHN: I'm capable of reading it. Thank you.

CAROL: We have a number of *texts* we need re...

JOHN: I see that.

CAROL: We're amenable to...

JOHN: Aha. Well, let me look over the...[*He reads.*]

CAROL: I think that...

JOHN: LOOK. I'm reading your demands. All right?! [*He reads*] [*Pause*] You want to ban my book?

CAROL: We do not...

JOHN: [*Of list*] It says here...

CAROL: ...We want it removed from inclusion as a representative example of the university.

JOHN: Get out of here.

CAROL: If you put aside the issues of personalities.

JOHN: Get the fuck out of my office.

CAROL: No, I think I would reconsider.

JOHN: ...you think you can.

CAROL: We can and we *will*. Do you want our support? That is the only quest...

JOHN: ...to ban my *book*...?

CAROL: ...that is correct...

JOHN: ...this...this is a *university*...we...

CAROL: ...and we have a statement...which we need you to...[*She hands him a sheet of paper.*]

JOHN: No, no. It's out of the question. I'm sorry, I don't know what I was thinking of. I want to tell you something. I'm a teacher. I am a teacher. Eh? It's my *name* on the door, and *I* teach the class, and that's what I do. I've got a book with my name on it. And my son will *see* that *book* someday. And I have a respon...No, I'm sorry I have a *responsibility*...to *myself*, to my *son*, to my *profession*.... I haven't been *home* for two days, do you know that? Thinking this out.

CAROL: ...you haven't?

JOHN: I've been, no. If it's of interest to you. I've been in a *hotel. Thinking.* [*The phone starts ringing.*] *Thinking*...

CAROL: ...you haven't been home?

JOHN: ...*thinking*, do you see?

CAROL: Oh.

JOHN: And, and, I owe you a debt, I see that now. [*Pause*] You're *dangerous,* you're *wrong* and it's my *job*…to say no to you. That's my job. You are absolutely right. You want to ban my book? Go to *hell,* and they can do whatever they want to me.

CAROL: …you haven't been home in two days…

JOHN: I think I told you that.

CAROL: …you'd better get that phone. [*Pause*] I think that you should pick up the phone. [*Pause*]

JOHN *picks up the phone.*

JOHN: [*on phone*] Yes. [*Pause*] Yes. Wh…I. I. I had to be away. All ri…did they wor…did they worry ab…No. I'm all right, now, Jerry. I'm f…I got a little turned *around,* but I'm *sitting* here and…I've got it figured out. I'm fine. I'm fine don't worry about me. I got a little bit mixed up. But I am not sure that it's not a blessing. It cost me my job? Fine. Then the job was not worth having. Tell Grace that I'm coming home and everything is fff…[*Pause*] What? [*Pause*] *What?* [*Pause*] What do you *mean?* WHAT? Jerry…
Jerry. They…Who, who, what can they do…? [*Pause*] NO. [*Pause*] NO. They can't do th…What do you mean? [*Pause*] But how…[*Pause*] She's, she's, she's *here* with me. To…Jerry. I don't underst…[*Pause*] [*He hangs up.*] [*To* CAROL:] What does this mean?

CAROL: I thought you knew.

JOHN: What. [*Pause*] What does it mean. [*Pause*]

CAROL: You tried to rape me. [*Pause*] According to the law. [*Pause*]

JOHN: …what…?

CAROL: You tried to rape me. I was leaving this office, you "pressed" yourself into me. You "pressed" your body into me.

JOHN: …I…

CAROL: My Group has told your lawyer that we may pursue criminal charges.

JOHN: …no…

CAROL: …under the statute. I am told. It was battery.

JOHN: …no…

CAROL: Yes. And attempted rape. That's right. [*Pause*]

JOHN: I think that you should go.

CAROL: Of course. I thought you knew.

JOHN: I have to talk to my lawyer.

CAROL: Yes. Perhaps you should. [*The phone rings again.*] [*Pause*]

JOHN: [*Picks up phone. Into phone:*] Hello? I…Hello…? I…Yes, he just called. No…I. I can't talk to you now, Baby. [*To* CAROL:] Get out.

CAROL: …your wife…?

JOHN: …who it is is no concern of yours. Get out. [*To phone:*] No, no, it's going to be all right. I. I can't talk now, Baby. [*To* CAROL:] Get out of here.

CAROL: I'm going.

JOHN: Good.

CAROL: [*exiting*] …and don't call your wife "baby."

JOHN: What?

CAROL: Don't call your wife baby. You heard what I said.

CAROL *starts to leave the room.* JOHN *grabs her and begins to beat her.*

JOHN: You vicious little bitch. You think you can come in here with your political correctness and destroy my life?

He knocks her to the floor.

> After how I treated you...? You should be...*Rape you...?* Are you kidding me...?

He picks up a chair, raises it above his head, and advances on her.

> I wouldn't touch you with a ten-foot pole. You little *cunt*...

She cowers on the floor below him. Pause. He looks down at her. He lowers the chair. He moves to his desk, and arranges the papers on it. Pause. He looks over at her.

> ...well...

Pause. She looks at him.

CAROL: Yes. That's right.

> [*She looks away from him, and lowers her head. To herself:*]...yes. That's right.

End

MAKING CONNECTIONS

1. Describe John and Carol. Did you find yourself favoring one or the other as the play progressed? Explain.
2. The entire play is set in John's office. Why? In what way is this setting important to the play?
3. At the beginning of both Act 2 and Act 3, time has passed, and we are presented with new and important information. Were you surprised or shocked by these revelations? Explain.
4. What is your reaction to the ending of the play? To the charge against John? To his physical attack of Carol?
5. Who do you think is right, John or Carol? Why?
6. What is the central idea or theme of this play? What does it mean?

MAKING AN ARGUMENT

1. Take a position in favor of [or against] John or Carol. Write an essay supporting your position. Cite the text of the play—and any other appropriate sources—to support your view.

JOHN MILLINGTON SYNGE [1871–1909]

Irish dramatist, poet, prose writer, and folklorist J. M. Synge was a major contributor to the Irish Literary Revival and one of the cofounders of the Abbey Theatre. He is best known for two critically acclaimed plays, Riders to the Sea *(1905) and* The Playboy of the Western World *(1907), which caused riots in Dublin during its opening run at the Abbey Theatre. Although he came from a middle-class Protestant background, Synge's writings focused on the*

lives of Catholic peasants on the Aran Islands off the west coast of Ireland—and their experience of a world dominated by a relentless struggle with the sea. Synge wrote four other notable plays during his brief, cancer-shortened life. In the Shadow of the Glen *and* The Well of the Saints *were produced in 1905. Two other plays,* Deirdre of the Sorrows *(1910) and* The Tinker's Wedding *(1912), were produced posthumously.*

RIDERS TO THE SEA   [1905]

LIST OF CHARACTERS
MAURYA, *an old woman*
BARTLEY, *her son*
CATHLEEN, *her daughter*
NORA, *a younger daughter*
MEN *and* WOMEN

SCENE: An island off the West of Ireland. Cottage kitchen, with nets, oil-skins, spinning-wheel, some new boards standing by the wall, etc. CATHLEEN, *a girl of about twenty, finishes kneading cake, and puts it down in the pot-oven by the fire; then wipes her hands, and begins to spin at the wheel.* NORA, *a young girl puts her head in at the door.*

NORA: [*in a low voice*] Where is she?

CATHLEEN: She's lying down, God help her, and may be sleeping, if she's able.

NORA *comes in softly, and takes a bundle from under her shawl.*

CATHLEEN [*spinning the wheel rapidly*]:   What is it you have?

NORA: The young priest is after bringing them. It's a shirt and a plain stocking were got off a drowned man in Donegal.

CATHLEEN *stops her wheel with a sudden movement, and leans out to listen.*

NORA: We're to find out if it's Michael's they are, some time herself will be down looking by the sea.

CATHLEEN: How would they be Michael's, Nora? How would he go the length of that way to the far north?

NORA: The young priest says he's known the like of it. "If it's Michael's they are," says he, "you can tell herself he's got a clean burial by the grace of God, and if they're not his, let no one say a word about them, for she'll be getting her death," says he, "with crying and lamenting."

The door which NORA *half-closed is blown open by a gust of wind.*

CATHLEEN [*looking out anxiously*]:   Did you ask him would he stop Bartley going this day with the horses to the Galway fair?

NORA: "I won't stop him," says he, "but let you not be afraid. Herself does be saying prayers half through the night and the Almighty God won't leave her destitute," says he, "with no son living."

CATHLEEN: Is the sea bad by the white rocks, Nora?

NORA: Middling bad, God help us. There's a great roaring in the west, and it's worse it'll be getting when the tide's turned to the wind. [*She goes over to the table with the bundle.*] Shall I open it now?

CATHLEEN: Maybe she'd wake up on us, and come in before we'd done. [*Coming to the table.*] It's a long time we'll be, and the two of us crying.

NORA [*goes to the inner door and listens*]:   She's moving about on the bed. She'll be coming in a minute.

CATHLEEN: Give me the ladder, and I'll put them up in the turf-loft, the way she won't know of them at all, and maybe when the tide turns she'll be going down to see would he be floating from the east.

They put the ladder against the gable of the chimney; CATHLEEN *goes up a few steps and hides the bundle in the turf-loft.* MAURYA *comes from the inner room.*

MAURYA [*looking up at* CATHLEEN *and speaking querulously*]:   Isn't it turf enough you have for this day and evening?

CATHLEEN: There's a cake baking at the fire for a short space [*throwing down the turf*] and Bartley will want it when the tide turns if he goes to Connemara.

NORA *picks up the turf and puts it round the pot-oven.*

MAURYA [*sitting down on a stool at the fire*]:   He won't go this day with the wind rising from the south and west. He won't go this day, for the young priest will stop him surely.

NORA: He'll not stop him, mother, and I heard Eamon Simon and Stephen Pheety and Colum Shawn saying he would go.

MAURYA: Where is he itself?

NORA: He went down to see would there be another boat sailing in the week, and I'm thinking it won't be long till he's here now, for the tide's turning at the green head, and the hooker's[1] tacking from the east.

CATHLEEN: I hear some one passing the big stones.

NORA [*looking out*]:   He's coming now, and he in a hurry.

BARTLEY [*comes in and looks round the room. Speaking sadly and quietly*]:   Where is the bit of new rope, Cathleen, was bought in Connemara?

CATHLEEN [*coming down*]:   Give it to him, Nora; it's on a nail by the white boards. I hung it up this morning, for the pig with the black feet was eating it.

NORA [*giving him a rope*]:   Is that it, Bartley?

MAURYA: You'd do right to leave that rope, Bartley, hanging by the boards. [BARTLEY *takes the rope.*] It will be wanting in this place, I'm telling you, if Michael is washed up tomorrow morning, or the next morning, or any morning in the week, for it's a deep grave we'll make him by the grace of God.

BARTLEY [*beginning to work with the rope*]:   I've no halter the way I can ride down on the mare, and I must go now quickly. This is the one boat going for two weeks or beyond it, and the fair will be a good fair for horses I heard them saying below.

MAURYA: It's a hard thing they'll be saying below if the body is washed up and there's no man in it to make the coffin, and I after giving a big price for the finest white boards you'd find in Connemara.

She looks round at the boards.

---

[1]**hooker** a small fishing boat

BARTLEY: How would it be washed up, and we after looking each day for nine days, and a strong wind blowing a while back from the west and south?

MAURYA: If it wasn't found itself, that wind is raising the sea, and there was a star up against the moon, and it rising in the night. If it was a hundred horses, or a thousand horses you had itself, what is the price of a thousand horses against a son where there is one son only?

BARTLEY [*working at the halter, to* CATHLEEN]:   Let you go down each day, and see the sheep aren't jumping in on the rye, and if the jobber comes you can sell the pig with the black feet if there is a good price going.

MAURYA: How would the like of her get a good price for a pig?

BARTLEY [*to* CATHLEEN]:   If the west wind holds with the last bit of the moon let you and Nora get up weed enough for another cock for the kelp:[2] It's hard set we'll be from this day with no one in it but one man to work.

MAURYA: It's hard set we'll be surely the day you're drownd'd with the rest! What way will I live and the girls with me, and I an old woman looking for the grave?

BARTLEY *lays down the halter, takes off his old coat, and puts on a newer one of the same flannel.*

BARTLEY [*to* NORA]:   Is she coming to the pier?

NORA [*looking out*]:   She's passing the green head and letting fall her sails.

BARTLEY [*getting his purse and tobacco*]:   I'll have half an hour to go down, and you'll see me coming again in two days, or in three days, or maybe in four days if the wind is bad.

MAURYA [*turning round to the fire, and putting her shawl over her head*]:   Isn't it a hard and cruel man won't hear a word from an old woman, and she holding him from the sea?

CATHLEEN: It's the life of a young man to be going on the sea, and who would listen to an old woman with one thing and she saying it over?

BARTLEY [*taking the halter*]:   I must go now quickly. I'll ride down on the red mare, and the gray pony'll run behind me.... The blessing of God on you.

He goes out.

MAURYA [*crying out as he is in the door*]:   He's gone now, God spare us, and we'll not see him again. He's gone now, and when the black night is falling I'll have no son left me in the world.

CATHLEEN: Why wouldn't you give him your blessing and he looking round in the door? Isn't it sorrow enough is on every one in this house without your sending him out with an unlucky word behind him, and a hard word in his ear?

MAURYA *takes up the tongs and begins raking the fire aimlessly without looking round.*

NORA [*turning towards her*]:   You're taking away the turf from the cake

CATHLEEN [*crying out*]:   The Son of God forgive us, Nora, we're after forgetting his bit of bread.

---

[2]**kelp** seaweed

She comes over to the fire.

NORA: And it's destroyed he'll be going till dark night, and he after eating nothing since the sun went up.

CATHLEEN [*turning the cake out of the oven*]:   It's destroyed he'll be, surely. There's no sense left on any person in a house where an old woman will be talking for ever.

MAURYA *sways herself on her stool.*

CATHLEEN [*cutting off some of the bread and rolling it in a cloth; to* MAURYA]:   Let you go down now to the spring well and give him this and he passing. You'll see him then and the dark word will be broken, and you can say "God speed you," the way he'll be easy in his mind.

MAURYA [*taking the bread*]:   Will I be in it as soon as himself?

CATHLEEN: If you go now quickly.

MAURYA [*standing up unsteadily*]:   It's hard set I am to walk.

CATHLEEN [*looking at her anxiously*]:   Give her the stick, Nora, or maybe she'll slip on the big stones.

NORA: What stick?

CATHLEEN: The stick Michael brought from Connemara.

MAURYA [*taking a stick* NORA *gives her*]:   In the big world the old people do be leaving things after them for their son and children, but in this place it is the young men do be leaving things behind for them that do be old.

She goes out slowly. NORA *goes over to the ladder.*

CATHLEEN: Wait, Nora, maybe she'd turn back quickly. She's that sorry, God help her, you wouldn't know the thing she'd do.

NORA: Is she gone around by the bush?

CATHLEEN [*looking out*]:   She's gone, now! Throw it down quickly, for the Lord knows when she'll be out of it again.

NORA [*getting the bundle from the loft*]:   The young priest said he'd be passing to-morrow; and we might go down and speak to him below if it's Michael's they are surely.

CATHLEEN [*taking the bundle*]:   Did he say what way they were found?

NORA [*coming down*]:   "There were two men" says he, "and they rowing round with poteen[3] before the cocks crowed and the oar of one of them caught the body, and they passing the black cliffs of the north."

CATHLEEN [*trying to open the bundle*]:   Give me a knife, Nora the strings perished with the salt water and there's a black knot on it you wouldn't loosen in a week.

NORA [*giving her a knife*]:   I've heard tell it was a long way to Donegal.

CATHLEEN [*cutting the string*]:   It is surely. There was a man in here a while ago— the man sold us that knife—and he said if you set off walking from the rock beyond, it would be seven days you'd be in Donegal.

NORA: And what time would a man take, and he floating?

---

[3]**poteen** whiskey

CATHLEEN *opens the bundle and takes out a bit of a stocking. They look at them eagerly.*

CATHLEEN [*in a low voice*]:   The Lord spare us, Nora! isn't it a queer hard thing to say if it's his they are surely?

NORA: I'll get his shirt off the hook the way we can put the one flannel on the other. [*She looks through some clothes hanging in the corner.*] It's not with them, Cathleen, and where will it be?

CATHLEEN: I'm thinking Bartley put it on him in the morning, for his own shirt was heavy with the salt in it. [*Pointing to the corner.*] There's a bit of a sleeve was of the same stuff. Give me that and it will do.

NORA *brings it to her and they compare the flannel.*

CATHLEEN: It's the same stuff, Nora; but if it is itself aren't there great rolls of it in the shops of Galway, and isn't it many another man may have a shirt of it as well as Michael himself?

NORA [*who has taken up the stocking and counted the stitches, crying out*]:   It's Michael, Cathleen, it's Michael; God spare his soul, and what will herself say when she hears this story, and Bartley on the sea?

CATHLEEN [*taking the stocking*]:   It's a plain stocking.

NORA: It's the second one of the third pair I knitted, and I put up three score stitches, and I dropped four of them.

CATHLEEN [*counts the stitches*]:   It's that number is in it. [*Crying out.*] Ah, Nora, isn't it a bitter thing to think of him floating that way to the far north, and no one to keen[4] him but the black hags that do be flying on the sea?

NORA [*swinging herself round, and throwing out her arms on the clothes*]:   And isn't it a pitiful thing when there is nothing left of a man who was a great rower and fisher, but a bit of an old shirt and a plain stocking?

CATHLEEN [*after an instant*]:   Tell me is herself coming, Nora? I hear a little sound on the path.

NORA [*looking out*]:   She is, Cathleen. She's coming up to the door.

CATHLEEN: Put these things away before she'll come in. Maybe it's easier she'll be after giving her blessing to Bartley, and we won't let on we've heard anything the time he's on the sea.

NORA [*helping* CATHLEEN *to close the bundle*]:   We'll put them here in the corner.

They put them into a hole in the chimney corner. CATHLEEN *goes back to the spinning-wheel.*

NORA: Will she see it was crying I was?

CATHLEEN: Keep your back to the door the way the light'll not be on you.

NORA *sits down at the chimney corner, with her back to the door.* MAURYA *comes in very slowly, without looking at the girls, and goes over to her stool at the other side of the fire. The cloth with the bread is still in her hand. The girls look at each other, and* NORA *points to the bundle of bread.*

CATHLEEN [*after spinning for a moment*]:   You didn't give him his bit of bread?

---

[4]**keen** a mournful weeping and wailing

MAURYA *begins to keen softly, without turning round*.

CATHLEEN: Did you see him riding down?

MAURYA *goes on keening*.

CATHLEEN [*a little impatiently*]:   God forgive you; isn't it a better thing to raise your voice and tell what you seen, than to be making lamentation for a thing that's done? Did you see Bartley, I'm saying to you.

MAURYA [*with a weak voice*]:   My heart's broken from this day.

CATHLEEN [*as before*]:   Did you see Bartley?

MAURYA: I seen the fearfulest thing.

CATHLEEN [*leaves her wheel and looks out*]:   God forgive you; he's riding the mare now over the green head, and the gray pony behind him.

MAURYA [*starts, so that her shawl falls back from her head and shows her white tossed hair. With a frightened voice*]:   The gray pony behind him.

CATHLEEN [*coming to the fire*]:   What is it ails you, at all?

MAURYA [*speaking very slowly*]:   I've seen the fearfulest thing any person has seen, since the day Bride Dara seen the dead man with the child in his arms.

CATHLEEN AND NORA: Uah.

They crouch down in front of the old woman at the fire.

NORA: Tell us what it is you seen.

MAURYA: I went down to the spring well, and I stood there saying a prayer to myself. Then Bartley came along, and he riding on the red mare with the gray pony behind him. [*She puts up her hands, as if to hide something from her eyes.*] The Son of God spare us, Nora!

CATHLEEN: What is it you seen?

MAURYA: I seen Michael himself.

CATHLEEN [*speaking softly*]:   You did not, mother, it wasn't Michael you seen, for his body is after being found in the far north, and he's got a clean burial by the grace of God.

MAURYA [*a little defiantly*]:   I'm after seeing him this day, and he riding and galloping. Bartley came first on the red mare; and I tried to say "God speed you," but something choked the words in my throat. He went by quickly; and "the blessing of God on you," says he, and I could say nothing. I looked up then, and I crying, at the gray pony, and there was Michael upon it—with fine clothes on him, and new shoes on his feet.

CATHLEEN [*begins to keen*]:   It's destroyed we are from this day. It's destroyed, surely.

NORA: Didn't the young priest say the Almighty God wouldn't leave her destitute with no son living?

MAURYA [*in a low voice, but clearly*]:   It's little the like of him knows of the sea....Bartley will be lost now, and let you call in Eamon and make me a good coffin out of the white boards, for I won't live after them. I've had a husband, and a husband's father, and six sons in this house—six fine men, though it was a hard birth I had with every one of them and they coming to the world—and some of them were found and some of them were not found, but they're gone now the lot of them.... There were Stephen and Shawn were lost in the great wind, and found after in the Bay of Gregory of the Golden Mouth, and carried up the two of them on the one plank, and in by that door.

She pauses for a moment, the girls start as if they heard something through the door that is half open behind them.

NORA [*in a whisper*]:   Did you hear that, Cathleen? Did you hear a noise in the north-east?

CATHLEEN [*in a whisper*]:   There's someone after crying out by the seashore.

MAURYA [*continues without hearing anything*]:   There was Sheamus and his father, and his own father again, were lost in a dark night, and not a stick or sign was seen of them when the sun went up. There was Patch after was drowned out of a curagh[5] that turned over. I was sitting here with Bartley, and he a baby, lying on my two knees, and I seen two women, and three women, and four women coming in, and they crossing themselves, and not saying a word. I looked out then, and there were men coming after them, and they holding a thing in the half of a red sail, and water dripping out of it—it was a dry day, Nora—and leaving a track to the door.

She pauses again with her hand stretched out towards the door. It opens softly and old women begin to come in, crossing themselves on the threshold, and kneeling down in front of the stage with red petticoats over their heads.

MAURYA [*half in a dream, to* CATHLEEN]:   Is it Patch, or Michael, or what is it at all?

CATHLEEN: Michael is after being found in the far north, and when he is found there how could he be here in this place?

MAURYA: There does be a power of young men floating round in the sea, and what way would they know if it was Michael they had, or another man like him, for when a man is nine days in the sea, and the wind blowing, it's hard set his own mother would be to say what man was in it.

CATHLEEN: It's Michael, God spare him, for they're after sending us a bit of his clothes from the far north.

She reaches out and hands MAURYA *the clothes that belonged to Michael.* MAURYA *stands up slowly and takes them in her hand.* NORA *looks out.*

NORA: They're carrying a thing among them and there's water dripping out of it and leaving a track by the big stones.

CATHLEEN [*in a whisper to the women who have come in*]:   Is it Bartley it is?

ONE OF THE WOMEN: It is surely, God rest his soul.

Two younger women come in and pull out the table. Then men carry in the body of BARTLEY, *laid on a plank, with a bit of sail over it, and lay it on the table.*

CATHLEEN [*to the women, as they are doing so*]:   What way was he drowned?

ONE OF THE WOMEN: The gray pony knocked him into the sea, and he was washed out where there is a great surf on the white rocks.

MAURYA *has gone over and knelt down at the head of the table. The women are keening softly and swaying themselves with a slow movement.* CATHLEEN *and* Nora *kneel at the other end of the table. The men kneel near the door.*

[5]**curagh** a canoe-like canvas-bottomed boat

MAURYA [*raising her head and speaking as if she did not see the people around her*]: They're all gone now, and there isn't anything more the sea can do to me....I'll have no call now to be up crying and praying when the wind breaks from the south, and you can hear the surf is in the east and the surf is in the west, making a great stir with the two noises, and they hitting one on the other. I'll have no call now to be going down and getting Holy Water in the dark nights after Samhain,[6] and I won't care what way the sea is when the other women will be keening. [*To* NORA] Give me the Holy Water, Nora, there is a small cup still on the dresser.

NORA *gives it to her.*

MAURYA: [*drops Michael's clothes across* BARTLEY'S *feet and sprinkles the Holy Water over him*] It isn't that I haven't prayed for you, Bartley, to the Almighty God. It isn't that I haven't said prayers in the dark night till you wouldn't know what I'd be saying; but it's a great rest I'll have now, and it's time surely. It's a great rest I'll have now, and great sleeping in the long nights after Samhain, if it's only a bit of wet flour we do have to eat, and maybe a fish that would be stinking.

She kneels down again, crossing herself, and saying prayers under her breath.

CATHLEEN [*to an old man*]: Maybe yourself and Eamon would make a coffin when the sun rises. We have fine white boards herself bought, God help her, thinking Michael would be found, and I have a new cake you can eat while you'll be working.

THE OLD MAN [*looking at the boards*]: Are there nails with them?

CATHLEEN: There are not, Colum; we didn't think of the nails.

ANOTHER MAN: It's a great wonder she wouldn't think of the nails, and all the coffins she's seen made already.

CATHLEEN: It's getting old she is, and broken.

MAURYA *stands up again very slowly and spreads out the pieces of Michael's clothes beside the body, sprinkling them with the last of the Holy Water.*

NORA [*in a whisper to* CATHLEEN]: She's quiet now and easy but the day Michael was drowned you could hear her crying out from this to the spring well. It's fonder she was of Michael, and would any one have thought that?

CATHLEEN [*slowly and clearly*]: An old woman will be soon tired with anything she will do, and isn't it nine days herself is after crying and keening, and making great sorrow in the house?

MAURYA [*puts the empty cup mouth downwards on the table and lays her hands together on* BARTLEY'S *feet*]: They're all together this time, and the end is come. May the Almighty God have mercy on Bartley's soul, and on Michael's soul, and on the souls of Sheamus and Patch, and Stephen and Shawn [*bending her head*]; and may He have mercy on my soul, Nora, and on the soul of every one is left living in the world.

She pauses, and the keen rises a little more loudly from the women, then sinks away.

[6]**Samhain** All Saints' Day, November 1st

MAURYA [*continuing*]:   Michael has a clean burial in the far north, by the grace of the Almighty God. Bartley will have a fine coffin out of the white boards, and a deep grave surely. What more can we want than that? No man at all can be living for ever, and we must be satisfied.

She kneels down again and the curtain falls slowly.

MAKING CONNECTIONS

1. Discuss the impact of the setting on conflict and characterization in this play.
2. Maurya says, "In the big world the old people do be leaving things after them for their son and children, but in this place it is the young men do be leaving things behind for them that be old." What does she mean? What difference does it make to the culture of these people?
3. Synge wrote the dialogue in this play to conform to the speech patterns of the people of the Aran islands. Do you think it is effective or do you think it would be just as effective to have them speak standard English—and be understood more easily? Explain.
4. Compare and contrast this play with Stephen Crane's poem "A Man Said to the Universe" on page 1172 or Thomas Hardy's "Hap" on page 1173.

MAKING AN ARGUMENT

1. At the end of the play, Maurya comments on the death and "clean" burial of her only remaining sons: "What more can we want than that? No man at all can be living for ever, and we must be satisfied." Do you agree? Write an essay that takes a position for or against her opinion. Cite the text of the play and [if appropriate] other sources to support your view.

Ten-Minute Plays

The two plays that follow, John Galsworthy's "The Sun" and Anton Chekhov's "The Swan Song," are so brief that—as the heading suggests, they might be performed—or read aloud in class in ten minutes.

JOHN GALSWORTHY [1867–1933]

As a novelist Galsworthy is chiefly known for The Forsyte Saga. *The first novel of this group,* The Man of Property, *appeared in 1906 and was a harsh criticism of the upper middle classes. It was fifteen years until he resumed work on the history of the Forsytes with* In Chancery *(1920) and* To Let *(1921). Meanwhile he had written a considerable number of novels, short stories, and plays.* The Forsyte Saga *continued with the four volumes of* A Modern Comedy, The White Monkey *(1924),* The Silver Spoon *(1926),* Swan Song *(1928), and its two interludes,* A Silent Wooing *and* Passersby *(1927). In 1930, he added a collection*

of short stories, On Forsyte Change. *Galsworthy's plays often took up social injustice as applied to the upper and lower classes in* The Silver Box *(1906),* Strife *(1909),* Justice *(1910),* The Mob *(1914), and* The Skin Game *(1920). He was awarded the Nobel Prize in Literature in 1932.*

THE SUN   [1921]

NOTE: This play is reprinted from *Six Short Plays.* John Galsworthy. London: Duckworth, 1921.

CHARACTERS

THE GIRL
THE MAN
THE SOLDIER

[A GIRL *sits crouched over her knees on a stile close to a river. A* MAN *with a silver badge stands beside her, clutching the worn top plank.* THE GIRL'S *level brows are drawn together; her eyes see her memories.* THE MAN'S *eyes see* THE GIRL; *he has a dark, twisted face. The bright sun shines; the quiet river flows, the cuckoo is calling; the mayflower is in bloom along the hedge that ends in the stile on the towing-path.]*

	THE GIRL:	God knows what 'e'll say, Jim.
	THE MAN:	Let 'im 'E's come too late, that's all.
	THE GIRL:	He couldn't come before. I'm frightened. 'E was fond o' me.
	THE MAN:	And aren't I fond of you?
5	THE GIRL:	I ought to a' waited, Jim; with 'im in the fightin'.
	THE MAN:	[*Passionately*] And what about me? Aren't I been in the fightin'—earned all I could get?
	THE GIRL:	[*Touching him*] Ah!
	THE MAN:	Did you—?

[He cannot speak the words.]

	THE GIRL:	Not like you, Jim—not like you.
10	THE MAN:	Have a spirit, then.
	THE GIRL:	I promised him.
	THE MAN:	One man's luck's another's poison.
	THE GIRL:	I ought to 'a waited. I never thought he'd come back from the fightin'.
	THE MAN:	[*Grimly*] Maybe 'e'd better not 'ave.
15	THE GIRL:	[*Looking back along the tow-path*] What'll he be like, I wonder?
	THE MAN:	[*Gripping her shoulder*] Daisy, don't you never go back on me, or I should kill you, and 'im too.

[THE GIRL *looks at him, shivers, and puts her lips to his.*]

	THE GIRL:	I never could.
	THE MAN:	Will you run for it? 'E'd never find us.

[THE GIRL *shakes her head.*]

	THE MAN:	[*Dully*] What's the good o' stayin'? The world's wide.
20	THE GIRL:	I'd rather have it off me mind, with him home.
	THE MAN:	[*Clenching his hands*] It's temptin' Providence.
	THE GIRL:	What's the time, Jim?

THE MAN: [*Glancing at the sun*] 'Alf past four.

THE GIRL: [*Looking along the towing-path*] He said four o' clock. Jim, you better go.

25   THE MAN: Not *I*. *I've* not got the wind up. I've seen as much of hell as he has, any
day. What like is he?

THE GIRL: [*Dully*] I dunno, just. I've not seen him these three years. I dunno no
more, since I've known you

THE MAN: Big or little chap?

THE GIRL: 'Bout your size. Oh! Jim, go along!

THE MAN: No fear! What's a blighter like that to old Fritz's shells? We didn't shift
when they was comin'. If you'll go, I'll go; not else.

[*Again she shakes her head.*]

30   THE GIRL: Jim, do you love me true?

[*For answer,* THE MAN *takes her avidly in his arms.*]

THE GIRL: I ain't ashamed—I ain't ashamed. If 'e could see me 'eart.

THE MAN: Daisy! If I'd known you out there, I never could 'a stuck it. They'd 'a got
me for a deserter. That's how I love you!

THE GIRL: Jim, don't lift your hand to 'im! Promise!

THE MAN: That's according.

35   THE GIRL: Promise!

THE MAN: If 'e keeps quiet, I won't. But I'm not accountable—not always, I tell you
straight—not since I've been through that.

THE GIRL: [*With a shiver*] Nor p'raps he isn't.

THE MAN: Like as not. It takes the linch pins out, I tell you.

THE GIRL: God 'elp us!

40   THE MAN: [*Grimly*] Ah! We said that a bit too often. What we want we take, now;
there's no one else to give it us, and there's no fear'll stop us; we seen the
bottom of things.

THE GIRL: P'raps he'll say that too.

THE MAN: Then it'll be 'im or me.

THE GIRL: I'm frightened.

THE MAN: [*Tenderly*] No, Daisy, no! The river's handy. One more or less. 'E shant
'arm you; nor me neither.

[*He takes out a knife.*]

45   THE GIRL: [*Seizing his hand*] Oh, no! Give it to me, Jim!

THE MAN: [*Smiling*] No fear! [*He puts it away*] Shan't 'ave no need for it like as not.
All right, little Daisy; you can't be expected to see things like we do. What's
life, anyway? I've seen a thousand lives taken in five minutes. I've seen dead
men on the wires like flies on a flypaper. I've been as good as dead meself a
hundred times. I've killed a dozen men. It's nothin'. He's safe, if 'e don't get
my blood up. If he does, nobody's safe; not 'im, nor anybody else; not even
you. I'm speakin' sober.

THE GIRL: [*Softly*] Jim, you won't go fightin' in the sun, with the birds all callin'?

THE MAN: That depends on 'im. I'm not lookin' for it. Daisy, I love you I love your
hair. I love your eyes. I love you.

THE GIRL: I love you, Jim I don't want nothin' more than you in all the world.

50   THE MAN: Amen to that, my dear. Kiss me!

[*The sound of a voice singing breaks in on their embrace.* THE GIRL *starts from his arms, and looks behind her along the towing-path.* THE MAN *draws back against the hedge, fingering his side, where the knife is hidden. The song comes nearer:*]

> "I'll be right there to-night,
> Where the fields are snowy white;
> Banjo's ringing, [people] singing,
> All the world seems bright."

THE GIRL: It's him!

THE MAN: Don't get the wind up, Daisy. I'm here!

[*The singing stops.*]

SOLDER: [*Offstage*] Christ! It's Daisy; it's little Daisy 'erself!

[THE GIRL *stands rigid. The figure of a* SOLDIER *appears on the other side of the stile. His cap is tucked into his belt, his hair is bright in the sunshine; he is lean, wasted, brown, and laughing.*]

SOLDIER: Daisy! Daisy! Hallo, old pretty girl!

[THE GIRL *does not move, barring the way, as it were.*]

55   THE GIRL: Hallo, Jack! [*Softly*] I got things to tell you.

SOLDIER: What sort o' things, this lovely day? Why, I got things that'd take me years to tell Have you missed me, Daisy?

THE GIRL: You been so long.

SOLDIER: So I 'ave. My Gawd! It's a way they 'ave in the Army. I said when I got out of it I'd laugh. Like as the sun itself I used to think of you, Daisy, when the crumps was comin' over, and the wind was up. D'you remember that last night in the wood? "Come back and marry me quick, Jack." Well, here I am—got me pass to heaven. No more fightin' no more drillin', no more sleepin' rough. We can get married now, Daisy. We can live soft an' 'appy. Give us a kiss, my dear.

THE GIRL: [*Drawing back*] No.

60   SOLDIER: [*Blankly*] Why not?

[THE MAN, *with a swift movement, steps along the hedge to* THE GIRL'S *side.*]

THE MAN: That's why, soldier.

SOLDIER: [*Leaping over the stile*] 'Oo are you, Pompey? The sun don't shine in your inside, do it? 'Oo is he, Daisy?

THE GIRL: My man.

SOLDIER: Your–man! Lummy! "Taffy was a Welshman, Taffy was a thief!" Well, mate! So you've been through it, too. I'm laughin' this mornin' as luck will 'ave it. Ah! I can see your knife.

65   THE MAN: [*Who has half-drawn his knife.*] Don't laugh at *me*, I tell you.

SOLDIER: Not at you, not at you [*He looks from one to the other.*] I'm laughin' at things in general. Where did *you* get it, mate?

THE MAN: [*Watchfully*] Through the lung.

SOLDIER: Think o' that! An' I never was touched. Four years an' never was touched. An' so you've come an' took my girl! Nothin' doin'! Ha! [*Again he looks from one to the other—then away*] Well! The world's before me! [*He laughs*] I'll give you Daisy for a lung protector.

THE MAN: [*Fiercely*] You won't. I've took her.

70 SOLDIER: That's all right, then. You keep 'er. I've got a laugh in me you can't put out, black as you look! Good-bye, little Daisy!

[THE GIRL *makes a movement towards him.*]

THE MAN: Don't touch 'im!

[THE GIRL *stands hesitating, and suddenly bursts into tears.*]

SOLDIER: Look 'ere, mate; shake 'ands! I don't want to see a girl cry, this day of all, with the sun shinin'. I seen too much of sorrer. You and me've been at the back of it. We've 'ad our whack. Shake!

THE MAN: Who are you kiddin'? *You* never loved 'er!

SOLDIER: [*After a long moment's pause*] Oh! I thought I did.

75 THE MAN: I'll fight you for her.

[*He drops his knife.*]

SOLDIER: [*Slowly*] Mate, you done your bit, an' I done mine. It's took us two ways, seemin'ly.

THE GIRL: [*Pleading*] Jim!

THE MAN: [*With clenched fists*] I don't want 'is charity. I only want what I can take.

SOLDIER: Daisy, which of us will you 'ave?

80 THE GIRL: [*Covering her face*] Oh! *Him!*

SOLDIER: You see, mate! Put your 'ands down. There's nothin' for it but a laugh. You an' me know that. Laugh, mate!

THE MAN: You blarsted—

[THE GIRL *springs to him and stops his mouth.*]

SOLDIER: It's no use, mate. I can't do it. I said I'd laugh today, and laugh I will. I've come through that, an' all the stink of it; I've come through sorrer. Never again! Cheerio, mate! The sun's a-shinin'!

[*He turns away.*]

THE GIRL: Jack, don't think too 'ard of me!

85 SOLDIER: [*Looking back*] No fear, my dear! Enjoy your fancy! So long! Gawd bless you both!

[*He sings and goes along the path, and the song:*]

> "I'll be right there to-night,
>   Where the fields are snowy white;
> Banjo's ringing, [people] singing,
>   All the world seems bright."

THE MAN: 'E's mad.

THE GIRL: [*Looking down the path with her hands clasped.*] The sun has touched 'im, Jim!

CURTAIN

MAKING CONNECTIONS

1. The characters in this play are English—but they have cockney accents. Why would that matter? To what extent are their accents part of the setting of the play—and part of the conflict?
2. Were you surprised that the soldier does not fight for the girl? Do you think he should have? Explain.
3. What do you think the girl means when she says of the soldier at the end of the play: "The sun has touched him"? Has he been touched by the sun? Explain.

MAKING AN ARGUMENT

1. To what extent is this a war story? Compare it to another work about World War I: "*Dulce et Decorum Est*" on page 1175 or any other depiction of war and its effects in this section. Based on these works and other research you have done, write an essay about the impact of war on the soldiers who survive it.

ANTON CHEKHOV [1860–1904]

THE SWAN SONG   [1887]

(See biography on p. 759.)

Translated by Marian Fell

NOTE: This translation by Marian Fell was originally published in 1912 by Charles Scribner's Sons. It is now a public domain work and may be performed without royalties.

CHARACTERS

VASILI SVIETLOVIDOFF, *a comedian, 68 years old*
NIKITA IVANITCH, *a prompter, an old man*

[*The scene is laid on the stage of a country theatre, at night, after the play. To the right a row of rough, unpainted doors leading into the dressing-rooms. To the left and in the background the stage is encumbered with all sorts of rubbish. In the middle of the stage is an overturned stool.*]

SVIETLOVIDOFF: [*With a candle in his hand, comes out of a dressing-room and laughs.*] Well, well, this is funny! Here's a good joke! I fell asleep in my dressing-room when the play was over, and there I was calmly snoring after everybody else had left the theatre. Ah! I'm a foolish old man, a poor old dodderer! I have been drinking again, and so I fell asleep in there, sitting up. That was clever! Good for you, old boy! [*Calls.*] Yegorka! Petrushka! Where the devil are you? Petrushka! The scoundrels must be asleep, and an earthquake wouldn't wake them now! Yegorka! [*Picks up the stool, sits down, and puts the candle on the floor.*] Not a sound! Only echoes answer me. I gave Yegorka and Petrushka each a tip today, and now they have disappeared without leaving a trace behind them. The rascals have gone off and have probably locked up the theatre. [*Turns his head about.*] I'm drunk! Ugh! The play tonight was for my benefit, and it is disgusting to think how much beer and wine I have poured down my throat in honour of the occasion. Gracious! My body is burning all over, and I feel as if I had twenty tongues in my mouth. It is horrid! Idiotic! This poor old sinner is drunk again, and doesn't even know what he has been celebrating! Ugh! My head is splitting, I am shivering all over, and I feel as dark and cold inside as a cellar! Even if I don't mind ruining my health, I ought at least to remember my age, old idiot that I am! Yes, my old age! It's no use! I can play the fool, and brag, and pretend to be young, but my life is really over now, I kiss my hand to the sixty-eight years that have gone by; I'll never see them again! I have drained the bottle, only a few little drops are left at the bottom, nothing but the dregs. Yes, yes, that's the case, Vasili, old boy. [*Stares ahead of him.*] It is strange, though, that I have been on the stage now for forty-five years, and this is the first time I have seen a theatre at night, after the lights have been put out. The first time. [*Walks up to the footlights.*] How dark it is! I can't see a thing. Oh, yes, I can just make out the prompter's box, and his desk; the rest is in pitch darkness, a black, bottomless pit, like a grave, in which death itself might be hiding.... Brrr.... How cold it is! The wind blows out of the empty theatre as though out of a stone flue. What a place for ghosts! The shivers are running up and down my back. [*Calls.*] Yegorka! Petrushka! Where are you both? What on earth makes me think of such gruesome things here? I must give up drinking; I'm an old man, I shan't live much longer. At sixty-eight people go to church and prepare for death, but here I am—heavens! A profane old drunkard in this fool's dress—I'm simply not fit to look at. I must go and change at once....This is a dreadful place, I should die of fright sitting here all night. [*Goes toward his dressing-room; at the same time* NIKITA IVANITCH *in a long white coat comes out of the dressing-room at the farthest end of the stage.* SVIETLOVIDOFF *sees* IVANITCH—*shrieks with terror and steps back.*] Who are you? What? What do you want? [*Stamps his foot.*] Who are you?

IVANITCH: It is I, sir.

SVIETLOVIDOFF: Who are you?

IVANITCH: [*Comes slowly toward him.*] It is I, sir, the prompter, Nikita Ivanitch. It is I, master, it is I!

5   SVIETLOVIDOFF: [*Sinks helplessly onto the stool, breathes heavily and trembles violently.*] Heavens! Who are you? It is you....you Nikitushka? What...what are you doing here?

IVANITCH: I spend my nights here in the dressing-rooms. Only please be good enough not to tell Alexi Fomitch, sir. I have nowhere else to spend the night; indeed, I haven't.

SVIETLOVIDOFF: Ah! It is you, Nikitushka, is it? Just think, the audience called me out sixteen times; they brought me three wreathes and lots of other things, too; they were all wild with enthusiasm, and yet not a soul came when it was all over to wake the poor, drunken old man and take him home. I am an old man, Nikitushka! I am sixty-eight years old, and I am ill. I haven't the heart left to go on. [*Falls on* IVANITCH'S *neck and weeps.*] Don't go away, Nikitushka; I am old and helpless, and I feel it is time for me to die. Oh, it is dreadful, dreadful!

IVANITCH: [*Tenderly and respectfully.*] Dear master! It is time for you to go home, sir!

SVIETLOVIDOFF: I won't go home; I have no home—none! none! none!

10 IVANITCH: Oh, dear! Have you forgotten where you live?

SVIETLOVIDOFF: I won't go there. I won't! I am all alone there. I have nobody, Nikitushka! No wife—no children. I am like the wind blowing across the lonely fields. I shall die, and no one will remember me. It is awful to be alone—no one to cheer me, no one to caress me, no one to help me to bed when I am drunk. Whom do I belong to? Who needs me? Who loves me? Not a soul, Nikitushka.

IVANITCH: [*Weeping.*]: Your audience loves you, master.

SVIETLOVIDOFF: My audience has gone home. They are all asleep, and have forgotten their old clown. No, nobody needs me, nobody loves me; I have no wife, no children.

IVANITCH: Oh, dear, Oh, dear! Don't be so unhappy about it.

15 SVIETLOVIDOFF: But I am a man, I am still alive. Warm, red blood is tingling in my veins, the blood of noble ancestors. I am an aristocrat, Nikitushka; I served in the army, in the artillery, before I fell as low as this, and what a fine young chap I was! Handsome, daring eager! Where has it all gone? What has become of those old days? There's the pit that has swallowed them all! I remember it all now. Forty-five years of my life buried there, and what a life, Nikitushka! I can see it as clearly as I see your face; the ecstasy of youth, faith, passion, the love of women—women, Nikitushka!

IVANITCH: It is time you went to sleep, sir.

SVIETLOVIDOFF: When I first went on the stage, in the first glow of passionate youth, I remember a woman loved me for my acting. She was beautiful, graceful as a poplar, young, innocent, pure, and radiant as a summer dawn. Her smile could charm away the darkest night. I remember, I stood before her once, as I am now standing before you. She had never seemed so lovely to me as she did then, and she spoke to me so with her eyes—such a look! I shall never forget it, no, not even in the grave; so tender, so soft, so deep, so bright and young! Enraptured, intoxicated, I fell on my knees before her, I begged for my happiness, and she said: "Give up the stage!" Give up the stage! Do you understand? She could love an actor, but marry him—never! I was acting that day, I remember—I had a foolish, clown's part, and as I acted, I felt my eyes being opened; I saw that the worship of the art I had held so sacred was a delusion and an empty dream; that I was a slave, a fool, the plaything of the idleness of strangers. I understood my audience at last, and since that day I have not believed in their applause, or in their wreathes, or in their enthusiasm. Yes, Nikitushka! The people applaud me, they buy my photograph, but I am a stranger to them. They don't know me, I am as the dirt beneath their feet. They are willing enough to meet me...but allow a daughter or a sister to marry me, an outcast, never! I have no faith in them [*Sinks onto the stool.*] No faith in them.

IVANITCH: Oh, sir! You look dreadfully pale, you frighten me to death! Come, go home, have mercy on me!

SVIETLOVIDOFF: I saw through it all that day, and the knowledge was dearly bought. Nikitushka! After that…when that girl…well, I began to wander aimlessly about, living from day to day without looking ahead. I took the parts of buffoons and low comedians, letting my mind go to wreck. Ah! but I was a great artist once, till little by little I threw away my talents, played the motley fool, lost my looks, lost the power of expressing myself, and became in the end a Merry Andrew instead of a man. I have been swallowed up in that great black pit. I never felt it before, but tonight, when I woke up, I looked back, and there behind me lay sixty-eight years. I have just found out what it is to be old! It is all over…[*Sobs.*]…all over.

20   IVANITCH: There, there, dear master! Be quiet…gracious! [*Calls.*] Petrushka! Yegorka!

SVIETLOVIDOFF: But what a genius I was! You cannot imagine what power I had, what eloquence; how graceful I was, how tender; how many strings [*Beats his breast.*] quivered in this breast! It chokes me to think of it! Listen now, wait, let me catch my breath, there; now listen to this:

> "The shade of bloody Ivan now returning
> Fans through my lips rebellion to a flame,
> I am the dead Dimitri! In the burning
> Boris shall perish on the throne I claim
> Enough! The heir of Czars shall not be seen
> Kneeling to yonder haughty Polish Queen!"

Is that bad, eh? [*Quickly.*] Wait, now, here's something from King Lear. The sky is black, see? Rain is pouring down, thunder roars, lightning—zzz zzz zzz—splits the whole sky, and then, listen:

> "Blow winds, and crack your cheeks! Rage! Blow!
> You cataracts and hurricanes spout
> Till you have drench'd our steeples, drown'd the cocks!
> You sulphurous thought-executing fires,
> Vaunt-couriers of oak-cleaving thunderbolts,
> Singe my white head! And thou, all shaking thunder,
> Strike flat the thick rotundity o' the world!
> Crack nature's moulds, all germens spill at once
> That make ungrateful man!"

[*Impatiently.*] Now take the part of the fool. [*Stamps his foot.*] Come take the fool's part! Be quick, I can't wait!

IVANITCH: [*Takes the part of the fool.*]

> "O, Nuncle, court holy-water in a dry house is better than rain-water out o' door. Good Nuncle, in; ask thy daughter's blessing here's a night pities neither wise men nor fools."

Svietlovidoff

> "Rumble thy bellyful! Spit, fire! Spout, rain!
> Nor rain, wind, thunder, fire, are my daughters;
> I tax not you, you elements, with unkindness;
> I never gave you kingdom, call'd you children."

Ah! there is strength, there is talent for you! I'm a great artist! Now, then, here's something else of the same kind, to bring back my youth to me. For instance, take this, from Hamlet, I'll begin...let me see, how does it go? Oh, yes, this is it. [*Takes the part of Hamlet.*] "O! the recorders, let me see one.—To withdraw with you. Why do you go about to recover the wind of me, as if you would drive me into a toil?"

IVANITCH: "O, my lord, if my duty be too bold, my love is too unmannerly."

SVIETLOVIDOFF: "I do not well understand that. Will you play upon this pipe?"

25   IVANITCH: "My lord, I cannot."

SVIETLOVIDOFF: "I pray you."

IVANITCH: "Believe me, I cannot."

SVIETLOVIDOFF: "I do beseech you."

IVANITCH: "I know no touch of it, my lord."

30   SVIETLOVIDOFF: "Tis as easy as lying: govern these ventages with your finger and thumb, give it breath with your mouth, and it will discourse most eloquent music. Look you, these are the stops."

IVANITCH: "But these I cannot command to any utterance of harmony: I have not the skill."

SVIETLOVIDOFF: Why, look you, how unworthy a thing you make of me. You would play upon me; you would seem to know my stops; you would pluck out the heart of my mystery; you would sound me from my lowest note to the top of my compass; and there is much music, excellent voice, in this little organ, yet cannot you make it speak. S'blood! Do you think I am easier to be played on than a pipe? Call me what instrument you will, though you can fret me, you cannot play upon me!" [*Laughs and claps.*] Bravo! Encore! Bravo! Where the devil is there any old age in that? I'm not old, that is all nonsense, a torrent of strength rushes over me; this is life, freshness, youth! Old age and genius can't exist together. You seem to be struck dumb, Nikitushka. Wait a second, let me come to my senses again. Oh! Good Lord! Now then, listen! Did you ever hear such tenderness, such music? Sh! Softly;

> "The moon had set. There was not any light,
> Save of the lonely legion'd watch-stars pale
> In outer-air, and what by fits made bright
> Hot oleanders in a rosy vale
> Searched by the lamping fly, whose little spark
> Went in and out, like passion's bashful hope."

[*The noise of opening doors is heard.*] What's that?

IVANITCH: There are Petrushka and Yegorka coming back. Yes, you have genius, genius, my master.

SVIETLOVIDOFF: [*Calls, turning toward the noise.*] Come here to me, boys! [*To* IVANITCH.] Let us go and get dressed. I'm not old! All that is foolishness, non-sense! [*Laughs gaily.*] What are you crying for? You poor old granny, you, what's the matter now? This won't do! There, there, this won't do at all! Come, come, old man, don't stare so! What makes you stare like that? There, there! [*Embraces him in tears.*] Don't cry! Where there is art and genius there can never be such things as old age or loneliness or sickness…and death itself is half…[*Weeps.*] No, no, Nikitushka! It is all over for us now! What sort of genius am I? I'm like a squeezed lemon, a cracked bottle, and you—you are the old rat of the theatre…a prompter! Come on! [*They go.*] I'm no ge-nius, I'm only fit to be in the suite of Fortinbras, and even for that I am too old.…Yes.…Do you remember those lines from Othello, Nikitushka?

> "Farewell the tranquil mind! Farewell content!
> Farewell the plumed troops and the big wars
> That make ambition virtue! O farewell!
> Farewell the neighing steed and the shrill trump,
> The spirit-stirring drum, the ear-piercing fife,
> The royal banner, and all quality,
> Pride, pomp and circumstance of glorious war!"

35   IVANITCH: Oh! You're a genius, a genius!
SVIETLOVIDOFF: And again this:

> "Away! the moor is dark beneath the moon,
> Rapid clouds have drunk the last pale beam of even:
> Away! the gathering winds will call the darkness soon,
> And profoundest midnight shroud the serene lights of heaven."

[*They go out together, the curtains fall slowly.*]

CURTAIN

MAKING CONNECTIONS

1. What is a "swan song"?
2. Are you sympathetic to the actor, Svietlovidoff? What is he complaining about? Is this his Swan Song? Explain.
3. What is the role of Ivanitch in the play? In Svietlovidoff's life?

MAKING AN ARGUMENT

1. Clearly, Shakespeare is a particular favorite of Svietlovidoff. It is Shakespeare who writes in *As You Like It*: "All the world's a stage / And all the men and women merely players." To what extent is this play an example of that? Do you agree with the quote? Write an argument for or against the statement.

◆ ESSAYS ◆

ALBERT CAMUS [1913–1960]

French philosopher, novelist, dramatist, and journalist Albert Camus was born and raised in Algeria. Though his family was not particularly well educated, Camus was an excellent student throughout his youth, graduating with honors from the University of Algiers in 1936. At the outbreak of World War II, he worked as a reporter first in Algeria and then in France. His greatest works, which are often characterized as "absurdist," were written during this period and include the novel The Stranger, *the essay "The Myth of Sisyphus," and the play* Caligula. *During the German occupation of France, Camus, together with his friend the existentialist philosopher Jean-Paul Sartre, became one of the intellectual leaders of the French resistance, working late at night on the newspaper* Combat, *which went on to became one of France's most important postwar newspapers. Following the war, the now-famous Camus turned away from journalism and concentrated on writing novels and plays. Although he was often called a philosopher or existentialist, Camus rejected all labels, defining himself simply as "a man with a passion for the human heart." He was awarded the Nobel Prize for literature in 1957. In 1960, he was killed in a car accident in the south of France.*

THE MYTH OF SISYPHUS   [1942]

The gods had condemned Sisyphus to ceaselessly rolling a rock to the top of a mountain, whence the stone would fall back of its own weight. They had thought with some reason that there is no more dreadful punishment than futile and hopeless labor.

If one believes Homer, Sisyphus was the wisest and most prudent of mortals. According to another tradition, however, he was disposed to practice the profession of highwayman. I see no contradiction in this. Opinions differ as to the reasons why he became the futile laborer of the underworld. To begin with, he is accused of a certain levity in regard to the gods. He stole their secrets. Aegina, the daughter of Aesopus, was carried off by Jupiter. The father was shocked by that disappearance and complained to Sisyphus. He, who knew of the abduction, offered to tell about it on condition that Aesopus would give water to the citadel of Corinth. To the celestial thunderbolts he preferred the benediction of water. He was punished for this in the underworld. Homer tells us also that Sisyphus had put Death in chains. Pluto could not endure the sight of his deserted, silent empire. He dispatched the god of war, who liberated Death from the hands of her conqueror.

It is said also that Sisyphus, being near to death, rashly wanted to test his wife's love. He ordered her to cast his unburied body into the middle of the public square. Sisyphus woke up in the underworld. And there, annoyed by an obedience so contrary to human love, he obtained from Pluto permission to return to earth in order to chastise his wife. But when he had seen again the face of this world, enjoyed water and sun, warm stones and the sea, he no longer wanted to go back to the infernal darkness. Recalls, signs of anger, warnings were of no avail. Many years more he lived facing the curve of the gulf, the sparkling sea, and the smiles of earth. A decree of the gods was necessary. Mercury came and seized the impudent man by the collar and, snatching him from his joys, led him forcibly back to the underworld, where his rock was ready for him.

You have already grasped that Sisyphus is the absurd hero. He *is,* as much through his passions as through his torture. His scorn of the gods, his hatred of death, and his passion for life won him that unspeakable penalty in which the whole being is exerted toward accomplishing nothing. This is the price that must be paid for the passions of this earth. Nothing is told us about Sisyphus in the underworld. Myths are made for the imagination to breathe life into them. As for this myth, one sees merely the whole effort of a body straining to raise the huge stone, to roll it and push it up a slope a hundred times over; one sees the face screwed up, the cheek tight against the stone, the shoulder bracing the clay-covered mass, the foot wedging it, the fresh start with arms outstretched, the wholly human security of two earth-clotted hands. At the very end of his long effort measured by skyless space and time without depth, the purpose is achieved. Then Sisyphus watches the stone rush down in a few moments toward that lower world whence he will have to push it up again toward the summit. He goes back down to the plain.

5   It is during that return, that pause, that Sisyphus interests me. A face that toils so close to stones is already stone itself! I see that man going back down with a heavy yet measured step toward the torment of which he will never know the end. That hour like a breathing-space which returns as surely as his suffering, that is the hour of con-sciousness. At each of those moments when he leaves the heights and gradually sinks toward the lairs of the gods, he is superior to his fate. He is stronger than his rock.

If this myth is tragic, that is because its hero is conscious. Where would his tor-ture be, indeed, if at every step the hope of succeeding upheld him? The workman of today works every day in his life at the same tasks, and his fate is no less absurd. But it is tragic only at the rare moments when it becomes conscious. Sisyphus, proletarian of the gods, powerless and rebellious, knows the whole extent of his wretched condition; it is what he thinks of during his descent. The lucidity that was to constitute his torture at the same time crowns his victory. There is no fate that cannot be surmounted by scorn.

If the descent is thus sometimes performed in sorrow, it can also take place in joy. This word is not too much. Again I fancy Sisyphus returning toward his rock, and the sorrow was in the beginning. When the images of earth cling too tightly to memory, when the call of happiness becomes too insistent, it happens that melancholy rises in man's heart: this is the rock's victory, this is the rock itself. The boundless grief is too heavy to bear. These are our nights of Gethsemane. But crushing truths perish from being acknowledged. Thus, Oedipus at the outset obeys fate without knowing it. But from the moment he knows, his tragedy begins. Yet at the same moment, blind and desperate, he realizes that the only bond linking him to the world is the cool hand of a girl. Then a tremendous remark rings out: "Despite so many ordeals, my advanced age and the nobility of my soul make me conclude that all is well." Sophocles' Oedipus, like Dostoevsky's Kirilov, thus gives the recipe for the absurd victory. Ancient wisdom confirms modern heroism.

One does not discover the absurd without being tempted to write a manual of happiness. "What! by such narrow ways—?" There is but one world, however. Happiness and the absurd are two sons of the same earth. They are inseparable. It would be a mistake to say that happiness necessarily springs from the absurd discovery. It happens as well that the feeling of the absurd springs from happiness. "I conclude that all is well," says Oedipus, and that remark is sacred. It echoes in the wild and limited universe of man. It teaches that all is not, has not been, exhausted. It drives out of this world a god who had come into it with dissatisfaction and a preference for futile sufferings. It makes of fate a human matter, which must be settled among men.

All Sisyphus' silent joy is contained therein. His fate belongs to him. His rock is his thing. Likewise, the absurd man, when he contemplates his torment, silences all the idols. In the universe suddenly restored to its silence, the myriad wondering little voices of the earth rise up. Unconscious, secret calls, invitations from all the faces, they are the necessary reverse and price of victory. There is no sun without shadow, and it is essential to know the night. The absurd man says yes and his effort will henceforth be unceasing. If there is a personal fate, there is no higher destiny, or at least there is but one which he concludes is inevitable and despicable. For the rest, he knows himself to be the master of his days. At that subtle moment when man glances backward over his life, Sisyphus returning toward his rock, in that slight pivoting he contemplates that series of unrelated actions which becomes his fate, created by him, combined under his memory's eye and soon sealed by his death. Thus, convinced of the wholly human origin of all that is human, a blind man eager to see who knows that the night has no end, he is still on the go. The rock is still rolling.

10   I leave Sisyphus at the foot of the mountain! One always finds one's burden again. But Sisyphus teaches the higher fidelity that negates the gods and raises rocks. He too concludes that all is well. This universe henceforth without a master seems to him neither sterile nor futile. Each atom of that stone, each mineral flake of that night-filled mountain, in itself forms a world. The struggle itself toward the heights is enough to fill a man's heart. One must imagine Sisyphus happy.

 ## MAKING CONNECTIONS

1. Sisyphus is condemned to roll the rock to the top of the hill, but never complete his task. Why is this such a terrible punishment?
2. Camus says, "The workman of today works every day in his life at the same tasks, and his fate is no less absurd [than that of Sisyphus]." What does he mean? Do you agree? Explain.

 ## MAKING AN ARGUMENT

1. In the opening quotes for this theme, Thoreau is quoted as writing, "The mass of men [and women] lead lives of quiet desperation." How is Camus suggesting we should lead our lives? Is it a solution to the "quiet desperation" that Thoreau suggests we suffer from? Write an essay that interprets what Camus is suggesting, and agree or disagree with his premise. Cite the text of the essay for support.

PLATO [427–347 BCE]

The philosopher Plato was born in Athens and founded a school there called the Academy circa 387 BCE. He presided over this Academy, an institution devoted to research and instruction in philosophy and the sciences, until his death. During this time he wrote approximately thirty dialogues. Though Plato himself is not named as a participant, his own teacher, Socrates, is the "I" in these dialogues and moves the discussion along with a series of well-aimed leading questions. It is through these dialogues that Plato presented his own theories on a variety of subjects. "The Allegory of the Cave" that follows is taken from those dialogues.

THE ALLEGORY OF THE CAVE   [C. 387 BCE]

And now, I said, let me show in a figure how far our nature is enlightened or un-enlightened;—Behold! human beings living in an underground den, which has a mouth open towards the light and reaching all along the den; here they have been from their childhood, and have their legs and necks chained so that they cannot move, and can only see before them, being prevented by the chains from turning round their heads. Above and behind them a fire is blazing at a distance, and between the fire and the prisoners there is a raised way; and you will see, if you look, a low wall built along the way, like the screen which marionette players have in front of them, over which they show the puppets.

I see.

And do you see, I said, men passing along the wall carrying all sorts of vessels, and statues and figures of animals made of wood and stone and various materials, which appear over the wall? Some of them are talking, others silent.

You have shown me a strange image, and they are strange prisoners.

5   Like ourselves, I replied; and they see only their own shadows, or the shadows of one another, which the fire throws on the opposite wall of the cave?

True, he said; how could they see anything but the shadows if they were never allowed to move their heads?

And of the objects which are being carried in like manner they would only see the shadows?

Yes, he said.

And if they were able to converse with one another, would they not suppose that they were naming what was actually before them?

10   Very true.

And suppose further that the prison had an echo which came from the other side, would they not be sure to fancy when one of the passers-by spoke that the voice which they heard came from the passing shadow?

No question, he replied.

To them, I said, the truth would be literally nothing but the shadows of the images.

That is certain.

15   And now look again, and see what will naturally follow if the prisoners are released and disabused of their error. At first, when any of them is liberated and compelled suddenly to stand up and turn his neck round and walk and look towards the light, he will suffer sharp pains; the glare will distress him, and he will be unable to see the realities of which in his former state he had seen the shadows; and then conceive some one saying to him, that what he saw before was an illusion, but that now, when he is approaching nearer to being and his eye is turned towards more real existence, he has a clearer vision—what will be his reply? And you may further imagine that his instructor is pointing to the objects as they pass and requiring him to name them,—will he not be perplexed? Will he not fancy that the shadows which he formerly saw are truer than the objects which are now shown to him?

    Far truer.

    And if he is compelled to look straight at the light, will he not have a pain in his eyes which will make him turn away to take refuge in the objects of vision which he can see, and which he will conceive to be in reality clearer than the things which are now being shown to him?

    True, he said.

    And suppose once more, that he is reluctantly dragged up a steep and rugged ascent, and held fast until he is forced into the presence of the sun himself, is he not likely to be pained and irritated? When he approaches the light his eyes will be dazzled, and he will not be able to see anything at all of what are now called realities.

20   Not all in a moment, he said.

    He will require to grow accustomed to the sight of the upper world. And first he will see the shadows best, next the reflections of men and other objects in the water, and then the objects themselves; then he will gaze upon the light of the moon and the stars and the spangled heaven; and he will see the sky and the stars by night better than the sun or the light of the sun by day?

    Certainly.

    Last of all he will be able to see the sun, and not mere reflections of him in the water, but he will see him in his own proper place, and not in another; and he will contemplate him as he is.

    Certainly.

25   He will then proceed to argue that this is he who gives the season and the years, and is the guardian of all that is in the visible world, and in a certain way the cause of all things which he and his fellows have been accustomed to behold?

    Clearly, he said, he would first see the sun and then reason about him.

    And when he remembered his old habitation, and the wisdom of the den and his fellow prisoners, do you not suppose that he would felicitate himself on the change, and pity them?

    Certainly, he would.

    And if they were in the habit of conferring honors among themselves on those who were quickest to observe the passing shadows and to remark which of them went before, and which followed after, and which were together; and who were therefore best able to draw conclusions as to the future, do you think that he would care for such honors and glories, or envy the possessors of them? Would he not say with Homer, Better to be the poor servant of a poor master, and to endure anything, rather than think as they do and live after their manner?

30   Yes, he said, I think that he would rather suffer anything than entertain these false notions and live in this miserable manner.

Imagine once more, I said, such a one coming suddenly out of the sun to be replaced in his old situation; would he not be certain to have his eyes full of darkness?

To be sure, he said.

And if there were a contest, and he had to compete in measuring the shadows with the prisoners who had never moved out of the den, while his sight was still weak, and before his eyes had become steady (and the time which would be needed to acquire this new habit of sight might be very considerable), would he not be ridiculous? Men would say of him that up he went and down he came without his eyes; and that it was better not even to think of ascending; and if any one tried to loose another and lead him up to the light, let them only catch the offender, and they would put him to death.

No question, he said.

35   This entire allegory, I said, you may now append, dear Glaucon, to the previous argument; the prison house is the world of sight, the light of the fire is the sun, and you will not misapprehend me if you interpret the journey upwards to be the ascent of the soul into the intellectual world according to my poor belief, which, at your desire, I have expressed—whether rightly or wrongly God knows. But, whether true or false, my opinion is that in the world of knowledge the idea of good appears last of all, and is seen only with an effort; and, when seen, is also inferred to be the universal author of all things beautiful and right, parent of light and of the lord of light in this visible world, and the immediate source of reason and truth in the intellectual; and that this is the power upon which he who would act rationally either in public or private life must have his eye fixed.

I agree, he said, as far as I am able to understand you.

Moreover, I said, you must not wonder that those who attain to this beatific vision are unwilling to descend to human affairs; for their souls are ever hastening into the upper world where they desire to dwell; which desire of theirs is very natural, if our allegory may be trusted.

Yes, very natural.

And is there anything surprising in one who passes from divine contemplations to the evil state of man, misbehaving himself in a ridiculous manner, if, while his eyes are blinking and before he has become accustomed to the surrounding darkness, he is compelled to fight in courts of law, or in other places, about the images or the shadows of images of justice, and is endeavoring to meet the conceptions of those who have never yet seen absolute justice?

40   Anything but surprising, he replied.

Anyone who has common sense will remember that the bewilderments of the eyes are two kinds, and arise from two causes, either from coming out of the light or from going into the light, which is true of the mind's eye, quite as much as of the bodily eye; and he who remembers this when he sees anyone whose vision is perplexed and weak, will not be too ready to laugh; he will first ask whether that soul of man has come out of the brighter life, and is unable to see because unaccustomed to the dark, or having turned from darkness to the day is dazzled by excess of light. And he will count the one happy in his condition and state of being, and he will pity the other; or, if he have a mind to laugh at the soul which comes from below into the light, there will be more reason in this than in the laugh which greets him who returns from above out of the light into the den.

That, he said, is a very just distinction.

But then, if I am right, certain professors of education must be wrong when they say that they can put a knowledge into the soul which was not there before, like sight into blind eyes.

They undoubtedly say this, he replied.

45   Whereas, our argument shows that the power and capacity of learning exists in the soul already; and that just as the eye was unable to turn from darkness to light without the whole body, so too the instrument of knowledge can only by the movement of the whole soul be turned from the world of becoming into that of being, and learn by degrees to endure the sight of being, and of the brightest and best of being, or in other words, of the good.

Very true.

And must there not be some art which will effect conversion in the easiest and quickest manner; not implanting the faculty of sight, for that exists already, but has been turned in the wrong direction, and is looking away from the truth?

Yes, he said, such an art may be presumed.

And whereas the other so-called virtues of the soul seem to be akin to bodily qualities, for even when they are not originally innate they can be implanted later by habit and exercise, the virtue of wisdom more than anything else contains a divine element which always remains, and by this conversion is rendered useful and profitable; or, on the other hand, hurtful and useless. Did you never observe the narrow intelligence flashing from the keen eye of a clever rogue—how eager he is, how clearly his paltry soul sees the way to his end; he is the reverse of blind, but his keen eyesight is forced into the service of evil, and he is mischievous in proportion to his cleverness?

50   Very true, he said.

But what if there had been a circumcision of such natures in the days of their youth; and they had been severed from those sensual pleasures, such as eating and drinking, which, like leaden weights, were attached to them at their birth, and which drag them down and turn the vision of their souls upon the things that are below—if, I say, they had been released from these impediments and turned in the opposite direction, the very same faculty in them would have seen the truth as keenly as they see what their eyes are turned to now.

Very likely.

Yes, I said; and there is another thing which is likely, or rather a necessary inference from what has preceded, that neither the uneducated and uninformed of the truth, nor yet those who never make an end of their education, will be able ministers of State; not the former, because they have no single aim of duty which is the rule of all their actions, private as well as public; nor the latter, because they will not act at all except upon compulsion, fancying that they are already dwelling apart in the islands of the blessed.

Very true, he replied.

55   Then, I said, the business of us who are the founders of the State will be to compel the best minds to attain that knowledge which we have already shown to be the greatest of all—they must continue to ascend until they arrive at the good; but when they have ascended and seen enough we must not allow them to do as they do now.

What do you mean?

I mean that they remain in the upper world: but this must not be allowed; they must be made to descend again among the prisoners in the den, and partake of their labors and honors, whether they are worth having or not.

But is not this unjust? he said; ought we to give them a worse life, when they might have a better?

You have again forgotten, my friend, I said, the intention of the legislator, who did not aim at making any one class in the State happy above the rest; the happiness was to be in the whole State, and he held the citizens together by persuasion and necessity, making them benefactors of the State, and therefore benefactors of one another; to this end he created them, not to please themselves, but to be his instruments in binding up the State.

60   True, he said, I had forgotten.

Observe, Glaucon, that there will be no injustice in compelling our philosophers to have a care and providence of others; we shall explain to them that in other States, men of their class are not obliged to share in the toils of politics: and this is reasonable, for they grow up at their own sweet will, and the government would rather not have them. Being self-taught, they cannot be expected to show any gratitude for a culture which they have never received. But we have brought you into the world to be rulers of the hive, kings of yourselves and of the other citizens, and have educated you far better and more perfectly than they have been educated, and you are better able to share in the double duty. Wherefore each of you, when his turn comes, must go down to the general underground abode, and get the habit of seeing in the dark. When you have acquired the habit, you will see ten thousand times better than the inhabitants of the den, and you will know what the several images are, and what they represent, because you have seen the beautiful and just and good in their truth. And thus our State, which is also yours, will be a reality, and not a dream only, and will be administered in a spirit unlike that of other States, in which men fight with one another about shadows only and are distracted in the struggle for power, which in their eyes is a great good. Whereas the truth is that the State in which the rulers are most reluctant to govern is always the best and most quietly governed, and the State in which they are most eager, the worst.

Quite true, he replied.

And will our pupils, when they hear this, refuse to take their turn at the toils of State, when they are allowed to spend the greater part of their time with one another in the heavenly light?

Impossible, he answered; for they are just men, and the commands which we impose upon them are just; there can be no doubt that every one of them will take office as a stern necessity, and not after the fashion of our present rulers of State.

65   Yes, my friend, I said; and there lies the point. You must contrive for your future rulers another and a better life than that of a ruler, and then you may have a well-ordered State; for only in the State which offers this, will they rule who are truly rich, not in silver and gold, but in virtue and wisdom, which are the true blessings of life. Whereas if they go to the administration of public affairs, poor and hungering after their own private advantage, thinking that hence they are to snatch the chief good, order there can never be; for they will be fighting about office, and the civil and domestic broils which thus arise will be the ruin of the rulers themselves and of the whole State.

Most true, he replied.

And the only life which looks down upon the life of political ambition is that of true philosophy. Do you know of any other?

Indeed, I do not, he said.

MAKING CONNECTIONS

1. An allegory is an extended metaphor. What is the cave a metaphor for? What is Plato really describing here?
2. Do you think this metaphor works—that the darkness and light of a cave can be applied so broadly to human knowledge? Explain.
3. According to the narrator, "the State in which the rulers are most reluctant to govern is always the best...and the State in which they are most eager, the worst." What does he mean? To what extent do you agree?

MAKING AN ARGUMENT

1. Write an essay that compares and contrasts "The Allegory of the Cave" with the excerpt from Thoreau's "Civil Disobedience" on page 1054. Do Plato and Thoreau agree about the purpose of government? About the rights of the individual? About the nature of knowledge? Cite the text of both pieces for support.

PHILIP SIMMONS [1958–2002]

In 1993, at the age of thirty-five, Philip Simmons, a professor of literature and creative writing at Lake Forest College, a literary critic, and a fiction writer, was diagnosed with ALS, or Lou Gehrig's disease. The essay that follows is taken from his collection Learning to Fall, *which was written and published during his illness. After an exceptionally long struggle with ALS, Simmons died in New Hampshire in 2002.*

Learning to Fall

[2000]

Because I've spent the happier parts of my life at the southern edge of New Hampshire's White Mountains, two peaks rule my imagination: Mount Washington for its sheer size, its record winds and killing weather, and Mount Chocorua for its noble profile and for the legend of the defiant Pequawket Indian chief who leaped to his death from its summit, cursing the white men who had pursued him there. I climbed Chocorua many times as a boy, and from the time of our courtship, my wife and I counted a hike to its summits as one of our annual rituals. On one such hike we made the romantic and wildly impractical decision to build a seasonal home here in New Hampshire, the place of my boyhood summers, over a thousand miles away from the Midwestern flatlands where we live and work most of the year. On the same hike, incidentally, I talked a teenage boy out of jumping off of the large angular boulder that perches just a few yards down from the summit on the east side. The boy had climbed atop the rock, about the size of a one-car garage, and then could not quite bring himself to climb down again. As he was on the point of leaping, encouraged by his friends below, I summoned my best classroom voice and said "Don't do that." I then talked him down the way he had come up. In the back of my mind I was thinking that this young man was not cut out for Chief Chocorua's fate.

Barring a miracle, I'll not climb Chocorua again. It's been almost four years since I was diagnosed with Lou Gehrig's disease, a degenerative and ultimately fatal neurological disease with no effective treatment and no cure. In that time, I've managed to finish climbing all 49 of the New Hampshire peaks above 4,000 feet, a task begun at age six with my first ascent of Mount Washington. Now, however, my legs won't go the distance, and I must content myself with the lesser triumphs of getting on my socks in the morning and making it down the stairs. On the day last summer when I began writing this essay, my wife Kathryn and our seven-year-old son Aaron were climbing Mount Washington without me. Unable to join them in body, I did a quick search of the Web and found a live view from a camera mounted in the observatory at the summit. Pointed north, the camera showed the darkly hunched peaks of the northern Presidential Range beneath blue sky. Another click of the mouse gave me the current weather conditions. A near perfect July day: visibility 80 miles, wind at 35 miles per hour, temperature 42 degrees. Satisfied that my wife and son would experience the summit at its best, I then set out to discover, in their honor, what it might be possible to say about climbing, and not climbing. About remaining upright, and learning to fall.

Actors and stunt men learn to fall: as kids we watched them leap from moving trains and stage coaches. I have a dim memory of an eighth grade acting class in which I was taught to fall, but I can't remember the technique. Athletes learn to fall, and most people who have played sports have at some point had a coach tell them how to dive and roll, an art I never mastered. Devotees of the martial arts learn to fall, as do dancers and rock climbers. Mostly, though, we learn to do it badly.

My earliest memory: I'm standing alone at the top of the stairs, looking down, scared. I call for my mother, but she doesn't come. I grip the banister and look down: I have never done this on my own before. It's the first conscious decision of my life. On some level I must know that by doing this I'm becoming something new: I am becoming an "I." The memory ends here: my hand gripping the rail above my head, one foot launched into space.

5   Forty years later, encroaching baldness has made it easier to see the scars I gained from that adventure. Still, I don't regret it. One has to start somewhere. Is not falling, as much as climbing, our birth right? In the Christian theology of the fall, we all suffer the fall from grace, the fall from our primordial connectedness with God. My little tumble down the stairs was my own expulsion from the Garden: ever after I have been falling forward and down into the scarred years of conscious life, falling into the knowledge of pain, grief, and loss.

We have all suffered, and will suffer, our own falls. The fall from youthful ideals, the waning of physical strength, the failure of a cherished hope, the loss of our near and dear, the fall into injury or sickness, and late or soon, the fall to our certain ends. We have no choice but to fall, and little say as to the time or the means.

Perhaps, however, we do have some say in the manner of our falling. That is, perhaps we have a say in matters of *style*. As kids we all played the game of leaping from a diving board or dock, and before hitting the water striking some outrageous or goofy pose: axe-murderer, Washington crossing the Delaware, rabid dog. Maybe it comes to no more than this. But I'd like to think that learning to fall is more than merely a matter of posing, more than an opportunity to play it for laughs. In fact I would have it that in the way of our falling we have the opportunity to express our essential humanity.

There's a well-known Zen parable about the man who was crossing a field when he saw a tiger charging at him. The man ran, but the tiger gained on him, chasing him toward the edge of a cliff. When he reached the edge, the man had no choice but to leap. He had one chance to save himself: a scrubby branch growing out of the side of the cliff about half way down. He grabbed the branch and hung on. Looking down, what did he see on the ground below? Another tiger.

Then the man saw that a few feet off to his left a small plant grew out of the cliff, and from it there hung one ripe strawberry. Letting go with one hand he found that he could stretch his arm out just far enough to pluck the berry with his fingertips and bring it to his lips.

10   How sweet it tasted!

I'm sure we've all found ourselves in this predicament.

I found myself in it summer before last, half way up the rock slide on the north peak of Mount Tripyramid. The north slide of Tripyramid is a mile of slick granite slabs and loose gravel partially grown over with scrubby spruce and birch on a pitch as steep as the roof of your house. I had done this hike as a boy, in canvas sneakers and long pants, but had not remembered how hard it was. Earlier that summer my weakening, wobbly legs had managed to get me up Chocorua with only a little trouble on the upper ledges. But here they had failed me. I had already fallen twice, bruising ribs, gashing knees, mashing one elbow to pulp. Standing there looking out over the valley, my legs shook and each breath brought pain. I had been in tight spots in the mountains before, but this was the closest I had ever felt to the entire wretched business of litters, rescue teams, and emergency vehicles. I looked out at the mountains because they were the only thing I could look at. The view down the slope at my feet was terrifying, the view up at the climb ahead intolerable.

there and whether I was all right. I wish I could have managed an answer such as "practicing my yoga" or "listening for hoofbeats." What I was doing was learning to fall. In the following days I did some thinking about the expression "watch your step," and even better, "mind your step." I thought about the Buddhist practice of walking meditation in which one becomes fully mindful of each step placed upon the earth. One of the blessings of my current stumbling condition is that I must practice this meditation continually, becoming mindful where I once was heedless. To walk upright upon the earth—what a blessing! When my wife and son left for their hike up Mount Washington and I set to work on this essay, I was also thinking about the expression "to fall on one's face," that perfect metaphor for those failures that cure us of complacency and pride.

The next day I learned that within minutes of my finishing a paragraph on these subjects and calling it quits for the afternoon, Kathryn found herself briefly airborne on Mount Washington. She and Aaron had made the summit, drunk in the gorgeous view I had peeped at via computer gimmickry, and then begun their descent down the treeless rock pile of the summit cone. Still well above treeline, on a steep slope approaching a precipice, her toe caught a rock and launched her up and out as though she intended a glider tour of the Great Gulf Wilderness. I can only imagine my son's thoughts as he watched his mother take flight, but surely my wife felt in those instants the pull toward twin possibilities for transcendence—upward toward some unearthly ascension and downward toward death—before crashing to the rocks, my son watching her bounce and roll toward the abyss, wondering if she would ever stop, Kathryn at last coming to rest, sorely convinced that her escape from earthy toil would not come so easily, in the meantime suffering the ordinary and decidedly untranscendent fate of three cracked ribs and a punctured lung.

What to make of all this? I'm a husband, but I'm also a writer, and even while making the necessary phone calls, dealing with the health insurance, and driving to the hospital, any writer worth his salt is on some level thinking "this is good material." Writers, like bears, are willing to feed on almost anything.

Think again of falling as a figure of speech. We fall on our faces, we fall for a joke, we fall for someone, we fall in love. In each of these falls, what do we fall away from? We fall from ego, we fall from our carefully constructed identities, our reputations, our precious selves. We fall from ambition, we fall from grasping, we fall, at least temporarily, from reason. And what do we fall into? We fall into passion, into terror, into unreasoning joy. We fall into humility, into compassion, into emptiness, into oneness with forces larger than ourselves, into oneness with others whom we realize are likewise falling. We fall, at last, into the presence of the sacred, into godliness, into mystery, into our better, diviner natures.

25   After a few nights in the hospital and two difficult months my wife's ribs have mended. And I did make it to the top of Mount Tripyramid that day, despite the storm that splattered the rocks and sent us scurrying for rain gear. For I was not alone: my wife was there, and two of my brothers, and two young friends who hauled me, bloody and bowed, to the summit.

But this is not a story of triumph over adversity. The man chased by tigers does not win in the end, at least not Hollywood fashion. In Christian theology we fall so that we can rise again later. That's a good story, too, but not the one I'm telling today. I would rather, at least for now, find victory in the falling itself, in learning how to live fully, consciously in the presence of mystery. When we learn to fall we learn to accept the vulnerability that is our human endowment, the cost of walking upright on the earth.

In the northern part of our town there's a stream that comes down out of the mountains, and at one place that we call the Pothole it makes a pool of emerald clear water ten feet deep. Every summer from my boyhood until quite recently I would climb the rocks high above that pool and fling my body into the air. A summer was not complete without the thrill of that rushing descent, the slap of the water, the shock of its icy embrace. I have a photograph, taken two years ago, of what would prove to be my last such jump. In the foreground, seen from the back, my wife stands waist deep in water, shading her eyes with one hand, watching. She has never approved of this ritual, something most grown men leave behind with their teenage years, but there I am, half way down, pale against the dark rocks that I rush past. You can see my wet footprints on the rock over my head that I've just left. My eyes are focused downward on the water rushing toward my feet, and I am happy, terrified, alive.

We are all—all of us—falling. We are all, now, this moment, in the midst of that descent, fallen from heights that may now seem only a dimly remembered dream, falling toward a depth we can only imagine, glimpsed beneath the water's surface shimmer. And so let us pray that if we are falling from grace, dear God let us also fall *with* grace, *to* grace. If we are falling toward pain and weakness, let us also fall toward sweetness and strength. If we are falling toward death, let us also fall toward life.

MAKING CONNECTIONS

1. Have you ever been faced with a debilitating illness or injury? If so, what did you find most frustrating in that experience? What most illuminating?

2. What does he mean by "When we learn to fall we learn to accept the vulnerability that is our human endowment, the cost of walking upright on the earth"? Do you agree? Explain.

MAKING AN ARGUMENT

1. Both Philip Simmons's "Learning to Fall" and Camus's "The Myth of Sisyphus" on page 1232 seem to be saying that "life is not a problem to be solved." Write an essay that compares and contrasts the way that these two pieces address this theme. Cite the text of both essays for support.

CASE STUDY IN CONTEXTUAL CRITICISM

The Poetry of Emily Dickinson

By presenting some insights into the life of Emily Dickinson, a rich sampling of her work, and representative critical commentary, this Case Study provides you with contextual material sufficient for a self-contained research unit.

HER LIFE [1830–1886]

Emily Dickinson was born to a well-to-do, well-known family in Amherst, Massachusetts. Her grandfather was one of the founders of Amherst College, and her father was a state senator, U.S. congressman, and the lawyer and treasurer of Amherst College. At home, her father created and dominated a highly conservative, religious atmosphere in which he read morning prayers and scripture to both family and servants. Dickinson attended Amherst Academy, but after a subsequent unhappy year at the Mount Holyoke Female Seminary (which would become Mount Holyoke College), she returned home and gradually removed herself from outside responsibilities. She traveled rarely and led an almost solitary existence.

In order to protect her from books that might "joggle" her mind, her father forbade the reading of novels—a prohibition that did not stop her from reading and admiring novelists like the Brontë sisters or George Eliot. She read the Bible, classical myths, and Shakespeare—and often made allusions to them in her poems. And she read and admired the poetry of Keats, Robert and Elizabeth Barrett Browning, Tennyson, and the work of American contemporaries like Hawthorne, Emerson, and Thoreau.

Although it was reported that she dressed only in white, and was known throughout Amherst as an eccentric recluse, she had ongoing relationships with a number of people who provided her with feedback about her poetry. Most notable among these contacts were her sister-in-law, Susan Gilbert Dickinson, with whom she had a close friendship, and Thomas Wentworth Higginson, the editor of the *Atlantic Monthly,* whom she considered her mentor. And there were other men in her life: Benjamin Newton, who worked for her father and with whom she discussed books;

Samuel Bowles, a newspaper editor and friend of the family; Charles Wadsworth, a Presbyterian minister; and widower and longtime friend Judge Otis Lord. But though Dickinson wrote powerful poems about the passion and disappointments of love, there is no evidence to indicate with whom she might have been in love—or that she had ever been physically intimate with any man. What little we know of her exterior life, however, her remarkably insightful poems tell us a great deal about her rich, reflective interior life.

HER WORK

Dickinson published very few of the nearly two thousand exquisitely crafted and startlingly original poems she composed during her lifetime, and she made her sister and brother promise to destroy her remaining work after her death. Her sister, Lavinia, did destroy her letters, but (fortunately) could not bring herself to destroy the poems—many of which were sewn into booklets or tied in bundles and hidden in bureau drawers. After numerous revisions in wording, punctuation, rhyme, and structure were made to Dickinson's poetry to "conform" her work to nineteenth-century sensibilities, nine volumes of her work were published in the 1890s—and in subsequent editions during the first half of the twentieth century. Not until Thomas H. Johnson published his three-volume edition of her work in 1955, however, did Dickinson's verses become available as she originally composed them.

Dickinson's stature continued to grow throughout the twentieth century, and today, along with Walt Whitman, she is considered one of the two great poetic geniuses of the nineteenth century and a cofounder of modern American poetry. But while Dickinson and Whitman both wrote unconventional poetry, and their work is filled with brilliant originality, their poems are quite different. Whitman's poetry is expansive and public; the verse lines are long—and his themes are large and broadly focused. Dickinson's poems are tightly compressed and inward with a focus on intensely felt moments.

Dickinson's poetry is complex yet wonderfully simple. Her vivid, penetrating language offers and suggests complex thought and emotion—intensifying, clarifying, and recreating experience. Her images, her timing, her sounds and structures, and her indirections are inner-life magical.

THE POEMS

If you are unfamiliar with her unique style, her poetry may provide some difficulty—at least initially. The word combinations in her lines sometimes leave spaces you are expected to fill, and her language anticipates your interpretation. The poems require active engagement—an engagement that will fill in the gaps. Read each poem several times—and out loud. Listen carefully, and give yourself time to sense the images; immerse yourself in them, feel them before you try to figure them out. Once they are felt—"where the meanings are"—you'll be well on your way to understanding them.

SUCCESS IS COUNTED SWEETEST   [c. 1859]

Success is counted sweetest
By those who ne'er succeed.
To comprehend a nectar
Requires sorest need.

Not one of all the purple Host   5
Who took the Flag today
Can tell the definition
So clear of Victory

As he defeated—dying—
On whose forbidden ear   10
The distant strains of triumph
Burst agonized and clear!

FAITH IS A FINE INVENTION   [c. 1861]

"Faith" is a fine invention
For gentlemen who *see*—
But *microscopes* are prudent
In an Emergency.

THERE'S A CERTAIN SLANT OF LIGHT   [c. 1861]

There's a certain Slant of light,
Winter Afternoons—
That oppresses, like the Heft
Of Cathedral Tunes—

Heavenly Hurt, it gives us—   5
We can find no scar,
But internal difference,
Where the Meanings, are—

None may teach it—Any—
'Tis the Seal Despair—   10
An imperial affliction
Sent us of the Air—

When it comes, the Landscape listens—
Shadows—hold their breath—
When it goes, 'tis like the Distance   15
On the look of Death—

I LIKE A LOOK OF AGONY   [c. 1861]

I like a look of Agony,
Because I know it's true—

Men do not sham Convulsion,
Nor simulate, a Throe—

The Eyes glaze once—and that is Death—   5
Impossible to feign
The Beads upon the forehead
By homely Anguish strung.

WILD NIGHTS — WILD NIGHTS!   [c. 1861]

Wild Nights—Wild Nights!
Were I with thee
Wild Nights should be
Our luxury!

Futile—the Winds—   5
To a heart in port—
Done with the Compass—
Done with the Chart!

Rowing in Eden—
Ah! the Sea!
Might I but moor—Tonight—   10
In Thee!

THE BRAIN — IS WIDER THAN THE SKY —   [c. 1862]

The Brain—is wider than the sky—
For—put them side by side—
The one the other will contain
With ease—and You—beside—

The Brain is deeper than the sea—   5
For—hold them—Blue to Blue—
The one the other will absorb—
As Sponges—buckets—do—

The Brain is just the weight of God—
For—Heft them—Pound for Pound—
And they will differ—if they do—   10
As syllable from Sound—

MUCH MADNESS IS DIVINEST SENSE —   [c. 1862]

Much Madness is divinest Sense—
To a discerning Eye—
Much Sense—the starkest Madness—
'Tis the Majority
In this, as All, prevail—   5

Assent—and you are sane—
Demur—you're straightway dangerous—
And handled with a Chain—

I'VE SEEN A DYING EYE   [c. 1862]

I've seen a Dying Eye
Run round and round a room—
In search of Something—as it seemed—
Then Cloudier become—
And then—obscure with Fog—   5
And then—be soldered down
Without disclosing what it be
'Twere blessed to have seen—

I HEARD A FLY BUZZ — WHEN I DIED —   [c. 1862]

I heard a Fly buzz—when I died—
The Stillness in the Room
Was like the Stillness in the Air—
Between the Heaves of Storm—

The Eyes around—had wrung them dry—   5
And Breaths were gathering firm
For that last Onset—when the King
Be witnessed—in the Room—

I willed my Keepsakes—Signed away
What portion of me be   10
Assignable—and then it was
There interposed a Fly—

With Blue—uncertain stumbling Buzz—
Between the light—and me—
And then the Windows failed—and then   15
I could not see to see—

AFTER GREAT PAIN, A FORMAL FEELING COMES —   [c. 1862]

After great pain, a formal feeling comes—
The Nerves sit ceremonious, like Tombs—
The stiff Heart questions was it He, that bore,
And Yesterday, or Centuries before?

The Feet, mechanical, go round—   5
Of Ground, or Air, or Ought—
A Wooden way
Regardless grown,
A Quartz contentment, like a stone—

This is the Hour of Lead— 10
Remembered, if outlived,
As Freezing persons, recollect the Snow—
First—Chill—then Stupor—then the letting go—

SOME KEEP THE SABBATH GOING TO CHURCH— [c. 1862]

Some keep the Sabbath going to Church—
I keep it, staying at Home—
With a Bobolink for a Chorister—
And an Orchard, for a Dome—

Some keep the Sabbath in Surplice— 5
I just wear my Wings—
And instead of tolling the Bell, for Church,
Our little Sexton—sings.

God preaches, a noted Clergyman—
And the sermon is never long, 10
So instead of getting to Heaven, at last—
I'm going, all along.

THIS WORLD IS NOT CONCLUSION [C. 1862]

This World is not Conclusion.
A Sequel stands beyond—
Invisible, as Music—
But positive, as Sound—
It beckons, and it baffles— 5
Philosophy—don't know—
And through a Riddle, at the last—
Sagacity, must go—
To guess it, puzzles scholars—
To gain it, Men have borne 10
Contempt of Generations
And Crucifixion, shown—
Faith slips—and laughs, and rallies—
Blushes, if any see—
Plucks at a twig of Evidence— 15
And asks a Vane, the way—
Much Gesture, from the pulpit—
Strong Hallelujahs roll—
Narcotics cannot still the Tooth
That nibbles at the soul— 20

THERE IS A PAIN—SO UTTER— [C. 1862]

There is a pain—so utter—
It swallows substance up—
Then covers the Abyss with Trance—

So memory can step
Around—across—upon it—   5
As one within a Swoon—
Goes safely—where an open eye—
Would drop Him—Bone by Bone.

BECAUSE I COULD NOT STOP FOR DEATH —   [c. 1863]

Because I could not stop for Death—
He kindly stopped for me—
The Carriage held but just Ourselves—
And Immortality.

We slowly drove—He knew no haste,   5
And I had put away
My labor and my leisure too,
For His Civility—

We passed the School, where Children strove
At Recess—in the Ring—   10
We passed the Fields of Gazing Grain—
We passed the Setting Sun—

Or rather—He passed Us—
the Dew drew quivering and chill—
For only Gossamer, my Gown—   15
My Tippet°—only Tulle°—

We paused before a House that seemed
A swelling of the Ground—
The Roof was scarcely visible—
The Cornice—in the Ground—   20

Since then—'tis Centuries—and yet
Feels shorter than the Day
I first surmised the Horses' Heads
Were toward Eternity—

THE BUSTLE IN A HOUSE   [c. 1866]

The Bustle in a House
The Morning after Death
Is solemnest of industries
Enacted upon Earth—

The Sweeping up the Heart   5
And putting love away
We shall not want to use again
Until Eternity.

16 Tippet shawl   **Tulle** silk netting

Tell all the Truth but tell it slant—   [c. 1868]

Tell all the Truth but tell it slant—
Success in Circuit lies
Too bright for our Infirm Delight
The Truth's superb surprise
As Lightning to the Children eased   5
With explanations kind
The Truth must dazzle gradually
Or every man be blind—

MAKING CONNECTIONS

1. What similarities in structure, rhythm, and word choice do you notice
   among Dickinson's poems?
2. The poems above are arranged chronologically. Do you see any evidence
   that Dickinson's work has evolved over time? Are there noticeable changes
   or developments in ideas or styles? Explain.
3. To what extent does your reading and understanding of earlier poems in
   the sequence help you read and understand some of the later ones?

Success is Counted Sweetest

1. Do you agree with the title? Explain.
2. To what extent does your own experience influence your response?

Faith is a Fine Invention

1. What does the speaker mean "For gentleman who *see*"?
2. In what way do microscopes represent a different way of seeing?

There's a Certain Slant of Light

1. What is the setting for this poem? Why does the speaker call it a "Slant of
   light" rather than a "light"?
2. What does she mean by "None may teach it"? To what extent can this apply
   to the subjects of her other poems as well?

I Like a Look of Agony

1. Do you find it startling that the speaker likes "a look of Agony"? Explain.
2. To what extent is this a poem about other "looks" the speaker has seen?

Wild Nights—Wild Nights!

1. How can we reconcile this poem with Dickinson's reclusive life?
2. What is the central metaphor of the poem? To what extent does it work?

The Brain—is Wider than the Sky—

1. How could the brain be "wider than the sky"?
2. To what extent does this poem represent Dickinson's life and writing?

Much madness is divinest Sense —

1. What do you think the speaker means by "Much Madness"? By "Much Sense"?
2. Who is the "Majority" that prevail? Do you think they should? Explain.

I've seen a Dying Eye

1. In what way is this poem more about those looking on than it is about the dying person?
2. In what way is the eye running around the room—and why?

I Heard a Fly buzz—when I died —

1. Who is the speaker in the poem?
2. Why do you think the poet chose a "fly" and not something more exotic?

After great pain, a formal feeling comes —

1. What kind of "great pain" does the speaker make reference to?
2. To what extent is your response affected by your own experience? How do the images convey the meaning?

Some keep the Sabbath going to Church —

1. Describe how the speaker keeps the Sabbath.
2. What does the speaker mean by "instead of getting to Heaven.../ I'm going, all along"?

This World is not Conclusion

1. What is the "Tooth / That nibbles at the soul"?
2. Compare this poem to "Faith is a fine invention."

There is a pain—so utter —

1. Why do you think the speaker seems unable to finish the first line?
2. Compare this poem with "The Bustle in a House" or "After great pain, a formal feeling comes."

Because I could not stop for Death —

1. To what extent is the title and first line of this poem ironic?
2. What concrete images in the poem signify death?

The Bustle in a House

1. Why do you think there is such a bustle in the house? Have you ever experienced one like it? Explain.
2. Compare this poem to "There is a pain—so utter—" or "After great pain, a formal feeling comes."

Tell all the Truth but tell it slant —

1. How does this poem compare with the popular saying "Honesty is the best policy"? Do you think it's right when telling the truth to "tell it slant"? Explain.
2. Consider the words and images in this brief poem. Do you think they convey the message of the poem effectively? How so?

MAKING AN ARGUMENT

1. The sixteen Dickinson poems in this Case Study are connected to the theme of this section—Faith and Doubt—but what other, more specific thematic connections can you find between and among her poems? Identify a consistent theme in her work, and write an essay that supports your view. Cite the text of the poems for support.

2. Both Emily Dickinson and Walt Whitman were innovative geniuses who transcended the poetic conventions of their age—but their work is very different. Write an essay that compares and contrasts the style, structure, and content of Dickinson's poems with Whitman's poems in this anthology: "When I Heard the Learn'd Astronomer" (p. 89), "There Was a Child Went Forth" (p. 476), and "Song of Myself 6" (p. 1164).

3. Given the unusual nature of her images and metaphors, Dickinson's work is often compared with that of John Donne. Write an essay that compares her poetry and her metaphors with those in Donne's poem "Death, Be Not Proud" (p. 1157).

4. Choose one poem to read closely. Discuss *how* this poem embodies such poetic features as metaphor/simile, imagery, diction, rhyme, alliteration, and structure; and how these elements create meaning and emotion in the poem.

5. Relate several poems and describe what they have in common as well as where they differ—not only in theme but language, style, point of view, tone.

6. What "voice" do you hear in Emily Dickinson's poetry? Is there a consistent personality or attitude that comes across? Explain.

7. Choose one of the subjects that the poet addresses in one or more poems and show how she treats this theme, what perspective she brings to such motifs as passion, death, faith, intelligence, honesty, and poetry itself.

8. What makes Emily Dickinson's poetry ? (Provide the adjective of your choice: strange, difficult, challenging, humorous, interesting, etc.) Explain your choice.

9. Read one or more of the commentaries, essays, and poems that follow the poetry as part of the case study unit, and relate the text(s) to your reading of Dickinson's poetry.

EMILY DICKINSON—IN HER OWN WORDS

TO SUSAN GILBERT (DICKINSON)

late APRIL 1852

So sweet and still, and Thee, Oh Susie, what need I more, to make my heaven whole?

Sweet Hour, blessed Hour, to carry me to you, and to bring you back to me, long enough to snatch one kiss, and whisper Good bye, again.

I have thought of it all day, Susie, and I fear of but little else, and when I was gone to meeting it filled my mind so full, I could not find a *chink* to put the worthy pastor; when he said "Our Heavenly Father," I said "Oh Darling Sue"; when he read the 100th Psalm, I kept saying your precious letter all over to myself, and Susie, when they sang—it would have made you laugh to hear one little voice, piping to the departed. I made up words and kept singing how I loved you, and you had gone, while all the rest of the choir were singing Hallelujahs. I presume nobody heard me, because I sang *so small,* but it was a kind of a comfort to think I might put them out, singing of you. I a'nt there this afternoon, tho', because I am here, writing a little letter to my dear Sue, and I am very happy. I think of ten weeks— Dear One, and I think of love, and you, and my heart grows full and warm, and my breath stands still. The sun does'nt shine at all, but I can feel a sunshine stealing into my soul and making it all summer, and every thorn, a *rose.* And I pray that such summer's sun shine on my Absent One, and cause her bird to sing!

You have been happy, Susie, and now are sad—and the whole world seems lone; but it wont be so always, "some days *must* be dark and dreary"! You wont cry any more, will you, Susie, for my father will be your father, and my home will be your home, and where you go, I will go, and we will lie side by side in the kirkyard.

5　　I have parents on earth, dear Susie, but your's are in the skies, and I have an earthly fireside, but you have one above, and you have a "Father in Heaven," where I have *none*—and *sister* in heaven, and I know they love you dearly, and think of you every day.

Oh I wish I had half so many dear friends as you in heaven—I could'nt spare them now—but to know they had got there safely, and should suffer nevermore— Dear Susie!…

Emilie—

To T. W. Higginson

25 April 1862

Mr Higginson,

Your kindness claimed earlier gratitude—but I was ill—and write today, from my pillow.

Thank you for the surgery—it was not so painful as I supposed. I bring you others—as you ask—though they might not differ—

While my thought is undressed—I can make the distinction, but when I put them in the Gown—they look alike, and numb.

You asked how old I was? I made no verse—but one or two—until this winter—Sir—

5　　I had a terror—since September—I could tell to none—and so I sing, as the Boy does by the Burying Ground—because I am afraid—You inquire my Books— For Poets—I have Keats—and Mr and Mrs Browning. For Prose—Mr Ruskin—Sir Thomas Browne—and the Revelations. I went to school—but in your manner of the phrase—had no education. When a little Girl, I had a friend, who taught me Immortality—but venturing too near, himself—he never returned—Soon after, my Tutor, died—and for several years, my Lexicon—was my only companion—Then I found one more—but he was not contented I be his scholar—so he left the Land.

You ask of my Companions Hills—Sir—and the Sundown—and a Dog—large as myself, that my Father bought me—They are better than Beings—because they know—but do not tell—and the noise in the Pool, at Noon—excels my Piano. I have a Brother and Sister—My Mother does not care for thought—and Father, too busy with his Briefs—to notice what we do—He buys me many Books—but begs me not to read them—because he fears they joggle the Mind. They are religious—except me—and address an Eclipse, every morning—whom they call their "Father." But I fear my story fatigues you—I would like to learn—Could you tell me how to grow—or is it unconveyed—like Melody—or Witchcraft?

You speak of Mr Whitman—I never read his Book—but was told that he was disgraceful—

I read Miss Prescott's "Circumstance," but it followed me, in the Dark—so I avoided her—

Two Editors of Journals came to my Father's House, this winter—and asked me for my Mind—and when I asked them "Why," they said I was penurious—and they, would use it for the World—

10   I could not weigh myself—Myself—

My size felt small—to me—I read your Chapters in the Atlantic—and experienced honor for you—I was sure you would not reject a confiding question—

Is this—Sir—what you asked me to tell you?

Your friend,

E—Dickinson.

IN OTHERS' WORDS

THOMAS WENTWORTH HIGGINSON [1823–1911]

ON MEETING DICKINSON FOR THE FIRST TIME   [1870]

A large county lawyer's house, brown brick, with great trees & a garden—I sent up my card. A parlor dark & cool & stiffish, a few books & engravings & an open piano....

A step like a pattering child's in entry & in glided a little plain woman with two smooth bands of reddish hair & a face a little like Belle Dove's; not plainer—with no good feature—in a very plain & exquisitely clean white pique & a blue net worsted shawl. She came to me with two day lilies which she put in a sort of childlike way into my hand & said "These are my introduction" in a soft frightened breathless childlike voice—& added under her breath Forgive me if I am frightened; I never see strangers & hardly know what I say—but she talked soon & thenceforward continuously—& deferentially—sometimes stopping to ask me to talk instead of her—but readily recommencing...thoroughly ingenuous & simple...& saying many things which you would have thought foolish & I wise—& some things you wd. hv. liked. I add a few over the page....

"Women talk; men are silent; that is why I dread women."

"My father only reads on Sunday—he reads *lonely* & *rigorous* books."

5   "If I read a book [and] it makes my whole body so cold no fire ever can warm me I know *that* is poetry. If I feel physically as if the top of my head were taken off, I know *that* is poetry. These are the only ways I know it. Is there any other way?"

"How do most people live without any thoughts? There are many people in the world (you must have noticed them in the street). How do they live? How do they get strength to put on their clothes in the morning?"

"When I lost the use of my Eyes it was a comfort to think there were so few real *books* that I could easily find some one to read me all of them"

"Truth is such a *rare* thing it is delightful to tell it."

"I find ecstasy in living—the mere sense of living is joy enough"

10   I asked if she never felt want of employment, never going off the place & never seeing any visitor "I never thought of conceiving that I could ever have the slightest approach to such a want in all future time" (& added) "I feel that I have not expressed myself strongly enough."

From a letter to his wife, August 16, 1870

MABEL LOOMIS TODD [1856–1932]

THE CHARACTER OF AMHERST [1881]

I must tell you about the *character* of Amherst. It is a lady whom the people call the *Myth*. She is a sister of Mr. Dickinson, & seems to be the climax of all the family oddity. She has not been outside of her own house in fifteen years, except once to see a new church, when she crept out at night, & viewed it by moonlight. No one who calls upon her mother & sister ever see her, but she allows little children once in a great while, & one at a time, to come in, when she gives them cake or candy, or some nicety, for she is very fond of little ones. But more often she lets down the sweetmeat by a string, out of a window, to them. She dresses wholly in white, & her mind is said to be perfectly wonderful. She writes finely, but no one *ever* sees her. Her sister, who was at Mrs. Dickinson's party, invited me to come & sing to her mother sometime....People tell me the *myth* will hear every note—she will be near, but unseen....Isn't that like a book? So interesting.

From a letter to her parents, November 6, 1881

RICHARD WILBUR [B. 1921]

ON DICKINSON'S SENSE OF PRIVATION [1960]

What did Emily Dickinson do, as a poet, with her sense of privation? One thing she quite often did was to pose as the laureate and attorney of the empty-handed, and question God about the economy of His creation. Why, she asked, is a fatherly God so sparing of His presence? Why is there never a sign that prayers are heard? Why does Nature tell us no comforting news of its Maker? Why do some receive a whole loaf, while others must starve on a crumb? Where is the benevolence in shipwreck and earthquake? By asking such questions as these, she turned complaint into critique, and used her own sufferings as experiential evidence about the nature of the deity. The God who emerges from these poems is a God who does not answer, an unrevealed God whom one cannot confidently approach through Nature or through doctrine.

But there was another way in which Emily Dickinson dealt with her sentiment of lack—another emotional strategy which was both more frequent and more fruitful. I refer to her repeated assertion of the paradox that privation is more plentiful than plenty; that to renounce is to possess the more; that "The Banquet of abstemiousness/Defaces that of wine." We all know how the poet illustrated this ascetic paradox in her behavior—how in her latter years she chose to live in relative retirement, keeping the world, even in its dearest aspects, at a physical remove. She would write her friends, telling them how she missed them, then flee upstairs when they came to see her; afterward, she might send a note of apology, offering the odd explanation that "We shun because we prize." Any reader of Dickinson biographies can furnish other examples, dramatic or homely, of this prizing and shunning, this yearning and renouncing: in my own mind's eye is a picture of Emily Dickinson watching a gay circus caravan from the distance of her chamber window.

From "Sumptuous Destitution" in *Emily Dickinson: Three Views*, by Richard Wilbur, Louise Bogan, and Archibald MacLeish

SANDRA M. GILBERT [b. 1936] AND SUSAN GUBAR [b. 1944]

ON DICKINSON'S WHITE DRESS   [1979]

Today a dress that the Amherst Historical Society assures us is *the* white dress Dickinson wore—or at least one of her "Uniforms of Snow"—hangs in a drycleaner's plastic bag in the closet of the Dickinson homestead. Perfectly preserved, beautifully flounced and tucked, it is larger than most readers would have expected this self-consciously small poet's dress to be, and thus reminds visiting scholars of the enduring enigma of Dickinson's central metaphor, even while it draws gasps from more practical visitors, who reflect with awe upon the difficulties of maintaining such a costume. But what exactly did the literal and figurative whiteness of this costume represent? What rewards did it offer that would cause an intelligent woman to overlook those practical difficulties? Comparing Dickinson's obsession with whiteness to Melville's, William R. Sherwood suggests that "it reflected in her case the Christian mystery and not a Christian enigma...a decision to announce...the assumption of a worldly death that paradoxically involved regeneration." This, he adds, her gown—"a typically slant demonstration of truth"—should have revealed "to anyone with the wit to catch on."

We might reasonably wonder, however, if Dickinson herself consciously intended her wardrobe to convey any one message. The range of associations her white poems imply suggests, on the contrary, that for her, as for Melville, white is the ultimate symbol of enigma, paradox, and irony, "not so much a color as the visible absence of color, and at the same time the concrete of all colors." Melville's question [in *Moby-Dick*] might, therefore, also be hers: "is it for these reasons that there is such a dumb blankness, full of meaning, in a wide landscape of snows—a colorless, all-color of atheism from which we shrink?" And his concluding speculation might be hers too, his remark "that the mystical cosmetic which produces every one of [Nature's] hues, the great principle of light, for ever remains white or colorless in itself, and if operating without medium upon matter, would touch all objects…with its own blank tinge." For white, in Dickinson's poetry, frequently represents both the energy (the white heat) of Romantic creativity, and the loneliness (the polar cold) of the renunciation or tribulation Romantic creativity may demand, both the white radiance of eternity—or Revelation—and the white terror of a shroud.

From The Madwoman in the Attic: The Woman Writer
and the Nineteenth-Century Literary Imagination

CRITICAL COMMENTARY ON HER POETRY

HELEN MCNEIL

DICKINSON'S METHOD   [1986]

Many Victorian poems describe unexamined abstractions, as if society agreed about what constituted sorrow or love. These could be personified, and their attributes could be listed and elaborated metaphorically. Dickinson takes on a frightening abstraction and evolves its attributes from experience, not tradition. In poetry and philosophy, the subject—the experiencing person—may wonder about the existence of other minds. Dickinson wrote many poems on this problem. In "Pain—has an Element of Blank," she contemplates the possibility that there may be circumstances in which the perceiving consciousness also does not exist, erased by its own emotion. "The Soul has Bandaged moments—" she begins another poem; the abstract soul is a bandaged body, in a metaphor which denies dualism. Time is also represented physically, bound up by pain. As Dickinson concludes at the end of "The Soul has Bandaged moments—," such recognitions "are not brayed of Tongue—" in the public discourse of her society, or, for that matter, our society either.

Dickinson wrote about feeling, but out of feeling she constructed a theory of knowledge—not *beyond* feeling, or free from it, or in any way separate, but using it as a kind of knowing. In effect—though not in conventional terms—she is an epistemological poet, a poet who advances a theory of knowledge. Dickinson made this concern explicit. After the forms of the verb "to be," "know" is the most frequently used verb in Dickinson's poetry, appearing 230 times, more even than any noun except "day."

Dickinson's constant pressure towards knowing means that she can treat even the most tormented situations with great calm. She can begin by writing "I felt a Funeral, in my Brain," or "Pain—has an Element of Blank—" or "I felt my life with both my hands—" and then proceed to delineate that state with a commanding accuracy. In a manner more resembling the Metaphysical poets than her Victorian contemporaries, male or female, she uses emotionally heightened states as occasions for clarity.

American poetry characteristically embodies acts of process: the Dickinsonian "process" is passionate investigation. Her investigative process often implies narrative by taking speaker and reader through a sequence of rapidly changing images, even when all the action is interior. These investigations structure Dickinson's poetry;

I suspect that the flexibility of her investigative movement is the major reason why Dickinson generally was contented with common meter. She may even have enjoyed the way her condensed discoveries press against the limits of a small form.

From Emily Dickinson

CYNTHIA GRIFFIN WOLFF [B. 1935]

ON THE MANY VOICES IN DICKINSON'S POETRY   [1986]

There were many "Voices." This fact has sometimes puzzled Dickinson's readers. One poem may be delivered in a child's Voice; another in the Voice of a young woman scrutinizing nature and the society in which she makes her place. Sometimes the Voice is that of a woman self-confidently addressing her lover in a language of passion and sexual desire. At still other times, the Voice of the verse seems so precariously balanced at the edge of hysteria that even its calmest observations grate like the shriek of dementia. There is the Voice of the housewife and the Voice that has recourse to the occasionally agonizing, occasionally regal language of the conversion experience of latter-day New England Puritanism. In some poems the Voice is distinctive principally because it speaks in the aftermath of wounding and can comprehend extremities of pain. Moreover, these Voices are not always entirely distinct from one another: the child's Voice that opens a poem may yield to the Voice of a young woman speaking the idiom of ardent love; in a different poem, the speaker may fall into a mood of almost religious contemplation in an attempt to analyze or define such abstract entities as loneliness or madness or eternity; the diction of the housewife may be conflated with the sovereign language of the New Jerusalem, and taken together, they may render some aspect of the wordsmith's labor. No manageable set of discrete categories suffices to capture the diversity of discourse, and any attempt to simplify Dickinson's methods does violence to the verse.

Yet there is a paradox here. This is, by no stretch of the imagination, a body of poetry that might be construed as a series of lyrics spoken by many different people. Disparate as these many Voices are, somehow they all appear to issue from the same "self."...It is the enigmatic "Emily Dickinson" readers suppose themselves to have found in this poetry, even in the extreme case when Dickinson's supposed speaker is male. One explanation for this sense of intrinsic unity in the midst of diversity is the persistence with which Dickinson addresses the same set of problems, using a remarkably durable repertoire of linguistic modes. Evocations of injury and wounding—threats to the coherence of the self—appear in the earliest poems and continue until the end; ways of rendering face-to-face encounters change, but this preoccupation with "interview" is sustained by metaphors of "confrontation" that weave throughout. The summoning of one or another Voice in a given poem, then, is not an unselfconscious emotive reflection of Emily Dickinson's mood at the moment of creation. Rather, each different Voice is a calculated tactic, an attempt to touch her readers and engage them intimately with the poetry. Each Voice had its unique advantages; each its limitations. A poet self-conscious in her craft, she calculated this element as carefully as every other.

From Emily Dickinson

ALLEN TATE

ON "BECAUSE I COULD NOT STOP FOR DEATH"   [1959]

If the word "great" means anything in poetry, this poem is one of the greatest in the English language. The rhythm charges with movement the pattern of suspended action back of the poem. Every image is precise and, moreover, not merely beautiful, but fused with the central idea. Every image extends and intensifies every other. The third stanza especially shows Miss Dickinson's power to fuse, into a single order of perception, a heterogeneous series: the children, the grain, and the setting sun (time) have the same degree of credibility; the first subtly preparing for the last. The sharp *gazing* before *grain* instills into nature a cold vitality of which the qualitative richness has infinite depth. The content of death in the poem eludes explicit definition. He is a gentleman taking a lady out for a drive. But note the restraint that keeps the poet from carrying this so far that it becomes ludicrous and incredible; and note the subtly interfused erotic motive, which the idea of death has presented to most romantic poets, love being a symbol interchangeable with death. The terror of death is objectified through this figure of the genteel driver, who is made ironically to serve the end of Immortality. This is the heart of the poem: she has presented a typical Christian theme in its final irresolution, without making any final statements about it. There is no solution to the problem; there can be only a presentation of it in the full context of intellect and feeling. A construction of the human will, elaborated with all the abstracting powers of the mind, is put to the concrete test of experience: the idea of immortality is confronted with the fact of physical disintegration. We are not told what to think; we are told to look at the situation.

The framework of the poem is, in fact, the two abstractions, mortality and eternity, which are made to associate in equality with the images: she sees the ideas, and thinks the perceptions. She did, of course, nothing of the sort; but we must use the logical distinctions, even to the extent of paradox, if we are to form any notion of this rare quality of mind. She could not in the proper sense think at all, and unless we prefer the feeble poetry of moral ideas that flourished in New England in the eighties, we must conclude that her intellectual deficiency contributed at least negatively to her great distinction. Miss Dickinson is probably the only Anglo-American poet of her century whose work exhibits the perfect literary situation—in which is possible the fusion of sensibility and thought. Unlike her contemporaries, she never succumbed to her ideas, to easy solutions, to her private desires...

Neither the feeling nor the style of Miss Dickinson belongs to the seventeenth century; yet between her and Donne there are remarkable ties. Their religious ideas, their abstractions, are momently toppling from the rational plane to the level of perception. The ideas, in fact, are no longer the impersonal religious symbols created anew in the heat of emotion, that we find in poets like Herbert and Vaughan. They have become, for Donne, the terms of personality; they are mingled with the miscellany of sensation. In Miss Dickinson, as in Donne, we may detect a singularly morbid concern, not for religious truth, but for personal revelation. The modern word is self-exploitation. It is egoism grown irresponsible in religion and decadent in morals. In religion it is blasphemy; in society it means usually that culture is not self-contained and sufficient, that the spiritual community is breaking up. This is, along with some other features that do not concern us here, the perfect literary situation.

From "Emily Dickinson," in *Collected Essays*

PAULA BENNETT [B. 1936]

ON "I HEARD A FLY BUZZ—WHEN I DIED—"   [1990]

Dickinson's rage against death, a rage that led her at times to hate both life and death, might have been alleviated, had she been able to gather hard evidence about an afterlife. But, of course, she could not. "The *Bareheaded life*—under the grass—," she wrote to Samuel Bowles in c. 1860, "worries one like a Wasp." If death was the gate to a better life in "the childhood of the kingdom of Heaven," as the sentimentalists—and Christ—claimed, then, perhaps, there was compensation and healing for life's woes....But how do we know? What can we know? In "I heard a Fly buzz—when I died," Dickinson concludes that we do not know much....

Like many people in her period, Dickinson was fascinated by death-bed scenes. How, she asked various correspondents, did this or that person die? In particular, she wanted to know if their deaths revealed any information about the nature of the afterlife. In this poem, however, she imagines her own death-bed scene, and the answer she provides is grim, as grim (and, at the same time, as ironically mocking), as anything she ever wrote.

In the narrowing focus of death, the fly's insignificant buzz, magnified tenfold by the stillness in the room, is all that the speaker hears. This kind of distortion in scale is common. It is one of the "illusions" of perception. But here it is horrifying because it defeats every expectation we have. Death is supposed to be an experience of awe. It is the moment when the soul, departing the body, is taken up by God. Hence the watchers at the bedside wait for the moment when the "King" (whether God or death) "be witnessed" in the room. And hence the speaker assigns away everything but that which she expects God (her soul) or death (her body) to take.

What arrives instead, however, is neither God nor death but a fly, "[w]ith Blue—uncertain—stumbling Buzz," a fly, that is, no more secure, no more sure, than we are. Dickinson had associated flies with death once before in the exquisite lament, "How many times these low feet / staggered." In this poem, they buzz "on the / chamber window," and speckle it with dirt, reminding us that the housewife, who once protected us from such intrusions, will protect us no longer. Their presence is threatening but only in a minor way, "dull" like themselves. They are a background noise we do not have to deal with yet.

5   In "I heard a Fly buzz," on the other hand, there is only one fly and its buzz is not only foregrounded. Before the poem is over, the buzz takes up the entire field of perception, coming between the speaker and the "light" (of day, of life, of knowledge). It is then that the "Windows" (the eyes that are the windows of the soul as well as, metonymically, the light that passes through the panes of glass) "fail" and the speaker is left in darkness—in death, in ignorance. She cannot "see" to "see" (understand).

Given that the only sure thing we know about "life after death" is that flies—in their adult form and more particularly, as maggots—devour us, the poem is at the very least a grim joke. In projecting her death-bed scene, Dickinson confronts her ignorance and gives back the only answer human knowledge can with any certainty give. While we may hope for an afterlife, no one, not even the dying, can prove it exists.

From *Emily Dickinson: Woman Poet*

POEMS ABOUT EMILY DICKINSON

LINDA PASTAN [B. 1932]

EMILY DICKINSON   [1971]

We think of her hidden in a white dress
among the folded linens and sachets
of well-kept cupboards, or just out of sight
sending jellies and notes with no address
to all the wondering Amherst neighbors.   5
Eccentric as New England weather
the stiff wind of her mind, stinging or gentle,
blew two half-imagined lovers off.
Yet legend won't explain the shear sanity
of vision, the serious mischief   10
of language, the economy of pain.

BILLY COLLINS [B. 1941]

TAKING OFF EMILY DICKINSON'S CLOTHES   [1998]

First, her tippet made of tulle,
easily lifted off her shoulders and laid
on the back of a wooden chair.

And her bonnet,
the bow undone with a light forward pull.   5

Then the long white dress, a more
complicated matter with mother-of-pearl
buttons down the back,
so tiny and numerous that it takes forever
before my hands can part the fabric,   10
like a swimmer's dividing water,
and slip inside.

You will want to know
that she was standing
by an open window in an upstairs bedroom,   15
motionless, a little wide-eyed,
looking out at the orchard below,
the white dress puddled at her feet
on the wide-board, hardwood floor.

The complexity of women's undergarments   20
in nineteenth-century America
is not to be waved off,
and I proceeded like a polar explorer
through clips, clasps, and moorings,
catches, straps, and whalebone stays   25
sailing toward the iceberg of her nakedness.

Later, I wrote in a notebook
it was like riding a swan into the night,
but, of course, I cannot tell you everything—
the way she closed her eyes to the orchard,   30
how her hair tumbled free of its pins,
how there were sudden dashes
whenever we spoke.

What I can tell you is
it was terribly quiet in Amherst   35
that Sabbath afternoon,
nothing but a carriage passing the house,
a fly buzzing in a windowpane.

So I could plainly hear her inhale
when I undid the very top   40
hook-and-eye fastener of her corset

and I could hear her sigh when finally it was unloosed,
the way some readers sigh when they realize
that Hope has feathers,
that reason is a plank,   45
that life is a loaded gun
that looks right at you with a yellow eye.

A Student's Argumentative Essay

In the argumentative essay that follows, Sophie Drake writes about the effectiveness
of an unusual poetic device—the dash—in the poetry of Emily Dickinson. Her thesis
is that while the dash does not convey much by itself, "placed strategically before and
after" Dickinson's often unusual images, it provides an essential "clarifying pause." It
is an argumentative essay because she supports her thesis by analyzing the texts of
four of Dickinson's poems and cites the text of each poem to prove her point.

Sophie Drake

Prof. Madden

English 102

September 26, 20XX

A Dash of Meaning

It is fortunate that Emily Dickinson's brother and sister did not destroy her poems after her death (as she had requested), or we would be without the work of a great American poet. When we consider the original condition of those poems, it is understandable that for their initial publication they were revised to fit the standards of the 1890s by removing dashes and "correcting" other forms of punctuation and structure. However, it is also fortunate that in the 1950s Thomas Johnson restored Emily Dickinson's poems to their original form (Madden, "Poetry" 1248). Very important among these restorations is the reinstatement of the dashes. By themselves, the dashes convey very little. But placed strategically before and after Dickinson's unusual images, they convey a great deal. The meaning they convey is in the clarifying pause, which prompts a personal response from the reader.

"There's a certain Slant of light" is a poem filled with dashes that encourage us to pause and digest unusual images by personalizing them. The first dash follows a capitalized (emphasized) "Winter Afternoons—" (2) and prompts us to recall our own experience of winter afternoons and the pale light of winter that seems only a "Slant" of light, but a slant of light that weighs on us like "the Heft / Of Cathedral Tunes—" (3–4). Each of the twelve dashes in this poem follows an image we are prompted to recall from our own experience, and the poem concludes with a haunting but familiar image of the dim light of a winter's day descending into night: "When it goes, 'tis like the Distance / on the look of Death—" (15–16).

Sometimes the dashes simply make us pause to understand a provocative opening statement: "I like a look of Agony, / Because I know it's true—" (1–2). We understand that Dickinson is not referring to everything about the look of agony but only one thing, its authenticity. She then follows with a similar sentiment about the look of death, "Impossible to feign" (6).

The dashes invite us to be part of a process of discovery. They seem to pause the poem for our response. It's almost as if we are having a conversation with the poet, a conversation that has us comparing our own internal responses to the world with hers, the dashes telling us when it's our turn. Helen McNeil supports the idea of this "internal" process when she says of Dickinson's poetry, "Her investigative process often [takes] speaker and reader through a sequence of rapidly changing images, even when all the action is interior" (1261–62).

In "I heard a Fly buzz—when I died—" (1), the dashes surround the key phrase in the poem. There is nothing special about hearing a fly buzz, but hearing a fly buzz at the moment of death, as the last event in one's life, is worthy of notice. The dashes before and after "when I died" let us pause and digest the irony and meaning of the moment. The fourteen other dashes in this poem work in a similar way. Many things are being described in this monumental moment, the "Stillness in the Air—" (3), "The Eyes around—" (5). They are the kind of images we would expect to see at such a moment, and we are given time to digest them with help from the dashes. These predictable images put us back in the death scene, until suddenly "— and then it was / There interposed a Fly—" (11–12). The preceding dash transitions us to the fly; the dash that follows gives us pause to imagine and reflect upon the usually unimportant fly that is now dominating the last vision of the speaker. As Paula Bennett describes it, the fly's buzz "is not only foregrounded. Before the poem is over, the buzz takes up the entire field of perception, coming between the speaker and the 'light' (of day, of life, of knowledge)" (1264). The dashes in the poem help us to experience that.

Allen Tate describes the poem "Because I could not stop for Death—" as "one of the greatest in the English language." He says that "Every image intensifies every other," and he praises the poet's power "to fuse, into a single order of perception, a heterogeneous series: the children, the grain, and the setting sun (time)" (1263). The poem's twenty-two strategically placed dashes help us to experience this singular vision and intensity. The poem is a journey toward eternity and the dashes connect each leg of the journey to the next; they connect us (by giving us time to pause and reflect) to each of those legs. Death is a coachman who (because "I could not stop") "kindly stopped for me—" (2). The dash lines (—) seem to extend the miles on our journey and what we see out the coach window as we encounter "the School" (9), "the Fields and Grazing Grain—" (11), "the Setting Sun—" (12) (as both distance and time pass) until we reach the grave, "A swelling of the Ground—" (18), and finally, after centuries, the realization that "the Horses'

Heads / Were toward Eternity—" (24). That last dash acts as a question mark—prompting our own thoughts on the matter of an afterlife.

It would be foolish to suggest that the dashes in Dickinson's poetry are as important as her words and the striking images that result from those words. What makes her a brilliant poet is her use of words. But the dashes matter. They prompt us to pause and to clarify our own thoughts on the image at hand and the subject of the poem at large. They put us in an interior dialogue with the speaker in the poem. They magnify and extend the poem's images—and our responses. They are dashes of meaning.

[New Page]

Works Cited

Bennett, Paula. "On 'I heard a Fly buzz—when I died—.'" Madden 1264–65.

Dickinson, Emily. "Because I could not stop for Death." Madden 1253.

--- "I heard a Fly buzz—when I died—." Madden 1251.

--- "I like a look of Agony." Madden 1249–50.

--- "There's a certain Slant of light." Madden 1249.

Madden, Frank, ed. *Exploring Literature*. 5th ed. New York: Longman, 2012. Print.

---. "The Poetry of Emily Dickinson." Madden 1247.

McNeil, Helen. "Dickinson's Method." Madden 1261–62.

Tate, Allen. "On 'Because I could not stop for Death.'" Madden 1263–64.

EXPLORING THE LITERATURE OF FAITH AND DOUBT: OPTIONS FOR MAKING CONNECTIONS, BUILDING ARGUMENTS, AND USING RESEARCH

MAKING CONNECTIONS

1. Consider the ways your beliefs and values have affected your life. Do any of the stories, poems, plays, or essays in this section remind you of your own experiences or circumstances in your life? If so, choose one or more of these works, and write a personal response essay that compares your experiences or circumstances with those in the literature.

2. Our own values, beliefs, and/or doubts affect the way we see the world and can strongly influence our response to the literature in this section. We may agree or disagree with what an author says or what characters say or do. So, too, this literature may influence us and the formation of our values and beliefs. Write an essay about the ways in which one or more works in this section either provoked a moral judgment on your part or helped you learn something.

MAKING AN ARGUMENT

1. In his 1788 work *Critique of Practical Reason,* Immanuel Kant wrote: "Morality is not properly the doctrine of how we may make ourselves happy, but how we make ourselves worthy of happiness." Do you agree? Consider this quote, and write an essay about how an author or a character in one or more works in this section defines morality or his or her values.

2. In his poem "In Memoriam," Alfred Lord Tennyson expresses his view of faith and doubt in the following lines: "There lives more faith in honest doubt, / Believe me, than in half the creeds." Do you agree? Write about this quote as it affects the way a character or an author in one or more works in this section sees the world.

3. Choose a quote (or quotes) in the introduction to this section on Faith and Doubt (pp. 1108–1109), and pair it (or them) with one of the longer pieces in this section that either supports it or argues against it. For example, Yamaga Soko's comment about the unquestioning loyalty of the samurai warrior might be paired with Wilfred Owen's *"Dulce et Decorum Est,"* which might be seen as an argument against it. If you choose R. D. Laing's comment about alienation, you might choose Matthew Arnold's poem "Dover Beach" to support it. Write an essay that compares or contrasts a quote (or quotes) from the introduction with a story, poem, play, or essay that supports it or argues against it.

Using Research

Nathaniel Hawthorne's story "Young Goodman Brown," Wilfred Owen's poem *"Dulce et Decorum Est,"* and David Mamet's play *Oleanna* all have something important to say about faith and doubt. Each of these works, however, springs from a very different historical, social, or political context. Expanding our exploration of literature to include the context in which these works were produced can be an enriching and enlightening experience.

1. Choose one or more of these or other works in this section, and write a research essay that includes secondary source material about the historical, social, or political background of the literature. However insightful each of these pieces is by itself, expanding our exploration of this literature by seeking, using, and citing relevant secondary sources can add support and credibility to our writing.

2. Because of the wars in Iraq and Afghanistan, much research has been done on post-traumatic stress syndrome. Consider the poems under the subtheme The Impact of War and the short story "The Things They Carried" on page 1132. Write a research essay that references both the literary works and recent research and addresses the impact of war on returning soldiers. Cite the texts of your sources for support.

3. Consider the relationship between human beings and nature. Many people would suggest that rather than seeing ourselves as part of nature, we take our natural surroundings for granted. Scientists suggest that one clear

example of our neglect of nature is global warming. Take a position on this issue. Are we compatible with and supportive of nature and its "other" living creatures or are we arrogant and neglectful? Cite the literature in this section—as well as current research in this area—to support your view.

Writing About Connections Across Themes

Most of the literature in the text has been organized into theme sections, but good literature is much too complex to be reduced to a single, broad theme. Many of the works included under Faith and Doubt could just as easily fit under other themes—and in many cases works appearing in other themes could fit here as well.

Choose one or more of the following works from earlier chapters or other themes, and consider how they can be linked to Faith and Doubt—and how this combination of the work with more than one theme provides additional insight into the literature and fresh topics for writing.

Collaboration: Writing and Revising with Your Peers

In addition to applying your own values and standards to writing about the
literature in this section, you may find it beneficial to share and discuss your
work with classmates. Getting feedback from others can help you generate and
clarify your ideas and revise and edit your writing more effectively. For details,
see pages 397–398.

A Writing/Research Portfolio Option

A portfolio is a collection of your work, related materials, and commentary about
your work collected over time. Gathering materials in a portfolio will provide you
with resources for research and development. See page 398 for details.

Appendix A

Critical Approaches to Literature

Earlier in the text you were introduced to four different perspectives from which to interpret literature: reader-based, text-based, context-based, and author-based approaches. In this section we take a closer look at each of these critical perspectives.

Try to keep in mind that these approaches may easily overlap, and critics will often combine them in their analyses. A reader-based approach, though emphasizing personal response, may call on the text for detailed support or make reference to contextual issues. Text-based approaches, though emphasizing the text, may interpret the elements of the text through contextual knowledge. Context-based approaches may consider the attitudes of the reader and the author and derive support from the text. Author-based criticism may consider the author's style and structure in the text and the influence of readers and contextual issues on the author.

The difference between one critical approach and another may be more a matter of emphasis than kind, and drawing upon several perspectives can yield a rich interpretation. What distinguishes one approach from another is the answer to a fundamental question: *Where is the meaning?* In the reader? In the text? In the world around the text? In the author? How we answer this question will determine the approach we take.

The explanations below will define each approach. To clarify their differences in practice, let's apply each of them to two works of literature: the modern poem "Those Winter Sundays" (p. 13) and the ancient Greek drama *Antigonê* (p. 113). As you read these applications, it will be clear that some works of literature yield better results with some approaches than others.

Further Reading: Introduction to Literary Theory

Bressler, Charles. *Literary Criticism: An Introduction to Theory and Practice.*
    Third Edition. 2002.
Dobie, Ann B. *Theory into Practice: Introduction to Literary Criticism.* 2001.
Eagleton, Terry. *Literary Theory: An Introduction.* 1983.

READER-BASED CRITICISM

The basic premise of **reader-based** or **reader-response** critical theory is that literature does not exist separate from those who read it. The critical approach reflected in this book is reader-based. Readers are encouraged to respond personally to literature, to think about the ways their backgrounds influence their responses, and to support their responses with reference to the literature itself.

Throughout this book, readers have been encouraged to supplement this reader-based approach with other perspectives. Discussions of the elements of literature and close reading and textual analysis in Chapters 3 and 4 rely on text-based practices. So, too, suggestions for secondary source research in Chapter 5 encourage an exploration of literature typical of context-based and author-based approaches.

A reader-response approach to "Those Winter Sundays" might emphasize the reader's identification with the speaker in the poem. The student writer of the response essay at the end of Chapter 2, for example, compares her relationship with her father to that of the father-son relationship in the poem. She cites words and lines that remind her of her own situation and draws ample support from both her own life and the text of the poem to illustrate similarities and differences.

An example of a reader-response approach to *Antigonê* might include identification with or personal reactions to Antigonê, Ismenê, Creon, or Haimon. Readers might pass judgments on Creon or imagine how they would have behaved when faced with Antigonê's predicament. They might address which character is most like them, identify characters that remind them of people they know, and comment on how these personal connections affect their responses.

Further Reading on Reader-Based Criticism

Bleich, David. *Subjective Criticism*. 1978.

Brenner, Gerry. *Performative Criticism: Experiments in Reader Response*. 2004.

Davis, Todd F., and Kenneth Womack. *Formalist Criticism and Reader-Response Theory*. 2002.

Holland, Norman N. *The Dynamics of Literary Response*. 1973, 1989.

Iser, Wolfgang. *The Act of Reading*. 1978.

Rabinowitz, Peter. *Before Reading*. 1987.

Rosenblatt, Louise. *The Reader, the Text, the Poem*. 1978.

Tompkins, Jane O. *Reader-Response Criticism: From Formalism to Post-Structuralism*. 1980.

TEXT-BASED CRITICISM

Formalism

Formalism seeks to *objectify* the text—to examine it in isolation from its reader, its context, and its author. **New Criticism,** the most popular type of formalism, is not new. It was given its name more than half a century ago as a reaction to the older biographical and historical approaches that preceded it. Though its popularity has now declined, it was the most dominant form of literary criticism in the twentieth century. As the designation "formalism" suggests, this approach closely examines elements of form/structure and language such as genre, plot, characterization, narration, tone, irony, diction, imagery, metaphor, and symbol. A formalist critic constructs meaning by focusing exclusively on the elements of the text and the way they work together to form a unified, coherent whole.

Because the background, values, and feelings of the reader and the author cannot be objectively evaluated, formalism sees them as irrelevant or erroneous in the construction of a stable meaning. It classifies reliance on a reader's emotional response as an **affective fallacy** and reliance on knowledge of an author's life or intentions as an **intentional fallacy.**

A formalist response to "Those Winter Sundays," for example, would stick closely to the text of the poem. It might try to establish the meaning of the poem through analysis of the language, the images, symbols, and speaker's tone, and how they work together to build and to support the speaker's concluding rhetorical question, "what did I know / of love's austere and lonely offices?" (13–14).

A similar approach to *Antigonê* might consider how well the play fulfills the definition of tragedy. It might examine the structure of the plot, details of characterization, function of the chorus, and the way these elements form an organic unity—how the structure of the play naturally culminates in the final lines of Choragos as he sums up the meaning of the play.

Further Reading on Formalist Criticism

Brooks, Cleanth, and Robert Penn Warren. *Understanding Poetry.* 1938.

Davis, Todd F., and Kenneth Womack. *Formalist Criticism and Reader-Response Theory.* 2002.

Empson, William. *Seven Types of Ambiguity.* 1958.

Ransom, John Crowe. *The New Criticism.* 1941.

Richards, I. A. *Practical Criticism.* 1928.

Wellek, Rene, and Austin Warren. *Theory of Literature.* 1949, 1973.

Deconstruction

Like formalism, **deconstruction** focuses exclusively on the text and requires close reading. Unlike formalism, however, which examines parts and relationships to construct a whole, the intention of deconstruction, as its name suggests, is to break down the whole—to deconstruct its meaning. While formalism emphasizes structure and the stability of interpreting the text in isolation, deconstruction insists on the instability and transitory nature of the text.

An early proponent of deconstruction was Jacques Derrida, who explained it through the French word *differance,* which means both "to differ" and "to defer." First, this view asserts that nothing can be known in isolation. We can only know the meaning of something by how it differs from something else to which it is related. All knowledge is based on difference, and all language is relational. We can only know "dark" in relation to "light," "up" to "down," "good" to "evil." Second, any stable or definitive meaning or interpretation must be deferred or put off perpetually because meaning, like the world, is always changing. What authors intend is different from what they write or what readers read. No text has a definitive meaning. So we cannot say one interpretation is right and another wrong.

Rather than attempting to construct an interpretation of its own, a deconstructionist approach to either "Those Winter Sundays" or *Antigonê* might try to reveal any number of alternative meanings for the poem or the play. It might question the credibility of the speaker in the poem and Choragos in the play and attempt to dismantle other interpretations by demonstrating the instability of their meaning.

Further Reading on Deconstruction

Berman, Art. *From the New Criticism to Deconstruction.* 1988.
Culler, Jonathan. *On Deconstruction: Theory and Criticism after Structuralism.* 1983.
de Man, Paul. *Allegories of Reading.* 1979.
Derrida, Jacques. *Of Grammatology.* Trans. Gayatri Spivak. 1974.
Hartmann, Geoffrey H., et al. *Deconstruction and Criticism.* 1979.
McQuillan, Martin, ed. *Deconstruction: A Reader.* 2001.
Norris, Christopher. *Deconstruction: Theory and Practice.* 1982, 1991.

CONTEXT-BASED CRITICISM

Historical Criticism

The basic premise of **historical criticism** is that literature benefits from being read in its own historical context. Important to this perspective are the political, economic, and psychological influences of the era that produced the literature and its author. The audience for whom it was written and how its meaning and the connotations of its language may have changed over time are among the factors important to this type of interpretation.

A development in historical criticism, **New Historicism,** questions the validity of traditional historical criticism and argues that we can only view the past from the "informed" present. It insists that we see the past through our own values and view the "official" history of the ruling classes with skepticism, that the history of those defeated and oppressed must also be revealed.

A historical critic's view of "Those Winter Sundays" might identify the period in which the poem was set and examine the forces at work in that era. For example, the author was an African American born in 1913. Research into the economic conditions and racial attitudes prevalent during the period when the poet was growing up might help the reader understand the nature of the father's work and the cold and sparse setting of the poem.

A similar view of *Antigonê* might focus on the structure of Greek government and the tenets of Greek religion when the play was written. It might consider the burial of Polyneices and compare the audience's expectations of that era with those of a modern audience and explore the significance of those differences.

Further Reading on Historical Criticism

Auerbach, Erich. *Mimesis: The Representation of Reality in Western Literature.* 1953.
Brannigan, John. *New Historicism and Cultural Materialism.* 1998.
Foucault, Michel. *Madness and Civilization.* Trans. Richard Howard. 1965.
Gallagher, Catherine, and Stephen Greenblatt. *Practicing New Historicism.* 2001.
Greenblatt, Stephen. *Marvellous Possessions.* 1991.
Hamilton, Paul. *Historicism.* 1996.
Herman, Peter C., ed. *Historicizing Theory.* 2004.
Veser, H. Aram. *The New Historicism.* 1989.

Gender (Feminist, Lesbian, Gay) Criticism

Gender criticism examines how literature reflects sexual identity or orientation. It may address the ways in which an author's gender has influenced his or her work. It may examine the gender-based portrayal of literary characters and their behavior. It may explore the way in which literature supports or rejects societal norms that foster gender stereotypes. It may emphasize gay and lesbian issues.

Its most popular form is **Feminist Criticism,** which has emerged as a powerful literary force during the last fifty years. Among the issues feminist critics address are literary depictions of women; assumptions about women generated by male writers; and the recurring patterns in literature of male dominance, female passivity, and sexism in literature as it reflects the societies that fostered it.

A feminist response to "Those Winter Sundays" might consider the restrained nature of a father-son relationship that seems to suppress the communication of feelings. It might question why there is no mother in this household or why this male speaker took so long to realize his feelings for his father.

A similar approach to *Antigonê* might emphasize the overtly sexist nature of Creon's response to Antigonê and Ismenê—how his sexist words and attitude echoed an assumption about the inequality of the sexes tacitly supported by ancient Greek society. It might scrutinize the causes of Ismenê's passivity and the consequences of Antigonê's assertiveness.

Further Reading on Gender Criticism

Abel, Elizabeth, ed. *Writing and Sexual Difference.* 1982.

Cosslet, Tess, et al. *Feminism and Autobiography.* 2000.

Fetterly, Judith. *The Resisting Reader: A Feminist Approach to American Fiction.* 1978.

Jagose, Annamarie. *Queer Theory: An Introduction.* 1996.

Kent, Kathryn R. *Making Girls into Women: American Women's Writing and the Rise of Lesbian Identity.* 2003.

Malinowski, Sharon, and Christa Brelin. *The Gay and Lesbian Literary Companion.* 1995.

Ruthven, K. K. *Feminist Literary Studies: An Introduction.* 1984.

Sedgwick, Eve. *Epistemology of the Closet.* 1991.

Showalter, Elaine. *The New Feminist Criticism.* 1986.

Political-Economic Criticism

Political-economic criticism focuses on the influence and the consequences of the economic social order in literature. Its most popular form is **Marxist Criticism,** which argues that literature reflects the class structure and class struggle that produced it. It emphasizes the social content of literature and scrutinizes the economic circumstances of literature for instances of exploitation. It also analyzes the ways in which text, author, and readers reveal class attitudes.

A Marxist view of "Those Winter Sundays" might emphasize the poor economic situation of this family—how their economic plight and its consequence, the unceasing labor of the father to make ends meet, has created circumstances that made it impossible for the father to have the time for meaningful communication with his son.

A similar view of *Antigonê* might expose the arrogance of Creon as typical of the ruling class—how he exploits and silences the proletariat/laboring class messengers and guards of Polyneices's body—and forces them to go against their own consciences.

Further Reading on Political-Economic Criticism

Eagleton, Terry. *Criticism and Ideology: A Study in Marxist Literary Theory*. 1976.
Howard, Jean E., and Scott Cutler Shershow. *Marxist Shakespeares*. 2001.
Lentricchia, Frank. *Criticism and Social Change*. 1983.
Sartre, Jean-Paul. *What Is Literature?* 1949.
Williams, Raymond. *Marxism and Literature*. 1977.

Psychoanalytic Criticism

Derived from the psychological theory of Sigmund Freud, **psychoanalytic criticism** emphasizes the underlying meaning in the narrative, actions, and dialogue of literature. Sexual symbols, dreams, and repressed feelings are central to a psychological analysis of the characters. The creative process and psychological makeup of the author may also be of special interest. An excellent example of psychoanalytic criticism in this text is "Hamlet's Oedipus Complex" by Ernest Jones on page 627.

A psychoanalytic view of "Those Winter Sundays," for example, might focus on the repressed speaker and question why his feelings of affection for his father have lain dormant for so many years. It might conjecture about the competition between father and son for the affection of the unnamed, unmentioned mother in this family.

Given the incestuous nature of the relationship between Antigonê's parents, Oedipus and Iocastê, a psychoanalytic critic might be overwhelmed with material for exploration here. For example, what psychological burden does Antigonê carry because of the bizarre relationship between her parents? Such a question might yield some very interesting ideas.

Further Reading on Psychoanalytic Criticism

Chodorow, Nancy. *Feminism and Psychoanalytic Theory*. 1990.
Crews, Frederick C., ed. *Psychoanalysis and Literary Process*. 1970.
Ellmann, Maud. *Psychoanalytic Literary Criticism*. 1995.
Frankland, Graham. *Freud's Literary Culture*. 2000.
Hartmann, Geoffrey. *Psychoanalysis and the Question of Text*. 1979.
Kurzweil, Edith, and William Phillips, eds. *Literature and Psychoanalysis*. 1983.
Trilling, Lionel. *Freud and the Crisis of Our Culture*. 1955.
Wright, Elizabeth. *Psychoanalytic Criticism: A Reappraisal*. 1998.

Archetypal Criticism

Derived from the theories of psychologist Carl Jung, this approach assumes that we share a "collective unconscious" that has been shaped by the repeated experiences of our ancestors. It asserts that through this collective unconscious we indirectly share a knowledge of **archetypes**—universal images, patterns, and forms like the seasons, the sun, the moon, the wise old man or woman, fire, night, and blood. Of special interest to an archetypal critic are images, descriptive detail, plot patterns, and types of characters that appear frequently in literature and that seem to evoke nonrational but powerful responses from our unconscious memory.

An archetypal critic, for example, might approach "Those Winter Sundays" by identifying some of the more powerful images and symbols in the poem. Both the speaker's and the reader's response to a father who "makes banked fires blaze," and "who had driven out the cold" as an archetypal image might prompt some rich exploration.

A similar view of *Antigonê* might explore connections between the play and the many haunting and powerful mythological images and references presented in the dialogue and choral odes throughout the play.

Further Reading on Archetypal Criticism

Bodkin, Maud. *Archetypal Patterns in Poetry.* 1958.
Brady, Patrick. *Memory and History as Fiction: An Archetypal Approach to the Historical Novel.* 1993.
Campbell, Joseph. *The Hero with a Thousand Faces.* 1949.
Frye, Northrop. *Anatomy of Criticism.* 1957.
Lentricchia, Frank. *After the New Criticism.* 1980.
Moon, Beverly. *An Encyclopedia of Archetypal Symbolism.* 1997.

Postcolonial Criticism

The field of postcolonial studies emerged in the wake of widespread European imperialism and colonization. For example, the British Empire was in place for more than 400 years—and so extensive that the English could accurately claim, "The sun never sets on the British Empire." Not only did European powers become very wealthy and powerful at the expense of their colonies, but their presence often overwhelmed the native cultures and forced the people to embrace the cultural imperatives of their colonizers.

With the fall of European imperialism, **postcolonial criticism** emerged as a way of assessing the damage that colonial education and language did to the culture and identity of the colonized. A core concern of Postcolonial critics is how to reclaim native values. The colonial establishment may be gone, but the colonial hegemony in literary values remains behind—and undo influence is often given to writers who were popularized by the colonial establishment.

Further Reading and Examples of Postcolonial Criticism

Achebe, Chinua. *Things Fall Apart* (A Novel). 1958.
Fanon, Frantz. *Black Skin, White Masks* (1952) and *The Wretched of the Earth* (1961).
Spivak, Gayatri Chakravorty. *The Post-Colonial Critic: Interviews, Strategies, Dialogues.* Ed. Sarah Harasym. 1990.
Loomba, Ania. *Shakespeare, Race, and Colonialism.* 2002.
Loomba, Ania. *Colonialism/Postcolonialism.* 1998.

Mohanty, C. T., Russo, Ann, and Lourdes Torres, eds. *Third World Women and the Politics of Feminism*. 1991.

Said, Edward. *Culture and Imperialism*. 1993.

———. *Orientalism*. 1979.

Minh-ha, Trinh T. *Woman, Native, Other: Writing Postcoloniality and Feminism*. 1989.

Mukherjee, Arun. *Towards an Aesthetic of Opposition: Essays on Literature, Criticism and Cultural Imperialism*. 1988.

Spivak, Gayatri Chakravorty. *Critique of Post-Colonial Reason: Toward a History of the Vanishing Present*. 1999.

Thiong'o, Ngũgĩ Wa. *Decolonizing the Mind: The Politics of Language in African Literature*. 1986.

Trivedi, Harish. *Colonial Transactions: English Literature and India*. 1993.

AUTHOR-BASED CRITICISM

Author-based or **biographical** criticism emphasizes the relationship between authors' lives and their works. Finding out about an author's life, of course, requires reading a **biography** or **autobiography** of the author. An effective literary biography brings the author's work and life together. And literary biographies can be highly controversial.

Of special interest in biographical criticism is the way in which authors' lives have influenced their writing—how details and people in their own lives have entered their work. Exploring these connections may lead to a deeper understanding of a work's meaning.

A biographical critic's response to "Those Winter Sundays," for example, might include research on Robert Hayden's growing up and his relationship with his father. A biographical critic might seek connections between the events in Hayden's life and his psychological or emotional state when he wrote the poem.

A similar view of *Antigonê* might search for whatever details are available about the life and career of its author, Sophocles. With few biographical details available, a biographical critic might look for clues about Sophocles and his opinions in this and other plays and conjecture about his background based on knowledge of his contemporaries.

Further Reading and Examples of Biographical Criticism

Ackroyd, Peter. *Shakespeare*. 2005.

Edel, Leon. *Literary Biography*. 1957.

Ellmann, Richard. *James Joyce*. 1983.

Farr, Judith. *The Passion of Emily Dickinson*. 1992.

Felber, Lynette. *Literary Liaisons: Auto/Biographical Appropriations in Modernist Women's Writing*. 2002.

Greenblatt, Stephen. *Will in the World*. 2004.

Jellinek, Estelle C. *Women's Autobiography: Essays in Criticism*. 1986.

Kaplan, Fred. *The Singular Mark Twain: A Biography*. 2003.

Shapiro, James. *A Year in the Life of William Shakespeare: 1599*. 2005.

Appendix B

Writing About Film

From earliest times, people have loved stories. Before books, stories were passed along by word of mouth. Great storytellers, like the Greek bard Homer or the Anglo-Saxon narrator of *Beowulf,* wove their tales in poetry, which was pleasurable to listen to and easy to remember. With the invention of writing, stories could be recorded on parchment or paper. Storytellers became writers, authors whose tales could be read far beyond the reach of their own voices. Today we get our stories from a variety of media, including radio, movies, television, video, and computers. New technologies keep widening the storytelling circle.

WHY WRITE ABOUT FILM?

For more than one hundred years, filmmakers have been part of this tradition. The art of motion pictures, while relatively crude and simple in its infancy, has matured into one of the most powerful and eloquent forms of literature. Although movies vary in purpose and quality, just as printed literature does, many movies are worth close attention. Writing about film is a good way to learn more about this important medium: how it works, why it affects us as it does, and what it means to others. And since the movie screen is a kind of mirror, reflecting our cultural values and individual dreams, writing about film is another way to learn about ourselves.

Like the stories, poems, plays, and essays in this book, films are fitting subjects to help you understand your personal responses; to develop your critical thinking skills; and to explore the world beyond your immediate experience through analysis, argument, and research. In this appendix, you'll learn how to write about film from a number of perspectives: through response essays, film reviews, critical essays, film comparisons, and research papers. You'll see what film and written literature have in common and how they differ. You'll review the tools used by filmmakers to tell their stories, and you'll learn how to prepare to write about their films.

The author of this book thanks William V. Costanzo for contributing this appendix on film. William Costanzo has a Ph.D. from Columbia University and has spoken and published widely on the use of film and technology in English classes. He is the author of four books on this topic: *Double Exposure: Composing Through Writing and Film* (1984), *The Electronic Text* (1989), *Reading the Movies* (1992), and *Great Films and How To Teach Them* (2004).

FILM AS LITERATURE

Fiction films—movies that tell stories, as opposed to documentary films, which are more like essays—depend on the same narrative elements as novels and short stories. They have characters, settings, and plots. They present events from particular points of view. They possess a certain structure, tone, style, and often symbolism. These are the basic elements of storytelling.

Filmmakers use different tools for handling these elements. Whereas a writer is limited to the written word, a director has cameras, actors, sets, lights, editing consoles, sound, and more. The actors represent characters through the repertoire of performance, including gesture, facial expression, intonation, make-up, and costumes. The setting is represented by actual locations or by sets constructed by a team of carpenters and designers. The plot—that chain of related events leading to the story's climax—is played out in a succession of scenes fashioned by scriptwriters, filmed by cinematographers under the director's watchful eye, and rearranged into a final sequence by film editors. While a writer might specify a particular point of view by using "I saw" or "she noticed," the filmmaker might use the camera to control perspective, framing the subject as a close-up or shooting the subject from different angles. To create tone and mood, a writer manipulates the instruments of language—atmospheric adjectives, sentence rhythm, muscular or supple verbs. The filmmaker creates these effects with lighting, color, music, and sound effects.

One big difference between written literature and film regards authorship. A story or a novel has one name on the title page, but who is the author of a movie? Sometimes the director has a strong hand in shaping the film, but often the actors, scriptwriters, cinematographers, or editors make equal or stronger contributions. Try counting all the names that roll by on the closing credits of a major feature film.

Another difference lies in the nature of language and the medium of film. A movie shows the characters, settings, and events as motion pictures and adds the auditory dimension of voice-over narration, music, dialogue, and sound effects. A writer must describe events in words. The reader must interpret those words, picturing a story's people and places in the mind's eye, thus transforming the written text into a movie directed by his or her own imagination.

PREPARING TO WRITE ABOUT FILMS

Before you launch into an essay or a film review, it helps to be clear about your topic, purpose, audience, format, scope, and slant. You might ask yourself the following questions:

- What film or films have I chosen to write about?
- What approach will I be taking? (For each purpose, there is probably a set of stylistic and structural expectations—a format—that you can follow.)
- Will I be examining my personal reactions (a response essay), summarizing and evaluating the film (film review), relating one film to other films by the same director (comparison essay), or finding out more about how the film was made (research essay)?

- Who is my intended audience? What are my readers likely to know about movies, and what will I need to tell them?
- How far beyond the film itself will my essay range (its scope)?
- What particular theories, opinions, or viewpoints (slant) will I be bringing to this film?

Because movies require some form of projection system, you'll need to be familiar with the technical features of the system you use. DVDs easily allow you to navigate scenes using a menu. Of course, if you've chosen to write about a film that hasn't been released yet for home viewing, you'll probably need to make several trips to the theatre. In this case, since you can't control the film, you need to rely on your memory, focused attention, and techniques for taking notes in the dark. However, viewing movies in a theatre setting can give you valuable information about audience response that you can't get when you're home alone. You can see for yourself how people react to different scenes and include these observations in your review.

When you take notes, decide ahead of time what you'll be looking for. Some of this is standard production information, but some helpful questions might include:

- Who are the directors, scriptwriters, cinematographers, editors, art directors, composers, and producers?
- Who are the principal performers, and what roles do they play?
- When was the film originally released, and what studio produced it?

Some information will help you summarize the story. Look for the chief features of the plot: the central conflict, the complications, high points, and final outcome.

- Are there any subplots (secondary stories going on at the same time as the main plot)?
- What are the key scenes? Where do they take place, and how does each scene develop the story or reveal something new about its characters?

Pay particular attention to the opening and closing shots because these are often carefully constructed to introduce the story's crucial elements or to tie them all together. Notice how the movie's title, cultural allusions, and symbolic details contribute to the story's theme or themes.

Sometimes it's a good idea to read something about a film before watching it. This helps to orient your expectations, to prepare you for the journey, so you can recognize the significance of events when they occur. It's easier to spot telling details like a shadow on the wall or an ominous gathering of birds when you know what you're looking for. After your first or second screening, you may want to do some serious research. Find out more about the director's life and other films. Read about the actors. Find a documentary on the making of the film. If the story relates to some real-life event, look for a factual account of the event.

The strategies that help you write essays about literature can serve you well when writing about film. Try brainstorming, listing, or freewriting to get down first impressions and ideas. Keep a viewing log or double-entry journal (one side for your first run through the film, the other side for reflections and re-screenings) to record your thoughts as they evolve over time. Make an outline or concept map to help organize all the information you have collected.

WRITING PERSONAL RESPONSE ESSAYS

A response essay describes your reactions to a film. It's a good way to explore the personal feelings, memories, and ideas that the film triggered for you—and to clarify them for your readers. Sometimes by explaining your responses to another person, you come to understand them better yourself.

You might begin simply by talking to your friends about the movie that you saw. Start with your general impressions. What words describe your overall response? Then get specific. Tell them what pleased or upset you most. Which characters were really interesting, funny, or weird? Which scenes had you enthralled? When were you aware of the music, photography, or special effects?

Now look for the reasons behind your responses. What explanations can you give for such strong or weak reactions? Did any of the characters or settings remind you of people or places in your life? Did you identify closely with any scenes? What additional associations—with other movies, historical events, or works of literature or art—might help to clarify the thoughts and feelings you experienced during the film?

The final format of a personal essay need not be formal. It may be conversational in tone, like a journal, but it should share something important about your film experience. It should both *show* and *tell* about the film as it occurred to you. If you're successful, your readers should be able to see what you saw, hear what you heard, and understand how you felt.

WRITING FILM REVIEWS

A film review introduces a new film to readers who might want to see it. Typically, film reviews include a plot summary, descriptions of the main performances, perhaps some references to interesting film techniques, background information on the production, and an account of the movie's themes. An important purpose of a film review is evaluation. Readers want to know whether this film is for them.

Keep your summary brief. Let your readers know what the movie is about without ruining it for them. Don't give away the ending or spoil any surprises along the way. Try to give them both the gist and flavor of the film. Compare it to other films that they might know. Is it a romantic comedy, a horror film, a film noir, or a quirky independent film? Does Brad Pitt play the usual heartthrob? Is Julia Roberts up to her performance in *Erin Brockovich* or just another pretty woman? What makes the film special and unique?

Evaluate the movie in specific terms. Describe one or two scenes in detail to convey a sense of the acting. In addition to particular performances, you might comment on the spectacular underwater photography, the musical score that swells unnecessarily behind every romantic moment, the fast-paced editing that propels the action forward, or the annoying use of handheld cameras to create a pseudo-documentary effect.

Nearly every newspaper, as well as many magazines and Web sites, publish film reviews. Sample a few before writing your final draft. Notice that they tend to be somewhat more formal than personal responses but less formal than critical or research essays. They follow the same general format and include the same kinds of information, yet they reflect the particular styles and interests of the author and the intended audience.

WRITING ARGUMENTATIVE ESSAYS

Argumentative essays go beyond description. They analyze a film and develop a thesis about it. The focus here is more on the text of the film itself than on your personal responses or evaluation. A formal analysis examines the film's formal aspects, or how it is constructed. This is an opportunity to notice the many technical and artistic decisions about casting, lighting, camera work, set design, editing, and sound that contribute to the film experience.

One way to begin a formal study is to analyze a particular scene shot by shot. Use a DVD to view the scene repeatedly.

- Number every shot, and jot down what you notice about each shot.
- Describe the action (what the characters do) and the setting (where and when the action takes place).
- Describe the camerawork—is it a close-up or long shot? A high angle (seen from above) or low angle (seen from below)? Does the camera pan (pivot horizontally) to the left, track forward (move closer to the subject), zoom in (adjust the lens so that objects seem to get closer)?
- Describe the lighting—is it bright and buoyant? Dark and mysterious? Glamorously illuminated from above?
- Describe the sound (dialogue, narration, music, sound effects).

You might also want to record the length of each shot because timing is an important feature of editing. A shot-by-shot analysis can help you appreciate a film's creative features, and it can provide you with evidence to support your broad claims about the film.

Any good analysis should have a payoff. There's little point in breaking something down into its component parts unless the process serves a bigger purpose. That's the function of your thesis—to clarify some larger understanding of the film. Your goal might be to show how *The Godfather* uses parallel editing to reveal Michael Corleone's hypocrisy. As support, you might analyze the scene in which Michael (played by Al Pacino) attends his godson's baptism while his henchmen slaughter all his rivals. Or your thesis might concern Steven Spielberg's use of black and white photography in *Schindler's List*. Here you might analyze the Krakow ghetto scene in which a little girl's red coat contrasts strikingly with the grim documentary tones of the liquidation.

When writing an argumentative essay, assume that readers are already familiar with the film. There's no need to worry about giving away the plot. Argumentative essays tend to be more formal than film reviews, introducing the thesis in the opening paragraph and developing it with the tools of argument: clear reasoning and supportive evidence. Your readers should be able to follow every turn of thought to your conclusion. At best, they will agree with you; at worst, they'll understand your point even if they disagree.

WRITING COMPARISON ESSAYS

While watching a film, you may be reminded of something else: a similar film, a work of literature, or maybe a current event. A comparison essay is one way to explore such similarities. There should be a solid basis for comparison. Two films may be by the same director, feature the same actor, take place in the same location, belong to the same genre (science fiction, black comedy, the Western), or focus on the same topic or theme. You might compare sequels to the original, or you might compare the movie and the book.

Comparison essays are usually organized in one of two ways—either they compare A and B separately, using a block format; or they compare A and B side by side, using a point-by-point strategy. For example, a block comparison of the three *Godfather* films would first describe the original *The Godfather* (1972) before moving on to *The Godfather II* (1979) and *The Godfather III* (1990). A point-by-point comparison might contrast the time frames for all three films before comparing their plots, then their characters, and so on. Either way, the final purpose of such comparisons is to learn something that might not be available by studying one film by itself.

Film adaptations are especially good subjects for a literature class. They give you a chance to compare the movie version to the original work. You get to notice what was added and left out. You get to judge the filmmaker's interpretation of characters, settings, and themes against your own visual imagination. Do the actors look and act as you pictured them when you read the book? Do the sets and locations live up to your expectations? Is the movie faithful to the spirit of the written work? How do the experiences of watching and reading differ? Ultimately, which experience is more satisfying for you?

Many of the stories in this book have been adapted for the screen. William Faulkner's "A Rose for Emily" (p. 907) and Nathaniel Hawthorne's "Young Goodman Brown" (p. 1122) are short films. Joyce Carol Oates's short story "Where Are You Going, Where Have You Been?" (p. 436) has been turned into a feature-length production, titled *Smooth Talk* (1985), with Laura Dern as Connie and Treat Williams as Arnold Friend. Since the story itself was based on actual events, you might compare both fictional versions to the newspaper accounts of what reporters called "The Pied Piper of Tucson."

Nearly all of the plays in *Exploring Literature* have been interpreted on film, some more than once. Read the section entitled "Desperately Seeking *Hamlet*: Four Interpretations" (pp. 620–23), which compares four filmed interpretations of

Hamlet. Since drama is meant to be performed rather than read, comparing a script to a movie of the play is a little like comparing sheet music to a concert. You can learn a lot about the play, the nature of performance, and yourself by comparing what you experience on the page and on the screen.

WRITING RESEARCH ESSAYS

At some point while watching a film you may want to know more than meets the eye. Perhaps you're interested in learning more about an actor, a director, or how the film was made. A film about prohibition in 1920s Chicago or drug trafficking in modern Argentina may arouse your curiosity about those places and events. The purpose of a research essay is to find out more about some aspect of the film by investigating outside sources. It's an opportunity to look behind the screen.

Lots of leading questions could be asked about the making of a film, such as:

- Where did the idea for this film originate?
- How did the final script come to be written?
- What technical innovations—in camera work, lighting, color, or special effects—were used during production, and how were they achieved?
- Were there special problems in shooting on location or creating the sets? How were they solved?
- What musical decisions were made for the sound track, and how do they contribute to the total film experience?
- What are the director's hallmarks in this and other films? How did the actors behave on and off the set?

You might also have questions about the economic, social, and cultural aspects of the film:

- How much did it cost to make, and how much did it earn?
- How important were the promotions, tie-ins, theatrical releases, and video sales?
- How did the public respond to the final film? What did the critics say?
- Do you see this film as part of a larger trend, perhaps a trend in ritualized violence or a growing fear of natural disasters? If so, what other films does it resemble, and what do these films say collectively about life today?
- How does the film represent different kinds of people: men and women, rich and poor, old and young, or various ethnic groups?
- What cultural beliefs about sexuality, politics, or family are challenged or confirmed by the film?

Such questions lead both inward to a closer look at the film itself and outward to the conditions that produced it. Your role as researcher and writer is to make meaningful connections between these two perspectives—the text and the cultural context. Although the information comes from primary and secondary sources, you're the one who puts it all together. Remember, the final essay represents *your* interpretation in *your* own voice. What makes it worth writing and reading are the insights you arrive at based on your research.

Review the sections on research in Chapter 5 and on documentation in Appendix C. These pages will guide you to reliable sources and remind you how to cite those sources in the body of your essay as well as on the Works Cited page. These days, excellent background material can be found on DVD editions of films, including documentaries, interviews, production notes, rehearsal footage, outtakes, production stills, and storyboards. The Internet offers a wealth of useful Web sites, though their quality and dependability varies widely. Don't overlook traditional print sources, either. Often the best information may come from a biography, film journal, or movie review.

As you write your essay, keep in mind all the people who make movies, enjoy them, and write about them. The circle of cinematic storytelling is an ever-widening community. What you write can be a ticket of admission to the circle.

By writing about movies, you also widen the circle of literature to include some of the best stories of our times. You get to apply much of what you've learned about good written literature to a new medium, and you begin to appreciate the differences between the media of print and film. At the same time, you get to sharpen the all-important skills of critical thinking, persuasive writing, and research. And, if you practice reading literature with a filmmaker's eye, you learn to enrich your reading with the powers of your visual imagination.

Appendix C

Documentation

A DIRECTORY OF MLA FORMATTING AND DOCUMENTATION

The Physical Layout of the Research Essay

Citing Sources in the Text of the Essay

Documenting the Works Cited
Books (Nonperiodical Print Publications)

Periodical Print Publications

The Physical Layout of the Research Essay

Individual course requirements may vary from MLA format, so check with your instructor before writing your essay.

Type of Paper   Your research essay should be typed on 8 1/2" × 11" unlined paper.

Margins   Top and bottom margins should be one inch from the edge of the paper. Left and right margins should be one inch from the edge of the paper.

Spacing   The text of your research essay should be double-spaced. Quotations should be double-spaced. Your Works Cited page should be double-spaced.

Page Numbers   Number all pages in the upper-right-hand corner about half an inch from the top edge of the paper. Type your name before the page number.

Heading and Title   Your research essay does not require a separate title page. At the top and left margin of your first page, print the following:

> Your Name
> Your Instructor's Name
> The Title and Number of the Course
> The Date
>   Center the Title
> (Do not underline, place in quotations, or capitalize all the letters in your
>   title. Double space between the title and the first line of your writing.)
>   The Text of Your Essay

Works Cited Page   The Works Cited page is a separate page at the end of the essay.

1. Works are listed in alphabetical order.
2. Each listing is double-spaced, and there is double-spacing between listings.
3. The first line of each listing begins at the left margin. All other lines are indented five spaces.
4. Only works cited in the text of your essay are included.

Documentation—MLA Style

Because it is the most popular form for those who do literary research, the style we use here for documentation is taken from the *MLA Handbook for Writers of Research Papers*, seventh edition.

This edition brings an important change in the way online sources are documented. Previously the assumption was, unless stated otherwise, the medium of the source was print. Given the widespread use of online sources, however, print is simply one medium among several others. Therefore, the medium should be indicated for each source. MLA style no longer requires URLs for online sources. (In the past, URLs were notoriously unreliable because Web sites would often change addresses.)

Citing Sources in the Text of the Essay

The source from which you have taken the information is cited in your essay through parenthetic reference in the following ways:

1. Ideas or information phrased in your own words
   The author's last name and the page number in parentheses: (Brown 253)
   Example: The conditions in those schools were reported as terrible (Brown 253).
2. Ideas or information put into your own words but with the author's name mentioned in your text
   Page number in parentheses: (253)
   Example: Brown reported that the conditions in the schools he visited were terrible (253).
3. Direct quotation—prose
   Direct prose quotations of *four lines or less* are put in quotation marks and integrated into the text of your writing.

Example: "I could not believe the appalling conditions I saw" (Brown 253).

or

Brown said, "I could not believe the appalling conditions I saw" (253).

4.   Direct quotation—prose with five or more lines

Direct prose quotations of *five or more lines* are double-spaced and separated from the text of your writing by starting the quote on a new line and indenting an inch from the left margin.

Example: It was very clear that Dr. Grantly was taking much longer to die than anyone expected:

> A month since the physicians had named four weeks as the outside period during which breath could be supported within the body of the dying man. At the end of the month the physicians wondered, and named another fortnight. The old man lived on wine alone, but at the end of the fortnight he still lived; and the tidings of the ministry became more frequent. (Trollope 3)

5.   Direct quotation—poetry

Direct quotations of *three lines or fewer* may be put in quotation marks and integrated into the text of your writing. Use a slash (/) with a space on each side to separate the lines of verse.

Example: I sense deep regret in Robert Hayden's last lines: "What did I know, what did I know / of love's austere and lonely offices?" (13–14).

6.   Direct quotation—poetry with four or more lines

Direct quotations of *more than three lines* should be double-spaced and begin on a new line. Indent all quoted lines one inch from the left margin and use no quotation marks.

Example: I was deeply affected by the scene described in William Stafford's poem:

> The car aimed ahead its lowered parking lights;
> under the hood purred the steady engine.
> I stood in the glare of the warm exhaust turning red;
> around our group I could hear the wilderness listen. (13–16)

7.   Direct quotation—drama

Quoted dialogue between two or more characters should be separated from the text. Begin each quote with the character's name indented one inch from the left margin, written in all capital letters, and followed by a period. All additional lines below that first line should be indented three additional spaces. Line-numbered verse plays are cited in parentheses by act, scene, and line numbers; prose plays by page numbers.

Example: In Sophocles' play, Ismenê's attempt to talk Antigonê out of her defiance is futile:

> ISMENÊ. But no one must hear of this, you must tell no one! I will keep
>   it a secret, I promise!
> ANTIGONÊ. Oh, tell it! Tell everyone!
>   Think how they'll hate you when it all comes out
>   If they learn that you knew about it all the time!
> ISMENÊ. So fiery! You should be cold with fear.
> ANTIGONÊ. Perhaps. But I am doing what I must. (Pro. 74–80)

Documenting the Works Cited

The descriptions and examples below will account for many of the sources you are likely to use, but this is not an exhaustive list. If the source you are using is not shown here, the best source of additional information is the *MLA Handbook for Writers of Research Papers,* seventh edition, 2009, published by the Modern Language Association of America.

Books (Nonperiodical Print Publications)

1. A Book by One Author
    Author's Name (reversed). *Title of Book* (italicized). City of Publication: Publisher, Year of Publication. Medium.
    Examples:
    Ellmann, Richard. *James Joyce.* New York: Oxford UP, 1959. Print.
    Sledge, Linda Ching. *A Map of Paradise.* New York: Bantam, 1997. Print.

2. A Book by Two or Three Authors
    Author's Name (reversed) and Second Author's Name. *Title of Book* (italicized). City of Publication: Publisher, Year of Publication. Medium.
    Examples:
    Desmond, Adrian, and James Moore. *Darwin.* New York: Warner, 1991. Print.
    Gilbert, Sandra, and Susan Gubar. *The Madwoman in the Attic: The Woman Writer and the Nineteenth Century Literary Imagination.* New Haven: Yale UP, 1979. Print.

3. A Work in an Anthology
    Author's Name (reversed). "Title of the Work" (in quotation marks). *Title of the Anthology* (italicized). Editor's name(s). Number of edition. City of Publication: Publisher, Year of Publication. Page Range. Medium.
    Examples:
    Chopin, Kate. "The Story of an Hour." *Literature for Composition.* Sylvan Barnet, William Burto, and Marcia Stubbs, eds. 6th ed. New York: Longman, 2003. 12–14. Print.
    Valdez, Luis. "Los Vendidos." *Exploring Literature.* Frank Madden, ed. New York: Longman, 2012. 1031–39. Print.

4. A Work in a Collection by the Same Author
    Author's Name (reversed). "Title of the Work" (in quotation marks). *Title of the Collection* (italicized). City of Publication: Publisher, Year of Publication. Page Range. Medium.
    Examples:
    Cheever, John. "The Enormous Radio." *The Stories of John Cheever.* New York: Knopf, 1978. 33–41. Print.
    Sontag, Susan. "The Aesthetics of Silence." *Styles of Radical Will.* New York: Farrar, 1969. 3–34. Print.

5. An Introduction, Foreword, or Afterword

Author's Name (reversed). Introduction. *Title of Book* (italicized). By (author of book if different). City of Publication: Publisher, Year of Publication. Page Range. Medium.

Examples:

Costanzo, William V. Introduction. *Reading the Movies*. Urbana: NCTE, 1992. Print.

Orne, Martin T. Foreword. *Anne Sexton*. By Dianne Wood Middlebrook. Boston: Houghton, 1991. xii–xxiii. Print.

6. A Reference Book (Encyclopedia, Dictionary, etc.)

"Title of Entry" (if a person, reverse the name). *Title of Reference Book* (italicized). Number and/or Year of Edition. Medium.

Examples:

"Symbol." *The New Encyclopaedia Britannica: Micropaedia*. 1974 ed. Print.

"Sheridan, Richard Brinsley." *The Oxford Companion to English Literature*. 5th ed. 1985. Print.

7. An Author with Two or More Works

Author's Name (reversed, in first entry of author only). Rest of Publication Information. Medium.

In subsequent listings, type three hyphens, followed by a period and the title.

Example:

Costanzo, William V. *The Electronic Text*. Englewood Cliffs: Educational Technology, 1989. Print.

———. *Reading the Movies*. Urbana: NCTE, 1992. Print.

8. A Translated Book

Author's Name (reversed). Title of Book (italicized). Translator. City of Publication: Publisher, Year of Publication. Medium.

Example:

Homer. *The Odyssey*. Trans. Robert Fagles. New York: Penguin, 1996. Print.

Periodical Print Publications

9. An Article in a Magazine

Author's Name (reversed). "Title of Article" (in quotation marks). *Title of Magazine* (italicized). Date of Publication (day, month, year): Page Range. Medium.

If monthly or bimonthly, list month(s) as date. If no author's name appears, begin with the title of the article (but not "A" or "The").

Examples:

Korda, Michael. "The Third Man." *New Yorker* 25 Mar. 1996: 44–51. Print.

Updike, John. "The Literary Life." *Civilization* Dec. 1996: 56–73. Print.

10. An Article in a Scholarly Journal

Author's Name (reversed). "Title of Article" (in quotation marks). *Title of Journal* (italicized) and Volume Number (year of publication, in parentheses): Page Range. Medium.

Examples:

Kamps, Ivo. "Possible Pasts: Historiography and Legitimation in *Henry VIII*." *College English* 58 (1996): 192–215. Print.

Wilkinson, James. "A Choice of Fictions: Historians, Memory, and Evidence." *PMLA* 111 (1996): 80–92. Print.

11. **An Article in a Newspaper**

Author's Name (reversed). "Title of Article" (in quotation marks). *Title of Newspaper* (italicized) and Date. Edition: Section Letter and Beginning Page Number. Medium.

Examples:

Grimes, William. "A Woman of Words That Win Pulitzers." *New York Times* 4 June 1996, natl. ed. C1. Print.

Wu, Jim. "Authors Praise New Forms." *New York Times* 8 Mar. 1987, Sec. 2:1. Print.

12. **A Review**

Reviewer's Name (reversed). "Title of Review" (in quotation marks). Rev. of *Title of Work Reviewed* (italicized), by Author of Work Reviewed. *Publication* (italicized) Publication Date: Inclusive Page Numbers. Medium.

Examples:

Fraser, Kennedy. "Piper Pipe That Song Again." Rev. of *Blake*, by Peter Ackroyd. *New Yorker* 27 May 1996: 127–31. Print.

Vendler, Helen. Rev. of *Essays on Style*, Roger Fowler, ed. *Essays in Criticism* 16 (1966): 457–63. Print.

Citing Internet Sources

While relevant information is not always available, it is essential that you give as much information as you can—at least enough information so that readers of your work can find the source themselves. To verify the quality and reliability of an online source, see the suggestions in the checklist in Chapter 5, pp. 191–92. For additional information, the Modern Language Association guidelines for citing Internet sources can be accessed at http://www.mla.org.

Citing Online Sources from a Nonperiodical Publication on the Internet (include as much of this information as available)

Author's Name (reversed).
Title (in quotation marks or italicized, as appropriate).
Print Publication Information, if appropriate.
Title of the overall Web site, Project, Database, etc. (italicized, if separate from the title).
Volume, Issue, or Identifying Number (if available).
Page, Paragraph, or Section Numbers.
Publisher or institution or organization sponsoring the site (if not available, use *N.p.*).
Date of Electronic Publication.

Medium.

Your Date of Access.

Each item is followed by a period except the publisher or sponsor, which is followed by a comma. Untitled works may be identified by genre. If not otherwise identified, the name of the Web site creator may be listed following the tite of the Web site. Whenever you cannot find this type on informaton, simpy cite what is available.

Citing Online Sources from a Nonperiodical Publication on the Internet with Print Publication Data

13. **An Entire Internet Database or Scholarly Project Site**
    Bartleby.com: Great Books Online. Steven van Leeuwen, ed. 2002. Web. 24 May 2003.

14. **A Document or Online Book within a Scholarly Project or Database**
    Austen, Jane. *Persuasion.* 1818. *Project Gutenberg.* Sharon Partridge, ed. Feb. 1994. Web. 18 May 2004.

15. **A Personal or Professional Site**
    Van Noate, Judith. *Theater Connections.* J. Murrey Atkins Library, U of North Carolina Charlotte. Web. 6 Apr. 2003.

16. **An Online Book**
    Twain, Mark. *The Adventures of Tom Sawyer.* Internet Wiretap Online. Carnegie-Mellon U. Web. 22 Feb. 2002.

17. **An Article in an Online Periodical**
    Sohmer, Steve. "Opening Day at Shakespeare's Globe." *Early Modern Literary Studies* 3.1 (1997): 46 pars. Web. 24 May 2003.

18. **An Article in an Encyclopedia on the Internet**
    "Hawthorne, Nathaniel." *Britannica Online.* Vers. 98.2. Apr. 1998. Encyclopaedia Britannica. Web. 16 Oct. 1998.

19. **An Article in a Newspaper on the Internet**
    Markon, Jerry. "Virginia Colleges May Bar Illegal Immigrants." *washingtonpost.com* 26 Feb. 2004. Web. 6 Apr. 2004.

20. **An Article in a Magazine on the Internet**
    Pitta, Julie. "Un-Wired?" *Forbes* 20 Apr. 1998. Web. 4 Sept. 2002.

21. **An E-mail**
    Courage, Richard. "Re: Assessment Rubric." Message to the author. 10 Mar. 2005. E-mail.

22. **An Online Posting**
    Lardaro, Barbara. "Reaction to Joyce's *Portrait of the Artist as a Young Man.*" WebCT. ENG 224H_XFM. Online posting. 5 Dec. 2004. Web. 6 Dec. 2004.

Other Electronic Sources

3. A Periodical CD-ROM Database
   Author's Name (reversed). "Title" (in quotation marks). *Name of Source* (electronic journal, conference, database, etc., italicized). Number of Volume or

Issue. Year or Date of Publication. Publication Medium (CD-ROM, diskette, tape). Vendor. Date of Electronic Publication.

Barron, James. "After 17 Years, Cicada Emerges for Ritual of Sex and Death." *New York Times On disc.* CD-ROM. UMI-Proquest. 4 June 1996.

24. **A Nonperiodical CD-ROM Publication**
Author's Name (reversed). *Title* (italicized). Medium of Publication. City of Publication. Publisher. Date of Publication.

Shakespeare, William. *All's Well That Ends Well. William Shakespeare: The Complete Works on CD-ROM.* CD-ROM. Abingdon, Eng.: Andromeda Interactive, 1994.

Other Sources

25. **A Personal Interview**
Person's Name (reversed). Type of Interview (telephone, mail, online, personal, etc.). Date.

Martin, James. Telephone interview. 3 June 2004.

26. **A Lecture**
Speaker's Name (reversed). "Title of the Lecture" (in quotation marks). Nature of the Meeting. Location. Date. Presentation.

Haynes, Terry. "The Problematic Essay: Right and Responsibility." Conference on College Composition and Communication. Hyatt Regency, Milwaukee. 28 Mar. 1996. Presentation.

Worley, Demetrice A. "Telling Tales in School: An African American Woman's Voice in Composition." MLA Convention. Sheraton Washington, Washington, D.C. 28 Dec. 1996. Presentation.

27. **A TV or Radio Program**
"Title of Episode or Segment" (in quotation marks). *Title of Program* (italicized). Name of the Network. Call Letters of the Local Station. Date of Broadcast. Medium.

"The Irish Question." *The Story of English.* PBS. WNET, New York. 6 Apr. 1985. Television.

Brideshead Revisited, Episode 4. With Anthony Andrews and Jeremy Irons. PBS. WETA, Washington, D.C. 24 July 1984. Television.

28. **A Sound Recording**
Name of Person (composer, conductor, performers—whoever should be emphasized). *Title of the Recording* (italicized). Manufacturer, Year of Issue. Medium (CD, LP, Audiocassette, Audiotape).

Mozart, Wolfgang Amadeus. *Symphony no. 40 in G minor.* Vienna Philharmonic. Cond. Leonard Bernstein. Deutsche Grammophon, 1984. Audiocassette.

Rea, Stephen. *James Joyce's Ulysses.* BBC Audio, 1993. CD.

29. **A Film or Video Recording**
Title of Film or Video (italicized). Director. Distributor, Year. Medium.

Agamemnon. By Aeschylus. Dir. Peter Hall. The National Theatre of Great
Britain, 1983. DVD.

Rozencrantz and Guildenstern Are Dead. Dir. Tom Stoppard. Perf. Gary
Oldman, Tim Roth, and Richard Dreyfuss. Cinecom Entertainment, 1990.
Videocassette.

Sample Works Cited Page

Works Cited

Agamemnon. By Aeschylus. Dir. Peter Hall. The National Theatre of Great
Britain, 1983. DVD.

Austen, Jane. *Persuasion.* 1818. *Project Gutenberg.* Sharon Partridge, ed.
Feb. 1994. Web. 18 May 2004.

Barron, James. "After 17 Years, Cicada Emerges for Ritual of Sex and Death."
New York Times On disc. CD-ROM. UMI-Proquest. 4 June 1996.

Cheever, John. "The Enormous Radio." *The Stories of John Cheever.* New York:
Knopf, 1978. 33–41. Print.

Costanzo, William V. *The Electronic Text.* Englewood Cliffs: Educational
Technology, 1989. Print.

———. *Reading the Movies.* Urbana: NCTE, 1992. Print.

Courage, Richard. "Re: Assessment Rubric." Message to the author. 10 Mar.
2005. E-mail.

Desmond, Adrian, and James Moore. *Darwin.* New York: Warner, 1991. Print.

Ellmann, Richard. *James Joyce.* New York: Oxford UP, 1959. Print.

Fraser, Kennedy. "Piper Pipe That Song Again." Rev. of *Blake,* by Peter
Ackroyd. *New Yorker* 27 May 1996: 127–131. Print.

Grimes, William. "A Woman of Words That Win Pulitzers." *New York Times*
4 June 1996: C1. Print.

"Hawthorne, Nathaniel." *Britannica Online.* Vers. 98.2. Apr. 1998.
Encyclopaedia Britannica. Web. 16 Oct. 1998.

Haynes, Terry. "The Problematic Essay: Right and Responsibility." Conference
on College Composition and Communication. Hyatt Regency, Milwaukee.
28 Mar. 1996. Presentation.

Homer. *The Odyssey.* Trans. Robert Fagles. New York: Penguin, 1996. Print.

"The Irish Question." *The Story of English.* PBS. WNET, New York. 6 Apr.
1985. Television.

Kamps, Ivo. "Possible Pasts: Historiography and Legitimation in *Henry VIII*." *College English* 58 (1996): 192–215. Print.

Korda, Michael. "The Third Man." *New Yorker* 25 Mar. 1996: 44–51. Print.

Lardaro, Barbara. "Reaction to Joyce's *Portrait of the Artist as a Young Man*." WebCT. ENG 224H_XFM. Online posting. 5 Dec. 2004. Web. 6 Dec. 2004.

Markon, Jerry. "Virginia Colleges May Bar Illegal Immigrants." *washingtonpost.com* 26 Feb. 2004. Web. 6 Apr. 2004.

Martin, James. Telephone interview, 3 June 2004.

Pitta, Julie. "Un-Wired?" *Forbes* 20 Apr. 1998. Web. 4 Sept. 2002.

Rea, Stephen. *James Joyce's Ulysses*. BBC Audio, 1993. Audiocassette.

"Sheridan, Richard Brinsley." *The Oxford Companion to English Literature*. 5th ed. 1985. Print.

Sledge, Linda Ching. *A Map of Paradise*. New York: Bantam, 1997. Print.

Twain, Mark. *The Adventures of Tom Sawyer*. Internet Wiretap Online Library. Carnegie-Mellon U. Web. 22 Feb. 1999.

Valdez, Luis. "Los Vendidos." *Exploring Literature*. Frank Madden, ed. 5th ed. New York: Longman, 2012. 1031–39. Print.

Van Noate, Judith. *Theater Connections*. J. Murrey Atkins Library, U of North Carolina, Charlotte. Web. 6 Apr. 2003.

Voice of the Shuttle English Literature. U of California, Santa Barbara. Rev. 1999. Web. 22 Feb. 1999.

GLOSSARY OF LITERARY TERMS

abstract language words that represent broad qualities or characteristics (e.g., interesting, good, fine, horrible, lovely)

allegory an extended metaphor

alliteration the repetition of initial consonant sounds in words close together (e.g., "sad Sunday school superintendent stare")

allusion a reference to another literary/artistic/historic work, author, character, or event (frequently biblical or mythological)

amphitheater a semicircular large, outdoor theater with seats rising in tiers from a central acting area

anecdote a brief personal story used to illustrate a point

antagonist a character who seems to be the major force in opposition to the protagonist or main character

archaic language language no longer in use

arena stage (or Theater in the Round) a theater with seats surrounding the stage

argumentative essay an essay that tries to prove a point by supporting it with evidence

aside a brief comment by an actor, heard by the audience, but not the other characters on stage

assonance the repetition of internal vowel sounds in words close together (time line, free and easy)

atmosphere the dominant mood or tone of setting

autobiography an account of the author's own life

ballad a narrative poem, usually sung or recited

blank verse unrhymed iambic pentameter

box set a stage set composed of "flats" or connected walls enclosing three sides of the stage, with an invisible "fourth wall" open to the audience

catastrophe the reversal of the tragic hero's good fortune in Greek tragedy

catharsis an emotional purging or cleansing experienced by an ancient Greek audience at the end of a tragedy

character a person in fiction, drama, or poetry

characterization the development of characters in fiction, drama, or poetry

chorus a group of actors in Greek drama who comment on the action of the play. The role of the chorus came directly from drama as religious ritual and dates from a time when there were no individual actors. What the chorus says about the action reflects the traditional values of ancient Greek culture. Chorus members chanted their lines together and moved as a unit from side to side on the stage.

climax the turning point of the plot in fiction or drama

closed form poetry that follows traditional patterns of rhyme, meter, and line groupings

comedy The traditional plot of comedy is the reverse of tragedy. The protagonist, usually an ordinary person, has a problem. The plot of the play is an extrication from the problem and improvement of circumstances. The reversal of fortune is from bad to good; the falling action becomes a rising action with a happy ending.

complication the building of the conflict in plot as part of the rising action

concrete language words that represent specific, particular, graphic qualities and characteristics

conflict the struggle of opposing external or internal forces. External conflict may be physical (characters against nature) or social (characters against each other or against society). Internal conflict is a struggle of opposing forces within a character.

connotation the personal definition or association triggered by a word

consonance   repetition of final consonant sounds in words close together
(**sh**ort and **sw**eet, st**ruts** and f**rets**)

convention   an accepted or traditional
feature of a work (e.g., the Greek
chorus, the Shakespearian aside,
blank verse)

couplet   a pair of rhyming verse lines

crisis   the turning point of a plot
(closely related to "climax," which
seems to complete its action)

critical essay   an essay that interprets
and/or evaluates

denotation   the literal, dictionary
definition of a word

denouement   the resolution of the plot
in fiction or drama (an "untying" of
the complications at the end of the
story line)

dialogue   conversation of characters in
fiction or drama

didactic   teaching a lesson or having a
"moral"

documentation   accounting for and
giving credit to the origin of a source

dramatic monologue   In a dramatic
monologue, the poet, like an actor in
a play, speaks through the voice and
personality of another person.

dramatis personae   the list of
characters in a play

Early Modern   a period in Western
European history (circa 1500–1800)

Elizabethan   the era beginning with the
reign of Elizabeth I, Queen of England
from 1558 to 1603 and ending with
the Puritans' closing of the theaters
in 1642

ellipsis   (…) indication of an omission
of words in a quote

epic   a long narrative poem, usually
depicting the values of a culture
through the adventures of a hero

explication   a line-by-line explanation
of a poem or other literary work

exposition   the introduction of essential characters, setting, circumstances
of a story or play

expository essay   an essay that
shares, explains, suggests, or
explores information, emotion,
and ideas

expressionism   a movement in drama
that emphasizes subjectivity of
perception

falling action   the action that follows
the crisis and climax (*see also*
catastrophe, denouement,
resolution, catharsis)

figurative language   language that
expresses more than a literal meaning (e.g., metaphor, simile)

flat character   a character not fully
developed who seems to represent a
"type" more than a real personality
(*see also* stock character)

foot   a combination of syllables that
represent one measure of meter in a
verse line

"fourth wall"   the invisible wall open
to the audience in a box set (*see also*
box set)

free verse   poetry without standardized
rhyme, meter, or structure. It is not
formless, however, but relies on its
own words and content to determine
its best form.

genre   a form or type of literature (e.g.,
fiction, poetry, drama, the essay)

groundlings   members of an Elizabethan audience who paid a very low
entrance fee and stood in the open
area below and around the stage.
Because they stood on the ground
unprotected from the weather, they
were called "groundlings," a term
meant to disparage their social
standing as much as to describe their
location in the theater.

hubris   excessive pride that usually
leads to the downfall of the tragic
hero in Greek drama

hyperbole   an exaggeration in figurative language

iambic   an unstressed/stressed combination of syllables in a metrical foot

image/imagery   descriptive language
that helps us see, hear, smell, taste,
or feel

inductive/deductive reasoning Inductive   reasoning moves from observation of specific circumstances and
makes a general conclusion; **deductive**
reasoning takes a general truth and
applies it to specific circumstances.

interpretation   an analysis of a work
to determine its meaning

irony   The two most popular forms of
irony are verbal irony and situational
irony. **Verbal irony** results from the

contrast between what is said by a character and what is meant. **Irony of situation** results from the contrast between what is expected and what actually happens.

limerick a five-line poem. The first, second, and fifth lines rhyme (aaa) and so do the third and fourth (bb). The first, third, and fifth have the same verbal rhythm (**meter**) and length, and so do the second and fourth.

lyric poetry characterized by the expression of the poet's innermost feelings, thoughts, and imagination

magical realism fiction that blends realistic or ordinary details and events with those that are magical or fantastic. Gabriel García Márquez's "The Handsomest Drowned Man in the World" (p. 924) exemplifies this form.

melodrama plays with elaborate but oversimplified plots, flat characters, excessive sentiment, and happy endings

metafiction fiction that explores the process of its own language and creation as it tells the story

metaphor an implied comparison of two apparently dissimilar things

meter describes rhythm in a poem. It refers to the pattern of stressed and unstressed syllables in a line of verse. The group of syllables making up one metrical unit is called a **foot**. The metrical feet most commonly used are **iambic** (unstressed-stressed), **trochaic** (stressed-unstressed), **anapestic** (two unstressed-one stressed), and **dactylic** (one stressed-two unstressed).

The number of feet in each line is described as **monometer** (one foot), **dimeter** (two feet), **trimeter** (three feet), **tetrameter** (four feet), **pentameter** (five feet), **hexameter** (six feet), **heptameter** (seven feet), and **octameter** (eight feet). The most common form of meter in poetry written in English is **iambic** (unstressed-stressed) pentameter (five feet).

microcosm a smaller version or "little world"

monologue a speech by a single character

mood the atmosphere or tone of a work

narrative essay an essay that tells a story. Most essays of this type spring from an event or experience in the writer's life.

narrative poem a poem that tells a story

narrator the voice of the speaker in a story

Neoclassicism a movement that dominated during the eighteenth century and was notable for its adherence to the "forms" of classical drama

ode a formal lyric poem recited for ceremonial occasions

onomatopoeia a word that sounds like what it represents (e.g., the "buzzing" of a bee)

open form poetry that does not follow traditional patterns of rhyme, meter, and line groupings (*see also* free verse)

orchestra the playing area in an ancient Greek theater

paraphrase to record someone else's words in the writer's own words

parodos the ode chanted by the chorus as they enter in Greek tragedy

pentameter five feet of verse line

personal essay an essay that emphasizes a personal, subjective view

personification giving human qualities to things non-human

Petrarchan Sonnet The oldest form of the sonnet is the Italian or Petrarchan Sonnet (named for its greatest practitioner—Petrarch). Its rhyme scheme is usually an octave (eight lines) and a sestet (six lines). The octave usually follows a pattern of **abbaabba**. The concluding sestet may be **cdecde** or **cdcdcd** or **cdedce**.

plot the structure of the story; the pattern of twists and turns the story takes

point of view the perspective from which the narrator speaks to us. Generally, the pronoun that dominates the narration will signal which point of view is represented. The terms most commonly used to identify point of view are **first person**, **third person**, **omniscient**, **objective**, and **shifting**.

primary/secondary sources   A primary source is the original text or materials. A secondary source is commentary about that original material.

props   objects or items used by the actors on the stage

proscenium arch   a frame around the stage that separates the actors and the set from the audience

protagonist   the main character in a story or drama

quatrain   a four-line stanza

Realism   a movement in literature to represent life as it really is. It is often characterized by accurate depiction of ordinary people in their natural surroundings.

recognition   the point near the end of a classic tragedy when the protagonist recognizes the causes and consequences of his reversal

resolution   the final phase of the falling action in plot when things are returned to normal

reversal   the change from good to bad fortune in classic tragedy; from bad to good fortune in classic comedy

rhyme   when final vowel and consonant sounds in the last syllable of one word match those of another, usually at the end of lines

rhythm   the pattern of sound in a poem. The most structured form of rhythm is meter, the pattern of stressed and unstressed syllables.

rising action   that point in the plot when conflict and our emotional involvement intensifies

Romanticism   a movement that values literature as an expression of unique feelings, attitudes, and experiences

round character   a fully developed character with the complexities of a real person

satire   ridiculing stupidity, vice, or folly through exaggeration and humor

scansion   analysis of the kind and number of metrical feet in a poem

script   the printed text of a drama

sentimentality   evoking a predictable emotional response with a clichéd prompt

set   structures on the stage that represent the setting of the play

setting   the environment in which the work takes place

Shakespearian Sonnet   The most popular form in English is the English or Shakespearian Sonnet. It is a fourteen-line poem of three quatrains (four-line units) and a final couplet (a two-line unit) in the rhyme scheme **abab cdcd efef gg**. It presents the content of the poem in predictable ways. The first two quatrains will often present a problem. The third quatrain is often pivotal and will begin a reversal. The final couplet most often suggests a solution.

simile   an announced comparison introduced with the words "like" or "as"

soliloquy   Delivered by a character alone on the stage, soliloquies are a "thinking out loud" shared with the audience. They are often statements of a philosophical, reflective nature, and they are highlights of Shakespeare's plays.

sonnet   a fourteen-line lyric poem usually in iambic pentameter

speaker   the narrator of a story or poem

stage directions   descriptions (in the text of the play) of the set, the props, voice and movements of the actors, and the lighting

stanza   a unit of lines in a poem that usually share a metrical or thematic pattern

stock character   a character not fully developed who seems to represent a "type" more than a real personality (*see also* flat character)

style   the choice of words and sentence structure that makes each author's writing different

summary   the material condensed to its main points

surrealistic drama   seeks its truth in the irrationality of the unconscious mind

symbol   an object or action that represents more than itself

symbolist drama   seeks its truth in symbols, myths, and dreams

syntax   the ordering of words in a sentence

theme   the overall meaning we derive from the poem, story, play, or essay

thesis   the point of the essay

thrust stage   a stage that extends into the audience

tone   the attitude expressed by the writer toward the subject

tragedy   Classic tragedy follows the plight of a noble person who is flawed by a defect and whose actions cause him to break some moral law and suffer downfall and destruction.

tragic flaw   the tragic hero's flaw (often excessive pride or hubris) that leads directly to a reversal of his good fortune (**catastrophe**)

tragic hero   as defined by Aristotle, a man of noble stature who is admired by society but flawed

tragicomedy   a play that combines the elements of tragedy and comedy

unities   The unities of time, place, and action as principles of dramatic composition have been hotly debated since Aristotle's *Poetics*. In brief, **unity of time** suggests that the action of the play occur in a twenty-four-hour period; **unity of place** suggests that the action occur in one place or location; and **unity of action** suggests that all parts of the play should be related in a clear causal pattern.

unreliable narrator   a narrator who tells the story from a biased, erroneous perspective

verse   a line or the form of poetry

villanelle   a nineteen-line poem having only two rhymes and repeating two of the lines in a set pattern. Dylan Thomas's "Do Not Go Gentle into That Good Night" (p. 1182) exemplifies this form.

voice   the personality or style of the writer or narrator that seems to come to life in the words

LITERARY AND PHOTO CREDITS

LITERARY CREDITS

Achebe, Chinua, "Marriage Is a Private Affair" from *Girls at War and Other Stories* by Chinua Achebe, copyright © 1972, 1973 by Chinua Achebe. Used by permission of Doubleday, a division of Random House, Inc.

Alexie, Sherman, "Evolution" reprinted from *The Business of Fancydancing.* © 1992 by Sherman Alexie, by permission of Hanging Loose Press.

Alvarez, Julia, "Dusting" from *Homecoming.* Copyright © 1984, 1996 by Julia Alvarez. Published by Plume, an imprint of The Penguin Group (USA), and originally published by Grove Press. By permission of Susan Bergholz Literary Services, New York, NY, and Lamy, NM. All rights reserved.

Alvarez, Julia, "Snow" from *How the Garcia Girls Lost Their Accents.* Copyright © 1991 by Julia Alvarez. Published by Plume, an imprint of The Penguin Group (USA), and originally in hardcover by Algonquin Books of Chapel Hill. By permission of Susan Bergholz Literary Services, New York, NY, and Lamy, NM. All rights reserved.

Anderson, Michael, "'A Raisin in the Sun': A Landmark Lesson in Being Black" by Michael Anderson from *The New York Times*, March 7, 1997. © 1997 by The New York Times Co. All rights reserved. Used by permission and protected by the Copyright Laws of the United States. The printing, copying, redistribution, or retransmission of the Content without express written permission is prohibited.

Angelou, Maya, "Phenomenal Woman" copyright © 1978 by Maya Angelou, from *And Still I Rise* by Maya Angelou. Used by permission of Random House, Inc.

Anzaldúa, Gloria, "To Live in the Borderlands Means You" from *Borderlands/La Frontera: The New Mestiza.* Copyright © 1987 by Gloria Andaldúa. Reprinted by permission of Aunt Lute Books.

Armas, José, "El Tonto del Barrio" by José Armas. Copyright © 1970. Reprinted by permission of the author.

Atwood, Margaret, "Siren Song" from *Selected Poems, 1965–1976* by Margaret Atwood. Copyright © 1976 by Margaret Atwood. Reprinted by permission of Houghton Mifflin Harcourt Publishing Company. All rights reserved. "You Fit Into Me" by Margaret Atwood from *Power Politics.* © 1971 by Margaret Atwood. Reprinted by permission of House of Anansi Press Ltd. Toronto, Ontario.

Auden, W. H., "Musée des Beaux Arts" and "The Unknown Citizen" copyright © 1940 and renewed 1968 by W. H. Auden, from *Collected Poems of W. H. Auden* by W. H. Auden. Used by permission of Random House.

Baldwin, James, "Sonny's Blues" © 1957 by James Baldwin was originally published in *Partisan Review.* Copyright renewed. Collected in *Going to Meet the Man*, published by Vintage Books. "Sweet Lorraine" © 1969 by James Baldwin was originally published in *Esquire.* Copyright renewed. Collected in *The Price of the Ticket*, published by St. Martin's.

Both selections are reprinted by arrangement with the James Baldwin Estate.

Bambara, Toni Cade, "The Lesson" copyright © 1972 by Toni Cade Bambara, from *Gorilla, My Love* by Toni Cade Bambara. Used by permission of Random House, Inc.

Basho, "A village without bells –" from THE ESSENTIAL HAIKU: VERSIONS OF BASHO, BUSON & ISSA, edited and with an Introduction by Robert Hass. Introduction and selection copyright © 1994 by Robert Hass. Unless otherwise noted, all translations copyright © 1994 by Robert Hass. Reprinted by permission of HarperCollins Publishers, Inc.

Bennett, Gwendolyn, "Heritage" by Gwendolyn Bennett from Opportunity Magazine, 1926.

Bennett, Paula, "On 'I Heard a Fly Buzz—When I Died'" from *Emily Dickinson, Woman Poet*, 1990. Reprinted by permission of Pearson Education Limited.

Bettelheim, Bruno, "Cinderella" from *The Uses of Enchantment* by Bruno Bettelheim. Copyright © 1975, 1976 by Bruno Bettelheim. Reprinted by permission of Raines & Raines.

Bishop, Elizabeth, "In the Waiting Room" from *The Complete Poems 1927–1979* by Elizabeth Bishop. Copyright © 1979, 1983 by Alice Helen Methfessel. Reprinted by permission of Farrar, Straus and Giroux, LLC.

Bloom, Claire, "Playing Gertrude on Television" from *Playing Gertrude for the BBC TV* by Claire Bloom, 1980 from BBC TV Shakespeare's Hamlet. Reprinted by permission.

Brooks, Gwendolyn, "We Real Cool" from *Blacks* by Gwendolyn Brooks. Copyright © 1991 by Gwendolyn Brooks. Published by Gwendolyn Brooks through Third World Press, Chicago, 1991. Reprinted by permission of the author.

Brutschy, Jennifer, "Born Again" by Jennifer Brutschy is reprinted by permission of the author.

Buson, "Listening to the moon…" from THE ESSENTIAL HAIKU: VERSIONS OF BASHO, BUSON & ISSA, edited and with an Introduction by Robert Hass. Introduction and selection copyright © 1994 by Robert Hass. Unless otherwise noted, all translations copyright © 1994 by Robert Hass. Reprinted by permission of HarperCollins Publishers, Inc.

Butler, Robert Olen, "Jealous Husband Returns in Form of Parrot" from the book *Tabloid Dreams* by Robert Olen Butler. Copyright © 1996 by Robert Olen Butler. Reprinted by permission of Henry Holt and Company, LLC.

Camus, Albert, "The Myth of Sisyphus" from *The Myth of Sisyphus* by Albert Camus, translated by Justin O'Brien. Translation copyright © 1955, copyright renewed 1983 by Alfred A. Knopf, a division of Random House, Inc. Used by permission of Alfred A. Knopf, a division of Random House, Inc.

Carter, Steven R., "Hansberry's Artistic Misstep" by Steven R. Carter from *Hansberry's Drama: Commitment Amid Complexity.* Champaign: University of Illinois Press, 1991.

1307

renewed 1990 by John Updike. Used by permission of Alfred A. Knopf, a division of Random House, Inc. "Ex-Basketball Player" from *Collected Poems 1953–1993* by John Updike, copyright © 1993 by John Updike. Used by permission of Alfred A. Knopf, a division of Random House, Inc.

Valdez, Luis, "Los Venididos" is reprinted with permission from the publisher of *Luis Valdez–Early Works* by Luis Valdez (© 1971 Arte Publico Press, University of Houston).

Walker, Alice, "Everyday Use" from *In Love & Trouble: Stories of Black Women,* copyright © 1973 by Alice Walker, reprinted by permission of Houghton Mifflin Harcourt Publishing Company. "Foreword: Zora Neale Hurston—A Cautionary Tale and a Partisan View" by Alice Walker from *Zora Neale Hurston: A Literary Biography* by Robert E. Hemenway. Copyright 1977 by the Board of Trustees of the University of Illinois. Used by permission of the author and the University of Illinois Press.

Wilbur, Richard, "On Dickinson's Sense of Privation" from "Sumptious Destitution" in *Emily Dickinson: Three Views* by Richard Wilbur, Louise Bogan and Archibald MacLeish, 1960 by Amherst College Press. Reprinted by permission of the author.

Williams, Tennessee, "The Glass Menagerie" by Tennessee Williams. Copyright © 1945, renewed 1973 The University of the South. Reprinted by permission of Georges Borchardt, Inc. for the Estate of Tennessee Williams.

Williams, William Carlos, "At the Ball Game" by William Carlos Williams from *The Collected Poems: Volume I 1909–1939,* copyright © 1938 by New Directions Publishing Corp. Reprinted by permission of New Directions Publishing Corp.

Wolff, Cynthia Griffin, Excerpt from *Emily Dickinson* by Cynthia Griffin Wolff, copyright © 1986 by Cynthia Griffin Wolff. Used by permission of Alfred A. Knopf, a division of Random House, Inc.

Woolf, Virginia, "Shakespeare's Sister" from *A Room of One's Own* by Virginia Woolf, copyright 1929 by Houghton Mifflin Harcourt Publishing Company and renewed 1957 by Leonard Woolf, reprinted by permission of the publisher.

Yellen, Samuel, "Nighthawks" by Samuel Yellen. First published in *Commentary,* 1951. Reprinted by permission of Marilyn Gaylin for the Estate of Samuel Yellen.

Zimmer, Paul, "Zimmer in Grade School" from *Crossing to Sunlight.* Copyright © 1976 by Paul Zimmer. Reprinted by permission of the author.

INDEX OF AUTHORS, TITLES, AND FIRST LINES OF POEMS

INDEX OF TERMS